The Philosophy of Mind

The Philosophy of Mind

Classical Problems/Contemporary Issues

second edition

edited by Brian Beakley and Peter Ludlow

A Bradford Book
The MIT Press
Cambridge, Massachusetts
London, England

MIT Press books may be purchased at special quantity discounts for business or sales promotional use. For information, please email special_sales@mitpress.mit.edu or write to Special Sales Department, The MIT Press, 55 Hayward Street, Cambridge, MA 02142.

This book was set in Stone Serif and Stone Sans on 3B2 by Asco Typesetters, Hong Kong, and was printed and bound in the United States of America.

Library of Congress Cataloging-in-Publication Data

The philosophy of mind : classical problems / contemporary issues / edited by Brian Beakley and Peter Ludlow.—2nd ed.
p. cm.
"A Bradford book."
Includes bibliographical references and index.
ISBN 0-262-02593-0 (hc. : alk. paper)—ISBN 0-262-52451-1 (pbk. : alk. paper)
1. Philosophy of mind. I. Beakley, Brian. II. Ludlow, Peter, 1957–.
BD418.3.P45 2006
128′.2—dc22 2005047924

10 9 8 7 6 5 4 3 2 1

Contents

Preface to the Second Edition

Hardly had the first edition of this book hit the shelves when we began considering the corrections, additions, and improvements we might make to it. And while any book offers opportunities to tweak after the fact, in a reader covering a variety of topics spanning 2,500 years the potential for tinkering is almost unlimited. In order to keep the book's size within practical limits (and deliver it to the press only a few years late), we have focused primarily on closing significant gaps on the historical side, and updating the contemporary selections. Though we think the historical selections in the first edition were judicious, we have found better examples of some historical positions, as well as some neglected precursors to views that are usually considered recent innovations. And while we naturally needed to keep the readings current in areas particularly close to empirical research (such as connectionism and innatism), in fact the dialogue has evolved in every area covered by the first edition.

The mind–body problem is typically the central topic in a philosophy of mind course, and one that frames the discussion of other subjects. With this in mind, we have expanded Part I more than any other, on both the historical and contemporary ends. In order to keep such a large collection of readings from appearing a disorganized grab-bag, we have divided it into three sections. We stress, however, that these subdivisions are intended primarily as a convenience for the reader, and not meant to suggest some strong claim about the nature of the mind–body problem. We realize that the sections overlap substantially (as do all five parts of the book, for that matter), and that other divisions of the material might have made just as much sense.

In one case we gave in to the temptation to add an entirely new section to the book, introducing in this edition a selection of readings on mental content. In light of the continuing importance of this topic in current philosophy, and the connections it has with most of the other subjects discussed here, we felt an understanding of different views on mental content would prove invaluable to anyone seeking a good introduction to the philosophy of mind. We extend to this section the blanket excuse we offer on all topics: should the reader not find her favorite author's view included here, we can only say that the array of readings is vast, and we realize with regret that we are bound to exclude many good works. But concerning the mental content section we must offer an additional apology: in order to include these new readings, we were forced to eliminate the section on mental imagery. This was a difficult decision for us; but in the end we concluded that mental imagery may not be quite as central to ongoing *philosophical* research and controversy as mental content. Whereas philosophers today continue to hotly debate questions of mental content, work on mental imagery has to a large degree become the domain of psychologists.

In addition, by way of better integrating the historical and contemporary works on innatism, and bringing out what we think are the central issues, we have rechristened Part IV with a longer, but we hope more useful, label: "Innateness and Modularity."

We note with appreciation several informative discussions of historical sources with Richard F. Foley, and a useful suggestion on mental causation from Gabriel Segal. As always, the folks at MIT Press—in particular Betty Stanton, Carolyn Gray Anderson, and more recently Thomas Stone, Jessica Lawrence-Hurt, Margy Avery, and Judy Feldmann—were very helpful (and patient). They have our sincere thanks. We have also received some welcome e-mail feedback from readers, for which we are grateful. And since nothing shows the limits of a text quite like road testing it in the classroom, we owe a unique debt to the many students who have used the first edition with us in our classes. We hope this new edition will fill in some of the blanks and answer some of the questions they have posed for us.

Finally, despite the many changes in this edition, one point remains very much unchanged: now, as before, we encourage readers to send us their comments, criticisms, and suggestions. Feel free to write us!

Brian Beakley bbeakley@eiu.edu

Peter Ludlow ludlow@umich.edu

Sources

Every effort was made to locate the owners of copyrighted material and to make full acknowledgment of its use. Errors or omissions will be corrected in subsequent editions if notification in writing is received by the publisher. Grateful acknowledgment is made for permission to include the following material.

Aristotle, *Metaphysics*, from W. D. Ross, trans. and ed., *The Works of Aristotle*, volume 8, 2d edition (Oxford: Clarendon Press, 1928). Reprinted by permission of the publisher.

Aristotle, *On the Soul*, from W. D. Ross, ed., and J. A. Smith, trans., *The Works of Aristotle*, volume 3 (Oxford: Clarendon Press, 1931). Reprinted by permission of Oxford University Press.

René Descartes, *Meditations on the First Philosophy*, from Elizabeth Haldane and G. R. T. Ross, ed. and trans., *The Philosophical Works of Descartes*, volume 1 (Cambridge: Cambridge Univ. Press, 1911 [reprinted with corrections, 1931]). Reprinted with the permission of Cambridge University Press.

René Descartes, *Objections and Replies*, from Elizabeth Haldane and G. R. T. Ross, eds. and trans., *The Philosophical Works of Descartes*, volume 2 (Cambridge: Cambridge Univ. Press, 1911 [reprinted with corrections, 1931]). Reprinted with the permission of Cambridge University Press.

John Locke, *An Essay Concerning Human Understanding*, ed. Peter H. Nidditch (Oxford: Oxford Univ. Press, 1975 [London, 1690]). Reprinted by permission of Oxford University Press.

George Berkeley, *A Treatise Concerning the Principles of Human Knowledge*, from G. N. Wright, ed., *The Works of George Berkeley* (London: Thomas Tegg, 1843).

Gottfried Wilhelm Leibniz, *Monadology*, trans. George P. Montgomery (LaSalle, Ill.: Open Court, 1902).

Julien Offray DeLaMettrie, *Man a Machine* (LaSalle, Ill.: Open Court, 1912).

Auguste Comte, *The Positive Philosophy of Auguste Comte*, trans. Harriet Martineau (London: Truebner, 1842).

John Stuart Mill, *A System of Logic, Ratiocinative and Inductive, Being a Connected View of the Principles of Evidence and the Methods of Scientific Investigation*, 8th edition (London: Longmans, Green, Reader, and Dyer, 1872).

William James, "Does Consciousness Exist?" *Journal of Philosophy, Psychology and Scientific Methods* 1 (September 1, 1904):18.

James Rowland Angell, "The Province of Functional Psychology," *Psychological Review* 14 (1906): 61–91.

Gilbert Ryle, *The Concept of Mind* (New York: Harper Collins, 1949). Reprinted by permission of HarperCollins Publishers.

Ullin Thomas Place, "Is Consciousness a Brain Process?" *British Journal of Psychology* 47 (1956): 44–50. Reprinted by permission of the author and publisher.

Hilary Putnam, "The Nature of Mental States," originally published as "Psychological Predicates" by Hilary Putnam in *Art, Mind, and Religion*, W. H. Capitan and D. D. Merrill, eds., © 1967 by the University of Pittsburgh Press. Reprinted by permission of the publisher.

Ned Block, "Troubles with Functionalism," from C. W. Savage, ed., *Perception and Cognition: Issues in the Foundations of Psychology*, Minnesota Studies in the Philosophy of Science, volume 9 (Minneapolis: Univ. of Minnesota Press, 1978). This version has been significantly revised by the author. Copyright 1978 by the University of Minnesota.

John Searle, "Minds, Brains, and Programs," *Behavioral and Brain Sciences* 3 (1980): 417–424. Reprinted with the permission of Cambridge University Press. Copyright 1980 Cambridge University Press.

Paul Churchland, "Eliminative Materialism and the Propositional Attitudes," *Journal of Philosophy* 78, 2 (1981): 67–90. Reprinted by permission of the author and *The Journal of Philosophy*.

Patricia Smith Churchland, *Neurophilosophy* (Cambridge, Mass.: MIT Press, 1986). © 1986 by The Massachusetts Institute of Technology.

Jaegwon Kim, "Multiple Realization and the Metaphysics of Reduction," *Philosophy and Phenomenological Research* 52 (1992): 1–26.

Noam Chomsky, *Language and Problems of Knowledge: The Managua Lectures* (Cambridge, Mass.: MIT Press, 1988). Reprinted by permission of The MIT Press.

Bas van Fraassen, *The Empirical Stance* (New Haven and London: Yale Univ. Press, 2002). Reprinted by permission of Yale University Press.

Clarence Irving Lewis, *Mind and the World Order* (London: Dover Books, 1929).

Herbert Feigl, "The Mental and the Physical," in H. Feigl, M. Scriven, and G. Maxwell, eds., *Minnesota Studies in the Philosophy of Science*, vol. II: *Concepts, Theories, and the Mind–Body Problem* (Minneapolis: Univ. of Minnesota Press: 1958); reprinted in Herbert Feigl, *The "Mental" and the "Physical"* (Minneapolis: Univ. of Minnesota Press: 1967). Copyright 1967 by the University of Minnesota.

John Jamieson Carswell Smart, "Sensations and Brain Processes," *Philosophical Review* 68, 2 (April 1959): 141–156. Reprinted by permission of *The Philosophical Review*.

Thomas Nagel, "What Is It Like to Be a Bat?" *Philosophical Review* 82 (1974): 435–450. Reprinted by permission of *The Philosophical Review*.

Sydney Shoemaker, "Functionalism and Qualia," *Philosophical Studies* 27 (1975): 291–315. © Kluwer Academic Publishers. Reprinted with kind permission from Springer Science and Business Media.

Saul Kripke, "Identity and Necessity," from Milton Munitz, ed., *Identity and Individuation* (New York: New York Univ. Press, 1971). Reprinted by permission of the author and NYU Press.

William Lycan, "Form, Function, and Feel," *Journal of Philosophy* 78 (1981): 24–50. Reprinted by permission of William Lycan and *The Journal of Philosophy*.

Frank Jackson, "Epiphenomenal Qualia," *Philosophical Quarterly* 32 (1982): 127–136. Reprinted by permission of Basil Blackwell Ltd.

Colin McGinn, "Can We Solve the Mind–Body Problem?" *Mind* 98 (1989): 349–366. Reprinted by permission of Oxford University Press.

Laurence Nemirow, "Physicalism and the Cognitive Role of Acquaintance," in William Lycan, ed., *Mind and Cognition: A Reader* (Oxford: Blackwell, 1990). Reprinted by permission of Blackwell Publishing.

René Descartes, *The Passions of the Soul*, from Elizabeth Haldane and G. R. T. Ross, eds. and trans., *The Philosophical Works of Descartes*, volume 1 (Cambridge: Cambridge Univ. Press, 1911 [reprinted with corrections, 1931]). Reprinted with the permission of Cambridge University Press.

Nicolas Malebranche, *The Search after Truth*, trans. Thomas Lennon and Paul Olscamp (Columbus: Ohio State Univ. Press, 1980). Reprinted by permission of the publisher.

Gottfried Wilhelm Leibniz, "The Nature and Communication of Substances," in Leroy Loemker, ed., *Philosophical Letters and Papers of Leibniz*, volume 2 (Chicago: Univ. of Chicago Press, 1956).

Immanuel Kant, *Critique of Pure Reason*, trans. Max Muller (New York: Macmillan, 1893).

Thomas Henry Huxley, "On the Hypothesis That Animals Are Automata," in his *Collected Essays*, volume 1 (London, 1893).

Donald Davidson, "Mental Events," reprinted from *Experience and Theory*, ed. Lawrence Foster and J. W. Swanson (Amherst: University of Massachusetts Press, 1970), copyright © 1970 by the University of Massachusetts Press.

Ernest LePore and Barry Loewer, "Mind Matters," *Journal of Philosophy* 84 (1987): 630–642. Reprinted by permission of the authors and *The Journal of Philosophy*.

Jerry A. Fodor, "Making Mind Matter More," *Philosophical Topics* 17 (1989): 59–79. Reprinted by permission of the author and publisher.

Jaegwon Kim, "The Myth of Non-Reductive Materialism," *Proceedings and Addresses of the American Philosophical Association* 63 (1989): 31–47. Reprinted by permission of the APA.

Frank Jackson and Philip Pettit, "Causation in the Philosophy of Mind," *Philosophy and Phenomenological Research* 50 (suppl., fall 1990): 195–214.

Elliott Sober, "Physicalism from a Probabilistic Point of View," *Philosophical Studies* 35 (1999): 135–174. © Kluwer Academic Publishers. Reprinted with kind permission from Springer Science and Business Media.

Aristotle, *On the Soul*, in W. D. Ross, ed., *The Works of Aristotle*, volume 3 (Oxford: Oxford Univ. Press, 1931). By permission of Oxford University Press.

René Descartes, *Meditations on the First Philosophy*, in Elizabeth Haldane and G. R. T. Ross, eds. and trans., *The Philosophical Works of Descartes*, volume 1 (Cambridge: Cambridge Univ. Press, 1911 [reprinted with corrections, 1931]). Reprinted with the permission of Cambridge University Press.

Rene Descartes, *Objections and Replies*, in Elizabeth Haldane and G. R. T. Ross, eds. and trans., *The Philosophical Works of Descartes*, volume 2 (Cambridge: Cambridge Univ. Press, 1911 [reprinted with corrections, 1931]). Reprinted with the permission of Cambridge University Press.

John Locke, *An Essay Concerning Human Understanding*, ed. Peter H. Nidditch (Oxford: Oxford Univ. Press, 1975 [London, 1690]). By Permission of Oxford University Press.

David Hume, *A Treatise of Human Nature*, ed. Peter H. Nidditch (Oxford: Oxford Univ. Press, 1978 [London, 1739]). By permission of Oxford University Press.

Gottfried Wilhelm Leibniz, *Discourse on Metaphysics and Correspondence with Arnauld*, trans. George P. Montgomery (LaSalle, Ill.: Open Court, 1902).

Charles Saunders Peirce, "How to Make Our Ideas Clear," *Popular Science Monthly* 12 (January 1878): 286–302.

Alexius Meinong, "The Theory of Objects," trans. Isaac Levi, D. B. Terrell, and Roderick M. Chisholm, in Roderick M. Chisholm, ed., *Realism and the Background of Phenomenology* (Glencoe, Ill.: Free Press, 1960). © 1960 by Ridgeview Publishing Co. Reproduced with permission of Ridgeview Publishing Co. via Copyright Clearance Center.

Bertrand Russell, *The Problems of Philosophy* (Oxford: Oxford Univ. Press: 1912). By permission of Oxford University Press.

Clarence Irving Lewis, *Mind and the World Order* (London: Dover Books: 1929).

Hilary Putnam, "The Meaning of 'Meaning,'" in Keith Gunderson, ed., *Language, Mind, and Knowledge: Minnesota Studies in the Philosophy of Science*, volume 7 (Minneapolis: Univ. of Minnesota Press, 1975). Copyright 1975 by the University of Minnesota.

Tyler Burge, "Individualism and the Mental," in Peter A. French, Theodore E. Uehling, Jr., and Howard K. Wettstein, eds., *Midwestern Studies in Philosophy*, vol. 4: *Studies in Metaphysics* (Minneapolis: Univ. of Minnesota Press, 1979). Copyright 1979 by the University of Minnesota.

Jerry A. Fodor, "Methodological Solipsism Considered as a Research Strategy in Cognitive Psychology," *Behavioral and Brain Sciences* 3 (1980): 63–73. Reprinted with the permission of Cambridge University Press.

Fred Dretske, "Misrepresentation," in Radu J. Bogdan, ed., *Belief: Form, Content, and Function* (Oxford: Clarendon Press, 1986). By permission of Oxford University Press.

Gilbert Harman, "(Nonsolipsistic) Conceptual Role Semantics," in Ernest LePore, ed., *New Directions in Semantics* (Orlando, Florida: Harcourt Brace Jovanovich, 1987). Reprinted by permission of the publisher.

Brian Loar, "Social Content and Psychological Content," reprinted from *Contents of Thought*, edited by Robert Grimm and Daniel Merrill, © 1988 The Arizona Board of Regents. Reprinted by permission of the University of Arizona Press.

Robert A. Wilson, "Wide Computationalism," *Mind* 103 (1994): 351–372. Reprinted by permission of Oxford University Press.

Gabriel M. A. Segal, *A Slim Book on Narrow Content* (Cambridge, Mass.: MIT Press, 2000). Reprinted by permission of MIT Press.

Plato, *The Meno*, trans. B. Jowett, in *The Dialogues of Plato*, volume 2 (New York: Random House, 1892).

Aristotle, *Posterior Analytics*, from W. D. Ross, ed., *The Works of Aristotle* (Oxford: Oxford Univ. Press, 1928). By permission of Oxford University Press.

René Descartes, *Objections and Replies*, from Elizabeth Haldane and G. R. T. Ross, eds. and trans., *The Philosophical Works of Descartes*, volume 2 (Cambridge: Cambridge Univ. Press, 1911 [reprinted with corrections, 1931]). Reprinted with the permission of Cambridge University Press.

René Descartes, *Notes Directed against a Certain Program*, from Elizabeth Haldane and G. R. T. Ross, eds. and trans., *The Philosophical Works of Descartes*, volume 1 (Cambridge: Cambridge Univ. Press,

1911 [reprinted with corrections, 1931]). Reprinted with the permission of Cambridge University Press.

John Locke, *An Essay Concerning Human Understanding*, ed. Peter H. Nidditch (Oxford: Oxford Univ. Press, 1975 [1690]). Reprinted by permission of Oxford University Press.

Gottfried Wilhelm Leibniz, *New Essays on Human Understanding*, trans. Peter Remnant and Jonathan Bennett (Cambridge: Cambridge Univ. Press, 1981). Reprinted with the permission of Cambridge University Press.

Johann Gaspar Spurzheim, *Phrenology* (Boston: Marsh, Capen, and Lyon, 1832).

Jerry A. Fodor, *The Language of Thought* (Cambridge, Mass.: Harvard Univ. Press, 1975). Copyright © 1975 by Thomas Y. Crowell Company, Inc. Reprinted by permission of Pearson Education, Inc.

Jean Piaget, "The Psychogenesis of Knowledge and Its Epistemological Significance," from Massimo Piatelli-Palmarini, ed., *The Debate between Noam Chomsky and Jean Piaget* (Cambridge, Mass.: Harvard Univ. Press, 1980). Copyright © 1980 by the President and Fellows of Harvard College and Routledge & Kegan Paul Ltd. Originally appeared in French as "Théories du language, theories de l'apprentissage." Copyright © 1979 Editions du Seuil. Reprinted by permission of Georges Borchardt, Inc., for Editions de Seuil.

Noam Chomsky, "On Cognitive Structures and Their Development: A Reply to Piaget," from Massimo Piatelli-Palmarini, ed., *The Debate between Noam Chomsky and Jean Piaget* (Cambridge, Mass.: Harvard Univ. Press, 1980). Copyright © 1980 by the President and Fellows of Harvard College and Routledge & Kegan Paul Ltd.

Hilary Putnam, "What Is Innate and Why: Comments on the Debate," from Massimo Piatelli-Palmarini, ed., *The Debate between Noam Chomsky and Jean Piaget* (Cambridge, Mass.: Harvard Univ. Press, 1980). Copyright © 1980 by the President and Fellows of Harvard College and Routledge & Kegan Paul Ltd.

Noam Chomsky, *Rules and Representations* (New York: Columbia Univ. Press, 1980). © 1980 by Noam Chomsky.

Jerry A. Fodor, *Modularity of Mind* (Cambridge, Mass.: MIT Press, 1983). © 1983 The Massachusetts Institute of Technology. Reprinted by permission of MIT Press.

William Marslen-Wilson and Lorraine Komisarjevsky Tyler, "Against Modularity," in J. Garfield, ed., *Modularity in Knowledge Representation and Natural-Language Understanding* (Cambridge, Mass.: MIT Press, 1987). © 1987 The Massachusetts Institute of Technology. Reprinted by permission of MIT Press.

Dan Sperber, "The Modularity of Thought and the Epidemiology of Representations," in Lawrence Hirshfield and Susan Gelman, eds., *Domain Specificity in Cognition and Culture* (Cambridge: Cambridge Univ. Press, 1994). Reprinted with the permission of Cambridge University Press.

Neil Smith, "Dissociation and Modularity: Reflections on Language and Mind." Reprinted from "Dissociation and Modularity: Reflections on Language and Mind," by Neil Smith, in *Mind, Brain, and Language: Multidisciplinary Perspectives*, Marie T. Banich and Molly A. Mack, eds. (Mahwah, N.J.: Lawrence Erlbaum, 2003). Reprinted by permission.

Thomas Hobbes, *Leviathan, or the Matter, Forme, and Power of a Commonwealth Ecclesiasticall and Civill* (New York: Macmillan, Collier Books, 1962). Reprinted with the permission of Scribner, an imprint of Simon & Schuster Adult Publishing Group, from *Leviathan* by Thomas Hobbes, edited by Michael Oakeshott. Copyright © 1962 by Macmillan Publishing Company.

John Stuart Mill, *A System of Logic, Ratiocinative and Inductive, Being a Connected View of the Principles of Evidence and the Methods of Scientific Investigation*, 8th edition (London: Longmans, Green, Reader, and Dyer, 1872).

William James, *The Principles of Psychology*, volume 1 (New York: Henry Holt, 1890).

James L. Rumelhart, David E. McClelland, and Geoffrey E. Hinton, "The Appeal of Parallel Distributed Processing," in David E. Rumelhart, James L. McClelland, and the PDP Research Group, *Parallel Distributed Processing: Explorations in the Microstructure of Cognition* (Cambridge, Mass.: MIT Press, 1986). Copyright 1986 by The Massachusetts Institute of Technology.

Jerry A. Fodor and Zenon W. Pylyshyn, "Connectionism and Cognitive Architecture: A Critical Analysis," *Cognition* 28 (1988): 2–71. Reprinted with permission from Elsevier.

Paul Smolensky, "The Constituent Structure of Connectionist Mental States: A Reply to Fodor and Pylyshyn," *Southern Journal of Philosophy* 26 (1987, suppl.): 137–161. Reprinted by permission of the publisher.

Jerry A. Fodor and Brian P. McLaughlin, "Connectionism and the Problem of Systematicity: Why Smolensky's Solution Doesn't Work," *Cognition* 35 (1990): 183–204. Reprinted with permission from Elsevier.

Tim van Gelder, "What Is the 'D' in 'PDP'? A Survey of the Concept of Distribution." Reprinted from "What Is the 'D' in 'PDP'? A Survey of the Concept of Distribution," by Timothy van Gelder, in *Philosophy and Connectionist Theory*, William Ramsey, Stephen P. Stich, and David E. Rumelhart, eds. (Mahwah, N.J.: Lawrence Erlbaum, 1991). Reprinted by permission.

William Ramsey, Stephen P. Stich, and Joseph Garon, "Connectionism, Eliminativism, and the Future of Folk Psychology." Reprinted from "Connectionism, Eliminativism, and the Future of Folk Psychology" by William Ramsey, Stephen P. Stich, and Joseph Garon, in *Philosophy and Connectionist Theory*, William Ramsey, Stephen P. Stich, and David E. Rumelhart, eds. (Mahwah, N.J.: Lawrence Erlbaum, 1991). Reprinted by permission.

The Philosophy of Mind

I The Mind–Body Problem

Introduction

This part of the book is devoted to what is no doubt one of the oldest philosophical topics: the "mind–body problem." The "problem" here is to explain what relation (if any) an individual's mind bears to the physical world—in particular, to his body. Certain answers suggest themselves even to someone entirely unfamiliar with the philosophical debate: that the mind (or "soul") is an immaterial thing, or that the mind is just the brain. But if the history of philosophy has not yielded a conclusive answer to this question, it has at least offered a surprising number of possible views. The major variations are surveyed in the first section, "Classic Positions." The second section, "Materialism(s)," focuses on what are perhaps the three most prevalent positions in recent philosophy of mind: functionalism, reductive materialism, and eliminative materialism. The third section, "Mind and Subjective Experience," explores a topic that many have taken to form the true puzzle (or even mystery) concerning the mind and its relation to the natural world: the first-person, subjective features of conscious experience (sometimes called "phenomenological" qualities, or "qualia"), and the enormous divide there seems to be between consciousness and unconscious matter.

A Classic Positions

Although the claim is controversial, Aristotle (384–322 B.C.E.) may be thought of as the first functionalist. In his discussion of definition—which he takes to express the formula, or essence, of a thing—Aristotle describes objects as combinations of *form* and *matter*. He argues that there are many cases where the form of the object is what's essential to being such an object, while the matter is not. For example, a sphere made of bronze has its geometrical shape as an essential part of being a sphere, but it is, as a sphere, only coincidentally made of bronze (since it would still be a sphere even if it were made of tin or marble). Because the form of a sphere can be realized in many different substances, we know that the form and the material substance are not identical. Contemporary philosophers would call this a *multiple instantiation* argument, for it appeals to the fact that a single form can be "instantiated" (realized) in many different physical substances. Although, as it turns out, the form of the soul is only realized in material like bones and muscle, Aristotle warns that we should not make the mistake of thinking of this matter as essential to the mind—just as, if the only spheres we ever saw were made of bronze, we would still not count the bronze as a defining aspect of spheres.

(It should be noted that while geometric shape is essential to spheres, Aristotle's concept of "form" does not always involve an object's *mathematical* features. For many types of objects, the form is the *purpose* of such an object, *what it's for*. For example, the *form* of the eye is seeing, because that's what eyes are *for*; and that is why objects that don't perform that function—for example, the "eyes" of a statue—don't count as real eyes. So in fact we find in Aristotle's theory hints of two *different* sorts of functionalism: the functionalism of abstract mathematical structure, which Putnam argues for; and the functionalism of purpose and biological "functions," promoted by authors such as James, Angell, and Lycan.)

René Descartes (1596–1650) provides perhaps the best-known statement of dualism—the view that minds and bodies are different sorts of things, made of different *substances*. Starting with the experience of his own mental existence, Descartes asks which features of himself, as a mind, he cannot conceivably lack—these being the essential features of a mind. He concludes that *thought* is the only feature essential to being a mind ("thought," for Descartes, including pretty much any conscious experience—emotions, sensations, deciding, remembering, etc.). Applying this same conceivability test to bodies (physical objects), Descartes concludes that only *spatial extension* is essential to being a body. Since minds and bodies have different essential features, Descartes concludes that they must be two different sorts of thing—in particular, that the mind is an immaterial object.

John Locke (1632–1704) opposes Descartes's appeal to *conceivability arguments*, insisting that our knowledge and concepts are far too limited to provide the kind of certainty that those arguments take for granted. According to Locke, our knowledge of the world is limited both by our *imperfect evidence* and by the *limited ideas* we use to understand this evidence. Even in an area like mathematics, where we have a perfectly clear idea of a triangle, we cannot easily understand everything involved in the idea—it took centuries of mathematical reasoning to deduce various truths about triangles from our idea of them. Our concept of matter is much more imperfect, and some of the most basic and universal features of matter that we know from experience (such as gravitational attraction) cannot simply be deduced from this concept. So, Locke insists, any attempt to stake out limits on what matter can do, through a conceivability argument, is simply idle speculation. He concludes that, *for all we know*, God could give matter the mysterious power of thought as easily as He gave it its known physical powers; so, *for all we know*, the mind *could* be just a material thing. (It is important to note that Locke does not claim to have *proven* materialism true—in fact, he preferred dualism—only that the issue cannot be decided through appeal to our bare *concepts* of mind and matter.)

George Berkeley (1685–1753) presents an argument for idealism. This is a form of monism—the view that everything in the universe is made of the same substance; and in the case of idealism, that one substance is *mind*. All we know about physical objects, Berkeley argues, is what we perceive—our entire concept of an apple, for instance, involves just the qualities of the apple that we see, taste, touch, etc. So, he concludes, the apple *is* nothing more than that group of sensory qualities. And since sensory qualities exist in sensations, the apple—and likewise all other objects of the senses—are really just clusters of sensations in our minds.

Although Gottfried Wilhelm Leibniz (1646–1716) was critical of Berkeley's views, his own position is similar in certain ways. In place of material atoms, he proposes that the world is composed of "monads"—basically, mental atoms, whose only features are *perceptions* of the world. Leibniz argues that nonliving, physical parts could never combine to form something living, or having perceptions; so the very stuff, or "material" that conscious, living beings are made of, must itself be alive and aware. He distinguishes, however, between those monads that merely perceive the world, and those that can also reflect on their perceptions and are aware that they perceive—a more advanced state which Leibniz calls "apperception." Humans, having apperception, are capable of rising above mere habitual association of ideas, to understand the eternal truths of mathematics, philosophy, and ethics. However, Leibniz holds that even in apperception, when I am reflectively aware of my perceptions, I do not have a perfect grasp of all the parts of my perception: the tiny, atomic perceptions making up my perceptual state are far too small for me to focus on, so that I am only aware of the large-scale layout of my perception. In this respect, Leibniz may have pioneered the view that we have mental representations outside the reach of conscious access—what we would now call "unconscious mental states."

Julien Offray DeLaMettrie (1709–1751), a French doctor who studied a variety of illnesses, argues here for reductive materialism (sometimes known as the "identity theory"). This is a form of *monism* that claims that everything in the universe is made of *matter*. Arguing that only factual data, from medical and anatomical case studies, can reveal the true nature of the mind, DeLaMettrie first cites the extensive *correlations* between bodily and mental conditions. For instance, anxiety can prevent the body from sleeping, while bodily exhaustion can prevent a sleeping soldier from perceiving the sounds of battle; fearful thoughts can increase heart rate; and drugs such as opium, alcohol, and caffeine can alter our mental states. In addition, he appeals to examples from comparative anatomy and ethology to stress the common elements between humans and other animals—for example, common brain structures matched by parallel cognitive functions, and evidence for a sense of values in animals similar to that of humans. On the basis of such correlations, DeLaMettrie concludes that everything in the universe—including the human mind—is made of a single, *physical* substance.

The reading by Auguste Comte (1798–1857) is part of a theory of scientific progress he calls "positive philosophy." On this view, the achievements of science so far (Comte was writing in the 1830s) assure us that we will eventually develop a complete, unified body of scientific theory covering every aspect of reality. Comte presents a model of this scientific knowledge where chemistry is built up from physics, biology from chemistry, and sociology (a science first suggested by Comte) from biology. Surprisingly, psychology has no place in this model, since Comte thinks psychology is far too unscientific to survive the march of progress. Traditional philosophical psychology, he argues, focuses at best only on the *intellectual* features of *normal humans*, thereby neglecting data available from studies of emotions and mental illness, and comparative studies of animals. As a result of this detachment from data, the traditional picture of the mind is populated with objects—for example, the (alleged) faculties of sensation, memory, imagination, and judgment, and a single, unified "self"—that, according to Comte, scientific developments are revealing to be mere fictions, relics of an outdated theory. In their place will be entirely new and different faculties that, he explains, are already being developed by the latest brain research—in particular, Gall and Spurzheim's theory of phrenology (discussed further in chapter 64). While Comte admits that these theories of the brain will require further revision—so much so that we cannot yet picture the final set of categories it will provide—he is confident that it will not include such traditional psychological objects and faculties.

Comte's view is like reductive materialism in rejecting a nonphysical second substance. Unlike the reductive materialist, however, he does *not* foresee a reduction of traditional psychological states and faculties to neuroscientific counterparts, since he thinks traditional psychological categories will be scrapped. In this sense his views seem closer to eliminative materialism (see chapter 16): he doubts that the traditional mental objects and faculties are composed of matter, because he thinks scientific progress will reveal that *they simply don't exist.*

John Stuart Mill (1806–1873) responds to Comte's attack on traditional psychology, providing a methodological argument that psychology will remain valuable as a separate science. While Mill agrees that materialism may be a plausible answer to the *ontological* question about the mind (the question of what the mind really is), he argues that we must not overlook the *methodological* question of how science should best proceed to study the mind. Even if we hold that mental states are brain states, the brain is so complex and so poorly understood that we will need to study mental regularities independently of brain research. Thus, Mill concludes, the study of mind (psychology) should continue to exist as a separate science, even if materialism turns out to be true.

William James (1842–1910) begins his essay by promoting a form of neutral monism. On this view, everything is made of the same substance (which James calls "experience"); but since that substance makes up both the mental and the physical equally, it is no more one than the other. What makes a (neutral) phenomenon *mental,* or *physical,* according to James, is not the *stuff* it is made of, but the other phenomena it is *connected with.* An imagined tree, for example, would be immediately followed by something else entirely—perhaps an imagined unicorn, or whatever I choose to think of—and is under the complete control of my will. But a "physical" tree-phenomenon is followed by other, closely related, tree-phenomena (what we call the "other sides" of the tree) and is disconnected from any of my attempts to will it to be something else. Given just one (split-second) tree-phenomenon in isolation, James argues, there would be nothing about it that would make it mental or physical. And that is because being *mental* or *physical* isn't a matter of some feature *inside* the tree-phenomenon, but rather a matter of the different relations it has to other things *outside* it. By the end of the essay, in fact, James has abandoned any real interest in the "substance" things are made of, and his view has shifted to a form of functionalism, where an object's nature is determined by the place that object holds in a network of relationships.

This early "functionalist" viewpoint was promoted in psychology as well as in philosophy, by largely the same group of people—most famously, William James, John Dewey, and James's student James Rowland Angell (1869–1949). Angell presents functionalist psychology as an alternative to what he calls "structuralism"—the introspectionism of psychologists like Wundt and Titchener, who focused exclusively on the immediate texture and experience of sensations. By contrast, psychological functionalism is inspired by evolutionary theory and views mental faculties (and even individual mental events) in terms of the *function* they play in the overall mental system.

As Angell points out, once mental states are defined in terms of what role they play, questions about *what they're made of* become relatively unimportant. For instance, my current memory of my tenth birthday might be "made up of" certain colors, feelings, and so on, while the memory I had twenty years ago of the same event was made up of different (perhaps more vivid) sensations. Still, since both streams of sensation served the same role in my mind (pointing to that past event), they both count as memories-of-my-tenth-birthday. So, Angell concludes, different individuals might have entirely different immediate experiences (colors, sounds, feelings, etc.)—what philosophers call "qualia"—but from a functionalist point of view, they could nonetheless have the same mental states. (Later philosophers will disagree as to whether leaving out the qualia in this way is a point in *favor* of functionalism, or a point *against* it—see chapters 14 and 28, below.)

The psychological functionalism of the early twentieth century gave way to a quite different approach, as Angell's own case illustrates: his most famous student, John Watson, broke away from functionalism to develop the theory of behaviorism. (In fact, a somewhat similar shift is suggested in the article by Peirce, in chapter 47.) Gilbert Ryle (1900–1976) likewise develops a basically behaviorist approach, though from a more philosophical angle. Noting how certain misunderstandings of ordinary language ("category mistakes") can lead people to draw bizarre conclusions, Ryle claims to find the origins of Descartes's dualism in just such a linguistic confusion. While our ordinary mental terminology of "belief" and "desire" actually refers to types of behavior and dispositions to behave, people misconstrue these phrases as referring to some invisible objects *behind* the behavior. As Ryle stresses at the end of this chapter, his view is (rather like the views of James and Angell) neutral about the *substance* of mind, and for that reason it supports neither idealism nor reductive materialism.

B Materialism(s): Function, Reduction, and Elimination

U. T. Place (1924–2000) attempts to defuse some of the objections to the identity theory (reductive materialism). Place argues that two things can turn out to be identical even if our concepts or definitions of them are different; the term "lightning," for example, may not *mean* the same thing as "electrical discharge," but we can still discover that lightning and electrical discharge are, as a matter of fact, identical. Likewise, though "mind" and "body" may have different definitions, we can nonetheless discover that mind and body are identical. According to Place, part of what makes us believe that lightning *is* an electrical discharge in the atmosphere—rather than being two different, but correlated, things—is that our scientific theory of electricity and optics *explains why* electrical discharge would yield the usual appearance of lightning. Likewise, he suggests, if our study of the brain can explain *why* our conscious states have their particular subjective, "phenomenological" qualities, then we would have strong evidence that such conscious states are just brain processes. Place holds (in an argument taken up by Smart, in chapter 23) that central to this explanation will be showing that common sorts of brain states underlie experiences with common subjective features—for example, that the brain states involved when I see an orange afterimage are relevantly similar to those involved in seeing an orange object.

In a very influential paper, Hilary Putnam argues against both philosophical behaviorism and reductive materialism, in favor of a view recent philosophers have come to call "functionalism." However, whereas earlier functionalists like James and Angell were inspired by the "functions" of evolutionary theory, Putnam is inspired more by the "functions" of mathematics, and particularly of *computing* theory. He suggests that the mind can be thought of as a *Turing machine*—a type of abstract computing device. Computing machines can be realized, or "instantiated," in many different kinds of hardware—silicon chips, Tinkertoy models, and, according to Putnam, the human body. Putnam argues that this "multiple instantiability" is evidence against reductive materialism: because a given psychological state (e.g., pain) can be realized in creatures with nervous systems quite different from our own, and indeed can presumably even be realized by the silicon-based creatures of science fiction, there is no single physical type that correlates with the psychological type *pain*. And if no chemical-physical "definition" of pain is possible, that means that the psychological state, pain, will not *reduce* to any particular neurophysiological state.

(It is worth noting that this sort of functionalism is *compatible* with everything in the universe being a material thing—it may be that the only hardware that exists in the universe, for our mental "program" to run on, is material. And in fact most philosophers who subscribe to computational functionalism do claim that everything in the universe is material. Indeed, the possibility of such a nonreductive materialism has been considered an especially attractive feature of this sort of functionalism: it claims to offer a materialist theory, taken to be compatible with a scientific worldview, but without mental states "reducing" to any particular chemical-physical state.)

Ned Block presents an attack on functionalism, arguing that any functional definition of mental states will be either too liberal (ascribing mental states to creatures that don't really have them), or too chauvinistic (failing to ascribe mental states to creatures that do have them). In setting up his argument, he surveys a number of concerns that have been raised against functionalism, including the problem of accounting for the phenomenology of mental states—the qualitiative features, or "qualia," which Block believes will be left out of the purely *relational* definitions of functional states.

John Searle argues against the functionalist view that mental states could reduce to computational states, by constructing a thought experiment (similar to one developed by Leibniz, in chapter 5). He pictures a system whose inputs and outputs are perfectly grammatical, coherent Chinese sentences, but containing only Searle and a large manual of input sentences and the appropriate output responses. In this case, Searle says, he and his manual together would perfectly model the computational states of a fluent Chinese speaker, even though Searle doesn't know any Chinese. Since, in this case, he would execute the right computational states and behavior, but *without* the matching mental states (of *understanding* what the Chinese words mean), Searle concludes that the functionalist account of the mind must be incorrect—being a mind cannot be *just* a matter of running a computer program.

Paul Churchland argues for eliminative materialism—a form of materialist monism that holds that the objects of traditional psychology will *not* reduce to material states, because such objects will turn out *not to exist* at all. Churchland uses the name "folk psychology" for our everyday psychological talk about beliefs, desires, hopes, decisions, and the like. (Philosophers call such states "propositional attitudes," because the target of these states is traditionally assumed to be some *sentence* or *proposition*—for example, the belief that *it will rain today*, the desire that *we have ice cream after dinner*, the hope that *we win the race*.) Churchland insists that folk psychology is a genuine *theory* about our inner life—a theory permitting us to predict and explain one another's behavior and inner states. But as a theory, it runs the risk of being factually wrong, just as many scientific theories of the past have turned out to be. As evidence that folk psychology may indeed be false, Churchland notes that the basic premises of folk psychology have not changed in over two thousand years; that it has retreated, rather than expanded, in the domain it covers (since, e.g., storms and earthquakes are no longer explained in terms of the beliefs and desires of gods); and that most of the phenomena of mental life (e.g., mental illness, sleep, learning, and vision) cannot be explained in terms of folk psychology. But while he recognizes that elimination of folk psychology by some superior, neuroscientific theory of the mind would involve an enormous conceptual upheaval, Churchland suggests that this would ultimately be a constructive step, opening the way to future possibilities that now seem only the stuff of science fiction.

Patricia Churchland presents an attack on the functionalist's multiple instantiation argument, claiming that the notion of reduction the functionalist uses is too restrictive—so restrictive, in fact, that by those standards it is not clear *any* science or theory could be said to have been reduced to a more fundamental one. The theory of thermodynamics, for instance, is widely taken to have been reduced to statistical mechanics; but as Churchland notes, a kind of multiple instantiation argument is possible here as well. For in gases, temperature is reduced to mean molecular kinetic energy, while in solids it is something else, and in a vacuum something else again. Yet we do not conclude from this that there was no reduction; instead, there were piecemeal, *domain-specific* reductions. Churchland argues that the same could occur for mental states—for example, reducing pain-in-a-human to one biological structure, pain-in-a-mollusk to some other structure, and so on. Noting as well that scientists will adjust higher-level theories to better match the lower, "reducing" theories, Churchland concludes that reductive materialism may be practically *inevitable*.

Jaegwon Kim has long been similarly critical of functionalism's antireductionist claims. Here he presents a dilemma for a functionalist who appeals to the *multiple realization* (or multiple instantiability) of mental states: *either* such states reduce in spite of their multiple realizations (by way of domain-specific reduction of the sort argued for in the previous chapter by Patricia Churchland, and in earlier work by Kim himself); *or* they are revealed as scientifically illegitimate, in the manner of eliminative materialism. While a mental state like pain might indeed be realized in many different physical "hardwares"—one sort for humans, another for robots, and a third type for certain aliens—Kim asks why we couldn't simply give a physical definition of pain as being "*either* the human hardware for pain, *or* the robot hardware for pain, *or* the alien hardware for pain." (Such a series of options, joined together with "or"—or with the "or"-symbol "$\vee$"—is called a *disjunction*; and a property consisting of *either* one physical property *or* a second physical property, *or* ... is a *disjunctive property*.) By way of blocking such physical "definitions" of the mental, functionalists have claimed that disjunctive properties are not real, scientific properties—because, for instance, such disjunctive properties don't show up in the laws of physical science. But Kim argues that functional states, which themselves straddle a wide disjunction of physical states, should then likewise be rendered unscientific. When, for example, it was discovered that jade is not one mineral, but two quite different (though similar-looking) minerals, jade was no longer taken to be an objective mineral family. And Kim suggests that if mental states like "pain" are likewise realized in very different chemical structures, then they should similarly be discarded as objective scientific objects—resulting in eliminative materialism. So, he concludes, the multiply realizable objects of functionalist psychology will either be *reduced* or *eliminated*; an independent, nonreducing science of psychology is not a genuine possibility.

Both Noam Chomsky and Bas van Fraassen hold that the argument over whether or not the mind is a material thing may ultimately be a *meaningless* dispute. According to Chomsky, since, as a matter of scientific methodology, we revise our theories to accommodate new data, the notion of "physical body" in particular is subject to ongoing revision by the sciences. So, although Descartes took himself to have found the correct concept of body, true for all time, that concept was soon superseded by the Newtonian notion of body, and research in particle physics during the last century has continued to alter our understanding of the nature of physical bodies. In light of this, Chomsky argues, the very notion of a "mind–body problem" is ill defined—for if certain facts about mental phenomena prove to be incompatible with our theory of physical body, we will simply change our understanding of the physical world to accommodate these facts. Since our scientific understanding of physical bodies is basically "whatever we need it to be, to fit all the data," there is no genuine possibility of a clash between features of the mind and the physical sciences—and so, no point to arguments over whether or not the mind will ultimately turn out to be a "physical" thing.

Philosopher of science Bas van Fraassen argues that self-proclaimed materialist philosophers (whether reductive materialists, eliminative materialists, or nonreductive materialists) are fundamentally confused as to the nature of the "materialism" they argue for. The history of science shows again and again that attempts to define the "physical" or "material" in specific, factual terms are contradicted by later scientific developments. For example, Descartes's definition of the material as something extended in space does not fit Hertz's point-particles; and defining the material as fundamental physical particles, and larger things built of these, would not count Newton's forces or Huyghen's light-waves as material. Even failure of the mental to correlate systematically with brain events (in the manner required for reduction or "supervenience") would not lead to the conclusion that the mental is nonphysical—since quantum mechanics claims a similar unpredictability for particle decay, yet no one has concluded from this that such particles are nonphysical. If the materialist tries to get around the problem by claiming that only the objects of future, completed physics exist, then he doesn't (before we reach such a scientific "golden age") know *what* he believes in. Moreover, if physics simply evolves forever, and there is no *final* theory, then someone believing that only the objects of "the final theory" exist would wind up believing that *nothing* exists.

Two things are striking about this, for van Fraassen: even though philosophers take materialism to lie at the heart of scientific inquiry, guiding and constraining which kinds of theories are possible, the development of physical theory repeatedly overflows and contradicts any statement of such "constraints"; and yet, even though each age's "materialism" ends up refuted by the development of later scientific theory, materialism in philosophy lives on. Van Fraassen explains both facts by arguing that materialism is not a set of factual claims at all, but a kind of "stance," a *commitment* to following the science of the time. Materialist philosophers, he thinks, suffer from "false consciousness," a confusion about what their view really is: while they think they are defending definite claims, they are in fact only expressing a certain *attitude* of admiration and obedience to whatever science says. And while they present materialism as a set of views guiding and constraining scientific theorizing, van Fraassen claims they are mistaken about what's guiding what: since materialism is really just a commitment to believe whatever current science says, scientific theory changes as required to fit new data, and materialism brings up the rear, simply shadowing the science of the day.

C Mind and Subjective Experience

C. I. Lewis (1883–1964) separates mental states into two components: the "immediately given," or "sensuous," which is the input to the mind not created by the mind; and the "form" or "interpretation," which the mind imposes on that "given." When looking at an ink pen, for instance, I may have the same "immediately given"—color, shape, and so on—that a baby, or someone ignorant of pens, would have; but by mentally putting it in the "pen" category, my awareness of the pen is different from theirs. And while I can categorize this "given" in different ways (looking at the pen as a cylinder, or as a bad bargain), I *must*, according to Lewis, always mentally fit it into *some* group or "category"; we *never* experience the "given" all by itself, stripped of any conceptual categorization (except perhaps in special aesthetic experiences). Specific "givens"—a shade of red, a musical note of a particular loudness—are what Lewis calls qualia. And while he believes we can recognize qualia when encountering them again, he insists that they are, in themselves, neither *communicable* nor *knowable*, since both language and knowledge always require use of categories that relate various experiences together (while the given in itself is independent of any categories). Though an immediate awareness, or "acquaintance," with qualia leaves no room for error, it yields knowledge only when the qualia are fit into some categories; but the act of categorizing introduces the possibility of error. For instance, by categorizing certain qualia as a "ripe apple," I commit myself to (risky) hypothetical claims about further experiences, such as that *if it is bitten, it will yield a sweet taste.*

By separating mental events into the two components of experience and categories, and recognizing categorization as an essential ingredient in knowledge and communication, Lewis believes we can resolve a number of puzzles that such immediate experience poses. On this view, for example, it is no longer a mystery why we find ourselves incapable of communicating our immediate experiences through language. We are also able to reconcile the traditional belief that we couldn't possibly be wrong about our immediate experience with the modern view that all knowledge claims are fallible, capable of turning out wrong. And since such qualia are not candidates for knowledge in the first place, it is unsurprising that we can't know whether one person's qualia are the same as another's.

Herbert Feigl (1902–1988) thinks qualia pose no problem for reductive materialism, once we resolve conceptual ambiguities in the concepts "subjective" and "physical." To call features of experience "subjective" is, on its most reasonable reading, simply to say they are *directly experienced* (as opposed to being inferred from other evidence) and *introspectible.* At the same time, Feigl isolates two different senses of "physical" terms or concepts: those used by the science of physics (what he calls "physical_2"); and, more broadly, anything in principle testable or detectable through public, intersubjective methods ("physical_1"). Feigl suspects that subjective experience can be known and described by way of physical_2 concepts (amounting to the *reduction* of such states to those studied in physics); but he argues that, even barring reduction, knowledge of such experiences in physical_1 terms (basically, *objective* knowledge of these experiences, in whatever terms) is all that is required to reconcile qualia with a purely physical world. Although our sensory experiences (with their qualitative features) are our normal point of entry into knowledge of objective reality, Feigl claims, it is the nature of objective (intersubjectively confirmable) knowledge that creatures with various sorts of qualia and perceptual systems can, in principle, all arrive at the same facts. The particular qualitative experiences used will, for the most part, make a difference only to *how quickly* such facts can be determined. For example, while a creature with microscopic vision could detect in a glance facts about microorganisms that I can only determine through complex labwork and theoretical inference, we could still both come to know those facts; likewise, a blind neuroscientist with enough equipment and theory could come to know facts about my visual experience (for example, the colors involved) that I am immediately aware of.

What is required for the identification of conscious states with physical states is, then, just sufficient evidence for correlation between the two. Feigl argues that the qualitative features of experience possess more structure than skeptics acknowledge—for example, visual experience is extended in a two-dimensional space, with colors further arranged along dimensions of hue, saturation, and brightness. He concludes that if the structural features we directly introspect can be systematically correlated with physical features of the nervous system, then the most reasonable scientific theory explaining these correlations will be that conscious states simply *are* states of the nervous system.

J. J. C. Smart continues Place's argument (chapter 12), responding to several variations on the Cartesian objection to reductive materialism. By providing features that the mind has, but physical bodies lack (and vice versa), Descartes (in chapter 2) concluded that mind and body cannot be the same thing. But a dualist could argue in the same way that when I see an orange afterimage, there is nothing orange in my brain to correspond with this—in fact, there may be nothing in the physical world corresponding to that orange patch; so there must be a nonreducing, *nonphysical* realm in which these features exist. By way of reply, Smart suggests that the word "seeing" is used in somewhat different (though related) ways here: there is talk about seeing a real object (such as an orange, in a bowl of fruit), and also "seeing" an orange afterimage. The connection between these two sorts of "seeing," according to Smart, is that when I see an orange afterimage, there is a process occurring in my brain similar to the process that occurs when I really do see an orange-colored object. In both cases what gets reduced, according to the reductive materialist, is just the *process of seeing.* So in the case of seeing an orange afterimage, it is the *process* of seeing that is identical to a *process* in the brain. Since the orange patch itself isn't being reduced to a brain state (only the *seeing-an-orange-patch*), nothing in the brain need correspond to the orange afterimage. Moreover, the reductive materialist is only claiming that, for example, seeing an afterimage is *in fact* identical to a brain process—*not* that the person experiencing it *realizes* it's a brain process, or uses the phrases "seeing an afterimage" and "brain process" with the same definitional meaning. Here again, Smart holds, dualist arguments can be answered: though "seeing an afterimage" is something ordinary people report, while "having a certain brain process" is not, this is only a reflection of ordinary language definitions, not a difference in the things themselves.

Thomas Nagel argues that the first-person, "phenomenological" experience of conscious states (what he calls the "subjective character" of mental states) is ignored by all current materialist attempts to reduce the mental—rendering any such account incomplete and leaving the mind–body problem an unsolved mystery. "What it's like" to have a certain conscious experience is, by its very nature, what it's like *for the experiencer*; so the subjective character of experience is intrinsically linked to a particular *point of view*. (This, Nagel believes, is why only someone who's had a similar experience can understand what a certain experience is like for a certain individual: because knowing what it's like is a matter of adopting that individual's point of view, and the points of view we can imagine are limited by the sorts of experience we have had.) But since what makes a scientific theory objective is precisely that it *doesn't* adopt any particular point of view, it appears impossible to faithfully translate subjective experience into the objective vocabulary of science. Nagel points out that none of this proves that the mind is not a material thing, only that we can't currently understand what is involved in such materialism if it is true. But until philosophers of mind face up to this problem of subjective experience, he insists, the mind–body problem will remain unsolved.

Sydney Shoemaker reviews two related arguments against functionalism, both appealing to qualia: the inverted spectrum and absent qualia arguments. In a case of inverted qualia, an individual would have exactly the functional structure as you (in terms of how each mental state is causally related to perceptions, behavior, and other internal states), but with all qualia reversed (so that, e.g., grass perceptions exhibit red qualia, and stop signs exhibit green qualia). In a case of absent qualia, the functional structure is accompanied by no qualia at all. Shoemaker argues that, although these cases might appear genuinely possibilities, in fact the presence (and nature) of qualia will show up within the functional structure after all. For a qualitative state causes a qualitative belief—a belief that one has that qualitative state; and such a belief clearly plays a role in the overall functional structure of the mind. So if a different qualitative state (or no qualitative state at all) were present, a different qualitative belief would be present as well, and the functional structure would not be the same. Shoemaker concludes that, if inverted or absent qualia are indeed reflected in functional structure in this way, qualia will not pose the problem for functionalism that critics have claimed.

By appealing to conceivability and possibility in a manner somewhat like Descartes, Saul Kripke presents an argument in support of dualism. While reductive materialists like Place and Smart took mental processes to be *contingently identical* to brain processes—just as lightning is said to be contingently identical to electrical discharge—Kripke argues that belief in "contingent identity" stems from a confusion between *what something is* and our *methods for detecting it*. Taking, for example, heat to be the motion of molecules, Kripke holds that such an identity is not at all contingent—the identity is a *necessary* fact about that thing. When people claim it possible for heat not to be such motion, they are in fact imagining a situation where our usual *ways of detecting heat* (bodily sensations of warmth, for example) don't accompany that motion. Although such a situation is certainly possible, according to Kripke, it shows only that such *methods of detection* are contingently linked to the motion of molecules—not that heat itself is. But then a puzzle arises for the claimed identity between conscious experiences, such as pain, and brain processes: whereas brain processes may likewise be only *contingently* linked to our method of detecting them (namely, through first-person awareness), it seems wrong to say that pains are only contingently linked to the painful way they feel to us; on the contrary, pains are, according to Kripke, by their nature (hence *necessarily*) painful-feeling things. But if pains are necessarily painful-feeling, while brain processes (and physical processes generally) are not, then we have evidence that pains (and other conscious states) are not physical processes.

William Lycan proposes a variation on functionalism that he thinks can address critics' concerns about qualia. Instead of the mathematical-computational concept of "function" (as formal mapping) which Putnam proposed (chapter 13), Lycan suggests that functionalism should be based on a "teleological" (purposive) concept of "function" (hence marking a return to something closer to the earlier functionalism of James and Angell). Lycan takes the mind to be an interlocking collection of agents, each serving some functional role—where each of these agents is itself a collection of yet smaller parts, each serving some purpose in that (smaller) system, and so on. At bottom the smallest actors serve functions so simple they can be performed by physical mechanisms, hence providing a lower limit to the levels of teleology. A functionalism of this sort, Lycan argues, addresses Ned Block's criticism (in chapter 14) that any level of functional description will either be too liberal or too restrictive—for on this model, there need not be any *one* level for functional descriptions. Beliefs, desires, and intentions may be states at a higher, more abstract level (allowing Martians and robots to have these states as well); while for other mental states (perhaps including qualia), the required level may be so low and specific that something like reductive materialism may be true of them. Another possibility this model offers is that a state with qualitative features, such as pain, may be properly defined as a *combination* of functional profile and instantiation base—in which case pain would come in different sorts, for Martians, for robots, and so on—but all still qualifying as pain. Dealt with in this fashion, Lycan concludes, qualitative conscious states pose no special threat to functionalism.

Frank Jackson argues that even a complete physical and functional description of an individual would not yield knowledge of what her experiences are like, and so he concludes that such qualitative features of mental life must be nonphysical. For example, if Mary is raised entirely in a black-and-white environment, she may know all about the mathematical features of light, the physiology of human vision, and so on; but even knowing all that, when she first sees colors, she learns something new—what they look like. So, Jackson concludes, these qualitative features of Mary's experience are something above and beyond all the *physical* facts about vision. In the end, Jackson claims these features may be epiphenomenal—having no causal effect on anything in the world, including our brains and behavior. (For more on *epiphenomenalism*, see Huxley's views in chapter 35.) Against those who claim that such epiphenomenal qualia have no place in our scientific theories of the world, Jackson replies that there may be many things in the universe that are beyond the understanding of the human mind (and the scientific theories it constructs)—and epiphenomenal qualia may be one of these things.

Colin McGinn draws a conclusion similar to Jackson's closing points, arguing that certain fundamental limitations of our minds may prevent us from ever understanding the relation of mind to matter. While McGinn feels it is obvious consciousness must stem from, and be explainable in terms of, some natural property—"natural" properties being roughly the same sort as those studied by the physical sciences—he argues that the sorts of concepts we use (or could ever use) will block us from understanding what this natural seat of consciousness is. He points out that not only are we perplexed when trying to understand how first-person qualities of consciousness arise from currently known material states, but that we draw just as much of a blank even when trying to conceive of some yet-to-be discovered physical states giving rise to consciousness; and this, he thinks, illustrates that future extensions of our natural scientific concepts will no better resolve the mystery of consciousness for us. McGinn stresses that this view is not entirely pessimistic: by tracing the mystery of consciousness back to our own conceptual limitations—rather than to any intrinsic peculiarity of consciousness—we explain why the mind–body problem lives on, without having to appeal to a mysterious, dualistic nature in consciousness itself.

Laurence Nemirow agrees with Nagel and Jackson (chapters 24 and 28) that someone who had never had any visual experiences of color would lack a certain kind of knowledge—for example, knowledge of *what it's like* to see red, knowledge of *what red is like*. But he thinks it is a mistake to conclude from this that there are some special types of properties—"purely subjective properties"—that fall outside the grasp of objective scientific theory. According to Nemirow, the mistake in Nagel's and Jackson's arguments lies in confusing *knowing some fact* (such as what 2+2 equals, or which city is the capital of Italy) with *knowing how to do something*. Knowing what red is like, he claims, is knowing how to do something—namely, *to imagine* red at will. And given the way humans are structured, it is true that someone (such as a blind person) who has never visually experienced red would indeed be unable to imagine red at will (and hence not "know what red is like"). Moreover, this ability to call up an experience in the imagination is involved in other abilities—for example, the ability to "picture" the burglar's face allows me to describe him to a police sketch artist (something not provided by mere ability to *recognize* him if I saw him again). Nemirow claims that this "ability" interpretation seems to fit the way we speak about knowledge of "what it's like" (for example, our saying of some experience that we know, forget, remember, or have discovered *what it's like* is mirrored in our saying that we know, forget, remember, or have discovered *how to do* certain things); and it accounts for this data without needing to postulate any special, nonobjective properties.

Further Reading

A number of more specialized essays on Aristotle's philosophy of mind can be found in *Essays on Aristotle's* De Anima, ed. Martha C. Nussbaum and Amelie Oksenberg Rorty (Clarendon Press: 1992).

In *Thinking Matter: Materialism in Eighteenth-Century Britain* (University of Minnesota Press: 1984), and *Locke and French Materialism* (Oxford University Press: 1991), John Yolton explores the controversy surrounding Locke's suggestion (in chapter 3) that God could give matter the power to think.

In his book *The Physical Basis of Mind* (Truebner: 1877), particularly *Problem III: Animal Automatism*, chapters I and III, George Henry Lewes develops an early version of neutral monism similar to James's view, though distinguishing mental from physical in terms of the *language used* to describe phenomena: the mental is described qualitatively, while the physical is described quantitatively.

Readings in the Philosophy of Psychology, volume I, ed. Ned Block (Harvard University Press: 1980), contains important essays on behaviorism, reductive materialism, and functionalism. Another useful collection of readings is found in William Lycan, ed., *Mind and Cognition* (Basil Blackwell: 1990).

A more detailed discussion of the metaphysics of functionalism and reduction is provided by Jaegwon Kim in *Supervenience and Mind* (Cambridge University Press: 1993). Part 1 of the book, in particular, provides a thorough (though at times technical) investigation of *supervenience* in the philosophy of mind. Kim's *Mind in a Physical World* (MIT Press: 1998) provides a compact overview of his positions on materialism, reductionism, and mental causation.

In somewhat the same way that U. T. Place, in seeking a "contingent" link between mind and body, appealed to the "'is' of composition," some philosophers have more recently explored "composition" or "constitution" as a way of explaining the relation of mind to body. A collection of essays on this topic is provided in Michael Rea, ed., *Material Constitution: A Reader* (Rowman and Littlefield: 1997).

Chomsky and His Critics, ed. Lousie Antony and Norbert Hornstein (Blackwell: 2003), includes an essay by William Lycan criticizing Chomsky's argument against the very idea of a "mind–body problem," as well as a reply by Chomsky.

In his early *Rules for the Direction of the Mind*, Descartes takes ideas of color to derive from the senses, and denies (in Rule 14) that we can "by force of argument" communicate the idea of color we have to a blind man; in his later *Fifth Set of Replies*, however, Descartes allows that a blind man might possibly have normal ideas of color after all. In keeping with his strong anti-innatism, Locke holds in his *Essay on Human Understanding* (book III, chapter 4) that a blind man cannot have the sighted person's ideas of colors. William James, in chapter 2 of his *Psychology: Briefer Course* (Henry Holt: 1892) likewise holds that no amount of physical knowledge will enable a blind man to know what sighted people know firsthand about colors.

In book II, chapter 32 of his *Essay*, Locke also recognizes the possibility of "inverted qualia," but concludes that such cases would be irrelevant for purposes of knowledge. Similarly, Bertrand Russell, in chapter 21 of *The Analysis of Matter* (Dover Books: 1927), holds that the "intrinsic character" of first-person experience (e.g., whether different people have inverted qualia) will fall outside of physical knowledge, but adds that this is unproblematic for scientific purposes.

In *Body and Mind* (Anchor Books: 1970) Keith Campbell presents an argument that qualia (including absent and inverted qualia) pose a problem for a materialist view of the mind, and settles on an epiphenomenalist theory of nonmaterial qualia similar to that of Frank Jackson (in chapter 28).

The Nature of Consciousness: Philosophical Debates, ed. Ned Block, Owen Flanagan, and Güven Güzeldere (MIT Press: 1997), offers a very useful collection of readings on the topic of consciousness, qualia, and related issues.

The "knowledge argument" that Frank Jackson presents in chapter 28 is discussed by numerous authors in Peter J. Ludlow, Yujin Nagasawa, and Daniel Stoljar, eds., *There's Something About Mary: Essays on Phenomenal Consciousness and Frank Jackson's Knowledge Argument* (MIT Press: 2004).

A Classic Positions

1 From *Metaphysics,* Book 7, and *On the Soul,* Book 2

Aristotle

Since a definition is a formula, and every formula has parts, and as the formula is to the thing, so is the part of the formula to the part of the thing, the question is already being asked whether the formula of the parts must be present in the formula of the whole or not. For in some cases the formulae of the parts are seen to be present, and in some not. The formula of the circle does not include that of the segments, but that of the syllable includes that of the letters; yet the circle is divided into segments as the syllable is into letters. And further if the parts are prior to the whole, and the acute angle is a part of the right angle and the finger a part of the animal, the acute angle will be prior to the right angle and the finger to the man. But the latter are thought to be prior; for in formula the parts are explained by reference to them, and in respect also of the power of existing apart from each other the wholes are prior to the parts.

... Let us inquire about the parts of which *substance* consists. If then matter is one thing, form another, the compound of these a third, and both the matter and the form and the compound are substance, even the matter is in a sense called part of a thing, while in a sense *it* is not, but only the elements of which the formula of the form consists. E.g., ... the bronze is a part of the concrete statue, but not of the statue when this is spoken of in the sense of the form. (For the form, or the thing as having form, should be said to be the thing, but the material element by itself must never be said to be so.) And so the formula of the circle does not include that of the segments, but the formula of the syllable includes that of the letters; for the letters are parts of the formula of the form, and not matter, but the segments are parts in the sense of matter on which the form supervenes; yet they are nearer the form than the bronze is when roundness is produced in bronze. But in a sense not even every kind of letter will be present in the formula of the syllable, e.g., particular waxen letters or the letters as movements in the air; for in these also we have already something that is part of the syllable only in the sense that it is its perceptible matter. For even if the line when divided passes away into its halves, or the man into bones and muscles and flesh, it does not follow that they are composed of these as parts of their essence, but rather as matter; and these are parts of the concrete thing, but not also of the form, i.e., of that to which the formula refers; wherefore also they are not present in the formulae. In one kind of formula, then, the formula of such parts will be present, but in another it must not be present, where the formula does not refer to the concrete object. For it is for this reason that some things have as their constituent principles parts into which they pass away, while some have not. Those things which are the form and the matter taken together, e.g., . . . the bronze circle, pass away into these materials, and the matter is a part of them; but those things which do not involve matter but are without matter, and whose formulae are formulae of the form only, do not pass away. . . . Therefore these materials are principles and parts of the concrete things, while of the form they are neither parts nor principles. And therefore the clay statue is resolved into clay and the ball into bronze and Callias into flesh and bones, and again the circle into its segments; for there is a sense of "circle" in which it involves matter. For "circle" is used ambiguously, meaning both the circle, unqualified, and the individual circle, because there is no name peculiar to the individuals.

The truth has indeed now been stated, but still let us state it yet more clearly, taking up the question again. The parts of the formula, into which the formula is divided, are prior to it, either all or some of them. . . . The circle and the semicircle also are in such a relation; for the semicircle is defined by the circle; and so is the finger by the whole body, for a finger is "such and such a part of a man." Therefore the parts which are of the nature of matter, and into which as its matter a thing is divided, are posterior; but those which are of the nature of parts of the formula, and of the substance according to its formula, are prior, either all or some of them. And since the soul of animals (for this is the substance of a living being) is their substance according to the formula, i.e., the form and the essence of a body of a certain kind (at least we shall define each part, if we define it well, not without reference to its function, and this cannot belong to it without perception), so that the parts of soul are prior, either all or some of them, to the concrete "animal," and so too with each individual animal; and the body and its parts are posterior to this, the essential substance, and it is not the substance but the concrete thing that is divided into these parts as its matter: this being so, to the concrete thing these are in a sense prior, but in a sense they are not. For they cannot even exist if severed from the whole; for it is not a finger in any and every state that is the finger of a living thing, but a dead finger is a finger only in name. . . . "A part" may be a part either of the form (i.e., of the essence), or of the compound of the form and the matter, or of the matter itself. But only the parts of the form are parts of the formula, and the formula is of the universal; for "being a circle" is the same as the circle, and "being a soul" the same as the soul. But when we come to the concrete thing, e.g., *this* circle, i.e., one of the individual circles, whether perceptible or intelligible (I mean by intelligible circles the mathematical, and by perceptible circles those of bronze and of wood)—of these there is no definition, but they are known by the aid of intuitive thinking or of perception. . . .

We have stated, then, how matters stand with regard to whole and part, and their priority and posteriority. But when any one asks whether the right angle and the circle and the animal are prior, or the things into which they are divided and of which they consist, i.e., the parts, we must meet the inquiry by saying that the question cannot be answered simply. For if even bare soul is the animal or the living thing, or the soul of each individual is the individual itself, and "being a circle" is the circle, and "being a right angle" and the essence of the right angle is the right angle, then the whole in one sense must be called posterior to the part in one sense, i.e., to the parts included in the formula and to the parts of the individual right angle (for both the material right angle which is made of bronze, and that which is formed by individual lines, are posterior to their parts); the immaterial right angle is posterior to the parts included in the formula, but prior to those included in the particular instance, and the question must not be answered simply. If the soul is something different and is not identical with the animal, even so some parts must, as we have maintained, be called prior and others must not.

... In the case of things which are found to occur in specifically different materials, as a circle may exist in bronze or stone or wood, it seems plain that these, the bronze or the stone, are no part of the essence of the circle, since it is found apart from them. Of things which are *not* seen to exist apart, [even here] there is no reason why the same may not be true, just as if all circles that had ever been seen were of bronze; for none the less the bronze would be no part of the form; but it is hard to eliminate it in thought. E.g., the form of man is always found in flesh and bones and parts of this kind; are these then also parts of the form and the formula? No, they are matter; but because man is not found also in other matters we are unable to perform the abstraction....

We are in the habit of recognizing, as one determinate kind of [being], substance, and that in several senses, (*a*) in the sense of matter or that which in itself is not "a [such-and-such]," and (*b*) in the sense of form or essence, which is that precisely in virtue of which a thing is called "a [such-and-such]," and thirdly (*c*) in the sense of that which is compounded of both (*a*) and (*b*). Now matter is potentiality, form actuality; of the latter there are two grades related to one another as, e.g., knowledge to the exercise of knowledge.

Substances are, by general consent, [taken to include] bodies and especially natural bodies; for they are the principles of all other bodies. Of natural bodies some have life in them, others not; by life we mean self-nutrition and growth (with its correlative decay). It follows that every natural body which has life in it is a substance in the sense of a composite.

But since it is also a *body* of such and such a kind, viz. having life, the *body* cannot be soul; the body is the subject, or matter, not what is attributed to it. Hence the soul must be a substance in the sense of the form of a natural body having life potentially within it. But form is actuality, and thus soul is the actuality of a body as above characterized. Now the word actuality has two senses corresponding respectively to the possession of knowledge and the actual exercise of knowledge. It is obvious that the soul is actuality in the first sense, viz. that of knowledge as possessed, for both sleeping and waking presuppose the existence of soul, and of these waking corresponds to actual knowing, sleeping to knowledge possessed but not employed, and, in the history of the individual, knowledge comes before its employment or exercise.

That is why the soul is the first grade of actuality of a natural body having life potentially in it. The body so described is a body which is organized. The parts of plants in spite of their extreme simplicity are "organs"; e.g., the leaf serves to shelter the pericarp, the pericarp to shelter the fruit, while the roots of plants are analogous to the mouth of animals, both serving for the absorption of food. If, then, we have to give a general formula applicable to all kinds of soul, we must describe it as the first grade of actuality of a natural organized body. That is why we can wholly dismiss as unnecessary the question whether the soul and the body are one: it is as meaningless as to ask whether the wax and the shape given to it by the stamp are one, or generally the matter of a thing and that of which it is the matter....

We have now given an answer to the question, What is soul?—an answer which applies to it in its full extent. It is substance in the sense which corresponds to the definitive formula of a thing's essence. That means that it is "the essential whatness" of a body of the character just assigned. . . . Suppose that the eye were an animal—sight would have been its soul, for sight is the substance, or *essence,* of the eye which corresponds to the formula, the eye being merely the matter of seeing; when seeing is removed the eye is no longer an eye, except in name—it is no more a real eye than the eye of a statue or of a painted figure. We must now extend out consideration from the "parts" to the whole living body; for what the departmental sense is to the bodily part which is its organ, that the whole faculty of sense is to the whole sensitive body as such. . . .

While waking is actuality in a sense corresponding to [actually] seeing, the soul is actuality in the sense corresponding to the power of sight . . . ; the body corresponds to what exists in potentiality; as the pupil *plus* the power of sight constitutes the eye, so the soul *plus* the body constitutes the animal.

From this it indubitably follows that the soul is inseparable from its body, or at any rate that certain parts of it are (if it has parts)—for the actuality of some of them is nothing but the actualities of their bodily parts.

2 From *Meditations on First Philosophy* II and VI and *Reply to Objections* II

René Descartes

By the body I understand all that which can be defined by a certain figure: something which can be confined in a certain place, and which can fill a given space in such a way that every other body will be excluded from it; which can be perceived either by touch, or by sight, or by hearing, or by taste, or by smell: which can be moved in many ways not, in truth, by itself, but by something which is foreign to it, by which it is touched [and from which it receives impressions[1]]: for to have the power of self-movement, as also of feeling or of thinking, I did not consider to appertain to the nature of body: on the contrary, I was rather astonished to find that faculties similar to them existed in some bodies.

But what am I, now that I suppose that there is a certain genius which is extremely powerful, and, if I may say so, malicious, who employs all his powers in deceiving me? Can I affirm that I possess the least of all those things which I have just said pertain to the nature of body? I pause to consider, I revolve all these things in my mind, and I find none of which I can say that it pertains to me. It would be tedious to stop to enumerate them. Let us pass to the attributes of soul and see if there is any one which is in me? What of nutrition or walking [the first mentioned]? But if it is so that I have no body it is also true that I can neither walk nor take nourishment. Another attribute is sensation. But one cannot feel without body, and besides I have thought I perceived many things during sleep that I recognised in my waking moments as not having been experienced at all. What of thinking? I find here that thought is an attribute that belongs to me; it alone cannot be separated from me. I am, I exist, that is certain. But how often? Just when I think; for it might possibly be the case if I ceased entirely to think, that I should likewise cease altogether to exist. I do not now admit anything which is not necessarily true: to speak accurately I am not more than a thing which thinks, that is to say a mind or a soul, or an understanding, or a reason, which are terms whose significance was formerly unknown to me. I am, however, a real thing and really exist; but what thing? I have answered: a thing which thinks....

And first of all, because I know that all things which I apprehend clearly and distinctly can be created by God as I apprehend them, it suffices that I am able to apprehend one thing apart from another clearly and distinctly in order to be certain that the one is different from the other, since they may be made to exist in separation at least by the omnipotence of God; and it does not signify by what power this separation is made in order to compel me to judge them to be different: and, therefore, just because I know certainly that I exist, and that meanwhile I do not remark that any other thing necessarily pertains to my nature or essence, excepting that I am a thinking thing, I rightly conclude that my essence consists solely in the fact that I am a thinking thing [or a substance whose whole essence or nature is to think]. And although possibly (or rather certainly, as I shall say in a moment) I possess a body with which I am very intimately conjoined, yet because, on the one side, I have a clear and distinct idea of myself inasmuch as I am only a thinking and unextended thing, and as, on the other, I possess a distinct idea of body, inasmuch as it is only an extended and unthinking thing, it is certain that this I [that is to say, my soul by which I am what I am], is entirely and absolutely distinct from my body, and can exist without it. . . .

Do you deny that in order to recognise a real distinctness between objects it is sufficient for us to conceive one of them clearly apart from the other? If so, offer us some surer token of real distinction. I believe that none such can be found. What will you say? That those things are really distinct each of which can exist apart from the other. But once more I ask how you will know that one thing can be apart form the other; this, in order to be a sign of the distinctness, should be known. Perhaps you will say that it is given to you by the senses, since you can see, touch, etc., the one thing while the other is absent. But the trustworthiness of the senses is inferior to that of the intellect, and it is in many ways possible for one and the same thing to appear under various guises or in several places or in different manners, and so to be taken to be two things. And finally if you bear in mind what was said at the end of the Second Meditation about wax, you will see that properly speaking not even are bodies themselves perceived by sense, but that they are perceived by the intellect alone, so that there is no difference between perceiving by sense one thing apart from another, and having an idea of one thing and understanding that that idea is not the same as an idea of something else. Moreover, this knowledge can be drawn from no other source than the fact that the one thing is perceived apart from the other; nor can this be known with certainty unless the ideas in each case are clear and distinct. Hence that sign you offer of real distinctness must be reduced to my criterion in order to be infallible.

But if any people deny that they have distinct ideas of mind and body, I can do nothing further than ask them to give sufficient attention to what is said in the Second Meditation. I beg them to note that the opinion they perchance hold, namely, that the parts of the brain join their forces with the soul to form thoughts, has not arisen from any positive ground, but only from the fact that they have never had experience of separation from the body, and have not seldom been hindered by it in their operations, and that similarly if anyone had from infancy continually worn irons on his legs, he would think that those irons were part of his own body and that he needed them in order to walk.

Note

1. All bracketed text is the translator's interpolation.—Eds.

3 From *An Essay Concerning Human Understanding*

John Locke

§1. Knowledge, as has been said, lying in the Perception of the Agreement, or Disagreement, of any of our *Ideas*, it follows from hence, That,

First, We can have *Knowledge* no farther than we have *Ideas*.

§2. *Secondly*, That we can have no *Knowledge* farther, than we can have Perception of that Agreement, or Disagreement: Which Perception being, 1. Either by *Intuition*, or the immediate comparing any two *Ideas*; or, 2. By *Reason*, examining the Agreement, or Disagreement of two *Ideas*, by the Intervention of some others: Or, 3. By *Sensation*, perceiving the Existence of particular Things. Hence it also follows,

§3. *Thirdly*, That we cannot have an *intuitive Knowledge*, that shall extend it self to all our *Ideas*, and all that we would know about them; because we cannot examine and perceive all the Relations they have one to another by *juxta*-position, or an immediate comparison one with another. Thus having the *Ideas* of an obtuse, and an acute angled Triangle, both drawn from equal Bases, and between Parallels, I can by intuitive Knowledge, perceive the one not to be the other; but cannot that way know, whether they be equal, or no; because their Agreement, or Disagreement in equality, can never be perceived by an immediate comparing them: The difference of Figure makes their parts uncapable of an exact immediate application; and therefore there is need of some intervening Quantities to measure them by, which is Demonstration, or rational Knowledge.

§4. *Fourthly*, It follows also, from what is above observed, that our *rational Knowledge*, cannot reach to the whole extent of our *Ideas*. Because between two different *Ideas* we would examine, we cannot always find such *Mediums*, as we can connect one to another with an intuitive Knowledge, in all the parts of the Deduction; and wherever that fails, we come short of Knowledge and Demonstration.

§5. *Fifthly*, *Sensitive Knowledge* reaching no farther than the Existence of Things actually present to our Senses, is yet much narrower than either of the former.

§6. From all which it is evident, that *the extent of our Knowledge* comes not only short of the reality of Things, but even of the extent of our own *Ideas*. Though our Knowledge be limited to our *Ideas*, and cannot exceed them either in extent, or perfection; and though these be very narrow bounds, in respect of the extent of Allbeing, and far short of what we may justly imagine to be in some even created understandings, not tied down to the dull and narrow Information, is to be received from some few, and not very acute ways of Perception, such as are our Senses; yet it would be well with us, if our Knowledge were but as large as our *Ideas*, and there were not many Doubts and Enquiries concerning the *Ideas* we have, whereof we are not, nor I believe ever shall be in this World, resolved. Nevertheless, I do not question, but that Humane Knowledge, under the present Circumstances of our Beings and Constitutions may be carried much farther, than it hitherto has been, if Men would sincerely, and with freedom of Mind, employ all that Industry and Labour of Thought, in improving the means of discovering Truth, which they do for the colouring or support of Falshood, to maintain a System, Interest, or Party, they are once engaged in. But yet after all, I think I may, without Injury to humane Perfection, be confident, that our Knowledge would never reach to all we might desire to know concerning those *Ideas* we have; nor be able to surmount all the Difficulties, and resolve all the Questions might arise concerning any of them. We have the *Ideas* of a *Square*, a *Circle*, and *Equality*; and yet, perhaps, shall never be able to find a Circle equal to a Square, and certainly know that it is so. We have the *Ideas* of *Matter* and *Thinking*, but possibly shall never be able to know, whether any mere material Being thinks, or no; it being impossible for us, by the contemplation of our own *Ideas*, without revelation, to discover, whether Omnipotency has not given to some Systems of Matter fitly disposed, a power to perceive and think, or else joined and fixed to Matter so disposed, a thinking immaterial Substance: It being, in respect of our Notions, not much more remote from our Comprehension to conceive, that GOD can, if he pleases, superadd to Matter a Faculty of Thinking, than that he should superadd to it another Substance, with a Faculty of Thinking; since we know not wherein Thinking consists, nor to what sort of Substances the Almighty has been pleased to give that Power, which cannot be in any created Being, but merely by the good pleasure and Bounty of the Creator. For I see no contradiction in it, that the first eternal thinking Being should, if he pleased, give to certain Systems of created sensless matter, put together as he thinks fit, some degrees of sense, perception, and thought: Though, as I think, I have proved, *Lib.* 4. *c.* 10*th.* it is no less than a contradiction to suppose matter (which is evidently in its own nature void of sense and thought) should be that Eternal first thinking Being. What certainty of Knowledge can any one have that some perceptions, such as *v.g.* pleasure and pain, should not be in some bodies themselves, after a certain manner modified and moved, as well as that they should be in an immaterial Substance, upon the Motion of the parts of Body: Body as far as we can conceive being able only to strike and affect body; and Motion, according to the utmost reach of our *Ideas*, being able to produce nothing but Motion, so that when we allow it to produce pleasure or pain, or the *Idea* of a Colour, or Sound, we are fain to quit our Reason, go beyond our *Ideas*, and attribute it wholly to the good Pleasure of our Maker. For since we must allow he has annexed Effects to Motion, which we can no way conceive Motion able to produce, what reason have we to conclude, that he could not order them as well to be produced in a Subject we cannot conceive capable of them, as well as in a Subject we cannot conceive the motion of Matter can any way operate upon? I say not this, that I would any way lessen the belief of the Soul's Immateriality: I am not here speaking of Probability, but Knowledge; and I think not only, that it becomes the Modesty of Philosophy, not to pronounce Magisterially, where we want that Evidence that can produce Knowledge; but also, that it is of use to us, to discern how far our Knowledge does reach; for the state we are at present in, not being that of Vision, we must, in many Things, content our selves with Faith and Probability: and in the present Question, about the immateriality of the Soul, if our Faculties cannot arrive at demonstrative Certainty, we need not think it strange. All the great Ends of Morality and Religion, are well enough secured, without philosophical Proofs of the Soul's Immateriality; since it is evident, that he who made us at first begin to subsist here, sensible intelligent Beings, and for several years continued us in such a state, can and will restore us to the like state of Sensibility in another World, and make us capable there to receive the Retribution he has designed to Men, according to their doings in this Life. And therefore 'tis not of such mighty necessity to determine one way or t'other, as some over zealous for, or against the Immateriality of the Soul, have been forward to make the World believe. Who, either on the one side, indulging too much to their Thoughts immersed altogether in Matter, can allow no existence to what is not material: Or, who on the other side, finding not *Cogitation* within the natural Powers of Matter, examined over and over again, by the utmost Intention of Mind, have the confidence to conclude, that Omnipotency it self, cannot give Perception and Thought to a Substance, which has the Modification of Solidity. He that considers how hardly Sensation is, in our Thoughts, reconcilable to extended Matter; or Existence to any thing that hath no Extension at all, will confess, that he is very far from certainly knowing what his Soul is, 'Tis a Point, which seems to me, to be put out of the reach of our Knowledge: And he who will give himself leave to consider freely, and look into the dark and intricate part of each Hypothesis, will scarce find his Reason able to determine him fixedly for, or against the Soul's Materiality. Since on which side soever he views it, either as an unextended Substance, or as a thinking extended Matter; the difficulty to conceive either, will, whilst either alone is in his Thoughts, still drive him to the contrary side. An unfair way which some Men take with themselves: who, because of the unconceivableness of something they find in one, throw themselves violently into the contrary Hypothesis, though altogether as unintelligible to an unbiassed Understanding. This serves, not only to shew the Weakness and the Scantiness of our Knowledge, but the insignificant Triumph of such sort of Arguments, which, drawn from our own Views, may satisfy us that we can find no certainty on one side of the Question; but do not at all thereby help us to Truth, by running into the opposite Opinion, which, on examination, will be found clogg'd with equal difficulties. For what Safety, what Advantage to any one is it, for the avoiding the seeming Absurdities, and, to him, unsurmountable Rubs he meets with in one Opinion, to take refuge in the contrary, which is built on something altogether as inexplicable, and as far remote from his Comprehension? 'Tis past controversy, that we have in us something that thinks, our very Doubts about what it is, confirm the certainty of its being, though we must content our selves in the Ignorance of what kind of *Being* it is: And 'tis in vain to go about to be sceptical in this, as it is unreasonable in most other cases to be positive against the being of any thing, because we cannot comprehend its Nature. For I would fain know what Substance exists that has not something in it, which manifestly baffles our Understandings. Other Spirits, who see and know the Nature and inward Constitution of things, how much must they exceed us in Knowledge? To which if we add larger Comprehension, which enables them at one Glance to see the Connexion and Agreement of very many *Ideas,* and readily supplys to them the intermediate Proofs, which we by single and slow Steps, and long poring in the dark, hardly at last find out, and are often ready to forget one before we have hunted out another, we may guess at some part of the Happiness of superior Ranks of Spirits, who have a quicker and more penetrating Sight, as well as a larger Field of Knowledge. But to return to the Argument in hand, our *Knowledge,* I say, is not only limited to the Paucity and Imperfections of the *Ideas* we have, and which we employ it about, but even comes short of that too. . . .

4 From *The Principles of Human Knowledge*

George Berkeley

It is evident to any one who takes a survey of the *objects* of human knowledge, that they are either ideas actually imprinted on the senses; or else such as are perceived by attending to the passions and operations of the mind; or lastly, ideas formed by help of memory and imagination—either compounding, dividing, or barely representing those originally perceived in the aforesaid ways. By sight I have the ideas of light and colours, with their several degrees and variations. By touch I perceive hard and soft, heat and cold, motion and resistance, and of all these more and less either as to quantity or degree. Smelling furnishes me with odours; the palate with tastes; and hearing conveys sounds to the mind in all their variety of tone and composition. And as several of these are observed to accompany each other, they come to be marked by one name, and so to be reputed as one thing. Thus, for example, a certain colour, taste, smell, figure and consistence having been observed to go together, are accounted one distinct thing, signified by the name *apple*; other collections of ideas constitute a stone, a tree, a book, and the like sensible things—which as they are pleasing or disagreeable excite the passions of love, hatred, joy, grief, and so forth.

But, besides all that endless variety of ideas or objects of knowledge, there is likewise something which knows or perceives them, and exercises divers operations, as willing, imagining, remembering, about them. This perceiving, active being is what I call *mind, spirit, soul,* or *myself*. By which words I do not denote any one of my ideas, but a thing entirely distinct from them, wherein they exist, or, which is the same thing, whereby they are perceived—for the existence of an idea consists in being perceived.

That neither our thoughts, nor passions, nor ideas formed by the imagination, exist without the mind, is what everybody will allow. And to me it is no less evident that the various sensations or ideas imprinted on the sense, however blended or combined together (that is, whatever objects they compose), cannot exist otherwise than in a mind perceiving them. I think an intuitive knowledge may be obtained of this by any one that shall attend to what is meant by the term *exist* when applied to sensible things. The table I write on I say exists, that is, I see and feel it; and if I were out of my study I should say it existed—meaning thereby that if I was in my study I might perceive it, or that some other spirit actually does perceive it. There was an odour, that is, it was smelt; there was a sound, that is, it was heard; a colour or figure, and it was perceived by sight or touch. This is all that I can understand by these and the like expressions. For as to what is said of the absolute existence of unthinking things without any relation to their being perceived, that is to me perfectly unintelligible. Their *esse* is *percipi,* nor is it possible they should have any existence out of the minds or thinking things which perceive them.

It is indeed an opinion strangely prevailing amongst men, that houses, mountains, rivers, and in a word all sensible objects, have an existence, natural or real, distinct from their being perceived by the understanding. But, with how great an assurance and acquiescence soever this principle may be entertained in the world, yet whoever shall find in his heart to call it in question may, if I mistake not, perceive it to involve a manifest contradiction. For, what are the forementioned objects but the things we perceive by sense? and what do we perceive besides our own ideas or sensations? and is it not plainly repugnant that any one of these, or any combination of them, should exist unperceived?

If we throughly examine this tenet it will, perhaps, be found at bottom to depend on the doctrine of *abstract ideas*. For can there be a nicer strain of abstraction than to distinguish the existence of sensible objects from their being perceived, so as to conceive them existing unperceived? Light and colours, heat and cold, extension and figures—in a word the things we see and feel—what are they but so many sensations, notions, ideas, or impressions on the sense? and is it possible to separate, even in thought, any of these from perception? For my part, I might as easily divide a thing from itself. I may, indeed, divide in my thoughts, or conceive apart from each other, those things which, perhaps, I never perceived by sense so divided. Thus, I imagine the trunk of a human body without the limbs, or conceive the smell of a rose without thinking on the rose itself. So far, I will not deny, I can abstract—if that may properly be called *abstraction* which extends only to the conceiving separately such objects as it is possible may really exist or be actually perceived asunder. But my conceiving or imagining power does not extend beyond the possibility of real existence or perception. Hence, as it is impossible for me to see or feel anything without an actual sensation of that thing, so is it impossible for me to conceive in my thoughts any sensible thing or object distinct from the sensation or perception of it. [In truth, the object and the sensation are the same thing, and cannot therefore be abstracted from each other.]

Some truths there are so near and obvious to the mind that a man need only open his eyes to see them. Such I take this important one to be, viz. that all the choir of heaven and furniture of the earth, in a word all those bodies which compose the mighty frame of the world, have not any subsistence without a mind, that their *being* is to be perceived or known; that consequently so long as they are not actually perceived by me, or do not exist in my mind or that of any other created spirit, they must either have no existence at all, or else subsist in the mind of some Eternal Spirit—it being perfectly unintelligible, and involving all the absurdity of abstraction, to attribute to any single part of them an existence independent of a spirit. [To be convinced of which, the reader need only reflect, and try to separate in his own thoughts the *being* of a sensible thing from its *being perceived*.]

From what has been said it is evident there is not any other Substance than *Spirit*, or that which perceives. But, for the fuller demonstration of this point, let it be considered the sensible qualities are colour, figure, motion, smell, taste, etc., i.e., the ideas perceived by sense. Now, for an idea to exist in an unperceiving thing is a manifest contradiction, for to have an idea is all one as to perceive; that therefore wherein colour, figure, etc. exist must perceive them; hence it is clear there can be no unthinking substance or *substratum* of those ideas.

But, say you, though the ideas themselves do not exist without the mind, yet there may be things like them, whereof they are copies or resemblances, which things exist without the mind in an unthinking substance. I answer, an idea can be like nothing but an idea; a colour or figure can be like nothing but another colour or figure. If we look but never so little into our thought, we shall find it impossible for us to conceive a likeness except only between our ideas. Again, I ask whether those supposed originals or external things, of which our ideas are the pictures or representations, be themselves perceivable or no? If they are, then they are ideas and we have gained our point; but if you say they are not, I appeal to any one whether it be sense to assert a colour is like something which is invisible; hard or soft, like something which is intangible; and so of the rest.

Some there are who make a distinction betwixt *primary* and *secondary* qualities. By the former they mean extension, figure, motion, rest, solidity or impenetrability, and number; by the latter they denote all other sensible qualities, as colours, sounds, tastes, and so forth. The ideas we have of these they acknowledge not to be the resemblances of anything existing without the mind, or unperceived, but they will have our ideas of the primary qualities to be patterns or images of things which exist without the mind, in an unthinking substance which they call Matter. By Matter, therefore, we are to understand an inert, senseless substance, in which extension, figure, and motion do actually subsist. But it is evident, from what we have already shewn, that extension, figure, and motion are only ideas existing in the mind, and that an idea can be like nothing but another idea, and that consequently neither they nor their archetypes can exist in an unperceiving substance. Hence, it is plain that the very notion of what is called *Matter* or *corporeal substance*, involves a contradiction in it. [Insomuch that I should not think it necessary to spend more time in exposing its absurdity. But, because the tenet of the existence of Matter seems to have taken so deep a root in the minds of philosophers, and draws after it so many ill consequences, I choose rather to be thought prolix and tedious than omit anything that might conduce to the full discovery and extirpation of that prejudice.]

5 From *The Monadology*

Gottfried Wilhelm Leibniz

1. The Monad, of which we will speak here, is nothing else than a simple substance, which goes to make up composites; by simple, we mean without parts.

2. There must be simple substances because there are composites; for a composite is nothing else than a collection or *aggregatum* of simple substances.

3. Now, where there are no constituent parts there is possible neither extension, nor form, nor divisibility. These Monads are the true Atoms of nature, and, in fact, the Elements of things.

4. Their dissolution, therefore, is not to be feared and there is no way conceivable by which a simple substance can perish through natural means.

5. For the same reason there is no way conceivable by which a simple substance might, through natural means, come into existence, since it can not be formed by composition.

6. We may say then, that the existence of Monads can begin or end only all at once, that is to say, the Monad can begin only through creation and end only through annihilation. Composites, however, begin or end gradually.

7. There is also no way of explaining how a Monad can be altered or changed in its inner being by any other created thing, since there is no possibility of transposition within it, nor can we conceive of any internal movement which can be produced, directed, increased or diminished there within the substance, such as can take place in the case of composites where a change can occur among the parts. The Monads have no windows through which anything may come in or go out. The Attributes are not liable to detach themselves and make an excursion outside the substance, as could *sensible species* of the Schoolmen. In the same way neither substance nor attribute can enter from without into a Monad....

9. Each Monad, indeed, must be different from every other. For there are never in nature two beings which are exactly alike, and in which it is not possible to find a difference either internal or based on an intrinsic property.

10. I assume it as admitted that every created being, and consequently the created Monad, is subject to change, and indeed that this change is continuous in each.

11. It follows from what has just been said, that the natural changes of the Monad come from an internal principle, because an external cause can have no influence upon its inner being....

14. The passing condition which involves and represents a multiplicity in the unity, or in the simple substance, is nothing else than what is called Perception. This should be carefully distinguished from Apperception or Consciousness, as will appear in what

follows. In this matter the Cartesians have fallen into a serious error, in that they treat as non-existent those perceptions of which we are not conscious. It is this also which has led them to believe that spirits alone are Monads and that there are no souls of animals or other Entelechies, and it has led them to make the common confusion between a protracted period of unconsciousness and actual death. They have thus adopted the Scholastic error that souls can exist entirely separated from bodies, and have even confirmed ill-balanced minds in the belief that souls are mortal.

15. The action of the internal principle which brings about the change or the passing from one perception to another may be called Appetition. It is true that the desire (*l'appetit*) is not always able to attain to the whole of the perception which it strives for, but it always attains a portion of it and reaches new perceptions.

16. We, ourselves, experience a multiplicity in a simple substance, when we find that the most trifling thought of which we are conscious involves a variety in the object. Therefore all those who acknowledge that the soul is a simple substance ought to grant this multiplicity in the Monad, and Monsieur Bayle should have found no difficulty in it, as he has done in his *Dictionary*, article "Rorarius."

17. It must be confessed, however, that Perception, and that which depends upon it, are inexplicable by mechanical causes, that is to say, by figures and motions. Supposing that there were a machine whose structure produced thought, sensation, and perception, we could conceive of it as increased in size with the same proportions until one was able to enter into its interior, as he would into a mill. Now, on going into it he would find only pieces working upon one another, but never would he find anything to explain Perception. It is accordingly in the simple substance, and not in the composite nor in a machine that the Perception is to be sought. Furthermore, there is nothing besides perceptions and their changes to be found in the simple substance. And it is in these alone that all the internal activities of the simple substance can consist.

18. All simple substances or created Monads may be called Entelechies, because they have in themselves a certain perfection (ἔχουσι τὸ ἐντελές). There is in them a sufficiency (αὐτάρκεια) which makes them the source of their internal activities, and renders them, so to speak, incorporeal Automatons.

19. If we wish to designate as soul everything which has perceptions and desires in the general sense that I have just explained, all simple substances or created Monads could be called souls. But since feeling is something more than a mere perception I think that the general name of Monad or Entelechy should suffice for simple substances which have only perception, while we may reserve the term Soul for those whose perception is more distinct and is accompanied by memory.

20. We experience in ourselves a state where we remember nothing and where we have no distinct perception, as in periods of fainting, or when we are overcome by a profound, dreamless sleep. In such a state the soul does not sensibly differ at all from a simple Monad. As this state, however, is not permanent and the soul can recover from it, the soul is something more.

21. Nevertheless it does not follow at all that the simple substance is in such a state without perception. This is so because of the reasons given above; for it cannot perish, nor on the other hand would it exist without some affection and the affection is noth-

ing else than its perception. When, however, there are a great number of weak perceptions where nothing stands out distinctively, we are stunned; as when one turns around and around in the same direction, a dizziness comes on, which makes him swoon and makes him able to distinguish nothing. Among animals, death can occasion this state for quite a period.

22. Every present state of a simple substance is a natural consequence of its preceding state, in such a way that its present is big with its future.

23. Therefore, since on awakening after a period of unconsciousness we become conscious of our perceptions, we must, without having been conscious of them, have had perceptions immediately before; for one perception can come in a natural way only from another perception, just as a motion can come in a natural way only from a motion.

24. It is evident from this that if we were to have nothing distinctive, or so to speak prominent, and of a higher flavor in our perceptions, we should be in a continual state of stupor. This is the condition of Monads which are wholly bare. . . .

51. In the case of simple substances, the influence which one Monad has upon another is only ideal. It can have its effect only through the mediation of God, in so far as in the Ideas of God each Monad can rightly demand that God, in regulating the others from the beginning of things, should have regarded it also. For, since one created Monad cannot have a physical influence upon the inner being of another, it is only through this primal regulation that one can have dependence upon another.

52. It is thus that among created things action and passion are reciprocal. For God, in comparing two simple substances, finds in each one reasons obliging him to adapt the other to it; and consequently that which is active in certain respects is passive from another point of view,—active in so far as that which we distinctly know in it serves to give a reason for that which occurs in another, and passive in so far as the reason for what transpires in it is found in that which is distinctly known in another. . . .

56. Now, this interconnection, relationship, or this adaptation of all things to each particular one, and of each one to all the rest, brings it about that every simple substance has relations which express all the others and that it is consequently a perpetual living mirror of the universe.

57. And as the same city regarded from different sides appears entirely different, and is, as it were, multiplied perspectively, so, because of the infinite number of simple substances, there are a similar infinite number of universes which are, nevertheless, only the aspects of a single one, as seen from the special point of view of each Monad. . . .

60. Besides, in what has just been said, can be seen the *a priori* reasons why things cannot be otherwise than they are. It is because God, in ordering the whole, has had regard to every part and in particular to each Monad whose nature it is to represent. Therefore, nothing can limit it to represent merely a part of the things. It is nevertheless true, that this representation is, as regards the details of the whole universe, only a confused representation, and is distinct only as regards a small part of them, that is to say, as regards those things which are nearest or most in relation to each Monad. If the representation were distinct as to the details of the entire universe, each Monad would be a Deity. It is not in the object represented that the Monads are limited, but in the modifications of their knowledge of the object. In a confused way they reach out to

infinity or to the whole, but are limited and differentiated in the degree of their distinct perceptions.

61. In this respect composites are like simple substances. For all space is filled up; therefore, all matter is connected; and in a plenum or filled space every movement has an effect upon bodies in proportion to their distance, so that not only is every body affected by those which are in contact with it, and responds in some way to whatever happens to them, but also by means of them the body responds to those bodies adjoining them, and their intercommunication can be continued to any distance at will. Consequently every body responds to all that happens in the universe, so that he who saw all, could read in each one what is happening everywhere, and even what has happened and what will happen. He can discover in the present what is distant both as regards space and as regards time; σύμπνοια πάντα, as Hippocrates said. A soul can, however, read in itself only what is there represented distinctly. It cannot all at once open up all its folds, because they extend to infinity.

62. Thus although each created Monad represents the whole universe, it represents more distinctly the body which specially pertains to it, and of which it constitutes the entelechy. And as the body expresses all the universe through the interconnection of all matter in the plenum, the soul also represents the whole universe in representing this body, which belongs to it in a particular way.

63. The body belonging to a Monad, which is its entelechy or soul, constitutes together with the entelechy what may be called a *living being,* and with a soul what is called an *animal.* Now, this body of a living being or of an animal is always organic, because every Monad is a mirror of the universe according to its own fashion, and, since the universe is regulated with perfect order, there must needs be order also in the representative, that is to say, in the perceptions of the soul and consequently in the body through which the universe is represented in the soul.

64. Therefore, every organic body of a living being is a kind of divine machine, or natural automaton, infinitely surpassing all artificial automatons. Because a machine constructed by man's skill is not a machine in each of its parts; for instance, the teeth of a brass wheel have parts or bits which to us are not artificial products and contain nothing in themselves to show the use to which the wheel was destined in the machine. The machines of nature, however, that is to say, living bodies, are still machines in their smallest parts *ad infinitum.* Such is the difference between nature and art, that is to say, between Divine art and ours.

65. The author of nature has been able to employ this divine and infinitely marvellous artifice, because each portion of matter is not only, as the ancients recognized, infinitely divisible, but also because it is really divided without end, every part into other parts, each one of which has its own proper motion. Otherwise it would be impossible for each portion of matter to express all the universe.

66. Whence we see that there is a world of created things, of living beings, of animals, of entelechies, of souls, in the minutest particle of matter.

67. Every portion of matter may be conceived as like a garden full of plants, and like a pond full of fish. But every branch of a plant, every member of an animal, and every drop of the fluids within it, is also such a garden or such a pond.

68. And although the ground and the air which lies between the plants of the garden, and the water which is between the fish in the pond, are not themselves plant or

fish, yet they nevertheless contain these, usually so small, however, as to be imperceptible to us.

69. There is, therefore, nothing uncultivated, or sterile or dead in the universe, no chaos, no confusion, save in appearance; somewhat as a pond would appear at a distance when we could see in it a confused movement, and so to speak, a swarming of the fish, without, however, discerning the fish themselves.

70. It is evident, then, that every living body has a dominating entelechy, which in animals is the soul. The parts, however, of this living body are full of other living beings, plants and animals, which, in turn, have each one its entelechy or dominating soul.

71. This does not mean, as some who have misunderstood my thought have imagined, that each soul has a quantity or portion of matter appropriated to it or attached to itself for ever, and that it consequently owns other inferior living beings destined to serve it always; because all bodies are in a state of perpetual flux like rivers, and the parts are continually entering in and passing out.

72. The soul, therefore, changes its body only gradually and by degrees, so that it is never deprived all at once of all its organs. There is frequently a metamorphosis in animals, but never metempsychosis or a transmigration of souls. Neither are there souls wholly separate from bodies, nor bodiless spirits. God alone is without body.

73. This is also why there is never absolute generation or perfect death in the strict sense, consisting in the separation of the soul from the body. That which we call generation is development and growth, and that which we call death is envelopment and diminution.

74. Philosophers have been much perplexed in accounting for the origin of forms, entelechies, or souls. To-day, however, when it has been learned through careful investigations made in plant, insect, and animal life, that the organic bodies of nature are never the product of chaos or putrefaction, but always come from seeds in which there was without doubt some *preformation*, it has been decided that not only is the organic body already present before conception, but also that a soul, in a word, the animal itself, is also in this body; and it has been decided that, by means of conception the animal is disposed for a great transformation, so as to become an animal of another species. We can see cases somewhat similar outside of generation when grubs become flies and caterpillars become butterflies. . . .

76. This, however, is only half the truth. I believe, therefore, that if the animal never actually commences in nature, no more does it by natural means come to an end. Not only is there no generation, but also there is no entire destruction or absolute death. These reasonings, carried on *a posteriori*, and drawn from experience, accord perfectly with the principles which I have above deduced *a priori*.

77. Therefore, we may say, that not only the soul (the mirror of an indestructible universe) is indestructible, but also the animal itself is, although its mechanism is frequently destroyed in parts and although it puts off and takes on organic coatings. . . .

82. Although I find that essentially the same thing is true of all living things and animals, which we have just said, namely, that animals and souls begin from the very commencement of the world and that they come to an end no more than does the world, there is, as far as minds or rational souls are concerned nevertheless, this thing peculiar, that their little spermatic progenitors, as long as they remain such, have only

ordinary or sensuous souls, but those of them which are, so to speak, elevated, attain by actual conception to human nature, and their sensuous souls are raised to the rank of reason and to the prerogative of minds.

83. Among the differences that there are between ordinary souls and spirits, some of which I have already instanced, there is also this that, while souls in general are living mirrors or images of the universe of created things, minds are also images of the Deity himself or of the author of nature. They are capable of knowing the system of the universe, and to imitate it somewhat by means of architectonic patterns, each mind being like a small divinity in its sphere. . . .

6 From *Man a Machine*

Julien Offray DeLaMettrie

. . . I reduce to two the systems of philosophy which deal with man's soul. The first and older system is materialism; the second is spiritualism.

The metaphysicians who have hinted that matter may well be endowed with the faculty of thought have perhaps not reasoned ill. For there is in this case a certain advantage in their inadequate way of expressing their meaning. In truth, to ask whether matter can think, without considering it otherwise than in itself, is like asking whether matter can tell time. . . .

The Leibnizians with their monads have set up an unintelligible hypothesis. They have rather spiritualized matter than materialized the soul. How can we define a being whose nature is absolutely unknown to us?

Descartes and all the Cartesians, among whom the followers of Malebranche have long been numbered, have made the same mistake. They have taken for granted two distinct substances in man, as if they had seen them, and positively counted them. . . .

The excellence of reason does not depend on a big word devoid of meaning (immateriality), but on the force, extent, and perspicuity of reason itself. Thus a "soul of clay" which should discover, at one glance, as it were, the relations and the consequences of an infinite number of ideas hard to understand, would evidently be preferable to a foolish and stupid soul, though that were composed of the most precious elements. . . . But as man, even though he should come from an apparently still more lowly source, would yet be the most perfect of all beings, so whatever the origin of his soul, if it is pure, noble, and lofty, it is a beautiful soul which dignifies the man endowed with it. . . .

. . . Experience and observation should therefore be our only guides here. Both are to be found throughout the records of the physicians who were philosophers, and not in the works of the philosophers who were not physicians. The former have traveled through and illuminated the labyrinth of man; they alone have laid bare to us those springs [of life] hidden under the external integument which conceals so many wonders from our eyes. They alone, tranquilly contemplating our soul, have surprised it, a thousand times, both in its wretchedness and in its glory, and they have no more despised it in the first estate, than they have admired it in the second. Thus, to repeat, only the physicians have a right to speak on this subject. What could the others, especially the theologians, have to say? Is it not ridiculous to hear them shamelessly coming to conclusions about a subject concerning which they have had no means of knowing anything, and from which on the contrary they have been completely turned aside by obscure studies that have led them to a thousand prejudiced opinions,—in a word, to fanaticism, which adds yet more to their ignorance of the mechanism of the body?

But even though we have chosen the best guides, we shall still find many thorns and stumbling blocks in the way.

Man is so complicated a machine that it is impossible to get a clear idea of the machine beforehand, and hence impossible to define it. For this reason, all the investigations have been vain, which the greatest philosophers have made *à priori*, that is to say, in so far as they use, as it were, the wings of the spirit. Thus it is only *à posteriori* or by trying to disentangle the soul from the organs of the body, so to speak, that one can reach the highest probability concerning man's own nature, even though one can not discover with certainty what his nature is.

Let us then take in our hands the staff of experience, paying no heed to the accounts of all the idle theories of philosophers. To be blind and to think that one can do without this staff is the worst kind of blindness. How truly a contemporary writer says that only vanity fails to gather from secondary causes the same lessons as from primary causes! One can and one even ought to admire all these fine geniuses in their most useless works, such men as Descartes, Malebranche, Leibniz, Wolff and the rest, but what profit, I ask, has any one gained from their profound meditations, and from all their works? Let us start out then to discover not what has been thought, but what must be thought for the sake of repose in life. . . .

In disease the soul is sometimes hidden, showing no sign of life; sometimes it is so inflamed by fury that it seems to be doubled; sometimes, imbecility vanishes and the convalescence of an idiot produces a wise man. Sometimes, again, the greatest genius becomes imbecile and loses the sense of self. Adieu then to all that fine knowledge, acquired at so high a price, and with so much trouble! Here is a paralytic who asks if his leg is in bed with him; there is a soldier who thinks that he still has the arm which has been cut off. The memory of his old sensations, and of the place to which they were referred by his soul, is the cause of his illusion, and of this kind of delirium. The mere mention of the member which he has lost is enough to recall it to his mind, and to make him feel all its motions; and this causes him an indefinable and inexpressible kind of imaginary suffering. This man cries like a child at death's approach, while this other jests. What was needed to change the bravery of Caius Julius, Seneca, or Petronius into cowardice or faintheartedness? Merely an obstruction in the spleen, in the liver, an impediment in the portal vein? Why? Because the imagination is obstructed along with the viscera, and this gives rise to all the singular phenomena of hysteria and hypochondria.

What can I add to the stories already told of those who imagine themselves transformed into wolf-men, cocks or vampires, or of those who think that the dead feed upon them? Why should I stop to speak of the man who imagines that his nose or some other member is of glass? The way to help this man regain his faculties and his own flesh-and-blood nose is to advise him to sleep on hay, lest he break the fragile organ, and then to set fire to the hay that he may be afraid of being burned—a fear which has sometimes cured paralysis. But I must touch lightly on facts which everybody knows.

Neither shall I dwell long on the details of the effects of sleep. Here a tired soldier snores in a trench, in the middle of the thunder of hundreds of cannon. His soul hears nothing; his sleep is as deep as apoplexy. A bomb is on the point of crushing him. He will feel this less perhaps than he feels an insect which is under his foot.

On the other hand, this man who is devoured by jealousy, hatred, avarice, or ambition, can never find any rest. The most peaceful spot, the freshest and most calming drinks are alike useless to one who has not freed his heart from the torment of passion.

The soul and the body fall asleep together. As the motion of the blood is calmed, a sweet feeling of peace and quiet spreads through the whole mechanism. The soul feels itself little by little growing heavy as the eyelids droop, and loses its tenseness, as the fibres of the brain relax; thus little by little it becomes as if paralyzed and with it all the muscles of the body. These can no longer sustain the weight of the head, and the soul can no longer bear the burden of thought; it is in sleep as if it were not.

Is the circulation too quick? the soul can not sleep. Is the soul too much excited? the blood can not be quieted: it gallops through the veins with an audible murmur. Such are the two opposite causes of insomnia. A single fright in the midst of our dreams makes the heart beat at double speed and snatches us from needed and delicious repose, as a real grief or an urgent need would do. Lastly as the mere cessation of the functions of the soul produces sleep, there are, even when we are awake (or at least when we are half awake), kinds of very frequent short naps of the mind, vergers' dreams, which show that the soul does not always wait for the body to sleep. For if the soul is not fast asleep, it surely is not far from sleep, since it can not point out a single object to which it has attended, among the uncounted number of confused ideas which, so to speak, fill the atmosphere of our brains like clouds.

Opium is too closely related to the sleep it produces, to be left out of consideration here. This drug intoxicates, like wine, coffee, etc., each in its own measure and according to the dose. It makes a man happy in a state which would seemingly be the tomb of feeling, as it is the image of death. How sweet is this lethargy! The soul would long never to emerge from it. For the soul has been a prey to the most intense sorrow, but now feels only the joy of suffering past, and of sweetest peace. Opium even alters the will, forcing the soul which wished to wake and to enjoy life, to sleep in spite of itself. I shall omit any reference to the effect of poisons.

Coffee, the well-known antidote for wine, by scourging the imagination, cures our headaches and scatters our cares without laying up for us, as wine does, other headaches for the morrow. But let us contemplate the soul in its other needs.

The human body is a machine which winds its own springs. It is the living image of perpetual movement. Nourishment keeps up the movements which fever excites. Without food, the soul pines away, goes mad, and dies exhausted. The soul is a taper whose light flares up the moment before it goes out. But nourish the body, pour into its veins life-giving juices and strong liquors, and then the soul grows strong like them, as if arming itself with a proud courage, and the soldier whom water would have made flee, grows bold and runs joyously to death to the sound of drums. Thus a hot drink sets into stormy movement the blood which a cold drink would have calmed....

Thus, the diverse states of the soul are always correlative with those of the body. But the better to show this dependence, in its completeness and its causes, let us here make use of comparative anatomy; let us lay bare the organs of man and of animals. How can human nature be known, if we may not derive any light from an exact comparison of the structure of man and of animals?

In general, the form and the structure of the brains of quadrupeds are almost the same as those of the brain of man; the same shape, the same arrangement everywhere, with this essential difference, that of all the animals man is the one whose brain is largest, and, in proportion to its mass, more convoluted than the brain of any other animal; then come the monkey, the beaver, the elephant, the dog, the fox, the cat. These animals are most like man, for among them, too, one notes the same progressive analogy in relation to the *corpus callosum* in which Lancisi—anticipating the late M. de la Peyronie—established the seat of the soul. . . .

I shall draw the conclusions which follow clearly from these incontestable observations: 1st, that the fiercer animals are, the less brain they have; 2d, that this organ seems to increase in size in proportion to the gentleness of the animal; 3d, that nature seems here eternally to impose a singular condition, that the more one gains in intelligence the more one loses in instinct. Does this bring gain or loss?

Do not think, however, that I wish to infer by that, that the size alone of the brain, is enough to indicate the degree of tameness in animals: the quality must correspond to the quantity, and the solids and liquids must be in that due equilibrium which constitutes health.

If, as is ordinarily observed, the imbecile does not lack brain, his brain will be deficient in its consistency—for instance, in being too soft. The same thing is true of the insane, and the defects of their brains do not always escape our investigation. But if the causes of imbecility, insanity, etc., are not obvious, where shall we look for the causes of the diversity of all minds? They would escape the eyes of a lynx and of an argus. A mere nothing, a tiny fibre, something that could never be found by the most delicate anatomy, would have made of Erasmus and Fontenelle two idiots, and Fontenelle himself speaks of this very fact in one of his best dialogues.

Willis has noticed in addition to the softness of the brain-substance in children, puppies, and birds, that the *corpora striata* are obliterated and discolored in all these animals, and that the striations are as imperfectly formed as in paralytics. . . .

However cautious and reserved one may be about the consequences that can be deduced from these observations, and from many others concerning the kind of variation in the organs, nerves, etc., [one must admit that] so many different varieties can not be the gratuitous play of nature. They prove at least the necessity for a good and vigorous physical organization, since throughout the animal kingdom the soul gains force with the body and acquires keenness, as the body gains strength. . . .

. . . Some say that there is in man a natural law, a knowledge of good and evil, which has never been imprinted on the heart of animals.

But is this objection, or rather this assertion, based on observation? Any assertion unfounded on observation may be rejected by a philosopher. Have we ever had a single experience which convinces us that man alone has been enlightened by a ray denied all other animals? If there is no such experience, we can no more know what goes on in animals' minds or even in the minds of other men, than we can help feeling what affects the inner part of our own being. We know that we think, and feel remorse—an intimate feeling forces us to recognize this only too well; but this feeling in us is insufficient to enable us to judge the remorse of others. That is why we have to take others at their word, or judge them by the sensible and external signs we have noticed in ourselves when we experienced the same accusations of conscience and the same torments.

In order to decide whether animals which do not talk have received the natural law, we must, therefore, have recourse to those signs to which I have just referred, if any such exist. The facts seem to prove it. A dog that bit the master who was teasing it, seemed to repent a minute afterwards; it looked sad, ashamed, afraid to show itself, and seemed to confess its guilt by a crouching and downcast air....

But since all the faculties of the soul depend to such a degree on the proper organization of the brain and of the whole body, that apparently they are but this organization itself, the soul is clearly an enlightened machine. For finally, even if man alone had received a share of natural law, would he be any less a machine for that? A few more wheels, a few more springs than in the most perfect animals, the brain proportionally nearer the heart and for this very reason receiving more blood—any one of a number of unknown causes might always produce this delicate conscience so easily wounded, this remorse which is no more foreign to matter than to thought, and in a word all the differences that are supposed to exist here. Could the organism then suffice for everything? Once more, yes; since thought visibly develops with our organs, why should not the matter of which they are composed be susceptible of remorse also, when once it has acquired, with time, the faculty of feeling?

The soul is therefore but an empty word, of which no one has any idea, and which an enlightened man should use only to signify the part in us that thinks. Given the least principle of motion, animated bodies will have all that is necessary for moving, feeling, thinking, repenting, or in a word for conducting themselves in the physical realm, and in the moral realm which depends upon it....

Grant only that organized matter is endowed with a principle of motion, which alone differentiates it from the inorganic (and can one deny this in the face of the most incontestable observation?) and that among animals, as I have sufficiently proved, everything depends upon the diversity of this organization: these admissions suffice for guessing the riddle of substances and of man. It [thus] appears that there is but one [type of organization] in the universe, and that man is the most perfect [example]....

To be a machine, to feel, to think, to know how to distinguish good from bad, as well as blue from yellow, in a word, to be born with an intelligence and a sure moral instinct, and to be but an animal, are therefore characters which are no more contradictory, than to be an ape or a parrot and to be able to give oneself pleasure.... I believe that thought is so little incompatible with organized matter, that it seems to be one of its properties on a par with electricity, the faculty of motion, impenetrability, extension, etc....

... We imagine, or rather we infer, a cause superior to that to which we owe all, and which truly has wrought all things in an inconceivable fashion. No; matter contains nothing base, except to the vulgar eyes which do not recognize her in her most splendid works; and nature is no stupid workman. She creates millions of men, with a facility and a pleasure more intense than the effort of a watchmaker in making the most complicated watch. Her power shines forth equally in creating the lowliest insect and in creating the most highly developed man; the animal kingdom costs her no more than the vegetable, and the most splendid genius no more than a blade of wheat. Let us then judge by what we see of that which is hidden from the curiosity of our eyes and of our investigations, and let us not imagine anything beyond. Let us observe the ape, the beaver, the elephant, etc., in their operations. If it is clear that these activities can not be performed without intelligence, why refuse intelligence to these animals?...

Break the chain of your prejudices, arm yourselves with the torch of experience, and you will render to nature the honor she deserves, instead of inferring anything to her disadvantage, from the ignorance in which she has left you. Only open wide your eyes, only disregard what you can not understand, and you will see that the ploughman whose intelligence and ideas extend no further than the bounds of his furrow, does not differ essentially from the greatest genius,—a truth which the dissection of Descartes's and of Newton's brains would have proved ... in short, you will learn that since everything depends absolutely on difference of organization, a well constructed animal which has studied astronomy, can predict an eclipse, as it can predict recovery or death when it has used its genius and its clearness of vision, for a time, in the school of Hippocrates and at the bedside of the sick. By this line of observations and truths, we come to connect the admirable power of thought with matter, without being able to see the links, because the subject of this attribute is essentially unknown to us....

Let us then conclude boldly that man is a machine, and that in the whole universe there is but a single substance differently modified. This is no hypothesis set forth by dint of a number of postulates and assumptions; it is not the work of prejudice, nor even of my reason alone; I should have disdained a guide which I think to be so untrustworthy, had not my senses, bearing a torch, so to speak, induced me to follow reason by lighting the way themselves. Experience has thus spoken to me in behalf of reason; and in this way I have combined the two.

But it must have been noticed that I have not allowed myself even the most vigorous and immediately deduced reasoning, except as a result of a multitude of observations which no scholar will contest; and furthermore, I recognize only scholars as judges of the conclusions which I draw from the observations; and I hereby challenge every prejudiced man who is neither anatomist, nor acquainted with the only philosophy which can here be considered, that of the human body. Against so strong and solid an oak, what could the weak reeds of theology, of metaphysics, and of the schools, avail,—childish arms, like our parlor foils, that may well afford the pleasure of fencing, but can never wound an adversary. Need I say that I refer to the empty and trivial notions, to the pitiable and trite arguments that will be urged (as long as the shadow of prejudice or of superstition remains on earth) for the supposed incompatibility of two substances which meet and move each other unceasingly? Such is my system, or rather the truth, unless I am much deceived. It is short and simple. Dispute it now who will.

7 From *Positivism*

Auguste Comte

The remaining portion of biological philosophy is that which relates to the study of the affective and intellectual faculties, which leads us over from individual physiology to Social Physics, as vegetative physiology does from the inorganic to the organic philosophy.

While Descartes was rendering to the world the glorious service of instituting a complete system of positive philosophy, the reformer, with all his bold energy, was unable to raise himself so far above his age as to give its complete logical extension to his own theory by comprehending in it the part of physiology that relates to intellectual and moral phenomena. After having instituted a vast mechanical hypothesis upon the fundamental theory of the most simple and universal phenomena, he extended in succession the same philosophical spirit to the different elementary notions relating to the inorganic world; and finally subordinated to it the study of the chief physical functions of the animal organism. But, when he arrived at the functions of the affections and the intellect, he stopped abruptly, and expressly constituted from them a special study, as an appurtenance of the metaphysico-theological philosophy, to which he thus endeavoured to give a kind of new life, after having wrought far more successfully in sapping its scientific foundations. We have an unquestionable evidence of the state of his mind in his celebrated paradox about the intelligence and instincts of animals. He called brutes automata, rather than allow the application of the old philosophy to them. Being unable to pursue this method with Man, he delivered him over expressly to the domain of metaphysics and theology. It is difficult to see how he could have done otherwise, in the then existing state of knowledge: and we owe to his strange hypothesis, which the physiologists went to work to confute, the clearing away of the partition which he set up between the study of animals and that of Man, and consequently, the entire elimination among the higher order of investigators, of theological and metaphysical philosophy. What the first contradictory constitution of the modern philosophy was, we may see in the great work of Malebranche, who was the chief interpreter of Descartes, and who shows how his philosophy continued to apply to the most complex parts of the intellectual system the same methods which had been shown to be necessarily futile with regard to the simplest subjects. It is necessary to indicate this state of things because it has remained essentially unaltered during the last two centuries, notwithstanding the vast progress of positive science, which has all the while been gradually preparing for its inevitable transformation.... It was not till our own time that modern science, with the illustrious Gall for its organ, drove the old philosophy from this last portion of its domain, and passed on in the inevitable course from the critical to the organic state, striving in its turn to treat in its own way the general theory of the highest vital functions. However imperfect the first attempts, the thing is done. Subjected for half a century to the most decisive tests, this new doctrine has clearly manifested all the indications which can guarantee the indestructible vitality of scientific conceptions. Neither enmity nor irrational advocacy has hindered the continuous spread, in all parts of the scientific world, of the new system of investigation of intellectual and moral man. All the signs of the progressive success of a happy philosophical revolution are present in this case.

The positive theory of the affective and intellectual functions is therefore settled, irreversibly, to be this:—it consists in the experimental and rational study of the phenomena of interior sensibility proper to the cerebral ganglions, apart from all immediate external apparatus. These phenomena are the most complex and the most special of all belonging to physiology; and therefore they have naturally been the last to attain to a positive analysis. . . .

We need not stop to draw out any parallel or contrast between phrenology and psychology. Gall has fully and clearly exposed the powerlessness of metaphysical methods for the study of intellectual and moral phenomena: and in the present state of the human mind, all discussion on this subject is superfluous. The great philosophical cause is tried and judged; and the metaphysicians have passed from a state of domination to one of protestation,—in the learned world at least, where their opposition would obtain no attention but for the inconvenience of their still impeding the progress of popular reason. The triumph of the positive method is so decided that it is needless to devote time and effort to any demonstration, except in the way of instruction: but, in order to characterize, by a striking contrast, the true general spirit of phrenological physiology, it may be useful here to analyse very briefly the radical vices of the pretended psychological method, considered merely in regard to what it has in common in the principal existing schools. . . .

As for their fundamental principle of *interior observation*, it would certainly be superfluous to add anything to what I have already said about the absurdity of the supposition of a man seeing himself think. It was well remarked by M. Broussais, on this point, that such a method, if possible, would extremely restrict the study of the understanding, by necessarily limiting it to the case of adult and healthy Man, without any hope of illustrating this difficult doctrine by any comparison of different ages, or consideration of pathological states, which yet are unanimously recognized as indispensable auxiliaries in the simplest researches about Man. But, further, we must be also struck by the absolute interdict which is laid upon all intellectual and moral study of animals, from whom the psychologists can hardly be expecting any *interior observation*. It seems rather strange that the philosophers who have so attenuated this immense subject should be those who are for ever reproaching their adversaries with a want of comprehensiveness and elevation. The case of animals is the rock on which all psychological theories have split, since the naturalists have compelled the metaphysicians to part with the singular expedient imagined by Descartes, and to admit that animals, in the higher parts of the scale at least, manifest most of our affective, and even intellectual faculties, with mere differences of degree; a fact which no one at this day ventures to deny, and which is enough of itself to demonstrate the absurdity of these idle conceptions.

Recurring to the first ideas of philosophical common sense, it is at once evident that no function can be studied but with relation to the organ that fulfils it, or to the phenomena of its fulfilment: and, in the second place, that the affective functions, and yet more the intellectual, exhibit in the latter respect this particular characteristic,—that they cannot be observed during their operation, but only in their results,—more or less immediate, and more or less durable. There are then only two ways of studying such an order of functions; either determining, with all attainable precision, the various organic conditions on which they depend,—which is the chief object of phrenological physiology; or in directly observing the series of intellectual and moral acts,—which belongs rather to natural history, properly so called: these two inseparable aspects of one subject being always so conceived as to throw light on each other. Thus regarded, this great study is seen to be indissolubly connected on the one hand with the whole of the foregoing parts of natural philosophy, and especially with the fundamental doctrines of biology; and, on the other hand, with the whole of history,—of animals as well as of man and of humanity. But when, by the pretended psychological method, the consideration of both the agent and the act is discarded altogether, what material can remain but an unintelligible conflict of words, in which merely nominal entities are substituted for real phenomena? The most difficult study of all is thus set up in a state of isolation, without any one point of support in the most simple and perfect sciences, over which it is yet proposed to give it a majestic sovereignty: and in this all psychologists agree, however extreme may be their differences on other points.

About the method of psychology or ideology, enough has been said. As to the doctrine, the first glance shows a radical fault in it, common to all sects,—a false estimate of the general relations between the affective and the intellectual faculties.... The intellect is almost exclusively the subject of their speculations, and the affections have been almost entirely neglected; and, moreover, always subordinated to the understanding. Now, such a conception represents precisely the reverse of the reality, not only for animals, but also for Man: for daily experience shows that the affections, the propensities, the passions, are the great springs of human life; and that, so far from resulting from intelligence, their spontaneous and independent impulse is indispensable to the first awakening and continuous development of the various intellectual faculties, by assigning to them a permanent end, without which—to say nothing of the vagueness of their general direction—they would remain dormant in the majority of men. It is even but too certain that the least noble and most animal propensities are habitually the most energetic, and therefore the most influential. The whole of human nature is thus very unfaithfully represented by these futile systems, which, if noticing the affective faculties at all, have vaguely connected them with one single principle, sympathy, and, above all, self-consciousness, always supposed to be directed by the intellect. Thus it is that, contrary to evidence, Man has been represented as essentially a reasoning being, continually carrying on, unconsciously, a multitude of imperceptible calculations, with scarcely any spontaneity of action, from infancy upwards. This false conception has doubtless been supported by a consideration worthy of all respect,—that it is by the intellect that Man is modified and improved; but science requires, before all things, the reality of any views, independently of their desirableness; and it is always this reality which is the basis of genuine utility. Without denying the secondary influence of such a view, we can show that two purely philosophical causes, quite unconnected with any idea of application, and inherent in the nature of the method, have led the metaphysicians of all sects to this hypothesis of the supremacy of the intellect. The first is the radical separation which it was thought necessary to make between brutes and man, and which would have been effaced at once by the admission of the preponderance of the affective over the intellectual faculties; and the second was the necessity that the metaphysicians found themselves under, of preserving the unity of what they called the *I*, that it might correspond with the unity of the *soul*, in obedience to the requisitions of the theological philosophy, of which metaphysics is, as we must ever bear in mind, the final transformation. But the positive philosophers, who approach the question with the simple aim of ascertaining the true state of things, and reproducing it with all possible accuracy in their theories, have perceived that, according to universal experience, human nature is so far from being single that it is eminently multiple; that is, usually induced in various directions by distinct and independent powers, among which equilibrium is established with extreme difficulty when, as usually happens in civilized life, no one of them is, in itself, sufficiently marked to acquire spontaneously any considerable preponderance over the rest. Thus, the famous theory of the *I* is essentially without a scientific object, since it is destined to represent a purely fictitious state. There is, in this direction, as I have already pointed out, no other real subject of positive investigation than the study of the equilibrium of the various animal functions,—both of irritability and of sensibility,—which marks the normal state, in which each of them, duly moderated, is regularly and permanently associated with the whole of the others, according to the laws of sympathy, and yet more of synergy. The very abstract and indirect notion of the *I* proceeds from the continuous sense of such a harmony; that is, from the universal accordance of the entire organism. Psychologists have attempted in vain to make out of this idea, or rather sense, an attribute of humanity exclusively. It is evidently a necessary result of all animal life; and therefore it must belong to all animals, whether they are able to discourse upon it or not. No doubt a cat, or any other vertebrated animal, without knowing how to say "I," is not in the habit of taking itself for another. Moreover, it is probable that among the superior animals the sense of personality is still more marked than in Man, on account of their more isolated life; though if we descended too far in the zoological scale we should reach organisms in which the continuous degradation of the nervous system attenuates this compound sense, together with the various simple feelings on which it depends.

It must not be overlooked that though the psychologists have agreed in neglecting the intellectual and moral faculties of brutes, which have been happily left to the naturalists, they have occasioned great mischief by their obscure and indefinite distinction between intelligence and instinct, thus setting up a division between human and animal nature which has had too much effect even upon zoologists to this day. The only meaning that can be attributed to the word *instinct*, is any spontaneous impulse in a determinate direction, independently of any foreign influence. In this primitive sense, the term evidently applies to the proper and direct activity of any faculty whatever, intellectual as well as affective; and it therefore does not conflict with the term *intelligence* in any way, as we so often see when we speak of those who, without any education, manifest a marked talent for music, painting, mathematics, etc. In this way there is instinct, or rather, there are instincts in Man, as much or more than in brutes. If, on the other hand, we describe *intelligence* as the aptitude to modify conduct in conformity to the circumstances of each case,—which, in fact, is the main practical attribute of *reason,* in its proper sense,—it is more evident than before that there is no other essential difference between humanity and animality than that of the degree of development admitted by a faculty which is, by its nature, common to all animal life, and without which it could not even be conceived to exist. Thus the famous scholastic definition of Man as a *reasonable animal* offers a real no-meaning, since no animal, especially in the higher parts of the zoological scale, could live without being to a certain extent reasonable, in proportion to the complexity of its organism.... An attentive examination of the facts therefore discredits the perversion of the word *instinct* when it is used to signify the fatality under which animals are impelled to the mechanical performance of *acts* uniformly determinate, without any possible modification from corresponding circumstances, and neither requiring nor allowing any education, properly so called. This gratuitous supposition is evidently a remnant of the automatic hypothesis of Descartes. Leroy has demonstrated that among mammifers and birds this ideal fixity in the construction of habitations, in the seeking of food by hunting, in the mode of migration, etc., exists only in the eyes of closet-naturalists or inattentive observers.

After thus much notice of the radical vice of all psychological systems, it would be departing from the object of this work to show how the intellectual faculties themselves have been misconceived. It is enough to refer to the refutation by which Gall and Spurzheim have introduced their labours: and I would particularly point out the philosophical demonstration by which they have exhibited the conclusion that sensation, memory, imagination, and even judgment,—all the scholastic faculties, in short,—are not, in fact, fundamental and abstract faculties, but only different degrees or consecutive modes of the same phenomenon, proper to each of the true elementary phrenological functions, and necessarily variable in different cases, with a proportionate activity....

... Dismissing all these for the present, we must examine the great attempt of Gall, in order to see what is wanting in phrenological philosophy to form it into the scientific constitution which is proper to it, and from which it is necessarily still more remote than organic, and even animal physiology.

Two philosophical principles, now admitted to be indisputable, serve as the immoveable basis of Gall's doctrine as a whole: viz., the innateness of the fundamental dispositions, affective and intellectual, and the plurality of the distinct and independent faculties, though real acts usually require their more or less complex concurrence. Within the limits of the human race, all cases of marked talents or character prove the first; and the second is proved by the diversity of such marked cases, and by most pathological states,—especially by those in which the nervous system is directly affected. A comparative observation of the higher animals would dispel all doubt, if any existed in either case.... [B]esides all guidance from analogy, after the study of the animal life, we derive confirmation from all the methods of investigation that physiology admits; from direct observation, experiment, pathological analysis, the comparative method and popular good sense,—all of which converge towards the establishment of this double principle. Such a collection of proofs secures the stability of this much of phrenological doctrine, whatever transformations other parts may have to undergo.

In the anatomical view, this physiological conception corresponds with the division of the brain into a certain number of partial organs, symmetrical like those of the animal life, and, though more contiguous and mutually resembling than in any other system, and therefore more adapted both for sympathy and synergy, still distinct and mutually independent, as we were already aware was the case with the ganglions appropriate to the external senses. In brief, the brain is no longer an organ, but an apparatus of organs, more complex in proportion to the degree of animality. The proper object of phrenological physiology thence consists in determining the cerebral organ appropriate to each clearly marked, simple disposition, affective or intellectual; or, reciprocally, which is more difficult, what function is fulfilled by any portion of the mass of the brain which exhibits the anatomical conditions of a distinct organ. The two processes are directed to develope the agreement between physiological and anatomical analysis which constitutes the true science of living beings. Unfortunately, our means are yet further from answering our aims than in the two preceding divisions of the science.

The scientific principle involved in the phrenological view is that the functions, affective and intellectual, are more elevated, more human, if you will, and at the same time less energetic, in proportion to the exclusiveness with which they belong to the higher part of the zoological series, their positions being in portions of the brain more and more restricted in extent, and further removed from its immediate origin....

A full contemplation of Gall's doctrine convinces us of its faithful representation of the intellectual and moral nature of Man and animals. All the psychological sects have misconceived or ignored the pre-eminence of the affective faculties, plainly manifest as it is in all the moral phenomena of brutes, and even of Man; but we find this fact placed on a scientific basis by the discovery that the affective organs occupy all the hinder and middle portion of the cerebral apparatus, while the intellectual occupy only the front portion, which, in extreme cases, is not more than a fourth, or even a sixth part of the whole. The difference between Gall and his predecessors was not in the separation of the two kinds of faculties, but that they assigned the brain to the intellectual faculties alone, regarding it as a single organ, and distributing the passions among the organs pertaining to the vegetative life,—the heart, the liver, etc....

Next comes the subdivision established by Gall and Spurzheim in each of these two orders. The affective faculties are divided into the propensities, and the affections or sentiments: the first residing in the hindmost and lowest part of the brain; and the other class in the middle portion. The intellectual faculties are divided into the various perceptive faculties, which together constitute the range of observation: and the small number of reflective faculties, the highest of all, constituting the power of combination, by comparison and co-ordination. The upper part of the frontal region is the seat of these last, which are the chief characteristic attribute of human nature. There is a certain deficiency of precision in this description; but, besides that we may expect improving knowledge to clear it up, we shall find, on close examination, that the inconvenience lies more in the language than in the ideas. The only language we have is derived from a philosophical period when all moral and even intellectual ideas were shrouded in a mysterious metaphysical unity, which allows us now no adequate choice of terms.

Taking the ordinary terms in their literal sense, we should misconceive the fundamental distinction between the intellectual faculties and the others. When the former are very marked, they unquestionably produce real inclinations or propensities, which are distinguished from the inferior passions only by their smaller energy. Nor can we deny that their action occasions true emotions or sentiments, more rare, more pure, more sublime than any other, and, though less vivid than others, capable of moving to tears; as is testified by so many instances of the rapture excited by the discovery of truth, in the most eminent thinkers that have done donour to their race—as Archimedes, Descartes, Kepler, Newton, etc. Would any thoughtful student take occasion, by such approximations, to deny all real distinction between the intellectual and affective faculties? The wiser conclusion to be drawn from the case is that we must reform our philosophical language, to raise it, by rigorous precision, to the dignity of scientific language. We may say as much about the subdivision of the affective faculties into propensities and sentiments, the distinction being, though less marked, by no means less real. Apart from all useless discussion of nomenclature, we may say that the real difference has not been clearly seized. . . .

A much more serious objection to Gall's doctrine arises out of the venturesome and largely erroneous localization of the faculties which he thought proper to propose. If we look at his position, we shall see that he merely used the right, common to all natural philosophers, of instituting a scientific hypothesis, in accordance with the theory on that subject which we examined in connection with Physics. He fulfilled the conditions of this theory; his subject being, not any imaginary fluids, ethers or the like, but tangible organs, whose hypothetical attributes admit of positive verifications. Moreover, none of those who have criticized his localization could have proposed any less imperfect, or, probably, so well indicated. The advice of prudent mediocrity, to abstain from hypothesis, is very easy to offer; but if the advice was followed, nothing would ever be done in the way of scientific discovery. It is doubtless inconvenient to have to withdraw or remake, at a subsequent period, the hypotheses to which a science owes its existence, and which, by that time, have been adopted by inferior inquirers with a blinder and stronger faith than that of the original proposers; but there is no use in dwelling upon a liability which arises from the infirmity of our intelligence. The practical point for the future is that strong minds, prepared by a suitable scientific education, should plant themselves on the two great principles which have been laid down as the foundation of the science, and thence explore the principal needs of cerebral physiology, and the character of the means by which it may be carried forwards. . . .

If metaphysicians have confounded all their psychological notions in an absurd unity, it is probable that the phrenologists have gone to the other extreme in multiplying elementary functions. Gall set up twenty-seven; which was, no doubt, an exaggeration to begin with. Spurzheim raised the number to thirty-five; and it is liable to daily increase for want of a rational principle of circumscription for the regulation of the easy enthusiasm of popular explorers. Unless a sound philosophy interposes, to establish some order, we may have as many faculties and organs as the psychologists of old made entities. However great may be the diversity of animal natures, or even of human types, it is yet to be conceived, (as real acts usually suppose the concurrence of several fundamental faculties,) that even a greater multiplicity might be represented by a very small number of elementary functions of the two orders. If, for instance, the whole number were reduced to twelve or fifteen well-marked faculties, their combinations, binary, ternary, quaternary, etc., would doubtless correspond to many more types than can exist, even if we restricted ourselves to distinguishing, in relation to the normal degree of activity of each function, two other degrees,—one higher and the other lower. But the exorbitant multiplication of faculties is not in itself so shocking as the levity of most of the pretended analyses which have regulated their distribution. In the intellectual order, especially, the aptitudes have been usually ill-described, apart from the organs: as when a mathematical aptitude is assigned on grounds which would justify our assigning a chemical aptitude, or an anatomical aptitude, if the whole bony casket had not been previously parcelled off into irremoveable compartments. If a man could do sums according to rules quickly and easily, he had the mathematical aptitude, according to those who do not suspect that mathematical speculations require any superiority of intellect. Though the analysis of the affective faculties, which are so much better marked, is less imperfect, there are several instances of needless multiplication in that department.

To rectify or improve this analysis of the cerebral faculties, it would be useful to add to the observation of Man and society a physiological estimate of the most marked individual cases,—especially in past times. The intellectual order, which most needs revision, is that which best admit of this procedure. If, for instance, it had been applied to the cases of the chief geometers, the absurd mistake that I have just pointed out could not have been committed; for it would have been seen what compass and variety of faculties are required to constitute mathematical genius, and how various are the forms in which that genius manifests itself. One great geometer has shone by the sagacity of his inventions; another by the strength and extent of his combinations; a third by the happy choice of his notations, and the perfection of his algebraic style, etc. We might discover, or at least verify, all the real fundamental intellectual faculties by the scientific class alone. In an inferior degree it would be the same with an analogous study of the most eminent artists. . . .

Phrenological analysis has, then, to be reconstituted; first in the anatomical, and then in the physiological order; and finally, the two must be harmonized; and not till then can phrenological physiology be established upon its true scientific basis. Such a procedure is fairly begun, as we have seen, with regard to the two preceding divisions of our science; but it is not yet even conceived of in relation to cerebral physiology, from its greater complexity and more recent positivity.

The phrenologists must make a much more extensive use than hitherto of the means furnished by biological philosophy for the advancement of all studies relating to living bodies: that is, of pathological, and yet more of comparative analysis. The luminous maxim of M. Broussais, which lies at the foundation of medical philosophy,—that the phenomena of the pathological state are a simple prolongation of the phenomena of the normal state, beyond the ordinary limits of variation,—has never been duly applied to intellectual and moral phenomena: yet it is impossible to understand anything of the different kinds of madness, if they are not examined on this principle. Here, as in a former division of the science, we see that the study of malady is the way to understand the healthy state. Nothing can aid us so well in the discovery of the fundamental faculties as a judicious study of the state of madness, when each faculty manifests itself in a degree of exaltation which separates it distinctly from others. . . . Humanity and animality ought reciprocally to cast light upon each other. If the whole set of faculties constitutes the complement of animal life, it must surely be that all that are fundamental must be common to all the superior animals, in some degree or other: and differences of intensity are enough to account for the existing diversities,—the association of the faculties being taken into the account, on the one hand, and, on the other, the improvement of Man in society being set aside. If there are any faculties which belong to Man exclusively, it can only be such as correspond to the highest intellectual aptitudes: and this much may appear doubtful if we compare, in an unprejudiced way, the actions of the highest mammifers with those of the least developed savages. It seems to me more rational to suppose that power of observation and even of combination exists in animals, though in an immeasurably inferior degree. . . .

We have now seen how irrational and narrow is the way in which intellectual and moral physiology is conceived of and studied: and that till this is rectified, the science, which really appears not to have advanced a single step since its institution, cannot make any true progress. We see how it requires, above even the other branches of physiology, the preparation of scientific habits, and familiarity with the foregoing departments of natural philosophy; and how, from its vicious isolation, it tends to sink to the level of the most superficial and ill-prepared minds, which will make it the groundwork of a gross and mischievous quackery, if the true scientific inquirers do not take it out of their hands. No inconveniences of this kind, however, should blind us to the eminent merits of a conception which will ever be one of the principal grounds of distinction of the philosophy of the nineteenth century, in comparison with the one which preceded it. . . .

8 From *A System of Logic*

John Stuart Mill

What Is Meant by Laws of Mind

What the Mind is, as well as what Matter is, or any other question respecting Things in themselves, as distinguished from their sensible manifestations, it would be foreign to the purposes of this treatise to consider. Here, as throughout our inquiry, we shall keep clear of all speculations respecting the mind's own nature, and shall understand by the laws of mind those of mental phenomena—of the various feelings or states of consciousness of sentient beings. These, according to the classification we have uniformly followed, consist of Thoughts, Emotions, Volitions, and Sensations; the last being as truly states of Mind as the three former. It is usual, indeed, to speak of sensations as states of body, not of mind. But this is the common confusion of giving one and the same name to a phenomenon and to the proximate cause or conditions of the phenomenon. The immediate antecedent of a sensation is a state of body, but the sensation itself is a state of mind. If the word mind means anything, it means that which feels. Whatever opinion we hold respecting the fundamental identity or diversity of matter and mind, in any case the distinction between mental and physical facts, between the internal and the external world, will always remain as a matter of classification; and in that classification, sensations, like all other feelings, must be ranked as mental phenomena. The mechanism of their production, both in the body itself and in what is called outward nature, is all that can with any propriety be classed as physical.

The phenomena of mind, then, are the various feelings of our nature, both those improperly called physical and those peculiarly designated as mental; and by the laws of mind I mean the laws according to which those feelings generate one another.

Is There a Science of Psychology?

All states of mind are immediately caused either by other states of mind or by states of body. When a state of mind is produced by a state of mind, I call the law concerned in the case a law of Mind. When a state of mind is produced directly by a state of body, the law is a law of Body, and belongs to physical science.

With regard to those states of mind which are called sensations, all are agreed that these have for their immediate antecedents states of body. Every sensation has for its proximate cause some affection of the portion of our frame called the nervous system, whether this affection originate in the action of some external object, or in some pathological condition of the nervous organisation itself. The laws of this portion of our nature—the varieties of our sensations and the physical conditions on which they proximately depend—manifestly belong to the province of Physiology.

Whether the remainder of our mental states are similarly dependent on physical conditions, is one of the *vexatae questiones* in the science of human nature. It is still disputed whether our thoughts, emotions, and volitions are generated through the intervention of material mechanism; whether we have organs of thought and of emotion in the same sense in which we have organs of sensation. Many eminent physiologists hold the affirmative. These contend that a thought (for example) is as much the result of nervous agency as a sensation; that some particular state of our nervous system, in particular of that central portion of it called the brain, invariably precedes, and is presupposed by, every state of our consciousness. According to this theory, one state of mind is never really produced by another; all are produced by states of body. When one thought seems to call up another by association, it is not really a thought which recalls a thought; the association did not exist between the two thoughts, but between the two states of the brain or nerves which preceded the thoughts: one of those states recalls the other, each being attended, in its passage, by the particular state of consciousness which is consequent on it. On this theory the uniformities of succession among states of mind would be mere derivative uniformities, resulting from the laws of succession of the bodily states which cause them. There would be no original mental laws, no Laws of Mind in the sense in which I use the term, at all; and mental science would be a mere branch, though the highest and most recondite branch, of the science of Physiology. M. Comte, accordingly, claims the scientific cognisance of moral and intellectual phenomena exclusively for physiologists; and not only denies to Psychology, or Mental Philosophy properly so called, the character of a science, but places it, in the chimerical nature of its objects and pretensions, almost on a par with astrology.

But, after all has been said which can be said, it remains incontestable that there exist uniformities of succession among states of mind, and that these can be ascertained by observation and experiment. Further, that every mental state has a nervous state for its immediate antecedent and proximate cause, though extremely probable, cannot hitherto be said to be proved, in the conclusive manner in which this can be proved of sensations; and even were it certain, yet every one must admit that we are wholly ignorant of the characteristics of these nervous states; we know not, and at present have no means of knowing, in what respect one of them differs from another; and our only mode of studying their successions or co-existences must be by observing the successions and co-existences of the mental states of which they are supposed to be the generators or causes. The successions, therefore, which obtain among mental phenomena do not admit of being deduced from the physiological laws of our nervous organisation; and all real knowledge of them must continue, for a long time at least, if not always, to be sought in the direct study, by observation and experiment, of the mental successions themselves. Since, therefore, the order of our mental phenomena must be studied in those phenomena, and not inferred from the laws of any phenomena more general, there is a distinct and separate Science of Mind.

The relations, indeed, of that science to the science of physiology must never be overlooked or undervalued. It must by no means be forgotten that the laws of mind may be derivative laws resulting from laws of animal life, and that their truth therefore may ultimately depend on physical conditions; and the influence of physiological states or physiological changes in altering or counteracting the mental successions is one of the most important departments of psychological study. But, on the other hand, to reject the resource of psychological analysis, and construct the theory of the mind solely on such data as physiology at present affords, seems to me as great an error in principle, and an even more serious one in practice. Imperfect as is the science of mind, I do not scruple to affirm that it is in a considerably more advanced state than the portion of physiology which corresponds to it; and to discard the former for the latter appears to me an infringement of the true canons of inductive philosophy, which must produce, and which does produce, erroneous conclusions in some very important departments of the science of human nature.

9 From "Does 'Consciousness' Exist?"

William James

"Thoughts" and "things" are names for two sorts of object, which common sense will always find contrasted and will always practically oppose to each other. Philosophy, reflecting on the contrast, has varied in the past in her explanations of it, and may be expected to vary in the future. At first, "spirit and matter," "soul and body," stood for a pair of equipollent substances quite on a par in weight and interest. But one day Kant undermined the soul and brought in the transcendental ego, and ever since then the bipolar relation has been very much off its balance. The transcendental ego seems nowadays in rationalist quarters to stand for everything, in empiricist quarters for almost nothing. In the hands of such writers as Schuppe, Rehmke, Natorp, Münsterberg—at any rate in his earlier writings, Schubert-Soldern and others, the spiritual principle attenuates itself to a thoroughly ghostly condition, being only a name for the fact that the "content" of experience *is known*. It loses personal form and activity—these passing over to the content—and becomes a bare *Bewusstheit* or *Bewusstsein überhaupt*, of which in its own right absolutely nothing can be said.

I believe that "consciousness," when once it has evaporated to this estate of pure diaphaneity, is on the point of disappearing altogether. It is the name of a nonentity, and has no right to a place among first principles. Those who still cling to it are clinging to a mere echo, the faint rumor left behind by the disappearing "soul" upon the air of philosophy. During the past year, I have read a number of articles whose authors seemed just on the point of abandoning the notion of consciousness,[1] and substituting for it that of an absolute experience not due to two factors. But they were not quite radical enough, not quite daring enough in their negations. For twenty years past I have mistrusted "consciousness" as an entity; for seven or eight years past I have suggested its non-existence to my students, and tried to give them its pragmatic equivalent in realities of experience. It seems to me that the hour is ripe for it to be openly and universally discarded.

To deny plumply that "consciousness" exists seems so absurd on the face of it—for undeniably "thoughts" do exist—that I fear some readers will follow me no farther. Let me then immediately explain that I mean only to deny that the word stands for an entity, but to insist most emphatically that it does stand for a function. There is, I mean, no aboriginal stuff or quality of being, contrasted with that of which material objects are made, out of which our thoughts of them are made; but there is a function in experience which thoughts perform, and for the performance of which this quality of being is invoked. That function is *knowing*. "Consciousness" is supposed necessary to explain the fact that things not only are, but get reported, are known. Whoever blots out the notion of consciousness from his list of first principles must still provide in some way for that function's being carried on.

I

My thesis is that if we start with the supposition that there is only one primal stuff or material in the world, a stuff of which everything is composed, and if we call that stuff "pure experience," then knowing can easily be explained as a particular sort of relation towards one another into which portions of pure experience may enter. The relation itself is a part of pure experience; one of its "terms" becomes the subject or bearer of the knowledge, the knower,[2] the other becomes the object known. This will need much explanation before it can be understood....

... [W]e are supposed by almost every one to have an immediate consciousness of consciousness itself. When the world of outer fact ceases to be materially present, and we merely recall it in memory, or fancy it, the consciousness is believed to stand out and to be felt as a kind of impalpable inner flowing, which, once known in this sort of experience, may equally be detected in presentations of the outer world. "The moment we try to fix our attention upon consciousness and to see *what*, distinctly, it is," says a recent writer, "it seems to vanish. It seems as if we had before us a mere emptiness. When we try to introspect the sensation of blue, all we can see is the blue; the other element is as if it were diaphanous. Yet it *can* be distinguished, if we look attentively enough, and know that there is something to look for."[3] "Consciousness" (Bewusstheit), says another philosopher, "is inexplicable and hardly describable, yet all conscious experiences have this in common that what we call their content has this peculiar reference to a centre for which 'self' is the name, in virtue of which reference alone the content is subjectively given, or appears.... While in this way consciousness, or reference to a self, is the only thing which distinguishes a conscious content from any sort of being that might be there with no one conscious of it, yet this only ground of the distinction defies all closer explanations. The existence of consciousness, although it is the fundamental fact of psychology, can indeed be laid down as certain, can be brought out by analysis, but can neither be defined nor deduced from anything but itself."[4]

"Can be brought out by analysis," this author says. This supposes that the consciousness is one element, moment, factor—call it what you like—of an experience of essentially dualistic inner constitution, from which, if you abstract the content, the consciousness will remain revealed to its own eye. Experience, at this rate, would be much like a paint of which the world pictures were made. Paint has a dual constitution, involving, as it does, a menstruum[5] (oil, size or what not) and a mass of content in the form of pigment suspended therein. We can get the pure menstruum by letting the pigment settle, and the pure pigment by pouring off the size or oil. We operate here by physical subtraction; and the usual view is, that by mental subtraction we can separate the two factors of experience in an analogous way—not isolating them entirely, but distinguishing them enough to know that they are two.

II

Now my contention is exactly the reverse of this. *Experience, I believe, has no such inner duplicity; and the separation of it into consciousness and content comes, not by way of subtraction, but by way of addition*—the addition, to a given concrete piece of it, of other sets of experiences, in connection with which severally its use or function may be of two different kinds. The paint will also serve here as an illustration. In a pot in a paint-shop, along with other paints, it serves in its entirety as so much saleable matter. Spread on a canvas, with other paints around it, it represents, on the contrary, a feature in a picture and performs a spiritual function. Just so, I maintain, does a given undivided portion of experience, taken in one context of associates, play the part of a knower, of a state of mind, of "consciousness"; while in a different context the same undivided bit of experience plays the part of a thing known, of an objective "content." In a word, in one group it figures as a thought, in another group as a thing. And, since it can figure in both groups simultaneously we have every right to speak of it as subjective and objective both at once. The dualism connoted by such double-barrelled terms as "experience," "phenomenon," "datum," "*Vorfindung*"—terms which, in philosophy at any rate, tend more and more to replace the single-barrelled terms of "thought" and "thing"—that dualism, I say, is still preserved in this account, but reinterpreted, so that, instead of being mysterious and elusive, it becomes verifiable and concrete. It is an affair of relations, it falls outside, not inside, the single experience considered, and can always be particularized and defined.

The entering wedge for this more concrete way of understanding the dualism was fashioned by Locke when he made the word "idea" stand indifferently for thing and thought, and by Berkeley when he said that what common sense means by realities is exactly what the philosopher means by ideas. Neither Locke nor Berkeley thought his truth out into perfect clearness, but it seems to me that the conception I am defending does little more than consistently carry out the "pragmatic" method which they were the first to use.

If the reader will take his own experiences, he will see what I mean. Let him begin with a perceptual experience, the "presentation," so called, of a physical object, his actual field of vision, the room he sits in, with the book he is reading as its centre; and let him for the present treat this complex object in the common-sense way as being "really" what it seems to be, namely, a collection of physical things cut out from an environing world of other physical things with which these physical things have actual or potential relations. Now at the same time it is just *those self-same things* which his mind, as we say, perceives; and the whole philosophy of perception from Democritus's time downwards has been just one long wrangle over the paradox that what is evidently one reality should be in two places at once, both in outer space and in a person's mind. "Representative" theories of perception avoid the logical paradox, but on the other hand they violate the reader's sense of life, which knows no intervening mental image but seems to see the room and the book immediately just as they physically exist.

The puzzle of how the one identical room can be in two places is at bottom just the puzzle of how one identical point can be on two lines. It can, if it be situated at their intersection; and similarly, if the "pure experience" of the room were a place of intersection of two processes, which connected it with different groups of associates respectively, it could be counted twice over, as belonging to either group, and spoken of loosely as existing in two places, although it would remain all the time a numerically single thing.

Well, the experience is a member of diverse processes that can be followed away from it along entirely different lines. The one self-identical thing has so many relations to the rest of experience that you can take it in disparate systems of association, and treat it as belonging with opposite contexts. In one of these contexts it is your "field of consciousness"; in another it is "the room in which you sit," and it enters both contexts in its wholeness, giving no pretext for being said to attach itself to consciousness by one of its parts or aspects, and to outer reality by another. What are the two processes, now, into which the room-experience simultaneously enters in this way?

One of them is the reader's personal biography, the other is the history of the house of which the room is part. The presentation, the experience, the *that* in short (for until we have decided *what* it is it must be a mere *that*) is the last term of a train of sensations, emotions, decisions, movements, classifications. expectations, etc., ending in the present, and the first term of a series of similar "inner" operations extending into the future, on the reader's part. On the other hand, the very same *that* is the *terminus ad quem* of a lot of previous physical operations, carpentering, papering, furnishing, warming, etc., and the *terminus a quo* of a lot of future ones, in which it will be concerned when undergoing the destiny of a physical room. The physical and the mental operations form curiously incompatible groups. As a room, the experience has occupied that spot and had that environment for thirty years. As your field of consciousness it may never have existed until now. As a room, attention will go on to discover endless new details in it. As your mental state merely, few new ones will emerge under attention's eye. As a room, it will take an earthquake, or a gang of men, and in any case a certain amount of time, to destroy it. As your subjective state, the closing of your eyes, or any instantaneous play of your fancy will suffice. In the real world, fire will consume it. In your mind, you can let fire play over it without effect. As an outer object, you must pay so much a month to inhabit it. As an inner content, you may occupy it for any length of time rent-free. If, in short, you follow it in the mental direction, taking it along with events of personal biography solely, all sorts of things are true of it which are false, and false of it which are true if you treat it as a real thing experienced, follow it in the physical direction, and relate it to associates in the outer world.

III

So far, all seems plain sailing, but my thesis will probably grow less plausible to the reader when I pass from percepts to concepts, or from the case of things presented to that of things remote. I believe, nevertheless, that here also the same law holds good. If we take conceptual manifolds, or memories, or fancies, they also are in their first intention mere bits of pure experience, and, as such, are single *thats* which act in one context as objects, and in another context figure as mental states. By taking them in their first intention, I mean ignoring their relation to possible perceptual experiences with which they may be connected, which they may lead to and terminate in, and which then they may be supposed to "represent." Taking them in this way first, we confine the problem to a world merely "thought-of" and not directly felt or seen. This world, just like the world of percepts, comes to us at first as a chaos of experiences, but lines of order soon get traced. We find that any bit of it which we may cut out as an example is connected with distinct groups of associates, just as our perceptual experiences are, that these associates link themselves with it by different relations,[6] and that one forms the inner history of a person, while the other acts as an impersonal "objective" world, either spatial and temporal, or else merely logical or mathematical, or otherwise "ideal." ...

... [W]hat I maintain is, that any single non-perceptual experience tends to get counted twice over, just as a perceptual experience does, figuring in one context as an object or field of objects, in another as a state of mind: and all this without the least internal self-diremption on its own part into consciousness and content. It is all consciousness in one taking; and, in the other, all content.

I find this objectivity of non-perceptual experiences, this complete parallelism in point of reality between the presently felt and the remotely thought, so well set forth in a page of Münsterberg's *Grundzüge,* that I will quote it as it stands.

"I may only think of my objects," says Professor Münsterberg; "yet, in my living thought they stand before me exactly as perceived objects would do, no matter how different the two ways of apprehending them may be in their genesis. The book here lying on the table before me, and the book in the next room of which I think and which I mean to get, are both in the same sense given realities for me, realities which I acknowledge and of which I take account. If you agree that the perceptual object is not an idea within me, but that percept and thing, as indistinguishably one, are really experienced *there, outside,* you ought not to believe that the merely thought-of object is hid away inside of the thinking subject. The object of which I think, and of whose existence I take cognizance without letting it now work upon my senses, occupies its definite place in the outer world as much as does the object which I directly see."

"What is true of the here and the there, is also true of the now and the then. I know of the thing which is present and perceived, but I know also of the thing which yesterday was but is no more, and which I only remember. Both can determine my present conduct, both are parts of the reality of which I keep account. It is true that of much of the past I am uncertain, just as I am uncertain of much of what is present if it be but dimly perceived. But the interval of time does not in principle alter my relation to the object, does not transform it from an object known into a mental state.... The things in the room here which I survey, and those in my distant home of which I think, the things of this minute and those of my long-vanished boyhood, influence and decide me alike, with a reality which my experience of them directly feels. They both make up my real world, they make it directly, they do not have first to be introduced to me and mediated by ideas which now and here arise within me.... This not-me character of my recollections and expectations does not imply that the external objects of which I am aware in those experiences should necessarily be there also for others. The objects of dreamers and hallucinated persons are wholly without general validity. But even were they centaurs and golden mountains, they still would be 'off there,' in fairy land, and not 'inside' of ourselves."[7]

This certainly is the immediate, primary, naïf, or practical way of taking our thought-of world. Were there no perceptual world to serve as its "reductive," in Taine's sense, by being "stronger" and more genuinely "outer" (so that the whole merely thought-of world seems weak and inner in comparison), our world of thought would be the only world, and would enjoy complete reality in our belief. This actually happens in our dreams, and in our day-dreams so long as percepts do not interrupt them.

And yet, just as the seen room (to go back to our late example) is *also* a field of consciousness, so the conceived or recollected room is *also* a state of mind; and the doubling-up of the experience has in both cases similar grounds.

The room thought-of, namely, has many thought-of couplings with many thought-of things. Some of these couplings are inconstant, others are stable. In the reader's personal history the room occupies a single date—he saw it only once perhaps, a year ago. Of the house's history, on the other hand, it forms a permanent ingredient. Some couplings have the curious stubbornness, to borrow Royce's term, of fact; others show the fluidity of fancy—we let them come and go as we please. Grouped with the rest of its house, with the name of its town, of its owner, builder, value, decorative plan, the room maintains a definite foothold, to which, if we try to loosen it, it tends to return, and to reassert itself with force.[8] With these associates, in a word, it coheres, while to other houses, other towns, other owners, etc., it shows no tendency to cohere at all. The two collections, first of its cohesive, and, second, of its loose associates, inevitably come to be contrasted. We call the first collection the system of external realities, in the midst of which the room, as "real," exists; the other we call the stream of our internal thinking, in which, as a "mental image," it for a moment floats.[9] The room thus again gets counted twice over. It plays two different rôles, being *Gedanke* and *Gedachtes*, the thought-of-an-object, and the object-thought-of, both in one; and all this without paradox or mystery, just as the same material thing may be both low and high, or small and great, or bad and good, because of its relations to opposite parts of an environing world.

As "subjective" we say that the experience represents; as "objective" it is represented. What represents and what is represented is here numerically the same; but we must remember that no dualism of being represented and representing resides in the experience *per se*. In its pure state, or when isolated, there is no self-splitting of it into consciousness and what the consciousness is "of." Its subjectivity and objectivity are functional attributes solely, realized only when the experience is "taken," *i.e.*, talked-of, twice, considered along with its two differing contexts respectively, by a new retrospective experience, of which that whole past complication now forms the fresh content.

The instant field of the present is at all times what I call the "pure" experience. It is only virtually or potentially either object or subject as yet. For the time being, it is plain, unqualified actuality, or existence, a simple *that*. In this *naïf* immediacy it is of course *valid*; it is *there*, we *act* upon it; and the doubling of it in retrospection into a state of mind and a reality intended thereby, is just one of the acts. The "state of mind," first treated explicitly as such in retrospection, will stand corrected or confirmed, and the retrospective experience in its turn will get a similar treatment; but the immediate experience in its passing is always "truth,"[10] practical truth, *something to act on*, at its own movement. If the world were then and there to go out like a candle, it would remain truth absolute and objective, for it would be "the last word," would have no critic, and no one would ever oppose the thought in it to the reality intended.[11]

I think I may now claim to have made my thesis clear. Consciousness connotes a kind of external relation, and does not denote a special stuff or way to being. *The peculiarity of our experiences, that they not only are, but are known, which their "conscious" quality is invoked to explain, is better explained by their relations—these relations themselves being experiences—to one another.*

IV

Were I now to go on to treat of the knowing of perceptual by conceptual experiences, it would again prove to be an affair of external relations. One experience would be the knower, the other the reality known; and I could perfectly well define, without the notion of "consciousness," what the knowing actually and practically amounts to—leading-towards, namely, and terminating-in percepts, through a series of transitional experiences which the world supplies. But I will not treat of this, space being insufficient.[12] I will rather consider a few objections that are sure to be urged against the entire theory as it stands.

V

First of all, this will be asked: "If experience has not 'conscious' existence, if it be not partly made of 'consciousness,' of what then is it made? Matter we know, and thought we know, and conscious content we know, but neutral and simple 'pure experience' is something we know not at all. Say *what* it consists of—for it must consist of something—or be willing to give it up!"

To this challenge the reply is easy. Although for fluency's sake I myself spoke early in this article of a stuff of pure experience, I have now to say that there is no *general* stuff of which experience at large is made. There are as many stuffs as there are "natures" in the things experienced. If you ask what any one bit of pure experience is made of, the answer is always the same: "It is made of *that,* of just what appears, of space, of intensity, of flatness, brownness, heaviness, or what not." Shadworth Hodgson's analysis here leaves nothing to be desired. Experience is only a collective name for all these sensible natures, and save for time and space (and, if you like, for "being") there appears no universal element of which all things are made.

VI

The next objection is more formidable, in fact it sounds quite crushing when one hears it first.

"If it be the self-same piece of pure experience, taken twice over, that serves now as thought and now as thing"—so the objection runs—"how comes it that its attributes should differ so fundamentally in the two takings. As thing, the experience is extended; as thought, it occupies no space or place. As thing, it is red, hard, heavy; but who ever heard of a red, hard or heavy thought? Yet even now you said that an experience is made of just what appears, and what appears is just such adjectives. How can the one experience in its things-function be made of them, consist of them, carry them as its own attributes, while in its thought-function it disowns them and attributes them elsewhere. There is a self-contradiction here from which the radical dualism of thought and thing is the only truth that can save us. Only if the thought is one kind of being can the adjectives exist in it 'intentionally' (to use the scholastic term); only if the thing is another kind, can they exist in it constitutively and energetically. No simple subject can take the same adjectives and at one time be qualified by it, and at another time be merely 'of' it, as of something only meant or known."

The solution insisted on by this objector, like many other common-sense solutions, grows the less satisfactory the more one turns it in one's mind. To begin with, *are* thought and thing as heterogeneous as is commonly said?

No one denies that they have some categories in common. Their relations to time are identical. Both, moreover, may have parts (for psychologists in general treat thoughts as having them); and both may be complex or simple. Both are of kinds, can be compared, added and subtracted and arranged in serial orders. All sorts of adjectives qualify our thoughts which appear incompatible with consciousness, being as such a bare diaphaneity. For instance, they are natural and easy, or laborious. They are beautiful, happy, intense, interesting, wise, idiotic, focal, marginal, insipid, confused, vague, precise, rational, casual, general, particular, and many things besides. Moreover, the chapters on "Perception" in the psychology-books are full of facts that make for the essential homogeneity of thought with thing. How, if "subject" and "object" were separated "by the whole diameter of being," and had no attributes in common, could it be so hard to tell, in a presented and recognized material object, what part comes in through the sense-organs and what part comes "out of one's own head"? Sensations and apperceptive ideas fuse here so intimately that you can no more tell where one begins and the other ends, than you can tell, in those cunning circular panoramas that have lately been exhibited, where the real foreground and the painted canvas join together.[13]

Descartes for the first time defined thought as the absolutely unextended, and later philosophers have accepted the description as correct. But what possible meaning has it to say that, when we think of a foot-rule or a square yard, extension is not attributable to our thought? Of every extended object the *adequate* mental picture must have all the extension of the object itself. The difference between objective and subjective extension is one of relation to a context solely. In the mind the various extents maintain no necessarily stubborn order relatively to each other, while in the physical world they bound each other stably, and, added together, make the great enveloping Unit which we believe in and call real Space. As "outer," they carry themselves adversely, so to speak, to one another, exclude one another and maintain their distances; while, as "inner," their order is loose, and they form a *durcheinander* in which unity is lost.[14] But to argue from this that inner experience is absolutely inextensive seems to me little short of absurd. The two worlds differ, not by the presence or absence of extension, but by the relations of the extensions which in both worlds exist.

Does not this case of extension now put us on the track of truth in the case of other qualities? It does; and I am surprised that the facts should not have been noticed long ago. Why, for example, do we call a fire hot, and water wet, and yet refuse to say that our mental state, when it is "of" these objects, is either wet or hot? "Intentionally," at any rate, and when the mental state is a vivid image, hotness and wetness are in it just as much as they are in the physical experience. The reason is this, that, as the general chaos of all our experiences gets sifted, we find that there are some fires that will always burn sticks and always warm our bodies, and that there are some waters that will always put out fires; while there are other fires and waters that will not act at all. The general group of experiences that *act*, that do not only possess their natures intrinsically, but wear them adjectively and energetically, turning them against one another, comes inevitably to be contrasted with the group whose members, having identically the same natures, fail to manifest them in the "energetic" way. I make for myself now an experience of blazing fire; I place it near my body; but it does not warm me in the least. I lay a stick upon it, and the stick either burns or remains green, as I please. I call up water, and pour it on the fire, and absolutely no difference ensues. I account for all such facts by calling this whole train of experiences unreal, a mental train. Mental fire is what won't burn real sticks; mental water is what won't necessarily (though of course it may) put out even a mental fire. Mental knives may be sharp, but they won't cut real wood. Mental triangles are pointed, but their points won't wound. With "real" objects, on the contrary, consequences always accrue; and thus the real experiences get sifted from the mental ones, the things from our thoughts of them, fanciful or true, and precipitated together as the stable part of the whole experience-chaos, under the name of the physical world. Of this our perceptual experiences are the nucleus, they being the originally *strong* experiences. We add a lot of conceptual experiences to them, making these strong also in imagination, and building out the remoter parts of the physical world by their means; and around this core of reality the world of laxly connected fancies and mere rhapsodical objects floats like a bank of clouds. In the clouds, all sorts of rules are violated which in the core are kept. Extensions there can be indefinitely located; motion there obeys no Newton's laws....

Notes

1. Articles by Baldwin, Ward, Bawden, King, Alexander and others. Dr. Perry is frankly over the border.

2. In my *Psychology* I have tried to show that we need no knower other than the "passing thought." [*Principles of Psychology*, vol. I, pp. 338 ff.]

3. G. E. Moore: *Mind*, vol. XII, N. S. [1903], p. 450.

4. Paul Natorp: *Einleitung in die Psychologie*, 1888, pp. 14, 112.

5. "Figuratively speaking, consciousness may be said to be the one universal solvent, or menstruum, in which the different concrete kinds of psychic acts and facts are contained, whether in concealed or in obvious form." G. T. Ladd: *Psychology, Descriptive and Explanatory*, 1894, p. 30.

6. Here as elsewhere the relations are of course *experienced* relations, members of the same originally chaotic manifold of non-perceptual experience of which the related terms themselves are parts.

7. Münsterberg: *Grundzüge der Psychologie*, vol. I, p. 48.

8. Cf. A. L. Hodder: *The Adversaries of the Sceptic*, pp. 94–99.

9. For simplicity's sake I confine my exposition to "external" reality. But there is also the system of ideal reality in which the room plays its part. Relations of comparison, of classification, serial order, value, also are stubborn, assign a definite place to the room, unlike the incoherence of its places in the mere rhapsody of our successive thoughts.

10. Note the ambiguity of this term, which is taken sometimes objectively and sometimes subjectively.

11. In the *Psychological Review* of July [1904], Dr. R. B. Perry has published a view of Consciousness which comes nearer to mine than any other with which I am acquainted. At present, Dr. Perry thinks, every field of experience is so much "fact." It becomes "opinion" or "thought" only in retrospection, when a fresh experience, thinking the same object, alters and corrects it. But the corrective experience becomes itself in turn corrected, and thus experience as a whole is a process in which what is objective originally forever turns subjective, turns into our apprehension of the object. I strongly recommend Dr. Perry's admirable article to my readers.

12. I have given a partial account of the matter in *Mind*, vol. X, p. 27, 1885 [reprinted in *The Meaning of Truth*, pp. 1–42], and in the *Psychological Review*, vol. II, p. 105, 1895 [partly reprinted in *The Meaning of Truth*, pp. 43–50]. See also C. A. Strong's article in the *Journal of Philosophy, Psychology and Scientific Methods*, vol. I, p. 253, May 12, 1904. I hope myself very soon to recur to the matter.

13. Spencer's proof of his "Transfigured Realism" (his doctrine that there is an absolutely non-mental reality) comes to mind as a splendid instance of the impossibility of establishing radical heterogeneity between thought and thing. All his painfully accumulated points of difference run gradually into their opposites, and are full of exceptions. [Cf. Spencer: *Principles of Psychology*, part VII, ch. XIX.]

14. I speak here of the complete inner life in which the mind plays freely with its materials. Of course the mind's free play is restricted when it seeks to copy real things in real space.

10 From "The Province of Functional Psychology"

James Rowland Angell

Functional psychology is at the present moment little more than a point of view, a program, an ambition. It gains its vitality primarily perhaps as a protest against the exclusive excellence of another starting point for the study of the mind, and it enjoys for the time being at least the peculiar vigor which commonly attaches to Protestantism of any sort in its early stages before it has become respectable and orthodox. The time seems ripe to attempt a somewhat more precise characterization of the field of functional psychology than has as yet been offered. What we seek is not the arid and merely verbal definition which to many of us is so justly anathema, but rather an informing appreciation of the motives and ideals which animate the psychologist who pursues this path. His status in the eye of the psychological public is unnecessarily precarious. The conceptions of his purposes prevalent in non-functionalist circles range from positive and dogmatic misapprehension, through frank mystification and suspicion up to moderate comprehension. Nor is this fact an expression of anything peculiarly abstruse and recondite in his intentions. It is due in part to his own ill-defined plans, in part to his failure to explain lucidly exactly what he is about. Moreover, he is fairly numerous and it is not certain that in all important particulars he and his confrères are at one in their beliefs. The considerations which are herewith offered suffer inevitably from this personal limitation. No psychological council of Trent has as yet pronounced upon the true faith. But in spite of probable failure it seems worth while to hazard an attempt at delineating the scope of functionalist principles. I formally renounce any intention to strike out new plans; I am engaged in what is meant as a dispassionate summary of actual conditions.

Whatever else it may be, functional psychology is nothing wholly new. In certain of its phases it is plainly discernible in the psychology of Aristotle and in its more modern garb it has been increasingly in evidence since Spencer wrote his *Psychology* and Darwin his *Origin of Species*. Indeed, as we shall soon see, its crucial problems are inevitably incidental to any serious attempt at understanding mental life. All that is peculiar to its present circumstances is a higher degree of self-consciousness than it possessed before, a more articulate and persistent purpose to organize its vague intentions into tangible methods and principles.

A survey of contemporary psychological writing indicates, as was intimated in the preceding paragraph, that the task of functional psychology is interpreted in several different ways. Moreover, it seems to be possible to advocate one or more of these conceptions while cherishing abhorrence for the others. I distinguish three principal forms of the functional problem with sundry subordinate variants. It will contribute to the clarification of the general situation to dwell upon these for a moment, after which I propose to maintain that they are substantially but modifications of a single problem.

I

There is to be mentioned first the notion which derives most immediately from contrast with the ideals and purposes of structural psychology so-called. This involves the identification of functional psychology with the effort to discern and portray the typical *operations* of consciousness under actual life conditions, as over against the attempt to analyze and describe its elementary and complex *contents*. The structural psychology of sensation, *e.g.*, undertakes to determine the number and character of the various unanalyzable sensory materials, such as the varieties of color, tone, taste, etc. The functional psychology of sensation would on the other hand find its appropriate sphere of interest in the determination of the character of the various sense activities as differing in their *modus operandi* from one another and from other mental processes such as judging, conceiving, willing and the like. . . .

The more extreme and ingenuous conceptions of structural psychology seem to have grown out of an unchastened indulgence in what we may call the "states of consciousness" doctrine. I take it that this is in reality the contemporary version of Locke's "idea." If you adopt as your material for psychological analysis the isolated "moment of consciousness," it is very easy to become so absorbed in determining its constitution as to be rendered somewhat oblivious to its artificial character. The most essential quarrel which the functionalist has with structuralism in its thoroughgoing and consistent form arises from this fact and touches the feasibility and worth of the effort to get at mental process as it *is* under the conditions of actual experience rather than as it *appears* to a merely postmortem analysis. It is of course true that for introspective purposes we must in a sense always work with vicarious representatives of the particular mental processes which we set out to observe. But it makes a great difference even on such terms whether one is directing attention primarily to the discovery of the way in which such a mental process operates, and what the conditions are under which it appears, or whether one is engaged simply in tearing apart the fibers of its tissues. The latter occupation is useful and for certain purposes essential, but it often stops short of that which is as a life phenomenon the most essential, *i.e.*, the *modus operandi* of the phenomenon. . . .

The fact that mental contents are evanescent and fleeting marks them off in an important way from the relatively permanent elements of anatomy. No matter how much we may talk of the preservation of psychical dispositions, nor how many metaphors we may summon to characterize the storage of ideas in some hypothetical deposit chamber of memory, the obstinate fact remains that when we are not experiencing a sensation or an idea it is, strictly speaking, non-existent. Moreover, when we manage by one or another device to secure that which we designate the same sensation or the same idea, we not only have no guarantee that our second edition is really a replica of the first, we have a good bit of presumptive evidence that from the content point of view the original never is and never can be literally duplicated.

Functions, on the other hand, persist as well in mental as in physical life. We may never have twice exactly the same idea viewed from the side of sensuous structure and composition. But there seems nothing whatever to prevent our having as often as we will contents of consciousness which *mean* the same thing. They function in one and the same practical way, however discrepant their momentary texture. The situation is rudely analogous to the biological case where very different structures may under different conditions be called on to perform identical functions; and the matter naturally harks back for its earliest analogy to the instance of protoplasm where functions seem very tentatively and imperfectly differentiated. Not only then are general functions like memory persistent, but special functions such as the memory of particular events are persistent and largely independent of the specific conscious contents called upon from time to time to subserve the functions. . . .

Substantially identical with this first conception of functional psychology, but phrasing itself somewhat differently, is the view which regards the functional problem as concerned with discovering how and why conscious processes are what they are, instead of dwelling as the structuralist is supposed to do upon the problem of determining the irreducible elements of consciousness and their characteristic modes of combination. I have elsewhere defended the view that however it may be in other sciences dealing with life phenomena, in psychology at least the answer to the question "what" implicates the answer to the questions "how" and "why."

Stated briefly the ground on which this position rests is as follows: In so far as you attempt to analyze any particular state of consciousness you find that the mental elements presented to your notice are dependent upon the particular exigencies and conditions which call them forth. Not only does the affective coloring of such a psychical moment depend upon one's temporary condition, mood and aims, but the very sensations themselves are determined in their qualitative texture by the totality of circumstances subjective and objective within which they arise. You cannot get a fixed and definite color sensation for example, without keeping perfectly constant the external and internal conditions in which it appears. The particular sense quality is in short functionally determined by the necessities of the existing situation which it emerges to meet. If you inquire then deeply enough what particular sensation you have in a given case, you always find it necessary to take account of the manner in which, and the reasons why, it was experienced at all. You may of course, if you will, abstract from these considerations, but in so far as you do so, your analysis and description is manifestly partial and incomplete. Moreover, even when you do so abstract and attempt to describe certain isolable sense qualities, your descriptions are of necessity couched in terms not of the experienced quality itself, but in terms of the conditions which produced it, in terms of some other quality with which it is compared, or in terms of some more overt act to which the sense stimulation led. That is to say, the very description itself is functionalistic and must be so. The truth of this assertion can be illustrated and tested by appeal to any situation in which one is trying to reduce sensory complexes, *e.g.*, colors or sounds, to their rudimentary components.

II

A broader outlook and one more frequently characteristic of contemporary writers meets us in the next conception of the task of functional psychology. This conception is in part a reflex of the prevailing interest in the larger formulæ of biology and particularly the evolutionary hypotheses within whose majestic sweep is nowadays included the history of the whole stellar universe; in part it echoes the same philosophical call to new life which has been heard as pragmatism, as humanism, even as functionalism itself. I should not wish to commit either party by asserting that functional psychology and pragmatism are ultimately one. Indeed, as a psychologist I should hesitate to bring down on myself the avalanche of metaphysical invective which has been loosened by pragmatic writers. To be sure pragmatism has slain its thousands, but I should cherish scepticism as to whether functional psychology would the more speedily slay its tens of thousands by announcing an offensive and defensive alliance with pragmatism. In any case I only hold that the two movements spring from similar logical motivation and rely for their vitality and propagation upon forces closely germane to one another.

The functional psychologist then in his modern attire is interested not alone in the operations of mental process considered merely of and by and for itself, but also and more vigorously in mental activity as part of a larger stream of biological forces which are daily and hourly at work before our eyes and which are constitutive of the most important and most absorbing part of our world. The psychologist of this stripe is wont to take his cue from the basal conception of the evolutionary movement, *i.e.*, that for the most part organic structures and functions possess their present characteristics by virtue of the efficiency with which they fit into the extant conditions of life broadly designated the environment. With this conception in mind he proceeds to attempt some understanding of the manner in which the psychical contributes to the furtherance of the sum total of organic activities, not alone the psychical in its entirety, but especially the psychical in its particularities—mind as judging, mind as feeling, etc.

This is the point of view which instantly brings the psychologist cheek by jowl with the general biologist. It is the presupposition of every philosophy save that of outright ontological materialism that mind plays the stellar rôle in all the environmental adaptations of animals which possess it. But this persuasion has generally occupied the position of an innocuous truism or at best a jejune postulate, rather than that of a problem requiring, or permitting, serious scientific treatment. At all events, this was formerly true.

This older and more complacent attitude toward the matter is, however, being rapidly displaced by a conviction of the need for light on the exact character of the accommodatory service represented by the various great modes of conscious expression. Such an effort if successful world not only broaden the foundations for biological appreciation of the intimate nature of accommodatory process, it would also immensely enchance the psychologist's interest in the exact portrayal of conscious life. It is of course the latter consideration which lends importance to the matter from our point of view. Moreover, not a few practical consequences of value may be expected to flow from this attempt, if it achieves even a measurable degree of success. Pedagogy and mental hygiene both await the quickening and guiding counsel which can only come from a psychology of this stripe. For their purposes a strictly structural psychology is as sterile in theory as teachers and psychiatrists have found it in practice.

As a concrete example of the transfer of attention from the more general phases of consciousness as accommodatory activity to the particularistic features of the case may be mentioned the rejuvenation of interest in the quasi-biological field which we designate animal psychology. This movement is surely among the most pregnant with which we meet in our own generation. Its problems are in no sense of the merely theoretical and speculative kind, although, like all scientific endeavor, it possesses an intellectual and methodological background on which such problems loom large. But the frontier upon which it is pushing forward its explorations is a region of definite, concrete fact, tangled and confused and often most difficult of access, but nevertheless a region of fact, accessible like all other facts to persistent and intelligent interrogation.

That many of the most fruitful researches in this field have been achievements of men nominally biologists rather than psychologists in no wise affects the merits of the case. A similar situation exists in the experimental psychology of sensation where not a little of the best work has been accomplished by scientists not primarily known as psychologists.

It seems hardly too much to say that the empirical conceptions of the consciousness of the lower animals have undergone a radical alteration in the past few years by virtue of the studies in comparative psychology. The splendid investigations of the mechanism of instinct, of the facts and methods of animal orientation, of the scope and character of the several sense processes, of the capabilities of education and the range of selective accommodatory capacities in the animal kingdom, these and dozens of other similar problems have received for the first time drastic scientific examination, experimental in character wherever possible, observational elsewhere, but observational in the spirit of conservative non-anthropomorphism as earlier observations almost never were. In most cases they have to be sure but shown the way to further and more precise knowledge, yet there can be but little question that the trail which they have blazed has success at its farther end.

One may speak almost as hopefully of human genetic psychology which has been carried on so profitably in our own country. As so often in psychology, the great desideratum here, is the completion of adequate methods which will insure really stable scientific results. But already our general psychological theory has been vitalized and broadened by the results of the genetic methods thus far elaborated. These studies constantly emphasize for us the necessity of getting the longitudinal rather than the transverse view of life phenomena. . . .

III

The third conception which I distinguish is often in practice merged with the second, but it involves stress upon a problem logically prior perhaps to the problem raised there and so warrants separate mention. Functional psychology, it is often alleged, is in reality a form of psychophysics. To be sure, its aims and ideals are not explicitly quantitative in the manner characteristic of that science as commonly understood. But it finds its major interest in determining the relations to one another of the physical and mental portions of the organism.

It is undoubtedly true that many of those who write under functional prepossessions are wont to introduce frequent references to the physiological processes which accompany or condition mental life. Moreover, certain followers of this faith are prone to declare forthwith that psychology is simply a branch of biology and that we are in consequence entitled, if not indeed obliged, to make use where possible of biological materials....

Whether or not one sympathizes with the views of that wing of the functionalist party to which our attention has just been directed it certainly seems a trifle unfair to cast up the mind–body difficulty in the teeth of the functionalist as such when on logical grounds he is no more guilty than any of his psychological neighbors. No courageous psychology of volition is possible which does not squarely face the mind–body problem, and in point of fact every important description of mental life contains doctrine of one kind or another upon this matter. A literally pure psychology of volition would be a sort of hanging-garden of Babylon, marvelous but inaccessible to psychologists of terrestrial habit. The functionalist is a greater sinner than others only in so far as he finds necessary and profitable a more constant insistence upon the translation of mental process into physiological process and conversely.

IV

... No description of the actual circumstances attending the participation of mind in the accommodatory activities of the organism could be other than a mere empty schematism without making reference to the manner in which mental processes eventuate in motor phenomena of the physiological organism. The overt accommodatory act is, I take it, always sooner or later a muscular movement. But this fact being admitted, there is nothing for it, if one will describe accommodatory processes, but to recognize the mind–body relations and in some way give expression to their practical significance. It is only in this regard ... that the functionalist departs a trifle in his practice and a trifle more in his theory from the rank and file of his colleagues.

11 From *The Concept of Mind*

Gilbert Ryle

The Official Doctrine

There is a doctrine about the nature and place of minds which is so prevalent among theorists and even among laymen that it deserves to be described as the official theory. Most philosophers, psychologists and religious teachers subscribe, with minor reservations, to its main articles and, although they admit certain theoretical difficulties in it, they tend to assume that these can be overcome without serious modifications being made to the architecture of the theory. It will be argued here that the central principles of the doctrine are unsound and conflict with the whole body of what we know about minds when we are not speculating about them.

The official doctrine, which hails chiefly from Descartes, is something like this. With the doubtful exceptions of idiots and infants in arms every human being has both a body and a mind. Some would prefer to say that every human being is both a body and a mind. His body and his mind are ordinarily harnessed together, but after the death of the body his mind may continue to exist and function.

Human bodies are in space and are subject to the mechanical laws which govern all other bodies in space. Bodily processes and states can be inspected by external observers. So a man's bodily life is as much a public affair as are the lives of animals and reptiles and even as the careers of trees, crystals and planets.

But minds are not in space, nor are their operations subject to mechanical laws. The workings of one mind are not witnessable by other observers; its career is private. Only I can take direct cognisance of the states and processes of my own mind. A person therefore lives through two collateral histories, one consisting of what happens in and to his body, the other consisting of what happens in and to his mind. The first is public, the second private. The events in the first history are events in the physical world, those in the second are events in the mental world.

It has been disputed whether a person does or can directly monitor all or only some of the episodes of his own private history; but, according to the official doctrine, of at least some of these episodes he has direct and unchallengeable cognisance. In consciousness, self-consciousness and introspection he is directly and authentically apprised of the present states and operations of his mind. He may have great or small uncertainties about concurrent and adjacent episodes in the physical world, but he can have none about at least part of what is momentarily occupying his mind.

It is customary to express this bifurcation of his two lives and of his two worlds by saying that the things and events which belong to the physical world, including his own body, are external, while the workings of his own mind are internal. This antithesis of outer and inner is of course meant to be construed as a metaphor, since minds, not being in space, could not be described as being spatially inside anything else, or as having things going on spatially inside themselves. But relapses from this good intention are common and theorists are found speculating how stimuli, the physical sources of which are yards or miles outside a person's skin, can generate mental responses inside his skull, or how decisions framed inside his cranium can set going movements of his extremities.

Even when "inner" and "outer" are construed as metaphors, the problem how a person's mind and body influence one another is notoriously charged with theoretical difficulties. What the mind wills, the legs, arms and the tongue execute; what affects the ear and the eye has something to do with what the mind perceives; grimaces and smiles betray the mind's moods and bodily castigations lead, it is hoped, to moral improvement. But the actual transactions between the episodes of the private history and those of the public history remain mysterious, since by definition they can belong to neither series. They could not be reported among the happenings described in a person's autobiography of his inner life, but nor could they be reported among those described in some one else's biography of that person's overt career. They can be inspected neither by introspection nor by laboratory experiment. They are theoretical shuttle-cocks which are forever being bandied from the physiologist back to the psychologist and from the psychologist back to the physiologist.

Underlying this partly metaphorical representation of the bifurcation of a person's two lives there is a seemingly more profound and philosophical assumption. It is assumed that there are two different kinds of existence or status. What exists or happens may have the status of physical existence, or it may have the status of mental existence. Somewhat as the faces of coins are either heads or tails, or somewhat as living creatures are either male or female, so, it is supposed, some existing is physical existing, other existing is mental existing. It is a necessary feature of what has physical existence that it is in space and time, it is a necessary feature of what has mental existence that it is in time but not in space. What has physical existence is composed of matter, or else is a function of matter; what has mental existence consists of consciousness, or else is a function of consciousness.

There is thus a polar opposition between mind and matter, an opposition which is often brought out as follows. Material objects are situated in a common field, known as "space," and what happens to one body in one part of space is mechanically connected with what happens to other bodies in other parts of space. But mental happenings occur in insulated fields, known as "minds," and there is, apart maybe from telepathy, no direct causal connection between what happens in one mind and what happens in another. Only through the medium of the public physical world can the mind of one person make a difference to the mind of another. The mind is its own place and in his inner life each of us lives the life of a ghostly Robinson Crusoe. People can see, hear and jolt one another's bodies, but they are irremediably blind and deaf to the workings of one another's minds and inoperative upon them.

What sort of knowledge can be secured of the workings of a mind? On the one side, according to the official theory, a person has direct knowledge of the best imaginable kind of the workings of his own mind. Mental states and processes are (or are normally) conscious states and processes, and the consciousness which irradiates them can engender no illusions and leaves the door open for no doubts. A person's present thinkings, feelings and willings, his perceivings, rememberings and imaginings are intrinsically "phosphorescent"; their existence and their nature are inevitably betrayed to their owner. The inner life is a stream of consciousness of such a sort that it would be absurd to suggest that the mind whose life is that stream might be unaware of what is passing down it.

True, the evidence adduced recently by Freud seems to show that there exist channels tributary to this stream, which run hidden from their owner. People are actuated by impulses the existence of which they vigorously disavow; some of their thoughts differ from the thoughts which they acknowledge; and some of the actions which they think they will to perform they do not really will. They are thoroughly gulled by some of their own hypocrisies and they successfully ignore facts about their mental lives which on the official theory ought to be patent to them. Holders of the official theory tend, however, to maintain that anyhow in normal circumstances a person must be directly and authentically seized of the present state and workings of his own mind.

Besides being currently supplied with these alleged immediate data of consciousness, a person is also generally supposed to be able to exercise from time to time a special kind of perception, namely inner perception, or introspection. He can take a (non-optical) "look" at what is passing in his mind. Not only can he view and scrutinize a flower through his sense of sight and listen to and discriminate the notes of a bell through his sense of hearing; he can also reflectively or introspectively watch, without any bodily organ of sense, the current episodes of his inner life. This self-observation is also commonly supposed to be immune from illusion, confusion or doubt. A mind's reports of its own affairs have a certainty superior to the best that is possessed by its reports of matters in the physical world. Sense-perceptions can, but consciousness and introspection cannot, be mistaken or confused.

On the other side, one person has no direct access of any sort to the events of the inner life of another. He cannot do better than make problematic inferences from the observed behaviour of the other person's body to the states of mind which, by analogy from his own conduct, he supposes to be signalised by that behaviour. Direct access to the workings of a mind is the privilege of that mind itself; in default of such privileged access, the workings of one mind are inevitably occult to everyone else. For the supposed arguments from bodily movements similar to their own to mental workings similar to their own would lack any possibility of observational corroboration. Not unnaturally, therefore, an adherent of the official theory finds it difficult to resist this consequence of his premisses, that he has no good reason to believe that there do exist minds other than his own. Even if he prefers to believe that to other human bodies there are harnessed minds not unlike his own, he cannot claim to be able to discover their individual characteristics, or the particular things that they undergo and do. Absolute solitude is on this showing the ineluctable destiny of the soul. Only our bodies can meet.

As a necessary corollary of this general scheme there is implicitly prescribed a special way of construing our ordinary concepts of mental powers and operations. The verbs, nouns and adjectives, with which in ordinary life we describe the wits, characters and higher-grade performances of the people with whom we have do, are required to be construed as signifying special episodes in their secret histories, or else as signifying tendencies for such episodes to occur. When someone is described as knowing, believing or guessing something, as hoping, dreading, intending or shirking something, as designing this or being amused at that, these verbs are supposed to denote the occurrence of specific modifications in his (to us) occult stream of consciousness. Only his own privileged access to this stream in direct awareness and introspection could provide authentic testimony that these mental-conduct verbs were correctly or incorrectly applied. The onlooker, be he teacher, critic, biographer or friend, call never assure himself that his comments have any vestige of truth. Yet it was just because we do in fact all know how to make such comments, make them with general correctness and correct them when they turn out to be confused or mistaken, that philosophers found it necessary to construct their theories of the nature and place of minds. Finding mental-conduct concepts being regularly and effectively used, they properly sought to fix their logical geography. But the logical geography officially recommended would entail that there could be no regular or effective use of these mental-conduct concepts in our descriptions of, and prescriptions for, other people's minds.

The Absurdity of the Official Doctrine

Such in outline is the official theory. I shall often speak of it, with deliberate abusiveness, as "the dogma of the Ghost in the Machine." I hope to prove that it is entirely false, and false not in detail but in principle. It is not merely an assemblage of particular mistakes. It is one big mistake and a mistake of a special kind. It is, namely, a category-mistake. It represents the facts of mental life as if they belonged to one logical type or category (or range of types or categories), when they actually belong to another. The dogma is therefore a philosopher's myth. In attempting to explode the myth I shall probably be taken to be denying well-known facts about the mental life of human beings, and my plea that I aim at doing nothing more than rectify the logic of mental-conduct concepts will probably be disallowed as mere subterfuge.

I must first indicate what is meant by the phrase "Category-mistake." This I do in a series of illustrations.

A foreigner visiting Oxford or Cambridge for the first time is shown a number of colleges, libraries, playing fields, museums, scientific departments and administrative offices. He then asks "But where is the University? I have seen where the members of the Colleges live, where the Registrar works, where the scientists experiment and the rest. But I have not yet seen the University in which reside and work the members of your University." It has then to be explained to him that the University is not another collateral institution, some ulterior counterpart to the colleges, laboratories and offices which he has seen. The University is just the way in which all that he has already seen is organized. When they are seen and when their co-ordination is understood, the University has been seen. His mistake lay in his innocent assumption that it was correct to speak of Christ Church, the Bodleian Library, the Ashmolean Museum *and* the University, to speak, that is, as if "the University" stood for an extra member of the class of which these other units are members. He was mistakenly allocating the University to the same category as that to which the other institutions belong.

The same mistake would be made by a child witnessing the march-past of a division, who, having had pointed out to him such and such battalions, batteries, squadrons, etc., asked when the division was going to appear. He would be supposing that a division was a counterpart to the units already seen, partly similar to them and partly unlike them. He would be shown his mistake by being told that in watching the battalions, batteries and squadrons marching past he had been watching the division marching past. The march-past was not a parade of battalions, batteries, squadrons *and* a division; it was a parade of the battalions, batteries and squadrons *of* a division.

One more illustration. A foreigner watching his first game of cricket learns what are the functions of the bowlers, the batsmen, the fielders, the umpires and the scorers. He then says "But there is no one left on the field to contribute the famous element of team-spirit. I see who does the bowling, the batting and the wicket-keeping; but I do not see whose role it is to exercise *esprit de corps.*" Once more, it would have to be explained that he was looking for the wrong type of thing. Team-spirit is not another cricketing-operation supplementary to all of the other special tasks. It is, roughly, the keenness with which each of the special tasks is performed, and performing a task keenly is not performing two tasks. Certainly exhibiting team-spirit is not the same thing as bowling or catching, but nor is it a third thing such that we can say that the bowler first bowls *and* then exhibits team-spirit or that a fielder is at a given moment *either* catching *or* displaying *esprit de corps.*

These illustrations of category-mistakes have a common feature which must be noticed. The mistakes were made by people who did not know how to wield the concepts *University, division* and *team-spirit.* Their puzzles arose from inability to use certain items in the English vocabulary.

The theoretically interesting category-mistakes are those made by people who are perfectly competent to apply concepts, at least in the situations with which they are familiar, but are still liable in their abstract thinking to allocate those concepts to logical types to which they do not belong. An instance of a mistake of this sort would be the following story. A student of politics has learned the main differences between the British, the French and the American Constitutions, and has learned also the differences and connections between the Cabinet, Parliament, the various Ministries, the Judicature and the Church of England. But he still becomes embarrassed when asked questions about the connections between the Church of England, the Home Office and the British Constitution. For while the Church and the Home Office are institutions, the British Constitution is not another institution in the same sense of that noun. So inter-institutional relations which can be asserted or denied to hold between the Church and the Home Office cannot be asserted or denied to hold between either of them and the British Constitution. "The British Constitution" is not a term of the same logical type as "the Home Office" and "the Church of England." In a partially similar way, John Doe may be a relative, a friend, an enemy or a stranger to Richard Roe; but he cannot be any of these things to the Average Taxpayer. He knows how to talk sense in certain sorts of discussions about the Average Taxpayer, but he is baffled to say why he could not come across him in the street as he can come across Richard Roe.

It is pertinent to our main subject to notice that, so long as the student of politics continues to think of the British Constitution as a counterpart to the other institutions, he will tend to describe it as a mysteriously occult institution; and so long as

John Doe continues to think of the Average Taxpayer as a fellow-citizen, he will tend to think of him as an elusive insubstantial man, a ghost who is everywhere yet nowhere.

My destructive purpose is to show that a family of radical category-mistakes is the source of the double-life theory. The representation of a person as a ghost mysteriously ensconced in a machine derives from this argument. Because, as is true, a person's thinking, feeling and purposive doing cannot be described solely in the idioms of physics, chemistry and physiology, therefore they must be described in counterpart idioms. As the human body is a complex organised unit, so the human mind must be another complex organised unit, though one made of a different sort of stuff and with a different sort of structure. Or, again, as the human body, like any other parcel of matter, is a field of causes and effects, so the mind must be another field of causes and effects, though not (Heaven be praised) mechanical causes and effects.

The Origin of the Category-Mistake

One of the chief intellectual origins of what I have yet to prove to be the Cartesian category-mistake seems to be this. When Galileo showed that his methods of scientific discovery were competent to provide a mechanical theory which should cover every occupant of space, Descartes found in himself two conflicting motives. As a man of scientific genius he could not but endorse the claims of mechanics, yet as a religious and moral man he could not accept, as Hobbes accepted, the discouraging rider to those claims, namely that human nature differs only in degree of complexity from clockwork. The mental could not be just a variety of the mechanical.

He and subsequent philosophers naturally but erroneously availed themselves of the following escape-route. Since mental-conduct words are not to be construed as signifying the occurrence of mechanical processes, they must be construed as signifying the occurrence of non-mechanical processes; since mechanical laws explain movements in space as the effects of other movements in space, other laws must explain some of the non-spatial workings of minds as the effects of other non-spatial workings of minds. The difference between the human behaviours which we describe as intelligent and those which we describe as unintelligent must be a difference in their causation; so, while some movements of human tongues and limbs are the effects of mechanical causes, others must be the effects of non-mechanical causes, i.e. some issue from movements of particles of matter, others from workings of the mind.

The differences between the physical and the mental were thus represented as differences inside the common framework of the categories of "thing," "stuff," "attribute," "state," "process," "change," "cause" and "effect." Minds are things, but different sorts of things from bodies; mental processes are causes and effects, but different sorts of causes and effects from bodily movements. And so on. Somewhat as the foreigner expected the University to be an extra edifice, rather like a college but also considerably different, so the repudiators of mechanism represented minds as extra centres of causal processes, rather like machines but also considerably different from them. Their theory was a para-mechanical hypothesis.

That this assumption was at the heart of the doctrine is shown by the fact that there was from the beginning felt to be a major theoretical difficulty in explaining how minds can influence and be influenced by bodies. How can a mental process, such as willing, cause spatial movements like the movements of the tongue? How can a physical change in the optic nerve have among its effects a mind's perception of a flash of light? This notorious crux by itself shows the logical mould into which Descartes pressed his theory of the mind. It was the self-same mould into which he and Galileo set their mechanics. Still unwittingly adhering to the grammar of mechanics, he tried to avert disaster by describing minds in what was merely an obverse vocabulary. The workings of minds had to be described by the mere negatives of the specific descriptions given to bodies; they are not in space, they are not motions, they are not modifications of matter, they are not accessible to public observation. Minds are not bits of clockwork, they are just bits of not-clockwork.

As thus represented, minds are not merely ghosts harnessed to machines, they are themselves just spectral machines. Though the human body is an engine, it is not quite an ordinary engine, since some of its workings are governed by another engine inside it—this interior governor-engine being one of a very special sort. It is invisible, inaudible and it has no size or weight. It cannot be taken to bits and the laws it obeys are not those known to ordinary engineers. Nothing is known of how it governs the bodily engine.

A second major crux points the same moral. Since, according to the doctrine, minds belong to the same category as bodies and since bodies are rigidly governed by mechanical laws, it seemed to many theorists to follow that minds must be similarly governed by rigid non-mechanical laws. The physical world is a deterministic system, so the mental world must be a deterministic system. Bodies cannot help the modifications that they undergo, so minds cannot help pursuing the careers fixed for them. *Responsibility, choice, merit* and *demerit* are therefore inapplicable concepts—unless the compromise solution is adopted of saying that the laws governing mental processes, unlike those governing physical processes, have the congenial attribute of being only rather rigid. The problem of the Freedom of the Will was the problem how to reconcile the hypothesis that minds are to be described in terms drawn from the categories of mechanics with the knowledge that higher-grade human conduct is not of a piece with the behaviour of machines.

It is an historical curiosity that it was not noticed that the entire argument was broken-backed. Theorists correctly assumed that any sane man could already recognise the differences between, say, rational and non-rational utterances or between purposive and automatic behaviour. Else there would have been nothing requiring to be salved from mechanism. Yet the explanation given presupposed that one person could in principle never recognise the difference between the rational and the irrational utterances issuing from other human bodies, since he could never get access to the postulated immaterial causes of some of their utterances. Save for the doubtful exception of himself, he could never tell the difference between a man and a Robot. It would have to be conceded, for example, that, for all that we can tell, the inner lives of persons who are classed as idiots or lunatics are as rational as those of anyone else. Perhaps only their overt behaviour is disappointing; that is to say, perhaps "idiots" are not really idiotic, or "lunatics" lunatic. Perhaps, too, some of those who are classed as sane are really idiots. According to the theory, external observers could never know how the overt behaviour of others is correlated with their mental powers and processes and so they could never know or even plausibly conjecture whether their applications of mental-conduct concepts to these other people were correct or incorrect. It would then be hazardous or impossible for a man to claim sanity or logical consistency even for himself, since he would be debarred from comparing his own performances with those of others. In short, our characterisations of persons and their performances as intelligent, prudent and virtuous or as stupid, hypocritical and cowardly could never have been made, so the problem of providing a special causal hypothesis to serve as the basis of such diagnoses would never have arisen. The question, "How do persons differ from machines?" arose just because everyone already knew how to apply mental-conduct concepts before the new causal hypothesis was introduced. This causal hypothesis could not therefore be the source of the criteria used in those applications. Nor, of course, has the causal hypothesis in any degree improved our handling of those criteria. We still distinguish good from bad arithmetic, politic from impolitic conduct and fertile from infertile imaginations in the ways in which Descartes himself distinguished them before and after he speculated how the applicability of these criteria was compatible with the principle of mechanical causation.

He had mistaken the logic of his problem. Instead of asking by what criteria intelligent behaviour is actually distinguished from non-intelligent behaviour, he asked "Given that the principle of mechanical causation does not tell us the difference, what other causal principle will tell it us?" He realised that the problem was not one of mechanics and assumed that it must therefore be one of some counterpart to mechanics. Not unnaturally psychology is often cast for just this role.

When two terms belong to the same category, it is proper to construct conjunctive propositions embodying them. Thus a purchaser may say that he bought a left-hand glove and a right-hand glove, but not that he bought a left-hand glove, a right-hand glove and a pair of gloves. "She came home in a flood of tears and a sedan-chair" is a well-known joke based on the absurdity of conjoining terms of different types. It would have been equally ridiculous to construct the disjunction "She came home either in a flood of tears or else in a sedan-chair." Now the dogma of the Ghost in the Machine does just this. It maintains that there exist both bodies and minds; that there occur physical processes and mental processes; that there are mechanical causes of corporeal movements and mental causes of corporeal movements. I shall argue that these and other analogous conjunctions are absurd; but, it must be noticed, the argument will not show that either of the illegitimately conjoined propositions is absurd in itself. I am not, for example, denying that there occur mental processes. Doing long division is a mental process and so is making a joke. But I am saying that the phrase "there occur mental processes" does not mean the same sort of thing as "there occur physical processes," and, therefore, that it makes no sense to conjoin or disjoin the two.

If my argument is successful, there will follow some interesting consequences. First, the hallowed contrast between Mind and Matter will be dissipated, but dissipated not by either of the equally hallowed absorptions of Mind by Matter or of Matter by Mind, but in quite a different way. For the seeming contrast of the two will be shown to be as illegitimate as would be the contrast of "she came home in a flood of tears" and "she came home in a sedan-chair." The belief that there is a polar opposition between Mind and Matter is the belief that they are terms of the same logical type.

It will also follow that both Idealism and Materialism are answers to an improper question. The "reduction" of the material world to mental states and processes, as well as the "reduction" of mental states and processes to physical states and processes, presuppose the legitimacy of the disjunction "Either there exist minds or there exist bodies (but not both)." It would be like saying, "Either she bought a left-hand and a right-hand glove or she bought a pair of gloves (but not both)."

It is perfectly proper to say, in one logical tone of voice, that there exist minds and to say, in another logical tone of voice, that there exist bodies. But these expressions do not indicate two different species of existence, for "existence" is not a generic word like "coloured" or "sexed." They indicate two different senses of "exist," somewhat as "rising" has different senses in "the tide is rising," "hopes are rising," and "the average age of death is rising." A man would be thought to be making a poor joke who said that three things are now rising, namely the tide, hopes and the average age of death. It would be just as good or bad a joke to say that there exist prime numbers and Wednesdays and public opinions and navies; or that there exist both minds and bodies.... I try to prove that the official theory does rest on a batch of category-mistakes by showing that logically absurd corollaries follow from it. The exhibition of these absurdities will have the constructive effect of bringing out part of the correct logic of mental-conduct concepts.

Historical Note

It would not be true to say that the official theory derives solely from Descartes' theories, or even from a more widespread anxiety about the implications of seventeenth century mechanics. Scholastic and Reformation theology had schooled the intellects of the scientists as well as of the laymen, philosophers and clerics of that age. Stoic-Augustinian theories of the will were embedded in the Calvinist doctrines of sin and grace; Platonic and Aristotelian theories of the intellect shaped the orthodox doctrines of the immortality of the soul. Descartes was reformulating already prevalent theological doctrines of the soul in the new syntax of Galileo. The theologian's privacy of conscience became the philosopher's privacy of consciousness, and what had been the bogy of Predestination reappeared as the bogy of Determinism.

It would also not be true to say that the two-worlds myth did no theoretical good. Myths often do a lot of theoretical good, while they are still new. One benefit bestowed by the para-mechanical myth was that it partly superannuated the then prevalent para-political myth. Minds and their Faculties had previously been described by analogies with political superiors and political subordinates. The idioms used were those of ruling, obeying, collaborating and rebelling. They survived and still survive in many ethical and some epistemological discussions. As, in physics, the new myth of occult Forces was a scientific improvement on the old myth of Final Causes, so, in anthropological and psychological theory, the new myth of hidden operations, impulses and agencies was an improvement on the old myth of dictations, deferences and disobediences.

B Materialism(s): Function, Reduction, and Elimination

12 Is Consciousness a Brain Process?

U. T. Place

Introduction

The view that there exists a separate class of events, mental events, which cannot be described in terms of the concepts employed by the physical sciences no longer commands the universal and unquestioning acceptance amongst philosophers and psychologists which it once did. Modern physicalism, however, unlike the materialism of the seventeenth and eighteenth centuries, is behaviouristic. Consciousness on this view is either a special type of behaviour, "sampling" or "running-back-and-forth" behaviour as Tolman (1932, p. 206) has it, or a disposition to behave in a certain way, an itch for example being a temporary propensity to scratch. In the case of cognitive concepts like "knowing," "believing," "understanding," "remembering" and volitional concepts like "wanting" and "intending," there can be little doubt, I think, that an analysis in terms of dispositions to behave (Wittgenstein 1953, Ryle 1949) is fundamentally sound. On the other hand, there would seem to be an intractable residue of concepts clustering around the notions of consciousness, experience, sensation and mental imagery, where some sort of inner process story is unavoidable (Place 1954). It is possible, of course, that a satisfactory behaviouristic account of this conceptual residuum will ultimately be found. For our present purposes, however, I shall assume that this cannot be done and that statements about pains and twinges, about how things look, sound and feel, about things dreamed of or pictured in the mind's eye, are statements referring to events and processes which are in some sense private or internal to the individual of whom they are predicated. The question I wish to raise is whether in making this assumption we are inevitably committed to a dualist position in which sensations and mental images form a separate category of processes over and above the physical and physiological processes with which they are known to be correlated. I shall argue that an acceptance of inner processes does not entail dualism and that the thesis that consciousness is a process in the brain cannot be dismissed on logical grounds.

The "Is" of Definition and the "Is" of Composition

I want to stress from the outset that in defending the thesis that consciousness is a process in the brain, I am not trying to argue that when we describe our dreams, fantasies and sensations we are talking about processes in our brains. That is, I am not claiming that statements about sensations and mental images are reducible to or analysable into statements about brain processes, in the way in which "cognition statements" are analysable into statements about behaviour. To say that statements about consciousness are statements about brain processes is manifestly false. This is shown (*a*) by the fact that you can describe your sensations and mental imagery without knowing anything about your brain processes or even that such things exist, (*b*) by the fact that statements about one's consciousness and statements about one's brain processes are verified in entirely different ways and (*c*) by the fact that there is nothing self-contradictory about the statement "*X* has a pain but there is nothing going on in his brain." What I do want to assert, however, is that the statement "consciousness is a process in the brain," although not necessarily true, is not necessarily false. "Consciousness is a process in the brain," on my view is neither self-contradictory nor self-evident; it is a reasonable scientific hypothesis, in the way that the statement "lightning is a motion of electric charges" is a reasonable scientific hypothesis.

The all but universally accepted view that an assertion of identity between consciousness and brain processes can be ruled out on logical grounds alone, derives, I suspect, from a failure to distinguish between what we may call the "is" of definition and the "is" of composition. The distinction I have in mind here is the difference between the function of the word "is" in statements like "a square is an equilateral rectangle," "red is a colour," "to understand an instruction is to be able to act appropriately under the appropriate circumstances," and its function in statements like "his table is an old packing case," "her hat is a bundle of straw tied together with string," "a cloud is a mass of water droplets or other particles in suspension." These two types of "is" statements have one thing in common. In both cases it makes sense to add the qualification "and nothing else." In this they differ from those statements in which the "is" is an "is" of predication; the statements "Toby is 80 years old and nothing else," "her hat is red and nothing else" or "giraffes are tall and nothing else," for example, are nonsense. This logical feature may be described by saying that in both cases both the grammatical subject and the grammatical predicate are expressions which provide an adequate characterization of the state of affairs to which they both refer.

In another respect, however, the two groups of statements are strikingly different. Statements like "a square is an equilateral rectangle" are necessary statements which are true by definition. Statements like "his table is an old packing case," on the other hand, are contingent statements which have to be verified by observation. In the case of statements like "a square is an equilateral rectangle" or "red is a colour," there is a relationship between the meaning of the expression forming the grammatical predicate and the meaning of the expression forming the grammatical subject, such that whenever the subject expression is applicable the predicate must also be applicable. If you can describe something as red then you must also be able to describe it as coloured. In the case of statements like "his table is an old packing case," on the other hand, there is no such relationship between the meanings of the expressions "his table" and "old packing case"; it merely so happens that in this case both expressions are applicable to and at the same time provide an adequate characterization of the same object. Those who contend that the statement "consciousness is a brain process" is logically untenable base their claim, I suspect, on the mistaken assumption that if the meanings of two statements or expressions are quite unconnected, they cannot both provide an adequate characterization of the same object or state of affairs: if something is a state of consciousness, it cannot be a brain process, since there is nothing self-contradictory in supposing that someone feels a pain when there is nothing happening inside his skull. By the same token we might be led to conclude that a table cannot be an old packing case, since there is nothing self-contradictory in supposing that someone has a table, but is not in possession of an old packing case.

The Logical Independence of Expressions and the Ontological Independence of Entities

There is, of course, an important difference between the table/packing case and the consciousness/brain process case in that the statement "his table is an old packing case" is a particular proposition which refers only to one particular case, whereas the statement "consciousness is a process in the brain" is a general or universal proposition applying to all states of consciousness whatever. It is fairly clear, I think, that if we lived in a world in which all tables without exception were packing cases, the concepts of "table" and "packing case" in our language would not have their present logically independent status. In such a world a table would be a species of packing case in much the same way that red is a species of colour. It seems to be a rule of language that whenever a given variety of object or state of affairs has two characteristics or sets of characteristics, one of which is unique to the variety of object or state of affairs in question, the expression used to refer to the characteristic or set of characteristics which defines the variety of object or state of affairs in question will always entail the expression used to refer to the other characteristic or set of characteristics. If this rule admitted of no exception it would follow that any expression which is logically independent of another expression which uniquely characterizes a given variety of object or state of affairs, must refer to a characteristic or set of characteristics which is not normally or necessarily associated with the object or state of affairs in question. It is because this rule applies almost universally, I suggest, that we are normally justified in arguing from the logical independence of two expressions to the ontological independence of the states of affairs to which they refer. This would explain both the undoubted force of the argument that consciousness and brain processes must be independent entities because the expressions used to refer to them are logically independent and, in general, the curious phenomenon whereby questions about the furniture of the universe are often fought and not infrequently decided merely on a point of logic.

The argument from the logical independence of two expressions to the ontological independence of the entities to which they refer breaks down in the case of brain processes and consciousness, I believe, because this is one of a relatively small number of cases where the rule stated above does not apply. These exceptions are to be found, I suggest, in those cases where the operations which have to be performed in order to verify the presence of the two sets of characteristics inhering in the object or state of affairs in question can seldom if ever be performed simultaneously. A good example here is the case of the cloud and the mass of droplets or other particles in suspension. A cloud is a large semi-transparent mass with a fleecy texture suspended in the atmosphere whose shape is subject to continual and kaleidoscopic change. When observed at close quarters, however, it is found to consist of a mass of tiny particles, usually water droplets, in continuous motion. On the basis of this second observation we conclude that a cloud is a mass of tiny particles and nothing else. But there is no logical connexion in our language between a cloud and a mass of tiny particles; there is nothing self-contradictory in talking about a cloud which is not composed of tiny particles in suspension. There is no contradiction involved in supposing that clouds consist of a dense mass of fibrous tissue; indeed, such a consistency seems to be implied by many of the functions performed by clouds in fairy stories and mythology. It is clear from this that the terms "cloud" and "mass of tiny particles in suspension" mean quite different things. Yet we do not conclude from this that there must be two things, the mass of particles in suspension and the cloud. The reason for this, I suggest, is that although the characteristics of being a cloud and being a mass of tiny particles in suspension are invariably associated, we never make the observations necessary to verify the statement "that is a cloud" and those necessary to verify the statement "this is a mass of tiny particles in suspension" at one and the same time. We can observe the micro-structure of a cloud only when we are enveloped by it, a condition which effectively prevents us from observing those characteristics which from a distance lead us to describe it as a cloud. Indeed, so disparate are these two experiences that we use different words to describe them. That which is a cloud when we observe it from a distance becomes a fog or mist when we are enveloped by it.

When Are Two Sets of Observations of the Same Event?

The example of the cloud and the mass of tiny particles in suspension was chosen because it is one of the few cases of a general proposition involving what I have called the "is" of composition which does not involve us in scientific technicalities. It is useful because it brings out the connexion between the ordinary everyday cases of the "is" of composition like the table/packing case example and the more technical cases like "lightning is a motion of electric charges" where the analogy with the consciousness/brain process case is most marked. The limitation of the cloud/tiny particles in suspension case is that it does not bring out sufficiently clearly the crucial problem of how the identity of the states of affairs referred to by the two expressions is established. In the cloud case the fact that something is a cloud and the fact that something is a mass of tiny particles in suspension are both verified by the normal processes of visual observation. It is arguable, moreover, that the identity of the entities referred to by the two expressions is established by the continuity between the two sets of observations as the observer moves towards or away from the cloud. In the case of brain processes and consciousness there is no such continuity between the two sets of observations involved. A closer introspective scrutiny will never reveal the passage of nerve impulses over a thousand synapses in the way that a closer scrutiny of a cloud will reveal a mass of tiny particles in suspension. The operations required to verify statements about consciousness and statements about brain processes are fundamentally different.

To find a parallel for this feature we must examine other cases where an identity is asserted between something whose occurrence is verified by the ordinary processes of observation and something whose occurrence is established by special scientific procedures. For this purpose I have chosen the case where we say that lightning is a motion of electric charges. As in the case of consciousness, however closely we scrutinize the lightning we shall never be able to observe the electric charges, and just as the operations for determining the nature of one's state of consciousness are radically different from those involved in determining the nature of one's brain processes, so the operations for determining the occurrence of lightning are radically different from those involved in determining the occurrence of a motion of electric charges. What is it, therefore, that leads us to say that the two sets of observations are observations of the same event? It cannot be merely the fact that the two sets of observations are systematically correlated such that whenever there is lightning there is always a motion of electric charges. There are innumerable cases of such correlations where we have no temptation to say that the two sets of observations are observations of the same event. There is a systematic correlation, for example, between the movement of the tides and the stages of the moon, but this does not lead us to say that records of tidal levels are records of the moon's stages or vice versa. We speak rather of a causal connexion between two independent events or processes.

The answer here seems to be that we treat the two sets of observations as observations of the same event, in those cases where the technical scientific observations set in the context of the appropriate body of scientific theory provide an immediate explanation of the observations made by the man in the street. Thus we conclude that lightning is nothing more than a motion of electric charges, because we know that a motion of electric charges through the atmosphere, such as occurs when lightning is reported, gives rise to the type of visual stimulation which would lead an observer to report a flash of lightning. In the moon/tide case, on the other hand, there is no such direct causal connexion between the stages of the moon and the observations made by the man who measures the height of the tide. The causal connexion is between the moon and the tides, not between the moon and the measurement of the tides.

The Physiological Explanation of Introspection and the Phenomenological Fallacy

If this account is correct, it should follow that in order to establish the identity of consciousness and certain processes in the brain, it would be necessary to show that the introspective observations reported by the subject can be accounted for in terms of processes which are known to have occurred in his brain. In the light of this suggestion it is extremely interesting to find that when a physiologist as distinct from a philosopher finds it difficult to see how consciousness could be a process in the brain, what worries him is not any supposed self-contradiction involved in such an assumption, but the apparent impossibility of accounting for the reports given by the subject of his conscious processes in terms of the known properties of the central nervous system. Sir Charles Sherrington has posed the problem as follows: "The chain of events stretching from the sun's radiation entering the eye to, on the one hand, the contraction of the pupillary muscles, and on the other, to the electrical disturbances in the brain-cortex are all straightforward steps in a sequence of physical 'causation,' such as, thanks to science, are intelligible. But in the second serial chain there follows on, or attends, the stage of brain-cortex reaction an event or set of events quite inexplicable to us, which both as to themselves and as to the causal tie between them and what preceded them science does not help us; a set of events seemingly incommensurable with any of the events leading up to it. The self 'sees' the sun; it senses a two-dimensional disc of brightness, located in the 'sky,' this last a field of lesser brightness, and overhead shaped as a rather flattened dome, coping the self and a hundred other visual things as well. Of hint that this is within the head there is none. Vision is saturated with this strange property called 'projection,' the unargued inference that what it sees is at a 'distance' from the seeing 'self.' Enough has been said to stress that in the sequence of events a step is reached where a physical situation in the brain leads to a psychical, which however contains no hint of the brain or any other bodily part.... The supposition has to be, it would seem, two continuous series of events, one physico-chemical, the other psychical, and at times interaction between them" (Sherrington, 1947, pp. xx–xxi).

Just as the physiologist is not likely to be impressed by the philosopher's contention that there is some self-contradiction involved in supposing consciousness to be a brain process, so the philosopher is unlikely to be impressed by the considerations which lead Sherrington to conclude that there are two sets of events, one physico-chemical, the other psychical. Sherrington's argument for all its emotional appeal depends on a fairly simple logical mistake, which is unfortunately all too frequently made by psychologists and physiologists and not infrequently in the past by the philosophers themselves. This logical mistake, which I shall refer to as the "phenomenological fallacy," is the mistake of supposing that when the subject describes his experience, when he describes how things look, sound, smell, taste or feel to him, he is describing the literal properties of objects and events on a peculiar sort of internal cinema or television screen, usually referred to in the modern psychological literature as the "phenomenal field." If we assume, for example, that when a subject reports a green after-image he is asserting the occurrence inside himself of an object which is literally green, it is clear that we have on our hands an entity for which there is no place in the world of physics. In the case of the green after-image there is no green object in the subject's environment corresponding to the description that he gives. Nor is there anything green in his brain; certainly there is nothing which could have emerged when he reported the appearance of the green after-image. Brain processes are not the sort of things to which colour concepts can be properly applied.

The phenomenological fallacy on which this argument is based depends on the mistaken assumption that because our ability to describe things in our environment depends on our consciousness of them, our descriptions of things are primarily descriptions of our conscious experience and only secondarily, indirectly and inferentially descriptions of the objects and events in our environments. It is assumed that because we recognize things in our environment by their look, sound, smell, taste and feel, we begin by describing their phenomenal properties, i.e., the properties of the looks, sounds, smells, tastes and feels which they produce in us, and infer their real properties from their phenomenal properties. In fact, the reverse is the case. We begin by learning to recognize the real properties of things in our environment. We learn to recognize them, of course, by their look, sound, smell, taste and feel; but this does not mean that we have to learn to describe the look, sound, smell, taste and feel of things before we can describe the things themselves. Indeed, it is only after we have learnt to describe the things in our environment that we can learn to describe our consciousness of them. We describe our conscious experience not in terms of the mythological "phenomenal properties" which are supposed to inhere in the mythological "objects" in the mythological "phenomenal field," but by reference to the actual physical properties of the concrete physical objects, events and processes which normally, though not perhaps in the present instance, give rise to the sort of conscious experience which we are trying to describe. In other words when we describe the after-image as green, we are not saying that there is something, the after-image, which is green, we are saying that we are having the sort of experience which we normally have when, and which we have learnt to describe as, looking at a green patch of light.

Once we rid ourselves of the phenomenological fallacy we realize that the problem of explaining introspective observations in terms of brain processes is far from insuperable. We realize that there is nothing that the introspecting subject says about his conscious experiences which is inconsistent with anything the physiologist might want to say about the brain processes which cause him to describe the environment and his consciousness of that environment in the way he does. When the subject describes his experience by saying that a light which is in fact stationary, appears to move, all the physiologist or physiological psychologist has to do in order to explain the subject's introspective observations, is to show that the brain process which is causing the subject to describe his experience in this way, is the sort of process which normally occurs when he is observing an actual moving object and which therefore normally causes him to report the movement of an object in his environment. Once the mechanism whereby the individual describes what is going on in his environment has been worked out, all that is required to explain the individual's capacity to make introspective observations is an explanation of his ability to discriminate between those cases where his normal habits of verbal description are appropriate to the stimulus situation and those cases where they are not and an explanation of how and why, in those cases where the appropriateness of his normal descriptive habits is in doubt, he learns to issue his ordinary descriptive protocols preceded by a qualificatory phrase like "it appears," "seems," "looks," "feels," etc.

Acknowledgments

I am greatly indebted to my fellow-participants in a series of informal discussions on this topic which took place in the Department of Philosophy, University of Adelaide, in particular to Mr. C. B. Martin for his persistent and searching criticism of my earlier attempts to defend the thesis that consciousness is a brain process, to Prof. D. A. T. Gasking, of the University of Melbourne, for clarifying many of the logical issues involved and to Prof. J. J. C. Smart for moral support and encouragement in what often seemed a lost cause.

References

Place, U. T. (1954). The concept of heed. *Brit. J. Psychol.* 45, 243–55.

Ryle, G. (1949). *The Concept of Mind.* London: Hutchinson.

Sherrington, Sir Charles (1947). Foreword to the 1947 edition of *The Integrative Action of the Nervous System.* Cambridge University Press.

Tolman, E. C. (1932). *Purposive Behaviour in Animals and Men.* Berkeley and Los Angeles: University of California Press.

Wittgenstein, L. (1953). *Philosophical Investigations.* Oxford: Blackwell.

13 The Nature of Mental States

Hilary Putnam

The typical concerns of the Philosopher of Mind might be represented by three questions: (1) How do we know that other people have pains? (2) Are pains brain states? (3) What is the analysis of the concept *pain*? I do not wish to discuss questions (1) and (3) in this chapter. I shall say something about question (2).

Identity Questions

"Is pain a brain state?" (Or, "Is the property of having a pain at time *t* a brain state?")[1] It is impossible to discuss this question sensibly without saying something about the peculiar rules which have grown up in the course of the development of "analytical philosophy"—rules which, far from leading to an end to all conceptual confusions, themselves represent considerable conceptual confusion. These rules—which are, of course, implicit rather than explicit in the practice of most analytical philosophers—are (1) that a statement of the form "being *A* is being *B*" (e.g., "being in pain is being in a certain brain state") can be *correct* only if it follows, in some sense, from the meaning of the terms *A* and *B*; and (2) that a statement of the form "being *A* is being *B*" can be philosophically *informative* only if it is in some sense reductive (e.g., "being in pain is having a certain unpleasant sensation" is not philosophically informative; "being in pain is having a certain behavior disposition" is, if true, philosophically informative). These rules are excellent rules if we still believe that the program of reductive analysis (in the style of the 1930s) can be carried out; if we don't, then they turn analytical philosophy into a mug's game, at least so far as "is" questions are concerned.

In this paper I shall use the term "property" as a blanket term for such things as being in pain, being in a particular brain state, having a particular behavior disposition, and also for magnitudes such as temperature, etc.—i.e., for things which can naturally be represented by one-or-more-place predicates or functors. I shall use the term "concept" for things which can be identified with synonymy-classes of expressions. Thus the concept *temperature* can be identified (I maintain) with the synonymy-class of the word "temperature."[2] (This is like saying that the number 2 can be identified with the class of all pairs. This is quite a different statement from the peculiar statement that 2 *is* the class of all pairs. I do not maintain that concepts *are* synonymy-classes, whatever that might mean, but that they can be identified with synonymy-classes, for the purpose of formalization of the relevant discourse.)

The question "What is the concept *temperature*?" is a very "funny" one. One might take it to mean "What is temperature? Please take my question as a conceptual one."

In that case an answer might be (pretend for a moment "heat" and "temperature" are synonyms) "temperature is heat," or even "the concept of temperature is the same concept as the concept of heat." Or one might take it to mean "What are *concepts*, really? For example, what is 'the concept of temperature'?" In that case heaven knows what an "answer" would be. (Perhaps it would be the statement that concepts *can be identified with* synonymy-classes.)

Of course, the question "What is the property temperature?" is also "funny." And one way of interpreting it is to take it as a question about the concept of temperature. But this is not the way a physicist would take it.

The effect of saying that the property P_1 can be identical with the property P_2 only if the terms P_1, P_2 are in some suitable sense "synonyms" is, to all intents and purposes, to collapse the two notions of "property" and "concept" into a single notion. The view that concepts (intensions) *are* the same as properties has been explicitly advocated by Carnap (e.g., in *Meaning and Necessity*). This seems an unfortunate view, since "temperature is mean molecular kinetic energy" appears to be a perfectly good example of a true statement of identity of properties, whereas "the concept of temperature is the same concept as a concept of mean molecular kinetic energy" is simply false.

Many philosophers believe that the statement "pain is a brain state" violates some rules or norms of English. But the arguments offered are hardly convincing. For example, if the fact that I can know that I am in pain without knowing that I am in brain state *S* shows that pain cannot be brain state *S*, then, by exactly the same argument, the fact that I can know that the stove is hot without knowing that the mean molecular kinetic energy is high (or even that molecules exist) shows that it is *false* that temperature is mean molecular kinetic energy, physics to the contrary. In fact, all that immediately follows from the fact that I can know that I am in pain without knowing that I am in brain state *S* is that the concept of pain is not the same concept as the concept of being in brain state *S*. But either pain, or the state of being in pain, or some pain, or some pain state, might still be brain state *S*. After all, the concept of temperature is not the same concept as the concept of mean molecular kinetic energy. But temperature is mean molecular kinetic energy.

Some philosophers maintain that both "pain is a brain state" and "pain states are brain states" are unintelligible. The answer is to explain to these philosophers, as well as we can, given the vagueness of all scientific methodology, what sorts of considerations lead one to make an empirical reduction (i.e., to say such things as "water is H_2O," "light is electromagnetic radiation," "temperature is mean molecular kinetic energy"). If, without giving reasons, he still maintains in the face of such examples that one cannot imagine parallel circumstances for the use of "pains are brain states" (or, perhaps, "pain states are brain states"), one has grounds to regard him as perverse.

Some philosophers maintain that "P_1 is P_2" is something that can be true, when the "is" involved is the "is" of empirical reduction, only when the properties P_1 and P_2 are (a) associated with a spatio-temporal region; and (b) the region is one and the same in both cases. Thus "temperature is mean molecular kinetic energy" is an admissible empirical reduction, since the temperature and the molecular energy are associated with the same space-time region, but "having a pain in my arm is being in a brain state" is not, since the spatial regions involved are different.

This argument does not appear very strong. Surely no one is going to be deterred from saying that mirror images are light reflected from an object and then from the surface of a mirror by the fact that an image can be "located" three feet *behind* the mirror! (Moreover, one can always find *some* common property of the reductions one is willing to allow—e.g., temperature is mean molecular kinetic energy—which is not a property of some one identification one wishes to disallow. This is not very impressive unless one has an argument to show that the very purposes of such identification depend upon the common property in question.)

Again, other philosophers have contended that all the predictions that can be derived from the conjunction of neurophysiological laws with such statements as "pain states are such-and-such brain states" can equally well be derived from the conjunction of the same neurophysiological laws with "being in pain is correlated with such-and-such brain states," and hence (*sic*!) there can be no methodological grounds for saying that pains (or pain states) *are* brain states, as opposed to saying that they are *correlated* (invariantly) with brain states. This argument, too, would show that light is only correlated with electromagnetic radiation. The mistake is in ignoring the fact that, although the theories in question may indeed lead to the same predictions, they open and exclude different *questions*. "Light is invariantly correlated with electromagnetic radiation" would leave open the questions "What is the light then, if it isn't the same as the electromagnetic radiation?" and "What makes the light accompany the electromagnetic radiation?"—questions which are excluded by saying that the light *is* the electromagnetic radiation. Similarly, the purpose of saying that pains are brain states is precisely to exclude from empirical meaningfulness the questions "What is the pain, then, if it isn't the same as the brain state?" and "What makes the pain accompany the brain state?" If there are grounds to suggest that these questions represent, so to speak, the wrong way to look at the matter, then those grounds are grounds for a theoretical identification of pains with brain states.

If all arguments to the contrary are unconvincing, shall we then conclude that it is meaningful (and perhaps true) to say either that pains are brain states or that pain states are brain states?

(1) It is perfectly meaningful (violates no "rule of English," involves no "extension of usage") to say "pains are brain states."

(2) It is not meaningful (involves a "changing of meaning" or "an extension of usage," etc.) to say "pains are brain states."

My own position is not expressed by either 1 or 2. It seems to me that the notions "change of meaning" and "extension of usage" are simply so ill defined that one cannot in fact say *either* 1 or 2. I see no reason to believe that either the linguist, or the man-on-the-street, or the philosopher possesses today a notion of "change of meaning" applicable to such cases as the one we have been discussing. The *job* for which the notion of change of meaning was developed in the history of the language was just a *much* cruder job than this one.

But, if we don't assert either 1 or 2—in other words, if we regard the "change of meaning" issue as a pseudo-issue in this case—then how are we to discuss the question with which we started? "Is pain a brain state?"

The answer is to allow statements of the form "pain is *A*," where "pain" and "*A*" are in no sense synonyms, and to see whether any such statement can be found which might be acceptable on empirical and methodological grounds. This is what we shall now proceed to do.

Is Pain a Brain State?

We shall discuss "Is pain a brain state?" then. And we have agreed to waive the "change of meaning" issue.

Since I am discussing not what the concept of pain comes to, but what pain is, in a sense of "is" which requires empirical theory-construction (or, at least, empirical speculation), I shall not apologize for advancing an empirical hypothesis. Indeed, my strategy will be to argue that pain is *not* a brain state, not on *a priori* grounds, but on the grounds that another hypothesis is more plausible. The detailed development and verification of my hypothesis would be just as Utopian a task as the detailed development and verification of the brain-state hypothesis. But the putting-forward, not of detailed and scientifically "finished" hypotheses, but of schemata for hypotheses, has long been a function of philosophy. I shall, in short, argue that pain is not a brain state, in the sense of a physical-chemical state of the brain (or even the whole nervous system), but another *kind* of state entirely. I propose the hypothesis that pain, or the state of being in pain, is a functional state of a whole organism.

To explain this it is necessary to introduce some technical notions. In previous papers I have explained the notion of a Turing Machine and discussed the use of this notion as a model for an organism. The notion of a Probabilistic Automaton is defined similarly to a Turing Machine, except that the transitions between "states" are allowed to be with various probabilities rather than being "deterministic." (Of course, a Turing Machine is simply a special kind of Probabilistic Automaton, one with transition probabilities 0, 1.) I shall assume the notion of a Probabilistic Automaton has been generalized to allow for "sensory inputs" and "motor outputs"—that is, the Machine Table specifies, for every possible combination of a "state" and a complete set of "sensory inputs," an "instruction" which determines the probability of the next "state," and also the probabilities of the "motor outputs." (This replaces the idea of the Machine as printing on a tape.) I shall also assume that the physical realization of the sense organs responsible for the various inputs, and of the motor organs, is specified, but that the "states" and the "inputs" themselves are, as usual, specified only "implicitly"—i.e., by the set of transition probabilities given by the Machine Table.

Since an empirically given system can simultaneously be a "physical realization" of many different Probabilistic Automata, I introduce the notion of a *Description* of a system. A Description of S where S is a system, is any true statement to the effect that S possesses distinct states $S_1, S_2 \ldots S_n$ which are related to one another and to the motor outputs and sensory inputs by the transition probabilities given in such-and-such a Machine Table. The Machine Table mentioned in the Description will then be called the Functional Organization of S relative to that Description, and the S_i such that S is in state S_i at a given time will be called the Total State of S (at the time) relative to that Description. It should be noted that knowing the Total State of a system relative to a

Description involves knowing a good deal about how the system is likely to "behave," given various combinations of sensory inputs, but does *not* involve knowing the physical realization of the S_i as, e.g., physical-chemical states of the brain. The S_i, to repeat, are specified only *implicitly* by the Description—i.e., specified *only* by the set of transition probabilities given in the Machine Table.

The hypothesis that "being in pain is a functional state of the organism" may now be spelled out more exactly as follows:

1. All organisms capable of feeling pain are Probabilistic Automata.
2. Every organism capable of feeling pain possesses at least one Description of a certain kind (i.e., being capable of feeling pain *is* possessing an appropriate kind of Functional Organization).
3. No organism capable of feeling pain possesses a decomposition into parts which separately possess Descriptions of the kind referred to in 2.
4. For every Description of the kind referred to in 2, there exists a subset of the sensory inputs such that an organism with that Description is in pain when and only when some of its sensory inputs are in that subset.

This hypothesis is admittedly vague, though surely no vaguer than the brain-state hypothesis in its present form. For example, one would like to know more about the kind of Functional Organization that an organism must have to be capable of feeling pain, and more about the marks that distinguish the subset of the sensory inputs referred to in 4. With respect to the first question, one can probably say that the Functional Organization must include something that resembles a "preference function," or at least a preference partial ordering and something that resembles an "inductive logic" (i.e., the Machine must be able to "learn from experience"). In addition, it seems natural to require that the Machine possess "pain sensors," i.e., sensory organs which normally signal damage to the Machine's body, or dangerous temperatures, pressures, etc., which transmit a special subset of the inputs, the subset referred to in 4. Finally, and with respect to the second question, we would want to require at least that the inputs in the distinguished subset have a high disvalue on the Machine's preference function or ordering (further conditions are discussed in the previous chapter). The purpose of condition 3 is to rule out such "organisms" (if they can count as such) as swarms of bees as single pain-feelers. The condition 1 is, obviously, redundant, and is only introduced for expository reasons. (It is, in fact, empty, since everything is a Probabilistic Automaton under *some* Description.)

I contend, in passing, that this hypothesis, in spite of its admitted vagueness, is far *less* vague than the "physical-chemical state" hypothesis is today, and far more susceptible to investigation of both a mathematical and an empirical kind. Indeed, to investigate this hypothesis is just to attempt to produce "mechanical" models of organisms—and isn't this, in a sense, just what psychology is about? The difficult step, of course, will be to pass from models to *specific* organisms to a *normal form* for the psychological description of organisms—for this is what is required to make 2 and 4 precise. But this too seems to be an inevitable part of the program of psychology.

I shall now compare the hypothesis just advanced with (a) the hypothesis that pain is a brain state, and (b) the hypothesis that pain is a behavior disposition.

Functional State versus Brain State

It may, perhaps, be asked if I am not somewhat unfair in taking the brain-state theorist to be talking about *physical-chemical* states of the brain. But (a) these are the only sorts of states ever mentioned by brain-state theorists. (b) The brain-state theorist usually mentions (with a certain pride, slightly reminiscent of the Village Atheist) the incompatibility of his hypothesis with all forms of dualism and mentalism. This is natural if physical-chemical states of the brain are what is at issue. However, functional states of whole systems are something quite different. In particular, the functional-state hypothesis is *not* incompatible with dualism! Although it goes without saying that the hypothesis is "mechanistic" in its inspiration, it is a slightly remarkable fact that a system consisting of a body and a "soul," if such things there be, can perfectly well be a Probabilistic Automaton. (c) One argument advanced by Smart is that the brain-state theory assumes only "physical" properties, and Smart finds "non-physical" properties unintelligible. The Total States and the "inputs" defined above are, of course, neither mental nor physical *per se*, and I cannot imagine a functionalist advancing this argument. (d) If the brain-state theorist does mean (or at least allow) states other than physical-chemical states, then his hypothesis is completely empty, at least until he specifies *what* sort of "states" he *does* mean.

Taking the brain-state hypothesis in this way, then, what reasons are there to prefer the functional-state hypothesis over the brain-state hypothesis? Consider what the brain-state theorist has to do to make good his claims. He has to specify a physical-chemical state such that *any* organism (not just a mammal) is in pain if and only if (a) it possesses a brain of a suitable physical-chemical structure; and (b) its brain is in that physical-chemical state. This means that the physical-chemical state in question must be a possible state of a mammalian brain, a reptilian brain, a mollusc's brain (octopuses are mollusca, and certainly feel pain), etc. At the same time, it must *not* be a possible (physically possible) state of the brain of any physically possible creature that cannot feel pain. Even if such a state can be found, it must be nomologically certain that it will also be a state of the brain of any extraterrestrial life that may be found that will be capable of feeling pain before we can even entertain the supposition that it may *be* pain.

It is not altogether impossible that such a state will be found. Even though octopus and mammal are examples of parallel (rather than sequential) evolution, for example, virtually identical structures (physically speaking) have evolved in the eye of the octopus and in the eye of the mammal, notwithstanding the fact that this organ has evolved from different kinds of cells in the two cases. Thus it is at least possible that parallel evolution, all over the universe, might *always* lead to *one and the same* physical "correlate" of pain. But this is certainly an ambitious hypothesis.

Finally, the hypothesis becomes still more ambitious when we realize that the brain-state theorist is not just saying that *pain* is a brain state; he is, of course, concerned to maintain that *every* psychological state is a brain state. Thus if we can find even one psychological predicate which can clearly be applied to both a mammal and an octopus (say "hungry"), but whose physical-chemical "correlate" is different in the two cases, the brain-state theory has collapsed. It seems to me overwhelmingly probable that we can do this. Granted, in such a case the brain-state theorist can save himself by *ad hoc* assumptions (e.g., defining the disjunction of two states to be a single "physical-chemical state"), but this does not have to be taken seriously.

Turning now to the considerations *for* the functional-state theory, let us begin with the fact that we identify organisms as in pain, or hungry, or angry, or in heat, etc., on the basis of their *behavior*. But it is a truism that similarities in the behavior of two systems are at least a reason to suspect similarities in the functional organization of the two systems, and a much *weaker* reason to suspect similarities in the actual physical details. Moreover, we expect the various psychological states—at least the basic ones, such as hunger, thirst, aggression, etc.—to have more or less similar "transition probabilities" (within wide and ill-defined limits, to be sure) with each other and with behavior in the case of different species, because this is an artifact of the way in which we identify these states. Thus, we would not count an animal as *thirsty* if its "unsatiated" behavior did not seem to be directed toward drinking and was not followed by "satiation for liquid." Thus any animal that we count as capable of these various states will at least *seem* to have a certain rough kind of functional organization. And, as already remarked, if the program of finding psychological laws that are not species-specific—i.e., of finding a normal form for psychological theories of different species—ever succeeds, then it will bring in its wake a delineation of the kind of functional organization that is necessary and sufficient for a given psychological state, as well as a precise definition of the notion "psychological state." In contrast, the brain-state theorist has to hope for the eventual development of neurophysiological laws that are species-independent, which seems much less reasonable than the hope that psychological laws (of a sufficiently general kind) may be species-independent, or, still waker, that a species-independent *form* can be found in which psychological laws can be written.

Functional State versus Behavior-Disposition

The theory that being in pain is neither a brain state nor a functional state but a behavior disposition has one apparent advantage: it appears to agree with the way in which we verify that organisms are in pain. We do not in practice know anything about the brain state of an animal when we say that it is in pain; and we possess little if any knowledge of its functional organization, except in a crude intuitive way. In fact, however, this "advantage" is no advantage at all: for, although statements about how we verify that *x* is *A* may have a good deal to do with what the concept of being *A* comes to, they have precious little to do with what the property *A is*. To argue on the ground just mentioned that pain is neither a brain state nor a functional state is like arguing that heat is not mean molecular kinetic energy from the fact that ordinary people do not (they think) ascertain the mean molecular kinetic energy of something when they verify that it is hot or cold. It is not necessary that they should; what is necessary is that the marks that they take as indications of heat should in fact be explained by the mean molecular kinetic energy. And, similarly, it is necessary to our hypothesis that the marks that are taken as behavioral indications of pain should be explained by the fact that the organism is a functional state of the appropriate kind, but not that speakers should *know* that this is so.

The difficulties with "behavior disposition" accounts are so well known that I shall do little more than recall them here. The difficulty—it appears to be more than a "difficulty," in fact—of specifying the required behavior disposition except as "the disposition of X to behave as if X were in *pain*," is the chief one, of course. In contrast, we *can* specify the functional state with which we propose to identify pain, at least roughly, without using the notion of pain. Namely, the functional state we have in mind is the state of receiving sensory inputs which play a certain role in the Functional Organization of the organism. This role is characterized, at least partially, by the fact that the sense organs responsible for the inputs in question are organs whose function is to detect damage to the body, or dangerous extremes of temperature, pressure, etc., and by the fact that the "inputs" themselves, whatever their physical realization, represent a condition that the organism assigns a high disvalue to. As I stressed in "The mental life of some machines," this does *not* mean that the Machine will always *avoid* being in the condition in question ("pain"); it only means that the condition will be avoided unless not avoiding it is necessary to the attainment of some more highly valued goal. Since the behavior of the Machine (in this case, an organism) will depend not merely on the sensory inputs, but also on the Total State (i.e., on other values, beliefs, etc.), it seems hopeless to make any general statement about how an organism in such a condition *must* behave; but this does not mean that we must abandon hope of characterizing the condition. Indeed, we have just characterized it.

Not only does the behavior-disposition theory seem hopelessly vague; if the "behavior" referred to is peripheral behavior, and the relevant stimuli are peripheral stimuli (e.g., we do not say anything about what the organism will do if its brain is operated upon), then the theory seems clearly false. For example, two animals with all motor nerves cut will have the same actual and potential "behavior" (namely, none to speak of); but if one has cut pain fibers and the other has uncut pain fibers, then one will feel pain and the other won't. Again, if one person has cut pain fibers, and another suppresses all pain responses deliberately due to some strong compulsion, then the actual and potential peripheral behavior may be the same, but one will feel pain and the other won't. (Some philosophers maintain that this last case is conceptually impossible, but the only evidence for this appears to be that *they* can't, or don't want to, conceive of it.) If, instead of pain, we take some sensation the "bodily expression" of which is easier to suppress—say, a slight coolness in one's left little finger—the case becomes even clearer.

Finally, even if there *were* some behavior disposition invariantly correlated with pain (species-independently!), and specifiable without using the term "pain," it would still be more plausible to identify being in pain with some state whose presence *explains* this behavior disposition—the brain state or functional state—than with the behavior disposition itself. Such considerations of plausibility may be somewhat subjective; but if other things *were* equal (of course, they aren't) why shouldn't we allow considerations of plausibility to play the deciding role?

Methodological Considerations

So far we have considered only what might be called the "empirical" reasons for saying that being in pain is a functional state, rather than a brain state or a behavior disposition; namely, that it seems more likely that the functional state we described is invariantly "correlated" with pain, species-independently, than that there is either a physical-chemical state of the brain (must an organism have a *brain* to feel pain? perhaps some ganglia will do) or a behavior disposition so correlated. If this is correct, then it follows that the identification we proposed is at least a candidate for consideration. What of methodological considerations?

The methodological considerations are roughly similar in all cases of reduction, so no surprises need be expected here. First, identification of psychological states with functional states means that the laws of psychology can be derived from statements of the form "such-and-such organisms have such-and-such Descriptions" together with the identification statements ("being in pain is such-and-such a functional state," etc.). Secondly, the presence of the functional state (i.e., of inputs which play the role we have described in the Functional Organization of the organism) is not merely "correlated with" but actually explains the pain behavior on the part of the organism. Thirdly, the identification serves to exclude questions which (if a naturalistic view is correct) represent an altogether wrong way of looking at the matter, e.g., "What *is* pain if it isn't either the brain state or the functional state?" and "What causes the pain to be always accompanied by this sort of functional state?" In short, the identification is to be tentatively accepted as a theory which leads to both fruitful predictions and to fruitful *questions*, and which serves to discourage fruitless and empirically senseless questions, where by "empirically senseless" I mean "senseless" not merely from the standpoint of verification, but from the standpoint of what there in fact *is*.

Notes

1. In this paper I wish to avoid the vexed question of the relation between *pains* and *pain states*. I only remark in passing that one common argument *against* identification of these two—namely, that a pain can be in one's arm but a state (of the organism) cannot be in one's arm—is easily seen to be fallacious.

2. There are some well-known remarks by Alonzo Church on this topic. Those remarks do not bear (as might at first be supposed) on the identification of concepts with synonymy-classes as such, but rather support the view that (in formal semantics) it is necessary to retain Frege's distinction between the normal and the "oblique" use of expressions. That is, even if we say that the concept of temperature *is* the synonymy-class of the word "temperature," we must not thereby be led into the error of supposing that "the concept of temperature" is synonymous with "the synonymy-class of the word 'temperature'"—for then "the concept of temperature" and "*der Begriff der Temperatur*" would not be synonymous, which they are. Rather, we must say that the concept of "temperature" *refers to* the synonymy-class of the word "temperature" (on this particular reconstruction); but that class is *identified* not as "the synonymy-class to which such-and-such a word belongs," but in another way (e.g., as the synonymy-class whose members have such-and-such a characteristic use).

14 Troubles with Functionalism (revised)

Ned Block

Functionalism, Behaviorism, and Physicalism

The functionalist view of the nature of the mind is now widely accepted.[1] Like behaviorism and physicalism, functionalism seeks to answer the question "What are mental states?" I shall be concerned with identity thesis formulations of functionalism. They say, for example, that pain is a functional state, just as identity thesis formulations of physicalism say that pain is a physical state.

I shall begin by describing functionalism, and sketching the functionalist critique of behaviorism and physicalism. Then I shall argue that the troubles ascribed by functionalism to behaviorism and physicalism infect functionalism as well.

One characterization of functionalism that is probably vague enough to be acceptable to most functionalists is: each type of mental state is a state consisting of a disposition to act in certain ways *and to have certain mental states*, given certain sensory inputs and certain mental states. So put, functionalism can be seen as a new incarnation of behaviorism. Behaviorism identifies mental states with dispositions to act in certain ways in certain input situations. But as critics have pointed out (Chisholm 1957, Geach 1957, Putnam 1963), desire for goal G cannot be identified with, say, the disposition to do A in input circumstances in which A leads to G, since, after all, the agent might not *know* that A leads to G and thus might not be disposed to do A. Functionalism replaces behaviorism's "sensory inputs" with "sensory inputs and mental states"; and functionalism replaces behaviorism's "dispositions to act" with "dispositions to act and have certain mental states." Functionalists want to individuate mental states causally, and since mental states have mental causes and effects as well as sensory causes and behavioral effects, functionalists individuate mental states partly in terms of causal relations to other mental states. One consequence of this difference between functionalism and behaviorism is that there are possible organisms that according to behaviorism, have mental states but, according to functionalism, do not have mental states.

So, necessary conditions for mentality that are postulated by functionalism are in one respect stronger than those postulated by behaviorism. According to behaviorism, it is necessary and sufficient for desiring that G that a system be characterized by a certain set (perhaps infinite) of input–output relations; that is, according to behaviorism, a system desires that G just in case a certain set of conditionals of the form "It will emit O given I" are true of it. According to functionalism, however, a system might have these input-output relations, yet not desire that G; for according to functionalism, whether a system desires that G depends on whether it has internal states which have certain causal relations to other internal states (and to inputs and outputs). Since behaviorism makes no such "internal state" requirement, there are possible systems of which behaviorism affirms and functionalism denies that they have mental states.[2] One way of stating this is that, according to functionalism, behaviorism is guilty of *liberalism*—ascribing mental properties to things that do not in fact have them.

Despite the difference just sketched between functionalism and behaviorism, functionalists and behaviorists need not be far apart in spirit.[3] Shoemaker (1975), for example, says, "On one construal of it, functionalism in the philosophy of mind is the doctrine that mental, or psychological, terms are, in principle, eliminable in a certain way" (pp. 306–307). Functionalists have tended to treat the mental-state terms in a functional characterization of a mental state quite differently from the input and output terms. Thus in the simplest Turing-machine version of the theory (Putnam 1967, Block and Fodor 1972), mental states are identified with the total Turing-machine states, which are themselves *implicitly* defined by a machine table that *explicitly* mentions inputs and outputs, described nonmentalistically.

In Lewis's version of functionalism, mental-state terms are defined by means of a modification of Ramsey's method, in a way that eliminates essential use of mental terminology from the definitions but does not eliminate input and output terminology. That is, "pain" is defined as synonymous with a definite description containing input and output terms but no mental terminology (see Lewis 1972).

Furthermore, functionalism in both its machine and nonmachine versions has typically insisted that characterizations of mental states should contain descriptions of inputs and outputs in *physical* language. Armstrong (1968), for example, says,

> We may distinguish between "physical behaviour," which refers to any merely physical action or passion of the body, and "behaviour proper" which implies relationship to mind.... Now, if in our formula ["state of the person apt for bringing about a certain sort of behaviour"] "behaviour" were to mean "behaviour proper," then we would be giving an account of mental concepts in terms of a concept that already presupposes mentality, which would be circular. So it is clear that in our formula, "behaviour" must mean "physical behaviour." (p. 84)

Therefore, functionalism can be said to "tack down" mental states only at the periphery—that is, through physical, or at least nonmental, specification of inputs and outputs. One major thesis of this article is that, because of this feature, functionalism fails to avoid the sort of problem for which it rightly condemns behaviorism. Functionalism, too, is guilty of liberalism, for much the same reasons as behaviorism. Unlike behaviorism, however, functionalism can naturally be altered to avoid liberalism—but only at the cost of falling into an equally ignominious failing.

The failing I speak of is the one that functionalism shows *physicalism* to be guilty of. By "physicalism," I mean the doctrine that pain, for example, is identical to a physical (or physiological) state.[4] As many philosophers have argued (notably Fodor 1965, Putnam 1966, see also Block and Fodor 1972), if functionalism is true, physicalism is probably false. The point is at its clearest with regard to Turing-machine versions of functionalism. Any given abstract Turing machine can be realized by a wide variety of physical devices; indeed, it is plausible that, given any putative correspondence between a Turing-machine state and a configurational physical (or physiological) state, there will be a possible realization of the Turing machine that will provide a counterexample to that correspondence. (See Kalke 1969, Gendron 1971, and Mucciolo 1974, for unconvincing arguments to the contrary; see also Kim 1972.) Therefore, if pain is a functional state, it cannot, for example, be a brain state, because creatures without brains can realize the same Turing machine as creatures with brains.

I must emphasize that the functionalist argument against physicalism does not appeal merely to the fact that one abstract Turing machine can be realized by systems of different *material composition* (wood, metal, glass, etc.). To argue this way would be like arguing that temperature cannot be a microphysical magnitude because the same temperature can be had by objects with *different* microphysical structures (Kim 1972). Objects with different microphysical structures, such as objects made of wood, metal, glass, etc., can have many interesting microphysical properties in common, such as molecular kinetic energy of the same average value. Rather, the functionalist argument against physicalism is that it is difficult to see how there *could be* a nontrivial first-order (see note 4) physical property in common to all and only the possible physical realizations of a given Turing-machine state. Try to think of a remotely plausible candidate! At the very least, the onus is on those who think such physical properties are conceivable to show us how to conceive of one.

One way of expressing this point is that, according to functionalism, physicalism is a *chauvinist* theory: it withholds mental properties from systems that in fact have them. In saying mental states are brain states, for example, physicalists unfairly exclude those poor brainless creatures who nonetheless have minds.

A second major point of this paper is that the very argument which functionalism uses to condemn physicalism can be applied equally well against functionalism; indeed, any version of functionalism that avoids liberalism falls, like physicalism, into chauvinism.

This article has three parts. The first argues that functionalism is guilty of liberalism, the second that one way of modifying functionalism to avoid liberalism is to tie it more closely to empirical psychology, and the third that no version of functionalism can avoid both liberalism and chauvinism.

More about What Functionalism Is

One way of providing some order to the bewildering variety of functionalist theories is to distinguish between those that are couched in terms of a Turing machine and those that are not.

A Turing-machine table lists a finite set of machine-table states, $S_1 \ldots S_n$; inputs, $I_1 \ldots I_m$; and outputs, $O_1 \ldots O_p$. The table specifies a set of conditionals of the form: if the machine is in state S_i and receives input I_j, it emits output O_k and goes into state S_1. That is, given any state and input, the table specifies an output and a next state. Any system with a set of inputs, outputs, and states related in the way specified by the table is described by the table and is a realization of the abstract automaton specified by the table.

To have the power for computing any recursive function, a Turing machine must be able to control its input in certain ways. In standard formulations, the output of a Turing machine is regarded as having two components. It prints a symbol on a tape, then moves the tape, thus bringing a new symbol into the view of the input reader. For the Turing machine to have full power, the tape must be infinite in at least one

Table 14.1

	S_1	S_2
nickel input	Emit no output Go to S_2	Emit a Coke Go to S_1
dime input	Emit a Coke Stay in S_1	Emit a Coke and a nickel Go to S_1

direction and movable in both directions. If the machine has no control over the tape, it is a "finite transducer," a rather limited Turing machine. Finite transducers need not be regarded as having tape at all. Those who believe that machine functionalism is true must suppose that just what power automaton we are is a substantive empirical question. If we are "full power" Turing machines, the environment must constitute part of the tape....

One very simple version of machine functionalism (Block and Fodor 1972) states that each system having mental states is described by at least one Turing-machine table of a specifiable sort and that each type of mental state of the system is identical to one of the machine-table states. Consider, for example, the Turing machine described in table 14.1 (cf. Nelson 1975). One can get a crude picture of the simple version of machine functionalism by considering the claim that S_1 = dime-desire, and S_2 = nickel-desire. Of course, no functionalist would claim that a Coke machine desires anything. Rather, the simple version of machine functionalism described above makes an analogous claim with respect to a much more complex hypothetical machine table. Notice that machine functionalism specifies inputs and outputs explicitly, internal states implicitly (Putnam 1967, p. 434) says: "The S_i, to repeat, are specified only *implicitly* by the description, i.e., specified *only* by the set of transition probabilities given in the machine table"). To be described by this machine table, a device must accept nickels and dimes as inputs and dispense nickels and Cokes as outputs. But the states S_1 and S_2 can have virtually any natures (even nonphysical natures), so long as those natures connect the states to each other and to the inputs and outputs specified in the machine table. All we are told about S_1 and S_2 are these relations; thus machine functionalism can be said to reduce mentality to input-output structures. This example should suggest the force of the functionalist argument against physicalism. Try to think of a first-order (see note 4) physical property that can be shared by all (and only) realizations of this machine table!

One can also categorize functionalists in terms of whether they regard functional identities as part of a priori psychology or empirical psychology.... The a priori functionalists (such as Smart, Armstrong, Lewis, Shoemaker) are the heirs of the logical behaviorists. They tend to regard functional analyses as analyses of the meanings of mental terms, whereas the empirical functionalists (such as Fodor, Putnam, Harman) regard functional analyses as substantive scientific hypotheses. In what follows, I shall refer to the former view as "Functionalism" and the latter as "Psychofunctionalism." (I shall use "functionalism" with a lowercase "f" as neutral between Functionalism and Psychofunctionalism. When distinguishing between Functionalism and Psychofunctionalism, I shall always use capitals.)

Functionalism and Psychofunctionalism and the difference between them can be made clearer in terms of the notion of the Ramsey sentence of a psychological theory. Mental-state terms that appear in a psychological theory can be defined in various ways by means of the Ramsey sentence of the theory.... All functional state identity theories ... can be understood as defining a set of functional states ... by means of the Ramsey sentence of a psychological theory—with one functional state corresponding to each mental state. The functional state corresponding to pain will be called the "Ramsey functional correlate" of pain, with respect to the psychological theory. In terms of the notion of a Ramsey functional correlate with respect to a theory, the distinction between Functionalism and Psychofunctionalism can be defined as follows: Functionalism identifies mental state S with S's Ramsey functional correlate with respect to a *common-sense* psychological theory; Psychofunctionalism identifies S with S's Ramsey functional correlate with respect to a *scientific* psychological theory.

This difference between Functionalism and Psychofunctionalism gives rise to a difference in specifying inputs and outputs. Functionalists are restricted to specification of inputs and outputs that are plausibly part of commonsense knowledge; Psychofunctionalists are under no such restriction. Although both groups insist on physical—or at least nonmental—specification on inputs and outputs, Functionalists require externally observable classifications (such as inputs characterized in terms of objects present in the vicinity of the organism, outputs in terms of movements of body parts). Psychofunctionalists, on the other hand, have the option to specify inputs and outputs in terms of internal parameters, such as signals in input and output neurons....

Let T be a psychological theory of either commonsense or scientific psychology. T may contain generalizations of the form: anyone who is in state w and receives input x emits output y, and goes into state z. Let us write T as

$$T(S_1 \ldots S_n, I_1 \ldots I_k, O_1 \ldots O_m)$$

where the Ss are mental states, the Is are inputs, and the Os are outputs. The "S"s are to be understood as mental state *constants* such as "pain," not variables, and likewise for the "I"s and "O"s. Thus, one could also write T as

T(pain ..., light of 400 nanometers entering left eye ..., left big toe moves 1 centimeter left ...)

To get the Ramsey sentence of T, replace the mental state terms—*but not the input and output terms*—by variables, and prefix an existential quantifier for each variable:

$$\exists F_1 \ldots \exists F_n T(F_1 \ldots F_n, I_1 \ldots I_k, O_1 \ldots O_m)$$

If "F_{17}" is the variable that replaced the word "pain" when the Ramsey sentence was formed, then we can define pain as follows in terms of the Ramsey sentence:

$$\text{x is in pain} \Leftrightarrow \exists F_1 \ldots \exists F_n T[(F_1 \ldots F_n, I_1 \ldots I_k, O_1 \ldots O_m) \text{ and x has } F_{17}]$$

The Ramsey functional correlate of pain is the property expressed by the predicate on the right hand side of this biconditional. Notice that this predicate contains input and output constants, but no mental constants since the mental constants were replaced by variables. The Ramsey functional correlate for pain is defined in terms of inputs and outputs, but not in mental terms.

For example, let T be the theory that pain is caused by skin damage and causes worry and the emission of "ouch," and worry, in turn, causes brow wrinkling. Then the Ramsey definition would be:

x is in pain ⇔ There are 2 states (properties), the first of which is caused by skin damage and causes both the emission of "ouch" and the second state, and the second state causes brow wrinkling, and x is in the first state.

The Ramsey functional correlate of pain with respect to this "theory" is the property of being in a state that is caused by skin damage and causes the emission of "ouch" and another state that in turn causes brow wrinkling. (Note that the words "pain" and "worry" have been replaced by variables, but the input and output terms remain.)

The Ramsey functional correlate of a state S is a state that has much in common with S. Specifically, S and its Ramsey functional correlate share the structural properties specified by the theory T. But, there are two reasons why it is natural to suppose that S and its Ramsey functional correlate will be distinct. First, the Ramsey functional correlate of S with respect to T can "include" at most those aspects of S that are captured by T; any aspects not captured by T will be left out. Second, the Ramsey functional correlate may even leave out some of what T does capture, for the Ramsey definition does not contain the "theoretical" vocabulary of T. The example theory of the last paragraph is true only of pain-feeling organisms—but trivially, in virtue of its use of the word "pain." However, the predicate that expresses the Ramsey functional correlate does not contain this word (since it was replaced by a variable), and so can be true of things that don't feel pain. It would be easy to make a simple machine that has some artificial skin, a brow, a tape-recorded "ouch," and two states that satisfy the mentioned causal relations, but no pain.

The bold hypothesis of functionalism is that for *some* psychological theory, this natural supposition that a state and its Ramsey functional correlate are distinct is false. Functionalism says that there is a theory such that pain, for example, *is* its Ramsey functional correlate with respect to that theory.

One final preliminary point: I have given the misleading impression that functionalism identifies *all* mental states with functional states. Such a version of functionalism is obviously far too strong. Let X be a newly created cell-for-cell duplicate of you (which, of course, is functionally equivalent to you). Perhaps you remember being bar mitzvahed. But X does not remember being bar mitzvahed, since X never was bar mitzvahed. Indeed, something can be functionally equivalent to you but fail to know what you know, or [verb], what you [verb], for a wide variety of "success" verbs. Worse still, if Putnam (1975b) is right in saying that "meanings are not in the head," systems functionally equivalent to you may, for similar reasons, fail to have many of your other propositional attitudes. Suppose you believe water is wet. According to plausible arguments advanced by Putnam and Kripke, a condition for the possibility of your believing water is wet is a certain kind of causal connection between you and water. Your "twin" on Twin Earth, who is connected in a similar way to XYZ rather than H_2O, would not believe water is wet.

If functionalism is to be defended, it must be construed as applying only to a subclass of mental states, those "narrow" mental states such that truth conditions for their application are in some sense "within the person." But even assuming that a notion of narrowness of psychological state can be satisfactorily formulated, the interest of functionalism may be diminished by this restriction. I mention this problem only to set it aside.

I shall take functionalism to be a doctrine about all "narrow" mental states.

Homunculi-Headed Robots

In this section I shall describe a class of devices that are prima facie embarrassments for all versions of functionalism in that they indicate functionalism is guilty of liberalism—classifying systems that lack mentality as having mentality.

Consider the simple version of machine functionalism already described. It says that each system having mental states is described by at least one Turing-machine table of a certain kind, and each mental state of the system is identical to one of the machine-table states specified by the machine table. I shall consider inputs and outputs to be specified by descriptions of neural impulses in sense organs and motor-output neurons. This assumption should not be regarded as restricting what will be said to Psychofunctionalism rather than Functionalism. As already mentioned, every version of functionalism assumes *some* specification of inputs and outputs. A Functionalist specification would do as well for the purposes of what follows.

Imagine a body externally like a human body, say yours, but internally quite different. The neurons from sensory organs are connected to a bank of lights in a hollow cavity in the head. A set of buttons connects to the motor-output neurons. Inside the cavity resides a group of little men. Each has a very simple task: to implement a "square" of an adequate machine table that describes you. On one wall is a bulletin board on which is posted a state card; that is, a card that bears a symbol designating one of the states specified in the machine table. Here is what the little men do: Suppose the posted card has a "G" on it. This alerts the little men who implement G squares—"G-men" they call themselves. Suppose the light representing input I_{17} goes on. One of the G-men has the following as his sole task: when the card reads "G" and the I_{17} light goes on, he presses output button O_{191} and changes the state card to "M." This G-man is called upon to exercise his task only rarely. In spite of the low level of intelligence required of each little man, the system as a whole manages to simulate you because the functional organization they have been trained to realize is yours. A Turing machine can be represented as a finite set of quadruples (or quintuples, if the output is divided into two parts): current state, current input; next state, next output. Each little man has the task corresponding to a single quadruple. Through the efforts of the little men, the system realizes the same (reasonably adequate) machine table as you do and is thus functionally equivalent to you.[5]

I shall describe a version of the homunculi-headed simulation, which has more chance of being nomologically possible. How many homunculi are required? Perhaps a billion are enough.

Suppose we convert the government of China to functionalism, and we convince its officials ... to realize a human mind for an hour. We provide each of the billion people in China (I chose China because it has a billion inhabitants) with a specially designed two-way radio that connects them in the appropriate way to other persons and to the artificial body mentioned in the previous example. We replace each of the little men with a citizen of China plus his or her radio. Instead of a bulletin board, we arrange to have letters displayed on a series of satellites placed so that they can be seen from anywhere in China.

The system of a billion people communicating with one another plus satellites plays the role of an external "brain" connected to the artifical body by radio. There is nothing absurd about a person being connected to his brain by radio. Perhaps the day will come when our brains will be periodically removed for cleaning and repairs. Imagine that this is done initially by treating neurons attaching the brain to the body with a chemical that allows them to stretch like rubber bands, thereby assuring that no brain–body connections are disrupted. Soon clever businessmen discover that they can attract more customers by replacing the stretched neurons with radio links so that brains can be cleaned without inconveniencing the customer by immobilizing his body.

It is not at all obvious that the China-body system is physically impossible. It could be functionally equivalent to you for a short time, say an hour.

"But," you may object, "how could something be functionally equivalent to me for *an hour*? Doesn't my functional organization determine, say, how I would react to doing nothing for a week but reading the *Reader's Digest*?" Remember that a machine table specifies a set of conditionals of the form: if the machine is in S_i and receives input I_j, it emits output O_k and goes into S_1. These conditionals are to be understood *subjunctively*. What gives a system a functional organization at a time is not just what it *does* at that time, but also the counterfactuals true of it at that time: what it *would* have done (and what its state transitions would have been) had it had a different input or been in a different state. If it is true of a system at time t that it *would* obey a given machine table no matter which of the states it is in and no matter which of the inputs it receives, then the system is described at t by the machine table (and realizes at t the abstract automaton specified by the table), even if it exists for only an instant. For the hour the Chinese system is "on," it *does* have a set of inputs, outputs, and states of which such subjunctive conditionals are true. This is what makes any computer realize the abstract automaton that it realizes.

Of course, there are signals the system would respond to that you would not respond to—for example, massive radio interference or a flood of the Yangtze River. Such events might cause a malfunction, scotching the simulation, just as a bomb in a computer can make it fail to realize the machine table it was built to realize. But just as the computer *without* the bomb *can* realize the machine table, the system consisting of the people and artificial body can realize the machine table so long as there are no catastrophic interferences, such as floods, etc.

"But," someone may object, "there is a difference between a bomb in a computer and a bomb in the Chinese system, for in the case of the latter (unlike the former), inputs as specified in the machine table can be the cause of the malfunction. Unusual neural activity in the sense organs of residents of Chungking Province caused by a bomb or by a flood of the Yangtze can cause the system to go haywire."

Reply: The person who says what system he or she is talking about gets to say what signals count as inputs and outputs. I count as inputs and outputs only neural activity in the artificial body connected by radio to the people of China. Neural signals in the people of Chungking count no more as inputs to this system than input tape jammed by a saboteur between the relay contacts in the innards of a computer counts as an input to the computer.

Of course, the object consisting of the people of China + the artificial body has *other* Turing-machine descriptions under which neural signals in the inhabitants of Chungking *would* count as inputs. Such a new system (that is, the object under such a new Turing-machine description) would not be functionally equivalent to you. Likewise, any commercial computer can be redescribed in a way that allows tape jammed into its innards to count as inputs. In describing an object as a Turing machine, one draws a line between the inside and the outside. (If we count only neural impulses as inputs and outputs, we draw that line inside the body; if we count only peripheral stimulations as inputs, . . . we draw that line at the skin.) In describing the Chinese system as a Turing machine, I have drawn the line in such a way that it satisfies a certain type of functional description—one that you *also* satisfy, and one that, according to functionalism, justifies attributions of mentality. Functionalism does not claim that every mental system has a machine table of a sort that justifies attributions of mentality with respect to *every* specification of inputs and outputs, but rather, only with respect to *some* specification.

Objection: The Chinese system would work too slowly. The kind of events and processes with which we normally have contact would pass by far too quickly for the system to detect them. Thus, we would be unable to converse with it, play bridge with it, etc.

Reply: It is hard to see why the system's time scale should matter. . . . Is it really contradictory or nonsensical to suppose we could meet a race of intelligent beings with whom we could communicate only by devices such as time-lapse photography? When we observe these creatures, they seem almost inanimate. But when we view the time-lapse movies, we see them conversing with one another. Indeed, we find they are saying that the only way they can make any sense of us is by viewing movies greatly slowed down. To take time scale as all important seems crudely behavioristic. . . .

What makes the homunculi-headed system (count the two systems as variants of a single system) just described a prima facie counterexample to (machine) functionalism is that there is prima facie doubt whether it has any mental states at all—especially whether it has what philosophers have variously called "qualitative states," "raw feels," or "immediate phenomenological qualities." (You ask: What is it that philosophers have called qualitative states? I answer, only half in jest: As Louis Armstrong said when asked what jazz is, "If you got to ask, you ain't never gonna get to know.") In Nagel's terms (1974), there is a prima facie doubt whether there is anything which it is like to be the homunculi-headed system.[6] . . .

Putnam's Proposal

One way functionalists can try to deal with the problem posed by the homunculi-headed counterexamples is by the ad hoc device of stipulating them away. For example, a functionalist might stipulate that two systems cannot be functionally equivalent if one contains parts with functional organizations characteristic of sentient beings and the other does not. In his article hypothesizing that pain is a functional state, Putnam stipulated that "no organism capable of feeling pain possesses a decomposition into parts which separately possess Descriptions" (as the sort of Turing machine which can be in the functional state Putnam identifies with pain). The purpose of this condition is "to rule out such 'organisms' (if they count as such) as swarms of bees as single pain feelers" (Putnam 1967, pp. 434–435).

One way of filling out Putnam's requirement would be: a pain-feeling organism cannot possess a decomposition into parts *all* of which have a functional organization characteristic of sentient beings. But this would not rule out my homunculi-headed example, since it has nonsentient parts, such as the mechanical body and sense organs. It will not do to go to the opposite extreme and require that *no* proper parts be sentient. Otherwise pregnant women and people with sentient parasites will fail to count as pain-feeling organisms. What seems to be important to examples like the homunculi-headed simulation I have described is that the sentient beings *play a crucial role* in giving the thing its functional organization. This suggests a version of Putnam's proposal which requires that a pain-feeling organism has a certain functional organization and that it has no parts which (1) themselves possess that sort of functional organization and also (2) play a crucial role in giving the whole system its functional organization.

Although this proposal involves the vague notion "crucial role," it is precise enough for us to see it will not do. Suppose there is a part of the universe that contains matter quite different from ours, matter that is infinitely divisible. In this part of the universe, there are intelligent creatures of many sizes, even humanlike creatures much smaller than our elementary particles. In an intergalactic expedition, these people discover the existence of our type of matter. For reasons known only to them, they decide to devote the next few hundred years to creating out of *their* matter substances with the chemical and physical characteristics (except at the subelementary particle level) of *our* elements. They build hordes of space ships of different varieties about the sizes of our electrons, protons, and other elementary particles, and fly the ships in such a way as to mimic the behavior of these elementary particles. The ships also contain generators to produce the type of radiation elementary particles give off. Each ship has a staff of experts on the nature of our elementary particles. They do this so as to produce huge (by our standards) masses of substances with the chemical and physical characteristics of oxygen, carbon, etc. Shortly after they accomplish this, you go off on an expedition to that part of the universe, and discover the "oxygen," "carbon," etc. Unaware of its real nature, you set up a colony, using these "elements" to grow plants for food, provide "air" to breathe, etc. Since one's molecules are constantly being exchanged with the environment, you and other colonizers come (in a period of a few years) to be composed mainly of the "matter" made of the tiny people in space ships. Would you be any less capable of feeling pain, thinking, etc. just because the matter of which you are composed contains (and depends on for its characteristics) beings who themselves have a functional organization characteristic of sentient creatures? I think not. The basic electrochemical mechanisms by which the synpase operates are now fairly well understood. As far as is known, changes that do not affect these electrochemical mechanisms do not affect the operation of the brain, and do not affect mentality. The electrochemical mechanisms in your synapses would be unaffected by the change in your matter.[7]

It is interesting to compare the elementary-particle-people example with the homunculi-headed examples the chapter started with. A natural first guess about the source of our intuition that the initially described homunculi-headed simulations lack mentality is that they have *too much* internal mental structure. The little men may be sometimes bored, sometimes excited. We may even imagine that they deliberate about the best way to realize the given functional organization and make changes intended to give them more leisure time. But the example of the elementary-particle people just described suggests this first guess is wrong. What seems important is *how* the mentality of the parts contributes to the functioning of the whole.

There is one very noticeable difference between the elementary-particle-people example and the earlier homunculus examples. In the former, the change in you as you become homunculus-infested is not one that makes any difference to your psychological processing (that is, information processing) or neurological processing but only to your microphysics. No techniques proper to human psychology or neurophysiology would reveal any difference in you. However, the homunculi-headed simulations described in the beginning of the chapter are not things to which neurophysiological theories true of us apply, and *if they are construed as Functional* (rather than Psychofunctional) simulations, they need not be things to which psychological (information-processing) theories true of us apply. This difference suggest that our intuitions are in part controlled by the not unreasonable view that our mental states depend on our having the psychology and/or neurophysiology we have. So something that differs markedly from us in both regards (recall that it is a Functional rather than Psychofunctional simulation) should not be assumed to have mentality just on the ground that it has been designed to be Functionally equivalent to us.

Is the Prima Facie Doubt Merely Prima Facie?

The Absent Qualia Argument rested on an appeal to the intuition that the homunculi-headed simulations lacked mentality or at least qualia. I said that this intuition gave rise to prima facie doubt that functionalism is true. But intuitions unsupported by principled argument are hardly to be considered bedrock. Indeed, intuitions incompatible with well-supported theory (such as the pre-Copernican intuition that the earth does not move) thankfully soon disappear. Even fields like linguistics whose data consist mainly in intuitions often reject such intuitions as that the following sentences are ungrammatical (on theoretical grounds):

The horse raced past the barn fell.

The boy the girl the cat bit scratched died.

These sentences are in fact grammatical though hard to process.[8]

Appeal to intuitions when judging possession of mentality, however, is *especially* suspicious. *No* physical mechanism seems very intuitively plausible as a seat of qualia, least of all a *brain*. Is a hunk of quivering gray stuff more intuitively appropriate as a seat of qualia than a covey of little men? If not, perhaps there is a prime facie doubt about the qualia of brain-headed systems too?

However, there is a very important difference between brain-headed and homunculi-headed systems. Since we know that *we are brain-headed systems*, and that *we* have qualia, we know that brain-headed systems can have qualia. So even though we have no theory of qualia which explains how this is *possible*, we have overwhelming reason to disregard whatever prima facie doubt there is about the qualia of brain-headed systems. Of course, this makes may argument partly *empirical*—it depends on knowledge of what makes us tick. But since this is knowledge we in fact possess, dependence on this knowledge should not be regarded as a defect.[9]

There is another difference between us meat-heads and the homunculi-heads: they are systems designed to mimic us, but we are not designed to mimic anything (here I rely on another empirical fact). This fact forestalls any attempt to argue on the basis of an inference to the best explanation for the qualia of homunculi-heads. The best explanation of the homunculi-heads' screams and winces is not their pains, but that they were designed to mimic our screams and winces.

Some people seem to feel that the complex and subtle behavior of the homunculi-heads (behavior just as complex and subtle—even as "sensitive" to features of the environment, human and nonhuman, as your behavior) is itself sufficient reason to disregard the prima facie doubt that homunculi-heads have qualia. But this is just crude behaviorism....

My case against Functionalism depends on the following principle: if a doctrine has an absurd conclusion which there is no independent reason to believe, and if there is no way of explaining away the absurdity or showing it to be misleading or irrelevant, and if there is no good reason to believe the doctrine that leads to the absurdity in the first place, then don't accept the doctrine. I claim that there is no independent reason to believe in the mentality of the homunculi-head, and I know of no way of explaining away the absurdity of the conclusion that it has mentality (though of course, my argument is vulnerable to the introduction of such an explanation). The issue, then, is whether there is any good reason to believe Functionalism. One argument for Functionalism is that it is the best solution available to the mind–body problem. I think this is a bad form of argument, but since I also think that Psychofunctionalism is preferable to Functionalism (for reasons to be mentioned below), I'll postpone consideration of this form of argument to the discussion of Psychofunctionalism.

The only other argument for Functionalism that I know of is that Functional identities can be shown to be true on the basis of analyses of the meanings of mental terminology. According to this argument, Functional identities are to be justified in the way one might try to justify the claim that the state of being a bachelor is identical to the state of being an unmarried man. A similar argument appeals to commonsense platitudes about mental states instead of truths of meaning. Lewis says that functional characterizations of mental states are in the province of "commonsense psychology—folk science, rather than professional science" (Lewis 1972, p. 250). (See also Shoemaker 1975, and Armstrong 1968. Armstrong equivocates on the analyticity issue. See Armstrong 1968, pp. 84–85, and p. 90.) And he goes on to insist that Functional characterizations should "include only platitudes which are common knowledge among us—everyone knows them, everyone knows that everyone else knows them, and so on" (Lewis 1972, p. 256). I shall talk mainly about the "platitude" version of the argument. The analyticity version is vulnerable to essentially the same considerations, as well as Quinean doubts about analyticity....

I am willing to concede, for the sake of argument, that it is possible to define any given mental state term in terms of platitudes concerning other mental state terms, input terms, and output terms. But this does not commit me to the type of definition of mental terms in which all mental terminology has been eliminated via Ramsification or some other device. It is simply a fallacy to suppose that if each mental term is definable in terms of the others (plus inputs and outputs), then each mental term is definable nonmentalistically. To see this, consider the example given earlier. Indeed, let's simplify matters by ignoring the inputs and outputs. Let's define pain as the cause of worry, and worry as the effect of pain. Even a person so benighted as to accept this needn't accept a definition of pain as *the cause of something*, or a definition of worry as *the effect of something*. Lewis claims that it is analytic that pain is the occupant of a certain causal role. Even if he is right about a causal role, specified in part mentalistically, one cannot conclude that it is analytic that pain is the occupant of any causal role, nonmentalistically specified.

I don't see any decent argument for Functionalism based on platitudes or analyticity. Further, the conception of Functionalism as based on platitudes leads to trouble with cases that platitudes have nothing to say about. Recall the example of brains being removed for cleaning and rejuvenation, the connections between one's brain and one's body being maintained by radio while one goes about one's business. The process takes a few days and when it is completed, the brain is reinserted in the body. Occasionally it may happen that a person's body is destroyed by an accident while the brain is being cleaned and rejuvenated. If hooked up to input sense organs (but not output organs) such a brain would exhibit *none* of the usual platitudinous connections between behavior and clusters of inputs and mental states. If, as seems plausible, such a brain could have almost all the same (narrow) mental states as we have (and since such a state of affairs could become typical), Functionalism is wrong.

It is instructive to compare the way Psychofunctionalism attempts to handle brains in bottles. According to Psychofunctionalism, what is to count as a system's inputs and outputs is an empirical question. Counting neural impulses as inputs and outputs would avoid the problems just sketched, since the brains in bottles and paralytics could have the right neural impulses even without bodily movements. Objection: There could be paralysis that affects the nervous system, and thus affects the neural impulses, so the problem which arises for Functionalism arises for Psychofunctionalism as well. Reply: Nervous system diseases can actually *change mentality*: for example they can render victims incapable of having pain. So it might actually be true that a widespread nervous system disease that caused intermittent paralysis rendered people incapable of certain mental states.

According to plausible versions of Psychofunctionalism, the job of deciding what neural processes should count as inputs and outputs is in part a matter of deciding *what malfunctions count as changes in mentality and what malfunctions count as changes in peripheral input and output connections*. Psychofunctionalism has a resource that Functionalism does not have, since Psychofunctionalism allows us to *adjust the line we draw between the inside and the outside of the organism so as to avoid problems of the sort discussed.* All versions of Functionalism go wrong in attempting to draw this line on the basis of only commonsense knowledge; "analyticity" versions of Functionalism go especially wrong in attempting to draw the line a priori.

Psychofunctionalism

In criticizing Functionalism, I appealed to the following principle: if a doctrine has an absurd conclusion which there is no independent reason to believe, and if there is no way of explaining away the absurdity or showing it to be misleading or irrelevant, and if there is no good reason to believe the doctrine that leads to the absurdity in the first place, then don't accept the doctrine. I said that there was no independent reason to believe that the homunculi-headed Functional simulation has any mental states.

However, there *is* an independent reason to believe that the homunculi-headed *Psycho*-functional simulation has mental states, namely that a Psychofunctional simulation of you would be Psychofunctionally equivalent to you, so any psychological theory true of you would be true of it too. What better reason could there be to attribute to it whatever mental states are in the domain of psychology?

This point shows that any Psychofunctional simulation of you shares your *non*-qualitative mental states. However, in the next section I shall argue that there is nonetheless some doubt that it shares your qualitative mental states.

Are Qualia Psychofunctional States?

I began this chapter by describing a homunculi-headed device and claiming there is prima facie doubt about whether it has any mental states at all, especially whether it has qualitative mental states like pains, itches, and sensations of red. The special doubt about qualia can perhaps be explicated by thinking about *inverted* qualia rather than *absent* qualia. It makes sense, or seems to make sense, to suppose that objects we both call green look to me the way objects we both call red look to you. It seems that we could be functionally equivalent even though the sensation fire hydrants evoke in you is qualitatively the same as the sensation grass evokes in me. Imagine an inverting lens which when placed in the eye of a subject results in exclamations like "Red things now look the way green things used to look, and vice versa." Imagine further, a pair of identical twins one of whom has the lenses inserted at birth. The twins grow up normally, and at age 21 are functionally equivalent. This situation offers at least some evidence that each's spectrum is inverted relative to the other's. (See Shoemaker 1975, note 17, for a convincing description of intrapersonal spectrum inversion.) However, it is very hard to see how to make sense of the analog of spectrum inversion with respect to nonqualitative states. Imagine a pair of persons one of whom believes that p is true and that q is false while the other believes that q is true and that p is false. Could these persons be functionally equivalent? It is hard to see how they could.[10] Indeed, it is hard to see how two persons could have only this difference in beliefs and yet there be no possible circumstance in which this belief difference would reveal itself in different behavior. Qualia seem to be supervenient on functional organization in a way that beliefs are not. . . .

There is another reason to firmly distinguish between qualitative and nonqualitative mental states in talking about functionalist theories: Psychofunctionalism avoids Functionalism's problems with nonqualitative states—for example propositional attitudes like beliefs and desires. But Psychofunctionalism may be no more able to handle qualitative states than is Functionalism. The reason is that qualia may well not be in the domain of psychology.

To see this let us try to imagine what a homunculi-headed realization of human psychology would be like. Current psychological theorizing seems directed toward the description of information-flow relations among psychological mechanisms. The aim seems to be to decompose such mechanisms into psychologically primitive mechanisms, "black boxes" whose internal structure is in the domain of physiology rather than in the domain of psychology. (See Fodor 1968, Dennett 1975, and Cummins 1975; interesting objections are raised in Nagel 1969.) For example, a near-primitive mechanism might be one that matches two items in a representational system and determines if they are tokens of the same type. Or the primitive mechanisms might be like those in a digital computer—for example, they might be (a) *add 1 to a given register,* and (b) *subtract 1 from a given register, or if the register contains 0, go to the nth (indicated) instruction.* (These operations can be combined to accomplish any digital computer operation; see Minsky 1967, p. 206.) Consider a computer whose machine-language code contains only two instructions corresponding to (a) and (b). If you ask how it multiplies or solves differential equations or makes up payrolls, you can be answered by being shown a program couched in terms of the two machine-language instructions. But if you ask how it adds 1 to a given register, the appropriate answer is given by a wiring diagram, not a program. The machine is hard-wired to add 1. When the instruction corresponding to (a) appears in a certain register, the contents of another register "automatically" change in a certain way. The computational structure of a computer is determined by a set of primitive operations and the ways nonprimitive operations are built up from them. Thus it does not matter to the computational structure of the computer whether the primitive mechanisms are realized by tube circuits, transistor circuits, or relays. Likewise, it does not matter to the psychology of a mental system whether its primitive mechanisms are realized by one or another neurological mechanism. Call a system a "realization of human psychology" if every psychological theory true of us is true of it. Consider a realization of human psychology whose primitive psychological operations are accomplished by little men, in the manner of the homunculi-headed simulations discussed. So, perhaps one little man produces items from a list, one by one, another compares these items with other representations to determine whether they match, etc.

Now there is good reason for supposing this system has some mental states. Propositional attitudes are an example. Perhaps psychological theory will identify remembering that P with having "stored" a sentencelike object which expresses the proposition that P (Fodor 1975). Then if one of the little men has put a certain sentencelike object in "storage," we may have reason for regarding the system as remembering that P. But unless having qualia is just a matter of having certain information processing (at best a controversial proposal), there is no such theoretical reason for regarding the system as having qualia. In short, there is perhaps as much doubt about the qualia of this homunculi-headed system as there was about the qualia of the homunculi-headed Functional simulation discussed early in the chapter.

But the system we are discussing is *ex hypothesi* something of which any true psychological theory is true. *So any doubt that it has qualia is a doubt that qualia are in the domain of psychology.*

It may be objected: "The kind of psychology you have in mind is *cognitive* psychology, that is, psychology of thought processes; and it is no wonder that qualia are not in the domain of *cognitive* psychology!" But I *do not* have cognitive psychology in mind, and if it sounds that way, this is easily explained: nothing we know about the psychological processes underlying our conscious mental life has anything to do with qualia. What passes for the "psychology" of sensation or pain, for example, is (a) physiology, (b) psychophysics (that is, the study of the mathematical functions relating stimulus variables and sensation variables; for example, the intensity of sound as a function of the amplitude of the sound waves), or (c) a grab bag of descriptive studies (see Melzack 1973, ch. 2). Of these, only psychophysics could be construed as being about qualia *per se*. And it is obvious that psychophysics touches only the *functional* aspect of sensation, not its qualitative character. Psychophysical experiments done on you would have the same results if done on any system Psychofunctionally equivalent to you, even if it had inverted or absent qualia. If experimental results would be unchanged whether or not the experimental subjects have inverted or absent qualia, they can hardly be expected to cast light on the nature of qualia.

Indeed, on the basis of the kind of conceptual apparatus now available in psychology, I do not see how psychology in anything like its present incarnation *could* explain qualia. We cannot now conceive how psychology could explain qualia, though we *can* conceive how psychology could explain believing, desiring, hoping, etc. (see Fodor 1975). That something is currently inconceivable is not a good reason to think it is impossible. Concepts could be developed tomorrow that would make what is now inconceivable conceivable. But all we have to go on is what we know, and on the basis of what we have to go on, it looks as if qualia are not in the domain of psychology....

It is no objection to the suggestion that qualia are not psychological entities that qualia are the very paradigm of something in the domain of psychology. As has often been pointed out, it is in part an empirical question what is in the domain of any particular branch of science. The liquidity of water turns out not to be explainable by chemistry, but rather by subatomic physics. Branches of science have at any given time a set of phenomena they seek to explain. But it can be discovered that some phenomenon which seemed central to a branch of science is actually in the purview of a different branch....

The Absent Qualia Argument exploits the possibility that the Functional or Psychofunctional state Functionalists or Psychofunctionalists would want to identify with pain can occur without any quale occurring. It also seems to be conceivable that the latter occur without the former. Indeed, there are facts that lend plausibility to this view. After frontal lobotomies, patients typically report that they still have pains, though the pains no longer bother them (Melzack 1973, p. 95). These patients show all the "sensory" signs of pain (such as recognizing pin pricks as sharp), but they often have little or no desire to avoid "painful" stimuli.

One view suggested by these observations is that each pain is actually a *composite* state whose components are a quale and a Functional or Psychofunctional state.[11] Or what amounts to much the same idea, each pain is a quale playing a certain Functional or Psychofunctional role. If this view is right, it helps to explain how people can have believed such different theories of the nature of pain and other sensations; they have emphasized one component at the expense of the other. Proponents of behaviorism and functionalism have had one component in mind; proponents of private ostensive definition have had the other in mind. Both approaches err in trying to give one account of something that has two components of quite different natures.

Chauvinism vs. Liberalism

It is natural to understand the psychological theories Psychofunctionalism adverts to as theories of *human* psychology. On Psychofunctionalism, so understood, it is impossible for a system to have beliefs, desires, etc., except in so far as psychological theories true of us are true of it. Psychofunctionalism (so understood) stipulates that Psychofunctional equivalence to us is necessary for mentality.

But even if Psychofunctional equivalence to us is a condition on our *recognition of mentality*, what reason is there to think it is a condition on mentality itself? Could there not be a wide variety of possible psychological processes that can underlie mentality, of which we instantiate only one type? Suppose we meet Martians and find that they are roughly Functionally (but not Psychofunctionally) equivalent to us. When we get to know Martians, we find them about as different from us as humans we know. We develop extensive cultural and commercial intercourse with them. We study each other's science and philosophy journals, go to each other's movies, read each other's novels, etc. Then Martian and Earthian psychologists compare notes, only to find that in underlying psychology, Martians and Earthians are very different. They soon agree that the difference can be described as follows. Think of humans and Martians as if they were products of conscious design. In any such design project, there will be various options. Some capacities can be built in (innate), others learned. The brain can be designed to accomplish tasks using as much memory capacity as necessary in order to minimize use of computation capacity; or, on the other hand, the designer could choose to conserve memory space and rely mainly on computation capacity. Inferences can be accomplished by systems which use a few axioms and many rules of inference, or, on the other hand, few rules and many axioms. Now imagine that what Martian and Earthian psychologists find when they compare notes is that Martians and Earthians differ as if they were the end products of maximally different design choices (compatible with rough Functional equivalence in adults). Should we reject our assumption that Martains can enjoy our films, believe their own apparent scientific results, etc.? Should they "reject" their "assumption" that we "enjoy" their novels, "learn" from their textbooks, etc.? Perhaps I have not provided enough information to answer this question. After all, there may be many ways of filling in the description of the Martian–human differences in which it would be reasonable to suppose there simply is no fact of the matter, or even to suppose that the Martians do not deserve mental ascriptions. But surely there are many ways of filling in the description of the Martian–Earthian difference I sketched on which it would be perfectly clear that even if Martians behave differently from us on subtle psychological experiments, they none the less think, desire, enjoy, etc. To suppose otherwise would be crude human chauvinism. (Remember theories are chauvinist in so far as they falsely *deny* that systems have mental properties and liberal in so far as they falsely *attribute* mental properties.) ...

An obvious suggestion of a way out of this difficulty is to identify mental states with Psychofunctional states, taking the domain of psychology to include *all creatures with mentality*, including Martians. The suggestion is that we define "Psychofunctionalism" in terms of "universal" or "cross-system" psychology, rather than the human psychology I assumed earlier. Universal psychology, however, is a suspect enterprise. For how are we to decide what systems should be included in the *domain* of universal psychology? One possible way of deciding what systems have mentality, and are thus in the domain of universal psychology, would be to use some *other* developed theory of mentality such as behaviorism or Functionalism. But such a procedure would be at least as ill-justified as the other theory used. Further, if Psychofunctionalism must presuppose some other theory of mind, we might just as well accept the other theory of mind instead.

Perhaps universal psychology will avoid this "domain" problem in the same way other branches of science avoid it or seek to avoid it. Other branches of science start with tentative domains based on intuitive and prescientific versions of the concepts the sciences are supposed to explicate. They then attempt to develop natural kinds in a way which allows the formulations of lawlike generalizations which apply to all or most of the entities in the prescientific domains. In the case of many branches of science—including biological and social sciences such as genetics and linguistics—the prescientific domain turned out to be suitable for the articulation of lawlike generalizations.

Now it may be that we shall be able to develop universal psychology in much the same way we develop Earthian psychology. We decide on an intuitive and prescientific basis what creatures to include in its domain, and work to develop natural kinds of psychological theory which apply to all or at least most of them. Perhaps the study of a wide range of organisms found on different worlds will one day lead to theories that determine truth conditions for the attribution of mental states like belief, desire, etc., applicable to systems which are pretheoretically quite different from us. Indeed, such cross-world psychology will no doubt require a whole new range of mentalistic concepts. Perhaps there will be families of concepts corresponding to belief, desire, etc.; that is, a family of belief-like concepts, desire-like concepts, etc. If so, the universal psychology we develop shall, no doubt, be somewhat dependent on which new organisms we discover first. Even if universal psychology is in fact possible, however, there will certainly be many possible organisms whose mental status is indeterminate.

On the other hand, it may be that universal psychology is *not* possible. Perhaps life in the universe is such that we shall simply have no basis for reasonable decisions about what systems are in the domain of psychology and what systems are not.

If universal psychology *is* possible, the problem I have been raising vanishes. Universal-Psychofunctionalism avoids the liberalism of Functionalism and the chauvinism of human-Psychofunctionalism. But the question of whether universal psychology is possible is surely one which we have no way of answering now.

Here is a summary of the argument so far:

1. Functionalism has the bizarre consequence that a homunculi-headed simulation of you has qualia. This puts the burden of proof on the Functionalist to give us some reason for believing his doctrine. However, the one argument for Functionalism in the literature is no good, and so Functionalism shows no sign of meeting the burden of proof.
2. Psychofunctional simulations of us share whatever states are in the domain of psychology, so the Psychofunctional homunculi-head does not cast doubt on Psychofunctional theories of cognitive states, but only on Psychofunctionalist theories of qualia, there being a doubt as to whether qualia are in the domain of psychology.
3. Psychofunctionalist theories of mental states that are in the domain of psychology, however, are hopelessly chauvinist.

So one version of functionalism has problems with liberalism, the other has problems with chauvinism. As to qualia, if they are in the domain of psychology, then Psychofunctionalism with respect to qualia is just as chauvinist as Psychofunctionalism with respect to belief. On the other hand, if qualia are not in the domain of psychology, the Psychofunctionalist homunculi-head can be used against Psychofunctionalism with respect to qualia. For the only thing that shields Psychofunctionalism with respect to mental state S from the homunculi-head argument is that if you have S, then any Psychofunctional simulation of you must have S, because the correct theory of S applies to it just as well as to you.

The Problem of the Inputs and the Outputs

I have been supposing all along (as Psychofunctionalists often do—see Putnam 1967) that inputs and outputs can be specified by neural impulse descriptions. But this is a chauvinist claim, since it precludes organisms without neurons (such as machines) from having functional descriptions. How can one avoid chauvinism with respect to specification of inputs and outputs? One way would be to characterize the inputs and outputs *only as* inputs and outputs. So the functional description of a person might list outputs by number: $output_1$, $output_2$, ... Then a system could be functionally equivalent to you if it had a set of states, inputs, and outputs causally related to one another in the way yours are, no matter what the states, inputs, and outputs were like. Indeed, though this approach violates the demand of some functionalists that inputs and outputs be physically specified, other functionalists—those who insist only that input and output descriptions be *nonmental*—may have had something like this in mind. This version of functionalism does not "tack down" functional descriptions at the periphery with relatively specific descriptions of inputs and outputs; rather, this version of functionalism treats inputs and outputs just as all versions of functionalism treat internal states. That is, this version specifies states, inputs, and outputs only by requiring that they *be* states, inputs, and outputs.

The trouble with this version of functionalism is that it is wildly liberal. Economic systems have inputs and outputs, such as influx and outflux of credits and debits. And economic systems also have a rich variety of internal states, such as having a rate of increase of GNP equal to double the Prime Rate. It does not seem impossible that a wealthy sheik could gain control of the economy of a small country, for example Bolivia, and manipulate its financial system to make it functionally equivalent to a person, for example himself. If this seems implausible, remember that the economic states, inputs, and outputs designated by the sheik to correspond to his mental states, inputs, and outputs need not be "natural" economic magnitudes. Our hypothetical sheik could pick *any* economic magnitudes at all—for example, the fifth time derivative of the balance of payments. His only constraint is that the magnitudes he picks be economic, that their having such-and-such values be inputs, outputs, and states, and that he be able to set up a financial structure which can be made to fit the intended formal mold. The mapping from psychological magnitudes to economic magnitudes could be as bizarre as the sheik requires.

This version of functionalism is far too liberal and must therefore be rejected. If there are any fixed points when discussing the mind–body problem, one of them is that the economy of Bolivia could not have mental states, no matter how it is distorted by powerful hobbyists. Obviously, we must be more specific in our descriptions of inputs and outputs. The question is: is there a description of inputs and outputs specific enough to avoid liberalism, yet general enough to avoid chauvinism? I doubt that there is.

Every proposal for a description of inputs and outputs I have seen or thought of is guilty of either liberalism or chauvinism. Though this paper has concentrated on liberalism, chauvinism is the more pervasive problem. Consider standard Functional and Psychofunctional descriptions. Functionalists tend to specify inputs and outputs in the manner of behaviorists: outputs in terms of movements of arms and legs, sound emitted and the like; inputs in terms of light and sound falling on the eyes and ears.... Such descriptions are blatantly *species-specific.* Humans have arms and legs, but snakes do not—and whether or not snakes have mentality, one can easily imagine snake-like creatures that do. Indeed, one can imagine creatures with all manner of input-output devices, for example creatures that communicate and manipulate by emitting strong magnetic fields. Of course, one could formulate Functional descriptions for each such species, and somewhere in disjunctive heaven there is a disjunctive description which will handle all species that ever actually exist in the universe (the description may be infinitely long). But even an appeal to such suspicious entities as infinite disjunctions will not bail out Functionalism, since even the amended view will not tell us what there is in common to pain-feeling organisms in virtue of which they all have pain. And it will not allow the ascription of pain to some hypothetical (but nonexistent) pain-feeling creatures. Further, these are just the grounds on which functionalists typically acerbically reject the disjunctive theories sometimes advanced by desperate physicalists. If functionalists suddenly smile on wildly disjunctive states to save themselves from chauvinism, they will have no way of defending themselves from physicalism.

Standard Psychofunctional descriptions of inputs and outputs are also species-specific (for example in terms of neural activity) and hence chauvinist as well.

The chauvinism of standard input-output descriptions is not hard to explain. The variety of possible intelligent life is enormous. Given any fairly specific descriptions of inputs and outputs, any high-school-age science-fiction buff will be able to describe a sapient sentient being whose inputs and outputs fail to satisfy that description.

I shall argue that *any physical description* of inputs and outputs (recall that many functionalists have insisted on physical descriptions) yields a version of functionalism that is inevitably chauvinist or liberal. Imagine yourself so badly burned in a fire that your optimal way of communicating with the outside world is via modulations of your EEG pattern in Morse Code. You find that thinking an exciting thought produces a pattern that your audience agrees to interpret as a dot, and a dull thought produces a "dash." Indeed, this fantasy is not so far from reality. According to a recent newspaper article (*Boston Globe,* 21 March 1976), "at UCLA scientists are working on the use of EEG to control machines.... A subject puts electrodes on his scalp, and thinks an object through a maze." The "reverse" process is also presumably possible: others communicating with you in Morse Code by producing bursts of electrical activity that affect your brain (for example causing a long or short afterimage). Alternatively, if the cerebroscopes that philosophers often fancy become a reality, your thoughts will be readable directly from your brain. Again, the reverse process also seems possible. In these cases, *the brain itself becomes an essential part of one's input and output devices.* This possibility has embarrassing consequences for functionalists. You will recall that functionalists pointed out that physicalism is false because a single mental state can be realized by an indefinitely large variety of physical states that have no necessary and sufficient physical characterization. But if this functionalist point against physicalism is right, *the same point applies to inputs and outputs*, since the physical realization of mental states can serve as an essential part of the input and output devices. That is, on any sense of "physical" in which the functionalist criticism of physicalism is correct, *there will be no physical characterization that applies to all and only mental systems' inputs and outputs*. Hence, any attempt to formulate a functional description with physical characterizations of inputs and outputs will inevitably either exclude some systems with mentality or include some systems without mentality. Hence,... *functionalists cannot avoid both chauvinism and liberalism.*

So physical specifications of inputs and outputs will not do. Moreover, mental or "action" terminology (such as "punching the offending person") cannot be used either, since to use such specifications of inputs or outputs would be to give up the functionalist program of characterizing mentality in nonmental terms. On the other hand, as you will recall, characterizing inputs and outputs simply *as* inputs and outputs is inevitably liberal. I, for one, do not see how there can be a vocabulary for describing inputs and outputs that avoids both liberalism and chauvinism. I do not claim that this is a conclusive argument against functionalism. Rather, like the functionalist argument against physicalism, it is best construed as a burden-of-proof argument. The functionalist says to the physicalist: "It is very hard to see how there could be a single physical characterization of the internal states of all and only creatures with mentality." I say to the functionalist: "It is very hard to see how there could be a single physical characterization of the inputs and outputs of all and only creatures with mentality." In both cases, enough has been said to make it the responsibility of those who think there could be such characterizations to sketch how they could be possible.[12]

Notes

1. See Fodor 1965; Lewis 1972; Putnam 1966, 1967, 1970, 1975a; Armstrong 1968; Locke 1968; perhaps Sellars 1968; perhaps Dennett 1969, 1978b; Nelson 1969, 1975 (but see also Nelson 1976); Pitcher 1971; Smart 1971; Block and Fodor 1972; Harman 1973; Grice 1975; Shoemaker 1975; Wiggins 1975.

2. The converse is also true.

3. Indeed, if one defines "behaviorism" as the view that mental terms can be defined in nonmental terms, then functionalism *is* a version of behaviorism....

4. State type, not state token. Throughout the chapter, I shall mean by "physicalism" the doctrine that says each distinct type of mental state is identical to a distinct type of physical state; for example, pain (the universal) is a physical state. Token physicalism, on the other hand, is the (weaker) doctrine that each particular datable pain is a state of some physical type or other. Functionalism shows that type physicalism is false, but it does not show that token physicalism is false.

By "physicalism," I mean *first-order* physicalism, the doctrine that, e.g., the property of being in pain is a first-order (in the Russell–Whitehead sense) physical property. (A first-order property is one whose definition does not require quantification over properties; a second-order property is one whose definition requires quantification over first-order properties—and not other properties.) The claim that being in pain is a second-order physical property is actually a (physicalist) form of functionalism. See Putnam 1970.

5. The basic idea for this example derives from Putnam (1967). I am indebted to many conversations with Hartry Field on the topic. Putnam's attempt to defend functionalism from the problem posed by such examples is discussed in the section entitled Putnam's Proposal of this chapter.

6. Shoemaker (1975) argues (in reply to Block and Fodor 1972) that absent qualia are logically impossible; that is, that it is logically impossible that two systems be in the same functional state yet one's state have and the other's state lack qualitative content. . . .

7. Since there is a difference between the role of the little people in producing your functional organization in the situation just described and the role of the homunculi in the homunculi-headed simulations this chapter began with, presumably Putnam's condition could be reformulated to rule out the latter without ruling out the former. But this would be a most *ad hoc* maneuver.

8. Compare the first sentence with "The fish eaten in Boston stank." The reason it is hard to process is that "raced" is naturally read as active rather than passive. See Fodor et al., 1974, p. 360. For a discussion of why the second sentence is grammatical, see Fodor and Garrett 1967, Bever 1970, and Fodor et al., 1974.

9. We often fail to be able to conceive of how something is possible because we lack the relevant theoretical concepts. For example, before the discovery of the mechanism of genetic duplication, Haldane argued persuasively that no conceivable physical mechanism could do the job. He was right. But instead of urging that scientists should develop ideas that would allow us to conceive of such a physical mechanism, he concluded that a *non*physical mechanism was involved. (I owe the example to Richard Boyd.)

10. Suppose a man who has good color vision mistakenly uses "red" to denote green and "green" to denote red. That is, he simply confuses the two words. Since his confusion is purely linguistic, though he says of a green thing that it is red, he does not *believe* that it is red, any more than a foreigner who has confused "ashcan" with "sandwich" believes people eat ashcans for lunch. Let us say that the person who has confused "red" and "green" in this way is a victim of Word Switching.

Now consider a different ailment: having red/green inverting lenses placed in your eyes without your knowledge. Let us say a victim of this ailment is a victim of Stimulus Switching. Like the victim of Word Switching, the victim of Stimulus Switching applies "red" to green things and vice versa. But the victim of Stimulus Switching *does* have false color beliefs. If you show him a green patch he says *and believes* that it is red.

Now suppose that a victim of Stimulus Switching suddenly becomes a victim of Word Switching as well. (Suppose as well that he is a lifelong resident of a remote Arctic village, and has no standing beliefs to the effect that grass is green, fire hydrants are red, and so forth.) He speaks normally, applying "green" to green patches and "red" to red patches. Indeed, he is functionally normal. But his *beliefs* are just as abnormal as they were before he became a victim of Word Switching. Before he confused the words "red" and "green," he applied "red" to a green patch, and mistakenly believed the patch to be red. Now he (correctly) says "red," but his belief is still wrong.

So two people can be functionally the same, yet have incompatible beliefs. Hence, the inverted qualia problem infects belief as well as qualia (though presumably only qualitative belief). This fact should be of concern not only to those who hold functional state identity theories of belief, but also to those who are attracted by Harman-style accounts of meaning as functional role. Our double victim—of Word and Stimulus Switching—is a counterexample to such accounts. For his word "green" plays the normal role in his reasoning and inference, yet since in saying of something that it "is green," he expresses his belief that it is *red,* he uses "green" with an abnormal meaning. I am indebted to Sylvain Bromberger for discussion of this issue.

11. The quale might be identified with a physico-chemical state. This view would comport with a suggestion Hilary Putnam made in the late 1960s in his philosophy of mind seminar. See also ch. 5 of Gunderson 1971.

12. I am indebted to Sylvain Bromberger, Hartry Field, Jerry Fodor, David Hills, Paul Horwich, Bill Lycan, Georges Rey, and David Rosenthal for their detailed comments on one or another earlier draft of this paper. Beginning in the fall of 1975, parts of earlier versions were read at Tufts University, Princeton University, the University of North Carolina at Greensboro, and the State University of New York at Binghamton.

References

Armstrong, D. (1968) *A Materialist Theory of Mind.* London: Routledge and Kegan Paul.

Bever, T. (1970) "The cognitive basis for linguistic structure," in J. R. Hayes (ed.), *Cognition and the Development of Language.* New York: Wiley.

Block, N. (1980) "Are absent qualia impossible?" *Philosophical Review,* 89(2).

Block, N. and Fodor, J. (1972) "What psychological states are not," *Philosophical Review,* 81, 159–81.

Chisholm, Roderick (1957) *Perceiving.* Ithaca: Cornell University Press.

Cummins, R. (1975) "Functional analysis," *Journal of Philosophy,* 72, 741–64.

Davidson, D. (1970) "Mental events," in L. Swanson and J. W. Foster (eds.), *Experience and Theory.* Amherst: University of Massachusetts Press.

Dennett, D. (1969) *Content and Consciousness.* London: Routledge and Kegan Paul.

Dennett, D. (1975) "Why the law of effect won't go away," *Journal for the Theory of Social Behavior,* 5, 169–87.

Dennett, D. (1978a) "Why a computer can't feel pain," *Synthese,* 38, 3.

Dennett, D. (1978b) *Brainstorms,* Montgomery, Vt.: Bradford.

Feldman, F. (1973) "Kripke's argument against materialism," *Philosophical Studies,* 416–19.

Fodor, J. (1965) "Explanations in psychology," in M. Black (ed.), *Philosophy in America.* London: Routledge and Kegan Paul.

Fodor, J. (1968) "The appeal to tacit knowledge in psychological explanation," *Journal of Philosophy,* 65, 627–40.

Fodor, J. (1974) "Special sciences," *Synthese,* 28, 97–115.

Fodor, J. (1975) *The Language of Thought.* New York: Crowell.

Fodor, J., Bever, T. and Garrett, M. (1974) *The Psychology of Language.* New York: McGraw-Hill.

Fodor, J. and Garrett, M. (1967) "Some syntactic determinants of sentential complexity," *Perception and Psychophysics,* 2, 289–96.

Geach, P. (1957) *Mental Acts.* London: Routledge and Kegan Paul.

Gendron, B. (1971) "On the relation of neurological and psychological theories: A critique of the hardware thesis," in R. C. Buck and R. S. Cohen (eds.), *Boston Studies in the Philosophy of Science VIII*. Dordrecht: Reidel.

Grice, H. P. (1975) "Method in philosophical psychology (from the banal to the bizarre)," *Proceedings and Addresses of the American Philosophical Association.*

Gunderson, K. (1971) *Mentality and Machines*. Garden City: Doubleday Anchor.

Harman, G. (1973) *Thought*. Princeton: Princeton University Press.

Hempel, C. (1970) "Reduction: Ontological and linguistic facets," in S. Morgenbesser, P. Suppes and M. White (eds.), *Essays in Honor of Ernest Nagel*. New York: St. Martins Press.

Kalke, W. (1969) "What is wrong with Fodor and Putnam's functionalism?" *Noûs*, 3, 83–93.

Kim, J. (1972) "Phenomenal properties, psychophysical laws, and the identity theory," *Monist*, 56(2), 177–92.

Lewis, D. (1972) "Psychophysical and theoretical identifications," *Australasian Journal of Philosophy*, 50(3), 249–58.

Locke, D. (1968) *Myself and Others*. Oxford: Oxford University Press.

Melzack, R. (1973) *The Puzzle of Pain*. New York: Basic Books.

Minsky, M. (1967) *Computation*. Englewood Cliffs, NJ: Prentice-Hall.

Mucciolo, L. F. (1974) "The identity thesis and neuropsychology," *Noûs*, 8, 327–42.

Nagel, T. (1969) "The boundaries of inner space," *Journal of Philosophy*, 66, 452–8.

Nagel, T. (1970) "Armstrong on the mind," *Philosophical Review*, 79, 394–403.

Nagel, T. (1972) "Review of Dennett's *Content and Consciousness*," *Journal of Philosophy*, 50, 220–34.

Nagel, T. (1974) "What is it like to be a bat?" *Philosophical Review*, 83, 435–50.

Nelson, R. J. (1969) "Behaviorism is false," *Journal of Philosophy*, 66, 417–52.

Nelson, R. J. (1975) "Behaviorism, finite automata and stimulus response theory," *Theory and Decision*, 6, 249–67.

Nelson, R. J. (1976) "Mechanism, functionalism, and the identity theory," *Journal of Philosophy*, 73, 365–86.

Oppenheim, P. and Putnam, H. (1958) "Unity of science as a working hypothesis," in H. Feigl, M. Scriven and G. Maxwell (eds.), *Minnesota Studies in the Philosophy of Science II*. Minneapolis: University of Minnesota Press.

Pitcher, G. (1971) *A Theory of Perception*. Princeton: Princeton University Press.

Putnam, H. (1963) "Brains and behavior"; reprinted as are all Putnam's articles referred to here (except "On properties") in *Mind, Language and Reality: Philosophical Papers*, vol. 2. London: Cambridge University Press, 1975.

Putnam, H. (1966) "The mental life of some machines."

Putnam, H. (1967) "The nature of mental states" (originally published under the title "Psychological Predicates").

Putnam, H. (1970) "On properties," in *Mathematics, Matter and Method: Philosophical Papers*, vol. 1. London: Cambridge University Press.

Putnam, H. (1975a) "Philosophy and our mental life."

Putnam, H. (1975b) "The meaning of 'meaning.'"

Rorty, R. (1972) "Functionalism, machines and incorrigibility," *Journal of Philosophy*, 69, 203–20.

Scriven, M. (1966) *Primary Philosophy*. New York: McGraw-Hill.

Sellars, W. (1956) "Empiricism and the philosophy of mind," in H. Feigl and M. Scriven (eds.), *Minnesota Studies in Philosophy of Science I*. Minneapolis: University of Minnesota Press.

Sellars, W. (1968) *Science and Metaphysics* (ch. 6). London: Routledge and Kegan Paul.

Shoemaker, S. (1975) "Functionalism and qualia," *Philosophical Studies*, 27, 271–315.

Shoemaker, S. (1976) "Embodiment and behavior," in A. Rorty (ed.), *The Identities of Persons*. Berkeley: University of California Press.

Shallice, T. (1972) "Dual functions of consciousness," *Psychological Review*, 79, 383–93.

Smart, J. J. C. (1971) "Reports of immediate experience," *Synthese*, 22, 346–59.

Wiggins, D. (1975) "Identity, designation, essentialism, and physicalism," *Philosophia*, 5, 1–30.

15 Minds, Brains, and Programs

John R. Searle

What psychological and philosophical significance should we attach to recent efforts at computer simulations of human cognitive capacities? In answering this question, I find it useful to distinguish what I will call "strong" AI from "weak" or "cautious" AI (Artificial Intelligence). According to weak AI, the principal value of the computer in the study of the mind is that it gives us a very powerful tool. For example, it enables us to formulate and test hypotheses in a more rigorous and precise fashion. But according to strong AI, the computer is not merely a tool in the study of the mind; rather, the appropriately programmed computer really *is* a mind, in the sense that computers given the right programs can be literally said to *understand* and have other cognitive states. In strong AI, because the programmed computer has cognitive states, the programs are not mere tools that enable us to test psychological explanations; rather, the programs are themselves the explanations.

I have no objection to the claims of weak AI, at least as far as this article is concerned. My discussion here will be directed at the claims I have defined as those of strong AI, specifically the claim that the appropriately programmed computer literally has cognitive states and that the programs thereby explain human cognition. When I hereafter refer to AI, I have in mind the strong version, as expressed by these two claims.

I will consider the work of Roger Schank and his colleagues at Yale (Schank & Abelson 1977), because I am more familiar with it than I am with any other similar claims, and because it provides a very clear example of the sort of work I wish to examine. But nothing that follows depends upon the details of Schank's programs. The same arguments would apply to Winograd's SHRDLU (Winograd 1973), Weizenbaum's ELIZA (Weizenbaum 1965), and indeed any Turing machine simulation of human mental phenomena.

Very briefly, and leaving out the various details, one can describe Schank's program as follows: the aim of the program is to simulate the human ability to understand stories. It is characteristic of human beings' story-understanding capacity that they can answer questions about the story even though the information that they give was never explicitly stated in the story. Thus, for example, suppose you are given the following story: "A man went into a restaurant and ordered a hamburger. When the hamburger arrived it was burned to a crisp, and the man stormed out of the restaurant angrily, without paying for the hamburger or leaving a tip." Now, if you are asked "Did the man eat the hamburger?" you will presumably answer, "No, he did not." Similarly, if you are given the following story: "A man went into a restaurant and ordered a hamburger; when the hamburger came he was very pleased with it; and as he left the restaurant he gave the waitress a large tip before paying his bill," and you are asked the question, "Did the man eat the hamburger?," you will presumably answer, "Yes, he ate the hamburger." Now Schank's machines can similarly answer questions about restaurants in this fashion. To do this, they have a "representation" of the sort of information that human beings have about restaurants, which enables them to answer such questions as those above, given these sorts of stories. When the machine is given the story and then asked the question, the machine will print out answers of the sort that we would expect human beings to give if told similar stories. Partisans of strong AI claim that in this question and answer sequence the machine is not only simulating a human ability but also

1. that the machine can literally be said to *understand* the story and provide the answers to questions, and
2. that what the machine and its program do *explains* the human ability to understand the story and answer questions about it.

Both claims seem to me to be totally unsupported by Schank's[1] work, as I will attempt to show in what follows.

One way to test any theory of the mind is to ask oneself what it would be like if my mind actually worked on the principles that the theory says all minds work on. Let us apply this test to the Schank program with the following *Gedankenexperiment*. Suppose that I'm locked in a room and given a large batch of Chinese writing. Suppose furthermore (as is indeed the case) that I know no Chinese, either written or spoken, and that I'm not even confident that I could recognize Chinese writing as Chinese writing distinct from, say, Japanese writing or meaningless squiggles. To me, Chinese writing is just so many meaningless squiggles. Now suppose further that after this first batch of Chinese writing I am given a second batch of Chinese script together with a set of rules for correlating the second batch with the first batch. The rules are in English, and I understand these rules as well as any other native speaker of English. They enable me to correlate one set of formal symbols with another set of formal symbols, and all that "formal" means here is that I can identify the symbols entirely by their shapes. Now suppose also that I am given a third batch of Chinese symbols together with some instructions, again in English, that enable me to correlate elements of this third batch with the first two batches, and these rules instruct me how to give back certain Chinese symbols with certain sorts of shapes in response to certain sorts of shapes given me in the third batch. Unknown to me, the people who are giving me all of these symbols call the first batch "a script," they call the second batch a "story," and they call the third batch "questions." Furthermore, they call the symbols I give them back in response to the third batch "answers to the questions," and the set of rules in English that they gave me, they call "the program." Now just to complicate the story a little, imagine that these people also give me stories in English, which I understand, and they then ask me questions in English about these stories, and I give them back answers in English. Suppose also that after a while I get so good at following the instructions for manipulating the Chinese symbols and the programmers get so good at writing the programs that from the external point of view—that is, from the point of view of somebody outside the room in which I am locked—my answers to the questions are absolutely indistinguishable from those of native Chinese speakers. Nobody just looking at my answers can tell that I don't speak a word of Chinese. Let us also suppose that my answers to the English questions are, as they no doubt would be, indistinguishable from those of other native English speakers, for the simple reason that I am a native English speaker. From the external point of view—from the point of view of someone reading my "answers"—the answers to the Chinese questions and the English questions are equally good. But in the Chinese case, unlike the English case, I produce the answers by manipulating uninterpreted formal symbols. As far as the Chinese is concerned, I simply behave like a computer; I perform computational operations on formally specified elements. For the purposes of the Chinese, I am simply an instantiation of the computer program.

Now the claims made by strong AI are that the programmed computer understands the stories and that the program in some sense explains human understanding. But we are now in a position to examine these claims in light of our thought experiment.

1. As regards the first claim, it seems to me quite obvious in the example that I do not understand a word of the Chinese stories. I have inputs and outputs that are indistinguishable from those of the native Chinese speaker, and I can have any formal program you like, but I still understand nothing. For the same reasons, Schank's computer understands nothing of any stories, whether in Chinese, English, or whatever, since in the Chinese case the computer is me, and in cases where the computer is not me, the computer has nothing more than I have in the case where I understand nothing.

2. As regards the second claim, that the program explains human understanding, we can see that the computer and its program do not provide sufficient conditions of understanding since the computer and the program are functioning, and there is no understanding. But does it even provide a necessary condition or a significant contribution to understanding? One of the claims made by the supporters of strong AI is that when I understand a story in English, what I am doing is exactly the same—or perhaps more of the same—as what I was doing in manipulating the Chinese symbols. It is simply more formal symbol manipulation that distinguishes the case in English, where I do understand, from the case in Chinese, where I don't. I have not demonstrated that this claim is false, but it would certainly appear an incredible claim in the example. Such plausibility as the claim has derives from the supposition that we can construct a program that will have the same inputs and outputs as native speakers, and in addition we assume that speakers have some level of description where they are also instantiations of a program. On the basis of these two assumptions we assume that even if Schank's program isn't the whole story about understanding, it may be part of the story. Well, I suppose that is an empirical possibility, but not the slightest reason has so far been given to believe that it is true, since what is suggested—though certainly not demonstrated—by the example is that the computer program is simply irrelevant to my understanding of the story. In the Chinese case I have everything that artificial intelligence can put into me by way of a program, and I understand nothing; in the English case I understand everything, and there is so far no reason at all to suppose that my understanding has anything to do with computer programs, that is, with computational operations on purely formally specified elements. As long as the program is defined in terms of computational operations on purely formally defined elements, what the example suggests is that these by themselves have no interesting

connection with understanding. They are certainly not sufficient conditions, and not the slightest reason has been given to suppose that they are necessary conditions or even that they make a significant contribution to understanding. Notice that the force of the argument is not simply that different machines can have the same input and output while operating on different formal principles—that is not the point at all. Rather, whatever purely formal principles you put into the computer, they will not be sufficient for understanding, since a human will be able to follow the formal principles without understanding anything. No reason whatever has been offered to suppose that such principles are necessary or even contributory, since no reason has been given to suppose that when I understand English I am operating with any formal program at all.

Well, then, what is it that I have in the case of the English sentences that I do not have in the case of the Chinese sentences? The obvious answer is that I know what the former mean, while I haven't the faintest idea what the latter mean. But in what does this consist and why couldn't we give it to a machine, whatever it is? I will return to this question later, but first I want to continue with the example.

I have had the occasions to present this example to several workers in artifical intelligence, and, interestingly, they do not seem to agree on what the proper reply to it is. I get a surprising variety of replies, and in what follows I will consider the most common of these (specified along with their geographic origins).

But first I want to block some common misunderstandings about "understanding": in many of these discussions one finds a lot of fancy footwork about the word "understanding." My critics point out that there are many different degrees of understanding; that "understanding" is not a simple two-place predicate; that there are even different kinds and levels of understanding, and often the law of excluded middle doesn't even apply in a straightforward way to statements of the form "x understands y"; that in many cases it is a matter for decision and not a simple matter of fact whether x understands y; and so on. To all of these points I want to say: of course, of course. But they have nothing to do with the points at issue. There are clear cases in which "understanding" literally applies and clear cases in which it does not apply; and these two sorts of cases are all I need for this argument.[2] I understand stories in English; to a lesser degree I can understand stories in French; to a still lesser degree, stories in German; and in Chinese, not at all. My car and my adding machine, on the other hand, understand nothing: they are not in that line of business. We often attribute "understanding" and other cognitive predicates by metaphor and analogy to cars, adding machines, and other artifacts, but nothing is proved by such attributions. We say, "The door *knows* when to open because of its photoelectric cell," "The adding machine *knows how* (*understands how*, is *able*) to do addition and subtraction but not division," and "The thermostat *perceives* changes in the temperature." The reason we make these attributions is quite interesting, and it has to do with the fact that in artifacts we extend our own intentionality;[3] our tools are extensions of our purposes, and so we find it natural to make metaphorical attributions of intentionality to them; but I take it no philosophical ice is cut by such examples. The sense in which an automatic door "understands instructions" from its photoelectric cell is not at all the sense in which I understand English. If the sense in which Schank's programmed computers understand stories is supposed to be the metaphorical sense in which the door understands, and not the sense in which I understand English, the issue would not be worth discussing. But Newell and Simon (1963) write that the kind of cognition they claim for computers is exactly the same as for human beings. I like the straightforwardness of this claim, and it is the sort of claim I will be considering. I will argue that in the literal sense the programmed computer understands what the car and the adding machine understand, namely, exactly nothing. The computer understanding is not just (like my understanding of German) partial or incomplete; it is zero.

Now to the replies:

I The Systems Reply (Berkeley) "While it is true that the individual person who is locked in the room does not understand the story, the fact is that he is merely part of a whole system, and the system does understand the story. The person has a large ledger in front of him in which are written the rules, he has a lot of scratch paper and pencils for doing calculations, he has 'data banks' of sets of Chinese symbols. Now, understanding is not being ascribed to the mere individual; rather it is being ascribed to this whole system of which he is a part."

My response to the systems theory is quite simple: let the individual internalize all of these elements of the system. He memorizes the rules in the ledger and the data banks of Chinese symbols, and he does all the calculations in his head. The individual then incorporates the entire system. There isn't anything at all to the system that he does not encompass. We can even get rid of the room and suppose he works outdoors. All the same, he understands nothing of the Chinese, and a fortiori neither does the system, because there isn't anything in the system that isn't in him. If he doesn't understand, then there is no way the system could understand because the system is just a part of him.

Actually I feel somewhat embarrassed to give even this answer to the systems theory because the theory seems to me so unplausible to start with. The idea is that while a person doesn't understand Chinese, somehow the *conjunction* of that person and bits of paper might understand Chinese. It is not easy for me to imagine how someone who was not in the grip of an ideology would find the idea at all plausible. Still, I think many people who are committed to the ideology of strong AI will in the end be inclined to say something very much like this; so let us pursue it a bit further. According to one version of this view, while the man in the internalized systems example doesn't understand Chinese in the sense that a native Chinese speaker does (because, for example, he doesn't know that the story refers to restaurants and hamburgers, etc.), still "the man as a formal symbol manipulation system" *really does understand Chinese.* The subsystem of the man that is the formal symbol manipulation system for Chinese should not be confused with the subsystem for English.

So there are really two subsystems in the man; one understands English, the other Chinese, and "it's just that the two systems have little to do with each other." But, I want to reply, not only do they have little to do with each other, they are not even remotely alike. The subsystem that understands English (assuming we allow ourselves to talk in this jargon of "subsystems" for a moment) knows that the stories are about restaurants and eating hamburgers, he knows that he is being asked questions about restaurants and that he is answering questions as best he can by making various inferences from the content of the story, and so on. But the Chinese system knows none of this. Whereas the English subsystem knows that "hamburgers" refers to hamburgers, the Chinese subsystem knows only that "squiggle squiggle" is followed by "squoggle squoggle." All he knows is that various formal symbols are being introduced at one end and manipulated according to rules written in English, and other symbols are going out at the other end. The whole point of the original example was to argue that such symbol manipulation by itself couldn't be sufficient for understanding Chinese in any literal sense because the man could write "squoggle squoggle" after "squiggle squiggle" without understanding anything in Chinese. And it doesn't meet that argument to postulate subsystems within the man, because the subsystems are no better off than the man was in the first place; they still don't have anything even remotely like what the English-speaking man (or subsystem) has. Indeed, in the case as described, the Chinese subsystem is simply a part of the English subsystem, a part that engages in meaningless symbol manipulation according to rules in English.

Let us ask ourselves what is supposed to motivate the systems reply in the first place; that is, what *independent* grounds are there supposed to be for saying that the agent must have a subsystem within him that literally understands stories in Chinese? As far as I can tell the only grounds are that in the example I have the same input and output as native Chinese speakers and a program that goes from one to the other. But the whole point of the examples has been to try to show that that couldn't be sufficient for understanding, in the sense in which I understand stories in English, because a person, and hence the set of systems that go to make up a person, could have the right combination of input, output, and program and still not understand anything in the relevant literal sense in which I understand English. The only motivation for saying there *must* be a subsystem in me that understands Chinese is that I have a program and I can pass the Turing test; I can fool native Chinese speakers. But precisely one of the points at issue is the adequacy of the Turing test. The example shows that there could be two "systems," both of which pass the Turing test, but only one of which understands; and it is no argument against this point to say that since they both pass the Turing test they must both understand, since this claim fails to meet the argument that the system in me that understands English has a great deal more than the system that merely processes Chinese. In short, the systems reply simply begs the question by insisting without argument that the system must understand Chinese.

Furthermore, the systems reply would appear to lead to consequences that are independently absurd. If we are to conclude that there must be cognition in me on the grounds that I have a certain sort of input and output and a program in between, then it looks like all sorts of noncognitive subsystems are going to turn out to be cognitive. For example, there is a level of description at which my stomach does information processing, and it instantiates any number of computer programs, but I take it we do not want to say that it has any understanding [cf. Pylyshyn: "Computation and Cognition" *BBS* 3(1) 1980]. But if we accept the systems reply, then it is hard to see how we avoid saying that stomach, heart, livers, and so on, are all understanding subsystems, since there is no principled way to distinguish the motivation for saying the Chinese subsystem understands from saying that the stomach understands. It is, by the way, not an answer to this point to say that the Chinese system has information as input and output and the stomach has food and food products as input and output, since from the point of view of the agent, from my point of view, there is no information in either the food or the Chinese—the Chinese is just so many meaningless squiggles. The information in the Chinese case is solely in the eyes of the programmers and the interpreters, and there is nothing to prevent them from treating the input and output of my digestive organs as information if they so desire.

This last point bears on some independent problems in strong AI, and it is worth digressing for a moment to explain it. If strong AI is to be a branch of psychology, then it must be able to distinguish those systems that are genuinely mental from those that are not. It must be able to distinguish the principles on which the mind works from those on which nonmental systems work; otherwise it will offer us no explanations of what is specifically mental about the mental. And the mental-nonmental distinction cannot be just in the eye of the beholder but it must be intrinsic to the systems; otherwise it would be up to any beholder to treat people as nonmental and, for example, hurricanes as mental if he likes. But quite often in the AI literature the distinction is blurred in ways that would in the long run prove disastrous to the claim that AI is a cognitive inquiry. McCarthy, for example, writes, "Machines as simple as thermostats can be said to have beliefs, and having beliefs seems to be a characteristic of most machines capable of problem solving performance" (McCarthy 1979). Anyone who thinks strong AI has a chance as a theory of the mind ought to ponder the implications of that remark. We are asked to accept it as a discovery of strong AI that the hunk of metal on the wall that we use to regulate the temperature has beliefs in exactly the same sense that we, our spouses, and our children have beliefs, and furthermore that "most" of the other machines in the room—telephone, tape recorder, adding machine, electric light switch,—also have beliefs in this literal sense. It is not the aim of this article to argue against McCarthy's point, so I will simply assert the following without argument. The study of the mind starts with such facts as that humans have beliefs, while thermostats, telephones, and adding machines don't. If you get a theory that denies this point you have produced a counterexample to the theory and the theory is false. One gets the impression that people in AI who write this sort of thing think they can get away with it because they don't really take it seriously, and they don't think anyone else will either. I propose for a moment at least, to take it seriously. Think hard for one minute about what would be necessary to establish that that hunk of metal on the wall over there had real beliefs, beliefs with direction of fit, propositional content, and conditions of satisfaction; beliefs that had the possibility of being strong beliefs or weak beliefs; nervous, anxious, or secure beliefs; dogmatic, rational, or superstitious beliefs; blind faiths or hesitant cogitations; any kind of beliefs. The thermostat is not a candidate. Neither is stomach, liver, adding machine, or telephone. However, since we are taking the idea seriously, notice that its truth would be fatal to strong AI's claim to be a science of the mind. For now the mind is everywhere. What we wanted to know is what distinguishes the mind from thermostats and livers. And if McCarthy were right, strong AI wouldn't have a hope of telling us that.

II The Robot Reply (Yale) "Suppose we wrote a different kind of program from Schank's program. Suppose we put a computer inside a robot, and this computer would not just take in formal symbols as input and give out formal symbols as output, but rather would actually operate the robot in such a way that the robot does something very much like perceiving, walking, moving about, hammering nails, eating, drinking—anything you like. The robot would, for example, have a television camera attached to it that enabled it to 'see,' it would have arms and legs that enabled it to 'act,' and all of this would be controlled by its computer 'brain.' Such a robot would, unlike Schank's computer, have genuine understanding and other mental states."

The first thing to notice about the robot reply is that it tacitly concedes that cognition is not soley a matter of formal symbol manipulation, since this reply adds a set of causal relation with the outside world [cf. Fodor: "Methodological Solipsism" *BBS* 3(1) 1980]. But the answer to the robot reply is that the addition of such "perceptual" and "motor" capacities adds nothing by way of understanding, in particular, or intentionality, in general, to Schank's original program. To see this, notice that the same thought experiment applies to the robot case. Suppose that instead of the computer inside the robot, you put me inside the room and, as in the original Chinese case, you give me more Chinese symbols with more instructions in English of matching Chinese symbols to Chinese symbols and feeding back Chinese symbols to the outside. Suppose, unknown to me, some of the Chinese symbols that come to me come from a television camera attached to the robot and other Chinese symbols that I am giving out serve to make the motors inside the robot move the robot's legs or arms. It is important to emphasize that all I am doing is manipulating formal symbols: I know none of these other facts. I am receiving "information" from the robot's "perceptual" apparatus, and I am giving out "instructions" to its motor apparatus without knowing either of these facts. I am the robot's homunculus, but unlike the traditional homunculus, I don't know what's going on. I don't understand anything except the rules for symbol manipulation. Now in this case I want to say that the robot has no intentional states at all; it is simply moving about as a result of its electrical wiring and its program. And furthermore, by instantiating the program I have no intentional states of the relevant type. All I do is follow formal instructions about manipulating formal symbols.

III The Brain Simulator Reply (Berkeley and M.I.T.) "Suppose we design a program that doesn't represent information that we have about the world, such as the information in Schank's scripts, but simulates the actual sequence of neuron firings at the synapses of the brain of a native Chinese speaker when he understands stories in Chinese and gives answers to them. The machine takes in Chinese stories and questions about them as input, it simulates the formal structure of actual Chinese brains in processing these stories, and it gives out Chinese answers as outputs. We can even imagine that the machine operates, not with a single serial program, but with a whole set of programs operating in parallel, in the manner that actual human brains presumably operate when they process natural language. Now surely in such a case we would have to say that the machine understood the stories; and if we refuse to say that, wouldn't we also have to deny that native Chinese speakers understood the stories? At the level of the synapses, what would or could be different about the program of the computer and the program of the Chinese brain?"

Before countering this reply I want to digress to note that it is an odd reply for any partisan of artificial intelligence (or functionalism, etc.) to make: I thought the whole idea of strong AI is that we don't need to know how the brain works to know how the mind works. The basic hypothesis, or so I had supposed, was that there is a level of mental operations consisting of computational processes over formal elements that constitute the essence of the mental and can be realized in all sorts of different brain processes, in the same way that any computer program can be realized in different computer hardwares: on the assumptions of strong AI, the mind is to the brain as the program is to the hardware, and thus we can understand the mind without doing neurophysiology. If we had to know how the brain worked to do AI, we wouldn't bother with AI. However, even getting this close to the operation of the brain is still not sufficient to produce understanding. To see this, imagine that instead of a monolingual man in a room shuffling symbols we have the man operate an elaborate set of water pipes with valves connecting them. When the man receives the Chinese symbols, he looks up in the program, written in English, which valves he has to turn on and off. Each water connection corresponds to a synapse in the Chinese brain, and the whole system is rigged up so that after doing all the right firings, that is after turning on all the right faucets, the Chinese answers pop out at the output end of the series of pipes.

Now where is the understanding in this system? It takes Chinese as input, it simulates the formal structure of the synapses of the Chinese brain, and it gives Chinese as output. But the man certainly doesn't understand Chinese, and neither do the water pipes, and if we are tempted to adopt what I think is the absurd view that somehow the *conjunction* of man *and* water pipes understands, remember that in principle the man can internalize the formal structure of the water pipes and do all the "neuron firings" in his imagination. The problem with the brain simulator is that it is simulating the wrong things about the brain. As long as it simulates only the formal structure of the sequence of neuron firings at the synapses, it won't have simulated what matters about the brain, namely its causal properties, its ability to produce intentional states. And that the formal properties are not sufficient for the causal properties is shown by the water pipe example: we can have all the formal properties carved off from the relevant neurobiological causal properties.

IV The Combination Reply (Berkeley and Stanford) "While each of the previous three replies might not be completely convincing by itself as a refutation of the Chinese room counterexample, if you take all three together they are collectively much more convincing and even decisive. Imagine a robot with a brain-shaped computer lodged in its cranial cavity, imagine the computer programmed with all the synapses of a human brain, imagine the whole behavior of the robot is indistinguishable from human behavior, and now think of the whole thing as a unified system and not just as a computer with inputs and outputs. Surely in such a case we would have to ascribe intentionality to the system."

I entirely agree that in such a case we would find it rational and indeed irresistible to accept the hypothesis that the robot had intentionality, as long as we knew nothing more about it. Indeed, besides appearance and behavior, the other elements of the combination are really irrelevant. If we could build a robot whose behavior was indistinguishable over a large range from human behavior, we would attribute intentionality to it, pending some reason not to. We wouldn't need to know in advance that its computer brain was a formal analogue of the human brain.

But I really don't see that this is any help to the claims of strong AI; and here's why: According to strong AI, instantiating a formal program with the right input and output is a sufficient condition of, indeed is constitutive of, intentionality. As Newell (1979) puts it, the essence of the mental is the operation of a physical symbol system. But the attributions of intentionality that we make to the robot in this example have nothing to do with formal programs. They are simply based on the assumption that if the robot looks and behaves sufficiently like us, then we would suppose, until proven otherwise, that it must have mental states like ours that cause and are expressed by its behavior and it must have an inner mechanism capable of producing such mental states. If we knew independently how to account for its behavior without such assumptions we would not attribute intentionality to it, especially if we knew it had a formal program. And this is precisely the point of my earlier reply to objection II.

Suppose we knew that the robot's behavior was entirely accounted for by the fact that a man inside it was receiving uninterpreted formal symbols from the robot's sensory receptors and sending out uninterpreted formal symbols to its motor mechanisms, and the man was doing this symbol manipulation in accordance with a bunch of rules. Furthermore, suppose the man knows none of these facts about the robot, all he knows is which operations to perform on which meaningless symbols. In such a case we would regard the robot as an ingenious mechanical dummy. The hypothesis that the dummy has a mind would now be unwarranted and unnecessary, for there is now no longer any reason to ascribe intentionality to the robot or to the system of which it is a part (except of course for the man's intentionality in manipulating the symbols). The formal symbol manipulations go on, the input and output are correctly matched, but the only real locus of intentionality is the man, and he doesn't know any of the relevant intentional states; he doesn't, for example, *see* what comes into the robot's eyes, he doesn't *intend* to move the robot's arm, and he doesn't *understand* any of the remarks made to or by the robot. Nor, for the reasons stated earlier, does the system of which man and robot are a part.

To see this point, contrast this case with cases in which we find it completely natural to ascribe intentionality to members of certain other primate species such as apes and monkeys and to domestic animals such as dogs. The reasons we find it natural are, roughly, two: we can't make sense of the animal's behavior without the ascription of intentionality, and we can see that the beasts are made of similar stuff to ourselves—that is an eye, that a nose, this is its skin, and so on. Given the coherence of the animal's behavior and the assumption of the same causal stuff underlying it, we assume both that the animal must have mental states underlying its behavior, and that the mental states must be produced by mechanisms made out of the stuff that is like our stuff. We would certainly make similar assumptions about the robot unless we had some reason not to, but as soon as we knew that the behavior was the result of a formal program, and that the actual causal properties of the physical substance were irrelevant we would abandon the assumption of intentionality. [See "Cognition and Consciousness in Nonhuman Species" *BBS* I(4) 1978.]

There are two other responses to my example that come up frequently (and so are worth discussing) but really miss the point.

V The Other Minds Reply (Yale) "How do you know that other people understand Chinese or anything else? Only by their behavior. Now the computer can pass the behavioral tests as well as they can (in principle), so if you are going to attribute cognition to other people you must in principle also attribute it to computers."

This objection really is only worth a short reply. The problem in this discussion is not about how I know that other people have cognitive states, but rather what it is that I am attributing to them when I attribute cognitive states to them. The thrust of the argument is that it couldn't be just computational processes and their output because the computational processes and their output can exist without the cognitive state. It is no answer to this argument to feign anesthesia. In "cognitive sciences" one presupposes the reality and knowability of the mental in the same way that in physical sciences one has to presuppose the reality and knowability of physical objects.

VI The Many Mansions Reply (Berkeley) "Your whole argument presupposes that AI is only about analogue and digital computers. But that just happens to be the present state of technology. Whatever these causal processes are that you say are essential for intentionality (assuming you are right), eventually we will be able to build devices that have these causal processes, and that will be artificial intelligence. So your arguments are in no way directed at the ability of artificial intelligence to produce and explain cognition."

I really have no objection to this reply save to say that it in effect trivializes the project of strong AI by redefining it as whatever artificially produces and explains cognition. The interest of the original claim made on behalf of artificial intelligence is that it was a precise, well defined thesis: mental processes are computational processes over formally defined elements. I have been concerned to challenge that thesis. If the claim is redefined so that it is no longer that thesis, my objections no longer apply because there is no longer a testable hypothesis for them to apply to.

Let us now return to the question I promised I would try to answer: granted that in my original example I understand the English and I do not understand the Chinese, and granted therefore that the machine doesn't understand either English or Chinese, still there must be something about me that makes it the case that I understand English and a corresponding something lacking in me that makes it the case that I fail to understand Chinese. Now why couldn't we give those somethings, whatever they are, to a machine?

I see no reason in principle why we couldn't give a machine the capacity to understand English or Chinese, since in an important sense our bodies with our brains are precisely such machines. But I do see very strong arguments for saying that we could not give such a thing to a machine where the operation of the machine is defined solely in terms of computational processes over formally defined elements; that is, where the operation of the machine is defined as an instantiation of a computer program. It is not because I am the instantiation of a computer program that I am able to understand English and have other forms of intentionality (I am, I suppose, the instantiation of any number of computer programs), but as far as we know it is because I am a certain sort of organism with a certain biological (i.e. chemical and physical) structure, and this structure, under certain conditions, is causally capable of producing perception, action, understanding, learning, and other intentional phenomena. And part of the point of the present argument is that only something that had those causal powers could have that intentionality. Perhaps other physical and chemical processes could produce exactly these effects; perhaps, for example, Martians also have intentionality but their brains are made of different stuff. That is an empirical question, rather like the question whether photosynthesis can be done by something with a chemistry different from that of chlorophyll.

But the main point of the present argument is that no purely formal model will ever be sufficient by itself for intentionality because the formal properties are not by themselves constitutive of intentionality, and they have by themselves no causal powers except the power, when instantiated, to produce the next stage of the formalism when the machine is running. And any other causal properties that particular realizations of the formal model have, are irrelevant to the formal model because we can always put the same formal model in a different realization where those causal properties are obviously absent. Even if, by some miracle, Chinese speakers exactly realize Schank's program, we can put the same program in English speakers, water pipes, or computers, none of which understand Chinese, the program notwithstanding.

What matters about brain operations is not the formal shadow cast by the sequence of synapses but rather the actual properties of the sequences. All the arguments for the strong version of artificial intelligence that I have seen insist on drawing an outline around the shadows cast by cognition and then claiming that the shadows are the real thing.

By way of concluding I want to try to state some of the general philosophical points implicit in the argument. For clarity I will try to do it in a question and answer fashion, and I begin with that old chestnut of a question:

"Could a machine think?"

The answer is, obviously, yes. We are precisely such machines.

"Yes, but could an artifact, a man-made machine, think?"

Assuming it is possible to produce artificially a machine with a nervous system, neurons with axons and dendrites, and all the rest of it, sufficiently like ours, again the answer to the question seems to be obviously, yes. If you can exactly duplicate the causes, you could duplicate the effects. And indeed it might be possible to produce consciousness, intentionality, and all the rest of it using some other sorts of chemical principles than those that human beings use. It is, as I said, an empirical question.

"OK, but could a digital computer think?"

If by "digital computer" we mean anything at all that has a level of description where it can correctly be described as the instantiation of a computer program, then again the answer is, of course, yes, since we are the instantiations of any number of computer programs, and we can think.

"But could something think, understand, and so on *solely* in virtue of being a computer with the right sort of program? Could instantiating a program, the right program of course, by itself be a sufficient condition of understanding?"

This I think is the right question to ask, though it is usually confused with one or more of the earlier questions, and the answer to it is no.

"Why not?"

Because the formal symbol manipulations by themselves don't have any intentionality; they are quite meaningless; they aren't even *symbol* manipulations, since the symbols don't symbolize anything. In the linguistic jargon, they have only a syntax but no semantics. Such intentionality as computers appear to have is solely in the minds of those who program them and those who use them, those who send in the input and those who interpret the output.

The aim of the Chinese room example was to try to show this by showing that as soon as we put something into the system that really does have intentionality (a man), and we program him with the formal program, you can see that the formal program carries no additional intentionality. It adds nothing, for example, to a man's ability to understand Chinese.

Precisely that feature of AI that seemed so appealing—the distinction between the program and the realization—proves fatal to the claim that simulation could be duplication. The distinction between the program and its realization in the hardware seems to be parallel to the distinction between the level of mental operations and the level of brain operations. And if we could describe the level of mental operations as a formal program, then it seems we could describe what was essential about the mind without doing either introspective psychology or neurophysiology of the brain. But the equation, "mind is to brain as program is to hardware" breaks down at several points, among them the following three:

First, the distinction between program and realization has the consequence that the same program could have all sorts of crazy realizations that had no form of intentionality. Weizenbaum (1976, Ch. 2), for example, shows in detail how to construct a computer using a roll of toilet paper and a pile of small stones. Similarly, the Chinese story understanding program can be programmed into a sequence of water pipes, a set of wind machines, or a monolingual English speaker, none of which thereby acquires an understanding of Chinese. Stones, toilet paper, wind, and water pipes are the wrong kind of stuff to have intentionality in the first place—only something that has the same causal powers as brains can have intentionality—and though the English speaker has the right kind of stuff for intentionality you can easily see that he doesn't get any extra intentionality by memorizing the program, since memorizing it won't teach him Chinese.

Second, the program is purely formal, but the intentional states are not in that way formal. They are defined in terms of their content, not their form. The belief that it is raining, for example, is not defined as a certain formal shape, but as a certain mental content with conditions of satisfaction, a direction of fit (see Searle 1979), and the like. Indeed the belief as such hasn't even got a formal shape in this syntactic sense, since one and the same belief can be given an indefinite number of different syntactic expressions in different linguistic systems.

Third, as I mentioned before, mental states and events are literally a product of the operation of the brain, but the program is not in that way a product of the computer.

"Well if programs are in no way constitutive of mental processes, why have so many people believed the converse? That at least needs some explanation."

I don't really know the answer to that one. The idea that computer simulations could be the real thing ought to have seemed suspicious in the first place because the computer isn't confined to simulating mental operations, by any means. No one supposes that computer simulations of a five-alarm fire will burn the neighborhood down or that a computer simulation of a rainstorm will leave us all drenched. Why on earth would anyone suppose that a computer simulation of understanding actually understood anything? It is sometimes said that it would be frightfully hard to get computers to feel pain or fall in love, but love and pain are neither harder nor easier than cognition or anything else. For simulation, all you need is the right input and output and a program in the middle that transforms the former into the latter. That is all the computer has for anything it does. To confuse simulation with duplication is the same mistake, whether it is pain, love, cognition, fires, or rainstorms.

Still, there are several reasons why AI must have seemed—and to many people perhaps still does seem—in some way to reproduce and thereby explain mental phenomena, and I believe we will not succeed in removing these illusions until we have fully exposed the reasons that give rise to them.

First, and perhaps most important, is a confusion about the notion of "information processing": many people in cognitive science believe that the human brain, with its mind, does something called "information processing," and analogously the computer with its program does information processing; but fires and rainstorms, on the other hand, don't do information processing at all. Thus, though the computer can simulate the formal features of any process whatever, it stands in a special relation to the mind and brain because when the computer is properly programmed, ideally with the same program as the brain, the information processing is identical in the two cases, and this information processing is really the essence of the mental. But the trouble with this argument is that it rests on an ambiguity in the notion of "information." In the sense in which people "process information" when they reflect, say, on problems in arithmetic or when they read and answer questions about stories, the programmed computer does not do "information processing." Rather, what it does is manipulate formal symbols. The fact that the programmer and the interpreter of the computer output use the symbols to stand for objects in the world is totally beyond the scope of the computer. The computer, to repeat, has a syntax but no semantics. Thus, if you type into the computer "2 plus 2 equals?" it will type out "4." But it has no idea that "4" means 4 or that it means anything at all. And the point is not that it lacks some second-order information about the interpretation of its first-order symbols, but rather that its first-order symbols don't have any interpretations as far as the computer is concerned. All the computer has is more symbols. The introduction of the notion of "information processing" therefore produces a dilemma: either we construe the notion of "information processing" in such a way that it implies intentionality as part of the process or we don't. If the former, then the programmed computer does not do information processing, it only manipulates formal symbols. If the latter, then, though the computer does information processing, it is only doing so in the sense in which adding machines, typewriters, stomachs, thermostats, rainstorms, and hurricanes do information processing; namely, they have a level of description at which we can describe them as taking information in at one end, transforming it, and producing information as output. But in this case it is up to outside observers to interpret the input and output as information in the ordinary sense. And no similarity is established between the computer and the brain in terms of any similarity of information processing.

Second, in much of AI there is a residual behaviorism or operationalism. Since appropriately programmed computers can have input-output patterns similar to those of human beings, we are tempted to postulate mental states in the computer similar to human mental states. But once we see that it is both conceptually and empirically possible for a system to have human capacities in some realm without having any intentionality at all, we should be able to overcome this impulse. My desk adding machine has calculating capacities, but no intentionality, and in this paper I have tried to show that a system could have input and output capabilities that duplicated those of a native Chinese speaker and still not understand Chinese, regardless of how it was programmed. The Turing test is typical of the tradition in being unashamedly behavioristic and operationalistic, and I believe that if AI workers totally repudiated behaviorism and operationalism much of the confusion between simulation and duplication would be eliminated.

Third, this residual operationalism is joined to a residual form of dualism; indeed strong AI only makes sense given the dualistic assumption that, where the mind is concerned, the brain doesn't matter. In strong AI (and in functionalism, as well) what matters are programs, and programs are independent of their realization in machines; indeed, as far as AI is concerned, the same program could be realized by an electronic machine, a Cartesian mental substance, or a Hegelian world spirit. The single most surprising discovery that I have made in discussing these issues is that many AI workers are quite shocked by my idea that actual human mental phenomena might be dependent on actual physical-chemical properties of actual human brains. But if you think about it a minute you can see that I should not have been surprised; for unless you accept some form of dualism, the strong AI project hasn't got a chance. The project is to reproduce and explain the mental by designing programs, but unless the mind is not only conceptually but empirically independent of the brain you couldn't carry out the project, for the program is completely independent of any realization. Unless you believe that the mind is separable from the brain both conceptually and empirically—dualism in a strong form—you cannot hope to reproduce the mental by writing and running programs since programs must be independent of brains or any other particular forms of instantiation. If mental operations consist in computational operations on formal symbols, then it follows that they have no interesting connection with the brain; the only connection would be that the brain just happens to be one of the indefinitely many types of machines capable of instantiating the program. This form of dualism is not the traditional Cartesian variety that claims there are two sorts of *substances*, but it is Cartesian in the sense that it insists that what is specifically mental about the mind has no intrinsic connection with the actual properties of the brain. This underlying dualism is masked from us by the fact that AI literature contains frequent fulminations against "dualism"; what the authors seem to be unaware of is that their position presupposes a strong version of dualism.

"Could a machine think?" My own view is that *only* a machine could think, and indeed only very special kinds of machines, namely brains and machines that had the same causal powers as brains. And that is the main reason strong AI has had little to tell us about thinking, since it has nothing to tell us about machines. By its own definition, it is about programs, and programs are not machines. Whatever else intentionality is, it is a biological phenomenon, and it is as likely to be as causally dependent on the specific biochemistry of its origins as lactation, photosynthesis, or any other biological phenomena. No one would suppose that we could produce milk and sugar by running a computer simulation of the formal sequences in lactation and photosynthesis, but where the mind is concerned many people are willing to believe in such a miracle because of a deep and abiding dualism: the mind they suppose is a matter of formal processes and is independent of quite specific material causes in the way that milk and sugar are not.

In defense of this dualism the hope is often expressed that the brain is a digital computer (early computers, by the way, were often called "electronic brains"). But that is no help. Of course the brain is a digital computer. Since everything is a digital computer, brains are too. The point is that the brain's causal capacity to produce intentionality cannot consist in its instantiating a computer program, since for any program you like it is possible for something to instantiate that program and still not have any mental states. Whatever it is that the brain does to produce intentionality, it cannot consist in instantiating a program since no program, by itself, is sufficient for intentionality.

Acknowledgments

I am indebted to a rather large number of people for discussion of these matters and for their patient attempts to overcome my ignorance of artificial intelligence. I would especially like to thank Ned Block, Hubert Dreyfus, John Haugeland, Roger Schank, Robert Wilensky, and Terry Winograd.

Notes

1. I am not, of course, saying that Schank himself is committed to these claims.

2. Also, "understanding" implies both the possession of mental (intentional) states and the truth (validity, success) of these states. For the purposes of this discussion we are concerned only with the possession of the states.

3. Intentionality is by definition that feature of certain mental states by which they are directed at or about objects and states of affairs in the world. Thus, beliefs, desires, and intentions are intentional states; undirected forms of anxiety and depression are not. For further discussion see Searle 1979c.

References

McCarthy, J. (1979) Ascribing Mental Qualities to Machines. In *Philosophical Perspectives in Artificial Intelligence*, ed. M. Ringle. Atlantic Highlands, N.J.: Humanities Press.

Newell, A. (1979) Physical Symbol Systems. Lecture at La Jolla Conference on Cognitive Science.

Newell, A. and Simon, H. A. (1963) GPS, A Program that Simulates Human Thought. In *Computers and Thought*, ed. A. Feigenbaum and V. Feldman, pp. 279–93. New York: McGraw Hill.

Pylyshyn, Z. W. (1980a) Computation and Cognition: Issues in the Foundations of Cognitive Science. *Behavioral and Brain Sciences* 3.

Schank, R. C. and Abelson, R. P. (1977) *Scripts, Plans, Goals, and Understanding*. Hillsdale, N.J.: Lawrence Erlbaum Press.

Searle, J. R. (1979a) Intentionality and the Use of Language. In *Meaning and Use*, ed. A. Margalit. Dordrecht: Reidel.

Searle, J. R. (1979b) The Intentionality of Intention and Action. *Inquiry* 22: 253–80.

Searle, J. R. (1979c) What Is an Intentional State? *Mind* 88: 74–92.

Weizenbaum, J. (1965) Eliza—A Computer Program for the Study of Natural Language Communication Between Man and Machine. *Communication of the Association for Computing Machinery* 9: 36–45.

Weizenbaum, J. (1976) *Computer Power and Human Reason.* San Francisco: W. H. Freeman.

Winograd, T. (1973) A Procedural Model of Language Understanding. In *Computer Models of Thought and Language*, ed. R. Schank and K. Colby. San Francisco: W. H. Freeman.

Winston, P. H. (1977) *Artificial Intelligence.* Reading, Mass. Addison-Wesley.

16 Eliminative Materialism and the Propositional Attitudes

Paul Churchland

Eliminative materialism is the thesis that our common-sense conception of psychological phenomena constitutes a radically false theory, a theory so fundamentally defective that both the principles and the ontology of that theory will eventually be displaced, rather than smoothly reduced, by completed neuroscience. Our mutual understanding and even our introspection may then be reconstituted within the conceptual framework of completed neuroscience, a theory we may expect to be more powerful by far than the common-sense psychology it displaces, and more substantially integrated within physical science generally. My purpose in this paper is to explore these projections, especially as they bear on (1) the principal elements of common-sense psychology: the propositional attitudes (beliefs, desires, etc.), and (2) the conception of rationality in which these elements figure.

This focus represents a change in the fortunes of materialism. Twenty years ago, emotions, qualia, and "raw feels" were held to be the principal stumbling blocks for the materialist program. With these barriers dissolving,[1] the locus of opposition has shifted. Now it is the realm of the intentional, the realm of the propositional attitude, that is most commonly held up as being both irreducible to and ineliminable in favor of anything from within a materialist framework. Whether and why this is so, we must examine.

Such an examination will make little sense, however, unless it is first appreciated that the relevant network of common-sense concepts does indeed constitute an empirical theory, with all the functions, virtues, *and perils* entailed by that status. I shall therefore begin with a brief sketch of this view and a summary rehearsal of its rationale. The resistance it encounters still surprises me. After all, common sense has yielded up many theories. Recall the view that space has a preferred direction in which all things fall; that weight is an intrinsic feature of a body; that a force-free moving object will promptly return to rest; that the sphere of the heavens turns daily; and so on. These examples are clear, perhaps, but people seem willing to concede a theoretical component within common sense only if (1) the theory and the common sense involved are safely located in antiquity, and (2) the relevant theory is now so clearly false that its speculative nature is inescapable. Theories are indeed easier to discern under these circumstances. But the vision of hindsight is always 20/20. Let us aspire to some foresight for a change.

I Why Folk Psychology Is a Theory

Seeing our common-sense conceptual framework for mental phenomena as a theory brings a simple and unifying organization to most of the major topics in the philosophy of mind, including the explanation and prediction of behavior, the semantics of mental predicates, action theory, the other-minds problem, the intentionality of mental states, the nature of introspection, and the mind–body problem. Any view that can pull this lot together deserves careful consideration.

Let us begin with the explanation of human (and animal) behavior. The fact is that the average person is able to explain, and even predict, the behavior of other persons with a facility and success that is remarkable. Such explanations and predictions standardly make reference to the desires, beliefs, fears, intentions, perceptions, and so forth, to which the agents are presumed subject. But explanations presuppose laws—rough and ready ones, at least—that connect the explanatory conditions with the behavior explained. The same is true for the making of predictions, and for the justification of subjunctive and counterfactual conditionals concerning behavior. Reassuringly, a rich network of common-sense laws can indeed be reconstructed from this quotidean commerce of explanation and anticipation; its principles are familiar homilies; and their sundry functions are transparent. Each of us understands others, as well as we do, because we share a tacit command of an integrated body of lore concerning the lawlike relations holding among external circumstances, internal states, and overt behavior. Given its nature and functions, this body of lore may quite aptly be called "folk psychology."[2]

This approach entails that the semantics of the terms in our familiar mentalistic vocabulary is to be understood in the same manner as the semantics of theoretical terms generally: the meaning of any theoretical term is fixed or constituted by the network of laws in which it figures. (This position is quite distinct from logical behaviorism. We deny that the relevant laws are analytic, and it is the lawlike connections generally that carry the semantic weight, not just the connections with overt behavior. But this view does account for what little plausibility logical behaviorism did enjoy.)

More importantly, the recognition that folk psychology is a theory provides a simple and decisive solution to an old skeptical problem, the problem of other minds. The problematic conviction that another individual is the subject of certain mental states is not inferred deductively from his behavior, nor is it inferred by inductive analogy from the perilously isolated instance of one's own case. Rather, that conviction is a singular *explanatory hypothesis* of a perfectly straightforward kind. Its function, in conjunction with the background laws of folk psychology, is to provide explanations/predictions/understanding of the individual's continuing behavior, and it is credible to the degree that it is successful in this regard over competing hypotheses. In the main, such hypotheses are successful, and so the belief that others enjoy the internal states comprehended by folk psychology is a reasonable belief.

Knowledge of other minds thus has no essential dependence on knowledge of one's own mind. Applying the principles of our folk psychology to our behavior, a Martian could justly ascribe to us the familiar run of mental states, even though his own psychology were very different from ours. He would not, therefore, be "generalizing from his own case."

As well, introspective judgments about one's own case turn out not to have any special status or integrity anyway. On the present view, an introspective judgment is just an instance of an acquired habit of conceptual response to one's internal states, and the integrity of any particular response is always contingent on the integrity of the acquired conceptual framework (theory) in which the response is framed. Accordingly, one's *introspective* certainty that one's mind is the seat of beliefs and desires may be as badly misplaced as was the classical man's *visual* certainty that the star-flecked sphere of the heavens turns daily.

Another conundrum is the intentionality of mental states. The "propositional attitudes," as Russell called them, form the systematic core of folk psychology; and their uniqueness and anomalous logical properties have inspired some to see here a fundamental contrast with anything that mere physical phenomena might conceivably display. The key to this matter lies again in the theoretical nature of folk psychology. The intentionality of mental states here emerges not as a mystery of nature, but as a structural feature of the concepts of folk psychology. Ironically, those same structural features reveal the very close affinity that folk psychology bears to theories in the physical sciences. Let me try to explain.

Consider the large variety of what might be called "numerical attitudes" appearing in the conceptual framework of physical science: "... has a mass_{kg} of *n*," "... has a velocity of *n*," "... has a temperature_{K} of *n*," and so forth. These expressions are predicate-forming expressions: when one substitutes a singular term for a number into the place held by "*n*," a determinate predicate results. More interestingly, the relations between the various "numerical attitudes" that result are precisely the relations between the numbers "contained" in those attitudes. More interesting still, the argument place that takes the singular terms for numbers is open to quantification. All this permits the expression of generalizations concerning the lawlike relations that hold between the various numerical attitudes in nature. Such laws involve quantification over numbers, and they exploit the mathematical relations holding in that domain. Thus, for example,

(1) $(x)(f)(m)[((x \text{ has a mass of } m) \ \& \ (x \text{ suffers a net force of } f)) \supset (x \text{ accelerates at } f/m)]$

Consider now the large variety of propositional attitudes: "... believes that *p*," "... desires that *p*," "... fears that *p*," "... is happy that *p*," etc. These expressions are predicate-forming expressions also. When one substitutes a singular term for a proposition into the place held by "*p*," a determinate predicate results, e.g., "... believes that Tom is tall." (Sentences do not generally function as singular terms, but it is difficult to escape the idea that when a sentence occurs in the place held by "*p*," it is there functioning as or like a singular term. On this, more below.) More interestingly, the relations between the resulting propositional attitudes are characteristically the relations that hold between the propositions "contained" in them, relations such as entailment, equivalence, and mutual inconsistency. More interesting still, the argument place that takes the singular terms for propositions is open to quantification. All this permits the expression of generalizations concerning the lawlike relations that hold among propositional attitudes. Such laws involve quantification over propositions, and they exploit various relations holding in that domain. Thus, for example,

(2) $(x)(p)[(x \text{ fears that } p) \supset (x \text{ desires that } \sim p)]$

(3) $(x)(p)[((x \text{ hopes that } p) \; \& \; (x \text{ discovers that } p)) \supset (x \text{ is pleased that } p)]$

(4) $(x)(p)(g)[((x \text{ believes that } p) \; \& \; (x \text{ believes that (if } p \text{ then } g))) \supset$ (barring confusion,distraction,etc., x believes that g)]

(5) $(x)(p)(g)[((x \text{ desires that } p) \; \& \; (x \text{ believes that (if } g \text{ then } p)) \; \& \; (x \text{ is able to bring it about that } g)) \supset$ (barring conflicting desires or preferred strategies, x brings it about that g)][3]

Not only is folk psychology a theory, it is so *obviously* a theory that it must be held a major mystery why it has taken until the last half of the twentieth century for philosophers to realize it. The structural features of folk psychology parallel perfectly those of mathematical physics; the only difference lies in the respective domain of abstract entities they exploit—numbers in the case of physics, and propositions in the case of psychology.

Finally, the realization that folk psychology is a theory puts a new light on the mind–body problem. The issue becomes a matter of how the ontology of one theory (folk psychology) is, or is not, going to be related to the ontology of another theory (completed neuroscience); and the major philosophical positions on the mind–body problem emerge as so many different anticipations of what future research will reveal about the intertheoretic status and integrity of folk psychology.

The identity theorist optimistically expects that folk psychology will be smoothly *reduced* by completed neuroscience, and its ontology preserved by dint of transtheoretic identities. The dualist expects that it will prove *ir*reducible to completed neuroscience, by dint of being a nonredundant description of an autonomous, nonphysical domain of natural phenomena. The functionalist also expects that it will prove irreducible, but on the quite different grounds that the internal economy characterized by folk psychology is not, in the last analysis, a law-governed economy of natural states, but an abstract organization of functional states, an organization instantiable in a variety of quite different material substrates. It is therefore irreducible to the principles peculiar to any of them.

Finally, the eliminative materialist is also pessimistic about the prospects for reduction, but his reason is that folk psychology is a radically inadequate account of our internal activities, too confused and too defective to win survival through intertheoretic reduction. On his view it will simply be displaced by a better theory of those activities.

Which of these fates is the real destiny of folk psychology, we shall attempt to divine presently. For now, the point to keep in mind is that we shall be exploring the fate of a theory, a systematic, corrigible, speculative *theory*.

II Why Folk Psychology Might (Really) Be False

Given that folk psychology is an empirical theory, it is at least an abstract possibility that its principles are radically false and that its ontology is an illusion. With the exception of eliminative materialism, however, none of the major positions takes this possibility seriously. None of them doubts the basic integrity or truth of folk psychology (hereafter, "FP"), and all of them anticipate a future in which its laws and categories are conserved. This conservatism is not without some foundation. After all, FP does enjoy a substantial amount of explanatory and predictive success. And what better grounds than this for confidence in the integrity of its categories?

What better grounds indeed? Even so, the presumption in FP's favor is spurious, born of innocence and tunnel vision. A more searching examination reveals a different picture. First, we must reckon not only with FP's successes, but with its explanatory failures, and with their extent and seriousness. Second, we must consider the long-term history of FP, its growth, fertility, and current promise of future development. And third, we must consider what sorts of theories are *likely* to be true of the etiology of our behavior, given what else we have learned about ourselves in recent history. That is, we must evaluate FP with regard to its coherence and continuity with fertile and well-established theories in adjacent and overlapping domains—with evolutionary theory, biology, and neuroscience, for example—because active coherence with the rest of what we presume to know is perhaps the final measure of any hypothesis.

A serious inventory of this sort reveals a very troubled situation, one which would evoke open skepticism in the case of any theory less familiar and dear to us. Let me sketch some relevant detail. When one centers one's attention not on what FP can explain, but on what it cannot explain or fails even to address, one discovers that there is a very great deal. As examples of central and important mental phenomena that remain largely or wholly mysterious within the framework of FP, consider the nature and dynamics of mental illness, the faculty of creative imagination, or the ground of intelligence differences between individuals. Consider our utter ignorance of the nature and psychological functions of sleep, that curious state in which a third of one's life is spent. Reflect on the common ability to catch an outfield fly ball on the run, or hit a moving car with a snowball. Consider the internal construction of a 3-D visual image from subtle differences in the 2-D array of stimulations in our respective retinas. Consider the rich variety of perceptual illusions, visual and otherwise. Or consider the miracle of memory, with its lightning capacity for relevant retrieval. On these and many other mental phenomena, FP sheds negligible light.

One particularly outstanding mystery is the nature of the learning process itself, especially where it involves large-scale conceptual change, and especially as it appears in its pre-linguistic or entirely nonlinguistic form (as in infants and animals), which is by far the most common form in nature. FP is faced with special difficulties here, since its conception of learning as the manipulation and storage of propositional attitudes founders on the fact that how to formulate, manipulate, and store a rich fabric of propositional attitudes is itself something that is learned, and is only one among many acquired cognitive skills. FP would thus appear constitutionally incapable of even addressing this most basic of mysteries.[4]

Failures on such a large scale do not (yet) show that FP is a false theory, but they do move that prospect well into the range of real possibility, and they do show decisively that FP is *at best* a highly superficial theory, a partial and unpenetrating gloss on a deeper and more complex reality. Having reached this opinion, we may be forgiven for exploring the possibility that FP provides a positively misleading sketch of our internal kinematics and dynamics, one whose success is owed more to selective application and forced interpretation on our part than to genuine theoretical insight on FP's part.

A look at the history of FP does little to allay such fears, once raised. The story is one of retreat, infertility, and decadence. The presumed domain of FP used to be much larger than it is now. In primitive cultures, the behavior of most of the elements of nature were understood in intentional terms. The wind could know anger, the moon jealousy, the river generosity, the sea fury, and so forth. These were not metaphors. Sacrifices were made and auguries undertaken to placate or divine the changing passions of the gods. Despite its sterility, this animistic approach to nature has dominated our history, and it is only in the last two or three thousand years that we have restricted FP's literal application to the domain of the higher animals.

Even in this preferred domain, however, both the content and the success of FP have not advanced sensibly in two or three thousand years. The FP of the Greeks is essentially the FP we use today, and we are negligibly better at explaining human behavior in its terms than was Sophocles. This is a very long period of stagnation and infertility for any theory to display, especially when faced with such an enormous backlog of anomalies and mysteries in its own explanatory domain. Perfect theories, perhaps, have no need to evolve. But FP is profoundly imperfect. Its failure to develop its resources and extend its range of success is therefore darkly curious, and one must query the integrity of its basic categories. To use Imre Lakatos' terms, FP is a stagnant or degenerating research program, and has been for millennia.

Explanatory success to date is of course not the only dimension in which a theory can display virtue or promise. A troubled or stagnant theory may merit patience and solicitude on other grounds; for example, on grounds that it is the only theory or theoretical approach that fits well with other theories about adjacent subject matters, or the only one that promises to reduce to or be explained by some established background theory whose domain encompasses the domain of the theory at issue. In sum, it may rate credence because it holds promise of theoretical integration. How does FP rate in this dimension?

It is just here, perhaps, that FP fares poorest of all. If we approach *Homo sapiens* from the perspective of natural history and the physical sciences, we can tell a coherent story of his constitution, development, and behavioral capacities which encompasses particle physics, atomic and molecular theory, organic chemistry, evolutionary theory, biology, physiology, and materialistic neuroscience. That story, though still radically incomplete, is already extremely powerful, outperforming FP at many points even in its own domain. And it is deliberately and self-consciously coherent with the rest of our developing world picture. In short, the greatest theoretical synthesis in the history of the human race is currently in our hands, and parts of it already provide searching descriptions and explanations of human sensory input, neural activity, and motor control.

But FP is no part of this growing synthesis. Its intentional categories stand magnificently alone, without visible prospect of reduction to that larger corpus. A successful reduction cannot be ruled out, in my view, but FP's explanatory impotence and long stagnation inspire little faith that its categories will find themselves neatly reflected in the framework of neuroscience. On the contrary, one is reminded of how alchemy must have looked as elemental chemistry was taking form, how Aristotelean cosmology must have looked as classical mechanics was being articulated, or how the vitalist conception of life must have looked as organic chemistry marched forward.

In sketching a fair summary of this situation, we must make a special effort to abstract from the fact that FP is a central part of our current *lebenswelt,* and serves as the principal vehicle of our interpersonal commerce. For these facts provide FP with a conceptual inertia that goes far beyond its purely theoretical virtues. Restricting ourselves to this latter dimension, what we must say is that FP suffers explanatory failures on an epic scale, that it has been stagnant for at least twenty-five centuries, and that its categories appear (so far) to be incommensurable with or orthogonal to the categories of the background physical science whose long-term claim to explain human behavior seems undeniable. Any theory that meets this description must be allowed a serious candidate for outright elimination.

We can of course insist on no stronger conclusion at this stage. Nor is it my concern to do so. We are here exploring a possibility, and the facts demand no more, and no less, than it be taken seriously. The distinguishing feature of the eliminative materialist is that he takes it very seriously indeed.

III Arguments against Elimination

Thus the basic rationale of eliminative materialism: FP is a theory, and quite probably a false one; let us attempt, therefore to transcend it.

The rationale is clear and simple, but many find it uncompelling. It will be objected that FP is not, strictly speaking, an *empirical* theory; that it is not false, or at least not refutable by empirical considerations; and that it ought not or cannot be transcended in the fashion of a defunct empirical theory. In what follows we shall examine these objections as they flow from the most popular and best-founded of the competing positions in the philosophy of mind: functionalism.

An antipathy toward eliminative materialism arises from two distinct threads running through contemporary functionalism. The first thread concerns the *normative* character of FP, or at least of that central core of FP which treats of the propositional attitudes. FP, some will say, is a characterization of an ideal, or at least praiseworthy mode of internal activity. It outlines not only what it is to have and process beliefs and desires, but also (and inevitably) what it is to be rational in their administration. The ideal laid down by FP may be imperfectly achieved by empirical humans, but this does not impugn FP as a normative characterization. Nor need such failures seriously impugn FP even as a descriptive characterization, for it remains true that our activities can be both usefully and accurately understood as rational *except for* the occasional lapse due to noise, interference, or other breakdown, which defects empirical research may eventually unravel. Accordingly, though neuroscience may usefully augment it, FP has no pressing need to be displaced, even as a descriptive theory; nor could it be replaced, qua normative characterization, by any descriptive theory of neural mechanisms, since rationality is defined over propositional attitudes like beliefs and desires. FP, therefore, is here to stay.

Daniel Dennett has defended a view along these lines.[5] And the view just outlined gives voice to a theme of the property dualists as well. Karl Popper and Joseph Margolis both cite the normative nature of mental and linguistic activity as a bar to their penetration or elimination by any descriptive/materialist theory.[6] I hope to deflate the appeal of such moves below.

The second thread concerns the *abstract* nature of FP. The central claim of functionalism is that the principles of FP characterize our internal states in a fashion that makes no reference to their intrinsic nature or physical constitution. Rather, they are characterized in terms of the network of causal relations they bear to one another, and to sensory circumstances and overt behavior. Given its abstract specification, that internal economy may therefore be realized in a nomically heterogeneous variety of physical systems. All of them may differ, even radically, in their physical constitution, and yet at another level, they will all share the same nature. This view, says Fodor, "is compatible with very strong claims about the ineliminability of mental language from behavioral theories."[7] Given the real possibility of multiple instantiations in heterogeneous physical substrates, we cannot eliminate the functional characterization in favor of any theory peculiar to one such substrate. That would preclude our being able to describe the (abstract) organization that any one instantiation shares with all the other. A functional characterization of our internal states is therefore here to stay.

This second theme, like the first, assigns a faintly stipulative character to FP, as if the onus were on the empirical systems to instantiate faithfully the organization that FP specifies, instead of the onus being on FP to describe faithfully the internal activities of a naturally distinct class of empirical systems. This impression is enhanced by the standard examples used to illustrate the claims of functionalism—mousetraps, valve-lifters, arithmetical calculators, computers, robots, and the like. These are artifacts, constructed to fill a preconceived bill. In such cases, a failure of fit between the physical system and the relevant functional characterization impugns only the former, not the latter. The functional characterization is thus removed from empirical criticism in a way that is most unlike the case of an empirical theory. One prominent functionalist—Hilary Putnam—has argued outright that FP is not a corrigible theory at all.[8] Plainly, if FP is construed on these models, as regularly it is, the question of its empirical integrity is unlikely ever to pose itself, let alone receive a critical answer.

Although fair to some functionalists, the preceding is not entirely fair to Fodor. On his view the aim of psychology is to find the *best* functional characterization of ourselves, and what that is remains an empirical question. As well, his argument for the ineliminability of mental vocabulary from psychology does not pick out current FP in particular as ineliminable. It need claim only that *some* abstract functional characterization must be retained, some articulation or refinement of FP perhaps.

His estimate of eliminative materialism remains low, however. First, it is plain that Fodor thinks there is nothing fundamentally or interestingly wrong with FP. On the contrary, FP's central conception of cognitive activity—as consisting in the manipulation of propositional attitudes—turns up as the central element in Fodor's own theory on the nature of thought (*The Language of Thought, op. cit.*). And second, there remains the point that, whatever tidying up FP may or may not require, it cannot be displaced by any naturalistic theory of our physical substrate, since it is the abstract functional features of his internal states that make a person, not the chemistry of his substrate.

All of this is appealing. But almost none of it, I think, is right. Functionalism has too long enjoyed its reputation as a daring and *avant garde* position. It needs to be revealed for the short-sighted and reactionary position it is.

IV The Conservative Nature of Functionalism

A valuable perspective on functionalism can be gained from the following story. To begin with, recall the alchemists' theory of inanimate matter. We have here a long and variegated tradition, of course, not a single theory, but our purposes will be served by a gloss.

The alchemists conceived the "inanimate" as entirely continuous with animated matter, in that the sensible and behavioral properties of the various substances are owed to the ensoulment of baser matter by various spirits or essences. These nonmaterial aspects were held to undergo development, just as we find growth and development in the various souls of plants, animals, and humans. The alchemist's peculiar skill lay in knowing how to seed, nourish, and bring to maturity the desired spirits enmattered in the appropriate combinations.

On one orthodoxy, the four fundamental spirits (for "inanimate" matter) were named "mercury," "sulphur," "yellow arsenic," and "sal ammoniac." Each of these spirits was held responsible for a rough but characteristic syndrome of sensible, combinatorial, and causal properties. The spirit mercury, for example, was held responsible for certain features typical of metallic substances—their shininess, liquefiability, and so forth. Sulphur was held responsible for certain residual features typical of metals, and for those displayed by the ores from which running metal could be distilled. Any given metallic substance was a critical orchestration principally of these two spirits. A similar story held for the other two spirits, and among the four of them a certain domain of physical features and transformations was rendered intelligible and controllable.

The degree of control was always limited, of course. Or better, such prediction and control as the alchemists possessed was owed more to the manipulative lore acquired as an apprentice to a master, than to any genuine insight supplied by the theory. The theory followed, more than it dictated, practice. But the theory did supply some rhyme to the practice, and in the absence of a developed alternative it was sufficiently compelling to sustain a long and stubborn tradition.

The tradition had become faded and fragmented by the time the elemental chemistry of Lavoisier and Dalton arose to replace it for good. But let us suppose that it had hung on a little longer—perhaps because the four-spirit orthodoxy had become a thumbworn part of everyman's common sense—and let us examine the nature of the conflict between the two theories and some possible avenues of resolution.

No doubt the simplest line of resolution, and the one which historically took place, is outright displacement. The dualistic interpretation of the four essences—as immaterial spirits—will appear both feckless and unnecessary given the power of the corpuscularian taxonomy of atomic chemistry. And a reduction of the old taxonomy to the new will appear impossible, given the extent to which the comparatively toothless old theory cross-classifies things relative to the new. Elimination would thus appear the only alternative—*unless* some cunning and determined defender of the alchemical vision has the wit to suggest the following defense.

Being "ensouled by mercury," or "sulphur," or either of the other two so-called spirits, is actually a *functional* state. The first, for example, is defined by the disposition to reflect light, to liquefy under heat, to unite with other matter in the same state, and so forth. And each of these four states is related to the others, in that the syndrome for each varies as a function of which of the other three states is also instantiated in the same substrate. Thus the level of description comprehended by the alchemical vocabulary is abstract: various material substances, suitably "ensouled," can display the features of a metal, for example, or even of gold specifically. For it is the total syndrome of occurrent and causal properties which matters, not the corpuscularian details of the substrate. Alchemy, it is concluded, comprehends a level of organization in reality distinct from and irreducible to the organization found at the level of corpuscularian chemistry.

This view might have had considerable appeal. After all, it spares alchemists the burden of defending immaterial souls that come and go; it frees them from having to meet the very strong demands of a naturalistic reduction; and it spares them the shock and confusion of outright elimination. Alchemical theory emerges as basically all right! Nor need they appear too obviously stubborn or dogmatic in this. Alchemy as it stands, they concede, may need substantial tidying up, and experience must be our guide. But we need not fear its naturalistic displacement, they remind us, since it is the particular orchestration of the syndromes of occurrent and causal properties which makes a piece of matter gold, not the idiosyncratic details of its corpuscularian substrate. A further circumstance would have made this claim even more plausible. For the fact is, the alchemists *did* know how to make gold, in this relevantly weakened sense of "gold," and they could do so in a variety of ways. Their "gold" was never as perfect, alas, as the "gold" nurtured in nature's womb, but what mortal can expect to match the skills of nature herself?

What this story shows is that it is at least possible for the constellation of moves, claims, and defenses characteristic of functionalism to constitute an outrage against reason and truth, and to do so with a plausibility that is frightening. Alchemy is a terrible theory, well-deserving of its complete elimination, and the defense of it just explored is reactionary, obfuscatory, retrograde, and wrong. But in historical context, that defense might have seemed wholly sensible, even to reasonable people.

The alchemical example is a deliberately transparent case of what might well be called "the functionalist strategem," and other cases are easy to imagine. A cracking good defense of the phlogiston theory of combustion can also be constructed along these lines. Construe being highly phlogisticated and being dephlogisticated as functional states defined by certain syndromes of causal dispositions; point to the great variety of natural substrates capable of combustion and calxification; claim an irreducible functional integrity for what has proved to lack any natural integrity; and bury the remaining defects under a pledge to contrive improvements. A similar recipe will provide new life for the four humors of medieval medicine, for the vital essence or archeus of pre-modern biology, and so forth.

If its application in these other cases is any guide, the functionalist strategem is a smokescreen for the preservation of error and confusion. Whence derives our assurance that in contemporary journals the same charade is not being played out on behalf of FP? The parallel with the case of alchemy is in all other respects distressingly complete, right down to the parallel between the search for artificial gold and the search for artificial intelligence!

Let me not be misunderstood on this last point. Both aims are worthy aims: thanks to nuclear physics, artificial (but real) gold is finally within our means, if only in submicroscopic quantities; and artificial (but real) intelligence eventually will be. But just as the careful orchestration of superficial syndromes was the wrong way to produce genuine gold, so may the careful orchestration of superficial syndromes be the wrong way to produce genuine intelligence. Just as with gold, what may be required is that our science penetrate to the underlying *natural* kind that gives rise to the total syndrome directly.

In summary, when confronted with the explanatory impotence, stagnant history, and systematic isolation of the intentional idioms of FP, it is not an adequate or responsive defense to insist that those idioms are abstract, functional, and irreducible in character. For one thing, this same defense could have been mounted with comparable plausibility no matter *what* haywire network of internal states our folklore had ascribed to us. And for another, the defense assumes essentially what is at issue: it assumes that it is the intentional idioms of FP, plus or minus a bit, that express the *important* features shared by all cognitive systems. But they may not. Certainly it is wrong to assume that they do, and then argue against the possibility of a materialistic displacement on grounds that it must descibe matters at a level that is different from the important level. This just begs the question in favor of the older framework.

Finally, it is very important to point out that eliminative materialism is strictly *consistent* with the claim that the essence of a cognitive system resides in the abstract functional organization of its internal states. The eliminative materialist is not committed to the idea that the correct account of cognition *must* be a naturalistic account, though he may be forgiven for exploring the possibility. What he does hold is that the correct account of cognition, whether functionalistic or naturalistic, will bear about as much resemblance to FP as modern chemistry bears to four-spirit alchemy.

Let us now try to deal with the argument, against eliminative materialism, from the normative dimension of FP. This can be dealt with rather swiftly, I believe.

First, the fact that the regularities ascribed by the intentional core of FP are predicated on certain logical relations among propositions is not by itself grounds for claiming anything essentially normative about FP. To draw a relevant parallel, the fact that the regularities ascribed by the classical gas law are predicated on arithmetical relations between numbers does not imply anything essentially normative about the classical gas law. And logical relations between propositions are as much an objective matter of abstract fact as are arithmetical relations between numbers. In this respect, the law

(4) $(x)(p)(g)[((x$ believes that $p)$ & $(x$ believes that (if p then $g))) \supset$ (barring confusion,distraction,etc., x believes that $g)]$

is entirely on a par with the classical gas law

(6) $(x)(P)(V)(\mu)[((x$ has a pressure $P)$ & $(x$ has a volume $V)$ & $(x$ has a quantity $\mu)) \supset$ (barring very high pressure or density, x has a temperature of $PV/\mu R)]$

A normative dimension enters only because we happen to *value* most of the patterns ascribed by FP. But we do not value all of them. Consider

(7) $(x)(p)[((x$ desires with all his heart that $p)$ & $(x$ learns that $\sim p)) \supset$ (barring unusual strength of character, x is shattered that $\sim p)]$

Moreover, and as with normative convictions generally, fresh insight may motivate major changes in what we value.

Second, the laws of FP ascribe to us only a very minimal and truncated rationality, not an ideal rationality as some have suggested. The rationality characterized by the set of all FP laws falls well short of an ideal rationality. This is not surprising. We have no clear or finished conception of ideal rationality anyway; certainly the ordinary man does not. Accordingly, it is just not plausible to suppose that the explanatory failures from which FP suffers are owed primarily to human failure to live up to the ideal standard it provides. Quite to the contrary, the conception of rationality it provides appears limping and superficial, especially when compared with the dialectical complexity of our scientific history, or with the ratiocinative virtuosity displayed by any child.

Third, even if our current conception of rationality—and more generally, of cognitive virtue—is largely constituted within the sentential/propositional framework of FP, there is no guarantee that this framework is adequate to the deeper and more accurate account of cognitive virtue which is clearly needed. Even if we concede the categorial integrity of FP, at least as applied to language-using humans, it remains far from clear that the basic parameters of intellectual virtue are to be found at the categorial level comprehended by the propositional attitudes. After all, language use is something that is learned, by a brain already capable of vigorous cognitive activity; language use is acquired as only one among a great variety of learned manipulative skills; and it is mastered by a brain that evolution has shaped for a great many functions, language use being only the very latest and perhaps the least of them. Against the background of these facts, language use appears as an extremely peripheral activity, as a racially idiosyncratic mode of social interaction which is mastered thanks to the versatility and power of a more basic mode of activity. Why accept then, a theory of cognitive activity that models its elements on the elements of human language? And why assume that the fundamental parameters of intellectual virtue are or can be defined over the elements at this superficial level?

A serious advance in our appreciation of cognitive virtue would thus seem to *require* that we go beyond FP, that we transcend the poverty of FP's conception of rationality by transcending its propositional kinematics entirely, by developing a deeper and more general kinematics of cognitive activity, and by distinguishing within this new framework which of the kinematically possible modes of activity are to be valued and encouraged (as more efficient, reliable, productive, or whatever). Eliminative materialism thus does not imply the end of our normative concerns. It implies only that they will have to be reconstituted at a more revealing level of understanding, the level that a matured neuroscience will provide.

What a theoretically informed future might hold in store for us, we shall now turn to explore. Not because we can foresee matters with any special clarity, but because it is important to try to break the grip on our imagination held by the propositional kinematics of FP. As far as the present section is concerned, we may summarize our conclusions as follows. FP is nothing more and nothing less than a culturally entrenched theory of how we and the higher animals work. It has no special features that make it empirically invulnerable, no unique functions that make it irreplaceable, no special status of any kind whatsoever. We shall turn a skeptical ear then, to any special pleading on its behalf.

V Beyond Folk Psychology

What might the elimination of FP actually involve—not just the comparatively straightforward idioms for sensation, but the entire apparatus of propositional attitudes? That depends heavily on what neuroscience might discover, and on our determination to capitalize on it. Here follow three scenarios in which the operative conception of cognitive activity is progressively divorced from the forms and categories that characterize natural language. If the reader will indulge the lack of actual substance, I shall try to sketch some plausible form.

First suppose that research into the structure and activity of the brain, both fine-grained and global, finally does yield a new kinematics and correlative dynamics for what is now thought of as cognitive activity. The theory is uniform for all terrestrial brains, not just human brains, and it makes suitable conceptual contact with both evolutionary biology and non-equilibrium thermodynamics. It ascribes to us, at any given time, a set or configuration of complex states, which are specified within the theory as figurative "solids" within a four- or five-dimensional phase space. The laws of the theory govern the interaction, motion, and transformation of these "solid" states within that space, and also their relations to whatever sensory and motor transducers the system possesses. As with celestial mechanics, the exact specification of the "solids" involved and the exhaustive accounting of all dynamically relevant adjacent "solids" is not practically possible, for many reasons, but here also it turns out that the obvious approximations we fall back on yield excellent explanations/predictions of internal change and external behavior, at least in the short term. Regarding long-term activity, the theory provides powerful and unified accounts of the learning process, the nature of mental illness, and variations in character and intelligence across the animal kingdom as well as across individual humans.

Moreover, it provides a straightforward account of "knowledge," as traditionally conceived. According to the new theory, any declarative sentence to which a speaker would give confident assent is merely a one-dimensional *projection*—through the compound lens of Wernicke's and Broca's areas onto the idiosyncratic surface of the speaker's language—a one-dimensional projection of a four- or five-dimensional "solid" that is an element in his true kinematical state. (Recall the shadows on the wall of Plato's cave.) Being projections of that inner reality, such sentences do carry significant information regarding it and are thus fit to function as elements in a communication system. On the other hand, being *sub*dimensional projections, they reflect but a narrow part of the reality projected. They are therefore *un*fit to represent the deeper reality in all its kinematically, dynamically, and even normatively relevant respects. That is to say, a system of propositional attitudes, such as FP, must inevitably fail to capture what is going on here, though it may reflect just enough superficial structure to sustain an alchemylike tradition among folk who lack any better theory. From the perspective of the newer theory, however, it is plain that there simply are no law-governed states of the kind FP postulates. The real laws governing our internal activities are defined over different and much more complex kinematical states and configurations, as are the normative criteria for developmental integrity and intellectual virtue.

A theoretical outcome of the kind just described may fairly be counted as a case of elimination of one theoretical ontology in favor of another, but the success here imagined for systematic neuroscience need not have any sensible effect on common practice. Old ways die hard, and in the absence of some practical necessity, they may not die at all. Even so, it is not inconceivable that some segment of the population, or all of it, should become intimately familiar with the vocabulary required to characterize our kinematical states, learn the laws governing their interactions and behavioral projections, acquire a facility in their first-person ascription, and displace the use of FP altogether, even in the marketplace. The demise of FP's ontology would then be complete.

We may now explore a second and rather more radical possibility. Everyone is familiar with Chomsky's thesis that the human mind or brain contains innately and uniquely the abstract structures for learning and using specifically human natural languages. A competing hypothesis is that our brain does indeed contain innate structures, but that those structures have as their original and still primary function the organization of perceptual experience, the administration of linguistic categories being an acquired and additional function for which evolution has only incidentally suited them.[9] This hypothesis has the advantage of not requiring the evolutionary saltation that Chomsky's view would seem to require, and there are other advantages as well. But these matters need not concern us here. Suppose, for our purposes, that this competing view is true, and consider the following story.

Research into the neural structures that fund the organization and processing of perceptual information reveals that they are capable of administering a great variety of complex tasks, some of them showing a complexity far in excess of that shown by natural language. Natural languages, it turns out, exploit only a very elementary portion of the available machinery, the bulk of which serves far more complex activities beyond the ken of the propositional conceptions of FP. The detailed unraveling of what that machinery is and of the capacities it has makes it plain that a form of language far more sophisticated than "natural" language, though decidedly "alien" in its syntactic and semantic structures, could also be learned and used by our innate systems. Such a novel system of communication, it is quickly realized, could raise the efficiency of information exchange between brains by an order of magnitude, and would enhance epistemic evaluation by a comparable amount, since it would reflect the underlying structure of our cognitive activities in greater detail than does natural language.

Guided by our new understanding of those internal structures, we manage to construct a new system of verbal communication entirely distinct from natural language, with a new and more powerful combinatorial grammar over novel elements forming novel combinations with exotic properties. The compounded strings of this alternative system—call them "übersatzen"—are not evaluated as true or false, nor are the relations between them remotely analogous to the relations of entailment, etc., that hold between sentences. They display a different organization and manifest different virtues.

Once constructed, this "language" proves to be learnable; it has the power projected; and in two generations it has swept the planet. Everyone uses the new system. The syntactic forms and semantic categories of so-called "natural" language disappear entirely. And with them disappear the propositional attitudes of FP, displaced by a more revealing scheme in which (of course) "übersatzenal attitudes" play the leading role. FP again suffers elimination.

This second story, note, illustrates a theme with endless variations. There are possible as many different "folk psychologies" as there are possible differently structured communication systems to serve as models for them.

A third and even stranger possibility can be outlined as follows. We know that there is considerable lateralization of function between the two cerebral hemispheres, and that the two hemispheres make use of the information they get from each other by way of the great cerebral commissure—the corpus callosum—a giant cable of neurons connecting them. Patients whose commissure has been surgically severed display a variety of behavioral deficits that indicate a loss of access by one hemisphere to information it used to get from the other. However, in people with callosal agenesis (a congenital defect in which the connecting cable is simply absent), there is little or no behavioral deficit, suggesting that the two hemisphere have learned to exploit the information carried in other less direct pathways connecting them through the subcortical regions. This suggests that, even in the normal case, a developing hemisphere *learns* to make use of the information the cerebral commissure deposits at its doorstep. What we have then, in the case of a normal human, is two physically distinct cognitive systems (both capable of independent function) responding in a systematic and learned fashion to exchanged information. And what is especially interesting about this case is the sheer amount of information exchanged. The cable of the commissure consists of ≈ 200 million neurons,[10] and even if we assume that each of these fibres is capable of one of only two possible states each second (a most conservative estimate), we are looking at a channel whose information capacity is $>2 \times 10^8$ binary bits/second. Compare this to the <500 bits/second capacity of spoken English.

Now, if two distinct hemispheres can learn to communicate on so impressive a scale, why shouldn't two distinct brains learn to do it also? This would require an artificial "commissure" of some kind, but let us suppose that we can fashion a workable transducer for implantation at some site in the brain that research reveals to be suitable, a transducer to convert a symphony of neural activity into (say) microwaves radiated from an aerial in the forehead, and to perform the reverse function of converting received microwaves back into neural activation. Connecting it up need not be an insuperable problem. We simply trick the normal processes of dendretic arborization into growing their own myriad connections with the active microsurface of the transducer.

Once the channel is opened between two or more people, they can learn (*learn*) to exchange information and coordinate their behavior with the same intimacy and virtuosity displayed by your own cerebral hemispheres. Think what this might do for hockey teams, and ballet companies, and research teams! If the entire population were thus fitted out, spoken language of any kind might well disappear completely, a victim of the "why crawl when you can fly?" principle. Libraries become filled not with books, but with long recordings of exemplary bouts of neural activity. These constitute a growing cultural heritage, an evolving "Third World," to use Karl Popper's terms. But they do not consist of sentence or arguments.

How will such people understand and conceive of other individuals? To this question I can only answer, "In roughly the same fashion that your right hemisphere 'understands' and 'conceives of' your left hemisphere—intimately and efficiently, but not propositionally!"

These speculations, I hope, will evoke the required sense of untapped possibilities, and I shall in any case bring them to a close here. Their function is to make some inroads into the aura of inconceivability that commonly surrounds the idea that we might reject FP. The felt conceptual strain even finds expression in an argument to the effect that the thesis of eliminative materialism is incoherent since it denies the very conditions presupposed by the assumption that it is meaningful. I shall close with a brief discussion of this very popular move.

As I have received it, the reductio proceeds by pointing out that the statement of eliminative materialism is just a meaningless string of marks or noises, unless that string is the expression of a certain *belief*, and a certain *intention* to communicate, and a *knowledge* of the grammar of the language, and so forth. But if the statement of eliminative materialism is true, then there are no such states to express. The statement at issue would then be a meaningless string of marks or noises. It would therefore *not* be true. Therefore it is not true. Q.E.D.

The difficulty with any nonformal reductio is that the conclusion against the initial assumption is always no better than the material assumptions invoked to reach the incoherent conclusion. In this case the additional assumptions involve a certain theory of meaning, one that presupposes the integrity of FP. But formally speaking, one can as well infer, from the incoherent result, that this theory of meaning is what must be rejected. Given the independent critique of FP leveled earlier, this would even seem the preferred option. But in any case, one cannot simply assume that particular theory of meaning without begging the question at issue, namely, the integrity of FP.

The question-begging nature of this move is most graphically illustrated by the following analogue, which I owe to Patricia Churchland.[11] The issue here, placed in the seventeenth century, is whether there exists such a substance as *vital spirit*. At the time, this substance was held, without significant awareness of real alternatives, to be that which distinguished the animate from the inanimate. Given the monopoly enjoyed by this conception, given the degree to which it was integrated with many of our other conceptions, and given the magnitude of the revisions any serious alternative conception would require, the following refutation of any anti-vitalist claim would be found instantly plausible.

> The anti-vitalist says that there is no such thing as vital spirit. But this claim is self-refuting. The speaker can expect to be taken seriously only if his claim cannot. For if the claim is true, then the speaker does not have vital spirit and must be *dead*. But if he is dead, then his statement is a meaningless string of noises, devoid of reason and truth.

The question-begging nature of this argument does not, I assume, require elaboration. To those moved by the earlier argument, I commend the parallel for examination.

The thesis of this paper may be summarized as follows. The propositional attitudes of folk psychology do not constitute an unbreachable barrier to the advancing tide of neuroscience. On the contrary, the principled displacement of folk psychology is not only richly possible, it represents one of the most intriguing theoretical displacements we can currently imagine.

Acknowledgments

An earlier draft of this paper was presented at the University of Ottawa, and to the *Brain, Mind, and Person* colloquium at SUNY/Oswego. My thanks for the suggestions and criticisms that have informed the present version.

Notes

1. See Paul Feyerabend, "Materialism and the Mind–Body Problem," *Review of Metaphysics*, XVII.1, 65 (September 1963): 49–66; Richard Rorty, "Mind–Body Identity, Privacy, and Categories," *ibid.*, XIX.1, 73 (September 1965): 24–54; and my *Scientific Realism and the Plasticity of Mind* (New York: Cambridge, 1979).

2. We shall examine a handful of these laws presently. For a more comprehensive sampling of the laws of folk psychology, see my *Scientific Realism and Plasticity of Mind, op. cit.*, ch. 4. For a detailed examination of the folk principles that underwrite action explanations in particular, see my "The Logical Character of Action Explanations," *Philosophical Review*, LXXIX, 2 (April 1970): 214–236.

3. Staying within an objectual interpretation of the quantifiers, perhaps the simplest way to make systematic sense of expressions like ⌜*x* believes that *p*⌝ and closed sentences formed therefrom is just to construe whatever occurs in the nested position held by "*p*," "*q*," etc. as there having the function of a singular term. Accordingly, the standard connectives, as they occur between terms in that nested position, must be construed as there functioning as operators that form compound singular terms from other singular terms, and not as sentence operators. The compound singular terms so formed denote the appropriate compound propositions. Substitutional quantification will of course underwrite a different interpretation, and there are other approaches as well. Especially appealing is the prosentential approach of Dorothy Grover, Joseph Camp, and Nuel Belnap, "A Prosentential Theory of Truth," *Philosophical Studies*, XXVII, 2 (February 1975): 73–125. But the resolution of these issues is not vital to the present discussion.

4. A possible response here is to insist that the cognitive activity of animals and infants is linguaformal in its elements, structures, and processing right from birth. J. A. Fodor, in *The Language of Thought* (New York: Crowell, 1975), has erected a positive theory of thought on the assumption that the innate forms of cognitive activity have precisely the form here denied. For a critique of Fodor's view, see Patricia Churchland, "Fodor on Language Learning," *Synthese*, XXXVIII, 1 (May 1978): 149–159.

5. Most explicitly in "Three Kinds of Intentional Psychology" [in *The Intentional Stance* (Cambridge, Mass.: MIT Press, 1987)] but this theme of Dennett's goes all the way back to his "Intentional Systems," this JOURNAL, LXVIII, 4 (Feb. 25, 1971): 87–106; reprinted in his *Brainstorms* (Montgomery, Vt.: Bradford Books, 1978).

6. Popper, *Objective Knowledge* (New York: Oxford, 1972); with J. Eccles, *The Self and Its Brain* (New York: Springer Verlag, 1978). Margolis, *Persons and Minds* (Boston: Reidel, 1978).

7. *Psychological Explanation* (New York: Random House, 1968), p. 116.

8. "Robots: Machines or Artificially Created Life?," *Journal of Philosophy*, LXI, 21 (Nov. 12, 1964): 668–691, pp. 675, 681 ff.

9. Richard Gregory defends such a view in "The Grammar of Vision," *Listener*, LXXXIII, 2133 (February 1970): 242–246; reprinted in his *Concepts and Mechanisms of Perception* (London: Duckworth, 1975), pp. 622–629.

10. M. S. Gazzaniga and J. E. LeDoux, *The Integrated Mind* (New York: Plenum Press, 1975).

11. "Is Determinism Self-Refuting?," *Mind* [90, 1981].

17 From *Neurophilosophy*

Patricia Smith Churchland

Antireductionism in Functionalist Theories of the Mind

Functional Types and Structural Implementations

The core idea of functionalism is the thesis that mental states are defined in terms of their abstract causal roles within the wider information-processing system. A given mental state is characterized in terms of its abstract causal relations to environmental input, to other internal states, and to output. Being in pain, on this account, is a state characterized by its causal relations to behavior such as wincing and crying out, by its causal relations to external input such as the skin being burned, by its causal relations to other internal states such as the desire to make the pain go away, beliefs about the source of the pain and about what will bring relief, and so forth. The characterization of having the goal of, say, finding a mate will follow a similar pattern: the goal state will be connected to a complex range of beliefs and desires, will prompt a diverse range of plans and actions, and will be connected in rich and complicated ways to perceptual states (Putnam 1967, Fodor 1975, Lycan 1981b).

In general, functional kinds are specified by reference to their roles or relational profiles, not by reference to the material structure in which they are instantiated. What makes a certain part of an engine a valve lifter is that, given a specified input, it has a certain output, namely the lifting of the valves, and it might be instantiated in various physical devices, such as a rotating camshaft or a hydraulic device. More humbly, "mousetrap" is a functional kind, being implementable in all manner of physically different devices: spring traps, assorted cage traps, a sack of grain falling when a trip line is wriggled, or perhaps even a cat or a specially bred killer rat. There is nothing in the specification "mousetrap" that says it must have a tin spring or a wooden housing. Being a mousetrap or a valve lifter is therefore a functional kind, not a physical kind, though mousetraps and valve lifters are implemented in physical stuff and every implementation or "token" is a physical device.

According to functionalism, then, mental states and processes are functional kinds. Functionalists have typically sided with physicalism by claiming that our mental states are implemented in neural stuff, not, as the dualist would have it, in spiritual stuff. At one level of description we can talk about the causal and logical relations among perceptions, beliefs, desires, and behavior, and at the structural level we can talk about spiking frequencies of neurons, patterns of excitations, and so forth. It is because neurons are orchestrated as they are that the system has the functional organization it does, and thus the physical substratum subserves the functional superstratum. In our case the functional organization that is our psychology is realized in our neural "gubbins." In similar fashion, it is because on–off switches in a computer are orchestrated as they are that it adds, finds square roots, and so forth. The computer's program is realized in its electronic "gubbins." The functionalist theory is thus as roundly physicalist as it can be, yet despite their adherence to physicalist principles, functionalists have typically rejected reductionism and ignored neuroscience. Why?

Plainly, it is not because functionalists suppose that mental states have no material realization. Rather, it is because they envision that types of mental states could have *too many* distinct material realizations for a reductive mold to fit. As functionalists see it, for a reductive strategy to succeed, a type of mental state must be identical to a type of physical state, but, they argue, the identities are not forthcoming. The reason is that one and the same cognitive organization might be realized or embodied in various ways in various stuffs, which entails that there cannot be one-to-one relations between functional types and structural types. A cognitive organization is like the computational organization of a computer executing a program: computational processes are logical, or at least semantically coherent, and they operate on symbols as a function of the symbol's meaning, not as a function of its physical etiology in the machine, and the same program can be run on different machines (Putnam 1967, Pylyshyn 1984). There is nothing in the specification of a cognitive organization, the functionalist will remind us, that says that pain must be subserved by substance P in a given set of neurons or that a goal-to-find-a-mate state must be linked to testosterone. This oversimplifies, of course, but the main point is clear enough.

In a general way one can imagine that on another planet there might have evolved creatures who, though very different from us in physical structure, might have a cognitive organization much like our own. Suppose, for example, they were silicon-based instead of carbon-based as we are. For these animals, having a goal will be functionally like our having a goal, but such a state will not be identical to having neurons *n–m* responding thus and so, though to be sure the goal state will be embodied in their physical structure. Or suppose that in time we figure out how to manufacture a robot that has the same functional organization as a human: it has goals, beliefs, and pains, and it solves problems, sees, and moves about. Its information-processing innards are not neurons but microchips, and its cognitive organization cannot therefore be identical to a particular neuronal organization, since *neural* stuff it has not got. Instead, its cognitive economy will be instantiated in electronic stuff. As we shall see, the plausibility of these thought-experiments depends on a crucial and highly suspect assumption—namely, that we know at what level the biology does not matter.

Fictional examples are not really needed to make the point anyhow, since there are certain to be neural (structural) differences between functionally identical states in distinct species. An echidna and a yak may both be in pain or have the goal of finding a mate and hence be in the same functional state, though the neural events and processes subserving their states may differ considerably. The same is probably true of more closely related species such as chimpanzees and gorillas. Moreover, it is continued, there may be nontrivial differences in structural detail between two *humans* in a functionally identical state: the neural events that subserve my adding 29 and 45 may not be the same as those in the brain of a calculating prodigy or a mathematician or a child or a street vendor. Indeed, on different occasions different neuronal events may realize *my* adding 29 and 45, depending on what else my brain is doing and heaven knows what other matters. We know quite well that two computers can be in the same type of functional state and yet have very different structural states. For example, two computers can be executing the same program written in BASIC, though their hardware and even their assembly language may be quite different (Fodor 1975).

Identity of functional-state types with structural-state types, argues the functionalist, is therefore hopelessly unrealistic, and since reduction requires such identities, *tant pis* for reduction. Physicalist principles are in no way sundered, however, for all that physicalism requires is that any given *instance* of a functional-state type (a token of that type) be realized in physical stuff, and this the functionalist heartily agrees to and insists upon. He therefore describes himself as espousing *token–token* identity of mental states with physical states, but denying *type–type* identity and therewith reductionism (Putnam 1967, Dennett 1978b).

This foray against the reductionist program is known as the argument from *multiple instantiability* or *multiple realizability*. Functional states are multiply instantiable, and the range of physical implementations will be so diverse that we cannot expect it to form a natural kind. Apart from its implications for the theory that mental states are identical with brain states, the argument has been deployed to methodological purpose in the following way.

If mental states and processes are functional kinds, then to understand how cognitively adept organisms solve problems, think, reason, and comport themselves intelligently, what we need to understand is their functional organization. Research on neurons is not going to reveal the nature of the functional organization, but only something about the embodiment of the functional organization—and just one sort of instantiation at that. Neuroscience, it has been argued, is focused on the engineering details rather than on the functional scheme, and to this extent it is removed from the level of description that is appropriate to answering questions concerning learning, intelligence, problem solving, memory, and so forth. Knowledge of the structural minutiae is important for repairs, of course, and to this extent neuroscience has obvious medical significance, but structural theory will not enlighten functional hypotheses and functional models. To put it crudely, it will not tell us how the mind works. Cognitive psychology, in contrast, is focused at the appropriate level of description, and in cooperation with research in artificial intelligence it constitutes the best strategy for devising a theory of our functional cognitive economy. Thus the crux of the argument.

As Pylyshyn (1980) sees it, the research labor can be divided along these lines: the cognitive scientists will figure out the functional/cognitive theory, and the neuroscientists can untangle the underlying physical devices that instantiate the cognitive "program." On an extreme version of this view, nothing much of the details of neuronal business need be known by the cognitive scientist—or the philosopher, either—since the way the functional organization is instantiated in the brain is a quite separate and *independent* matter from the way our cognitive economy is organized. Pylyshyn comes close to this in his claim that computational questions can be addressed exclusively at a privileged (functional) level of algorithms and symbolic manipulation (1980: 111). He says, "... in studying computation it is possible, and in certain respects essential, to factor apart the nature of the symbolic process from the properties of the physical device in which it is realized" (p. 115).

Neuroscience, on this picture, is irrelevant to the computational questions of cognitive science. What it is relevant to are implementation issues, such as whether a particular computational model of cognitive business is in fact implemented in the neural structure. Computational (functional) psychology is thus conceived as an *autonomous* science, with its proprietary vocabulary and its own domain of questions, the answers to which, as Pylyshyn remarks, "... can be given without regard to the material or hardware properties of the device on which these processes are executed" (p. 115). It may even be suggested that the less known about the actual pumps and pulleys of the embodiment of mental life, the better, for the less there is to clutter up one's functionally oriented research.

Whether anyone really holds the extreme version of the research ideology is doubtful, but certainly milder versions have won considerable sympathy, and sometimes cognitive science programs permit or encourage neglect of neuroscience, where the autonomy of psychology is the rationale. How influential the view is I cannot estimate, but some philosophers are still wont to excuse those colleagues who take neuroscience seriously as having not quite managed to master the distinction between functional and structural descriptions. The methodological point should be taken seriously because functionalism is now the dominant theory of the mind espoused by philosophers as well as by many cognitive scientists. Even so, there are significant differences among functionalists on a number of issues, including the relevance of theories of brain function to theories of psychological function. Dissent from the methodological point is not without voice in cognitive psychology (for example, McClelland and Rumelhart 1981, Posner, Pea, and Volpe 1982), philosophy (for example, Enç 1983, Hooker 1981, Paul M. Churchland 1981), and computer science (for example, Anderson and Hinton 1981). My lot is thrown in with the dissenters, because I think both the antireductionist argument and the research ideology it funds are theoretically unjustified and pragmatically unwise to boot. In what follows I shall try to show why.

In Defense of Reductionism

There are two principal sources of error in the antireductionist views I have outlined. The first concerns the background assumptions about the nature of intertheoretic reduction; the second concerns the conception of levels—how many there are, their nature, their discovery, and their interconnections. These sources of error will be considered in sequence.

Intertheoretic Reduction and Functionalism

Functionalists appear to assume that intertheoretic reduction cannot come off unless the properties in the reduced theory have a *unique* realization in physical stuff. This assumption is crucial in the case against reduction, and it is what floats the methodological claim for the autonomy of cognitive psychology. Is the assumption justified?

One way to test the claim is to see whether it conflicts with or comports with the paradigm cases of reduction in the history of science. "Temperature" is a predicate of thermodynamics, and as thermodynamics and molecular theory co-evolved, the temperature of gases was found to reduce to the mean kinetic energy of the constituent molecules. That is, a corrected version of the classical ideal gas law was derived from statistical mechanics together with certain assumptions. Several features of this case are immediately relevant to the issue at hand. Notice that what was reduced was not temperature tout court, but temperature of a gas. The temperature of a gas *is* mean kinetic energy of the constituent molecules, but the temperature of a solid is something else again; the temperature of a plasma cannot be a matter of kinetic energy of the molecules, because plasmas are high-energy states consisting not of molecules but of dissociated atoms; the temperature of empty space as embodied in its transient electromagnetic radiation is different yet again. (Paul M. Churchland 1984 and Enç 1983 also make this point.) And perhaps there are states as yet undiscovered for which temperature is specified in none of these ways. The initial reduction in thermodynamics was relative to a certain domain of phenomena, to wit, gases, but it was a bona fide reduction for all that. Nor is this domain-relativity used as grounds for saying that thermodynamics is an autonomous science, independent and separate from physics. Quite the contrary, the co-evolution of corpuscular physics and thermodynamics was of the first importance to both physics and thermodynamics.

Yet if we heed the functionalist assumption at issue, we ought to withhold the stamp of reduction on grounds that temperature must be a functional property that is multiply realized in distinct physical structures. Now, however, this looks like a merely verbal recommendation about what to call reductions in cases where the predicates in the reducing theory are relativized to certain domains (cf. Cummins 1983). As such, it implies nothing about the derivation of one theory from another or about the autonomy of the sciences. No grand methodological strictures about what is and is not relevant to the "functional" theory will be in order. As a merely verbal recommendation it is not especially objectionable, but it has no obvious utility either.

Dialectically, it does the functionalist no good to deny reduction in thermodynamics, for then he loses the basis for saying that psychology is on an entirely different footing from the rest of science (Enç 1983). After all, if psychology is no worse off than thermodynamics, then reductionists can be cheerful indeed. At any rate, the requirements for the reduction of psychology should not be made stiffer than those for intertheoretic reduction elsewhere in science. (See also Richardson 1979, Paul M. Churchland 1984.)

The main point of the example drawn from thermodynamics is that reductions may be reductions *relative to a domain of phenomena*. Though this is called "multiple instantiability" and is draped in black by the functionalist, it is seen as part of normal business in the rest of science. By analogy with the thermodynamics example, if human brains and electronic brains both enjoy a certain type of cognitive organization, we may get two distinct, domain-relative reductions. Or we may, in the fullness of time and after much co-evolution in theories, have one reductive account of, say, goals or pain in vertebrates, a different account for invertebrates, and so forth. In and of itself, the mere fact that there are differences in hardware has no implications whatever for whether the psychology of humans will eventually be explained in neuroscientific terms, whether the construction of psychological theories can benefit from neuroscientific information, and whether psychology is an autonomous and independent science. That reductions are domain-relative does not mean they are phony reductions or reductions manqué, and it certainly does not mean that psychology can justify methodological isolation from neuroscience.

Enç (1983) draws a further point out of the thermodynamics case. Two volumes of a gas might have the same temperature, but the distributions of velocities of their constituent molecules will be quite different even while their mean value is the same. To be consistent, functionalists should again deny reductive success to statistical mechanics since, as they would put it, *temperature of a gas* is differently realized in the two cases. If, on the other hand, they want to concede reduction here but withhold its possibility from psychology, they need to do more than merely predict hardware differences between species or between individuals.

If it turns out that we are lucky enough to get a reduction (domain-relative) of *human* psychology to neuroscience, what does this do to the thesis that mental kinds are functional kinds? Nothing, for that thesis is independent of the antireductionist argument, and it stands on its own feet after the argument from multiple instantiability falls. The thesis that mental states are identified in terms of their abstract causal roles in the wider information-processing system is the core conception that makes functionalism functionalism, and it is entirely neutral on the question of reducibility. Functionalists can be true blue functionalists without naysaying reduction. Functionalism as it lives and breathes, however, is another matter, and frequently functionalists have wished to argue for a package: the functional characterization of mental states, the nonreducibility of psychology, and the autonomy (in some degree) of psychology from the more basic sciences. As a result, the term "functionalism" is typically if inappropriately associated with the whole package.

The point of this section has been a very general one: intertheoretic reductions are not conditional on a one-to-one mapping of predicates of the higher-level theory onto predicates of the reducing theory. Antireductionists may wish to concede the general point but to continue by arguing that the details of the case at hand rule out reduction. In so arguing, they will point to radical differences between the neuronal level of explanation and the functional-computational level, and they will point out that the multiplicity of instantiations of psychological predicates can be so profuse, diverse, and arbitrary that the case cannot be likened to the thermodynamics-statistical mechanics example. In a word, they claim that the case of psychology is special.

Levels of Organization in the Mind–Brain

There is a good deal that is uncontroversial in the antireductionist's appreciation that there must *be* a set of levels of organization. A theory of cellular and synaptic changes occurring during learning will be more fine-grained than a theory of how an interactive network learns, which will be more fine-grained than a theory of what anatomical structures subserve learning, which will be more fine-grained than a theory that postulates a coding mechanism, retrieval mechanisms, and so forth. What is controversial is the assumption that the trilevel model suitable to von Neumann computers is also suitable to organic brains. That there should be some division of labor is also beyond dispute; no one since Bacon could take all knowledge as his province. Indeed, no one since Helmholtz could take even all of neuroscience as his province. What is regrettable, however, is the divisive research ideology based on the trilevel model.

As we have seen, the hypothesis based on the computer analogy is that the mind–brain has three levels of organization: the semantic, the syntactic, and the mechanistic—the level of *content*, the level of the *algorithm*, and the level of *structural implementation*. The principal problem with the computer metaphor is that on the basis of the complexity we already know to be found in the brain, it is evident that there are *many* levels of organization between the topmost level and the level of intracellular dynamics. (See also Lycan 1981a.) And even if there were just three, neurobiological theory challenges that way of specifying their organizational description. How many levels there are, and how they should be described, is not something to be decided in advance of empirical theory. Pretheoretically, we have only rough and ready—and eminently revisable—hunches about what constitutes a level of organization.

As a first approximation, we can distinguish the following levels of organization: the membrane, the cell, the synapse, the cell assembly, the circuit, the behavior. And within each level further substrata can be distinguished. If, however, neurons are organized into modules, each perhaps playing a role in several distinct information-processing modules, and if modules themselves are members of higher-order "meta-modules," again with membership being a diverse and distributed affair, or if some cell assemblies or modules have a transient membership or a transient existence, we may then find a description of levels that is orthogonal to the first.

Another preliminary and related way to demarcate a level is to characterize it in terms of the research methods used. Certainly this is a very rough way of defining levels of organization, but it may be useful until the research reveals enough for us to see what the levels really are. For example, in research on learning and memory one can discern many different methods that, compared to one another, are more or less fine-grained. The cellular approach taken by Kandel and his colleagues (Hawkins and Kandel 1984) showing modification in presynaptic neurotransmitter release in habituation is in some sense at a lower level than studies by Lynch and his colleagues (Lee et al. 1980) showing modification of synapse numbers and synaptic morphology correlated with plasticity in behavior, which in turn is at a (slightly) lower level than the studies by Greenough and his colleagues (Greenough, Juraska, and Volkmar 1979) on the effect of maze training on dendritic branching. We then ascend to the multicellular studies in the hippocampus done by Berger, Latham, and Thompson (1980), and from there up (a bit) to the cell assembly studies in the olfactory bulb by Freeman (1979), which uses an 8×8 electrode array and evoked response potential averaging techniques. Upward again to the studies of Nottebohm (1981) on the seasonal changes in the "songster" nuclei of the canary brain or to the animal models of human amnesia studied by Zola-Morgan and Squire (1984). At yet a different level are the studies by Jernigan (1984) and Volpe et al. (1983) of correlations between neural tissue atrophy and memory performance using neural imaging techniques (CBF, PET). Finally there are neurological studies of human amnesia (Weiskrantz 1978, Squire and Cohen 1984), ethological studies of such things as how bees remember flowers (Gould 1985), and psychological studies of memory capacities and skills of college undergraduates (Norman 1973, Tulving 1983). This is obviously a very fast Cook's ascent at just one point through the research strata, but a more leisurely tour will reinforce the impressions.

It is simply not rewarding to sort out this research in terms of the trilevel computer analogy, nor is there any useful purpose to be served by trying to force a fit. Moreover, at each of the research levels one can distinguish among questions concerning the nature of the capacity, questions concerning the processes subserving the capacity, and the matter of the physical implementation. The point is, even at the level of *cellular* research, one can view the cell as being the functional unit with a certain input–output profile, as having a specifiable dynamics, and as having a structural implementation in certain proteins and other subcellular structures.

What this means is that one cannot foist on the brain a monolithic distinction between function and structure, and then appoint psychologists to attend to function and neuroscientists to attend to structure. Relative to a lower research level a neuroscientist's research can be considered functional, and relative to a higher level it can be considered structural. Thus, Thompson's work on multicellular response profiles in the hippocampus is perhaps structural relative to Squire's work on the recognition capacities of amnesic humans but functional relative to Lynch's work on plasticity of synaptic morphology. The structure–function distinction, though not without utility, is a *relative*, not an absolute, distinction, and even then it is insufficiently precise to support any sweeping research ideology.

In addition, we simply do not know at what level of organization one can assume that the physical implementation can vary but the capacities will remain the same. In brief, it may be that if we had a complete cognitive neurobiology we would find that to build a computer with the same capacities as the human brain, we had to use as structural elements things that behaved very like neurons. That is, the artificial units would have to have both action potentials and graded potentials, and a full repertoire of synaptic modifiability, dendritic growth, and so forth, though unlike neurons they might not need to have, say, mitochondria or ribosomes. But, for all we know now, to mimic nervous plasticity efficiently, we might have to mimic very closely even certain subcellular structures.

There is a further assumption, usually unstated, that lends credence to the ideology of autonomy and should be debunked. This assumption is that neuroscience, because it tries to understand the physical device—the brain itself—will not produce *theories* of functional organization. Now we have already seen that the functional–structural distinction will not support the simplistic idea that psychology does functional analysis and neuroscience does structural analysis, and that there are bound to be many levels of organization between the level of the single cell and the level at which most cognitive psychologists work. It is important as well to emphasize that when neuroscientists do address such questions as how neurons manage to store information, or how cell assemblies do pattern recognition, or how they manage to effect sensorimotor control, they are addressing questions concerning neurodynamics—concerning information and how the brain processes it. In doing so, they are up to their ears in theorizing, and even more shocking, in theorizing about representations and computations. If the representations postulated are not sentencelike, and if the transformation postulated do not resemble reasoning, this does not mean the theory is not functional theory, or not real theory, or not relevant to theories at a higher level. . . . The existence of bona fide *neurofunctional* theorizing is perhaps the most resounding refutation of the second assumption.

My general conclusion, therefore, is that it is supremely naive to assume that we know what level is functional and what is structural, and that neurons can be ignored as we get on with the functional specification of the mind-brain. This explains my earlier warning about the multiple instantiation thought-experiments that are endlessly invoked by antireductionists. Nevertheless, antireductionists will argue for the autonomy of cognitive psychology not merely on the basis of the trilevel hypothesis but also on the grounds that the categories and generalizations appropriate to the cognitive levels are special. For reasons to be examined, these categories are believed to have an invulnerable theoretical integrity and to be irreducible to physical categories.

References

Anderson, James A. and Geoffrey Hinton, 1981. "Models of Information Processing in the Brain." In Hinton and Anderson, eds., *Parallel Models of Associative Memory*. Hillsdale NJ: Erlbaum.

Berger, T. W., R. I. Latham, and R. F. Thomson, 1980. "Hippocampal Unit Behavior Correlations During Classical Conditioning," *Brain Research* 193: 483–85.

Churchland, Paul M., 1981. "Eliminative Materialism and the Propositional Attitudes." *Journal of Philosophy* 78, no. 2, 67–90.

Churchland, Paul M., 1984. *Matter and Consciousness: A Contemporary Introduction to the Philosophy of Mind*. Cambridge MA: MIT Press.

Cummins, Robert, 1983. *The Nature of Psychological Explanation*. Cambridge MA: MIT Press.

Dennett, Daniel C., 1978b. *Brainstorms: Philosophical Essays on Mind and Psychology*. Cambridge MA: MIT Press.

Enç, Berent, 1983. "In Defense of the Identity Theory," *Journal of Philosophy* 80: 279–98.

Fodor, Jerry A., 1975. *The Language of Thought*. New York: Crowell.

Freeman, Walter, 1979. "Nonlinear dynamics of paleocortex manifested in the olfactory EEG," *Biological Cybernetics* 3: 21–37.

Gould, James L., 1985. "How Bees Remember Flower Shapes," *Science* 227: 1492–94.

Greenough, W. T., J. M. Juraska, and F. R. Volkmar, 1979. "Maze Training Effects on Dendritic Branching in Occipital Cortex of Adult Rats," *Behavioral and Neural Biology* 26: 287–97.

Hawkins, Robert D., and Eric R. Kandel, 1984. "Steps Toward a Cell-Biological Alphabet for Elementary Forms of Learning." In G. Lynch, J. L. McGaugh, and N. M. Weinberger, eds., *Neurobiology of Learning and Memory*. New York: Guilford.

Hooker, Clifford A., 1981. "Toward a General Theory of Reduction," *Dialogue* 20: 38–59, 201–236, 496–529.

Jernigan, Terry L., 1984. "The Study of Human Memory with Neuro-Imaging Techniques." In L. R. Squire and N. Butters, eds., *Neuropsychology of Memory*. New York: Guilford.

Lee, K. S., F. Schottler, M. Oliver, and G. Lynch, 1980. "Brief Bursts of High-Frequency Produce Two Types of Structural Change in Rat Hippocampus," *Journal of Neurophysiology* 44: 247–58.

Lycan, William G., 1981a. "Form, Function, and Feel," *Journal of Philosophy* 78: 24–50.

Lycan, William G., 1981b. "Toward a Homuncular Theory of Believing," *Cognition and Brain Theory* 4: 139–59.

McClelland, James L., and David E. Rumelhart, 1981. "An Interactive Activation Model of the Effect of Context in Letter Perception. Part I: An Account of Basic Findings," *Psychological Review* 88: 375–407.

Norman, D. A., 1973. "Memory, Knowledge, and the Answering of Questions." In R. Solso, ed., *The Loyola Symposium on Cognitive Psychology*. Washington D.C.: Winston.

Nottebohm, F., 1981. "Laterality, Seasons, and Space Governing the Learning of a Motor Skill," *Trends in Neuroscience* 4, no. 5: 104–6.

Posner, Michael I., Roy Pea, and Bruce Volpe, 1982. "Cognitive Neuroscience: Developments Toward a Science of Synthesis." In J. Mehler, E. Walker, and M. Garrett, eds., *Perspectives on Mental Representation*. Hillsdale NJ: Erlbaum.

Putnam, Hilary, 1967. "The Nature of Mental States." In W. H. Capitan and D. D. Merrill, eds., *Art, Mind, and Religion*. Pittsburgh: Univ. Pittsburgh Press.

Pylyshyn, Zenon, 1980. "Computation and Cognition: Issues in the Foundation of Cognitive Science," *Behavioral and Brain Sciences* 3, no. 1: 111–34.

Pylyshyn, Zenon, 1984. *Computation and Cognition*. Cambridge MA: MIT Press.

Richardson, Robert, 1979. "Functionalism and Reduction," *Philosophy of Science* 46: 533–58.

Squire, Larry R., and Neal J. Cohen, 1984. "Human Memory and Amnesia." In G. Lynch, J. L. McGaugh, and N. M. Weinberger, eds., *Neurobiology of Learning and Memory*. New York: Guilford.

Tulving, Endel, 1983. *Elements of Episodic Memory*. Oxford: Clarendon Press.

Volpe, B. T., P. Herscovitch, M. E. Raichle, M. S. Gazzaniga, and W. Hirst, 1983. "Cerebral Blood Flow and Metabolism in Human Amnesia," *Journal of Cerebral Blood Flow and Metabolism* 3: 5.

Weiskrantz, L., 1978. "A Comparison of Hippocampal Pathology in Man and Other Animals." In *Functions of the Septo-Hippocampal System*. Amsterdam: Elsevier.

Zola-Morgan, S., and L. R. Squire, 1984. "Preserved Learning in Monkeys with Medial Temporal Lesions: Sparing of Motor and Cognitive Skills," *Journal of Neuroscience* 4: 1072–85.

18 Multiple Realization and the Metaphysics of Reduction

Jaegwon Kim

I Introduction

It is part of today's conventional wisdom in philosophy of mind that psychological states are "multiply realizable," and are in fact so realized, in a variety of structures and organisms. We are constantly reminded that any mental state, say pain, is capable of "realization," "instantiation," or "implementation" in widely diverse neural-biological structures in humans, felines, reptiles, mollusks, and perhaps other organisms further removed from us. Sometimes we are asked to contemplate the possibility that extraterrestrial creatures with a biochemistry radically different from the earthlings', or even electro-mechanical devices, can "realize the same psychology" that characterizes humans. This claim, to be called hereafter "the Multiple Realization Thesis" ("MR,"[1] for short), is widely accepted by philosophers, especially those who are inclined to favor the functionalist line on mentality. I will not here dispute the truth of MR, although what I will say may prompt a reassessment of the considerations that have led to its nearly universal acceptance.

And there is an influential and virtually uncontested view about the philosophical significance of MR. This is the belief that MR refutes psychophysical reductionism once and for all. In particular, the classic psychoneural identity theory of Feigl and Smart, the so-called "type physicalism," is standardly thought to have been definitively dispatched by MR to the heap of obsolete philosophical theories of mind. At any rate, it is this claim, that MR proves the physical irreducibility of the mental, that will be the starting point of my discussion.

Evidently, the current popularity of antireductionist physicalism is owed, for the most part, to the influence of the MR-based antireductionist argument originally developed by Hilary Putnam and elaborated further by Jerry Fodor[2]—rather more so than to the "anomalist" argument associated with Donald Davidson.[3] For example, in their elegant paper on nonreductive physicalism,[4] Geoffrey Hellman and Frank Thompson motivate their project in the following way:

> Traditionally, physicalism has taken the form of reductionism—roughly, that all scientific terms can be given explicit definitions in physical terms. Of late there has been growing awareness, however, that reductionism is an unreasonably strong claim.

But why is reductionism "unreasonably strong"? In a footnote Hellman and Thompson explain, citing Fodor's "Special Sciences":

Doubts have arisen especially in connection with functional explanation in the higher-level sciences (psychology, linguistics, social theory, etc.). Functional predicates may be physically realizable in heterogeneous ways, so as to elude physical definition.

And Ernest LePore and Barry Loewer tell us this:[5]

It is practically received wisdom among philosophers of mind that psychological properties (including content properties) are not identical to neurophysiological or other physical properties. The relationship between psychological and neurophysiological properties is that the latter *realize* the former. Furthermore, a single psychological property might (in the sense of conceptual possibility) be realized by a large number, perhaps an infinitely many, of different physical properties and even by non-physical properties.

They then go on to sketch the reason why MR, on their view, leads to the rejection of mind–body reduction:[6]

If there are infinitely many physical (and perhaps nonphysical) properties which can realize *F* then *F* will not be reducible to a basic physical property. Even if *F* can only be realized by finitely many basic physical properties it might not be reducible to a basic physical property since the disjunction of these properties might not itself be a basic physical property (i.e., occur in a fundamental physical law). We will understand "multiple realizability" as involving such irreducibility.

This antireductionist reading of MR continues to this day; in a recent paper, Ned Block writes:[7]

Whatever the merits of physiological reductionism, it is not available to the cognitive science point of view assumed here. According to cognitive science, the essence of the mental is computational, and any computational state is "multiply realizable" by physiological or electronic states that are not identical with one another, and so content cannot be identified with any one of them.

Considerations of these sorts have succeeded in persuading a large majority of philosophers of mind[8] to reject reductionism and type physicalism. The upshot of all this has been impressive: MR has not only ushered in "non-reductive physicalism" as the new orthodoxy on the mind–body problem, but in the process has put the very word "reductionism" in disrepute, making reductionisms of all stripes an easy target of disdain and curt dismissals.

I believe a reappraisal of MR is overdue. There is something right and instructive in the antireductionist claim based on MR and the basic argument in its support, but I believe that we have failed to follow out the implications of MR far enough, and have as a result failed to appreciate its full significance. One specific point that I will argue is this: the popular view that psychology constitutes an *autonomous special science*, a doctrine heavily promoted in the wake of the MR-inspired antireductionist dialectic, may in fact be inconsistent with the real implications of MR. Our discussion will show that MR, when combined with certain plausible metaphysical and methodological assumptions, leads to some surprising conclusions about the status of the mental and the nature of psychology as a science. I hope it will become clear that the fate of type physicalism is not among the more interesting consequences of MR.

II Multiple Realization

It was Putnam, in a paper published in 1967,[9] who first injected MR into debates on the mind–body problem. According to him, the classic reductive theories of mind presupposed the following naive picture of how psychological kinds (properties, event and state types, etc.) are correlated with physical kinds:

For each psychological kind M there is a unique physical (presumably, neurobiological) kind P that is *nomologically coextensive* with it (i.e., as a matter of law, any system instantiates M at t iff that system instantiates P at t).

(We may call this "the Correlation Thesis.") So take pain: the Correlation Thesis has it that pain as an event kind has a neural substrate, perhaps as yet not fully and precisely identified, that, as a matter of law, always co-occur with it in all pain-capable organisms and structures. Here there is no mention of species or types of organisms or structures: the neural correlate of pain is invariant across biological species and structure types. In his 1967 paper, Putnam pointed out something that, in retrospect, seems all too obvious:[10]

Consider what the brain-state theorist has to do to make good his claims. He has to specify a physical-chemical state such that any organism (not just a mammal) is in pain if and only if (a) it possesses a brain of a suitable physical-chemical structure; and (b) its brain is in that physical-chemical state. This means that the physical-chemical state in question must be a possible state of a mammalian brain, a reptilian brain, a mollusc's brain (octopuses are mollusca, and certainly feel pain), etc. At the same time, it must not be a possible brain of any physically possible creature that cannot feel pain.

Putnam went on to argue that the Correlation Thesis was *empirically false*. Later writers, however, have stressed the multiple realizability of the mental as a *conceptual* point: it is a priori, conceptual fact about psychological properties that they are "second-order" physical properties, and that their specification does not include constraints on the manner of their physical implementation.[11] Many proponents of the functionalist account of psychological terms and properties hold such a view.

Thus, on the new, improved picture, the relationship between psychological and physical kinds is something like this: there is no single neural kind N that "realizes" pain, across all types of organisms or physical systems; rather, there is a multiplicity of neural-physical kinds, $N_h, N_r, N_m, \ldots$ such that N_h realizes pain in humans, N_r realizes pain in reptiles, N_m realizes pain in Martians, etc. Perhaps, biological species as standardly understood are too broad to yield unique physical-biological realization bases; the neural basis of pain could perhaps change even in a single organism over time. But the main point is clear: any system capable of psychological states (that is, any system that "has a psychology") falls under some structure type T such that systems with structure T share the same physical base for each mental state-kind that they are capable of instantiating (we should regard this as relativized with respect to time to allow for the possibility that an individual may fall under different structure types at different times). Thus physical realization bases for mental states must be relativized to species or, better, physical structure-types. We thus have the following thesis:

If anything has mental property M at time t, there is some physical structure type T and physical property P such that it is a system of type T at t and has P at t, and it holds as a matter of law that all systems of type T have M at a time just in case they have P at the time.

We may call this "the Structure-Restricted Correlation Thesis" (or "the Restricted Correlation Thesis" for short).

It may have been noticed that neither this nor the correlation thesis speaks of "realization."[12] The talk of "realization" is not metaphysically neutral: the idea that mental properties are "realized" or "implemented" by physical properties carries with it a certain ontological picture of mental properties as derivative and dependent. There is the suggestion that when we look at concrete reality there is nothing over and beyond instantiations of physical properties and relations, and that the instantiation on a given occasion of an appropriate physical property in the right contextual (often causal) setting simply *counts as*, or *constitutes*, an instantiation of a mental property on that occasion. An idea like this is evident in the functionalist conception of a mental property as *extrinsically* characterized in terms of its "causal role," where what fills this role is a physical (or, at any rate, nonmental) property (the latter property will then be said to "realize" the mental property in question). The same idea can be seen in the related functionalist proposal to construe a mental property as a "second-order property" consisting in the having of a physical property satisfying certain extrinsic specifications. We will recur to this topic later; however, we should note that someone who accepts either of the two correlation theses need not espouse the "realization" idiom. That is, it is prima facie a coherent position to think of mental properties as "first-order properties" in their own right, characterized by their intrinsic natures (e.g., phenomenal feel), which, as it happens, turn out to have nomological correlates in neural properties. (In fact, anyone interested in defending a serious dualist position on the mental should eschew the realization talk altogether and consider mental properties as first-order properties on a par with physical properties.) The main point of MR that is relevant to the antireductionist argument it has generated is just this: *mental properties do not have nomically coextensive physical properties, when the latter are appropriately individuated.* It may be that properties that are candidates for reduction must be thought of as being realized, or implemented, by properties in the prospective reduction base;[13] that is, if we think of certain properties as having their own intrinsic characterizations that are entirely independent of another set of properties, there is no hope of *reducing* the former to the latter. But this point needs to be argued, and will, in any case, not play a role in what follows.

Assume that property M is realized by property P. How are M and P related to each other and, in particular, how do they covary with each other? LePore and Loewer say this:[14]

> The usual conception is that *e*'s being P realizes *e*'s being F iff e is P and there is a strong connection of some sort between P and F. We propose to understand this connection as a necessary connection which is *explanatory*. The existence of an explanatory connection between two properties is stronger than the claim that $P \rightarrow F$ is physically necessary since not every physically necessary connection is explanatory.

Thus, LePore and Loewer require only that the realization base of M be *sufficient* for M, not both necessary and sufficient. This presumably is in response to *MR*: if pain is multiply realized in three ways as above, each of N_h, N_r, and N_m will be sufficient for pain, and none necessary for it. This I believe is not a correct response, however; the correct response is not to weaken the joint necessity and sufficiency of the physical base, but rather to *relativize* it, as in the Restricted Correlation Thesis, with respect to species or structure types. For suppose we are designing a physical system that will instantiate a certain psychology, and let $M_1, \ldots, M_n$ be the psychological properties required by this psychology. The design process must involve the specification of an n-tuple of physical properties, $P_1, \ldots, P_n$, all of them instantiable by the system, such that for each i, P_i constitutes a *necessary and sufficient* condition *in this system* (and others of relevantly similar physical structure), not merely a sufficient one, for the occurrence of M_i. (Each such n-tuple of physical properties can be called a "physical realization" of the psychology in question.[15]) That is, for each psychological state we must design into the system a nomologically coextensive physical state. We must do this *if we are to control both the occurrence and non-occurrence of the psychological states involved*, and control of this kind is necessary if we are to ensure that the physical device will properly instantiate the psychology. (This is especially clear if we think of building a computer; computer analogies loom large in our thoughts about "realization.")

But isn't it possible for multiple realization to occur "locally" as well? That is, we may want to avail ourselves of the flexibility of allowing a psychological state, or function, to be instantiated by alternative mechanisms within a single system. This means that P_i can be a *disjunction* of physical properties; thus, M_i is instantiated in the system in question at a time if and only if at least one of the disjuncts of P_i is instantiated at that time. The upshot of all this is that LePore and Loewer's condition that $P \rightarrow M$ holds as a matter of law needs to be upgraded to the condition that, *relative to the species or structure-type in question (and allowing P to be disjunctive)*, $P \leftrightarrow M$ holds as a matter of law.[16]

For simplicity let us suppose that pain is realized in three ways as above, by N_h in humans, N_r in reptiles, and N_m in Martians. The finitude assumption is not essential to any of my arguments: if the list is not finite, we will have an infinite disjunction rather than a finite one (alternatively, we can talk in terms of "sets" of such properties instead of their disjunctions). If the list is "open-ended," that's all right, too; it will not affect the metaphysics of the situation. We allowed above the possibility of a realization base of a psychological property itself being disjunctive; to get the discussion going, though, we will assume that these *N*s, the three imagined physical realization bases of pain, are not themselves disjunctive—or, at any rate, that their status as properties is not in dispute. The propriety and significance of "disjunctive properties" is precisely one of the principal issues we will be dealing with below, and it will make little difference just as what stage this issue is faced.

III Disjunctive Properties and Fodor's Argument

An obvious initial response to the MR-based argument against reducibility is "the disjunction move": Why not take the disjunction, $N_h \vee N_r \vee N_m$, as the single physical substrate of pain? In his 1967 paper, Putnam considers such a move but dismisses it out of hand: "Granted, in such a case the brain-state theorist can save himself by ad hoc assumptions (e.g., defining the disjunction of two states to be a single 'physical-chemical state'), but this does not have to be taken seriously."[17] Putnam gives no hint as to why he thinks the disjunction strategy does not merit serious consideration.

If there is something deeply wrong with disjunctions of the sort involved here, that surely isn't obvious; we need to go beyond a sense of unease with such disjunctions and develop an intelligible rationale for banning them. Here is where Fodor steps in, for he appears to have an argument for disallowing disjunctions. As I see it, Fodor's argument in "Special Sciences" depends crucially on the following two assumptions:

(1) To reduce a special-science theory T_M to physical theory T_p, each "kind" in T_M (presumably, represented by a basic predicate of T_M) must have a nomologically coextensive "kind" in T_p;

(2) A disjunction of heterogeneous kinds is not itself a kind.

Point (1) is apparently prompted by the derivational model of intertheoretic reduction due to Ernest Nagel:[18] the reduction of T_2 to T_1 consists in the derivation of laws of T_2 from the laws of T_1, in conjunction with "bridge" laws or principles connecting T_2-terms with T_1-terms. Although this characterization does not in general require that each T_2-term be correlated with a *coextensive* T_1-term, the natural thought is that the existence of T_1-coextensions for T_2-terms would in effect give us definitions of T_2-terms in T_1-terms, enabling us to rewrite T_2-laws exclusively in the vocabulary of T_1; we could then derive these rewrites of T_2-laws from the laws of T_1 (if they cannot be so derived, we can add them as additional T_1-laws—assuming both theories to be true).

Another thought that again leads us to look for T_1-coextensions for T_2-terms is this: for genuine reduction, the bridge laws must be construed as *property identities*, not mere *property correlations*—namely, we must be in a position to identify the property expressed by a given T_2-term (say, water-solubility) with a property expressed by a term in the reduction base (say, having a certain molecular structure). This of course requires that each T_2-term have a nomic (or otherwise suitably modalized) coextension in the vocabulary of the reduction base. To put it another way, ontologically significant reduction requires the reduction of higher-level *properties*, and this in turn requires (unless one takes an eliminativist stance) that they be identified with complexes of lower-level properties. Identity of properties of course requires, at a minimum, an appropriately modalized coextensivity.[19]

So assume M is a psychological kind, and let us agree that to reduce M, or to reduce the psychological theory containing M, we need a physical coextension, P, for M. But why should we suppose that P must be a physical "kind"? But what is a "kind," anyway? Fodor explains this notion in terms of *law*, saying that a given predicate P is a "kind predicate" of a science just in case the science contains a law with P as its antecedent or consequent.[20] There are various problems with Fodor's characterization, but we don't need to take its exact wording seriously; the main idea is that kinds, or kind predicates, of a science are those that figure in the laws of that science.

To return to our question, why should "bridge laws" connect kinds to kinds, in this special sense of "kind"? To say that bridge laws are "laws" and that, by definition, only kind predicates can occur in laws is not much of an answer. For that only invites the further question why "bridge laws" ought to be "laws"—what would be lacking in a reductive derivation if bridge laws were replaced by "bridge principles" which do not necessarily connect kinds to kinds.[21] But what of the consideration that these principles must represent property identities? Does this force on us the requirement that each reduced kind must find a coextensive kind in the reduction base? No; for it isn't obvious why it isn't perfectly proper to reduce kinds by identifying them with properties expressed by non-kind (disjunctive) predicates in the reduction base.

There is the following possible argument for insisting on kinds: if M is identified with non-kind Q (or M is reduced via a biconditional bridge principle "$M \leftrightarrow Q$", where Q is a non-kind), M could no longer figure in special science laws; e.g., the law, "$M \rightarrow R$", would in effect reduce to "$Q \rightarrow R$", and therefore loses its status as a law on account of containing Q, a non-kind.

I think this is a plausible response—at least, the beginning of one. As it stands, though, it smacks of circularity: "$Q \rightarrow R$" is not a law because a non-kind, Q, occurs in it, and Q is a non-kind because it cannot occur in a law and "$Q \rightarrow R$", in particular, is not a law. What we need is an *independent* reason for the claim that the sort of Q we are dealing with under MR, namely a badly heterogeneous disjunction, is unsuited for laws.

This means that point (1) really reduces to point (2) above. For, given Fodor's notion of a kind, (2) comes to this: disjunctions of heterogeneous kinds are unfit for laws. What we now need is an *argument* for this claim; to dismiss such disjunctions as "wildly disjunctive" or "heterogeneous and unsystematic" is to label a problem, not to offer a diagnosis of it.[22] In the sections to follow, I hope to take some steps toward such a diagnosis and draw some implications which I believe are significant for the status of mentality.

IV Jade, Jadeite, and Nephrite

Let me begin with an analogy that will guide us in our thinking about multiply realizable kinds.

Consider *jade*: we are told that jade, as it turns out, is not a mineral kind, contrary to what was once believed; rather, jade is comprised of two distinct minerals with dissimilar molecular structures, *jadeite* and *nephrite*. Consider the following generalization:

(L) Jade is green

We may have thought, before the discovery of the dual nature of jade, that (L) was a law, a law about jade; and we may have thought, with reason, that (L) had been strongly confirmed by all the millions of jade samples that had been observed to be green (and none that had been observed not to be green). We now know better: (L) is really a conjunction of these two laws:

(L_1) Jadeite is green

(L_2) Nephrite is green

But (L) itself might still be a law as well; is that possible? It has the standard basic form of a law, and it apparently has the power to support counterfactuals: if anything were jade—that is, if anything were a sample of jadeite or of nephrite—then, in either case, it would follow, by law, that it was green. No problem here.

But there is another standard mark of lawlikeness that is often cited, and this is "projectibility," the ability to be confirmed by observation of "positive instances." Any generalized conditional of the form "All Fs are G" can be confirmed by the *exhaustion* of the class of Fs—that is, by eliminating all of its potential falsifiers. It is in this sense that we can verify such generalizations as "All the coins in my pockets are copper" and "Everyone in this room is either first-born or an only child." Lawlike generalizations, however, are thought to have the following further property: observation of positive instances, Fs that are Gs, can strengthen our credence in the next F's being G. It is this kind of instance-to-instance accretion of confirmation that is supposed to be the hallmark of lawlikeness; it is what explains the possibility of confirming a generalization about an indefinitely large class of items on the basis of a finite number of favorable observations. This rough characterization of projectibility should suffice for our purposes.

Does (L), "Jade is green," pass the projectibility test? Here we seem to have a problem.[23] For we can imagine this: on re-examining the records of past observations, we find, to our dismay, that all the positive instances of (L), that is, all the millions of observed samples of green jade, turn out to have been samples of jadeite, and none of nephrite! If this should happen, we clearly would not, and should not, continue to think of (L) as well confirmed. All we have is evidence strongly confirming (L_1), and none having anything to do with (L_2). (L) is merely a conjunction of two laws, one well confirmed and the other with its epistemic status wholly up in the air. But all the millions of green jadeite samples *are* positive instances of (L): they satisfy both the antecedent and the consequent of (L). As we have just seen, however, (L) is not confirmed by them, at least not in the standard way we expect. And the reason, I suggest, is that jade is a true disjunctive kind, a disjunction of two heterogeneous nomic kinds which, however, is not itself a nomic kind.[24]

That disjunction is implicated in this failure of projectibility can be seen in the following way: inductive projection of generalizations like (L) with disjunctive antecedents would sanction a cheap, and illegitimate, confirmation procedure. For assume that "All *F*s are *G*" is a law that has been confirmed by the observation of appropriately numerous positive instances, things that are both *F* and *G*. But these are also positive instances of the generalization "All things that are *F or H* are *G*," for any *H* you please. So, if you in general permit projection of generalizations with a disjunctive antecedent, this latter generalization is also well confirmed. But "All things that are *F or H* are *G*" logically implies "All *H*s are *G*." Any statement implied by a well confirmed statement must itself be well confirmed.[25] So "All *H*s are *G*" is well confirmed—in fact, it is confirmed by the observation of *F*s that are *G*s!

One might protest: "Look, the very same strategy can be applied to something that is a genuine law. We can think of any nomic kind—say, being an emerald—as a disjunction, being an African emerald or a non-African emerald. This would make 'All emeralds are green' a conjunction of two laws, 'All African emeralds are green' and 'All non-African emeralds are green.' But surely this doesn't show there is anything wrong with the lawlikeness of 'All emeralds are green.'" Our reply is obvious: the disjunction, "being an African emerald or non-African emerald," does not denote some heterogeneously disjunctive, nonnomic kind; it denotes a perfectly well-behaved nomic kind, that of being an emerald! There is nothing wrong with disjunctive predicates as such; the trouble arises when the kinds denoted by the disjoined predicates are heterogeneous, "wildly disjunctive," so that instances falling under them do not show the kind of "similarity," or unity, that we expect of instances falling under a single kind.

The phenomenon under discussion, therefore, is related to the simple maxim sometimes claimed to underlie inductive inference: "similar things behave in similar ways," "same cause, same effect," and so on. The source of the trouble we saw with instantial confirmation of "All jade is green" is the fact, or belief, that samples of jadeite and sample of nephrite do not exhibit an appropriate "similarity" with respect to each other to warrant inductive projections from the observed samples of jadeite to unobserved samples of nephrite. But similarity of the required sort presumably holds for African emeralds and non-African emeralds—at least, that is what we believe, and that is what makes the "disjunctive kind," being an African emerald or a non-African emerald, a single nomic kind. More generally, the phenomenon is related to the point often made about disjunctive properties: disjunctive properties, unlike conjunctive properties, do not guarantee similarity for instances falling under them. And similarity, it is said, is the core of our idea of a property. If that is your idea of a property, you will believe that there are no such things as disjunctive properties (or "negative properties"). More precisely, though, we should remember that properties are not inherently disjunctive or conjunctive any more than classes are inherently unions or intersections, and that any property can be expressed by a disjunctive predicate. Properties of course can be conjunctions, or disjunctions, *of* other properties. The point about disjunctive properties is best put as a closure condition on properties: the class of properties is not closed under disjunction (presumably, nor under negation). Thus, there may well be properties *P* and *Q* such that *P or Q* is also a property, but its being so doesn't follow from the mere fact that *P* and *Q* are properties.[26]

V Jade and Pain

Let us now return to pain and its multiple realization bases, N_h, N_r, and N_m. I believe the situation here is instructively parallel to the case of jade in relation to jadeite and nephrite. It seems that we think of jadeite and nephrite as distinct kinds (and of jade not as kind) because they are different chemical kinds. But why is their being distinct as chemical kinds relevant here? Because many important properties of minerals, we think, are supervenient on, and explainable in terms of, their microstructure, and chemical kinds constitute a microstructural taxonomy that is explanatorily rich and powerful. Microstructure is important, in short, because macrophysical properties of substances are determined by microstructure. There ideas make up our "metaphysics" of microdetermination for properties of minerals and other substances, a background of partly empirical and partly metaphysical assumptions that regulate our inductive and explanatory practices.

The parallel metaphysical underpinnings for pain, and other mental states in general, are, first, the belief, expressed by the Restricted Correlation Thesis, that pain, or any other mental state, occurs in a system when, and only when, appropriate physical conditions are present in the system, and, second, the corollary belief that significant properties of mental states, in particular nomic relationships amongst them, are due to, and explainable in terms of, the properties and causal-nomic connections among their physical "substrates." I will call the conjunction of these two beliefs "the Physical Realization Thesis".[27] Whether or not the microexplanation of the sort indicated in the second half of the thesis amounts to a "reduction" is a question we will take up later. Apart from this question, though, the Physical Realization Thesis is widely accepted by philosophers who talk of "physical realization," and this includes most functionalists; it is all but explicit in LePore and Loewer, for example, and in Fodor.[28]

Define a property, N, by disjoining N_h, N_r, and N_m; that is, N has a disjunctive definition, $N_h \vee N_r \vee N_m$. If we assume, with those who endorse the MR-based antireductionist argument, that N_h, N_r, and N_m are a heterogeneous lot, we cannot make the heterogeneity go away merely by introducing a simpler expression, "N"; if there is a problem with certain disjunctive properties, it is not a *linguistic* problem about the form of expressions used to refer to them.

Now, we put the following question to Fodor and like-minded philosophers: If pain is nomically equivalent to N, the property claimed to be wildly disjunctive and obviously nonnomic, *why isn't pain itself equally heterogeneous and nonnomic as a kind?* Why isn't pain's relationship to its realization bases, N_h, N_r, and N_m analogous to jade's relationship to jadeite and nephrite? If jade turns out to be nonnomic on account of its dual "realizations" in distinct microstructures, why doesn't the same fate befall pain? After all, the group of actual and nomologically possible realizations of pain, as they are described by the MR enthusiasts with such imagination, is far more motley than the two chemical kinds comprising jade.

I believe we should insist on answers to these questions from those functionalists who view mental properties as "second-order" properties, i.e., properties that consist in having a property with a certain functional specification.[29] Thus, pain is said to be a second-order property in that it is the *property of having some property with a certain specification* in terms of its typical causes and effects and its relation to other mental properties; call this "specification H." The point of MR, on this view, is that there is more than one property that meets specification H—in fact, an open-ended set of such properties, it will be said. But pain itself, it is argued, is a more abstract but well-behaved property at a higher level, namely the property of having one of these properties meeting specification H. It should be clear why a position like this is vulnerable to the questions that have been raised. For the property of having property P is exactly identical with P, and the property of having *one* of the properties, $P_1, P_2, \ldots, P_n$, is exactly identical with the disjunctive property, $P_1 \vee P_2 \vee \cdots \vee P_n$. On the assumption that N_h, N_r, and N_m are all the properties satisfying specification H, the property of having a property with H, namely pain, is none other than the property of having either N_h or N_r or N_m[30]—namely, the *disjunctive* property, $N_h \vee N_r \vee N_m$! We cannot hide the disjunctive character of pain behind the second-order *expression*, "the property of having a property with specification H." Thus, on the construal of mental properties as second-order properties, mental properties will in general turn out to be disjunctions of their physical realization bases. It is difficult to see how one could have it both ways—that is, to castigate $N_h \vee N_r \vee N_m$ as unacceptably disjunctive while insisting on the integrity of pain as a scientific kind.

Moreover, when we think about making projections over pain, very much the same worry should arise about their propriety as did for jade. Consider a possible law: "Sharp pains administered at random intervals cause anxiety reactions". Suppose this generalization has been well confirmed for humans. Should we expect *on that basis* that it will hold also for Martians whose psychology is implemented (we assume) by a vastly different physical mechanism? Not if we accept the Physical Realization Thesis, fundamental to functionalism, that psychological regularities hold, to the extent that they do, in virtue of the causal-nomological regularities at the physical implementation level. The reason the law is true for humans is due to the way the human brain is "wired"; the Martians have a brain with a different wiring plan, and we certainly should not expect the regularity to hold for them just because it does for humans.[31] "Pains cause anxiety reactions" may turn out to possess no more unity as a scientific law than does "Jade is green".

Suppose that in spite of all this Fodor insists on defending pain as a nomic kind. It isn't clear that that would be a viable strategy. For he would then owe us an explanation of why the "wildly disjunctive" *N*, which after all is equivalent to pain, is not a nomic kind. If a predicate is nomically equivalent to a well-behaved predicate, why isn't that enough to show that it, too, is well behaved, and expresses a well-behaved property? To say, as Fodor does,[32] that "it is a law that . . ." is "intensional" and does not permit substitution of equivalent expressions ("equivalent" in various appropriate senses) is merely to locate a potential problem, not to resolve it.

Thus, the nomicity of pain may lead to the nomicity of *N*; but this isn't very interesting. For given the Physical Realization Thesis, and the priority of the physical implicit in it, our earlier line of argument, leading from the nonnomicity of *N* to the nonnomicity of pain, is more compelling. We must, I think, take seriously the reasoning leading to the conclusion that pain, and other mental states, might turn out to be nonnomic. If this turns out to be the case, it puts in serious jeopardy Fodor's contention that its physical irreducibility renders psychology an autonomous special science. If pain fails to be nomic, it is not the sort of property in terms of which laws can be formulated; and "pain" is not a predicate that can enter into a scientific theory that seeks to formulate causal laws and causal explanations. And the same goes for all multiply realizable psychological kinds—which, according to MR, means *all* psychological kinds. There are no scientific theories of jade, and we don't need any; if you insist on having one, you can help yourself with the *conjunction* of the theory of jadeite and the theory of nephrite. In the same way, there will be theories about human pains (instances of N_h), reptilian pains (instances of N_r), and so on; but there will be no unified, integrated theory encompassing all pains in all pain-capable organisms, only a conjunction of pain theories for appropriately individuated biological species and physical structure-types. Scientific psychology, like the theory of jade, gives way to a conjunction of structure-specific theories. If this is right, the correct conclusion to be drawn from the MR-inspired antireductionist argument is not the claim that psychology is an irreducible and autononomous science, but something that contradicts it, namely that it cannot be a science with a unified subject matter. This is the picture that is beginning to emerge from MR when combined with the Physical Realization Thesis.

These reflections have been prompted by the analogy with the case of jade; it is a strong and instructive analogy, I think, and suggests the possibility of a general argument. In the following section I will develop a direct argument, with explicit premises and assumptions.

VI Causal Powers and Mental Kinds

One crucial premise we need for a direct argument is a constraint on concept formation, or kind individuation, in science that has been around for many years; it has lately been resurrected by Fodor in connection with content externalism.[33] A precise statement of the constraint may be difficult and controversial, but its main idea can be put as follows:

[Principle of Causal Individuation of Kinds] Kinds in science are individuated on the basis of causal powers; that is, objects and events fall under a kind, or share in a property, insofar as they have similar causal powers.

I believe this is a plausible principle, and it is, in any case, widely accepted.

We can see that this principle enables us to give a specific interpretation to the claim that N_h, N_r, and N_m are *heterogeneous* as kinds: the claim must mean that they are *heterogeneous as causal powers*—that is, they are diverse as causal powers and enter into diverse causal laws. This must mean, given the Physical Realization Thesis, that pain itself can show no more unity as a causal power than the disjunction, $N_h \vee N_r \vee N_m$. This becomes especially clear if we set forth the following principle, which arguably is implied by the Physical Realization Thesis (but we need not make an issue of this here):

[The Causal Inheritance Principle] If mental property M is realized in a system at t in virtue of physical realization base P, the causal powers of *this instance* of M are identical with the causal powers of P.[34]

It is important to bear in mind that this principle only concerns the causal powers of *individual instances* of M; it does not identify the causal powers of mental property M *in general* with the causal powers of some physical property P; such identification is precluded by the multiple physical realizability of M.

Why should we accept this principle? Let us just note that to deny it would be to accept *emergent* causal powers: causal powers that magically emerge at a higher-level and of which there is no accounting in terms of lower-level properties and their causal powers and nomic connections. This leads to the notorious problem of "downward causation" and the attendant violation of the causal closure of the physical domain.[35] I believe that a serious physicalist would find these consequences intolerable.

It is clear that the Causal Inheritance Principle, in conjunction with the Physical Realization Thesis, has the consequence that mental kinds cannot satisfy the Causal Individuation Principle, and this effectively rules out mental kinds as scientific kinds. The reasoning is simple: instances of M that are realized by the same physical base must be grouped under one kind, since *ex hypothesi* the physical base is a causal kind; and instances of M with different realization bases must be grouped under distinct kinds, since, again *ex hypothesi*, these realization bases are distinct as causal kinds. Given that mental kinds are realized by diverse physical causal kinds, therefore, it follows that mental kinds are not causal kinds, and hence are disqualified as proper scientific kinds. Each mental kind is sundered into as many kinds as there are physical realization bases for it, and the psychology as a science with disciplinary unity turns out to be an impossible project.

What is the relationship between this argument and the argument adumbrated in our reflections based on the jade analogy? At first blush, the two arguments might seem unrelated: the earlier argument depended chiefly on epistemological considerations, considerations on inductive projectibility of certain predicates, whereas the crucial premise of the second argument is the Causal Kind Individuation Principle, a broadly metaphysical and methodological principle about science. I think, though, that the two arguments are closely related, and the key to seeing the relationship is this: causal powers involve laws, and laws are regularities that are projectible. Thus, if pain (or jade) is not a kind over which inductive projections can be made, it cannot enter into laws, and therefore cannot qualify as a causal kind; and this disqualifies it as a scientific kind. If this is right, the jade-inspired reflections provide a possible rationale for the Causal Individuation Principle. Fleshing out this rough chain of reasoning in precise terms, however, goes beyond what I can attempt in this paper.

VII The Status of Psychology: Local Reductions

Our conclusion at this point, therefore, is this: If MR is true, psychological kinds are not scientific kinds. What does this imply about the status of psychology as a science? Do our considerations show that psychology is a pseudo-science like astrology and alchemy? Of course not. The crucial difference, from the metaphysical point of view, is that psychology has physical realizations, but alchemy does not. To have a physical realization is to be physically grounded and explainable in terms of the processes at an underlying level. In fact, if each of the psychological kinds posited in a psychological theory has a physical realization for a fixed species, the theory can be "locally reduced" to the physical theory of that species, in the following sense. Let S be the species involved; for each law L_m of psychological theory T_m, $S \rightarrow L_m$ (the proposition that L_m holds for members of S) is the "S-restricted" version of L_m; and $S \rightarrow T_m$ is the S-restricted version of T_m, the set of all S-restricted laws of T_m. We can then say that T_m is "locally reduced" for species S to an underlying theory, T_p, just in case $S \rightarrow T_m$ is reduced to T_p. And the latter obtains just in case each S-restricted law of T_m, $S \rightarrow L_m$,[36] is derivable from the laws of the reducing theory T_p, taken together with bridge laws. What bridge laws suffice to guarantee the derivation? Obviously, an array of S-restricted bridge laws of the form, $S \rightarrow (M_i \leftrightarrow P_i)$, for each mental kind M_i. Just as unrestricted psychophysical bridge laws can underwrite a "global" or "uniform" reduction of psychology, species- or structure-restricted bridge laws sanction its "local" reduction.

If the same psychological theory is true of humans, reptiles, and Martians, the psychological kinds posited by that theory must have realizations in human, reptilian, and Martian physiologies. This implies that the theory is locally reducible in three ways, for humans, reptiles, and Martians. If the dependence of the mental on the physical means anything, it must mean that the regularities posited by this common psychology must have divergent physical explanations for the three species. The very idea of physical realization involves the possibility of physically explaining psychological properties and regularities, and the supposition of multiple such realizations, namely MR, involves a commitment to the possibility of multiple explanatory reductions of psychology.[37] The important moral of MR we need to keep in mind is this: *if psychological properties are multiply realized, so is psychology itself.* If physical realizations of psychological properties are a "wildly heterogeneous" and "unsystematic" lot, psychological theory itself must be realized by an equally heterogeneous and unsystematic lot of physical theories.

I am inclined to think that multiple local reductions, rather than global reductions, are the rule, even in areas in which we standardly suppose reductions are possible. I will now deal with a possible objection to the idea of local reduction, at least as it is applied to psychology. The objection goes like this: given what we know about the differences among members of a single species, even species are too wide to yield determinate realization bases for psychological states, and given what we know about the phenomena of maturation and development, brain injuries, and the like, the physical bases of mentality may change even for a single individual. This throws into serious doubt, continues the objection, the availability of species-restricted bridge laws needed for local reductions.

The point of this objection may well be correct as a matter of empirical fact. Two points can be made in reply, however. First, neurophysiological research goes on because there is a shared, and probably well grounded, belief among the workers that there are not huge individual differences within a species in the way psychological kinds are realized. Conspecifics must show important physical-physiological similarities, and there probably is good reason for thinking that they share physical realization bases to a sufficient degree to make search for species-wide neural substrates for mental states feasible and rewarding. Researchers in this area evidently aim for neurobiological explanations of psychological capacities and processes that are generalizable over all or most ("normal") members of a given species.

Second, even if there are huge individual differences among conspecifics as to how their psychology is realized, that does not touch the metaphysical point: as long as you believe in the Physical Realization Thesis, you must believe that every organism or system with mentality falls under a physical structure-type such that its mental states are realized by determinate physical states of organisms with that structure. It may be that these structures are so finely individuated and so few *actual* individuals fall under them that research into the neural bases of mental states in these structures is no longer worthwhile, theoretically or practically. What we need to recognize here is that the scientific possibility of, say, human psychology is a contingent fact (assuming it is a fact); it depends on the fortunate fact that individual humans do not show huge physiological-biological differences that are psychologically relevant. But if they did, that would not change the metaphysics of the situation one bit; it would remain true that the psychology of each of us was determined by, and locally reducible to, his neurobiology.

Realistically, there are going to be psychological differences among individual humans: it is a commonsense platitude that no two persons are exactly alike—either physically or psychologically. And individual differences may be manifested not only in particular psychological facts but in psychological regularities. If we believe in the Physical Realization Thesis, we must believe that our psychological differences are rooted in, and explainable by, our physical differences, just as we expect our psychological similarities to be so explainable. Humans probably are less alike among themselves than, say, tokens of a Chevrolet model.[38] And psychological laws for humans, at a certain level of specificity, must be expected to be statistical in character, not deterministic—or, if you prefer, "ceteris paribus laws" rather than "strict laws." But this is nothing peculiar to psychology; these remarks surely apply to human physiology and anatomy as much as human psychology. In any case, none of this affects the metaphysical point being argued here concerning microdetermination and microreductive explanation.

VIII Metaphysical Implications

But does local reduction have any interesting philosophical significance, especially in regard to the status of mental properties? If a psychological property has been multiply locally reduced, does that mean that the property itself has been reduced? Ned Block has raised just such a point, arguing that species-restricted reductionism (or species-restricted type physicalism) "sidesteps the main metaphysical question: 'What is common to the pains of dogs and people (and all other species) in virtue of which they are pains?'"[39]

Pereboom and Kornblith elaborate on Block's point as follows:

> ... even if there is a single type of physical state that normally realizes pain in each type of organism, or in each structure type, this does not show that pain, *as a type of mental state*, is reducible to physical states. Reduction, in the present debate, must be understood as reduction of types, since the primary object of reductive strategies is explanations and theories, and explanations and theories quantify over types.... The suggestion that there are species-specific reductions of pain results in the claim that pains in different species have nothing in common. But this is just a form of eliminativism.[40]

There are several related but separable issues raised here. But first we should ask: Must all pains have "something in common" in virtue of which they are pains?

According to the phenomenological conception of pain, all pains do have something in common: they all *hurt*. But as I take it, those who hold this view of pain would reject any reductionist program, independently of the issues presently on hand. Even if there were a species-invariant uniform bridge law correlating pains with a single physical substrate across all species and structures, they would claim that the correlation holds as a brute, unexplainable matter of fact, and that pain as a qualitative event, a "raw feel," would remain irreducibly distinct from its neural substrate. Many emergentists apparently held a view of this kind.

I presume that Block, and Pereboom and Kornblith, are speaking not from a phenomenological viewpoint of this kind but from a broadly functionalist one. But from a functionalist perspective, it is by no means clear how we should understand the question "What do all pains have in common in virtue of which they are all pains?" Why should all pains have "something in common"? As I understand it, at the core of the functionalist program is the attempt to explain the meanings of mental terms *relationally*, in terms of inputs, outputs, and connections with other mental states. And on the view, discussed briefly earlier, that mental properties are second-order properties, pain is the property of having a property with a certain functional specification H (in terms of inputs, outputs, etc.). This yields a short answer to Block's question: what all pains have in common is the pattern of connections as specified by H. The local reductionist is entitled to that answer as much as the functionalist is. Compare two pains, an instance of N_h and one of N_m: what they have in common is that each is an instance of a property that realizes pain—that is, they exhibit the same pattern of input-output-other internal state connections, namely the pattern specified by H.

But some will say: "But H is only an *extrinsic* characterization; what do these instances of pain have in common that is *intrinsic* to them?" The local reductionist must grant that on his view there is nothing intrinsic that all pains have in common in virtue of which they are pains (assuming that N_h, N_r, and N_m "have nothing intrinsic in common"). But that is also precisely the consequence of the functionalist view. That, one might say, is the whole point of functionalism: the functionalist, especially one who believes in MR, would not, and should not, look for something common to all pains over and above H (the heart of functionalism, one might say, is the belief that mental states have no "intrinsic essence").

But there is a further question raised by Block et al.: What happens to properties that have been locally reduced? Are they still with us, distinct and separate from the underlying physical-biological properties? Granted: human pain is reduced to N_h, Martian pain to N_m, and so forth, but what of *pain itself*? It remains unreduced. Are we still stuck with the dualism of mental and physical properties?

I will sketch two possible ways of meeting this challenge. First, recall my earlier remarks about the functionalist conception of mental properties as second-order properties: pain is *the property of having a property with specification H*, and, given that N_h, N_r, and N_m are the properties meeting H, pain turns to be the disjunctive property, $N_h \vee N_r \vee N_m$. If you hold the second-order property view of mental properties, pain has been reduced to, and survives as, this disjunctive physical kind. Quite apart from considerations of local reduction, the very conception of pain you hold commits you to the conclusion that pain is a disjunctive kind, and if you accept any form of respectable physicalism (in particular, the Physical Realization Thesis), it is a disjunctive *physical* kind. And even if you don't accept the view of mental properties as second-order properties, as long as you are comfortable with disjunctive kinds and properties, you can, in the aftermath of local reduction, identify pain with the disjunction of its realization bases. On this approach, then, you have another, more direct, answer to Block's question: what all pains have in common is that they all fall under the disjunctive kind, $N_h \vee N_r \vee N_m$.

If you are averse to disjunctive kinds, there is another more radical, and in some ways more satisfying, approach. The starting point of this approach is the frank acknowledgement that MR leads to the conclusion that pain as a property or kind must go. Local reduction after all is reduction, and to be reduced is to be eliminated as an *independent* entity. You might say: global reduction is different in that it is also *conservative*—if pain is globally reduced to physical property P, pain survives as P. But it is also true that under local reduction, pain survives as N_h in humans, as N_r in reptiles, and so on. It must be admitted, however, that pain as a kind does not survive multiple local reduction. But is this so bad?

Let us return to jade once again. Is jade a *kind*? We know it is not a mineral kind; but is it any kind of a kind? That of course depends on what we mean by "kind." There are certain shared criteria, largely based on observable macroproperties of mineral samples (e.g., hardness, color, etc.), that determine whether something is a sample of jade, or whether the predicate "is jade" is correctly applicable to it. What all samples of jade have in common is just these observable macrophysical properties that define the applicability of the predicate "is jade." In this sense, speakers of English who have "jade" in their repertoire associate the same *concept* with "jade"; and we can recognize the existence of the concept of jade and at the same time acknowledge that the concept does not pick out, or answer to, a property or kind in the natural world.

I think we can say something similar about pain and "pain": there are shared criteria for the application of the predicate "pain" or "is in pain," and these criteria may well be for the most part functionalist ones. These criteria generate for us a *concept of pain*, a concept whose clarity and determinacy depend, we may assume, on certain characteristics (such as explicitness, coherence, and completeness) of the criteria governing the application of "pain." But the concept of pain, on this construal, need not pick out an objective kind any more than the concept of jade does.

All this presupposes a distinction between concepts and properties (or kinds). Do we have such a distinction? I believe we do. Roughly, concepts are in the same ball park as predicates, meanings (perhaps, something like Fregean *Sinnen*), ideas, and the like; Putnam has suggested that concepts be identified with "synonymy classes of predicates",[41] and that comes close enough to what I have in mind. Properties and relations, on the other hand, are "out there in the world"; they are features and characteristics of things and events in the world. They include fundamental physical magnitudes and quantities, like mass, energy, size, and shape, and are part of the causal structure of the world. The property of being water is arguably identical with the property of being H_2O, but evidently the concept of water is distinct from the concept of H_2O (Socrates had the former but not the latter). Most of us would agree that ethical predicates are meaningful, and that we have the concepts of "good," "right," etc.; however, it is a debatable issue, and has lately been much debated, whether there are such properties as goodness and rightness.[42] If you find that most of these remarks make sense, you understand the concept–property distinction that I have in mind. Admittedly, this is all a little vague and programmatic, and we clearly need a better articulated theory of properties and concepts; but the distinction is there, supported by an impressively systematic set of intuitions and philosophical requirements.[43]

But is this second approach a form of mental eliminativism? In a sense it is: as I said, on this approach no properties in the world answer to general, species-unrestricted mental concepts. But remember: there still are pains, and we sometimes are in pain, just as there still are samples of jade. We must also keep in mind that the present approach is not, in its ontological implications, a form of the standard mental eliminativism currently on the scene.[44] Without elaborating on what the differences are, let us just note a few important points. First, the present view does not take away species-restricted mental properties, e.g., human pain, Martian pain, canine pain, and the rest, although it takes away "pain as such." Second, while the standard eliminativism consigns mentality to the same ontological limbo to which phlogiston, witches, and magnetic effluvia, have been dispatched, the position I have been sketching views it on a par with jade, tables, and adding machines. To see jade as a nonkind is not to question the existence of jade, or the legitimacy and utility of the concept of jade. Tables do not constitute a scientific kind; there are no laws about tables as such, and being a table is not a causal-explanatory kind. But that must be sharply distinguished from the false claim that there are no tables. The same goes for pains. These points suggest the following difference in regard to the status of psychology: the present view allows, and in fact encourages, "species-specific psychologies," but the standard eliminativism would do away with all things psychological—species-specific psychologies as well as global psychology.[45]

To summarize, then, the two metaphysical schemes I have sketched offer these choices: either we allow disjunctive kinds and construe pain and other mental properties as such kinds, or else we must acknowledge that our general mental terms and concepts do not pick out properties and kinds in the world (we may call this "mental property irrealism"). I should add that I am not interested in promoting either disjunctive kinds or mental irrealism, a troubling set of choices to most of us. Rather, my main interest has been to follow out the consequences of MR and try to come to terms with them within a reasonable metaphysical scheme.

I have already commented on the status of psychology as a science under MR. As I argued, MR seriously compromises the disciplinary unity and autonomy of psychology as a science. But that does not have to be taken as a negative message. In particular, the claim does not imply that a scientific study of psychological phenomena is not possible or useful; on the contrary, MR says that psychological processes have a foundation in the biological and physical processes and regularities, and it opens the possibility of enlightening explanations of psychological processes at a more basic level. It is only that at a deeper level, psychology becomes sundered by being multiply locally reduced. However, species-specific psychologies, e.g., human psychology, Martian psychology, etc., can all flourish as scientific theories. Psychology remains *scientific*, though perhaps not *a science*. If you insist on having a global psychology valid for all species and structures, you can help yourself with that, too; but you must think of it as a *conjunction* of species-restricted psychologies and be careful, above all, with your inductions.[46]

Notes

1. On occasion, "MR" will refer to the *phenomenon* of multiple realization rather than the *claim* that such a phenomenon exists; there should be no danger of confusion.

2. Jerry Fodor, "Special Sciences, or the Disunity of Science as a Working Hypothesis" (hereafter, "Special Sciences"), *Synthese* 28 (1974): 97–115; reprinted in *Representations* (MIT Press: Cambridge, 1981), and as the introductory chapter in Fodor, *The Language of Thought* (New York: Crowell, 1975).

3. Donald Davidson, "Mental Events" reprinted in *Essays on Actions and Events* (Oxford: Oxford University Press, 1980).

4. "Physicalism: Ontology, Determination, and Reduction," *Journal of Philosophy* 72 (1975): 551–64. The two quotations below are from p. 551.

5. "More on Making Mind Matter," *Philosophical Topics* 17 (1989): 175–92. The quotation is from p. 179.

6. "More on Making Mind Matter," p. 180.

7. In "Can the Mind Change the World?," *Meaning and Method: Essays in Honor of Hilary Putnam*, ed. George Boolos (Cambridge University Press: Cambridge, 1990), p. 146.

8. They include Richard Boyd, "Materialism Without Reductionism: What Physicalism Does Not Entail," in Block, *Readings in Philosophy of Psychology*, vol. 1; Block, in "Introduction: What is

Functionalism?" in his anthology just cited, pp. 178–79; John Post, *The Faces of Existence* (Ithaca: Cornell University Press, 1987); Derk Pereboom and Hilary Kornblith, "The Metaphysics of Irreducibility" (*Philosophical Studies* 63 (1991): 125–145). One philosopher who is not impressed by the received view of MR is David Lewis; see his "Review of Putnam" in Block, *Readings in Philosophy of Psychology*, vol. 1.

9. Hilary Putnam, "Psychological Predicates," in W. H. Capitan and D. D. Merrill, eds., *Art, Mind, and Religion* (Pittsburgh: University of Pittsburgh, 1967); reprinted with a new title, "The Nature of Mental States," in Ned Block, ed., *Readings in Philosophy of Psychology*, vol. 1 (Cambridge: Harvard University Press, 1980).

10. "The Nature of Mental States," p. 228 (in the Block volume).

11. Thus, Post says, "Functional and intentional states are defined without regard to their physical or other realizations," *The Faces of Existence*, p. 161. Also compare the earlier quotation from Block.

12. As far as I know, the term "realization" was first used in something like its present sense by Hilary Putnam in "Minds and Machines," in Sydney Hook, ed., *Dimensions of Mind* (New York: New York University Press, 1960).

13. On this point see Robert Van Gulick, "Nonreductive Materialism and Intertheoretic Constraints," in *Emergence or Reduction?*, ed. Ansgar Beckemann, Hans Flohr, and Jaegwon Kim (De Gruyter, 1992).

14. "More on Making Mind Matter," p. 179.

15. Cf. Hartry Field, "Mental Representation," in Block, *Readings in Philosophy of Psychology* (Cambridge: Harvard University Press, 1981), vol. 2.

16. What of LePore and Loewer's condition (ii), the requirement that the realization basis "explain" the realized property? Something like this explanatory relation may well be entailed by the realization relation; however, I do not believe it should be part of the definition of "realization"; that such an explanatory relation holds should be a consequence of the realization relation, not constitutive of it.

17. "The Nature of Mental States," p. 228 (in the Block volume).

18. *The Structure of Science* (New York: Harcourt, Brace and World, 1961), chap. 11.

19. My remarks here and the preceding paragraph assume that the higher-level theory requires no "correction" in relation to the base theory. With appropriate caveats and qualifications, they should apply to models of reduction that allow such corrections, or models that only require the deduction of a suitable analogue, or "image", in the reduction base—as long as the departures are not so extreme as to warrant talk of replacement or elimination rather than reduction. Cf. Patricia Churchland, *Neurophilosophy* (Cambridge: The MIT Press, 1986), chap. 7.

20. See "Special Sciences," pp. 132–33 (in *Representations*).

21. Fodor appears to assume that the requirement that bridge laws must connect "kinds" to "kinds" is part of the classic positivist conception of reduction. I don't believe there is any warrant for this assumption, however.

22. See Pereboom and Kornblith, "The Metaphysics of Irreducibility" in which it is suggested that laws with disjunctive predicates are not "explanatory." I think, though, that this suggestion is not fully developed there.

23. The points to follow concerning disjunctive predicates were developed about a decade ago; however, I have just come across some related and, in some respects similar, points in David Owens's interesting paper "Disjunctive Laws," *Analysis* 49 (1989): 197–202. See also William Seager, "Disjunctive Laws and Supervenience," *Analysis* 51 (1991): 93–98.

24. This can be taken to define one useful sense of kind heterogeneity: two kinds are heterogeneous with respect to each other just in case their disjunction is not a kind.

25. Note: this doesn't say that for any *e*, if *e* is "positive evidence" for *h* and *h* logically implies *j*, then *e* is positive evidence for *j*. About the latter principle there is some dispute; see Carl G. Hempel, "Studies in the Logic of Confirmation," reprinted in Hempel, *Aspects of Scientific Explanation* (New York: The Free Press, 1965), especially pp. 30–35; Rudolf Carnap, *Logical Foundations of Probability* (Chicago: University of Chicago Press, 1950), pp. 471–76.

26. On issues concerning properties, kinds, similarity, and lawlikeness, see W. V. Quine, "Natural Kinds" in *Ontological Relativity and Other Essays* (New York: Columbia University Press, 1969); David Lewis, "New Work for a Theory of Universals," *Australasian Journal of Philosophy* 61 (1983): 347–77; D. M. Armstrong, *Universals* (Boulder, Colorado: Westview Press, 1989).

27. This term is a little misleading since the two subtheses have been stated without the term "realization" and may be acceptable to those who would reject the "realization" idiom in connection with the mental. I use the term since we are chiefly addressing philosophers (mainly functionalists) who construe the psychophysical relation in terms of realization, rather than, say, emergence or brute correlation.

28. See "Special Sciences," and "Making Mind Matter More," *Philosophical Topics* 17 (1989): 59–79.

29. See, e.g., Block, "Can the Mind Change the World?," p. 155.

30. We might keep in mind the close relationship between disjunction and the existential quantifier standardly noted in logic textbooks.

31. It may be a complicated affair to formulate this argument within certain functionalist schemes; if, for example, mental properties are functionally defined by Ramseyfying a total psychological theory, it will turn out that humans and Martians cannot share any psychological state unless the same total psychology (including the putative law in question) is true (or held to be true) for both.

32. "Special Sciences," p. 140 (in *Representations*).

33. See, e.g., Carl G. Hempel, *Fundamentals of Concept Formation in Empirical Science* (Chicago: University of Chicago Press, 1952); W. V. Quine, "Natural Kinds." Fodor gives it an explicit statement in *Psychosemantics* (Cambridge: MIT Press, 1988), chap. 2. A principle like this is often invoked in the current externalism/internalism debate about content; most principal participants in this debate seem to accept it.

34. A principle like this is sometimes put in terms of "supervenience" and "supervenience base" rather than "realization" and "realization base". See my "Epiphenomenal and Supervenient Causation," *Midwest Studies in Philosophy* 9 (1984): 257–70. Fodor appears to accept just such a principle of supervenient causation for mental properties in chap. 2 of his *Psychosemantics*. In "The Metaphysics of Irreducibility" Pereboom and Kornblith appear to reject it.

35. For more details see my "'Downward Causation' in Emergentism and Nonreductive Physicalism," in *Emergence or Reduction?*, ed. Beckermann, Flohr, and Kim, and "The Nonreductivist's

Troubles with Mental Causation," in *Mental Causation*, ed. John Heil and Alfred Mele (Oxford University Press).

36. Or an appropriately corrected version thereof (this qualification applies to the bridge laws as well).

37. In "Special Sciences" and "Making Mind Matter More" Fodor appears to accept the local reducibility of psychology and other special sciences. But he uses the terminology of local *explanation*, rather than reduction, of psychological regularities in terms of underlying microstructure. I think this is because his preoccupation with Nagelian uniform reduction prevents him from seeing that this is a form of inter-theoretic reduction if anything is.

38. Compare J. J. C. Smart's instructive analogy between biological organisms and superheterodyne radios, in *Philosophy and Scientific Realism* (London: Routledge & Kegan Paul, 1963), pp. 56–57. Smart's conception of the relation between physics and the special sciences, such as biology and psychology, is similar in some respects to the position I am defending here.

39. "Introduction: What is Functionalism?" in *Readings in Philosophy of Psychology*, pp. 178–79.

40. In their "The Metaphysics of Irreducibility." See also Ronald Endicott, "On Physical Multiple Realization," *Pacific Philosophical Quarterly* 70 (1989): 212–224, and "Species-Specific Properties and More Narrow Reductive Strategies," *Erkenntnis* 38 (1993): 303–321. In personal correspondence Earl Conee and Joe Mendola have raised similar points. There is a useful discussion of various metaphysical issues relating to MR in Cynthia Macdonald, *Mind–Body Identity Theories* (London and New York: Routledge, 1989).

41. In "The Nature of Mental States."

42. I of course have in mind the controversy concerning moral realism; see essays in Geoffrey Sayre-McCord, ed., *Essays on Moral Realism* (Ithaca: Cornell University Press, 1988).

43. On concepts and properties, see, e.g., Hilary Putnam, "On Properties," *Mathematics, Matter and Method* (Cambridge: Cambridge University Press, 1975); Mark Wilson, "Predicate Meets Property," *Philosophical Review* 91 (1982): 549–90, especially, section III.

44. Such as the versions favored by W. V. Quine, Stephen Stich, and Paul Churchland.

45. The approach to the mind–body problem being adumbrated here is elaborated in my "Functionalism as Mental Irrealism" (in preparation).

46. This paper is descended from an unpublished paper, "The Disunity of Psychology as a Working Hypothesis?," which was circulated in the early 1980s. I am indebted to the following persons, among, others, for helpful comments: Fred Feldman, Hilary Kornblith, Barry Loewer, Brian McLaughlin, Joe Mendola, Marcelo Sabates, and James Van Cleve.

19 From *Language and Problems of Knowledge*

Noam Chomsky

It is interesting to observe the fate of the Cartesian version of the mind–body problem and the problem of the existence of other minds. The mind–body problem can be posed sensibly only insofar as we have a definite conception of body. If we have no such definite and fixed conception, we cannot ask whether some phenomena fall beyond its range. The Cartesians offered a fairly definite conception of body in terms of their contact mechanics, which in many respects reflects commonsense understanding. Therefore they could sensibly formulate the mind–body problem and the problem of other minds. There was important work attempting to develop the concept of mind further, including studies by British Neoplatonists of the seventeenth century that explored the categories and principles of perception and cognition along lines that were later extended by Kant and that were rediscovered, independently, in twentieth-century Gestalt psychology.

Another line of development was the "general and philosophical grammar" (in our terms, scientific grammar) of the seventeenth, eighteenth, and early nineteenth centuries, which was much influenced by Cartesian conceptions, particularly in the early period. These inquiries into universal grammar sought to lay bare the general principles of language. These were regarded as not essentially different from the general principles of thought, so that language is "a mirror of mind," in the conventional phrase. For various reasons—some good, some not—these inquiries were disparaged and abandoned for a century, to be resurrected, again independently, a generation ago, though in quite different terms and without recourse to any dualist assumptions.

It is also interesting to see how the Cartesian conception of body and mind entered social thought, most strikingly in the libertarian ideas of Jean-Jacques Rousseau, which were based on strictly Cartesian conceptions of body and mind. Because humans, possessing minds, are crucially distinct from machines (including animals), so Rousseau argued, and because the properties of mind crucially surpass mechanical determinacy, therefore any infringement on human freedom is illegitimate and must be confronted and overcome. Although the later development of such thinking abandoned the Cartesian framework, its origins lie in significant measure in these classical ideas.

The Cartesian conception of a second substance was generally abandoned in later years, but it is important to recognize that it was not the theory of mind that was refuted (one might argue that it was hardly clear enough to be confirmed or refuted). Rather, the Cartesian concept of *body* was refuted by seventeenth-century physics, particularly in the work of Isaac Newton, which laid the foundations for modern science. Newton demonstrated that the motions of the heavenly bodies could not be explained by the principles of Descartes's contact mechanics, so that the Cartesian concept of body must be abandoned. In the Newtonian framework there is a "force" that one body exerts on another, without contact between them, a kind of "action at a distance." Whatever this force may be, it does not fall within the Cartesian framework of contact mechanics. Newton himself found this conclusion unsatisfying. He sometimes referred to gravitational force as "occult" and suggested that his theory gave only a mathematical description of events in the physical world, not a true "philosophical" (in more modern terminology, "scientific") explanation of these events. Until the late nineteenth century it was still widely held that a true explanation must be framed somehow in mechanical or quasi-mechanical terms. Others, notably the chemist and philosopher Joseph Priestley, argued that bodies themselves possess capacities that go beyond the limits of contact mechanics, specifically the property of attracting other bodies, but perhaps far more. Without pursuing subsequent developments further, the general conclusion is that the Cartesian concept of body was found to be untenable.

What is the concept of body that finally emerged? The answer is that there is no clear and definite concept of body. If the best theory of the material world that we can construct includes a variety of forces, particles that have no mass, and other entities that would have been offensive to the "scientific common sense" of the Cartesians, then so be it: We conclude that these are properties of the physical world, the world of body. The conclusions are tentative, as befits empirical hypotheses, but are not subject to criticism because they transcend some a priori conception of body. There is no longer any definite conception of body. Rather, the material world is whatever we discover it to be, with whatever properties it must be assumed to have for the purposes of explanatory theory. Any intelligible theory that offers genuine explanations and that can be assimilated to the core notions of physics becomes part of the theory of the material world, part of our account of body. If we have such a theory in some domain, we seek to assimilate it to the core notions of physics, perhaps modifying these notions as we carry out this enterprise. In the study of human psychology, if we develop a theory of some cognitive faculty (the language faculty, for example) and find that this faculty has certain properties, we seek to discover the mechanisms of the brain that exhibit these properties and to account for them in the terms of the physical sciences—keeping open the possibility that the concepts of the physical sciences might have to be modified, just as the concepts of Cartesian contact mechanics had to be modified to account for the motion of the heavenly bodies, and as has happened repeatedly in the evolution of the natural sciences since Newton's day.

In short, there is no definite concept of body. Rather, there is a material world, the properties of which are to be discovered, with no a priori demarcation of what will count as "body." The mind–body problem can therefore not even be formulated. The problem cannot be solved, because there is no clear way to state it. Unless someone proposes a definite concept of body, we cannot ask whether some phenomena exceed its bounds. Similarly, we cannot pose the problem of other minds. We can, and I think should, continue to use mentalistic terminology, as I have done throughout in discussing mental representations and operations that form and modify them in mental computation. But we do not see ourselves as investigating the properties of some "second substance," something crucially distinct from body that interacts with body in some mysterious way, perhaps through divine intervention. Rather, we are studying the properties of the material world at a level of abstraction at which we believe, rightly or wrongly, that a genuine explanatory theory can be constructed, a theory that provides genuine insight into the nature of the phenomena that concern us. These phenomena, in fact, are of real intellectual interest not so much in themselves but in the avenue that they provide for us to penetrate into the deeper workings of the mind. Ultimately, we hope to assimilate this study to the mainstream of the natural sciences, much as the study of genes or of valence and the properties of the chemical elements was assimilated to more fundamental sciences. We recognize, however, that, as in the past, it may turn out that these fundamental sciences must be modified or extended to provide foundations for the abstract theories of complex systems, such as the human mind.

Our task, then, is to discover genuine explanatory theories and to use these discoveries to facilitate inquiry into physical mechanisms with the properties outlined in these theories. Wherever this inquiry leads, it will be within the domain of "body." Or more accurately, we simply abandon the whole conception of body as possibly distinct from something else and use the methods of rational inquiry to learn as much as we can about the world—what we call the material world, whatever exotic properties it turns out to have.

The mind–body problem remains the subject of much controversy, debate, and speculation, and in this regard the problem is still very much alive. But the discussion seems to me incoherent in fundamental respects. Unlike the Cartesians, we have no definite concept of body. It is therefore quite unclear how we can even ask whether some phenomena lie beyond the range of the study of body, falling within the separate study of mind.

Recall the logic of Descartes's argument for the existence of a second substance, *res cogitans*. Having defined "body" in terms of contact mechanics, he argued that certain phenomena lie beyond its domain, so that some new principle was required; given his metaphysics, a second substance must be postulated. The logic is essentially sound; it is, in fact, much like Newton's, when he demonstrated the inadequacy of Cartesian contact mechanics for the explanation of the motion of the heavenly bodies so that a new principle, the principle of gravitational attraction, had to be postulated. The crucial difference between the Cartesian and the Newtonian enterprises was that the latter offered a genuine explanatory theory of the behavior of bodies, whereas the Cartesian theory offered no satisfactory account of properties such as the creative aspect of language use that lie beyond mechanical explanation in Descartes's view. Therefore Newton's conceptions came to be the "scientific common sense" of later generations of scientists, while Descartes's fell by the wayside.

20 From *The Empirical Stance*

Bas van Fraassen

One popular plea for metaphysics rests on the idea that for the good of science, scientists must start with provisional realism—there are unobservable causes for all observable phenomena or some such thesis—and presumptive materialism—matter is all there is, so those causes are all material mechanisms of some sort. I will concentrate here on materialism. Physicalism and naturalism are not precisely the same as old-fashioned materialism (all these isms come in various flavors and colors), but in the present context, the differences will not matter much. The argument will go through, mutatis mutandis, if we substitute, for example, "physical" or "supervenient on the physical" for "material."[1]

To begin, then, let us take the putative metaphysical theory summed up in the thesis: matter is all there is. This may sound a little dated, but is actually not far from current formulations.[2]

12 Is This a Factual Claim?

This thesis certainly sounds debatable: surely it must be either so or not so. . . . But appearances are deceiving. Genuine debatability presumes understanding of what the suggestion actually means. A much more basic presupposition is at stake: Does presumptive materialism in this sense make any difference to science at all? By "in this sense" I mean, in the sense of assumptions, theses, factual claims about what there is and what there is not.

13 What Is Matter?

Does the thesis that matter is all there is rule out at least some kinds of theories, so that they are not even candidates for scientific exploration? I will argue that this is quite illusory. There may, however, be a certain orientation, attitude, or stance associated with this thesis—which does affect science as well as practical and intellectual life generally—for which this thesis functions as code. If that is so, then materialism may be a prime example of false consciousness in philosophy. For in that case materialists may take themselves to be maintaining a theory while they are in reality merely expressing attitudes, in ways that lend themselves to such expression only under conditions of confusion and unclarity.

The thesis "matter is all there is" certainly sounds like a substantive factual claim. Does it not rule out Descartes's mind–body dualism, Aquinas's souls, spirits, entelechies, cosmic purpose? If those are substantive factual claims, then a thesis that contradicts them must be, too.

But we cannot simply assume that all those putative metaphysical theories really are what they sound like, if we are about to question the status of any one of them. The contradiction may also be just appearance. A contradiction may be merely verbal. For example, if a Cartesian says to a materialist "Matter is not all there is," then of course there is a contradiction on the syntactic level. One uses a sentence that is the negation of the other one. This syntactic contradiction is there, then, regardless of whether either materialist or Cartesian is making any sense at all. The materialist thesis will genuinely rule out the Cartesian view only if each can be made clear enough so that the denial has some genuine content (and even then it may not).[3] The precise truth conditions for these various claims require at least that there is a genuine, and not just a verbal, distinction between what is material and what is not material.

Suppose that the thesis is indeed the important part of materialism. Then something follows from this about what materialists will find it important to do. In that case they will certainly not rest until the distinction between matter and what is not matter has been made so clear that the thesis is a factual claim, which can clearly be either true or false. But if they do not, then by *modus tollens* we should conclude ... what?

What would count as something that is not material? Descartes said that matter is extended and mind is not; mind thinks. But if that is not a stipulative definition, it is certainly wrong. Otherwise we would have to say that Hertz's massive point particles, if they exist, are not material. Equally we would have to say that Hartry Field denies materialism when he claims that space-time points are real, concrete individuals. And Field is well known for his insistence that any philosophical account he would accept must be compatible with materialism.

It may be unfair to take Descartes as our whipping boy. Do more recent putative statements of materialism fare much better? Typically they start from some version of received scientific opinion, perhaps with some anxiety about being up to date. They will not say that atoms or elementary particles are all there is, since they know that there are trees, persons, and rocks as well. But they will say that everything is composed solely of atoms or elementary particles. If we take this seriously we shall, I wager, once more land in an untenable historical parochialism. When Newton introduced forces in addition to bodies, did he deny the thesis? Forces are not composed of particles. When Huyghens's waves-in-the-ether theory defeated Newton's particle theory of light, was that a setback for materialism? Surely not, although the ether was a continuous medium, not particulate. When a recent article in a physics journal bore the title "Particles Do Not Exist," was that a denial of materialism? The author's argument was that particle number is not relativistically invariant, so how many particles there are is as relative as left/right, up/down, rest/motion.[4]

There are, of course, still other attempts to identify precisely what it is to be physical or material. One to be found quite often is to equate the material or physical—almost nonchalantly—with what is located in space and time. Is that a good criterion for distinguishing what is material or physical from what is not? There does not seem to be a satisfactory conceptual connection. First of all, angels, demons, and God himself have been said to appear fully at certain places and times, although they are usually cited as paradigm examples of the nonphysical. These are, of course, examples of entities that are able to manifest themselves in space-time but are not at all times localized there. Should we then refine the criterion to something like "what is physical is precisely what is at all times fully localized in space"? It does not seem so, for elementary particles as conceived by the Copenhagen school of quantum mechanics are presumably physical but do not meet that criterion. As the electron is captured when it hits the television monitor screen, it has a particular location, but it did not have a well-defined spatio-temporal trajectory beforehand. Indeed, it is easy to show in the quantum mechanics developed at that time that if a particle's location is at a given moment in a well-defined finite spatial region, that condition will not last very long at all. So the electron is, as it were, going in and out of space. Is this, then, an example of the nonphysical? Did these physicists introduce immaterial substances into physics? It seems better to conclude that the spatio-temporal location criterion does not match materialists' understanding of their own thesis, either.

Whenever philosophers take some general feature of physics and use it to identify what is material, what happens? Physics soon goes on to describe things that lack that feature and are altogether different. When that happens, does materialism bite the dust? Surely not! But if materialism were really, purely and simply, some such thesis as "everything is composed of elementary particles," I could not so readily say "Surely not"!

14 Two Moves for Materialists

Soi-disant materialists have certainly taken cognizance of this difficulty. When their most important terms are tied to current scientific theories, they must die with those theories; but if not, they seem to lack content altogether. That is a dilemma. In response, they have opted for one of two moves. Some have attempted to formulate very specific theses relating to the putative subject matter of psychology, argued that these are empirical, and offered the results as a specific version of materialism. Others have pinned the thesis down by nailing it to a specific science such as physics, by means of a completeness claim for that science. It seems to me, and I will try to show, that neither move leaves us with materialism as an identifiable substantive thesis.

The First Move: Materialism as Scientific Hypothesis

Place argued that it is tenable to say that certain events and processes traditionally classified as mental (for example, sensation) are identical with events and processes in the brain.[5] That this is indeed so he labeled as materialism and argued that it is in fact a scientific, empirical hypothesis.[6] The described "mental" events and processes have a certain complexity, which brain events and processes may or may not have. Empirical evidence for such higher complexity would disconfirm the hypothesis. The name "materialism" is also given to this or closely similar claims about the psychological by, for example, David Armstrong.[7]

I have three preliminary questions. First, not every replacement for what I have called the thesis can be accepted as the "real" materialism; can this one? The principal question before us is what exactly the materialist's main thesis could be. We should perhaps accept any seriously offered contender. But if we could identify certain familiar psychological events and processes with physiological ones, we would hardly be finished with the traditional concerns of materialism. That a person has a purpose, for example, does not consist in any specific type of occurrent event or process; nor that her sins are forgiven, that she is in a state of grace, or that she is precious beyond rubies. And these are only examples about persons; what else may there not be between heaven and earth never dreamt of in materialist philosophy? I don't want to be fanciful, but merely establishing that sensations are brain states seems hardly more than a drop in the bucket for the materialist. The virtue of such a ringing thesis as "matter is all" was to settle the hash of all such stuff once and for all.

The second preliminary question: Does the description of the "mental" or the psychological in terms of which the replacement thesis is formulated do justice to its intended concern? Armstrong was rather more conscious than was Place of the second preliminary question when he was debating Malcolm, a Wittgensteinian. Today he would also have to contend with putative failures of functionalism, arguments that no computational theory of consciousness could even in principle be successful, and demonstrations that truth conditions for belief attributions must have historical and social parameters outside the believer.

But leave these debates aside. Here is the main question: Supposing the empirical claim is false or is scientifically investigated and found wanting, will there or will there not be a fall-back position to call "the real materialism after all"?

It would be a poor game if after much scientific strife the loser could say, "that's not it at all, that is not what I meant at all." Well, what if we accept Place's or Armstrong's formulation, and their empirical claims are found wanting? Suppose, for example, that no neurological process can be identified that can even in principle predict human decisions. The next empirical question would be: What probabilities can be assigned to the (neutrally described) actions being decided on, conditional on the states of the central nervous system? If these probabilities cannot even in principle be made as near zero and one as we would like, is that the end of materialism?

Think of the exact parallel: no quantum state will predict the exact time of radioactive decay. The probability of decay within a given time period cannot be brought arbitrarily close to zero or one no matter how much information we get about the physical situation. Is that the end of materialism? It is not; and neither would materialism come to an end if what humans do could be related only probabilistically to their brain states. People would simply be more like bits of radium than we had suspected. A favorite belief of the materialists would have to be relinquished, but they would all know how to retrench. Human behavior would simply be more like radioactive decay than we had thought, that is all. The spirit of materialism is never exhausted in piece-meal empirical claims.[8]

The Second Move: Whatever It Takes

If you press a materialist, you quickly find the most important constraint on the meaning of the thesis. That constraint is simply that it should be compatible with science, whatever science comes up with. That is contrary to what some of them say. If, they say, certain phenomena could not be explained purely in terms of material factors, then the scientific thing to do would be to give up materialism. But, holding the thesis, they make the bold conjecture that this will never happen. That what would never happen?

If that question cannot be answered with a precise and independent account of what material factors are, there is still one option. That is to nail a completeness claim to science or to a specific science such as physics. The instructive example here is Smart, who begins his essay "Materialism" with an offer to explain what he means: "By 'materialism' I mean the theory that there is nothing in the world over and above those entities which are postulated by physics (or, or course, those entities which will be postulated by future and more adequate physical theories)."[9] He quickly discusses some older and more recent postulations in actual physics, which make that "theory" look substantive. But of course the parenthetical qualification makes that discussion completely irrelevant!

Smart may believe, or think that he believes, the "theory" here formulated, but if he does, he certainly does not know what he believes. For of course he has no more idea than you or I of what physics will postulate in the future. It is a truly courageous faith that believes in an "I know not what"—is it not?

Indeed, in believing this, Smart cannot be certain that he believes anything at all. Suppose science goes on forever, and every theory is eventually succeeded by a better one. That has certainly been the case so far, and always some accepted successor has implied that the previously postulated fundamental entities (known, after all, only by description) do not exist. If that is also how it will continue, world without end, then Smart's so-called theory—as formulated above—entails that there is nothing at all. Let's not be too quick to celebrate this demonstration of clear empirical content.

In a clear indication that he is at least subliminally aware of the problem, Smart quickly adds some extra content. Not content with his initial formulation once he realizes that it is compatible with emergent properties, holism, and the irreducibility of biology to physics, he says, "I wish to lay down that it is incompatible with materialism that there should be any irreducibly emergent laws or properties, say in biology or psychology.... I also want to deny any theory of 'emergent properties'" (ibid., pp. 203–4). We should read this as an *amendment* of the above definition of materialism. The "theory" formulated above, taken by itself, did not imply any of that. Just how does Smart know that his initial formulation was inadequate? Is he telling us that he knows that either physics will forever eschew emergent properties or else materialism is false? Since quantum physics may provide, at this point, a clear example of holism (as argued, for example, by Paul Teller), should we conclude that materialism may already have come to an end?

Of course not. Faced with the consequences of his own idea—that materialism should be whatever it takes to be a completeness claim for physics—Smart started backpedaling. Everything that is "repugnant" to him (to use his phrase) may eventually come to be incorporated in future physics. So Smart adds, in effect, that physics will be false if that happens. But faced with that consequence, no materialists will stick by him if he sticks by that. They'll point out, quite rightly, that he was of a "classical" mind, and as so often happens with the older generation in physics itself, quite unable to assimilate new visions of the structure of the *material* world.[10]

15 Materialism as False Consciousness

So is it all just a matter of scientific reactionaries with their self-trivializing theses dressed up as uncompromising metaphysical constraints on science? No, it is not. All this effort to codify materialism bespeaks something much more important: the spirit of materialism. Materialism is a hardy philosophical tradition that appears differently substantiated in each philosophical era. Each instantiation has its empirical as well as its nonempirical claims, which interpret for that era, in its own terms, the invariant attitudes and convictions that I call here the "spirit of materialism."

How shall we identify what is really involved in materialism? Our great clue is the apparent ability of materialists to revise the content of their main thesis as science changes. If we took literally the claim of a materialist that his position is a simple belief, we would be faced with an insoluble mystery, for that belief would then consist in the claim that all is matter, as currently construed. If that were all there was to it, how would such a materialist know how to retrench when his favorite scientific hypotheses fail? How did the eighteenth-century materialists know that gravity, or forces in general, were material? By the end of that century, Baron d'Holbach's *Système de la Nature* defined materialism on the European continent, but it had become scientifically obsolete only a generation or two later. Nothing in d'Holbach's description of nature allowed for the new theories of light, electricity, and magnetism.[11] How did the materialists know in the nineteenth century that the electromagnetic field was material, and how did later materialists persist in this conviction after the ether had been sent packing?

Perhaps a materialist could reply that it is possible to measure certain quantities and that this is his cue to what is material. But that cannot provide the criterion needed. Just think again of the transition from Cartesian to Newtonian physics. Newton identified forces as the causes of changes in states of motion. Accordingly, if you measure the direction and rate of change of momentum, you obtain a description of that cause in terms of its effects. The recipe for measuring force direction and magnitude is exactly to measure those effects. But even if the effects are motions of material bodies, it does not follow logically that the cause is material. As far as logic is concerned, one could add consistently that these causes are immaterial, spiritual—even mental, if Mind does not need to be someone's mind. But instead the forces are said to be material just like the extended bodies so classified before. If this is a claim to knowledge, the materialist must seemingly have some rather mysterious power: a knowledge that the newly introduced entities have the *je ne sais quoi* that makes for materiality.

It is quite clear now: the new conclusion that the newly introduced entities are material too is not a matter of knowledge at all. But what is it, then, in this metaphysical position, that guides the change in content, which it would be pedantic to signal with a change in name? If the "physicalist" or "naturalist" part of this philosophical position is mainly the desire or commitment to have metaphysics guided by physics, then it is something that cannot be captured in any thesis or factual belief. If the position does not mainly consist in such a desire or commitment, then what is it? This knowing how to retrench cannot derive from the substantive belief which is (at that time) identified with the view that all is physical. So what does it derive from? Whatever the answer is, that, and not the explicit thesis, is the real answer to what materialism is.

Hence I propose the following diagnosis of materialism: it is not identifiable with a theory about what there is but only with an attitude or cluster of attitudes. These attitudes include strong deference to the current content of science in matters of opinion about what there is. They include also an inclination (and perhaps a commitment, at least an intention) to accept (approximative) completeness claims for science as actually constituted at any given time.[12] Let us call these the first and second characteristics of materialism. Given this diagnosis, the apparent knowledge of what is and what is not material among newly hypothesized entities is mere appearance. The ability to adjust the content of the thesis that all is matter again and again is explained instead by a knowing-how to retrench that derives from invariant attitudes.

This does not reflect badly on materialism; on the contrary, it gives materialism its due.[13] But it does imply that only the confusion of theses held with attitudes expressed, which yields false consciousness, can account for the conviction that science requires or implies materialism.

16 Materialism without False Consciousness?

I mean the above as a diagnosis of materialism, not an indictment or refutation. Its incarnation at any moment will be some position distinguished by certain empirical consequences, and these will either stand or fall as science evolves. But whether they stand or fall, materialism as general philosophical position, as historical tradition in philosophy, will survive. Given this, however, there can, for that very reason, be no question of regarding materialism as an assumption at the foundations of science. There is no "presumptive materialism" that constrains scientific theories to consistency with certain determinate factual theses. Materialism itself is not so constrained, and it survives by changing so as to accommodate the new sciences.

We may take this in part as explanation of something that materialism has in common with other hardy perennials of philosophy. Besides the theses on which the day's materialists take their stand, and which vary with time, there is also such a thing as the "spirit of materialism," which never dies. False consciousness can be avoided in two ways:

(1) the philosopher may lack that spirit and be genuinely concerned solely with certain definite factual questions about what there is, or

(2) the philosopher may have that spirit and not confuse its expression with any particular view of what the world is like.

The latter, however, may never yet have been instantiated among philosophers.[14]

Nevertheless, the second option is the really interesting one and similar to the one I would favor for any attempt to continue the empiricist tradition. The problem for materialists will then be to identify the true materialist stance and for the empiricist to identify the true empiricist stance (or the spectrum of true empiricist stances). Being or becoming an empiricist will then be similar or analogous to conversion to a cause, a religion, an ideology, to capitalism or to socialism, to a worldview such as Dawkins's selfish gene view or the view Russell expressed in "Why I Am Not a Christian." That is so, and not perhaps a prospect to everyone's liking. But let us not color the project with guilt by association. If I am right, all the great philosophical movements have really been of this sort, at heart, even if different in purport; what I favor is that we should do what we do without false purport. . . .

Notes

1. I will focus on a distinctly old-fashioned but straightforward sort of materialism. The argument seems to me not affected by such questions as whether the psychological reduces to or is merely supervenient on the physical. It also seems rather amusing to me that lately materialism has gone to formulations that presuppose just the sort of metaphysics that earlier materialists classed with the occult, such as realism about modalities. For a relevant critique of how contemporary materialists think to help themselves to bits of metaphysics, see Putnam, "After Empiricism" (a review of Ayer's *Philosophy in the Twentieth Century*), especially pp. 26–28. For a critical look at "supervenience" and the body–mind problem in the late twentieth century, with strong arguments against "token-identity" theories of mind, see Kim, *Mind in a Physical World*. But see also Clark Glymour's review of Kim's book, with its reflections on the ingression of analytic metaphysics into questions that properly belong to the empirical sciences.

2. Thus Galen Strawson's "Real Materialism" begins with "Materialism is the view that every thing and event in the universe is physical in every respect, that 'physical phenomenon' is coextensive with 'real phenomenon' or at least with 'real, concrete phenomenon.'"

3. Eleonore Stump's paper on Aquinas ("Non-Cartesian Substance Dualism and Materialism Without Reductionism") is very instructive here. If Aquinas's doctrine on souls is coherent it is at least not a mind–body dualism.

4. Davies, "Particles Do Not Exist."

5. Place, "Is Consciousness a Brain Process?"

6. Smart, "Sensations and Brain Processes"; Place, "Materialism as a Scientific Hypothesis." Place agreed in response to Smart that the conditions required for the assertability of such a hypothesis—conditions under which alone such an identity statement can be true—are subject to philosophical debate rather than empirical testing. But once such conditions are specified, the remaining question is empirical.

7. See, e.g., Armstrong's half of Armstrong and Malcolm, *Consciousness and Causality*, and his *Materialist Theory of Mind*.

8. Not to be forgotten in this connection is eliminative materialism, which is an option even if the logical structures of psychological and physicalist discourse are so mismatched as to preclude any form of reduction or supervenience. That was a great insight of Feyerabend, Sellars, Rorty, and Churchland, who did not care to play for such "small" stakes as Place did. Armstrong, however, says that if he were to be convinced of the irreducibility he would reluctantly become a dualist. I wonder if this means that he knows of a coherent and at least minimally adequate mind–body dualism? (For a critique of eliminative materialism, see Philipse, "Absolute Network Theory of Language and Traditional Epistemology.")

9. "Materialism," ch. 16 of his *Essays Metaphysical and Moral*; the paper was originally published in 1963. The passage quoted could be, for greater clarity, followed by David Lewis's acknowledgment that as physics changes, so must any such thesis: "[Materialism] was so named when the best physics of the day was the physics of matter alone. Now our best physics acknowledges other bearers of fundamental properties. . . . But it would be pedantry to change the name on that ac-

count" ("Reduction of Mind," p. 413). This is at the same time the continuation of Lewis's "Argument for the Identity Theory," which clearly belongs to the tradition of "Australian materialism" we are here examining.

10. A robust materialism may of course include a whole-hearted endorsement of the current physics as correct or essentially so. Thus David Lewis characterizes the materialism to which he subscribes as "metaphysics built to endorse the truth and descriptive completeness of physics more or less as we know it" (*Philosophical Papers* 2:x, n.). Galen Strawson cites this in his "Real Materialism" and disputes it, not wishing materialism to be saddled with so much faith in physics as it presently stands, but does not provide an alternative way to demarcate the physical from the nonphysical.

11. A century later Ludwig Buechner's *Force and Matter* compares very favorably with d'Holbach's work as far as knowledge of the sciences of the day was concerned. But Buechner belonged to that triumphal, scientifically enlightened part of the nineteenth century that was just about to see its most fundamental views of nature abandoned in the physical sciences. Again, in Buechner's writings, the position was presented as a view of what there is in the universe, oblivious to such possibilities of change in science.

12. The attitudes described here contrast with those I take to be typical of empiricism, of deference to or admiration for science as a paradigm of rational inquiry, characterized by mutual and self-criticism. The empiricist attitude does not imply deference to science in matters of opinion but rather a certain epistemic detachment with respect to the content of current or even ideal science. I will return to this below.

13. What exactly is the spirit of materialism? I will try to say a little more later on. The making explicit of materialism, however, in the sense of a perennial philosophy, or support for the conclusion that it can exist without false consciousness, is properly a task for the materialists themselves. I would ask the reader to compare here two instances of recent work, both historically conscious and well-informed, but one of them naïve (in the sense of being directly vulnerable to the above sort of critique) and the other more sophisticated. The first is Vitzthum's *Materialism: An Affirmative History and Definition*. To see quite clearly how his view is posed on the edge between a strong commitment and a factual thesis about nature, turn first to chapter 6, "A Summary Definition of Materialism." The second is Jean Bricmont's reply, "Qu'est-ce que le matérialisme scientifique?," to a review of his joint book with Sokal. Read this in conjunction with his "Comment peut-on être 'positiviste'?" to see how a large part of his position allies closely with what I characterize as empiricism, while not leaving the materialist tradition as I view it here.

14. As final sidelight on this I would refer to Paul Feyerabend's early essay on materialism (1963, with 1980 postscript, in *Realism, Rationalism, and Scientific Method*). At the outset he specifies that the argument might as well focus on ancient atomism as on contemporary science, and his phrasing suggests that any materialist thesis takes the form of a completeness claim for a certain scientific description of the world. It also suggests that philosophical disputes concerning materialism are entirely independent of the content of the thesis in question. If both suggestions are correct, there is already a serious question whether there is any such thing as the philosophical thesis that materialism purports to be. In the note added in 1980 he arrives at something like the conception of materialism as stance: "It may well be that a materialistic language ... is richer in cognitive content than commonsense.... But it will be much poorer in other respects. For example, it will lack the associations which now connect mental events with emotions, our relations to others, and which are the basis of the arts and the humanities." He adds, "The choice concerns the quality of our lives—it is a moral choice."

References

Armstrong, David M. *A Materialist Theory of Mind* (London: Routledge and Kegan Paul, 1968).

Armstrong, David M., and Norman Malcolm. *Consciousness and Causality* (Oxford: Blackwell, 1984).

Bricmont, Jean. "Comment Peut-On Être 'Positiviste'?" In Francis Martens, ed., *Psychanalyse, Que Reste-t-il de Nos Amours?* (Brussells: Revue de l'Université de Bruxelles, Editions Complexe, 2000), 71–90.

Bricmont, Jean. "Q'est-ce Que Le Matérialisme Scientifique?" Part 1, *La Raison* 441 (May 1999): 19–20; Part II, *La Raison* 442 (June 1999): 20–21.

Ludwig Buechner. *Kraft und Stoff* (Frankfurt: Meidinger, 1855); trans. J. F. Collingwood as *Force and Matter: Empirico-Philosophical Studies Intelligibly Rendered* (London, 1870).

Davies, P. C. W. "Particles Do Not Exist." In S. Christensen, ed., *Quantum Theory of Gravity* (Bristol: Hilger, 1984), 66–77.

Baron D'Holbach. *Système de la Nature* (1770).

Feyerabend, Paul. "Materialism and the Mind Body/Problem." *Review of Metaphysics* 17 (1963); reprinted with postscript in *Realism, Rationalism, and Scientific Method: Philosophical Papers,* volume 1 (Cambridge: Cambridge University Press, 1980).

Glymour, Clark. "A Mind Is a Terrible Thing to Waste: Review of Jaegwon Kim, *Mind in a Physical World.*" *Philosophy of Science* 66 (1999): 455–471.

Kim, Jaegwon. *Mind in a Physical World* (Cambridge, Mass.: MIT Press, 1998).

Lewis, David. "Reduction of Mind." In S. Guttenplan, ed., *A Companion to the Philosophy of Mind* (Oxford: Blackwell, 1994).

Lewis, David. "An Argument for the Identity Theory." *Journal of Philosophy* 63 (1966): 17–25; reprinted with additions in Lewis, *Philosophical Papers,* volume 1 (Oxford: Oxford University Press, 1983).

Lewis, David. *Philosophical Papers,* volume 2 (Oxford: Oxford University Press, 1986).

Philipse, Herman. "The Absolute Network Theory of Language and Traditional Epistemology." *Inquiry* 33 (1990): 127–178.

Place, U. T. "Is Consciousness a Brain Process?" *British Journal of Psychology* 47 (1956): 44–50.

Place, U. T. "Materialism as a Scientific Hypothesis." *Philosophical Review* 69 (1960): 101–104.

Putnam, Hilary. "After Empiricism." In John Rachman and Cornell West, eds., *Post-Analytic Philosophy* (New York: Columbia University Press, 1985), 20–30.

Sokal, Alan, and Jean Bricmont. *Fashionable Nonsense* (Picador, 1999).

Strawson, Galen. "Real Materialism." In Louise Antony and Norbert Hornstein, eds., *Chomsky and His Critics* (Oxford: Blackwell, 2003).

Smart, J. J. C. "Sensations and Brain Processes." *Philosophical Review* 68 (1959); revised version in Smart, *Essays Metaphysical and Moral* (Oxford: Blackwell, 1987).

Smart, J. J. C. "Materialism." *Journal of Philosophy* 60 (1963): 651–662; reprinted in Smart, *Essays Metaphysical and Moral* (Oxford: Blackwell, 1987).

Stump, Eleonore. "Non-Cartesian Substance Dualism and Materialism without Reductionism." *Faith and Philosophy* 12 (1999): 505–531.

Vitzthum, Richard C. *Materialism: An Affirmative History and Definition* (Amherst, N.Y.: Prometheus, 1995).

C Mind and Subjective Experience

21 From *Mind and the World Order*

C. I. Lewis

There are, in our cognitive experience, two elements; the immediate data, such as those of sense, which are presented or given to the mind, and a form, construction, or interpretation, which represents the activity of thought. Recognition of this fact is one of the oldest and most universal of philosophic insights. However, the manner in which these elements, and their relation to one another, are conceived, varies in the widest possible manner, and divergence on this point marks a principal distinction amongst theories of knowledge. As a result, even the most general attempt to designate these two elements—as by the terms used above—is likely to be objected to. Nevertheless this distinction, in some terms or other, is admitted to a place in almost every philosophy. To suppress it altogether, would be to betray obvious and fundamental characteristics of experience....

There is, in all experience, that element which we are aware that we do not create by thinking and cannot, in general, displace or alter. As a first approximation, we may designate it as "the sensuous."

At the moment, I have a fountain pen in my hand. When I so describe this item of my present experience, I make use of terms whose meaning I have learned. Correlatively I abstract this item from the total field of my present consciousness and relate it to what is not just now present in ways which I have learned and which reflect modes of action which I have acquired. It might happen that I remember my first experience of such a thing. If so, I should find that this sort of presentation did not then mean "fountain pen" to me. I bring to the present moment something which I did not then bring; a relation of this to other actual and possible experiences, and a classification of what is here presented with things which I did not then include in the same group. This present classification depends on that learned relation of this experience to other possible experience and to my action, which the shape, size, etc., of this object was not then a sign of. A savage in New Guinea, lacking certain interests and habits of action which are mine, would not so classify it. There is, to be sure, something in the character of this thing as a merely presented colligation of sense-qualities which is for me the clue to this classification or meaning; but that just this complex of qualities should be due to a "pen" character of the object is something which has been acquired. Yet what I refer to as "the given" in this experience is, in broad terms, qualitatively no different than it would be if I were an infant or an ignorant savage.

Again, suppose my present interest to be slightly altered. I might then describe this object which is in my hand as "a cylinder" or "hard rubber" or "a poor buy." In each case the thing is somewhat differently related in my mind, and the connoted modes of my possible behavior toward it, and my further experience of it, are different. Something called "given" remains constant, but its character as sign, its classification, and its relation to other things and to action are differently taken.

In whatever terms I describe this item of my experience, I shall not convey it *merely* as given, but shall supplement this by a meaning which has to do with relations, and particularly with relation to other experiences which I regard as possible but which are not just now actual. The manner of this supplementation reflects my habitual interests and modes of activity, the nature of my mind. The infant may see it much as I do, but still it will mean to him none of these things I have described it as being, but merely "plaything" or "smooth biteable." But for any mind whatever, it will be more than what is merely given if it be noted at all. Some meaning of it also will be contained in the experience. All that comes under this broad term "meaning" (unless immediate value or the specificity of sense-quality should be included) is brought to this experience by the mind, as is evidenced by the fact that in this respect the experience is alterable to my interest and my will. . . .

My designation of this thing as "pen" reflects my purpose to write; as "cylinder" my desire to explain a problem in geometry or mechanics; as "a poor buy" my resolution to be more careful hereafter in my expenditures. These divergent purposes are anticipatory of certain different future contingencies which are expected to accrue, in each case, partly as a result of my own action.

The distinction between this element of interpretation and the given is emphasized by the fact that the latter is what remains unaltered, no matter what our interests, no matter how we think or conceive. I can apprehend this thing as pen or rubber or cylinder, but I cannot, by taking thought, discover it as paper or soft or cubical.

While we can thus isolate the element of the given by these criteria of its unalterability and its character as sensuous feel or quality, we cannot describe any particular given *as such,* because in describing it, in whatever fashion, we qualify it by bringing it under some category or other, select from it, emphasize aspects of it, and relate it in particular and avoidable ways. If there be states of pure esthesis, in violent emotion or in the presence of great art, which are unqualified by thought, even these can be conveyed—and perhaps even retained in memory—only when they have been rendered articulate by thought. So that in a sense the given is ineffable, always. It is that which remains untouched and unaltered, however it is construed by thought. Yet no one but a philosopher could for a moment deny this immediate presence in consciousness of that which no activity of thought can create or alter. . . .

The given, as here conceived, is certainly an abstraction. Unless there be such a thing as pure esthesis (and I should join with the critic in doubting this), the given never exists in isolation in any experience or state of consciousness. Any Kantian "manifold" as a psychic datum or moment of experience, is probably a fiction, and the assumption of it as such is a methodological error. The given is *in,* not before, experience. But the condemnation of abstractions is the condemnation of thought itself. Nothing that thought can ever comprise is other than some abstraction which cannot exist in isolation. . . . Thought can do just two things: it can separate, by analysis, entities which in their temporal or spatial existence are not separated, and it can conjoin, by synthesis, entities which in their existence are disjoined. Only the mystic or those who conceive that man would be better off without an upper-brain, have ground for objection to analysis and abstractions. The only important question is whether this abstracted element, the "given," is genuinely to be discovered in experience. On this point I can, of course, only appeal to the reader. I shall hope that he has already identified provisionally what the word intends, and proceed upon that basis. . . .

Even in that sense in which the given is always one whole, it is not important for our purpose of analyzing knowledge that we should dwell upon this integrality of it. Our interest is, rather, in the *element* of givenness in what we may, for usual and commonplace reasons, mark off as "an experience" or "an object." This given element in a single experience of an object is what will be meant by "a presentation." Such a presentation is, obviously, an event and historically unique. But for most of the purposes of analyzing knowledge one presentation of a half-dollar held at right angles to the line of vision, etc., will be as good as another. If, then, I speak of "*the* presentation" of this or that, it will be on the supposition that the reader can provide his own illustration. No identification of the event itself with the repeatable content of it is intended.

In any presentation, this content is either a specific quale (such as the immediacy of redness or loudness) or something analyzable into a complex of such. The presentation as an event is, of course, unique, but the qualia which make it up are not. They are recognizable from one to another experience. . . .

. . . As will be pointed out later, what any concept denotes—or any adjective such as "red" or "round"—is something more complex than an identifiable sense-quale. In particular, the object of the concept must always have a time-span which extends beyond the specious present; this is essential to the cognitive significance of concepts. The qualia of sense as something given do not, in the nature of the case, have such temporal spread. Moreover, such qualia, though repeatable in experience and intrinsically recognizable, have no names. They are fundamentally different from the "universals" of logic and of traditional problems concerning these. . . .

It is of the essence of what will here be meant by "the given" that it should be *given*. We need not say that what is given is a "mental state" or even "in the mind" in any more explicit sense than is itself implied in such givenness. Nor should it be presumed that what is thus in mind is *exclusively* mental. The nature of that interpretation or construction by which we come to know objects suggests that the given must be, in some sense or other, a constituent of objective reality as well. All such questions are simply *later questions*. If there should be metaphysical problems concerning the kind of reality which what is "in mind" may have, it is not necessary to anticipate the solution of these beyond what may be verified in the discovery that certain items or aspects of the content of experience satisfy the criteria of givenness. These are, first, its specific sensuous or feeling-character, and second, that the mode of thought can neither create nor alter it—that it remains unaffected by any change of mental attitude or interest. It is the second of these criteria which is definitive; the first alone is not sufficient, for reasons which will appear.

This given element is never, presumably, to be discovered in isolation. If the content of perception is first given and then, in a later moment, interpreted, we have no consciousness of such a first state of intuition unqualified by thought, though we *do* observe *alteration* and *extension* of interpretation of given content as a psychological temporal process. A state of intuition utterly unqualified by thought is a figment of the metaphysical imagination, satisfactory only to those who are willing to substitute a dubious hypothesis for the analysis of knowledge as we find it. The given is admittedly an excised element or abstraction; all that is here claimed is that it is not an "unreal" abstraction, but an identifiable constituent in experience. . . .

Psychological differences of individuals are indeed impressive. Long before scientific psychology was thought of, the skeptic appealed to them to prove the impossibility of knowledge or the communication of ideas. For imagery and feeling, and even to some extent for sensation, idiosyncrasy is the rule. Furthermore, as the ancient skeptic was fond of pointing out, there can be no final verification of any community in these respects. The sense-quality of green cannot be conveyed to the congenitally blind; and if I suppose some idiosyncrasy of sense which makes my perception of green unique, I shall never discover that peculiarity provided it does not impair my powers to discriminate and relate as others do. In brief, there can be no verification of community between minds so far as it is a question of the feeling side of experience, though the assumption that there is no community here seems fantastic. . . .

. . . Knowledge must always concern principally the relations which obtain between one experience and another, particularly those relations into which the knower himself may enter as an active factor. It is the given as thus conceptually interpreted which is envisaged as the real object.

. . . Words represent rather large and ready-made wholes—relatively stable and relatively simple concepts which are a somewhat loose fit for the precise and complex knowledge of perceived objects. In a glance of the eye, so to speak, we apprehend what whole paragraphs will do no more than suggest. Language is primarily useful for conveying *generalizations* or else very specific abstracted items of experience. Not only is that knowledge of an object which is mediated by perception something which is usually difficult to convey precisely in words but usually it is not important to convey it in more than very partial fashion, since those who are required to act directly toward what is presented to us are usually those who are also present to it themselves.

In fact, this difference between what words convey and what perception mediates is so marked that it may suggest a distinction of two kinds of knowledge; direct knowledge of objects (acquaintance with), gained by the presentation of them in experience and immediately verifiable, and propositional knowledge or generalization (knowledge about) which concerns more than can be given at one time and thus requires some mental synthesis of what is temporally disjoined.

Such a dichotomy, however, would be falsely taken. It is the first thesis of this chapter that there is no knowledge merely by acquaintance; that knowledge *always* transcends the immediately given. The merely contemplated or enjoyed may possess esthetic significance, but if it is to have cognitive meaning this immediacy must become the subject of an interpretation which transcends it; we must take toward the given some attitude which serves practical action and relates it to what is not given. . . .

. . . This interpretation has the character of a generalization which has been learned. I phrase it by saying "That (denoting the given presentation) is a sweet apple (connoting among other things the possible taste)." If I should be completely absorbed in the first given, as an infant might, then I should frame no concept, it would have no meaning, and no action, unless a merely instinctive one, would be evoked. An object such as an apple is never given; between the real apple in all its complexity and this fragmentary presentation, lies that interval which only interpretation can bridge. The "objectivity" of this experience means *the verifiability of a further possible experience which is attributed by this interpretation.*

The notion that there is a simple sort of knowledge, gained by direct apprehension alone, has two major sources. In the first place it is falsely supposed that there are some concepts at least which denote "simple qualities"—something which can be directly exhibited in a single experience. And second, the word "knowledge" is sometimes used for that enjoyment or contemplation which projects no purposes but is completely absorbed in the given as an esthetic object. (Whether there are any experiences which have exclusively this character is open to doubt, but at least experience may have this ingredient or this aspect.) Putting these two together, it is easy to arrive at the erroneous conclusion that there is a kind of cognitive apprehension—of simple qualities or essences—which terminates directly in the given; it may even be supposed that other knowledge rises out of this by some kind of complication and thus that direct awareness is the simplest and the basic type of knowledge.

That there is direct apprehension of the immediate, it would be absurd to deny; but confusion is likely to arise if we call it "knowledge." There are no "simple qualities" which are named by any name; there is no concept the denotation of which does not extent beyond the immediately given, and beyond what *could be* immediately given. And without concepts, there is no knowledge.

There *are* recognizable qualitative characters of the given, which may be repeated in different experiences, and are thus a sort of universals; I call these "qualia." But although such qualia are universals, in the sense of being recognized from one to another experience, they must be distinguished from the properties of objects. Confusion of these two is characteristic of many historical conceptions, as well as of current essence-theories. The quale is directly intuited, given, and is not the subject of any possible error because it is purely subjective. The property of an object is objective; the ascription of it is a judgment which may be mistaken; and what the predication of it asserts is something which transcends what could be given in any single experience....

Qualia are universals, and they are universals such that without the recognition of them by the individual nothing presented in experience could be named or understood or known at all....

Qualia are subjective; they have no names in ordinary discourse but are indicated by some circumlocution such as "looks like"; they are ineffable, since they might be different in two minds with no possibility of discovering that fact and no necessary inconvenience to our knowledge of objects or their properties. All that can be done to designate a quale is, so to speak, to locate it in experience, that is, to designate the conditions of its recurrence or other relations of it. Such location does not touch the quale itself; if one such could be lifted out of the network of its relations, in the total experience of the individual, and replaced by another, no social interest or interest of action would be affected by such substitution. What is essential for understanding and for communication is not the quale as such but that pattern of its stable relations in experience which is what is implicitly predicated when it is taken as the sign of an objective property.

Apprehension of the presented quale, being immediate, stands in no need of verification; it is impossible to be mistaken about it. Awareness of it is not judgment in any sense in which judgment may be verified; it is not knowledge in any sense in which "knowledge" connotes the opposite of error....

An immediate quale apart from some relational context which "locates" it in experience is intrinsically and absolutely inarticulate. It is inarticulate not only in the sense that it cannot be expressed to another; it would be impossible for it to be abstracted and envisaged as an object of our own thought. Imagine a man to suffer all his life from toothache, but in such wise that no pressure on the jaw, no change of temperature or of the heart-beat, no behavior of himself or difference of surroundings would ever alter it. Not only would a person so afflicted be unaware that he suffered toothache—it would not in fact *be a toothache*; he could not even become conscious of the *ache* as a distinct fact of his experience. He would be aware of it as the cow is aware of hunger, perhaps, but it would never become for him an explicit object of thought. Such an all-pervasive ingredient of experience could never become articulate, because it would lack the ground of any possible discrimination and relation. No language could express it; there would be no thinking to be done about it; there would be no possibility of bounding it or eliciting it as a separate fact. For the person in question, it would be a part of his life or a coloring of reality but no part of his knowledge. The concept of a toothache does not consist of the ache but—broadly speaking—in the apprehension of what brought it on and the formula for getting rid of it. All that is intelligible about it is the set of relations in which it stands.

There are no concepts of immediate qualia as such—not because the word "concept" as here used has any unnecessary connotation of the verbal, but because articulation is the setting of bounds and establishing of connections; because what does not affect discrimination and relation has no handle by which the mind can take hold of it. It would be erroneous to take this fact to mean some positive bafflement in the presence of the immediate, because there is here no question we can ask which fails to find an answer; there is no interest which is baffled. The interest of knowledge is for action, and action proceeds by way of relation.

If, then, we take "simple ideas" such as "blue" and "round" as, so to speak, the least concepts that there are, we find that what such concepts embrace is not an immediate quale as such but some stable pattern of relations. We have concepts of objective properties—these are indicated by the manner in which we should proceed to verify the blueness of the blue blotter or the roundness of the penny. The manner in which such verification must take place is obvious. To verify a shape, we walk around the object or manipulate it. Its successive perspectives and their relation to our behavior meanwhile, must present a certain order of temporal relationships. If it is a small object, we may corroborate the visual by tactile and kinesthetic impressions. If a large one, we may measure it. Feeling the roundness of a marble as we roll it between thumb and fingers, or measuring a house, is again a temporally extended and ordered relation of apprehended qualia. To verify a color, we change the conditions of illumination or alter the angle so as to get rid of the sheen, or we bring the thing into juxtaposition with some object whose color has previously been tested or is accepted as a standard of comparison. When we thus manipulate the object or behave toward it, we must know what we expect if it really is round or blue, or what not. If what is thus predicted does not supervene, then our first ascription of the objective property will be withdrawn as proven false. The objective reality of the property consists, of course, from the point of view of knowledge, of what would verify it, and includes everything the failure of which would lead to the withdrawal of the judgment as mistaken. The concept of the blueness or roundness of an object which is presented includes all that is essential to the truth of the predication of the property. Thus what constitutes the existence of an objective property and the applicability of a concept—even of the simplest sort—is not a given quale alone but an ordered relation of different qualia, relative to different conditions or behavior. This pattern or order, which is what the adjective names, will always be *temporally extended* (which is the same as to say that the predication of the property is something *verifiable*), and always it will have relation to our own possible ways of acting toward the presented object.

... If concepts are to be articulate and meaningful, then the application of them must be something verifiable; which means that what they denote must have a temporal spread. Not a momentary presented quale but an ordered relationship of such, is the least that can be meaningfully named. The predication of a property on the basis of momentarily presented experience, is in the nature of an hypothesis, which predicts something definitely specifiable in further possible experience, and something which such experience may corroborate or falsify. The identifiable character of presented qualia is *necessary to* the predication of objective properties and to the recognition of objects, but it is not *sufficient for* the verification of what such predication and recognition implicitly assert, both because what is thus asserted transcends the given and has the significance of the prediction of further possible experience, and because the *same* property may be validly predicated on the basis of *different* presented qualia, and *different* properties may be signalized by the *same* presented quale. If the denotation of any concept were an immediately apprehensible quale or complex of such, then the ascription of this concept when such qualia were presented could not conceivably be in error. That the predication of a property may be mistaken, or the perception of it illusory, corroborates the fact that what is involved in the cognition of the property transcends the given. One cannot be mistaken about the content of an immediate awareness. If I have bitten an apple, I cannot be mistaken about the taste in my mouth. But I may conceivably fall into error in predicating sweetness of the apple or expecting a similar taste from another bite. The only sense in which apprehension could be illusory or erroneous is just this sense of including a meaning which is not given but is added to the given and must be verified, if at all, in some other experience.

It is evident that the considerations here brought forward with reference to the knowledge of objective properties will hold for the knowledge of objects in general. Knowledge *always* transcends the immediately given. It begins with the recognition of a qualitatively specific presentation, but even that minimum of cognition which consists in naming is an interpretation which implicitly asserts certain relations between the given and further experience. The ascription of a substantive or an adjective is the hypothesis of some sequence in possible experience or a multiplicity of such sequences.... The criterion of the objectivity of what is presented is always such a relation to further experience. In the nature of the case, the difference between veridical perception and an experience which is genuinely illusory (really deceptive to the individual in question) is never to be discovered within what is strictly given in the presentation. When we distinguish one experience as illusory, another as presentation of the real, we can intend nothing even conceivably verifiable except that, starting from the given experience and proceeding in certain ways, we reach other experience which is predictable in the one case and not in the other. *Thus "acquaintance with," the recognition of what is presented as a real object of a certain kind, has already the significance of prediction and asserts the same general type of temporal connection as our knowledge of law, the "knowledge about" which is stated in generalizations....*

On the other hand, that kind of knowledge which may strike us as more truly conceptual must always—if it be knowledge of reality—come down to just such interconnectedness of experience and must be verifiable in the pattern of presented experiences. It is this which is affirmed in the dictum of Charles Peirce: "Consider what effects that might conceivably have practical bearings you conceive the objects of your conception to have. Then, your conception of those effects is the whole of your conception of the object." "Effects" which are *verifiable* can, in the end, mean nothing more than actual or possible presentations....

... When I interpret a certain round ruddy presentation as "sweet apple," I implicitly predict that if I should bite, then I should get a certain taste. But perhaps I am not hungry now, so I merely file away this possibility for future reference. The "if" clause of my prediction is allowed to remain contrary to fact. Precisely here, in this apparently commonplace fact that the meanings ascribed in our recognition of objects and predications of properties must be *verifiable*, yet are commonly not *verified* or only verified in part, is something of great importance both for understanding the relation of knowledge to our ways of acting and for the nature of objectivity or thinghood....

To ascribe an objective quality to a thing means implicitly the prediction that if I act in certain ways, specifiable experience will eventuate: if I should bite this, it would taste sweet; if I should pinch it, it would feel moderately soft; if I should eat it, it would digest and not poison me; if I should turn it over, I should perceive another rounded surface much like this; if I should put it on the scales, they would register about three ounces. These and a hundred other such hypothetical propositions constitute my knowledge of the apple in my hand. These are *the meaning which this presentation has to me now*, but it may be that neither now nor in the immediate future do I actually verify these possibilities.

It is only because we are active beings that our world is bigger than the content of our actual experience. For the active being, reality is as much bigger than the content of given experience as is measured by the totality of all that is related to what is presented by those propositions of the type "If I should ... then ..." which he takes to be true. All that "more" which belongs to the objects presented to him, over and above what is immediately given, and all the rest of reality, as it stands related to his object but not presented with it, resides in this potency of possible experience....

The whole content of our knowledge of reality is the truth of such "If—then" propositions, in which the hypothesis is something we conceive could be made true by our mode of acting and the consequent presents a content of experience which, though not actual now and perhaps not to become actual, is a possible experience connected with the present. For the active being such hypothetical propositions can be meaningful and true when the hypothesis is false.[1] The attribution to what is given of connection with such a content of further possible experience is the conceptual interpretation of the presentation and our knowledge of the object....

Knowledge of objects, then, knowledge of the real, involves always two elements, the element of given and ineffable presentation, and the element of conceptual interpretation which represents the mind's response. . . .

. . . [T]he given is not formless in the sense of being indefinite. One kind of definiteness which the given has—its qualitative specificity—is too obvious to need pointing out. Further, it is not formless in the sense that this qualitative and ineffable character of it is indifferent for knowledge. If there were no correlation in the individual mind between the concept and particular qualia, then no experience could be the signal of any particular meaning. It is also to the point that the implicitly predicted relationships, comprised in the conceptual interpretation of what is presented, must be such that further possible experience could verify or fail to verify them. Without the correlation of concept and qualia, no experience could verify or fail to verify anything. My presently given experience leads me to say that if I should move ten feet to the left I should reach the wall. If the visual presentation interpreted as "wall" were not identifiable by its sensory qualities, or if stepping and contact did not have this identifiable qualitative specificity, then my statement could have no meaning. For another person, the sensory qualia which would be in point when he saw the wall from this chair might be different from mine. But for each of us, within his individual experience, if we did not correlate certain concepts with certain identifiable feelings, there could be no knowledge of objects at all.

The intelligibility of experience consists precisely in this; that between the specific quality of what is given and the pattern of its context in possible experience there is some degree of stable correlation. . . .

Note

1. The significance of knowledge depends upon the significance of possibility that is not actual. Possibility and impossibility—hence necessity and contingency, consistency and inconsistency, and various other fundamental notions—require that there should be "If—then—" propositions whose truth or falsity is independent of the truth or falsity of the condition stated in their antecedent clauses. Those readers who happen to be familiar with my doctrine of "strict implication" will find here a motive for the distinction of "strict" from "material" implication and for other basic conceptions of the system of "strict implication." A "material" implication represents an "If—then—" proposition the truth of which is *not* independent of the *truth* of its antecedent clause.

22 From "The 'Mental' and the 'Physical'"

Herbert Feigl

The physicalist views of Lashley (192), Carnap (62, 64, 66, 67), Hempel (146), Black (37, 38), Quine (268), Ryle (294), Skinner (321), and Wilfrid Sellars (315), though differing in many more or less important respects one from another, are primarily motivated by a basic doubt about the possibility of a purely phenomenal language. The observation language of everyday life, we are told, is rooted in the intersubjective terms whose usage we acquired in the learning situations of a common, public context of labeling things, properties, relations, states, events, processes, and dispositions. Subjective or "mentalistic" terms, this group of thinkers claims, are introduced and their usage learned on an intersubjective basis. Remove this intersubjective basis and not only have you deprived psychological concepts of their scientific significance, but you are left with nothing more than ineffable raw feels or with exclamations devoid of cognitive significance.

But the problems will not completely yield to this reductive approach. Introspection, though admittedly often unreliable, does enable us to describe elements, aspects, and configurations in the phenomenal fields of direct experience. When the doctor asks me whether I have a pain in my chest, whether my mood is gloomy, or whether I can read the fine print, *he* can afford to be a behaviorist and test for these various experiences in a perfectly objective manner. But *I have* (or do not have) the pain, the depressed mood, or the visual sensations; and I can report them on the basis of direct experience and introspection. Thus the question arises inevitably: how are the raw feels related to behavioral (or neurophysiological) states? Or, if we prefer the formal mode of speech to the material mode, what are the *logical* relations of raw-feel-talk (phenomenal terms, if not phenomenal language) to the terms and statements in the language of behavior (or of neurophysiology)?

No matter how sophisticated we may be in logical analysis or epistemology, the old perplexities center precisely around this point and they will not down. Many philosophical positions at least since the eighteenth century were primarily motivated, I strongly suspect, by the wish to avoid the mind–body problem. Moreover, the central significance of the problem for any *Weltanschauung* burdens its clarification with powerful emotions, be they engendered by materialistic, idealistic or theological prepossessions. Schopenhauer rightly viewed the mind–body problem as the "*Weltknoten*" (world knot). It is truly a cluster of intricate puzzles—some scientific, some epistemological, some syntactical, some semantical, and some pragmatic. Closely related to these are the equally sensitive and controversial issues regarding teleology, purpose, intentionality, and free will.

I am convinced, along with many contemporary philosophical analysts and logicians of science, that *all* of these problems have been unnecessarily complicated by conceptual confusions, and to that extent are gratuitous puzzles and pseudoproblems. But I feel that we have not yet done *full* justice to any of them....

... By "physical" I mean[1] the type of concepts and laws which suffice in principle for the explanation and prediction of inorganic processes. If emergentism is *not* required for the phenomena of organic life, "physical" would mean those concepts and laws sufficient for the explanation of inorganic as well as of biological phenomena. In accordance with the terminology of Meehl and Sellars (221), I shall henceforth designate *this* concept by "*physical*$_2$" in contradistinction to "*physical*$_1$," which is practically synonymous with "scientific," i.e., with being an essential part of the coherent and adequate descriptive and explanatory account of the spatio-temporal-causal world.

In view of what was said above about the *empirical* character of the interaction and the emergence problems, the concepts of mental states might well be *physical*$_1$ concepts, in that they could be introduced on the basis of the intersubjective observation language of common life (and this includes the observation language of science). Just as the concept of the magnetic field, while not denoting anything directly observable, can be introduced with the help of postulates and correspondence rules (cf. Carnap, 73), so it is conceivable that concepts of vital forces, entelechies, "diathetes" (cf. Kapp, 172, 173, 174), and mental events might be given their respective meanings by postulates and correspondence rules. Of course, the question remains whether such ("emergent") concepts are really needed and whether they will do the expected job in the explanation and prediction of the behavior of organisms, subhuman or human. My personal view, admittedly tentative and based on the progress and partial success of physicalistic microexplanation (implemented by Gestalt and cybernetic considerations), is to the effect that *physical*$_2$ laws will prove sufficient....

But scientists are radically opposed to the admission of *purely subjective* factors or data (conceived as in principle inaccessible to intersubjective confirmation) as a basis for prediction or explanation. This would indeed be scientifically meaningless, if not even statistical relations of subjective states to antecedent or consequent intersubjective observables could be assumed. If they *are* assumed, then the subjective states are not *purely* subjective or "private" in the radical sense intended by some interactionists. The "emergent" raw feels in the interpretation by Meehl and Sellars are of course subjective only in the sense that they can be the objects of direct introspective verification, but they are also intersubjective (physical$_1$) in the sense that they can be assumed (posited, inferred, hypothetically constructed) by scientists who do not have the same sort of raw feels in the repertory of their own direct experience. This is so, for example, in the case of a congenitally blind scientist equipped with modern electronic instruments who could establish the (behavioristic) psychology of vision for subjects endowed with eyesight. The blind scientist could thus confirm all sorts of statements about visual sensations and qualities—which in his knowledge would be represented by "hypothetical constructs." But if *ex hypothesi* all connections of the subjective raw feels with the intersubjectively accessible facts are radically severed, then such raw feels are, I should say by definition, excluded from the scope of science. The question whether discourse about such absolutely private raw feels makes sense in any sense of "sense" will be discussed later. . . .

. . . The juxtaposition of "subjective" and "objective" has been the source of endless and badly confused controversies throughout the ages. There is nevertheless something significant and worth preserving in this distinction. To say that a twinge of pain experienced by person A is "subjective" or "private" to him may simply mean that another person B, observing A's behavior, may *infer* A's pain, but does not *have* it, i.e. he does not directly experience it. Dentists do not have the toothaches of their patients. In one sense this is clearly analytic (tautological).[2] It is analytic for reasons analogous to those which make it self-contradictory to say that I am growing my wife's hair. (Schizophrenics are known to make assertions of this sort.) "I am eating with my wife's teeth" is merely funny, but not self-contradictory. "Dentists always suffer toothaches when their drill comes near the pulpa of their patient's tooth" is synthetic, but empirically false. "I am listening through my wife's ears" if meant literally (not metaphorically) is a border line case, depending on specific detailed interpretation. "I am enjoying Mozart's music exactly as my wife does" is synthetic and may even be rendered as "I have the *same* musical experience as does my wife." (Remarks about the two meanings of "same" will follow presently.)

The case is a trifle more complex for perception. Two persons sitting next to each other in the concert hall are said to hear the same music, or at a given moment the same tones or chords, produced by the pianist on the stage. But the facts of the case are really not fundamentally different from the first example. A does not *have* B's musical experience (or vice versa), even if their auditory discrimination, musical appreciation, etc., does not differ in any discernible way. They may be said to hear the same sounds, to be both equally impressed or thrilled by them; but common sense as well as scientific reasoning clearly indicates that their *experiences* are numerically different. Fundamentally this case does not differ from, e.g., the case of two thermometers immersed next to each other in the same glass of water. It is perfectly proper to say that these instruments indicate the *same* physical condition. It is also perfectly proper to say that the two thermometers not only indicate *but also* "have" the "same" temperature. (This is logically quite like saying that two marbles have the same color.) But it would be most improper and paradoxical to say that the *events* taking place in the one thermometer are *identical* with those in the other. This is not the place for a discussion of Plato's problem of the "one and the many." Suffice it to point out that the phrases "the same as" and "identical with" are ambiguously used. "Sameness" or "identity" may mean complete similarity, as in the case of the two musical experiences, or in the case of the two thermometric indications. But "sameness" or "identity" in other contexts means the numerical oneness of the individual referent of, e.g., two different names, or of two different unique characterizations (Russellian descriptions). I conclude then that it makes perfectly good sense to speak of the subjectivity or privacy of immediate experience. *Numerically* different but *qualitatively* identical (indistinguishable) experiences may be had by two or more persons, the experiential events being "private" to each of the distinct persons.

Terminological trouble, however, arises immediately when we take a scientific attitude toward direct experience and try to confirm, describe, or explain it "objectively."

Is it not an "objective" fact of the world that Eisenhower experienced severe pain when he had his heart attack? Is it not a public item of the world's history that Churchill during a certain speech experienced intense sentiments of indignation and contempt for Hitler? Of course! What is meant here is simply that statements about facts of this sort are in principle *intersubjectively confirmable* and could thus be incorporated in a complete historical account of the events of our universe....

There is, however, also a philosophical and speculatively extended sense of "subjective" or "private". In this very special and highly problematic sense it is assumed that there may be subjective states which are in principle inaccessible to intersubjective confirmation. Here we had better speak explicitly of "*absolute* subjectivity" or "*absolute* privacy." It is *this* sense which is entertained in some of the more radically interactionstic forms of dualism. And it is this sense which by definition is incompatible with "objectivity" understood as intersubjective confirmability. As I have indicated before, I no longer insist that a doctrine involving the notion of *absolute* privacy is entirely devoid of *cognitive* meaning. But I am inclined to regard it as *scientifically* meaningless. To recapitulate: if the scientific enterprise is defined as necessarily requiring *intersubjective* confirmability of knowledge claims, then this follows immediately and quite trivially.

Now, I think it is an essential aspect of the basic working program and of the working hypotheses of science that there is nothing in existence which would in principle escape intersubjective confirmation. Allowances have already been made for the (sometimes) insuperable *practical* difficulties of even the most incomplete and indirect confirmations. But the optimistic outlook that inspires the advance of science and informs its heuristic principles,[3] does not tolerate the (objectively) unknowable or "un-get-at-able." No matter how distant, complicated, or indirect the connection of scientific concepts with some (intersubjective) evidential bases may be, they would not be concepts of *empirical* science (as contrasted with the concepts of pure logic or mathematics) unless they could in some such fashion be "fixed" by "triangulation in logical space." The "fix" we are able to obtain may be as indefinite as it is when theoretical concepts (like those of the positron, the neutrino, or the meson in physics; that of the unit of heredity; or of memory traces; of the superego, of general paresis, or of schizophrenia in biology, psychology, or psychiatry) were *first* tentatively introduced by only very sketchily formulated postulates. The concepts of absolutely subjective or completely private data, however, are so conceived that they can be applied only on the basis of the direct experiences contained in a given stream of consciousness. A completely "captive mind"[4] might experience senselike qualities, thoughts, emotions, volitions, etc., but they would (*ex hypothesi*) not in any way, i.e., not even through weak statistical correlations, be connected with the publicly observable behavior or the neurophysiological processes of an organism....

It is time to draw some conclusions from this discussion. There is one meaning of "mental" in which it coincides with one meaning of "subjective." Let us call this meaning "phenomenal." In so calling it we may leave for later the question as to whether what is phenomenally given and phenomenally labeled is always also indirectly characterizable in an intersubjectively meaningful terminology. In any case we have isolated one contrasting (though not necessarily incompatible) pair of meanings for "mental" and "physical": the phenomenal (i.e., the subjectively confirmable) and the intersubjectively confirmable (i.e., the $physical_1$ in the terminology suggested above)....

... Emergence as conceived by most dualists,... refers to the evolutionary novelty and the ($physical_2$) underivability of *sentience* or *raw feels*. The whole issue therefore turns again upon the criterion of *subjective experience*. The issue can be brought out by questions such as the following: Suppose we could predict the detailed chemical structure of an entirely new perfume which will be manufactured in Paris in the year 1995. Suppose, furthermore, that we could equally exactly predict the neurophysiological effects of this perfume on the mucous membranes of a human nose, as well as the resulting cortical processes in the person thus smelling the perfume. Could we then also predict the quality of the experienced fragrance? The usual answer to this question is in the negative, because it is assumed that the fragrance in question will be an "emergent novelty." But behaviorists, and physicalists generally, need not take such a pessimistic view. For given the presuppositions of our questions it should also be possible to predict the answers to questionnaire items like "Is the fragrance more similar to Chanel 5 or to Nuit d'Amour?" That is to say, we should be able to predict the location of the quality in the topological space of odors, provided we have a sufficiency of psychophysiological correlation laws to make this particular case one of interpolation or (limited) extrapolation.

The issue can however be made more poignant if we are concerned with the prediction of qualities within an entirely new modality. In the case of the congenitally blind who by a cataract operation suddenly attain eyesight, the experience of colors and (visual) shapes is a complete novelty. Suppose that all of mankind had been completely blind up to a certain point in history, and then acquired vision. Presupposing $physical_2$ determinism we should (according to my basic conjecture) in principle be able to predict the relevant neural and behavioral processes, and thus to foretell all the discriminatory and linguistic behavior which depends upon the new cortical processes (which correspond to the emergent, novel qualities of experience). What is it then that we would not or could not know at the time of the original prediction? I think the answer is obvious. We would not and could not know (then) the color experiences *by acquaintance*; i.e., (1) we would not *have* them; (2) we could not *imagine* them; (3) we could not *recognize* (or *label*) them as "red," "green," etc., even if by some miracle we suddenly *had* them, except by completely new stipulations of designation rules.[5]

I conclude that the central puzzle of the mind–body problem is the logical nature of the correlation laws connecting raw feel qualities with neurophysiological processes....

But now to complete our analysis of the meanings of "physical": We have distinguished "$physical_1$" and "$physical_2$." By "$physical_1$ terms" I mean *all* (empirical) terms whose specification of meaning essentially involves logical (necessary or, more usually, probabilistic) connections with the intersubjective observation language, as well as the terms of this observation language itself. Theoretical concepts in physics, biology, psychology, and the social sciences hence are all—at least—$physical_1$ concepts. By "$physical_2$" I mean the kind of theoretical concepts (and statements) which are sufficient for the *explanation*, i.e., the deductive or probabilistic derivation, of the observation statements regarding the inorganic (lifeless) domain of nature. If my conjecture (discussed above) is correct, then the scopes of *theoretical* "$physical_1$" and "$physical_2$" terms are the same. *If*, however, there is genuine emergence, i.e., logical underivability, in the domains of organic, mental, and/or social phenomena, then the scope of "physical_2" terms is clearly narrower than that of "physical_1" theoretical terms. . . .

. . . *[I]f* there is no genuine emergence in the logical sense above the level of lifeless phenomena, then there is no basic distinction between the theoretical terms of the physical_1 and physical_2 languages. That is to say that the theoretical terms of biology and psychology are explicitly definable on the basis of the theoretical concepts of physics in the same sense as the theoretical terms of chemistry (e.g., the chemical bond) are nowadays explicitly definable on the basis of the theoretical terms of the physical_2 language (i.e., of the atomic and quantum theories).

The central questions of the mind–body problem then come down to this: are the concepts of introspective psychology—relating to phenomenal data or phenomenal fields—definable on the basis of physical_1 theoretical terms, and if so, are they also definable on the basis of physical_2 (theoretical) terms? The first question is a matter for *philosophical* analysis. The second question is, at the present level of scientific research, undecided, though my personal (admittedly bold and risky) guess is that future scientific progress will decide it affirmatively. . . .

. . . Our present concern is with the roles of acquaintance and of knowledge by acquaintance in the enterprise of science, especially in psychology. The first question I wish to discuss concerns the cognitive "plus," i.e., the alleged advantages of knowledge by acquaintance over knowledge by description. We may ask, for example, what does the seeing man know that the congenitally blind man could not know. Or, to take two examples from Eddington (93, 94), What could a man know about the effects of jokes if he had no sense of humor? Could a Martian, entirely without sentiments of compassion or piety, know about what is going on during a commemoration of the armistice? For the sake of the argument, we assume complete physical (1 or 2) predictability and explainability of the behavior of humans equipped with vision, a sense of humor, and sentiments of piety. The Martian could then predict all responses, including the linguistic utterances of the earthlings in the situations which involve their visual perceptions, their laughter about jokes, or their (solemn) behavior at the commemoration. But *ex hypothesi*, the Martian would be lacking completely in the sort of *imagery* and *empathy* which depends on familiarity (direct acquaintance) with the kinds of *qualia* to be imaged or empathized.

As we have pointed out before, "knowledge *of*," i.e., "acquaintance with," qualia is not a necessary condition for "knowledge *about*" (or knowledge by inference of) those qualia. A psychiatrist may know a great deal *about* extreme states of manic euphoria or of abject melancholic depression, without ever having experienced anything anywhere near them himself. In this case, of course, it must be admitted that the psychiatrist can get an "idea" of these extreme conditions by imaginative extrapolation from the milder spells of elation or depression which he, along with all human beings, does know by acquaintance. But the case is different for observers who are congenitally deprived of acquaintance with an entire modality of direct experience. This is the case of the congenitally blind or deaf, or that of our fancied Martian who has no emotions or sentiments of any kind. But I think it is also the case of human beings endowed with the entire repertory of normal sensory and emotional experience, when they introduce theoretical concepts in their science, such as the electromagnetic or gravitational fields, electric currents, and nuclear forces. We are "acquainted" with the perceptible things, properties, and relations on the relevant evidential bases which suggest the introduction of these concepts into the system of science generally, or which justify their special application in particular instances of observation.

In the context of the present discussion it does not matter very much whether we use the narrower, philosophical notion of direct acquaintance (restricted to the qualia of raw feels) or the wider commonsense or physicalistic notion of acquaintance (which includes the directly observable properties and relations of the objects in our everyday life environment). I think it does make sense to say that we do not know by acquaintance the "nature" of electric currents or of the forces within the nuclei of atoms. And although the congenitally blind have no acquaintance with color qualities or visual shapes, they may nevertheless come to have knowledge by inference at least of the neural correlates among the processes in the occipital lobes of the brains of persons with eyesight. The "intrinsic nature" of those neural processes remains unknown by acquaintance to the blind scientist, just as the "intrinsic nature" of electric currents remains unknown to scientists who have eyesight, and who have seen electrical machines and wires, have been tickled or shocked by electric currents, have seen electric sparks, have felt the heat produced by electric currents, have read voltmeters and ammeters, have observed the chemical and magnetic effects of electric currents, etc.

I trust my readers will not charge me with obscurantist tendencies. I do not at all share the view (e.g., Bergson's) that *genuine* knowledge is to be found only in direct acquaintance or intuition. Bergson, in his *Introduction to Metaphysics*, paradoxically claimed that metaphysics—the intuitive knowledge of intrinsic reality—is "the science that dispenses with symbols altogether." I wish to assert, quite to the contrary, that genuine knowledge is *always symbolic*, be it knowledge by acquaintance as formulated in direct introspective report sentences, or be it knowledge by description as, e.g., in the hypotheses of modern nuclear physics. If we knew all *about* electricity, magnetism, nuclear forces, etc., i.e., if we had a complete set of laws concerning those matters—this would be all we could possibly wish to know within the scientific enterprise. Anything added to this by way of "acquaintance" would be cognitively irrelevant imagery. Such imagery might be welcome from a poetic or artistic point of view. It might occasionally be helpful heuristically or didactically, but even in this regard it amounts only to pictorial bywork, and is often dangerously misleading. "Thou shalt not make unto thee any graven image . . ."

Our world, being what it is, can of course be known by description, in any of its parts or aspects, only on the basis of a foothold somewhere in direct acquaintance. This, it seems to me, is one of the cornerstones of any empiricist epistemology, old or new. But the new empiricism of recent times has come to recognize that it matters little just which areas of acquaintance are available or actually utilized for the "triangulation" of facts or entities outside the scope of direct acquaintance. The congenitally blind-deaf person, I stress again, could in principle construct and confirm a complete system of the natural sciences (including astronomy!) and the social sciences (including the psychology of vision and hearing, as well as the psychology of art and music appreciation!). It should go without saying that such a person, like Helen Keller, would normally depend upon information received from persons endowed with visual and auditory perception.

But, supposing such a human being could survive a long time as a solitary observer and was equipped with supreme intelligence and ingenuity, then one can well conceive of various modern instruments and devices (involving photoelectric cells, amplifiers, electromagnetic indicators, etc.) he could invent which would serve him in the detection of the stars, the chemical constitution of various substances, the behavior of animals, and so on—all accessible to him ultimately through, e.g., tactual pointer readings of one sort or another. All this is merely a picturesque way of saying that the "nomological net," i.e., the system of scientific concepts and laws, may be "tacked down" in a variety of alternative ways, either in several sense modalities (as in the normal case), or even in only one of them. To be sure, "triangulation of entities in logical space" is much easier and much more secure in the normal case. But, as we have pointed out, normal, unaided perception by itself is also quite insufficient for the confirmation of our knowledge regarding radio waves, infrared, ultraviolet, gamma radiations, cosmic rays, the molecular and atomic structure of matter, the motions and other physical and chemical characteristics of stars and galaxies, etc. Intricate instruments and ingenious theoretical constructions are indispensable in the case of normal (multimodal) perception as well. The difference between persons equipped with all normal sense organs and the deaf-blind is only one of degree, or of the speed with which they would, respectively, attain knowledge about the world in which they are embedded and of which they are parts.

Similar considerations apply to the advantages held by fully equipped persons in regard to psychological and linguistic or desciptive-semantical knowledge. If I have been trained by normal education to apply phenomenal terms (like "red," "green," "lilac fragrance," "rose fragrance," "sweet," "sour," etc.) to qualia of my own direct experience, then I can predict much more readily the application of these terms by other persons in the presence of certain specifiable visual, olfactory or gustatory stimuli. But predictions of this sort are based upon analogical inference; and they are in principle dispensable, because the discriminatory and verbal behavior of other persons is open to intersubjective test. Moreover, if we had a complete neurophysiological explanation of discriminatory and verbal responses we could derive these responses from the cerebral states which initiate them, and which, in turn were engendered by sensory stimulation. Analogously, whatever reliability empathetic understanding in common life, or "clinical intuition" in the psychologist's practice, may have is ultimately to be appraised by intersubjective tests. But the speed with which empathy or intuition do their work depends upon the breadth and the richness of the "experience" of the judge. It also depends upon his use of critical controls.

If the psychologist's personality type is radically different from that of his subject, he will have to correct (often to the point of complete reversal) his first intuitions. For example, an extremely extrovert person will find it difficult to "understand" an extreme introvert, and vice versa. If, however, the personalities are very similar, intuition may "click" readily, and it may even be frequently quite correct. The role of direct acquaintance in all these cases simply amounts to having in one's own experience features and regularities with which one is quite familiar, and which are hence speedily projected and utilized in the interpretation of the behavior of other persons. I conclude that the advantages of direct acquaintance pertain to the *context of discovery* (cf. Reichenbach, 273) and not to the context of justification. All the examples discussed do not differ in principle from the obvious examples of persons with "wide experience" as contrasted with persons with "narrow experience," in the most ordinary meaning of these terms. Someone thoroughly familiar with the weather patterns of Minnesota, or with the conduct of business in the Congress of the United States (to take two very different illustrations of the same point) will have the advantages of much speedier inferences and (usually) more reliable predictions than someone who has had no opportunity of long range observations in either case.

The philosophically intriguing questions regarding acquaintance are, I think, of a different sort. They are best expressed by asking, e.g., What is it that the blind man cannot know concerning color qualities? What is it that the (emotionless) Martian could not know about human feelings and sentiments? If we assume complete physical (i.e., at least $physical_1$) predictability of human behavior, i.e., as much predictability as the best developed physical science of the future could conceivably provide, then it is clear that the blind man or the Martian would lack only *acquaintance* and *knowledge by acquaintance* in certain areas of the realm of qualia. Lacking acquaintance means *not having* those experiential qualia; and the consequent lack of knowledge by acquaintance simply amounts to being unable to label the qualia with terms used previously by the subject (or by some other subject) when confronted with their occurrence in direct experience. Now, mere *having* or *living through* ("erleben") is not *knowledge* in any sense. "Knowledge by acquaintance," however, as we understand it here, is propositional, it does make truth claims; and although it is not infallible, it is under favorable circumstances so reliable that we rarely hesitate to call it "certain." It remains in any case the ultimate confirmation basis of *all* knowledge claims.

In many of the foregoing discussions we have suggested that what one person *has* and *knows by acquaintance* may be identical with what someone else knows by description. The color experiences of the man who can see are known to him by acquaintance, but the blind man *can* have inferential knowledge, or knowledge by description *about* those same experiences. After all, this is true as regards an individual color experience even if the other person *is* endowed with eyesight. The other person does not and could not conceivably *have* the numerically identical experience.... Why should we then not conclude that the behavioristic psychologist can "triangulate" the direct experiences of others? I think that indeed he does just that if he relinquishes the narrow peripheralist position, i.e., if he allows himself the introduction of theoretical concepts which are only logically connected with, but never explicitly definable in terms of, concepts pertaining to overt molar behavior. These acquaintancewise possibly unknown states which the behaviorist must introduce for the sake of a theoretical explanation of overt behavior, and to which he (no longer a "radical" behaviorist) refers as the central causes of the peripheral behavior symptoms and manifestations, may well be *identical* with the referents of the phenomenal (acquaintance) terms used by his subject in introspective descriptions of his (the subject's) direct experience. As remarked before, in ordinary communication about our respective mental states, we make this assumption of identity quite unquestioningly. It took a great deal of training in philosophical doubt for learned men to call this assumption into question.

But philosophical doubt, here as elsewhere,[6] while stimulating in the search for clarity, is ultimately due to conceptual confusions. We have learned how to avoid these confusions, and thus to return with a good philosophical conscience to (at least *some* of) the convictions of commonsense. We have learned that philosophical doubts, unlike ordinary empirical doubts, cannot be removed by logical or experimental demonstration. What *can* be demonstrated logically is only the exploitation of certain misleading extensions of, or deviations from, the sensible and fruitful use of terms in ordinary or scientific language. Thus to doubt whether we can at all have knowledge about the "private" experience of other persons is merely the philosophical extension of the ordinary and quite legitimate doubts that we may have in specific instances, for example, when we ask "Is he really as disappointed as his behavior would seem to indicate?" This is to confuse practical difficulties of knowing with (allegedly) basic impossibilities. Once one becomes fully aware of the disease of philosophical skepticism, it becomes possible to cure oneself of it by a sort of self-analysis (*logical* analysis is what I have in mind here; but in certain cases psychoanalysis may help too, or may even be indispensable).

Granting then that the *referents* of acquaintance terms and physical_1 theoretical terms may in some cases be identical, this does not by itself decide the issue between monism and dualism. As we have seen in the previous subsection, the inference to other persons' raw feels can be *logically* differentiated from the inference to their central nervous processes. Dualistic parallelism or epiphenomenalism is entirely compatible with the assertion of the identity of the subjectively labeled mental state with the intersubjectively inferred state which is needed for the explanation of molar behavior. The mental state is logically distinguishable from the "correlated" neurophysiological state. Indeed ... it makes no sense to talk of *correlation*, or in any case not the usual sense, if the relation of "correlation" were that of *identity*. We shall tackle this crucial point [below].

Before we proceed to the discussion of identity and identification, let us however summarize some important conclusions from our discussion of *acquaintance*. The data of direct experience function in three roles: First, in the use of typical patterns and regularities of one person's data for the intuitive or empathetic ascription of similar patterns and regularities of direct experience (or even of unconscious processes) to other persons, these data *suggest*, but by themselves are never a sufficiently strong *basis of validation* for knowledge claims about the mental life of other persons. Further clinical, experimental, or statistical studies of the behavior of those persons are needed in order to obtain a scientifically respectable degree of confirmation for such inferences. Second, nevertheless, and this is philosophically even more important, the first-person data of direct experience are, in the ultimate epistemological analysis, the *confirmation basis* of *all* types of factual knowledge claims. This is simply the core of the empiricist thesis over again. But third, the data are *also objects* (targets, referents) of *some* knowledge claims, viz. of those statements which concern nothing but the occurrence of raw feels or whatever regularities (if any!) can be formulated about raw feels in purely phenomenal terms. For examples of the latter, I mention the three-dimensional ordering of color qualia according to hue, brightness, and saturation; the regularities regarding the gradual (temporal) fading of intense emotions like joy, rage, exultation, embarrassment, regret, grief, etc.; the lawful correlations between, e.g., the experienced contents of daydreams and the attendant emotions of hope or fear. In all these cases, no matter whether the raw feels are our own or someone else's, *they* are the *objects* of our knowledge claims or the *referents* of certain terms in the sentences which describe them....

The identity thesis which I wish to clarify and to defend asserts that the states of direct experience which conscious human beings "live through," and those which we confidently ascribe to some of the higher animals, are identical with certain (presumably configurational) aspects of the neural processes in those organisms. To put the same idea in the terminology explained previously, we may say, what is *had-in-experience*, and (in the case of human beings) *knowable by acquaintance*, is identical with the object of *knowledge by description* provided first by molar behavior theory and this is in turn identical with what the science of neurophysiology *describes* (or, rather, will describe when sufficient progress has been achieved) as processes in the central nervous system, perhaps especially in the cerebral cortex. In its basic core this is the "double knowledge" theory held by many modern monistic critical realists.[7] ...

The empirical character of the identification rests upon the extensional equivalences, or extensional implications, which hold between statements about the behavioral and the neurophysiological evidence. In our example this means that all persons to whom we ascribe an after-image, as evidenced by certain stimulus and response conditions, also have cerebral processes of a certain kind, and vice versa. In view of the uncertainties and inaccuracies of our experimental techniques we can at present, of course, assert only a statistical correlation between the two domains of evidence. That is to say, the equivalences or implications are, practically speaking, only probabilistic. But in any case, the correlations as well as the theoretical identification of the referents indicated by various items of evidence are formulated in *intersubjectively* confirmable statements.

The identification of raw feels with neural states, however, crosses what in metaphysical phraseology is sometimes called an "ontological barrier." It connects the "subjective" with the "intersubjective." It *identifies* the referents of subjective terms with the referents of certain objective terms. But in my view of the matter there is here no longer an unbridgeable gulf, and hence no occasion for metaphysical shudders. Taking into account the conclusions of the preceding analyses of "privacy," "acquaintance," "physical," and of "identification," private states known by direct acquaintance and referred to by phenomenal (subjective) terms *can* be described in a public (at least physical$_1$) language and may thus be empirically identifiable with the referents of certain neurophysiological terms. Privacy is capable of public (intersubjective) description, and the objects of intersubjective science can be evidenced by data of private experience....

... We have stressed that the (empirical!) identification of the mental with the physical consists in regarding what is labeled in knowledge by acquaintance as a quale of direct experience as identical with the denotatum of some neurophysiological concept. The scientific evidence for parallelism or isomorphism is then *interpreted* as the *empirical* basis for the identification. The step from parallelism to the identity view is essentially a matter of philosophical interpretation. The principle of parsimony as it is employed in the sciences contributes only one reason in favor of monism. If isomorphism is admitted, the dualistic (parallelistic) position may be retained, but no good grounds can be adduced for such a duplication of realities, or even of "aspects" of reality. The principle of parsimony or of inductive (or hypothetico-deductive) simplicity does oppose the operationistic predilection for speaking of *two* (or more) concepts if the evidential facts, though completely correlated, are qualitatively heterogeneous....

Notes

1. In this context only; other meanings of "physical" will be listed and discussed [below].

2. This is now even admitted by Ayer (18) who had earlier (15) held it was synthetic. His earlier position was, however, incisively criticized by Pap (243, 248) and Wating (341).

3. Some philosophers rather speak of them as "metaphysical presuppositions"; for my criticisms of this interpretation of science cf. (110, 114).

4. The idea and the phrase are Hilary Putnam's.

5. Cf. Pap's discussion of absolute emergence (244).

6. As, e.g., in the problems of induction, the trustworthiness of memory, the veridicality of perception, etc.

7. Especially Alois Riehl, Moritz Schlick, Richard Gätschenberger, H. Reichenbach, Günther Jacoby, Bertrand Russell, Roy W. Sellars, Durant Drake, and C. A. Strong. To be sure, there are very significant differences among these thinkers. Russell has never quite freed himself from the neutral monism (phenomenalism) of his earlier neorealistic phase. R. W. Sellars and, following him on a higher level of logical sophistication, his son, Wilfrid, have combined their realistic, double-knowledge view with a doctrine of evolutionary emergence. Opposing the emergence view, Strong and Drake, originally influenced by F. Paulsen, adopted a panpsychistic metaphysics. My own view is a development in more modern terms of the epistemological outlook common to Riehl, Schlick, Russell, and to some extent of that of the erratic but brilliant Gätschenbeger. The French philosopher Raymond Ruyer (289, 290) especially before he turned to a speculative and questionable neovitalism (293) held a similar view. Among psychologists W. Köhler (182, 183), E. G. Boring (40), and D. K. Adams (1), again differing in many important respects, hold similar monistic positions. Personally, I consider sections 22–35 in Schlick (298) as the first genuinely perspicacious, lucid and convincing formulation of the realistic-monistic point of view here defended. It is to be hoped that an English translation of this classic in modern epistemology will eventually become available.

References

1. Adams, D. K. "Learning and Explanation," *Learning Theory, Personality Theory, and Clinical Research: The Kentucky Symposium*, pp. 66–80. New York: Wiley; London: Chapman and Hall, Ltd., 1954.

18. Ayer, A. J. *The Problem of Knowledge*. New York: St. Martin's Press, 1956.

37. Black, M. "Linguistic Method in Philosophy," *Philosophical and Phenomenological Research*, 8: 4 (1948). Reprinted in M. Black, *Language and Philosophy*. Ithaca: Cornell Univ. Press, 1949.

38. Black, M. "Symposium: Phenomenalism." *Science, Language, and Human Rights*. American Philosophical Association, vol. 1. Philadelphia: Univ. of Pennsylvania Press, 1952.

40. Boring, E. G. *The Physical Dimensions of Consciousness*. New York, London: The Century Co., 1933.

62. Carnap, R. "Psychologie in Physikalischer Sprache," *Erkenntnis*, 3: 107–142 (1933).

64. Carnap, R. "Testability and Meaning," *Philosophy of Science*, 3: 420–468 (1936); 4: 1–10 (1937). Also reprinted in H. Feigl and M. Brodbeck (eds.), *Readings in the Philosophy of Science*, pp. 47–92. New York: Appleton-Century-Crofts.

66. Carnap, R. *The Unity of Science*. London: Kegan Paul, 1938.

67. Carnap, R. "Logical Foundations of the Unity of Science," *International Encyclopedia of Unified Science*, vol. I, no. 1 (R. Carnap and C. W. Morris, eds.). Chicago: Univ. of Chicago Press, 1938, 42–62. Reprinted in H. Feigl and W. Sellars (eds.), *Readings in Philosophical Analysis*, pp. 408–423. New York: Appleton-Century-Crofts, 1949.

73. Carnap, R. "The Methodological Character of Theoretical Concepts," in *Minnesota Studies in the Philosophy of Science*, vol. I, pp. 38–76. Minneapolis: Univ. of Minnesota Press, 1956.

93. Eddington, A. S. *The Nature of the Physical World*. New York: Macmillan, 1928.

94. Eddington, A. S. *Science and the Unseen World*. New York: Macmillan, 1929.

109. Feigl, H. "De Principiis Non Disputandum . . . ? On the Meaning and the Limits of Justification," in M. Black (ed.), *Philosophical Analysis*, pp. 119–156. Ithaca, N.Y.: Cornell University Press, 1950.

110. Feigl, H. "Existential Hypotheses: Realistic versus Phenomenalistic Interpretations," *Philosophy of Science*, 17: 35–62 (1950).

114. Feigl, H. "Scientific Method without Metaphysical Presuppositions," *Philosophical Studies*, 5: 17–19 (1954). Reprinted with minor alterations in H. Feigl and M. Scriven (eds.), *Minnesota Studies in the Philosophy of Science*, vol. I, pp. 22–37. Minneapolis: Univ. of Minnesota Press, 1956.

146. Hempel, C. G. "The Logical Analysis of Psychology," *Revue de Synthèse*, 10: 27–42 (1935). Reprinted in H. Feigl and W. Sellars (eds.), *Readings in Philosophical Analysis*, pp. 373–384. New York: Appleton-Century-Crofts, 1949.

172. Kapp, R. O. *Science vs. Materialism*. London: Methuen, 1940.

173. Kapp, R. O. *Mind, Life, and Body*. London: Constable, 1951.

174. Kapp, R. O. *Facts and Faith: The Dual Nature of Reality*. New York: Oxford Univ. Press, 1955.

182. Köhler, W. "Ein Altes Scheinproblem," *Die Naturwissenschaften*, 17: 395–401 (1929).

183. Köhler, W. *The Place of Values in a World of Facts*. New York: Liveright, 1938.

192. Lashley, K. S. "Behaviorism and Consciousness," *Psychological Review*, 30: 346 (1923).

221. Meehl, P. E., and W. Sellars. "The Concept of Emergence," in H. Feigl and M. Scriven (eds.), *Minnesota Studies in the Philosophy of Science*, vol. I, pp. 239–252. Minneapolis: Univ. of Minnesota Press, 1956.

243. Pap, A. "Other Minds and the Principle of Verifiability," *Revue Internationale de Philosophie*, no. 17–18, fasc. 3–4 (1951).

244. Pap, A. "The Concept of Absolute Emergence," *British Journal for the Philosophy of Science*, 2: 8 (1952).

248. Pap, A. *Analytische Erkenntnistheorie*. Vienna: Springer, 1955.

268. Quine, W. V. "On Mental Entities," in *Proceedings of the American Academy of Arts and Sciences*, 80: 3 (1950), Contributions to the Analysis and Synthesis of Knoweldge.

273. Reichenbach, H. *Experience and Prediction*. Chicago: Univ. of Chicago Press, 1938.

289. Ruyer, R. *Esquisse d'une Philosophy de la Structure*. Paris: F. Alcan, 1930.

290. Ruyer, R. "Les Sensations Sont-Elles Dans Notre Tête?" *Journal de Psychologie*, 31: 555–580 (1934).

291. Ruyer, R. *Néo-Finalisme.* Paris: Presses Univ. de France, 1952.

294. Ryle, G. *The Concept of Mind.* London: Hutchinson's Universal Library, 1949.

298. Schlick, M. *Allgemeine Erkentnislehre.* Berlin: Springer, 1925.

315. Sellars, W. "Empiricism and the Philosophy of Mind," in H. Feigl and M. Scriven (eds.), *Minnesota Studies in the Philosophy of Science,* vol. I, pp. 253–329. Minneapolis: Univ. of Minnesota Press, 1956.

321. Skinner, B. F. *Science and Human Behavior.* New York: Macmillan, 1953.

341. Wating, A. "Ayer on Other Minds," *Theoria,* 20: 175–180 (1954).

23 Sensations and Brain Processes

J. J. C. Smart

Suppose that I report that I have at this moment a roundish, blurry-edged after-image which is yellowish towards its edge and is orange towards its centre. What is it that I am reporting?[1] One answer to this question might be that I am not reporting anything, that when I say that it looks to me as though there is a roundish yellowy orange patch of light on the wall I am expressing some sort of *temptation*, the temptation to say that there *is* a roundish yellowy orange patch on the wall (though I may know that there is not such a patch on the wall). This is perhaps Wittgenstein's view in the *Philosophical Investigations* (see paragraphs 367, 370). Similarly, when I "report" a pain, I am not really reporting anything (or, if you like, I am reporting in a queer sense of "reporting"), but am doing a sophisticated sort of wince. (See paragraph 244: "The verbal expression of pain replaces crying and does not describe it." Nor does it describe anything else?)[2] I prefer most of the time to discuss an after-image rather than a pain, because the word "pain" brings in something which is irrelevant to my purpose: the notion of "distress." I think that "he is in pain" entails "he is in distress," that is, that he is in a certain agitation-condition.[3] Similarly, to say "I am in pain" may be to do more than "replace pain behavior": it may be partly to report something, though this something is quite nonmysterious, being an agitation-condition, and so susceptible of behavioristic analysis. The suggestion I wish if possible to avoid is a different one, namely that "I am in pain" is a genuine report, and that what it reports is an irreducibly psychical something. And similarly the suggestion I wish to resist is also that to say "I have a yellowish orange after-image" is to report something irreducibly psychical.

Why do I wish to resist this suggestion? Mainly because of Occam's razor. It seems to me that science is increasingly giving us a viewpoint whereby organisms are able to be seen as physico-chemical mechanisms:[4] it seems that even the behavior of man himself will one day be explicable in mechanistic terms. There does seem to be, so far as science is concerned, nothing in the world but increasingly complex arrangements of physical constituents. All except for one place: in consciousness. That is, for a full description of what is going on in a man you would have to mention not only the physical processes in his tissue, glands, nervous system, and so forth, but also his states of consciousness: his visual, auditory, and tactual sensations, his aches and pains. That these should be *correlated* with brain processes does not help, for to say that they are *correlated* is to say that they are something "over and above." You cannot correlate something with itself. You correlate footprints with burglars, but not Bill Sikes the burglar with Bill Sikes the burglar. So sensations, states of consciousness, do seem to be the one sort of thing left outside the physicalist picture, and for various reasons I just cannot believe that this can be so. That everything should be explicable in terms of physics (together of course with descriptions of the ways in which the parts are put together—roughly, biology is to physics as radio-engineering is to electro-magnetism) except the occurrence of sensations seems to me to be frankly unbelievable. Such sensations would be "nomological danglers," to use Feigl's expression.[5] It is not often realized how odd would be the laws whereby these nomological danglers would dangle. It is sometimes asked, "Why can't there be psycho-physical laws which are of a novel sort, just as the laws of electricity and magnetism were novelties from the standpoint of Newtonian mechanics?" Certainly we are pretty sure in the future to come across new ultimate laws of a novel type, but I expect them to relate simple constituents: for example, whatever ultimate particles are then in vogue. I cannot believe that ultimate laws of nature could relate simple constituents to configurations consisting of perhaps billions of neurons (and goodness knows how many billion billions of ultimate particles) all put together for all the world as though their main purpose in life was to be a negative feedback mechanism of a complicated sort. Such ultimate laws would be like nothing so far known in science. They have a queer "smell" to them. I am just unable to believe in the nomological danglers themselves, or in the laws whereby they would dangle. If any philosophical arguments seemed to compel us to believe in such things, I would suspect a catch in the argument. In any case it is the object of this paper to show that there are no philosophical arguments which compel us to be dualists.

The above is largely a confession of faith, but it explains why I find Wittgenstein's position (as I construe it) so congenial. For on this view there are, in a sense, no sensations. A man is a vast arrangement of physical particles, but there are not, over and above this, sensations or states of consciousness. There are just behavioral facts about this vast mechanism, such as that it expresses a temptation (behavior disposition) to say "there is a yellowish-red patch on the wall" or that it goes through a sophisticated sort of wince, that is, says "I am in pain." Admittedly Wittgenstein says that though the sensation "is not a something," it is nevertheless "not a nothing either" (paragraph 304), but this need only mean that the word "ache" has a use. An ache is a thing, but only in the innocuous sense in which the plain man, in the first paragraph of Frege's *Foundations of Arithmetic*, answers the question "what is the number one?" by "a thing." It should be noted that when I assert that to say "I have a yellowish-orange after-image" is to express a temptation to assert the physical-object statement "there is a yellowish-orange patch on the wall," I mean that saying "I have a yellowish-orange after-image" is (partly) the exercise of the disposition[6] which is the temptation. It is not to *report* that I have the temptation, any more than is "I love you" normally a report that I love someone. Saying "I love you" is just part of the behavior which is the exercise of the disposition of loving someone.

Though, for the reasons given above, I am very receptive to the above "expressive" account of sensation statements, I do not feel that it will quite do the trick. Maybe this is because I have not thought it out sufficiently, but it does seem to me as though, when a person says "I have an after-image," he *is* making a genuine report, and that when he says "I have a pain," he *is* doing more than "replace pain-behavior," and that "this more" is not just to say that he is in distress. I am not so sure, however, that to admit this is to admit that there are nonphysical correlates of brain processes. Why should not sensations just be brain processes of a certain sort? There are, of course, well-known (as well as lesser-known) philosophical objections to the view that reports of sensations are reports of brain-processes, but I shall try to argue that these arguments are by no means as cogent as is commonly thought to be the case.

Let me first try to state more accurately the thesis that sensations are brain processes. It is not the thesis that, for example, "after-image" or "ache" means the same as "brain process of sort *X*" (where "*X*" is replaced by a description of a certain sort of brain process). It is that, in so far as "after-image" or "ache" is a report of a process, it is a report of a process that *happens to be* a brain process. It follows that the thesis does not claim that sensation statements can be *translated* into statements about brain processes.[7] Nor does it claim that the logic of a sensation statement is the same as that of a brain-process statement. All it claims is that in so far as a sensation statement is a report of something, that something is in fact a brain process. Sensations are nothing over and above brain processes. Nations are nothing "over and above" citizens, but this does not prevent the logic of nation statements being very different from the logic of citizen statements, nor does it insure the translatability of nation statements into citizen statements. (I do not, however, wish to assert that the relation of sensation statements to brain-process statements is very like that of nation statements to citizen statements. Nations do not just *happen to be* nothing over and above citizens, for example. I bring in the "nations" example merely to make a negative point: that the fact that the logic of A-statements is different from that of B-statements does not insure that A's are anything over and above B's.)

Remarks on Identity When I say that a sensation is a brain process or that lightning is an electric discharge, I am using "is" in the sense of strict identity. (Just as in the—in this case necessary—proposition "7 is identical with the smallest prime number greater than 5.") When I say that a sensation is a brain process or that lightning is an electric discharge I do not mean just that the sensation is somehow spatially or temporally continuous with the brain process or that the lightning is just spatially or temporally continuous with the discharge. When on the other hand I say that the successful general is the same person as the small boy who stole the apples I mean only that the successful general I see before me is a time slice[8] of the same four-dimensional object of which the small boy stealing apples is an earlier time slice. However, the four-dimensional object which has the general-I-see-before-me for its late time slice is identical in the strict sense with the four-dimensional object which has the small-boy-stealing-apples for an early time slice. I distinguish these two senses of "is identical with" because I wish to make it clear that the brain-process doctrine asserts identity in the *strict* sense.

I shall now discuss various possible objections to the view that the processes reported in sensation statements are in fact processes in the brain. Most of us have met some of these objections in our first year as philosophy students. All the more reason to take a good look at them. Others of the objections will be more recondite and subtle.

Objection 1 Any illiterate peasant can talk perfectly well about his after-images, or how things look or feel to him, or about his aches and pains, and yet he may know nothing whatever about neurophysiology. A man may, like Aristotle, believe that the brain is an organ for cooling the body without any impairment of his ability to make true statements about his sensations. Hence the things we are talking about when we describe our sensations cannot be processes in the brain.

Reply You might as well say that a nation of slug-abeds, who never saw the morning star or knew of its existence, or who had never thought of the expression "the Morning Star," but who used the expression "the Evening Star" perfectly well, could not use this expression to refer to the same entity as we refer to (and describe as) "the Morning Star."[9]

You may object that the Morning Star is in a sense not the very same thing as the Evening Star, but only something spatio-temporally continuous with it. That is, you may say that the Morning Star is not the Evening Star in the strict sense of "identity" that I distinguished earlier. I can perhaps forestall this objection by considering the slug-abeds to be New Zealanders and the early risers to be Englishmen. Then the thing the New Zealanders describe as "the Morning Star" could be the very same thing (in the strict sense) as the Englishmen describe as "the Evening Star." And yet they could be ignorant of this fact.

There is, however, a more plausible example. Consider lightning.[10] Modern physical science tells us that lightning is a certain kind of electrical discharge due to ionization of clouds of water-vapor in the atmosphere. This, it is now believed, is what the true nature of lightning is. Note that there are not two things: a flash of lightning and an electrical discharge. There is one thing, a flash of lightning, which is described scientifically as an electrical discharge to the earth from a cloud of ionized water-molecules. The case is not at all like that of explaining a footprint by reference to a burglar. We say that what lightning really is, what its true nature as revealed by science is, is an electric discharge. (It is not the true nature of a footprint to be a burglar.)

To forestall irrelevant objections, I should like to make it clear that by "lightning" I mean the publicly observable physical object, lightning, not a visual sense-datum of lightning. I say that the publicly observable physical object lightning is in fact the electric discharge, not just a correlate of it. The sense-datum, or at least the having of the sense-datum, the "look" of lightning, may well in my view be a correlate of the electric discharge. For in my view it is a brain state *caused* by the lightning. But we should no more confuse sensations of lightning with lighting than we confuse sensations of a table with the table.

In short, the reply to Objection 1 is that there can be contingent statements of the form "A is identical with B," and a person may well know that something is an A without knowing that it is a B. An illiterate peasant might well be able to talk about his sensations without knowing about his brain processes, just as he can talk about lightning though he knows nothing of electricity.

Objection 2 It is only a contingent fact (if it is a fact) that when we have a certain kind of sensation there is a certain kind of process in our brain. Indeed it is possible, though perhaps in the highest degree unlikely, that our present physiological theories will be as out of date as the ancient theory connecting mental processes with goings on in the heart. It follows that when we report a sensation we are not reporting a brain-process.

Reply The objection certainly proves that when we say "I have an after-image" we cannot *mean* something of the form "I have such and such a brain-process." But this does not show that what we report (having an after-image) is not *in fact* a brain process. "I see lightning" does not *mean* "I see an electric discharge." Indeed, it is logically possible (though highly unlikely) that the electrical discharge account of lightning might one day be given up. Again, "I see the Evening Star" does not *mean* the same as "I see the Morning Star," and yet "the Evening Star and the Morning Star are one and the same thing" is a contingent proposition. Possibly Objection 2 derives some of its apparent strength from a "Fido"–Fido theory of meaning. If the meaning of an expression were what the expression named, then of course it *would* follow from the fact that "sensation" and "brain-process" have different meanings that they cannot name one and the same thing.

Objection 3[11] Even if Objections 1 and 2 do not prove that sensations are something over and above brain-processes, they do prove that the qualities of sensations are something over and above the qualities of brain-processes. That is, it may be possible to get out of asserting the existence of irreducibly psychic processes, but not out of asserting the existence of irreducibly psychic *properties*. For suppose we identify the Morning Star with the Evening Star. Then there must be some properties which logically imply that of being the Morning Star, and quite distinct properties which entail that of being the Evening Star. Again, there must be some properties (for example, that of being a yellow flash) which are logically distinct from those in the physicalist story.

Indeed, it might be thought that the objection succeeds at one jump. For consider the property of "being a yellow flash." It might seem that this property lies inevitably outside the physicalist framework within which I am trying to work (either by "yellow" being an objective emergent property of physical objects, or else by being a power to produce yellow sense-data, where "yellow," in this second instantiation of the word, refers to a purely phenomenal or introspectible quality). I must therefore digress for a moment and indicate how I deal with secondary qualities. I shall concentrate on color.

First of all, let me introduce the concept of a normal percipient. One person is more a normal percipient than another if he can make color discriminations that the other cannot. For example, if A can pick a lettuce leaf out of a heap of cabbage leaves, whereas B cannot though he can pick a lettuce leaf out of a heap of beetroot leaves, then A is more normal than B. (I am assuming that A and B are not given time to distinguish the leaves by their slight difference in shape, and so forth.) From the concept of "more normal than" it is easy to see how we can introduce the concept of "normal." Of course, Eskimos may make the finest discriminations at the blue end of the spectrum, Hottentots at the red end. In this case the concept of a normal percipient is a slightly idealized one, rather like that of "the mean sun" in astronomical chronology. There is no need to go into such subtleties now. I say that "This is red" means something roughly like "A normal percipient would not easily pick this out of a clump of geranium petals though he would pick it out of a clump of lettuce leaves." Of course it does not exactly mean this: a person might know the meaning of "red" without knowing anything about geraniums, or even about normal percipients. But the point is that a person can be *trained* to say "This is red" of objects which would not easily be picked out of geranium petals by a normal percipient, and so on. (Note that even a color-blind person can reasonably assert that something is red, though of course he needs to use another human being, not just himself, as his "color meter.") This account of secondary qualities explains their unimportance in physics. For obviously the discriminations and lack of discriminations made by a very complex neurophysiological mechanism are hardly likely to correspond to simple and nonarbitrary distinctions in nature.

I therefore elucidate colors as powers, in Locke's sense, to evoke certain sorts of discriminatory responses in human beings. They are also, of course, powers to cause sensations in human beings (an account still nearer Locke's). But these sensations, I am arguing, are identifiable with brain processes.

Now how do I get over the objection that a sensation can be identified with a brain process only if it has some phenomenal property, not possessed by brain processes, whereby one-half of the identification may be, so to speak, pinned down?

My suggestion is as follows. When a person says, "I see a yellowish-orange after-image," he is saying something like this: "*There is something going on which is like what is going on when* I have my eyes open, am awake, and there is an orange illuminated in good light in front of me, that is, when I really see an orange." (And there is no reason why a person should not say the same thing when he is having a veridical sense-datum, so long as we construe "like" in the last sentence in such a sense that something can be like itself.) Notice that the italicized words, namely "there is something going on which is like what is going on when," are all quasi-logical or topic-neutral words. This explains why the ancient Greek peasant's reports about his sensations can be neutral between dualistic metaphysics or my materialistic metaphysics. It explains how sensations can be brain-processes and yet how those who report them need know nothing about brain-processes. For he reports them only very abstractly as "something going on which is like what is going on when . . ." Similarly, a person may say "someone is in the room," thus reporting truly that the doctor is in the room, even though he has never heard of doctors. (There are not two people in the room: "someone" *and* the doctor.) This account of sensation statements also explains the singular elusiveness of "raw feels"—why no one seems to be able to pin any properties on them.[12] Raw feels, in my view, are colorless for the very same reason that *something* is colorless. This does not mean that sensations do not have properties, for if they are brain-processes they certainly have properties. It only means that in speaking of them as being like or unlike one another we need not know or mention these properties.

This, then, is how I would reply to Objection 3. The strength of my reply depends on the possibility of our being able to report that one thing is like another without being able to state the respect in which it is like. I am not sure whether this is so or not, and that is why I regard Objection 3 as the strongest with which I have to deal.

Objection 4 The after-image is not in physical space. The brain-process is. So the after-image is not a brain-process.

Reply This is an *ignoratio elenchi*. I am not arguing that the after-image is a brain-process, but that the experience of having an after-image is a brain-process. It is the *experience* which is reported in the introspective report. Similarly, if it is objected that the after-image is yellowy-orange but that a surgeon looking into your brain would see nothing yellowy-orange, my reply is that it is the experience of seeing yellowy-orange that is being described, and this experience is not a yellowy-orange something. So to say that a brain-process cannot be yellowy-orange is not to say that a brain-process cannot in fact be the experience of having a yellowy-orange after-image. There is, in a sense, no such thing as an after-image or a sense-datum, though there is such a thing as the experience of having an image, and this experience is described indirectly in material object language, not in phenomenal language, for there is no such thing.[13] We describe the experience by saying, in effect, that it is like the experience we have when, for example, we really see a yellowy-orange patch on the wall. Trees and wallpaper can be green, but not the experience of seeing or imagining a tree or wallpaper. (Or if they are described as green or yellow this can only be in a derived sense.)

Objection 5 It would make sense to say of a molecular movement in the brain that it is swift or slow, straight or circular, but it makes no sense to say this of the experience of seeing something yellow.

Reply So far we have not given sense to talk of experiences as swift or slow, straight or circular. But I am not claiming that "experience" and "brain-process" mean the same or even that they have the same logic. "Somebody" and "the doctor" do not have the same logic, but this does not lead us to suppose that talking about somebody telephoning is talking about someone over and above, say, the doctor. The ordinary man when he reports an experience is reporting that something is going on, but he leaves it open as to what sort of thing is going on, whether in a material solid medium, or perhaps in some sort of gaseous medium, or even perhaps in some sort of nonspatial medium (if this makes sense). All that I am saying is that "experience" and "brain-process" may in fact refer to the same thing, and if so we may easily adopt a convention (which is not a change in our present rules for the use of experience words but an addition to them) whereby it would make sense to talk of an experience in terms appropriate to physical processes.

Objection 6 Sensations are private, brain processes are *public*. If I sincerely say, "I see a yellowish-orange after-image" and I am not making a verbal mistake, then I cannot be wrong. But I can be wrong about a brain-process. The scientist looking into my brain might be having an illusion. Moveover, it makes sense to say that two or more people are observing the same brain-process but not that two or more people are reporting the same inner experience.

Reply This shows that the language of introspective reports has a different logic from the language of material processes. It is obvious that until the brain-process theory is much improved and widely accepted there will be no *criteria* for saying "Smith has an experience of such-and-such a sort" *except* Smith's introspective reports. So we have adopted a rule of language that (normally) what Smith says goes.

Objection 7 I can imagine myself turned to stone and yet having images, aches, pains, and so on.

Reply I can imagine that the electrical theory of lightning is false, that lightning is some sort of purely optical phenomenon. I can imagine that lightning is not an electrical discharge. I can imagine that the Evening Star is not the Morning Star. But it is. All the objection shows is that "experience" and "brain-process" do not have the same meaning. It does not show that an experience is not in fact a brain process.

This objection is perhaps much the same as one which can be summed up by the slogan: "What can be composed of nothing cannot be composed of anything."[14] The argument goes as follows: on the brain-process thesis the identity between the brain-process and the experience is a contingent one. So it is logically possible that there should be no brain-process, and no process of any other sort, either (no heart process, no kidney process, no liver process). There would be the experience but no "corresponding" physiological process with which we might be able to identify it empirically.

I suspect that the objector is thinking of the experience as a ghostly entity. So it is composed of something, not of nothing, after all. On his view it is composed of ghost stuff, and on mine it is composed of brain stuff. Perhaps the counter-reply will be[15] that the experience is simple and uncompounded, and so it is not composed of anything after all. This seems to be a quibble, for, if it were taken seriously, the remark "What can be composed of nothing cannot be composed of anything" could be recast as an a priori argument against Democritus and atomism and for Descartes and infinite divisibility. And it seems odd that a question of this sort could be settled a priori. We must therefore construe the word "composed" in a very weak sense, which would allow us to say that even an indivisible atom is composed of something (namely, itself). The dualist cannot really say that an experience can be composed of nothing. For he holds that experiences are something over and above material processes, that is, that they are a sort of ghost stuff. (Or perhaps ripples in an underlying ghost stuff.) I say that the dualist's hypothesis is a perfectly intelligible one. But I say that experiences are not to be identified with ghost stuff but with brain stuff. This is another hypothesis, and in my view a very plausible one. The present argument cannot knock it down a priori.

Objection 8 The "beetle in the box" objection (see Wittgenstein, *Philosophical Investigations*, paragraph 293). How could descriptions of experiences, if these are genuine reports, get a foothold in language? For any rule of language must have public criteria for its correct application.

Reply The change from describing how things are to describing how we feel is just a change from uninhibitedly saying "this is so" to saying "this looks so." That is, when the naive person might be tempted to say, "There is a patch of light on the wall which moves whenever I move my eyes" or "A pin is being stuck into me," we have learned how to resist this temptation and say "It *looks as though* there is a patch of light on the wallpaper" or "It *feels as though* someone were sticking a pin into me." The introspective account tells us about the individual's state of consciousness in the same way as does "I see a patch of light" or "I feel a pin being stuck into me": it differs from the corresponding perception statement in so far as (a) in the perception statement the individual "goes beyond the evidence of his senses" in describing his environment and (b) in the introspective report he withholds descriptive epithets he is inclined to ascribe to the environment, perhaps because he suspects that they may not be appropriate to the actual state of affairs. Psychologically speaking, the change from talking about the environment to talking about one's state of consciousness is simply a matter of inhibiting descriptive reactions not justified by appearances alone, and of disinhibiting descriptive reactions which are normally inhibited because the individual has learned that they are unlikely to provide a reliable guide to the state of the environment in the prevailing circumstances.[16] To say that something looks green to me is to say that my experience is like the experience I get when I see something that really is green. In my reply to Objection 3, I pointed out the extreme openness or generality of statements which report experiences. This explains why there is no language of private qualities. (Just as "someone," unlike "the doctor," is a colorless word.)[17]

If it is asked what is the difference between those brain processes which, in my view, are experiences and those brain processes which are not, I can only reply that this is at present unknown. But it does not seem to me altogether fanciful to conjecture that the difference may in part be that between perception and reception (in Dr. D. M. MacKay's terminology) and that the type of brain process which is an experience might be identifiable with MacKay's active "matching response."[18]

I have now considered a number of objections to the brain-process thesis. I wish now to conclude by some remarks on the logical status of the thesis itself. U. T. Place seems to hold that it is a straight-out scientific hypothesis.[19] If so, he is partly right and partly wrong. If the issue is between (say) a brain-process thesis and a heart thesis, or a liver thesis, or a kidney thesis, then the issue is a purely empirical one, and the verdict is overwhelmingly in favor of the brain. The right sorts of things don't go on in the heart, liver, or kidney, nor do these organs possess the right sort of complexity of structure. On the other hand, if the issue is between a brain-or-heart-or-liver-or-kidney thesis (that is, some form of materialism) on the one hand and epiphenomenalism on the other hand, then the issue is not an empirical one. For there is no conceivable experiment which could decide between materialism and epiphenomenalism. This latter issue is not like the average straight-out empirical issue in science, but like the issue between the nineteenth-century English naturalist Philip Gosse[20] and the orthodox geologists and paleontologists of his day. According to Gosse, the earth was created about 4000 B.C. exactly as described in *Genesis*, with twisted rock strata, "evidence" of erosion, and so forth, and all sorts of fossils, all in their appropriate strata, just as if the usual evolutionist story had been true. Clearly this theory is in a sense irrefutable: no evidence can possibly tell against it. Let us ignore the theological setting in which Philip Gosse's hypothesis had been placed, thus ruling out objections of a theological kind, such as "what a queer God who would go to such elaborate lengths to deceive us." Let us suppose that it is held that the universe just *began* in 4004 B.C. with the initial conditions just everywhere as they were in 4004 B.C., and in particular that our own planet began with sediment in the rivers, eroded cliffs, fossils in the rocks, and so on. No scientist would ever entertain this as a serious hypothesis, consistent though it is with all possible evidence. The hypothesis offends against the principles of parsimony and simplicity. There would be far too many brute and inexplicable facts. Why are pterodactyl bones just as they are? No explanation in terms of the evolution of pterodactyls from earlier forms of life would any longer be possible. We would have millions of facts about the world as it was in 4004 B.C. that just have to be *accepted.*

The issue between the brain-process theory and epiphenomenalism seems to be of the above sort. (Assuming that a behavioristic reduction of introspective reports is not possible.) If it be agreed that there are no cogent philosophical arguments which force us into accepting dualism, and if the brain process theory and dualism are equally consistent with the facts, then the principles of parsimony and simplicity seem to me to decide overwhelmingly in favor of the brain-process theory. As I pointed out earlier, dualism involves a large number of irreducible psychophysical laws (whereby the "nomological danglers" dangle) of a queer sort, that just have to be taken on trust, and are just as difficult to swallow as the irreducible facts about the paleontology of the earth with which we are faced on Philip Gosse's theory.

Notes

1. This paper takes its departure from arguments to be found in U. T. Place's "Is Consciousness a Brain Process?" (*British Journal of Psychology*, XLVII, 1956, 44–50). I have had the benefit of discussing Place's thesis in a good many universities in the United States and Australia, and I hope that the present paper answers objections to his thesis which Place has not considered, and presents his thesis in a more nearly unobjectionable form. This paper is meant also to supplement "The 'Mental' and the 'Physical,'" by H. Feigl (in *Minnesota Studies in the Philosophy of Science*, II, 370–497), which argues for much the same thesis as Place's.

2. Some philosophers of my acquaintance, who have the advantage over me in having known Wittgenstein, would say that this interpretation of him is too behavioristic. However, it seems to me a very natural interpretation of his printed words, and whether or not it is Wittgenstein's real view it is certainly an interesting and important one. I wish to consider it here as a possible rival both to the "brain-process" thesis and to straight-out old-fashioned dualism.

3. See Ryle, *Concept of Mind* (New York, 1949), p. 93.

4. On this point see Paul Oppenheim and Hilary Putnam, "Unity of Science as a Working Hypothesis," in *Minnesota Studies in the Philosophy of Science*, II, 3–36; also my note "Plausible Reasoning in Philosophy," *Mind*, LXVI (1957), 75–78.

5. Feigl, *op. cit.*, p. 428.

6. Wittgenstein did not like the word "disposition." I am using it to put in a nutshell (and perhaps inaccurately) the view which I am attributing to Wittgenstein. I should like to repeat that I do not wish to claim that my interpretation of Wittgenstein is correct. Some of those who knew him do not interpret him in this way. It is merely a view which I find myself extracting from his printed words and which I think is important and worth discussing for its own sake.

7. See Place, *op. cit.*, p. 45, near top, and Feigl, *op. cit.*, p. 390, near top.

8. See J. H. Woodger, *Theory Construction* (Chicago, 1939), p. 38 (International Encyclopedia of Unified Science, Vol. 2, No. 5). I here permit myself to speak loosely. For warnings against possible ways of going wrong with this sort of talk, see my note "Spatialising Time," *Mind*, LXIV (1955), 239–41.

9. Cf. Feigl, *op. cit.*, p. 439.

10. See Place, *op. cit.*, p. 47; also Feigl, *op. cit.*, p. 438.

11. I think this objection was first put to me by Professor Max Black. I think it is the most subtle of any of those I have considered, and the one which I am least confident of having satisfactorily met.

12. See B. A. Farrell, "Experience," *Mind*, LIX (1950), especially 174.

13. Dr. J. R. Smythies claims that a sense-datum language could be taught independently of the material object language ("A Note on the Fallacy of the 'Phenomenological Fallacy,'" *British Journal of Psychology*, XLVIII, 1957, 141–144.) I am not so sure of this: there must be some public criteria for a person having got a rule wrong before we can teach him the rule. I suppose someone might *accidentally* learn color words by Dr. Smythies' procedure. I am not, of course, denying that we can learn a sense-datum language in the sense that we can learn to report our experience. Nor would Place deny it.

14. I owe this objection to Mr. C. B. Martin. I gather that he no longer wishes to maintain this objection, at any rate in its present form.

15. Martin did not make this reply, but one of his students did.

16. I owe this point to Place, in correspondence.

17. The "beetle in the box" objection is, *if it is sound*, an objection to *any* view, and in particular the Cartesian one, that introspective reports are genuine reports. So it is no objection to a weaker thesis that I would be concerned to uphold, namely, that if introspective reports of "experiences" are genuinely reports, then the things they are reports of are in fact brain processes.

18. See his article "Towards an Information-Flow model of Human Behaviour," *British Journal of Psychology*, XLVII (1956), 30–43.

19. *Op. cit.*

20. See the entertaining account of Gosse's book *Omphalos* by Martin Gardner in *Fads and Fallacies in the Name of Science* (2nd ed., New York, 1957).

24 What Is It Like to Be a Bat?

Thomas Nagel

Consciousness is what makes the mind–body problem really intractable. Perhaps that is why current discussions of the problem give it little attention or get it obviously wrong. The recent wave of reductionist euphoria has produced several analyses of mental phenomena and mental concepts designed to explain the possibility of some variety of materialism, psychophysical identification, or reduction.[1] But the problems dealt with are those common to this type of reduction and other types, and what makes the mind–body problem unique, and unlike the water–H_2O problem or the Turing machine–IBM machine problem or the lightning–electrical discharge problem or the gene–DNA problem or the oak tree–hydrocarbon problem, is ignored.

Every reductionist has his favorite analogy from modern science. It is most unlikely that any of these unrelated examples of successful reduction will shed light on the relation of mind to brain. But philosophers share the general human weakness for explanations of what is incomprehensible in terms suited for what is familiar and well understood, though entirely different. This has led to the acceptance of implausible accounts of the mental largely because they would permit familiar kinds of reduction. I shall try to explain why the usual examples do not help us to understand the relation between mind and body—why, indeed, we have at present no conception of what an explanation of the physical nature of a mental phenomenon would be. Without consciousness the mind–body problem would be much less interesting. With consciousness it seems hopeless. The most important and characteristic feature of conscious mental phenomena is very poorly understood. Most reductionist theories do not even try to explain it. And careful examination will show that no currently available concept of reduction is applicable to it. Perhaps a new theoretical form can be devised for the purpose, but such a solution, if it exists, lies in the distant intellectual future.

Conscious experience is a widespread phenomenon. It occurs at many levels of animal life, though we cannot be sure of its presence in the simpler organisms, and it is very difficult to say in general what provides evidence of it. (Some extremists have been prepared to deny it even of mammals other than man.) No doubt it occurs in countless forms totally unimaginable to us, on other planets in other solar systems throughout the universe. But no matter how the form may vary, the fact that an organism has conscious experience *at all* means, basically, that there is something it is like to *be* that organism. There may be further implications about the form of the experience; there may even (though I doubt it) be implications about the behavior of the organism. But fundamentally an organism has conscious mental states if and only if there is something that it is like to *be* that organism—something it is like *for* the organism.

We may call this the subjective character of experience. It is not captured by any of the familiar, recently devised reductive analyses of the mental, for all of them are logically compatible with its absence. It is not analyzable in terms of any explanatory system of functional states, or intentional states, since these could be ascribed to robots or automata that behaved like people though they experienced nothing.[2] It is not analyzable in terms of the causal role of experiences in relation to typical human behavior—for similar reasons.[3] I do not deny that conscious mental states and events cause behavior, nor that they may be given functional characterizations. I deny only that this kind of thing exhausts their analysis. Any reductionist program has to be based on an analysis of what is to be reduced. If the analysis leaves something out, the problem will be falsely posed. It is useless to base the defense of materialism on any analysis of mental phenomena that fails to deal explicitly with their subjective character. For there is no reason to suppose that a reduction which seems plausible when no attempt is made to account for consciousness can be extended to include consciousness. Without some idea, therefore, of what the subjective character of experience is, we cannot know what is required of a physicalist theory.

While an account of the physical basis of mind must explain many things, this appears to be the most difficult. It is impossible to exclude the phenomenological features of experience from a reduction in the same way that one excludes the phenomenal features of an ordinary substance from a physical or chemical reduction of it—namely, by explaining them as effects on the minds of human observers.[4] If physicalism is to be defended, the phenomenological features must themselves be given a physical account. But when we examine their subjective character it seems that such a result is impossible. The reason is that every subjective phenomenon is essentially connected with a single point of view, and it seems inevitable that an objective, physical theory will abandon that point of view.

Let me first try to state the issue somewhat more fully than by referring to the relation between the subjective and the objective, or between the *pour-soi* and the *en-soi*. This is far from easy. Facts about what it is like to be an *X* are very peculiar, so peculiar that some may be inclined to doubt their reality, or the significance of claims about them. To illustrate the connection between subjectivity and a point of view, and to make evident the importance of subjective features, it will help to explore the matter in relation to an example that brings out clearly the divergence between the two types of conception, subjective and objective.

I assume we all believe that bats have experience. After all, they are mammals, and there is no more doubt that they have experience than that mice or pigeons or whales have experience. I have chosen bats instead of wasps or flounders because if one travels too far down the phylogenetic tree, people gradually shed their faith that there is experience there at all. Bats, although more closely related to us than those other species, nevertheless present a range of activity and a sensory apparatus so different from ours that the problem I want to pose is exceptionally vivid (though it certainly could be raised with other species). Even without the benefit of philosophical reflection, anyone who has spent some time in an enclosed space with an excited bat knows what it is to encounter a fundamentally *alien* form of life.

I have said that the essence of the belief that bats have experience is that there is something that it is like to be a bat. Now we know that most bats (the microchiroptera, to be precise) perceive the external world primarily by sonar, or echolocation, detecting the reflections, from objects within range, of their own rapid, subtly modulated, high-frequency shrieks. Their brains are designed to correlate the outgoing impulses with the subsequent echoes, and the information thus acquired enables bats to make precise discriminations of distance, size, shape, motion, and texture comparable to those we make by vision. But bat sonar, though clearly a form of perception, is not similar in its operation to any sense that we possess, and there is no reason to suppose that it is subjectively like anything we can experience or imagine. This appears to create difficulties for the notion of what it is like to be a bat. We must consider whether any method will permit us to extrapolate to the inner life of the bat from our own case,[5] and if not, what alternative methods there may be for understanding the notion.

Our own experience provides the basic material for our imagination, whose range is therefore limited. It will not help to try to imagine that one has webbing on one's arms, which enables one to fly around at dusk and dawn catching insects in one's mouth; that one has very poor vision, and perceives the surrounding world by a system of reflected high-frequency sound signals; and that one spends the day hanging upside down by one's feet in an attic. In so far as I can imagine this (which is not very far), it tells me only what it would be like for *me* to behave as a bat behaves. But that is not the question. I want to know what it is like for a *bat* to be a bat. Yet if I try to imagine this, I am restricted to the resources of my own mind, and those resources are inadequate to the task. I cannot perform it either by imagining additions to my present experience, or by imagining segments gradually subtracted from it, or by imagining some combination of additions, subtractions, and modifications.

To the extent that I could look and behave like a wasp or a bat without changing my fundamental structure, my experiences would not be anything like the experiences of those animals. On the other hand, it is doubtful that any meaning can be attached to the supposition that I should possess the internal neurophysiological constitution of a bat. Even if I could by gradual degrees be transformed into a bat, nothing in my present constitution enables me to imagine what the experiences of such a future stage of myself thus metamorphosed would be like. The best evidence would come from the experiences of bats, if we only knew what they were like.

So if extrapolation from our own case is involved in the idea of what it is like to be a bat, the extrapolation must be incompletable. We cannot form more than a schematic conception of what it *is* like. For example, we may ascribe general *types* of experience on the basis of the animal's structure and behavior. Thus we describe bat sonar as a form of three-dimensional forward perception; we believe that bats feel some versions of pain, fear, hunger, and lust, and that they have other, more familiar types of perception besides sonar. But we believe that these experiences also have in each case a specific subjective character, which it is beyond our ability to conceive. And if there is conscious life elsewhere in the universe, it is likely that some of it will not be describable even in the most general experiential terms available to us.[6] (The problem is not confined to exotic cases, however, for it exists between one person and another. The subjective character of the experience of a person deaf and blind from birth is not accessible to me, for example, nor presumably is mine to him. This does not prevent us each from believing that the other's experience has such a subjective character.)

If anyone is inclined to deny that we can believe in the existence of facts like this whose exact nature we cannot possibly conceive, he should reflect that in contemplating the bats we are in much the same position that intelligent bats or Martians[7] would occupy if they tried to form a conception of what it was like to be us. The structure of their own minds might make it impossible for them to succeed, but we know they would be wrong to conclude that there is not anything precise that it is like to be us: that only certain general types of mental state could be ascribed to us (perhaps perception and appetite would be concepts common to us both; perhaps not). We know they would be wrong to draw such a skeptical conclusion because we know what it is like to be us. And we know that while it includes an enormous amount of variation and complexity, and while we do not possess the vocabulary to describe it adequately, its subjective character is highly specific, and in some respects describable in terms that can be understood only by creatures like us. The fact that we cannot expect ever to accommodate in our language a detailed description of Martian or bat phenomenology should not lead us to dismiss as meaningless the claim that bats and Martians have experiences fully comparable in richness of detail to our own. It would be fine if someone were to develop concepts and a theory that enabled us to think about those things; but such an understanding may be permanently denied to us by the limits of our nature. And to deny the reality or logical significance of what we can never describe or understand is the crudest form of cognitive dissonance.

This brings us to the edge of a topic that requires much more discussion than I can give it here: namely, the relation between facts on the one hand and conceptual schemes or systems of representation on the other. My realism about the subjective domain in all its forms implies a belief in the existence of facts beyond the reach of human concepts. Certainly it is possible for a human being to believe that there are facts which humans never *will* possess the requisite concepts to represent or comprehend. Indeed, it would be foolish to doubt this, given the finiteness of humanity's expectations. After all, there would have been transfinite numbers even if everyone had been wiped out by the Black Death before Cantor discovered them. But one might also believe that there are facts which *could* not ever be represented or comprehended by human beings, even if the species lasted forever—simply because our structure does not permit us to operate with concepts of the requisite type. This impossibility might even be observed by other beings, but it is not clear that the existence of such beings, or the possibility of their existence, is a precondition of the significance of the hypothesis that there are humanly inaccessible facts. (After all, the nature of beings with access to humanly inaccessible facts is presumably itself a humanly inaccessible fact.) Reflection on what it is like to be a bat seems to lead us, therefore, to the conclusion that there are facts that do not consist in the truth of propositions expressible in a human language. We can be compelled to recognize the existence of such facts without being able to state or comprehend them.

I shall not pursue this subject, however. Its bearing on the topic before us (namely, the mind–body problem) is that it enables us to make a general observation about the subjective character of experience. Whatever may be the status of facts about what it is like to be a human being, or a bat, or a Martian, these appear to be facts that embody a particular point of view.

I am not adverting here to the alleged privacy of experience to its possessor. The point of view in question is not one accessible only to a single individual. Rather it is a *type*. It is often possible to take up a point of view other than one's own, so the comprehension of such facts is not limited to one's own case. There is a sense in which phenomenological facts are perfectly objective: one person can know or say of another what the quality of the other's experience is. They are subjective, however, in the sense that even this objective ascription of experience is possible only for someone sufficiently similar to the object of ascription to be able to adopt his point of view—to understand the ascription in the first person as well as in the third, so to speak. The more different from oneself the other experiencer is, the less success one can expect with this enterprise. In our own case we occupy the relevant point of view, but we will have as much difficulty understanding our own experience properly if we approach it from another point of view as we would if we tried to understand the experience of another species without taking up *its* point of view.[8]

This bears directly on the mind–body problem. For if the facts of experience—facts about what it is like *for* the experiencing organism—are accessible only from one point of view, then it is a mystery how the true character of experiences could be revealed in the physical operation of that organism. The latter is a domain of objective facts *par excellence*—the kind that can be observed and understood from many points of view and by individuals with differing perceptual systems. There are no comparable imaginative obstacles to the acquisition of knowledge about bat neurophysiology by human scientists, and intelligent bats or Martians might learn more about the human brain than we ever will.

This is not by itself an argument against reduction. A Martian scientist with no understanding of visual perception could understand the rainbow, or lightning, or clouds as physical phenomena, though he would never be able to understand the human concepts of rainbow, lightning, or cloud, or the place these things occupy in our phenomenal world. The objective nature of the things picked out by these concepts could be apprehended by him because, although the concepts themselves are connected with a particular point of view and a particular visual phenomenology, the things apprehended from that point of view are not: they are observable from the point of view but external to it; hence they can be comprehended from other points of view also, either by the same organisms or by others. Lightning has an objective character that is not exhausted by its visual appearance, and this can be investigated by a Martian without vision. To be precise, it has a *more* objective character than is revealed in its visual appearance. In speaking of the move from subjective to objective characterization, I wish to remain noncommittal about the existence of an end point, the completely objective intrinsic nature of the thing, which one might or might not be able to reach. It may be more accurate to think of objectivity as a direction in which the understanding can travel. And in understanding a phenomenon like lightning, it is legitimate to go as far away as one can from a strictly human viewpoint.[9]

In the case of experience, on the other hand, the connection with a particular point of view seems much closer. It is difficult to understand what could be meant by the *objective* character of an experience, apart from the particular point of view from which its subject apprehends it. After all, what would be left of what it was like to be a bat if one removed the viewpoint of the bat? But if experience does not have, in addition to its subjective character, an objective nature that can be apprehended from many different points of view, then how can it be supposed that a Martian investigating my brain might be observing physical processes which were my mental processes (as he might observe physical processes which were bolts of lightning), only from a different point of view? How, for that matter, could a human physiologist observe them from another point of view?[10]

We appear to be faced with a general difficulty about psychophysical reduction. In other areas the process of reduction is a move in the direction of greater objectivity, toward a more accurate view of the real nature of things. This is accomplished by reducing our dependence on individual or species-specific points of view toward the object of investigation. We describe it not in terms of the impressions it makes on our senses, but in terms of its more general effects and of properties detectable by means other than the human senses. The less it depends on a specifically human viewpoint, the more objective is our description. It is possible to follow this path because although the concepts and ideas we employ in thinking about the external world are initially applied from a point of view that involves our perceptual apparatus, they are used by us to refer to things beyond themselves—toward which we *have* the phenomenal point of view. Therefore we can abandon it in favor of another, and still be thinking about the same things.

Experience itself, however, does not seem to fit the pattern. The idea of moving from appearance to reality seems to make no sense here. What is the analogue in this case to pursuing a more objective understanding of the same phenomena by abandoning the initial subjective viewpoint toward them in favor of another that is more objective but concerns the same thing? Certainly it *appears* unlikely that we will get closer to the real nature of human experience by leaving behind the particularity of our human point of view and striving for a description in terms accessible to beings that could not imagine what it was like to be us. If the subjective character of experience is fully comprehensible only from one point of view, then any shift to greater objectivity—that is, less attachment to a specific viewpoint—does not take us nearer to the real nature of the phenomenon: it takes us farther away from it.

In a sense, the seeds of this objection to the reducibility of experience are already detectable in successful cases of reduction; for in discovering sound to be, in reality, a wave phenomenon in air or other media, we leave behind one viewpoint to take up another, and the auditory, human or animal viewpoint that we leave behind remains unreduced. Members of radically different species may both understand the same physical events in objective terms, and this does not require that they understand the phenomenal forms in which those events appear to the senses of members of the other species. Thus it is a condition of their referring to a common reality that their more particular viewpoints are not part of the common reality that they both apprehend. The reduction can succeed only if the species-specific viewpoint is omitted from what is to be reduced.

But while we are right to leave this point of view aside in seeking a fuller understanding of the external world, we cannot ignore it permanently, since it is the essence of the internal world, and not merely a point of view on it. Most of the neobehaviorism of recent philosophical psychology results from the effort to substitute an objective concept of mind for the real thing, in order to have nothing left over which cannot be reduced. If we acknowledge that a physical theory of mind must account for the subjective character of experience, we must admit that no presently available conception gives us a clue how this could be done. The problem is unique. If mental processes are indeed physical processes, then there is something it is like, intrinsically,[11] to undergo certain physical processes. What it is for such a thing to be the case remains a mystery.

What moral should be drawn from these reflections, and what should be done next? It would be a mistake to conclude that physicalism must be false. Nothing is proved by the inadequacy of physicalist hypotheses that assume a faulty objective analysis of mind. It would be truer to say that physicalism is a position we cannot understand because we do not at present have any conception of how it might be true. Perhaps it will be thought unreasonable to require such a conception as a condition of understanding. After all, it might be said, the meaning of physicalism is clear enough: mental states are states of the body; mental events are physical events. We do not know *which* physical states and events they are, but that should not prevent us from understanding the hypothesis. What could be clearer than the words "is" and "are"?

But I believe it is precisely this apparent clarity of the word "is" that is deceptive. Usually, when we are told that *X* is *Y* we know *how* it is supposed to be true, but that depends on a conceptual or theoretical background and is not conveyed by the "is" alone. We know how both "*X*" and "*Y*" refer, and the kinds of things to which they refer, and we have a rough idea how the two referential paths might converge on a single thing, be it an object, a person, a process, an event, or whatever. But when the two terms of the identification are very disparate it may not be so clear how it could be true. We may not have even a rough idea of how the two referential paths could converge, or what kind of things they might converge on, and a theoretical framework may have to be supplied to enable us to understand this. Without the framework, an air of mysticism surrounds the identification.

This explains the magical flavor of popular presentations of fundamental scientific discoveries, given out as propositions to which one must subscribe without really understanding them. For example, people are now told at an early age that all matter is really energy. But despite the fact that they know what "is" means, most of them never form a conception of what makes this claim true, because they lack the theoretical background.

At the present time the status of physicalism is similar to that which the hypothesis that matter is energy would have had if uttered by a pre-Socratic philosopher. We do not have the beginnings of a conception of how it might be true. In order to understand the hypothesis that a mental event is a physical event, we require more than an understanding of the word "is." The idea of how a mental and a physical term might refer to the same thing is lacking, and the usual analogies with theoretical identification in other fields fail to supply it. They fail because if we construe the reference of mental terms to physical events on the usual model, we either get a reappearance of separate subjective events as the effects through which mental reference to physical events is secured, or else we get a false account of how mental terms refer (for example, a causal behaviorist one).

Strangely enough, we may have evidence for the truth of something we cannot really understand. Suppose a caterpillar is locked in a sterile safe by someone unfamiliar with insect metamorphosis, and weeks later the safe is reopened, revealing a butterfly. If the person knows that the safe has been shut the whole time, he has reason to believe that the butterfly is or was once the caterpillar, without having any idea in what sense this might be so. (One possibility is that the caterpillar contained a tiny winged parasite that devoured it and grew into the butterfly.)

It is conceivable that we are in such a position with regard to physicalism. Donald Davidson has argued that if mental events have physical causes and effects, they must have physical descriptions. He holds that we have reason to believe this even though we do not—and in fact *could* not—have a general psychophysical theory.[12] His argument applies to intentional mental events, but I think we also have some reason to believe that sensations are physical processes, without being in a position to understand how. Davidson's position is that certain physical events have irreducibly mental properties, and perhaps some view describable in this way is correct. But nothing of which we can now form a conception corresponds to it; nor have we any idea what a theory would be like that enabled us to conceive of it.[13]

Very little work has been done on the basic question (from which mention of the brain can be entirely omitted) whether any sense can be made of experiences' having an objective character at all. Does it make sense, in other words, to ask what my experiences are *really* like, as opposed to how they appear to me? We cannot genuinely understand the hypothesis that their nature is captured in a physical description unless we understand the more fundamental idea that they *have* an objective nature (or that objective processes can have a subjective nature).[14]

I should like to close with a speculative proposal. It may be possible to approach the gap between subjective and objective from another direction. Setting aside temporarily the relation between the mind and the brain, we can pursue a more objective understanding of the mental in its own right. At present we are completely unequipped to think about the subjective character of experience without relying on the imagination—without taking up the point of view of the experiential subject. This should be regarded as a challenge to form new concepts and devise a new method—an objective phenomenology not dependent on empathy or the imagination. Though presumably it would not capture everything, its goal would be to describe, at least in part, the subjective character of experiences in a form comprehensible to beings incapable of having those experiences.

We would have to develop such a phenomenology to describe the sonar experiences of bats; but it would also be possible to begin with humans. One might try, for example, to develop concepts that could be used to explain to a person blind from birth what it was like to see. One would reach a blank wall eventually, but it should be possible to devise a method of expressing in objective terms much more than we can at present, and with much greater precision. The loose intermodal analogies—for example, "Red is like the sound of a trumpet"—which crop up in discussions of this subject are of little use. That should be clear to anyone who has both heard a trumpet and seen red. But structural features of perception might be more accessible to objective description, even though something would be left out. And concepts alternative to those we learn in the first person may enable us to arrive at a kind of understanding even of our own experience which is denied us by the very ease of description and lack of distance that subjective concepts afford.

Apart from its own interest, a phenomenology that is in this sense objective may permit questions about the physical[15] basis of experience to assume a more intelligible form. Aspects of subjective experience that admitted this kind of objective description might be better candidates for objective explanations of a more familiar sort. But whether or not this guess is correct, it seems unlikely that any physical theory of mind can be contemplated until more thought has been given to the general problem of subjective and objective. Otherwise we cannot even pose the mind–body problem without sidestepping it.[16]

Notes

1. Examples are J. J. C. Smart, *Philosophy and Scientific Realism* (London, 1963); David K. Lewis, "An Argument for the Identity Theory," *Journal of Philosophy*, 63 (1966), reprinted with addenda in David M. Rosenthal, *Materialism and the Mind–Body Problem* (Englewood Cliffs, N.J., 1971); Hilary Putnam, "Psychological Predicates" in Capitan and Merrill, *Art, Mind, and Religion* (Pittsburgh, 1967), reprinted in Rosenthal, *op. cit.*, as "The Nature of Mental States"; D. M. Armstrong, *A Materialist Theory of the Mind* (London, 1968); D. C. Dennett, *Content and Consciousness* (London, 1969). I have expressed earlier doubts in "Armstrong on the Mind," *Philosophical Review*, 79 (1970), 394–403; "Brain Bisection and the Unity of Consciousness," *Synthese*, 22 (1971); and a review of Dennett, *Journal of Philosophy*, 69 (1972). See also Saul Kripke, "Naming and Necessity" in Davidson and Harman, *Semantics of Natural Language* (Dordrecht, 1972), esp. pp. 334–342; and M. T. Thornton, "Ostensive Terms and Materialism," *The Monist*, 56 (1972).

2. Perhaps there could not actually be such robots. Perhaps anything complex enough to behave like a person would have experiences. But that, if true, is a fact which cannot be discovered merely by analyzing the concept of experience.

3. It is not equivalent to that about which we are incorrigible, both because we are not incorrigible about experience and because experience is present in animals lacking language and thought, who have no beliefs at all about their experiences.

4. Cf. Richard Rorty, "Mind–Body Identity, Privacy, and Categories," *Review of Metaphysics*, 19 (1965), esp. 37–38.

5. By "our own case" I do not mean just "my own case," but rather the mentalistic ideas that we apply unproblematically to ourselves and other human beings.

6. Therefore the analogical form of the English expression "what it is *like*" is misleading. It does not mean "what (in our experience) it *resembles*," but rather "how it is for the subject himself."

7. Any intelligent extraterrestrial beings totally different from us.

8. It may be easier than I suppose to transcend inter-species barriers with the aid of the imagination. For example, blind people are able to detect objects near them by a form of sonar, using vocal clicks or taps of a cane. Perhaps if one knew what that was like, one could by extension imagine roughly what it was like to possess the much more refined sonar of a bat. The distance between oneself and other persons and other species can fall anywhere on a continuum. Even for other persons the understanding of what it is like to be them is only partial, and when one moves to species very different from oneself, a lesser degree of partial understanding may still be available. The imagination is remarkably flexible. My point, however, is not that we cannot *know* what it is like to be a bat. I am not raising that epistemological problem. My point is rather that even to form a *conception* of what it is like to be a bat (and a fortiori to know what it is like to be a

bat) one must take up the bat's point of view. If one can take it up roughly, or partially, then one's conception will also be rough or partial. Or so it seems in our present state of understanding.

9. The problem I am going to raise can therefore be posed even if the distinction between more subjective and more objective descriptions or viewpoints can itself be made only within a larger human point of view. I do not accept this kind of conceptual relativism, but it need not be refuted to make the point that psychophysical reduction cannot be accommodated by the subjective-to-objective model familiar from other cases.

10. The problem is not just that when I look at the *Mona Lisa*, my visual experience has a certain quality, no trace of which is to be found by someone looking into my brain. For even if he did observe there a tiny image of the *Mona Lisa*, he would have no reason to identify it with the experience.

11. The relation would therefore not be a contingent one, like that of a cause and its distinct effect. It would be necessarily true that a certain physical state felt a certain way. Saul Kripke (*op. cit.*) argues that causal behaviorist and related analyses of the mental fail because they construe, e.g., "pain" as a merely contingent name of pains. The subjective character of an experience ("its immediate phenomenological quality" Kripke calls it [p. 340]) is the essential property left out by such analyses, and the one in virtue of which it is, necessarily, the experience it is. My view is closely related to his. Like Kripke, I find the hypothesis that a certain brain state should *necessarily* have a certain subjective character incomprehensible without further explanation. No such explanation emerges from theories which view the mind–brain relation as contingent, but perhaps there are other alternatives, not yet discovered.

A theory that explained how the mind–brain relation was necessary would still leave us with Kripke's problem of explaining why it nevertheless appears contingent. That difficulty seems to me surmountable, in the following way. We may imagine something by representing it to ourselves either perceptually, sympathetically, or symbolically. I shall not try to say how symbolic imagination works, but part of what happens in the other two cases is this. To imagine something perceptually, we put ourselves in a conscious state resembling the state we would be in if we perceived it. To imagine something sympathetically, we put ourselves in a conscious state resembling the thing itself. (This method can be used only to imagine mental events and states—our own or another's.) When we try to imagine a mental state occurring without its associated brain state, we first sympathetically imagine the occurrence of the mental state: that is, we put ourselves into a state that resembles it mentally. At the same time, we attempt to perceptually imagine the non-occurrence of the associated physical state, by putting ourselves into another state unconnected with the first: one resembling that which we would be in if we perceived the non-occurrence of the physical state. Where the imagination of physical features is perceptual and the imagination of mental features is sympathetic, it appears to us that we can imagine any experience occurring without its associated brain state, and vice versa. The relation between them will appear contingent even if it is necessary, because of the independence of the disparate types of imagination.

(Solipsism, incidentally, results if one misinterprets sympathetic imagination as if it worked like perceptual imagination: it then seems impossible to imagine any experience that is not one's own.)

12. See "Mental Events" in Foster and Swanson, *Experience and Theory* (Amherst, 1970); though I don't understand the argument against psychophysical laws.

13. Similar remarks apply to my paper "Physicalism," *Philosophical Review* 74 (1965), 339–356, reprinted with postscript in John O'Connor, *Modern Materialism* (New York, 1969).

14. This question also lies at the heart of the problem of other minds, whose close connection with the mind–body problem is often overlooked. If one understood how subjective experience could have an objective nature, one would understand the existence of subjects other than oneself.

15. I have not defined the term "physical." Obviously it does not apply just to what can be described by the concepts of contemporary physics, since we expect further developments. Some may think there is nothing to prevent mental phenomena from eventually being recognized as physical in their own right. But whatever else may be said of the physical, it has to be objective. So if our idea of the physical ever expands to include mental phenomena, it will have to assign them an objective character—whether or not this is done by analyzing them in terms of other phenomena already regarded as physical. It seems to me more likely, however, that mental–physical relations will eventually be expressed in a theory whose fundamental terms cannot be placed clearly in either category.

16. I have read versions of this paper to a number of audiences, and am indebted to many people for their comments.

25 Functionalism and Qualia

Sydney Shoemaker

1. In their recent paper "What Psychological States are Not" N. J. Block and J. A. Fodor raise a number of objections to the "functional state identity theory" (FSIT), which says that "for any organism that satisfies psychological predicates at all, there exists a unique best *description* such that each psychological state of the organism is identical with one of its machine states relative to that description."[1] FSIT is a version of "functionalism," which they characterize as the more general doctrine that "the type-identity conditions for psychological states refer only to their relations to inputs, outputs, and one another."[2] Most of the objections Block and Fodor raise they take to be objections only to FSIT, and not to functionalism more broadly construed. I shall not be concerned with these objections here. But they raise one objection which, they say, "might be taken to show that psychological states cannot be functionally defined *at all* and that they cannot be put into correspondence with *any* properties definable over abstract automata."[3] Briefly put, the objection is that the way of "type-identifying" psychological states proposed by FSIT, and by functionalism generally, "fails to accommodate a feature of at least some such states that is critical for determining their type: namely their 'qualitative' character."[4]

Block and Fodor devote only a couple of pages to this objection, and raise it in a fairly tentative way; so it is quite likely that the length of my discussion of it here is disproportionate to the importance they put on it. But they have given a concise and vivid formulation to an objection which is felt, and voiced in conversation, more often than it is expressed in print, and which seems to me to raise fundamental issues. Other philosophers have raised much the same objection by saying that functionalism (or behaviorism, or materialism, or "causal" theories of the mind—the objection has been made against all of these) cannot account for the "raw feel" component of mental states, or for their "internal," or "phenomenological," character. My primary concern here is not with whether this objection is fatal to FSIT; if I understand that theory correctly, it is sufficiently refuted by the other objections Block and Fodor raise against it. But as they characterize functionalism "in the broad sense," it is, while vague, a view which many philosophers, myself included, find attractive; and it seems to me worth considering whether it can be defended against this objection.

I shall follow Block and Fodor in speaking of mental states (or rather, of some mental states) as having "qualitative character(s)" or "qualitative content." I hope that it will emerge in the ensuing discussion that this does not commit me to anything which a clear headed opponent of "private objects," or of "private language," should find objectionable.

2. Block and Fodor develop their objection in two stages. The first of these they call the "inverted qualia argument," and the second can be called the "absent qualia argument."

Because they are unpersuaded by the familiar "verificationist" arguments against the conceptual coherence of the "inverted spectrum hypothesis," Block and Fodor are inclined to think that cases of "inverted qualia" may be possible. They take it that there would be qualia inversion (presumably an extreme case of it) if it were true that "every person does, in fact, have slightly different qualia (or, better still, grossly different qualia) when in whatever machine table state is alleged to be identical to pain."[5] The possibility of this is incompatible with functionalism on the plausible assumption that "nothing would be a token of the type 'pain state' unless it felt like a pain, . . . even if it were connected to all of the other psychological states of the organism in whatever ways pains are."[6]

Block and Fodor do not regard the possibility of qualia inversion as constituting by itself a decisive objection to functionalism, for they think that it may be open to the functionalist to deny the *prima facie* plausible assumption that pains must be qualitatively similar (and, presumably, the related assumption that anything qualitatively identical to a pain is itself a pain).[7] If qualia inversion actually occurred in the case of pain (i.e., if a state functionally identical to a pain differed from it in qualitative character), then, they say, "it might be reasonable to say that the character of an organism's qualia is irrelevant to whether it is in pain or (equivalently) that pains feel quite different to different organisms."[8] Such a view is not in fact unheard of. According to Don Locke, "A sensation's being a pain sensation is not a matter of how it feels, but a matter of its being of the sort caused by bodily damage and leading to pain behavior."[9] And Alan Donagan has attributed to Wittgenstein the view that "you and I correctly say that we have the same sensation, say toothache, if we both have something frightful that we would naturally express by holding and rubbing our jaws, by certain kinds of grimace, and the like. Whether the internal character of what is expressed in these ways is the same for you as for me is irrelevant to the meaning of the word 'toothache.'"[10]

But while Block and Fodor do not dismiss this response to the inverted qualia argument as obviously mistaken, they see it as possibly opening the door to an argument much more damaging to functionalism, namely the absent qualia argument. Their thought may be that once it is admitted that a given functional state can exist without having a given "qualitative content," it will be difficult to deny the possibility that it might exist without having any qualitative content (or character) at all. At any rate, they go on to say that

> For all that we know, it may be nomologically possible for two psychological states to be functionally identical (that is, to be identically connected with inputs, outputs, and successor states), even if only one of the states has a qualitative content. In this case, FSIT would require us to say that an organism might be in pain even though it is feeling *nothing at all*, and this consequence seems totally unacceptable.[11]

And if cases of "absent qualia" are possible, i.e., if a state can be functionally identical to a state having a qualitative character without itself having a qualitative content, then not only FSIT, but also functionalism in the broad sense, would seem to be untenable.

3. If mental states can be alike or different in "qualitative character," we should be able to speak of a class of states, call them "qualitative states," whose "type-identity conditions" could be specified in terms of the notion of qualitative (or "phenomenological") similarity. For each determinate qualitative character a state can have, there is (i.e., we can define) a determinate qualitative state which a person has just in case he has a state having precisely that qualitative character. For example, there is a qualitative state someone has just in case he has a sensation that feels exactly the way my most recent headache felt. Qualitative states will presumably be "mental," or "psychological," states. And this calls into question the suggestion of Block and Fodor that a functionalist could deal with the "inverted qualia argument" by maintaining that "the character of an organism's qualia is irrelevant to whether it is in pain." It would of course be self-contradictory to hold that the character of an organism's qualia is irrelevant to what qualitative states it has. And Block and Fodor are presumably committed to the claim that qualitative states cannot themselves be functionally defined, or at least that this is so if there can be cases of "inverted qualia." For if qualitative states could be functionally defined, the fact that mental states have qualitative character would provide no problem for functionalism. Thus (assuming the possibility of qualia inversion) there will be one class of mental states, namely the qualitative states themselves, that cannot be functionally defined.

This raises questions which I shall return to in later sections, namely (a) in what sense are qualitative states not functionally definable (or, in what sense are they not functionally definable if qualia inversion is possible), and (b) is their being functionally undefinable (in whatever sense they are) seriously damaging to functionalism? As we shall see in the remainder of the present section, this question is also raised by a consideration of the alleged possibility of "absent qualia."

We can establish the impossibility of cases of "absent qualia" if we can show that if a state is functionally identical to a state having qualitative content then it must itself have qualitative content. One might try to do this by construing the notion of functional identity in such a way that qualitative states are included among the "other psychological states" by relation to which, along with input and output, the "type-identity" of a given psychological state is to be defined. Thus one might argue that if a given psychological state has a certain qualitative character, this involves its standing in some determinate relationship to some particular qualitative state (namely the qualitative state a person is in just in case he is in a state having that qualitative character), and that any state functionally identical to it must stand in the same relationship to that qualitative state, and so must have the same qualitative character.[12] But this argument is not very convincing. One objection that is likely to be made to it is that since qualitative states cannot themselves be functionally defined (assuming the possibility of *inverted* qualia), it is illegitimate to include them among the psychological states by reference to which other psychological states are functionally defined, or in terms of which "functional identity" is defined. I shall return to this objection later, since it is also a *prima facie* objection against the more plausible argument I shall present next. Another objection is that the relationship which a state has to a qualitative state, in having the "qualitative character" corresponding to that qualitative state, is not anything like a causal relationship and so is not the sort of relationship in terms of which a psychological state can be functionally defined. But the argument I shall present next is not open to this objection, and does seem to me to show that on any plausible construal of the notion of functional identity a state cannot be functionally identical to a state having qualitative character without itself having qualitative character.

One important way in which pains are related to other psychological states is that they give rise, under appropriate circumstances, to introspective awareness of themselves as having certain qualitative characters, i.e., as feeling certain ways. I shall assume that the meaning of this can be partially unpacked by saying that being in pain typically gives rise, given appropriate circumstances, to what I shall call a "qualitative belief," i.e., a belief to the effect that one feels a certain way (or, more abstractly, is in a state having a certain qualitative character, or, in still other terms, has a certain qualitative state). Any state functionally identical to a pain state will share with the pain state not only (1) its tendency to influence overt behavior in certain ways, and (2) its tendency to produce in the person the belief that there is something organically wrong with him (e.g., that he has been cut or burnt), but also (3) its tendency to produce qualitative beliefs in the person, i.e., to make him think that he has a pain having a certain qualitative character (one that he dislikes). According to the "absent qualia argument," such a state may nevertheless lack qualitative character, and so fail to be a pain. Let us consider whether this is plausible.

Supposing such cases of "absent qualia" are possible, how might we detect such a case if it occurred? And with what right does each of us reject the suggestion that perhaps his own case is such a case, and that he himself is devoid of states having qualitative character? Indeed, with what right do we reject the suggestion that perhaps no one ever has any feelings (or other states having qualitative character) at all? It is, of course, a familiar idea that behavior provides inconclusive evidence as to what qualitative character, if any, a man's mental states have. But what usually underlies this is the idea that the man himself has a more "direct" access to this qualitative character than behavior can possibly provide, namely introspection. And introspection, whatever else it is, is the link between a man's mental states and his beliefs about (or his knowledge or awareness of) those states. So one way of putting our question is to ask whether anything could be evidence (for anyone) that someone was not in pain, given that it follows from the states he is in, plus the psychological laws that are true of him (the laws which describe the relationships of his states to one another and to input and output), that the totality of possible behavioral evidence *plus* the totality of possible introspective evidence points unambiguously to the conclusion that he is in pain? I do not see how anything could be. To be sure, we can imagine (perhaps) that "cerebroscopes" reveal that the person is not in some neurophysiological state that we ourselves are always in when we are (so we think) in pain. But this simply raises the question, on what basis can we say that *we* have genuine pain (i.e., a state having a qualitative character as well as playing the appropriate functional role in its relationships to input, output, and other psychological states)? Here it seems that if the behavioral and introspective evidence are not enough, nothing could be enough. But if they are enough in the case of us, they are enough in the case of our hypothetical man. In any event, if we are given that a man's state is functionally identical with a state that in us is pain, it is hard to see how a physiological difference between him and us could be any evidence at all that his states lack qualitative character; for if anything can be evidence for us about his psychological state, the evidence that his state is functionally equivalent to ours is *ipso facto* evidence that any physiological difference between us and him is irrelevant to whether, although not to how, the state of pain is realized in him.

To hold that it is logically possible (or, worse, nomologically possible) that a state lacking qualitative character should be functionally identical to a state having qualitative character is to make qualitative character irrelevant both to what we can take ourselves to know in knowing about the mental states of others and also to what we can take ourselves to know in knowing about our own mental states. There could (on this view) be no possible physical effects of any state from which we could argue by an "inference to the best explanation" that it has qualitative character; for if there were, we could give at least a partial functional characterization of the having of qualitative character by saying that it tends to give rise, in such and such circumstances, to those physical effects, and could not allow that a state lacking qualitative character could be functionally identical to a state having it. And for reasons already given, if cases of "absent qualia" were possible, qualitative character would be necessarily inaccessible to introspection. If qualitative character were something that is irrelevant in this way to all knowledge of minds, self-knowledge as well as knowledge of others, it would not be at all "unacceptable," but would instead be just good sense, to deny that pains must have qualitative character. But of course it is absurd to suppose that ordinary people are talking about something that is in principle unknowable by anyone when they talk about how they feel, or about how things look, smell, sound, etc. to them. (Indeed, just as a causal theory of knowledge would imply that states or features that are independent of the causal powers of the things they characterize would be in principle unknowable, so a causal theory of reference would imply that such states and features are in principle unnamable and inaccessible to reference.) And if, to return to sanity, we take qualitative character to be something that can be known in the ways we take human feelings to be knowable (at a minimum, if it can be known introspectively), then it is not possible, not even logically possible, for a state that lacks qualitative character to be functionally identical to a state that has it.

This is not a "verificationist" argument. It does not assume any general connection between meaningfulness and verifiability (or knowability). What it does assume is that if there is to be any reason for supposing (as the "absent qualia argument" does) that it is essential to pain and other mental states that they have "qualitative character," then we must take "qualitative character" to refer to something which is knowable in at least some of the ways in which we take pains (our own and those of others) to be knowable. It also assumes that if there could be a feature of some mental state that was entirely independent of the causal powers of the state (i.e., was such that its presence or absence would make no difference to the state's tendencies to bring about other states, and so forth), and so was irrelevant to its "functional identity," then such a feature would be totally unknowable (if you like, this assumes a causal theory of knowledge).

Against this argument, as against an earlier one, it may be objected that the other psychological states by relation to which (along with inputs and outputs) a given psychological state is functionally defined must not include any states that cannot themselves be functionally defined. For, it may be said, the states I have called "qualitative beliefs" can no more be functionally defined than can qualitative states themselves. The most important relationship of these states to other states would appear to be their relationship to the qualitative states that characteristically give rise to them, yet (so the argument goes) the latter cannot be functionally defined and so cannot legitimately be referred to in functional definitions of the former. Moreover (remembering that the possibility of cases of *inverted* qualia is not here being questioned), it seems plausible to suppose that if two people differed in the qualitative character of their pains, but in such a way that the difference would not be revealed in any possible behavior, then they would also differ in their qualitative beliefs, and this difference too would be such that its existence could not be revealed in any possible behavior. And if this is possible, there seems as much reason to deny that qualitative beliefs are capable of functional definition as there is to deny that qualitative states are capable of functional definition.

This objection does not touch one important point implicit in my argument, namely that we cannot deny, without being committed to an intolerable skepticism about the pains of others, that someone's saying that he feels a sharp pain is good evidence that he has some qualitative state or other, and is so because someone's saying this is, normally, an *effect* of his having a state having qualitative character—and this by itself strongly suggests that if a mental state of one person has qualitative character, and an otherwise similar state of another person lacks qualitative character, then the states differ in the ways they tend to influence behavior ("output") and hence differ functionally. Still, the possibility of "inverted qualia" does seem to imply that qualitative states, and hence qualitative beliefs, cannot be functionally defined. To see whether this is compatible with functionalism, and whether it undercuts the argument given above, we need to consider in what sense it is true that qualitative states (and qualitative beliefs) are not functionally definable, and what limits there are on the ways in which reference to mental states that are not functionally definable can enter into functional definitions of other mental states.

In order to consider these questions I wish to change examples, and shift our consideration from the case of pain to that of visual experience. There are two reasons why such a shift is desirable. First, the possibility of "spectrum inversion" (one person's experience of colors differing systematically, in its qualitative or phenomenological character, from another person's experience of the same colors) seems to me far less problematical than the possibility of "qualia inversion" in the case of pain (pain feeling radically different to different persons). Second, and related to this, it is much easier to distinguish seeing blue (for example) from its qualitative character than it is to distinguish pain from its qualitative character, and accordingly much easier to consider how reference to qualitative states might enter into a functional account of seeing colors than it is to consider how reference to such states might enter into a functional account of pain.

4. If I see something, it looks somehow to me, and the way it looks resembles and differs, in varying degrees and various respects, the ways other things look to me or have looked to me on other occasions. It is because similarities and differences between these "ways of being appeared to" correlate in systematic ways with similarities and differences between objects we see that we are able to see these objects and the properties of them in virtue of which the similarities and differences obtain.[13] Being appeared to in a certain way, e.g., things looking to one the way things now look to me as I stare out my window, I take to be a qualitative state. So seeing essentially involves the occur-

rence of qualitative states. Moreover, reference to these qualitative states enters into what looks very much like a functional account of seeing. For it would seem that what it means to say that someone sees something to be blue is something like the following:

S sees something to be blue if and only if
(1) *S* has a repertory of qualitative states which includes a set of states *K* which are associated with the colors of objects in such a way that (a) visual stimulation by an object of a certain color under "standard conditions" produces in the person the associated qualitative state, and (b) the degrees of "qualitative" or "phenomenological" similarity between the states in *K* correspond to the degrees of similarity between the associated colors, and (2) person *S* (a) is at present in the qualitative state associated with the color blue, (b) is so as the result of visual stimulation by something blue and (c) believes, because of (a) and (b), that there is something blue before him.[14]

I must now qualify the assertion that "being appeared to" in a certain way is a qualitative state. If asked to describe how he is appeared to, or, more naturally, how things look to him, a man might say, among other things, that a certain object looks blue to him, or that it looks to him as if he were seeing something blue, or (if he is a philosopher who speaks the "language of appearing") that he is "appeared-blue-to." And it is natural to make it a condition of someone's being appeared-blue-to that he be in the qualitative state that is, in him at that time, associated with visual stimulation by blue things; that is, it is natural to give an analysis of "*S* is appeared-blue-to" which is the same as the above analysis of "*S* sees something to be blue" except that clauses (b) and (c) of condition (2) are deleted. But if we do this, then being appeared-blue-to will not itself be a qualitative state. Or at any rate, this will be so if spectrum inversion is possible. We might sum up the situation by saying that being appeared-blue-to is, on the proposed analysis, a functional state whose functional characterization requires it always to have some qualitative character (or other) but does not require it to have the same qualitative character in different persons (assuming the possibility of intersubjective spectrum inversion) or in the same person at different times (assuming the possibility of intrasubjective spectrum inversion). But this raises again the question of whether qualitative states are themselves functionally definable and, if they are not, whether they can legitimately be referred to in functional characterizations of other mental states.

The expression "appeared-blue-to" could, I think, have a use in which it would stand for a qualitative state. I could "fix the reference" of this expression by stipulating that it refers to (or, since it is a predicate rather than a singular term, that it predicates or ascribes) that qualitative state which is at the present time (April, 1974) associated in me with the seeing of blue things.[15] Understanding the expression in this way, if I underwent spectrum inversion tomorrow it would cease to be the case that I am normally appeared-blue-to when I see blue things, and might become the case that I am normally appeared-yellow-to on such occasions.[16] (By contrast, in the "functional" sense of "appeared-blue-to" sketched above, it could be true before and after intrasubjective spectrum inversion that I am normally appeared-blue-to when I see blue things, although of course being appeared-blue-to would have the qualitative character at the later time which another visual state, say, being appeared-yellow-to, had at the earlier time.) I do not think that there would be much utility in having expressions that were, in this way, "rigid designators" (or "rigid predicators") of visual qualia. On the other hand, I see no reason in principle why we could not have them. But if we did have them, they could not be functionally defined. Such terms would have to be introduced by Kripkean "reference fixing" or (what is a special case of this) ostensive definition. To be sure, there is the theoretical possibility of giving a verbal definition of one of these expressions by making use of other expressions of the same sort; just as I might define "blue" by means of a description of the form "the color that is not yellow, or red, or green ... etc.," so I might define "being appeared-blue-to" as equivalent to a description of the form "the color qualia which is neither being appeared-yellow-to, nor being appeared-red-to, nor being appeared-green-to, ... etc." But this is of very little interest, since it is obviously impossible that names (or predicates) for all visual qualia should be defined in this way without circularity. So, assuming that talk of defining functional states is equivalent to talk of defining names or "rigid designators" for qualitative states, there seems to be a good sense in which qualitative states cannot be functionally defined.

But what seems to force us to this conclusion is the seeming possibility of spectrum inversion. I think that what (if anything) forces us to admit the possibility of spectrum inversion is the seeming conceivability and detectability of *intra*subjective spectrum inversion. And if we reflect on the latter, we will see, I believe, that while we cannot functionally define particular qualitative states, there is a sense in which we can functionally define the *class* of qualitative states—we can functionally define the identity conditions for members of this class, for we can functionally define the relationships of qualitative (phenomenological) similarity and difference. This is what I shall argue in the following section.

5. Taken one way, the claim that spectrum inversion is possible implies a claim that may, for all I know, be empirically false, namely that there is a way of mapping determinate shades of color onto determinate shades of color which is such that (1) every determinate shade (including "muddy" and unsaturated colors as well as the pure spectral colors) is mapped onto some determinate shade, (2) at least some of the shades are mapped onto shades other than themselves, (3) the mapping preserves, for any normally sighted person, all of the "distance" and "betweenness" relationships between the colors (so that if shades *a*, *b* and *c* are mapped onto shades *d*, *e* and *f*, respectively, then a normally sighted person will make the same judgments of comparative similarity about *a* in relation to *b* and *c* as about *d* in relation to *e* and *f*), and (4) the mapping preserves all of our intuitions, except those that are empirically conditioned by knowledge of the mixing properties of pigments and the like, about which shades are "pure" colors and which have other colors "in" them (so that, for example, if shades *a* and *b* are mapped onto shades of orange and red, respectively, we will be inclined to say that *a* is less pure than *b* and perhaps that it has *b* in it). But even if our color experience is not in fact such that a mapping of this sort is possible, it seems to me conceivable that it might have been—and that is what matters for our present philosophical purposes. For example, I think we know well enough what it would be like to see the world nonchromatically, i.e., in black, white, and the various shades of grey—for we frequently do see it in this way in photographs, moving pictures, and television. And there is an obvious mapping of the nonchromatic shades onto each other which satisfies the conditions for inversion. In the discussion that follows I shall assume, for convenience,

that such a mapping is possible for the full range of colors—but I do not think that anything essential turns on whether this assumption is correct.

Supposing that there is such a mapping (and, a further assumption of convenience, that there is only one), let us call the shade onto which each shade is mapped the "inverse" of that shade. We will have *inter*subjective spectrum inversion if the way each shade of color looks to one person is the way its inverse looks to another person, or, in other words, if for each shade of color the qualitative state associated in one person with the seeing of that shade is associated in another person with the seeing of the inverse of that shade. And we will have *intra*subjective spectrum inversion if there is a change in the way the various shades of color look to someone, each coming to look the way its inverse previously looked.

What strikes us most about spectrum inversion is that if it can occur intersubjectively there would appear to be no way of telling whether the color experience of two persons is the same or whether their color spectrums are inverted relative to each other. The systematic difference between experiences in which intersubjective spectrum inversion would consist would of course not be open to anyone's introspection. And there would appear to be no way in which these differences could manifest themselves in behavior—the hypothesis that your spectrum is inverted relative to mine and the hypothesis that our color experience is the same seem to give rise to the same predictions about our behavior. Here, of course, we have in mind the hypothetical case in which the various colors have always looked one way to one person and a different way to another person. And the situation seems very different when we consider the case of *intra*subjective spectrum inversion. In the first place, it seems that such a change would reveal itself to the introspection, or introspection *cum* memory, of the person in whom it occurred. But if this is so, other persons could learn of it through that person's reports. Moreover, and this is less often noticed, there is non-verbal behavior, as well as verbal behavior, that could indicate such a change. If an animal has been trained to respond in specific ways to objects of certain colors, and then begins, spontaneously, to respond in those ways to things of the inverse colors, and if it shows surprise that its responses are no longer rewarded in the accustomed ways, this will surely be some evidence that it has undergone spectrum inversion. In the case of a person we could have a combination of this sort of evidence and the evidence of the person's testimony.[17]

If we did not think that we could have these kinds of evidence of intrasubjective spectrum inversion, I think we would have no reason at all for thinking that spectrum inversion of any sort, intrasubjective or intersubjective, is even logically possible. To claim that spectrum inversion is possible but that it is undetectable even in the intrasubjective case would be to sever the connection we suppose to hold between qualitative states and introspective awareness of them (between them and the qualitative beliefs to which they give rise), and also their connections to perceptual beliefs about the world and, *via* these beliefs, to behavior. No doubt one could so *define* the term "qualitative state" as to make it inessential to qualitative states that they have these sorts of connections. But then it would not be in virtue of similarities and differences between "qualitative states" (in that defined sense) that things look similar and different to people, and the hypothesis that people differ radically in what "qualitative states" they have when they see things of various colors would be of no philosophical interest, and would not be the "inverted spectrum hypothesis" as usually understood. Indeed, the supposition that intrasubjective spectrum inversion could occur, but would be undetectable, is incoherent in much the same way as the "absent qualia hypothesis," i.e., the supposition that states "functionally identical" to states having qualitative content might themselves lack qualitative content. Neither supposition makes sense unless the crucial notions in them are implicitly defined, or redefined, so as to make the supposition empty or uninteresting.

But what, then, are we supposing about qualitative states, and about the relationships of qualitative or phenomenological similarity and difference between these states, in supposing that intrapersonal spectrum inversion *would* be detectable? In what follows I shall speak of token qualitative states as "experiences," and will say that experiences are "co-conscious" if they are conscious to a person at the same time, where an experience counts as conscious to a person when he correctly remembers it as well as when he is actually having it. One thing we are supposing, if we take intrasubjective spectrum inversion to be detectable in the ways I have indicated, is that when experiences are co-conscious the similarities between them tend to give rise to belief in the existence of objective similarities in the physical world, namely similarities between objects in whose perception the experiences occurred, and differences between them tend to give rise to belief in the existence of objective differences in the world. And these beliefs, in turn, give rise (in combination with the person's wants and other mental states) to overt behavior which is appropriate to them. This explains how there can be non-verbal behavior that is evidence of spectrum inversion; the behavior will be the manifestation of mistaken beliefs about things which result from the fact that, in cases of intrasubjective spectrum inversion, things of the same color will produce qualitatively different experiences after the inversion than they did before, while things of each color will produce, after the inversion, experiences qualitatively like those produced by things of a different color before the inversion.

But even if, for some reason, a victim of spectrum inversion were not led to have and act on mistaken beliefs about objective similarities and dissimilarities in this way, we could still have evidence that his spectrum had inverted—for he could tell us that it had. And in supposing that *he* can know of the spectrum inversion in such a case, and so be in a position to inform us of it, we are supposing something further about the relationships of qualitative similarity and difference, namely that when they hold between co-conscious experiences, this tends to give rise to introspective awareness of the holding of these very relationships, i.e., it tends to give rise to correct "qualitative beliefs" to the effect that these relationships hold.

Philosophers who talk of mental states as having behavioral "criteria" have sometimes said that the criterion of experiences being similar is their subject's sincerely reporting, or being disposed to report, that they are. If we recast this view in functionalist terms, it comes out as the view that what constitutes experiences being qualitatively similar is, in part anyhow, that they give rise, or tend to give rise, to their subject's having a qualitative belief to the effect that such a similarity holds, and, in virtue of this belief, a disposition to make verbal reports to this effect. But as a functional *definition* of qualitative similarity this would of course be circular. If we are trying to explain what it means for experiences to be similar, we cannot take as already understood, and as available for use in our explanation, the notion of believing experiences to be similar.

But no such circularity would be involved in functionally defining the notions of qualitative similarity and difference in terms of the first sort of relationship I mentioned, namely between, on the one hand, a person's experiences being qualitatively similar or different in certain ways, and, on the other, his believing in the existence of certain sorts of objective similarities or differences in the world, and, ultimately, his behaving in certain ways. I believe that a case can be made, although I shall not attempt to make it here, for saying that the tendency of sensory experiences to give rise to introspective awareness of themselves, and of their similarities and differences, is, for creatures having the conceptual capacities of humans, an inevitable by-product of their tendency to give rise to perceptual awareness of objects in the world, and of similarities and differences between these objects. And my suggestion is that what makes a relationship between experiences the relationship of qualitative (phenomenological) similarity is precisely its playing a certain "functional" role in the perceptual awareness of objective similarities, namely its tending to produce perceptual beliefs to the effect that such similarities hold. Likewise, what makes a relationship between experiences the relationship of qualitative difference is its playing a corresponding role in the perceptual awareness of objective differences.

This suggestion is, of course, vague and sketchy. But all that I have to maintain here is that the claim that we can give a functional account of qualitative similarity and difference along these lines is no less plausible than the claim that such mental states as belief and desire can be functionally defined. For my aim is not the ambitious one of showing that functionalism provides a fully satisfactory philosophy of mind; it is the much more modest one of showing that the fact that some mental states have "qualitative character" need not pose any special difficulties for a functionalist. And an important step toward showing the latter is to show that the notions of qualitative similarity and difference are as plausible candidates for functional definition as other mental notions. I conceded earlier that there is a sense in which particular qualitative states cannot be functionally defined. But it will be remembered that what distinguishes qualitative states from other sorts of mental states is that their "type-identity conditions" are to be given in terms of the notion of qualitative similarity. At the beginning of our discussion, specifying identity conditions in such terms seemed to contrast sharply with specifying them in functional terms. But this contrast becomes blurred if, as I have suggested, the notion of qualitative similarity can itself be defined in functional terms. And if the latter is so, and hence the identity conditions for qualitative states can be specified in functional terms, it seems not inappropriate to say, as I did earlier, that while particular qualitative states cannot be functionally defined, the *class* of qualitative states can be functionally defined.

6. Now let us return to the question of whether it is legitimate to make reference to qualitative states in giving functional definitions of other sorts of mental states.

On one construal of it, functionalism in the philosophy of mind is the doctrine that mental, or psychological, terms are, in principle, eliminable in a certain way. If, to simplify matters, we take our mental vocabulary to consist of names of mental states and relationships (rather than predicates ascribing such states and relationships), the claim will be that these names can be treated as synonymous with definite descriptions, each such description being formulable, in principle, without the use of any of the mental vocabulary. Mental states will indeed be quantified over, and in some cases identifyingly referred to, in these definite descriptions; but when they are, they will be characterized and identified, not in explicitly mentalistic terms, but in terms of their causal and other "topic neutral" relations to one another and to physical inputs and outputs.[18]

Now what I have already said implies that names of qualitative states (if we had them) could not be defined as equivalent to such definite descriptions—on the assumption, of course, that "qualia inversion" is possible. If the causal role played by a given qualitative state (in conjunction with other mental states) in mediating connections between input and output could be played by another qualitative state, and if that qualitative state could play a different role, then it is not essential to the state that it plays that causal role and it cannot be part of the meaning, or sense, of a term that rigidly designates it that the state so designated is *the* state that plays such a causal role. Moreover, since such a term could not be eliminated in this way in favor of a definite description, it could not occur within the definite description which functionally defines the name of some other mental state—assuming that the aim of such functionalist definitions is to eliminate mental terminology in favor of physical and topic neutral terminology.

But there is nothing in this to imply that qualitative states cannot be among the states quantified over in the definite descriptions that define other sorts of mental states. And it seems that it would be quantification over such states, rather than reference to particular states of this kind, that would be needed in the defining of other mental states. If spectrum inversion is possible, we do not want to make the occurrence of any particular qualitative state a necessary condition of seeing (or seeming to see) something blue, but we do want to require that at any given time in the history of a person there is some qualitative state or other that is (at that time) standardly involved in his seeing (or seeming to see) blue things. The specification of the roles of qualitative states in the seeing of blue things will no doubt invoke the notions of qualitative similarity and difference; but this causes no difficulties for a functionalist if, as I have suggested, these notions can themselves be functionally defined.

There would appear, however, to be some mental states (other than qualitative states) that cannot be functionally defined in the strong sense here under consideration, namely in such a way that there is no essential (uneliminable) use of mental terminology in the *definiens*. For consider the states I have called "qualitative beliefs," i.e., beliefs about qualitative states and in particular beliefs to the effect that one is in a particular qualitative state. Qualitative beliefs can be divided into two groups, those in whose propositional content there is reference to particular qualitative states, and those in whose propositional content there is quantification over qualitative states but no reference to particular qualitative states. So far as I can see, qualitative beliefs of the second sort provide no special difficulties for the functionalist; if other sorts of beliefs can be functionally defined, so can these. But qualitative beliefs of the first sort do seem to resist functional definition. Consider the belief I would express if I said "I am in the state of being appeared-blue-to," using the phrase "state of being appeared-blue-to" to rigidly designate a particular qualitative state. If we tried to characterize this state of believing functionally, i.e., in terms of its relationships to other mental states and to input and output, it would seem that we would have to make reference in our characterization to the qualitative state the belief is about—we would have to say that the state of believing that one is appeared-blue-to is typically the result of the state of being appeared-blue-to. If so, it is impossible to define such states (qualitative beliefs of the first sort) without making essential use of mental terms.

But this constitutes no obstacle to our functionally defining other sorts of mental states. For while we may want to include in our functional characterizations of some kinds of mental states that they give rise to qualitative beliefs of the first sort (i.e., those in whose propositional content there is reference to particular qualitative states), this need not involve our making identifying reference to beliefs of this sort in our functional characterizations; all that this need involve is quantifying over such beliefs. Thus, for example, we can build it into our functional characterization of pain that being in pain typically results in some qualitative belief to the effect that one has some specific qualitative state, without saying of any specific qualitative state that being in pain tends to give rise to a belief about it. And if quantifying over qualitative states is permissible in giving functional definitions, I see no reason why quantifying over functional beliefs should not be permissible as well.

Now let us return briefly to my argument in section 3 against the possibility of cases of "absent qualia." In that argument I pointed out that it is characteristic of pains to give rise to introspective awareness of themselves as having particular qualitative characters, and so to give rise to "qualitative beliefs," and I used this to argue that any state functionally identical to a state having qualitative character (e.g., a pain) must itself have qualitative character. The objection was raised to this argument that since qualitative beliefs, like qualitative states, cannot be functionally defined, they cannot legitimately enter into a functional account of the "type-identity conditions" for other mental states. We can now answer this objection. No doubt pains give rise to qualitative beliefs of the sort that (so I am allowing) cannot be functionally defined, i.e., beliefs to the effect that one is having some specific qualitative state. But they also give rise to beliefs to the effect that one is in pain—and if (as the "absent qualia argument" apparently assumes) pain is necessarily a state having qualitative character, then the belief that one is in pain presumably involves (at least in the case of a reflective person) the belief that one is in a state having some qualitative state or other. And while the latter belief is a qualitative belief, its propositional content quantifies over qualitative states rather than involving reference to particular qualitative states. No reason has been given why qualitative beliefs of this sort should not be regarded as functionally definable. And if they are functionally definable, there is no reason why the tendency of other states to give rise to such beliefs should not be part of what constitutes the functional identity of those other states. And this is all the argument of section 3 requires.

7. Over the last few decades, much of the controversy in the philosophy of mind has involved a battle between two seemingly conflicting sets of intuitions. On the one hand there is the intuition that mental states are somehow logically, or conceptually, connected with physical states of affairs, in particular the behaviors that are taken to manifest them. This intuition has found expression in a succession of different philosophical positions—logical behaviorism, the "criteriological" views inspired by Wittgenstein, and, most recently, functional or causal analyses of mental states (these

usually being combined with some form of materialism or physicalism).[19] On the other hand there is the intuition that connections between mental states and behavior are, at bottom, contingent; that under the most "intrinsic" descriptions of mental states, it is a contingent fact that they are related as they are to behavior and to other sorts of physical states. And a common expression of this view has been the claim that spectrum inversion and other sorts of "qualia inversion" are logically possible; for to say that these are logically possible is apparently to say that what intrinsic, internal character these mental states have, their "qualitative content," is logically irrelevant to their being related as they are to their bodily causes and behavioral manifestations. I have conceded that there is a substantial element of truth in this view. For I have allowed that spectrum inversion is a possibility, and have allowed that this implies that at least some qualitative states (and qualitative beliefs) cannot be functionally defined. But I believe that there is a substantial element of truth in the other view as well. I think that where the other view—the view that mental states are "logically" or "conceptually" connected with behavior—has its greatest plausibility is in its application to such states as desire and belief, and I think that these states do not have "qualitative character" in the sense that here concerns us, although they may sometimes be accompanied by qualitative states. But as I have tried to show, I think that even qualitative states can be accommodated within the framework of a functional, or causal, analysis of mental states. While it may be of the essence of qualitative states that they are "ineffable" in the sense that one cannot say in general terms, or at any rate in general terms that do not include names of qualitative states, what it is for a person to be in a particular qualitative state, this does not prevent us from giving a functional account of what it is for a state to be a qualitative state, and of what the identity conditions for qualitative states are. Thus it may be possible to reconcile these firmly entrenched, and seemingly conflicting, intuitions about the contingency or otherwise of relations between mental states and the physical world.

There are a number of issues that would have to be investigated before it could be claimed that this attempted reconciliation is successful. The account of qualitative similarity and difference that I have suggested was tailored to the case of perceptual experiences, and it needs to be considered whether it can be plausibly applied to sensations like pains. What its application to the case of pain may require is the acceptance of the view of pains as somatic sense impressions, i.e., impressions (which need not be veridical) of bodily injuries and the like.[20] Also, this account of qualitative similarity and difference is tailored to the case in which the experiences being compared are experiences of one and the same person, and it needs to be considered whether it gives sense, and the right sort of sense, to intersubjective comparisons of experiences. This would involve, among other things, a consideration of whether it is possible for experiences of different persons to be "co-conscious" in the sense defined earlier; and I think this reduces to the question of whether it is possible for there to be "fusion" between persons of the sort envisaged in some recent discussions of personal identity, i.e., a merging of two persons into a single person (or single subject of consciousness) who then remembers, and is able to compare, the experiences the persons had prior to the fusion. (It is worth noting that if fusion is possible, then it is not after all the case that no possible behavior would reveal whether the color experience of two persons was the same or whether their color spectrums were inverted relative to each other;

for were the persons to fuse, the behavior of the resulting person could presumably settle this question.) But these are all complex issues, and I shall not attempt to discuss them here.[21]

Notes

1. N. J. Block and J. A. Fodor, "What Psychological States are Not," *Philosophical Review* LXXXI (1972), p. 165.

2. *Op. cit.*, p. 173.

3. *Op. cit.*, pp. 173–174.

4. *Op. cit.*, p. 172.

5. *Op. cit.*, p. 173.

6. *Op. cit.*, p. 172. It is worth noting that this assumption, or one very much like it, plays a crucial role in Saul Kripke's recent arguments against the psychophysical identity theory; Kripke expresses it by saying that pain "is not picked out by one of its accidental properties; rather it is picked out by the property of being pain itself, by its immediate phenomenological quality. Thus pain ... is not rigidly designated by 'pain' but the reference of the designator is determined by an essential property of the referent" ("Naming and Necessity," in D. Davidson and H. Harman (eds.) *Semantics of Natural Language* (D. Reidel Publ. Co., Dordrecht-Holland, 1972, p. 340).

7. Block and Fodor mention another way, besides that mentioned in the text, in which a functionalist might try to meet the inverted qualia argument; he might maintain that "though inverted qualia, *if they occurred*, would provide counterexamples to his theory, as a matter of nomological fact it is impossible that functionally identical psychological states should be qualitatively distinct" (p. 172). The thought here must be that the mere logical, or conceptual, possibility of qualia inversion is not incompatible with functionalism. It would seem, however, that if the actual occurrence of inverted qualia would provide counterexamples to functionalism (as the envisioned reply concedes), then the mere logical possibility of inverted qualia is incompatible with functionalism; pain cannot be *identical* with a given functional state if there is a possible world, even a logically but not nomologically possible world, in which the functional state exists without pain existing, or *vice versa*. (On the general claim about identity here being invoked, namely that if *a* and *b* are identical they must be identical in any logically possible world in which either exists, see Kripke's "Naming and Necessity," already cited, and his "Identity and Necessity," in Milton K. Munitz, ed., *Identity and Individuation*, New York, 1971.)

8. Block and Fodor, *op. cit.*, p. 173.

9. Don Locke, *Myself and Others*, Oxford, 1968, p. 101.

10. Alan Donagan, "Wittgenstein on Sensations," in G. Pitcher (ed.), *Wittgenstein: The Philosophical Investigations*, Garden City, New York, 1966.

11. Block and Fodor, *loc. cit.*

12. Just what is the relationship that a state must have to a qualitative state in order to have the qualitative character corresponding to that state? It cannot be, in the cases that concern us, the relationship of identity (that would permit only qualitative states to have qualitative character, and would not permit us to speak of the qualitative character of states whose "type-identity" conditions are given in functional terms). And presumably it must be something stronger than the relationship "is accompanied by," or "is coinstantiated with." The best I can do is to say that a

particular token of a state *S* had the qualitative character corresponding to qualitative state *Q* if on the occasion in question the tokening (instantiation) of *S* essentially involved the tokening (instantiation) of *Q*. Possibly, but I am not sure of this, we could strengthen this, and make it less vague, by saying that on such occasions the token of *S is* a token of *Q*.

13. The "being appeared to" terminology I take from Roderick Chisholm; see his "'Appear,' 'Take,' and 'Evident,'" in R. J. Swartz (ed.), *Perceiving, Sensing and Knowing,* Garden City, New York, 1965, especially p. 480, footnote 6. One is "appeared to" both in cases of veridical perception and in cases of illusion and hallucination, and can be appeared to in the same ways in all of these sorts of cases. The technical locution "appeared-blue-to" is used in the text as an abbreviation for the locution "sees or seems to see something blue" (on a "nonepistemic" understanding of that locution).

14. As an analysis this will not quite do. I can see something to be blue even though it looks green (i.e., even if my visual qualitative state is that associated with green), if I have been "tipped off" that in these circumstances blue things look green.

15. I take the notion of "reference fixing," and the notion of a "rigid designator" employed below, from Saul Kripke; see his "Naming and Necessity," pp. 269–275 and *passim.* The use of a definite description "the *x* such that *Fx*" to "fix the reference" of a term *T* contrasts with defining *T* as equivalent in meaning to, i.e., as an abbreviation of, the definite description; in the former case, but not in the latter, the statement "if *T* exists, then *T* is the *x* such that *Fx*" will be contingently rather than necessarily true. An expression is a rigid designator if it designates the same object in all possible worlds (or in all possible worlds in which it designates anything). According to Kripke, ordinary names are rigid designators, while definite descriptions are not. When a definite description is used to introduce a name (and hence a rigid designator), it is used to "fix its reference" rather than to "define" it or give its "meaning."

16. My distinction between the "functional" sense of "appeared-blue-to" and a (possible) sense in which it rigidly designates (or, better, rigidly predicates) a qualitative state is similar to Chisholm's distinction between the "comparative" and "noncomparative" senses of expressions like "looks blue." See his *Perceiving: A Philosophical Study*, Ithaca, 1957, Chapter Four.

17. Sometimes it is suggested that if someone reported having undergone spectrum inversion, the most reasonable thing for us to conclude would be that something had gone awry with his grasp of the color vocabulary. This overlooks the fact that such a report could be backed up by behavioral evidence of a non-verbal sort. And I think we can imagine a series of events that would leave us no alternative but to conclude that spectrum inversion had occurred. Let us represent the color spectrum by a vertical line, and let us, arbitrarily, divide the line into six equal segments, labeling these from top to bottom with the first six letters of the alphabet. And now consider the case of George. At time t_1 George's color experience, and his use of color words, was perfectly normal. But at time t_2 he tells us that a remarkable change has occurred; while most things look to him just as they used to, or look different only in ways that might be expected (e.g., if there is painting being done), a sizable minority of objects look to him very different than they did before, and he knows, from consulting other persons and from spectroscopic evidence, that in fact these objects have not undergone any significant change in color. George describes the change by saying that if he now looks at what we would regard as a normal spectrum, it looks the way a spectrum would have looked at t_1 if the end segments, *A* and *F*, had been interchanged and rotated one hundred and eighty degrees, the positions of the other segments remaining unchanged. According to this, the structure of George's color experience at t_2 is different from its structure at t_1. And since the putative change involves a change in structure, our evidence that it occurred need not be limited to George's testimony. George's claim will be supported by his recognitional and discriminatory be-

havior if, as we will suppose, he finds it easy to discriminate certain shades of color, for example those on either side of the boundary between segments A and B of the spectrum, which he formerly found it difficult to discriminate (and which the rest of us still find it difficult to discriminate), and sometimes finds it difficult to discriminate between different shades, for example if one is near the bottom boundary of segment A and the other is near the bottom boundary of segment E, which he formerly found it easy to discriminate (and which the rest of us still find it easy to discriminate). To continue the story, at time t_3 George tells us that another such change has occurred and added itself, as it were, to the first one; this time it is as if segments B and E of the spectrum had been interchanged and rotated. Again we can suppose that there is behavioral evidence to substantiate his claim. Finally, at time t_4 he tells us that still another such change has occurred; this time it is as if segments C and D had been interchanged and rotated. And again there is the substantiating behavioral evidence. But at t_4, unlike at t_2 and t_3, George's judgments of color similarity and difference will coincide with ours and with those he made at t_1 (allowing, of course, for whatever objective changes in color may have occurred in the interim); at t_4 the "structure" of George's color experience will be the same as it was at t_1. Yet George reports that his color experience is systematically different from what it was at t_1; each color looks the way its inverse looked previously. And this claim of George's seems to be supported by the behavioral evidence that supported his claims that there were changes in his color experience between t_1 and t_2, between t_2 and t_3, and between t_3 and t_4; for these partial changes add up to a total spectrum inversion.

18. This account of what functional definition would amount to, and the elaboration of it that follows, is based loosely on David Lewis' account in "Psychophysical and Theoretical Identification," *Australasian Journal of Philosophy* **50** (December, 1972), pp. 249–258.

Starting with the "theory" which consists of the set of "platitudes" about relations of mental states to one another and to input and output which it is plausible to regard as analytic or quasi-analytic, we can define the mental terms in that theory (supposing them, for simplicity, to be names of mental states) in the following way. We first write the theory as a single conjunctive sentence. We then replace each of the mental terms in the theory with a different variable, forming an open sentence. We then prefix quantifiers which transform the open sentence into the "modified Ramsey sentence" of the theory, which says (in effect) that there exists a unique n-tuplet of states satisfying the open sentence. We are now in a position to define any of the mental terms that occurred in the original theory. Supposing that T_i is the term we wish to define, and y_i is the variable we replaced it with in forming the modified Ramsey sentence, we can turn the modified Ramsey sentence into a definite description by (1) adding to the open sentence within the scope of the initial quantifiers the conjunct "$y_i = x$," where "x" is a variable that does not occur in the modified Ramsey sentence, and (2) prefixing the whole sentence with a definite description operator binding "x." What we then get is something of the form: $(\iota x)\ (Ely_1)\ldots(Ely_i)\ldots(Ely\mathbf{a})$ $(\ldots\ldots y_i\ldots\ldots\ \&\ y_i = x)$. In this description there will occur no mental terms. And we can define T_i as being synonymous with this description.

I should emphasize that what I am characterizing here is only one version of functionalism. Many philosophers who would regard themselves as functionalists would disavow any intention of giving, or providing a recipe for giving, any sort of meaning analysis of psychological terms.

19. Some advocates of causal or functional theories of the mind, especially those who would not accept the characterization of functionalism in section 6 and footnote 18, would object to being put in this company. But others have clearly seen their accounts as incorporating what is correct in, or as explaining the intuitions which make plausible, behavioristic and criteriological views. See, for example, David Lewis, *op. cit.*, p. 257, David Armstrong, *A Materialist Theory of the Mind*, London, 1968, p. 92, and Alvin Goldman, *A Theory of Human Action*, Englewood Cliffs, N.J., 1970, p. 112.

20. Such a view has in fact been advanced by D. M. Armstrong and by George Pitcher. See Armstrong, *op. cit.*, p. 313ff., and Pitcher's "Pain Perception," *Philosophical Review* LXXIX (1970), pp. 368–393.

21. I have benefited from discussions on this topic with Jonathan Bennett and Keith Lehrer, and am grateful to Bennett, and to N. L. Block, for criticisms of an earlier version of the paper. The paper was written while I was a Fellow at the Center for Advanced Study in the Behavioral Sciences, in Stanford, California, and I would like to express my gratitude to that institution.

26 From "Identity and Necessity"

Saul Kripke

Let me turn to the case of heat and the motion of molecules. Here surely is a case that is contingent identity! Recent philosophy has emphasized this again and again. So, if it is a case of contingent identity, then let us imagine under what circumstances it would be false. Now, concerning this statement I hold that the circumstances philosophers apparently have in mind as circumstances under which it would have been false are not in fact such circumstances. First, of course, it is argued that "Heat is the motion of molecules" is an a posteriori judgment; scientific investigation might have turned out otherwise. As I said before, this shows nothing against the view that it is necessary—at least if I am right. But here, surely, people had very specific circumstances in mind under which, so they thought, the judgment that heat is the motion of molecules would have been false. What were these circumstances? One can distill them out of the fact that we found out empirically that heat is the motion of molecules. How was this? What did we find out first when we found out that heat is the motion of molecules? There is a certain external phenomenon which we can sense by the sense of touch, and it produces a sensation which we call "the sensation of heat." We then discover that the external phenomenon which produces this sensation, which we sense, by means of our sense of touch, is in fact that of molecular agitation in the thing that we touch, a very high degree of molecular agitation. So, it might be thought, to imagine a situation in which heat would not have been the motion of molecules, we need only imagine a situation in which we would have had the very same sensation and it would have been produced by something other than the motion of molecules. Similarly, if we wanted to imagine a situation in which light was not a stream of photons, we could imagine a situation in which we were sensitive to something else in exactly the same way, producing what we call visual experiences, though not through a stream of photons. To make the case stronger, or to look at another side of the coin, we could also consider a situation in which we *are* concerned with the motion of molecules but in which such motion does not give us the sensation of heat. And it might also have happened that we, or, at least, the creatures inhabiting this planet, might have been so constituted that, let us say, an increase in the motion of molecules did not give us this sensation but that, on the contrary, a slowing down of the molecules did give us the very same sensation. This would be a situation, so it might be thought, in which heat would not be the motion of molecules, or, more precisely, in which temperature would not be mean molecular kinetic energy.

But I think it would not be so. Let us think about the situation again. First, let us think about it in the actual world. Imagine right now the world invaded by a number of Martians, who do indeed get the very sensation that we call "the sensation of heat" when they feel some ice which has slow molecular motion, and who do not get a sensation of heat—in fact, maybe just the reverse—when they put their hand near a fire which causes a lot of molecular agitation. Would we say, "Ah, this casts some doubt on heat being the motion of molecules, because there are these other people who don't get the same sensation"? Obviously not, and no one would think so. We would say instead that the Martians somehow feel the very sensation we get when we feel heat when they feel cold and that they do not get a sensation of heat when they feel heat. But now let us think of a counterfactual situation.[1] Suppose the earth had from the very beginning been inhabited by such creatures. First, imagine it inhabited by no creatures at all: then there is no one to feel any sensations of heat. But we would not say that under such circumstances it would necessarily be the case that heat did not exist; we would say that heat might have existed, for example, if there were fires that heated up the air.

Let us suppose the laws of physics were not very different: Fires do heat up the air. Then there would have been heat even though there were no creatures around to feel it. Now let us suppose evolution takes place, and life is created, and there are some creatures around. But they are not like us, they are more like the Martians. Now would we say that heat has suddenly turned to cold, because of the way the creatures of this planet sense it? No, I think we should describe this situation as a situation in which, though the creatures on this planet got our sensation of heat, they did not get it when they were exposed to heat. They got it when they were exposed to cold. And that is something we can surely well imagine. We can imagine it just as we can imagine our planet being invaded by creatures of this sort. Think of it in two steps. First there is a stage where there are no creatures at all, and one can certainly imagine the planet still having both heat and cold, though no one is around to sense it. Then the planet comes through an evolutionary process to be peopled with beings of different neural structure from ourselves. Then these creatures could be such that they were insensitive to heat; they did not feel it in the way we do; but on the other hand, they felt cold in much the same way that we feel heat. But still, heat would be heat, and cold would be cold. And particularly, then, this goes in no way against saying that in this counterfactual situation heat would still *be* the molecular motion, *be* that which is produced by fires, and so on, just as it would have been if there had been no creatures on the planet at all. Similarly, we could imagine that the planet was inhabited by creatures who got visual sensations when there were sound waves in the air. We should not therefore say, "Under such circumstances, sound would have been light." Instead we should say, "The planet was inhabited by creatures who were in some sense visually sensitive to sound, and maybe even visually sensitive to light." If this is correct, it can still be and will still be a necessary truth that heat is the motion of molecules and that light is a stream of photons.

To state the view succinctly: we use both the terms "heat" and "the motion of molecules" as rigid designators for a certain external phenomenon. Since heat is in fact the motion of molecules, and the designators are rigid, by the argument I have given here, it is going to be *necessary* that heat is the motion of molecules. What gives us the illusion of contingency is the fact we have identified the heat by the contingent fact that there happen to be creatures on this planet—(namely, ourselves) who are sensitive to it in a certain way, that is, who are sensitive to the motion of molecules or to heat—these are one and the same thing. And this is contingent. So we use the description, "that which causes such and such sensations, or that which we sense in such and such a way," to identify heat. But in using this fact we use a contingent property of heat, just as we use the contingent property of Cicero as having written such and such works to identify him. We then use the terms "heat" in the one case and "Cicero" in the other *rigidly* to designate the objects for which they stand. And of course the term "the motion of molecules" is rigid; it always stands for the motion of molecules, never for any other phenomenon. So, as Bishop Butler said, "everything is what it is and not another thing." Therefore, "Heat is the motion of molecules" will be necessary, not contingent, and one only has the *illusion* of contingency in the way one could have the illusion of contingency in thinking that this table might have been made of ice. We might think one could imagine it, but if we try, we can see on reflection that what we are really imagining is just there being another lectern in this very position here which was in fact made of ice. The fact that we may identify this lectern by being the object we see and touch in such and such a position is something else.

Now how does this relate to the problem of mind and body? It is usually held that this is a contingent identity statement just like "Heat is the motion of molecules." That cannot be. It cannot be a contingent identity statement just like "Heat is the motion of molecules" because, if I am right, "Heat is the motion of molecules" is not a contingent identity statement. Let us look at this statement. For example, "My being in pain at such and such a time is my being in such and such a brain state at such and such a time," or, "Pain in general is such and such a neural (brain) state."

This is held to be contingent on the following grounds. First, we can imagine the brain state existing though there is no pain at all. It is only a scientific fact that whenever we are in a certain brain state we have a pain. Second, one might imagine a creature being in pain, but not being in any specified brain state at all, maybe not having a brain at all. People even think, at least prima facie, though they may be wrong, that they can imagine totally disembodied creatures, at any rate certainly not creatures with bodies anything like our own. So it seems that we can imagine definite circumstances under which this relationship would have been false. Now, if these circumstances are circumstances, notice that we cannot deal with them simply by saying that this is just an illusion, something we can apparently imagine, but in fact cannot in the way we thought erroneously that we could imagine a situation in which heat was not the motion of molecules. Because although we can say that we pick out heat contingently by the contingent property that it affects us in such and such a way, we cannot similarly say that we pick out pain contingently by the fact that it affects us in such and such a way. On such a picture there would be the brain state, and we pick it out by the contingent fact that it affects us as pain. Now that might be true of the brain state, but it cannot be true of the pain. The experience itself has to be *this experience*, and I cannot say that it is contingent property of the pain I now have that it is a pain.[2] In fact, it would seem that both the terms, "my pain" and "my being in such and such a brain state" are, first of all, both rigid designators. That is, whenever anything is such and such a pain, it is essentially that very object, namely, such and such a pain, and wherever anything is such and such a brain state, it is essentially that very object, namely, such and such a brain state. So both of these are rigid designators. One cannot say this pain might have been something else, some other state. These are both rigid designators.

Second, the way we would think of picking them out—namely, the pain by its being an experience of a certain sort, and the brain state by its being the state of a certain material object, being of such and such molecular configuration—both of these pick out their objects essentially and not accidentally, that is, they pick them out by essential properties. Whenever the molecules *are* in this configuration, we *do* have such and such a brain state. Whenever you feel *this*, you do have a pain. So it seems that the identity theorist is in some trouble, for, since we have two rigid designators, the identity statement in question is necessary. Because they pick out their objects essentially, we cannot say the case where you seem to imagine the identity statement false is really an illusion like the illusion one gets in the case of heat and molecular motion, because that illusion depended on the fact that we pick out heat by a certain contingent property. So there is very little room to maneuver; perhaps none.[3] The identity theorist, who holds that pain is the brain state, also has to hold that it necessarily is the brain state. He therefore cannot concede, but has to deny, that there would have been situations under which one would have had pain but not the corresponding brain state. Now usually in arguments on the identity theory, this is very far from being denied. In fact, it is conceded from the outset by the materialist as well as by his opponent. He says, "Of course, it *could* have been the case that we had pains without the brain states. It is a contingent identity." But that cannot be. He has to hold that we are under some illusion in thinking that we can imagine that there could have been pains without brain states. And the only model I can think of for what the illusion might be, or at least the model given by the analogy the materialists themselves suggest, namely, heat and molecular motion, simply does not work in this case. So the materialist is up against a very stiff challenge. He has to show that these things we think we can see to be possible are in fact not possible. He has to show that these things which we can imagine are not in fact things we can imagine. And that requires some very different philosophical argument from the sort which has been given in the case of heat and molecular motion. And it would have to be a deeper and subtler argument than I can fathom and subtler than has ever appeared in any materialist literature that I have read. So the conclusion of this investigation would be that the analytical tools we are using go against the identity thesis and so go against the general thesis that mental states are just physical states.[4]

The next topic would be my own solution to the mind–body problem, but that I do not have.

Notes

1. Isn't the situation I just described also counterfactual? At least it may well be, if such Martians never in fact invade. Strictly speaking, the distinction I wish to draw compares how we *would* speak *in* a (possibly counterfactual) situation, *if* it obtained, and how we *do* speak *of* a counterfactual situation, knowing that it does not obtain—i.e., the distinction between the language we would have used in a situation and the language we *do* use to describe it. (Consider the description: "Suppose we all spoke German." This description is in English.) The former case can be made vivid by imagining the counterfactual situation to be actual.

2. The most popular identity theories advocated today explicitly fail to satisfy this simple requirement. For these theories usually hold that a mental state is a brain state, and that what makes the brain state into a mental state is its "causal role," the fact that it tends to produce certain behavior (as intentions produce actions, or pain, pain behavior) and to be produced by certain stimuli (e.g., pain, by pinpricks). If the relations between the brain state and its causes and effects are regarded as contingent, then *being such-and-such-a-mental state* is a contingent property of the brain state. Let *X* be a pain. The causal-role identity theorist holds (1) that *X* is a brain state, (2) that the fact that *X* is a pain is to be analyzed (roughly) as the fact that *X* is produced by certain stimuli and produces certain behavior. The fact mentioned in (2) is, of course, regarded as contingent: the brain state *X* might well exist and not tend to produce the appropriate behavior in the absence of other conditions. Thus (1) and (2) assert that a certain pain *X* might have existed, yet not have been a pain. This seems to me self-evidently absurd. Imagine any pain: is it possible that *it itself* could have existed, yet not have been a pain?

If $X = Y$, then *X* and *Y* share all properties, including modal properties. If *X* is a pain and *Y* the corresponding brain state, then *being a pain* is an essential property of *X*, and *being a brain state* is an essential property of *Y*. If the correspondence relation is, in fact, identity, then it must be *necessary* of *Y* that it corresponds to a pain, and *necessary* of *X* that it correspond to a brain state, indeed to this particular brain state, *Y*. Both assertions seem false; it *seems* clearly possible that *X* should have existed without the corresponding brain state; or that the brain state should have existed without being felt as pain. Identity theorists cannot, contrary to their almost universal present practice, accept these intuitions; they must deny them, and explain them away. This is none too easy a thing to do.

3. A brief restatement of the argument may be helpful here. If "pain" and "C-fiber stimulation" are rigid designators of phenomena, one who identifies them must regard the identity as necessary. How can this necessity be reconciled with the apparent fact that C-fiber stimulation might have turned out not to be correlated with pain at all? We might try to reply by analogy to the case of heat and molecular motion; the latter identity, too, is necessary, yet someone may believe that, before scientific investigation showed otherwise, molecular motion might have turned out not to be heat. The reply is, of course, that what really is possible is that people (or some rational sentient beings) could have been in the *same epistemic situation* as we actually are, and identify *a phenomenon* in the same way we identify heat, namely, by feeling it by the sensation we call "the sensation of heat," without the phenomenon being molecular motion. Further, the beings might not have been sensitive to molecular motion (i.e., to heat) by any neural mechanism whatsoever. It is impossible to explain the apparent possibility of C-fiber stimulations not having been pain in the same way. Here, too, we would have to suppose that we could have been in the same epistemological situation, and identify something in the same way we identify pain, without its corresponding to C-fiber stimulation. But the way we identify pain is by feeling it, and if a C-fiber stimulation could have occurred without our feeling any pain, then the C-fiber stimulation would have occurred without there *being* any pain, contrary to the necessity of the identity. The trouble is that although "heat" is a rigid designator, heat is picked out by the contingent property of its being felt in a certain way; pain, on the other hand, is picked out by an essential (indeed necessary and sufficient) property. For a sensation to be *felt* as pain is for it to *be* pain.

4. All arguments against the identity theory which rely on the necessity of identity, or on the notion of essential property, are, of course, inspired by Descartes' argument for his dualism. The earlier arguments which superficially were rebutted by the analogies of heat and molecular motion, and the bifocals inventor who was also Postmaster General, had such an inspiration; and so does my argument here. R. Albritton and M. Slote have informed me that they independently have attempted to give essentialist arguments against the identity theory, and probably others have done so as well.

The simplest Cartesian argument can perhaps be restated as follows: Let "*A*" be a *name* (rigid designator) of Descartes' body. Then Descartes argues that since he could exist even if *A* did not, $\Diamond$ (Descartes $\neq A$), hence Descartes $\neq A$. Those who have accused him of a modal fallacy have forgotten that "*A*" is rigid. His argument is valid, and his conclusion is correct, provided its (perhaps dubitable) premise is accepted. On the other hand, provided that Descartes is regarded as having ceased to exist upon his death, "Descartes $\neq A$" can be established without the use of a modal argument; for if so, no doubt *A* survived Descartes when *A* was a corpse. Thus *A* had a property (existing at a certain time) which Descartes did not. The same argument can establish that a statue is not the hunk of stone, or the congery of molecules, of which it is composed. Mere non-identity, then, may be a weak conclusion. (See D. Wiggins, *Philosophical Review*, Vol. 77 (1968), pp. 90 ff.) The Cartesian modal argument, however, surely can be deployed to maintain relevant stronger conclusions as well.

27 Form, Function, and Feel

William Lycan

In the 1950s, U. T. Place and J. J. C. Smart proposed to identify mental states and events with neurophysiological states and events. A main advantage claimed for this identification was its avoidance of certain troublesome objections to earlier, behaviorist versions of materialism, objections designed to enforce our recalcitrant feeling that at least some mental states are genuinely *inner* states of persons and have distinctive, introspectible phenomenal characters. But complaints of this type have stayed with us, and are still raised against contemporary materialist views of all sorts. My purpose in this paper is to formulate and defend the materialist theory that I think has the best chance of turning aside these criticisms for good and all.

I The Identity Theory and Machine Functionalism

In defiance of the behaviorists, it was insisted that there is an "intractable residue"[1] of conscious mental states which bear only slack and indefinitely defeasible relations to overt behavior of any sort. Perhaps the best examples of such states are those which we usually describe in terms of their qualitative phenomenal characters, or "raw feels"; typically they involve sensory experience or mental imagery. By way of illustrating their resistance to explication wholly in terms of dispositions to behave, opponents complained that the behaviorist could not account for the apparent possibility of systematic variation in an organism's mental states (such as spectrum inversion[2]) which is not even counterfactually reflected in behavioral responses to stimuli.

The identity theorists, in particular, though approving of the behaviorists' anti-Cartesian stand, suggested that the behaviorist had mislocated the mental among the physical aspects of human beings. Mental states are undeniably inner after all; they are the states that *mediate* between stimulus and response and are *responsible for* the overt input-output functions so dear to the behaviorist.

This shift of location, from peripheral transactions to neurophysiological activity, was felt to be a great theoretical advance. But in the 1960s Hilary Putnam and others[3] exposed a presumptuous implication of the identity thesis construed as a theory of mental *types* or kinds: that any conceivable being (mammal, mollusc, or Martian) would have to have a neurophysiology just like ours in order to have beliefs, to suffer pain, or what have you. By specifying the scientific natures of mental states as narrowly as Place and Smart seemed to intend (in terms of specific sorts of neural fibers in the brain), the identity theorist[4] placed indefensibly strong constraints on the biology of any entity that was to be admitted as a possible subject of mental states or events, and so became a species chauvinist. It became clear that the identity theorists had overreacted to the behaviorist's difficulties and become far *too* concerned with the specifics of humans' actual inner state-tokens. We may hold onto our anti-Cartesian claim that mental state- and event-*tokens* are identical with organic state- and event-tokens in their owners, but we would do better to individuate mental types more abstractly, in terms (let us say) of the functional roles their tokens play in mediating between stimuli and responses. Putnam proposed to identify mental state- and event-types with roles of this sort, rather than with whatever various physiological states or events happened to play these roles in various humans and nonhumans from occasion to occasion; thus, he moved back in the direction of behaviorism in order to correct the identity theorists' overreaction.

Encouraged by the fruitfulness of comparing humans and other sentient organisms to computing machines, Putnam and others implemented their functionalist idea in terms of machine programs that would detail the functional relations between possible "inputs," possible "outputs," and the various inner states of the organism which figure abstractly in the production of outputs from inputs; Putnam envisioned a theory of mind whose explications of individual mental state-types would take the form, "To be in a mental state *M* is to realize or instantiate machine program *P* and be in functional state *S* relative to *P*." Let us call the view that some such set of explications is correct *machine functionalism*.

For reasons which I have developed elsewhere,[5] I do not believe any version of machine functionalism can succeed. Rather, I shall defend an ontology of the mental which is functionalist in a more robust sense of the term "function" than that employed by the machine theorist.

II Homuncular Functionalism

The multiple ambiguity of "function," "functional," *inter alia* has been widely noted. Prompted by Ernest Nagel, W. C. Wimsatt[6] distinguishes six senses and four "secondary uses" of "function," at least three of which are directly relevant here:

(i) The mathematical sense, in which "function" is synonymous with "mapping"

(ii) The "perspectival" sense, attributed to S. A. Kauffman, in which "the functions of an entity in a system are to be evaluated *relative to a view or perspective of what the system is doing*" (Wimsatt, 4)

(iii) The teleological sense, in which an entity has a "function" just in case that entity is "useful for or [contributes] to the attainment of some end or purpose of some user or system" (Wimsatt, 4/5)

The first point to notice is that the mathematical sense appears to have little to do with either the perspectival or the teleological sense; mathematical entities do not *do* anything nor in any active sense contribute to the fulfillment of anything's purposes. And yet it is precisely the mathematical sense of "function," in the guise of Turing machines, which occupied most of our attention in the early discussion of functionalist theories of the mental. I suspect that Putnam, and consequently others, were led to this as a result of being beguiled by the superficial similarity of a Turing machine table to a (behavioral) stimulus-and-response chart that takes inner states or intervening variables into account. But this superficial similarity need not tie us to the Turing machine model, or to any machine-functionalist model, for that matter.

The view I shall defend is "functionalist" in a looser sense amalgamated from senses (ii) and (iii) above. I shall take literally the idea that mental entities are to be characterized functionally, not in the mathematical sense as by the machine functionalist, but in the sense that we identify mental entities (as a first step in the direction of structural concreteness) by reference to the roles they play in furthering the goals and strategies of the systems in which they occur or obtain. In developing an ontology based on this idea I shall take my cue from D. C. Dennett's *homuncular* theory of psychological activity, outlined in a recent collection of papers,[7] to point directly toward this hybrid kind of view. Dennett takes his cue in turn from the methodology of certain AI research projects:

> The AI researcher *starts* with an intentionally characterized problem (e.g., how can I get a computer to *understand* questions of English?), breaks it down into sub-problems that are also intentionally characterized (e.g., how do I get the computer to *recognize* questions, *distinguish* subjects from predicates, *ignore* irrelevant parsings?) and then breaks these problems down still further until finally he reaches problem or task descriptions that are obviously mechanistic. (80)

As I read him, Dennett goes on to suggest that we view a *person* as a sort of corporate entity which corporately performs many immensely complex functions—functions of the sort usually called "mental" or "psychological." A psychologist who adopts Dennett's AI-inspired methodology will describe this person by means of a flow chart, which depicts the person's subpersonal agencies and their many and various routes of "access" to each other (see ch. 9) which enable them to cooperate in carrying out the purposes of the containing "institution" or organism that that person is. Each of these subpersonal agencies, represented by a "black box" on the original flow chart, is in turn describable by a flow chart that breaks *it* into further, subsubpersonal agencies which cooperate to fulfill *its* purposes, etc. On this view, the psychological capacities of a person and the various administrative units of a corporate organization stand in functional hierarchies of just the same type and in just the same sense.

To characterize the psychologists' quest in the way I have is to see them as first noting some intentionally or psychologically characterized abilities of the human being at the level of data or phenomena, and positing—as theoretical entities—the homunculi or subpersonal agencies which are needed to explain the human being's having those abilities. Then the psychologists posit further, smaller homunculi in order to explain the previously posited molar behavior of the original homunculi, and so on. It is this feature of Dennett's model that ingeniously blocks the traditional infinite-regress objection to homuncular theories in psychology:[8] We explain the successful activity of one homunculus, not by idly positing a second homunculus within it that successfully performs that activity, but by positing *a team* consisting of several smaller, individually less talented and more specialized homunculi; and detailing the ways in which the team members cooperate in order to produce their joint or corporate output.[9]

Cognitive psychologists have a reasonably good idea of the *sorts* of subpersonal agencies that will have to be assumed to be functioning within a human being in order for that human being to be able to perform the actions and other functions that it performs. Dennett mentions, at the immediately subpersonal level, a "print-out component" or speech center, a "higher executive or *Control* component," a "short-term memory store or buffer memory," a "perceptual analysis component," and a "problem-solving component" (ch. 9). And in chapter 11 he examines, in some clinical detail, a subsubpersonal structure which models the "behavior" involved with human pain. I put "behavior" in scare quotes because what is striking about Dennett's approach here is that he scrupulously takes into account, not just the usual sorts of overt behavior that are common coin among philosophical behaviorists, but subtler phenomena as well: very small differences in our phenomenological descriptions of pain; infrequently remarked phenomena such as the felt time lag between our feeling that we have been burnt and our feeling the deep pain of the burn; and (most interesting from the functionalist's point of view) the richly varied effects of a number of different kinds of anaesthetics and other drugs on a patient's live and retrospective reports concerning his pain. All these various sorts of consideration serve the psychologist (and Dennett) as vivid pointers toward complexities in the relevant functional organization of the human nervous system, indicating the distinct sub ... subpersonal agencies or black-box components we must represent in our flow diagrams—the kinds of receptors, inhibitors, filters, damping mechanisms, triggers, and so on that we must posit—and the comparably various sorts of pathways that connect these components with each other and with the grosser functional components of their owners such as perceptual analyzers, information stores, and the speech center.

The complexity of the functional sketch occasioned by Dennett's phenomena offers three noteworthy advantages: First, it enables a *homunctionalist theory* of such a state as pain to avoid some of the difficulties that afflict, say, Turing machine functionalism in virtue of the latter theory's evident oversimplicity.[10] Second, it nudges functionalism as a metaphysical theory of the mental toward the actual methods, practice, and results of researchers in artificial intelligence, neuropsychology, and medicine. Third, it renders functionalism as a philosophical view strikingly more testable, since (a) a sketch such as Dennett's suggests new experiments and crisply predicts their results, (b) the sketch makes more substantive predictions as regards what sorts of realizing or role-instantiating structures are in fact to be found in the brain, and (c) Dennett's data are characterized in rather specific physiological and chemical terms, which gives us a head start on tracing the realizing neurophysiological structures.

Now, if we accept Dennett's picture of the person as corporate institution, with what shall we as reductionistic philosophers of mind identify individual mental states and events? Dennett rightly warns against our positing a "pain center" functionally located between the subject's afferent and efferent devices and supposing that the subject's pain is an otherwise unanalyzed state of that organ. Homunctionally speaking, it seems to me, this would be tantamount to saying that to be in pain is to have a little man in one's head who is in pain. And in his most recent writings,[11] Dennett himself opts for an "instrumentalistic" ontology of the mental which I take to fall somewhere between Davidson's "anomalous monism" and Putnam's even more nihilistic view: he holds that beliefs, for example, have nothing characteristically in common and do not admit of reduction to anything more tractable; although they are "real" to the extent that some ascriptions of beliefs to people are loose approximations to the truth, they are not determinate inner states of persons, but are merely calculational devices used in prediction and control.

I propose to resist this instrumentalist/nihilist turn of Dennett's, and to pursue a reductive type-identification of beliefs and other mental items, including perceptual and other "qualitative" states, with homunctional states. Putting my cards on the table, I suggest we identify a mental state-type with the property of having such-and-such an institutionally characterized state of affairs obtaining in one (or more) of one's appropriate homunctional "departments" or subagencies. (The subagencies are those which would be depicted in the flow charts associated with their owners at various levels of institutional abstraction.) And so on for mental events, processes, and properties. To be in pain of type T, we might say, is for one's subsubpersonal ϕ-er to be in a characteristic state $S_T(\phi)$, or for a characteristic activity $A_T(\phi)$ to be going on in one's ϕ-er.

Of course, it would be difficult to predict a priori which levels of abstraction would, respectively, be the loci of the many different kinds of mental goings-on, or even in what way we should choose to cut up the subject organism into subpersonal and subsubpersonal agencies in the first place. I will say a good deal more about this below, for it is crucial to the solution of several problems faced by standard functionalist theories to date.

III Homunculi and Teleology

It may be protested that the characterizations "ϕ-er" and "$S_T(\phi)$" are themselves only implicitly defined by a teleological map of the organism, and that explications of them in turn would contain ultimately ineliminable references to other teleologically characterized agencies and states of the organism. This is plausible, but relatively harmless. Our job as philosophers of mind was to explicate the mental in a reductive (and noncircular) way, and this I have done, by reducing mental characterizations to homuncular institutional ones, which are teleological characterizations at various levels of functional abstraction. I am not additionally required to reduce the institutional characterizations to "nicer," more structural ones; if there were a reduction of institutional types to, say, physiological types, then on homunctionalism the identity theory would be true. Institutional *types* (at any given hierarchical level of abstraction) are irreducible, though I assume throughout that institutional *tokens* are reducible in the sense of strict identity, all the way down to the subatomic level.

In fact, the irreducibility of institutional types makes for a mark in favor of homunctionalism as a philosophical theory of the mental. As Donald Davidson and Wilfrid Sellars have both observed, an adequate theory of mind must, among its other tasks, explain the existence of the mind–body problem itself; this would involve explaining why the mental *seems* so different from the physical as to occasion Cartesianism in the naive, why it has historically proved so difficult even for the sophisticated to formulate a plausible reduction of the mental to the physical, and why our mental concepts as a family seem to comprise a "seamless whole," conceptually quite unrelated to the physiological or the physical family.[12] Homunctionalism provides the rudiments of such explanations. The apparent irreducibility of the mental is the genuine irreducibility of institutional types to the less teleological.[13] The difficulty of outlining a tenable reduction of the mental even to the institutional is due to our ignorance of the organizational workings of the institution itself at a sufficiently low level of abstraction. Nor is the irreducibility of institutional types to more physiological types an embarrassment, so long as our system of institutional categories, our system of physiological categories, and our system of physical categories are just alternative groupings of the same tokens. And finally, as Dennett urges in Chapter 1, the intentionality of mental ascriptions may be explained as ultimately being that of teleological ascriptions, though there are still plenty of obstacles to understanding the semantics and the metaphysics of intentionality itself.

Some philosophers might find the homunctionalist "reduction" very cold comfort. Certainly it would bore anyone who antecedently understands teleological characterizations of things *in terms of* mental items such as desires or intentions. Of course, as the foregoing discussion implies, I do not understand teleological talk in that way; rather, I am taking mental types to form a small subclass of teleological types occurring for the most part at a high level of functional abstraction. But if so, then how *do* I understand the teleological?

On this general issue I have little of my own to contribute. I hope, and am inclined to believe, that the teleological characterizations that homunctionalism requires can be independently explained in evolutionary terms. This hope is considerably encouraged by the work of Karl Popper, Wimsatt, and other philosophers of biology;[14] I cannot improve on their technical discussions. However, I do want to make one theoretical point, and then offer one example to back it up.

The theoretical point is that the teleologicalness of characterizations is a matter of degree: some characterizations of a thing are more teleological than others. One and the same space-time slice may be occupied by a collection of molecules, a piece of very hard stuff, a metal strip with an articulated flange, a mover of tumblers, a key, an unlocker of doors, an allower of entry to hotel rooms, a facilitator of adulterous liaisons, a destroyer of souls. Thus, we cannot split our theory of nature neatly into a well-behaved, purely mechanistic part and a dubious, messy vitalistic part better ignored or done away with. And for this reason we cannot maintain that a reduction of the mental to the teleological is no gain in ontological tractability; highly teleological characterizations, unlike naive and explicated mental characterizations, have the virtue of shading off fairly smoothly into (more) brutely physical ones.[15]

Let me give one illustration pertinent to psychology. Consider an organism capable of *recognizing faces* (to take one of Dennett's nice examples of a programmable psychological capacity). There is plenty of point to the question of *how* the organism does its job; the creature might accomplish its face-recognizing by being built according to any of a number of entirely dissimilar functional plans (cf. *Brainstorms, op. cit.*). Suppose the particular plan it does use is as follows: It will accept the command to identify only when it is given as input a front view, right profile, or left profile. The executive routine will direct a *viewpoint locator* to look over the perceptual display, and the viewpoint locator will sort the input into one of the three possible orientation categories. The display will then be shown to the appropriate *analyzer*, which will produce as output a coding of the display's content. A *librarian* will check this code formula against the stock of similarly coded visual reports already stored in the organism's *memory*; if it finds a match, it will look at the identification tag attached to the matching code formula and show the tag to the organism's *public relations officer*, who will give phonological instructions to the *motor subroutines* that will result in the organism's publicly and loudly pronouncing a name.

Knowing that this is the way in which our particular face-recognizer performs its job, we may want to ask for further details. We may want to know how the viewpoint locator works (is it a simple template?), or how the PR office is organized, or what kinds of subcomponents the analyzer employs. Suppose the analyzer is found to consist of a *projector* which imposes a grid on the visual display, and a *scanner* which runs through the grid a square at a time and produces a binary code number. We may go on to ask how the scanner works, and be told that it consists mainly of a light meter which registers a certain degree of darkness at a square and reports "0" or "1" accordingly; we may ask how the light meter works and be told some things about photosensitive chemicals, etc., etc. Now, at what point in this descent through the institutional hierarchy (from *recognizer* to *scanner* to *light meter* to *photosensitive substance*, and as much further down as one might care to go) does our characterization stop being teleological, period, and start being purely mechanical, period? I think it is clear that there is no such point, but rather a finely grained continuum connecting the abstract and highly teleological to the grittily concrete and only barely teleological. And this is why the mental can *seem* totally distinct and cut off from the physiochemical without *being*, ontologically, any such thing.

I shall now turn (at last) to some problems concerning felt phenomenal characters, and offer solutions. I shall discuss some "qualia"-based objections that have been raised against standard functionalist theories, and show that my version of homunctionalism avoids them in what I think is an illuminating way.

IV "Absent Qualia"

In section I above I construed Putnam as accusing the identity theorist of overreacting to the behaviorist's difficulties in allowing for the innerness and introspectibility of qualitative mental states. Jerry Fodor and N. J. Block (*op. cit.*) have made, in effect, a counteraccusation: that Putnam himself overreacted to the identity theorists' excesses and moved too far back toward behaviorism. Putnam and other functionalists characterize mental types in purely *relational* terms; therefore, say Fodor and Block, the functionalists are unable to account for the purely monadic qualitative natures of those states, viz., their phenomenal feels. Block in particular has offered two alleged counterexamples to the thesis, entailed by any version of functionalism, that any physical state of a person that bears the appropriate relations to inputs, outputs, and other states would *be* a pain or a visual sensation or what have you, complete with its smooth, homogeneous qualitative character.[16] The hypothetical cases go as follows:

> Imagine a body externally like a human body, say yours, but internally quite different. The neurons from sensory organs are connected to a bank of lights in a hollow cavity in the head. A set of buttons connects to the motor output neurons. Inside the cavity reside a group of little men. Each has a very simple task: to implement a "square" of a reasonably adequate machine table [program] which describes you. On one wall is a bulletin board on which is posted a state card, i.e., a card that bears a symbol designating one of the states specified in the machine table.... Each little

man has the task corresponding to a single quadruple [= square of a Turing Machine table]. Through the efforts of the little men, the system described realizes the same (reasonably adequate) machine table as you do and is thus functionally equivalent to you. . . .

Suppose we convert the government of China to functionalism, and we convince them that it would enormously enhance their international prestige if they realized a human mind for an hour. We provide each of the billion people in China . . . with a specially designed two-way radio which connects them in the appropriate way to other persons and to the artificial body mentioned in the previous example. We replace the little men [of the previous example] with a radio transmitter and receiver connected to the input and output neurons. Instead of a bulletin board, we arrange to have letters displayed on a series of satellites placed so that they can be seen from anywhere in China. Surely such a system is not physically impossible. It could be functionally equivalent to you for a short time, say an hour. (279)

Block holds that it is simply and straightforwardly absurd to suppose that either of these two group "organisms" is a conscious being or has qualitative, feely inner states. For each consists merely of a corps of clerical workers who pass written or spoken messages to one another: how could any amount of activity of this kind alone, no matter how skillful or complex, suffice to generate a visual field suffused with vivid yellow, or the rich, sweet taste of strawberry shortcake?

I have discussed Block's two cases in a previous paper (*op. cit.*), arguing at some length that Block begs the question against the functionalist; in that paper I also provided one positive reason for believing that group organisms of the type Block describes *would* be conscious and have qualitative states, silly as this may sound at first hearing. But I left the issue officially as a stalemate between attractive theory and persuasive intuition. I am now prepared to take the offensive and argue on more substantive grounds that Block's intuitions about his two cases, seductive as the cases may be, are untenable and have no force at all against homunctionalism. I shall begin by calling our attention to an offsetting counterintuition. Then I shall offer what I think is an accurate diagnosis of Block's intuitions, and explain them away. Later, in section VI below, I shall pose a dilemma for Block which should remove any remaining temptation to accept his cases as counterexamples.

The counterintuition is well expressed in an appeal of Dennett's (ch. 11). Again rejecting the suggestion that we account for the feel of pain by positing an otherwise useless "pain center" in our flow diagram, Dennett adds:

Suppose there were a person of whom our sub-personal account (or a similar one) *without the pain center* were true. What are we to make of the supposition that he does not experience pain, because the sub-personal theory he instantiates does not provide for it? First we make the behaviorist's point that it will be hard to pick him out of a crowd, for his pain behavior will be indistinguishable from that of normal people. But also, it appears *he* will not know the difference, for after all, under normally painful circumstances he believes he is in pain, he finds he is not immune to torture, he gladly takes aspirin and tells us, one way or another, of the relief it provides. I would not want to take on the task of telling him how fortunate he was to be lacking the *je ne sais quoi* that constituted real pain. (219–220)

The same may be said of a person suspected of being a homunculi-head, particularly when we remember the complexity and subtlety of all the variegated "behavior" that a homunctionalist theory is determined to take into account. The case of the population of China is intuitively less vulnerable to this kind of appeal to our sympathy and fellow feeling, since, unlike the homunculi-head, it is not humanoid and, hence, does not so easily stir tenderness and pity. But if we were able to translate the Chinese giant's verbal or "verbal" output well enough to engage it in conversation and philosophical discussion, the same point could be made: we would have a hard time persuading it that there was something forever inaccessible to it which we have no means of conveying to it or causing in it, or (worse) that despite all its protests there is "nothing it is like to be" it. At best, it seems to me, we would have to concede that, although the giant is not really in pain, it thinks it is, and this belief is entirely unshakeable though utterly false.[17] To this extent at least, Block's case as *he* describes it is bizarre, and this bizarreness dims its appeal considerably, at least for me.

Now to diagnosis. If I am right in maintaining that Block's intuition is simply mistaken, what accounts for the intuition in the first place? I suggest that Block and those who share his skepticism concerning our two group organisms are the victims of a kind of Gestalt blindness. This takes a bit of explaining.

Let us begin by taking note of the fact, hinted at by Block himself on page 293, that if his pejorative intuition were sound, an exactly similar intuition would impugn brain matter in just the same way that his impugns little bureaucrats: "A *neuron* is just a simple little piece of insensate stuff that does nothing but let electrical current pass through it from one point in space to another; by merely stuffing an empty brainpan with neurons, you couldn't produce *qualia—immediate phenomenal feels!*"—But I could and would produce feels, if I knew how to string the neurons together in the right way; the intuition expressed here, despite its evoking a perfectly appropriate sense of the *eeriness* of the mental, is just wrong.[18] (Notice carefully that in saying this I am not assuming the truth of materialism. I am assuming only that the mental *supervenes on* the neuroanatomical, as even Descartes conceded. This supervenience is no surprise to Block; I am arguing that the supervenience of the mental on the psychofunctional should not be surprising either.) Let me expand on this point.

Suppose that you were a little, tiny person—say, just ten times the size of a smallish molecule. And suppose that you were located somewhere within Ned Block's brain, perhaps standing somewhere in his left occipital lobe. What would you see? It would seem to you that you were standing in the middle of a vast and largely empty space. Occasionally a molecule (looking something like a cluster of basketballs) would whiz by at a terrific rate; sometimes you would see two or more of these clusters collide and rebound. Now suppose someone were to suggest to you that in fact you were standing inside the body, indeed inside the visual system, of a huge conscious being, whose body consisted just of the aggregate of all those basketball clusters, and that that being at that moment was experiencing a vividly and homogeneously red visual sensation, just in virtue of those otherwise inert basketball clusters' whizzing and bouncing around in the way they are. This would probably seem totally absurd to you, in just the way (I submit) that the example of the population of China seems absurd to Block. *And you would be wrong,* if Block were standing before a smooth red wall in good light.

Why would you be so prone to make this mistake? Why should the truth seem so absurd and unbelievable to you? Presumably because you would be too small to see the forest for the trees. You would be unable to see Block as a person rather than as an aggregate of inert chunks of stuff. Were you to move across the room, grow in size, and look back at Block, you would automatically undergo Gestalt shift, and (according to etiquette) exclaim "Aha!" Similarly, Block is too small to see the Chinese mainland's inputs and outputs, respectively, as psychological stimuli and behavior to which he could relate; were he larger he would be able to see the population of China as a person, with the aid of a suitable translation manual. (As Dennett recently noted in conversation, it is not an aggregate of items which is the subject of conscious states, but the person whose body the aggregate constitutes.) In the case of the homunculi-head, I suggest, the same Gestalt failure obtains even though Block is not smaller than the organism; Block's attention is focused on the hectic activities of the little men, and so he is seeing the homunculi-head as if through a microscope, rather than as a whole macroscopic person whose inner mechanisms are so finely articulated as not even to appear articulated at all.[19]

In diagnosing Block's intuition I have tried to show that it was to be expected even though it is wrong. If this claim is correct (if Block would have his elitist intuitions about the homunculi-head and Chinese-giant cases *whether or not* the homunculi-head or the giant were conscious), then the intuitions have no force against homunctionalism. And after developing my homunctionalist ontology a bit more, I shall return to Block's intuition and deal it a final blow. Meanwhile, however, a third alleged counterexample must be dealt with, put to me by Ian Hinckfuss:

Suppose a transparent plastic pail of spring water is sitting in the sun. At the micro level, a vast seething complexity of things are going on: convection currents, frantic breeding of bacteria and other minuscule life forms, and so on. These things in turn require even more frantic activity at the molecular level to sustain them. Now is all this activity not complex enough that, simply by chance, it might realize a human program for a brief period (given suitable correlations between certain micro-events and the requisite input-, output-, and state-symbols of the program)? And if so, must the functionalist not conclude that the water in the pail briefly constitutes the body of a conscious being, and has thoughts and feelings and so on? Indeed, virtually any physical object under any conditions has enough activity going on within it at the molecular level that, if Hinckfuss is right about the pail of water, the functionalist quickly slips into a panpsychism that does seem obviously absurd; our feeling that pails of water, rocks, and piles of sand are not conscious cannot be diagnosed away as easily as Block's intuitions were. So it seems the onus is on me either to show that Hinckfuss's case could not really occur or to formulate homunctionalism in such a way as to exclude entities of this sort from the community of sentient beings.

I have no crushing instance of either strategy to offer, at least until I have developed homunctionalism a bit further. What I would like to say is that any "realization" of a human program by, say, H_2O atoms would be *fortuitous*. Relative to all normal (and some abnormal) purposes, the motion of atoms through the void is random, and the degree of randomness present at the micro level, for me, removes any temptation to concede that Hinckfuss's quantity of water is realizing the relevant program in any interesting or useful sense.[20] What is missing, I think, is the idea of functional *organization*. In Block's two cases, the homunculi and the Chinese workers, respectively, are *cooperating* in a real sense, according to a prearranged plan, to translate inputs into ultimate outputs. Nothing of this sort is going on within the pail of water. If I am right in identifying mental entities with items teleologically characterized, we see at once why

Block's group organisms are admissible as sentient beings but Hinckfuss's pail of water is not: the homunculi-head and the population of China incorporate ϕ-ers, ψ-ers, and "-ers" of countless other types, courtesy of the bureaucrats who are doing all the work; the pail of water does not contain "-ers" of any kind that is mentioned in a homunctionalist program, precisely because it is not organized in the relevant way, even if the de facto motions of some of the molecules in the pail happen to ape the motions that would be made by an organism that *was* functionally organized on the human model. (Of course, the pail of water does contain "-ers" of various other kinds: microorganisms, the cells of which they are made, and the molecules, or "moleculers," themselves which [in groups] are busily realizing the "cell" programs.)

So far I have simply asserted that the pail of water is not "organized" in the appropriate way, and so my response is not conclusive even though it seems right. In order to vindicate my suggestion, we would need a theory of what it is for a physical entity to constitute a *system*, organism, or bureaucracy. But these are paradigmatically teleological terms; so what we really need is a theory of teleologicalness, and we needed that anyway. If my earlier suggestion—that teleological notions are to be cashed in evolutionary terms—is correct, then we shall have an even easier time distinguishing between humans, animals, group organisms, etc., on the one hand, and Hinckfuss's pail of water on the other, for there is a fairly clear sense in which things of the former sort and their capacities are products of evolutionary processes, but the pail of water and its microactivities are not. Certainly the former items exhibit a continually improving adaptation of means to ends, and the pail does not. However this distinction may eventually be spelled out, I think we can be confident for now that Hinckfuss's pail does not meet proper homunctional standards for sentience and so is not a counterexample to homunctionalism.

V The Problem of the Inputs and the Outputs

In defending homunctionalism against "absent qualia" objections, I do not mean to imply that the task of accounting for qualia is easy or trivial. Aside from all the monstrous technical and methodological obstacles facing the psychology of sensation, there are at least two philosophical reasons why a homunctional theorist would have to do substantive, hard work in order to produce even prototheories of the feel of pain, of the smoothness of colored visual expanses, and the like. First, the functionalist model applies paradigmatically to information-bearing, cognitive states that are rather obviously computational in character. To be sure, there are "wantings to say" closely associated with sensations and their qualitative features. But it is hard to imagine how one might give a positive account of homogeneous phenomenal characters by explicating them entirely in terms of mechanical information accessing.[21] This is not because qualia enthusiasts such as Block are still in search of an extraneous light bulb or traditional homuncular locum or personal ghost in the skull, as I think Dennett supposes in his chapter 9; I believe it is because Block and other philosophers quite naturally have a hard time seeing how such a thing as a sweet taste or a static, homogeneous expanse of phenomenal color, in what Sellars calls the "aesthetically interesting" sense, could be explicable in purely relational terms. And making sense of this possibility requires positive effort on the homunctionalist's part.

The second reason why the friends of qualia are right to demand such effort is that even if Block's two hypothetical cases have failed to refute homunctionalism, some problems of chauvinism and liberalism remain to be resolved. Whether or not Fodor and Block are right in suggesting that Putnam moved too far back toward behaviorism in backing off from the identity theory, the functionalist certainly bears the responsibility of finding a level of characterization of mental states which is neither so abstract or behavioristic as to rule out the possibility of inverted spectrum, etc., *nor* so specific and structural as to fall into chauvinism. Block himself goes on to argue that this problem is insoluble.

He raises the dilemma for the characterization of *inputs* and *outputs* in particular. Plainly, inputs and outputs cannot be characterized in human neural terms; this would chauvinistically preclude our awarding mental descriptions to machines, Martians, and other creatures who differ from us biologically, no matter what convincing credentials they might offer in defense of their sentience. On the other hand, inputs and outputs cannot be characterized in purely abstract terms (i.e., merely as "inputs" and "outputs"), since this will lead to the sort of ultraliberalism that Block has disparaged by means of his earlier examples, and also by means of new ones, such as that of an economic system which has very complex inputs, outputs, and internal states but which certainly has no mental characteristics. Nor can we appeal to any particular sorts of interactions of the sentient being with its environment via inputs and outputs, since in a few cases (those of paralytics, brains *in vitro*, and the like) we want to award mental descriptions to objects that cannot succeed in interacting with their environments in any way. Block concludes:

> Is there a description of inputs and outputs specific enough to avoid liberalism, yet general enough to avoid chauvinism? I doubt that there is.
>
> Every proposal for a description of inputs and outputs I have seen or thought of is guilty of either liberalism or chauvinism. Though this paper has focussed on liberalism, chauvinism is the more pervasive problem.
>
> ... *there will be no physical characterizations that apply to all mental systems' inputs and outputs. Hence, any attempt to formulate a functional description with physical characterizations of inputs and outputs will exclude some* [*possible*] *systems with mentality, and thus will be chauvinist.*
>
> ... On the other hand, you recall, characterizing inputs and outputs simply *as* inputs and outputs is inevitably liberal. I, for one, do not see how functionalism can describe inputs and outputs without falling afoul of either liberalism or chauvinism, or abandoning the original project of characterizing mentality in nonmental terms. I do not claim that this is a conclusive argument against functionalism. Rather, like the functionalist argument against physicalism, it is perhaps best construed as a burden of proof argument. (315–318)

I am not sure how detailed a plan Block is demanding of the functionalist here, though I have agreed that, on a mild-mannered understanding of "burden of proof," Block's challenge is one that the functionalist does bear the burden of meeting. The question is whether this burden is as prohibitively heavy as Block seems to assume. And there are at least three factors which I think lighten it considerably and give us some cause for optimism:

First, there is a line of argument that offers at least some slight positive reason or natural motivation for thinking that the dilemma of chauvinism and liberalism (either in regard to inputs and outputs or in regard to the inner states that the functionalist identifies with our mental states) does admit a solution. It begins as a slippery-slope argument. Block has stated the dilemma very uncompromisingly, implying that one's only choices are (a) to characterize inputs and outputs physiologically and be a chauvinist, or (b) to characterize inputs and outputs "purely abstractly" and be a bleeding heart. But this brutal statement of the alternatives overlooks the fact that functional abstraction is a matter of degree. Purely physiological characterization is an extreme, lying at the lower or "more structural" end of the spectrum; "purely abstract" characterization is the opposite extreme, lying at the higher or "more functional" end. Notice that (as I hinted in discussing Hinckfuss's pail) there are characterizations that are even *more* "structural" than physiological ones are, such as microphysical ones, relative to which physiological ones are "functional"; similarly, there are really more abstract characterizations than "input" and "output" themselves, such as "transfer," "motion," or even "occurrence." If it is true, as it seems to be, that "purely abstract" characterizations and physiological characterizations merely lie near the two ends of a continuum of functional abstraction, then it is reasonable to expect that there exists some intermediate level of abstraction which would yield characterizations that ruled out economic systems and their ilk but made room for human beings, molluscs, Martians, and brains *in vitro*.

Now, intuitively, many of the items that would figure in psychologists' descriptions of inputs and outputs, such as sentences, have highly significant structure for which our developed psychology would require some *semantical* mode of representation, and that system of semantical description might well help us articulate our needed intermediate level of functional characterization. In fact, I suspect that a great preponderance of the functional descriptions that would figure in the kind of psychology I am envisaging will be semantical description. I have several reasons for suspecting and for hoping this. (i) Jerry Fodor[22] has argued fairly persuasively that the computational processes carried out by any interesting agency of the brain (in our model, by the person's subordinate homunculi), being computational, must be couched in some system of representation, and that this system of representation will need to share enough of the characteristic features of natural languages so as to count as an internal language itself. It follows that the inputs and outputs over which the computations are defined will have semantical structure of some kind, and that this semantical level of structure will be the level that is relevant to psychological description and explanation. (For some criticisms of Fodor's argument, however, see Dennett, ch. 6.) (ii) If we describe propositional attitudes such as beliefs and desires, and the inputs and outputs germane to them, in semantical terms, we will be able (à la Sellars) to understand the intentionality of the attitudes as being a special case of the intentionality of sentences, a move whose explanatory value has been considerably increased by the recent elaboration of causal theories of referring. We may also account for beliefs' and thoughts' having truth values, exploiting the recursions that we suppose effect the truth valuations of sentences of formal and natural languages. (iii) In trying to work out a homuncular map of the human speech center,[23] I have come to think that sentential structures *cannot be created within the speech center itself*. If this is right, then (since the speech center *ipso facto* produces sententially structured items as outputs) it must antecedently accept them as inputs. But its inputs come largely from cognitive and conative components whose trade goods are beliefs, perceptual states, and other propositional attitudes. So it is likely that at least the beliefs and thoughts, and perhaps other states among this group, are sententially structured. If the beliefs have semantical structure of some sort, then, as Fodor points out (ch. 2), it is enormously probable that perceptual states also have semantical structure, since otherwise we would have a hard time explaining how it is that perceptual states seemingly give rise directly and immediately to beliefs. And so, finally, it is not unreasonable to suggest that perceptual inputs and outputs *can* be characterized in semantical terms of some sort even though we do not normally so characterize them and may not immediately see how such characterizations would optimally be formulated.

It might be replied that even if overtly sentencelike inputs and outputs were to be represented in psychology as having characteristic structures, economic events and the like are complex enough to instantiate those structures. Possibly so. But let us remember in addition (here is my second point in response to Block's challenge) that nothing forces us to assume that all the different kinds of mental states occur at the *same* level of functional abstraction. The intuitively "more behavioral" sorts of mental states, such as beliefs and desires and intentions, presumably occur at a relatively high level of abstraction, and this makes it easy for us to ascribe beliefs and desires and intentions to Martians whose overt behavior and very superficial psychology match ours; the same is true of highly "informational" mental activities such as remembering and (literal) computing. Intuitively, "less behavioral," more qualitative mental states probably occur at a much lower level of abstraction; sensings that have certain particular kinds of qualitative characters probably *are* quite specific to species (at least, we should not be very surprised to find out that this was so), and quite possibly our Martian's humanoid behavior *is* prompted by his having sensations (or possibly "schmensations") somewhat unlike ours, despite his superficial behavioral similarities to us.

Third, it might be profitable for us simply to stand by the "purely abstract" characterization of inputs and outputs, throwing the whole problem of chauvinism and liberalism back onto our characterization of internal states and events. There are so many possibilities, so many different levels of abstraction in the functional hierarchy as it applies to the brain (many of which overlap and cut across each other), that it seems quite reasonable to expect there to be, for each mental state-type, some middle way between chauvinism and liberalism—not necessarily the *same* middle way for each state-type. For the "more functional," nearly behavioristic mental states, perhaps we would not even mind admitting that an economic system or the population of China could have such states (say, dispositional beliefs), if it were to come to that. And possibly at the least functional end of the continuum there are even mental state-types of which the identity theory is true, though it is hard to think of any mental state that is as "qualitative" as that.

The foregoing remarks suggest a final additional response to Block's "absent qualia" arguments, one which I think is virtually conclusive. Earlier I characterized Block's intuitive disquiet over functionalism as being a matter of feeling the incongruity between the *relationalness* of functionalist explications and the homogeneous, primitively *monadic* qualitative characters of their explicanda; I gather that this incongruity seems to him absolute. Notice that evidently he has no similar objection to the identity theory; like any other materialist, he would simply charge the identity theorist with chauvinism and raise no further complaint. After all, one of the theory's main advantages was its ability to account for the possibility of inverted spectrum or other inner variation despite outward conformity. But if we also accept my claim that homunctional characterizations and physiological characterizations of states of persons reflect merely different levels of abstraction within a surrounding functional hierarchy or continuum, then we can no longer distinguish the functionalist from the identity theorist in any absolute way. "Neuron," for example, may be understood either as a physiological term (denoting a kind of human cell) or as a (teleo-) functional term (denoting a relayer of electrical charge); on *either* construal it stands for an instantiable—if you like, for a role being played by a group of more fundamental objects. Thus, *even the identity theorist is a functionalist*—one who locates mental entities at a very low level of abstraction. The moral is that if Block does want to insist that functionalist psychology is stymied by a principled incongruity of the sort I have mentioned and that a philosophy of mind that explicates mental items in terms of relational roles or instantiables cannot in principle accommodate the intractable monadicity of qualia, then one would have to make the same charge against the identity theorist as well, and this, I trust, he feels no intuitive compulsion to do.[24]

VI Two Alternative Strategies

I have recommended one way of solving the problems of chauvinism and liberalism concerning qualia within a functionalist ontology of the mental. There are alternative possible strategies. One alternative approach would be to bifurcate our view of the mental, by simply taking over the distinction between a mental state and its qualitative character, explicating the states in functional terms and the characters in rather broad physiological terms, tolerating the consequence that inverted spectrum or lesser intrapersonal differences in qualia might be more prevalent than we think (viz., exactly as prevalent as are intrapersonal physiological differences of comparable magnitude).[25]

Pain would present a useful test case for this second suggested way of accommodating qualia. An interesting and distinctive thing about pain is that (unlike most other mental states) it has both a strongly associated behavior pattern *and* vivid introspectible feely properties. This means, on the present proposal, that pain states may receive *multi-leveled* analyses. For example (just to speculate a bit), we might end up wanting to classify any internal state of an organism that played pain's usual "gross" behavioral role (that of being caused by damage and producing withdrawal-*cum*-favoring) as being *a* pain, but to distinguish the feels of pains according to the states' physiological bases.[26] It would follow that, although molluscs and Martians have pains, their pains probably feel differently to them from the ways in which our pains feel to us. It would also follow that a state that feels like a pain state of mine might in a differently organized creature be a mental state of some kind other than pain; some philosophers may find this crassly counterintuitive.

A third alternative approach suggests itself for the case of bodily sensations (though I doubt whether it could easily be applied to perceptual qualia). It is to suppose that feelings which seem phenomenally to be simple are actually complex and that the distinctive quale associated with a feeling of a certain type is really the coincidence or superimposition of a number of distinct, individually manageable homunctional features. I think this line, rather than that adumbrated in the foregoing paragraph, is the most plausible to take for the case of pain, because it is strongly suggested by the anaesthesiological data collected and summarized by Dennett in his chapter 11. What these data seem to indicate is that chemically different anaesthetics and analgesics disrupt subjects' normal "pain" subroutines at different functional junctures, eliciting from the subjects quite different verbal reports of their effects. Of a group of subjects suffering pain of roughly the same kind and same intensity, one subgroup given drug *A* may report that the pain has diminished or gone away entirely; whereas a subgroup given drug *B* may report that although they know that the pain is still there, they cannot feel it; a subgroup given drug *C* may say that although they can still feel the pain just as intensely as ever, they do not *mind* any more; and so on. That some of these reports sound funny to us (they would be pooh-poohed as "unintelligible" by some Wittgensteinians) naturally reflects the fact that the subjects' normal inner workings are being disrupted, and their normal inner experience of pain being altered, by the drugs. What the drugs seem to be doing is *splitting off components* of the subjects' phenomenal experience of the pain, by splitting off component subsubroutines of its rather complicated functional basis. And if this is so, it follows that our phenomenal experience of pain *has* components—it is a complex, consisting (perhaps) of urges, desires, impulses, and beliefs, probably occurring at quite different levels of institutional abstraction. If these components can individually be split off from each other by drugs, then we may perform a *Gedankenexperiment* in which we hypothetically take a suffering subject, split off one component of his pain by administering drug *A*, then split off another component by administering drug *B*, and repeat this process, eliciting reports as we go to keep track of how we are doing. It seems to me plausible to think that if we were to keep this up, disrupting one access pathway after another and eliminating the component urges, desires, and beliefs one by one, we would sooner or later succeed in eliminating the pain itself; it also seems that if we were to reverse the process—to begin restoring the pathways by withholding the various drugs one by one—the subject would necessarily come to feel the full-fledged pain again (provided his damaged tissues had not been repaired in the meantime). I believe this makes it reasonable to suppose that some proper (again) *multileveled* subsequence of the relevant complex of functional goings-on is both necessary and sufficient for the occurrence of the pain, contrary to the spirit of Block's antiliberalism.

I do not know how to make a conclusive choice among the three alternative approaches I have described, or what sorts of further evidence we might seek. I have run through some of the options only in order to show that the homunctionalist has fairly rich resources which can be brought to bear both on the dilemma of chauvinism and liberalism and on the positive task of accounting for qualia. On the basis of these resources I believe we are entitled to conclude that Block's pessimism about qualia is unwarranted.

Acknowledgments

Earlier versions of this paper have been presented at Tufts University, the University of Western Australia, and the 1978 Australasian Association of Philosophy Conference. I owe thanks to many people, especially to Dan Dennett, Ned Block, and David Armstrong for prolonged discussion of the issues treated here, and to the students and colleagues who attended my 1978 seminar at the University of Sydney for their many useful comments.

Notes

1. U. T. Place, "Is Consciousness a Brain Process?" in V. C. Chappell, ed., *The Philosophy of Mind* (Englewood Cliffs, N.J.: Prentice-Hall, 1962), p. 101.

2. Some philosophers have seen fit to deny that this apparent possibility is real. I have tried to rebut this denial in "Inverted Spectrum," *Ratio*, xv, 2 (December 1973): 315–319; though a recent unpublished paper by Michael DePaul has given me cause to worry anew.

3. Putnam, "Psychological Predicates," in W. H. Capitan and D. D. Merrill, eds., *Art, Mind, and Religion* (Pittsburgh, Pa.: University Press, 1967). See also my "Mental States and Putnam's Functionalist Hypothesis," *Australasian Journal of Philosophy*, LII, (1974).

4. In this paper I shall reserve the term 'the identity theory' to refer to Smart's *type–type* identification of the mental with the neurophysiological ["Sensations and Brain Processes," *Philosophical Review*, LXVIII, 2 (April 1959): 141–156]. For some identity theorists, a main motivation has been to explain supposed type–type correlations discovered by laboratory experiment (cf. Jaegwon Kim, "On the Psycho-physical Identity Theory," *American Philosophical Quarterly*, III, 3 (July 1966): 227–235), though Smart has protested to me in correspondence that he did not share this motivation and did not mean to insist on as broad a type–type identification as that which Putnam attacked.

5. "A New Lilliputian Argument against Machine Functionalism," *Philosophical Studies*, XXXV, 3 (April 1979): 279–287. And see n 20 below.

6. Wimsatt, "Teleology and the Logical Structure of Function Statements," *Studies in History and Philosophy of Science*, III (1972); Nagel, *The Structure of Science* (New York: Harcourt, 1961).

7. *Brainstorms* (Montgomery, Vt.: Bradford Books, 1978).

8. In fact, as David Armstrong has pointed out to me, Dennett's sort of maneuver blocks a number of standard infinite-regress arguments in traditional philosophy of mind, such as Ryle's complaint against volitional theories of deciding. Dennett himself wields it against a regress problem concerning mental representation that he attributes to Hume (pp. 122ff).

9. Imagine that you are a cost-benefit analyst from Harvard Business School, hired by some corporation to lift its sagging profits. On an inspection tour you are introduced to each of the various vice-presidents who head the corporation's major divisions. You ask one of the vice-presidents how his particular division is organized; he introduces you to each of his department heads. One of the departments interests you, and you ask how *it* corporately performs its job. This process continues until at one final point you are shown a large room full of clerks, each of whom does nothing but sort numbered index cards into pigeon-holes. "Here's the problem!" you cry. "These people should be replaced by machines!"

10. See, e.g., Fodor and Block, "What Psychological States Are Not," *Philosophical Review*, LXXXI, 2 (April 1972): 159–181.

11. Pages xvi–xvii, 28, and 105 of *Brainstorms, op. cit.*; "Three Kinds of Intentional Psychology," unpublished; and "Beyond Belief," unpublished. See also Donald Davidson, "Mental Events," in

Lawrence Foster and W. J. Swanson, eds., *Experience and Theory* (Amherst: Univ. of Massachusetts Press, 1970), and Putnam, *Meaning and the Moral Sciences* (Boston: Routledge & Kegan Paul, 1978).

12. For stout insistence on this, see Davidson, "Mental Events," *op. cit.*

13. Thus, Smart's example of the logic of "nation" statements' being different from the logic of "citizen" statements may have been more apropos than he imagined.

14. Popper, "Of Clouds and Clocks: An Approach to the Problem of Rationality and the Freedom of Man," reprinted in *Objective Knowledge: An Evolutionary Approach* (New York: Oxford, 1972); Wimsatt, "Teleology and the Logical Structure of Statements," *op. cit.*

15. Characterizations of the contents of our space-time slice may thus be arranged in a continuum, from the least teleological to the most (highly) teleological. This continuum corresponds fairly neatly to the hierarchy of functional instantiation or realization. The molecules jointly realize, or play the role of, the piece of metal; the piece of metal plays the role of the key; the key serves as our door-unlocker; and so on. The prevalence of functional hierarchies of this kind, I believe, is what encourages ontological reduction and the idea that "everything is ultimately a matter of physics." On the relations between teleology viewed from an evolutionary perspective, functional hierarchies, ontology, and the methodology of scientific reduction, see W. C. Wimsatt's brilliant essay, "Reductionism, Levels of Organization, and the Mind–Body Problem," in Gordon G. Globus, Grover Maxwell, and Irwin Savodnik, eds., *Consciousness and the Brain* (New York: Plenum, 1976). I have also profited from reading David Mellick's Ohio State University doctoral dissertation, *Behavioral Strata*, 1973.

16. Block, "Troubles with Functionalism," in C. Wade Savage, ed., *Perception and Cognition: Minnesota Studies in the Philosophy of Science*, vol. IX (Minneapolis: Univ. of Minnesota Press, 1978); page references in my text are to this work. Counterexamples of Block's type have been wielded against behaviorism by various authors, against Smart's program of topic-neutral translations by M. C. Bradley in his Critical Notice on Smart's *Philosophy and Scientific Realism* [*Australasian Journal of Philosophy*, XLII, 2 (August 1964): 262–283], and against D. M. Armstrong's causal analysis of the mental by Keith Campbell in *Body and Mind* (New York: Doubleday, 1970). Saul Kripke raised a distinct but closely related objection against Armstrong in "Naming and Necessity," in D. Davidson and G. Harman, eds., *Semantics of Natural Language* (Boston: Reidel, 1972); I have discussed Kripke's reasoning in "Kripke and the Materialists," *Journal of Philosophy*, LXXI, 18 (Oct. 24, 1974): 677–689.

The moral dimension of individuating mental types purely relationally is explored in Stanislaw Lem's "The Seventh Sally, or How Trurl's Own Perfection Led to No Good" [in *The Cyberiad*, tr. Michael Kandel (New York: Seabury Press, 1974)]; I am grateful to Jan Szrednicki for recommending Lem's writings to me. See also my "Abortion and the Civil Rights of Machines," unpublished Xerox.

17. Lawrence Davis has made a similar point, in more detail, in "Functional Definitions and How It Feels to Be in Pain," mimeo, 1976. Both Davis's discussion and the foregoing counterintuition reinforce the positive argument I made in favor of Block's group organisms in "A New Lilliputian Argument against Machine Functionalism," *op. cit.* That argument ran in outline as follows: Normally a being's engaging in elaborate *M*-behavior in appropriate circumstances, where '*M*' stands for some mental state, is excellent evidence that that being is in state *M*—in most cases, the best evidence we could possibly have, though of course still defeasible. When convincing *M*-behavior is forthcoming, a heavy burden of proof rests on the skeptic to come up with impressive defeating evidence in order to overrule the presumption that the *M*-behaving being is indeed in state *M*. By hypothesis, Block's group organisms engage in extremely sophisticated behavior indicating mental activity of all sorts. Where is Block's impressive defeating evidence?

18. Notice the absurdity of saying, "If we were to scoop the neurons out of your head and then stuff the empty brainpan with nothing but neurons arranged in the same way, you would cease to have phenomenal experience."

19. Michael DePaul has pointed out a difference between a homunculi-head and a normal human being which might be relevant: if the homunculi are really little people working in more or less the same way as do the Chinese workers in Block's other example, they cannot work nearly so *rapidly* as the standard neural realization of the human program. So both the homunculi-head and the population of China would respond only very slowly to stimuli. This drastic slowing of their computational activity, though it seemingly would not affect relatively nonfeely cognitive processes, *might* somehow affect phenomenal experience. But this would need to be shown.

20. The water might be "realizing" the program in the bare sense of there existing a one-one correspondence between the discrete (possible) physical "inputs," physical states, and physical "outputs" of the water and the abstract input-letters, logical-state symbols, and output-letters, respectively, appearing in the program. But I have argued in "A New Lilliputian Argument against Machine Functionalism" that this mathematical notion of "realization" is useless to the functionalist because such "realization" is too easy to achieve. Suppose, for example, that Harriet is a group organism. (On my view we are all group organisms, but let Harriet be a homunculi-head of Block's type.) It is relatively easy to show that, for any of Harriet's constituent homunculi *h* and for any machine program state *S*, if *h* "realizes" *S*, then Harriet does also. It follows from machine functionalism, therefore, that, if one of her homunculi is thinking consciously that broccoli is awful, then Harriet is thinking that too; and if another of Harriet's homunculi is suffering sciatic pain, then Harriet is too; and so on. The absurdity of this result convinces me that machine functionalism *is* too liberal (though Ray Elugardo has protested to me that he does not find the result all that absurd and that he thinks I have begged the question).

Now, the homunctionalist employs a more robust notion of realization, and so is able to avoid this objection. By individuating mental entities according to what they respectively *do for* their owners, we are able to prevent Harriet's overdose of mental activity. For a physiological state of one of her constituent homunculi, though *a fortiori* a physiological state of Harriet herself as well, need not be performing that service *for Harriet.* A state of one of the little women in her head which helps to purify the little woman's blood need have nothing at all to do with Harriet's circulatory system. And the physiological device that serves the little woman as her sciatic nerve does not also function as Harriet's sciatic nerve. (Notice how peculiar it is to credit Harriet with conscious awareness of sciatic pain if Harriet's *own* executive routine had no functional or physical route of access to the source of the trouble.) Likewise: suppose the homunctionalist locates the state of thinking that broccoli is awful as a state $S_i(\psi)$ of one's ψ-er. Then our friend *h* must have a ψ-er as a subsub ... personal component of herself, and her ψ-er must be in state $S_i(\psi)$. But whatever more structural mechanism it is in *h* that serves as her ψ-er would not also be serving Harriet as *her* ψ-er. So it does not follow (as it did from machine functionalism) that Harriet's ψ-er is in state $S_i(\psi)$ or even that she has a ψ-er at all; the objection is blocked.

21. In his ch. 9, Dennett makes an attempt at explicating consciousness in precisely these terms; he analyzes the notion of conscious awareness in terms of inclinations to say things, and identifies such inclinations with inputs to the "printout component," via the "*Control* component," from the short-term or buffer memory that holds the content of our present experience. This Rylean account has some plausibility, though I think doubt is shed on the letter of its sufficiency by the well-known "blindsight" phenomenon, in which subjects whose visual fields have been truncated as a result of brain surgery and who report a total lack of visual experience on one side nevertheless pick up considerable information about the colors and shapes of objects facing them on that side. [See Pöppel, Held, and Frost, "Residual Function after Brain Wounds Involving the

Central Visual Pathways in Man," *Nature*, CCXLIII (1973): 295/6 and L. Weiskrantz *et al.*, "Visual Capacity in the Hemianopic Field Following a Restricted Occipital Ablation," *Brain*, XCVII, 4 (December 1974): 709–728.]

What bothers me more about Dennett's account is that it deals only with awareness qua propositional attitude, and does not even address the kind of difficulty that I think Block is trying to bring out. The feel of pain, the sweetness of a taste, and the grainlessness of phenomenal color are not, or at least not prima facie, propositional at all.

It is important to distinguish a number of quite separate concerns that recent philosophers have expressed in qualia-based objections to materialist theories of the mental; materialists quite frequently and mistakenly think that in speaking to just one or the other of these concerns they have solved or dissolved the problem of qualia in its entirety. I catalogue them in "Sellars on Sensa and Second-guessing" [unpublished].

22. *The Language of Thought* (New York: Crowell, 1975).

23. "A Preliminary Functional Model of an English Speaker," unpublished handout.

24. Wilfrid Sellars does. But that is another story.

25. Block hints on p. 309 that he might not find this suggestion entirely uncongenial.

26. This move would take some of the sting out of what I take to be an antifunctionalist argument in David Lewis's "Mad Pain and Martian Pain," in Ned Block, ed., *Readings in Philosophy of Psychology*, vol. I (Cambridge, Mass.: Harvard University Press, 1980).

28 Epiphenomenal Qualia

Frank Jackson

It is undeniable that the physical, chemical and biological sciences have provided a great deal of information about the world we live in and about ourselves. I will use the label "physical information" for this kind of information, and also for information that automatically comes along with it. For example, if a medical scientist tells me enough about the processes that go on in my nervous system, and about how they relate to happenings in the world around me, to what has happened in the past and is likely to happen in the future, to what happens to other similar and dissimilar organisms, and the like, he or she tells me—if I am clever enough to fit it together appropriately—about what is often called the functional role of those states in me (and in organisms in general in similar cases). This information, and its kin, I also label "physical."

I do not mean these sketchy remarks to constitute a definition of "physical information," and of the correlative notions of physical property, process, and so on, but to indicate what I have in mind here. It is well known that there are problems with giving a precise definition of these notions, and so of the thesis of Physicalism that all (correct) information is physical information.[1] But—unlike some—I take the question of definition to cut across the central problems I want to discuss in this paper.

I am what is sometimes known as a "qualia freak." I think that there are certain features of the bodily sensations especially, but also of certain perceptual experiences, which no amount of purely physical information includes. Tell me everything physical there is to tell about what is going on in a living brain, the kind of states, their functional role, their relation to what goes on at other times and in other brains, and so on and so forth, and be I as clever as can be in fitting it all together, you won't have told me about the hurtfulness of pains, the itchiness of itches, pangs of jealousy, or about the characteristic experience of tasting a lemon, smelling a rose, hearing a loud noise or seeing the sky.

There are many qualia freaks, and some of them say that their rejection of Physicalism is an unargued intuition.[2] I think that they are being unfair to themselves. They have the following argument. Nothing you could tell of a physical sort captures the smell of a rose, for instance. Therefore, Physicalism is false. By our lights this is a perfectly good argument. It is obviously not to the point to question its validity, and the premise is intuitively obviously true both to them and to me.

I must, however, admit that it is weak from a polemical point of view. There are, unfortunately for us, many who do not find the premise intuitively obvious. The task then is to present an argument whose premises are obvious to all, or at least to as many as possible. This I try to do in §I with what I will call "the Knowledge argument." In §II I contrast the Knowledge argument with the Modal argument and in §III with the "What is it like to be" argument. In §IV I tackle the question of the causal role of qualia. The major factor in stopping people from admitting qualia is the belief that they would have to be given a causal role with respect to the physical world and especially the brain;[3] and it is hard to do this without sounding like someone who believes in fairies. I seek in §IV to turn this objection by arguing that the view that qualia are epiphenomenal is a perfectly possible one.

I The Knowledge Argument for Qualia

People vary considerably in their ability to discriminate colours. Suppose that in an experiment to catalogue this variation Fred is discovered. Fred has better colour vision than anyone else on record; he makes every discrimination that anyone has ever made, and moreover he makes one that we cannot even begin to make. Show him a batch of ripe tomatoes and he sorts them into two roughly equal groups and does so with complete consistency. That is, if you blindfold him, shuffle the tomatoes up, and then remove the blindfold and ask him to sort them out again, he sorts them into exactly the same two groups.

We ask Fred how he does it. He explains that all ripe tomatoes do not look the same colour to him, and in fact that this is true of a great many objects that we classify together as red. He sees two colours where we see one, and he has in consequence developed for his own use two words "red_1" and "red_2" to mark the difference. Perhaps he tells us that he has often tried to teach the difference between red_1 and red_2 to his friends but has got nowhere and has concluded that the rest of the world is red_1-red_2 colour-blind—or perhaps he has had partial success with his children, it doesn't matter. In any case he explains to us that it would be quite wrong to think that because "red" appears in both "red_1" and "red_2" that the two colours are shades of the one colour. He only uses the common term "red" to fit more easily into our restricted usage. To him red_1 and red_2 are as different from each other and all the other colours as yellow is from blue. And his discriminatory behaviour bears this out: he sorts red_1 from red_2 tomatoes with the greatest of ease in a wide variety of viewing circumstances. Moreover, an investigation of the physiological basis of Fred's exceptional ability reveals that Fred's optical system is able to separate out two groups of wavelengths in the red spectrum as sharply as we are able to sort out yellow from blue.[4]

I think that we should admit that Fred can see, really see, at least one more colour than we can; red_1 is a different colour from red_2. We are to Fred as a totally red-green colour-blind person is to us. H. G. Wells' story "The Country of the Blind" is about a sighted person in a totally blind community.[5] This person never manages to convince them that he can see, that he has an extra sense. They ridicule this sense as quite inconceivable, and treat his capacity to avoid falling into ditches, to win fights and so on as precisely that capacity and nothing more. We would be making their mistake if we refused to allow that Fred can see one more colour than we can.

What kind of experience does Fred have when he sees red_1 and red_2? What is the new colour or colours like? We would dearly like to know but do not; and it seems that no amount of physical information about Fred's brain and optical system tells us.

We find out perhaps that Fred's cones respond differentially to certain light waves in the red section of the spectrum that make no difference to ours (or perhaps he has an extra cone) and that this leads in Fred to a wider range of those brain states responsible for visual discriminatory behaviour. But none of this tells us what we really want to know about his colour experience. There is something about it we don't know. But we know, we may suppose, everything about Fred's body, his behaviour and dispositions to behaviour and about his internal physiology, and everything about his history and relation to others that can be given in physical accounts of persons. We have all the physical information. Therefore, knowing all this is *not* knowing everything about Fred. It follows that Physicalism leaves something out.

To reinforce this conclusion, imagine that as a result of our investigations into the internal workings of Fred we find out how to make everyone's physiology like Fred's in the relevant respects; or perhaps Fred donates his body to science and on his death we are able to transplant his optical system into someone else—again the fine detail doesn't matter. The important point is that such a happening would create enormous interest. People would say, "At last we will know what it is like to see the extra colour, at last we will know how Fred has differed from us in the way he has struggled to tell us about for so long." Then it cannot be that we knew all along all about Fred. But *ex hypothesi* we did know all along everything about Fred that features in the physicalist scheme; hence the physicalist scheme leaves something out.

Put it this way. *After* the operation, we will know *more* about Fred and especially about his colour experiences. But beforehand we had all the physical information we could desire about his body and brain, and indeed everything that has ever featured in physicalist accounts of mind and consciousness. Hence there is more to know than all that. Hence Physicalism is incomplete.

Fred and the new colour(s) are of course essentially rhetorical devices. The same point can be made with normal people and familiar colours. Mary is a brilliant scientist who is, for whatever reason, forced to investigate the world from a black and white room *via* a black and white television monitor. She specialises in the neurophysiology of vision and acquires, let us suppose, all the physical information there is to obtain about what goes on when we see ripe tomatoes, or the sky, and use terms like "red," "blue," and so on. She discovers, for example, just which wave-length combinations from the sky stimulate the retina, and exactly how this produces *via* the central nervous system the contraction of the vocal chords and expulsion of air from the lungs that results in the uttering of the sentence "The sky is blue." (It can hardly be denied that it is in principle possible to obtain all this physical information from black and white television, otherwise the Open University would *of necessity* need to use colour television.)

What will happen when Mary is released from her black and white room or is given a colour television monitor? Will she *learn* anything or not? It seems just obvious that she will learn something about the world and our visual experience of it. But then it is inescapable that her previous knowledge was incomplete. But she had *all* the physical information. *Ergo* there is more to have than that, and Physicalism is false.

Clearly the same style of Knowledge argument could be deployed for taste, hearing, the bodily sensations and generally speaking for the various mental states which are said to have (as it is variously put) raw feels, phenomenal features or qualia. The conclusion in each case is that the qualia are left out of the physicalist story. And the polemical strength of the Knowledge argument is that it is so hard to deny the central claim that one can have all the physical information without having all the information there is to have.

II The Modal Argument

By the Modal Argument I mean an argument of the following style.[6] Sceptics about other minds are not making a mistake in deductive logic, whatever else may be wrong with their position. No amount of physical information about another *logically entails* that he or she is conscious or feels anything at all. Consequently there is a possible world with organisms exactly like us in every physical respect (and remember that includes functional states, physical history, *et al.*) but which differ from us profoundly in that they have no conscious mental life at all. But then what is it that we have and they lack? Not anything physical *ex hypothesi*. In all physical regards we and they are exactly alike. Consequently there is more to us than the purely physical. Thus Physicalism is false.[7]

It is sometimes objected that the Modal argument misconceives Physicalism on the ground that that doctrine is advanced as a *contingent* truth.[8] But to say this is only to say that physicalists restrict their claim to *some* possible worlds, including especially ours; and the Modal argument is only directed against this lesser claim. If we in *our* world, let alone beings in any others, have features additional to those of our physical replicas in other possible worlds, then we have non-physical features or qualia.

The trouble rather with the Modal argument is that it rests on a disputable modal intuition. Disputable because it is disputed. Some sincerely deny that there can be physical replicas of us in other possible worlds which nevertheless lack consciousness. Moreover, at least one person who once had the intuition now has doubts.[9]

Head-counting may seem a poor approach to a discussion of the Modal argument. But frequently we can do no better when modal intuitions are in question, and remember our initial goal was to find the argument with the greatest polemical utility.

Of course, *qua* protagonists of the Knowledge argument we may well accept the modal intuition in question; but this will be a *consequence* of our already having an argument to the conclusion that qualia are left out of the physicalist story, not our ground for that conclusion. Moreover, the matter is complicated by the possibility that the connection between matters physical and qualia is like that sometimes held to obtain between aesthetic qualities and natural ones. Two possible worlds which agree in all "natural" respects (including the experiences of sentient creatures) must agree in all aesthetic qualities also, but it is plausibly held that the aesthetic qualities cannot be reduced to the natural.

III The "What Is It Like to Be" Argument

In "What is it like to be a bat?" Thomas Nagel argues that no amount of physical information can tell us what it is like to be a bat, and indeed that we, human beings, cannot imagine what it is like to be a bat.[10] His reason is that what this is like can only be understood from a bat's point of view, which is not our point of view and is not something capturable in physical terms which are essentially terms understandable equally from many points of view.

It is important to distinguish this argument from the Knowledge argument. When I complained that all the physical knowledge about Fred was not enough to tell us what his special colour experience was like, I was not complaining that we weren't finding out what it is like to *be* Fred. I was complaining that there is something *about* his experience, a property of it, of which we were left ignorant. And if and when we come to know what this property is we still will not know what it is like to *be* Fred, but we will know more *about* him. No amount of knowledge about Fred, be it physical or not, amounts to knowledge "from the inside" concerning Fred. We are not Fred. There is thus a whole set of items of knowledge expressed by forms of words like "that it is *I myself* who is ..." which Fred has and we simply cannot have because we are not him.[11]

When Fred sees the colour he alone can see, one thing he knows is the way his experience of it differs from his experience of seeing red and so on, *another* is that he himself is seeing it. Physicalist and qualia freaks alike should acknowledge that no amount of information of whatever kind that *others* have *about* Fred amounts to knowledge of the second. My complaint though concerned the first and was that the special quality of his experience is certainly a fact about it, and one which Physicalism leaves out because no amount of physical information told us what it is.

Nagel speaks as if the problem he is raising is one of extrapolating from knowledge of one experience to another, of imagining what an unfamiliar experience would be like on the basis of familiar ones. In terms of Hume's example, from knowledge of some shades of blue we can work out what it would be like to see other shades of blue. Nagel argues that the trouble with bats *et al.* is that they are too unlike us. It is hard to see an objection to Physicalism here. Physicalism makes no special claims about the imaginative or extrapolative powers of human beings, and it is hard to see why it need do so.[12]

Anyway, our Knowledge argument makes no assumptions on this point. If Physicalism were true, enough physical information about Fred would obviate any need to extrapolate or to perform special feats of imagination or understanding in order to know all about his special colour experience. *The information would already be in our possession.* But it clearly isn't. That was the nub of the argument.

IV The Bogey of Epiphenomenalism

Is there any really *good* reason for refusing to countenance the idea that qualia are causally impotent with respect to the physical world? I will argue for the answer no, but in doing this I will say nothing about two views associated with the classical epiphenomenalist position. The first is that mental *states* are inefficacious with respect to the physical world. All I will be concerned to defend is that it is possible to hold that certain *properties* of certain mental states, namely those I've called qualia, are such that their possession or absence makes no difference to the physical world. The second is that the mental is *totally* causally inefficacious. For all I will say it may be that you have to hold that the instantiation of *qualia* makes a difference to *other mental states* though not to anything physical. Indeed general considerations to do with how you could come to be aware of the instantiation of qualia suggest such a position.[13]

Three reasons are standardly given for holding that a quale like the hurtfulness of a pain must be causally efficacious in the physical world, and so, for instance, that its instantiation must sometimes make a difference to what happens in the brain. None, I will argue, has any real force. (I am much indebted to Alec Hyslop and John Lucas for convincing me of this.)

(i) It is supposed to be just obvious that the hurtfulness of pain is partly responsible for the subject seeking to avoid pain, saying "It hurts" and so on. But, to reverse Hume, anything can fail to cause anything. No matter how often *B* follows *A*, and no matter how initially obvious the causality of the connection seems, the hypothesis that *A* causes *B* can be overturned by an over-arching theory which shows the two as distinct effects of a common underlying causal process.

To the untutored the image on the screen of Lee Marvin's fist moving from left to right immediately followed by the image of John Wayne's head moving in the same general direction looks as causal as anything.[14] And of course throughout countless Westerns images similar to the first are followed by images similar to the second. All this counts for precisely nothing when we know the over-arching theory concerning how the relevant images are both effects of an underlying causal process involving the projector and the film. The epiphenomenalist can say exactly the same about the connection between, for example, hurtfulness and behaviour. It is simply a consequence of the fact that certain happenings in the brain cause both.

(ii) The second objection relates to Darwin's Theory of Evolution. According to natural selection the traits that evolve over time are those conducive to physical survival. We may assume that qualia evolved over time—we have them, the earliest forms of life do not—and so we should expect qualia to be conducive to survival. The objection is that they could hardly help us to survive if they do nothing to the physical world.

The appeal of this argument is undeniable, but there is a good reply to it. Polar bears have particularly thick, warm coats. The Theory of Evolution explains this (we suppose) by pointing out that having a thick, warm coat is conducive to survival in the Arctic. But having a thick coat goes along with having a heavy coat, and having a heavy coat is *not* conducive to survival. It slows the animal down.

Does this mean that we have refuted Darwin because we have found an evolved trait—having a heavy coat—which is not conducive to survival? Clearly not. Having a heavy coat is an unavoidable concomitant of having a warm coat (in the context, modern insulation was not available), and the advantages for survival of having a warm coat outweighed the disadvantages of having a heavy one. The point is that all we can extract from Darwin's theory is that we should expect any evolved characteristic to be *either* conducive to survival *or* a by-product of one that is so conducive. The epiphenomenalist holds that qualia fall into the latter category. They are a by-product of certain brain processes that are highly conducive to survival.

(iii) The third objection is based on a point about how we come to know about other minds. We know about other minds by knowing about other behaviour, at least in part. The nature of the inference is a matter of some controversy, but it is not a matter of controversy that it proceeds from behaviour. That is why we think that stones do not feel and dogs do feel. But, runs the objection, how can a person's behaviour provide any reason for believing he has qualia like mine, or indeed any qualia at all, unless this behaviour can be regarded as the *outcome* of the qualia. Man Friday's footprint was evidence of Man Friday because footprints are causal outcomes of feet attached to people. And an epiphenomenalist cannot regard behaviour, or indeed anything physical, as an outcome of qualia.

But consider my reading in *The Times* that Spurs won. This provides excellent evidence that *The Telegraph* has also reported that Spurs won, despite the fact that (I trust) *The Telegraph* does not get the results from *The Times*. They each send their own reporters to the game. *The Telegraph*'s report is in no sense an outcome of *The Times*', but the latter provides good evidence for the former nevertheless.

The reasoning involved can be reconstructed thus. I read in *The Times* that Spurs won. This gives me reason to think that Spurs won because I know that Spurs' winning is the most likely candidate to be what caused the report in *The Times*. But I also know that Spurs' winning would have had many effects, including almost certainly a report in *The Telegraph*.

I am arguing from one effect back to its cause and out again to another effect. The fact that neither effect causes the other is irrelevant. Now the epiphenomenalist allows that qualia are effects of what goes on in the brain. Qualia cause nothing physical but are caused by something physical. Hence the epiphenomenalist can argue from the behaviour of others to the qualia of others by arguing from the behaviour of others back to its causes in the brains of others and out again to their qualia.

You may well feel for one reason or another that this is a more dubious chain of reasoning than its model in the case of newspaper reports. You are right. The problem of other minds is a major philosophical problem, the problem of other newspaper reports is not. But there is no special problem of Epiphenomenalism as opposed to, say, Interactionism here.

There is a very understandable response to the three replies I have just made. "All right, there is no knockdown refutation of the existence of epiphenomenal qualia. But the fact remains that they are an excrescence. They *do* nothing, they *explain* nothing, they serve merely to soothe the intuitions of dualists, and it is left a total mystery how they fit into the world view of science. In short we do not and cannot understand the how and why of them."

This is perfectly true; but is no objection to qualia, for it rests on an overly optimistic view of the human animal, and its powers. We are the products of Evolution. We understand and sense what we need to understand and sense in order to survive. Epiphenomenal qualia are totally irrelevant to survival. At no stage of our evolution did natural selection favour those who could make sense of how they are caused and the laws governing them, or in fact why they exist at all. And that is why we can't.

It is not sufficiently appreciated that Physicalism is an extremely optimistic view of our powers. If it is true, we have, in very broad outline admittedly, a grasp of our place in the scheme of things. Certain matters of sheer complexity defeat us—there are an awful lot of neurons—but in principle we have it all. But consider the antecedent probability that everything in the Universe be of a kind that is relevant in some way or other to the survival of *Homo sapiens*. It is very low surely. But then one must admit that it is very likely that there is a part of the whole scheme of things, maybe a big part, which no amount of evolution will ever bring us near to knowledge about or understanding. For the simple reason that such knowledge and understanding is irrelevant to survival.

Physicalists typically emphasise that we are a part of nature on their view, which is fair enough. But if we are a part of nature, we are as nature has left us after however many years of evolution it is, and each step in that evolutionary progression has been a matter of chance constrained just by the need to preserve or increase survival value. The wonder is that we understand as much as we do, and there is no wonder that there should be matters which fall quite outside our comprehension. Perhaps exactly how epiphenomenal qualia fit into the scheme of things is one such.

This may seem an unduly pessimistic view of our capacity to articulate a truly comprehensive picture of our world and our place in it. But suppose we discovered living on the bottom of the deepest oceans a sort of sea slug which manifested intelligence. Perhaps survival in the conditions required rational powers. Despite their intelligence, these sea slugs have only a very restricted conception of the world by comparison with ours, the explanation for this being the nature of their immediate environment. Nevertheless they have developed sciences which work surprisingly well in these restricted terms. They also have philosophers, called slugists. Some call themselves tough-minded slugists, others confess to being soft-minded slugists.

The tough-minded slugists hold that the restricted terms (or ones pretty like them which may be introduced as their sciences progress) suffice in principle to describe everything without remainder. These tough-minded slugists admit in moments of weakness to a feeling that their theory leaves something out. They resist this feeling and their opponents, the soft-minded slugists, by pointing out—absolutely correctly—that no slugist has ever succeeded in spelling out how this mysterious residue fits into the highly successful view that their sciences have and are developing of how their world works.

Our sea slugs don't exist, but they might. And there might also exist super beings which stand to us as we stand to the sea slugs. We cannot adopt the perspective of these super beings, because we are not them, but the possibility of such a perspective is, I think, an antidote to excessive optimism.[15]

Notes

1. See, e.g., D. H. Mellor, "Materialism and Phenomenal Qualities," *Aristotelian Society Supp. Vol.* 47 (1973), 107–19; and J. W. Cornman, *Materialism and Sensations* (New Haven and London, 1971).

2. Particularly in discussion, but see, e.g., Keith Campbell, *Metaphysics* (Belmont, 1976), p. 67.

3. See, e.g., D. C. Dennett, "Current Issues in the Philosophy of Mind," *American Philosophical Quarterly*, 15 (1978), 249–61.

4. Put this, and similar simplifications below, in terms of Land's theory if you prefer. See, e.g., Edwin H. Land, "Experiments in Color Vision," *Scientific American*, 200 (5 May 1959), 84–99.

5. H. G. Wells, *The Country of the Blind and Other Stories* (London, n.d.).

6. See, e.g., Keith Campbell, *Body and Mind* (New York, 1970); and Robert Kirk, "Sentience and Behaviour," *Mind*, 83 (1974), 43–60.

7. I have presented the argument in an inter-world rather than the more usual intra-world fashion to avoid inessential complications to do with supervenience, causal anomalies and the like.

8. See, e.g., W. G. Lycan, "A New Lilliputian Argument Against Machine Functionalism," *Philosophical Studies*, 35 (1979), 279–87, p. 280; and Don Locke, "Zombies, Schizophrenics and Purely Physical Objects," *Mind*, 85 (1976), 97–9.

9. See R. Kirk, "From Physical Explicability to Full-Blooded Materialism," *Philosophical Quarterly*, 29 (1979), 229–37. See also the arguments against the modal intuition in, e.g., Sydney Shoemaker, "Functionalism and Qualia," *Philosophical Studies*, 27 (1975), 291–315.

10. *Philosophical Review*, 83 (1974), 435–50. Two things need to be said about this article. One is that, despite my dissociations to come, I am much indebted to it. The other is that the emphasis changes through the article, and by the end Nagel is objecting not so much to Physicalism as to all extant theories of mind for ignoring points of view, including those that admit (irreducible) qualia.

11. Knowledge *de se* in the terms of David Lewis, "Attitudes De Dicto and De Se," *Philosophical Review*, 88 (1979), 513–43.

12. See Laurence Nemirow's comments on "What is it . . ." in his review of T. Nagel, *Mortal Questions*, in *Philosophical Review*, 89 (1980), 473–7. I am indebted here in particular to a discussion with David Lewis.

13. See my review of K. Campbell, *Body and Mind*, in *Australasian Journal of Philosophy*, 50 (1972), 77–80.

14. Cf. Jean Piaget, "The Child's Conception of Physical Causality," reprinted in *The Essential Piaget* (London, 1977).

15. I am indebted to Robert Pargetter for a number of comments and, despite his dissent, to §IV of Paul E. Meehl, "The Compleat Autocerebroscopist" in *Mind, Matter, and Method*, ed. Paul Feyerabend and Grover Maxwell (Minneapolis, 1966).

29 Can We Solve the Mind–Body Problem?

Colin McGinn

How it is that anything so remarkable as a state of consciousness comes about as a result of initiating nerve tissue, is just as unaccountable as the appearance of the Djin, where Aladdin rubbed his lamp in the story . . .

—Julian Huxley

We have been trying for a long time to solve the mind–body problem. It has stubbornly resisted our best efforts. The mystery persists. I think the time has come to admit candidly that we cannot resolve the mystery. But I also think that this very insolubility—or the reason for it—removes the philosophical problem. In this paper I explain why I say these outrageous things.

The specific problem I want to discuss concerns consciousness, the hard nut of the mind–body problem. How is it possible for conscious states to depend upon brain states? How can technicolour phenomenology arise from soggy grey matter? What makes the bodily organ we call the brain so radically different from other bodily organs, say the kidneys—the body parts without a trace of consciousness? How could the aggregation of millions of individually insentient neurons generate subjective awareness? We know that brains are the *de facto* causal basis of consciousness, but we have, it seems, no understanding whatever of how this can be so. It strikes us as miraculous, eerie, even faintly comic. Somehow, we feel, the water of the physical brain is turned into the wine of consciousness, but we draw a total blank on the nature of this conversion. Neural transmissions just seem like the wrong kind of materials with which to bring consciousness into the world, but it appears that in some way they perform this mysterious feat. The mind–body problem is the problem of understanding how the miracle is wrought, thus removing the sense of deep mystery. We want to take the magic out of the link between consciousness and the brain.[1]

Purported solutions to the problem have tended to assume one of two forms. One form, which we may call constructive, attempts to specify some natural property of the brain (or body) which explains how consciousness can be elicited from it. Thus functionalism, for example, suggests a property—namely, causal role—which is held to be satisfied by both brain states and mental states; this property is supposed to explain how conscious states can come from brain states.[2] The other form, which has been historically dominant, frankly admits that nothing merely natural could do the job, and suggests instead that we invoke supernatural entities or divine interventions. Thus we have Cartesian dualism and Leibnizian pre-established harmony. These "solutions" at least recognize that something pretty remarkable is needed if the mind–body relation is to be made sense of; they are as extreme as the problem. The approach I favour is naturalistic but not constructive: I do not believe we can ever specify what it is about the brain that is responsible for consciousness, but I am sure that whatever it is it is not inherently miraculous. The problem arises, I want to suggest, because we are cut off by our very cognitive constitution from achieving a conception of that natural property of the brain (or of consciousness) that accounts for the psychophysical link. This is a kind of causal nexus that we are precluded from ever understanding, given the way we have to form our concepts and develop our theories. No wonder we find the problem so difficult!

Before I can hope to make this view plausible, I need to sketch the general conception of cognitive competence that underlies my position. Let me introduce the idea of *cognitive closure*. A type of mind *M* is cognitively closed with respect to a property *P* (or theory *T*) if and only if the concept-forming procedures at *M*'s disposal cannot extend to a grasp of *P* (or an understanding of *T*). Conceiving minds come in different kinds, equipped with varying powers and limitations, biases and blindspots, so that properties (or theories) may be accessible to some minds but not to others. What is closed to the mind of a rat may be open to the mind of a monkey, and what is open to us may be closed to the monkey. Representational power is not all or nothing. Minds are biological products like bodies, and like bodies they come in different shapes and sizes, more or less capacious, more or less suited to certain cognitive tasks.[3] This is particularly clear for perceptual faculties, of course: perceptual closure is hardly to be denied. Different species are capable of perceiving different properties of the world, and no species can perceive every property things may instantiate (without artificial instrumentation anyway). But such closure does not reflect adversely on the reality of the properties that lie outside the representational capacities in question; a property is no less real for not being reachable from a certain kind of perceiving and conceiving mind. The invisible parts of the electromagnetic spectrum are just as real as the visible parts, and whether a specific kind of creature can form conceptual representations of these imperceptible parts does not determine whether they exist. Thus cognitive closure with respect to *P* does not imply irrealism about *P*. That *P* is (as we might say) *noumenal* for *M* does not show that *P* does not occur in some naturalistic scientific theory *T*—it shows only that *T* is not cognitively accessible to *M*. Presumably monkey minds and the property of being an electron illustrate this possibility. And the question must arise as to whether human minds are closed with respect to certain true explanatory theories. Nothing, at least, in the concept of reality shows that everything real is open to the human concept-forming faculty—if, that is, we are realists about reality.[4]

Consider a mind constructed according to the principles of classical empiricism, a Humean mind. Hume mistakenly thought that human minds were Humean, but we can at least conceive of such a mind (perhaps dogs and monkeys have Humean minds). A Humean mind is such that perceptual closure determines cognitive closure, since "ideas" must always be copies of "impressions"; therefore the concept-forming system cannot transcend what can be perceptually presented to the subject. Such a mind will be closed with respect to unobservables; the properties of atoms, say, will not be representable by a mind constructed in this way. This implies that explanatory theories in which these properties are essentially mentioned will not be accessible to a Humean mind.[5] And hence the observable phenomena that are explained by allusion to unobservables will be inexplicable by a mind thus limited. But notice: the incapacity to explain certain phenomena does not carry with it a lack of recognition of the theoretical problems the phenomena pose. You might be able to appreciate a problem without being able to formulate (even in principle) the solution to that problem (I suppose human children are often in this position, at least for a while). A Humean mind cannot solve the problems that our physics solves, yet it might be able to have an inkling of what needs to be explained. We would expect, then, that a moderately intelligent enquiring Humean mind will feel permanently perplexed and mystified by the physical world, since the correct science is forever beyond its cognitive reach. Indeed, something like this was precisely the view of Locke. He thought that our ideas of matter are quite sharply constrained by our perceptions and so concluded that the true science of matter is eternally beyond us—that we could never remove our perplexities about (say) what solidity ultimately is.[6] But it does not follow for Locke that nature is itself inherently mysterious; the felt mystery comes from our own cognitive limitations, not from any objective eeriness in the world. It looks today as if Locke was wrong about our capacity to fathom the nature of the physical world, but we can still learn from his fundamental thought—the insistence that our cognitive faculties may not be up to solving every problem that confronts us. To put the point more generally: the human mind may not conform to empiricist principles, but it must conform to *some* principles—and it is a substantive claim that these principles permit the solution of every problem we can formulate or sense. Total cognitive openness is not guaranteed for human beings and it should not be expected. Yet what is noumenal for us may not be miraculous in itself. We should therefore be alert to the possibility that a problem that strikes us as deeply intractable, as utterly baffling, may arise from an area of cognitive closure in our ways of representing the world.[7] That is what I now want to argue is the case with our sense of the mysterious nature of the connection between consciousness and the brain. We are biased away from arriving at the correct explanatory theory of the psychophysical nexus. And this makes us prone to an illusion of objective mystery. Appreciating this should remove the philosophical problem: consciousness does not, in reality, arise from the brain in the miraculous way in which the Djin arises from the lamp.

I now need to establish three things: (i) there exists some property of the brain that accounts naturalistically for consciousness; (ii) we are cognitively closed with respect to that property; but (iii) there is no philosophical (as opposed to scientific) mind–body problem. Most of the work will go into establishing (ii).

Resolutely shunning the supernatural, I think it is undeniable that it must be in virtue of *some* natural property of the brain that organisms are conscious. There just *has* to be some explanation for how brains subserve minds. If we are not to be eliminativists about consciousness, then some theory must exist which accounts for the psychophysical correlations we observe. It is implausible to take these correlations as ultimate and inexplicable facts, as simply brute. And we do not want to acknowledge radical emergence of the conscious with respect to the cerebral: that is too much like accepting miracles *de re*. Brain states cause conscious states, we know, and this causal nexus must proceed through necessary connections of some kind—the kind that would make the nexus intelligible *if* they were understood.[8] Consciousness is like life in this respect. We know that life evolved from inorganic matter, so we expect there to be some explanation of this process. We cannot plausibly take the arrival of life as a primitive brute fact, nor can we accept that life arose by some form of miraculous emergence. Rather, there must be some natural account of how life comes from matter, whether or not we can know it. Eschewing vitalism and the magic touch of God's finger, we rightly insist that it must be in virtue of some natural property of (organized) matter that parcels of it get to be alive. But consciousness itself is just a further biological development, and so it too must be susceptible of some natural explanation—whether or not human beings are capable of arriving at this explanation. Presumably there exist objective natural laws that somehow account for the upsurge of consciousness. Consciousness, in short, must be a natural phenomenon, naturally arising from certain organizations of matter. Let us then say that there exists some property *P*, instantiated by the brain, in virtue of which the brain is the basis of consciousness. Equivalently, there exists some theory *T*, referring to *P*, which fully explains the dependence of conscious states on brain states. If we knew *T*, then we would have a constructive solution to the mind–body problem. The question then is whether we can ever come to know *T* and grasp the nature of *P*.

Let me first observe that it is surely *possible* that we could never arrive at a grasp of *P*; there is, as I said, no guarantee that our cognitive powers permit the solution of every problem we can recognize. Only a misplaced idealism about the natural world could warrant the dogmatic claim that everything is knowable by the human species at this stage of its evolutionary development (consider the same claim made on behalf of the intellect of cro-Magnon man). It *may* be that every property for which we can form a concept is such that *it* could never solve the mind–body problem. We *could* be like five-year-old children trying to understand Relativity Theory. Still, so far this is just a possibility claim: what reason do we have for asserting, positively, that our minds are closed with respect to *P*?

Longstanding historical failure is suggestive, but scarcely conclusive. Maybe, it will be said, the solution is just around the corner, or it has to wait upon the completion of the physical sciences? Perhaps we simply have yet to produce the Einstein-like genius who will restructure the problem in some clever way and then present an astonished world with the solution?[9] However, I think that our deep bafflement about the problem, amounting to a vertiginous sense of ultimate mystery, which resists even articulate formulation, should at least encourage us to explore the idea that there is something terminal about our perplexity. Rather as traditional theologians found themselves conceding cognitive closure with respect to certain of the properties of God, so we should look seriously at the idea that the mind–body problem brings us bang up against the limits of our capacity to understand the world. That is what I shall do now.

There seem to be two possible avenues open to us in our aspiration to identify *P*: we could try to get to *P* by investigating consciousness directly, or we could look to the study of the brain for *P*. Let us consider these in turn, starting with consciousness. Our acquaintance with consciousness could hardly be more direct; phenomenological description thus comes (relatively) easily. "Introspection" is the name of the faculty through which we catch consciousness in all its vivid nakedness. By virtue of possessing this cognitive faculty we ascribe concepts of consciousness to ourselves; we thus have "immediate access" to the properties of consciousness. But does the introspective faculty reveal property *P*? Can we tell just by introspecting what the solution to the mind–body problem is? Clearly not. We have direct cognitive access to one term of the mind–brain relation, but we do not have such access to the nature of the link. Introspection does not present conscious states *as* depending upon the brain in some intelligible way. We cannot therefore introspect *P*. Moreover, it seems impossible that we should ever augment our stock of introspectively ascribed concepts with the concept *P*—that is, we could not acquire this concept simply on the basis of sustained and careful introspection. Pure phenomenology will never provide the solution to the mind–body problem. Neither does it seem feasible to try to extract *P* from the concepts of consciousness we now have by some procedure of conceptual analysis—any more than we could solve the life–matter problem simply by reflecting on the concept *life*.[10] *P* has to lie outside the field of the introspectable, and it is not implicitly contained in the concepts we bring to bear in our first-person ascriptions. Thus the faculty of introspection, as a concept-forming capacity, is cognitively closed with respect to *P*; which is not surprising in view of its highly limited domain of operation (*most* properties of the world are closed to introspection).

But there is a further point to be made about *P* and consciousness, which concerns our restricted access to the concepts of consciousness themselves. It is a familiar point that the range of concepts of consciousness attainable by a mind *M* is constrained by the specific forms of consciousness possessed by *M*. Crudely, you cannot form concepts of conscious properties unless you yourself instantiate those properties. The man born blind cannot grasp the concept of a visual experience of red, and human beings cannot conceive of the echolocatory experiences of bats.[11] These are cases of cognitive closure within the class of conscious properties. But now this kind of closure will, it seems, affect our hopes of access to *P*. For suppose that we were cognitively open with respect to *P*; suppose, that is, that we had the solution to the problem of how specific forms of consciousness depend upon different kinds of physiological structure. Then, of course, we would understand how the brain of a bat subserves the subjective experiences of bats. Call this type of experience *B*, and call the explanatory property that links *B* to the bat's brain P_I. By grasping P_I it would be perfectly intelligible to us how the bat's brain generates *B*-experiences; we would have an explanatory theory of the causal nexus in question. We would be in possession of the same kind of understanding we would have of our own experiences if we had the correct psychophysical theory of them. But then it seems to follow that grasp of the theory that explains *B*-experiences would *confer* a grasp of the nature of those experiences: for how could we understand that theory without understanding the concept *B* that occurs in it? How could we grasp the *nature* of *B*-experiences without grasping the *character* of those experiences? The true psychophysical theory would seem to provide a route to a grasp of the subjective form of the bat's experiences. But now we face a dilemma, a dilemma which threatens to become a reductio: either we *can* grasp this theory, in which case the property *B* becomes open to us; or we *cannot* grasp the theory, simply because property *B* is *not* open to us. It seems to me that the looming reductio here is compelling: our concepts of consciousness just *are* inherently constrained by our own form of consciousness, so that any theory the understanding of which required us to transcend these constraints would *ipso facto* be inaccessible to us. Similarly, I think, any theory that required us to transcend the finiteness of our cognitive capacities would *ipso facto* be a theory we could not grasp—and this despite the fact that it might be needed to explain something we can see needs explaining. We cannot simply stipulate that our concept-forming abilities are indefinitely plastic and unlimited just because they would have to be to enable us to grasp the truth about the world. We constitutionally lack the concept-forming capacity to encompass all possible types of conscious state, and this obstructs our path to a general solution to the mind–body problem. Even if we could solve it for our own case, we could not solve it for bats and Martians. *P* is, as it were, too close to the different forms of subjectivity for it to be accessible to all such forms, given that one's form of subjectivity restricts one's concepts of subjectivity.[12]

I suspect that most optimists about constructively solving the mind–body problem will prefer to place their bets on the brain side of the relation. Neuroscience is the place to look for property *P*, they will say. My question then is whether there is any conceivable way in which we might come to introduce *P* in the course of our empirical investigations of the brain. New concepts have been introduced in the effort to understand the workings of the brain, certainly: could not *P* then occur in conceivable extensions of this manner of introduction? So far, indeed, the theoretical concepts we ascribe to the brain seem as remote from consciousness as any ordinary physical properties are, but perhaps we might reach *P* by diligent application of essentially the same procedures: so it is tempting to think. I want to suggest, to the contrary, that such procedures are inherently closed with respect to *P*. The fundamental reason for this, I think, is the role of *perception* in shaping our understanding of the brain—the way that our perception of the brain constrains the concepts we can apply to it. A point whose significance it would be hard to overstress here is this: the property of consciousness itself (or specific conscious states) is not an observable or perceptible property of the brain. You can stare into a living conscious brain, your own or someone else's, and see there a wide variety of instantiated properties—its shape, colour, texture, etc.—but you will not thereby *see* what the subject is experiencing, the conscious state itself. Conscious states are simply not potential objects of perception: they depend upon the brain but they cannot be observed by directing the senses onto the brain. In other words, consciousness is noumenal with respect to perception of the brain.[13] I take it this is obvious. So we know there *are* properties of the brain that are necessarily closed to perception of the brain; the question now is whether *P* is likewise closed to perception.

My argument will proceed as follows. I shall first argue that *P* is indeed perceptually closed; then I shall complete the argument to full cognitive closure by insisting that no form of *inference* from what is perceived can lead us to *P*. The argument for perceptual closure starts from the thought that nothing we can imagine perceiving in the brain would ever convince us that we have located the intelligible nexus we seek. No matter what recondite property we could see to be instantiated in the brain we would always be baffled about how it could give rise to consciousness. I hereby invite you to try to conceive of a perceptible property of the brain that might allay the feeling of mystery that attends our contemplation of the brain–mind link: I do not think you will be able to do it. It is like trying to conceive of a perceptible property of a rock that would render it perspicuous that the rock was conscious. In fact, I think it is the very impossibility of this that lies at the root of the felt mind–body problem. But why is this? Basically, I think, it is because the senses are geared to representing a spatial world; they essentially present things in space with spatially defined properties. But it is precisely *such* properties that seem inherently incapable of resolving the mind–body problem: we cannot link consciousness to the brain in virtue of spatial properties of the brain. There the brain is, an object of perception, laid out in space, containing spatially distributed processes; but consciousness defies explanation in such terms. Consciousness does not seem made up out of smaller spatial processes; yet perception of the brain seems limited to revealing such processes.[14] The senses are responsive to certain *kinds* of properties—those that are essentially bound up with space—but these properties are of the wrong sort (the wrong *category*) to constitute *P*. Kant was right, the form of outer sensibility is spatial; but if so, then *P* will be noumenal with respect to the senses, since no spatial property will ever deliver a satisfying answer to the mind–body problem. We simply do not understand the idea that conscious states might intelligibly arise from spatial configurations of the kind disclosed by perception of the world.

I take it this claim will not seem terribly controversial. After all, we do not generally expect that every property referred to in our theories should be a potential object of human perception: consider quantum theory and cosmology. Unrestricted perceptual openness is a dogma of empiricism if ever there was one. And there is no compelling reason to suppose that the property needed to explain the mind–brain relation should be in principle perceptible; it might be essentially "theoretical," an object of thought not sensory experience. Looking harder at nature is not the only (or the best) way of discovering its theoretically significant properties. Perceptual closure does not entail cognitive closure, since we have available the procedure of hypothesis formation, in which *un*observables come to be conceptualized.

I readily agree with these sentiments, but I think there are reasons for believing that no coherent method of concept introduction will ever lead us to *P*. This is because a certain principle of *homogeneity* operates in our introduction of theoretical concepts on the basis of observation. Let me first note that consciousness itself could not be introduced simply on the basis of what we observe about the brain and its physical effects. If our data, arrived at by perception of the brain, do not include anything that brings in conscious states, then the theoretical properties we need to explain these data will not include conscious states either. Inference to the best explanation of purely physical data will never take us outside the realm of the physical, forcing us to introduce concepts of consciousness.[15] Everything physical has a purely physical explanation. So the property of consciousness is cognitively closed with respect to the introduction of concepts by means of inference to the best explanation of perceptual data about the brain.

Now the question is whether *P* could ever be arrived at by this kind of inference. Here we must be careful to guard against a form of magical emergentism with respect to concept formation. Suppose we try out a relatively clear theory of how theoretical concepts are formed: we get them by a sort of analogical extension of what we observe. Thus, for example, we arrive at the concept of a molecule by taking our perceptual representations of macroscopic objects and conceiving of smaller scale objects of the same general kind. This method seems to work well enough for unobservable material objects, but it will not help in arriving at *P*, since analogical extensions of the entities we observe in the brain are precisely as hopeless as the original entities were as solutions to the mind–body problem. We would need a method that left the base of observational properties behind in a much more radical way. But it seems to me that even a more unconstrained conception of inference to the best explanation would still not do what is required: it would no more serve to introduce *P* than it serves to introduce the property of consciousness itself. To explain the observed physical data we need only such theoretical properties as bear upon those data, not the property that explains consciousness, which does not occur in the data. Since we do not need consciousness to explain those data, we do not need the property that explains consciousness. We will never get as far away from the perceptual data in our explanations of those data as we need to get in order to connect up explanatorily with consciousness. This is, indeed, why it seems that consciousness is theoretically epiphenomenal in the task of accounting for physical events. No concept needed to explain the workings of the physical world will suffice to explain how the physical world produces consciousness. So if *P* is perceptually noumenal, then it will be noumenal with respect to perception-based explanatory inferences. Accordingly, I do not think that *P* could be arrived at by empirical studies of the brain alone. Nevertheless, the brain *has* this property, as it has the property of consciousness. Only a magical idea of how we come by concepts could lead one to think that we can reach *P* by first perceiving the brain and then asking what is needed to explain what we perceive.[16] (The mind–body problem tempts us to magic in more ways than one.)

It will help elucidate the position I am driving towards if I contrast it with another view of the source of the perplexity we feel about the mind–brain nexus. I have argued that we cannot know which property of the brain accounts for consciousness, and so we find the mind–brain link unintelligible. But, it may be said, there is another account of our sense of irremediable mystery, which does not require positing properties our minds cannot represent. This alternative view claims that, even if we *now* had a grasp of *P*, we would *still* feel that there is something mysterious about the link, because of a special epistemological feature of the situation. Namely this: our acquaintance with the brain and our acquaintance with consciousness are necessarily mediated by distinct cognitive faculties, namely perception and introspection. Thus the faculty through which we apprehend one term of the relation is necessarily distinct from the faculty through which we apprehend the other. In consequence, it is not possible for us to use one of these faculties to apprehend the nature of the psychophysical nexus. No single faculty will enable us ever to apprehend the fact that consciousness depends upon the brain in virtue of property *P*. Neither perception alone nor introspection alone will ever enable us to witness the dependence. And this, my objector insists, is the real reason we find the link baffling: we cannot make sense of it in terms of the deliverances of a single cognitive faculty. So, even if we now had concepts for the properties of the brain that explain consciousness, we would still feel a residual sense of unintelligibility; we would still take there to be something mysterious going on. The necessity to shift from one faculty to the other produces in us an illusion of inexplicability. We might in fact have the explanation right now but be under the illusion that we do not. The right diagnosis, then, is that we should recognize the peculiarity of the epistemological situation and stop trying to make sense of the psychophysical nexus in the way we make sense of other sorts of nexus. It only *seems* to us that we can never discover a property that will render the nexus intelligible.

I think this line of thought deserves to be taken seriously, but I doubt that it correctly diagnoses our predicament. It is true enough that the problematic nexus is essentially apprehended by distinct faculties, so that it will never reveal its secrets to a single faculty; but I doubt that our intuitive sense of intelligibility is so rigidly governed by the "single-faculty condition." Why *should* facts only seem intelligible to us if we can conceive of apprehending them by one (sort of) cognitive faculty? Why not allow that we can recognize intelligible connections between concepts (or properties) even when those concepts (or properties) are necessarily ascribed using different faculties? Is it not suspiciously empiricist to insist that a causal nexus can only be made sense of by us if we can conceive of its being an object of a single faculty of apprehension? Would we think this of a nexus that called for touch and sight to apprehend each term of the relation? Suppose (*per impossible*) that we were offered *P* on a plate, as a gift from God: would we still shake our heads and wonder how that could resolve the mystery, being still the victims of the illusion of mystery generated by the epistemological duality in question? No, I think this suggestion is not enough to account for the miraculous appearance of the link: it is better to suppose that we are permanently blocked from forming a concept of what accounts for that link.

How strong is the thesis I am urging? Let me distinguish *absolute* from *relative* claims of cognitive closure. A problem is absolutely cognitively closed if no possible mind could resolve it; a problem is relatively closed if minds of some sorts can in principle solve it while minds of other sorts cannot. Most problems we may safely suppose, are only relatively closed: armadillo minds cannot solve problems of elementary arithmetic but human minds can. Should we say that the mind–body problem is only relatively closed or is the closure absolute? This depends on what we allow as a possible concept-forming mind, which is not an easy question. If we allow for minds that form their concepts of the brain and consciousness in ways that are quite independent of perception and introspection, then there may be room for the idea that there are possible minds for which the mind–body problem is soluble, and easily so. But if we suppose that *all* concept formation is tied to perception and introspection, however loosely, then *no* mind will be capable of understanding how it relates to its own body—the insolubility will be absolute. I think we can just about make sense of the former kind of mind, by exploiting our own faculty of a priori reasoning. Our mathematical concepts (say) do not seem tied either to perception or to introspection, so there does seem to be a mode of concept formation that operates without the constraints I identified earlier. The suggestion might then be that a mind that formed all of its concepts in this way—including its concepts of the brain and consciousness—would be free of the biases that prevent *us* from coming up with the right theory of how the two connect. Such a mind would have to be able to think of the brain and consciousness in ways that utterly prescind from the perceptual and the introspective—in somewhat the way we now (it seems) think about numbers. This mind would conceive of the psychophysical link in totally a priori terms. Perhaps this is how we should think of God's mind, and God's understanding of the mind–body relation. At any rate, something pretty radical is going to be needed if we are to devise a mind that can escape the kinds of closure that make the problem insoluble for us—if I am right in my diagnosis of our difficulty. *If* the problem is only relatively insoluble, then the type of mind that can solve it is going to be very different from ours and the kinds of mind we can readily make sense of (there may, of course, be cognitive closure here too). It certainly seems to me to be at least an open question whether the problem is absolutely insoluble; I would not be surprised if it were.[17]

My position is both pessimistic and optimistic at the same time. It is pessimistic about the prospects for arriving at a constructive solution to the mind–body problem, but it is optimistic about our hopes of removing the philosophical perplexity. The central point here is that I do not think we need to do the former in order to achieve the latter. This depends on a rather special understanding of what the philosophical problem consists in. What I want to suggest is that the nature of the psychophysical connection has a full and non-mysterious explanation in a certain science, but that this science is inaccessible to us as a matter of principle. Call this explanatory scientific theory *T*: *T* is as natural and prosaic and devoid of miracle as any theory of nature; it describes the link between consciousness and the brain in a way that is no more remarkable (or alarming) than the way we now describe the link between the liver and bile.[18] According to *T*, there is nothing eerie going on in the world when an event in my visual cortex causes me to have an experience of yellow—however much it seems to *us* that there is. In other words, there is no intrinsic conceptual or metaphysical difficulty about how consciousness depends on the brain. It is not that the correct science is compelled to postulate miracles *de re*; it is rather that the correct science lies in the dark part of the world for us. We confuse our own cognitive limitations with objective eeriness. We are like a Humean mind trying to understand the physical world, or a creature without spatial concepts trying to understand the possibility of motion. This removes the philosophical problem because it assures us that the entities *themselves* pose no inherent philosophical difficulty. The case is unlike, for example, the problem of how the abstract world of numbers might be intelligibly related to the world of concrete knowing subjects: here the mystery seems intrinsic to the entities, not a mere artefact of our cognitive limitations or biases in trying to understand the relation.[19] It would not be plausible to suggest that there exists a science, whose theoretical concepts we cannot grasp, which completely resolves any sense of mystery that surrounds the question how the abstract becomes an object of knowledge for us. In this case, then, eliminativism seems a live option. The *philosophical* problem about consciousness and the brain arises from a sense that we are compelled to accept that nature contains miracles—as if the merely metallic lamp of the brain could really spirit into existence the Djin of consciousness. But we do not need to accept this: we can rest secure in the knowledge that some (unknowable) property of the brain makes everything fall into place. What creates the philosophical puzzlement is the assumption that the problem must somehow be scientific but that any science *we* can come up with will represent things as utterly miraculous. And the solution is to recognize that the sense of miracle comes from us and not from the world. There is, in reality, nothing mysterious about how the brain generates consciousness. There is no *metaphysical* problem.[20]

So far that deflationary claim has been justified by a general naturalism and certain considerations about cognitive closure and the illusions it can give rise to. Now I want to marshall some reasons for thinking that consciousness is actually a rather simple natural fact; objectively, consciousness is nothing very special. We should now be comfortable with the idea that our own sense of difficulty is a fallible guide to objective complexity: what is hard for us to grasp may not be very fancy in itself. The grain of our thinking is not a mirror held up to the facts of nature.[21] In particular, it may be that the extent of our understanding of facts about the mind is not commensurate with some objective estimate of their intrinsic complexity: we may be good at understanding the mind in some of its aspects but hopeless with respect to others, in a way that cuts across objective differences in what the aspects involve. Thus we are adept at understanding action in terms of the folk psychology of belief and desire, and we seem not entirely out of our depth when it comes to devising theories of language. But our understanding of how consciousness develops from the organization of matter is nonexistent. But now, think of these various aspects of mind from the point of view of evolutionary biology. Surely language and the propositional attitudes are more complex and advanced evolutionary achievements than the mere possession of consciousness by a physical organism. Thus it seems that we are better at understanding some of the more complex aspects of mind than the simpler ones. Consciousness arises early in evolutionary history and is found right across the animal kingdom. In some respects it seems that the biological engineering required for consciousness is less fancy than that needed for certain kinds of complex motor behaviour. Yet we can come to understand the latter while drawing a total blank with respect to the former. Conscious states seem biologically quite primitive, comparatively speaking. So the theory *T* that explains the occurrence of consciousness in a physical world is very probably less objectively complex (by some standard) than a range of other theories that do not defy our intellects. If only we could know the psychophysical mechanism it might surprise us with its simplicity, its utter naturalness. In the manual that God consulted when he made the earth and all the beasts that dwell thereon the chapter about how to engineer consciousness from matter occurs fairly early on, well before the really difficult later chapters on mammalian reproduction and speech. It is not the *size* of the problem but its *type* that makes the mind–body problem so hard for us. This reflection should make us receptive to the idea that it is something about the tracks of our thought that prevents us from achieving a science that relates consciousness to its physical basis: the enemy lies within the gates.[22]

The position I have reached has implications for a tangle of intuitions it is natural to have regarding the mind–body relation. On the one hand, there are intuitions, pressed from Descartes to Kripke, to the effect that the relation between conscious states and bodily states is fundamentally contingent.[23] It can easily seem to us that there is no necessitation involved in the dependence of the mind on the brain. But, on the other hand, it looks absurd to try to dissociate the two entirely, to let the mind float completely free of the body. Disembodiment is a dubious possibility at best, and some kind of necessary supervenience of the mental on the physical has seemed undeniable to many. It is not my aim here to adjudicate this longstanding dispute; I want simply to offer a diagnosis of what is going on when one finds oneself assailed with this flurry of conflicting intuitions. The reason we feel the tug of contingency, pulling consciousness loose from its physical moorings, may be that we do not and cannot grasp the nature of the property that intelligibly links them. The brain has physical properties we can grasp, and variations in these correlate with changes in consciousness, but we cannot draw the veil that conceals the manner of their connection. Not grasping the nature of the connection, it strikes us as deeply contingent; we cannot make the assertion of a necessary connection intelligible to ourselves. There *may* then be a real necessary connection; it is just that it will always strike us as curiously brute and unperspicuous. We may thus, as upholders of intrinsic contingency, be the dupes of our own cognitive blindness. On the other hand, we are scarcely in a position to assert that there *is* a necessary connection between the properties of the brain we can grasp and states of consciousness, since we are so ignorant (and irremediably so) about the character of the connection. For all we know, the connection may be contingent, as access to *P* would reveal if we could have such access. The link between consciousness and property *P* is not, to be sure, contingent—virtually by definition—but we are not in a position to say exactly how *P* is related to the "ordinary" properties of the brain. It may be necessary or it may be contingent. Thus it is that we tend to vacillate between contingency and necessity; for we lack the conceptual resources to decide the question—or to understand the answer we are inclined to give. The indicated conclusion appears to be that we can never really know whether disembodiment is metaphysically possible, or whether necessary supervenience is the case, or whether spectrum inversion could occur. For these all involve claims about the modal connections between properties of consciousness and the ordinary properties of the body and brain that we can conceptualize; and the real nature of these connections is not accessible to us. Perhaps *P* makes the relation between C-fibre firing and pain necessary or perhaps it does not: we are simply not equipped to know. We are like a Humean mind wondering whether the observed link between the temperature of a gas and its pressure (at a constant volume) is necessary or contingent. To know the answer to that you need to grasp atomic (or molecular) theory, and a Humean mind just is not up to attaining the requisite theoretical understanding. Similarly, we are constitutionally ignorant at precisely the spot where the answer exists.

I predict that many readers of this paper will find its main thesis utterly incredible, even ludicrous. Let me remark that I sympathize with such readers: the thesis is not easily digestible. But I would say this: if the thesis *is* actually true, it will still strike us as hard to believe. For the idea of an explanatory property (or set of properties) that is noumenal for us, yet is essential for the (constructive) solution of a problem we face, offends a kind of natural idealism that tends to dominate our thinking. We find it taxing to conceive of the existence of a real property, under our noses as it were, which we are built not to grasp—a property that is responsible for phenomena that we observe in the most direct way possible. This kind of realism, which brings cognitive closure so close to home, is apt to seem both an affront to our intellects and impossible to get our minds around. We try to think of this unthinkable property and understandably fail in the effort; so we rush to infer that the very supposition of such a property is nonsensical. Realism of the kind I am presupposing thus seems difficult to hold in focus, and any philosophical theory that depends upon it will also seem to rest on something systematically elusive.[24] My response to such misgivings, however, is unconcessive: the limits of our minds are just not the limits of reality. It is deplorably anthropocentric to insist that reality be constrained by what the human mind can conceive. We need to cultivate a vision of reality (a metaphysics) that makes it truly independent of our given cognitive powers, a conception that includes these powers as a proper part. It is just that, in the case of the mind–body problem, the bit of reality that systematically eludes our cognitive grasp is an aspect of our own nature. Indeed, it is an aspect that makes it possible for us to have minds at all and to think about how they are related to our bodies. This particular transcendent tract of reality happens to lie within our own heads. A deep fact about our own nature as a form of embodied consciousness is thus necessarily hidden from us. Yet there is nothing inherently eerie or bizarre about this embodiment. We are much more straightforward than we seem. Our weirdness lies in the eye of the beholder.

The answer to the question that forms my title is therefore "No and Yes."[25]

Notes

1. One of the peculiarities of the mind–body problem is the difficulty of formulating it in a rigorous way. We have a sense of the problem that outruns our capacity to articulate it clearly. Thus we quickly find ourselves resorting to invitations to look inward, instead of specifying precisely *what* it is about consciousness that makes it inexplicable in terms of ordinary physical properties. And this can make it seem that the problem is spurious. A creature without consciousness would not properly appreciate the problem (assuming such a creature could appreciate other problems). I think an adequate treatment of the mind–body problem should explain why it is so hard to state the problem explicitly. My treatment locates our difficulty in our inadequate conceptions of the nature of the brain and consciousness. In fact, if we knew their natures fully we would already have solved the problem. This should become clear later.

2. I would also classify panpsychism as a constructive solution, since it attempts to explain consciousness in terms of properties of the brain that are as natural as consciousness itself. Attributing specks of proto-consciousness to the constituents of matter is not supernatural in the way postulating immaterial substances or divine interventions is; it is merely extravagant. I shall here be assuming that panpsychism, like all other extant constructive solutions, is inadequate as an answer to the mind–body problem—as (of course) are the supernatural "solutions." I am speaking to those who still feel perplexed (almost everyone, I would think, at least in their heart).

3. This kind of view of cognitive capacity is forcefully advocated by Noam Chomsky in *Reflections on Language*, Patheon Books, 1975, and by Jerry Fodor in *The Modularity of Mind*, Cambridge, Mass., MIT Press, 1983. Chomsky distinguishes between "problems," which human minds are in principle equipped to solve, and "mysteries," which systematically elude our understanding; and he envisages a study of our cognitive systems that would chart these powers and limitations. I am here engaged in such a study, citing the mind–body problem as falling on the side of the mysteries.

4. See Thomas Nagel's discussion of realism in *The View From Nowhere*, Oxford, Oxford University Press, 1986, ch. VI. He argues there for the possibility of properties we can never grasp. Combining Nagel's realism with Chomsky–Fodor cognitive closure gives a position looking very much like Locke's in the *Essay Concerning Human Understanding*: the idea that our God-given faculties do not equip us to fathom the deep truth about reality. In fact, Locke held precisely this about the relation between mind and brain: only divine revelation could enable us to understand how 'perceptions' are produced in our minds by material objects.

5. Hume, of course, argued, in effect, that no theory essentially employing a notion of objective causal necessitation could be grasped by our minds—and likewise for the notion of objective persistence. We might compare the frustrations of the Humean mind to the conceptual travails of the pure sound beings discussed in Ch. II of P. F. Strawson's *Individuals*, London, Methuen, 1959; both are types of mind whose constitution puts various concepts beyond them. We can do a lot better than these truncated minds, but we also have our constitutional limitations.

6. See the *Essay*, Book II, ch. IV. Locke compares the project of saying what solidity ultimately is to trying to clear up a blind man's vision by talking to him.

7. Some of the more arcane aspects of cosmology and quantum theory might be thought to lie just within the bounds of human intelligibility. Chomsky suggests that the causation of behaviour might be necessarily mysterious to human investigators: see *Reflections on Language*, p. 156. I myself believe that the mind–body problem exhibits a qualitatively different level of mystery from this case (unless it is taken as an aspect of that problem).

8. Cf. Nagel's discussion of emergence in "Panpsychism," in *Mortal Questions*, Cambridge, Cambridge University Press, 1979. I agree with him that the apparent radical emergence of mind from matter has to be epistemic only, on pain of accepting inexplicable miracles in the world.

9. Despite his reputation for pessimism over the mind–body problem, a careful reading of Nagel reveals an optimistic strain in his thought (by the standards of the present paper): see, in particular, the closing remarks of "What is it Like to be a Bat?," in *Mortal Questions*. Nagel speculates that we might be able to devise an "objective phenomenology" that made conscious states more amenable to physical analysis. Unlike me, he does not regard the problem as inherently beyond us.

10. This is perhaps the most remarkably optimistic view of all—the expectation that reflecting on the ordinary concept of pain (say) will reveal the manner of pain's dependence on the brain. If I am not mistaken, this is in effect the view of common-sense functionalists: they think that *P* consists in causal role, and that this can be inferred analytically from the concepts of conscious states. This would make it truly amazing that we should ever have felt there to be a mind–body problem at all, since the solution is already contained in our mental concepts. What optimism!

11. See Nagel, "What is it Like to be a Bat?" Notice that the fugitive character of such properties with respect to our concepts has nothing to do with their "complexity"; like fugitive colour properties, such experiential properties are "simple." Note too that such properties provide counter-examples to the claim that (somehow) rationality is a faculty that, once possessed, can be extended to encompass all concepts, so that if *any* concept can be possessed then *every* concept can.

12. It might be suggested that we borrow Nagel's idea of "objective phenomenology" in order to get around this problem. Instead of representing experiences under subjective descriptions, we should describe them in entirely objective terms, thus bringing them within our conceptual ken. My problem with this is that, even allowing that there could be such a form of description, it would not permit us to understand how the subjective aspects of experience depend upon the brain—which is really the problem we are trying to solve. In fact, I doubt that the notion of objective phenomenology is any more coherent than the notion of subjective physiology. Both involve trying to bridge the psychophysical gap by a sort of stipulation. The lesson here is that the gap cannot be bridged just by applying concepts drawn from one side to items that belong on the other side; and this is because neither sort of concept could ever do what is needed.

13. We should distinguish two claims about the imperceptibility of consciousness: (i) consciousness is not perceivable by directing the senses onto the brain; (ii) consciousness is not perceivable by directing the senses anywhere, even towards the behaviour that 'expresses' conscious states. I believe both theses, but my present point requires only (i). I am assuming, of course, that perception cannot be unrestrictedly theory-laden; or that if it can, the infusions of theory cannot have been originally derived simply be looking at things or tasting them or touching them or . . .

14. Nagel discusses the difficulty of thinking of conscious processes in the spatial terms that apply to the brain in *The View From Nowhere*, pp. 50–1, but he does not draw my despairing conclusion. The case is exactly *unlike* (say) the dependence of liquidity on the properties of molecules, since here we do think of both terms of the relation as spatial in character; so we can simply employ the idea of spatial composition.

15. Cf. Nagel: "it will never be legitimate to infer, as a theoretical explanation of physical phenomena alone, a property that includes or implies the consciousness of its subject," "Panpsychism," p. 183.

16. It is surely a striking fact that the microprocesses that have been discovered in the brain by the usual methods seem no nearer to consciousness than the gross properties of the brain open to casual inspection. Neither do more abstract "holistic" features of brain function seem to be on the right lines to tell us the nature of consciousness. The deeper science probes into the brain the more remote it seems to get from consciousness. Greater knowledge of the brain thus destroys our illusions about the kinds of properties that might be discovered by travelling along this path. Advanced neurophysiological theory seems only to deepen the miracle.

17. The kind of limitation I have identified is therefore not the kind that could be remedied simply by a large increase in general intelligence. No matter how large the frontal lobes of our biological descendants may become, they will still be stumped by the mind–body problem, so long as they form their (empirical) concepts on the basis of perception and introspection.

18. Or again, no more miraculous than the theory of evolution. Creationism is an understandable response to the theoretical problem posed by the existence of complex organisms; fortunately, we now have a theory that renders this response unnecessary, and so undermines the theism required by the creationist thesis. In the case of consciousness, the appearance of miracle might also tempt us in a "creationist" direction, with God required to perform the alchemy necessary to transform matter into experience. Thus the mind–body problem might similarly be used to prove the existence of God (no miracle without a miracle-maker). We cannot, I think, refute this argument in the way we can the original creationist argument, namely by actually producing a non-miraculous explanatory theory, but we can refute it by arguing that such a naturalistic theory must *exist.* (It is a condition of adequacy upon any account of the mind–body relation that it avoid assuming theism.)

19. See Paul Benacerraf, "Mathematical Truth," *Journal of Philosophy*, 1973, for a statement of this problem about abstract entities. Another problem that seems to me to differ from the mind–body problem is the problem of free will. I do not believe that there is some unknowable property *Q* which reconciles free will with determinism (or indeterminism); rather, the concept of free will contains internal incoherencies—as the concept of consciousness does not. This is why it is much more reasonable to be an eliminativist about free will than about consciousness.

20. A test of whether a proposed solution to the mind–body problem is adequate is whether it relieves the pressure towards eliminativism. If the data can only be explained by postulating a miracle (i.e. not explained), then we must repudiate the data—this is the principle behind the impulse to deny that conscious states exist. My proposal passes this test because it allows us to resist the postulation of miracles; it interprets the eeriness as merely epistemic, though deeply so. Constructive solutions are not the only way to relieve the pressure.

21. Chomsky suggests that the very faculties of mind that make us good at some cognitive tasks may make us poor at others; see *Reflections on Language*, pp. 155–6. It seems to me possible that what makes us good at the science of the purely physical world is what skews us away from developing a science of consciousness. Our faculties bias us towards understanding matter in motion, but it is precisely this kind of understanding that is inapplicable to the mind–body problem. Perhaps, then, the price of being good at understanding matter is that we cannot understand mind. Certainly our notorious tendency to think of everything in spatial terms does not help us in understanding the mind.

22. I get this phrase from Fodor, *The Modularity of Mind*, p. 121. The intended contrast is with kinds of cognitive closure that stem from exogenous factors—as, say, in astronomy. Our problem

with *P* is not that it is too distant or too small or too large or too complex; rather, the very structure of our concept-forming apparatus points us away from *P*.

23. Saul Kripke, *Naming and Necessity*, Oxford, Blackwell, 1980. Of course, Descartes explicitly argued from (what he took to be) the essential natures of the body and mind to the contingency of their connection. If we abandon the assumption that we know these natures, then agnosticism about the modality of the connection seems the indicated conclusion.

24. This is the kind of realism defended by Nagel in ch. VI of *The View From Nowhere*: to be is not to be conceivable by us. I would say that the mind–body problem provides a demonstration that there *are* such concept-transcending properties—not merely that there *could* be. I would also say that realism of this kind should be accepted precisely because it helps solve the mind–body problem; it is a metaphysical thesis that pulls its weight in coping with a problem that looks hopeless otherwise. There is thus nothing "epiphenomenal" about such radical realism: the existence of a reality we cannot know can yet have intellectual significance for us.

25. Discussions with the following people have helped me work out the ideas of this paper: Anita Avramides, Jerry Katz, Ernie Lepore, Michael Levin, Thomas Nagel, Galen Strawson, Peter Unger. My large debt to Nagel's work should be obvious throughout the paper: I would not have tried to face the mind–body problem down had he not first faced up to it.

30 Physicalism and the Cognitive Role of Acquaintance

Laurence Nemirow

I Some Theories of the Cognitive Role of Acquaintance

In a classical essay on the mind–body problem, Herbert Feigl briefly raises a perplexing problem for physicalism in the philosophy of mind, the view that a physical theory of nature can fully describe mental activity.[1] The problem is to fit the epistemology of experience into a physicalist frame of reference, and to capture, within the framework of physical science, the cognitive role of direct acquaintance with experience.

The physicalist framework, according to Feigl, is essentially *objective*, in that creatures with diverse sensory systems can formulate and test a physical hypothesis. In theory, no particular sensory organs are crucial to the capacity to advance physical science. Even a congenitally deaf-blind person "could in principle construct and confirm a complete system of the natural sciences ..."[2] Feigl pictures the method of science as the "triangulation of entities in logical space" grounded on types of sensory input none of which is, by itself, indispensable to the formulation and testing of the hypothesis.[3]

By contrast, the most remarkable information about a sensory experience appears to be *subjective*—accessible only to those who can employ a sensory organ of the same type as the one that produces the experience. As Feigl observes, the "philosophically intriguing problems" regarding direct acquaintance with experience "are best expressed by asking, e.g., 'What is it that the blind man cannot know concerning color qualities?'"[4] The problem for physicalism is to account for the salient knowledge of visual experience that a scientist without eyes could not infer.

Feigl attacks the problem by denying the premise that there is such knowledge. According to him, a blind person must lack only acquaintance with the experience of sight and knowledge by acquaintance of it. Although acquaintance is not knowledge (because "mere having or living through is not knowledge in any sense"), knowledge by acquaintance "is propositional, and does make truth claims."[5] Someone might know by acquaintance that he is seeing a bright color, for example. But that knowledge, Feigl observes, could be inferred by a blind psychologist, incapable of experiencing color, who examines the behavior and anatomy of the subject of experience.

Feigl underestimates the difficulty. Even if we grant that a congenitally blind psychologist might triangulate the experience of sight, thus confirming that it occurs and discerning all of its physiological aspects, he would not thereby learn what the experience of seeing is *like*. Knowledge of what seeing is like cannot be inferred from nonvisual sensory input.

Nor could Feigl plausibly assert that "knowledge of what an experience is like" amounts to mere acquaintance and thus fails to stand for genuine knowledge. Such an assertion would fail to account for our use of the vocabulary of knowledge in talking about what an experience is like. We speak of "knowing" what an experience is like, as well as "realizing," "discovering," "learning," "remembering" and "forgetting" what an experience is like, and in so doing we describe a common yet elusive kind of knowledge. Plainly, there is knowledge of what it's like to see that can be learned, remembered and forgotten, but it eludes those who are uninitiated to the experience of sight.

Knowledge of what an experience is like signifies genuine knowledge that does not yield to the method of triangulation. Some opponents of physicalism rely on this fact to show that physical science can never completely explain experience.

In what I shall call the "subjective qualities hypothesis," Thomas Nagel analyzes knowing what an experience is like as an act of appreciating its *subjective qualities*—qualities, that is, the attributions of which express subjective information, as defined above.[6] According to him, information about subjective qualities may be understood only from the "point of view of the experiencer." For Nagel, this means that a person must imagine an experience in order to understand its subjective quality.[7] Such understanding, he contends, evades creatures whose sensory apparatus is so unlike that of the experiencer that they cannot imagine from his point of view. Nagel thus concludes that physicalism is false, for he agrees with Feigl that physical science presupposes no particular sensory capacities.[8]

Frank Jackson engages a less burdened account of the argument against physicalism, which is referred to below as the "knowledge argument."[9] Declining to demarcate the class of physical properties (hence dispensing with the notion of objectivity), and making no attempt to explain what is peculiarly nonphysical about the mental (thus avoiding the concept of subjectivity), he merely observes that no amount of physical theorizing will convey to the uninitiated what it's like to see in color. Hypothetical neurophysiologists who could make observations only in black and white would learn less about the world than if they could learn what seeing in color is like. Yet no physical understanding would elude them by reason of their optical disability. So it must follow that physical science cannot describe the way things are mentally.

Nagel and Jackson are right to disagree with Feigl, but their own accounts of the cognitive role of acquaintance are nevertheless flawed. Contrary to Feigl, what the blind cannot know about seeing escapes scientific triangulation. But Nagel and Jackson too quickly conclude that what the blind cannot know is physically indescribable goings-on. That conclusion, I shall argue, is based on three familiar philosophical errors. The first mistake is to confound distinct types of knowledge by treating an ability as propositional knowledge. A second mistake is to confuse grammar and logic by assuming that a grammatical singular term must function as a referring term. The third mistake—and, arguably, the philosophically deep mistake—is to mischaracterize imagining, by equating the act of imagining the experience of a quality with the act of intellectually apprehending the quality itself.

II The Ability Equation

The knowledge argument rests on a shaky inference. From the premise that knowing what it's like escapes physical theorizing, the inference is made that there is information about what it's like that escapes physical science. In short, it is assumed that knowledge of what it's like must be knowledge of the way things are. But that assumption ignores the fact that the vocabulary of knowledge also applies to abilities.[10]

As Nagel's own theory provides, however, knowing what it's like essentially correlates with knowing how to imagine. Ask Harry if he knows what seeing chartreuse is like. If he takes you seriously, he may make an effort to imagine the sight of chartreuse. If he believes that he can imagine seeing chartreuse, he will affirm that he knows what seeing chartreuse is like; otherwise, he will deny that he knows it. It would be nonsense for Harry to insist that he can easily visualize chartreuse, but does not know what seeing it is like, or to maintain that he knows just what it's like, but cannot visualize it. (Throughout this paper, I use the expressions "visualizing a color" and "imagining the sight of a color" interchangeably. Visualizing is not identical to imagining, but visualizing is the special type of imagining that one must be able to perform in order to know what seeing a color is like.)

The correlation stated above suggests an equation: Knowing what it's like may be identified with knowing how to imagine.

The more seriously we take this ability equation, the easier it becomes to resist the knowledge argument. The latter assumes that science cannot convey what it's like to see red. The premise is uncontentious, for science does not seek to instill imaginative abilities. But the knowledge argument concludes that physical science cannot describe certain information about seeing red. The inference is invalid because it presumes that knowing what it's like is propositional knowledge rather than an ability.

The ability equation is confirmed by its explanatory power. It accounts for several facts that, considered together, threaten to undermine physicalism. First, the equation explains why it is appropriate to use the vocabulary of knowledge in discussing what an experience is like. It may be appropriate to speak of "discovering," "knowing," "remembering," "forgetting" what an experience is like because such expressions are used to speak about abilities.

Moreover, the ability equation obviates the need to attribute subjectivity to experience on the ground that knowing what it's like belongs only to those who are able to imagine having the experience (only to those who, as Nagel puts it, can "adopt the experiencer's point of view"). The ability equation avoids having to explain the correlation by transforming it into an equation, and thus circumvents the subjective qualities hypothesis.

The ability equation further explains the linguistic inexpressibility of knowing what it's like. It is a perennial philosophical puzzle that the congenitally blind cannot be told what seeing red is like. Opponents of physicalism may explain the puzzle by referring to inexpressible qualities of experience. But a more elegant explanation is that knowing what it's like is a linguistically inexpressible ability, like the ability to wiggle your ears or the ability to ride a bicycle.

But more must be said. After all, many kinds of knowing how can be expressed verbally. A complete resolution of the puzzle, then, will require a description of the conditions of inexpressibility, together with a demonstration that knowing what it's like satisfies the conditions.

How are abilities communicated? As R. M. Hare tells us, "knowing how to do something is normally communicated, *where it can be communicated at all*, by means of imperative sentences, as can be seen by looking at a cookery book."[11] Putting it schematically, we tell someone how to do A by telling him to do B, where the expression "B" is within the student's repertoire. A description of an action may be said to fall within a person's repertoire provided (i) the person has the ability to perform the action as described, and (ii) the person understands the description: that is, he understands that he can act so as to satisfy it.

Specifically, the ability to imagine a color (that is, knowing what the color is like) may be communicated to someone who has within his repertoire a description of an action by which visualizing can be accomplished. Normally, the ability to visualize a color can be exercised only by the performance of one of three mental actions:

1. Directly visualizing the color itself.
2. Remembering a visual experience of the color.
3. Visualizing or remembering similar colors and interpolating. (This third way of visualizing is, of course, Hume's way.)

It is only contingently true that this list is exhaustive. Someone with an abnormal imaginative capacity might provide a counterexample: Perhaps he could visualize green by banging his head against a wall, or by remembering a humiliating experience. But for most of us, the only activities that amount to visualizing a given color are the activities on the list. Consequently, we may tell those who are able to visualize or remember similar colors that they can imagine by visualizing or remembering and interpolating; and we may instruct others to refresh their recollection by remembering previous experiences of the color. As for those who are unable to follow any of these instructions, imagining is expressible only as such. These uninitiated, therefore, cannot be told what it's like to see green.

This account generalizes to all cases of knowing what its's like. It is generally, albeit contingently, true that imagining an experience may be accomplished only by (1) imagining the experience itself, (2) remembering previous experiences, or (3) imagining or remembering similar experiences and interpolating. So the ability to imagine an experience is describable only *as* imagining for those who cannot do (2) or (3). Those people might be able to imagine, and imagining might be expressible to them as such. But they cannot be told how if they do not already know. Accordingly, the uninitiated cannot be told what it's like.

In sum, the advantages of the ability equation are these: Forgoing nonphysical aspects of experience,[12] it renders the knowledge argument invalid. It also explains the pertinence of the vocabulary of knowledge, the essential connection between knowing what it's like and imaginative capacities, and the inexpressibility of knowing what it's like.

III The Ability Analysis

The ability equation prompts an ability analysis. The expression "x knows how to visualize red" either should replace or can be used to paraphrase "x knows what the experience of seeing red is like." This analysis demystifies the subexpression "what the experience of seeing red is like." On a naive reading, the subexpression is a name for a quality of experience. The latter must be subjective (in Nagel's terms) because only those who are able to visualize red can understand what seeing red is like. Under the analysis, however, the subexpression is a "pseudo-singular term"—an expression that has the grammatical form of a singular term, but, on analysis, does not even purport to refer. Like some other pseudo-singular terms (such as the term "sake" in the sentence, "she did it for her country's sake") the term "what it's like" is syncategoramatic; in other words, it is not separately analyzed.

Although the ability analysis palpably parses the meaning of the phrase "knowing what it's like," those who generally doubt the meaningfulness of synonymy may view the analysis as a possible linguistic reform that would preserve the explanatory power of the phrase while eliminating the use of a misleading singular term. In any event, the analysis should forestall the temptation to treat the expression "what it's like" as a referring expression in virtue of its grammatical form.[13]

IV The Cognitive Role of Imagining: Some Metaphysical Apprehensions

A polemically successful answer to the subjective qualities hypothesis and the knowledge argument must explain the intuitive appeal of the contention that what it's like is irreducibly nonphysical information about experience. The following points together may help accomplish that task:

i. Knowing what an experience is like is the same as knowing how to imagine having the experience.
ii. It is intuitively appealing, albeit incorrect, to analyze the act of imagining an experience of an instance of a certain universal as the intellectual apprehension of the universal itself.

Sentence (i), of course, repeats the ability equation, elaborated in the earlier parts of this paper. Sentence (ii) expresses a familiar point that underlies several classical discussions of universals.[14]

Sentence (ii) incorporates the thesis of Berkeley and Hume that the imagination represents particulars rather than apprehends universals. To visualize red, for example, is to apprehend neither the quality of being red nor the quality of seeing red; it is only to represent particular perceptions of a particular shade of red. Similarly, to imagine pain is not intellectually to apprehend the quality of being in pain; it is to represent a particular painful experience. "For myself, I find indeed I have a faculty of imagining, or representing to myself, the idea of those *particular* things I have perceived ..."[15]

Berkeley and Hume dispelled the philosophical clouds surrounding imaginative representation.[16] Quite obviously, however, an intuitive fog persists. Imagining pain just seems to reveal its painful nature.

The persistent illusion that imagination grants direct access to universals may be explained by what gives imagining its functional utility. We can begin to understand imagination functionally by considering its role in our reasoning, both propositional and practical. Berkeley illuminated that role when he wrote: "[A]n idea which, considered in itself, is particular, becomes general by being made to represent or stand for all other particular ideas of the same sort."[17]

Successfully visualizing a color, for example, engenders the ability to compare the color to other colors. So visualizing a color permits us to draw conclusions (or reason propositionally) about other colors as if we were seeing the imagined color. (I might conclude that the color I am imagining is a deeper shade of purple than the color I am witnessing.) Imagining seeing a color thus functionally represents seeing the color in our propositional reasoning about colors.

So too, successfully imagining a pain of a certain intensity enables us to consider what we would accept as compensation for agreeing to undergo pain of the same degree of intensity. By imagining pain we are able to draw conclusions (or reason practically) about whether to avoid impending pain as if we were experiencing ongoing pain. (I might conclude that the pain that I imagine the dentist would inflict upon me is not worth the intended benefits of a trip to the dentist.) Imagining pain thus functionally represents actual pain in our reasoning about future pain. Part of the functional utility of imagining, then, is that it engenders abilities to reason about experiences, both propositionally and practically, as if we were having an experience of the sort imagined.

We can explain the role of imagining in reasoning by invoking a notion of triangulation, although one that differs from Feigl's concept of triangulation. A key difference is the direction of the inferences in each case. For Feigl, triangulation in physical science involves inferences from sensory experiences, no one of which is critical, to an hypothesis of physical events. Such patterns of inference account for the capacity of scientific inquiry to reach objective generalizations. In reasoning from what an experience is like, a person begins by imagining particular experiences, and draws specific inferences about actual or future sensory experiences, none of which is itself critical to the function of the imagination. Such lines of inference in turn begin to account for the general utilities of imagining that cause imagining to appear to grant direct access to the essential qualities of experience.

Sentences (i) and (ii) together produce the conclusion that knowing what it's like to be in pain is an ability that is appealingly analyzed as the ability to apprehend a universal. If we were to treat what is appealing as fact, Nagel's theory of subjective qualities would follow. We would attribute a special understanding of what pain *is* only to those who know what it's *like*.

V Objections and Replies

One objection to the ability equation is that knowing how to imagine is too sophisticated an ability to attribute to everyone (or thing) who may know what it's like. For such an ability is, for all we know, well beyond the capabilities of creatures to whom we may on occasion attribute knowledge of what an experience is like—creatures such as cats and infants. But anything that is true of mature persons by reason of knowing what an experience is like should also be true of cats and infants who know what it's like—a point that apparently refutes the ability equation.

Rather than providing counterexamples to the ability equation, however, these hard cases suggest only that there are auxiliary concepts of "what it's like" that are triggered by nonparadigmatic applications of the phrase, and which would often be inapposite to use when speaking of mature persons.

If we say of a cat that it knows what the smell of abalone is like, for example, we might mean merely that, exposed to the smell, it will come running to its dish. The proposition apparently does not imply that the cat knows how to imagine the smell.

To apply the mature concept of knowing what the smell of abalone is like to a person, however, is not to assume any such behavioral correlation. Such an attribution directly describes what a person knows how to do in the privacy of his own mind, not how he would behave when exposed to the smell.

Similarly, we might say of an infant that he knows what a certain taste is like, without intending to imply that the infant knows how to imagine the taste. We may mean only that he can recognize the taste. On the other hand, when we use the mature concept of knowing what a taste is like, we mean more than that. We additionally attribute the ability to imagine. Someone might appropriately claim, "I can recognize the taste of chestnuts, I feel sure, but I have forgotten just what the taste is like." Similarly, no one is surprised to forget how to imagine a certain melody (what it's like to hear the melody), while remembering how to recognize the melody; or to forget what someone's face is like (what it's like to see his face), without forgetting how to recognize the face.

Someone might question the recognition examples by asking what the ability to imagine amounts to over and above the ability to recognize. As explained in the previous section of this paper, the ability to imagine is, at least in part, an ability to reason propositionally and practically as if one were having an experience of the sort imagined. The recognition examples suggest also that the ability to imagine produces certain other practical abilities that do not ordinarily fall under the rubric of practical reasoning. For example, if Beth can recognize but not imagine a melody, then she cannot imagine variations on it either. But if Beth can imagine the melody, not only can she imagine variations on it (assuming she has some modest musical talent), she can also ascertain whether one note of the melody is higher or lower than the next. Further, she can tap its beat or hum the tune. And she might even try to imagine hearing the notes in reverse order. But Beth could perform none of these tasks if she could only recognize without imagining. Similarly, if Frank can vividly imagine what the burglar looks like, then he can describe his looks so that a police artist might render a likeness. But if he could only recognize without imagining, he would be unable to describe in any detail how the burglar looks.

In any event, as the examples of sophisticated attributions of knowing what it's like show, such attributions do ascribe imaginative abilities, while the auxiliary concepts of knowing what it's like, such as conditioned response or recognitional ability do not.[18]

A second objection to the ability equation relies on the concept of *successful* imagining. Successful imagining, so the objection goes, presupposes subjective qualities (or qualities the attribution of which may be understood only by those with the right sensory capacities) for this reason: the ability successfully to imagine is the ability to entertain a truly representative state; but representation is a relationship between imagined and imagining states based on the similarity of their subjective qualities.

The crucial point in this objection is unmotivated. Assume for argument's sake, both that imagining constitutes mental representation, and that the relationship of representation holds between imagined and imagining states just in case they are similar with respect to certain qualities. What argument demonstrates that those qualities are subjective? The case had better not be that knowledge of what those qualities are like depends on acquaintance. That would merely repeat the knowledge argument, which the ability equation renders invalid. To be sure, an understanding of imaginative representation might require acquaintance with it; but such understanding itself consists of imaginative abilities rather than knowledge that may be summarized propositionally.

VI Final Remarks

The principal importance of acquaintance in cognition is the production of sophisticated imaginative abilities that give rise to an elaborate network of other abilities, including abilities to reason, both propositionally and practically, and to behave as if the person doing the imagining were having an experience of the sort imagined. These imaginative abilities are of such importance cognitively that they may properly be characterized as constituting a deep understanding of experience. Thus it does justice to the cognitive significance of acquaintance to equate knowledge of what an experience is like with the ability to imagine.

Acknowledgments

I am deeply grateful to David Lewis for his support, and to Joanne Kadish for discussion and for detailed comments on earlier drafts.

Notes

1. Feigl, *The "Mental" and the "Physical,"* Minneapolis: University of Minnesota, 1967, especially pp. 66–9.

2. Ibid., p. 66.

3. Ibid., pp. 66–8.

4. Ibid., p. 68.

5. Ibid.

6. See "What is it like to be a bat?" *Philosophical Review* 84 (1974), pp. 435–50; reprinted in Nagel, *Mortal Questions*, Cambridge: Cambridge University Press, 1979, pp. 165–81. (All page references are to *Mortal Questions*.)

7. Nagel equates the act of taking up the experiencer's point of view with the act of imagining having the experience many times throughout "What is it like to be a bat?" See, for example, p. 178.

8. Ibid., p. 172.

9. Frank Jackson, "Epiphenomenal qualia," *Philosophical Quarterly* 32 (1982), pp. 127–36. For a less sympathetic presentation of the argument against physicalism based on what the blind cannot know, see section IV of Paul E. Meehl, "The compleat autocerebroscopist," in Paul Feyerabend and Grover Maxwell (eds.), *Mind, Matter and Method*, Minneapolis: U. of Minn. Press, 1966.

10. See Gilbert Ryle, *The Concept of Mind*, New York: Barnes & Noble, 1949, pp. 27–32.

11. R. M. Hare, *Practical Inferences*, Berkeley: University of California Press, 1972, p. 3. (Emphasis added.)

12. It should be considered an advantage of an explanatory hypothesis if it facilitates physicalist reduction. Such a contribution is praiseworthy from the point of view of advancing systematization, which is an important criterion of theory selection. See Oppenheim and Kemeny, "On reduction," *Philosophical Studies* 7 (1956), pp. 9–16.

13. Frank Jackson and David Lewis have observed that the ability analysis may be read either as countenancing, or as not countenancing, an inference from "Sam knows how to imagine seeing chartreuse" to "Sam knows that he knows how to imagine seeing chartreuse." The analysandum shares the same ambiguity, which is excellent confirmation of the analysis.

14. Berkeley, *A Treatise Concerning the Principles of Human Knowledge,* especially the Introduction; and Hume, *A Treatise of Human Nature,* part 1, section VII.

15. *A Treatise Concerning the Principles of Human Knowledge,* paragraph 10 of the Introduction. (Emphasis added.)

16. I find the Berkeley–Hume argument, so construed, to be compelling, but I do not believe that there is a knockdown refutation of the view that the imagination apprehends universals. My own prejudice is based on a preference for explanatory simplicity. See note 12.

17. *A Treatise Concerning the Principles of Human Knowledge,* paragraph 12 of the Introduction.

18. A phrase of the form "knowing what it's like to be a ———" expresses the sophisticated concept of knowing what it's like because it entails complex imaginative capabilities rather than any characteristic recognitional or conditioned responses. Assuming that cats do not know how to imagine (which is consistent with, but not necessarily entailed by, auxiliary attributions to cats of knowing what it's like), it would follow that a cat does not know what it's like to be a cat. Or, more to the point, there is no knowledge of what it's like to be a cat.

II Mental Causation

Introduction

Whereas part I of this book was concerned with what mental states *are*, this section considers the question of how mental states can *have causal powers*. In the seventeenth century most philosophers were dualists, but this agreement did not by itself answer the question of how mind influences the body and vice versa. Likewise, most contemporary philosophers of mind are materialists, yet the problem of what role, if any, mental states play in causing our behavior remains open. So while the mind–body problem is concerned with the *nature* of mental states, the question of mental causation turns on the *causal powers* of mental states (whatever their nature). One's position on the first question certainly constrains the possible answers one can give to the second, but it falls far short of determining a specific answer.

René Descartes (1596–1650) argues for interactionism, insisting that the nonphysical mind interacts causally with the body. On his view the mind can affect most parts of the body and receive sensations from these parts, but it does so indirectly, by way of direct interaction with a small gland in the center of the brain—what we now know as the *pineal gland*.

Both Malebranche and Leibniz retain Descartes's *dualism*, but reject his straightforward *interactionism*. Nicolas Malebranche (1638–1715) argues for occasionalism: mind and body are incapable of directly influencing one another, but God intervenes to bring about the effect, giving the appearance that one has directly affected the other. For example, if I will my arm to move, this willing is itself powerless; but on each such occasion God raises my arm for me.

Gottfried Wilhelm Leibniz (1646–1716), while agreeing with Malebranche that mind and body cannot causally interact directly, suggests that the system of occasional causes is not a plausible strategy for an intelligent God. Instead, Leibniz argues that God instituted a "preestablished harmony" at the beginning of time, such that each object would react in the appropriate way at the appropriate time. While we might, for example, believe that one billiard ball caused another to move, in fact God "programmed" the second ball to move at exactly the same moment the first ball contacted it. Likewise, while I may believe that my mind caused my arm to move, Leibniz holds that in fact God designed my arm so that it would move spontaneously exactly when I will it to move—once again creating the illusion of direct causation.

Since the position Immanuel Kant (1724–1804) takes on mental causation forms part of his general system of philosophy, a bit of background is called for in explaining it. Kant argues that space and time are not objects in themselves, but subjective conditions of our "sensible intuition"—that is, part of the very structure of our sense perception. Since ordinary spatiotemporal objects are the objects of our knowledge, it follows that we know things only through these conditions. Hence Kant calls objects as known by us "appearances," or "phenomena." At the same time he holds that appearances must be appearances *of* something, so he postulates a "thing in itself" or "noumenon" behind these appearances; but since the thing in itself falls outside the conditions of knowledge (space and time), Kant concludes that we can know nothing about it. The fact that problems in classical metaphysics never find solutions is, according to Kant, a predictable consequence of the mind's attempt to go beyond the appearances and have knowledge of things in themselves. Arguments concerning the existence of God or the immortality of the soul, for example, are forever inconclusive because they ignore the fact that we can only know phenomena, and try instead to talk about noumena. In the passage included here, Kant demonstrates the dead-end nature of such arguments by showing how both sides of a metaphysical debate look equally reasonable: he sets up the argument that only physical causation exists, against the opposing view that free will constitutes a second kind of causation. We can never resolve this debate, since it concerns things in themselves; but Kant argues that in any case, the two views are compatible. Within the realm of space and time—that is, on the level of *appearances*—my action is entirely caused by past conditioning, brain states, and so forth. But at the same time, rational behavior *may* still reflect free will operating on the level of *things in themselves*.

Most recent philosophers, while adopting Kant's deterministic view of the universe, steer clear of his two-world metaphysics. Thomas Huxley (1825–1895) argues for epiphenomenalism: the view that mental states have *no* causal powers, but that they do nonetheless exist. Huxley is led to the conclusion that consciousness is a mere *epiphenomenon* (a causally inert accompanying factor) of brain states: just as my shadow accompanies my movements without being able to affect them, so my conscious states accompany my brain states but are powerless to influence them causally in any way.

The positions of Kant and (perhaps) Huxley have faint echoes in the writings of Donald Davidson (1917–2003). According to Davidson, causation requires strict (exceptionless) laws. But whereas physics can offer such strict laws, a theory of psychology, using mentalistic terms, cannot; so while we can describe an event in either physical or mental terms, the causal powers of the event hold by virtue of its physical properties alone. Nor, Davidson claims, are there any strict "psychophysical" laws linking the mental to the physical. Nonetheless, he insists that our ordinary claims that mental and physical events interact causally are correct. Because such causation can hold only for physically describable events, Davidson concludes that these facts about mental causation provide a kind of "proof" that every mental event must also be a physical event. Since his view holds that mental events do not, as mental, fall under strict laws (therefore being "anomalous," or lawless), and also that all mental events are physical events (hence amounting to a nonreductive form of materialist monism), he calls his position "anomalous monism."

Many writers have claimed that Davidson's view ultimately amounts to a new form of epiphenomenalism. Ernest LePore and Barry Loewer argue, however, that the mental aspects of events can be causally relevant within anomalous monism. They agree that if "being causally relevant" amounts to *appearing in strict laws*—what they call "relevance$_1$"—then mental features of events could not be causally relevant on Davidson's view, since he denies that they appear in strict laws. But if instead we use a "counterfactual" standard of causal relevance—what they call "relevance$_2$"—then anomalous monism does leave room for mental features to be causally relevant. By this second standard of causal relevance, a feature F of the cause is relevant to the effect's having feature G, if: F and G are distinct features; the cause does in fact have feature F, and the effect has feature G; and if the cause *hadn't* had F, then the effect *wouldn't have* had G. (For example: one event involves my wanting water, followed by a second involving my reaching out for a cup; and if the first event *hadn't* involved my wanting water, then the second *wouldn't have* been a case of my reaching out for a cup.) Arguing that critics of Davidson have used either the "strict law" standard of causal relevance ("relevance$_1$") or a counterfactual standard that wrongly discounts mental properties, Lepore and Loewer conclude that anomalous monism does leave room for the causal relevance of the mental after all, and so escapes the charge of epiphenomenalism.

Jerry Fodor is critical of LePore and Loewer's account of mental causation, arguing that causation-by-way-of-laws better fits what we naturally take causes to be. Yet while he agrees with Davidson that to be causally relevant, an event must fall under a causal law, Fodor argues that the laws in question need not be the strict, exceptionless sort required by Davidson; in particular, the more limited laws of sciences other than physics are sufficient for causation. These higher-level "special sciences" differ from physics in requiring certain lower-level conditions for their instantiation (whereas physics, being on the lowest level, requires no such conditions). Thus special science laws hold only *ceteris paribus* ("all else being equal"); but, Fodor insists, this does *not* block them from being genuine causal laws. And while he notes that removing the "strict law" requirement for causation undermines Davidson's "proof" of materialist monism, Fodor concludes that getting the facts right about mental causation is more important than trying to prove that everything is physical.

Continuing his critique of nonreductive materialism (from chapter 18), Jaegwon Kim argues that the problem of mental causation provides an additional reason why views such as functionalism, and Davidson's "anomalous monism," lead to either reductive or eliminative materialism. Although Kim again makes a case for "domain-specific" reductions compatible with multiple instantiability, he goes on to suggest that the mental states postulated by nonreductive materialism will ultimately prove devoid of any "causal powers." At the center of his argument is a *Causal Exclusion Principle,* which rules out more than one "full or sufficient" and "independent" cause of an event. Since nonreductive materialists are materialists, they will agree that mental states (taken as functional states) are realized in some physical "hardware"; and Kim holds that they should also agree with the *Causal Closure of the Physical,* whereby a causal explanation of any event can be given in purely physical terms. But if the physical hardware itself provides a "full or sufficient" cause for every bit of behavior, then the Causal Exclusion principle blocks the (functional) mental states from *also* being causally relevant. Kim adds that to believe in the reality of such functional states amounts to believing that they play a *causal role* somewhere in the world. So from the previous conclusion that functional states are without causal powers, we should conclude that mental states, as the functionalist conceives of them, *do not exist*—hence supporting a form of eliminative materialism.

Frank Jackson and Philip Pettit argue that although mental causation might seem a problem for functionalist accounts of mind, a more subtle understanding of the different varieties of causal connection can resolve this. In the case of human behavior specifically, they hold, each bit of behavior can be "completely explained" in terms of the physical events. But (as with Kim's Causal Exclusion Principle) once these physical features have completely explained the effect, all other features—including all functional, mental properties of the person, such as "wanting a cup of coffee"—are revealed as "causally irrelevant." However, Jackson and Pettit argue that this can be reconciled with the genuinely explanatory nature of functional states and properties: while only the fundamental properties of physics (something like the subatomic features) are *causally efficacious*, other properties can still be *causally relevant* by providing unifying explanations that apply to a wide number of (physically different) cases. Mental explanations of behavior are causally relevant in this way, because functional features apply not simply to the "hardware" states that the individual *actually has*, but (thanks to multiple instantiability) also to many different physical states the person *might have had* instead. The authors argue that, since our everyday causal explanations are really referring to causally relevant features, functionalist mental states can be appealed to unproblematically in ordinary causal explanations.

Philosopher of science Elliot Sober argues that if we examine causation within a probabilistic framework, we will find that worries about functionalist epiphenomenalism are ungrounded. He agrees with Kim that, if nonreducing mental states depend systematically on the physical—in technical terminology: if they "supervene" on the physical states—then once we have fixed the physical facts, we have fixed all the causal facts (Kim's Causal Closure of the Physical). But in the end, he claims, this systematic dependence of the functional on the physical is precisely what *prevents* functionalist epiphenomenalism. After illustrating how both supervenience and the "causal closure of the physical" can be represented in a probabilistic framework, Sober considers how causally relevant (or "causally efficacious") factors would look within this framework. Intuitively, causally relevant factors should raise the probability of the effect, compared to what happens when that factor is not present—for example, if cigarette smoking is a positively relevant causal factor for lung cancer, then lung cancer should be more likely among smokers than among nonsmokers. However, the probability of lung cancer among smokers must be compared against the probability for nonsmokers *who are otherwise the same*. It would not, for example, be accurate to measure incidence of lung cancer in smokers with the incidence in nonsmokers who breathe coal dust or asbestos. In order to ensure a fair comparison, *all other factors must be held fixed* when seeing if a certain factor raises the probability of some effect.

But, Sober notes, if cigarette smoke is made of chemicals XYZ, then inhalation of XYZ can't be one of the factors included in these background factors. Indeed, if it *were* included—so that everyone in the test population inhaled the same amount of XYZ—it would make no sense to try to compare those in the population who inhale cigarette smoke with those who don't. But Sober argues that, if (in light of supervenience) physical properties completely determine the mental properties, then it is equally improper to ask if mental properties make a causal difference, while including the physical properties among the fixed background factors. Here again, we would be trying to compare the probability of the effect when both the physical and mental properties are present, with its probability when the physical properties are present but the mental aren't—yet claiming (thanks to supervenience) that there are *no* possible cases where the physical properties occur without the mental. Appreciating in this way how supervenience and measures of causal factors combine, Sober concludes that the causal closure of the physical is no obstacle to saying that supervening mental states cause behavior.

Further Reading

Mental Causation, ed. John Heil and Alfred Mele (Oxford University Press, 1995) includes a number of recent works on mental causation, including Davidson's response to accusations of epiphenomenalism.

Jaegwon Kim, *Supervenience and Mind* (Cambridge University Press, 1993) focuses, in part II of the book, on the topic of mental causation. Kim's *Mind in a Physical World* (MIT Press, 1998) provides a compact overview of Kim's positions on materialism, reductionism, and mental causation.

31 From *The Passions of the Soul*

René Descartes

Article V

That it is an error to believe that the soul supplies the movement and heat to body.

By this means we shall avoid a very considerable error into which many have fallen; so much so that I am of opinion that this is the primary cause which has prevented our being able hitherto satisfactorily to explain the passions and the other properties of the soul. It arises from the fact that from observing that all dead bodies are devoid of heat and consequently of movement, it has been thought that it was the absence of soul which caused these movements and this heat to cease; and thus, without any reason, it was thought that our natural heat and all the movements of our body depend on the soul: while in fact we ought on the contrary to believe that the soul quits us on death only because this heat ceases, and the organs which serve to move the body disintegrate.

Article VI

The difference that exists between a living body and a dead body.

In order, then, that we may avoid this error, let us consider that death never comes to pass by reason of the soul, but only because some one of the principal parts of the body decays; and we may judge that the body of a living man differs from that of a dead man just as does a watch or other automaton (i.e., a machine that moves of itself), when it is wound up and contains in itself the corporeal principle of those movements for which it is designed along with all that is requisite for its action, from the same watch or other machine when it is broken and when the principle of its movement ceases to act....

Article XIII

That this action of outside objects may lead the spirits into the muscles in diverse ways.

And I have explained in the Dioptric how all the objects of sight communicate themselves to us only through the fact that they move locally by the intermission of transparent bodies which are between them and us, the little filaments of the optic nerves which are at the back of our eyes, and then the parts of the brain from which these nerves proceed; I explained, I repeat, how they move them in as many diverse ways as the diversities which they cause us to see in things, and that it is not immediately the movements which occur in the eye, but those that occur in the brain which represent these objects to the soul. To follow this example, it is easy to conceive how sounds, scents, tastes, heat, pain, hunger, thirst and generally speaking all objects of our other external senses as well as of our internal appetites, also excite some movement in our nerves which by their means pass to the brain; and in addition to the fact that these diverse movements of the brain cause diverse perceptions to become evident to our soul, they can also without it cause the spirits to take their course towards certain muscles rather than towards others, and thus to move our limbs, which I shall prove here by one example only. If someone quickly thrusts his hand against our eyes as if to strike us, even though we know him to be our friend, that he only does it in fun, and that he will take great care not to hurt us, we have all the same trouble in preventing ourselves from closing them; and this shows that it is not by the intervention of our soul that they close, seeing that it is against our will, which is its only, or at least its principal activity; but it is because the machine of our body is so formed that the movement of this hand towards our eyes excites another movement in our brain, which conducts the animal spirits into the muscles which cause the eyelids to close....

Article XVI

How all the members may be moved by the objects of the senses and by the animal spirits without the aid of the soul.

We must finally remark that the machine of our body is so formed that all the changes undergone by the movement of the spirits may cause them to open certain pores in the brain more than others, and reciprocally that when some one of the pores is opened more or less than usual (to however small a degree it may be) by the action of the nerves which are employed by the senses, that changes something in the movement of the spirits and causes them to be conducted into the muscles which serve to move the body in the way in which it is usually moved when such an action takes place. In this way all the movements which we make without our will contributing thereto (as frequently happens when we breathe, walk, eat, and in fact perform all those actions which are common to us and to the brutes), only depend on the conformation of our members, and on the course which the spirits, excited by the heat of the heart, follow naturally in the brain, nerves, and muscles, just as the movements of a watch are produced simply by the strength of the springs and the form of the wheels.

Article XVII

What the functions of the soul are.

After having thus considered all the functions which pertain to the body alone, it is easy to recognise that there is nothing in us which we ought to attribute to our soul excepting our thoughts, which are mainly of two sorts, the one being the actions of the soul, and the other its passions. Those which I call its actions are all our desires, because we find by experience that they proceed directly from our soul, and appear to depend on it alone: while, on the other hand, we may usually term one's passions all those kinds of perception or forms of knowledge which are found in us, because it is often not our soul which makes them what they are, and because it always receives them from the things which are represented by them.

Article XVIII

Of the Will.

Our desires, again, are of two sorts, of which the one consists of the actions of the soul which terminate in the soul itself, as when we desire to love God, or generally speaking, apply our thoughts to some object which is not material; and the other of the actions which terminate in our body, as when from the simple fact that we have the desire to take a walk, it follows that our legs move and that we walk. . . .

Article XXX

That the soul is united to all the portions of the body conjointly.

But in order to understand all these things more perfectly, we must know that the soul is really joined to the whole body, and that we cannot, properly speaking, say that it exists in any one of its parts to the exclusion of the others, because it is one and in some manner indivisible, owing to the disposition of its organs, which are so related to one another that when any one of them is removed, that renders the whole body defective; and because it is of a nature which has no relation to extension, nor dimensions, nor other properties of the matter of which the body is composed, but only to the whole conglomerate of its organs, as appears from the fact that we could not in any way conceive of the half or the third of a soul, nor of the space it occupies, and because it does not become smaller owing to the cutting off of some portion of the body, but separates itself from it entirely when the union of its assembled organs is dissolved.

Article XXXI

That there is a small gland in the brain in which the soul exercises its functions more particularly than in the other parts.

It is likewise necessary to know that although the soul is joined to the whole body, there is yet in that a certain part in which it exercises its functions more particularly than in all the others; and it is usually believed that this part is the brain, or possibly the heart: the brain, because it is with it that the organs of sense are connected, and the heart because it is apparently in it that we experience the passions. But, in examining the matter with care, it seems as though I had clearly ascertained that the part of the body in which the soul exercises its functions immediately is in nowise the heart, nor the whole of the brain, but merely the most inward of all its parts, to wit, a certain very small gland which is situated in the middle of its substance and so suspended above the duct whereby the animal spirits in its anterior cavities have communication with those in the posterior, that the slightest movements which take place in it may alter very greatly the course of these spirits; and reciprocally that the smallest changes which occur in the course of the spirits may do much to change the movements of this gland.

Article XXXII

How we know that this gland is the main seat of the soul.

The reason which persuades me that the soul cannot have any other seat in all the body than this gland wherein to exercise its functions immediately, is that I reflect that the other parts of our brain are all of them double, just as we have two eyes, two hands, two ears, and finally all the organs of our outside senses are double; and inasmuch as we have but one solitary and simple thought of one particular thing at one and the same moment, it must necessarily be the case that there must somewhere be a place where the two images which come to us by the two eyes, where the two other impressions which proceed from a single object by means of the double organs of the other senses, can unite before arriving at the soul, in order that they may not represent to it two objects instead of one. And it is easy to apprehend how these images or other impressions might unite in this gland by the intermission of the spirits which fill the cavities of the brain; but there is no other place in the body where they can be thus united unless they are so in this gland....

Article XXXIV

How the soul and the body act on one another.

Let us then conceive here that the soul has its principal seat in the little gland which exists in the middle of the brain, from whence it radiates forth through all the remainder of the body by means of the animal spirits, nerves, and even the blood, which, participating in the impressions of the spirits, can carry them by the arteries into all the members. And recollecting what has been said above about the machine of our body, i.e., that the little filaments of our nerves are so distributed in all its parts, that on the occasion of the diverse movements which are there excited by sensible objects, they open in diverse ways the pores of the brain, which causes the animal spirits contained in these cavities to enter in diverse ways into the muscles, by which means they can move the members in all the different ways in which they are capable of being moved; and also that all the other causes which are capable of moving the spirits in diverse ways suffice to conduct them into diverse muscles; let us here add that the small gland which is the main seat of the soul is so suspended between the cavities which contain the spirits that it can be moved by them in as many different ways as there are sensible diversities in the object, but that it may also be moved in diverse ways by the soul, whose nature is such that it receives in itself as many diverse impressions, that is to say, that it possesses as many diverse perceptions as there are diverse movements in this gland. Reciprocally, likewise, the machine of the body is so formed that from the simple fact that this gland is diversely moved by the soul, or by such other cause, whatever it is, it thrusts the spirits which surround it towards the pores of the brain, which conduct them by the nerves into the muscles, by which means it causes them to move the limbs.

Article XXXV

Example of the mode in which the impressions of the objects unite in the gland which is in the middle of the brain.

Thus, for example, if we see some animal approach us, the light reflected from its body depicts two images of it, one in each of our eyes, and these two images form two others, by means of the optic nerves, in the interior surface of the brain which faces its cavities; then from there, by means of the animal spirits with which its cavities are filled, these images so radiate towards the little gland which is surrounded by these spirits, that the movement which forms each point of one of the images tends towards the same point of the gland towards which tends the movement which forms the point of the other image, which represents the same part of this animal. By this means the two images which are in the brain form but one upon the gland, which, acting immediately upon the soul, causes it to see the form of this animal. . . .

Article XLI

The power of the soul in regard to the body.

But the will is so free in its nature, that it can never be constrained; and of the two sorts of thoughts which I have distinguished in the soul (of which the first are its actions, i.e., its desires, the others its passions, taking this word in its most general significance, which comprises all kinds of perceptions), the former are absolutely in its power, and can only be indirectly changed by the body, while on the other hand the latter depend absolutely on the actions which govern and direct them, and they can only indirectly be altered by the soul, excepting when it is itself their cause. And the whole action of the soul consists in this, that solely because it desires something, it causes the little gland to which it is closely united to move in the way requisite to produce the effect which relates to this desire.

Article XLII

How we find in the memory the things which we desire to remember.

Thus when the soul desires to recollect something, this desire causes the gland, by inclining successively to different sides, to thrust the spirits towards different parts of the brain until they come across that part where the traces left there by the object which we wish to recollect are found; for these traces are none other than the fact that the pores of the brain, by which the spirits have formerly followed their course because of the presence of this object, have by that means acquired a greater facility than the others in being once more opened by the animal spirits which come towards them in the same way. Thus these spirits in coming in contact with these pores, enter into them more easily than into the others, by which means they excite a special movement in the gland which represents the same object to the soul, and causes it to know that it is this which it desired to remember. . . .

Article XLVII

In what the strife consists which we imagine to exist between the lower and higher part of the soul.

And it is only in the repugnance which exists between the movements which the body by its animal spirits, and the soul by its will, tend to excite in the gland at the same time, that all the strife which we are in the habit of conceiving to exist between the inferior part of the soul, which we call the sensuous, and the superior which is rational, or as we may say, between the natural appetites and the will, consists. For there is within us but one soul, and this soul has not in itself any diversity of parts; the same part that is subject to sense impressions is rational, and all the soul's appetites are acts of will. The error which has been committed in making it play the part of various personages, usually in opposition one to another, only proceeds from the fact that we have not properly distinguished its functions from those of the body, to which alone we must attribute every thing which can be observed in us that is opposed to our reason; so that there is here no strife, excepting that the small gland which exists in the middle of the brain, being capable of being thrust to one side by the soul, and to the other by the animal spirits, which are mere bodies, as I have said above, it often happens that these two impulses are contrary, and that the stronger prevents the other from taking effect. We may, however, distinguish two sorts of movement excited by the animal spirits in the gland—the one sort represents to the soul the objects which move the senses, or the impressions which are met with in the brain, and makes no attempt to affect its will; the others do make an effort to do so—i.e., those which cause the passions or the movements of the body which accompany the passions. And as to the first, although they often hinder the actions of the soul, or else are hindered by them, yet, because they are not directly contrary to them, we do not notice any strife between them. We only notice the strife between the latter and the acts of will which conflict with them: e.g., between the effort with which the spirits impel the gland in order to cause a desire for something in the soul, and that with which the soul repels it again by the desire which it has to avoid the very same thing. And what causes this strife to come into evidence for the most part is that the will, not having the power to excite the passions directly, as has just been said, is constrained to use its best endeavours, and to apply itself to consider successively several things as to which, though it happens that one has the power to change for a moment the course taken by the spirits, it may come to pass that that which succeeds does not have it, and that they immediately afterwards revert to that same course because the disposition which has before held its place in the nerves, heart, and blood has not changed, and thus it comes about that the soul feels itself almost at the same time impelled to desire and not to desire the same thing. It is from this that occasion has been taken to imagine in the soul two powers which strive one with the other. At the same time we may still conceive a sort of strife to exist, inasmuch as often the same cause which excites some passion in the soul, also excites certain movements in the body to which the soul does not contribute, and which it stops, or tries to stop, directly it perceives them; as we see when what excites fear also causes the spirits to enter into the muscles which serve to move the legs with the object of flight, and when the wish which we have to be brave stops them from doing so.

32 From *The Search after Truth*

Nicolas Malebranche

One need not imagine, as do most philosophers, that the mind becomes material when united with the body, and that the body becomes mind when it unites with the mind. The soul is not spread through all parts of the body, in order to give life and movement to it, as the imagination might have it; and the body does not become capable of sensation through its union with the mind, as our false and misleading senses seem to convince us. Each substance remains what it is, and as the soul is incapable of extension and movement, so the body is incapable of sensation and inclinations. The only alliance of mind and body known to us consists in a natural and mutual correspondence of the soul's thoughts with the brain traces, and of the soul's emotions with the movements of the animal spirits.

As soon as the soul receives some new ideas, new traces are imprinted in the brain: and as soon as objects produce new traces, the soul receives new ideas. It is not that it considers these traces, since it has no knowledge of them; nor that these traces include these ideas, for they have no relation to them; nor, finally, that the soul receives its ideas from these traces: for, as we shall explain in the third book, it is inconceivable that the mind receive anything from the body and become more enlightened by turning toward it, as these philosophers claim who would have it that it is by *transformation* to fantasms, or brain traces, *per conversionem ad phantasmata*, that the mind perceives all things. But that all takes place according to the general laws of the union of soul and body, which I shall also explain in the third book.

Likewise as soon as the soul wills that the arm be moved, it is moved, even though the soul does not know what it must do in order to move it; and as soon as the animal spirits are agitated, the soul is affected, even though it might not even know whether there are animal spirits in its body.

When I come to speak of the passions, I shall talk about the connection between the brain traces and the movements of the spirits, and that between the ideas and the emotions of the soul, for all the passions depend on them. Right now, I need only mention the connection between the ideas and the traces, and the connection of the traces with each other.

There are three very important causes of the connection of ideas with traces. The first, and the one the others presuppose, is nature, or the constant and immutable will of the Creator. There is, for example, a natural connection, independent of our will, between the traces producing a tree or a mountain we see and the ideas of tree or mountain, between the traces that produce in our brain the cry of a suffering man or animal and our understanding him to complain, between the expression of a man who threatens or fears us and the ideas of pain, strength, weakness, and even among the feelings of compassion, fear, and courage arising in us.

These natural connections are the strongest of all. They are generally similar in all men, and they are absolutely necessary for the preservation of life. This is why they do not depend at all upon our wills. For, if the connection of ideas with sounds and certain characters is weak, and quite different in different countries, it is because it depends upon the weak and changeable will of men. And the reason why this connection depends upon it is that this connection is not absolutely necessary for living, but only for living as men, who should form a rational society among themselves. . . .

The *passions* of the soul are impressions from the Author of nature that incline us toward loving our body and all that might be of use in its preservation. . . . It is through this continuous action by God that our volitions are followed by all those movements in the body designed to carry them out, and that the movements of our body that are mechanically excited in us at the sight of some object are accompanied by a passion of our soul that inclines us to will what seems to be useful to the body.

It is this continuous and efficacious impression of the will of God on us that binds us so closely to one part of matter, and if this impression of His will should cease for but a moment, we would immediately be freed from our dependence upon the body and all the changes it undergoes. For I cannot understand how certain people imagine that there is an absolutely necessary relation between the movements of the spirits and blood and the emotions of the soul. A few tiny particles of bile are rather violently stirred up in the brain—therefore, the soul must be excited by some passion, and the passion must be anger rather than love. What relation can be conceived between the idea of an enemy's faults, or a passion of contempt or hatred, on the one hand, and the corporeal movement of the blood's parts striking against certain parts of the brain on the other? How can they convince themselves that the one depends on the other, and that the union or connection of two things so remote and incompatible as mind and matter could be caused and maintained in any way other than by the continuous and all-powerful will of the Author of nature?

. . . Now it appears to me quite certain that the will of minds is incapable of moving the smallest body in the world; for it is clear that there is no necessary connection between our will to move our arms, for example, and the movement of our arms. It is true that they are moved when we will it, and that thus we are the natural cause of the movement of our arms. But *natural* causes are not true causes; they are only *occasional* causes that act only through the force and efficacy of the will of God, as I have just explained.

For how could we move our arms? To move them, it is necessary to have animal spirits, to send them through certain nerves toward certain muscles in order to inflate and contract them, for it is thus that the arm attached to them is moved; or according to the opinion of some others, it is still not known how that happens. And we see that men who do not know that they have spirits, nerves, and muscles move their arms, and even move them with more skill and ease than those who know anatomy best. Therefore, men will to move their arms, and only God is able and knows how to move them. If a man cannot turn a tower upside down, at least he knows what must be done to do so; but there is no man who knows what must be done to move one of his fingers by means of animal spirits. How, then, could men move their arms? These things seem obvious to me and, it seems to me, to all those willing to think, although they are perhaps incomprehensible to all those willing only to sense.

But not only are men not the true causes of the movements they produce in their bodies, there even seems to be some contradiction (in saying) that they could be. A true cause as I understand it is one such that the mind perceives a necessary connection between it and its effect. Now the mind perceives a necessary connection only between the will of an infinitely perfect being and its effects. Therefore, it is only God who is the true cause and who truly has the power to move bodies. I say further (a) that it is inconceivable that God could communicate His power to move bodies to men or angels, and (b) that those who claim that our power to move our arms is a true power should admit that God can also give to minds the power to create, annihilate, and to do all possible things; in short, that He can render them omnipotent, as I shall show.

God needs no instruments to act; it suffices that He wills[1] in order that a thing be, because it is a contradiction that He should will and that what He wills should not happen. Therefore, His power is His will, and to communicate His power is to communicate the efficacy of His will. But to communicate this efficacy to a man or an angel signifies nothing other than to will that when a man or an angel shall will this or that body to be moved it will actually be moved. Now in this case, I see two wills concurring when an angel moves a body; that of God and that of the angel; and in order to know which of the two is the true cause of the movement of this body, it is necessary to know which one is efficacious. There is a necessary connection between the will of God and the thing He wills. God wills in this case that, when an angel wills this or that body be moved, it will be moved. Therefore, there is a necessary connection between the will of God and the movement of the body; and consequently it is God who is the true cause of its movement, whereas the will of the angel is only the occasional cause.

But to show this still more clearly, let us suppose that God wills to produce the opposite of what some minds will, as might be thought in the case of demons or some other minds that deserve this punishment. One could not say in this case that God would communicate His power to them, since they could do nothing they willed to do. Nevertheless, the wills of these minds would be the natural causes of the effects produced. Such bodies would be moved to the right only because these minds willed them moved to the left; and the volitions of these minds would determine the will of God to act, as our willing to move the parts of our bodies determines the first cause to move them. Thus, all the volitions of minds are only occasional causes....

There is therefore only one single true God and one single cause that is truly a cause, and one should not imagine that what precedes an effect is its true cause. God cannot even communicate His power to creatures, if we follow the lights of reason; He cannot make true causes of them, He cannot make them gods. But even if He could, we cannot conceive why He would. Bodies, minds, pure intelligences, all these can do nothing. It is He who made minds, who enlightens and activates them. It is He who created the sky and the earth, and who regulates their motions. In short, it is the Author of our being who executes our wills: *semel jussit, semper paret.* He moves our arms even when we use them against His orders; for He complains through His prophet that we make Him serve our unjust and criminal desires....

If religion teaches us that there is only one true God, this philosophy shows us that there is only one true cause. If religion teaches us that all the divinities of paganism are merely stones and metals without life or motion, this philosophy also reveals to us that all secondary causes, or all the divinities of philosophy, are merely matter and inefficacious wills. Finally, if religion teaches us that we must not genuflect before false gods, this philosophy also teaches us that our imaginations and minds must not bow before the imaginary greatness and power of causes that are not causes at all; that we must neither love nor fear them; that we must not be concerned with them; that we must think only of God alone, see God in all things, fear and love God in all things.

Note

1. It is clear that I am speaking here about practical volitions, or those God has when He wills to act.

33 A New System of the Nature and the Communication of Substances

Gottfried Wilhelm Leibniz

When I began to think about the union of the soul with the body, it was like casting me back into the open sea, for I found no way to explain how the body causes anything to take place in the soul, or vice versa, or how one substance can communicate with another created substance. So far as we can know from his writings, Descartes gave up the struggle over this problem. But seeing that the common opinion is inconceivable, his disciples concluded that we sense the qualities of bodies because God causes thoughts to arise in our soul on the occasion of material movements and that, when our soul in its turn wishes to move the body, God moves the body for it. And since the communication of motion also seemed inconceivable to them, they believed that God imparts motion to a body on the occasion of the motion of another body. This they call the *System of Occasional Causes*; it has had great vogue as a result of the beautiful reflections of the author of the *Recherche de la vérite*.

It must be admitted that this has definitely penetrated the difficulty in showing us what cannot take place. But it does not seem to have removed the difficulty by showing us what actually does happen. It is quite true that, speaking with metaphysical rigor, there is no real influence of one created substance upon another and that all things, with all their reality, are continually produced by the power of God. But problems are not solved merely by making use of a general cause and calling in what is called the *deus ex machina*. To do this without offering any other explanation drawn from the order of secondary causes is, properly speaking, to have recourse to miracle. In philosophy we must try to give a reason which will show how things are brought about by the Divine Wisdom in conformity with the particular concept of the subject in question.

Being constrained, then, to admit that it is impossible for the soul or any other true substance to receive something from without, except by the divine omnipotence, I was led insensibly to an opinion which surprised me, but which seems inevitable, and which has in fact very great advantages and very significant beauties. This is that we must say that God has originally created the soul, and every other real unity, in such a way that everything in it must arise from its own nature by a perfect *spontaneity* with regard to itself, yet by a perfect *conformity* to things without. And thus, since our internal sensations, that is, those which are in the soul itself and not in the brain or in the subtle parts of the body, are merely phenomena which follow upon external events or, better, are really appearances or like well-ordered dreams, it follows that these perceptions internal to the soul itself come to it through its own original constitution, that is to say, through its representative nature, which is capable of expressing entities outside of itself in agreement with its organs—this nature having been given it from its creation and constituting its individual character. It is this that makes each substance represent the entire universe accurately in its own way and according to a definite point of view. And the perceptions or expressions of external things reach the soul at the proper time by virtue of its own laws, as in a world apart, and as if there existed nothing but God and itself (to make use of the expression of a person of exalted mind and renowned piety). So there will be a perfect accord between all these substances which produces the same effect that would be noticed if they all communicated with each other by a transmission of species or of qualities, as the common run of philosophers imagine. Furthermore, the organized mass in which the point of view of the soul is found is itself expressed more immediately by the soul and is in turn ready to act by itself following the laws of the corporeal mechanism, at the moment at which the soul wills but without either disturbing the laws of the other, the animal spirits and the blood taking on, at exactly the right moment, the motions required to correspond to the passions and the perceptions of the soul. It is this mutual agreement, regulated in advance in every substance of the universe, which produces what we call their communication and which alone constitutes the union of soul and body. This makes it clear how the soul has its seat in the body by an immediate presence which could not be closer, since the soul is in it as a unity is in the resultant of unities which is a multitude.

This hypothesis is entirely possible. For why should God be unable to give to substance in the beginning a nature or internal force which enables it to produce in regular order—as in an *automaton that is spiritual or formal but free* in the case of that substance which has a share of reason—everything which is to happen to it, that is, all the appearances or expressions which it is to have, and this without the help of any created being? Especially since the nature of substance necessarily demands and essentially involves progress or change and would have no force of action without it. And since it is the nature of the soul to represent the universe in a very exact way, though with relative degrees of distinctness, the sequence of representations which the soul produces will correspond naturally to the sequence of changes in the universe itself. So the body, in turn, has also been adapted to the soul to fit those situations in which the soul is thought of as acting externally. This is all the more reasonable inasmuch as bodies are made solely for the spirits themselves, who are capable of entering into a society with God and of extolling his glory. Thus as soon as one sees the possibility of this *hypothesis of agreement*, one sees also that it is the most reasonable one and that it gives a wonderful idea of the harmony of the universe and of the perfection of the works of God.

There is also in it the great advantage that, instead of saying that we are free only in appearance and in a manner adequate for practical purposes, as several intelligent persons have thought, we must rather say that we are determined only in appearance and that in metaphysical strictness we are in a state of perfect independence as concerns the influence of all the other created beings. This throws a wonderful light on the immortality of our soul as well and on the always uniform conservation of our individual being, which is perfectly regulated by its own nature and fully sheltered from all accidents from without, whatever appearance there may be to the contrary. Never has a system so clearly exhibited our elevation. Since each mind is as a world apart and sufficient unto itself, independent of every other created being, enveloping the infinite and expressing the universe, it is as durable, as subsistent, as absolute as the universe of creatures itself. We must therefore conclude that it must always play such a part as is most fitting to contribute to the perfection of the society of all minds, which is their moral union in the City of God. A new proof of the existence of God can also be found here, one of surprising clarity. For the perfect agreement of so many substances which have no communication whatever with each other can come only from a common source....

Imagine two clocks or watches which are in perfect agreement. Now this can happen in *three ways*. The *first* is that of a natural influence. This is the way with which Mr. Huygens experimented, with results that greatly surprised him. He suspended two pendulums from the same piece of wood. The continued strokes of the pendulums transmitted similar vibrations to the particles of wood, but these vibrations could not continue in their own frequency without interfering with each other, at least when the two pendulums did not beat together. The result, by a kind of miracle, was that even when their strokes had been intentionally disturbed, they came to beat together again, somewhat like two strings tuned to each other. The *second* way of making two clocks, even poor ones, agree always is to assign a skilled craftsman to them who adjusts them and constantly sets them in agreement. The *third* way is to construct these two timepieces at the beginning with such skill and accuracy that one can be assured of their subsequent agreement.

Now put the soul and the body in the place of these two timepieces. Then their agreement or sympathy will also come about in one of these three ways. The *way of influence* is that of the common philosophy. But since it is impossible to conceive of material particles or of species or immaterial qualities which can pass from one of these substances into the other, this view must be rejected. The *way of assistance* is that of the system of occasional causes. But I hold that this makes a *deus ex machina* intervene in a natural and ordinary matter where reason requires that God should help only in the way in which he concurs in all other natural things. Thus there remains only my hypothesis, that is, the *way of preestablished harmony*, according to which God has made each of the two substances from the beginning in such a way that, though each follows only its own laws which it has received with its being, each agrees throughout with the other, entirely as if they were mutually influenced or as if God were always putting forth his hand, beyond his general concurrence. I do not think that there is anything more than this that I need to prove—unless someone should demand that I prove that God is skilful enough to make use of this foresighted artifice, of which we see samples even among men, to the extent that they are able men. And, assuming that God can do it, it is clear that this way is the most beautiful and the most worthy of him. You had suspected that my explanation would be opposed to the different idea we have of the mind and of the body. But now you clearly see that no one could establish their independence more effectively. For as long as one was obliged to explain their communication by means of a miracle, one always gave opportunity for some people to fear that the distinction between body and soul is not as real as is thought, since we were forced to go to such lengths to maintain it. Now all these scruples will cease.

34 From *Critique of Pure Reason*

Immanuel Kant

The Antinomy of Pure Reason

Third Conflict of the Transcendental Ideas

Thesis

Causality, according to the laws of nature, is not the only causality from which all the phenomena of the world can be deduced. In order to account for these phenomena it is necessary also to admit another causality, that of freedom.

Proof

Let us assume that there is no other causality but that according to the laws of nature. In that case everything that *takes place,* presupposes an anterior state, on which it follows inevitably according to a rule. But that anterior state must itself be something which has taken place (which has come to be in time, and did not exist before), because, if it had always existed, its effect too would not have only just arisen, but have existed always. The causality, therefore, of a cause, through which something takes place, is itself an *event,* which again, according to the law of nature, presupposes an anterior state and its causality, and this again an anterior state, and so on. If, therefore, everything takes place according to mere laws of nature, there will always be a secondary only, but never a primary beginning, and therefore no completeness of the series, on the side of successive causes. But the law of nature consists in this, that

Antithesis

There is no freedom, but everything in the world takes place entirely according to the laws of nature.

Proof

If we admit that there is *freedom,* in the transcendental sense, as a particular kind of causality, according to which the events in the world could take place, that is a faculty of absolutely originating a state, and with it a series of consequences, it would follow that not only a series would have its absolute beginning through this spontaneity, but the determination of that spontaneity itself to produce the series, that is, the causality, would have an absolute beginning, nothing preceding it by which this act is determined according to permanent laws. Every beginning of an act, however, presupposes a state in which the cause is not yet active, and a dynamically primary beginning of an act presupposes a state which has no causal connection with the preceding state of that cause, that is, in no wise follows from it. Transcendental freedom is therefore opposed to the law of causality, and represents such a nothing takes place without a cause sufficiently determined *a priori*. Therefore the proposition, that all causality is possible according to the laws of nature only, contradicts itself, if taken in unlimited generality, and it is impossible, therefore, to admit that causality as the only one.

We must therefore admit another causality, through which something takes place, without its cause being further determined according to necessary laws by a preceding cause, that is, an *absolute spontaneity* of causes, by which a series of phenomena, proceeding according to natural laws, begins by itself; we must consequently admit transcendental freedom, without which, even in the course of nature, the series of phenomena on the side of causes, can never be perfect.

connection of successive states of effective causes, that no unity of experience is possible with it. It is therefore an empty fiction of the mind, and not to be met with in any experience.

We have, therefore, nothing but *nature*, in which we must try to find the connection and order of events. Freedom (independence) from the laws of nature is no doubt a *deliverance* from restraint, but also from the *guidance* of all rules. For we cannot say that, instead of the laws of nature, laws of freedom may enter into the causality of the course of the world, because, if determined by laws, it would not be freedom, but nothing else but nature. Nature, therefore, and transcendental freedom differ from each other like legality and lawlessness. The former, no doubt, imposes upon the understanding the difficult task of looking higher and higher for the origin of events in the series of causes, because their causality is always conditioned. In return for this, however, it promises a complete and well-ordered unity of experience; while, on the other side, the fiction of freedom promises, no doubt, to the enquiring mind, rest in the chain of causes, leading him up to an unconditioned causality, which begins to act by itself, but which, as it is blind itself, tears the thread of rules by which alone a complete and coherent experience is possible.

Observation on the Third Antinomy

I On the Thesis

The transcendental idea of freedom is … the real stone of offence in the eyes of philosophy, which finds its unsurmountable difficulties in admitting this kind of unconditioned causality. That element in the question of the freedom of the will, which has always so much embarrassed speculative reason, is therefore in reality *transcendental* only, and refers merely to

II On the Antithesis

He who stands up for the omnipotence of nature (transcendental *physiocracy*), in opposition to the doctrine of freedom, would defend his position against the sophistical conclusions of that doctrine in the following manner. *If you do not admit something mathematically the first in the world with reference to time, there is no necessity why you should look for something* the question whether we must admit a faculty of *spontaneously* originating a series of successive things or states. How such a faculty is possible need not be answered, because, with regard to the causality, according to the laws of nature also, we must be satisfied to know *a priori* that such a causality has to be admitted, though we can in no wise understand the possibility how, through one existence, the existence of another is given, but must for that purpose appeal to experience alone. The necessity of a first beginning of a series of phenomena from freedom has been proved so far only as it is necessary in order to comprehend an origin of the world, while all successive states may be regarded as a result in succession according to mere laws of nature. But as the faculty of originating a series in time by itself has been proved, though by no means understood, it is now permitted also to admit, within the course of the world, different series, beginning by themselves, with regard to their causality, and to attribute to their substances a faculty of acting with freedom. But we must not allow ourselves to be troubled by a misapprehension, namely that, as every successive series in the world can have only a relatively primary beginning, some other state of things always preceding in the world, therefore no absolutely primary beginning of different series is possible in the course of the world. For we are speaking here of the absolutely first beginning, *not according to time,* but *according to causality.* If, for instance, at this moment I rise from my chair with perfect freedom, without the necessary determining influence of natural causes, a new series has its absolute beginning in this event, with all its natural consequences *ad infinitum,* although, *with regard to time,* this event is only the continuation of a preceding series. For this *dynamically the first with reference to causality.* Who has told you to invent an absolutely first state of the world, and with it an absolute beginning of the gradually progressing series of phenomena, and to set limits to unlimited nature in order to give to your imagination something to rest on? As substances have always existed in the world, or as the unity of experience renders at least such a supposition necessary, there is no difficulty in assuming that a change of their states, that is, a series of their changes, has always existed also, so that there is no necessity for looking for a first beginning either mathematically or dynamically. It is true we cannot render the possibility of such an infinite descent comprehensible without the first member to which everything else is subsequent. But, if for this reason you reject this riddle of nature, you will feel yourselves constrained to reject many fundamental properties (natural forces), which you cannot comprehend any more....

And, even if the transcendental faculty of freedom might somehow be conceded to start the changes of the world, such faculty would at all events have to be outside the world (though it would always remain a bold assumption to admit, outside the sum total of all possible intuitions, an object that cannot be given in any possible experience). But to attribute in the world itself a faculty to substances can never be allowed, because in that case the connection of phenomena determining each other by necessity and according to general laws, which we call nature, and with it the test of empirical truth, which distinguishes experience from dreams, would almost entirely disappear. For by the side of such a lawless faculty of freedom, nature could hardly be conceived any longer, because the laws of the latter would be constantly changed determination and this act do not belong to the succession of merely natural effects, nor are they a mere continuation of them, but the determining natural causes completely stop before it, so far as this event is concerned, which no doubt follows them, and does not *result* from them, and may therefore be called an absolutely first beginning in a series of phenomena, not with reference to time, but with reference to causality.

This requirement of reason to appeal in the series of natural causes to a first and free beginning is fully confirmed if we see that, with the exception of the Epicurean school, all philosophers of antiquity have felt themselves obliged to admit, for the sake of explaining all cosmical movements, a *prime mover*, that is, a freely acting cause which, first and by itself, started this series of states. They did not attempt to make a first beginning comprehensible by an appeal to nature only.

III

Solution of the Cosmological Ideas with Regard to the Totality of the Derivation of Cosmical Events from their Causes We can conceive two kinds of causality only with reference to events, causality either of *nature* or of *freedom*. The former is the connection of one state in the world of sense with a preceding state, on which it follows according to a rule. As the *causality* of phenomena depends on conditions of time, and as the preceding state, if it had always existed, could not have produced an effect, which first takes place in time, it follows that the causality of the cause of that which happens or arises must, according to the principle of the understanding, have itself *arisen* and require a cause.

By freedom, on the contrary, in its cosmological meaning, I understand the faculty of beginning a state *spontaneously*. Its causality, therefore, does not depend, according to the law of nature, on another cause, by which it is determined in time. In this sense freedom is a purely transcendental idea, which, first, contains nothing derived from *experience*, and, secondly, the object of which cannot be determined in any *experience*; because it is a general rule, even of the possibility of all *experience*, that everything which happens has a cause, and that therefore the causality also of the cause, which *itself* has happened or arisen, must again have a cause. In this manner the whole field of experience, however far it may extend, has been changed into one great whole of nature. As, however, it is impossible in this way to arrive at an absolute totality of the conditions

through the influence of the former, and the play of phenomena which, according to nature, is regular and uniform, would become confused and incoherent.

in causal relations, reason creates for itself the idea of spontaneity, or the power of beginning by itself, without an antecedent cause determining it to action, according to the law of causal connection.

It is extremely remarkable, that the practical concept of freedom is founded on the *transcendental idea of freedom*, which constitutes indeed the real difficulty which at all times has surrounded the question of the possibility of freedom. *Freedom*, in its *practical sense*, is the independence of our (arbitrary) will from the *coercion* through sensuous impulses....

It can easily be seen that, if all causality in the world of sense belonged to nature, every event would be determined in time through another, according to necessary laws. As therefore the phenomena, in determining the will, would render every act necessary as their natural effect, the annihilation of transcendental freedom would at the same time destroy all practical freedom. Practical freedom presupposes that, although something has not happened, it *ought* to have happened, and that its cause therefore had not that determining force among phenomena, which could prevent the causality of our will from producing, independently of those natural causes, and even contrary to their force and influence, something determined in the order of time, according to empirical laws, and from originating *entirely by itself* a series of events.

What happens here is what happens generally in the conflict of reason venturing beyond the limits of possible experience, namely, that the problem is not *physiological*, but *transcendental*. Hence the question of the possibility of freedom concerns no doubt psychology; but its solution, as it depends on dialectical arguments of pure reason, belongs entirely to transcendental philosophy. In order to enable that philosophy to give a satisfactory answer, which it cannot decline to do, I must first try to determine more accurately its proper procedure in this task.

If phenomena were things in themselves, and therefore space and time forms of the existence of things in themselves, the conditions together with the conditioned would always belong, as members, to one and the same series.... All depends here only on the dynamical relation of conditions to the conditioned, so that in the question on nature and freedom we at once meet with the difficulty, whether freedom is indeed possible, and whether, if it is possible, it can exist together with the universality of the natural law of causality. The question in fact arises, whether it is a proper disjunctive proposition to say, that every effect in the world must arise, *either* from nature, *or* from freedom, or whether *both* cannot coexist in the same event in different relations. The correctness of the principle of the unbroken connection of all events in the world of sense, according to unchangeable natural laws, is firmly established ... and admits of no limitation. The question, therefore, can only be whether, in spite of it, freedom also can be found in the same effect which is determined by nature; or whether freedom is entirely excluded by that inviolable rule? Here the common but fallacious supposition of the *absolute reality* of phenomena shows at once its pernicious influence in embarrassing reason. For if phenomena are things in themselves, freedom cannot be saved. Nature in that case is the complete and sufficient cause determining every event, and its condition is always contained in that series of phenomena only which, together with their effect, are necessary under the law of nature. If, on the contrary, phenomena are taken for nothing except what they are in reality, namely, not things in themselves, but representations only, which are connected with each other according to empirical laws, they must themselves have causes, which are not phenomenal. Such an intelligible cause, however, is not determined with reference to its causality by phenomena, although its effects become phenomenal, and can thus be determined by other phenomena. That intelligible cause, therefore, with its causality, is outside the series, though its *effects* are to be found *in* the series of empirical conditions. The effect therefore can, with reference to its *intelligible* cause, be considered as free, and yet at the same time, with reference to *phenomena*, as resulting from them according to the necessity of nature; a distinction which, if thus represented, in a general and entirely abstract form, may seem extremely subtle and obscure, but will become clear in its practical application. Here I only wished to remark that, as the unbroken *connection* of all phenomena in the context of nature, is an unalterable law, it would necessarily destroy all freedom, if we were to defend obstinately the reality of phenomena. Those, therefore, who follow the common opinion on this subject, have never been able to reconcile nature and freedom.

Possibility of a Causality through Freedom, in Harmony with the Universal Law of Natural Necessity Whatever in an object of the senses is not itself phenomenal, I call *intelligible*. If, therefore, what in the world of sense must be considered as phenomenal, possesses in itself a faculty which is not the object of sensuous intuition, but through which it can become the cause of phenomena, the *causality* of that being may be considered from *two sides*, as *intelligible* in its *action*, as the causality of a thing in itself, and as *sensible* in the *effects* of the action, as the causality of a phenomenon in the world of sense. Of the faculty of such a being we should have to form both an *empirical* and an *intellectual concept* of its causality, both of which consist together in one and the same effect. This twofold way of conceiving the faculty of an object of the senses does not contradict any of the concepts which we have to form of phenomena and of a possible experience. For since all phenomena, not being things in themselves, must have for their foundation a transcendental object, determining them as mere representations, there is nothing to prevent us from attributing to that transcendental object, besides the quality through which it becomes phenomenal, a *causality* also which is not phenomenal, although its *effect* appears in the phenomenon. Every efficient cause, however, must have a *character*, that is, a rule according to which it manifests its causality, and without which it would not be a cause. According to this we should have in every subject of the world of sense, first, an *empirical character*, through which its acts, as phenomena, stand with other phenomena in an unbroken connection, according to permanent laws of nature, and could be derived from them as their conditions, and in connection with them form the links of one and the same series in the order of nature. Secondly, we should have to allow to it an *intelligible character* also, by which, it is true, it becomes the cause of the same acts as phenomena, but which itself is not subject to any conditions of sensibility, and never phenomenal. We might call the former the character of such a thing as a phenomenon, in the latter the character of the thing in itself.

According to its intelligible character, this active subject would not depend on conditions of time, for time is only the condition of phenomena, and not of things in themselves. In it no *act* would *arise* or *perish*, neither would it be subject therefore to the law of determination in time and of all that is changeable, namely, that everything *which happens* must have its cause in *the phenomena* (of the previous state). In one word its causality, so far as it is intelligible, would not have a place in the series of empirical conditions by which the event is rendered necessary in the world of sense. It is true that that intelligible character could never be known immediately, because we cannot perceive anything, except so far as it appears, but it would nevertheless have to be conceived, according to the empirical character, as we must always admit in thought a transcendental object, as the foundation of phenomena, though we know nothing of what it is by itself.

In its empirical character, therefore, that subject, as a phenomenon, would submit, according to all determining laws, to a causal nexus, and in that respect it would be nothing but a part of the world of sense, the effects of which, like every other phenomenon, would arise from nature without fail. As soon as external phenomena began to influence it, and as soon as its empirical character, that is the law of its causality, had been known through experience, all its actions ought to admit of explanation, according to the laws of nature, and all that is requisite for its complete and necessary determination would be found in a possible experience.

In its intelligible character, however (though we could only have a general concept of it), the same subject would have to be considered free from all influence of sensibility, and from all determination through phenomena: and as in it, so far as it is a *noumenon*, nothing *happens*, and no change which requires dynamical determination of time, and therefore no connection with phenomena as causes, can exist, that active being would so far be quite independent and free in its acts from all natural necessity, which can exist in the world of sense only. One might say of it with perfect truth that it originates its effects in the world of sense *by itself*, though the act does not begin *in itself*. And this would be perfectly true, though the effects in the world of sense need not therefore originate by themselves, because in it they are always determined previously through empirical conditions in the previous time, though only by means of the empirical character (which is the phenomenal appearance of the intelligible character), and therefore impossible, except as a continuation of the series of natural causes. In this way freedom and nature, each in its complete signification, might exist together and without any conflict in the same action, according as we refer it to its intelligible or to its sensible cause.

Explanation of the Cosmological Idea of Freedom in Connection with the General Necessity of Nature I thought it best to give first this sketch of the solution of our transcendental problem, so that the course which reason has to adopt in its solution might be more clearly surveyed. We shall now proceed to explain more fully the points on which the decision properly rests, and examine each by itself.

That our reason possesses causality, or that we at least represent to ourselves such a causality in it, is clear from the *imperatives* which, in all practical matters, we impose as rules on our executive powers. The *ought* expresses a kind of necessity and connection with causes, which we do not find elsewhere in the whole of nature. The understanding can know in nature only what is present, past, or future. It is impossible that anything in it *ought to be* different from what it is in reality, in all these relations of time. Nay, if we only look at the course of nature, the ought has no meaning whatever. We cannot ask, what ought to be in nature, as little as we can ask, what qualities a circle ought to possess. We can only ask what happens in it, and what qualities that which happens has.

This ought expresses a possible action, the ground of which cannot be anything but a mere concept; while in every merely natural action the ground must always be a phenomenon. Now it is quite true that the action to which the ought applies must be possible under natural conditions, but these natural conditions do not affect the determination of the will itself, but only its effects and results among phenomena. There may be ever so many natural grounds which impel me to *will* and ever so many sensuous temptations, but they can never produce the *ought*, but only a willing which is always conditioned, but by no means necessary, and to which the ought, pronounced by reason, opposes measure, ay, prohibition and authority. Whether it be an object of the senses merely (pleasure), or of pure reason (the good), reason does not yield to the impulse that is given empirically, and does not follow the order of things, as they present themselves as phenomena, but frames for itself, with perfect spontaneity, a new order according to ideas to which it adapts the empirical conditions, and according to which it declares actions to be necessary, even though they *have not taken place*, and, maybe, never will take place. Yet it is presupposed that reason may have causality with respect to them, for otherwise no effects in experience could be expected to result from these ideas.

Now let us take our stand here and admit it at least as possible, that reason really possesses causality with reference to phenomena. In that case, reason though it be, it must show nevertheless an empirical character, because every cause presupposes a rule according to which certain phenomena follow as effects, and every rule requires in the effects a homogeneousness, on which the concept of cause (as a faculty) is founded. This, so far as it is derived from mere phenomena, may be called the empirical character, which is *permanent*, while the effects, according to a diversity of concomitant, and in part, restraining conditions, appear in *changeable* forms.

Every man therefore has an empirical character of his (arbitrary) will, which is nothing but a certain causality of his reason, exhibiting in its phenomenal actions and effects a rule, according to which one may infer the motives of reason and its actions, both in kind and in degree, and judge of the subjective principles of his will. As that empirical character itself must be derived from phenomena, as an effect, and from their rule which is supplied by experience, all the acts of a man, so far as they are phenomena, are determined from his empirical character and from the other concomitant causes, according to the order of nature; and if we could investigate all the manifestations of his will to the very bottom, there would be not a single human action which we could not predict with certainty and recognise from its preceding conditions as necessary. There is no freedom therefore with reference to this empirical character, and yet it is only with reference to it that we can consider man, when we are merely *observing*, and, as is the case in anthropology, trying to investigate the motive causes of his actions physiologically.

If, however, we consider the same actions with reference to reason ... solely so far as reason is the cause which *produces* them; in one word, if we compare actions with reason, with reference to *practical* purposes, we find a rule and order, totally different from the order of nature. For, from this point of view, everything, it may be, *ought not to have happened,* which according to the course of nature *has happened,* and according to its empirical grounds, was inevitable. And sometimes we find, or believe at least that we find, that the ideas of reason have really proved their causality with reference to human actions as phenomena, and that these actions have taken place, not because they were determined by empirical causes, but by the causes of reason.

Now supposing one could say that reason possesses causality in reference to phenomena, could the action of reason be called free in that case, as it is accurately determined by the empirical character (the disposition) and rendered necessary by it? That character again is determined in the intelligible character (way of thinking). The latter, however, we do not know, but signify only through phenomena, which in reality give us immediately a knowledge of the disposition (empirical character) only.[1] . . . Pure reason, as a simple intelligible faculty, is not subject to the form of time, or to the conditions of the succession of time. The causality of reason in its intelligible character does *not arise* or begin at a certain time in order to produce an effect; for in that case it would be subject to the natural law of phenomena, which determines all causal series in time, and its causality would then be nature and not freedom. What, therefore, we can say is, that if reason can possess causality with reference to phenomena, it is a faculty *through which* the sensuous condition of an empirical series of effects first begins. For the condition that lies in reason is not sensuous, and therefore does itself not begin. Thus we get what we missed in all empirical series, namely, that the *condition* of a successive series of events should itself be empirically unconditioned. For here the condition is really *outside* the series of phenomena (in the intelligible), and therefore not subject to any sensuous condition, nor to any temporal determination through preceding causes.

Nevertheless the same cause belongs also, in another respect, to the series of phenomena. Man himself is a phenomenon. His will has an empirical character, which is the (empirical) cause of all his actions. There is no condition, determining man according to this character, that is not contained in the series of natural effects and subject to their law, according to which there can be no empirically unconditioned causality of anything that happens in time. No given action therefore (as it can be perceived as a phenomenon only) can begin absolutely by itself. Of pure reason, however, we cannot say that the state in which it determines the will is preceded by another in which that state itself is determined. For as reason itself is not a phenomenon, and not subject to any of the conditions of sensibility, there exists in it, even in reference to its causality, no succession of time, and the dynamical law of nature, which determines the succession of time according to rules, cannot be applied to it.

Reason is therefore the constant condition of all free actions by which man takes his place in the phenomenal world. Every one of them is determined beforehand in his empirical character, before it becomes actual. With regard to the intelligible character, however, of which the empirical is only the sensuous schema, there is neither *before* nor *after*; and every action, without regard to the temporal relation which connects it with other phenomena, is the immediate effect of the intelligible character of pure reason. That reason therefore acts freely, without being determined dynamically, in the chain of natural causes, by external or internal conditions, anterior in time. That freedom must then not only be regarded negatively, as independence of empirical conditions (for in that case the faculty of reason would cease to be a cause of phenomena), but should be determined positively also, as the faculty of beginning spontaneously a series of events. Hence nothing begins in reason itself, and being itself the unconditioned condition of every free action, reason admits of no condition antecedent in time above itself, while nevertheless its effect takes its beginning in the series of phenomena, though it can never constitute in that series an *absolutely* first beginning.

In order to illustrate the regulative principle of reason by an example of its empirical application, not in order to confirm it (for such arguments are useless for transcendental propositions), let us take a voluntary action, for example, a malicious lie, by which a man has produced a certain confusion in society, and of which we first try to find out the motives, and afterwards try to determine how far it and its consequences may be imputed to the offender. With regard to the first point, one has first to follow up his empirical character to its very sources, which are to be found in wrong education, bad society, in part also in the viciousness of a natural disposition, and a nature insensible to shame, or ascribed to frivolity and heedlessness, not omitting the occasioning causes at the time. In all this the procedure is exactly the same as in the investigation of a series of determining causes of a given natural effect. But although one believes that the act was thus determined, one nevertheless blames the offender, and not on account of his unhappy natural disposition, not on account of influencing circumstances, not even on account of his former course of life, because one supposes one might leave entirely out of account what that course of life may have been, and consider the past series of conditions as having never existed, and the act itself as totally unconditioned by previous states, as if the offender had begun with it a new series of effects, quite by himself. This blame is founded on a law of reason, reason being considered as a cause which, independent of all the before-mentioned empirical conditions, would and should have determined the behaviour of the man otherwise. Nay, we do not regard the causality of reason as a concurrent agency only, but as complete in itself, even though the sensuous motives did not favour, but even oppose it. The action is imputed to a man's intelligible character. At the moment when he tells the lie, the guilt is entirely his; that is, we regard reason, in spite of all empirical conditions of the act, as completely free, and the act has to be imputed entirely to a fault of reason.

Such an imputation clearly shows that we imagine that reason is not affected at all by the influences of the senses, and that it does not change (although its manifestations, that is the mode in which it shows itself by its effects, do change): that in it no state precedes as determining a following state, in fact, that reason does not belong to the series of sensuous conditions which render phenomena necessary, according to laws of nature. Reason, it is supposed, is present in all the actions of man, in all circumstances of time, and always the same; but it is itself never in time, never in a new state in which it was not before; it is *determining*, never *determined*. . . .

We thus see that, in judging of voluntary actions, we can, so far as their causality is concerned, get only so far as the intelligible cause, but not beyond. We can see that that cause is free, that it determines as independent of sensibility, and therefore is capable of being the sensuously unconditioned condition of phenomena. To explain why that intelligible character should, under present circumstances, give these phenomena and this empirical character, and no other, transcends all the powers of our reason, nay, all its rights of questioning, as if we were to ask why the transcendental object of our external sensuous intuition gives us intuition in *space* only and no other.

But the problem which we have to solve does not require us to ask or to answer such questions. Our problem was, whether freedom is contradictory to natural necessity in one and the same action: and this we have sufficiently answered by showing that freedom may have relation to a very different kind of conditions from those of nature, so that the law of the latter does not affect the former, and both may exist independent of, and undisturbed by, each other.

It should be clearly understood that, in what we have said, we had no intention of establishing the *reality* of freedom, as one of the faculties which contain the cause of the phenomenal appearances in our world of sense. For not only would this have been no transcendental consideration at all, which is concerned with concepts only, but it could never have succeeded, because from experience we can never infer anything but what must be represented in thought according to the laws of experience. It was not even our intention to prove the *possibility* of freedom, for in this also we should not have succeeded, because from mere concepts *a priori* we can never know the possibility of any real ground or any causality. We have here treated freedom as a transcendental idea only, which makes reason imagine that it can absolutely begin the series of phenomenal conditions through what is sensuously unconditioned, but by which reason becomes involved in an antinomy with its own laws, which it had prescribed to the empirical use of the understanding. That this antinomy rests on a mere illusion, and that nature does *not contradict* the causality of freedom, that was the only thing which we could prove, and cared to prove.

Note

1. The true morality of actions (merit or guilt), even that of our own conduct, remains therefore entirely hidden. Our imputations can refer to the empirical character only. How much of that may be the pure effect of freedom, how much should be ascribed to nature only, and to the faults of temperament, for which man is not responsible, or its happy constitution (*merito fortunae*), no one can discover, and no one can judge with perfect justice.

35 From "On the Hypothesis That Animals Are Automata"

Thomas Henry Huxley

Descartes' line of argument is perfectly clear. He starts from reflex action in man, from the unquestionable fact that, in ourselves, co-ordinate, purposive actions may take places, without the intervention of consciousness or volition, or even contrary to the latter. As actions of a certain degree of complexity are brought about by mere mechanism, why may not actions of still greater complexity be the result of a more refined mechanism? What proof is there that brutes are other than a superior race of marionettes, which eat without pleasure, cry without pain, desire nothing, know nothing, and only simulate intelligence as a bee simulates a mathematician?

The Port Royalists adopted the hypothesis that brutes are machines, and are said to have carried its practical applications so far as to treat domestic animals with neglect, if not with actual cruelty. As late as the middle of the eighteenth century, the problem was discussed very fully and ably by Bouillier, in his "*Essai philosophique sur l'Âme des Bêtes,*" while Condillac deals with it in his "*Traité des Animaux;*" but since then it has received little attention. Nevertheless, modern research has brought to light a great multitude of facts, which not only show that Descartes' view is defensible, but render it far more defensible than it was in his day....

... And would Descartes not have been justified in asking why we need deny that animals are machines, when men, in a state of unconsciousness, perform, mechanically, actions as complicated and as seemingly rational as those of any animals?

But though I do not think that Descartes' hypothesis can be positively refuted, I am not disposed to accept it. The doctrine of continuity is too well established for it to be permissible to me to suppose that any complex natural phenomenon comes into existence suddenly, and without being preceded by simpler modifications; and very strong arguments would be needed to prove that such complex phenomena as those of consciousness, first make their appearance in man. We know, that, in the individual man, consciousness grows from a dim glimmer to its full light, whether we consider the infant advancing in years, or the adult emerging from slumber and swoon. We know, further, that the lower animals possess, though less developed, that part of the brain which we have every reason to believe to be the organ of consciousness in man; and as, in other cases, function and organ are proportional, so we have a right to conclude it is with the brain; and that the brutes, though they may not possess our intensity of consciousness, and though, from the absence of language, they can have no trains of thoughts, but only trains of feelings, yet have a consciousness which, more or less distinctly, foreshadows our own.

I confess that, in view of the struggle for existence which goes on in the animal world, and of the frightful quantity of pain with which it must be accompanied, I should be glad if the probabilities were in favour of Descartes' hypothesis; but, on the other hand, considering the terrible practical consequences to domestic animals which might ensue from any error on our part, it is as well to err on the right side, if we err at all, and deal with them as weaker brethren, who are bound, like the rest of us, to pay their toll for living, and suffer what is needful for the general good. As Hartley finely says, "We seem to be in the place of God to them"; and we may justly follow the precedents He sets in nature in our dealings with them.

But though we may see reason to disagree with Descartes' hypothesis that brutes are unconscious machines, it does not follow that he was wrong in regarding them as automata. They may be more or less conscious, sensitive, automata; and the view that they are such conscious machines is that which is implicitly, or explictly, adopted by most persons. When we speak of the actions of the lower animals being guided by instinct and not by reason, what we really mean is that, though they feel as we do, yet their actions are the results of their physical organisation. We believe, in short, that they are machines, one part of which (the nervous system) not only sets the rest in motion, and co-ordinates its movements in relation with changes in surrounding bodies, but is provided with special apparatus, the function of which is the calling into existence of those states of consciousness which are termed sensations, emotions, and ideas. I believe that this generally accepted view is the best expression of the facts at present known.

It is experimentally demonstrable—any one who cares to run a pin into himself may perform a sufficient demonstration of the fact—that a mode of motion of the nervous system is the immediate antecedent of a state of consciousness. All but the adherents of "Occasionalism," or of the doctrine of "Pre-established Harmony" (if any such now exist), must admit that we have as much reason for regarding the mode of motion of the nervous system as the cause of the state of consciousness, as we have for regarding any event as the cause of another. How the one phenomenon causes the other we know, as much or as little, as in any other case of causation; but we have as much right to believe that the sensation is an effect of the molecular change, as we have to believe that motion is an effect of impact; and there is as much propriety in saying that the brain evolves sensation, as there is in saying that an iron rod, when hammered, evolves heat.

As I have endeavoured to show, we are justified in supposing that something analogous to what happens in ourselves takes place in the brutes, and that the affections of their sensory nerves give rise to molecular changes in the brain, which again give rise to, or evolve, the corresponding states of consciousness. Nor can there be any reasonable doubt that the emotions of brutes, and such ideas as they possess, are similarly dependent upon molecular brain changes. Each sensory impression leaves behind a record in the structure of the brain—an "ideagenous" molecule, so to speak, which is competent, under certain conditions, to reproduce, in a fainter condition, the state of consciousness which corresponds with that sensory impression; and it is these "ideagenous molecules" which are the physical basis of memory.

It may be assumed, then, that molecular changes in the brain are the causes of all the states of consciousness of brutes. Is there any evidence that these states of consciousness may, conversely, cause those molecular changes which give rise to muscular motion? I see no such evidence. The frog walks, hops, swims, and goes through his gymnastic performances quite as well without consciousness, and consequently without volition, as with it; and, if a frog, in his natural state, possesses anything corresponding with what we call volition, these is no reason to think that it is anything but a concomitant of the molecular changes in the brain which form part of the series involved in the production of motion.

The consciousness of brutes would appear to be related to the mechanism of their body simply as a collateral product of its working, and to be as completely without any power of modifying that working as the steam-whistle which accompanies the work of a locomotive engine is without influence upon it machinery. Their volition, if they have any, is an emotion indicative of physical changes, not a cause of such changes.

This conception of the relations of states of consciousness with molecular changes in the brain—of *psychoses* with *neuroses*—does not prevent us from ascribing free will to brutes. For an agent is free when there is nothing to prevent him from doing that which he desires to do. If a greyhound chases a hare, he is a free agent, because his action is in entire accordance with his strong desire to catch the hare; while so long as he is held back by the leash he is not free, being prevented by external force from following his inclination. And the ascription of freedom to the greyhound under the former circumstances is by no means inconsistent with the other aspect of the facts of the case—that he is a machine impelled to the chase, and caused, at the same time, to have the desire to catch the game by the impression which the rays of light proceeding from the hare make upon his eyes, and through them upon his brain.

Much ingenious argument has at various times been bestowed upon the question: How is it possible to imagine that volition, which is a state of consciousness, and, as such, has not the slightest community of nature with matter in motion, can act upon the moving matter of which the body is composed, as it is assumed to do in voluntary acts? But if, as is here suggested, the voluntary acts of brutes—or, in other words, the acts which they desire to perform—are as purely mechanical as the rest of their actions, and are simply accompanied by the state of consciousness called volition, the inquiry, so far as they are concerned, becomes superfluous. Their volitions do not enter into the chain of causation of their actions at all.

The hypothesis that brutes are conscious automata is perfectly consistent with any view that may be held respecting the often discussed and curious question whether they have souls or not; and, if they have souls, whether those souls are immortal or not. It is obviously harmonious with the most literal adherence to the text of Scripture concerning "the beast that perisheth"; but it is not inconsistent with the amiable conviction ascribed by Pope to his "untutored savage," that when he passes to the happy hunting-grounds in the sky, "his faithful dog shall bear him company." If the brutes have consciousness and no souls, then it is clear that, in them, consciousness is a direct function of material changes; while, if they possess immaterial subjects of consciousness, or souls, then, as consciousness is brought into existence only as the consequence of molecular motion of the brain, it follows that it is an indirect product of material changes. The soul stands related to the body as the bell of a clock to the works, and consciousness answers to the sound which the bell gives out when it is struck.

Thus far I have strictly confined myself to the problem with which I proposed to deal at starting—the automatism of brutes. The question is, I believe, a perfectly open one, and I feel happy in running no risk of either Papal or Presbyterian condemnation for the views which I have ventured to put forward. And there are so very few interesting questions which one is, at present, allowed to think out scientifically—to go as far as reason leads, and stop where evidence comes to an end—without speedily being deafened by the tattoo of "the drum ecclesiastic"—that I have luxuriated in my rare freedom, and would now willingly bring the disquisition to an end if I could hope that other people would go no father. Unfortunately, past experience debars me from entertaining any such hope, even if

that drum's discordant sound
Parading round and round and round,

were not, at present, as audible to me as it was to the mild poet who ventured to express his hatred of drums in general, in that well-known couplet.

It will be said, that I mean that the conclusions deduced from the study of the brutes are applicable to man, and that the logical consequences of such application are fatalism, materialism, and atheism—whereupon the drums will beat the *pas de charge.*

One does not do battle with drummers; but I venture to offer a few remarks for the calm consideration of thoughtful persons, untrammelled by foregone conclusions, unpledged to shore-up tottering dogmas, and anxious only to know the true bearings of the case.

It is quite true that, to the best of my judgment, the argumentation which applies to brutes holds equally good of men; and, therefore, that all states of consciousness in us, as in them, are immediately caused by molecular changes of the brain-substances. It seems to me that in men, as in brutes, there is no proof that any state of consciousness is the cause of change in the motion of the matter of the organism. If these positions are well based, it follows that our mental conditions are simply the symbols in consciousness of the changes which take place automatically in the organism; and that, to take an extreme illustration, the feeling we call volition is not the cause of a voluntary act, but the symbol of that state of the brain which is the immediate cause of that act. We are conscious automata, endowed with free will in the only intelligible sense of that much-abused term—inasmuch as in many respects we are able to do as we like—but nonetheless parts of the great series of causes and effects which, in unbroken continuity, composes that which is, and has been, and shall be—the sum of existence.

36 Mental Events

Donald Davidson

Mental events such as perceivings, rememberings, decisions, and actions resist capture in the nomological net of physical theory.[1] How can this fact be reconciled with the causal role of mental events in the physical world? Reconciling freedom with causal determinism is a special case of the problem if we suppose that causal determinism entails capture in, and freedom requires escape from, the nomological net. But the broader issue can remain alive even for someone who believes a correct analysis of free action reveals no conflict with determinism. *Autonomy* (freedom, self-rule) may or may not clash with determinism; *anomaly* (failure to fall under a law) is, it would seem, another matter.

I start from the assumption that both the causal dependence, and the anomalousness, of mental events are undeniable facts. My aim is therefore to explain, in the face of apparent difficulties, how this can be. I am in sympathy with Kant when he says,

> it is as impossible for the subtlest philosophy as for the commonest reasoning to argue freedom away. Philosophy must therefore assume that no true contradiction will be found between freedom and natural necessity in the same human actions, for it cannot give up the idea of nature any more than that of freedom. Hence even if we should never be able to conceive how freedom is possible, at least this apparent contradiction must be convincingly eradicated. For if the thought of freedom contradicts itself or nature ... it would have to be surrendered in competition with natural necessity.[2]

Generalize human actions to mental events, substitute anomaly for freedom, and this is a description of my problem. And of course the connection is closer, since Kant believed freedom entails anomaly.

Now let me try to formulate a little more carefully the "apparent contradiction" about mental events that I want to discuss and finally dissipate. It may be seen as stemming from three principles.

The first principle asserts that at least some mental events interact causally with physical events. (We could call this the Principle of Causal Interaction.) Thus for example if someone sank the *Bismarck*, then various mental events such as perceivings, nothings, calculations, judgments, decisions, intentional actions and changes of belief played a causal role in the sinking of the *Bismarck*. In particular, I would urge that the fact that someone sank the *Bismarck* entails that he moved his body in a way that was caused by mental events of certain sorts, and that this bodily movement in turn caused the *Bismarck* to sink.[3] Perception illustrates how causality may run from the physical to the mental: if a man perceives that a ship is approaching, then a ship approaching must have caused him to come to believe that a ship is approaching. (Nothing depends on accepting these as examples of causal interaction.)

Though perception and action provide the most obvious cases where mental and physical events interact causally, I think reasons could be given for the view that all mental events ultimately, perhaps through causal relations with other mental events, have causal intercourse with physical events. But if there are mental events that have no physical events as causes or effects, the argument will not touch them.

The second principle is that where there is causality, there must be a law: events related as cause and effect fall under strict deterministic laws. (We may term this the Principle of the Nomological Character of Causality.) This principle, like the first, will be treated here as an assumption, though I shall say something by way of interpretation.[4]

The third principle is that there are no strict deterministic laws on the basis of which mental events can be predicated and explained (the Anomalism of the Mental).

The paradox I wish to discuss arises for someone who is inclined to accept these three assumptions or principles, and who thinks they are inconsistent with one another. The inconsistency is not, of course, formal unless more premises are added. Nevertheless it is natural to reason that the first two principles, that of causal interaction, and that of the nomological character of causality, together imply that at least some mental events can be predicted and explained on the basis of laws, while the principle of the anomalism of the mental denies this. Many philosophers have accepted, with or without argument, the view that the three principles do lead to a contradiction. It seems to me, however, that all three principles are true, so that what must be done is to explain away the appearance of contradiction; essentially the Kantian line.

The rest of this paper falls into three parts. The first part describes a version of the identity theory of the mental and the physical that shows how the three principles may be reconciled. The second part argues that there cannot be strict psychophysical laws; this is not quite the principle of the anomalism of the mental, but on reasonable assumptions entails it. The last part tries to show that from the fact that there can be no strict psychophysical laws, and our other two principles, we can infer the truth of a version of the identity theory, that is, a theory that identifies at least some mental events with physical events. It is clear that this "proof" of the identity theory will be at best conditional, since two of its premises are unsupported, and the argument for the third may be found less than conclusive. But even someone unpersuaded of the truth of the premises may be interested to learn how they may be reconciled and that they serve to establish a version of the identity theory of the mental. Finally, if the argument is a good one, it should lay to rest the view, common to many friends and some foes of identity theories, that support for such theories can come only from the discovery of psychophysical laws.

I

The three principles will be shown consistent with one another by describing a view of the mental and the physical that contains no inner contradiction and that entails the three principles. According to this view, mental events are identical with physical events. Events are taken to be unrepeatable, dated individuals such as the particular eruption of a volcano, the (first) birth or death of a person, the playing of the 1968 World Series, or the historic utterance of the words, "You may fire when ready, Gridley." We can easily frame identity statements about individual events; examples (true or false) might be:

The death of Scott = the death of the author of *Waverley*;
The assassination of the Archduke Ferdinand = the event that started the First World War;
The eruption of Vesuvius in A.D. 79 = the cause of the destruction of Pompeii.

The theory under discussion is silent about processes, states, and attributes if these differ from individual events.

What does it mean to say that an event is mental or physical? One natural answer is that an event is physical if it is describable in a purely physical vocabulary, mental if describable in mental terms. But if this is taken to suggest that an event is physical, say, if some physical predicate is true of it, then there is the following difficulty. Assume that the predicate "*x* took place at Noosa Heads" belongs to the physical vocabulary; then so also must the predicate "*x* did not take place at Noosa Heads" belong to the physical vocabulary. But the predicate "*x* did or did not take place at Noosa Heads" is true of every event, whether mental or physical.[5] We might rule out predicates that are tautologically true of every event, but this will not help since every event is truly describable either by "*x* took place at Noosa Heads" or by "*x* did not take place at Noosa Heads." A different approach is needed.[6]

We may call those verbs mental that express propositional attitudes like believing, intending, desiring, hoping, knowing, perceiving, noticing, remembering, and so on. Such verbs are characterized by the fact that they sometimes feature in sentences with subjects that refer to persons, and are completed by embedded sentences in which the usual rules of substitution appear to break down. This criterion is not precise, since I do not want to include these verbs when they occur in contexts that are fully extensional ("He knows Paris," "He perceives the moon" may be cases), nor exclude them whenever they are not followed by embedded sentences. An alternative characterization of the desired class of mental verbs might be that they are psychological verbs as used when they create apparently nonextensional contexts.

Let us call a description of the form "the event that is M" or an open sentence of the form "event *x* is M" a *mental description* or a *mental open sentence* if and only if the expression that replaces "M" contains at least one mental verb essentially. (Essentially, so as to rule out cases where the description or open sentence is logically equivalent to one not containing mental vocabulary.) Now we may say that an event is mental if and only if it has a mental description, or (the description operator not being primitive) if there is a mental open sentence true of that event alone. Physical events are those picked out by descriptions or open sentences that contain only the physical vocabulary essentially. It is less important to characterize a physical vocabulary because relative to the mental it is, so to speak, recessive in determining whether a description is mental or physical. (There will be some comments presently on the nature of a physical vocabulary, but these comments will fall far short of providing a criterion.)

On the proposed test of the mental, the distinguishing feature of the mental is not that it is private, subjective, or immaterial, but that it exhibits what Brentano called intentionality. Thus intentional actions are clearly included in the realm of the mental along with thoughts, hopes, and regrets (or the events tied to these). What may seem doubtful is whether the criterion will include events that have often been considered paradigmatic of the mental. Is it obvious, for example, that feeling a pain or seeing an afterimage will count as mental? Sentences that report such events seem free from taint of nonextensionality, and the same should be true of reports of raw feels, sense data, and other uninterpreted sensations, if there are any.

However, the criterion actually covers not only the havings of pains and afterimages, but much more besides. Take some event one would intuitively accept as physical, let's say the collision of two stars in distant space. There must be a purely physical predicate "P*x*" true of this collision, and of others, but true of only this one at the time it occurred. This particular time, though, may be pinpointed as the same time that Jones notices that a pencil starts to roll across his desk. The distant stellar collision is thus *the* event *x* such that P*x* and *x* is simultaneous with Jones' noticing that a pencil starts to roll across his desk. The collision has now been picked out by a mental description and must be counted as a mental event.

This strategy will probably work to show every event to be mental; we have obviously failed to capture the intuitive concept of the mental. It would be instructive to try to mend this trouble, but it is not necessary for present purposes. We can afford Spinozistic extravagance with the mental since accidental inclusions can only strengthen the hypothesis that all mental events are identical with physical events. What would matter would be failure to include bona fide mental events, but of this there seems to be no danger.

I want to describe, and presently to argue for, a version of the identity theory that denies that there can be strict laws connecting the mental and the physical. The very possibility of such a theory is easily obscured by the way in which identity theories are commonly defended and attacked. Charles Taylor, for example, agrees with protagonists of identity theories that the sole "ground" for accepting such theories is the supposition that correlations or laws can be established linking events described as mental with events described as physical. He says, "It is easy to see why this is so: unless a given mental event is invariably accompanied by a given, say, brain process, there is no ground for even mooting a general identity between the two."[7] Taylor goes on (correctly, I think) to allow that there may be identity without correlating laws, but my present interest is in noticing the invitation to confusion in the statement just quoted. What can "a given mental event" mean here? Not a particular, dated, event, for it would not make sense to speak of an individual event being "invariably accompanied" by another. Taylor is evidently thinking of events of a given *kind*. But if the only identities are of kinds of events, the identity theory presupposes correlating laws.

One finds the same tendency to build laws into the statement of the identity theory in these typical remarks:

> When I say that a sensation is a brain process or that lightning is an electrical discharge, I am using "is" in the sense of strict identity ... there are not two things: a flash of lightning and an electrical discharge. There is one thing, a flash of lightning, which is described scientifically as an electrical discharge to the earth from a cloud of ionized water molecules.[8]

The last sentence of this quotation is perhaps to be understood as saying that for every lightning flash there exists an electrical discharge to the earth from a cloud of ionized water molecules with which it is identical. Here we have a honest ontology of individual events and can make literal sense of identity. We can also see how there could be identities without correlating laws. It is possible, however, to have an ontology of events with the conditions of individuation specified in such a way that any identity implies a correlating law. Kim, for example, suggests that F*a* and G*b* "describe or refer to the same event" if and only if $a = b$ and the property of being F = the property of being G. The identity of the properties in turn entails that $(x)(Fx \leftrightarrow Gx)$.[9] No wonder Kim says:

> If pain is identical with brain state *B*, there must be a concomitance between occurrences of pain and occurrences of brain state *B*.... Thus, a necessary condition of the pain-brain state *B* identity is that the two expressions "being in pain" and "being in brain state *B*" have the same extension.... There is no conceivable observation that would confirm or refute the identity but not the associated correlation.[10]

It may make the situation clearer to give a fourfold classification of theories of the relation between mental and physical events that emphasizes the independence of claims about laws and claims of identity. On the one hand there are those who assert, and those who deny, the existence of psychophysical laws; on the other hand there are those who say mental events are identical with physical and those who deny this. Theories are thus divided into four sorts: *Nomological monism*, which affirms that there are correlating laws and that the events correlated are one (materialists belong in this category); *nomological dualism*, which comprises various forms of parallelism, interactionism, and epiphenomenalism; *anomalous dualism*, which combines ontological dualism with the general failure of laws correlating the mental and the physical (Cartesianism). And finally there is *anomalous monism*, which classifies the position I wish to occupy.[11]

Anomalous monism resembles materialism in its claim that all events are physical, but rejects the thesis, usually considered essential to materialism, that mental phenomena can be given purely physical explanations. Anomalous monism shows an ontological bias only in that it allows the possibility that not all events are mental, while insisting that all events are physical. Such a bland monism, unbuttressed by correlating laws or conceptual economies, does not seem to merit the term "reductionism"; in any case it is not apt to inspire the nothing-but reflex ("Conceiving the *Art of the Fugue* was nothing but a complex neural event," and so forth).

Although the position I describe denies there are psychophysical laws, it is consistent with the view that mental characteristics are in some sense dependent, or supervenient, on physical characteristics. Such supervenience might be taken to mean that there cannot be two events alike in all physical respects but differing in some mental respect, or that an object cannot alter in some mental respect without altering in some physical respect. Dependence or supervenience of this kind does not entail reducibility through law or definition: if it did, we could reduce moral properties to descriptive, and this there is good reason to *believe* cannot be done; and we might be able to reduce truth in a formal system to syntactical properties, and this we *know* cannot in general be done.

This last example is in useful analogy with the sort of lawless monism under consideration. Think of the physical vocabulary as the entire vocabulary of some language L with resources adequate to express a certain amount of mathematics, and its own syntax. L′ is L augmented with the truth predicate "true-in-L," which is "mental." In L (and hence L′) it is possible to pick out, with a definite description or open sentence, each sentence in the extension of the truth predicate, but if L is consistent there exists no predicate of syntax (of the "physical" vocabulary), no matter how complex, that applies to all and only the true sentences of L. There can be no "psychophysical law" in the form of a biconditional, "(x) (x is true-in-L if and only if x is ϕ)" where "ϕ" is replaced by a "physical" predicate (a predicate of L). Similarly, we can pick out each mental event using the physical vocabulary alone, but no purely physical predicate, no matter how complex, has, as a matter of law, the same extension as a mental predicate.

It should now be evident how anomalous monism reconciles the three original principles. Causality and identity are relations between individual events no matter how described. But laws are linguistic; and so events can instantiate laws, and hence be explained or predicted in the light of laws, only as those events are described in one or another way. The principle of causal interaction deals with events in extension and is therefore blind to the mental–physical dichotomy. The principle of the anomalism of the mental concerns events described as mental, for events are mental only as described. The principle of the nomological character of causality must be read carefully: it says that when events are related as cause and effect, they have descriptions that instantiate a law. It does not say that every true singular statement of causality instantiates a law.[12]

II

The analogy just bruited, between the place of the mental amid the physical, and the place of the semantical in a world of syntax, should not be strained. Tarski proved that a consistent language cannot (under some natural assumptions) contain an open sentence "Fx" true of all and only the true sentences of that language. If our analogy were pressed, then we would expect a proof that there can be no physical open sentence "Px" true of all and only the events having some mental property. In fact, however, nothing I can say about the irreducibility of the mental deserves to be called a proof; and the kind of irreducibility is different. For if anomalous monism is correct, not only can every mental event be uniquely singled out using only physical concepts, but since the number of events that falls under each mental predicate may, for all we know, be finite, there may well exist a physical open sentence coextensive with each mental predicate, though to construct it might involve the tedium of a lengthy and uninstructive alternation. Indeed, even if finitude is not assumed, there seems no compelling reason to deny that there could be coextensive predicates, one mental and one physical.

The thesis is rather that the mental is nomologically irreducible: there may be *true* general statements relating the mental and the physical, statements that have the logical form of a law; but they are not *lawlike* (in a strong sense to be described). If by absurdly remote chance we were to stumble on a nonstochastic true psychophysical generalization, we would have no reason to believe it more than roughly true.

Do we, by declaring that there are no (strict) psychophysical laws, poach on the empirical preserves of science—a form of *hubris* against which philosophers are often warned? Of course, to judge a statement lawlike or illegal is not to decide its truth outright; relative to the acceptance of a general statement on the basis of instances, ruling it lawlike must be a priori. But such relative apriorism does not in itself justify philosophy, for in general the grounds for deciding to trust a statement on the basis of its instances will in turn be governed by theoretical and empirical concerns not to be distinguished from those of science. If the case of supposed laws linking the mental and the physical is different, it can only be because to allow the possibility of such laws would amount to changing the subject. By changing the subject I mean here: deciding not to accept the criterion of the mental in terms of the vocabulary of the propositional attitudes. This short answer cannot prevent further ramifications of the problem, however, for there is no clear line between changing the subject and changing what one says on an old subject, which is to admit, in the present context at least, that there is no clear line between philosophy and science. Where there are no fixed boundaries only the timid never risk trespass.

It will sharpen our appreciation of the anomological character of mental-physical generalizations to consider a related matter, the failure of definitional behaviorism. Why are we willing (as I assume we are) to abandon the attempt to give explicit definitions of mental concepts in terms of behavioral ones? Not, surely, just because all actual tries are conspicuously inadequate. Rather it is because we are persuaded, as we are in the case of so many other forms of definitional reductionism (naturalism in ethics, instrumentalism and operationalism in the sciences, the causal theory of meaning, phenomenalism, and so on—the catalogue of philosophy's defeats), that there is system in the failures. Suppose we try to say, not using any mental concepts, what it is for a man to believe there is life on Mars. One line we could take is this: when a certain sound is produced in the man's presence ("Is there life on Mars?") he produces another ("Yes"). But of course this shows he believes there is life on Mars only if he understands English, his production of the sound was intentional, and was a response to the sounds as meaning something in English; and so on. For each discovered deficiency, we add a new proviso. Yet no matter how we patch and fit the nonmental conditions, we always find the need for an additional condition (provided he *notices*, *understands*, etc.) that is mental in character.[13]

A striking feature of attempts at definitional reduction is how little seems to hinge on the question of synonymy between definiens and definiendum. Of course, by imagining counterexamples we do discredit claims of synonymy. But the pattern of failure prompts a stronger conclusion: if we were to find an open sentence couched in behavioral terms and exactly coextensive with some mental predicate, nothing could reasonably persuade us that we had found it. We know too much about thought and behavior to trust exact and universal statements linking them. Beliefs and desires issue in behavior only as modified and mediated by further beliefs and desires, attitudes and attendings, without limit. Clearly this holism of the mental realm is a clue both to the autonomy and to the anomalous character of the mental.

These remarks apropos definitional behaviorism provide at best hints of why we should not expect nomological connections between the mental and the physical. The central case invites further consideration.

Lawlike statements are general statements that support counterfactual and subjunctive claims, and are supported by their instances. There is (in my view) no nonquestionbegging criterion of the lawlike, which is not to say there are no reasons in particular cases for a judgment. Lawlikeness is a matter of degree, which is not to deny that there may be cases beyond debate. And within limits set by the conditions of communication, there is room for much variation between individuals in the pattern of statements to which various degrees of nomologicality are assigned. In all these respects, nomologicality is much like analyticity, as one might expect since both are linked to meaning.

"All emeralds are green" is lawlike in that its instances confirm it, but "all emeralds are grue" is not, for "grue" means "observed before time *t* and green, otherwise blue," and if our observations were all made before *t* and uniformly revealed green emeralds, this would not be a reason to expect other emeralds to be blue. Nelson Goodman has suggested that this shows that some predicates, "grue" for example, are unsuited to laws (and thus a criterion of suitable predicates could lead to a criterion of the lawlike). But it seems to me the anomalous character of "All emeralds are grue" shows only that the predicates "is an emerald" and "is grue" are not suited to one another: grueness is not an inductive property of emeralds. Grueness *is* however an inductive property of entities of other sorts, for instance of emerires. (Something is an emerire if it is examined before *t* and is an emerald, and otherwise is a sapphire.) Not only is "All emerires are grue" entailed by the conjunction of the lawlike statements "All emeralds are green" and "All sapphires are blue," but there is no reason, as far as I can see, to reject the deliverance of intuition, that it is itself lawlike.[14] Nomological statements bring together predicates that we know a priori are made for each other—know, that is, independently of knowing whether the evidence supports a connection between them. "Blue," "red," and "green" are made for emeralds, sapphires, and roses; "grue," "bleen," and "gred" are made for sapphalds, emerires, and emeroses.

The direction in which the discussion seems headed is this: mental and physical predicates are not made for one another. In point of lawlikeness, psychophysical statements are more like "All emeralds are grue" than like "All emeralds are green."

Before this claim is plausible, it must be seriously modified. The fact that emeralds examined before *t* are grue not only is no reason to believe all emeralds are grue; it is not even a reason (if we know the time) to believe *any* unobserved emeralds are grue. But if an event of a certain mental sort has usually been accompanied by an event of a certain physical sort, this often is a good reason to expect other cases to follow suit roughly in proportion. The generalizations that embody such practical wisdom are assumed to be only roughly true, or they are explicitly stated in probabilistic terms, or they are insulated from counterexample by generous escape clauses. Their importance lies mainly in the support they lend singular causal claims and related explanations of particular events. The support derives from the fact that such a generalization, however crude and vague, may provide good reason to believe that underlying the particular case there is a regularity that could be formulated sharply and without caveat.

In our daily traffic with events and actions that must be foreseen or understood, we perforce make use of the sketchy summary generalization, for we do not know a more accurate law, or if we do, we lack a description of the particular events in which we are interested that would show the relevance of the law. But there is an important distinction to be made within the category of the rude rule of thumb. On the one hand, there are generalizations whose positive instances give us reason to believe the generalization itself could be improved by adding further provisos and conditions stated in the same general vocabulary as the original generalization. Such a generalization points to the form and vocabulary of the finished law: we may say that it is a *homonomic* generalization. On the other hand there are generalizations which when instantiated may give us reason to believe there is a precise law at work, but one that can be stated only by shifting to a different vocabulary. We may call such generalizations *heteronomic*.

I suppose most of our practical lore (and science) is heteronomic. This is because a law can hope to be precise, explicit, and as exceptionless as possible only if it draws its concepts from a comprehensive closed theory. This ideal theory may or may not be deterministic, but it is if any true theory is. Within the physical sciences we do find homonomic generalizations, generalizations such that if the evidence supports them, we then have reason to believe they may be sharpened indefinitely by drawing upon further physical concepts: there is a theoretical asymptote of perfect coherence with all the evidence, perfect predictability (under the terms of the system), total explanation (again under the terms of the system). Or perhaps the ultimate theory is probabilistic, and the asymptote is less than perfection; but in that case there will be no better to be had.

Confidence that a statement is homonomic, correctible within its own conceptual domain, demands that it draw its concepts from a theory with strong constitutive elements. Here is the simplest possible illustration; if the lesson carries, it will be obvious that the simplification could be mended.

The measurement of length, weight, temperature, or time depends (among many other things, of course) on the existence in each case of a two-place relation that is transitive and asymmetric: warmer than, later than, heavier than, and so forth. Let us take the relation *longer than* as our example. The law or postulate of transitivity is this:

(L) $L(x, y)$ and $L(y, z) \rightarrow L(x, z)$

Unless this law (or some sophisticated variant) holds, we cannot easily make sense of the concept of length. There will be no way of assigning numbers to register even so much as ranking in length, let alone the more powerful demands of measurement on a ratio scale. And this remark goes not only for any three items directly involved in an intransitivity: it is easy to show (given a few more assumptions essential to measurement of length) that there is no consistent assignment of a ranking to any item unless (L) holds in full generality.

Clearly (L) alone cannot exhaust the import of "longer than"—otherwise it would not differ from "warmer than" or "later than." We must suppose there is some empirical content, however difficult to formulate in the available vocabulary, that distinguishes "longer than" from the other two-place transitive predicates of measurement and on the basis of which we may assert that one thing is longer than another. Imagine this empirical content to be partly given by the predicate "$O(x, y)$." So we have this "meaning postulate":

(M) $L(x, y) \rightarrow O(x, y)$

that partly interprets (L). But now (L) and (M) together yield an empirical theory of great strength, for together they entail that there do not exist three objects *a*, *b*, and *c* such that $O(a,b)$, $O(b,c)$, and $O(c,a)$. Yet what is to prevent this happening if "$O(x, y)$" is a predicate we can ever, with confidence, apply? Suppose we *think* we observe an intransitive triad; what do we say? We could count (L) false, but then we would have no application for the concept of length. We could say (M) gives a wrong test for length; but then it is unclear what we thought was the *content* of the idea of one thing being longer than another. Or we could say that the objects under observation are not, as the theory requires, *rigid* objects. It is a mistake to think we are forced to accept some one of these answers. Concepts such as that of length are sustained in equilibrium by a number of conceptual pressures, and theories of fundamental measurement are distorted if we force the decision, among such principles as (L) and (M): analytic or synthetic. It is better to say the whole set of axioms, laws, or postulates for the measurement of length is partly constitutive of the idea of a system of macroscopic, rigid, physical objects. I suggest that the existence of lawlike statements in physical science depends upon the existence of constitutive (or synthetic a priori) laws like those of the measurement of length within the same conceptual domain.

Just as we cannot intelligibly assign a length to any object unless a comprehensive theory holds of objects of that sort, we cannot intelligibly attribute any propositional attitude to an agent except within the framework of a viable theory of his beliefs, desires, intentions, and decisions.

There is no assigning beliefs to a person one by one on the basis of his verbal behavior, his choices, or other local signs no matter how plain and evident, for we make sense of particular beliefs only as they cohere with other beliefs, with preferences, with intentions, hopes, fears, expectations, and the rest. It is not merely, as with the measurement of length, that each case tests a theory and depends upon it, but that the content of a propositional attitude derives from its place in the pattern.

Crediting people with a large degree of consistency cannot be counted mere charity: it is unavoidable if we are to be in a position to accuse them meaningfully of error and some degree of irrationality. Global confusion, like universal mistake, is unthinkable, not because imagination boggles, but because too much confusion leaves nothing to be confused about and massive error erodes the background of true belief against which alone failure can be construed. To appreciate the limits to the kind and amount of blunder and bad thinking we can intelligibly pin on others is to see once more the inseparability of the question what concepts a person commands and the question what he does with those concepts in the way of belief, desire, and intention. To the extent that we fail to discover a coherent and plausible pattern in the attitudes and actions of others we simply forego the chance of treating them as persons.

The problem is not bypassed but given center stage by appeal to explicit speech behavior. For we could not begin to decode a man's sayings if we could not make out his attitudes towards his sentences, such as holding, wishing, or wanting them to be true. Beginning from these attitudes, we must work out a theory of what he means, thus simultaneously giving content to his attitudes and to his words. In our need to make him make sense, we will try for a theory that finds him consistent, a believer of truths, and a lover of the good (all by our own lights, it goes without saying). Life being what it is, there will be no simple theory that fully meets these demands. Many theories will effect a more or less acceptable compromise, and between these theories there may be no objective grounds for choice.

The heteronomic character of general statements linking the mental and the physical traces back to this central role of translation in the description of all propositional attitudes, and to the indeterminacy of translation.[15] There are no strict psychophysical laws because of the disparate commitments of the mental and physical schemes. It is a feature of physical reality that physical change can be explained by laws that connect it with other changes and conditions physically described. It is a feature of the mental that the attribution of mental phenomena must be responsible to the background of reasons, beliefs, and intentions of the individual. There cannot be tight connections between the realms if each is to retain allegiance to its proper source of evidence. The nomological irreducibility of the mental does not derive merely from the seamless nature of the world of thought, preference and intention, for such interdependence is common to physical theory, and is compatible with there being a single right way of interpreting a man's attitudes without relativization to a scheme of translation. Nor is the irreducibility due simply to the possibility of many equally eligible schemes, for this is compatible with an arbitrary choice of one scheme relative to which assignments of mental traits are made. The point is rather that when we use the concepts of belief, desire and the rest, we must stand prepared, as the evidence accumulates, to adjust our theory in the light of considerations of overall cogency: the constitutive ideal of rationality partly controls each phase in the evolution of what must be an evolving theory. An arbitrary choice of translation scheme would preclude such opportunistic tempering of theory; put differently, a right arbitrary choice of a translation manual would be of a manual acceptable in the light of all possible evidence, and this a choice we cannot make. We must conclude, I think, that nomological slack between the mental and the physical is essential as long as we conceive of man as a rational animal.

III

The gist of the foregoing discussion, as well as its conclusion, will be familiar. That there is a categorial difference between the mental and the physical is a commonplace. It may seem odd that I say nothing of the supposed privacy of the mental, or the special authority an agent has with respect to his own propositional attitudes, but this appearance of novelty would fade if we were to investigate in more detail the grounds for accepting a scheme of translation. The step from the categorial difference between the mental and the physical to the impossibility of strict laws relating them is less common, but certainly not new. If there is a surprise, then, it will be to find the lawlessness of the mental serving to help establish the identity of the mental with that paradigm of the lawlike, the physical.

The reasoning is this. We are assuming, under the Principle of the Causal Dependence of the Mental, that some mental events at least are causes or effects of physical events; the argument applies only to these. A second Principle (of the Nomological Character of Causality) says that each true singular causal statement is backed by a strict law connecting events of kinds to which the events mentioned as cause and effect belong. Where there are rough, but homonomic, laws, there are laws drawing on concepts from the same conceptual domain and upon which there is no improving in point of precision and comprehensiveness. We urged in the last section that such laws occur in the physical sciences. Physical theory promises to provide a comprehensive closed system guaranteed to yield a standardized, unique description of every physical event couched in a vocabulary amenable to law.

It is not plausible that mental concepts alone can provide such a framework, simply because the mental does not, by our first principle, constitute a closed system. Too much happens to affect the mental that is not itself a systematic part of the mental. But if we combine this observation with the conclusion that no psychophysical statement is, or can be built into, a strict law, we have the Principle of the Anomalism of the Mental: there are no strict laws at all on the basis of which we can predict and explain mental phenomena.

The demonstration of identity follows easily. Suppose *m*, a mental event, caused *p*, a physical event; then under some description *m* and *p* instantiate a strict law. This law can only be physical, according to the previous paragraph. But if *m* falls under a physical law, it has a physical description; which is to say it is a physical event. An analogous argument works when a physical event causes a mental event. So every mental event that is causally related to a physical event is a physical event. In order to establish anomalous monism in full generality it would be sufficient to show that every mental event is cause or effect of some physical event; I shall not attempt this.

If one event causes another, there is a strict law which those events instantiate when properly described. But it is possible (and typical) to know of the singular causal relation without knowing the law or the relevant descriptions. Knowledge requires reasons, but these are available in the form of rough heteronomic generalizations, which are lawlike in that instances make it reasonable to expect other instances to follow suit without being lawlike in the sense of being indefinitely refinable. Applying these facts to knowledge of identities, we see that it is possible to know that a mental event is identical with some physical event without knowing which one (in the sense of being able to give it a unique physical description that brings it under a relevant law). Even if someone knew the entire physical history of the world, and every mental event were identical with a physical, it would not follow that he could predict or explain a single mental event (so described, of course).

Two features of mental events in their relation to the physical—causal dependence and nomological independence—combine, then, to dissolve what has often seemed a paradox, the efficacy of thought and purpose in the material world, and their freedom from law. When we portray events as perceivings, rememberings, decisions and actions, we necessarily locate them amid physical happenings through the relation of cause and effect; but that same mode of portrayal insulates mental events, as long as we do not change the idiom, from the strict laws that can in principle be called upon to explain and predict physical phenomena.

Mental events as a class cannot be explained by physical science; particular mental events can when we know particular identities. But the explanations of mental events in which we are typically interested relate them to other mental events and conditions. We explain a man's free actions, for example, by appeal to his desires, habits, knowledge and perceptions. Such accounts of intentional behavior operate in a conceptual framework removed from the direct reach of physical law by describing both cause and effect, reason and action, as aspects of a portrait of a human agent. The anomalism of the mental is thus a necessary condition for viewing action as autonomous. I conclude with a second passage from Kant:

It is an indispensable problem of speculative philosophy to show that its illusion respecting the contradiction rests on this, that we think of man in a different sense and relation when we call him free, and when we regard him as subject to the laws of nature.... It must therefore show that not only can both of these very well co-exist, but that both must be thought *as necessarily united* in the same subject....[16]

Notes

1. I was helped and influenced by Daniel Bennett, Sue Larson, and Richard Rorty, who are not responsible for the result. My research was supported by the National Science Foundation and the Center for Advanced Study in the Behavioral Sciences.

2. *Fundamental Principles of the Metaphysics of Morals*, trans. T. K. Abbott (London, 1909), pp. 75–76.

3. These claims are defended in my "Actions, Reasons and Causes," *Journal of Philosophy*, LX (1963), pp. 685–700 and in "Agency," a paper forthcoming in the proceedings of the November, 1968, colloquium on Agent, Action, and Reason at the University of Western Ontario, London, Canada.

4. In "Causal Relations," *Journal of Philosophy*, LXIV (1967), pp. 691–703, I elaborate on the view of causality assumed here. The stipulation that the laws be deterministic is stronger than required by the reasoning, and will be relaxed.

5. The point depends on assuming that mental events may intelligibly be said to have a location; but it is an assumption that must be true if an identity theory is, and here I am not trying to prove the theory but to formulate it.

6. I am indebted to Lee Bowie for emphasizing this difficulty.

7. Charles Taylor, "Mind–Body Identity, a Side Issue?" *Philosophical Review*, LXXVI (1967), p. 202.

8. J. J. C. Smart, "Sensations and Brain Processes," *Philosophical Review*, LXVIII (1959), pp. 141–56. The quoted passages are on pp. 163–165 of the reprinted version in *The Philosophy of Mind*, ed. V. C. Chappell (Englewood Cliffs, N. J., 1962). For another example, see David K. Lewis, "An Argument for the Identity Theory," *Journal of Philosophy*, LXIII (1966), pp. 17–25. Here the assumption is made explicit when Lewis takes events as universals (p. 17, footnotes 1 and 2). I do not suggest that Smart and Lewis are confused, only that their way of stating the identity theory tends to obscure the distinction between particular events and kinds of events on which the formulation of my theory depends.

9. Jaegwon Kim, "On the Psycho-Physical Identity Theory," *American Philosophical Quarterly*, III (1966), p. 231.

10. Ibid., pp. 227–228. Richard Brandt and Jaegwon Kim propose roughly the same criterion in "The Logic of the Identity Theory," *Journal of Philosophy*, LIV (1967), pp. 515–537. They remark that on their conception of event identity, the identity theory "makes a stronger claim than merely that there is a pervasive phenomenal-physical correlation" (p. 518). I do not discuss the stronger claim.

11. Anomalous monism is more or less explicitly recognized as a possible position by Herbert Feigl, "The 'Mental' and the 'Physical,'" in *Concepts, Theories and the Mind–Body Problem*, vol. II,

Minnesota Studies in the Philosophy of Science (Minneapolis, 1958); Sydney Shoemaker, "Ziff's Other Minds," *Journal of Philosophy*, LXII (1965), pp. 589; David Randall Luce, "Mind–Body Identity and Psycho-Physical Correlation," *Philosophical Studies*, XVII (1966), pp. 1–7; Charles Taylor, op. cit., p. 207. Something like my position is tentatively accepted by Thomas Nagel, "Physicalism," *Philosophical Review*, LXXIV (1965), pp. 339–356, and briefly endorsed by P. F. Strawson in *Freedom and the Will*, ed. D. F. Pears (London, 1963), pp. 63–67.

12. The point that substitutivity of identity fails in the context of explanation is made in connection with the present subject by Norman Malcolm, "Scientific Materialism and the Identity Theory," *Dialogue*, III (1964–65), pp. 123–124. See also my "Actions, Reasons and Causes," *Journal of Philosophy*, LX (1963), pp. 696–699 and "The Individuation of Events" in *Essays in Honor of Carl G. Hempel*, ed. N. Rescher, et al. (Dordrecht, 1969).

13. The theme is developed in Roderick Chisholm, *Perceiving* (Ithaca, New York, 1957), chap. 11.

14. This view is accepted by Richard C. Jeffrey, "Goodman's Query," *Journal of Philosophy*, LXII (1966), p. 286 ff., John R. Wallace, "Goodman, Logic, Induction," same journal and issue, p. 318, and John M. Vickers, "Characteristics of Projectible Predicates," *Journal of Philosophy*, LXIV (1967), p. 285. On pp. 328–329 and 286–287 of these journal issues respectively Goodman disputes the lawlikeness of statements like "All emerires are grue." I cannot see, however, that he meets the point of my "Emeroses by Other Names," *Journal of Philosophy*, LXIII (1966), pp. 778–780.

15. The influence of W. V. Quine's doctrine of the indeterminacy of translation, as in chap. 2 of *Word and Object* (MIT Press: Cambridge, Mass., 1960), is, I hope, obvious. In §45 Quine develops the connection between translation and the propositional attitudes, and remarks that "Brentano's thesis of the irreducibility of intentional idioms is of a piece with the thesis of indeterminacy of translation" (p. 221).

16. Op. cit., p. 76.

37 Mind Matters

Ernest LePore and Barry Loewer

Who knows what I want to do?... Isn't it all a question of brain chemistry, signals going back and forth, electrical energy in the cortex?... Some minor little activity takes place somewhere in this unimportant place in one of the brain hemispheres and suddenly I want to go to Montana or I don't want to go to Montana. Maybe it's just an accidental flash in the medulla and suddenly there I am in Montana and I find out I really didn't want to go there in the first place ... It's all this activity in the brain and you don't know what's you as a person and what's the brain and what's some neuron that just happens to fire or just happens to misfire ...

—Don DeLillo, *White Noise*

Consider the following, admittedly imprecise claims:

(1) The mental and the physical are distinct.

(2) The mental and the physical causally interact.

(3) The physical is causally closed.

Much can be said in favor of each of these. In support of (1), we can point to the failure of attempts to reduce the phenomenal and the intentional to the physical, and to arguments from Descartes to Donald Davidson which purport to show that such reductions are, in principle, impossible. (2) is supported by our everyday experience and by various theories of perception and action. (3) means that every physical event or fact has, in its causal history, only physical events and facts. Both (3) and its cousin:

(3′) All causation is reducible to, or grounded in, physical causation,

where "grounded" means, roughly, that causal relations supervene on noncausal physical facts and laws, have seemed to many philosophers to be supported by the development of the sciences.

The trouble is that it seems (1), (2), and (3) are incompatible. To be a bit more definite, consider their application to events. (1) then says that no mental event is a physical event; (2), that some mental events cause physical events and vice versa; and (3), that all the causes of physical events are physical events. The inconsistency is obvious. If mental events are distinct from physical events and sometimes cause them, then obviously the physical is not causally closed. The dilemma posed by the plausibility of each of these claims and by their apparent incompatibility is, of course, the mind–body problem.[1]

Our primary concern here is how Davidson's[2] account of the relation between the mental and the physical, which he calls "anomalous monism" (*AM*), attempts to resolve the dilemma. AM consists of the following three theses:

(4) There are no strict psychophysical or psychological laws and in fact all strict laws are expressed in a purely physical vocabulary (the anomalousness of the mental).

(5) Mental events causally interact with physical events.

(6) Event *c* causes event *e* only if there is a strict causal law which subsumes *c* and *e* (entails that *c* causes *e*) (the nomological character of causality).

(4) is a version of (1). It is commonly held that a property expressed by *M* is reducible to a property expressed by *P* (where *M* and *P* are not analytically connected) only if there is an exceptionless bridge law that links them.[3] So it follows from (4) that (intentional) mental and physical properties are distinct.[4] (6) says that *c* causes *e* only if there are singular descriptions *D* of *c* and *D′* of *e* and a strict causal law *L* such that *L* and "*D* occurred" entail "*D* caused *D′*" ("Causal Relations," p. 158). (6) and the second part of (4) entail that physical events have only physical causes and that all event causation is physically grounded.[5]

The notion of a law being *strict* figures prominently both in Davidson's affirmation of the distinctness of the mental and the physical and in his account of causation. Davidson's notion of a strict law is best explained by contrast with nonstrict laws. A nonstrict law is a generalization that contains a *ceteris paribus* qualifier that specifies that the law holds under "normal or ideal conditions," where the relevant notions of normal or ideal are specified by the theoretical context of the law. The generalizations one finds in the special sciences are mostly of this kind. In contrast, a strict law is one that contains no *ceteris paribus* qualifiers; it is exceptionless not just *de facto* but as a matter of law. A nonstrict law may be improved upon by explicitly including some of its *ceteris paribus* conditions in its antecedents. Davidson's view is that psychophysical laws of the form—whenever a person is in physical state *P*, then he is in intentional state *M*—are *essentially* nonstrict. That is, no matter how many conditions are added to the antecedent, short of trivializing the generalization, it will not be strict.[6]

Given the parallel between (4)–(6) and (1)–(3), it may seem that the former are also incompatible. But they are not. Davidson shows that they all can be true if (and only if) mental events are identical to physical events ("Mental Events," p. 215). Let us say that an event *e* is a physical event just in case *e* satisfies a basic physical predicate (that is, a physical predicate appearing in a strict law). Since only physical predicates (or predicates expressing properties reducible to basic physical properties) appear in strict laws, it follows that every event that enters into causal relations satisfies a basic physical predicate. So, those mental events which enter into causal relations are also physical events.

AM is committed only to a partial endorsement of (1). The mental and physical are distinct insofar as they are not linked by strict law—mental properties are not reducible to physical properties—but they are not distinct insofar as mental events are physical events. This being so, one might wonder whether AM also only partially endorses claims (2) and (3). In fact, Davidson's views have been criticized precisely on the point of (2). Ernest Sosa[7] writes: "I conclude that … anomalous monism is [not] really compatible with the full content of our deep and firm conviction that the mind and body each acts causally on the other" (*ibid.*, p. 278). Ted Honderich[8] goes even further charging that AM is really a form of epiphenomenalism: "I went on … to claim that [AM] was epiphenomenalist; it did not make the mental as mental an ineliminable part of the explanation of actions" (*ibid.*, p. 88).

If Honderich means that Davidson's views are committed to epiphenomenalism with respect to mental events, he is clearly mistaken, since, according to AM, mental events do cause other events. They *are* physical events and so can, like any event, have consequences. It is rather that, on AM, as he puts it, the mental *as* mental—some writers use the expressions "*qua* mental" and "*in virtue of being* mental"—is causally irrelevant. In defense of Davidson, one might reply that, although it is correct to say it is not *c* as mental that causes *e*, this has nothing to do with any epiphenomenalism on the part of the mental, but simply reflects the fact that it is not events *as* mental or *as* physical or *as* anything else which cause other events. Causation is a relation between events, not between events *as Fs*. It seems to Davidson's critics, however, to make sense to distinguish some features of an event as causally relevant and others as causally irrelevant. It is this distinction which underlies the locution that it is *c as F* (not *as F′*) that causes *e* (to be *G*). Sosa and Fred Dretske[9] illustrate their understanding of the distinction in the following passages, respectively:

> A gun goes off, a shot is fired and it kills someone. The loud noise is the shot. Thus if the victim is killed by the shot it is the loud noise that kills the victim.... In a certain sense the victim is killed by the loud noise. Not by the loud noise as a loud noise but only by the loud noise as a shot, or the like.... The loudness of the shot has no causal relevance to the death of the victim. Had the gun been equipped with a silencer the shot would have killed the victim just the same. (*op. cit.*, pp. 277/8)

> Meaningful sounds, if they occur at the right pitch and amplitude, can shatter glass, but the fact that these sounds have a meaning is irrelevant to their having this effect. The glass would shatter if the sounds meant something completely different or if they meant nothing at all. (*op. cit.*)

Sosa, Honderich, Jaegwon Kim, Dretske, (among others)[10] think that, once we have made the distinction between the causally relevant and irrelevant features of an event, we will see that it is a consequence of AM that mental features are never causally relevant. Why is the causal irrelevance of the mental supposed to be entailed by AM? Kim[11] reasons as follows:

> Consider Davidson's account: whether or not a given event had a mental description ... seems entirely irrelevant to what causal relations it enters into. Its causal powers are wholly determined by the physical description or characteristic that holds for it; for it is under its physical description that it may be subsumed under a causal law. And Davidson explicitly denies any possibility of a nomological connection between an event's mental description and its physical description that could bring the mental into the causal picture. (*ibid.*, p. 267)

The argument is that, since, according to AM, *c* causes *e* only if there is a strict law that subsumes *c* and *e* and since strict laws contain only physical (never mental) predicates, it follows that the mental features of events *c* and *e* are irrelevant to whether they are causally connected. The physical features of events suffice to fix, given the strict laws, *all* causal connections. Mental features neither suffice nor are required to fix causal connections. The argument is powerful. The conclusion the authors draw from it is that on AM *the mind does not matter*; that a neural event has a certain intentional content is as irrelevant to its effect as the fact that the sounds are meaningful is to the sounds causing the glass to break.

But is this criticism of AM correct? We claim that it is not, and that it rests on a simple, but perhaps not obvious, confusion. The confusion is between two ways in which properties of an event *c* may be said to be causally relevant and irrelevant. Consider the following locutions:

(a) Properties *F* and *G* are relevant$_1$ to making it the case that *c* causes *e*,

and

(b) *c*'s possessing property *F* is causally relevant$_2$ to *e*'s possessing property *G*.

We will say that (a) holds iff *c* has *F* and *e* has *G*, and there is a strict law that entails *F*s cause *G*s. It is in this sense that it is *c*'s having *F* and *e*'s having *G* "make it the case" that *c* causes *e*. Relevance$_2$ is a relation among *c*, one of its properties *F*, *e*, and one of its properties *G*. It holds when *c*'s being *F* brings it about that *e* is *G*. We shall argue that those who charge AM with epiphenomenalism are guilty of confusing relevance$_1$ with relevance$_2$.

None of the authors we have been considering defines the sense of causal relevance they have in mind when they accuse AM of rendering the mental causally inefficacious. Their discussions, though, do suggest a *test* for causal irrelevance. Recall Sosa's remark that "had the gun been equipped with a silencer it would have killed the victim just the same" (278); and Dretske's remark that "the glass would shatter if the sounds meant something completely different." So it may be that Sosa and Dretske (and others) think that AM entails the causal irrelevance of the mental, because they think that it entails the falsity of such mentalistic counterfactuals as: if Fred had not believed that Jerry would attend the conference, he would not have come.

In view of this counterfactual test for causal irrelevance$_2$, we suggest that the authors who propose it may have in mind the following characterization of causal relevance$_2$.[12]

(I) *c*'s being *F* is causally relevant$_2$ to *e*'s being *G* iff

i. *c* causes *e*.

ii. *Fc* and *Ge*.

iii. $-Fc > -Ge$.

iv. *Fc* and *Ge* are logically and metaphysically independent.[13]

Condition (iv) is intended to exclude cases in which the connection between *F* and *G* is conceptual/metaphysical rather than causal, e.g., *c*'s being the cause of *e* is causally relevant$_2$ to *e*'s being caused by *c*, when *c* does cause *e*.

The heart of our response to the claim that AM is committed to epiphenomenalism is this: AM entails that mental features are causally irrelevant$_1$, but does not entail that they are causally irrelevant$_2$. Before arguing these claims, we need to discuss the interpretation of the counterfactual:

(*Q*) If event *c* were not *F*, then event *e* would not be *G*.

We will adopt the Lewis–Stalnaker[14] account of counterfactuals, according to which $A > B$ is true iff *B* is true at all the worlds most similar to the actual world at which *A* is true (or *A* is true at no such world). We will suppose that an event *e* that occurs at the actual world may occur or have counterparts that occur at others. "*c*" and "*e*" are to be understood as rigid designators of events. In evaluating (*Q*), we need to look at the most similar worlds to the actual world at which *c* fails to be *F*. *c* may fail to be *F* at *w* either by existing there and not being *F* or failing to occur at *w* (or have a counterpart) at all. (*Q*) is true just in case the most similar worlds at which counterparts to *c* fail to have F or at which c fails to have a counterpart are such that counterparts to e fail to have G or e fails to have a counterpart.

The irrelevance$_1$ of the mental follows immediately from the definition of relevance$_1$ and from AM's (4) and (6). The irrelevance$_1$ of psychological predicates, however, is perfectly compatible with the truth of counterfactuals $-Fc > -Ge$, where F and G are predicates that do not occur in strict laws. That is, the set of strict laws and basic physical facts do not by themselves settle the truth values of counterfactuals.

We can see that this is so as follows: consider the set of worlds W at which all the strict laws hold. (This set includes the actual world α.) Until a *similarity order*, $\geq\alpha$, is placed on W, the truth values of almost all counterfactuals are indeterminate. Only those counterfactuals $A > B$ such that the strict laws and noncounterfactual statements true at α entail $A \rightarrow B$ or $-(A \rightarrow B)$ have determinate truth values, since any similarity ordering $\geq \alpha$ will make the former true and the latter false. This is just the lesson of Nelson Goodman's[15] failed attempts to analyze counterfactuals in terms of laws. What Goodman found is that laws and noncounterfactual truths are themselves not sufficient to settle the truth value of any but a limited set of counterfactuals. It follows that the truth of counterfactuals of the sort needed to establish causal relevance$_2$ (since neither they nor their negations are entailed by the strict physical laws and noncounterfactual truths) are compatible with AM.

Of course, it is one thing to show that mentalistic counterfactuals are compatible with AM. It is quite another thing to produce an account of what makes these counterfactuals true and also show that this account is compatible with AM. The question of what makes counterfactuals true is a general one which concerns all counterfactuals and not just mentalistic ones. We shall briefly address it toward the end of our discussion.

To this point, we have shown that, if (I) supplies sufficient conditions for causal relevance$_2$, then there is no incompatibility between AM and the causal relevance$_2$ of the mental.[16] This is important, since, as we have seen, many of Davidson's critics seem to think there is such an incompatibility. There are two further related questions we need to address. One is whether causal irrelevance$_1$ alone is sufficient to sustain a charge of epiphenomenalism. A second is whether there are some further conditions on (I) such that, once added, AM does entail the causal irrelevance$_2$ of the mental.

Why would anyone think that irrelevance$_1$ of the mental entails epiphenomenalism? Honderich[17] formulates a principle he calls "the principle of the nomological character of causally relevant properties," according to which c's having F is causally relevant to e's having G, iff there is a law of the form Fs cause Gs (62). If one thinks, as Honderich does, that AM implies that psychological predicates never appear in causal laws, then one might conclude that psychological features have no causal role to play and indeed that psychology could not be a science. But, as Davidson has been careful to observe (240), there may very well be psychological and psychophysical causal laws that support counterfactuals and other subjunctive conditionals; it is just that such laws cannot be *strict*. If Honderich intends for the principle of nomological relevance to include nonstrict as well as strict laws, then AM is compatible with the causal relevance (in Honderich's sense) of psychological properties. If he intends for the principle to include only strict laws, then it is an unacceptable principle. It is implausible that there are any strict laws linking "is a match striking" with "is a match lighting." So, on the strict law construal of Honderich's principle, being a match striking is not causally relevant to the match's lighting. On this construal, Honderich's principle would render virtually all properties of events causally irrelevant$_2$. This certainly seems wrong.

In arguing that AM entails the causal irrelevance of the mental, some authors have suggested a strengthened account of causal relevance$_2$. For example, Sosa writes:

I extend my hand because of a certain neurological event. That event is my sudden desire to quench my thirst. Thus, if my grasping is caused by that neurological event, it's my sudden desire that causes my grasping.... Assuming the anomalism of the mental, though extending my hand is, in a certain sense, caused by my sudden desire to quench my thirst, it is not caused by my desire qua desire but only by desire qua *neurological* of a certain sort.... [T]he being a desire of my desire has no causal relevance to my extending my hand (if the mental is indeed anomalous): *if the event that is in fact my desire had not been my desire but had remained a neurological event of a certain sort, then it would have caused my extending my hand just the same.* (277/8, our emphasis)

This passage suggests the following as a sufficient condition for causal irrelevance$_2$:

(II) c's being F is causally irrelevant$_2$ to e's being G, if there is a property $F*$ of c such that $(F * c \ \& \ -Fc) > Ge$ holds nonvacuously.

Even when $-Fc > -Ge$ holds, there may be a property $F*$ of c such that $(F * c \ \& \ -Fc) > Ge$. In this case, it may seem that it is in virtue of c's being $F*$, not F, that e is G. When this holds, we will say that $F * c$ "screens off" Fc from Ge. Converting (II) into a necessary condition for causal relevance$_2$ and adding it to (I), we obtain the following proposal:

(III) c's being F is relevant$_2$ to e's being G iff the conditions in (I) are satisfied and there is *no* property $F*$ of c such that $(F * c \ \& \ -Fc) > Ge$ holds nonvacuously.

Sosa seems to think that it follows from AM that c's being a certain neural state, Nc, *screens off* c's being a desire to quench thirst, Mc, from e's being an extending of the hand, Be. More generally, he seems to think that neural properties screen off intentional mental properties. Presumably, Sosa thinks that this follows from AM, because he thinks there are strict laws connecting neural properties with behavioral properties. Since mental properties are not reducible to neural properties, it follows that there are physically possible worlds in which Nc, Mc, and in *all* such worlds Be.

It is not at all clear that there are strict laws connecting neural properties with mental properties (and so that AM *entails* that the neural property screens off the mental property), but it does seem that, as a matter of fact in a case like Sosa's, the neural property does screen off the mental property. The worry then is that, if (II) is kept as a condition on causal irrelevance$_2$, then the causal irrelevance$_2$ of the mental will follow from AM after all.[18]

In response to this, notice first that (II)'s rendering the mental causally irrelevant$_2$ is independent of AM, at least to the extent that the problem-creating counterfactual, $(Nc \ \& \ -Mc) > Be$, holds whether or not there is a strict law linking N with B. So anyone who adopts (II) as a condition on causal irrelevance$_2$ will be committed to the causal irrelevance$_2$ of the mental in this case. But it seems to us that (II) is not a correct condition on irrelevance$_2$. It renders even properties connected by strict law causally irrelevant$_2$. To see this, consider the neural event c and the behavioral event e in Sosa's example. c possesses basic physical property P and mental property M (being a desire to quench his thirst), and e possesses the property B (being a certain movement of the hand). Assuming a strict law between P and B, it follows that:

(S) $(-Mc \,\&\, Pc) > Be$.

So, P screens off M from B. Now consider the counterfactual:

(T) $(-Pc \,\&\, Mc) > Be$.

It can be shown that (T) is compatible with AM *and* (S). Furthermore, it is plausible that (T) is in fact true. If c had been a desire to quench thirst but had not been P, it would have had some other property $P*$. Furthermore, c still would have resulted in an e that has the property B. That is, in the closest possible world in which Sosa desires to quench his thirst but this desire is not a P, it still causes him to extend his hand. Supporting this claim there may be a law, though not strict, to the effect that, when someone experiences a sudden desire to quench his thirst and believes there is a glass of water in front of him which he can reach by extending his hand, then, *ceteris paribus*, his hand will extend. When we consider the possibility that c is M but not P, this law "takes over" so that c still causes an event that is B. Here is a nonpsychological example which will, perhaps, help elucidate our claim.

Consider the event of hurricane Donald striking the coast causing the streets to be flooded. That event is identical to the event of certain air and water molecules moving in various complex ways. Call the property of consisting of molecules moving in such ways P. It is perfectly possible for the following counterfactual to be true: if hurricane Donald had not had property P (that is, if a hurricane as much like Donald as possible, though without P, had occurred), then is still would have caused the streets to be flooded. Indeed, it would have had some property $P*$ sufficiently similar to P, and $P*$ events (under the relevant conditions) cause floodings. The result is that Donald's being a hurricane would be said to be causally irrelevant to its flooding the streets. We think that examples such as this one show that (III) is too strong a requirement on causal relevance$_2$.[19]

A fully adequate account of causal relevance$_2$ should show how mentalistic counterfactuals are grounded. What is it about Sosa, his situation, etc., that makes it true that, if he had not experienced a sudden desire to quench his thirst, he would not have extended his hand? We do not have such an account, but we do want to suggest an approach that fits within the framework of AM. As we have observed already, the existence of nonstrict psychophysical and psychological laws is compatible with AM. A nonstrict law is one which has a *ceteris paribus* qualifier. The interesting thing about such laws is the ways in which they can support counterfactuals. We will illustrate this by building upon a suggestion by Lewis.[20] Let R, W, and B be the statements that a red block, a white block, and a blue block is placed in front of Donald and S_r, S_w, and S_b be the statements that Donald sees a red block, a white block, and a blue block. We will suppose, as is plausible, that there are nonstrict laws of the form:

(L) If X and C, then S_x,

where C are conditions like lighting is good, Donald is awake and paying attention, and so on. Even with such conditions added, the law is a *ceteris paribus* one and, if AM is correct, it will be impossible to add explicit conditions that turn it into a strict law.

When the laws (L) hold, we will say that the statements describing what Donald sees *depend nomically* on the statements describing the blocks in front of him. Call conditions C *counterfactually independent* of the family of statements $\{R, W, B\}$, if C would continue to hold no matter which member of $\{R, W, B\}$ is true. Lewis shows that, if C and the *ceteris paribus* conditions associated with (L) are counterfactually independent of $\{R, W, B\}$, then S_x will depend counterfactually on X. That is, each of the counterfactuals, $R > S_r$, $W > S_w$, $B > S_b$, will be true. If we further assume that a block which has one of three colors will be placed in front of Donald [and that this statement is also counterfactually independent of (R, W, B)], then the statement $-X > -S_x$ will also be true. Suppose a red block is placed in front of Donald, and this event causes the event of his seeing a red block. It will follow that, if the first event had not been a placing of a red block, then the second event would not have been Donald's seeing a red block. As Lewis points out, this "grounding" of counterfactuals in laws fails to *reduce* counterfactuals to laws, since the assumption of counterfactual independence is essential. It does show, however, how laws, including *ceteris paribus* laws, can support counterfactuals. The program for a psychology compatible with AM is the discovery and the systematization of such nonstrict laws (at various levels) connecting psychological and/or behavioral properties.

We have seen that AM attempts to resolve the mind–body problem by endorsing (2), (3), and (3′), denying (1) with respect to events, and affirming (1) with respect to properties. Davidson is silent on (2) and (3) with respect to properties, leading to the accusation that AM is committed to epiphenomenalism. We rebutted this charge by showing that AM is compatible with there being counterfactual dependencies between events in virtue of their mental properties. To do this is to affirm (2) with respect to properties but, of course, to deny (3) with respect to properties. An event's physical features may counterfactually depend on another event's mental features. But, interestingly, we need not deny (3′) for our account of causal relevance$_2$. It may be that all counterfactuals *supervene* on basic physical truths and strict laws. That is, if two possible worlds are exactly alike with respect to basic physical facts and strict laws, they are exactly alike with respect to counterfactuals. This fairly strong physicalism still allows sufficient autonomy of the mental so that it is not reducible to the physical and it has a genuine explanatory and causal role to play.

Acknowledgments

Thanks are due to Jonathan Adler, John Biro, Paul Boghossian, Donald Davidson, Fred Dretske, Ray Elugardo, Jerry Fodor, Richard Foley, Terry Horgan, Brian McLaughlin, Alexander Rosenberg, Stephen Schiffer, and John Searle.

Notes

1. Similar characterizations of the mind–body problem can be found in J. L. Mackie, "Mind, Brain and Causation," *Midwest Studies in Philosophy*, VI (1979): 19–29; and Anthony Skillen, "Mind and Matter: A Problem that Refuses Dissolution," *Mind*, XCIII (1984): 514–526.

2. This view is given in three places in Davidson's *Essays on Actions and Events* (New York: Oxford, 1980); at the beginning and end of "Mental Events," pp. 208, 223; and in "Psychology as Philos-

ophy," p. 231. Where nothing else is said, all page references in the text of our paper are to this book.

3. Davidson's argument against psychophysical laws is restricted to laws whose psychological predicates express propositional attitudes.

4. We shall typically speak of features, aspects, and properties of events. For present purposes, however, unless we indicate otherwise, what we say can be recast in terms of events satisfying descriptions or predicates.

5. Davidson never provides an example of a strict causal law. And there are some philosophers who think his account of causation is much too stringent, because there may be too few strict causal laws. (The best candidates for such laws are basic laws of quantum mechanics.) It is not our aim here to defend Davidson's metaphysical account of causation.

6. For an explication and defense of Davidson's arguments for the impossibility of strict psychophysical laws, see Jaegwon Kim, "Psychophysical Laws," *Actions and Events: Perspectives on the Philosophy of Donald Davidson*, LePore and Brian McLaughlin, eds. (London: Basil Blackwell, 1986), pp. 369–386, and also the introduction by McLaughlin in the same volume. Cf. also LePore and Loewer, "Davidson and the Anomalousness of the Mental," *Philosophical Perspectives on the Philosophy of Mind*, J. Tomberlin, ed., forthcoming.

7. "Mind–body Interaction and Supervenient Causation," *Midwest Studies in Philosophy*, IX (1984): 271–282.

8. "Smith and the Champion of the Mauve," *Analysis*, XLIV, 2 (1984): 86–89.

9. "Reasons and Causes," manuscript presented at the Chapel Hill Colloquium. For similar characterizations and examples of causal relevance, see Ted Hoderich, "The Argument for Anomalous Monism," *Analysis*, XLII, 1 (January 1982): 61; John Searle, *Intentionality* (New York: Cambridge, 1983), pp. 155–157; Elizabeth Anscombe, "Causality and Extensionality," *Causation and Conditionals*, E. Sosa, ed. (New York: Oxford, 1975), p. 178; and Peter Achenstein, "The Causal Relation," *Midwest Studies in Philosophy*, IV (1977): 368.

10. Others who have argued that AM is epiphenomenalist include: F. Stoutland, "The Causation of Behavior," *Essays on Wittgenstein in Honor of G. H. von Wright* (Acta Philosophica Fennica, 1976), p. 307; Dagfinn Føllesdal, "Causation and Explanation: A Problem in Davidson's View on Action and Mind," *Action and Events: Perspectives on the Philosophy of Donald Davidson, op. cit.*, p. 315; Mark Johnston, "Why the Mind Matters," *ibid.*, p. 423; and Skillen, *op. cit.*, p. 520.

11. "Epiphenomenal and Supervenient Causation," *Midwest Studies in Philosophy*, IX (1984), 257–270.

12. While many philosophers appeal to the notion of causal relevance, it is far from clear that there is a single or well-characterizable notion that underlies the locution that *c* qua *F* causes *e* to be *G*. We are here interested only in sketching enough of an account to refute the charge that AM is committed to epiphenomenalism. Anyone interested in a thorough explication of causal relevance would have to show how to accommodate familiar difficulties involving pre-emption, overdetermination, and so on. But these are problems which confront every account of causation and we will not discuss them here.

13. *c*'s being *F* and *e*'s being *G* are metaphysically independent, iff there is a possible world in which *c* (or a counterpart of *c*) is *F* but *e* (or a counterpart of *e*) fails to occur or fails to be *G* and vice versa.

14. See David Lewis, *Counterfactuals* (Oxford: Blackwell, 1973); and Robert Stalnaker, "A Theory of Conditionals," *Studies in Logical Theory*, N. Rescher, ed. (New York: Oxford, 1968). There are differences between the two accounts irrelevant to our discussion.

15. *Fact, Fiction and Forecast*, 4th ed. (Cambridge, Mass.: Harvard, 1982).

16. Although there is a tradition in the philosophy of action arguing that there are conceptual connections between propositional attitudes and actions, this does not entail that particular propositional attitude properties are conceptually connected. For example, suppose that John believes that Mary is across the street and, for this reason, waves his hand. Let *c* be John's thought, *e* his action, *F* the property of his believing Mary is across the street, and *G* the property of being a waving hand. Clearly, we can have *c*'s being *F* causally relevant_2 to *e*'s being *G*, since *c*'s being *F* can obtain without *e*'s being *G* and vice versa in some metaphysically possible world.

17. "The Argument for Anomalous Monism," *Analysis*, XLII, 1 (January 1982): 59–64.

18. Jerry Fodor has argued that a taxonomy of propositional attitude states in terms of their truth conditions is not a taxonomy in terms of causal powers. See his *Psychosemantics* (Cambridge, Mass.: MIT Press, 1987), ch. 2. Condition (III) may be involved in the view of some philosophers that scientific psychology requires a notion of narrow content. Thus, Fodor seems to hold that Oscar's belief that water quenches thirst is not causally relevant_2 to Oscar's behavior, since, if Oscar were in the same neural state as he is in but had not believed that water quenches his thirst, he would have behaved identically. The antecedent of this counterfactual is thought to be metaphysically possible for Putnamian reasons: if Oscar has lived in an environment containing XYZ and not H_2O his neural state would have been a belief that twin-water quenches thirst. One might conclude that, if we want a notion of content such that propositional attitudes are causally relevant_2 in virtue of their contents, then we need a notion of content which makes propositional attitudes supervene on neural states.

19. It may be that there is some account of causal relevance_2 midway in strength between (I) and (III) which captures what some of Davidson's critics have in mind. We leave to them the task of formulating it and attempting to demonstrate that AM entails the irrelevance_2 of the mental so characterized.

20. "Causation," *Causation and Conditionals*, E. Sosa, ed. (Oxford, New York: 1975), pp. 180–191.

38 Making Mind Matter More

Jerry A. Fodor

An outbreak of epiphobia (epiphobia is the fear that one is turning into an epiphenomenalist) appears to have much of the philosophy of mind community in its grip. Though it is generally agreed to be compatible with physicalism that intentional states should be causally responsible for behavioral outcomes, epiphobics worry that it is *not* compatible with physicalism that intentional states should be causally responsible for behavioral outcomes *qua intentional*. So they fear that the very successes of a physicalistic (and/or a computational) psychology will entail the causal inertness of the mental. Fearing this makes them unhappy.

In this paper, I want to argue that epiphobia is a neurotic worry; if there is a problem, it is engendered not by the actual-or-possible successes of physicalistic psychology, but by two philosophical mistakes: (a) a wrong idea about what it is for a property to be causally responsible; and (b) a complex of wrong ideas about the relations between special-science laws and the events that they subsume.[1] Here's how I propose to proceed: First, we'll have a little psychodrama; I want to give you a feel for how an otherwise healthy mind might succumb to epiphobia. Second, I'll provide a brief, sketchy, but I hope good-enough-for-present-purposes account of what it is for a property to be causally responsible. It will follow from this account that intentional properties are causally responsible if there are intentional causal laws. I'll then argue that (contrary to the doctrine called "anomalous monism") there is no good reason to doubt that there are intentional causal laws. I'll also argue that, so far as the matter affects the cluster of issues centering around epiphenomenalism, the sorts of relations that intentional causal laws can bear to the individuals they subsume are much the same as the sorts of relations that *non*intentional causal laws can bear to the individuals that they subsume. So then everything will be all right.

I Causal Responsibility

There are many routes to epiphobia. One of them runs via two premises and a stipulation.

1. Premise (Supervenience of Causal Powers): The causal powers of an event are entirely determined by its physical properties. Suppose two events are identical in their physical properties; then all causal hypotheticals true of one event are true of the other. If, for example, e1 and e2 are events identical in their physical properties, then all hypotheticals of the form "if e1 occurred in situation S, it would cause...." remain true if "e2" is substituted for "e1" and vice versa.

2. Premise (Property Dualism): Intentional properties supervene on physical properties, but no intentional property is identical to any physical property. (A physical property is a property expressible in the vocabulary of physics. Never mind, for now, what the vocabulary of physics is; just assume that it contains no intentional terms.)
3. Stipulation: A property is "causally responsible" iff it affects the causal powers of things that have it. And (also by stipulation) all properties that aren't causally responsible are epiphenomenal.

But then, consider the mental event *m* (let's say, an event which consists of you desiring to lift your arm) which is the cause of the behavioral event *b* (let's say, an event which consists of you lifting your arm). *m* does, of course, have certain intentional properties. But, according to 2, none of its intentional properties is identical to any of its physical properties. And, according to 1, *m*'s physical properties fully determine its causal powers (including, of course, its power to cause *b*). So, it appears that *m*'s being the cause of your lifting your arm doesn't depend on its being a desire to lift your arm; *m* would have caused your lifting of your arm even if it hadn't had its intentional properties, so long as its physical properties were preserved.[2] So it appears that *m*'s intentional properties don't affect its causal powers. So it appears that *m*'s intentional properties are causally inert. Clearly, this argument iterates to *any* intentional property of the cause of any behavioral effect. So the intentional properties of mental events are epiphenomenal. Epiphobia!

Now, the first thing to notice about this line of argument is that it has *nothing to do with intentionality as such*. On the contrary, it applies equally happily to prove the epiphenomenality of *any* non-physical property, so long as property dualism is assumed. Consider, for example, the property of being a mountain; and suppose (what is surely plausible) that being a mountain isn't a physical property. (Remember, this just means that "mountain" and its synonyms aren't items in the lexicon of physics.) Now, untutored intuition might suggest that many of the effects of mountains are attributable *to their being* mountains. Thus, untutored intuition suggests, it is because Mt. Everest is a mountain that Mt. Everest has glaciers on its top; and it is because Mt. Everest is a mountain that it casts such a long shadow; and it is because Mt. Everest is a mountain that so many people try to climb Mt. Everest ... and so on. But not so according to the present line of argument. For surely the causal powers of Mt. Everest are fully determined by its physical properties, and we've agreed that *being a mountain* isn't one of the physical properties of mountains. So then Mt. Everest's being a mountain doesn't affect its causal powers. So then—contrary to what one reads in geology books—the property of being a mountain is causally inert. Geoepiphobia!

No doubt there will be those who are prepared to bite this bullet. Such folk may either (i) deny that property dualism applies to mountainhood (because, on reflection, *being a mountain* is a physical property after all) or (ii) assert that it *is* intuitively plausible that *being a mountain* is causally inert (because, on reflection, it is intuitively plausible that it's not *being a mountain* but some other of Mt. Everest's properties—specifically, some of its physical properties—that are causally responsible for its effects). So be it; I do not want this to turn into a squabble about cases. Instead, let me emphasize that there are lots and lots and *lots* of examples where, on the one hand, considerations like multiple realizability make it implausible that a certain property is expressible in physical vocabulary; and, on the other hand, claims for the causal inertness of the property appear to be wildly implausible, at least prima facie.

Consider the property of being a sail. I won't bore you with the fine points (terribly tempted, though I am, to exercise my hobbyhorse[3]). Suffice it that sails are *airfoils* and there is quite a nice little theory about the causal properties of airfoils. Typically, airfoils generate lift in a direction, and in amounts, that are determined by their geometry, their rigidity, and many, many details of their relations to the (liquid or gaseous) medium through which they move. The basic idea is that lift is propagated at right angles to the surface of the airfoil along which the medium flows fastest, and is proportional to the relative velocity of the flow. Hold a flat piece of paper by one edge and blow across the top. The free side of the paper will move *up* (i.e., towards the air flow), and the harder you blow, the more it will do so. (*Ceteris paribus*.)

Now, the relative velocity of the airfoil may be increased by forcing the medium to flow through a "slot" (a constriction, one side of which is formed by the surface of the airfoil). The controlling law is that the narrower the slot, the faster the flow. (On sailboats of conventional Bermuda rig, the slot is the opening between the jib and the main. But perhaps you didn't want to know that.) Anyhow, airfoils and slots can be made out of all sorts of things; sails are airfoils, but so are keel-wings, and airplane wings and bird's wings. Slots are multiply realizable too: You can have a slot both sides of which are made of sailcloth, as in the jib/mainsail arrangement, but you can also have a slot one side of which is made of sailcloth and the other side of which is made of *air*. (That's part of the explanation of why you can sail towards the wind even if you haven't got a jib.) So then, if one of your reasons for doubting that *believing that P* is a physical property is that believing is multiply realizable, then you have the same reason for doubting that *being an airfoil* or *being a slot* counts as a physical property.

And yet, of course, it would seem to be quite mad to say that *being an airfoil* is causally inert. Airplanes fall down when you take their wings off; and sailboats come to a stop when you take down their sails. Everybody who isn't a philosopher agrees that these and other such facts are explained by the story about lift being generated by causal interactions between the airfoil and the medium. If that *isn't* the right explanation, what keeps the plane up? If that *is* the right explanation, how could it be that *being an airfoil* is causally inert?

Epiphobics primarily concerned with issues in the philosophy of mind might well stop here. The geological and aerodynamic analogies make it plausible that if there's a case for epiphenomenalism in respect of psychological properties, then there is the same case for epiphenomenalism in respect of *all* the non-physical properties mentioned in theories in the special sciences. I pause, for a moment, to moralize about this.

Many philosophers have the bad habit of thinking about only two sciences when they think about sciences at all; these being psychology and physics. When in the grip of this habit, they are likely to infer that if psychological theories have some property that physical theories don't, that must be because psychological states (qua psychological) are intentional and physical states (qua physical) are not. In the present case, if there's an argument that psychological properties are epiphenomenal, and no corresponding argument that physical properties are epiphenomenal, that must show that there is something funny about intentionality.

But we now see that it shows no such thing since, if the causal inertness of psychological properties is maintained along anything like the lines of 1–3, there are likely to be parallel arguments that *all properties are causally inert except those expressed by the vocabulary of physics*. In which case, *why should anybody care* whether psychological properties are epiphenomenal? All that anybody could reasonably want for psychology is that its constructs should enjoy whatever sort of explanatory/causal role is proper to the constructs of the special sciences. If beliefs and desires are as well off ontologically as mountains, wings, spiral nebulas, trees, gears, levers and the like, then surely they're as well off as anyone could need them to be.

But, in fact, we shouldn't stop here. Because, though it's true that claims for the epiphenomenality of mountainhood and airfoilhood and, in general, of any nonphysical-property-you-like-hood will follow from the same sorts of arguments that imply claims for the epiphenomenality of beliefhood and desirehood, it's also true that such claims are prima facie absurd. Whatever you may think about beliefs and desires and the other paraphernalia of intentional psychology, it's a fact you have to live with that there are all these *non*intentional special sciences around; and that many, many—maybe even all—of the properties that figure in their laws are nonphysical too. Surely something *must* have gone wrong with arguments that show that all these properties are epiphenomenal. How could there be laws about airfoils (notice, laws about *the causal consequences of something's being an airfoil*) if airfoilhood is epiphenomenal? How could there be a science of geology if geological properties are causally inert?

It seems to me, in light of the foregoing, that it ought to be a minimal condition upon a theory of what it is for something to be a causally responsible property that it does not entail the epiphenomenality of winghood, mountainhood, gearhood, leverhood, beliefhood, desirehood and the like. I'm about to propose a theory which meets this condition, and thereby commends itself as a tonic for epiphobics. It isn't, as you will see, very shocking, or surprising or anything; actually it's pretty dull. Still, I need a little stage setting before I can tell you about it. In particular, I need some caveats and some assumptions.

Caveats First, curing epiphobia requires making it plausible that intentional properties can meet sufficient conditions for causal responsibility; but one is not also required to show that they can meet *necessary and sufficient* conditions for causal responsibility. This is just as well, since necessary and sufficient conditions for causal responsibility might be sort of hard to come by (necessary and sufficient conditions for *anything* tend to be sort of hard to come by) and I, for one, don't claim to have any.

Second, the question "What makes a property causally responsible?" needs to be distinguished from the probably much harder question. "What determines which property is responsible in a given case when one event causes another?" Suppose that e1 causes e2; then, trivially, it must do so in virtue of some or other of its causally responsible properties; i.e., in virtue of some or other property in virtue of which it is able to be a cause. But it may be that e1 has many—perhaps many, many—such properties; so it must not be assumed that if e1 is capable of being a cause in virtue of having a certain property P, then P is ipso facto the property in virtue of which e1 is the cause of e2. Indeed, it must not even be assumed that if e1 is capable of being a cause of e2 in virtue of its having P, then P is ipso facto the property in virtue of which e1 causes e2.

For again it may be that e1 has many—even many, many—properties in virtue of which it is capable of being the cause of e2, and it need not be obvious which one of these properties is the one in virtue of which it actually *is* the cause of e2. At least, I can assure you, it need not be obvious to me.

It is, to put all this a little less pedantically, one sort of success to show that it was in virtue of its intentional content that your desire to raise your hand made something happen. It is another, and lesser, sort of success to show that *being a desire to raise your hand* is the kind of property in virtue of which things *can* be made to happen. Curing epiphobia requires only a success of the latter, lesser sort.

Assumptions I assume that singular causal statements need to be covered by causal laws. That means something like:

4. Covering Principle: If an event e1 causes an event e2, then there are properties F, G such that:
4.1. e1 instantiates F;
4.2. e2 instantiates G;
and
4.3. "F instantiations and sufficient for G instantiations" is a causal law.[4]

When a pair of events bears this relation to a law, I'll say that the individuals are each *covered* or *subsumed* by that law and I'll say that the law *projects* the properties in virtue of which the individuals are subsumed by it. Notice that when an individual is covered by a law, it will always have some property in virtue of which the law subsumes it. If, for example, the covering law is that Fs cause Gs, then individuals that get covered by this law do so either in virtue of being Fs (in case they are subsumed by its antecedent) or in virtue of being Gs (in case they are subsumed by its consequent). This could all be made more precise, but I see no reason to bother.

OK, I can now tell you my sufficient condition for a property to be causally responsible:

5. P is a causally responsible property if it's a property in virtue of which individuals are subsumed by causal laws; or, equivalently,
5.1. P is a causally responsible property if it's a property projected by a causal law; or, equivalently (since the satisfaction of the antecedent of a law is ipso facto nomologically sufficient for the satisfaction of its consequent),
5.2. P is a causally responsible property if it's a property in virtue of the instantiation of which the occurrence of one event is nomologically sufficient for the occurrence of another.[5]

If this is right, then intentional properties are causally responsible in case there are intentional causal laws; aerodynamic properties are causally responsible in case there are aerodynamic causal laws; geological properties are causally responsible in case there are geological causal laws . . . and so forth. To all intents and purposes, on this view the question whether the property P is causally responsible *reduces to* the question whether there are causal laws about P. To settle the second question *is* to settle the first.

I don't mind if you find this proposal dull, but I would be distressed if you found it circular. How, you might ask, can one possibly make progress by defining "*causally* responsible property" in terms of "covering *causal* law"? And yet it's unclear that we can just drop the requirement that the covering law *be* causal because there are *non*-causal laws (e.g., the gas law about pressure and volume varying inversely) and perhaps an event's being covered by those sorts of laws *isn't* sufficient for its having a causally responsible property.

I can think of two fairly plausible ways out of this. First, it may be that any property in virtue of which some law covers an individual will be a property in virtue of which some causal law covers an individual;[6] i.e., that no property figures *only* in noncausal laws. This is, I think, an interesting metaphysical possibility; if it is true, then we can just identify the causally responsible properties with the properties in virtue of which individuals are covered by laws.

And, even if it's not true, it may be that what makes a law causal can itself be specified in noncausal terms. Perhaps it involves such properties as covering temporal successions, being asymmetric, and the like. In that case it would be okay to construe "causally responsible" in terms of "causal law" since the latter could be independently defined. Barring arguments to the contrary, I'm prepared to suppose that this will work.

We're now in a position to do a little diagnosis. According to the present view, the properties projected in the laws of basic science are causally responsible, and so too are the properties projected in the laws of the special sciences. This is truistic since the present view just is that being projected is sufficient for being causally responsible. Notice, in particular, that even if the properties that the special sciences talk about are supervenient upon the properties that the basic sciences talk about, that does *not* argue that the properties that the special sciences talk about are epiphenomenal. Not, at least, if there are causal laws of the special sciences. The causal laws of the special sciences and causal laws of basic sciences have in common that they *both* license ascriptions of causal responsibility. Or so, at least, the present view would have it.

This is not, however, to deny that there are metaphysically interesting differences between special-science laws and basic science laws. Let me introduce here a point that I propose to make a fuss of later.

Roughly, the satisfaction of the antecedent of a law is nomologically sufficient for the satisfaction of its consequent.[7] (I'll sometimes say that the truth of the antecedent of a law *nomologically necessitates* the truth of its consequent.) But a metaphysically interesting difference between basic and nonbasic laws is that, in the case of the latter but not the former, there always has to be a *mechanism in virtue of which* the satisfaction of its antecedent brings about the satisfaction of its consequent. If "Fs cause Gs" is basic, then there is no answer to the question *how* do Fs cause Gs; they just do, and that they do is among the not-to-be-further-explained facts about the way the world is put together. Whereas, if "Fs cause Gs" is *non*basic, then there is always a story about what goes on when—and in virtue of which—Fs cause Gs.

Sometimes it's a microstructure story: Meandering rivers erode their outside banks; facts about the abrasive effects of particles suspended in moving water explain why there is erosion; and the Bernouli effect explains why it's the *outside* banks that get eroded most. Sometimes there's a story about chains of macrolevel events that intervene between F-instantiations and G-instantiations. Changes in CO_2 levels in the atmosphere cause changes in fauna. There's a story about how CO_2 blocks radiation from the earth's surface; and there's a story about how the blocked radiation changes the air temperature; and there's a story about how changes in the air temperature cause climactic changes; and there's a (Darwinian) story about how climactic changes have zoological impacts. (I try to be as topical as I can.)

Or, to get closer home, consider the case in computational psychology: There are—so I fondly suppose—intentional laws that connect, for example, states of believing that P & (P → Q) to states of believing that Q. (*Ceteris paribus*, of course. More of that later.) Because there are events covered by such laws, it follows (trivially) that intentional properties (like *believing that P & (P → Q)*) are causally responsible. And because nobody (except, maybe, panpsychists; who I am prepared not to take seriously for present purposes) thinks that intentional laws are basic, it follows that there must be a mechanism in virtue of which believing that P & (P → Q) *brings it about* that one believes Q.

There are, as it happens, some reasonably persuasive theories about the nature of such mechanisms currently on offer. The one I like best says that the mechanisms that implement intentional laws are computational. Roughly, the story goes: believing (etc.) is a relation between an organism and a mental representation. Mental representations have (*inter alia*) syntactic properties; and the mechanisms of belief-change are defined over the syntactic properties of mental representations. Let's not worry, for the moment, about whether this story is right; let's just worry about whether it's epiphobic.

Various philosophers have supposed that it is. Steven Stich, for example, has done some public handwringing about how anybody (a fortiori, how *I*) could hold *both* that intentional properties are causally responsible *and* the ("methodologically solipsistic") view that mental processes are entirely computational (/syntactic). And Norbert Hornstein[8] has recently ascribed to me the view that "the generalizations of psychology, the laws and the theories, are stated over syntactic objects, i.e., it is over syntactic representations that computations proceed" (p. 18). But: THE CLAIM THAT MENTAL PROCESSES ARE SYNTACTIC DOES NOT ENTAIL THE CLAIM THAT THE LAWS OF PSYCHOLOGY ARE SYNTACTIC. On the contrary THE LAWS OF PSYCHOLOGY ARE INTENTIONAL THROUGH AND THROUGH. This is a point to the reiteration of which my declining years seems somehow to have become devoted. What's syntactic is not the laws of psychology but the mechanisms by which the laws of psychology are implemented. Cf: The mechanisms of geological processes are—as it might be—chemical and molecular; it does not follow that chemical or molecular properties are projected by geological laws (on the contrary, it's geological properties that are projected by geological laws); and it does not follow that geological properties are causally inert (on the contrary, it's because Mt. Everest is such a very damned big mountain that it's so very damned cold on top).

It is, I should add, not in the least unusual to find that the vocabulary that's appropriate to articulate a special-science law is systematically different from the vocabulary that's appropriate to articulate its implementing mechanism(s). Rather, shift of vocabulary as one goes from the law to the mechanism is the *general* case. If you want to talk laws of inheritance, you talk recessive traits and dominant traits and homozygotes and heterozygotes; if you want to talk mechanisms of inheritance, you talk chromosomes and genes and how the DNA folds. If you want to talk psychological law, you talk intentional vocabulary; if you want to talk psychological mechanism, you talk syntactic (or maybe neurological) vocabulary. If you want to talk geological law, you talk mountains and glaciers; if you want to talk geological mechanism, you talk abrasion coefficients and cleavage planes. If you want to talk aerodynamic law, you talk airfoils and lift forces; if you want to talk aerodynamic mechanism, you talk gas pressure and laminar flows. It doesn't follow that the property of being a belief or an airfoil or a recessive trait is causally inert; all that follows is that *specifying the causally responsible macroproperty isn't the same as specifying the implementing micromechanism.*

It's a confusion to suppose that, if there's a law, then there needn't be an implementing mechanism; and it's a confusion to suppose that, if there's a mechanism that implements a law, then the properties that the law projects must be causally inert. If you take great care to avoid both these confusions, you will be delighted to see how rapidly your epiphobia disappears. You really will. Trust me.

II Intentional Laws

According to the position just developed, the question whether a property is causally responsible reduces to the question whether it is a property in virtue of which individuals are subsumed by covering causal laws. So, in particular, if there are intentional laws, then it follows that intentional properties aren't epiphenomenal. But maybe there aren't intentional laws; or, if there are, maybe they can't cover individual causes in the way that causal laws are supposed to cover the events that they subsume. The view that this is so is widespread in recent philosophy of mind. Clearly, if intentional covering doesn't actually happen, the question whether it would be sufficient for the causal responsibility of the mental is academic even by academic standards. And the treatment for epiphobia that I prescribed in part I won't work. The rest of the paper will be devoted to this issue, with special attention to a very interesting recent discussion by Barry Loewer and Ernie LePore.

There seems to be some tension between the following three principles, each of which I take to be prima facie sort of plausible:

6. Strict covering: Just like 4 except with the following in place of 4.3; "P1 instantiations are causally sufficient for P2 instantiations" is a *strict* causal law.
7. Anomia of the mental: The only strict laws are laws of physics. Specifically, there are no strict "psychophysical" laws relating types of brain states to types of intentional states; and there are no strict "psychological" laws relating types of mental events to one another or to types of behavioral outcomes.
8. Causal responsibility of the mental: Intentional properties aren't epiphenomenal.

6 means something like: Causal transactions must be covered by exceptionless laws; the satisfaction of the antecedent of a covering law has to provide literally nomologically sufficient conditions for the satisfaction of its consequent so that its consequent is satisfied in every nomologically possible situation in which its antecedent is satisfied.

7 means something like this: The laws of physics differ in a characteristic way from the laws of the special sciences (notably including psychology). Special science laws are typically hedged with 'ceteris paribus' clauses, so that whereas physical laws say what

has to happen come what may, special-science laws only say what has to happen all else being equal.[9]

How we should construe 8 has, of course, been a main concern throughout; but, according to the account of causal responsibility that I've been trying to sell you, it effectively reduces to the requirement that mental causes be covered by intentional laws. So now we can see where the tension between the three principles (6–8) arises. The responsibility of the mental requires covering by intentional laws. But given the revised notion of covering, according to which causes have to be covered by *strict* laws, it must be *physical* laws, and not intentional ones, that cover mental causes. So it turns out that the intentional properties are causally inert even according to the count of causal responsibility commended in part I.[10]

Something has to be done, and I assume it has to be done to 6 or 8 (or both) since 7 would seem to be okay. It is quite generally true about special-science laws that they hold only "barring breakdowns," or "under appropriately idealized conditions," or "when the effects of interacting variables are ignored." If even geological laws have to be hedged—as indeed they do—then it's more than plausible that the "all else equal" proviso in psychological laws will prove not to be eliminable. On balance, we had best assume that 7 stays.

What about 8 then? Surely we want 8 to come out true on *some* reasonable construal. I've opted for a robust reading: mental properties are causally responsible because they are the properties in virtue of which mental causes are subsumed by covering laws; which is to say that mental properties are causally responsible because there are intentional generalizations which specify nomologically sufficient conditions for behavioral outcomes. But this reading of 8 looks to be incompatible with 7.7 suggests that there *aren't* intentionally specifiable sufficient conditions for behavioral outcomes since, at best, intentional laws hold only ceteris paribus. So, maybe the notion of causal responsibility I've been selling is too strong. Maybe we could learn to make do with less.[11]

This is, more or less explicitly, the course that LePore and Loewer recommend in "Mind Matters": If the causal *responsibility* of the intentional can somehow be detached from its causal *sufficiency* for behavioral outcomes, we could then maybe reconcile causal responsibility with anomicness. In effect, L&L's idea is to hold on to 6 and 7 at the cost of not adopting a nomological subsumption reading of 8. Prima facie, this strategy is plausible in light of a point that L&L emphasize in their discussion of Sosa: The very fact that psychological laws are hedged would seem to rule out any construal of causal responsibility that requires mental causes qua mental to be nomologically sufficient for behavior. If it's only true ceteris paribus that someone who wants a drink reaches for the locally salient glass of water, then it's epiphobic to hold that desiring is causally responsible for reaching only if literally everyone who desires would thereupon reach. After all, quite aside from what you think of 6, it's simply not coherent to require the antecedents of hedged laws to provide literally nomologically sufficient conditions for the satisfaction of their consequents.

That's the stick; but Loewer and LePore also have a carrot on offer. They concede that, if the only strict laws are physical, then instantiations of intentional properties are not strictly sufficient for determining behavioral outcomes. But they observe that granting 6 and 7 *doesn't* concede that the *physical* properties of mental events are *necessary* for their behavioral effects. To see this, assume an event *m* which instantiates the mental property M and the physical property P. Assume that *m* has the behavioral outcome *b*, an event with the behavioral property B, and that it does so in virtue of a physical law which strictly connects the instantiation of P with the instantiation of B. LePore and Loewer point out that all this is fully compatible with the truth of the counterfactual: $-Pm$ & $Mm \rightarrow Bb$ (i.e., with it being the case that *m* would have caused B*b* even if it hadn't been P). Think of the case where M events are "multiply realized," e.g., not just by P instantiations but also by P∗ instantiations. And suppose that there's a strict law connecting P∗ events with B events. Then $Mm \rightarrow Bb$ will be true not only when *m* is a P instantiation, but also when *m* is a P∗ instantiation. The point is that *one* way that $-Pm$ & $Mm \rightarrow Bb$ can be true is if there are strict psychological laws; i.e., if being an M instantiation is strictly sufficient for being a B instantiation. But the counterfactual could also be true on the assumption that B instantiations have *disjoint physically sufficient conditions*. And that assumption can be allowed by someone who claims that only physical laws can ground mental causes (e.g., because he claims that only physical laws articulate strictly sufficient conditions for behavioral outcomes).

In short, LePore and Loewer show us that we can get quite a lot of what we want from the causal responsibility of the mental without assuming that intentional events are nomologically sufficient for behavioral outcomes; i.e., without assuming that intentional laws nomologically necessitate their consequents; i.e., without denying that the mental is anomic. Specifically, we can get that the particular constellation of physical properties that a mental cause exhibits needn't be necessary for its behavioral outcomes. I take LePore and Loewer's advice to be that we should settle for this; that we should construe the causal responsibility of the mental in some way that doesn't require mental events to be nomologically sufficient for their behavioral consequences. In effect, given a conflict between 6 and a covering law construal of 8, LePore and Loewer opt for 6; keep the idea that causes have to be strictly covered, and give up on the idea that the causal responsibility of the mental is the nomological necessitation of the behavioral by the intentional.

Now, this may be good advice, but I seem to detect a not-very-hidden agenda. Suppose, just for the sake of argument, that there *is* some way of providing intentionally sufficient conditions for behavioral outcomes. Then this would not only allow for an intuitively satisfying construal of the causal responsibility of the mental (viz., mental properties are causally responsible if mental causes are covered by intentional laws, as per part I), it would also undermine the idea that mental causes have to be covered by *physical* laws. If the laws of psychology have in common with the laws of physics that both strictly necessitate their consequents, then presumably either would do equally well to satisfy the constraints that 6 imposes on the laws that cover mental causes. But the idea that mental causes have to be covered by physical laws is the key step in the famous Davidsonian argument from the anomia of the mental to physicalism. It may be that LePore and Loewer would like to hang onto the Davidsonian argument; it's pretty clear that Davidson would.

I take Davidson's argument to go something like this:

9.1. Mental causes have to be covered by some strict law (strict covering);
9.2. but not by intentional laws because intentional laws aren't strict; the satisfaction of their antecedents isn't nomologically sufficient for the satisfaction of their consequents (anomia of the mental);

9.3. so mental causes must be covered by physical laws;
9.4. so they must have physical properties. Q.E.D.

But if there are intentionally sufficient conditions for behavioral outcomes you lose step 9.2; and if you lose step 9.2, you lose the argument. It appears that the cost of an intuitively adequate construal of mental responsibility is that there's no argument from mental causation to physicalism.

Well, so much for laying out the geography. Here's what happens next: First, I'll try to convince you that your intuitions really do cry out for some sort of causal sufficiency account of causal responsibility; something like that if it's *m*'s being M that's causally responsible for *b*'s being B, then *b* is B in all nearby worlds where *m* is M. (This is, to repeat, a consequence of defining causal responsibility in terms of strict covering laws, since it is a defining property of such laws that the satisfaction of their antecedents necessitates the satisfaction of their consequents.) I'll then suggest that, appearances to the contrary, it really isn't very hard to square such an account with the admission that even the best psychological laws are very likely to be hedged. In effect, I'm claiming that, given a conflict between 6 and 8, there's a natural replacement for 8. At this point the question about physicalism becomes moot since it will no longer be clear why hedged psychological laws can't ground mental causes; and, presumably, if hedged psychological laws can, then strict physical laws needn't. It still might turn out, however, that you can get a physicalist conclusion from considerations about mental causation, though by a slightly different route from the one that Davidson follows—a route that doesn't require the subsumption of causes by strict laws as a lemma.

My first point, then, is that, Loewer and LePore to the contrary notwithstanding, the notion of the causal responsibility of the mental that your intuitions demand is that Ms should be a nomologically sufficient condition for Bs. Accept no substitutes, is what I say. I'm not, however, exactly sure how to convince you that this is indeed what your intuitions cry out for; perhaps the following considerations will seem persuasive.

There aren't, of course, any reliable procedures of scientific discovery. But one might think of the procedures that have sometimes been proposed as, in effect, codifying our intuitions about causal responsibility. For example, it's right to say that Pasteur used the "method of differences" to discover that contact with stuff in the air—and not spontaneous generation in the nutrient—is responsible for the breeding of maggots. This is not, however, a comment on how Pasteur went about thinking up his hypotheses or his experiments. The method of differences doesn't tell you *how* to find out what is causally responsible. Rather, it tells you *what* to find out to find out what's causally responsible. It says: thrash about in the nearby nomologically possible worlds and find a property such that you get the maggots just when you get that property instantiated. *That* will be the property whose instantiation is causally responsible for the maggots.

I'm claiming that Pasteur had in mind to assign causal responsibility for the maggots, and that, in doing so, it was preeminantly reasonable of him to have argued according to the method of differences: viz., that if the infestation is airborne, then fitting a gauze top to the bottle should get rid of the maggots, and taking the gauze top off the bottle should bring the maggots back again. Assigning causal responsibility to contact with stuff in the air involved showing that such contact is necessary *and sufficient* for getting the maggots; that was what the method of differences required, and that was what Pasteur figured out how to do. If those intuitions about causal responsibility were good enough for Pasteur, I guess they ought to be good enough for you and me.

So then, I assume that the method of differences codifies our intuitions about causal responsibility. But this implies that assigning causal responsibility to the mental requires the truth of more counterfactuals than L&L are prepared to allow. Intuitively, what we need is that *m*'s being M is what *makes the difference* in determining whether *b* is B, hence that "B*b* whenever M*m*" is true in all nearby worlds. If the method of differences tells us what causal responsibility is, then what it tells us is that causal responsibility requires nomological sufficiency.[12] So the causal responsibility of the mental must be the nomological sufficiency of intentional states for producing behavioral outcomes.

The first—and crucial—step in getting what a robust construal of the causal responsibility of the mental requires is to square the idea that Ms are nomologically sufficient for Bs with the fact that psychological laws are hedged. How can you have it *both* that special laws only necessitate their consequents ceteris paribus *and* that we must get Bs *whenever* we get Ms. Answer: you can't. But what you can have is just as good: viz., that if it's a law that M → B ceteris paribus, then it follows that you get Bs whenever you get Ms *and* the ceteris paribus conditions are satisfied.[13] This shows us how ceteris paribus laws can do serious scientific business, since it captures the difference between the (substantive) claim that Fs cause Gs ceteris paribus, and the (empty) claim that Fs cause Gs except when they don't.

So, it's sufficient for M to be a causally responsible property if it's a property in virtue of which Ms cause Bs. And here's what it is for M to be a property in virtue of which Ms cause Bs:

10.1. Ms cause Bs;
10.2. "M → B ceteris paribus" is a law;[14] and
10.3. the ceteris paribus conditions are satisfied in respect of some Ms.

I must say, the idea that hedged (including intentional) laws necessitate their consequents when their ceteris paribus clauses are discharged seems to me to be so obviously the pertinent proposal that I'm hard put to see how anybody could seriously object to it. But no doubt somebody will.

One might, I suppose, take the line that there's no fact of the matter about whether, in a given case, the ceteris paribus conditions on a special science law are satisfied. Or that, even if there is a fact of the matter, still one can't ever know what the fact of the matter is. But, surely that would be mad. After all, Pasteur did demonstrate, to the satisfaction of all reasonable men, that ceteris paribus you get maggots when and only when the nutrients are in contact with stuff in the air. And presumably he did it *by* investigating experimental environments in which the ceteris paribus condition was satisfied and known to be so. Whatever is actual is possible; what Pasteur could do in fact, even you and I can do in principle.

I remark, in passing, that determining that ceteris paribus stuff in the air causes maggots did not require that Pasteur be able to *enumerate* the ceteris paribus conditions, only that he be able to recognize some cases in which they were in fact satisfied. *Sufficient* conditions for the satisfaction of ceteris paribus clauses may be determinate and epistemically accessible even when *necessary and sufficient* conditions for their satisfaction aren't. A fortiori, hedged laws whose ceteris paribus conditions cannot be enumerated may nevertheless be satisfied in particular cases. Perhaps we should say that M is causally responsible only if Ms cause Bs in *any* world in which the ceteris paribus clause of "M → B all else equal" is discharged. This would leave it open, and not very important, whether "*all and only* the worlds in which the ceteris paribus conditions are discharged" is actually well defined. It's not very important because what determines whether a given law can cover a given event is whether the law is determinately satisfied by the event. It is not also required that it be determinate whether the law would be satisfied by arbitrary other events (or by that same event in arbitrary other worlds). It seems to me that the plausibility of Davidson's assumption that hedged laws can't ground causes may depend on overlooking this point.

Finally, it might be argued that, although the ceteris paribus conditions on other special-science laws are sometimes known to be satisfied, there is nevertheless something peculiar about *intentional* laws, so that their ceteris paribus conditions can't be. I take it that Davidson thinks that something of this sort is true; but I have never been able to follow the arguments that are supposed to show that it is. And I notice (with approval) that LePore and Loewer are apparently not committed to any such claim.

Where does all this leave us with respect to the classical Davidsonian argument that infers physicalism from the anomalousness of the mental? It seems to me that we are now lacking any convincing argument for accepting principle 6. Suppose it's true that causes need to be covered by laws that necessitate their consequents; it doesn't follow that they need to be covered by *strict* laws. Hedged laws necessitate their consequents in worlds where their ceteris paribus conditions are satisfied. Why, then, should mental causes that are covered by hedged intentional laws with satisfied antecedents and satisfied ceteris paribus conditions require *further* covering by a strict law of physics?

The point till now has been that if strict laws will do to cover causes, so too will hedged laws in worlds where the hedges are discharged. I digress to remark that hedged laws can play the same role as strict ones in covering law explanations, so long as it's part of the explanation that the ceteris paribus conditions are satisfied.

When the antecedent of a strict law is satisfied, you are *guaranteed* the satisfaction of its consequent, and the operation of strict laws in covering law explanations depends on this. What's typically in want of a covering law explanation is some such fact as that an event *m* caused an event *b* (and not, nb, that an event *m* caused an event *b* ceteris paribus).[15] Indeed, it's not clear to me that there are facts of this latter sort. Hedged generalizations are one thing; hedged singulary causal statements would be quite another. Well, the point is that strict laws can explain *m*'s causing *b* precisely because if it's strict that Ms cause Bs and it's true that there is an M, then it *follows* that there is an M-caused *b*. "You got a B because you had an M, and it's a law that you get a B *whenever* you get an M." But if that sort of explanation is satisfying, then so too ought to be: "You got a B in world *w* because you had an M in world *w*, and it's a law that ceteris paribus you get a B whenever you have an M, and the ceteris paribus conditions were satisfied in world *w*." The long and short is: One reason you might think that causes have to be covered by strict laws is that covering law explanations depend on this being so. But they don't. Strict laws and hedged laws with satisfied ceteris paribus conditions operate alike in respect of their roles in covering causal relations and in respect of their roles in covering law explanations. Surely this is as it should be: Strict laws are just the special case of hedged laws where the ceteris paribus clauses are discharged *vacuously*; they're the hedged laws for which 'all else' is *always* equal.

Still, I think that there is *something* to be said for the intuition that strict physical laws play a special role in respect of the metaphysical under-pinnings of causal relations, and I think there may after all be a route from considerations about mental causation to physicalism. I'll close by saying a little about this.

In my view, the metaphysically interesting fact about special-science laws isn't that they're hedged; it's that they're *not basic*. Correspondingly, the metaphysically interesting contrast isn't between physical laws and special science laws; it's between basic laws and the rest. For present purposes, I need to remind you of a difference between special laws and basic laws that I remarked on in part I: If it's nonbasically lawful that Ms cause Bs, there's always a story to tell about how (typically, by what transformations of microstructures) instantiating M brings about the instantiation of B. Nonbasic laws want implementing mechanisms; basic laws don't. (That, I imagine, is what makes them basic.)

It is therefore surely no accident that *hedged* laws are typically—maybe always—*not* basic. On the one hand, it's intrinsic to a law being hedged that it is nomologically possible for its ceteris paribus conditions not to be satisfied. And, on the other hand, a standard way to account for the failure of a ceteris paribus condition is to point to the breakdown of an intervening mechanism. Thus, meandering rivers erode their outside banks ceteris paribus, but not when the speed of the river is artificially controlled (no Bernoulli effect); and not when the river is chemically pure (no suspended particles); and not when somebody has built a wall on the outside bank (not enough abrasion to overcome adhesion). In such cases, the ceteris paribus clause fails to be satisfied *because* an intervening mechanism fails to operate. By contrast, this strategy is unavailable in the case of *non*basic laws; basic laws don't rely on mechanisms of implementation, so if they have exceptions that must be because they're nondeterministic.

We see here one way in which ceteris paribus clauses do their work. Nonbasic laws *rely on* mediating mechanisms which they do not, however, *articulate* (sometimes because the mechanisms aren't known; sometimes because As can cause Bs in many different ways, so that the same law has a variety of implementations). Ceteris paribus clauses can have the effect of existentially quantifying over these mechanisms, so that "As cause Bs ceteris paribus" can mean something like "There exists an intervening mechanism such that As cause Bs when it's intact." I expect that the ceteris paribus clauses in special science laws can do other useful things as well. It is a scandal of the philosophy of science that we haven't got a good taxonomy of their functions.

However, I digress. The present point is that:

11. non-basic laws require mediation by intervening mechanisms; and
12. there are surely no basic laws of psychology.

Let us now make the following bold assumption: all the mechanisms that mediate the operation of nonbasic laws are eventually physical.[16] I don't, I confess, know exactly what this bold assumption means (because I don't know exactly what it *is* for a mechanism to be physical as opposed, say, to spiritual); and I confess that I don't know exactly why it seems to me to be a reasonable bold assumption to make. But I do suspect that if it could be stated clearly, it would be seen to be a sort of bold assumption for which the past successes of our physicalistic world view render substantial inductive support.

Well, if all the mechanisms that nonbasic laws rely on are eventually physical, then the mechanisms of mental causation must be eventually physical, too. For, on the current assumptions, mental causes have their effects in virtue of being subsumed by psychological laws and, since psychological laws aren't basic, they require mediation by intervening mechanisms. However, it seems to me that to admit that mental causes must be related to their effects (including, notice, their *mental* effects) by physical mechanisms *just is* to admit that mental causes are physical. Or, if it's not, then it's to admit something so close that I can't see why the difference matters.

So, then, perhaps there's a route to physicalism from stuff about mental causation that *doesn't* require the claim that ceteris paribus laws can't ground mental causes. If so, then my story gives us both physicalism and a reasonable account of the causal responsibility of the mental; whereas Davidson's story gives us at most the former.[17] But if we *can't* get both the causal responsibility of the mental and an argument for physicalism, then it seems to me that we ought to give up the argument for physicalism. I'm not really convinced that it matters very much whether the mental is physical; still less that it matters very much whether we can prove that it is. Whereas, if it isn't literally true that my wanting is causally responsible for my reaching, and my itching is causally responsible for my scratching, and my believing is causally responsible for my saying.... if none of that is literally true, then practically everything I believe about anything is false and it's the end of the world.

Acknowledgments

This paper is a revised and extended version of some remarks presented at an APA symposium on December 30, 1987, in reply to Ernest LePore and Barry Loewer's "Mind Matters," *Journal of Philosophy* 84.11 (Nov. 1987): 630–642. I am grateful to them and to Brian McLaughlin, for much stimulating conversation on these and related issues.

Notes

1. I shall more or less assume, in what follows, that events are the individuals that causal laws subsume and to which causal powers are ascribed. Nothing will turn on this; it's just a bore to always be having to say "events, or situations, or things or whatever...."

2. It facilitates the discussion not to worry about which of their properties events have essentially. In particular, I shall assume that we can make sense of counterfactuals in which a certain mental event is supposed to have *no* intentional content, or an intentional content or a physical constituency different from its actual content or constituency. Nothing germane to the present issues hangs on this since, as far as I can tell, the same sorts of points I'll be making about counterfactual properties of events could just as well be made about relations between events and their counterparts.

3. What follows is a very crude approximation of the aerodynamic facts. Enthusiasts will find a serious exposition in W. Ross, *Sail Power* (New York: Alfred A. Knopf, 1975).

4. The Covering Principle is generally in the spirit of the proposals of Donald Davidson, except that, unlike Davidson, I'm prepared to be shameless about properties.

5. 5.2 is in the text to emphasize that the nomological subsumption account of the causal responsibility of the mental is closely connected to the idea that mental events are nomologically sufficient for behavioral outcomes. We will thus have to consider how to square the nomological subsumption story with the fact that the antecedents of psychological laws generally do *not* specify nomologically sufficient conditions for the satisfaction of their consequents (because, like the laws of the other special sciences, the laws of psychology typically have essential ceteris paribus causes). See part II.

6. I'm leaving statistical laws out of consideration. If some laws are irremediably statistical, then the proposal in the text should be changed to read: "any property in virtue of which some deterministic law covers an individual will be a property in virtue of which some causal law covers an individual."

7. But this will have to be hedged to deal with ceteris paribus laws. Part II is about what's the right way to hedge it.

8. N. Hornstein, "The Heartbreak of Semantics," *Mind and Language* 3 (1988): 18.

9. Special science laws are unstrict not just de facto, but in principle. Specifically, they are characteristically "*heteronomic*": You can't convert them into strict laws by elaborating their antecedents. One reason why this is so is that special science laws typically fail in limiting conditions, or in conditions where the idealizations presupposed by the science aren't approximated; and, generally speaking, you have to go outside the vocabulary of the science to say what these conditions are. Old rivers meander, but not when somebody builds a levee. Notice that "levee" is not a *geological* term. (Neither, for that matter, is "somebody.")

I emphasize this point because it's sometimes supposed that heteronomicity is a proprietary feature of *intentional* laws qua intentional. Poppycock.

10. It could, no doubt, be said that accepting 6 doesn't really make the mental properties drop out of the picture because, even if mental causes have to be covered by physical laws, it can still be true that they are *also* covered by intentional laws (*viz.*, in the old 4.3 sense of "covering" which didn't require covering laws to be strict). As Brian McLaughlin (ms) has rightly pointed out, it's perfectly consistent to hold that covering by strict laws is necessary and sufficient for causal relations and *also to hold that covering by loose laws is necessary, or even sufficient, for causal relations*, so long as you are prepared to assume that every cause that is loosely covered is strictly covered, too.

However, it is not clear that this observation buys much relief from epiphobia. After all, if mental properties really are causally active, why isn't intentional covering *all by itself* sufficient to ground the causal relations of mental events? I've been urging that intentional properties are causally responsible if mental causes are covered by intentional laws. But that seems plausible only if mental events are causes *in virtue of* their being covered by intentional laws. But how could mental causes be causes qua intentionally covered if, in order to *be* causes, they are further required to be subsumed by nonintentional laws? Taken together, 6 and 7 make it look as though, even if mental events are covered qua intentional, they're causes only qua physical. So again it looks like the intentional properties of mental events aren't doing any of the work.

11. I'm doing a little pussyfooting here, so perhaps I'd better put the point exactly: On the view that I will presently commend, there *are* circumstances in which instantiations of mental proper-

ties nomologically necessitate behavioral outcomes. What isn't, however, quite the case is that these circumstances are fully specified by the antecedents of intentional laws. On my view, only *basic* laws have the property that their antecedents fully specify the circumstances that nomologically necessitate the satisfaction of their consequents (and then only if they're deterministic).

12. It will be noticed that I'm stressing the importance of causal sufficiency for causal responsibility, whereas it was causal necessity that Pasteur cared about most. Pasteur was out to show that contact with stuff in the air and *only* contact with stuff in the air is causally responsible for maggots; specifically that contact with stuff in the air accounts for *all* of the maggots, hence that spontaneous generation accounts for none. I take it that it is *not* among our intuitions that a certain mental property is causally responsible for a certain behavior only if that sort of behavior can have no other sort of cause.

13. So, what I said above—that a law is a hypothetical the satisfaction of whose antecedent nomologically necessitates the satisfaction of its consequent—wasn't quite true since it doesn't quite apply to hedged laws. What *is* true is that a law is a hypothetical the satisfaction of whose antecedent nomologically necessitates the satisfaction of its consequent *when its ceteris paribus conditions are satisfied.*

14. If it's a strict law, then the ceteris paribus clause is vacuously satisfied.

15. To put it another way: Suppose you're feeling Hempelian about the role of covering laws in scientific explanations. Then you might worry that (i) ceteris paribus As cause Bs together with (ii) Aa yields something like (iii) ceteris paribus Bb which isn't strong enough to explain the datum (Bb). "Ceteris paribus Bb" doesn't look to have the form of a possible data statement. I wonder in the text whether it even has the form of a possible truth.

16. "Eventually" means: either the law is implemented by a physical mechanism, or its implementation depends on a lower level law which is itself either implemented by a physical mechanism or is dependent on a still lower level law which is itself either implemented by a physical mechanism or . . . , etc. Since only finite chains of implementation are allowed, you have to get to a physical mechanism "eventually."

We need to put it this way because, as we've been using it, a "physical" mechanism is one whose means of operation is covered by a physical law (i.e., by a law articulated in the language of physics). And though, presumably, physical mechanisms implement every high-level law, they usually do so via lots of levels of intermediate laws and implementations. So, for example, intentional laws are implemented by syntactic mechanisms that are governed by syntactic laws that are implemented by neurological mechanisms that are governed by neurological laws that are implemented by biochemical mechanisms that . . . and so on down to physics.

None of this really matters for present purposes, of course. A demonstration that mental events have neural properties would do to solve the mind/body problem since nobody doubts that neural events have physical properties.

17. On the other hand, I don't pretend to do what Davidson seems to think he can: viz., to get physicalism *just* from considerations about the constraints that causation places on covering laws together with the truism that psychological laws aren't strict. That project was breathtakingly ambitious but maybe not breathtakingly well advised. My guess is: If you want to get a lot of physicalism out, you're going to have to put a lot of physicalism in; what I put in was the independent assumption that the mechanism of intentional causation is physical.

39 The Myth of Nonreductive Materialism

Jaegwon Kim

I

Reductionism of all sorts has been out of favor for many years. Few among us would now seriously entertain the possibility that ethical expressions are definable, or reducible in some broader sense, in terms of "descriptive" or "naturalistic" expressions. I am not sure how many of us can remember, in vivid enough detail, the question that was once vigorously debated as to whether so-called "physical-object statements" are translatable into statements about the phenomenal aspects of perceptual experience, whether these are conceived as "sense data" or as some manner of "being appeared to." You may recall the idea that concepts of scientific theories must be reduced, via "operational definitions," to intersubjectively performable procedures whose results can be ascertained through observation. This sounded good—properly tough-minded and hard-nosed—but it didn't take long for philosophers and scientists to realize that a restrictive constraint of this sort was neither enforceable nor necessary—not necessary to safeguard science from the threat of metaphysics and pseudo-science. These reductionisms are now nothing but museum pieces.

In philosophy of mind, too, we have gone through many reductionisms; some of these, such as logical behaviorism, have been defunct for many years; others, most notably the psychoneural identity theory, have been repeatedly declared dead; and still others, such as versions of functionalism, are still hanging on, though with varying degrees of difficulty. Perhaps as a result of the singular lack of success with which our earlier reductionist efforts have been rewarded, a negative image seems to have emerged for reductionisms in general. Many of us have the feeling that there is something rigid and narrow-minded about reductionist strategies. Reductionisms, we tend to feel, attempt to impose on us a monolithic, strait-jacketed view of the subject matter, the kind of cleansed and tidy picture that appeals to those obsessed with orderliness and discipline. Perhaps this impression has something to do with the reductionists' ritual incantations of slogans like "parsimony," "simplicity," "economy," and "unity," all of them virtues of a rather puritanical sort. Perhaps, too, reductionisms are out of step with the intellectual style of our times: we strive for patterns of life and thought that are rich in diversity and complexity and tolerant of disagreement and multiplicity. We are apt to think that the real world is a messy place and resists any simplistic drive, especially one carried on from the armchair, toward simplification and unification. In fact, the word "reductionism" seems by now to have acquired a negative, faintly disreputable flavor—at least in philosophy of mind. Being a reductionist is a bit like being a logical positivist or member of the Old Left—an aura of doctrinaire naivete hangs over such a person.

At any rate, reductionism in the mind–body problem has been out of fashion for two decades; it has been about that long since the unexpectedly early demise of the psychoneural identity theory, a doctrine advertised by its proponents as the one that was in tune with a world view adequately informed by the best contemporary science. Surprisingly, the abandonment of psychoneural reductionism has not led to a resurgence of dualism. What is curious, at least in terms of the expectations set by the earlier mind–body debates, is the fact that those who renounced reductionism have stayed with physicalism. The distinctive feature of the mind–body theories that have sprung up in the wake of the identity theory is the belief, or hope, that one can be an honest-to-goodness physicalist without at the same time being a reductionist. In fact, a correct and realistic view of science as it is practiced will show us, the new physicalists assure us, that as an account of the "cross-level" relation between theories, classical reductionism is untenable everywhere, not just about the psychophysical relation. The leading idea in all this has been the thought that we can assuage our physicalist qualms by embracing "ontological physicalism,"[1] the claim that all that exists in spacetime is physical, but, at the same time, accept "property dualism," a dualism about psychological and physical attributes, insisting that psychological concepts or properties form an irreducible, autonomous domain. The issue I want to explore here is whether or not a robust physicalist can, consistently and plausibly, swear off reductionism—that is, whether or not a substantial form of physicalism can be combined with the rejection of psychophysical reduction.

To lay my cards on the table, I will argue that a middle-of-the road position of the sort just described is not available. More specifically, I will claim that a physicalist has only two genuine options, eliminativism and reductionism. That is, if you have already made your commitment to a version of physicalism worthy of the name, you must accept the reducibility of the psychological to the physical, or, failing that, you must consider the psychological as falling outside your physicalistically respectable ontology. Of course, you might decide to reconsider your commitment to physicalism; but I will not here consider what dualist alternatives there might be which are still live options for us. So if I am right, the choices we face concerning the mind–body problem are rather stark: there are three—dualism, reductionism, and eliminativism.

II

Pressures from two sources have been largely responsible, I believe, for the decline of reductionism in philosophy of mind, a decline that began in the late 1960's. One was Donald Davidson's "anomalism of the mental," the doctrine that there are no precise or strict laws about mental events.[2] According to Davidson, the mental is anomalous not only in that there are no laws relating mental events to other mental events but none relating them to physical events either. This meant that no nomological linkages between the mental and the physical were available to enable the reduction of the former to the latter. The second antireductionist pressure came from a line of argument based on the phenomenon of "multiple realizability" of mental states which Hilary Putnam forcefully brought to philosophical attention, claiming that it directly refuted the reductive materialism of Smart and Feigl.[3] Jerry Fodor and others have developed this idea as a general antireductionist argument, advancing the claim that the "special sciences," such as psychology, sociology, and economics, are in general irreducible to physical theory, and that reductive materialism, or "type identity theory," is generally false as a theory about science.[4] Earlier physicalists would have regarded the irreducibility as evidence showing the mental to be beyond the pale of a scientifically respectable ontology; that is, they would have inferred eliminativism from the irreducibility. This in fact was Quine's response to the problem of intentionality.[5] But not for the latter-day physicalists: for them, the irreducibility only meant that psychology, and other special sciences, are "autonomous," and that a physicalist can, in consistency and good conscience, accept the existence of these isolated autonomous domains within science.

Let us begin with Davidson. As noted, the anomalism of the mental can be thought of as the conjunction of two claims: first, the claim that there are no purely psychological laws, that is, laws connecting psychological events with other psychological events, and second, the claim that there are no laws connecting psychological events; with physical events. The second claim, which we might call "psychophysical anomalism," is what underlies Davidson's argument against reductionism. The argument is simple and direct: the demise of analytical behaviorism scotched the idea that the mental could be definitionally reduced to the physical. Further, psychophysical anomalism shows that a nomological reduction of the mental isn't in the offing either. The implicit assumption about reduction in this argument is one that is widely shared: reduction of one theory to another requires the derivation of the laws of the reduced theory from those of the reducer, and for this to be possible, terms of the first theory must be appropriately connected via "bridge principles," with those of the second. And the bridge principles must be either conceptually underwritten as definitions, or else express empirical lawlike correlations ("bridge laws" or "theoretical identities").[6]

This is all pretty straightforward. What was striking was the further philosophical conclusions Davidson inferred from these considerations. Far from deriving some sort of dualism, he used them to argue for a materialist monism. His argument is well known, but it bears repeating. Mental events, Davidson observed, enter into causal relations with physical events.[7] But causal relations must be backed by laws; that is, causal relations between individual events must instantiate lawful regularities. Since there are no laws about the mental, either psychophysical or purely psychological, any causal relation involving a mental event must instantiate a physical law, from which it follows that the mental event has a physical description, or falls under a physical event kind. From this it further follows that the event is a physical event. For an event is physical (or mental) if it falls under a physical event kind (or a mental event kind).

It follows then that all events are physical events—on the assumption that every event enters into at least one causal relation. This assumption seems entirely unproblematic, for it only leaves out events that are both *causeless* and *effectless*. If there are any such events, it is difficult to see how their existence can be known to us; I believe we could safely ignore them. So imagine a Davidsonian universe of events: all these events are physical events, and some of them are also mental. That is to say, all events have physical properties, and some have mental properties as well. Such is Davidson's celebrated "anomalous monism."

Davidson's ontology recognizes individual events as spatiotemporal particulars. And the principal structure over these events is causal structure; the network of causal relations that interconnect events is what gives intelligible structure to this universe of events. What role does mentality play, on Davidson's anomalous monism, in shaping this structure? The answer: None whatever.

For anomalous monism entails this: the very same network of causal relations would obtain in Davidson's world if you were to redistribute mental properties over its events any way you like; you would not disturb a single causal relation if you randomly and arbitrarily reassigned mental properties to events, or even removed mentality entirely from the world. The fact is that under Davidson's anomalous monism, mentality does no causal work. Remember: on anomalous monism, events are causes or effects only as they instantiate physical laws, and this means that an event's mental properties make no causal difference. And to suppose that altering an event's mental properties would also alter its physical properties and thereby affect its causal relations is to suppose that psychophysical anomalism, a cardinal tenet of anomalous monism, is false.[8]

Anomalous monism, therefore, permits mental properties no causal role, not even in relation to other mental properties. What does no causal work does no explanatory work either; it may as well not be there—it's difficult to see how we could miss it if it weren't there at all. That there are in this world just these mental events with just these mental characteristics is something that makes no causal difference to anything. On anomalous monism, that an event falls under a given mental kind is a causally irrelevant fact; it is also something that is entirely inexplicable in causal terms. Given all this, it's difficult to see what point there is in recognizing mentality as a feature of the world. I believe that if we push anomalous monism this way, we will find that it is a doctrine virtually indistinguishable from outright eliminativism.

Thus, what we see is this: anomalous monism, rather than giving us a form of nonreductive physicalism, is essentially a form of eliminativism. Unlike eliminativism, it allows mentality to exist; but mentality is given no useful work and its occurrence is left wholly mysterious and causally inexplicable. This doesn't strike me as a form of existence worth having. In this respect, anomalous monism does rather poorly even in comparison with epiphenomenalism as a realism about the mental. Epiphenomenalism gives the mental a place in the causal network of events; the mind is given a well-defined place, if not an active role, in the causal structure of the world.

These observations highlight the importance of *properties*; for it is in terms of properties and their interrelations that we make sense of certain concepts that are crucial in this context, such as law, causality, explanation, and dependence. Thus, the anomalousness of mental properties has far-reaching consequences within Davidson's framework: within it, anomalous properties are causally and explanatorily impotent, and it is doubtful that they can have any useful role at all. The upshot is that we don't get in Davidson's anomalous monism a plausible form of nonreductive physicalism; his anomalous monism comes perilously close to eliminativism.[9]

III

Let us now turn to the multiple realizability (or "compositional plasticity") of psychological events and its implications for psychophysical reduction. In a passage that turned out to have a profound impact on the discussions of the mind–body problem, Putnam wrote:[10]

> Consider what the brain-state theorist has to do to make good his claims. He has to specify a physical-chemical state such that *any* organism (not just a mammal) is in pain if and only if (a) it possesses a brain of a suitable physical-chemical structure; and (b) its brain is in that physical-chemical state. This means that the physical-chemical state in question must be a possible state of a mammalian brain, a reptilian brain, a mollusc's brain (octopuses are mollusca, and certainly feel pain), etc. At the same time, it must *not* be a possible (physically possible) state of the brain of any physically possible creature that cannot feel pain. Even if such a state can be found, it must be nomologically certain that it will also be a state of the brain of any extraterrestrial life that may be found that will be capable of feeling pain before we can even entertain the supposition that it may *be* pain.

This paragraph helped bring on an unexpectedly early demise of the psychoneural identity theory of Smart and Feigl and inspired a new theory of the mental, functionalism, which in spite of its assorted difficulties is still the most influential position on the nature of the mental.[11] Putnam's basic point is that any psychological event-type can be "physically realized" or "instantiated" or "implemented" in endlessly diverse ways, depending on the physical-biological nature of the organism or system involved, and that this makes it highly implausible to expect the event to correlate uniformly with, and thus be identifiable with, some "single" type of neural or physical state. This idea has been used by Fodor to formulate a general antireductionist argument, whose gist can be quickly summarized.

As we have seen, reduction of one theory to another is thought to require the derivation of the laws of the reduced theory from the laws of the reducer via "bridge laws." If a predicate of the theory being reduced has a nomologically coextensive predicate in the reducing theory, the universally quantified biconditional connecting the two predicates will be available for use as a bridge law.[12] Let us say that the vocabulary of the reduced theory is "strongly connected" with that of the reducing theory if such a biconditional bridge law correlates each predicate of the former with a predicate of the latter. It is clear that the condition of strong connectibility guarantees reduction (on the assumption that the theory being reduced is a true theory). For it would enable us to rewrite basic laws of the target theory in the vocabulary of the reducer, using these biconditional laws in effect as definitions. Either these rewrites are derivable from the laws of the reducing theory, or else they can be added as additional basic laws. In the latter case, the reducer theory has been expanded; but that does not diminish the ontological and conceptual import of the reductive procedure.

But what multiple realization puts in doubt, according to the antireductionist, is precisely the strong connectibility of mental predicates vis-à-vis physical-neural predicates. For any psychological property, there is in principle an endless sequence of nomologically possible physical states such that, though each of them "realizes" or "implements" it, none of them will by itself be coextensive with it. Why can't we take the *disjunction* of these physical states as the physical coextension of the mental property? Putnam somewhat disdainfully dismisses this move, saying only that "this does not have to be taken seriously."[13] I think there are some complex issues here about disjunctive predicates vs. disjunctive properties, complexity of predicates vs. that of properties, etc.; but these are likely to be contentious issues that can only distract us at present.[14] So let us go along with Putnam here and disregard the disjunctive solution to the multiple realization problem.

In rejecting the disjunction move, however, Putnam appears to be assuming this: *a physical state that realizes a mental event is at least nomologically sufficient for it.* For if this assumption were rejected, the disjunction move couldn't even get started. This generates laws of the form "Pi → M," where M is a mental state and Pi is a physical state that realizes it. Thus, where there is multiple realization, there must be psychophysical laws, each specifying a physical state as nomologically sufficient for the given mental state. Moreover, Putnam's choice of examples in the quotation above, which are either biological species or determinate types of physical structures ("extraterrestrials"), and his talk of "species-specificity" and "species-independence"[15] suggest that he is thinking of laws of a somewhat stronger form, "Si → (M ↔ Pi)," which, *relative to species or structure* Si, specifies a physical state, Pi, as *both necessary and sufficient* for the occurrence of mental state M. A law of this form states that any organism or system, belonging to a certain species, is such that it has the given mental property at a time if and only if it is in a certain specified physical state at that time. We may call laws of this form "species-specific biconditional laws."

In order to generate laws of this kind, biological species may turn out to be too wide; individual differences in the localization of psychological functions in the brain are well known. Moreover, given the phenomena of learning and maturation, injuries to the brain, and the like, the neural structure that subserves a psychological state or function may change for an individual over its lifetime. What is important then is that these laws are relative to physical-biological structure-types, although for simplicity I will continue to put the matter in terms of species. The substantive theoretical assumption here is the belief that for each psychological state there are physical-biological structure types, at a certain level of description or specification, that generate laws of this form. I think an assumption of this kind is made by most philosophers who speak of multiple realizations of psychological states, and it is in fact a plausible assumption for a physicalist to make.[16] Moreover, such an assumption seems essential to the very idea of a physical realization; what else could "physical realization" mean?

So what I am saying is this: the multiple realization argument perhaps shows that the strong connectibility of mental properties vis-à-vis physical properties does not obtain: however, it *presupposes* that *species-specific strong connectibility* does hold. Merely to defeat the antireductionist argument, I need not make this second claim; all I need is the weaker claim that the phenomenon of multiple realization is *consistent* with the species-specific strong connectibility, and it seems to me that that is plainly true.

The point of all this is that the availability of species-specific biconditional laws linking the mental with the physical breathes new life into psychophysical reductionism. Unlike species-independent laws, these laws cannot buy us a *uniform* or *global* reduction of psychology, a reduction of every psychological state to a uniform physical-biological base across all actual and possible organisms; however, these laws will buy us a series of *species-specific* or *local* reductions. If we had a law of this form for each psychological state-type for humans, we would have a physical reduction of human psychology; this reduction would tell us how human psychology is physically implemented, how the causal connections between our psychological events and processes work at the physical-biological level, what biological subsystems subserve our cognitive capacities and functions, and so forth. This is reduction in a full-blown sense, except that it is limited to individuals sharing a certain physical-biological structure. I believe "local reductions" of this sort are the rule rather than the exception in all of science, not just in psychology.[17] In any case, this is a plausible picture of what in fact goes on in neurobiology, physiological psychology and cognitive neuroscience. And it seems to me that any robust physicalist must expect, and demand, the possibility of local reductions of psychology just in this sense.[18]

Thus, the conclusion we must draw is that the multiple realizability of the mental has no antireductionist implications of great significance; on the contrary, it entails, or at least is consistent with, the local reducibility of psychology, local relative to species or physical structure-types. If psychological states are multiply realized, that only means that we shall have multiple local reductions of psychology. The multiple realization argument, if it works, shows that a global reduction is not in the offing; however, local reductions are reduction enough, by any reasonable scientific standards and in their philosophical implications.

IV

Some have looked to the idea of "supervenience" for a formulation of physicalism that is free of reductionist commitments. The promise of supervenience in this area appears to have been based, at least in part, on the historical circumstance that some prominent ethical theorists, such as G. E. Moore and R. M. Hare, who constructed classic arguments against naturalistic reductionism in ethics, at the same time held the view that moral properties are "supervenient" upon descriptive or naturalistic properties. So why not think of the relation between psychological and physical properties in analogy with the relation, as conceived by these ethical theorists, between moral and descriptive properties? In each instance, the supervenient properties are in some substantive sense dependent on, or determined by, their subvenient, base properties and yet, it is hoped, irreducible to them. This was precisely the line of thinking that appears to have prompted Davidson to inject supervenience into the discussion of the mind–body problem. He wrote:[19]

> Although the position I describe denies there are psychophysical laws, it is consistent with the view that mental characteristics are in some sense dependent, or supervenient, on physical characteristics. Such supervenience might be taken to mean that there cannot be two events alike in all physical respects but differing in some mental respects, or that an object cannot alter in some mental respect without altering in some physical respect. Dependence or supervenience of this kind does not entail reducibility through law or definition: if it did, we could reduce moral properties to descriptive, and this there is good reason to *believe* cannot be done....

Although Davidson himself did not pursue this idea further, many other philosophers have tried to work this suggestive idea into a viable form of nonreductive materialism.

The central problem in implementing Davidson's suggestion has been that of defining a supervenience relation that will fill the twin requirements he set forth: first, the relation must be *nonreductive*; that is, a given domain can be supervenient on another without being reducible to it. Second, the relation must be one of *dependence*: if a domain supervenes on another, there must be a sturdy sense in which the first is dependent on the second, or the second determines the first. But it has not been easy to find such a relation. The main difficulty has been this: if a relation is weak enough to be nonreductive, it tends to be too weak to serve as a dependence relation; conversely, when a relation is strong enough to give us dependence, it tends to be too strong—strong enough to imply reducibility.

I will not rehearse here the well known arguments pro and con concerning various supervenience relations that have been proposed. I will instead focus on one supervenience relation that has seemed to several philosophers[20] to hold the most promise as a nonreductive dependency relation, viz., "global supervenience." The generic idea of supervenience is that things that are indiscernible in respect of the "base" (or "subvenient") properties cannot differ in respect of the supervenient properties. Global supervenience applies this consideration to "worlds," giving us the following formulation of psychophysical supervenience:

Worlds that are indiscernible in all physical respects are indiscernible in mental respects; in fact, physically indiscernible worlds are one and the same world.

Thus, any world that is just like this world in all physical details must be just like it in all psychological respects as well. This relation of supervenience is appropriately called "global" in that worlds rather than individuals within worlds are compared for discernibility or indiscernibility in regard to sets of properties. What is it for two worlds to be physically, or mentally, indiscernible? For simplicity let us assume that the same individuals exist in all the worlds:[21] We may then say that two worlds are indiscernible with respect to a set of properties just in case these properties are distributed over individuals in the same way in the two worlds.

It can be shown that, as hoped, the global supervenience of the mental on the physical does not entail the existence of psychophysical laws;[22] thus, global supervenience is consistent with the nomological irreducibility of the mental to the physical. The only question then is whether it yields an appropriate relation of dependency between the mental and the physical, one that is strong enough to qualify it as a physicalism. The answer, I will argue, is in the negative.

We may begin by observing that the global supervenience of the mental permits the following: Imagine a world that differs from the actual world in some minute physical detail. We may suppose that in that world one lone hydrogen atom somewhere in deep space is slightly displaced relative to its position in this world. This world with one wayward hydrogen atom could, consistently with the global supervenience of the mental, be as different as you please from the actual world in any mental respect (thus, in that world nothing manifests mentality, or mentality is radically redistributed in other ways). The existence of such a world and other similarly aberrant worlds does not violate the constraints of global supervenience; since they are not physically indiscernible from the actual world, they could, under global supervenience, differ radically from this world in psychological characteristics.[23]

If that doesn't convince you of the weakness of global supervenience as a determination or dependency relation, consider this: it is consistent with global supervenience for there to be two organisms in our actual world which, though wholly indiscernible physically, are radically different in mental respects (say, your molecule-for-molecule duplicate is totally lacking in mentality). This is consistent with global supervenience because there might be no other possible world that is just like this one physically and yet differing in some mental respect.[24]

It seems to me that indiscernibility considerations at the global level, involving whole worlds, are just too coarse to give us the kind of dependency relation we should demand if the mental is truly dependent on the physical. Like it or not, we treat individuals, and perhaps also aggregates of individuals smaller than total worlds, as psychological units, and it seems to me that if psychophysical determination or dependence means anything, it ought to mean that the psychological nature of each such unit is wholly determined by its physical nature. That is, dependency or determination must hold at the local as well as the global level.

Moreover, talk of whole worlds in this connection, unless it is anchored in determinative relations obtaining at the local level, has little verifiable content; it is difficult to see how there can be empirical evidence for the global supervenience thesis that is not based in evidence about specific psychophysical dependencies—dependencies and correlations between specific psychological and physical properties. In fact, it seems to me that we must look to local dependencies for an *explanation* of global supervenience as well as its evidence. Why is it the case that no two worlds can exist that are indiscernible physically and yet discernible psychologically? Or why is it the case that "physical truths determine all the truths,"[25] as some prefer to put it? I think this is a legitimate question to raise, and as far as I can see the only answer, other than the response that it is a brute, unexplainable metaphysical fact, is in terms of local correlations and dependencies between specific mental and physical properties. If the global supervenience of the mental on the physical were to be proposed as an unexplainable fact that we must accept on faith, I doubt that we need to take the proposal seriously. Specific psychophysical dependencies holding for individuals, and other proper parts of the world, are both evidence for, and an explanatory ground of, global supervenience.

The trouble is that once we begin talking about correlations and dependencies between specific psychological and physical properties, we are in effect talking about psychophysical laws, and these laws raise the specter of unwanted physical reductionism. Where there are psychophysical laws, there is always the threat, or promise, of psychophysical reduction. We must conclude that supervenience is not going to deliver to us a viable form of nonreductive materialism.

V

So far I have reviewed three influential formulations of nonreductive materialism—Davidson's anomalous monism, the Putnam-Fodor doctrine of psychological autonomy, and supervenient physicalism—and found each of them wanting either as a materialism or as an antireductionism. In this final section, I want to advance a direct argument to show why the prospects for a nonreductive physicalism are dim.

Let us first of all note that nonreductive physicalism is not to be a form of eliminativism; that is, it acknowledges the mental as a legitimate domain of entities. What sort of entities? Here let us, for convenience, make use of the Davidsonian scheme of individual events, thinking of mentality to be exhibited as properties of these events. Thus, as a noneliminativist, the nonreductive physicalist believes that there are events in her ontology that have mental properties (e.g., being a pain, being a belief that snow is cold, etc.). I argued earlier, in discussing Davidson's anomalous monism, that if your noneliminativism is to be more than a token gesture, you had better find some real causal work for your mental properties. The fact that a given event is a mental event of a certain kind must play some causal-explanatory role in what other events occur and what properties they have. Thus, I am supposing that a nonreductive physicalist is a mental realist, and that to be a mental realist, your mental properties must be *causal properties*—properties in virtue of which an event enters into causal relations it would otherwise not have entered into.

Let me now make another assumption: psychophysical causation takes place—that is, some mental events cause physical events. For example, a sudden sharp pain felt in my hand causes a jerky withdrawal of the hand. It is true that in a Davidsonian domain, all events are physical; that is, every event has some physical property. But when I say that mental events cause physical events, something stronger is intended, namely that an event, *in virtue of its mental property*, causes another event to have a certain physical property. I believe that this assumption will be granted by most of us—it will be granted by anyone who believes that at least sometimes our limbs move because we have certain desires and beliefs.[26] When I walk to the water fountain for a drink of water, my legs move in the way they do in part because of my desire for water and my belief that there is water to be had at the water fountain.

There is a further assumption that I believe any physicalist would grant. I call this "the causal closure of the physical domain"; roughly, it says this: *any physical event that has a cause at time t has a physical cause at t*. This is the assumption that if we trace the causal ancestry of a physical event, we need never go outside the physical domain. To deny this assumption is to accept the Cartesian idea that some physical events have only nonphysical causes, and if this is true there can in principle be no complete and self-sufficient physical theory of the physical domain. If the causal closure failed, our physics would need to refer in an essential way to nonphysical causal agents, perhaps Cartesian souls and their psychic properties, if it is to give a complete account of the physical world. I think most physicalists would find that picture unacceptable.

Now we are ready to derive some consequences from these assumptions. Suppose that a certain event, in virtue of its mental property, causes a physical event. The causal closure of the physical domain says that this physical event must also have a physical cause. We may assume that this physical cause, in virtue of its physical property, causes the physical event. The following question arises: *What is the relationship between these two causes, one mental and the other physical?* Each is claimed to be a cause of the physical effect. There are two initial possibilities that we can consider.

First, when we are faced with two purported causes of a single event, we could entertain the possibility that each is only a *partial cause*, the two together making up a full or sufficient cause, as when a car crash is said to be caused by the driver's careless braking and the icy condition of the road. Applied to our case, it says that the mental cause and the physical cause are each only a partial cause, and that they *together* make up one sufficient cause. This seems like an absurd thing to say, and in any case it violates the causal closure principle in that it regards the mental event as a necessary constituent of a full cause of a physical event; thus, on this view, a full causal story of how this physical event occurs must, at least partially, go outside the physical domain.

Could it be that the mental cause and the physical cause are each an *independent sufficient* cause of the physical effect? The suggestion then is that the physical effect is *overdetermined*. So if the physical cause hadn't occurred, the mental cause by itself would have caused the effect. This picture is again absurd: from what we know about the physiology of limb movement, we must believe that if the pain sensation causes my hand to withdraw, the causal chain from the pain to the limb motion must somehow make use of the causal chain from an appropriate central neural event to the muscle contraction; it makes no sense to think that there was an independent, perhaps telekinetic, causal path from the pain to the limb movement. Moreover, the overdetermination idea seems to violate the causal closure principle as well: in the counterfactual situation in which the physical cause does not occur, the closure principle is violated. For the idea that the mental and the physical cause are each an independent sufficient cause involves the acceptance of the counterfactual that if the physical cause had not occurred, the mental cause would have occurred and caused the physical effect. This is in violation of the causal closure principle.

These two ways of looking at the situation are obvious nonstarters. We need a more plausible answer to the question, how are the mental cause and the physical cause of the single physical effect related to each other? Given that any physical event has a physical cause, how is a mental cause *also* possible? This I call "the problem of causal-explanatory exclusion," for the problem seems to arise from the fact that a cause, or causal explanation, of an event, when it is regarded as a full, sufficient cause or explanation, appears to *exclude* other *independent* purported causes or causal explanations of it.[27]

At this point, you might want to protest: why all this beating around the bush? Why not just say the mental cause and the physical cause are one and the same? Identification simplifies ontology and gets rid of unwanted puzzles. Consider saying that there are in this glass two distinct substances, H_2O and water; that is, consider saying that water and H_2O co-occur everywhere as a matter of law but that they are distinct substances nonetheless. This would invite a host of unwanted and unnecessary puzzles: given that what is in the glass weighs a total of ten ounces, how much of the weight is to be attributed to the water and how much to the H_2O? By dropping a lighted match in the glass, I extinguish it. What caused it? Was it the water or the H_2O? Were they each only a partial cause, or was the extinguishing of the match overdetermined? The identification of the water with the H_2O puts all these questions to rest in a single stroke: there is here one thing, not two. The identity solution can work similar magic in our present case: the pain *is* a neural state—here there is one cause, not two. The limb motion was caused by the pain, that is to say, by a neural state. The unwanted puzzles vanish.

All this is correct. But what does the identity solution involve? Remember that what is for us at issue is the causal efficacy of *mental properties* of events vis-à-vis their physical properties. Thus, the items that need to be identified are properties—that is, we would need to identify mental properties with physical properties. If this could be done, that would be an excellent way of vindicating the causal powers of mentality.

But this is precisely the route that is barred to our nonreductivist friends. The identification of mental properties with physical properties is the heart of reductionist "type physicalism." These property identities would serve as bridge laws par excellence, enabling a derivational reduction of psychology to physical theory. The identities entail psychophysical correlations of biconditional form, stable over possible, or nomologically possible, worlds, and this, we have been told, is excluded by Davidson's mental anomalism and Putnam's multiple realization argument. So the identity solution is out of the question for the nonreductive materialist. Is there any other way to respond to the causal exclusion problem, a way that falls short of identifying mental with physical attributes?

There is one, but it isn't something that would be palatable to the nonreductivist. I believe that the only way other than the identity solution is to give a general account of causal relations involving macro-events as "supervenient causal relations," causal relations that are supervenient on micro-causal processes. You put a kettle of water on the stove and turn on the burner; and soon the water starts to boil. Heating the water caused it to boil. That is a causal relation at the macro-level. It is natural to think of this causal relation as supervenient on certain underlying causal processes at the micro-level. The heating of water supervenes on the increasing kinetic energy of water molecules, and when their mean kinetic energy reaches a certain level, water molecules begin to move in turbulence, some of them being ejected into the air. Boiling is a macro-state that supervenes on just these micro-processes. A sharp pain causes an anxiety attack five seconds later. What's going on? Again, it is tempting, and natural, to think thus: the pain is supervenient on a certain underlying neural activity, and this neural event causes another neural event to occur. The anxiety attack occurs because it is supervenient on this second neural event.

The general model of supervenient causation applied to macro-causal relations is this: macro-event **m** is a cause or effect of event **E** in virtue of the fact that **m** is supervenient on some micro-event, **n**, which is a cause or effect of event **E**.[28] The suggestion then is that we use this model to explain mental causation: a mental event is a cause, or an effect, of another event in virtue of the fact that it is supervenient on some physical event standing in an appropriate causal relation to this event. Thus, mental properties are seen as deriving their causal potential from the physical properties on which they supervene. That is the main idea.

But what sort of supervenience relation is involved in this picture? Global supervenience we considered above obviously will not do; it does not give us a way of speaking of supervenience of specific mental properties on specific physical properties, since it only refers to indiscernibility holding for worlds. Supervenient causation in my sense requires talk of specific mental properties supervening on specific physical base properties, and this is possible only if there are laws correlating psychological with physical properties. This is what I have called elsewhere "strong supervenience," and it can be argued plausibly that supervenience of this strength entails the possibility of reducing the supervenient to the subvenient.[29] I will spare you the details here, but the fact that this form of supervenience directly involves psychophysical laws would be enough to give pause to any would-be nonreductive physicalist. I am not entirely certain that this supervenience solution will suffice; that is, I am not certain that anything short of the identity solution will resolve the exclusion problem. However, I believe that it is the only alternative to explore if, for whatever reason, you are unwilling or unable to go for psychophysical attribute identities. But I doubt that this solution will be found acceptable by the nonreductivist any more than the identity solution.

If nonreductive physicalists accept the causal closure of the physical domain, therefore, they have no visible way of accounting for the possibility of psychophysical causation. This means that they must either give up their antireductionism or else reject the possibility of psychophysical causal relations. The denial of psychophysical causation can come about in two ways: first, you make such a denial because you don't believe there are mental events; or second, you keep faith with mental events even though you acknowledge that they never enter into causal transactions with physical processes, constituting their own autonomous causal world. So either you have espoused eliminativism, or else you are moving further in the direction of dualism, a dualism that posits a realm of the mental in total causal isolation from the physical realm. This doesn't look to me much like materialism.

Is the abandonment of the causal closure of the physical domain an option for the materialist? I think not: to reject the closure principle is to embrace irreducible nonphysical causes of physical phenomena. It would be a retrogression to Cartesian interactionist dualism, something that is definitive of the *denial* of materialism.

Our conclusion, therefore, has to be this: nonreductive materialism is not a stable position. There are pressures of various sorts that push it either in the direction of outright eliminativism or in the direction of an explicit form of dualism.[30]

Notes

1. Throughout I will be using "physicalism" and "materialism" (and their cognates) interchangeably; similarly, "mental" and "psychological."

2. See Davidson, "Mental Events" in *Essays on Actions and Events* (Oxford: Oxford University Press, 1980). This paper was first published in 1970.

3. See Putnam, "The Nature of Mental States" in *Mind, Language, and Reality: Philosophical Papers*, vol. II (Cambridge: Cambridge University Press, 1975). This article was first published in 1967.

4. Jerry Fodor, "Special Sciences, or the Disunity of Science as a Working Hypothesis," *Synthese* 28 (1974): 97–115. See also Richard Boyd, "Materialism without Reductionism: What Physicalism Does Not Entail," *Readings in Philosophy of Psychology*, ed. Ned Block (Cambridge: Harvard University Press, 1980).

5. As it is the response of some recent eliminativists; see, e.g., Paul Churchland, "Eliminative Materialism and the Propositional Attitudes," *Journal of Philosophy* 78 (1981): 67–90.

6. The classic source on reduction is Ernest Nagel, *The Structure of Science* (New York: Harcourt, Brace & World, 1961), ch. 11.

7. Actually the argument can proceed with a weaker premise to the effect that mental events enter into causal relations, either with physical events or with other mental events.

8. Davidson says in "Mental Events" that he believes in the "supervenience" of the mental on the physical, and this does introduce a constraint on the distribution of physical properties when the distribution of mental properties is altered. This, however, does not detract substantively from the point being made here. For one, it remains true, on the notion of supervenience Davidson favors (which corresponds to "weak supervenience"; see his "Reply to Essays X–XII" in *Essays on Davidson: Actions and Events*, ed. Bruce Vermazen and Merrill B. Hintikka [Oxford: Oxford University Press, 1985]), that the removal of *all* mental properties from events of this world would have no consequence whatever on how physical properties are distributed over them. For another, the supervenience of the mental is best regarded as an independent thesis, and my present remarks only concern the implications of anomalous monism. I consider the supervenience view below in IV.

9. Davidson's overall views of the mental are richer and more complex than the present discussion might seem to indicate. I believe that they contain some distinctly dualistic elements; for a discussion of this aspect of Davidson, see my "Psychophysical Laws" in Ernest LePore and Brain McLaughlin, eds., *Actions and Events: Perspectives on the Philosophy of Donald Davidson* (Oxford: Blackwell, 1984). There have been some interesting recent attempts, which I cannot discuss here, to reconcile anomalous monism with the possibility of mental causation; see, e.g., Ernest LePore and Barry Loewer, "Mind Matters," *Journal of Philosophy* 84 (1987): 630–642; Brian McLaughlin, "Type Epiphenomenalism, Type Dualism, and the Causal Priority of the Physical," *Philosophical Perspectives* 3 (1989): 109–136; Terence Horgan, "Mental Quasation," *Philosophical Perspectives* 3 (1989): 47–76.

10. Putnam, "The Nature of Mental States."

11. Putnam himself has abandoned functionalism; see his *Representation and Reality* (Cambridge: MIT Press, 1988), chs. 5 and 6.

12. There are some complex logical and ontological details we are leaving our here. See, for details, Robert L. Causey, *Unity of Science* (Dordrecht: Reidel, 1977).

13. "The Nature of Mental States," p. 437.

14. Note also that derivational reduction does not *require* strong connectibility; any set of bridge laws, of whatever form and strength, will do as long as it enables the required derivation. But this obviously depends on the strength of the two theories involved, and there seems to be little of interest that is sufficiently general to say about this. There are also philosophical considerations for thinking that biconditionals and attribute identities are important in reduction. Cf. Lawrence Sklar, "Types of Inter-Theoretic Reduction," *British Journal for the Philosophy of Science* 18 (1967): 109–124.

15. "The Nature of Mental States," p. 437.

16. Ned Block says, "Most functionalists are willing to allow ... that for each type of pain-feeling organism, there is (perhaps) a single type of physical state that realizes pain in that type of organism," in his "Introduction: What is Functionalism?" in Block, ed., *Readings in Philosophy of Psychology*, vol. 1 (Cambridge: Harvard University Press, 1980), p. 172. Such a law would have exactly the form under discussion.

17. See on this point Berent Enc, "In Defense of the Identity Theory," *Journal of Philosophy* 80 (1983): 279–98.

18. This point, and some related points, are elaborated in *Supervenience and Mind* (Cambridge: Cambridge University Press, 1993).

19. "Mental Events," in Davidson, *Essays on Actions and Events*, p. 214.

20. Including Terence Horgan in his "Supervenience and Microphysics," *Pacific Philosophical Quarterly* 63 (1982): 29–43; John Haugeland in "Weak Supervenience," *American Philosophical Quarterly* 19 (1982): 93–103; John Post in *The Faces of Existence* (Ithaca: Cornell University Press, 1987); and Bradford Petrie, "Global Supervenience and Reduction," *Philosophy and Phenomenological Research* 48 (1987): 119–130. The model-theoretic notion of determination worked out by Geoffrey Hellman and Frank Thompson, in "Physicalism: Ontology, Determination, and Reduction," *Journal of Philosophy* 72 (1975): 551–564, is closely related to global supervenience.

21. Even with this simplifying assumption certain complications arise; however, we may disregard them for the present purposes. For further details see my "Supervenience for Multiple Domains," *Philosophical Topics* 16 (1988): 129–150.

22. At least not in a straightforward way. See my "'Strong' and 'Global' Supervenience Revisited," *Philosophy and Phenomenological Research* 48 (1987): 315–326.

23. This particular difficulty can be largely met by formulating global supervenience in terms of *similarity* between worlds rather than indiscernibility. See my "'Strong' and 'Global' Supervenience Revisited."

24. This shows that global supervenience is consistent with the failure of "weak supervenience." See my "'Strong' and 'Global' Supervenience Revisited."

25. See Hellman and Thompson, "Physicalism: Ontology, Determination, and Reduction"; Post, *The Faces of Existence.*

26. For a forceful statement of this point see Fred Dretske, *Explaining Behavior: Reasons in a World of Causes* (Cambridge: MIT Press, 1988).

27. This idea is developed in greater detail in my "Mechanism, Purpose, and Explanatory Exclusion," *Philosophical Perspectives* 3 (1989): 381–405.

28. For critical discussions of this model, see Brian McLaughlin, "Event Supervenience and Supervenient Causation," *Southern Journal of Philosophy* 22, *The Spindel Conference Supplement on Supervenience* (1984): 71–91; Peter Menzies, "Against Causal Reductionism," *Mind* 97 (1988): 560–574.

29. I am putting the point somewhat tentatively here because it involves several currently contentious issues. For a general argument for this point, see my "Concepts of Supervenience," *Philosophy and Phenomenological Research* 45 (1984): 153–176; especially, section III; and "Supervenience as a Philosophical Concept," *Metaphilosophy* 21 (1990): 1–27. However, this argument makes use of infinite disjunctions and conjunctions (actually, infinite disjunctions are all one needs; see "Supervenience as a Philosophical Concept"). If the argument is found objectionable because of this feature, it could be supplemented with an argument modeled on my argument in section III above against the Putnam–Fodor antireductionist thesis. This means that the supervenience relation needed for the model of supervenient causation sketched here must require that each supervenient property have a *nomologically coextensive base property relative to the given physical structure.* There are, I believe, plausible considerations in favor of this stronger supervenience relation as a basis for the concept of supervenient causation (or the reduction of causal relations); however, I cannot go into the details here.

30. My thanks to Richard Brandt, Sydney Shoemaker, and Ernest Sosa for helpful comments on earlier versions, and to David Benfield, Barry Loewer, and Brian McLaughlin for discussing with me some of the topics of this paper.

40 Causation in the Philosophy of Mind

Frank Jackson and Philip Pettit

Causation has come to play an increasingly important role in the philosophy of mind, reaching its apotheosis in the doctrine that to be a mental state of kind K is to fill the causal role definitive of that kind of mental state: the typology of mental states is a typology of causal roles. However, ironically, there is, from this very functionalist perspective, a problem about how to understand the causal role of mental properties, those properties which make a mental state the kind of mental state that it is. This problem surfaces in one way or another in the debates over the language of thought (for instance, in the argument that only if intentional states have syntactic-like structure can they play the required causal roles); over the explanatory role of broad content (for instance, in the argument that broad content is explanatorily irrelevant to behaviour because doppelgängers behave alike while possibly differing in broad content); and over the eliminativist implications of connectionism (for instance, in the argument that certain versions of connectionism falsify the propositional modularity component of the folk conception of the causes of behaviour). We wish, however, to reverse the usual order of discussion. Instead of entering directly into one or another of these fascinating debates, we want to raise the problem of how to understand the causal role of mental properties as an issue in its own right. We will then offer a solution to the problem which seems to us plausible independently of those debates. The final stage of our discussion will be a brief application of the proffered solution to argue that connectionism does not have the eliminativist implications sometimes associated with it.[1]

1 The Problem

How things were at some earlier time is succeeded by how things are at subsequent times, and we distinguish the way and extent to which how things were is causally responsible or relevant to how they are or will be. For instance, one aspect of how things were a little while ago is that there was a sharp drop in atmospheric pressure, and another aspect of how things were a little while ago is that a man with an odd number of freckles scratched his nose; the first aspect of how things were is causally relevant to the fact that it is now raining, the second is not.

But how things were, are or will be at a time is a matter of which properties are instantiated at that time. So our commonplace observation amounts to noting that we can and must distinguish a relation of (positive) causal relevance among *properties*. Those who hold to a fine-grained or relatively fine-grained conception of events, which broadly places them in the category of property instances, or of property instances of some favoured class of properties, will see this as really nothing more than the familiar doctrine that (singular) causation relates events.[2] But for those who hold to a coarse-grained conception of events which places them in the category of concrete particulars which have or instantiate properties, but are quite distinct from, and much more sparse than, properties or their instances, our commonplace must be seen as an addition to the story about causation being a relation between events. In addition to asking which events are causally relevant to which other events, we can and must ask which properties of events are causally relevant to which other properties. But surely this must, or should, have been an implicit ingredient in the story about singular causation all along.[3] Surely not even the most robust defender of a concrete conception of events supposed that *featureless* events might do some causing. Their events caused what they did because of how they were—that is to say, because of which properties they possessed.

Accordingly, we are going to take as a datum the idea that we can distinguish among properties in respect of their causal relevance to the obtaining of some effect or other. Exactly how to fit this fact into an event metaphysics of causation is left as a question for another time. We should emphasise that by "causal relevance" in what follows we mean positive, actual causal relevance. We mean what might best have been called "causal responsibility" except that "relevance" has become somewhat entrenched in the literature, and "responsibility" perhaps carries a connotation of sufficiency, whereas we are talking about the idea of a property being *a* factor, and typically one factor among many, in the causing of something.

We are now in a position to state our problem. Perhaps we can say a priori that a number's being prime cannot be causally relevant to any physical occurrence, but most often the question of whether a property is causally relevant to some effect is an a posteriori one. It was, for example, an empirical discovery that the mass of a body is irrelevant to its rate of acceleration under gravity in a vacuum, and that the density of a medium is relevant to the speed of light through that medium.

How do we establish that some property or set of properties is causally irrelevant to some effect? An attractive answer is that we do so by completely explaining the effect in terms of properties distinct from that property or set of properties. This is the point behind the familiar argument—sometimes referred to as "the shadow of physiology" argument—against dualist interactionist theories of mind.[4] It is observed that it is very plausible that in principle a complete explanation of each and every bodily movement of a person can be given in terms of their internal physiology, with their neurophysiology playing a particularly important role, along with interactions of a physical kind between their physiological states and their environment. There are no mysterious, unclosable-in-principle gaps in the story medical science tells about what makes a person's arm go up. The conclusion then is that the sort of properties that feature in the dualist story are causally irrelevant to behaviour; and we are led to the familiar objection to dualism that the interactionist variety of dualism has to give way to an epiphenomenalist variety—and so much the worse for dualism![5]

Our problem is that if the popular functionalist approach to mental properties is correct, the very same style of argument appears to be available to cast doubt on the causal relevance of mental properties. The shadow of physiology seems to raise a problem for functionalists as well as for dualists despite the fact that functionalism is compatible with a purely materialistic view of the mind. Take, for instance, content and our commonsense conviction that content is causally relevant to behaviour, our conviction that the fact that a certain state of mine has the property of being the belief *that p* or of being the desire *that q* is causally relevant to my arm moving in a certain way. (We will stick with this example from now on in order to avoid the difficult problem of *qualia* or raw feels. We take it for granted that a materialistic account of an essentially naturalistic variety can be given of intentional states and their contents.) How can that be, given the just discussed fact that a complete explanation in principle entirely in physiological terms of my behaviour is possible? For the kind of property content is identified with in the functionalist story will not appear anywhere in that story. What will matter at the various points in that story will be the physiological, and particularly neurophysiological, properties involved, whereas, as has so often been emphasised, what matters from the functionalist perspective for being a certain kind of mental state is not the nature of the state neurophysiologically speaking but rather the functional role occupied by that state. One way of putting the point is by saying that what drives behaviour is the physiological nature of the various states, not the functional roles they fill. How then can functional role, and so content according to functionalism, be a causally relevant property?

Some have concluded from considerations like these—so much the worse for functionalism as an account of content, in somewhat the same way that an earlier generation of philosophers concluded—so much the worse for dualism.[6] We think, however, that there is an important error in the line of thought that suggests that functionalism makes content (and mental properties in general) causally irrelevant or epiphenomenal. Before we say what it is, we need to say why, as it seems to us, two initially attractive responses to our problem fail. The first response appeals to a type–type version of mind–brain identity theory based on functionalism; the second to the fact that functional role is supervenient on physiology plus physical environment.

The Identity Theory Response to Our Problem

The identity theory as originally presented was a type–type identity theory. Mental properties, including the possession of some particular content, were identified with neurophysiological properties.[7] Functionalists sometimes speak as if the familiar and correct point that the kind of functional role definitive of content (to stick with that example) can be, and most likely is, variously realized in different sentient organisms refuted this theory.[8] We agree, however, with the unrepentant type–type theorists that the point about the possibility of different neurophysiological states realizing a given content in different species, or even in different members of the same species, or even in a given individual at different times, only shows that different properties may be a given content in different species, or in different members of the same species, or in the one individual at different times.[9] Does this mean that we should espouse a simple answer to our question about the causal relevance of being in a state with a certain content—namely, the answer that being in that state is precisely as causally relevant to the action it putatively explains as is the neurophysiological property the relevant content property is identical with?

We think that this reply evades the crucial question of concern. When I explain your behaviour by citing your belief that it is about to rain, I am surely explaining your behaviour in terms of something I know about you, or at least that I think that I know about you. I am not saying that there is some internally realized property, I know not what, which is causally relevant to your behaviour. That would be hardly more than a declaration that your action is not a random occurrence. I am rather explaining your behaviour in terms of something I know about you; and as I do not know, and know that I do not know, about the nature of your internal physiological states, it can only be the relevant functional role which I am citing as the property which you instantiate which is causally relevant to your behaviour. When we explain behaviour in terms of the contents of beliefs and desires, the properties we are invoking must be the known or guessed about functional roles, not the unknown nature of the occupiers of those roles. Moreover, even though type–type theorists identify a given belief content in a given organism on a given occasion with a neurophysiological state (type) rather than a functional state, they must and do hold that it is the functional role the state occupies, not the kind of neurophysiological state it is, which gives that state the belief content it has. Functional role is the final arbiter. The upshot is that we need to vindicate the causal relevance of functional role—it is what we know about and what in the final analysis matters—in order to justify the commonsense attitude to causal explanations in terms of content.[10]

The Supervenience Response to Our Problem

Our problem was framed in the following terms. The whole causal story about the origins of behaviour can be told in terms of the neurophysiological nature of our internal workings combined with environmental considerations—where then is there room for functional properties to do any causal work? Ergo, functional properties are causally irrelevant. Our model was the familiar argument which forces dualists into embracing an epiphenomenalist position on the mind.

There is, however, a major difference between dualism and functionalism. Although both see properties other than neurophysiological ones as what is crucial to being minded, the properties functionalism sees as crucial *supervene* on physiology, or at least on physiology together with the relevant laws and, if we are dealing with broad functional roles, certain environmental and historical factors, whereas the properties dualists see as crucial are *emergent* ones. There is a sense, that is, in which the crucial properties according to functionalists, namely, the functional properties, are not *wholly* distinct from the neurophysiological ones. Although no functional property is identical with any neurophysiological one, enough by way of neurophysiological properties when combined with environmental facts (and perhaps laws of nature) fully determines the functional properties. The supervenience reply to our problem, thus, is the observation that from the fact that the whole causal story can be told in neurophysiological terms, and that no functional property is any neurophysiological property, it does not follow that the functional properties do not appear in the story. They appear in the story by supervening on the neurophysiological properties (in the same way though less transparently, that you and I being the same height appears in a story that includes your being 182 cms and my being 182 cms in height).

This reply wins the battle but not the war. Our problem is not how to reply to scepticism about whether functional properties are instantiated, but how to reply to scepticism about their causal relevance. Some philosophers have worried about whether we should acknowledge truth and reference as features of the world on the ground that neither the fact that some sentence is true nor the fact that some word has a certain reference plays a role in explaining the causal order of the natural world.[11] The reply to this worry is that truth and reference supervene on what does feature in the best explanations of the natural world. Similarly, the fact that a person's behaviour can be explained in full without explicit reference to the functional properties as such of their internal states does not show that we should be sceptics about their states instantiating functional properties. The functional properties supervene on the properties we do explicitly invoke in our explanations. It is, though, one thing to be reassured about the presence of certain properties, and another to be reassured about their causal relevance. The point about supervenience leaves open the question of the causal relevance of the functional properties.

It might be thought easy to close this question by appeal to the following principle: If being F is causally relevant to some effect E, and being G supervenes on being F, then being G is causally relevant to E. The idea would be that we solve our problem by observing (a) that physiological properties are non-controversially causally relevant to behaviour, (b) that functional properties supervene on them, perhaps in combination with other matters, and then (c) use the principle to obtain the desired result that functional properties, and so, contents, are causally relevant to behaviour.[12] The principle is, however, false. In general for any property or property complex which is causally relevant to the obtaining of some effect E, there will be indefinitely many properties which supervene on that property or property complex, and it would be absurdly generous to count all and sundry as causally relevant. Examples bear this general observation out.

Consider a machine with two weighing platforms set up to respond whenever the weight on one platform is half that on the other. In that case alone a circuit in the machine closes causing a bell to ring, and further suppose that on some particular occasion a weight of three grams is placed on one platform and a weight of six on the other causing the bell to ring. Clearly none of, one weight's being a prime number of grams, one weight's being one less than seven, or one weight's being divisible by three or the weight of the Prime Minister is causally relevant to the bell's ringing. And yet all these properties supervene on the properties that on the occasion were causally relevant—namely, one weight's being three grams when the other was six grams. As we might naturally say it, one weight's being three grams and the other's being six grams was relevant because three is half six and not, for instance, because three is a prime number, or because six is one less that seven. Or again suppose that the fact that someone lives in a particular suburb on the North side of town is causally relevant to their being happy about where they live. Their living *somewhere* on the North side of town supervenes on their living in the particular Northern suburb that they do live in, yet it need not be the case that their living somewhere on the North side of town causally explains their contentment. Perhaps they particularly dislike all the other Northern suburbs apart from the one they live in—in this case it would not be their living somewhere on the North side, but only their living just where they do in fact live which would be causally relevant. Or again, going to twenty committee meetings may be causally relevant to Jones's sorry state of mind in a way in which going to at least two is not, yet going to at least two supervenes on going to twenty.[13]

A Solution to Our Problem

We can think of functional properties as a more complex and general case of dispositional properties, and as our problem has a simplified analogue in the case of dispositional properties, we will start with them.

Dispositional properties are causally relevant: a glass breaks because it is fragile; Fred is saved because his seat belt has the right degree of elasticity; Mary dies because the ladder she allows to touch power lines is a good conductor of electricity; a kingdom is lost because a monarch is intemperate; and so and so forth.[14] And yet a full account of how these various events come about can be given in terms of the dispositions's categorical bases rather than the dispositions themselves. It is this point that lies behind the familiar doctrine that dispositions are, as it is sometimes put, causally impotent.[15] How then can they be causally relevant?

It can be tempting to think that there is a simple solution to this puzzle.[16] A dispositional property may be properly invoked in a causal explanation despite its impotence provided that its categorical basis is causally relevant to what is being explained.[17] This is the analogue for dispositions to the identity solution to our problem discussed above, and we could simply repeat, suitably modified, our objections to that solution. However, there happens to be a simple and decisive counterexample to the solution as applied to dispositions. It is the case of conductivity.[18] The categorical basis in metals of the different dispositional properties of electrical conductivity, thermal conductivity, ductility, metallic lustre and opacity is essentially the same, namely, the nature of the cloud of free electrons that permeates the metal. Nevertheless, the person who dies because she allows her aluminium ladder to touch power lines does not die because her ladder is a good conductor of heat, or because it is lustrous or ductile or highly opaque; she dies because her ladder is a good electrical conductor. Although one and the same property is the categorical basis of all these dispositions, out of these dispositions it is only being a good electrical conductor which is causally relevant to her death. This is a contingent fact, of course. It might have been the fact that the ladder obscured someone's view which was crucial, in which case the ladder's opacity would have been the causally relevant property; or it might have been the opacity together with the good electrical conductivity which was the real problem, or.... The point of importance for us is that the fact that there is one categorical basis for the various dispositions does not mean that the various dispositions are alike in causal relevance.

We propose in place of an "identity theory," that the causal relevance of dispositions can be captured in terms of what might be called invariance of effect under variation of realization. Here is a simple non-dispositional example to illustrate the central idea. Smith takes ten grains of arsenic which causes him to die about ten minutes later. Jones takes ten grains of arsenic which causes him to die in about ten minutes also. When is it right to say that the fact that they both died in about the same time is explained by the fact that they both took the same amount of arsenic? Well, suppose the time to die after taking a given dose of arsenic is given by a complicated formula involving body weight, and that this formula gives in the case of Smith and Jones very different times to die for a given identical dose *except* when the dose is ten grains. In that case the explanation of their taking the same time to die would be their both taking ten grains, and not their taking identical doses. After all, if the one and only case where the same dose is followed by the same time to die is the single case where the doses are both ten grains, it is a fluke—the fluke that the sameness in doses happened to be constituted or realized by their both taking ten grains—that the sameness in dose was followed by their taking the same time to die. Only if its being ten grains in both cases does not matter to their dying in about the same time, that is if they would take about the same time to die after the same dose pretty much regardless of the dose provided it was lethal, is it correct to explain their dying in the same time as being due to the doses being the same. We can view the matter in terms of realizations. There are many ways of realizing taking the same doses—by both taking ten grains, by both taking nine grains,.... If any of a good range of these realizations, including the actual one, would lead to death in the same time for each person, then it is correct to explain the sameness in times to die in terms of the sameness of doses, and taking the same dose is causally relevant to dying in the same time. For then the doses each being 10 grains is not what is crucial for Smith and Jones dying in the same time, but rather the doses each being the same number of grains.

We suggest a similar approach to causal explanation by citing dispositional properties. The reason being a good conductor of electricity is causally relevant to Mary's death is that it did not matter (within reason) what the categorical basis of that disposition was, for provided the causal role definitive of good electrical conductivity was occupied by a state of the ladder she would have died. We move from the non-contentious causal relevance of the categorical basis to the causal relevance of the disposition via the facts that (a) the actual categorical basis was causally relevant to the death by electrocution, and (b) had the good electrical conductivity of the ladder had a different categorical basis, then that basis would have been causally relevant to the death. And, of course, the reason opacity, say, is not causally relevant to her dying is that it might easily have been realized without her dying—as would, for instance, have been the case had the ladder been wooden.

The explanatory interest of an explanation in terms of a dispositional property is now clear. We are often interested not merely in how something in fact came about but also in how it would have come about. That is why, paradoxically, we can sometimes improve an explanation by, in a sense, saying less. An elevator has a safety device which holds it at a given floor if more than ten people step into it at that floor. Twenty people step into it on the ground floor and as a result it does not move. In explaining what has happened to the disappointed customers, it will be better for me to say that the reason that the elevator is not moving is because more than ten people stepped into it, than to say that it is not moving because twenty people stepped into it. How so—after all, that twenty people stepped into the elevator entails, but is not entailed by and so is logically stronger than, that at least ten people stepped into it? The answer, of course, is that in giving the explanation in terms of at least ten, I tell the customers what would have happened had, say, fifteen people stepped into the elevator.

Our account of how functional properties, and so in particular content, can be causally relevant to behaviour will by now come as no surprise. A certain piece of behaviour will have a certain property, say that of being in the direction of a certain cup of coffee, as a result of the concatenation of very many neurophysiological states which will have given rise to that piece of behaviour by virtue of their natures, that is, by virtue of the neurophysiological properties they instantiate. But, of course, there will be other ways that behaviour with the property of being towards the coffee could have been caused, other neurophysiological ways, or even, other non-neurophysiological ways if we allow ourselves Martian speculations. Is there anything interesting that we can say about resemblances between these various actual and possible ways of getting behaviour towards the coffee? The answer is that it may be that many of these ways, including the actual way, are united by the functional properties they realize, and in particular by the functional properties definitive of contents that they realize. In that case, an explanation in terms of content-bearing states will apply and its explanatory interest will lie in the fact that it tells us about what would happen in addition to what did happen. That is how the content properties may be causally relevant.

Have We Really Laid the Demon to Rest: The Metaphysics of Causation?

The intuition that functionalist accounts of content make content epiphenomenal is a strong one.[19] We have encountered the following response to our defence of the causal relevance of content properties. "You have shown how the fact that a certain piece of behaviour follows the instantiation of certain content properties need not be a fluke. For (a) it is not a fluke that the behaviour follows a certain concatenation of neurophysiological states, (b) this concatenation is, at the least, a major part of what the relevant functional properties supervene on, and (c) it may be that many different complexes of neurophysiological states alike in the having the relevant functional properties supervening on them would also be followed by behaviour exemplifying the feature we are seeking to explain. (Often the behaviours will count as different under some natural taxonomy, but this is, of course, consistent with their being alike in the respect of interest.) But all that that shows is the non-flukey nature of a certain sequence, and the explanatory value of content ascriptions. It does not show that content properties conceived functionally do the *driving* of behaviour. The fact remains that that is done by neurophysiological (or least relatively intrinsic structural or syntactic) properties; yet surely the commonsense intuition that cries out for vindication is that content drives behaviour."

Now of course it is true that some non-flukey sequences are not causal. That possibility lies at the heart of classical epiphenomenalism. According to epiphenomenalism, a certain kind of mental event regularly precedes a certain kind of brain event which leads on to the behaviour we associate with that mental event; but this is not because the first event causes the second but because both are caused by a third, earlier brain event. But it is essential to this story that according to classical epiphenomenalism the mental event is indeed caused by the earlier brain event. But if caused then distinct, whereas a key part of our account of how content properties are causally relevant to behaviour is that they are not completely distinct from the relevant neurophysiology; they instead supervene on it. We would be in trouble if our story was that the neurophysiological properties are causally relevant both to the content properties and to the behaviour. But our view is rather that the connection between neurophysiology and content is that the latter supervenes on the former, and supervenience is incompatible with causation. More precisely, enough by way of neurophysiology and the relevant laws together possibly with environmental setting and history (how much of the latter two you need to include depends on whether and to what extent the content is broad) *logically* fixes the content, and therefore is not *causally* responsible for it. Accordingly, as the neurophysiology is a proper part of what the content logically supervenes on (we might put this by saying that the content contingently supervenes on the neurophysiology), the neurophysiology is not causally relevant to the content. This is why the content is not possessed a moment after the relevant neurophysiological facts obtain, as would have to be the case were the connection causal.

Nevertheless, there is more to say about the objection, for behind it lies an attractive view about the metaphysics of causation.[20] Suppose that in a laboratory in Russia electron A is acted on by a force of value four and accelerates at rate seven (all in some suitable units). At the same time in a laboratory in America electron B is also acted upon by a force of value four and as a result it too accelerates at rate seven. Suppose that the sameness of the resultant accelerations is in no way dependent on the fact that the impressed forces were of value four. All that mattered (within limits, of course) for the sameness of the accelerations was the sameness of the impressed forces. Then clearly the sameness of the impressed forces is causally relevant to the sameness of the resultant accelerations. The sameness of the first causally explains the sameness of the second. (The situation is in essentials the same as in the arsenic example described earlier.)

Suppose, however, we think of causation as a matter of production or efficacy which does not reduce sooner or later to nothing more than nomological sequence: according to this view, a sequence is nomological because of underlying causal productivities, not conversely.[21] Then it is plausible that in some sense the sameness of the impressed forces does not actually *produce* the sameness of the resultant accelerations.[22] Consider electron A. It is acted upon by a force which both has the property of taking the value four and the relational property of being the same in value as the force acting on electron B. Does the latter fact actually have any influence on the way the electron moves off under the impact of the force? Surely not. All the work is done by the force acting on A taking the value four; how things are with B, which after all is a very long way away, is surely in *some* sense irrelevant. Perhaps the sharpest way of putting the point is the Occamist one. Supposing that the force taking the value four produces the acceleration of value seven in both cases is enough to explain (because it entails) the fact that sameness of impressed force on A and B is in fact followed by sameness of acceleration by A and B. There is no need in addition to give having the same impressed force per se a productive or efficacious role with respect to the sameness of the resultant accelerations.[23]

The idea then is that we can distinguish as a special case of causal relevance among properties, causal efficacy. Every case where an instance of F is causally efficacious with respect to an instance of G is a case of causal relevance, but some cases where an instance of F is causally relevant to an instance of G are cases of relevance without efficacy.[24] The objection under discussion can now be put as follows: our defence of the explanatory role of content from the functionalist perspective only shows causal relevance (and indeed we used that very term to describe matters earlier); it does not show that content properties are causally efficacious with respect to behaviour, and it is the latter which is integral to the common intuition about content's role with respect to behaviour.

Our reply turns on the point that the Occamist thought that lies behind distinguishing causal efficacy as a special case of causal relevance has farreaching ramifications. It has been widely noted how plausible is the idea that everything about the way our bodies move, including everything by way of the causal relations involved, supervenes on how things, including the laws, are at the most fundamental micro-physical level. If this is right, then the Occamist attitude combined with the view of causation which does not reduce it to nothing more than nomological sequences, enjoins us to restrict relations of causal efficacy to certain properties in fundamental Physics—which properties exactly is a matter for empirical science—and to see all the causal relevancies "higher up" as, strictly speaking, nonefficacious.[25] For we do not need to believe in any fundamental efficacies over and above those between properties at the micro-level in order to explain the regularities, actual and counterfactual, all the way up, because supervenience tells us that they are fixed by how things are at the bottom (*if* there is a bottom). But then the neurophysiological properties are not causally efficacious in the special sense any more than are the content properties. And more generally there will not be a contrast between the causal relationship that content and functional properties generally have to behaviour, and the causal relationship that taking arsenic has to death, that lying in the sun has to getting hot, that rising inflation has to falling living standards, and so on and so forth. These cases will be all alike in being cases of causal relevance without causal efficacy. Ergo, the functionalist account of content does not downgrade its causal role, rather it leaves it in the excellent company of everything except for certain members of that most exclusive of clubs, the properties of fundamental physics.[26]

We suspect that the thought behind the view that we functionalists have made content epiphenomenal is that we have somehow taken the "push" out of content. But consider someone being torn apart by an imbalance of forces acting on him (as happens if you step into Space without a space suit on). The imbalance of forces has plenty of push but plausibly is not efficacious, for the simple reason that it is a "convenient fiction." It is plausible that the resultant force in the familiar parallelogram of forces is a convenient fiction. It is the component forces which really exist (or rather certain of the component forces, the component forces in a parallelogram of forces can of course themselves be resultants in some other parallelogram of forces), and so it is they at most which can stand in relations of causal efficacy.[27]

Application to an Argument for Eliminativism

We can now see the mistake in an interesting and initially appealing line of argument for eliminativism about the propositional attitudes.

Eliminativists see the apparatus of beliefs and desires with their associated contents as part of an ancient (and so prima facie suspect, but that is another story) theory—dubbed "folk psychology"—which we invoke to explain and predict inter alia and especially behaviour. But to explain behaviour is to say something about the causes of behaviour and, runs the argument we wish to reply to, what folk psychology says about the causes of behaviour may turn out as a matter of empirical fact to be mistaken in an important respect, a respect important enough to justify describing what has happened as a refutation, rather than, say, an elaboration, of folk psychology. What is meant here by "as a matter of empirical fact" is not as a matter of abstractly possible empirical fact—it is common ground (or ought to be) that it is logically possible that the causal story about our behaviour be incompatible with folk psychology. What these eliminativists have in mind is the causal story implied by certain connectionist views about information processing in the brain, which they take to be very much live options. Eliminativists see folk psychology as committed to beliefs and desires being properly described as propositional attitudes. This combined with the idea that folk psychology is an explanatory theory leads to the doctrine that the folk are committed to the idea that the internal causes of behaviour can be illuminatingly divided up in terms of the propositions which are the objects of our beliefs and desires. Folk psychology carries with it its own way of taxonomizing the causes of behaviour in terms of contents given typically by indicative natural language sentences prefixed by "that"—propositional modularity, as it is sometimes called. The eliminativist argument is that if developments in neuroscience confirm certain connectionist views, then this will show that propositional modularity is false, and so will be nothing less than an empirical refutation of the folk taxonomy of the causes of behaviour, and so of folk psychology with its apparatus of beliefs and desires.[28]

One might quarrel with one or another detail of the eliminativists's account of folk psychology, but the general picture is highly plausible. For consider Jill, who believes that a book relevant to her current research has arrived in the library and also believes that it will rain later today. We folk do distinguish these two beliefs precisely because they differ in content, and that is a matter at least very closely connected with the propositions expressed by the embedded sentences.[29] And further we do distinguish the causal role that the two beliefs play with respect to her behaviour. Unless we have reason to attribute somewhat bizarre desires to Jill, the belief about a book relevant to her current research is most likely to be appealed to in order to explain her going to the library, and the belief that it will rain later is most likely to be appealed to in order to explain her taking an umbrella to work.

Our reply to the eliminativist argument takes this general picture for granted. We grant that we folk distinguish the two beliefs by distinguishing their propositional objects and that we folk give the distinguished beliefs distinct causal roles in explaining Jill's behaviour precisely in accord with their distinct propositional objects (and the same goes for desires, of course). Our quarrel is with the claim that there is an incompatibility between this picture and certain connectionist views about information processing in the brain.

Why do eliminativists see an incompatibility between connectionism and folk propositional modularity? Well, if beliefs are anything like stored sentences in the brain, then it is plausible that there will be in Jill's brain two distinct bits of storing, one of the sentence about the book, the other of the sentence about the rain, and eliminativists observe that consequently in this case we can sensibly suppose that the first bit of storing has a special causal relationship to Jill's movements towards the library that the second lacks, and that the second bit of storing has a special relationship to her umbrella-taking that the first lacks. But, runs the argument, if certain versions of connectionism are correct, it will be impossible to isolate in any way one part of the brain or its activities and see this as one of the beliefs, at the same time as isolating something else in the brain and seeing that as the other belief. Information processing is a completely holistic and distributed matter on these versions of connectionism. There will be nothing in the brain, at the neurophysiological level or at the level of cognitive architecture, to be isolated as one belief as opposed to the other.[30] How then can the folk hypothesis about distinctness of causal roles be true?

Our reply is that our approach to the causal relevance of content properties in terms of invariance of effect under variation of realization of that content, shows how one and the same underlying state (be it widely distributed or localized) can realize two different contents, one of which is, and the other of which is not, causally relevant to a given piece of behaviour. We do not need to find distinct states at, say, the brain level—distinct encodings, or whatever—to be the two beliefs in order to vindicate the commonsense conviction that my belief that p may differ in its causal relevancies from my belief that q. For on our approach, a certain content is causally relevant to a certain effect if (a) a state occupying the role definitive of that content is causally relevant to that effect, and (b) had that content been differently realized, then other things being equal the counterfactual realizer state would have been causally relevant to that effect. Now it is clearly a live possibility that a single state S be such that it occupies the role definitive of different contents, C_1 and C_2, and yet for some effect E other ways of realizing C_1 would ceteris paribus have been causally relevant to E, whereas other ways of realizing C_2 would not. Indeed, the dispositional correlate of this live possibility actually obtains in the case of conductivity discussed earlier (and remember we noted that it is wrong to conclude from the fact that we cannot pick out distinct underlying states of Mary's ladder to be the bases of the various distinct dispositional properties of her ladder, that all the dispositions are equally causally relevant to what happened to her).

This story fits well with our everyday approach to our case of Jill who believes both that a book relevant to her current research has just arrived in the library and that it will rain. Although she has both beliefs, we take it that it is the first that is causally relevant to her movement towards the library, because we take it that she would have moved towards the library whether or not she had had the belief that it will rain; whereas she would have taken an umbrella whether or not she had believed that a book especially relevant to her research had just arrived in the library, and so this belief is not why she took an umbrella.[31]

It might well be objected that when we explain Jill's movement towards the library in terms of her belief that a book especially relevant to her research has just arrived, we are giving that belief an active role in the story.[32] It is not a standing condition but rather a state being activated in the context of a set of standing conditions. The same point applies when we explain Fred's survival in terms of his seat belt having the right degree of elasticity. The seat belt presumably had that right degree of elasticity from the day of its manufacture, but something happened at a certain moment during the accident which brought that degree of elasticity into play in a way which led to his survival. A fair question, therefore, is whether in the supposed connectionist case where there is no isolating one belief from the other in different encodings, we can give Jill's belief that a book especially relevant to her research has just arrived in the library an active role in explaining her movement towards the library without at the same time giving the intuitively irrelevant belief that it will rain the same role? But consider our ladder example again. Mary's aluminium ladder was a good conductor of electricity from the day it was made. When its being so was actively causally relevant to her death by electrocution what happened was that the nature of the cloud of free electrons in the matter of the ladder occupied the role definitive of being a good electrical conductor in a special way. The set of subjunctive conditionals definitive of that role contained a member which, in addition to being itself true, had a true antecedent and a true consequent. It was true that for some salient-to-being-an-electrical-conductor conditional "had so and so happened, then such and such would have happened" that, not only was it the case that it obtained by virtue of the nature of those electrons, in addition, on the occasion in question, so and so actually happened and, by virtue of the nature of those electrons, such and such followed in a way which contributed to Mary's death. In brief, the disposition manifested itself; and the crucial point is that, although the underlying basis for being a good electrical conductor in the ladder is one and the same as that for, for instance, being opaque and being a good heat conductor, being a good electrical conductor can, and did in the case we are imagining, manifest itself without the other dispositions manifesting themselves. The same can be said in the case where Jill's belief about the book played an active role in getting her to the library. It did so by virtue of certain of the inputs and outputs salient in the specification of the functional role corresponding to having that belief actually obtaining, and, of course, that can happen without the differently specified inputs and outputs constitutive of having the belief that it will rain actually obtaining.

Conclusion

Functionalism specifies mental properties in terms of causal roles. The irony is that it then appears to be the case that functionalism deprives mental properties of causal relevance. It appears that it is the properties in virtue of which the relevant states occupy the relevant causal roles, and not the roles themselves, which are causally relevant to behaviour. Our aim in this paper has been to rebut this beguiling argument, and to do so in a way which shows the flaw in the equally beguiling argument that connectionism supports eliminativism.[33]

Notes

1. For the application to how broad content can explain see, e.g., Martin Davies, "Individualism and Supervenience," *Proceedings of the Aristotelian Society*, supp. vol. 60 (1986): 263–83, Frank Jackson and Philip Pettit, "Functionalism and Broad Content," *Mind*, XCVII, 387 (1988): 381–400, and the references therein. The bearing of the issue about the causal role of mental properties, and of content properties especially, to the debate over the language of thought is central in Jerry Fodor, *Psychosemantics* (Cambridge: MIT Press, 1987). See also D. R. Braddon Mitchell and J. B. Fitzpatrick, "Explanation and the Language of Thought," *Synthese* 83 (1990): 3–29.

2. For different versions of this approach see, e.g., Jaegwon Kim, "Events as Property Exemplifications" in *Action Theory*, ed. M. Brand and D. Walton (Dordrecht: Reidel, 1976), pp. 159–77, David Lewis, "Events," in *Philosophical Papers*, vol. II (Oxford: Oxford University Press, 1986), pp. 241–69, and David Sanford, "Causal Relata," in *Actions and Events*, Ernest LePore and Brian McLaughlin,

eds. (Oxford: Basil Blackwell, 1985), pp. 282–93. But note that property instances in these approaches need to be distinguished from property instances in the sense of the tropes of Donald Williams, "The Elements of Being" in *Principles of Empirical Realism* (Springfield: Thomas, 1966). For in these approaches, when one and the same person at one and the same time says hullo loudly and thereby says hullo, the instance of saying hello is distinguished from that of a saying hello loudly—that is essential to allowing them to stand in different causal relations. Whereas Williams's tropes are absolutely specific; and so, if the saying hullo is a property instance in his trope sense, it is identical with saying hullo in some absolutely specific manner, and, therefore, in the case in question, to saying hullo loudly. On the absolutely specific nature of property instances on the Williams's scheme, see Keith Campbell, *Metaphysics* (Belmont, California: Dickenson, 1976), chap. 14. As a result of this point, a trope approach to the relata of the causal relation will, like the Davidsonian approach discussed next in the text, need to regard our commonplace as something to be added to the story about causation.

3. And is, we think, though under a different guise, in Donald Davidson's adumbration of the view that causation is a relation between events concretely conceived in his "Causal Relations," *Journal of Philosophy*, 64 (1967): 691–703. For, first, he holds that singular causal relations hold in virtue of causal laws (while holding that exactly how to spell this out is no easy matter), and, secondly, in discussing the kinds of examples which lead other writers to make events property-like, he admits in effect that we can, when dealing with what is in his view one and the same event, discriminate which properties of the single event play a special role in a causal explanation: although the bolt's giving way is one and the same event as its giving way suddenly in his view, the special place we may well give the latter in explaining the tragedy is accommodated by giving the correlative property a special place in the causal explanation of the tragedy. Davidson may well wish to urge that this special place is a place in a causal *law*, not in a singular causal relation. But for our purposes what is central is the partition of properties into causally relevant and causally irrelevant ones with respect to some effect, not whether this partition is a topic in the theory of singular causation or the theory of causal laws. We are indebted here to a discussion with Peter Menzies.

4. See, e.g., Keith Campbell, *Body and Mind* (London: Macmillan, 1971), chap. 3.

5. But see Campbell, *Body and Mind*, and Frank Jackson, "Epiphenomenal Qualia," *Philosophical Quarterly*, 32, 127: 127–36, for reservations about the decisiveness of this argument when (and only when) directed at qualia.

6. Most recently, Ned Block, "Can the Mind Change the World?" in George Boolos, ed., *Meaning and Method: Essays in Honour of Hilary Putnam* (Cambridge: Cambridge University Press), forthcoming. See also Hartry Field, "Mental Representation," reprinted in Ned Block, *Readings in Philosophical Psychology*, vol. 2 (Cambridge: Harvard University Press, 1981), pp. 78–114, see esp. pp. 88–96; Jerry Fodor, "Introduction: Something on the State of the Art" in his *Representations* (Sussex: Harvester, 1981), but see his *Psychosemantics* (Cambridge: MIT Press, 1987), p. 140 for what we take to be something akin to the supervenience approach we describe below. The problem and the associated issues would, of course, be much the same for views which regard functional role as a major ingredient, along with evolutionary history or whatever, in determining content. To keep things simple, we will set these hybrid views to one side.

7. See, e.g., J. J. C. Smart, "Sensations and Brain Processes," *Philosophical Review*, LXVIII, 1959: 141–56, D. M. Armstrong, *A Materialist Theory of the Mind* (London: Routledge & Kegan Paul, 1968), and, most explicitly, David Lewis, "An Argument for the Identity Theory," *Journal of Philosophy*, 63, 1 (1966): 17–25.

8. See, e.g., Hilary Putnam, "The Mental Life of Some Machines," reprinted in his *Mind, Language and Reality* (Cambridge: Cambridge University Press, 1975). Putnam is, of course, no longer a functionalist, see, e.g., chap. 5 of *Representation and Reality* (Cambridge: MIT Press, 1989), but the point is widely accepted; see, e.g., Dan Dennett, "Current Issues in the Philosophy of Mind," *American Philosophical Quarterly*, 15, 4 (1978): 249–61.

9. See, e.g., David Lewis, "Review of Putnam," reprinted in *Readings in Philosophical Psychology*, vol. 1 (London: Methuen, 1980), ed. Ned Block, 1980, pp. 232–33, and Frank Jackson, Robert Pargetter and Elizabeth Prior, "Functionalism and Type–Type Identity Theories," *Philosophical Studies*, 42 (1982): 209–23.

10. We take it that our objections here are essentially the same as Block's, "Can Content Change the World?"

11. See, e.g., Michael Devitt, *Realism and Truth* (Oxford: Basil Blackwell, 1984), chap. 6.

12. The principle would be a kind of converse of that espoused by Jaegwon Kim, see, e.g., "Epiphenomenal and Supervenient Causation," *Midwest Studies in Philosophy* 9 (1984): 257–70, and, for a recent critical discussion of the surrounding issues to which we are indebted, Peter Menzies, "Against Causal Reductionism," *Mind*, XCVII (1988): 551–74. The "perhaps in combination with other matters" is included in (b) to cover the possibility that the functional properties are broad ones tailored to capture broad content. Also, a full specification of the supervenience base should include the relevant laws.

13. Examples such as these abound in the literature, but the focus is most often not so much on whether causal relevance among properties is transmitted over supervenience, but rather on whether it is events concretely conceived or whether it is property-like entities (be they called "events" or not), which are the relata of the causal relation. See, e.g., Kim, "Events as Property Exemplifications," Lewis, "Events," Alvin Goldman, *A Theory of Human Action*, Princeton: Princeton University Press, 1970, and Sanford, "Causal Relata."

14. Why does the first example in this list have so much less force than the others? Because being fragile is in part defined in terms of a certain relation to breaking; in consequence, being told that a glass broke because it is fragile is not particularly informative. Some have gone further and held that being fragile is no explanation. We disagree but do not pursue the point because the other examples will serve.

15. See, e.g., Roger Squires, "Are Dispositions Causes?" *Analysis*, 29, 1 (1968): 45–7, and Elizabeth Prior, Robert Pargetter, and Frank Jackson, "Three Theses about Dispositions," *American Philosophical Quarterly*, 19, 3 (1982): 251–57.

16. One of us was tempted, see Prior, Pargetter, and Jackson, "Three Theses about Dispositions."

17. We agree with D. M. Armstrong, *A Materialist Theory of the Mind* (London: Routledge & Kegan Paul, 1968), p. 85f, though for reasons different from his, that it is necessarily true that a disposition has a categorical basis. However, the argument needs only the weaker doctrine that there is in fact a categorical basis. Moreover, we can regard the term "categorical basis" as a tag phrase, and so do not need to buy into the debate about exactly how "categorical" it must be.

18. We owe the example to Peter Menzies, "Against Causal Reductionism," who owes it in turn to David Lewis. We are much indebted to them for it. They should not be held responsible for the use we make of it.

19. As Ned Block and Paul Boghossian convinced us.

20. One author (F. J.) finds it more attractive than does the other (P. P.).

21. This is a view forced on us if (but *not* only if) we accept the non-Humean idea that there can be strongly singularist causation in the sense of one event causing another which does not fall under a law, either deterministic or indeterministic. For defences of strongly singularist causation, see G. E. M. Anscombe, "Causality and Determination," in *Causation and Conditionals*, E. Sosa, ed. (Oxford University Press, 1975), pp. 63–81, and Michael Tooley, "The Nature of Causation: A Singularist Account," *Canadian Journal of Philosophy*, suppl. 16 (1990): 271–322.

22. Of course, from a purely nomic point of view, and provided the details are sufficiently filled out, the sequence: same forces, same accelerations, may be just as "good" as the sequence: force four, acceleration seven.

23. We are here in agreement with Block, "Can the Mind Change the World?"

24. Elsewhere, we refer to cases of causal relevance without causal efficacy as cases of causal programming, see "Functionalism and Broad Content"; see also "Program Explanation: A General Perspective," *Analysis*, forthcoming.

25. For a defence of the view, to put it in our terms, that the answer science delivers is that causal efficacy is a relation between forces, see John Bigelow and Robert Pargetter, "The Metaphysics of Causation," *Erkenntnis* 33 (1990): 89–119.

26. We are not, of course, saying that most of our commonsense convictions about causal connections expressed in everyday language are false. When we use terms like "efficacious" and "productive" in everyday talk, they mean roughly what we are using "causal relevance" for (perhaps restricted to causal relevance between relatively intrinsic properties, see Lewis, "Events"). Our thesis is a thesis in (a posteriori) Metaphysics which holds, not that most of our convictions are mistaken, but rather that what makes the true ones true is a relation between properties in fundamental Physics. We take this general way of looking at the matter to be consonant with D. M. Armstrong's species of realism about universals, as expressed for instance in his *A Theory of Universals* (Cambridge: Cambridge University Press, 1978), see particularly chap. 24 for the connection with causality. What becomes of the doctrine that dispositions are causally impotent on this metaphysics of causation? *If* "causally impotent" is given the special sense given to "causally inefficacious," then the doctrine is true; but it is also true that a disposition's categorical basis is impotent unless specified micro-physically.

27. On the existence of component forces, see John Bigelow and Robert Pargetter, "Forces," *Philosophy of Science* 55 (1988): 614–630.

28. The most explicit development of this argument that we know is in William Ramsey, Stephen Stich and Joseph Garon, "Connectionism, Eliminativism and the Future of Folk Psychology," in *Philosophy and Connectionist Theory*, W. Ramsey, D. Rumelhart, and S. Stich, eds. (New Jersey: Erlbaum, 1991), but see also Paul Churchland, *Scientific Realism and the Plasticity of Mind* (Cambridge University Press, 1979), §18 ff, and "Eliminative Materialism and the Propositional Attitudes," *Journal of Philosophy*, 78, 1981, 67–90.

29. See David Lewis, *On the Plurality of Worlds* (Oxford: Blackwell, 1986), for arguments that the connection between the objects of beliefs and the embedded sentences in our reports of belief is more complicated than one might have hoped.

30. See Ramsey et al., "Connectionism, Eliminativism and the Future of Folk Psychology," and Andy Clark, *Microcognition* (Cambridge: MIT Press, 1989), and the references therein to the connectionist literature. Clark is with us in denying that connectionism implies eliminativism.

31. We are supposing that the important problems of overdetermination and causal preemption are separate ones from those under discussion here.

32. As Andy Clark reminded us.

33. This paper arose out of discussions engendered by the notion of a program explanation in "Functionalism and Broad Content." In addition to the acknowledgments already made, we can remember the changes forced by talking to Martin Davies and Robert Pargetter. No doubt there are more than we can remember.

41 From "Physicalism from a Probabilistic Point of View"

Elliott Sober

Physicalism—like other *isms*—has meant different things to different people. The main physicalistic theses I will discuss here is the claim that all occurrences *supervene* on physical occurrences—that the physical events and states of affairs at a time *determine* everything that happens at that time. This synchronic claim has been discussed most in the context of the mind/body problem, but it is fruitful to consider as well how the supervenience thesis applies to what might be termed the organism/body problem. How are the biological properties of a system at a time related to its physical properties at that time?

Philosophers have discussed the meaning of supervenience claims at considerable length, mainly with an eye to getting clear on modal issues. Less ink has been spilled on the question of why anyone should believe this physicalistic thesis. In what follows, I'll discuss both the metaphysics and the epistemology of supervenience from a probabilistic point of view....

Preliminaries

What, exactly, is the supervenience thesis supposed to mean? It adverts to "physical" properties, but what are these? This question apparently leads to a dilemma (Hempel, 1969; Hellman, 1985; Crane and Mellor, 1990). If the supervenience thesis presupposes that the list of fundamental magnitudes countenanced by present physics is true and complete, then the claim is almost certainly false, since physics is probably not over as a subject. Alternatively, if we interpret "physical property" to mean what an ideally complete physics would describe, then the supervenience thesis lapses into vagueness. What does it mean to say of some future scientific theory that it is part of the discipline we now call "physics"?

Papineau (1990, 1991) suggests one way to address this dilemma. Rather than worry about what "physics" means, we should instead exploit the fact that we know what it is for a property to be mental. Human beings have beliefs, desires, and sensations, but the very small physical parts (cells, molecules, atoms, etc.) of which human bodies and their environments are made do not. The claim of interest is that mental properties supervene on non-mental properties. In reply, it should be noted that worries about the meaning of "physical property" also can be conjured up in connection with the concept of the mental. Our current list of mental properties—both those used in folk psychology and the ones at work in science—may well undergo change. Can we really say with any precision what makes a future scientific predicate "psychological"?

I think the right response is simply to admit that we know how to apply the concepts of mental and physical property only in so far as the properties in question resemble those that we currently call mental and physical. If future science departs dramatically from current conceptions, it may be impossible to say whether that science ends up vindicating or overturning what we now call physicalism. However, this possible indeterminacy does not deprive physicalism of its philosophical interest. There is still a point to the question of whether psychological properties, as we currently understand them, supervene on physical properties, where the later are understood in terms of our current best physical theories. Current physics does not include belief, desire, or sensation in its list of fundamental properties. Do these properties supervene on space-time curvature, mass-energy, and the other properties that are discussed in current physics? We miss an interesting philosophical question if we reject the question by pointing out that current physics is probably wrong or incomplete in some respect we know not what.

Above, I described supervenience as endorsing a determination claim. A system's mental properties at a time are a function (in the mathematical sense of a mapping) of its physical properties at that time. This way of putting the point leaves open that the converse relation may also obtain—that a system's physical properties are a function of its mental properties. This raises the question of whether the concept of supervenience offers any prospect of identifying an asymmetry between the mental and the physical.

It is tempting to use the idea of multiple realizability to argue that a system's mental properties don't determine its physical properties. If a system can have mental property M by having any of several physical properties $P_1, P_2, \ldots, P_n$, then each P_i determines that M will be present, but M does not determine which of the P_i is present. Quite so, but this settles the matter only if one assumes that disjunctions of physical properties aren't physical properties; after all, M *does* guarantee that the disjunction (P_1 or P_2 or ... or P_n) is instantiated.

A simpler and less metaphysically weighty way of locating an asymmetry is available. Even if multiple realizability were false, the physical still would not, *in general*, supervene on the mental. The reason is that there are lots of physical things that don't have any mental properties at all. The sun and Lake Michigan and alike psychologically—neither has beliefs, neither has desires, neither has sensations, and so on. Yet, they differ physically. Even if there were a one-to-one mapping between mental and physical properties in the domain of individuals who have minds, there is no such mapping that covers mindless individuals. From this more general perspective, in which both minded and mindless individuals are taken into account, supervenience involves an asymmetry. A system's physical properties uniquely determine its mental properties, but not, in general, conversely.[1]

I have described supervenience as a synchronic relation between instantaneous states—the physical properties at time t determine the nonphysical properties at time t. However, a moment's reflection shows that many of the properties we attribute to systems are temporally "thick." For example, when we say that Sally saw the moon at time t, we are describing a relationship between what is going on in Sally's mind at time t and the state of the moon some time earlier. Her seeing the moon entails that a process took place that lasted from t-dt to t. A supervenience thesis should cover attributions of this sort. The easy solution is to let talk of "time t" denote intervals as well as instants. Supervenience remains a synchronic relations, and so it contrasts with the similar sounding diachronic relation of causal determination.

What I've just said about time also applies to space. Philosophical discussion of supervenience has examined the question of how much of the physical world at a time is needed to determine the state of a given supervening property that attaches to an individual at the same time. Surface grammar is a poor guide to this issue. Biologists talk about the fitness of organisms, and philosophers of biology have often claimed that fitness supervenes on physical properties. However, the supervenience base has to include properties of the environment as well as properties of the organism. The fitness of an organism supervenes on the properties of a larger, containing, system. Parallel points have been emphasized by philosophers of mind who think that the semantic content of a mental representation is "wide"—that it depends on features of the organism's environment. My discussion in what follows won't be affected by how large the containing system has to be when one considers whether this or that property of an organism supervenes on properties of the containing system. For convenience, I'll usually talk of a system's mental or biological properties supervening on the system's physical properties, but this is solely for the sake of convenience.

Supervenience Entails the Causal Completeness of Physics, but not Conversely

Let M = a mental property of a system at time t, P = all the physical properties of the system at time t, and B = a behavior of the system at time t + dt. I understand the supervenience claim to assert that:

(S) $\Pr(M \mid P) = 1.0$.

That P confers on M a probability of 1.0 is a reasonable representation of the idea that P necessitates M, as long as there are finitely many states that M and P might occupy; if P is true, there is no chance that M will be false.[2]

The thesis that physics is causally complete says that

(CCP) $\Pr(B \mid P) = \Pr(B \mid P\&M)$.

That is, the chance at time t that B will occur at time t + dt is fixed by the physical properties that the system has at time t; the value is unaffected by taking account of the system's mental properties at time t as well.[3] (CCP) says that the physical properties instantiated at time t "screen off" the mental properties instantiated at that time from behaviors that occur afterwards. Although (CCP) is an ontological, not an epistemological, thesis, it has a natural epistemological reading—knowing the mental properties of the system is superfluous, once you know the physical properties, if the goal is to predict whether the behavior will occur.

Thus defined, supervenience entails the causal completeness of physics. To see why, consider the following expansion of the expression $\Pr(B \mid P)$:

$$\begin{aligned}\Pr(B \mid P) &= \Pr(B\&P)/\Pr(P)\\ &= [\Pr(B\&P\&M) + \Pr(B\&P\&\text{not-}M)]/\Pr(P)\end{aligned}$$

$$= [\Pr(B \mid P\&M) \Pr(P\&M) + \Pr(B\&\text{not-}M \mid P) \Pr(P)]/\Pr(P)$$

$$= \Pr(B \mid P\&M) \Pr(M \mid P) + \Pr(B\&\text{not-}M \mid P)$$

From this last equation, it is clear that if $\Pr(M \mid P) = 1.0$, then $\Pr(B \mid P) = \Pr(B \mid P\&M)$.

What about the converse? Does (CCP) entail (S)? The answer is no. To see why, suppose that supervenience is false, in the $0 < \Pr(M \mid P) < 1.0$. This allows us to expend $\Pr(B \mid P)$ as follows:

$$\Pr(B \mid P) = \Pr(B \mid P\&M) \Pr(M \mid P) + \Pr(B \mid P\&\text{not-}M) \Pr(\text{not-}M \mid P).$$

If we substitute r for $\Pr(B \mid P)$, for $\Pr(B \mid P\&M)$, and for $\Pr(B \mid P\&\text{not-}M)$, as (CCP) allows, we obtain

$$r = r[\Pr(M \mid P)] + r[\Pr(\text{not-}M \mid P)].$$

Notice that this equation is true, regardless of the value assigned to $\Pr(M \mid P)$....

Emergent Causation and Diachronic Determinism

Let the thesis of emergent causation assert that the occurrence of the mental property M at time t makes a difference in the probability that behavior B will occur at time $t + dt$, even after all the physical properties P at time t are taken into account:

(EC) $\Pr(B \mid P\&M) \neq \Pr(B \mid P)$.

(EC) is the denial of (CCP). It follows that (EC) must be incompatible with any proposition that entails (CCP)—specifically with (S). Causal emergentists must deny supervenience.

How is the synchronic thesis of supervenience related to the diachronic thesis of causal determinism? We have already seen that if $\Pr(M \mid P) = 1$, then $\Pr(B \mid P) = \Pr(B \mid P\&M)$. That is, supervenience entails that the physical facts at time t "screen off" the mental facts at time t from behaviors that occur at $t + dt$. However, nothing follows from this as to what value $\Pr(B \mid P)$ has; it could be unity, and it could also be less. Supervenience does not entail causal determinism. If so, causal indeterminism does not entail that the supervenience thesis is false (contrary to Crane and Mellor, 1990).

Does the conjunction of causal determinism and (CCP) entail supervenience? The answer is, again, no. Even if $\Pr(B \mid P) = \Pr(B \mid P\&M) = 1.0$, $\Pr(M \mid P)$ can still take on any value at all....

Causal Efficacy and Causal Completeness

Although emergent causation (EC) and the causal completeness of physics (CCP) are incompatible, the claim that mental properties are causally efficacious and the claim that physical properties are causally efficacious are perfectly compatible. To see why, we must consider how claims of causal efficacy are understood in a probabilistic framework.

The basic idea in probabilistic representations of causality is that a positive causal factor must raise the probability of the effect, when other simultaneously instantiated causal factors are "held fixed." Conjunctions of these other simultaneous factors are called "background contexts." The idea is that

C is a positive causal factor for E if and only if $\Pr(E \mid C \& X_i) \geq \Pr(E \mid \text{not-}C \& X_i)$ for all background contexts X_i, with strict inequality for at least one X_i.

The causal claim is assumed to be about the individuals in a specific population. So the idea that smoking is a positive causal factor for the production of lung cancer in the population of human beings alive now in the US means that smoking increases the chance of lung cancer for people with at least one constellation of other properties, and doesn't lower it for any one else. If smoking raises for some and lowers for others, smoking is said to be a "mixed" causal factor, not a positive one (Eells, 1991). My point here is not to insist that this probabilistic representation of what causality means is exactly right, but to discuss what is involved in talking about a "background context."

A background context is a conjunction of properties. Inhaling asbestos particles might be one of the conjuncts. If smoking is a positive causal factor for lung cancer, then smoking must raise (or at least not lower) the probability of lung cancer among individuals who have the same level of asbestos exposure. This other factor is "held fixed"; against this homogeneous background, one sees whether smoking makes a difference in the chance of lung cancer.

What one doesn't do is hold fixed the chemical composition of cigarette smoke. To simplify discussion, let's pretend that cigarette smoke always consists of three types of particles (X, Y, and Z) in equal proportions. To find out whether smoking cigarettes is a positive causal factor for lung cancer, one doesn't see whether smoking raises the probability of cancer among people who inhale the same amount of XYZ. By hypothesis, it won't, but that doesn't show that smoking doesn't promote lung cancer. Given the composition of cigarettes in the real world, cigarette smoke automatically contains XYZ. This means that neither is part of the background contexts that have to be considered when the causal efficacy of the other is under discussion.

To see whether inhaling cigarette smoke promotes lung cancer, you investigate whether smoking cigarettes increases the risk of lung cancer among individuals who all inhale the same *other* things. To see whether inhaling XYZ promotes lung cancer, you investigate whether inhaling XYZ increases the risk of lung cancer among individuals who all inhale the same *other* things. But if you are studying cigarette smoke, XYZ does not count as "another inhalant." And if you are studying XYZ, cigarette smoke does not count as "another inhalant."

This fact about scientific practice stands on its own, but it also is reflected in the probabilistic criterion described before. If the presence or absence of XYZ is to be part of the background contexts against which the impact of smoking cigarettes (C) on some effect variable is tested (or vice versa), then all conditional probabilities of the form $\Pr(- \mid \pm XYZ \,\&\, \pm C)$ must be well defined. This will not be true if $\Pr(C \,\&\, \text{not-}XYZ)$ or $\Pr(\text{not-}C \,\&\, XYZ)$ have values of zero.

I hope the parallel point about the relevance of mental and physical properties to the causation of behavior is clear. If I walk from my office to the Student Union, it may be asked why I did so. Consider the hypothesis that this behavior was caused by my believing that the Student Union sells coffee and by my wanting to buy a cup of coffee. To see whether this belief/desire pair is a positive causal factor in the production of that type of behavior, one determines whether the belief/desire pair increases the probability of walking to the Union in different background contexts. These background contexts presumably would include the other beliefs and desires that individuals might have. However, suppose that $P_1, P_2, \ldots, P_n$ are the (physically specified) supervenience bases that provide different realizations of the belief/desire pair. It would be a mistake to judge the causal efficacy of the belief/desire pair by seeing whether it raises the probability of strolls to the Union among people who have a given P_i.

Thus, the idea that physics is causally complete and that the mental supervenes on the physical does not entail that mental properties are causally inert. In fact, (CCP) and (S), when brought in contact with a probabilistic conception of causality, explain why a certain argument against the causal efficacy of mental properties is invalid. One cannot argue that a property M plays no causal role in producing B by showing that P screens off M from B, if in fact P is a supervenience base of M.

These remarks are not intended to explain how the semantic properties of mental states manage to be causally efficacious. Rather, they bear on how that problem should be formulated. The issue isn't how mental features at time t can make a difference in what happens later, even after all the physical properties at time t are taken into account. They can't—not if supervenience is right. But that doesn't show that the mental is causally inert. You don't need emergent causation for mental properties to be causally efficacious; supervenience, the causal completeness of physics, and the causal efficacy of the mental are perfectly compatible, contrary to Kim (1989a, 1989b, 1990)....

Acknowledgments

I thank Martin Barrett, Tom Bontly, Tim Crane, Ellery Eells, Berent Enç, Branden Fitelson, Malcolm Forster, Peter Godfrey-Smith, Leslie Graves, Daniel Hausman, Terry Horgan, Jaegwon Kim, Barry Loewer, Brian McLaughlin, Hugh Mellor, Greg Mougin, David Papineau, John Post, Alan Sidelle, Larry Shapiro, and Dennis Stampe for comments on an earlier draft.

Notes

1. I don't deny that there may be further asymmetries between mental and physical properties. For example, Enç (1986) has discussed the intuition that a system's physical properties at a time "determine" its mental properties at that time, but not conversely, even in a domain in which there is a one-to-one mapping. I have nothing to say about how this intuition might be clarified, or on whether it is ultimately correct.

2. This probabilistic formulation of the supervenience thesis should be understood as a quantified statement: For any system, and for any mental property M, if the system has M at a given time, then there exists a set of physical properties P such that the system has P at that time and $Pr(M \mid P) = 1.0$. Notice that no mention of "completeness" is needed here, since if $Pr(M \mid P) = 1.0$, then $Pr(M \mid P\&Q) = 1.0$ also. The idea of listing "all" the physical features of the system isn't essential. Note, in addition, that the conditional used in the supervenience thesis, like those in the other doctrines I'll discuss, should not be understood truth-functionally. It isn't enough for the supervenience thesis to be true that all actual objects that differ mentally also happen to differ physically.

3. As was true for the supervenience thesis, (CCP) is a quantified statement. It has the quantifier order $(\forall)(\exists)(\forall)$: For every property B, if the system has B at time $t + dt$, then there exists a set of physical properties P that the system has at time t, such that for all other properties M that the system has at time t, $Pr(B \mid P) = Pr(B \mid P\&M)$.

References

Crane, T., and Mellor, H. (1990). "There Is No Question of Physicalism." *Mind* 99: 185–206.

Eells, E. (1991). *Probabilistic Causality*. Cambridge: Cambridge University Press.

Enç, B. (1986). "Essentialism without Individual Essences—Causation, Kinds, Supervenience, and Restricted Identities." In P. French, T. Uehling and H. Wettstein (eds.), *Midwest Studies in Philosophy*, vol. 11, pp. 403–426. Minneapolis: University of Minnesota Press.

Hellman, G. (1985). "Determination and Logical Truth." *Journal of Philosophy* 82: 607–616.

Hempel, C. (1969). "Reduction—Ontological and Linguistic Facts." In S. Morgenbesser, P. Suppes, and M. White (eds.), *Philosophy, Science, and Method*. New York: St. Martin's.

Kim, J. (1989a). "The Myth of Non-reductive Materialism." *Proceedings of the American Philosophical Association* 63: 31–47.

Kim, J. (1989b). "Mechanism, Purpose, and Explanatory Exclusion." In J. Tomberlin (ed.), *Philosophical Perspectives*, vol. 3, pp. 77–108. Atascadero, Calif.: Ridgeview Press.

Kim, J. (1990). "Explanatory Exclusion and the Problem of Mental Causation." In E. Villanueva (ed.), *Information, Semantics, and Epistemology*, pp. 36–56. Oxford: Blackwell.

Papineau, D. (1990). "Why Supervenience?" *Analysis* 50: 66–71.

Papineau, D. (1991). "The Reason Why—Response to Crane." *Analysis* 51: 37–40.

III Mental Content

Introduction

One of the most fundamental features of mental states (some have argued that it is *the* defining feature) is that they are *about* things. Sensory perceptions are typically perceptions *of* the things around us; in fact, even hallucinations are hallucinations *of* something—a pink elephant, or an evil voice. Likewise, doubts, beliefs, memories, and desires are doubts, beliefs, memories, or desires *about* some (actual or possible) thing or situation. Philosophers call this feature of "being about something" *intentionality*. And it seems that mental states provide one of the only sources of intentionality, or "aboutness," in the universe. Moreover, the other obvious examples of things that represent are human-made representations such as sentences and pictures. For this reason, some have claimed that mental states are the sole origin of *all* representative powers in the world.

But although it is intuitively clear that mental states have things they are about—the *content* of mental states—it's not nearly so easy to say *how* they manage to be about anything. This is the question of mental content: what is it that makes a mental state (for example, a desire *that there be sunny weather tomorrow*, or a belief *that some infinite sets are bigger than others*) about *that* thing or situation, and not some other thing or situation? The fact that mental states have content seems obvious, but stating what is involved in having such content turns out to be surprisingly difficult. As the readings in this section show, this central feature of the mind continues to challenge philosophers.

Aristotle (384–322 B.C.E.) applies his theory of form and matter (from chapter 1 of this volume) to explain the content of mental states. Every object, for Aristotle, is composed of form (containing its essential, defining qualities) and matter (the material that has these qualities)—for example, a bronze sphere has its geometrical shape as form, and bronze as matter. The same form can be embodied in different types of matter, however, and this provides Aristotle's theory of content: a mental state is *about* an object by having the same *form* as that object (though the form then exists in the "matter" of the mind). It is in this sense that Aristotle says the mind "is" the object it thinks about; and in making judgments about objects, those objects (as forms) are "linked together" in the mind.

René Descartes (1596–1650) provides a theory of mental content similar in certain ways to Aristotle's, leaning as it does on different "realizations" of one and the same form. Descartes explains that we can view a mental state in two different ways: either *materially* or *formally*. Considering a mental state "materially" amounts to considering it *without* appeal to its meaning (what it's about). Looked at materially, a mental state is simply a process in the mind, so that *materially* all mental states are on a par. But when considering a mental state in terms of its content, the state is viewed "formally." And this mental content, according to Descartes, is the *form* of the mental state. When thinking about the sun, for instance, the form of the thought (which makes it a thought *about* the sun) is simply *the sun itself* existing within that mental process. As Descartes makes clear, this sun existing in my mental state is *the very same sun* that exists in the sky—though the sun exists one way ("objectively") in my mind, and in a different way ("formally") in the sky. By postulating different *types* of existence (objective vs. formal existence), Descartes can explain how one and the same sun can exist in space and in the mind. And as in Aristotle's account, Descartes holds that in making mental judgments, we link the objects themselves (existing objectively) together in the mind.

John Locke (1632–1704) begins with the view that complex ideas are built up out of simpler ideas, rather like molecules are built up out of smaller molecules or atoms. Since Locke is an empiricist and thus insists that we have no innate ideas (chapter 62), the simplest, "atomic" ideas must come from experience—from our five external senses and our inner sense of self-awareness. All our concepts, then, follow a simple principle of "mental chemistry": each idea must ultimately break down entirely into simple ideas acquired from the senses. But whereas later empiricists like Berkeley and Hume hold that the empirical properties of, say, apples or gold are all there is to apples or gold (so that apples and gold are nothing more than "clouds" of such properties, held together for simplicity by a single blanket name, "apple" or "gold"), Locke is not happy with that conclusion. He insists that there is also a "substance" underlying these features, which they all "adhere" to, and that such a substance is what an apple perception or apple thought is ultimately *about*. This combination of views leads Locke to a striking conclusion: since ideas must break down into "atomic" ideas from the senses, and yet this "substance" is by its nature *behind* all such empirical features, Locke must in the end describe this substance as an indescribable "I know not what."

A similar sort of split occurs in Locke's theory of the essential (or defining) features of objects. The *nominal essence* of, for example, gold is just a set of empirical properties—the cloud of properties that appear together so systematically that our English-speaking ancestors dubbed it "gold." At the same time, Locke admits that what our senses can detect may only be the tip of the iceberg concerning all the properties gold may have, and that our senses may detect only superficial properties of gold, not the features that determine its nature. So Locke postulates in addition the *real essence* of a natural kind like gold, which he takes to be the hidden microscopic structure *causing* the empirical properties detected by our senses. According to Locke, the *nominal essence* of gold is the handiwork of the human mind: we consider a cloud of features as all one thing, simply for convenience (because these properties run in a herd together, and having one shorthand name for all of them is simpler than listing each property). Yet, because nominal essences are based only on the surface features of objects, Locke insists that they may not reflect the true structure, or the real natural kinds, in the world. On the other hand, while *real essences* are based on the ultimate structure of the world—and so will carve up nature correctly into its natural kinds—Locke (writing in the late 1600s) is skeptical that scientific research will *ever* be capable of detecting the microstructure of reality; so he believes real essences may be forever out of the reach of human knowledge.

David Hume (1711–1776) provides an "atomistic," empiricist theory of mental states, following Locke's model. Here, as in Locke, some mental states, such as memories or imaginings, are copies of earlier representations, always tracing back sooner or later to originals supplied by sense perception or inner self-awareness. But Hume simplifies Locke's picture by declaring that sensory perceptions—the "Impressions of Sensation"—are simply "from unknown causes"; and such external causes play no role in his account of mental states. In this way, his entire theory of mind, and whatever meaning mental states may have, is described without reference to things outside the mind, making it what later writers such as Putnam and Fodor would call a "solipsistic" theory.

Gottfried Wilhelm Leibniz (1646–1716) offers a well-known account of our concepts of *specific individuals*, such as Adam, or Benjamin Franklin, and how a thought (or sentence) can succeed in being about just that individual and no one else. Leibniz claims that each individual has a set of essential qualities, so that thinking of someone with just those qualities will succeed in picking out that individual from all others. As to *which* qualities of an individual are essential—its defining qualities—Leibniz has a simple and striking answer: *all* of an individual's qualities are essential to being that person. In effect, God has a kind of mental dictionary containing each individual's name, and an infinitely long definition attached to that name, including every feature the individual will ever have at any time; and with such infinite detail, such a "complete concept" will pick out that person from all the people who ever exist, or could possibly exist.

Leibniz recognizes a problem with this view, presented in a letter from Antoine Arnauld: if *everything* about Adam is true "by definition," as Leibniz claims, then it would be a *contradiction* to think about Adam possibly being any different. Being expelled from the Garden of Eden, for instance, is a defining feature of "Adam"; so a thought or sentence about what it would be like if Adam *wasn't* expelled would involve a *contradiction in terms*—like talking about a married bachelor, or a four-sided triangle. Yet surely it seems that we *can* coherently think and talk about Adam not being expelled, not eating the apple, and so on. Leibniz agrees, and explains that, since we are finite mortals, we cannot possibly handle God's infinitely long concepts. Instead, we must use a shortened list of defining qualities—including perhaps only two or three features in our concept of "Adam," and thereby allowing us to consistently consider Adam having been different. By arguing that our concepts of individuals amount to a list of defining features, Leibniz provides a simple account of how each of those concepts succeeds in picking out exactly that person and no one else. (A later version of this "description" theory of names and individual concepts is presented by Bertrand Russell, in chapter 49.)

Charles Saunders Peirce (1839–1914) begins with a functional-role description of mental states, similar to his fellow pragmatists Angell and James (chapters 9 and 10): *thought*—which for Peirce means something like reasoning, or inference—and *belief* are defined in terms of their respective functions, the role each plays in the mind. As Peirce notes, defining these mental processes in a functional manner makes them independent of the particular sensations they are "composed" of, in the same way that a melody can be transposed into different notes, while remaining the same melody. Thought functions to resolve indecision or doubt, by settling on a definite belief; while belief itself is a habit, a rule of action. The functional profile of a habit, for Peirce, is entirely a matter of the "when" and "how" it operates: the "when" of the habit is the perception that triggers its exercise, while the "how" is the result—the observable action(s) that it produces. This is clearly an *empiricist* theory of meaning, tying down concepts as it does to perceptible qualities. For example, if certain observable qualities—the colors and textures—of certain objects lead Protestants to call the objects bread and wine, but lead Catholics to call them flesh and blood—then, Peirce concludes, their beliefs are in fact the same, despite the different wording. (Moreover, since all perceptual stimuli and behavioral responses are actual events, this theory seems—as Peirce recognizes—to find no meaning in talk about other possibilities, other ways things could be.) But since both the "input" and "output" of a habit is something detectible by the senses, his view also ends up looking somewhat like a *behaviorist* theory of meaning. (It should be noted that this is a rather early paper by Peirce, and that his later views on these matters were quite different.)

Alexius Meinong (1853–1920) begins with what he considers the defining feature of the mental: *intentionality*, being *about* something. Mental states like perceptions, memories, and desires must by their very nature be perceptions of something, memories of something, desires for something; whereas nonmental things like rocks and planets are not about anything. Mental states can be about an Object (like a perception of an *apple*), or about an "Objective," a situation (like a belief that *the apple is on the table*). But if we take the content of mental states to be a matter of reference (pointing at that thing), we are faced with a puzzle: a perception of the apple is about an existing object, a real apple; but a thought about Santa Claus doesn't have any existing object it is about, since Santa Claus doesn't exist. Now, if a thought about Santa Claus has no object, it looks like there isn't anything it's *about*. But if that thought isn't about anything, then (lacking intentionality) it wouldn't qualify as a mental state for Meinong. In response to this problem, Meinong makes the bold metaphysical move of postulating *nonexisting* objects: a thought about Santa Claus is certainly *about* something (namely, Santa Claus); it just so happens that the object of this thought is a nonexisting thing. This allows for a fairly simple theory of mental content: a mental state is about an object or situation, because it refers to (points at) that object or situation. But most philosophers are unhappy with postulating a realm of nonexisting objects, and therefore reject Meinong's answer to the question of mental content.

Bertrand Russell (1872–1970) seeks to show how a belief about an individual like Santa Claus can be meaningful, without appealing to Meinong's nonexisting objects. In addition, Russell wants to explain how our thoughts can be about things far *outside* our immediate experience, while still grounding our knowledge of the world strictly within the realm of our experience (following more or less the empiricist model of knowledge spelled out by Locke and Hume, in chapters 44 and 45). The most basic and direct form of knowledge for Russell is direct acquaintance: an immediate contact with the object of knowledge, about which we cannot be mistaken. But the range of knowledge by acquaintance is extremely limited, since we are acquainted only with sense data, our own mental states, and general concepts. Thanks to our acquaintance with concepts, however, we are able to build descriptions that pick out objects in the world outside our acquaintance. In particular, we can string together concepts into a "definite description"—a description of the form "*the* so-and-so"—that will pick out a unique individual. For example, although I have never come in contact with Benjamin Franklin, I can still have a thought about him, by using a definite description in my thought such as "the inventor of bifocals and first president of Pennsylvania"—a description that in fact applies only to Benjamin Franklin, thereby successfully making my thought *about* him. Russell holds that almost all "proper names" are really shorthand for an associated definite description, in the sense that only such a description expresses the thought in the mind of the person using the name. (Later writers, such as Kripke and Putnam, will strongly oppose Russell's "description" theory.)

C. I. Lewis (1883–1964) develops a theory of meaning out of his theory of knowledge and qualitative experience (chapter 21). According to Lewis, immediate first-person experience ("qualia") are, outside of any conceptual classification, not themselves describable or capable of being communicated from one person to another. But *within* a person's mind, concepts are correlated with specific qualia or patterns of qualia—and these concepts *can* be communicated and shared among many minds. Concepts come to have their specific meanings through definition—definitions that never appeal to anything except further concepts, and make no use of the immediate qualitative features of experience. As Lewis notes, each word in a dictionary is defined in terms of other words in that same dictionary, so that ultimately definitions don't form a hierarchy (with some basic terms at the bottom that go undefined) but rather a web or network of interconnections. Each concept is "defined" entirely by the place it holds in our conceptual network of interrelated concepts; and as long as my concept holds the same place in my conceptual network as yours holds in your conceptual network, we have the same meaning in mind. As a self-proclaimed pragmatist, Lewis is here spelling out in some detail the "conceptual role" theory of meaning suggested by earlier pragmatists such as Angell and Peirce (chapters 10 and 47). And like these writers, Lewis argues that worries about different (possibly inverted) qualia between different people is irrelevant to our having concepts in common—since, according to Lewis, qualia play no role in this theory of meaning.

Hilary Putnam presents a discussion of linguistic meaning that has exercised a great influence on theories of mental content. He begins by noting the traditional division of meaning into two parts, or varieties: the *extension* of a term (e.g., a predicate or a natural kind term), and the *sense* of that term. Philosophers have assumed that the sense of the term is a concept grasped (or possessed) in the mind of the speaker, and that this sense provides the information necessary to pick out the extension in the world. (For example, the sense of the natural kind word "water" might be a description—"clear, tasteless liquid that fills our rivers and lakes, and quenches thirst"; and this description will pick out all and only the water in the world.) If these assumptions were true, Putnam says, then meaning would be contained entirely in the mind of the individual speaker, and would be the same regardless of how the external world was, or even *if* there was an external world at all. Such a view of meaning is "solipsistic" (not assuming the existence of anything outside the person's mind). But in a now-famous thought experiment, Putnam challenges this individualist, solipsistic view of meaning. Assume there is a planet just like Earth—call it "Twin Earth"—and that each of us has a perfect twin on that planet, who acts the same, thinks the same, and speaks English just like we do. But suppose the clear, tasteless, thirst-quenching liquid on Twin Earth is not made of H_2O like on Earth, but some other chemical compound, XYZ. If neither Oscar, nor his twin on Twin Earth, know any chemistry (perhaps they live in 1750, before the chemistry of water is known), then they will both use the word "water" *with the same beliefs and thoughts* about what they're talking about. Still, Putnam insists, "water" spoken by Oscar points to H_2O, while "water" for Twin Oscar points to XYZ. Our use of a term like "water," he says, is based on the assumption that when our ancestors first pointed at some clear liquid and dubbed it "water," they intended the term to apply to all other samples of the same stuff (even though they might not have known the chemical make-up of that stuff at the time). Since Oscar's ancestors on Earth were pointing out H_2O when they began using the word "water," while Twin Oscar's ancestors were pointing out XYZ, the words pick out different liquids for the (psychologically identical) twins. Therefore, *psychological state alone does not settle the meaning of a person's words*, and the solipsistic tradition in meaning must be false.

Putnam argues further that an individual's *social group* shapes his meaning as well. For instance, while I don't know the difference between elms and beeches (I can't pick out one over the other, my description of them is the same, etc.), the two terms still *mean* different things in English, even when I utter them. Again, a factor outside the individual's mind—my social group of fellow English speakers, including tree experts—determines what I mean by my words. Once we recognize the contribution that external environment and social group make to a person's meaning, Putnam concludes, we must admit that "meanings just ain't in the head." He also notes, in closing, some peculiar consequences of this view. In particular, someone who speaks both English and German might know words such as "beech" and "Buche," but not know that their meanings (as fixed by English and German social groups, respectively) are the same. So he might think *one and the same claim* is *true and false at the same time*, by thinking it in two different languages ("This tree is a beech," "This tree is a Buche"). (This paradoxical result is discussed further by Loar, in chapter 56.)

The nonindividualistic ("nonsolipsistic") sort of content that Putnam argues for is what philosophers have come to call "*wide content*." Tyler Burge makes an argument similar to Putnam's, but argues for a "wide" theory of *mental*, rather than just *linguistic*, content. Burge argues that certain aspects of mental content reveal a social element essential to mental states, which has been overlooked by leading models of the mind (such as functionalism and reductive materialism). For the most part, we attribute ("ascribe") mental states to one another using a two-part terminology: we specify the type of mental state (belief, doubt, memory, hope, want), and specify the "target" or *content* of that mental state, using a "clause" (sentence), often preceded by a word such as "that." For example, we attribute to someone the belief *that it will rain*; remembering *that the previous picnic was rained out*; a doubt *whether we should cancel the picnic*; or a hope *that the weather will be good*. Being describable in terms of such a "content clause" (or "'that'-clause") seems essential to making a mental state the particular state it is. A belief *that it will rain*, for instance, and a belief *that zebras are mammals*, are clearly two different mental states, even though they are both beliefs; and what makes them different mental states is that they are beliefs about different things. But Burge insists that in many cases we find it perfectly appropriate to state an individual's mental content (in a content clause) using terms that the person himself does not fully understand. For example, if Bert sincerely tells his doctor "I believe that I have arthritis in my thigh," he obviously does not fully understand the concept "arthritis" (since arthritis is an illness of the joints). Yet, Burge argues, Bert clearly intends to use the term "arthritis" the way his linguistic community does—in particular, the way medical experts do. And in light of this conformity to social convention concerning word use, we should resist coining some new concept that Bert attaches to the word "arthritis," instead of the standard concept of his linguistic community. Bert means—and his *mental state* is *about*—what his community means, even if Bert himself doesn't fully understand what that is.

Although this may seem unexceptional, Burge spells out some far-reaching consequences. First, one ingredient in an individual's mental content will be the usage of the surrounding linguistic community. So, as in Putnam's argument, meanings—here, *mental* contents—aren't entirely "in the head." In some cases, a person may not even be the best authority on what he's thinking. Second, if Bert has a molecule-for-molecule twin (who therefore also has all the same internal *functional* states), yet Twin Bert lives in a linguistic community where "arthritis" is defined more broadly (to include ailments of the thigh), then Twin Bert would have a *different mental content* when he says "I believe I have arthritis in my thigh." But if mental content is an essential ingredient in determining which mental state a person has, this means that Bert and his physical-functional twin, simply by being in different linguistic communities, would have *different mental states*. (Note that here Burge breaks with Putnam: according to Burge, because Oscar and Twin Oscar come from communities that use the word "water" in entirely different ways, Oscar and his twin *don't even have the same mental state*—despite Putnam's assumption to the contrary.) Burge concludes that any theory of mind that leaves the social community out of its definition of mental state—theories such as functionalism, or reductive materialism—must give an incorrect account of mental states.

Jerry Fodor, on the contrary, argues that a computational model of the mind requires a type of mental content making no reference to objects outside of the mind—a "narrow," or "solipsistic" form of mental content. In the representational theory of mind (which, Fodor argues, is central to cognitive science), mental states are taken as relations to contents—so that, for instance, to the sentence-like content *"it is raining,"* one can hold the *believing* relation, the *doubting* relation, the *wondering* relation, and so on; and mental processes are operations on such contents. But while a representational theory of mind requires such content, a *computational* theory requires that mental states and processes be identified *solely* in terms of the formal, computational features of mental symbols (their "syntactic" features), making no appeal to anything else. The only way to satisfy both these requirements, Fodor argues, is to have mental content correspond exactly to the formal, computational features of mental states—so that any differences in meaning must be reflected in a formal difference in mental symbols, and symbols that are formally the same have the same mental content. Fodor concludes that this requirement—which he calls the "formality condition"—is essential for a theory of content for a computational theory of mind. And since the formal, computational features of a mind are purely internal to that mind (reflecting nothing about a world outside the mind), a theory of mental content obeying the formality condition must be "solipsistic," defining mental content without assuming anything about the world outside the mind. Since the computational ("functional") properties of mental states and processes define how they interact, lead to behavior, and so on, Fodor thinks such *"narrow content"* is required in order for mental content to play a role in psychological explanation. Recognizing that his view is directly opposed to the "wide" theories of content promoted by Putnam and Burge, Fodor argues that "wide content" cannot work for mental states; for if mental content were defined (at least partly) in terms of the nature of the world outside the mind, then we could not develop a theory of mental content—or a representational theory of mind—until the facts were in about the structure of the external world. For instance, if the content of my "water" thoughts depends partly on the chemical structure of water, then a theory of mental content must wait until our theories of chemistry and physics are complete—meaning we might *never* have a theory of "wide" mental content. (It is worth noting that, since writing this article, Fodor has gone on to hold different views on mental content—most recently, ones similar to those of Burge.)

Fred Dretske approaches the mind's special ability to represent, through studying the ability to *misrepresent*—to have *false* representations of the world. An object or system can exhibit a kind of "natural meaning," if what it's representing is what causes that representation—for example, spots mean a person has a certain disease, because the disease caused those spots. But such "natural meaning" seems incapable of misrepresenting the world; for if the person has spots without having that disease, then that disease isn't causing the spots—so the spots won't have that disease as their "natural meaning." Hence the ability to misrepresent (which our minds certainly possess) marks a more advanced form of representation, requiring a more complicated explanation. Dretske thinks a promising approach lies in "functional meaning," where a state of an organism has, as its biological function, the representation of something in the world. While noting that a very simple function might not suffice, Dretske holds that a system with multiple ways of representing the same thing, and at least a moderate capacity for conditioned response, will possess powers of representation complete with the ability to misrepresent—and all explainable in purely "naturalistic" (scientific) terms.

In light of Fodor's claim that a computational, *functional* theory of mind requires "narrow" content, and Burge's criticism of functionalism for not involving "wide" content, one might conclude that a "conceptual role" approach to mental content would by its nature be a theory of narrow content. But the reading by Gilbert Harman illustrates that this is not the case: Harman argues that the role of one concept must involve not simply the relation to other concepts, but to perception and action as well. The concept of *greenness*, for example, is clearly linked to perception, but also to inference and decisions—the greenness of a piece of fruit, for instance, leading to the conclusion that it is unripe, and perhaps the decision not to eat it. Even a highly theoretical concept such as quark may be implicated not only in mental inference, but in perception and actions—for example, in reading diagrams properly. Harman argues moreover that conceptual content, conceived of in terms of its perceptual, inferential, and behavioral function, must be understood against the background of its normal use—for instance, a creature's concept of food is to be understood through its normal behavior (attempting to eat) toward objects correctly perceived. But because conceptual role so crucially involves perception, behavior, and background of normal use in this way, Harman insists that conceptual role must be "wide" or nonsolipsistic, including many factors outside the individual.

Brian Loar seeks to defend a "narrow" type of mental content—a content specified in terms of functional role, which can vary from one individual to the next—while acknowledging many of the points that Burge makes about the social nature of content. Burge sought to drive a wedge between mental content and (individual) functional role by presenting cases where functional role is the same, while psychological contents are different (for example, Twin Earth cases, where my functional twin has "water" beliefs functionally the same as mine, but with different content), and cases where mental content is the same even though the mental states with that content can still lead to different inferences, utterances, and so on (e.g., Bert, who believes arthritis can occur in his thigh, and his doctor who knows that it can't). But, Loar notes, in these arguments Burge relies on agreement about *the meaning of words* used in "that"-clauses—a kind of *linguistic* meaning that Loar calls "social content"—to argue for sameness of *psychological content*. By attempting to break the link between social content (as used in "that"-clauses) and psychological content, Loar seeks to undermine Burge's anti-individualistic conclusion about mental content.

Loar presents thought experiments meant to illustrate that agreement about sameness of content in "that"-clauses does not automatically translate into a sameness of mental content. For example, if Pierre knows of a town called "London," and one called (in French) "Londres," but doesn't realize they're the same, then we would say his belief *that London is pretty* is not the same as his belief *that Londres est jolie*—even though the linguistic content of these two "that"-clauses is the same. Likewise, Loar argues, differences in (linguistic) content of "that"-clauses might fit cases where the mental contents reported on are still the same. For instance, if a commuter between Earth and Twin Earth, who is ignorant of chemistry, sincerely claims that "Water is thirst-quenching," we can't identify his mental content with those of either an Earthling or a Twin Earthling; but we can still perfectly well explain his behavior (e.g., why, when thirsty, he drinks a clear liquid from a bottle label "water"), appealing to the fact that he has a psychological state that plays the same role as the mental state of an Earthling or Twin Earthling, in terms of drawing inferences, guiding actions, and so on. Loar agrees with Burge that "that"-clauses, on their own, report a common social content—factoring out individual peculiarities (e.g., about beliefs concerning "arthritis"), in order to provide a common ground for practical communication. But Loar insists we can still use a common language to report narrow psychological content, by using a "that"-clause along with additional context—for example, by noting the different linguistic communities the individual belongs to, or the unusual beliefs the individual holds about the subject matter.

Robert A. Wilson challenges the assumption, made by Fodor and others, that the computational states of an organism (such as a human being) are defined entirely in terms of what goes on inside that organism. Instead, Wilson proposes what he calls "wide computation"—computation that is defined in terms of objects outside, as well as inside, an individual. As a simple example, he notes that when a person does complicated arithmetic, she may use a pencil and paper to work out the solution. Since the representations on the paper play a crucial role in completing that computational task,

Wilson holds that the computation took place in a larger system made of person-plus-paper; and since the computation went beyond the borders of the individual, it is a case of "wide computation." Moreover, he finds evidence of wide computation in current cognitive theory, citing examples from visual perception and animal navigation. And while Wilson views computation as a nonsemantic concept—so that, as he notes, wide computation by itself doesn't take a stand on the debate over wide vs. narrow content—it is still relevant to discussions of mental content. In particular, while Fodor's argument for "narrow content" (chapter 53) relied on content mirroring the nature of the computational process, the possibility of wide computation implies that such mirroring will provide no evidence that content must be "narrow," defined solely in terms of processes within the individual.

Gabriel Segal, promoting a view similar to Loar's, presents a critique of arguments for the "wide content" meaning of natural kind terms and concepts, as well as a defense of "narrow" mental content. First, Segal believes that the sort of argument Putnam made for kind terms like "gold" (and which Burge adapts to mental states about gold) will stumble over empty (nonreferring) concepts like "ghost," or the "phlogiston" of early chemical theory. We now suppose these concepts (and terms) do not really refer to anything (since ghosts, and the liquid-like phlogiston, do not really exist); but in order for a psychologist or anthropologist to explain the behavior of people who do believe in ghosts or phlogiston, she will have to appeal to mental states *about* ghosts or phlogiston. This explanation will, according to Segal, identify a concept in terms of its cognitive role—the causal role it plays in the individual's overall psychology; and this cognitive role will be just the same in "twin" individuals, even if one lives in a world where his concept refers, while the other lives in a world where his concept is empty (nonreferring). Therefore reference (or lack of such) should not affect mental content. Segal likewise provides a number of objections to arguments that mental content depends on social usage, where Putnam and Burge argue that we defer, in our meanings, to the usage of experts. Segal claims that such arguments must unlink word-meaning and mental content in a way that ultimately undermines the argument itself (since agreement about word content would then reflect nothing about mental content), and that such a view still cannot handle cases where an individual, deferring to experts, nonetheless ends up having two different concepts where the experts have only one.

In the end, Segal concludes, a theory of content must be based on how we actually introduce meanings and concepts; and he feels the theories of Putnam and Burge are not faithful to the facts. While Putnam assumed that if "water" first applied to samples of H_2O, it would apply in the future only to H_2O, Segal counters that actual usage does not always follow the contour of chemical theory; for instance, even in a case where the term first applied to H_2O, it might end up referring to all "watery" liquids. Likewise, considering a number of examples of British and American usage of English, Segal argues that Burge's theory of deferring to accepted usage won't be able to provide a theory of content for a nonexpert member of both groups. Considering cases of actual practice in psychology and other sciences, Segal claims that researchers fix an individual's content by examining his speech and behavior, and attributing whatever concept makes best sense of him—even to the point of coining "neologisms" (new terms) like "prelief" if his concept of "belief" is different from our normal concept. Following scientific methodology of this sort, Segal claims, leads to a kind of "functional role" theory of narrow content.

Further Readings

An "anti-Russellian" theory of meaning, of the sort employed by Putnam and Burge above, is set out in Saul Kripke's very influential series of lectures, *Naming and Necessity* (Cambridge, Mass.: Harvard University Press, 1980).

Burge also argues for a "wide" theory of perceptual content, in "Individualism and Psychology," *Philosophical Review* 95: 3–45. A shorter paper by Burge, promoting similar points, is included in Jay L. Garfield, ed., *Modularity in Knowledge Representation and Natural-Language Understanding* (Cambridge, Mass.: MIT Press, 1987).

One of the main objections to Burge's argument is that it seems to undermine self-knowledge and a person's privileged access to his own mental states (basically, the idea that I know better than anyone else what my mental states are about). This topic is explored in a number of papers in the following two books:

Peter Ludlow and Norah Martin, eds., *Externalism and Self-Knowledge* (Cambridge: Cambridge University Press, 1998).

Crispin Wright, Barry C. Smith, and Cynthia Macdonald, eds., *Knowing Our Own Minds* (Oxford: Oxford University Press, 2000).

42 From *On the Soul*, Book 3

Aristotle

... Turning now to the part of the soul with which the soul knows and thinks (whether this is separable from the others in definition only, or spatially as well) we have to inquire (1) what differentiates this part, and (2) how thinking can take place.

If thinking is like perceiving, it must be either a process in which the soul is acted upon by what is capable of being thought, or a process different from but analogous to that. The thinking part of the soul must therefore be, while impassible, capable of receiving the form of an object; that is, must be potentially identical in character with its object without being the object. Mind must be related to what is thinkable, as sense is to what is sensible.

Therefore, since everything is a possible object of thought, mind in order, as Anaxagoras says, to dominate, that is, to know, must be pure from all admixture; for the copresence of what is alien to its nature is a hindrance and a block: it follows that it too, like the sensitive part, can have no nature of its own, other than that of having a certain capacity. Thus that in the soul which is called mind (by mind I mean that whereby the soul thinks and judges) is, before it thinks, not actually any real thing. For this reason it cannot reasonably be regarded as blended with the body: if so, it would acquire some quality, e.g. warmth or cold, or even have an organ like the sensitive faculty: as it is, it has none. It was a good idea to call the soul "the place of forms," though (1) this description holds only of the intellective soul, and (2) even this is the forms only potentially, not actually.

Observation of the sense-organs and their employment reveals a distinction between the impassibility of the sensitive and that of the intellective faculty. After strong stimulation of a sense we are less able to exercise it than before, as e.g. in the case of a loud sound we cannot hear easily immediately after, or in the case of a bright colour or a powerful odour we cannot see or smell, but in the case of mind thought about an object that is highly intelligible renders it more and not less able afterwards to think objects that are less intelligible: the reason is that while the faculty of sensation is dependent upon the body, mind is separable from it.

Once the mind has become each set of its possible objects, as a man of science has, when this phrase is used of one who is actually a man of science (this happens when he is now able to exercise the power on his own initiative), its condition is still one of potentiality, but in a different sense from the potentiality which preceded the acquisition of knowledge by learning or discovery: the mind too is then able to think *itself*....

The problem might be suggested: if thinking is a passive affection, then if mind is simple and impassible and has nothing in common with anything else, as Anaxagoras says, how can it come to think at all? For interaction between two factors is held to require a precedent community of nature between the factors. Again it might be asked, is mind a possible object of thought to itself? For if mind is thinkable *per se* and what is thinkable is in kind one and the same, then either (*a*) mind will belong to everything, or (*b*) mind will contain some element common to it with all other realities which makes them all thinkable.

(1) Have not we already disposed of the difficulty about interaction involving a common element, when we said that mind is in a sense potentially whatever is thinkable, though actually it is nothing until it has thought? What it thinks must be in it just as characters may be said to be on a writing-tablet on which as yet nothing actually stands written: this is exactly what happens with mind.

(2) Mind is itself thinkable in exactly the same way as its objects are. For (*a*) in the case of objects which involve no matter, what thinks and what is thought are identical; for speculative knowledge and its object are identical. (Why mind is not always thinking we must consider later) (*b*) In the case of those which contain matter each of the objects of thought is only potentially present. It follows that while *they* will not have mind in them (for mind is a potentiality of them only in so far as they are capable of being disengaged from matter) mind may yet be thinkable.

Since in every class of things, as in nature as a whole, we find two factors involved, (1) a matter which is potentially all the particulars included in the class, (2) a cause which is productive in the sense that it makes them all (the latter standing to the former, as e.g. an art to its material), these distinct elements must likewise be found within the soul.

And in fact mind as we have described it is what it is by virtue of becoming all things, while there is another which is what it is by virtue of making all things: this is a sort of positive state like light; for in a sense light makes potential colours into actual colours.

Mind in this sense of it is separable, impassible, unmixed, since it is in its essential nature activity (for always the active is superior to the passive factor, the originating force to the matter which it forms).

Actual knowledge is identical with its object: in the individual, potential knowledge is in time prior to actual knowledge, but in the universe as a whole it is not prior even in time. Mind is not at one time knowing and at another not. When mind is set free from its present conditions it appears as just what it is and nothing more: this alone is immortal and eternal (we do not, however, remember its former activity because, while mind in this sense is impassible, mind as passive is destructible), and without it nothing thinks.

The thinking then of the simple objects of thought is found in those cases where falsehood is impossible: where the alternative of true or false applies, there we always find a putting together of objects of thought in a quasi-unity. As Empedocles said that "where heads of many a creature sprouted without necks" they afterwards by Love's power were combined, so here too objects of thought which were given separate are combined, e.g. "incommensurate" and "diagonal": if the combination be of objects past or future the combination of thought includes in its content the date. For falsehood always involves a synthesis; for even if you assert that what is white is not white you have included not-white in a synthesis. It is possible also to call all these cases division as well as combination. However that may be, there is not only the true or false assertion that Cleon is white but also the true or false assertion that he *was* or *will be* white. In each and every case that which unifies is mind....

Assertion is the saying of something concerning something, e.g. affirmation, and is in every case either true or false: this is not always the case with mind: the thinking of the definition in the sense of the constitutive essence is never in error nor is it the assertion of something concerning something, but, just as while the seeing of the special object of sight can never be in error, the belief that the white object seen is a man may be mistaken, so too in the case of objects which are without matter....

To the thinking soul images serve as if they were contents of perception (and when it asserts or denies them to be good or bad it avoids or pursues them). That is why the soul never thinks without an image....

The faculty of thinking then thinks the forms in the images, and as in the former case what is to be pursued or avoided is marked out for it, so where there is no sensation and it is engaged upon the images it is moved to pursuit or avoidance. E.g. perceiving by sense that the beacon is fire, it recognizes in virtue of the general faculty of sense that it signifies an enemy, because it sees it moving; but sometimes by means of the images or thoughts which are within the soul, just as if it were seeing, it calculates and deliberates what is to come by reference to what is present; and when it makes a pronouncement, as in the case of sensation it pronounces the object to be pleasant or painful, in this case it avoids or pursues; and so generally in cases of action.

That too which involves no action, i.e. that which is true or false, is in the same province with what is good or bad: yet they differ in this, that the one set imply and the other do not a reference to a particular person.

The so-called abstract objects the mind thinks just as, if one had thought of the snub-nosed not as snub-nosed but as hollow, one would have thought of an actuality without the flesh in which it is embodied: it is thus that the mind when it is thinking the objects of Mathematics thinks as separate elements which do not exist separate. In every case the mind which is actively thinking is the objects which it thinks. Whether it is possible for it while not existing separate from spatial conditions to think anything that is separate, or not, we must consider later.

Let us now summarize our results about soul, and repeat that the soul is in a way all existing things; for existing things are either sensible or thinkable, and knowledge is in a way what is knowable, and sensation is in a way what is sensible: in *what* way we must inquire.

Knowledge and sensation are divided to correspond with the realities, potential knowledge and sensation answering to potentialities, actual knowledge and sensation to actualities. Within the soul the faculties of knowledge and sensation are *potentially* these objects, the one what is knowable, the other what is sensible. They must be either the things themselves or their forms. The former alternative is of course impossible: it is not the stone which is present in the soul but its form.

It follows that the soul is analogous to the hand; for as the hand is a tool of tools, so the mind is the form of forms and sense the form of sensible things.

Since according to common agreement there is nothing outside and separate in existence from sensible spatial magnitudes, the objects of thought are in the sensible forms, viz. both the abstract objects and all the states and affections of sensible things. Hence (1) no one can learn or understand anything in the absence of sense, and (2) when the mind is actively aware of anything it is necessarily aware of it along with an image; for images are like sensuous contents except in that they contain no matter....

43 From *Meditations on First Philosophy* and *Replies to Objections* I–IV

René Descartes

... [I]t is requisite that I should here divide my thoughts into certain kinds, and that I should consider in which of these kinds there is, properly speaking, truth or error to be found. Of my thoughts some are, so to speak, images of the things, and to these alone is the title "idea" properly applied; examples are my thought of a man or of a chimera, of heaven, of an angel, or [even] of God....

Now as to what concerns ideas, if we consider them only in themselves and do not relate them to anything else beyond themselves, they cannot properly speaking be false; for whether I imagine a goat or a chimera, it is not less true that I imagine the one than the other....

... If ideas are only taken as certain modes of thought, I recognise amongst them no difference or inequality, and all appear to proceed from me in the same manner; but when we consider them as images, one representing one thing and the other another, it is clear that they are very different one from the other. There is no doubt that those which represent to me substances are something more, and contain so to speak more objective reality within them [that is to say, by representation participate in a higher degree of being or perfection] than those that simply represent modes or accidents; and that idea again by which I understand a supreme God, eternal, infinite, [immutable], omniscient, omnipotent, and Creator of all things which are outside of Himself, has certainly more objective reality in itself than those ideas by which finite substances are represented....

... [S]ince ideas themselves are forms, and are never composed of any matter, when we take them as representing something, we regard them not *in a material guise* but *formally*; but if we were to consider them not in so far as they represent this or that other thing, but in the respect in which they are operations of the intellect, it might be said that they were taken materially, but then they would have no reference to the truth or falsity of objects....

... [W]hat I speak of is the idea, which at no time exists outside the mind, and in the case of which "*objective existence*" is indistinguishable from being in the understanding in that way in which objects are wont to be there.... Hence the idea of the sun will be the sun itself existing in the mind, not indeed formally, as it exists in the sky, but objectively, i.e. in the way in which objects are wont to exist in the mind; and this mode of being is truly much less perfect than that in which things exist outside the mind, but it is not on that account mere nothing, as I have already said....

... [I]n reasoning we unite not names but the things signified by the names; and I marvel that the opposite can occur to anyone. For who doubts whether a Frenchman and a German are able to reason in exactly the same way about the same things, though they yet conceive the words in an entirely diverse way? And has not my opponent condemned himself in talking of conventions arbitrarily made about the meanings of words? For, if he admits that words signify anything, why will he not allow our reasonings to refer to this something that is signified, rather than to the words alone?...

I. *Thought* is a word that covers everything that exists in us in such a way that we are immediately conscious of it. Thus all the operations of will, intellect, imagination, and of the senses are thoughts. But I have added *immediately*, for the purpose of excluding that which is a consequence of our thought; for example, voluntary movement, which, though indeed depending on thought as on a causal principle, is yet itself not thought.
II. *Idea* is a word by which I understand the form of any thought, that form by the immediate awareness of which I am conscious of that said thought; in such a way that, when understanding what I say, I can express nothing in words, without that very fact making it certain that I possess the idea of that which these words signify....
III. By the *objective reality of an idea* I mean that in respect of which the thing represented in the idea is an entity, in so far as that exists in the idea; and in the same way we can talk of objective perfection, objective device, etc. For whatever we perceive as being as it were in the objects of our ideas, exists in the ideas themselves objectively....

44 From *An Essay Concerning Human Understanding*

John Locke

Let us then suppose the Mind to be, as we say, white Paper, void of all Characters, without any *Ideas*; How comes it to be furnished? Whence comes it by that vast store, which the busy and boundless Fancy of Man has painted on it, with an almost endless variety? Whence has it all the materials of Reason and Knowledge? To this I answer, in one word, From *Experience*: In that, all our Knowledge is founded; and from that it ultimately derives it self. Our Observation employ'd either about *external, sensible Objects; or about the internal Operations of our Minds, perceived and reflected on by our selves, is that, which supplies our Understandings with all the materials of thinking.* These two are the Fountains of Knowledge, from whence all the *Ideas* we have, or can naturally have, do spring.

First, *Our Senses*, conversant about particular sensible Objects, do *convey into the Mind*, several distinct *Perceptions* of things, according to those various ways, wherein those Objects do affect them: And thus we come by those *Ideas*, we have of *Yellow, White, Heat, Cold, Soft, Hard, Bitter, Sweet*, and all those which we call sensible qualities, which when I say the senses convey into the mind, I mean, they from external Objects convey into the mind what produces there those *Perceptions*. This great Source, of most of the *Ideas* we have, depending wholly upon our Senses, and derived by them to the Understanding, I call *SENSATION*.

Secondly, The other Fountain, from which Experience furnisheth the Understanding with *Ideas*, is the *Perception of the Operations of our own Minds* within us, as it is employ'd about the *Ideas* it has got; which Operations, when the Soul comes to reflect on, and consider, do furnish the Understanding with another set of *Ideas*, which could not be had from things without: and such are, *Perception, Thinking, Doubting, Believing, Reasoning, Knowing, Willing*, and all the different actings of our own Minds; which we being conscious of, and observing in our selves, do from these receive into our Understandings, as distinct *Ideas*, as we do from Bodies affecting our Senses. This Source of *Ideas*, every Man has wholly in himself: And though it be not Sense, as having nothing to do with external Objects; yet it is very like it, and might properly enough be call'd internal Sense. But as I call the other *Sensation*, so I call this *REFLECTION*, the *Ideas* it affords being such only, as the Mind gets by reflecting on its own Operations within it self. By *REFLECTION* then, in the following part of this Discourse, I would be understood to mean, that notice which the Mind takes of its own Operations, and the manner of them, by reason whereof, there come to be *Ideas* of these Operations in the Understanding. These two, I say, *viz.* External, Material things, as the Objects of *SENSATION*;

and the Operations of our own Minds within, as the Objects of *REFLECTION*, are, to me, the only Originals, from whence all our *Ideas* take their beginnings. The term *Operations* here, I use in a large sence, as comprehending not barely the Actions of the Mind about its *Ideas*, but some sort of Passions arising sometimes from them, such as is the satisfaction or uneasiness arising from any thought.

The Understanding seems to me, not to have the least glimmering of any *Ideas*, which it doth not receive from one of these two. *External Objects furnish the Mind with the* Ideas *of sensible qualities*, which are all those different perceptions they produce in us: And the *Mind furnishes the Understanding with* Ideas *of its own Operations*.

These, when we have taken a full survey of them, and their several Modes, Combinations, and Relations, we shall find to contain all our whole stock of *Ideas*; and that we have nothing in our Minds, which did not come in, one of these two ways. Let any one examine his own Thoughts, and throughly search into his Understanding, and then let him tell me, Whether all the original *Ideas* he has there, are any other than of the Objects of his *Senses*; or of the Operations of his Mind, considered as Objects of his *Reflection*: and how great a mass of Knowledge soever he imagines to be lodged there, he will, upon taking a strict view, see, that he has *not any* Idea *in his Mind, but what one of these two have imprinted*; though, perhaps, with infinite variety compounded and enlarged by the Understanding, as we shall see hereafter. . . .

The better to understand the Nature, Manner, and Extent of our Knowledge, one thing is carefully to be observed, concerning the *Ideas* we have; and that is, That *some* of them are *simple*, and *some complex*.

Though the Qualities that affect our Senses, are, in the things themselves, so united and blended, that there is no separation, no distance between them; yet 'tis plain, the *Ideas* they produce in the Mind, enter by the Senses simple and unmixed. For though the Sight and Touch often take in from the same Object, at the same time, different *Ideas*; as a Man sees at once Motion and Colour; the Hand feels Softness and Warmth in the same piece of Wax: Yet the simple *Ideas* thus united in the same Subject, are as perfectly distinct, as those that come in by different Senses. The coldness and hardness, which a Man feels in a piece of *Ice*, being as distinct *Ideas* in the Mind, as the Smell and Whiteness of a Lily; or as the taste of Sugar, and smell of a Rose: And there is nothing can be plainer to a Man, than the clear and distinct Perception he has of those simple *Ideas*; which being each in it self uncompounded, contains in it nothing but *one uniform Appearance*, or Conception in the mind, and is not distinguishable into different *Ideas*.

These simple *Ideas*, the Materials of all our Knowledge, are suggested and furnished to the Mind, only by those two ways above mentioned, *viz. Sensation* and *Reflection*. When the Understanding is once stored with these simple *Ideas*, it has the Power to repeat, compare, and unite them even to an almost infinite Variety, and so can make at Pleasure new complex *Ideas*. But it is not in the Power of the most exalted Wit, or enlarged Understanding, by any quickness or variety of Thought, to *invent or frame one new simple* Idea in the mind, not taken in by the ways before mentioned: nor can any force of the Understanding, *destroy* those that are there. The Dominion of Man, in this little World of his own Understanding, being muchwhat the same, as it is in the great World of visible things; wherein his Power, however managed by Art and Skill, reaches no farther, than to compound and divide the Materials, that are made to his

Hand; but can do nothing towards the making the least Particle of new Matter, or destroying one Atome of what is already in Being. The same inability, will every one find in himself, who shall go about to fashion in his Understanding any simple *Idea*, not received in by his Senses, from external Objects; or by reflection from the Operations of his own mind about them. I would have any one try to fancy any Taste, which had never affected his Palate; or frame the *Idea* of a Scent, he had never smelt: And when he can do this, I will also conclude, that a blind Man hath *Ideas* of Colours, and a deaf Man true distinct Notions of Sounds.

This is the Reason why, though we cannot believe it impossible to God, to make a Creature with other Organs, and more ways to convey into the Understanding the notice of Corporeal things, than those five, as they are usually counted, which he has given to Man: Yet I think, it is *not possible*, for any one *to imagine* any other *Qualities* in Bodies, howsoever constituted, whereby they can be taken notice of, besides Sounds, Tastes, Smells, visible and tangible Qualities. And had Mankind been made with but four Senses, the Qualities then, which are the Object of the Fifth Sense, had been as far from our Notice, Imagination, and Conception, as now any *belonging to a Sixth, Seventh, or Eighth Sense*, can possibly be: which, whether yet some other Creatures, in some other Parts of this vast, and stupendious Universe, may not have, will be a great Presumption to deny. He that will not set himself proudly at the top of all things; but will consider the Immensity of this Fabrick, and the great variety, that is to be found in this little and inconsiderable part of it, which he has to do with, may be apt to think, that in other Mansions of it, there may be other, and different intelligent Beings, of whose Faculties, he has as little Knowledge or Apprehension, as a Worm shut up in one drawer of a Cabinet, hath of the Senses or Understanding of a Man; Such Variety and Excellency, being suitable to the Wisdom and Power of the Maker. I have here followed the common Opinion of Man's having but five Senses; though, perhaps, there may be justly counted more; but either Supposition serves equally to my present purpose. . . .

The Mind being, as I have declared, furnished with a great number of the simple *Ideas*, conveyed in by the *Senses*, as they are found in exteriour things, or by *Reflection* on its own Operations, takes notice also, that a certain number of these simple *Ideas* go constantly together; which being presumed to belong to one thing, and Words being suited to common apprehensions, and made use of for quick dispatch, are called so united in one subject, by one name; which by inadvertency we are apt afterward to talk of and consider as one simple *Idea*, which indeed is a complication of many *Ideas* together; Because, as I have said, not imagining how these simple *Ideas* can subsist by themselves, we accustom our selves, to suppose some *Substratum*, wherein they do subsist, and from which they do result, which therefore we call *Substance*.

So that if any one will examine himself concerning his *Notion of pure Substance in general*, he will find he has no other *Idea* of it at all, but only a Supposition of he knows not what support of such Qualities, which are capable of producing simple *Ideas* in us; which Qualities are commonly called Accidents. If any one should be asked, what is the subject wherein Colour or Weight inheres, he would have nothing to say, but the solid extended parts: And if he were demanded, what is it, that that Solidity and Extension inhere in, he would not be in a much better case, than the *Indian* before mentioned; who, saying that the World was supported by a great Elephant, was asked, what the Elephant rested on; to which his answer was, a great Tortoise: But being again pressed to know what gave support to the broad-back'd Tortoise, replied, something, he knew not what. And thus here, as in all other cases, where we use Words without having clear and distinct *Ideas,* we talk like Children; who, being questioned, what such a thing is, which they know not, readily give this satisfactory answer, That it is *something;* which in truth signifies no more, when so used, either by Children or Men, but that they know not what; and that the thing they pretend to know, and talk of, is what they have no distinct *Idea* of at all, and so are perfectly ignorant of it, and in the dark. The *Idea* then we have, to which we give the general name Substance, being nothing, but the supposed, but unknown support of those Qualities, we find existing, which we imagine cannot subsist, *sine re substante,* without something to support them, we call that Support *Substantia;* which, according to the true import of the Word, is in plain *English, standing under,* or *upholding.*

An obscure and relative *Idea* of Substance in general being thus made, we come to have the *Ideas of particular sorts of Substances,* by collecting such Combinations of simple *Ideas,* as are by Experience and Observation of Men's Senses taken notice of to exist together, and are therefore supposed to flow from the particular internal Constitution, or unknown Essence of that Substance. Thus we come to have the *Ideas* of a Man, Horse, Gold, Water, *etc.* of which Substances, whether any one has any other clear *Idea,* farther than of certain simple *Ideas* coexisting together, I appeal to every one's own Experience. 'Tis the ordinary Qualities, observable in Iron, or a Diamond, put together, that make the true complex *Idea* of those Substances, which a Smith, or a Jeweller, commonly knows better than a Philosopher; who, whatever substantial forms he may talk of, has no other *Idea* of those Substances, than what is framed by a collection of those simple *Ideas* which are to be found in them; only we must take notice, that our complex *Ideas* of Substances, besides all these simple *Ideas* they are made up of, have always the confused *Idea* of *something* to which they belong, and in which they subsist: and therefore when we speak of any sort of Substance, we say it is a *thing* having such or such Qualities, as Body is a *thing* that is extended, figured, and capable of Motion; a Spirit a *thing* capable of thinking; and so Hardness, Friability, and Power to draw Iron, we say, are Qualities to be found in a Loadstone. These, and the like fashions of speaking intimate, that the Substance is supposed always *something* besides the Extension, Figure, Solidity, Motion, Thinking, or other observable *Ideas,* though we know not what it is.

Hence when we talk or think of any particular sort of corporeal Substances, as *Horse, Stone, etc.* though the *Idea,* we have of either of them, be but the Complication, or Collection of those several simple *Ideas* of sensible Qualities, which we use to find united in the thing called *Horse* or *Stone,* yet because we cannot conceive, how they should subsist alone, nor one in another, we suppose them existing in, and supported by some common subject; *which Support we denote by the name Substance,* though it be certain, we have no clear, or distinct *Idea* of that *thing* we suppose a Support.

The same happens concerning the Operations of the Mind, *viz.* Thinking, Reasoning, Fearing, *etc.* which we concluding not to subsist of themselves, nor apprehending how they can belong to Body, or be produced by it, we are apt to think these the Actions of some other *Substance,* which we call *Spirit;* whereby yet it is evident, that having no other *Idea* or Notion, of Matter, but *something* wherein those many sensible Qualities, which affect our Senses, do subsist; by supposing a Substance, wherein *Thinking, Knowing, Doubting,* and a power of Moving, *etc.* do subsist, *We have as clear a Notion of the Substance of Spirit, as we have of Body*; the one being supposed to be (without knowing what it is) the *Substratum* to those simple *Ideas* we have from without; and the other supposed (with a like ignorance of what it is) to be the *Substratum* to those Operations, which we experiment in our selves within. 'Tis plain then, that the *Idea* of corporeal *Substance* in Matter is as remote from our Conceptions, and Apprehensions, as that of Spiritual *Substance,* or *Spirit*; and therefore from our not having any notion of the *Substance* of Spirit, we can no more conclude its non-Existence, than we can, for the same reason, deny the Existence of Body: It being as rational to affirm, there is no Body, because we have no clear and distinct *Idea* of the *Substance* of Matter; as to say, there is no Spirit, because we have no clear and distinct *Idea* of the *Substance* of a Spirit.

Whatever therefore be the secret and abstract Nature of *Substance* in general, all *the* Ideas *we have of particular distinct sorts of Substances,* are nothing but several Combinations of simple *Ideas,* coexisting in such, though unknown, Cause of their Union, as makes the whole subsist of itself. 'Tis by such Combinations of simple *Ideas* and nothing else, that we represent particular sorts of *Substances* to our selves; such are the *Ideas* we have of their several species in our Minds; and such only do we, by their specifick Names, signify to others, *v.g. Man, Horse, Sun, Water, Iron,* upon hearing which Words, every one who understands the Language, frames in his Mind a Combination of those several simple *Ideas,* which he has usually observed, or fancied to exist together under that denomination; all which he supposes to rest in, and be, as it were, adherent to that unknown common Subject, which inheres not in any thing else. Though in the mean time it be manifest, and every one upon Enquiry into his own thoughts, will find that he has no other *Idea* of any *Substance, v.g.* let it be *Gold, Horse, Iron, Man, Vitriol, Bread,* but what he has barely of those sensible Qualities, which he supposes to inhere, with a supposition of such a *Substratum,* as gives as it were a support to those Qualities, or simple *Ideas,* which he has observed to exist united together. Thus the *Idea* of the *Sun,* What is it, but an aggregate of those several simple *Ideas*, Bright, Hot, Roundish, having a constant regular motion, at a certain distance from us, and, perhaps, some other: as he who thinks and discourses of the *Sun,* has been more or less accurate, in observing those sensible Qualities, *Ideas,* or Properties, which are in that thing, which he calls the *Sun*....

The common Names of Substances, as well as other general Terms, *stand for Sorts*: which is nothing else but the being made signs of such complex *Ideas,* wherein several particular Substances do, or might agree, by virtue of which, they are capable to be comprehended in one common Conception, and be signified by one Name. I say, do or might agree: for though there be but one Sun existing in the World, yet the *Idea* of it being abstracted, so that more Substances (if there were several) might each agree in it; it is as much a Sort, as if there were as many Suns, as there are Stars. They want not their Reasons, who think there are, and that each fixed Star, would answer the *Idea* the name *Sun* stands for, to one who were placed in a due distance; which, by the way, may shew us how much the Sorts, or, if you please, *Genera* and *Species* of Things (for those Latin Terms signify to me, no more than the English word *Sort*) depend on such Collections of *Ideas*, as Men have made; and not on the real Nature of Things: since 'tis not impossible, but that in propriety of Speech, that might be a Sun to one, which is a Star to another.

The measure and boundary of each Sort, or *Species*, whereby it is constituted that particular Sort, and distinguished form others, is that we call its *Essence*, which *is* nothing but that *abstract* Idea *to which the Name is annexed*: So that every thing contained in that *Idea*, is essential to that Sort. This, though it be all the *Essence* of natural Substances, that we know, or by which we distinguish them into Sorts; yet I call it by a peculiar name, the *nominal Essence*, to distinguish it from that real Constitution of Substances, upon which depends this *nominal Essence*, and all the Properties of that Sort; which therefore, as has been said, may be called the *real Essence*: *v.g.* the *nominal Essence* of *Gold*, is that complex *Idea* the word *Gold* stands for, let it be, for instance, a Body yellow, of a certain weight, malleable, fusible, and fixed. But the *real Essence* is the constitution of the insensible parts of that Body, on which those Qualities, and all the other Properties of *Gold* depend. How far these two are different, though they are both called *Essence*, is obvious, at first sight, to discover.

For though, perhaps, voluntary Motion, with Sense and Reason, join'd to a Body of a certain shape, be the complex *Idea*, to which I, and others, annex the name *Man*; and so be the *nominal Essence* of the *Species* so called: yet no body will say, that that complex *Idea* is the *real Essence* and Source of all those Operations, which are to be found in any Individual of that Sort. The foundation of all those Qualities, which are the Ingredients of our complex *Idea*, is something quite different: And had we such a Knowledge of that Constitution of *Man*, from which his Faculties of Moving, Sensation, and Reasoning, and other Powers flow; and on which his so regular shape depends, as 'tis possible Angels have, and 'tis certain his Maker has, we should have a quite other *Idea* of his *Essence*, than what now is contained in our Definition of that *Species*, be it what it will: And our *Idea* of any individual *Man* would be as far different from what it now is, as is his, who knows all the Springs and Wheels, and other contrivances within, of the famous Clock at *Strasburg*, from that which a gazing Country-man has of it, who barely sees the motion of the Hand, and hears the Clock strike, and observes only some of the outward appearances.

That *Essence*, in the ordinary use of the word, relates to *Sorts*, and that it is considered in particular Beings, no farther than as they are ranked into *Sorts*, appears from hence: That take but away the abstract *Ideas*, by which we sort Individuals, and rank them under common Names, and then the thought of any thing *essential* to any of them, instantly vanishes: we have no notion of the one, without the other: which plainly shews their relation. 'Tis necessary for me to be as I am; GOD and Nature has made me so: But there is nothing I have, is essential to me. An Accident, or Disease, may very much alter my Colour, or Shape; a Fever, or Fall, may take away my Reason, or Memory, or both; and an Apoplexy leave neither Sense, nor Understanding, no nor Life. Other Creatures of my shape, may be made with more, and better, or fewer, and worse Faculties than I have: and others may have Reason, and Sense, in a shape and body very different from mine. None of these are essential to the one, or the other, or to any Individual whatsoever, till the Mind refers it to some Sort or *Species* of things; and then presently, according to the abstract *Idea* of that sort, something is found *essential*. Let any one examine his own Thoughts, and he will find, that as soon as he supposes or speaks of *Essential,* the consideration of some *Species,* or the complex *Idea,* signified by some general name, comes into his Mind: And 'tis in reference to that, that this or that Quality is said to be *essential.* So that if it be asked, whether it be *essential* to me, or any other particular corporeal Being to have Reason? I say no; no more than it is *essential* to this white thing I write on, to have words in it. But if that particular Being, be to be counted of the sort *Man,* and to have the name *Man* given it, then Reason is *essential* to it, supposing Reason to be a part of the complex *Idea* the name *Man* stands for: as it is *essential* to this thing I write on, to contain words, if I will give it the name *Treatise,* and rank it under that *Species.* So that *essential, and not essential, relate only to our abstract Ideas, and the names annexed to them;* which amounts to no more but this, That whatever particular Thing, has not in it those Qualities, which are contained in the abstract *Idea,* which any general Term stands for, cannot be ranked under that *Species,* nor be called by that name, since that abstract *Idea* is the very *Essence* of that *Species.*

Thus if the *Idea* of *Body,* with some People, be bare Extension, or Space, then Solidity is not *essential* to Body: If others make the *Idea,* to which they give the name *Body,* to be Solidity and Extension, then Solidity is essential to *Body.* That therefore, and *that alone is* considered as *essential, which makes a part of the complex* Idea *the name of a Sort stands for,* without which, no particular Thing can be reckoned of that Sort, nor be intituled to that name. Should there be found a parcel of Matter, that had all the other Qualities that are in *Iron,* but wanted Obedience to the Load-stone; and would neither be drawn by it, nor receive Direction from it, Would any one question, whether it wanted any thing *essential*? It would be absurd to ask, Whether a thing really existing, wanted any thing *essential* to it. Or could it be demanded, Whether this made an *essential* or *specifick* difference, or no; since we have no other measure of *essential* or *specifick,* but our abstract *Ideas*? And to talk of specifick Differences in Nature, without reference to general *Ideas* and Names, is to talk unintelligibly. For I would ask any one, What is sufficient to make an *essential* difference in Nature, between any two particular Beings, without any regard had to some abstract *Idea,* which is looked upon as the Essence and Standard of a *Species*? All such Patterns and Standards, being quite laid aside, particular Beings, considered barely in themselves, will be found to have all their Qualities equally *essential;* and every thing, in each Individual, will be *essential* to it, or, which is more true, nothing at all. For though it may be reasonable to ask, Whether obeying the Magnet, be *essential* to *Iron*? yet, I think, it is very improper and insignificant to ask, Whether it be *essential* to the particular parcel of Matter I cut my Pen with, without considering it under the name *Iron,* or as being of a certain *Species*? And if, as has been said, our abstract *Ideas,* which have names annexed to them, are the Boundaries of *Species,* nothing can be *essential* but what is contained in those *Ideas.*

'Tis true, I have often mentioned a *real Essence,* distinct in Substances, from those abstract *Ideas* of them, which I call their *nominal Essence.* By this *real Essence,* I mean, that real constitution of any Thing, which is the foundation of all those Properties, that are combined in, and are constantly found to co-exist with the *nominal Essence;* that particular constitution, which every Thing has within it self, without any relation to any thing without it. But *Essence,* even in this sense, *relates to a Sort,* and supposes a *Species*: For being that real Constitution, on which the Properties depend, it necessarily supposes a sort of Things, Properties belonging only to *Species,* and not to Individuals; *v.g.*

Supposing the nominal Essence of *Gold,* to be Body of such a peculiar Colour and Weight, with Malleability and Fusibility, the real Essence is that Constitution of the parts of Matter, on which these Qualities, and their Union, depend; and is also the foundation of its Solubility in *Aqua Regia,* and other Properties accompanying that complex *Idea.* Here are *Essences* and *Properties,* but all upon supposition of a Sort, or general abstract *Idea,* which is considered as immutable: but there is no individual parcel of Matter, to which any of these Qualities are so annexed, as to be *essential* to it, or inseparable from it. That which is *essential,* belongs to it as a Condition, whereby it is of this or that Sort: But take away the consideration of its being ranked under the name of some abstract *Idea,* and then there is nothing necessary to it, nothing inseparable from it. Indeed, as to the *real Essences* of Substances, we only suppose their Being, without precisely knowing what they are: But that which annexes them still to the *Species,* is the nominal Essence, of which they are the supposed foundation and cause.

The next thing to be considered is, by which of those Essences it is, that *Substances are determined into* Sorts, or *Species*; and that 'tis evident, is *by the nominal Essence.* For 'tis that alone, that the name, which is the mark of the Sort, signifies. 'Tis impossible therefore, that any thing should determine the Sorts of Things, which we rank under general Names, but that *Idea,* which that Name is design'd as a mark for; which is that, as has been shewn, which we call the *Nominal Essence.* Why do we say, This is a *Horse,* and that a *Mule*; this is an *Animal,* that an *Herb*? How comes any particular Thing to be of this or that *Sort,* but because it has that nominal Essence, Or, which is all one, agrees to that abstract *Idea,* that name is annexed to? And I desire any one but to reflect on his own Thoughts, when he hears or speaks any of those, or other Names of Substances, to know what sort of *Essences* they stand for.

And that the *Species of Things to us, are nothing but the ranking them under distinct Names, according to the complex* Ideas *in us*; and not according to precise, distinct, real *Essences* in them, is plain from hence; That we find many of the Individuals that are ranked into one Sort, called by one common Name, and so received as being of one *Species,* have yet Qualities depending on their real Constitutions, as far different one from another, as from others, from which they are accounted to differ *specifically.* This, as it is easy to be observed by all, who have to do with natural Bodies; so Chymists especially are often, by sad Experience, convinced of it, when they, sometimes in vain, seek for the same Qualities in one parcel of Sulphur, Antimony, or Vitriol, which they have found in others. For though they are Bodies of the same *Species,* having the same nominal *Essence,* under the same Name; yet do they often, upon severe ways of examination, betray Qualities so different one from another, as to frustrate the Expectation and Labour of very wary Chymists. But if Things were distinguished into *Species,* according to their real Essences, it would be as impossible to find different Properties in any two individual Substances of the same *Species,* as it is to find different Properties in two Circles, or two equilateral Triangles. That is properly the *Essence* to us, which determines every particular to this or that *Classis*; or, which is the same Thing, to this or that general Name: And what can that be else, but that abstract *Idea,* to which that name is annexed? and so has, in truth, a reference, not so much to the being of particular Things, as to their general Denominations.

Nor indeed *can we* rank, and *sort Things,* and consequently (which is the end of sorting) denominate them *by their real Essences,* because we know them not. Our Faculties carry us no farther towards the knowledge and distinction of Substances, than a Collection of those sensible *Ideas*, which we observe in them; which however made with the greatest diligence and exactness, we are capable of, yet is more remote from the true internal Constitution, from which those Qualities flow, than, as I said, a Countryman's *Idea* is from the inward contrivance of that famous Clock at *Strasburg*, whereof he only sees the outward Figure and Motions. There is not so contemptible a Plant or Animal, that does not confound the most inlarged Understanding. Though the familiar use of Things about us, take off our Wonder; yet it cures not our Ignorance. When we come to examine the Stones, we tread on; or the Iron, we daily handle, we presently find, we know not their Make; and can give no Reason, of the different Qualities we find in them. 'Tis evident the internal Constitution, whereon their Properties depend, is unknown to us. For to go no farther than the grossest and most obvious we can imagine amongst them, What is that Texture of Parts, that real *Essence*, that makes Lead, and Antimony fusible; Wood, and Stones not? What makes Lead, and Iron malleable; Antimony, and stones not? And yet how infinitely these come short, of the fine Contrivances, and unconceivable *real Essences* of Plants and Animals, every one knows. The Workmanship of the All-wise, and Powerful God, in the great Fabrick of the Universe, and every part thereof, farther exceeds the Capacity and Comprehension of the most inquisitive and intelligent Man, than the best contrivance of the most ingenious Man, doth the Conceptions of the most ignorant of rational Creatures. Therefore we in vain pretend to range Things into sorts, and dispose them into certain Classes, under Names, by their *real Essences*, that are so far from our discovery or comprehension. A blind Man may as soon sort Things by their Colours, and he that has lost his Smell, as well distinguish a Lily and a Rose by their Odors, as by those internal Constitutions which he knows not. He that thinks he can distinguish Sheep and Goats by their real Essences, that are unknown to him, may be pleased to try his Skill in those *Species*, called *Cassiowary*, and *Querechinchio*; and by their internal real Essences, determine the boundaries of those *Species*, without knowing the complex *Idea* of sensible Qualities, that each of those Names stands for, in the Countries where those Animals are to be found. . . .

But supposing that the *real Essences* of Substances were discoverable, by those, that would severely apply themselves to that Enquiry; yet we could not reasonably think, that the *ranking of things under general Names, was regulated by* those internal real Constitutions, or any thing else but *their obvious appearances*. Since Languages, in all Countries, have been established long before Sciences. So that they have not been Philosophers, or Logicians, or such who have troubled themselves about *Forms* and *Essences*, that have made the general Names, that are in use amongst the several Nations of Men: But those, more or less comprehensive terms, have, for the most part, in all Languages, received their Birth and Signification, from ignorant and illiterate People, who sorted and denominated Things, by those sensible Qualities they found in them, thereby to signify them, when absent, to others, whether they had an occasion to mention a Sort, or a particular Thing. . . .

45 From *A Treatise of Human Nature*

David Hume

All the perceptions of the human mind resolve themselves into two distinct kinds, which I shall call IMPRESSIONS and IDEAS. The difference betwixt these consists in the degrees of force and liveliness, with which they strike upon the mind, and make their way into our thought or consciousness. Those perceptions, which enter with most force and violence, we may name *impressions*; and under this name I comprehend all our sensations, passions and emotions, as they make their first appearance in the soul. By *ideas* I mean the faint images of these in thinking and reasoning; such as, for instance, are all the perceptions excited by the present discourse, excepting only, those which arise from the sight and touch, and excepting the immediate pleasure or uneasiness it may occasion. I believe it will not be very necessary to employ many words in explaining this distinction. Every one of himself will readily perceive the difference betwixt feeling and thinking. The common degrees of these are easily distinguished; tho' it is not impossible but in particular instances they may very nearly approach to each other. Thus in sleep, in a fever, in madness, or in any very violent emotions of soul, our ideas may approach to our impressions: As on the other hand it sometimes happens, that our impressions are so faint and low, that we cannot distinguish them from our ideas. But notwithstanding this near resemblance in a few instances, they are in general so very different, that no-one can make a scruple to rank them under distinct heads, and assign to each a peculiar name to mark the difference.[1]

There is another division of our perceptions, which it will be convenient to observe, and which extends itself both to our impressions and ideas. This division is into SIMPLE and COMPLEX. Simple perceptions or impressions and ideas are such as admit of no distinction nor separation. The complex are the contrary to these, and may be distinguished into parts. Tho' a particular colour, taste, and smell are qualities all united together in this apple, 'tis easy to perceive they are not the same, but are at least distinguishable from each other.

Having by these divisions given an order and arrangement to our objects, we may now apply ourselves to consider with the more accuracy their qualities and relations. The first circumstance, that strikes my eye, is the great resemblance betwixt our impressions and ideas in every other particular, except their degree of force and vivacity. The one seem to be in a manner the reflexion of the other; so that all the perceptions of the mind are double, and appear both as impressions and ideas. When I shut my eyes and think of my chamber, the ideas I form are exact representations of the impressions I felt; nor is there any circumstance of the one, which is not to be found in the other. In running over my other perceptions, I find still the same resemblance and representation. Ideas and impressions appear always to correspond to each other. This circumstance seems to me remarkable, and engages my attention for a moment.

Upon a more accurate survey I find I have been carried away too far by the first appearance, and that I must make use of the distinction of perceptions into *simple and complex*, to limit this general decision, *that all our ideas and impressions are resembling*. I observe, that many of our complex ideas never had impressions, that corresponded to them, and that many of our complex impressions never are exactly copied in ideas. I can imagine to myself such a city as the *New Jerusalem*, whose pavement is gold and walls are rubies, tho' I never saw any such. I have seen *Paris*; but shall I affirm I can form such an idea of that city, as will perfectly represent all its streets and houses in their real and just proportions?

I perceive, therefore, that tho' there is in general a great resemblance betwixt our *complex* impressions and ideas, yet the rule is not universally true, that they are exact copies of each other. We may next consider how the case stands with our *simple* perceptions. After the most accurate examination, of which I am capable, I venture to affirm, that the rule here holds without any exception, and that every simple idea has a simple impression, which resembles it; and every simple impression a correspondent idea. That idea of red, which we form in the dark, and that impression, which strikes our eyes in sun-shine, differ only in degree, not in nature. That the case is the same with all our simple impressions and ideas, 'tis impossible to prove by a particular enumeration of them. Every one may satisfy himself in this point by running over as many as he pleases. But if any one should deny this universal resemblance, I know no way of convincing him, but by desiring him to shew a simple impression, that has not a correspondent idea, or a simple idea, that has not a correspondent impression. If he does not answer this challenge, as 'tis certain he cannot, we may from his silence and our own observation establish our conclusion.

Thus we find, that all simple ideas and impressions resemble each other; and as the complex are formed from them, we may affirm in general, that these two species of perception are exactly correspondent. Having discover'd this relation, which requires no farther examination, I am curious to find some other of their qualities. Let us consider how they stand with regard to their existence, and which of the impressions and ideas are causes and which effects.

The *full* examination of this question is the subject of the present treatise; and therefore we shall here content ourselves with establishing one general proposition, *That all our simple ideas in their first appearance are deriv'd from simple impressions, which are correspondent to them, and which they exactly represent.*

In seeking for phænomena to prove this proposition, I find only those of two kinds; but in each kind the phænomena are obvious, numerous, and conclusive. I first make myself certain, by a new review, of what I have already asserted, that every simple impression is attended with a correspondent idea, and every simple idea with a correspondent impression. From this constant conjunction of resembling perceptions I immediately conclude, that there is a great connexion betwixt our correspondent impressions and ideas, and that the existence of the one has a considerable influence upon that of the other. Such a constant conjunction, in such an infinite number of instances, can never arise from chance; but clearly proves a dependence of the impressions on the ideas, or of the ideas on the impressions. That I may know on which side this dependence lies, I consider the order of their *first appearance*; and find by constant experience, that the simple impressions always take the precedence of their correspondent ideas, but never appear in the contrary order. To give a child an idea of scarlet or orange, of sweet or bitter, I present the objects, or in other words, convey to him these impressions; but proceed not so absurdly, as to endeavour to produce the impressions by exciting the ideas. Our ideas upon their appearance produce not their correspondent impressions, nor do we perceive any colour, or feel any sensation merely upon thinking of them. On the other hand we find, that any impressions either of the mind or body is constantly followed by an idea, which resembles it, and is only different in the degrees of force and liveliness. The constant conjunction of our resembling perceptions, is a convincing proof, that the one are the causes of the other; and this priority of the impressions is an equal proof, that our impressions are the causes of our ideas, not our ideas of our impressions.

To confirm this I consider another plain and convincing phænomenon; which is, that where-ever by any accident the faculties, which give rise to any impressions, are obstructed in their operations, as when one is born blind or deaf; not only the impressions are lost, but also their correspondent ideas; so that there never appear in the mind the least traces of either of them. Nor is this only true, where the organs of sensation are entirely destroy'd, but likewise where they have never been put in action to produce a particular impression. We cannot form to ourselves a just idea of the taste of a pine-apple, without having actually tasted it.

There is however one contradictory phænomenon, which may prove, that 'tis not absolutely impossible for ideas to go before their correspondent impressions. I believe it will readily be allow'd, that the several distinct ideas of colours, which enter by the eyes, or those of sounds, which are convey'd by the hearing, are really different from each other, tho' at the same time resembling. Now if this be true of different colours, it must be no less so of the different shades of the same colour, that each of them produces a distinct idea, independent of the rest. For if this shou'd be deny'd, 'tis possible, by the continual gradation of shades, to run a colour insensibly into what is most remote from it; and if you will not allow any of the means to be different, you cannot without absurdity deny the extremes to be the same. Suppose therefore a person to have enjoyed his sight for thirty years, and to have become perfectly well acquainted with colours of all kinds, excepting one particular shade of blue, for instance, which it never has been his fortune to meet with. Let all the different shades of that colour, except that single one, be plac'd before him, descending gradually from the deepest to the lightest; 'tis plain, that he will perceive a blank, where that shade is wanting, and will be sensible, that there is a greater distance in that place betwixt the contiguous colours, than in any other. Now I ask, whether 'tis possible for him, from his own imagination, to supply this deficiency, and raise up to himself the idea of that particular shade, tho' it had never been conveyed to him by his senses? I believe there are few but will be of opinion that he can; and this may serve as a proof, that the simple ideas are not always derived from the correspondent impressions; tho' the instance is so particular and singular, that 'tis scarce worth our observing, and does not merit that for it alone we should alter our general maxim.

But besides this exception, it may not be amiss to remark on this head, that the principle of the priority of impressions to ideas must be understood with another limitation, *viz.* that as our ideas are images of our impressions, so we can form secondary ideas, which are images of the primary; as appears from this very reasoning concerning them. This is not, properly speaking, an exception to the rule so much as an explanation of it. Ideas produce the images of themselves in new ideas; but as the first ideas are supposed to be derived from impressions, it still remains true, that all our simple ideas proceed either mediately or immediately, from their correspondent impressions.

This then is the first principle I establish in the science of human nature; nor ought we to despise it because of the simplicity of its appearance. For 'tis remarkable, that the present question concerning the precedency of our impressions or ideas, is the same with what has made so much noise in other terms, when it has been disputed whether there be any *innate ideas*, or whether all ideas be derived from sensation and reflexion. We may observe, that in order to prove the ideas of extension and colour not to be innate, philosophers do nothing but shew, that they are conveyed by our senses. To prove the ideas of passion and desire not to be innate, they observe that we have a preceding experience of these emotions in ourselves. Now if we carefully examine these arguments, we shall find that they prove nothing but that ideas are preceded by other more lively perceptions, from which they are derived, and which they represent. I hope this clear stating of the question will remove all disputes concerning it, and will render this principle of more use in our reasonings, than it seems hitherto to have been. . . .

Since it appears, that our simple impressions are prior to their correspondent ideas, and that the exceptions are very rare, method seems to require we should examine our impressions, before we consider our ideas. Impressions may be divided into two kinds, those of Sensation and those of Reflexion. The first kind arises in the soul originally, from unknown causes. The second is derived in a great measure from our ideas, and that in the following order. An impression first strikes upon the senses, and makes us perceive heat or cold, thirst or hunger, pleasure or pain of some kind or other. Of this impression there is a copy taken by the mind, which remains after the impression ceases; and this we call an idea. This idea of pleasure or pain, when it returns upon the soul, produces the new impressions of desire and aversion, hope and fear, which may properly be called impressions of reflexion, because derived from it. These again are copied by the memory and imagination, and become ideas; which perhaps in their turn give rise to other impressions and ideas. So that the impressions of reflexion are only antecedent to their correspondent ideas; but posterior to those of sensation, and deriv'd from them. The examination of our sensations belongs more to anatomists and natural philosophers than to moral; and therefore shall not at present be enter'd upon. And as the impressions of reflexion, *viz.* passions, desires, and emotions, which principally deserve our attention, arise mostly from ideas, 'twill be necessary to reverse that method, which at first sight seems most natural; and in order to explain the nature and principles of the human mind, give a particular account of ideas, before we proceed to impressions. For this reason I have here chosen to begin with ideas. . . .

Note

1. I here make use of these terms, *impression and idea*, in a sense different from what is usual, and I hope this liberty will be allowed me. Perhaps I rather restore the word, idea, to its original sense, from which Mr. *Locke* had perverted it, in making it stand for all our perceptions. By the term of impression I would not be understood to express the manner, in which our lively perceptions are produced in the soul, but merely the perceptions themselves; for which there is no particular name either in the *English* or any other language, that I know of.

46 From *Discourse on Metaphysics* and *Correspondence with Arnauld*

Gottfried Wilhelm Leibniz

... Now it is evident that every true predication has some basis in the nature of things, and even when a proposition is not identical, that is, when the predicate is not expressly contained in the subject, it is still necessary that it be virtually contained in it, and this is what the philosophers call *in-esse*, saying thereby that the predicate is in the subject. Thus the content of the subject must always include that of the predicate in such a way that if one understands perfectly the concept of the subject, he will know that the predicate appertains to it also. This being so, we are able to say that this is the nature of an individual substance or of a complete being, namely, to afford a conception so complete that the concept shall be sufficient for the understanding of it and for the deduction of all the predicates of which the substance is or may become the subject. Thus the quality of king, which belonged to Alexander the Great, an abstraction from the subject, is not sufficiently determined to constitute an individual, and does not contain the other qualities of the same subject, nor everything which the idea of this prince includes. God, however, seeing the individual concept, or hæcceity, of Alexander, sees there at the same time the basis and the reason of all the predicates which can be truly uttered regarding him; for instance that he will conquer Darius and Porus, even to the point of knowing *a priori* (and not by experience) whether he died a natural death or by poison,—facts which we can learn only through history. When we carefully consider the connection of things we see also the possibility of saying that there was always in the soul of Alexander marks of all that had happened to him and evidences of all that would happen to him and traces even of everything which occurs in the universe, although God alone could recognize them all....

I have said that the supposition from which all human events can be deduced is not simply that of the creation of an undetermined Adam but the creation of a particular Adam, determined to all the circumstances, chosen out of an infinity of possible Adams. This has given M. Arnaud opportunity to object, not without reason, that it is as little possible to conceive several Adams, understanding Adam as a particular nature, as to conceive of several me's. I agree, but yet, in speaking of several Adams, I do not take Adam for a determined individual. I must, therefore, explain. This is what I meant. When we consider in Adam a part of his predicates, for example, that he was the first man, put into a garden of enjoyment, and that, from his side, God took a woman, and, if we consider similar things, conceived *sub ratione generalitatis* (that is to say, without mentioning Eve or Paradise, or the other circumstances which constitute his individuality), and if we call the person to whom these predicates are attributed Adam, all this does not suffice to determine the individual, for there might be an infinity of Adams, that is to say, of possible persons to whom these would apply who would, nevertheless, differ among themselves. Far from disagreeing with M. Arnaud, in what he says against the plurality of the same individual, I would myself, employ the idea to make it clearer that the nature of an individual should be complete and determined. I am quite convinced in regard to what St. Thomas has taught about intelligences, and what I hold to be a general truth, namely, that it is not possible for two individuals to exist wholly alike, that is, differing *solo numero.* We must, therefore, not conceive of a vague Adam or of a person to whom certain attributes of Adam appertain when we try to determine him, if we would hold that all human events follow from the one presupposition, but we must attribute to him a concept so complete that all which can be attributed to him may be derived from his. . . .

It follows, also, that if he had had other circumstances, this would not have been our Adam, but another, because nothing prevents us from saying that this would be another. He is, therefore, another. It indeed appears to us that this block of marble brought from Genoa would be wholly the same if it had been left there, because our senses cause us to judge only superficially, but in reality, because of the interconnection of things, the universe, with all its parts, would be wholly different and would have been wholly different from the very commencement if the least thing in it happened otherwise than it has. . . .

. . . There must then be some reason *a priori* independent of my existence why we may truly say that it was I who was at Paris and that it is still I and not another who am now in Germany and consequently it must be that the concept of myself unites or includes different conditions. Otherwise it could be said that it is not the same individual although it appears to be the same and in fact certain philosophers who have not understood sufficiently the nature of substance and of individual beings or of beings *per se* have thought that nothing remained actually the same. It is for this, among other reasons, that I have come to the conclusion that bodies would not be substances if they had only extension in them.

I think, Monsieur, that I have sufficiently met the difficulties regarding the principal proposition, but, as you have made in addition some important remarks in regard to certain incidental expressions, which I used, I will attempt to explain them also. I said that the presupposition from which all human events could be deduced, was not that of the creation of an undetermined Adam but of the creation of a certain Adam determined in all circumstances, selected out of an infinity of possible Adams. In regard to this you make two important remarks, the one against the plurality of Adams and the other against the reality of substances which are merely possible. In regard to the first point, you say with good reason that it is as little possible to think of several possible Adams, taking Adam for a particular nature, as to conceive of several me's. I agree, but in speaking of several Adams I do not take Adam for a determined individual but for a certain person conceived *sub ratione generalitatis* under the circumstances which appear to us to determine Adam as an individual but which do not actually determine him sufficiently. As if we should mean by Adam the first man, whom God set in a garden of pleasure whence he went out because of sin, and from whose side God fashioned a woman. All this would not sufficiently determine him and there might have been several Adams separately possible or several individuals to whom all that would apply. This is true, whatever finite number of predicates incapable of determining all the rest might be taken, but that which determines a certain Adam ought to involve absolutely all his predicates. And it is this complete concept which determines the particular individual. . . .

47 From "How to Make Our Ideas Clear"

Charles S. Peirce

... The principles set forth in the first of these papers lead, at once, to a method of reaching a clearness of thought of a far higher grade than the "distinctness" of the logicians. We have there found that the action of thought is excited by the irritation of doubt, and ceases when belief is attained; so that the production of belief is the sole function of thought. All these words, however, are too strong for my purpose. It is as if I had described the phenomena as they appear under a mental microscope. Doubt and Belief, as the words are commonly employed, relate to religious or other grave discussions. But here I use them to designate the starting of any question, no matter how small or how great, and the resolution of it. If, for instance, in a horse-car, I pull out my purse and find a five-cent nickel and five coppers, I decide, while my hand is going to the purse, in which way I will pay my fare. To call such a question Doubt, and my decision Belief, is certainly to use words very disproportionate to the occasion. To speak of such a doubt as causing an irritation which needs to be appeased, suggests a temper which is uncomfortable to the verge of insanity. Yet, looking at the matter minutely, it must be admitted that, if there is the least hesitation as to whether I shall pay the five coppers or the nickel (as there will be sure to be, unless I act from some previously contracted habit in the matter), though irritation is too strong a word, yet I am excited to such small mental activity as may be necessary to deciding how I shall act. Most frequently doubts arise from some indecision, however momentary, in our action. Sometimes it is not so. I have, for example, to wait in a railway-station, and to pass the time I read the advertisements on the walls, I compare the advantages of different trains and different routes which I never expect to take, merely fancying myself to be in a state of hesitancy, because I am bored with having nothing to trouble me. Feigned hesitancy, whether feigned for mere amusement or with a lofty purpose, plays a great part in the production of scientific inquiry. However the doubt may originate, it stimulates the mind to an activity which may be slight or energetic, calm or turbulent. Images pass rapidly through consciousness, one incessantly melting into another, until at last, when all is over—it may be in a fraction of a second, in an hour, or after long years—we find ourselves decided as to how we should act under such circumstances as those which occasioned our hesitation. In other words, we have attained belief.

In this process we observe two sorts of elements of consciousness, the distinction between which may best be made clear by means of an illustration. In a piece of music there are the separate notes, and there is the air. A single tone may be prolonged for an hour or a day, and it exists as perfectly in each second of that time as in the whole taken together; so that, as long as it is sounding, it might be present to a sense from which everything in the past was as completely absent as the future itself. But it is different with the air, the performance of which occupies a certain time, during the portions of which only portions of it are played. It consists in an orderliness in the succession of sounds which strike the ear at different times; and to perceive it there must be some continuity of consciousness which makes the events of a lapse of time present to us. We certainly only perceive the air by hearing the separate notes; yet we cannot be said to directly hear it, for we hear only what is present at the instant, and an orderliness of succession cannot exist in an instant. These two sorts of objects, what we are *immediately* conscious of and what we are *mediately* conscious of, are found in all consciousness. Some elements (the sensations) are completely present at every instant so long as they last, while others (like thought) are actions having beginning, middle, and end, and consist in a congruence in the succession of sensations which flow through the mind. They cannot be immediately present to us, but must cover some portion of the past or future. Thought is a thread of melody running through the succession of our sensations.

We may add that just as a piece of music may be written in parts, each part having its own air, so various systems of relationship of succession subsist together between the same sensations. These different systems are distinguished by having different motives, ideas, or functions. Thought is only one such system, for its sole motive, idea, and function, is to produce belief, and whatever does not concern that purpose belongs to some other system of relations. The action of thinking may incidentally have other results; it may serve to amuse us, for example ... But the soul and meaning of thought, abstracted from the other elements which accompany it, though it may be voluntarily thwarted, can never be made to direct itself toward anything but the production of belief. Thought in action has for its only possible motive the attainment of thought at rest; and whatever does not refer to belief is no part of the thought itself.

And what, then, is belief? It is the demi-cadence which closes a musical phrase in the symphony of our intellectual life. We have seen that it has just three properties: First, it is something that we are aware of; second, it appeases the irritation of doubt; and, third, it involves the establishment in our nature of a rule of action, or, say for short, a *habit*. As it appeases the irritation of doubt, which is the motive for thinking, thought relaxes, and comes to rest for a moment when belief is reached. But, since belief is a rule for action, the application of which involves further doubt and further thought, at the same time that it is a stopping-place, it is also a new starting-place for thought. That is why I have permitted myself to call it thought at rest, although thought is essentially an action. The *final* upshot of thinking is the exercise of volition, and of this thought no longer forms a part; but belief is only a stadium of mental action, an effect upon our nature due to thought, which will influence future thinking.

The essence of belief is the establishment of a habit, and different beliefs are distinguished by the different modes of action to which they give rise. If beliefs do not differ in this respect, if they appease the same doubt by producing the same rule of action, then no mere differences in the manner of consciousness of them can make them different beliefs, any more than playing a tune in different keys is playing different tunes. Imaginary distinctions are often drawn between beliefs which differ only in their mode of expression;—the wrangling which ensues is real enough, however. To believe that

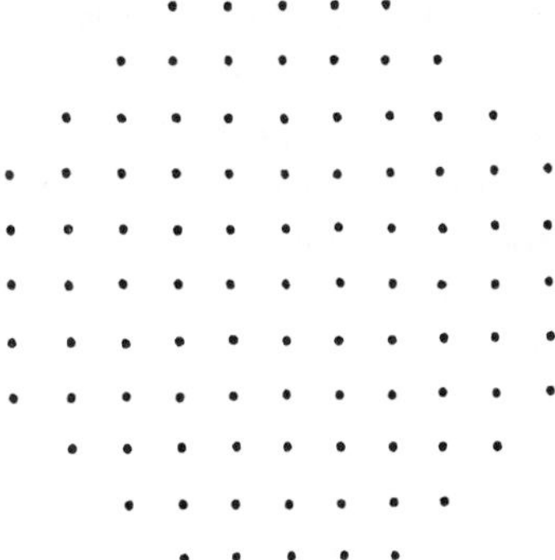

Figure 47.1

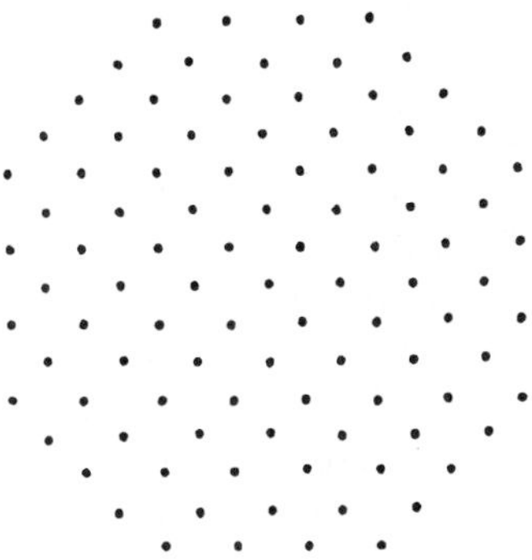

Figure 47.2

any objects are arranged as in Fig. 47.1, and to believe that they are arranged in Fig. 47.2, are one and the same belief; yet it is conceivable that a man should assert one proposition and deny the other. Such false distinctions do as much harm as the confusion of beliefs really different, and are among the pitfalls of which we ought constantly to beware, especially when we are upon metaphysical ground....

From all these sophisms we shall be perfectly safe so long as we reflect that the whole function of thought is to produce habits of action; and that whatever there is connected with a thought, but irrelevant to its purpose, is an accretion to it, but no part of it. If there be a unity among our sensations which has no reference to how we shall act on a given occasion, as when we listen to a piece of music, why we do not call that thinking. To develop its meaning, we have, therefore, simply to determine what habits it produces, for what a thing means is simply what habits it involves. Now, the identity of a habit depends on how it might lead us to act, not merely under such circumstances as are likely to arise, but under such as might possibly occur, no matter how improbable they may be. What the habit is depends on *when* and *how* it causes us to act. As for the *when*, every stimulus to action is derived from perception; as for the *how*, every purpose of action is to produce some sensible result. Thus, we come down to what is tangible and practical, as the root of every real distinction of thought, no matter how subtile it may be; and there is no distinction of meaning so fine as to consist in anything but a possible difference of practice.

To see what this principle leads to, consider in the light of it such a doctrine as that of transubstantiation. The Protestant churches generally hold that the elements of the sacrament are flesh and blood only in a tropical sense; they nourish our souls as meat and the juice of it would our bodies. But the Catholics maintain that they are literally just that; although they possess all the sensible qualities of wafer-cakes and diluted wine. But we can have no conception of wine except what may enter into a belief, either—

1. That this, that, or the other, is wine; or,
2. That wine possesses certain properties.

Such beliefs are nothing but self-notifications that we should, upon occasion, act in regard to such things as we believe to be wine according to the qualities which we believe wine to possess. The occasion of such action would be some sensible perception, the motive of it to produce some sensible result. Thus our action has exclusive reference to what affects the senses, our habit has the same bearing as our action, our belief the same as our habit, our conception the same as our belief; and we can consequently mean nothing by wine but what has certain effects, direct or indirect, upon our senses; and to talk of something as having all the sensible characters of wine, yet being in reality blood, is senseless jargon. Now, it is not my object to pursue the theological question; and having used it as a logical example I drop it, without caring to anticipate the theologian's reply. I only desire to point out how impossible it is that we should have an idea in our minds which relates to anything but conceived sensible effects of things. Our idea of anything *is* our idea of its sensible effects; and if we fancy that we have any other we deceive ourselves, and mistake a mere sensation accompanying the thought for a part of the thought itself. It is absurd to say that thought has any meaning unrelated to its only function. It is foolish for Catholics and Protestants to fancy themselves in disagreement about the elements of the sacrament, if they agree in regard to all their sensible effects, here or hereafter.

It appears, then, that the rule for attaining the third grade of clearness of apprehension is as follows: Consider what effects, which might conceivably have practical bearings, we conceive the object of our conception to have. Then, our conception of these effects is the whole of our conception of the object....

But I may be asked what I have to say to all the minute facts of history, forgotten never to be recovered, to the lost books of the ancients, to the buried secrets.

Full many a gem of purest ray serene
The dark, unfathomed caves of ocean bear;
Full many a flower is born to blush unseen,
And waste its sweetness on the desert air.

Do these things not really exist because they are hopelessly beyond the reach of our knowledge? And then, after the universe is dead (according to the prediction of some scientists), and all life has ceased forever, will not the shock of atoms continue though there will be no mind to know it? To this I reply that, though in no possible state of knowledge can any number be great enough to express the relation between the amount of what rests unknown to the amount of the known, yet it is unphilosophical to suppose that, with regard to any given question (which has any clear meaning), investigation would not bring forth a solution of it, if it were carried far enough. Who would have said, a few years ago, that we could ever know of what substances stars are made whose light may have been longer in reaching us than the human race has existed? Who can be sure of what we shall not know in a few hundred years? Who can guess what would be the result of continuing the pursuit of science for ten thousand years, with the activity of the last hundred? And if it were to go on for a million, or a billion, or any number of years you please, how is it possible to say that there is any question which might not ultimately be solved?

But it may be objected, "Why make so much of these remote considerations, especially when it is your principle that only practical distinctions have a meaning?" Well, I must confess that it makes very little difference whether we say that a stone on the bottom of the ocean, in complete darkness, is brilliant or not—that is to say, that it *probably* makes no difference, remembering always that that stone *may* be fished up tomorrow. But that there are gems at the bottom of the sea, flowers in the untraveled desert, etc., are propositions which, like that about a diamond being hard when it is not pressed, concern much more the arrangement of our language than they do the meaning of our ideas. . . .

48 From "The Theory of Objects"

Alexius Meinong

1 The Problem

That knowing is impossible without something being known, and more generally, that judgments and ideas or presentations (*Vorstellungen*) are impossible without being judgments about and presentations of something, is revealed to be self-evident by a quite elementary examination of these experiences. I have been able to show, almost without special investigation, that this is also true in the realm of assumptions (*Annahmen*), even though psychological research has but recently turned in their direction.[1] The situation is more complicated in this respect, however, in the case of feelings. There is no doubt that language is somewhat misleading in referring to joy or grief, or to pity or envy, and the like, as being that which one feels. There are also complications in the area of desires, insofar as we think from time to time that we should revert to the possibility of desires which are not desires for anything, despite the linguistic evidence, which is here once again entirely unambiguous. However, even one who would disagree with my view that feelings, like desires, are dependent psychological states insofar as they have ideas as their indispensable "psychological presuppositions,"[2] would unhesitatingly concede that we are happy about something, interested in something, and, at least in the majority of cases, do not wish or intend without wishing for or intending something. To put it briefly, no one fails to recognize that psychological events so very commonly have this distinctive "character of being directed to something" (*auf etwas Gerichtetsein*) as to suggest very strongly (at least) that we should take it to be a characteristic aspect of the psychological as opposed to the non-psychological.

The purpose of the following remarks is, nevertheless, not to explain why I hold this way of looking at the matter to be firmly established, despite the many difficulties confronting it. There are so many cases in which reference, indeed explicit directedness (*Gerichtetsein*), to that "something," or (as we say quite naturally) to an object, unquestionably forces itself upon our attention that, even if they alone were to be considered, the question would soon be answered for anyone who investigated these matters scientifically.

The partitioning of whatever deserves and needs theoretical consideration into different scientific realms, and the careful delimitation of these realms, may often be of little practical importance in advancing the research connected with it. What matters in the final analysis is the work that is accomplished, and not the banner under which it is done. However, obscurities as to the boundaries of the diverse areas of science can become significant in two contrasting ways: either the areas which are actually investigated encroach upon one another, or they are separated from each other, and consequently leave an intermediate area untouched. The significance of such obscurities, within the sphere of our theoretical interest, is exactly the opposite of their significance within the sphere of practical affairs. In the latter, the "neutral zone" is a guarantee (always desired but rarely capable of being realized) of amicable neighborly relations, while the overlapping of territorial claims presents the typical case of conflict of interests. But in the realm of theoretical activity, where such conflicts, at least, have no justification, it is a gain, objectively considered, if the frontier districts coincide, for as a result they are investigated from different sides. A separation, on the other hand, is always a disadvantage, the seriousness of which depends on the size and significance of the intermediate territory.

The intent of the problem raised here is to call attention to just such an area of knowledge, which is sometimes overlooked, sometimes not sufficiently appreciated in its distinctive character. The question concerns the proper place for the scientific investigation of the Object (*Gegenstand*) taken as such and in general—we wish to know whether, among the sciences that are accredited by scientific tradition, there is one within which we could attempt a theoretical consideration of the Object as such, or from which we could at least demand this.

2 The Prejudice in Favor of the Actual

It was no accident that the foregoing account took cognition as its starting point in order to arrive at the Object. To be sure, cognition is not unique in "having" an Object. It has it in such a distinctive manner, however, that whenever we are speaking of Objects, we are influenced to think first of all of the Object of cognition. For, to be precise, the psychological event we call cognition does not constitute the cognitive situation in and of itself: knowledge is, so to speak, a double fact (*Doppeltatsache*) in which what is known confronts the act of knowing as something relatively independent. The act of knowing is not merely directed toward what is known, in the way in which a false judgment may be directed toward its Object. In knowing, on the contrary, it is as though what is known were seized or grasped by the psychological act, or however else one might attempt to describe, in an unavoidably pictorial way, something which is indescribable. If one concentrates exclusively on the Object of knowledge, the problem about the science of Objects which was raised above is initially placed in a rather unfavorable light. A science of the Objects of cognition: does this mean anything more than the demand that what is already known as the Object of cognition be now made the Object of a science, and thus the Object of cognition for a second time? In other words, are we not asking for a science which either is made up of the sum-total of the sciences taken together, or one which would have to accomplish all over again what the recognized sciences jointly accomplish anyway?

We should guard ourselves against concluding from these considerations that the idea of a universal science, in addition to the special sciences, is absurd. This understanding of the nature of the world in its entirety and of its ultimate foundations, which the best minds have always considered to be the final and most estimable goal of their pursuit of knowledge, can only be the subject of a comprehensive science *in addition to* the special sciences. Indeed, the discipline which goes under the name of metaphysics has been thought to be exactly such a science. No matter how many disappointments have been associated with this name, and are associated with it, the responsibility for them lies with our intellectual capacities, and not with the idea of such a science. May one go so far, therefore, as to take metaphysics to be the science whose legitimate function is to deal with Objects as such—or Objects in their totality?

If we remember how metaphysics has always been conceived as including in its subject matter the farthest and the nearest, the greatest and the smallest alike, we may be surprised to be told that metaphysics cannot take on such a task. It may sound strange to hear that metaphysics is not universal enough for a science of Objects, and hence cannot take on the task just formulated. For the intentions of metaphysics have been universal (a fact which has so often been disastrous to its success). Without doubt, metaphysics has to do with everything that exists. However, the totality of what exists, including what has existed and will exist, is infinitely small in comparison with the totality of the Objects of knowledge. This fact easily goes unnoticed, probably because the lively interest in reality which is part of our nature tends to favor that exaggeration which finds the non-real a mere nothing—or, more precisely, which finds the non-real to be something for which science has no application at all or at least no application of any worth.

How little truth there is in such a view is most easily shown by ideal Objects[3] which do indeed subsist (*bestehen*), but which do not by any means exist (*existieren*), and consequently cannot in any sense be real (*wirklich*). Similarity and difference are examples of objects of this type: perhaps, under certain circumstances, they subsist between realities; but they are not a part of reality themselves. That ideas, as well as assumptions and judgments, are nevertheless concerned with such Objects (and often have reason to be very intimately concerned with them) is, of course, beyond question. Similarly, number does not exist in addition to what is numbered, supposing the latter does exist; this we clearly know from the fact that we can also count what does not exist. Again, a connection does not exist in addition to what is connected, supposing the latter does exist: That their existence is not indispensable is proven by the connection between the equilaterality and equiangularity of a triangle. Moreover, where existing objects are concerned, such as atmospheric and thermometric or barometric conditions, the connectedness does not unite these realities themselves so much as it does their being or even their non-being. In knowing such a connection, we are already dealing with that special type of Object (*mit jenem eigentumlichen Gegenstandartigen*), which, as I hope I have shown,[4] is related to judgment and assumptions (*Urteilen und Annahmen*) in the way in which the Object, in a strict sense, (*der eigentliche Gegenstand*) is related to presentations (*Vorstellungen*). I have recommended the name "Objective" (*Objetkiv*) for this type of Object, and I have shown that the Objective itself can assume the functions of an Object in the strict sense. In particular, it can become the Object (*Gegenstand*) of a new judgment, or of some other intellectual operation, which is related to it as to an ordinary object (*Objekt*). If I say, "It is true that the antipodes exist," truth is ascribed not to the antipodes, but to the Objective, "that the antipodes exist." But this existence of the antipodes is a fact (*Tatsache*) which, as everyone sees immediately, can very well have a subsistent status, but cannot be still another existent entity in its own turn, as it were [*dass sie zwar sehr wohl bestehen, aber nicht ihrerseits sozusagen noch einmal existieren kann*]. This holds, likewise, for all other objectives, so that every cognitive act which has an Objective as its Object represents thereby a case of knowing something which does not exist.

What has been stated here only in terms of isolated examples is supported by the testimony of a very highly developed science—indeed the most highly developed one: mathematics. We would surely not want to speak of mathematics as alien to reality, as though it had nothing to do with what exists. Indeed, we cannot fail to recognize that mathematics is assured of an extensive sphere of application in practical life no less than in the theoretical treatment of reality. However, pure mathematical knowledge is never concerned with anything which must, in the nature of the case, be actual. The form of being (*Sein*) with which mathematics as such is occupied is never existence (*Existenz*). In this respect, mathematics never transcends subsistence (*Bestand*): a straight line has no more existence than a right angle; a regular polygon, no more than a circle. It can be regarded only as a peculiarity of the mathematical use of language that this usage makes quite explicit existence-claims.[5] Even though the mathematician may use the term "existence," he cannot but concede that what we would otherwise call "possibility" is, in the final analysis, all that he requires of the objects of his theoretical consideration; it is very noteworthy, however, that a positive turn is being given to this ordinarily merely negative concept.

Together with the prejudice in favor of our knowledge of reality, alluded to previously, the basic independence of mathematics from existence enables us to understand a fact which would be fairly surprising if these points were not considered. Attempts to systematize the sciences as parts of a whole usually find themselves in an embarrassing position in connection with mathematics, and they must be extricated, with varying degrees of success, by more or less artificial expedients. This is in striking contrast to the recognition—one might straightaway say popularity—which mathematics has acquired for itself even in lay circles by its achievements. But the organization of all knowledge into the science of nature and the science of mind (*Natur- und Geisteswissenschaft*), appearing to be an exhaustive disjunction, really takes into account only the sort of knowledge which has to do with reality (*Wirklichkeit*). Consequently, when we look at the matter more closely, we should not be at all surprised to find that this organization does not do full justice to mathematics.

3 *Sosein* and *Nichtsein*

There is thus not the slightest doubt that what is supposed to be the Object of knowledge need not exist at all. But our account up to now may seem to leave room for the conjecture that wherever existence is absent, it not only *can* be but *must* be replaced by subsistence. But even this restriction is inadmissable, as may be seen by contrasting the characteristic functions of judging and assuming, a distinction I have attempted to maintain by contrasting the "thetic and synthetic function" of thought.[6] In the former case, the act of thought grasps a *Sein*, in the latter a "*Sosein*." In each case, naturally, it is an Objective that is grasped; it is reasonable to speak of a *Seinsobjektiv* and of a *Soseinsobjektiv*, respectively. Now it would accord very well with the aforementioned prejudice in favor of existence to hold that we may speak of a *Sosein* only if a *Sein* is presupposed. There would, indeed, be little sense in calling a house large or small, a region fertile or unfertile, before one knew that the house or the land does exist, has existed, or will exist. However, the very science from which we were able to obtain the largest number of instances counter to this prejudice shows clearly that any such principle is untenable. As we know, the figures with which geometry is concerned do not exist. Nevertheless, their properties, and hence their *Sosein*, can be established. Doubtless, in the area of what can be known merely *a posteriori*, a claim as to *Sosein* will be completely unjustifiable if it is not based on knowledge of a *Sein;* it is equally certain that a *Sosein* which does not rest on a *Sein* may often enough be utterly lacking in natural interest. None of this alters the fact that the *Sosein* of an Object is not affected by its *Nichtsein*. The fact is sufficiently important to be explicitly formulated as the principle of the independence of *Sosein* from *Sein*.[7] The area of applicability of this principle is best illustrated by consideration of the following circumstance: the principle applies, not only to Objects which do not exist in fact, but also to Objects which could not exist because they are impossible. Not only is the much heralded gold mountain made of gold, but the round square is as surely round as it is square. To be sure, insights of actual importance regarding such Objects have been noted only in exceptional cases. Nevertheless, even from them some light might be shed on domains which are especially important for us to know.

But such things may be alien to our natural way of thinking; it is even more instructive to recall this trivial fact, which does not yet go beyond the realm of the *Seinsobjektiv*: Any particular thing that isn't real (*Nichtseiendes*) must at least be capable of serving as the Object for those judgments which grasp its *Nichtsein*. It does not matter whether this *Nichtsein* is necessary or merely factual; nor does it matter in the first case whether the necessity stems from the essence of the Object or whether it stems from aspects which are external to the Object in question. In order to know that there is no round square, I must make a judgment about the round square. If physics, physiology, and psychology agree in asserting the so-called ideal character of sense-qualities, they implicitly assert something about color as well as about sound, namely, that the one exists no more than the other. Those who like paradoxical modes of expression could very well say: "There are objects of which it is true that there are no such objects." The fact, familiar the world over, which is meant by this statement throws such a bright light on the relation of objects to reality, or their relation to being, generally, that a somewhat closer examination of the matter, which is of fundamental importance in its own right, is entirely in place in our present study.

4 The *Aussersein* of the Pure Object

A recourse to certain psychological experiences suggests itself as a natural way of resolving the paradox which seems to lie before us. I have attempted to present the most essential points pertaining to this problem in another work.[8] But, according to my account here, if we were now to maintain the aforementioned subjectivity of sense-qualities, we could speak of the object of a presentation of blue only in the sense of something which is a capacity of that presentation, from which reality withholds, as it were, the opportunity for its realization. Considered from the standpoint of the presentation, this still seems to me to touch on something of essential significance. However, I cannot conceal from myself at present the fact that it is no more necessary to an Object that it be presented in order not to exist than it is in order for it to exist. Further, even if there were a reference to it, the most that could result from its being presented would be a sort of existence—"existence by way of idea (*in der Vorstellung*)"—and so, more precisely, "pseudo-existence."[9] To express it more exactly: If I say, "Blue does not exist," I am thinking just of blue, and not at all of a presentation and the capacities it may have. It is as if the blue must have being in the first place, before we can raise the question of its being (*Sein*) or non-being (*Nichtsein*). But in order not to fall into new paradoxes or actual absurdities, perhaps the following turn of expression may be appropriate: Blue, or any other Object whatsoever, is somehow given prior to our determination of its being or non-being, in a way that does not carry any prejudice to its non-being. We could also describe the situation from its psychological side in this way: if I should be able to judge that a certain Object is not, then I appear to have had to grasp the Object in some way beforehand, in order to say anything about its non-being, or more precisely, in order to affirm or to deny the ascription of non-being to the Object.

This fact, despite its commonplace character, is seen to be of a very peculiar type. We could hope to do justice to it with somewhat greater theoretical rigor by means of the following considerations. As I have stated elsewhere,[10] that a certain thing, A, is not—more briefly, the *Nichtsein* of A—is just as much an Objective as is the *Sein* of A. And the degree of certainty with which I am justified in saying that A "is not" is the degree of certainty that the Objective, "*Nichtsein* of A," itself has a *Sein* (or, more precisely, as mentioned above, that it has subsistence *[Bestand]*). Now an Objective, whether it is a *Seinsobjektiv* or *Nichtseinsobjektiv*, stands in relation to its Object (*Objekt*), albeit *cum grano salis*, as the whole to its parts. But if the whole has being, so must its parts. This seems to mean, when it is extended to the case of the Objective: if the Objective has being (*ist*), so, in some sense or other, must the object which belongs to it, even when the Objective is an objective of non-being (*Nichtseinsobjektiv*). Furthermore, since the Objective strictly prevents us from assuming that A has being, (being, as we have seen, can sometimes be understood as existence, sometimes as subsistence), it appears that the requirement that the Object have being (which was inferred from the being of the *Nichtseinsobjektiv*) makes sense only insofar as the being in question is neither existence nor subsistence—only insofar as a third order of being, if one may speak this way, is adjoined to existence and subsistence. This sort of being must belong, therefore, to every Object as such. A *Nichtsein* of the same type cannot be set in opposition to it, for a *Nichtsein* even in this new sense would have to immediately produce difficulties analogous to those which arise from *Nichtsein* in its ordinary sense, and which the new concept was to have eliminated. The term "*Quasisein*" seemed to me for a while to be a completely suitable expression for this rather oddly constituted type of being.

This designation, however, like others that were approved earlier (for instance, "*Pseudoexistenz*" and "*Quasitranszendenz*"[11]), runs the risk of causing confusion. More important, meanwhile, are the following pertinent considerations. Can being which is in principle unopposed by non-being be called being at all? However much we are permitted in this connection to judge that there is a being which is neither existence nor subsistence, nowhere else do we find grounds for such a postulate. Must we not take thought to avoid it in our case also wherever it is possible? The consideration which seems to force us to such a postulate is, to be sure, an experience which is easily observed. As we have seen, A must be "given" to me in some way or other if I am to grasp its non-being. This produces, however, as I have already shown elsewhere,[12] an assumption (*Annahme*) possessing affirmative quality: in order to deny A, I must first assume the being of A. What I refer to, so far as the being of A is concerned, is thus something which is to a certain extent only a claimant to being (*ein gewissermassen vorgegebenes Sein des A*). But it is of the essence of assumption that it direct itself upon a being which itself does not need to be.

Without a doubt, it would be comforting to be able to say that the strange kind of being which belongs to that which does not have being (*Sein des Nichtseiendes*) is just as absurd as it sounds. Such a view could recommend itself to us were it not for the fact that the Objective, which has being, always seems to require in turn an Object which has being. For the present, this requirement is based solely on the analogy to the part-whole relation: an Objective is thereby treated as a complex of some kind and the Object belonging to it as a kind of component. In many respects this may be in accordance with our insight into the nature of an Objective, which is as yet still exceedingly defective. However, no one will deny that this analogy is only an initial expedient in our embarrassment and that there would be no grounds for following this analogy rigorously even for part of the way. Thus, instead of deriving the being of an Object from the being of an Objective, even on the basis of a questionable analogy where the Objective is an Objective of non-being, it would be better to conclude from the facts with which we are concerned that this analogy does not apply to the Objective of non-being—i.e., that the being of the Objective is not by any means universally dependent upon the being of its Object.

This is a position which speaks for itself without any further ado. If the opposition of being and non-being is primarily a matter of the Objective and not of the Object, then it is, after all, clearly understandable that neither being nor non-being can belong essentially to the Object in itself. This is not to say, of course, that an Object can neither be nor not be. Nor is it to say that the question, whether or not the Object has being, is purely accidental to the nature of every Object. An absurd Object such as a round square carries in itself the guarantee of its own non-being in every sense; an ideal Object, such as diversity, carries in itself the guarantee of its own non-existence. Anyone who seeks to associate himself with models which have become famous could formulate what has been shown above by saying that the Object as such (without considering the occasional peculiarities or the accompanying Objective-clause which is always present) stands "beyond being and non-being." This may also be expressed in the following less engaging and also less pretentious way, which is in my opinion, however, a more appropriate one: The Object is by nature indifferent to being (*ausserseiend*), although at least one of its two Objectives of being, the Object's being or non-being, subsists.

What one could thus call with propriety the principle of the indifference of pure Objects to being (*den Satz vom Aussersein des reinen Gegenstandes*) finally eliminates the appearance of a paradox which was the immediate occasion for the assertion of this principle. As soon as it is recognized that, apart from special cases, both being and non-being are equally external to an Object, it is then understandable that nothing more, so to speak, is involved in comprehending the non-being of the Object than there is in comprehending its being. The above-mentioned principle of the independence of *Sosein* from *Sein* now presents a welcome supplement to this view. It tells us that that which is not in any way external to the Object, but constitutes its proper essence, subsists in its *Sosein*—the *Sosein* attaching to the Object whether the object has being or not. We are finally in a position to see with sufficient clarity what confronted us above as the prejudice in favor of the existence, or at least the being, of all possible Objects of knowledge. Being is not the presupposition under which knowledge finds, as it were, its point of attack; it is itself such a point of attack. Non-being is equally as good a point of attack. Furthermore, in the *Sosein* of each Object, knowledge already finds a field of activity to which it may have access without first answering the question concerning being or non-being, or without answering this question affirmatively.

Notes

1. *Über Annahmen* (Leipzig, 1902), pp. 256 f. [The references in the present selection to *Über Annahmen* are to the first edition, not to the second, revised edition of 1910.]

2. See my *Psychologisch-ethischen Untersuchungen zur Werttheorie* (Graz, 1894), pp. 34 f. Also Höfler, *Psychologie,* p. 389.

3. Concerning the sense in which I intend to employ the expression "ideal," which unfortunately is ambiguous in ordinary language, see my essay, "Über Gegenstände höherer Ordnung, etc.," *Zeitschrift für Psychologie,* XXI, 198. [This essay appears in Volume II of Meinong's collected works. . . .]

4. *Über Annahmen,* chap. vii.

5. Cf. K. Zindler: "Beiträge zur Theorie der mathematischen Erkenntnis," *Sitzungsberichte der kais. Akademie der Wissenschaften in Wien, phil. hist. Kl.,* CXVIII (1889), p. 33 and 53 f.

6. *Über Annahmen,* pp. 142 ff.

7. This principle was first enunciated by E. Mally in his treatise which was honored by the Wartinger prize in 1903, and which appears in completely revised form as No. III of these papers; see chap. i, §3, of Mally's paper. [Meinong here refers to the volume in which his own essay originally appeared. Mally's paper is entitled "Untersuchungen zur Gegenstandstheorie des Messens."]

8. *Über Annahmen,* pp. 98 ff.

9. See "Über Gegenstände höherer Ordnung," *loc. cit.,* pp. 186 f.

10. *Über Annahmen,* chap. vii.

11. *Über Annahmen,* p. 95.

12. *Loc. cit.,* pp. 105 ff.

49 From *The Problems of Philosophy*

Bertrand Russell

Knowledge by Acquaintance and Knowledge by Description

In the preceding chapter we saw that there are two sorts of knowledge: knowledge of things, and knowledge of truths. In this chapter we shall be concerned exclusively with knowledge of things, of which in turn we shall have to distinguish two kinds. Knowledge of things, when it is of the kind we call knowledge by *acquaintance*, is essentially simpler than any knowledge of truths, and logically independent of knowledge of truths, though it would be rash to assume that human beings ever, in fact, have acquaintance with things without at the same time knowing some truth about them. Knowledge of things by *description*, on the contrary, always involves, as we shall find in the course of the present chapter, some knowledge of truths as its source and ground. But first of all we must make clear what we mean by "acquaintance" and what we mean by "description."

We shall say that we have *acquaintance* with anything of which we are directly aware, without the intermediary of any process of inference or any knowledge of truths. Thus in the presence of my table I am acquainted with the sense-data that make up the appearance of my table—its colour, shape, hardness, smoothness, etc.; all these are things of which I am immediately conscious when I am seeing and touching my table. The particular shade of colour that I am seeing may have many things said about it—I may say that it is brown, that it is rather dark, and so on. But such statements, though they make me know truths *about* the colour, do not make me know the colour itself any better than I did before: so far as concerns knowledge of the colour itself, as opposed to knowledge of truths about it, I know the colour perfectly and completely when I see it, and no further knowledge of it itself is even theoretically possible. Thus the sense-data which make up the appearance of my table are things with which I have acquaintance, things immediately known to me just as they are.

My knowledge of the table as a physical object, on the contrary, is not direct knowledge. Such as it is, it is obtained through acquaintance with the sense-data that make up the appearance of the table. We have seen that it is possible, without absurdity, to doubt whether there is a table at all, whereas it is not possible to doubt the sense-data. My knowledge of the table is of the kind which we shall call "knowledge by description." The table is "the physical object which causes such-and-such sense-data." This *describes* the table by means of the sense-data. In order to know anything at all about the table, we must know truths connecting it with things with which we have acquaintance: we must know that "such-and-such sense-data are caused by a physical object." There is no state of mind in which we are directly aware of the table; all our knowledge of the table is really knowledge of *truths*, and the actual thing which is the table is not, strictly speaking, known to us at all. We know a description, and we know that there is just one object to which this description applies, though the object itself is not directly known to us. In such a case, we say that our knowledge of the object is knowledge by description.

All our knowledge, both knowledge of things and knowledge of truths, rests upon acquaintance as its foundation. It is therefore important to consider what kinds of things there are with which we have acquaintance.

Sense-data, as we have already seen, are among the things with which we are acquainted; in fact, they supply the most obvious and striking example of knowledge by acquaintance. But if they were the sole example, our knowledge would be very much more restricted than it is. We should only know what is now present to our senses: we could not know anything about the past—not even that there was a past—nor could we know any truths about our sense-data, for all knowledge of truths, as we shall show, demands acquaintance with things which are of an essentially different character from sense-data, the things which are sometimes called "abstract ideas," but which we shall call "universals." We have therefore to consider acquaintance with other things besides sense-data if we are to obtain any tolerably adequate analysis of our knowledge.

The first extension beyond sense-data to be considered is acquaintance by *memory*. It is obvious that we often remember what we have seen or heard or had otherwise present to our senses, and that in such cases we are still immediately aware of what we remember, in spite of the fact that it appears as past and not as present. This immediate knowledge by memory is the source of all our knowledge concerning the past: without it, there could be no knowledge of the past by inference, since we should never know that there was anything past to be inferred.

The next extension to be considered is acquaintance by *introspection*. We are not only aware of things, but we are often aware of being aware of them. When I see the sun, I am often aware of my seeing the sun; thus "my seeing the sun" is an object with which I have acquaintance. When I desire food, I may be aware of my desire for food; thus "my desiring food" is an object with which I am acquainted. Similarly we may be aware of our feeling pleasure or pain, and generally of the events which happen in our minds. This kind of acquaintance, which may be called self-consciousness, is the source of all our knowledge of mental things. It is obvious that it is only what goes on in our own minds that can be thus known immediately. What goes on in the minds of others is known to us through our perception of their bodies, that is, through the sense-data in us which are associated with their bodies. But for our acquaintance with the contents of our own minds, we should be unable to imagine the minds of others, and therefore we could never arrive at the knowledge that they have minds. It seems natural to suppose that self-consciousness is one of the things that distinguish men from animals: animals, we may suppose, though they have acquaintance with sense-data, never become aware of this acquaintance. I do not mean that they *doubt* whether they exist, but that they have never become conscious of the fact that they have sensations and feelings, nor therefore of the fact that they, the subjects of their sensations and feelings, exist.

We have spoken of acquaintance with the contents of our minds as *self*-consciousness, but it is not, of course, consciousness of our *self*: it is consciousness of particular thoughts and feelings. The question whether we are also acquainted with our bare selves, as opposed to particular thoughts and feelings, is a very difficult one, upon which it would be rash to speak positively. When we try to look into ourselves we always seem to come upon some particular thought or feeling, and not upon the "I" which has the thought or feeling. Nevertheless there are some reasons for thinking that we are acquainted with the "I," though the acquaintance is hard to disentangle from other things. To make clear what sort of reason there is, let us consider for a moment what our acquaintance with particular thoughts really involves.

When I am acquainted with "my seeing the sun," it seems plain that I am acquainted with two different things in relation to each other. On the one hand there is the sense-datum which represents the sun to me, on the other hand there is that which sees this sense-datum. All acquaintance, such as my acquaintance with the sense-datum which represents the sun, seems obviously a relation between the person acquainted and the object with which the person is acquainted. When a case of acquaintance is one with which I can be acquainted (as I am acquainted with my acquaintance with the sense-datum representing the sun), it is plain that the person acquainted is myself. Thus, when I am acquainted with my seeing the sun, the whole fact with which I am acquainted is "Self-acquainted-with-sense-datum."

Further, we know the truth "I am acquainted with this sense-datum." It is hard to see how we could know this truth, or even understand what is meant by it, unless we were acquainted with something which we call "I." It does not seem necessary to suppose that we are acquainted with a more or less permanent person, the same to-day as yesterday, but it does seem as though we must be acquainted with that thing, whatever its nature, which sees the sun and has acquaintance with sense-data. Thus, in some sense it would seem we must be acquainted with our Selves as opposed to our particular experiences. But the question is difficult, and complicated arguments can be adduced on either side. Hence, although acquaintance with ourselves seems *probably* to occur, it is not wise to assert that it undoubtedly does occur.

We may therefore sum up as follows what has been said concerning acquaintance with things that exist. We have acquaintance in sensation with the data of the outer senses, and in introspection with the data of what may be called the inner sense—thoughts, feelings, desires, etc.; we have acquaintance in memory with things which have been data either of the outer senses or of the inner sense. Further, it is probable, though not certain, that we have acquaintance with Self, as that which is aware of things or has desires towards things.

In addition to our acquaintance with particular existing things, we also have acquaintance with what we shall call *universals*, that is to say, general ideas, such as *whiteness*, *diversity*, *brotherhood*, and so on. Every complete sentence must contain at least one word which stands for a universal, since all verbs have a meaning which is universal.... For the present, it is only necessary to guard against the supposition that whatever we can be acquainted with must be something particular and existent. Awareness of universals is called *conceiving*, and a universal of which we are aware is called a *concept*.

It will be seen that among the objects with which we are acquainted are not included physical objects (as opposed to sense-data), nor other people's minds. These things are known to us by what I call "knowledge by description," which we must now consider.

By a "description" I mean any phrase of the form "a so-and-so" or "the so-and-so." A phrase of the form "a so-and-so" I shall call an "ambiguous" description; a phrase of the form "the so-and-so" (in the singular) I shall call a "definite" description. Thus "a man" is an ambiguous description, and "the man with the iron mask" is a definite description. There are various problems connected with ambiguous descriptions, but I pass them by, since they do not directly concern the matter we are discussing, which is the nature of our knowledge concerning objects in cases where we know that there is an object answering to a definite description, though we are not *acquainted* with any such object. This is a matter which is concerned exclusively with *definite* descriptions. I shall therefore, in the sequel, speak simply of "descriptions" when I mean "definite descriptions." Thus a description will mean any phrase of the form "the so-and-so" in the singular.

We shall say that an object is "known by description" when we know that it is "the so-and-so," i.e. when we know that there is one object, and no more, having a certain property; and it will generally be implied that we do not have knowledge of the same object by acquaintance. We know that the man with the iron mask existed, and many propositions are known about him; but we do not know who he was. We know that the candidate who gets the most votes will be elected, and in this case we are very likely also acquainted (in the only sense in which one can be acquainted with some one else) with the man who is, in fact, the candidate who will get most votes; but we do not know which of the candidates he is, i.e. we do not know any proposition of the form "A is the candidate who will get most votes" where A is one of the candidates by name. We shall say that we have "merely descriptive knowledge" of the so-and-so when, although we know that the so-and-so exists, and although we may possibly be acquainted with the object which is, in fact, the so-and-so, yet we do not know any proposition "*a* is the so-and-so," where *a* is something with which we are acquainted.

When we say "the so-and-so exists," we mean that there is just one object which is the so-and-so. The proposition "*a* is the so-and-so" means that *a* has the property so-and-so, and nothing else has. "Mr. A. is the Unionist candidate for this constituency" means "Mr. A. is a Unionist candidate for this constituency, and no one else is." "The Unionist candidate for this constituency exists" means "some one is a Unionist candidate for this constituency, and no one else is." Thus, when we are acquainted with an object which is the so-and-so, we know that the so-and-so exists; but we may know that the so-and-so exists when we are not acquainted with any object which we know to be the so-and-so, and even when we are not acquainted with any object which, in fact, is the so-and-so.

Common words, even proper names, are usually really descriptions. That is to say, the thought in the mind of a person using a proper name correctly can generally only be expressed explicitly if we replace the proper name by a description. Moreover, the description required to express the thought will vary for different people, or for the same person at different times. The only thing constant (so long as the name is rightly used) is the object to which the name applies. But so long as this remains constant, the particular description involved usually makes no difference to the truth or falsehood of the proposition in which the name appears.

Let us take some illustrations. Suppose some statement made about Bismarck. Assuming that there is such a thing as direct acquaintance with oneself, Bismarck himself might have used his name directly to designate the particular person with whom he was acquainted. In this case, if he made a judgement about himself, he himself might be a constituent of the judgement. Here the proper name has the direct use which it always wishes to have, as simply standing for a certain object, and not for a description of the object. But if a person who knew Bismarck made a judgement about him, the case is different. What this person was acquainted with were certain sense-data which he connected (rightly, we will suppose) with Bismarck's body. His body, as a physical object, and still more his mind, were only known as the body and the mind connected with these sense-data. That is, they were known by description. It is, of course, very much a matter of chance which characteristics of a man's appearance will come into a friend's mind when he thinks of him; thus the description actually in the friend's mind is accidental. The essential point is that he knows that the various descriptions all apply to the same entity, in spite of not being acquainted with the entity in question.

When we, who did not know Bismarck, make a judgement about him, the description in our minds will probably be some more or less vague mass of historical knowledge—far more, in most cases, than is required to identify him. But, for the sake of illustration, let us assume that we think of him as "the first Chancellor of the German Empire." Here all the words are abstract except "German." The word "German" will, again, have different meanings for different people. To some it will recall travels in Germany, to some the look of Germany on the map, and so on. But if we are to obtain a description which we know to be applicable, we shall be compelled, at some point, to bring in a reference to a particular with which we are acquainted. Such reference is involved in any mention of past, present, and future (as opposed to definite dates), or of here and there, or of what others have told us. Thus it would seem that, in some way or other, a description known to be applicable to a particular must involve some reference to a particular with which we are acquainted, if our knowledge about the thing described is not to be merely what follows *logically* from the description. For example, "the most long-lived of men" is a description involving only universals, which must apply to some man, but we can make no judgements concerning this man which involve knowledge about him beyond what the description gives. If, however, we say, "The first Chancellor of the German Empire was an astute diplomatist," we can only be assured of the truth of our judgement in virtue of something with which we are acquainted—usually a testimony heard or read. Apart from the information we convey to others, apart from the fact about the actual Bismarck, which gives importance to our judgement, the thought we really have contains the one or more particulars involved, and otherwise consists wholly of concepts.

All names of places—London, England, Europe, the Earth, the Solar System—similarly involve, when used, descriptions which start from some one or more particulars with which we are acquainted. I suspect that even the Universe, as considered by metaphysics, involves such a connexion with particulars. In logic, on the contrary, where we are concerned not merely with what does exist, but with whatever might or could exist or be, no reference to actual particulars is involved.

It would seem that, when we make a statement about something only known by description, we often *intend* to make our statement, not in the form involving the description, but about the actual thing described. That is to say, when we say anything about Bismarck, we should like, if we could, to make the judgement which Bismarck alone can make, namely, the judgement of which he himself is a constituent. In this we are necessarily defeated, since the actual Bismarck is unknown to us. But we know that there is an object B, called Bismarck, and that B was an astute diplomatist. We can thus *describe* the proposition we should like to affirm, namely, "B was an astute diplomatist," where B is the object which was Bismarck. If we are describing Bismarck as "the first Chancellor of the German Empire," the proposition we should like to affirm may be described as "the proposition asserting, concerning the actual object which was the first Chancellor of the German Empire, that this object was an astute diplomatist." What enables us to communicate in spite of the varying descriptions we employ is that we know there is a true proposition concerning the actual Bismarck, and that however we may vary the description (so long as the description is correct) the proposition described is still the same. This proposition, which is described and is known to be true, is what interests us; but we are not acquainted with the proposition itself, and do not know *it*, though we know it is true.

It will be seen that there are various stages in the removal from acquaintance with particulars: there is Bismarck to people who knew him; Bismarck to those who only know of him through history; the man with the iron mask; the longest-lived of men. These are progressively further removed from acquaintance with particulars; the first comes as near to acquaintance as is possible in regard to another person; in the second, we shall still be said to know "who Bismarck was"; in the third, we do not know who was the man with the iron mask, though we can know many propositions about him which are not logically deducible from the fact that he wore an iron mask; in the fourth finally, we know nothing beyond what is logically deducible from the definition of the man. There is a similar hierarchy in the region of universals. Many universals, like many particulars, are only known to us by description. But here, as in the case of particulars, knowledge concerning what is known by description is ultimately reducible to knowledge concerning what is known by acquaintance.

The fundamental principle in the analysis of propositions containing descriptions is this: *Every proposition which we can understand must be composed wholly of constituents with which we are acquainted.*

We shall not at this stage attempt to answer all the objections which may be urged against this fundamental principle. For the present, we shall merely point out that, in some way or other, it must be possible to meet these objections, for it is scarcely conceivable that we can make a judgement or entertain a supposition without knowing what it is that we are judging or supposing about. We must attach *some* meaning to the words we use, if we are to speak significantly and not utter mere noise; and the meaning we attach to our words must be something with which we are acquainted. Thus when, for example, we make a statement about Julius Caesar, it is plain that Julius Caesar himself is not before our minds, since we are not acquainted with him.

We have in mind some *description* of Julius Caesar: "the man who was assassinated on the Ides of March," "the founder of the Roman Empire," or, perhaps, merely "the man whose name was *Julius Caesar*." (In this last description, *Julius Caesar* is a noise or shape with which we are acquainted.) Thus our statement does not mean quite what it seems to mean, but means something involving, instead of Julius Caesar, some description of him which is composed wholly of particulars and universals with which we are acquainted.

The chief importance of knowledge by description is that it enables us to pass beyond the limits of our private experience. In spite of the fact that we can only know truths which are wholly composed of terms which we have experienced in acquaintance, we can yet have knowledge by description of things which we have never experienced. In view of the very narrow range of our immediate experience, this result is vital, and until it is understood, much of our knowledge must remain mysterious and therefore doubtful.

50 From *Mind and the World Order*

C. I. Lewis

The word "concept" is used, in philosophic discussion, in many different senses, three of which it is particularly important to distinguish. It may signify (1) the psychological state of mind when one uses a word or phrase to designate some individual thing or some class of objects. Or (2) it may refer to the meaning of a word or phrase throughout some period of the development of the individual's thought, or some period of the development of a science, of a given culture, or even of humanity altogether. Or, (3) it may signify the logical intension or connotation of a term. This third meaning is exemplified by dictionary definitions where these are satisfactory—and is the usual signification of "concept" in the study of logic.

The use of any substantive phrase or term ordinarily undergoes a process of development, both in the history of society and in the history of any individual who uses it. Usually, though not always, the denotation of the term remains unchanged throughout this process; we apply it to the same class of objects, but our realization of what is essential to these things reflects a process of learning. Such learning may consist in an enlargement of our experience of the class of things in question, or it may occasionally represent simply our more accurate apprehension of what are the universal properties and relations of the familiar objects thus classified. But if the meaning of a word or phrase undergo evolution, then, however normal or inevitable or commendable this process may be, we must, for the sake of clarity, recognize that this meaning is one unitary entity only in some generic and genetic sense, and that logically what we have is a succession of different meanings, related in ways which may be important. The recognition of their historical continuity must not obscure the fact of their logical distinctness.

. . . Here a meaning must be precise and clear, or be capable of being made so, and must remain unaltered throughout any discussion in which it occurs. No psychological or historical process is legislated out of existence by this restriction in the use of the word, but if there should be development or learning which affects the connotation of a term, then, from this point of view, we have *another* meaning; that is all.

Again, the psychological state is not the object in which we are here primarily interested. If a psychologist, thinking in terms of a context-theory of meaning, says, "Infinity means to me the image of the blue-black, dense, arched sky,"[1] then we must observe that such a psychologist blurs over the distinction between what is essential and what is non-essential in meaning. He is in no danger of misunderstanding one who talks about what the symbol ∞ denotes to be referring to the heavens, nor does he, even in his own thinking, suppose that infinity is blue-black. To use "concept" to designate such a psychological state or association-complex, is to fail to mark the distinction between what is objective in meaning and what is adventitious or purely personal. Indeed, the question how meaning *can* be objective and shared, when the psychological states which are bearers of this meaning are separate existences and not even identical in their qualitative content, is one of the important problems of meaning.

Because it is our main interest here to isolate that element in knowledge which we can with certainty maintain to be objective and impersonal, we shall define the pure concept as "that meaning which must be common to two minds when they understand each other by the use of a substantive or its equivalent." ...

That meanings may have this sort of objectivity, is a fundamental assumption of science or of any other intellectual enterprise. If there is nothing objective about propositions and concepts, then there is no such thing as truth and there can be no serious purpose in reflection or discussion. There must be meanings which are common to minds when they coöperate in scientific or even in merely practical endeavors. Otherwise the coöperation is illusory; and one cannot escape the question how such common meaning stands related to different minds or psychological states which mean....

... [I]t is obvious that common meanings do transcend such individual differences of perception and imagery. We use language to convey thought. If language really conveys anything, then there must be something which is identical in your mind and in mine when we understand each other. And if our thought is objective and not merely a report of introspection, then what is identical in our two minds must also be somehow germane to that objective reality as we know it.

Suppose we talk of physical things in physical terms, and our discussion involves physical measurement. Presumably we have the same ideas of feet and pounds and seconds. If not, the thing is hopeless. But in psychological terms, my notion of a foot goes back to some immediate image of visual so-long-ness, or the movements which I make when I put my hands so far apart, or a relation between these two. Distances in general mean quite complex relationships between such visual images, muscle and contact-sensations, the feeling of fatigue, and so on. Weight goes back to muscle-sensations, the "heft" of the thing. And our direct apprehension of time is that feeling of duration which is so familiar but so difficult to describe.

Now in such terms, will your sensory image of a foot or a pound coincide with mine? I am near-sighted; your eyes are good. My arms are long; yours are short. If we lift a weight, there is the difference in strength between us to take into account. So it is with everything. In acuity of perception and power to discriminate, there is almost always some small difference between the senses of two individuals, and frequently these discrepancies are marked. It is only in rough and ready terms that we can reasonably suppose that our direct intuitions and images are alike. That so often theories of knowledge have ignored such differences, which are the rule and not the exception, or have proceeded as if our common and supposedly veridical knowledge depended on coincidence of such sensory content, is really a frightful scandal.

Even for the large and crude distinctions, what assurance is there that our impressions coincide? Suppose it should be a fact that I get the sensation you signalize by saying "red" whenever I look at what you call "green" and vice versa. Suppose that in the

Psychologically, this conceptual pattern of relations is, of course, an abstraction; no such concept ever existed, apart from imagery and sensory material, in any human mind. *For each individual* there must be a correlation of concept with specific sense-quality. But this correlation of concept and sense is intrinsically individual; if it, too, should be shared, we could not verify that fact, and it is not in the least essential to common understanding that it should be. The concept, so defined, is precisely that abstraction which it is *necessary* to make if we are to discover the basis of our common understanding of that reality which we all know. On a day which is terribly long to me and abominably short to you, we meet, by agreement, at three o'clock, and thus demonstrate that we have a world in common. An "hour" is not a feeling of tedium or vivacity, but sixty minutes, one round of the clock, a pattern of relations which we have established between chronometers and distances and rates of movement, and so on.

Defining, like logical analysis in general, sets up a pattern of relationships. We are all of us fond of what Bosanquet called the "linear" mode of thinking in such matters, and we might easily suppose that definition chases a conceptual meaning back into other such concepts, and these into still others, until finally it is brought to bay in some first (or last) identity of meaning which is identity of sensation or imagery. So far as meaning within the individual mind is concerned, I should suppose this is precisely what takes place; we analyze the meaning back until we come to rest in familiar imagery. But the end-terms, which for us are thus understood directly by reference to sense and feeling, have still a conceptual meaning; they are not indefinable. This conceptual meaning is shareable; our imagery essentially not. Thus the end-terms of such analysis are no different than the beginning terms; they have meaning in two senses—the logical, shareable meaning of further conceptual relations, and the direct, non-shareable meaning of reference to some complex of sense-qualities.

The notion that the analysis of meaning must, in linear fashion, go back eventually to ultimate constituents whose meaning *cannot* in turn be thus relational, is a prejudice which is very largely due to a false metaphor. Logical analysis is conceived after the fashion of the physical dissection of a whole into parts, or the chemical analysis of a compound into elements. But it will not escape the thoughtful reader that all definition is eventually circular. It is often the case that *A* can be defined in terms of *B* and *C*, *B* in terms of *A* and *C*, or *C* in terms of *A* and *B*. Where the circle is so small, and the defined meaning so promptly returns upon itself, the analysis is likely to be inadequate. But this circularity would never be possible at all, if the relation of defining to defined were that of part to whole. Moreover, the difference between a good and a bad definition, on this point, is only, so to speak, in the diameter of the circle. All the terms in the dictionary, however ideal its definitions, will be themselves defined.

Logical analysis is not dissection but relation; the analysis of *A* into *B* and *C* does not divide *A* into constituents *B* and *C* but merely traces a pattern of relations connecting *A* with *B* and *C*. As regards their conceptual meaning, terms are very closely analogous to points in space. A point is nothing whatever apart from its relation to other points; its very essence is relational. Likewise the conceptual meaning of a term is nothing whatever apart from other such meanings. Also it is true that if point *A* is located by reference to *B* and *C*, *B* and *C* in turn, and the other points in any spatial array, have their position eventually, in circularwise, in their relation to *A* and to one another. The positional relationships of any point are internal to its nature and constitute that nature. Likewise, the definitive relations of a term, signifying a concept, are internal to the meaning of that term and constitute it. The nature of a concept as such is its internal (essential or definitive) relationships with other concepts. All points have their positions eventually in terms of the array of all space: no point or set of points has any primal position in any other fashion; we merely choose as an arbitary basis of reference some set which is convenient or marks the place where we happen to be. All terms or concepts similarly have their meaning eventually in the array of all meanings, and no member of this array is intrinsically primal or privileged.

Concerning this interpretation of the concept as consisting in relational structures of meaning, there can be two doubts. We seldom "have in mind" any such conceptual pattern of definition. When we reflect upon the manner in which coincidence in the meaning of one term involves coincidence in the meaning of others, we see that such an ideal pattern of meaning goes far beyond what anyone could consciously have in mind at any one time. Again, we often coincide in our use of terms, and thus seem to possess meanings in common, when the definition of our terms would be a matter of some doubt and one holding possibility of disagreement. . . .

If I talk with a chemist about helium or with a biologist about cells, we may understand each other perfectly. But without recourse to some reference book, I could not define "helium" or "cell" in a fashion which the specialist would accept as adequate. To me "helium" means "a non-inflammable gas a little lighter than hydrogen (or a little heavier—I forget which), produced in the disintegration of alpha-particles and found in the sun." I could not specify either atomic-weight or spectrum characteristics, one or other of which the chemist will regard as essential to a sufficiently guarded definition. But as long as we converse together without misunderstanding, the *common* meaning of "helium" is just what is set down above. This is a less specific meaning than the chemist's, but included in it, and sufficient for our present purposes. If our discussion should touch upon more recondite matters, he might need to instruct me about helium, and thus establish a more specific common concept, before we could go on. I recognize his authority to do so, and should accept his definition (which I cannot now give) as the "true" meaning of the word "helium." But this does not alter the fact that, for the time being, the common concept which serves our purposes is my looser understanding of the term. Such is quite commonly the case. Our actual meanings, the concepts we are concerned to convey, are more restricted than the true or full or dictionary meanings of the terms we use. Most words may convey any one of a whole range of more or less full and accurate meanings. It is, thus, quite possible that we may understand each other perfectly even when we should disagree about the definition of our terms, because only some restricted meaning, covered in both our definitions, is required by our discussion.

Second, it is obvious that in some sense or other we may have a meaning in mind when we could not state it without further thought. Any true account of thought and speech must recognize this. The ruling interest in knowledge is the practical interest of action. A meaning may be implicitly present in the consistency of behavior when confronted with experience of a certain type without the explicit recognition of what this behavior implies having come into consciousness or even been brought in question. Such we must suppose to be the child's early use of language. And in this sense, we may perhaps say that meanings must be implicit in the mind before they can become conscious. In fact, we may doubt whether any meaning would ever become conscious if it were not for the practical difficulties which arise when meanings are not thus explicit—the difficulties of hesitant or inconsistent behavior in border-line cases, and the social difficulty of misunderstanding, that is, of incongruous behavior when the same term has been used with apparently the same meaning.

Josiah Royce used to speak to his classes of the three grades of clearness about the meanings of terms.[2] We have the first grade of clearness when we are able appropriately to accept or reject any object of our acquaintance as belonging or not belonging to the class in question. The second grade of clearness involves, further, the preparedness to classify correctly objects not precisely like those with which we have previously been acquainted; that is, to make the dichotomy, *X* or not-*X*, not only for familiar but also for unfamiliar things, not only for all actual but also for all conceivable objects. The third grade of clearness consists in the ability to specify the criteria by which such classification is determined. This last, of course, is equivalent to definition, the explicit possession of the concept. That the mind may have the first or second grade of clearness without the third, is obvious. It is also evident without discussion, that even when we have, in the ordinary sense, this highest grade of clearness, we do not have this definition explicitly in mind whenever we use a term with understanding. . . .

Common meaning may override all idiosyncrasy of feeling or sense, so far as such idiosyncrasy does not prevent congruous distinction and relations. It may even override differences which are reflected in failure of discrimination and relation, in ways which have already been commented on. In fact, I think we may fairly be impressed with the tremendous achievement which our common meanings and our intellectual coöperation represent in the life of the race. Community of meaning may also override much idiosyncrasy of behavior. But eventually the very purposes for which communication exists insure a certain congruity of behavior when meanings are the same.

Berkeley pointed out that we can never test the validity of knowledge by comparing an idea in the mind with an object outside the mind. We can only compare ideas among themselves. This is a pertinent consideration about the *criteria* of knowledge, whether one agrees with Berkeley's idealism or not. What I would here point out about the concept has a certain similarity. We cannot test community of meaning, even eventually, by comparing the immediate experience in our own mind with the immediate experience in another mind, nor by comparing another's concepts, conveyed to us, with his immediate feelings and sensations. We can only compare meanings among themselves, as purely conceptual and abstracted from the character of any experience beyond our own. We can only grasp another's meanings by observing the relation of his meanings to one another and to his behavior. . . .

Suppose two men speaking different languages but having a few words in common to be chained to the opposite walls of a dark cell, so that the possibility of establishing common meanings by such methods as pointing and naming would be at a minimum. With good luck in the initial common concepts, and with a high enough order of intelligence, they might eventually establish a very large range of common notions by methods which the reader can imagine for himself.

The actual case of Miss Helen Keller, in which a normal range of understanding has been developed from original coincidence in kinesthetic and contact-sensation (*absolute* coincidence even in these being somewhat doubtful) need only be mentioned.

Or suppose there should be creatures on Mars of a high order of mentality. They might be psychologically rather different from ourselves and have senses and experience largely incomparable with our own. Yet if we could establish some initial common understanding (say if we should signal to them in light-flashes -, --, ---, and they should eventually respond with ----, -----, ------), then in spite of our differences from them, it would be hard to set a limit beyond which it could be said with certainty that our common understanding could not go.

In fact, it is just this indefinite extensibility of conceptual understanding which is exhibited by abstract mathematical systems. To take the best illustration; by a miracle of patience and insight, Mr. Russell and Mr. Whitehead have achieved, in "Principia Mathematica," such an analysis of various branches that the whole field of this subject (excepting the geometrical, so far omitted) can be developed from seven initial concepts. These undefined ideas are of such a sort that they must almost inevitably belong to any creature which should be conscious of its own ways of acting and should possess the habit of communication—ideas such as "proposition" and "either-or." Supposing these notions to be common to two minds—in any terms you please—these two minds could, if their patience and intelligence should be sufficient, arrive eventually at a common understanding of the whole of mathematics.

So far, I am only concerned to point out that an initial community could extend itself extraordinarily. The exigencies of common life, the need of coöperation, the tendency to imitation in behavior, and the enormously developed institution of human education—using the term in its widest meaning—all go to enforce just this sort of elaboration and extension of any initial mutuality of human understanding. Idiosyncrasy is pretty systematically suppressed. And what cannot be suppressed (abnormalities and deficiencies) we go about it most earnestly and ingeniously to get around. A relatively meager mutuality of concepts, given human powers of discrimination, abstraction and relation, and our human social habits, would be sufficient as the initial foundation for our actual and most elaborate mutual understanding. I am not trying to argue that it *is* from such a meager basis of initial mutuality that the community of understanding actually develops, though obviously one could make out a pretty good case from the manner in which the infant acquires his social inheritance of ideas. I wish only to point out the fact that, given such a meager mutuality, elaborate common understanding could develop; and that to argue straight from our elaborate common understanding to an equally extended coincidence of felt qualities or given experience, is unnecessary and fallacious. . . .

Notes

1. The reference is, of course, to Titchener.

2. He used to attribute this to Charles Peirce, but Peirce's discussion in "How to Make Our Ideas Clear," does not so precisely cover the point.

51 From "The Meaning of 'Meaning'"

Hilary Putnam

Meaning and Extension

Since the Middle Ages at least, writers on the theory of meaning have purported to discover an ambiguity in the ordinary concept of meaning, and have introduced a pair of terms—*extension* and *intension*, or *Sinn* and *Bedeutung*, or whatever—to disambiguate the notion. The *extension* of a term, in customary logical parlance, is simply the set of things the term is true of. Thus, "rabbit," in its most common English sense, is true of all and only rabbits, so the extension of "rabbit" is precisely the set of rabbits. Even this notion—and it is the *least* problematical notion in this cloudy subject—has its problems, however. Apart from problems it inherits from its parent notion of *truth*, the foregoing example of "rabbit" *in its most common English sense* illustrates one such problem: strictly speaking, it is not a term, but an ordered pair consisting of a term and a "sense" (or an occasion of use, or something else that distinguishes a term in one sense from the same term used in a different sense) that has an extension. Another problem is this: a "set," in the mathematical sense, is a "yes–no" object; any given object either definitely belongs to *S* or definitely does not belong to *S*, if *S* is a set. But words in a natural language are not generally "yes–no": there are things of which the description "tree" is clearly true and things of which the description "tree" is clearly false, to be sure, but there are a host of borderline cases. Worse, the line between the clear cases and the borderline cases is itself fuzzy. Thus the idealization involved in the notion of *extension*—the idealization involved in supposing that there is such a thing as the set of things of which the term "tree" is true—is actually very severe....

The problem of a word's having more than one sense is standardly handled by treating each of the senses as a different word (or rather, by treating the word as if it carried invisible subscripts, thus: "rabbit_1"—animal of a certain kind; "rabbit_2"—coward; and as if "rabbit_1" and "rabbit_2" or whatever were different words entirely). This again involves two very severe idealizations (at least two, that is): supposing that words have discretely many senses, and supposing that the entire repertoire of senses is fixed once and for all. Paul Ziff has recently investigated the extent to which both of these suppositions distort the actual situation in natural language;[1] nevertheless, we will continue to make these idealizations here.

Now consider the compound terms "creature with a heart" and "creature with a kidney." Assuming that every creature with a heart possesses a kidney and vice versa, the extension of these two terms is exactly the same. But they obviously differ in meaning.

Supposing that there is a sense of "meaning" in which meaning = extension, there must be another sense of "meaning" in which the meaning of a term is not its extension but something else, say the "concept" associated with the term. Let us call this "something else" the *intension* of the term. The concept of a creature with a heart is clearly a different concept from the concept of a creature with a kidney. Thus the two terms have different intension. When we say they have different "meaning," meaning = intension.

Intension and Extension

... Unclear as it is, the traditional doctrine that the notion "meaning" possesses the extension/intension ambiguity has certain typical consequences. Most traditional philosophers thought of concepts as something *mental*. Thus the doctrine that the meaning of a term (the meaning "in the sense of intension," that is) is a concept carried the implication that meanings are mental entities. Frege and more recently Carnap and his followers, however, rebelled against this "psychologism," as they termed it. Feeling that meanings are *public* property—that the *same* meaning can be "grasped" by more than one person and by persons at different times—they identified concepts (and hence "intensions" or meanings) with abstract entities rather than mental entities. However, "grasping" these abstract entities was still an individual psychological act. None of these philosophers doubted that understanding a word (knowing its intension) was just a matter of being in a certain psychological state (somewhat in the way in which knowing how to factor numbers in one's head is just a matter of being in a certain very complex psychological state).

Secondly, the timeworn example of the two terms "creature with a kidney" and "creature with a heart" does show that two terms can have the same extension and yet differ in intension. But it was taken to be obvious that the reverse is impossible: two terms cannot differ in extension and have the same intension. Interestingly, no argument for this impossibility was ever offered. Probably it reflects the tradition of the ancient and medieval philosophers who assumed that the concept corresponding to a term was jut a conjunction of predicates, and hence that the concept corresponding to a term must *always* provide a necessary and sufficient condition for falling into the extension of the term.[2] For philosophers like Carnap, who accepted the verifiability theory of meaning, the concept corresponding to a term provided (in the ideal case, where the term had "complete meaning") a *criterion* for belonging to the extension (not just in the sense of "necessary and sufficient condition," but in the strong sense of *way of recognizing* if a given thing falls into the extension or not). Thus these positivistic philosophers were perfectly happy to retain the traditional view on this point. So theory of meaning came to rest on two unchallenged assumptions:

(I) That knowing the meaning of a term is just a matter of being in a certain psychological state (in the sense of "psychological state," in which states of memory and psychological dispositions are "psychological states"; no one thought that knowing the meaning of a word was a continuous state of consciousness, of course).

(II) That the meaning of a term (in the sense of "intension") determines its extension (in the sense that sameness of intension entails sameness of extension).

I shall argue that these two assumptions are not jointly satisfied by *any* notion, let alone any notion of meaning. The traditional concept of meaning is a concept which rests on a false theory.

"Psychological State" and Methodological Solipsism

... When traditional philosophers talked about psychological states (or "mental" states), they made an assumption which we may call the assumption of methodological solipsism. This assumption is the assumption that no psychological state, properly so called, presupposes the existence of any individual other than the subject to whom that state is ascribed. (In fact, the assumption was that no psychological state presupposes the existence of the subject's *body* even: if *P* is a psychological state, properly so called, then it must be logically possible for a "disembodied mind" to be in *P*.) This assumption is pretty explicit in Descartes, but it is implicit in just about the whole of traditional philosophical psychology. Making this assumption is, of course, adopting a *restrictive program*—a program which deliberately limits the scope and nature of psychology to fit certain mentalistic preconceptions or, in some cases, to fit an idealistic reconstruction of knowledge and the world. Just *how* restrictive the program is, however, often goes unnoticed. Such common or garden variety psychological states as *being jealous* have to be reconstructed, for example, if the assumption of methodological solipsism is retained. For, in its ordinary use, *x is jealous of y* entails that *y* exists, and *x is jealous of y's regard for z* entails that both *y* and *z* exist (as well as *x*, of course). Thus *being jealous* and *being jealous of someone's regard for someone else* are not psychological states permitted by the assumption of methodological solipsism. (We shall call them "psychological states in the wide sense" and refer to the states which are permitted by methodological solipsism as "psychological states in the narrow sense.") The reconstruction required by methodological solipsism would be to reconstrue *jealousy* so that I can be jealous of my own hallucinations, or of figments of my imagination, etc. Only if we assume that psychological states in the narrow sense have a significant degree of causal closure (so that restricting ourselves to psychological states in the narrow sense will facilitate the statement of psychological *laws*) is there any point in engaging in this reconstruction, or in making the assumption of methodological solipsism. But the three centuries of failure of mentalistic psychology is tremendous evidence against this procedure, in my opinion.

Be that as it may, we can now state more precisely what we claimed at the end of the preceding section. Let *A* and *B* be any two terms which differ in extension. By assumption (II) they must differ in meaning (in the sense of "intension"). By assumption (I), *knowing the meaning of A* and *knowing the meaning of B* are psychological states *in the narrow sense*—for this is how we shall construe assumption (I). *But these psychological states must determine the extension of the terms A and B just as much as the meanings ("intensions") do.*

To see this, let us try assuming the opposite. Of course, there cannot be two terms *A* and *B* such that *knowing the meaning of A* is the same state as *knowing the meaning of B* even though *A* and *B* have different extensions. For *knowing the meaning of A* isn't just "grasping the intension" of *A*, whatever that may come to; it is also knowing that the "intension" that one has "grasped" *is* the intension of *A*. (Thus, someone who knows the meaning of "wheel" presumably "grasps the intension" of its German synonym *Rad*; but if he doesn't know that the "intension" in question is the intension of *Rad* he isn't said to "know the meaning of *Rad*.") If *A* and *B* are different terms, then *knowing the meaning of A* is a different state from *knowing the meaning of B* whether the meanings of *A* and *B* be themselves the same or different. But by the same argument, if I_1 and I_2 are different *intensions* and *A* is a term, then *knowing that* I_1 *is the meaning of A* is a different psychological state from *knowing that* I_2 *is the meaning of A*. Thus, there cannot be two different logically possible worlds L_1 and L_2 such that, say, Oscar is in the *same* psychological state (in the narrow sense) in L_1 and in L_2 (in all respects), but in L_1 Oscar understands *A* as having the meaning I_1 and in L_2 Oscar understands *A* as having the meaning I_2. (For, if there were, then in L_1 Oscar would be in the psychological state *knowing that* I_1 *is the meaning of A* and in L_2 Oscar would be in the psychological state *knowing that* I_2 *is the meaning of A*, and these are different and even—assuming that *A* has just *one* meaning for Oscar in each world—incompatible psychological states in the narrow sense.)

In short, if *S* is the sort of psychological state we have been discussing—a psychological state of the form *knowing that* I *is the meaning of A*, where *I* is an "intension" and *A* is a term—then the *same* necessary and sufficient condition for falling into the extension of *A* "works" in *every* logically possible world in which the speaker is in the psychological state *S*. For the state *S determines* the intension *I*, and by assumption (II) the intension amounts to a necessary and sufficient condition for membership in the *extension*.

If our interpretation of the traditional doctrine of intension and extension is fair to Frege and Carnap, then the whole psychologism/Platonism issue appears somewhat a tempest in a teapot, as far as meaning-theory is concerned. (Of course, it is a very important issue as far as general philosophy of mathematics is concerned.) For even if meanings are "Platonic" entities rather than "mental" entities on the Frege–Carnap view, "grasping" those entities is presumably a psychological state (in the narrow sense). Moreover, the psychological state uniquely determines the "Platonic" entity. So whether one takes the "Platonic" entity or the psychological state as the "meaning" would appear to be somewhat a matter of convention. And taking the psychological state to be the meaning would hardly have the consequence that Frege feared, that meanings would cease to be public. For psychological states are "public" in the sense that different people (and even people in different epochs) can be in the *same* psychological state. Indeed, Frege's argument against psychologism is only an argument against identifying concepts with mental particulars, not with mental entities in general.

The "public" character of psychological states entails, in particular, that if Oscar and Elmer understand a word *A* differently, then they must be in *different* psychological states. For the state of *knowing the intension of* A *to be, say, I* is the *same* state whether Oscar or Elmer be in it. Thus two speakers cannot be in the same psychological state in all respects and understand the term *A* differently; the psychological state of the speaker determines the intension (and hence, by assumption (II), the extension) of *A*.

It is this last consequence of the joint assumptions (I), (II) that we claim to be false. We claim that it is possible for two speakers to be in exactly the *same* psychological state (in the narrow sense), even though the extension of the term *A* in the idiolect of the one is different from the extension of the term *A* in the idiolect of the other. Extension is *not* determined by psychological state.

This will be shown in detail in later sections. If this is right, then there are two courses open to one who wants to rescue at least one of the traditional assumptions; to give up the idea that psychological state (in the narrow sense) determines *intension*, or to give up the idea that intension determines extension. We shall consider these alternatives later.

Are Meanings in the Head?

That psychological state does not determine extension will now be shown with the aid of a little science-fiction. For the purpose of the following science-fiction examples, we shall suppose that somewhere in the galaxy there is a planet we shall call Twin Earth. Twin Earth is very much like Earth; in fact, people on Twin Earth even speak *English*. In fact, apart from the differences we shall specify in our science-fiction examples, the reader may suppose that Twin Earth is *exactly* like Earth. He may even suppose that he has a *Doppelgänger*—an identical copy—on Twin Earth, if he wishes, although my stories will not depend on this.

Although some of the people on Twin Earth (say, the ones who call themselves "Americans" and the ones who call themselves "Canadians" and the ones who call themselves "Englishmen," etc.) speak English, there are, not surprisingly, a few tiny differences which we will now describe between the dialects of English spoken on Twin Earth and Standard English. These differences themselves depend on some of the peculiarities of Twin Earth.

One of the peculiarities of Twin Earth is that the liquid called "water" is not H_2O but a different liquid whose chemical formula is very long and complicated. I shall abbreviate this chemical formula simply as *XYZ*. I shall suppose that *XYZ* is indistinguishable from water at normal temperatures and pressures. In particular, it tastes like water and it quenches thirst like water. Also, I shall suppose that the oceans and lakes and seas of Twin Earth contain *XYZ* and not water, that it rains *XYZ* on Twin Earth and not water, etc.

If a spaceship from Earth ever visits Twin Earth, then the supposition at first will be that "water" has the same meaning on Earth and on Twin Earth. This supposition will be corrected when it is discovered that "water" on Twin Earth is *XYZ*, and the Earthian spaceship will report somewhat as follows:

On Twin Earth the word "water" means *XYZ*.

(It is this sort of use of the word "means" which accounts for the doctrine that extension is one sense of "meaning," by the way. But note that although "means" does mean something like *has as extension* in this example, one would *not* say

On Twin Earth the meaning of the word "water" is *XYZ*.

unless, possibly, the fact that "water is *XYZ*" was known to every adult speaker of English on Twin Earth. We can account for this in terms of the theory of meaning we develop below; for the moment we just remark that although the verb "means" sometimes means "has as extension," the nominalization "meaning" *never* means "extension.")

Symmetrically, if a spaceship from Twin Earth ever visits Earth, then the supposition at first will be that the word "water" has the same meaning on Twin Earth and on Earth. This supposition will be corrected when it is discovered that "water" on Earth is H_2O, and the Twin Earthian spaceship will report:

On Earth[3] the word "water" means H_2O.

Note that there is no problem about the extension of the term "water." The world simply has two different meanings (as we say): in the sense in which it is used on Twin Earth, the sense of $water_{TE}$, what *we* call "water" simply isn't water; while in the sense in which it is used on Earth, the sense of $water_E$, what the Twin Earthians call "water" simply isn't water. The extension of "water" in the sense of $water_E$ is the set of all wholes consisting of H_2O molecules, or something like that; the extension of water in the sense of $water_{TE}$ is the set of all wholes consisting of *XYZ* molecules, or something like that.

Now let us roll the time back to about 1750. At that time chemistry was not developed on either Earth or Twin Earth. The typical Earthian speaker of English did not know water consisted of hydrogen and oxygen, and the typical Twin Earthian speaker of English did not know "water" consisted of *XYZ*. Let $Oscar_1$ be such a typical Earthian English speaker, and let $Oscar_2$ be his counterpart on Twin Earth. You may suppose that there is no belief that $Oscar_1$ had about water that $Oscar_2$ did not have about "water." If you like, you may even suppose that $Oscar_1$ and $Oscar_2$ were exact duplicates in appearance, feelings, thoughts, interior monologue, etc. Yet the extension of the term "water" was just as much H_2O on Earth in 1750 as in 1950; and the extension of the term "water" was just as much *XYZ* on Twin Earth in 1750 as in 1950. $Oscar_1$ and $Oscar_2$ understood the term "water" differently in 1750 *although they were in the same psychological state*, and although, given the state of science at the time, it would have taken their scientific communities about fifty years to discover that they understood the term "water" differently. Thus the extension of the term "water" (and, in fact, its "meaning" in the intuitive preanalytical usage of that term) is *not* a function of the psychological state of the speaker by itself.

But, it might be objected, why should we accept it that the term "water" has the same extension in 1750 and in 1950 (on both Earths)? The logic of natural-kind terms like "water" is a complicated matter, but the following is a sketch of an answer. Suppose I point to a glass of water and say "this liquid is called water" (or "this is called water," if the marker "liquid" is clear from the context). My "ostensive definition" of water has the following empirical presupposition: that the body of liquid I am pointing to bears a certain sameness relation (say, *x is the same liquid as y*, or *x is the* $same_L$ *as y*) to most of the stuff I and other speakers in my linguistic community have on other occasions called "water." If this presupposition is false because, say, I am without knowing it pointing to a glass of gin and not a glass of water, then I do not intend my ostensive definition to be accepted. Thus the ostensive definition conveys what might be called a defeasible necessary and sufficient condition: the necessary and sufficient condition for being water is bearing the relation $same_L$ to the stuff in the glass; but this is the necessary and sufficient condition only if the empirical presupposition is satisfied. If it is not satisfied, then one of a series of, so to speak, "fallback" conditions becomes activated.

The key point is that the relation $same_L$ is a *theoretical* relation: whether something is or is not the same liquid as *this* may take an indeterminate amount of scientific investigation to determine. Moreover, even if a "definite" answer has been obtained either through scientific investigation or through the application of some "common sense" test, the answer is *defeasible*: future investigation might reverse even the most "certain" example. Thus, the fact that an English speaker in 1750 might have called *XYZ* "water," while he or his successors would not have called *XYZ* water in 1800 or 1850 does not mean that the "meaning" of "water" changed for the average speaker in the interval. In 1750 or in 1850 or in 1950 one might have pointed to, say, the liquid in Lake Michigan as an example of "water." What changed was that in 1750 we would have mistakenly thought that *XYZ* bore the relation $same_L$ to the liquid in Lake Michigan, while in 1800 or 1850 we would have known that it did not (I am ignoring the fact that the liquid in Lake Michigan was only dubiously water in 1950, of course).

Let us now modify our science-fiction story. I do not know whether one can make pots and pans out of molybdenum; and if one can make them out of molybdenum, I don't know whether they could be distinguished easily from aluminum pots and pans. (I don't know any of this even though I have acquired the word "molybdenum.") So I shall suppose that molybdenum pots and pans *can't* be distinguished from aluminum pots and pans save by an expert. (To emphasize the point, I repeat that this could be true for all I know, and *a fortiori* it could be true for all I know by virtue of "knowing the meaning" of the words *aluminum* and *molybdenum*.) We will now suppose that molybdenum is as common on Twin Earth as aluminum is on Earth, and that aluminum is as rare on Twin Earth as molybdenum is on Earth. In particular, we shall assume that "aluminum" pots and pans are made of molybdenum on Twin Earth. Finally, we shall assume that the words "aluminum" and "molybdenum" are *switched* on Twin Earth: "aluminum" is the name of *molybdenum* and "molybdenum" is the name of *aluminum*.

This example shares some features with the previous one. If a spaceship from Earth visited Twin Earth, the visitors from Earth probably would not suspect that the "aluminum" pots and pans on Twin Earth were not made of aluminum, especially when the Twin Earthians *said* they were. But there is one important difference between the two cases. An Earthian metallurgist could tell very easily that "aluminum" was molybdenum, and a Twin Earthian metallurgist could tell equally easily that aluminum was "molybdenum." (The shudder quotes in the preceding sentence indicate Twin Earthian usages.) Whereas in 1750 no one on either Earth or Twin Earth could have distinguished water from "water," the confusion of aluminum with "aluminum" involves only a part of the linguistic communities involved.

The example makes the same point as the preceding one. If $Oscar_1$ and $Oscar_2$ are standard speakers of Earthian English and Twin Earthian English respectively, and neither is chemically or metallurgically sophisticated, then there may be no difference at all in their psychological state when they use the word "aluminum"; nevertheless we have to say that "aluminum" has the extension *aluminum* in the idiolect of $Oscar_1$ and the extension *molybdenum* in the idiolect of $Oscar_2$. (Also we have to say that $Oscar_1$ and $Oscar_2$ mean different things by "aluminum," that "aluminum" has a different meaning on Earth than it does on Twin Earth, etc.) Again we see that the psychological state of the speaker does *not* determine the extension (*or* the "meaning," speaking preanalytically) of the word.

Before discussing this example further, let me introduce a *non*-science-fiction example. Suppose you are like me and cannot tell an elm from a beech tree. We still say that the extension of "elm" in my idiolect is the same as the extension of "elm" in anyone else's, viz., the set of all elm trees, and that the set of all beech trees is the extension of "beech" in *both* of our idiolects. Thus "elm" in my idiolect has a different extension from "beech" in your idiolect (as it should). Is it really credible that this difference in extension is brought about by some difference in our *concepts*? My *concept* of an elm tree is exactly the same as my concept of a beech tree (I blush to confess). (This shows that the identification of meaning "in the sense of intension" with *concept* cannot be correct, by the way.) If someone heroically attempts to maintain that the difference between the extension of "elm" and the extension of "beech" in *my* idiolect is explained by a difference in my psychological state, then we can always refute him by constructing a "Twin Earth" example—just let the words "elm" and "beech" be switched on Twin Earth (the way "aluminum" and "molybdenum" were in the previous example.) Moreover, I suppose I have a *Doppelgänger* on Twin Earth who is molecule for molecule "identical" with me (in the sense in which two neckties can be "identical"). If you are a dualist, then also suppose my *Doppelgänger* thinks the same verbalized thoughts I do, has the same sense data, the same dispositions, etc. It is absurd to think *his* psychological state is one bit different from mine: yet he "means" *beech* when he says "elm" and *I* "mean" *elm* when I say elm. Cut the pie any way you like, "meanings" just ain't in the *head*!

A Socio-Linguistic Hypothesis

The last two examples depend upon a fact about language that seems, surprisingly, never to have been pointed out: that there is *division of linguistic labor*. We could hardly use such words as "elm" and "aluminum" if no one possessed a way of recognizing elm trees and aluminum metal; but not everyone to whom the distinction is important has to be able to make the distinction. Let us shift the example: consider *gold*. Gold is important for many reasons: it is a precious metal, it is a monetary metal, it has symbolic value (it is important to most people that the "gold" wedding ring they wear *really* consist of gold and not just *look* gold), etc. Consider our community as a "factory": in this "factory" some people have the "job" of *wearing gold wedding rings*, other people have the "job" of *selling gold wedding rings*, still other people have the "job" of *telling whether or not something is really gold*. It is not at all necessary or efficient that everyone who wears a gold ring (or a gold cufflink, etc.), or discusses the "gold standard," etc., engage in buying and selling gold. Nor is it necessary or efficient that everyone who buys and sells gold be able to tell whether or not something is really gold in a society where this form of dishonesty is uncommon (selling fake gold) and in which one can easily consult an expert in case of doubt. And it is *certainly* not necessary or efficient that everyone who has occasion to buy or wear gold be able to tell with any reliability whether or not something is really gold.

The foregoing facts are just examples of mundane division of labor (in a wide sense). But they engender a division of linguistic labor: everyone to whom gold is important for any reason has to *acquire* the word "gold"; but he does not have to acquire the *method of recognizing* if something is or is not gold. He can rely on a special subclass of speakers. The features that are generally thought to be present in connection with a general name—necessary and sufficient conditions for membership in the extension, ways of recognizing if something is in the extension ("criteria"), etc.—are all present in the linguistic community *considered as a collective body*; but that collective body divides the "labor" of knowing and employing these various parts of the "meaning" of "gold."

This division of linguistic labor rests upon and presupposes the division of *non*-linguistic labor, of course. If only the people who know how to tell if some metal is really gold or not have any reason to have the word "gold" in their vocabulary, then the word "gold" will be as the word "water" was in 1750 with respect to that subclass of speakers, and the other speakers just won't acquire it at all. And some words do not exhibit any division of linguistic labor: "chair," for example. But with the increase of division of labor in the society and the rise of science, more and more words begin to exhibit this kind of division of labor. "Water," for example, did not exhibit it at all prior to the rise of chemistry. Today it is obviously necessary for every speaker to be able to recognize water (reliably under normal conditions), and probably every adult speaker even knows the necessary and sufficient condition "water is H_2O," but only a few adult speakers could distinguish water from liquids which superficially resembled water. In case of doubt, other speakers would rely on the judgement of these "expert" speakers. Thus the way of recognizing possessed by these "expert" speakers is also, through them, possessed by the collective linguistic body, even though it is not possessed by each individual member of the body, and in this way the most recherché fact about water may become part of the *social* meaning of the word while being unknown to almost all speakers who acquire the word.

It seems to me that this phenomenon of division of linguistic labor is one which it will be very important for sociolinguistics to investigate. In connection with it, I should like to propose the following hypothesis:

Hypothesis of the Universality of the Division of Linguistic Labor Every linguistic community exemplifies the sort of division of linguistic labor just described: that is, possesses at least some terms whose associated "criteria" are known only to a subset of the speakers who acquire the terms, and whose use by the other speakers depends upon a structured cooperation between them and the speakers in the relevant subsets.

It would be of interest, in particular, to discover if extremely primitive peoples were sometimes exceptions to this hypothesis (which would indicate that the division of linguistic labor is a product of social evolution), or if even they exhibit it. In the latter case, one might conjecture that division of labor, including linguistic labor, is a fundamental trait of our species.

It is easy to see how this phenomenon accounts for some of the examples given above of the failure of the assumptions (1), (2). Whenever a term is subject to the division of linguistic labor, the "average" speaker who acquires it does not acquire anything that fixes its extension. In particular, his individual psychological state *certainly* does not fix its extension; it is only the sociolinguistic state of the collective linguistic body to which the speaker belongs that fixes the extension.

We may summarize this discussion by pointing out that there are two sorts of tools in the world: there are tools like a hammer or a screwdriver which can be used by one person; and there are tools like a steamship which require the cooperative activity of a number of persons to use. Words have been thought of too much on the model of the first sort of tool.

Indexicality and Rigidity[4]

The first of our science-fiction examples—"water" on Earth and on Twin Earth in 1750—does not involve division of linguistic labor, or at least does not involve it in the same way the examples of "aluminum" and "elm" do. There were not (in our story, anyway) any "experts" on water on Earth in 1750, nor any experts on "water" on Twin Earth. (The example *can* be construed as involving division of labor *across time*, however. I shall not develop this method of treating the example here.) The example *does* involve things which are of fundamental importance to the theory of reference and also to the theory of necessary truth, which we shall now discuss.

There are two obvious ways of telling someone what one means by a natural-kind term such as "water" or "tiger" or "lemon." One can give him a so-called ostensive definition—"this (liquid) is water"; "this (animal) is a tiger"; "this (fruit) is a lemon"; where the parentheses are meant to indicate that the "markers" *liquid, animal, fruit,* may be either explicit or implicit. Or one can give him a *description*. In the latter case the description one gives typically consists of one or more markers together with a *stereotype* ... —a standardized description of features of the kind that are typical, or "normal," or at any rate stereotypical. The central features of the stereotype generally are *criteria*—features which in normal situations constitute ways of recognizing if a thing belongs to the kind or, at least, necessary conditions (or probabilistic necessary conditions) for membership in the kind. Not all criteria used by the linguistic community as a collective body are included in the stereotype, and in some cases the stereotypes may be quite weak. Thus (unless I am a very atypical speaker), the stereotype of an elm is just that of a common deciduous tree. These features are indeed necessary conditions for membership in the kind (I mean "necessary" in a loose sense; I don't think "elm trees are deciduous" is *analytic*), but they fall far short of constituting a way of recognizing elms. On the other hand, the stereotype of a tiger does enable one to recognize tigers (unless they are albino, or some other atypical circumstance is present), and the stereotype of a lemon generally enables one to recognize lemons. In the extreme case, the stereotype may be *just* the marker: the stereotype of molybdenum might be *just* that molybdenum is a *metal*. Let us consider both of these ways of introducing a term into someone's vocabulary.

Suppose I point to a glass of liquid and say "*this* is water," in order to teach someone the word "water." We have already described some of the empirical presuppositions of this act, and the way in which this kind of meaning-explanation is defeasible. Let us now try to clarify further how it is supposed to be taken.

In what follows, we shall take the notion of "possible world" as primitive. We do this because we feel that in several senses the notion makes sense and is scientifically important even if it needs to be made more precise. We shall assume further that in at least some cases it is possible to speak of the same individual as existing in more than one possible world.[5] Our discussion leans heavily on the work of Saul Kripke, although the conclusions were obtained independently.

Let W_1 and W_2 be two possible worlds in which I exist and in which this glass exists and in which I am giving a meaning explanation by pointing to this glass and saying "this is water." (We do *not* assume that the *liquid* in the glass is the same in both worlds.) Let us suppose that in W_1 the glass is full of H_2O and in W_2 the glass is full of *XYZ*. We shall also suppose that W_1 is the *actual* world and that *XYZ* is the stuff typically called "water" in the world W_2 (so that the relation between English speakers in W_1 and English speakers in W_2 is exactly the same as the relation between English speakers on Earth and English speakers on Twin Earth). Then there are two theories one might have concerning the meaning of "water."

(1) One might hold that "water" was *world-relative* but *constant* in meaning (i.e. the word has a *constant relative meaning*). In this theory, "water" *means the same* in W_1 and W_2; it's just that water is H_2O in W_1 and water is *XYZ* in W_2.
(2) One might hold that water is H_2O in all worlds (the stuff called "water" in W_2 isn't water), but "water" doesn't have the same meaning in W_1 and W_2.

If what was said before about the Twin Earth case was correct, then (2) is clearly the correct theory. When I say "*this* (liquid) is water," the "this" is, so to speak, a *de re* "this"—i.e. the force of my explanation is that "water" is whatever bears a certain equivalence relation (the relation we called "same_L" above) to the piece of liquid referred to as "this" *in the actual world*. . . .

Kripke calls a designator "rigid" (in a given sentence) if (in that sentence) it refers to the same individual in every possible world in which the designator designates. If we extend the notion of rigidity to substance names, then we may express Kripke's theory and mine by saying that the term "water" is *rigid*. . . .

We may also say, following Kripke, that when I give the ostensive definition "*this* (liquid) is water," the demonstrative "this" is *rigid*. . . .

Suppose, now, that I discover the microstructure of water—that water is H_2O. At this point I will be able to say that the stuff on Twin Earth that I earlier *mistook* for water isn't really water. In the same way, if you describe not another planet in the actual universe, but another possible universe in which there is stuff with the chemical formula *XYZ* which passes the "operational test" for *water*, we shall have to say that that stuff isn't water but merely *XYZ*. You will not have described a possible world in which "water is *XYZ*," but merely a possible world in which there are lakes of *XYZ*, people drink *XYZ* (and not water), or whatever. In fact, once we have discovered the nature of water, nothing counts as a possible world in which water doesn't have that nature. Once we have discovered that water (in the actual world) is H_2O, *nothing counts as a possible world in which water isn't* H_2O. In particular, if a "logically possible" statement is one that holds in some "logically possible world," *it isn't logically possible that water isn't* H_2O.

On the other hand, we can perfectly well imagine having experiences that would convince us (and that would make it rational to believe that) water *isn't* H_2O. In that sense, it is conceivable that water isn't H_2O. It is conceivable but it isn't logically possible! Conceivability is no proof of logical possibility.

Kripke refers to statements which are rationally unrevisable (assuming there are such) as *epistemically necessary*. Statements which are true in all possible worlds he refers to simply as necessary (or sometimes as "metaphysically necessary"). In this terminology, the point just made can be restated as: a statement can be (metaphysically) necessary and epistemically contingent. Human intuition has no privileged access to metaphysical necessity....

In this paper our interest is in theory of meaning, however, and not in theory of necessary truth. Points closely related to Kripke's have been made in terms of the notion of *indexicality*.[6] Words like "now," "this," "here," have long been recognized to be *indexical*, or *token-reflexive*—i.e. to have an extension which varied from context to context or token to token. For these words no one has ever suggested the traditional theory that "intension determines extension." To take our Twin Earth example: if I have a *Doppelgänger* on Twin Earth, then when I think "I have a headache," *he* thinks "I have a headache." But the extension of the particular token of "I" in his verbalized thought is himself (or his unit class, to be precise), while the extension of the token of "I" in *my* verbalized thought is *me* (or my unit class, to be precise). So the same word, "I," has two different extensions in two different idiolects; but it does not follow that the concept I have of myself is in any way different from the concept my *Doppelgänger* has of himself.

Now then, we have maintained that indexicality extends beyond the *obviously* indexical words and morphemes (e.g. the tenses of verbs). Our theory can be summarized as saying that words like "water" have an unnoticed indexical component: "water" is stuff that bears a certain similarity relation to the water *around here*. Water at another time or in another place or even in another possible world has to bear the relation $same_L$ to *our* "water" *in order to be water*. Thus the theory that (1) words have "intensions," which are something like concepts associated with the words by speakers; and that (2) intension determines extension—cannot be true of natural-kind words like "water" for the same reason the theory cannot be true of obviously indexical words like "I."

The theory that natural-kind words like "water" are indexical leaves it open, however, whether to say that "water" in the Twin Earth dialect of English has the same *meaning* as "water" in the Earth dialect and a different extension (which is what we normally say about "I" in different idiolects), thereby giving up the doctrine that "meaning (intension) determines extension"; or to say, as we have chosen to do, that difference is extension is *ipso facto* a difference in meaning for natural-kind words, thereby giving up the doctrine that meanings are concepts, or, indeed, mental entities of *any* kind....

Another misunderstanding that should be avoided is the following: to take the account we have developed as implying that the members of the extension of a natural-kind word necessarily *have* a common hidden structure. It could have turned out that the bits of liquid we call "water" had *no* important common physical characteristics *except* the superficial ones. In that case the necessary and sufficient condition for being "water" would have been possession of sufficiently many of the superficial characteristics.

Incidentally, the last statement does not imply that water could have failed to have a hidden structure (or that water could have been anything but H_2O). When we say that it could have *turned out* that water had no hidden structure what we mean is that a liquid with no hidden structure (i.e. many bits of different liquids, with nothing in common *except* superficial characteristics) could have looked like water, tasted like water, and have filled the lakes, etc., that are actually full of water. In short, we could have been in the same epistemological situation with respect to a liquid with no hidden structure as we were actually with respect to water at one time. Compare Kripke on the "lectern made of ice" (Kripke, 1972).

There are, in fact, almost continuously many cases. Some diseases, for example, have turned out to have no hidden structure (the only thing the paradigm cases have in comon is a cluster of symptoms), while others have turned out to have a common hidden structure in the sense of an etiology (e.g. tuberculosis). Sometimes we still don't know; there is a controversy still raging about the case of multiple sclerosis.

An interesting case is the case of *jade*. Although the Chinese do not recognize a difference, the term "jade" applies to two minerals: jadeite and nephrite. Chemically, there is a marked difference. Jadeite is a combination of sodium and aluminum. Nephrite is made of calcium, magnesium, and iron. These two quite different microstructures produce the same unique textural qualities!

Coming back to the Twin Earth example, for a moment; if H_2O and *XYZ* had both been plentiful on Earth, then we would have had a case similar to the jadeite/nephrite case: it would have been correct to say that there were *two kinds of "water."* And instead of saying that "the stuff on Twin Earth turned out not to really be water," we would have to say "it turned out to be the *XYZ kind of water.*"

To sum up: if there is a hidden structure, then generally it determines what it is to be a member of the natural kind, not only in the actual world, but in all possible worlds. Put another way, it determines what we can and cannot counterfactually suppose about the natural kind ("water could have all been vapor?" yes/"water could have been *XYZ*" no). But the local water, or whatever, may have two or more hidden structures—or so many that "hidden structure" becomes irrelevant, and superficial characteristics become the decisive ones....

Meaning

Let us now see where we are with respect to the notion of meaning. We have now seen that the extension of a term is not fixed by a concept that the individual speaker has in his head, and this is true both because extension is, in general, determined *socially*—there is division of linguistic labor as much as of "real" labor—and because extension is, in part, determined *indexically*. The extension of our terms depends upon the actual nature of the particular things that serve as paradigms,[7] and this actual nature is not, in general, fully known to the speaker. Traditional semantic theory leaves out only two contributions to the determination of extension—the contribution of society and the contribution of the real world!

We saw at the outset that meaning cannot be identified with extension. Yet it cannot be identified with "intension" either, if intension is something like an individual speaker's *concept*. What are we to do?

There are two plausible routes that we might take. One route would be to retain the identification of meaning with concept and pay the price of giving up the idea that meaning determines extension. If we followed this route, we might say that "water" has the same *meaning* on Earth and on Twin Earth, but a different *extension*. (Not just a different *local* extension but a different *global* extension. The *XYZ* on Twin Earth isn't in the extension of the tokens of "water" that I utter, but it is in the extension of the tokens of "water" that my *Doppelgänger* utters, and this isn't just because Twin Earth is far away from me, since molecules of H_2O are in the extension of the tokens of "water" that I utter no matter how far away from me they are in space and time. Also, what I can counterfactually suppose water to be is different from what my *Doppelgänger* can counterfactually suppose "water" to be.) While this is the correct route to take for an *absolutely* indexical word like "I," it seems incorrect for the words we have been discussing. Consider "elm" and "beech," for example. If these are "switched" on Twin Earth, then surely we would *not* say that "elm" has the same meaning on Earth and Twin Earth, even if my *Doppelgänger's* stereotype of a beech (or an "elm," as he calls it) is identical with my stereotype of an elm. Rather, we would say that "elm" in my *Doppelgänger's* idiolect means *beech*. For this reason, it seems preferable to take a different route and identify "meaning" with an ordered pair (or possibly an ordered *n-tuple*) of entities, *one of which is the extension.* (The other components of the, so to speak, "meaning vector" will be specified later.) Doing this makes it trivially true that *meaning determines extension* (i.e. difference in extension is *ipso facto* difference in meaning), but totally abandons the idea that if there is a difference in the meaning my *Doppelgänger* and I assign to a word, then there *must* be some difference in our concepts (or in our psychological state). Following this route, we can say that my *Doppelgänger* and I *mean something different* when we say "elm," but this will not be an assertion about our psychological states. All this means is that the tokens of the word he utters have a different extension than the tokens of the word I utter; but this difference in extension is not a reflection of any difference in our individual linguistic competence considered in isolation.

If this is correct, and I think it is, then the traditional problem of meaning splits into two problems. The first problem is to account for the *determination of extension*. Since, in many cases, extension is determined socially and not individually, owing to the division of linguistic labor, I believe that this problem is properly a problem for sociolinguistics. Solving it would involve spelling out in detail exactly how the division of linguistic labor works....

The other problem is to describe *individual competence*. Extension may be determined socially, in many cases, but we don't assign the standard extension to the tokens of a word *W* uttered by Jones *no matter how* Jones uses *W*. Jones has to have some particular ideas and skills in connection with *W* in order to play his part in the linguistic division of labor. Once we give up the idea that individual competence has to be so strong as to actually determine extension, we can begin to study it in a fresh frame of mind....

The Meaning of "Meaning"

... Briefly, my proposal is to define "meaning" not by picking out an object which will be identified with the meaning (although that might be done in the usual set-theoretic style if one insists), but by specifying a normal form (or, rather, a *type* of normal form) for the description of meaning. If we know what a "normal form description" of the meaning of a word should be, then, as far as I am concerned, we know what meaning *is* in any scientifically interesting sense.

My proposal is that the normal form description of the meaning of a word should be a finite sequence, or "vector," whose components should certainly include the following (it might be desirable to have other types of components as well): (1) the syntactic markers that apply to the word, e.g. "noun"; (2) the semantic markers that apply to the word, e.g. "animal," "period of time"; (3) a description of the additional features of the stereotype, if any; (4) a description of the extension.

The following convention is a part of this proposal: the components of the vector all represent a hypothesis about the individual speaker's competence, *except the extension*. Thus the normal form description for "water" might be, in part:

Syntactic Markers	*Semantic Markers*	*Stereotype*	*Extension*
mass noun, concrete;	natural kind; liquid;	colorless; transparent; tasteless; thirst-quenching; etc.	H_2O (give or take impurities)

—this does *not* mean that knowledge of the fact that water is H_2O is being imputed to the individual speaker or even to the society. It means that (*we* say) the extension of the term "water" as *they* (the speakers in question) use it is *in fact* H_2O....

In particular the representation of the words "water" in Earth dialect and "water" in Twin Earth dialect would be the same except that in the last column the normal form description of the Twin Earth word "water" would have *XYZ* and not H_2O. This means, in view of what has just been said, that we are ascribing the *same* linguistic competence to the typical Earthian/Twin Earthian speaker, but a different extension to the word, nonetheless.

This proposal means that we keep assumption (II) of our early discussion. Meaning determines extension—by construction, so to speak. But (I) is given up; the psychological state of the individual speaker does not determine "what he means."

In most contexts this will agree with the way we speak, I believe. But one paradox: suppose Oscar is a German–English bilingual. In our view, in his total collection of dialects, the words "beech" and *Buche* are *exact synonyms*. The normal form descriptions of their meanings would be identical. But he might very well not know that they are synonyms! A speaker can have two synonyms in his vocabulary and not know that they are synonyms!...

On just about any materialist theory, believing a proposition is likely to involve processing some *representation* of that proposition, be it a sentence in a language, a piece of "brain code," a thought form, or whatever. Materialists, and not only materialists, are reluctant to think that one can believe propositions *neat*. But even materialists tend to believe that, if one believes a proposition, *which* representation one employs is (pardon the pun) immaterial. If S_1 and S_2 are both representations that are *available* to me, then if I believe the proposition expressed by S_1 under the representation S_1, I must also believe it under the representation S_2—at least, I must do this if I have any claim to rationality. But, as we have just seen, this isn't right. Oscar may well believe that *this* is a "beech" (it has a sign on it that says "beech"), but not believe or disbelieve that this is a "*Buche*." It is not just that belief is a process involving representations; he believes the proposition (if one wants to introduce "propositions" at all) under one representation and not under another.

The amazing thing about the theory of meaning is how long the subject has been in the grip of philosophical misconceptions, and how strong these misconceptions are. Meaning has been identified with a necessary and sufficient condition by philosopher after philosopher. In the empiricist tradition, it has been identified with method of verification, again by philosopher after philosopher. Nor have these misconceptions had the virtue of exclusiveness; not a few philosophers have held that meaning = method of verification = necessary and sufficient condition.

On the other side, it is amazing how weak the grip of the facts has been. After all, what have been pointed out in this essay are little more than home truths about the way we use words and how much (or rather, how little) we actually know when we use them. My own reflection on these matters began after I published a paper in which I confidently maintained that the meaning of a word was "a battery of semantical rules," ... and then began to wonder how the meaning of the common word "gold" could be accounted for in this way. And it is not that philosophers had never considered such examples: Locke, for example, uses this word as an example and is not troubled by the idea that its meaning is a necessary and sufficient condition!

If there is a reason for both learned and lay opinion having gone so far astray with respect to a topic which deals, after all, with matters which are in everyone's experience, matters concerning which we all have more data than we know what to do with, matters concerning which we have, if we shed preconceptions, pretty clear intuitions, it must be connected to the fact that the grotesquely mistaken views of language which are and always have been current reflect two specific and very central philosophical tendencies: the tendency to treat cognition as a purely *individual* matter and the tendency to ignore the *world*, insofar as it consists of more than the individual's "observations." Ignoring the division of linguistic labor is ignoring the social dimension of cognition; ignoring what we have called the *indexicality* of most words is ignoring the contribution of the environment. Traditional philosophy of language, like much traditional philosophy, leaves out other people and the world; a better philosophy and a better science of language must encompass both.

Notes

1. This is discussed by Ziff (1972) especially chapter VIII.

2. This tradition grew up because *the* term whose analysis provoked all the discussion in medieval philosophy was the term "God," and the term "God" was thought to be defined through the conjunction of the terms "Good," "Powerful," "Omniscient," etc.—the so called "Perfections." There was a problem, however, because God was supposed to be a Unity, and Unity was thought to exclude His essence being complex in *any* way—i.e. "God" was defined through a conjunction of terms, but God (without quotes) could not be the logical product of properties, nor could He be the unique thing exemplifying the logical product of two or more *distinct* properties, because even this highly abstract kind of "complexity" was held to be incompatible with His perfection of Unity. This is a theological paradox with which Jewish, Arabic, and Christian theologians wrestled for centuries (e.g. the doctrine of the Negation of Privation in Maimonides and Aquinas). It is amusing that theories of contemporary interest, such as conceptualism and nominalism, were first proposed as solutions to the problem of predication in the case of God. It is also amusing that the favorite model of definition in all of this theology—the conjunction-of-properties model—should survive, at least through its consequences, in philosophy of language until the present day.

3. Or rather, they will report: "On Twin Earth (*the Twin Earthian name for Terra*—H.P.) the word 'water' means H_2O."

4. The substance of this section was presented at a series of lectures I gave at the University of Washington (Summer Institute in Philosophy) in 1968, and at a lecture at the University of Minnesota.

5. This assumption is not actually needed in what follows. What *is* needed is that the same *natural kind* can exist in more than one possible world.

6. These points were made in my 1968 lectures at the University of Washington and the University of Minnesota.

7. I *don't* have in mind the Flewish notion of "paradigm" in which any paradigm of a *K* is *necessarily* a *K* (in reality).

52 From "Individualism and the Mental"

Tyler Burge

Since Hegel's *Phenomenology of Spirit,* a broad, inarticulate division of emphasis between the individual and his social environment has marked philosophical discussions of mind. On one hand, there is the traditional concern with the individual subject of mental states and events. In the elderly Cartesian tradition, the spotlight is on what exists or transpires "in" the individual—his secret cogitations, his innate cognitive structures, his private perceptions and introspections, his grasping of ideas, concepts, or forms. More evidentially oriented movements, such as behaviorism and its liberalized progeny, have highlighted the individual's publicly observable behavior—his input-output relations and the dispositions, states, or events that mediate them. But both Cartesian and behaviorist viewpoints tend to feature the individual subject. On the other hand, there is the Hegelian preoccupation with the role of social institutions in shaping the individual and the content of his thought. This tradition has dominated the continent since Hegel. But is has found echoes in English-speaking philosophy during this century in the form of a concentration on language. Much philosophical work on language and mind has been in the interests of Cartesian or behaviorist viewpoints that I shall term "individualistic." But many of Wittgenstein's remarks about mental representation point up a social orientation that is discernible from his flirtations with behaviorism. And more recent work on the theory of reference has provided glimpses of the role of social cooperation in determining what an individual thinks.

In many respects, of course, these emphases within philosophy—individualistic and social—are compatible. To an extent, they may be regarded simply as different currents in the turbulent stream of ideas that has washed the intellectual landscape during the last hundred and some odd years. But the role of the social environment has received considerably less clear-headed philosophical attention (though perhaps not less philosophical attention) than the role of the states, occurrences, or acts in, on, or by the individual. Philosophical discussions of social factors have tended to be obscure, evocative, metaphorical, or platitudinous, or to be bent on establishing some large thesis about the course of history and the destiny of man. There remains much room for sharp delineation. I shall offer some considerations that stress social factors in descriptions of an individual's mental phenomena. These considerations call into question individualistic presuppositions of several traditional and modern treatments of mind. I shall conclude with some remarks about mental models.

I Terminological Matters

Our ordinary mentalistic discourse divides broadly into two sorts of idiom. One typically makes reference to mental states or events in terms of sentential expressions. The other does not. A clear case of the first kind of idiom is "Alfred thinks that his friends' sofa is ugly." A clear case of the second sort is "Alfred is in pain." Thoughts, beliefs, intentions, and so forth are typically specified in terms of subordinate sentential clauses, that-clauses, which may be judged as true or false. Pains, feels, tickles, and so forth have no special semantical relation to sentences or to truth or falsity. There are intentional idioms that fall in the second category on this characterization, but that share important semantical features with expressions in the first—idioms like "Al worships Buicks." But I shall not sort these out here. I shall discuss only the former kind of mentalistic idiom. The extension of the discussion to other intentional idioms will not be difficult.

In an ordinary sense, the noun phrases that embed sentential expressions in mentalistic idioms provide the *content* of the mental state or event. We shall call that-clauses and their grammatical variants *"content clauses."* Thus the expression "that sofas are more comfortable than pews" provides the content of Alfred's belief that sofas are more comfortable than pews. My phrase "provides the content" represents an attempt at remaining neutral, at least for present purposes, among various semantical and metaphysical accounts of precisely how that-clauses function and precisely what, if anything, contents are.

Although the notion of content is, for present purposes, ontologically neutral, I do think of it as holding a place in a systematic *theory* of mentalistic language. The question of when to count contents different, and when the same, is answerable to theoretical restrictions. It is often remarked that in a given context we may ascribe to a person two that-clauses that are only loosely equivalent and count them as attributions of the "same attitude." We may say that Al's intention to climb Mt. McKinley and his intention to climb the highest mountain in the United States are the "same intention." (I intend the terms for the mountain to occur obliquely here. See later discussion.) This sort of point extends even to content clauses with extensionally non-equivalent counterpart notions. For contextually relevant purposes, we might count a thought that the glass contains some water as "the same thought" as a thought that the glass contains some thirst-quenching liquid, particularly if we have no reason to attribute either content as opposed to the other, and distinctions between them are contextually irrelevant. Nevertheless, in both these examples, every systematic theory I know of would want to represent the semantical contribution of the content-clauses in distinguishable ways—as "providing different contents."

One reason for doing so is that the person himself is capable of having different attitudes described by the different content-clauses, even if these differences are irrelevant in a particular context. (Al might have developed the intention to climb the highest mountain before developing the intention to climb Mt. McKinley—regardless of whether he, in fact, did so.) A second reason is that the counterpart components of the that-clauses allude to distinguishable elements in people's cognitive lives. "Mt. McKinley" and "the highest mountain in the U.S." serve, or might serve, to indicate cognitively different notions. This is a vague, informal way of generalizing Frege's point: the thought that Mt. McKinley is the highest mountain in the U.S. is potentially interesting or informative. The thought that Mt. McKinley is Mt. McKinley is not. Thus when we say in a given context that attribution of different contents is attribution of the "same attitude," we use "same attitude" in a way similar to the way we use "same car" when we say that people who drive Fords (or green 1970 Ford Mavericks) drive the "same car." For contextual purposes different cars are counted as "amounting to the same."

Although this use of "content" is theoretical, it is not I think theoretically controversial. In cases where we shall be counting contents different, the cases will be uncontentious: On any systematic theory, differences in the *extension*—the actual denotation, referent, or application—of counterpart expressions in that-clauses will be semantically represented, and will, in our terms, make for differences in content. I shall be avoiding the more controversial, but interesting, questions about the general conditions under which sentences in that-clauses can be expected to provide the same content.

I should also warn of some subsidiary terms. I shall be (and have been) using the term *"notion"* to apply to components or elements of contents. Just as whole that-clauses provide the content of a person's attitude, semantically relevant components of that-clauses will be taken to indicate notions that enter into the attitude (or the attitude's content). This term is supposed to be just as ontologically neutral as its fellow. When I talk of understanding or mastering the notion of contract, I am not relying on any special epistemic or ontological theory, except insofar as the earlier-mentioned theoretical restrictions on the notion of content are inherited by the notion of notion. The expression, *"understanding (mastering) a notion"* is to be construed more or less intuitively. Understanding the notion of contract comes roughly to knowing what a contract is. One can master the notion of contract without mastering the term "contract"—at the very least if one speaks some language other than English that has a term roughly synonymous with "contract." (An analogous point holds for my use of "mastering a content.") Talk of notions is roughly similar to talk of concepts in an informal sense. "Notion" has the advantage of being easier to separate from traditional theoretical commitments.

I speak of *attributing* an attitude, content, or notion, and of *ascribing* a that-clause or other piece of language. Ascriptions are the linguistic analogs of attributions. This use of "ascribe" is nonstandard, but convenient and easily assimilated.

There are semantical complexities involving the behavior of expressions in content clauses, most of which we can skirt. But some must be touched on. Basic to the subject is the observation that expressions in content clauses are often not intersubstitutable with extensionally equivalent expressions in such a way as to maintain the truth value of the containing sentence. Thus from the facts that water is H_2O and that Bertrand thought that water is not fit to drink, it does not follow that Bertrand thought that H_2O is not fit to drink. When an expression like "water" functions in a content clause so that it is not freely exchangeable with all extensionally equivalent expressions, we shall say that it has *oblique occurrence*. Roughly speaking, the reason why "water" and "H_2O" are not interchangeable in our report of Bertrand's thought is that "water" plays a role in characterizing a different mental act or state from that which "H_2O" would play a role in characterizing. In this context at least, thinking that water is not fit to drink is different from thinking that H_2O is not fit to drink.

By contrast, there are non-oblique occurrences of expressions in content clauses. One might say that some water—say, the water in the glass over there—is thought by Bertrand to be impure; or that Bertrand thought that *that* water is impure. And one might intend to make no distinction that would be lost by replacing "water" with "H_2O"—or "that water" with "that H_2O" or "that common liquid," or any other expression extensionally equivalent with "that water." We might allow these exchanges even though Bertrand had never heard of, say, H_2O. In such purely nonoblique occurrences, "water" plays *no role* in providing the *content* of Bertrand's thought, *on our use of "content,"* or (in any narrow sense) in characterizing Bertrand or his mental state. Nor is the water part of Bertrand's thought content. We speak of Bertrand *thinking his content of* the water. At its nonoblique occurrence, the term "that water" simply isolates, in one of many equally good ways, a portion of wet stuff to which Bertrand or his thought is related or applied. In certain cases, it may also mark a context in which Bertrand's thought is applied. But it is expressions at oblique occurrences within content clauses that primarily do the job of providing the content of mental states or events, and in characterizing the person.

Mentalistic discourse containing obliquely occurring expressions has traditionally been called *intentional discourse*. The historical reasons for this nomenclature are complex and partly confused. But roughly speaking, grammatical contexts involving oblique occurrences have been fixed upon as specially relevant to the representational character (sometimes called "intentionality") of mental states and events. Clearly oblique occurrences in mentalistic discourse have something to do with characterizing a person's epistemic perspective—how things seem to him, or in an informal sense, how they are represented to him. So without endorsing all the commitments of this tradition, I shall take over its terminology....

II A Thought Experiment

IIa First Case

We now turn to a three-step thought experiment. Suppose first that:

> A given person has a large number of attitudes commonly attributed with content clauses containing "arthritis" in oblique occurrence. For example, he thinks (correctly) that he has had arthritis for years, that his arthritis in his wrists and fingers is more painful than his arthritis in his ankles, that it is better to have arthritis than cancer of the liver, that stiffening joints is a symptom of arthritis, that certain sorts of aches are characteristic of arthritis, that there are various kinds of arthritis, and so forth. In short, he has a wide range of such attitudes. In addition to these unsurprising attitudes, he thinks falsely that he has developed arthritis in the thigh.

Generally competent in English, rational and intelligent, the patient exports to his doctor his fear that his arthritis has now lodged in his thigh. The doctor replies by telling him that this cannot be so, since arthritis is specifically an inflammation of joints. Any dictionary could have told him the same. The patient is surprised, but relinquishes his view and goes on to ask what might be wrong with his thigh.

The second step of the thought experiment consists of a counterfactual supposition. We are to conceive of a situation in which the patient proceeds from birth through the same course of physical events that he actually does, right to and including the time at which he first reports his fear to his doctor. Precisely the same things (non-intentionally described) happen to him. He has the same physiological history, the same diseases, the same internal physical occurrences. He goes through the same motions, engages in the same behavior, has the same sensory intake (physiologically described). His dispositions to respond to stimuli are explained in physical theory as the effects of the same proximate causes. All of this extends to his interaction with linguistic expressions. He says and hears the same words (word forms) at the same times he actually does. He develops the disposition to assent to "Arthritis can occur in the thigh" and "I have arthritis in the thigh" as a result of the same physically described proximate causes. Such dispositions might have arisen in a number of ways. But we can suppose that in both actual and counterfactual situations, he acquires the word "arthritis" from casual conversation or reading, and never hearing anything to prejudice him for or against applying it in the way that he does, he applies the word to an ailment in his thigh (or to ailments in the limbs of others) which seems to produce pains or other symptoms roughly similar to the disease in his hands and ankles. In both actual and counterfactual cases, the disposition is never reinforced or extinguished up until the time when he expresses himself to his doctor. We further imagine that the patient's non-intentional, phenomenal experience is the same. He has the same pains, visual fields, images, and internal verbal rehearsals. The *counterfactuality* in the supposition touches only the patient's social environment. In actual fact, "arthritis," as used in his community, does not apply to ailments outside joints. Indeed, it fails to do so by a standard, non-technical dictionary definition. But in our imagined case, physicians, lexicographers, and informed laymen apply "arthritis" not only to arthritis but to various other rheumatoid ailments. The standard use of the term is to be conceived to encompass the patient's actual misuse. We could imagine either that arthritis had not been singled out as a family of diseases, or that some other term besides "arthritis" were applied, though not commonly by laymen, specifically to arthritis. We may also suppose that this difference and those necessarily associated with it are the only differences between the counterfactual situation and the actual one. (Other people besides the patient will, of course, behave differently.) To summarize the second step:

> The person might have had the same physical history and non-intentional mental phenomena while the word "arthritis" was conventionally applied, and defined to apply, to various rheumatoid ailments, including the one in the person's thigh, as well as to arthritis.

The final step is an interpretation of the counterfactual case, or an addition to is as so far described. It is reasonable to suppose that:

> In the counterfactual situation, the patient lacks some—probably *all*—of the attitudes commonly attributed with content clauses containing "arthritis" in oblique occurrence. He lacks the occurrent thoughts or beliefs that he has arthritis in the thigh, that he has had arthritis for years, that stiffening joints and various sorts of aches are symptoms of arthritis, that his father had arthritis, and so on.

We suppose that in the counterfactual case we cannot correctly ascribe any content clause containing an oblique occurrence of the term "arthritis." It is hard to see how the patient could have picked up the notion of arthritis. The word "arthritis" in the counterfactual community does not mean *arthritis*. It does not apply only to inflammations of joints. We suppose that no other word in the patient's repertoire means *arthritis*. "Arthritis," in the counterfactual situation, differs both in dictionary definition and in extension from "arthritis" as we use it. Our ascriptions of content clauses to the patient (and ascriptions within his community) would not constitute attributions of the same contents we actually attribute. For counterpart expressions in the content clauses that are actually and counterfactually ascribable are not even extensionally equivalent. However we describe the patient's attitudes in the counterfactual situation, it will not be with a term or phrase extensionally equivalent with "arthritis." So the patient's counterfactual attitude contents differ from his actual ones.

The upshot of these reflections is that the patient's mental contents differ while his entire physical and non-intentional mental histories, considered in isolation from their social context, remain the same. (We could have supposed that he dropped dead at the time he first expressed his fear to the doctor.) The differences seem to stem from differences "outside" the patient considered as an isolated physical organism, causal mechanism, or seat of consciousness. The difference in his mental contents is attributable to differences in his social environment. In sum, the patient's internal qualitative experiences, his physiological states and events, his behaviorally described stimuli and responses, his dispositions to behave, and whatever sequences of states (non-intentionally described) mediated his input and output—all these remain constant, while his attitude contents differ, even in the extensions of counterpart notions. As we observed at the outset, such differences are ordinarily taken to spell differences in mental states and events.

IIb Further Exemplifications

The argument has an extremely wide application. It does not depend, for example, on the kind of word "arthritis" is. We could have used an artifact term, an ordinary natural kind word, a color adjective, a social role term, a term for a historical style, an abstract noun, an action verb, a physical movement verb, or any of various other sorts of words. I prefer to leave open precisely how far one can generalize the argument. But I think it has a very wide scope. The argument can get under way in any case where it is intuitively possible to attribute a mental state or event whose content involves a notion that the subject incompletely understands. As will become clear, this possibility is the key to the thought experiment....

IIc Expansion and Delineation of the Thought Experiment

As I have tried to suggest in the preceding examples, the relevant attributions in the first step of the thought experiment need not display the subject's error. They may be attributions of a true content. We can begin with a propositional attitude that involved the misconceived notion, but in a true, unproblematic application of it: for example, the patient's belief that he, like his father, developed arthritis in the ankles and wrists at age 58 (where "arthritis" occurs obliquely).

One need not even rely on an underlying *mis*conception in the thought experiment. One may pick a case in which the subject only partially understands an expression. He may apply it firmly and correctly in a range of cases, but be unclear or agnostic about certain of its applications or implications which, in fact, are fully established in common practice. Most of the examples we gave previously can be reinterpreted in this way. To take a new one, imagine that our protagonist is unsure whether his father has mortgages on the car and house, or just one on the house. He is a little uncertain about exactly how the loan and collateral must be arranged in order for there to be a mortgage, and he is not clear abut whether one may have mortgages on anything other than houses. He is sure, however, that Uncle Harry paid off his mortgage. Imagine our man constant in the ways previously indicated and that "mortgage" commonly applied only to mortgages on houses. But imagine banking practices themselves to be the same. Then the subject's uncertainty would plausibly not involve the notion of mortgage. Nor would his other propositional attitudes be correctly attributed with the term "mortgage" in oblique position. Partial understanding is as good as misunderstanding for our purposes.

On the other hand, the thought experiment does appear to depend on the possibility of someone's having a propositional attitude despite an incomplete mastery of some notion in its content. To see why this appears to be so, let us try to run through a thought experiment, attempting to avoid any imputation of incomplete understanding. Suppose the subject thinks falsely that all swans are white. One can certainly hold the features of swans and the subject's non-intentional phenomenal experience, physical history, and non-intentional dispositions constant, and imagine that "swan" meant "white swan" (and perhaps some other term, unfamiliar to the subject, meant what "swan" means). Could one reasonably interpret the subject as having different attitude contents without at some point invoking a misconception? The questions to be asked here are about the subject's dispositions. For example, in the actual case, if he were shown a black swan and told that he was wrong, would he fairly naturally concede his mistake? Or would he respond, "I'm doubtful that that's a swan," until we brought in dictionaries, encyclopedias, and other native speakers to correct his usage? In the latter case, his understanding of "swan" would be deviant. Suppose then that in the actual situation he would respond normally to the counterexample. Then there is reason to say that he understands the notion of swan correctly; and his error is not conceptual or linguistic, but empirical in an ordinary and narrow sense. (Of course, the line we are drawing here is pretty fuzzy.) When one comes to the counterfactual stage of the thought experiment, the subject has the same dispositions to respond pliably to the presentation of a black specimen. But such a response would suggest a misunderstanding of the term "swan" as counterfactually used. For in the counterfactual community, what they call "swans" could not fail to be white. The mere presentation of a black swan would be irrelevant to the definitional truth "All swans are white." I have not set this case up as an example of the thought experiment's going through. Rather I have used it to support the conjecture that *if* the thought experiment is to work, one must at some stage find the subject believing (or having some attitude characterized by) a content, despite an incomplete understanding or misapplication. An ordinary empirical error appears not to be sufficient.

It would be a mistake, however, to think that incomplete understanding, in the sense that the argument requires, is in general an unusual or even deviant phenomenon. *What I have called "partial understanding" is common or even normal in the case of a large number of expressions in our vocabularies.* "Arthritis" is a case in point. Even if by the grace of circumstance a person does not fall into views that run counter to the term's meaning or application, it would not be in the least deviant or "socially unacceptable" to have no clear attitude that would block such views. "Brisket," "contract," "recession," "sonata," "deer," "elm" (to borrow a well-known example), "preamplifier," "carburetor," "gothic," "fermentation," probably provide analogous cases. Continuing the list is largely a matter of patience. The sort of "incomplete understanding" required by the thought experiment includes quite ordinary, nondeviant phenomena.

It is worth remarking that the thought experiment as originally presented might be run in reverse. The idea would be to start with an ordinary belief or thought involving no incomplete understanding. Then we find the incomplete understanding in the second step. For example, properly understanding "arthritis," a patient may think (correctly) that he has arthritis. He happens to have heard of arthritis only occurring in joints, and he correctly believes that that is where arthritis always occurs. Holding his physical history, dispositions, and pain constant, we imagine that "arthritis" commonly applies to rheumatoid ailments of all sorts. Arthritis has not been singled out for special mention. If the patient were told by a doctor "You also have arthritis in the thigh," the patient would be disposed (as he is in the actual case) to respond, "Really? I didn't know that one could have arthritis except in joints." The doctor would answer, "No, arthritis occurs in muscles, tendons, bursas, and elsewhere." The patient would stand corrected. The notion that the doctor and patient would be operating with in such a case would not be that of arthritis....

Even *apart* from reversals of the thought experiment, it is plausible (in the light of its original versions) that our well-understood propositional attitudes depend partly for their content on social factors independent of the individual, asocially and nonintentionally construed. For each of us can reason as follows. Take a set of attitudes that involve a given notion and whose contents are well-understood by me. It is only contingent that I understand that notion as well as I do. Now holding my community's practices constant, imagine that I understand the given notion incompletely, but that the deficient understanding is such that it does not prevent my having attitude contents involving that notion. In fact, imagine that I am in the situation envisaged in the first step of one of the original thought experiments. In such a case, a proper subset of the original set of my actual attitude contents would, or might, remain the same—intuitively, at least those of my actual attitudes whose justification or point is untouched by my imagined deficient understanding. (In the arthritis case, an example would be a true belief that many old people have arthritis.) These attitude contents remain constant despite the fact that my understanding, inference patterns, behavior, dispositions, and so on would in important ways be different and partly inappropriate to applications of the given notion. What is it that enables these unaffected contents to remain applications of the relevant notion? It is not *just* that my understanding, inference patterns, behavior, and so forth are enough like my actual understanding, inference patterns, behavior, and so forth. For if communal practice had *also* varied so as to apply the relevant notion as I am imagining I misapply it, then my attitude contents would not involve the relevant notion at all. This argument suggests that communal practice is a factor (in addition to my understanding, inference patterns, and perhaps behavior, physical activity, and other features) in fixing the contents of my attitudes, even in cases where I fully understand the content.

IId Independence from Factive-Verb and Indexical-Reference Paradigms

The thought experiment does not play on psychological "success" verbs or "factive" verbs—verbs like "know," "regret," "realize," "remember," "foresee," "perceive." This point is important for our purposes because such verbs suggest an easy and clearcut distinction between the contribution of the individual subject and the objective, "veridical" contribution of the environment to making the verbs applicable. (Actually the mater becomes more complicated on reflection, but we shall stay with the simplest cases.) When a person knows that snow is common in Greenland, his knowledge obviously depends on more than the way the person is. It depends on there actually being a lot of snow in Greenland. His mental state (belief that snow is common in Greenland) must be successful in a certain way (true). By changing the environment, one could change the truth value of the content, so that the subject could no longer be said to know the content. It is part of the burden of our argument that even intentional mental states of the individual like beliefs, which carry no implication of veridicality or success, cannot be understood by focusing purely on the individual's acts, dispositions, and "inner" goings on.

The thought experiment also does not rest on the phenomenon of indexicality, or on *de re* attitudes, in any direct way. When Alfred refers to an apple, saying to himself "That is wholesome," what he refers to depends not just on the content of what he says or thinks, but on what apple is before him. Without altering the meaning of Alfred's utterance, the nature of his perceptual experiences, or his physical acts or dispositions, we could conceive an exchange of the actual apple for another one that is indistinguishable to Alfred. We would thereby conceive him as referring to something different and even as saying something with a different truth value....

It seems to me clear that the thought experiment need not rely on *de re* attitudes at all. The subject need not have entered into special *en rapport* or quasi-indexical relations with objects that the misunderstood term applies to in order for the argument to work. We can appeal to attitudes that would usually be regarded as paradigmatic cases of *de dicto*, non-indexical, *non-de-re*, mental attitudes or events. The primary mistake in the contract example is one such, but we could choose others to suit the reader's taste. To insist that such attitudes must all be indexically infected or *de re* would, I think, be to trivialize and emasculate these notions, making nearly all attitudes *de re*. All *de dicto* attitudes presuppose *de re* attitudes. But it does not follow that indexical or *de re* elements survive in every attitude....

I shall not, however, argue this point here. The claim that is crucial is not that our argument does not fix on *de re* attitudes. It is, rather, that the social differences between the actual and counterfactual situations affect the *content* of the subject's attitudes. That is, the difference affects standard cases of obliquely occurring, cognitive-content-conveying expressions in content clauses. For example, still with his misunderstanding, the subject might think that this (referring to his disease in his hands) is arthritis. Or he might think *de re* of the disease in his ankle (or of the disease in his thigh) that his arthritis is painful. It does not really matter whether the relevant attitude is *de re* or purely *de dicto*. What is crucial to our argument is that the occurrence of "arthritis" is oblique and contributes to a characterization of the subject's mental content. One might even hold, implausibly I think, that all the subject's attitudes involving the notion of arthritis are *de re*, that "arthritis" in that-clauses *indexically* picks out the property of being arthritis, or something like that. The fact remains that the term occurs obliquely in the relevant cases and serves in characterizing the *dicta* or contents of the subject's attitudes. The thought experiment exploits this fact.

Approaches to the mental that I shall later criticize as excessively individualistic tend to assimilate environmental aspects of mental phenomena to either the factive-verb or indexical-reference paradigm.... This sort of assimilation suggests that one might maintain a relatively clearcut distinction between extramental and mental aspects of mentalistic attributions. And it may encourage the idea that the distinctively mental aspects can be understood fundamentally in terms of the individual's abilities, dispositions, states, and so forth, considered in isolation from his social surroundings. Our argument undermines this latter suggestion. Social context infects even the distinctively mental features of mentalistic attributions. No man's intentional mental phenomena are insular. Every man is a piece of the social continent, a part of the social main.

III Reinterpretations

IIIa Methodology

I find that most people unspoiled by conventional philosophical training regard the three steps of the thought experiment as painfully obvious. Such folk tend to chafe over my filling in details or elaborating on strategy. I think this naivete appropriate. But for sophisticates the three steps require defense.

Before launching a defense, I want to make a few remarks about its methodology. My objective is to better understand our common mentalistic notions. Although such notions are subject to revision and refinement, I take it as evident that there is philosophical interest in theorizing about them as they now are. I assume that a primary way of achieving theoretical understanding is to concentrate on our *discourse* about mentalistic notions. Now it is, of course, never obvious at the outset how much idealization, regimentation, or special interpretation is necessary in order to adequately understand ordinary discourse. Phenomena such as ambiguity, ellipsis, indexicality, idioms, and a host of others certainly demand some regimentation or special interpretation for purposes of linguistic theory. Moreover, more global considerations—such as simplicity in accounting for structural relations—often have effects on the cast of one's theory. For all that, there is a methodological bias in favor of taking natural discourse literally, other things being equal. For example, unless there are clear reasons for construing discourse as ambiguous, elliptical or involving special idioms, we should not so construe it. Literal interpretation is *ceteris paribus* preferred. My defense of the thought experiment, as I have interpreted it, partly rests on this principle....

IIIb Incomplete Understanding and Standard Cases of Reinterpretation

The first step, as I have interpreted it, is the most likely to encounter opposition. In fact, there is a line of resistance that is second nature to linguistically oriented philosophers. According to this line, we should deny that, say, the patient really believed or thought that arthritis can occur outside of joints because he misunderstood the word "arthritis." More generally, we should deny that a subject could have any attitudes whose contents he incompletely understands.

What a person understands is indeed one of the chief factors that bear on what thoughts he can express in using words. If there were not deep and important connections between propositional attitudes and understanding, one could hardly expect one's attributions of mental content to facilitate reliable predictions of what a person will do, say, or think. But our examples provide reason to believe that these connections are not simple entailments to the effect that having a propositional attitude strictly implies full understanding of its content.

There are, of course, numerous situations in which we normally reinterpret or discount a person's words in deciding what he thinks. Philosophers often invoke such cases to bolster their animus against such attributions as the ones we made to our subjects: "If a foreigner were to mouth the words 'arthritis may occur in the thigh' or 'my father had arthritis,' not understanding what he uttered in the slightest, we would not say that he believed that arthritis may occur in the thigh, or that his father had arthritis. So why should we impute the belief to the patient?" Why, indeed? Or rather, why do we?

The question is a good one. We do want a general account of these cases. But the implied argument against our attribution is anemic. We tacitly and routinely distinguish between the cases I described and those in which a foreigner (or anyone) utters something without any comprehension. The best way to understand mentalistic notions is to recognize such differences in standard practice and try to account for them. One can hardly justify the assumption that full understanding of a content is in general a necessary condition for believing the content by appealing to some cases that tend to support the assumption in order to reject others that conflict with it.

It is a good method of discovery, I think, to note the sorts of cases philosophers tend to gravitate toward when they defend the view that the first step in the thought experiment should receive special interpretation. By reflecting on the differences between these cases and the cases we have cited, one should learn something about principles controlling mentalistic attribution.

I have already mentioned foreigners without command of the language. A child's imitation of our words and early attempts to use them provide similar examples. In these cases, mastery of the language and responsibility to its precepts have not been developed; and mental content attribution based on the meaning of words uttered tends to be precluded.

There are cases involving regional dialects. A person's deviance or ignorance judged by the standards of the larger community may count as normality or full mastery when evaluated from the regional perspective. Clearly, the regional standards tend to be the relevant ones for attributing content when the speaker's training or intentions are regionally oriented. The conditions for such orientation are complex, and I shall touch on them again in Section V. But there is no warrant in actual practice for treating each person's idiolect as always analogous to dialects whose words we automatically reinterpret—for purposes of mental content attribution—when usage is different. People are frequently held, and hold themselves, to the standards of their community when misuse or misunderstanding are at issue. One should distinguish these cases, which seem to depend on a certain *responsibility* to communal practice, from cases of automatic reinterpretation.

Tongue slips and Spoonerisms form another class of example where reinterpretation of a person's words is common and appropriate in arriving at an attribution of mental content. In these cases, we tend to exempt the speaker even from commitment to a homophonically formulated assertion content, as well as to the relevant mental content. The speaker's own behavior usually follows this line, often correcting himself when what he uttered is repeated back to him.

Malapropisms form a more complex class of examples. I shall not try to map it in detail. But in a fairly broad range of cases, we reinterpret a person's words at least in attributing mental content. If Archie says, "Lead the way and we will precede," we routinely reinterpret the words in describing his expectations. Many of these cases seem to depend on the presumption that there are simple, superficial (for example, phonological) interference or exchange mechanisms that account for the linguistic deviance.

There are also examples of quite radical misunderstandings that sometimes generate reinterpretation. If a generally competent and reasonable speaker thinks that "orangutan" applies to a fruit drink, we would be reluctant, and it would unquestionably be misleading, to take his words as revealing that he thinks he has been drinking orangutans for breakfast for the last few weeks. Such total misunderstanding often *seems* to block literalistic mental content attribution, at least in cases where we are not directly characterizing his mistake. (Contrary to philosophical lore, I am not convinced that such a man cannot correctly and literally be attributed a belief that an orangutan is a kind of fruit drink. But I shall not deal with the point here.)

There are also some cases that do not seem generally to prevent mental content attribution on the basis of literal interpretation of the subject's words in quite the same way as the others, but which deserve some mention. For almost any content except for those that directly display the subject's incomplete understanding, there will be many contexts in which it would be misleading to attribute that content to the subject without further comment. Suppose I am advising you about your legal liabilities in a situation where you have entered into what may be an unwritten contract. You ask me what Al would think. It would be misleading for me to reply that Al would think that you do not have a contract (or even do not have any legal problems), if I know that Al thinks a contract must be based on a formal document. Your evaluation of Al's thought would be crucially affected by his inadequate understanding. In such cases, it is incumbent on us to cite the subject's eccentricity: "(He would think that you do not have a contract, but then) he thinks that there is no such thing as a verbally based contract."

Incidentally, the same sort of example can be constructed using attitudes that are abnormal, but that do not hinge on misunderstanding of any one notion. If Al had thought that only traffic laws and laws against violent crimes are ever prosecuted, it would be misleading for me to tell you that Al would think that you have no legal problems.

Both sorts of cases illustrate that in reporting a single attitude content, we typically suggest (implicate, perhaps) that the subject has a range of other attitudes that are normally associated with it. Some of these may provide reasons for it. In both sorts of cases, it is usually important to keep track of, and often to make explicit, the nature and extent of the subject's deviance. Otherwise, predictions and evaluations of his thought and action, based on normal background assumptions, will go awry. When the deviance is huge, attributions demand reinterpretation of the subject's words. Radical misunderstanding and mental instability are cases in point. But frequently, common practice seems to allow us to cancel the misleading suggestions by making explicit the subject's deviance, retaining literal interpretation of his words in our mentalistic attributions all the while.

All of the foregoing phenomena are relevant to accounting for standard practice. But they are no more salient than cases of straightforward belief attribution where the subject incompletely understands some notion in the attributed belief content. I think any impulse to say that common practice is *simply* inconsistent should be resisted (indeed, scorned). We cannot expect such practice to follow general principles rigorously. But even our brief discussion of the matter should have suggested the beginnings of generalizations about differences between cases where reinterpretation is standard and cases where it is not. A person's overall linguistic competence, his allegiance and responsibility to communal standards, the degree, source, and type of misunderstanding, the purposes of the report—all affect the issue. From a theoretical point of view, it would be a mistake to try to assimilate the cases in one direction or another. We do not want to credit a two-year-old who memorizes "$e = mc^2$" with belief in relativity theory. But the patient's attitudes involving the notion of arthritis should not be assimilated to the foreigner's uncomprehending pronunciations.

For purposes of defending the thought experiment and the arguments I draw from it, I can afford to be flexible about exactly how to generalize about these various phenomena. The thought experiment depends only on there being some cases in which a person's incomplete understanding does not force reinterpretation of his expressions in describing his mental contents. Such cases appear to be legion. . . .

IV Applications

I want to turn now to a discussion of how our argument bears on philosophical approaches to the mental that may be termed *individualistic*. I mean this term to be somewhat vague. But roughly, I intend to apply it to philosophical treatments that seek to see a person's intentional mental phenomena ultimately and purely in terms of what happens to the person, what occurs within him, and how he responds to his physical environment, without any essential reference to the social context in which he or the interpreter of his mental phenomena are situated. How I apply the term "individualistic" will perhaps become clearer by reference to the particular cases that I shall discuss.

a. As I have already intimated, the argument of the preceding sections affects the traditional intro- (or extro-) spectionist treatments of the mind, those of Plato, Descartes, Russell, and numerous others. These treatments are based on a model that likens the relation between a person and the contents of his thought to seeing, where seeing is taken to be a kind of direct, immediate experience. On the most radical and unqualified versions of the model, a person's inspection of the contents of his thought is infallible: the notion of incompletely understanding them has no application at all.

The model tends to encourage individualistic treatments of the mental. For it suggests that what a person thinks depends on what occurs or "appears" within his mind. Demythologized, what a person thinks depends on the power and extent of his comprehension and on his internal dispositions toward the comprehended contents. The model is expressed in perhaps its crudest and least qualified form in a well-known passage by Russell:

> Whenever a relation of supposing or judging occurs, the terms to which the supposing or judging mind is related by the relation of supposing or judging must be terms with which the mind in question is acquainted.... It seems to me that the truth of this principle is evident as soon as the principle is understood.[1]

Acquaintance is (for Russell) direct, infallible, non-propositional, non-perspectival knowledge. "Terms" like concepts, ideas, attributes, forms, meanings, or senses are entities that occur in judgments more or less immediately before the mind on a close analogy to the way sensations are supposed to....

The history of the model makes an intricate subject. My remarks are meant merely to provide a suggestive caricature of it. It should be clear, however, that in broad outline the model mixes poorly with the thought experiment of Section II, particularly its first step. The thought experiment indicates that certain "linguistic truths" that have often been held to be indubitable can be thought yet doubted. And it shows that a person's thought *content* is not fixed by what goes on in him, or by what is accessible to him simply by careful reflection. The reason for this last point about "accessibility" need not be that the content lies too deep in the unconscious recesses of the subject's psyche. Contents are sometimes "inaccessible" to introspection simply because much mentalistic attribution does not presuppose that the subject has fully mastered the content of his thought....

b. This century's most conspicuous attempt to replace the traditional Cartesian model has been the behaviorist movement and its heirs. I take it as obvious that the argument of Section II provides yet another reason to reject the most radical version of behaviorism—"philosophical," "logical" or "analytical" behaviorism. This is the view that mentalistic attributions can be "analytically" defined, or given strict meaning equivalences, purely in non-mental, behavioral terms. No analysis resting purely on the individual's dispositions to behavior can give an "analytic" definition of a mental content attribution because we can conceive of the behavioral definiens applying while the mentalistic definiendum does not. But a new argument for this conclusion is hardly needed since "philosophical" behaviorists are, in effect, extinct.

There is, however, an heir of behaviorism that I want to discuss at somewhat greater length. The approach sometimes goes by the name "functionalism," although that term is applied to numerous slogans and projects, often vaguely formulated. Even views that seem to me to be affected by our argument are frequently stated so sketchily that one may be in considerable doubt about what is being proposed. So my remarks should be taken less as an attempt to refute the theses of particular authors than as an attack on a way of thinking that seems to inform a cluster of viewpoints....

Any attempt to give an account of specific beliefs and thoughts along the lines I have indicated will come up short. For we may fix the input, output, and total array of dispositional or functional states of our subject, as long as these are non-intentionally described and are limited to what is relevant to accounting for his activity taken in isolation from that of his fellows. But we can still conceive of his mental contents as varying. Functionally equivalent people—on any plausible notion of functional equivalence that has been sketched—may have non-equivalent mental-state and event contents, indicated by obliquely non-equivalent content clauses. Our argument indicates a systematic inadequacy in attempts of the sort I described.

Proponents of functionalist accounts have seen them as revealing the true nature of characteristic marks of the mental and as resolving traditional philosophical issues about such marks. In the case of beliefs, desires, and thoughts, the most salient mark is intentionality—the ill-specified information-bearing, representational feature that seems to invest these mental states and events.[2] In our terminology, accounting for intentionality largely amounts to accounting for the content of mental states and events. (There is also, of course, the application of content in *de re* cases. But we put this aside here.) Such content is clearly part of what the functional roles of our subjects' states fail to determine....

Our ordinary method of identifying occurrent thought events and differentiating between them is to make reference to the person or organism to whom the thought occurs, the time of its occurrence, and the content of the thought. If person, time, and content are the same, we would normally count the thought event the same. If any one of these parameters differs in descriptions of thought events (subject to qualifications about duration), then the events or occurrences described are different. Of course, we can differentiate between events using descriptions that do not home in on these particular parameters. But these parameters are dominant. (It is worth noting that differentiations in terms of causes and effects usually tend to rely on the content of mental events or states at some point, since mental states or events are often among the causes or effects of a given mental event, and these causes or effects will usually be identified partly in terms of their content.) The important point for our purposes is that in ordinary practice, sameness of thought content (or at least some sort of strong equivalence of content) is taken as a necessary condition for sameness of thought occurrence.

Now one might codify and generalize this point by holding that no occurrence of a thought (that is, no token thought event) could have a different (or extensionally non-equivalent) content and be the very same token event. If this premise is accepted, then our argument of Section II can be deployed to show that a person's thought event is not *identical* with any event in him that is described by physiology, biology, chemistry, or physics. For let *b* be any given event described in terms of one of the physical sciences that occurs in the subject while he thinks the relevant thought. Let "*b*" be such that it denotes the same physical event occurring in the subject in our counterfactual situation. (If you want, let "*b*" be rigid in Kripke's sense, though so strong a stipulation is not needed.) The second step of our argument in Section II makes it plausible that *b* need not be affected by counterfactual differences in the communal use of the word "arthritis." Actually, the subject thinks that his ankles are stiff from arthritis, while *b* occurs. But we can conceive of the subject's *lacking* a thought event that his ankles are stiff from arthritis, while *b* occurs. Thus in view of our initial premise, *b* is not identical with the subject's occurrent thought.[3] ...

The recent prosperity of materialist-functionalist ways of thinking has been so great that it is often taken for granted that a given thought event might have been a thought with a different, obliquely non-equivalent content. Any old event, on this view, could have a different content, a different significance, if its surrounding context were changed. But in the case of occurrent thoughts—and intentional mental events generally—it is hardly obvious, or even initially plausible, that anything is more essential to the identity of the event than the content itself. Materialist identity theories have schooled the imagination to picture the content of a mental event as varying while the event remains fixed. But whether such imaginings are possible fact or just philosophical fancy is a separate question.[4]

At any rate, functionalist accounts have not provided adequate specification of what it is to be a thought that ______, for particular fillings of the blank. So a specification of a given thought event in functionalist terms does not reveal the contingency of the usual, undisputed intentional specifications. . . .

. . . The authority of a person's reports about his thoughts and beliefs (*modulo* sincerity, lack of subconscious interference, and so forth) does not issue from a special intellectual vision of the contents of those thoughts and beliefs. It extends even to some cases in which the subject incompletely understands those contents. And it depends partly on the social advantages of maintaining communally established standards of communication and mentalistic attribution. Likewise, the descriptive and explanatory role of mental discourse is not adequately modeled by complex non-intentional mechanisms or programs for the production of an individual's physical movement and behavior. Attributing intentional mentalistic phenomena to individuals serves not only to explain their behavior viewed in isolation but also to chart their activity (intentional, verbal, behavioral, physical) by complex comparison to others—and against socially established standards.[5] Both traditional metaphors make the mistake, among others, of treating intentional mental phenomena individualistically. New approaches must do better. The sense in which man is a social animal runs deeper than much mainstream philosophy of mind has acknowledged.[6]

Notes

1. Bertrand Russell, *Mysticism and Logic* (London, 1959), p. 221. Although Russell's statement is unusually unqualified, its kinship to Descartes' and Plato's model is unmistakable. Cf. Plato, *Phaedrus*, 249b–c, *Phaedo*, 47b6–c4; Descartes, *Philosophical Works*, eds. Haldane and Ross 2 vols. (New York, 1955), *Rules for the Direction of the Mind*, section XII, Vol. I, pp. 41–42, 45; *Principles of Philosophy*, Part I, XXXII–XXXV. Vol. I, pp. 232–33; *Replies*, Vol. II, 52; Hume, *A Treatise of Human Nature*, I, 3,5; II, 2,6; Kant, *A Critique of Pure Reason*, A7–B11; Frege, *The Foundations of Arithmetic*, section 105; G. E. Moore, *Principia Ethica*, 86.

2. Often functionalists give mental contents only cursory discussion, if any at all. But claims that a functional account explains intentionality by accounting for all specific intentional states and events in non-intentional, functional language occur in the following: Daniel Dennett, *Content and Consciousness* (London, 1969), Chapter II and *passim*; Harman, *Thought*, for example, p. 60: "To specify the meaning of a sentence used in communication is partly to specify the belief or other mental state expressed; and the representative character of that state is determined by its functional role"; Fodor, *The Language of Thought*, Chapters I and II, for example, p. 75: "The way that information is stored, computed . . . or otherwise processed by the organism explains its cognitive states and in particular, its propositional attitudes"; Smart, "Further Thoughts on the Identity Theory"; Hartry Field, "Mental Representation," *Erkenntnis* 13 (1978): 9–61. I shall confine

discussion to the issue of intentionality. But it seems to me that the individualistic cast of functionalist accounts renders them inadequate in their handling of another major traditional issue about intentional mental states and events—first-person authority.

3. The argument is basically Cartesian in style, (cf. *Meditations* II), though the criticism of functionalism, which is essential to its success, is not in any obvious sense Cartesian.... Also the conclusion gives no special support to Cartesian ontology. The terminology of rigidity is derived from Saul Kripke, "Naming and Necessity," *Semantics of Natural Language*, eds., Davidson and Harman (Dordrecht, 1972), though as mentioned above, a notion of rigidity is not essential for the argument. Kripke has done much to clarify the force of the Cartesian sort of argument. He gives such an argument aimed at showing the non-identity of sensations with brain processes. The argument as presented seems to suffer from a failure to criticize materialistic accounts of sensation language and from not indicating clearly how token physical events and token sensation events that are *prima facie* candidates for identification could have occurred independently. For criticism of Kripke's argument, see Fred Feldman, "Kripke on the Identity Theory," *The Journal of Philosophy* 71 (1974): 665–76; William G. Lycan, "Kripke and the Materialists," *Ibid.*, pp. 677–89; Richard Boyd, "What Physicalism Does Not Entail," *Readings in the Philosophy of Psychology*, ed. N. Block (forthcoming); Colin McGinn, "Anomalous Monism and Kripke's Cartesian Intuitions," *Analysis* 37 (1977): 78–80. It seems to me, however, that these issues are not closed.

4. There are *prima facie* viable philosophical accounts that take sentences (whether tokens or types) as truth bearers. One might hope to extend such accounts to mental contents. On such treatments, contents are not things over and above sentences. They simply *are* sentences interpreted in a certain context, treated in a certain way. Given a different context of linguistic interpretation, the content of the same sentence might be different. One could imagine mental events to be analogous to the sentences on this account. Indeed, some philosophers have thought of intentional mental events as being inner, physical sentence (or symbol) tokens—a sort of brain writing. Here again, there is a picture according to which the same thought event might have had a different content. But here again the question is whether there is any reason to think it is a true picture. There is the prior question of whether sentences can reasonably be treated as contents. (I think sentence types probably can be; but the view has hardly been established, and defending it against sophisticated objections is treacherous.) Even if this question is answered affirmatively, it is far from obvious that the analogy between sentences and contents, on the one hand, and thought events and contents, on the other, is a good one. Sentences (types or tokens) are commonly identified independently of their associated contents (as evidenced by inter- and intra-linguistic ambiguity). It is *relatively* uncontroversial that sentences can be identified by syntactical, morphemic, or perceptual criteria that are in principle specifiable independently of what particular content the sentence has. The philosophical question about sentences and contents is whether discourse about contents can be reasonably interpreted as having an ontology of nothing more than sentences (and intentional agents). The philosophical question about mental events and contents is "What is the nature of the events?" "Regardless of what contents are, could the very same thought event have a different content?" The analogous question for sentences—instead of thought events—has an uncontroversial affirmative answer. Of course, we know that when and where non-intentionally identifiable physical events have contents, the same physical event could have had a different content. But it can hardly be *assumed* for purposes of arguing a position on the mind-body problem that mental events are non-intentionally identifiable physical events.

5. In emphasizing social and pragmatic features in mentalistic attributions, I do not intend to suggest that mental attributions are any the less objective, descriptive, or on the ontological up and up. There are substantial arguments in the literature that might lead one to make such inferences. But my present remarks are free of such implications. Someone might want to insist that from a

"purely objective viewpoint" one can describe "the phenomena" equally well in accord with common practice, literally interpreted, or in accord with various reinterpretation strategies. Then our arguments would, perhaps, show only that it is "objectively indeterminate" whether functionalism and the identity theory are true. I would be inclined to question the application of the expressions that are scare-quoted.

6. I am grateful to participants at a pair of talks given at the University of London in the spring of 1978, and to Richard Rorty for discussions earlier. I am also indebted to Robert Adams and Rogers Albritton whose criticisms forced numerous improvements. I appreciatively acknowledge support of the John Simon Guggenheim Foundation.

53 Methodological Solipsism Considered as a Research Strategy in Cognitive Psychology

Jerry A. Fodor

... to form the idea of an object and to form an idea simply is the same thing; the reference of the idea to an object being an extraneous denomination, of which in itself it bears no mark or character.

—Hume's *Treatise*, Book I

Your standard contemporary cognitive psychologist—your thoroughly modern mentalist—is disposed to reason as follows. To think (e.g.) that Marvin is melancholy is to represent Marvin in a certain way; viz., as being melancholy (and not, for example, as being maudlin, morose, moody, or merely moping and dyspeptic). But surely we cannot represent Marvin as being melancholy except as we are in some or other relation to a representation of Marvin; and not just to *any* representation of Marvin, but, in particular, to a representation the content of which is *that* Marvin is melancholy; a representation which, as it were, expresses the proposition that Marvin is melancholy. So, a fortiori, at least some mental states/processes are or involve at least some relations to at least some representations. Perhaps, then, this is the *typical* feature of such mental states/processes as cognitive psychology studies; perhaps all such states can be viewed as relations to representations and all such processes as operations defined on representations.

This is, prima facie, an appealing proposal since it gives the psychologist two degrees of freedom to play with and they seem, intuitively, to be the right two. On the one hand, mental states are distinguished by the *content* of the associated representations, so we can allow for the difference between thinking that Marvin is melancholy and thinking that Sam is (or that Albert isn't, or that it sometimes snows in Cincinnati); and, on the other hand, mental states are distinguished by the *relation* that the subject bears to the associated representation (so we can allow for the difference between thinking, hoping, supposing, doubting and pretending that Marvin is melancholy). It's hard to believe that a serious psychology could make do with fewer (or less refined) distinctions than these, and it's hard to believe that a psychology that makes these distinctions could avoid taking the notion of mental representation seriously. Moreover, the burden of argument is clearly upon anyone who claims that we need *more* degrees of freedom than just these two: the least hypothesis that is remotely plausible is that a mental state is (type) individuated by specifying a relation and a representation such that the subject bears the one to the other.[1]

I'll say that any psychology that takes this line is a version of the REPRESENTATIONAL THEORY OF THE MIND. I think that it's reasonable to adopt some such theory as a sort of working hypothesis, if only because there aren't any alternatives which seem to be even remotely plausible and because empirical research carried out within this framework has, thus far, proved interesting and fruitful.[2] However, my present concern is neither to attack nor to defend this view, but rather to distinguish it from something other—and stronger—that modern cognitive psychologists *also* hold. I shall put this stronger doctrine as the view that mental states and processes are COMPUTATIONAL. Much of what is characteristic of cognitive psychology is a consequence of adherence to this stronger view. What I want to do in this paper is to say something about what this stronger view is, something about why I think it's plausible, and, most of all, something about the ways in which it shapes the cognitive psychology we have.

I take it that computational processes are both *symbolic* and *formal*. They are symbolic because they are defined over representations, and they are formal because they apply to representations, in virtue of (roughly) the *syntax* of the representations. It's the second of these conditions that makes the claim that mental processes are computational stronger than the representational theory of the mind. Most of this paper will be a meditation upon the consequences of assuming that mental processes are formal processes.

I'd better cash the parenthetical "roughly." To say that an operation is formal isn't the same as saying that it is syntactic since we could have formal processes defined over representations which don't, in any obvious sense, *have* a syntax. Rotating an image would be a timely example. What makes syntactic operations a species of formal operations is that being syntactic is a way of *not* being semantic. Formal operations are the ones that are specified without reference to such semantic properties of representations as, for example, truth, reference and meaning. Since we don't know how to complete this list (since, that is, we don't know what semantic properties there are), I see no responsible way of saying what, in general, formality amounts to. The notion of formality will thus have to remain intuitive and metaphoric, at least for present purposes: formal operations apply in terms of the, as it were, "shapes" of the objects in their domains.[3]

To require that mental processes be computational (viz., formal-syntactic) is thus to require something not very clear. Still, the requirement has some clear consequences, and they are striking and tendentious. Consider that we started by assuming that the *content* of representations is a (type) individuating feature of mental states. So far as the *representational* theory of the mind is concerned, it's possibly the *only* thing that distinguishes Peter's thought that Sam is silly from his thought that Sally is depressed. But, now, if the *computational* theory of the mind is true (and if, as we may assume, content is a semantic notion par excellence) it follows that content alone cannot distinguish thoughts. More exactly, the computational theory of the mind requires that two thoughts can be distinct in content only if they can be identified with relations to formally distinct representations. More generally: fix the subject and the relation, and then mental states can be (type) distinct only if the representations which constitute their objects are formally distinct.

Again, consider that accepting a formality condition upon mental states implies a drastic narrowing of the ordinary ontology of the mental; all sorts of states which look, prima facie, to be mental states in good standing are going to turn out to be none of the psychologist's business if the formality condition is endorsed. This point is one that philosophers have made in a number of contexts, and usually in a deprecating tone of voice. Take, for example, knowing that such-and-such and assume that you can't know what's not the case. Since, on that assumption, knowledge is involved with truth, and since truth is a semantic notion, it's going to follow that there can't be a psychology of *knowledge* (even if it is consonant with the formality condition to hope for a psychology of *belief*). Similarly, it's a way of making a point of Ryle's to say that, strictly speaking, there can't be a psychology of perception if the formality condition is to be complied with. Seeing is an achievement; you can't see what's not there. From the point of view of the representational theory of the mind, this means that seeing involves relations between mental representations *and their referents*; hence, semantic relations within the meaning of the act.

I hope that such examples suggest (what, in fact, I think is true) that even if the formality condition isn't very clear, it is quite certainly very strong. In fact, I think it's not all *that* anachronistic to see it as the central issue which divides the two main traditions in the history of psychology: "Rational psychology" on the one hand, and "Naturalism" on the other. Since this is a mildly eccentric way of cutting the pie, I'm going to permit myself a semihistorical excursus before returning to the main business of the paper.

Descartes argued that there is an important sense in which how the world is makes no difference to one's mental states. Here is a well-known passage from the *Meditations*:

> At this moment it does indeed seem to me that it is with eyes awake that I am looking at this paper; that this head which I move is not asleep, that it is deliberately and of set purpose that I extend my hand and perceive it.... But in thinking over this I remind myself that on many occasions I have been deceived by similar illusions, and in dwelling on this reflection I see so manifestly that there are no certain indications by which we may clearly distinguish wakefulness from sleep that I am lost in astonishment. And my astonishment is such that it is almost capable of persuading me that I now dream. (Descartes 1931)

At least three sorts of reactions to this kind of argument are distinguishable in the philosophical literature. First, there's a long tradition, including both Rationalists and Empiricists, which takes it as axiomatic that one's experiences (and, a fortiori, one's beliefs) might have been just as they are even if the world had been quite different from the way that it is. See, for example, the passage from Hume which serves as an epigraph to this paper. Second, there's a vaguely Wittgensteinian mood in which one argues that it's just *false* that one's mental states might have been what they are had the world been relevantly different. For example, if there had been a dagger there, Macbeth would have been *seeing*, not just hallucinating. And what could be more different than that? If the Cartesian feels that this reply misses the point, he is at least under an obligation to say precisely which point it misses; in precisely *which* respects the way the world is irrelevant to the character of one's beliefs, experiences, etc. Finally there's a tradition which argues that—epistemology to one side—it is at best a strategic mistake to attempt to develop a psychology which individuates mental states without reference to their environmental causes and effects; (e.g., which counts the state that Macbeth *was* in as type-identical to the state he would have been in had the dagger been supplied.) I have in mind the tradition which includes the American Naturalists (notably Pierce and Dewey), all the learning theorists, and such contemporary representatives as Quine in philosophy and Gibson in psychology. The recurrent theme here is that psychology is a branch of biology, hence that one must view the organism as embedded in a physical environment. The psychologist's job is to trace those organism/environment interactions which constitute its behavior. A passage from William James (1890, p. 6) will serve to give the feel of the thing:

> On the whole, few recent formulas have done more service of a rough sort in psychology than the Spencerian one that the essence of mental life and of bodily life are one, namely, "the adjustment of inner to outer relations." Such a formula is vagueness incarnate; but because it takes into account the fact that minds inhabit environments which act on them and on which they in turn react; because, in short, it takes mind in the midst of all its concrete relations, it is immensely more fertile than the old-fashioned "rational psychology" which treated the soul as a detached existent, sufficient unto itself, and assumed to consider only its nature and its properties.

A number of adventitious intrusions have served to muddy the issues in this long-standing dispute. On the one hand, it may well be that Descartes was relying on a specifically introspectionist construal of the claim that the individuation of mental states is independent of their environmental causes. That is, Descartes' point may have been that (a) mental states are (type) identical if and only if (iff) they are introspectively indistinguishable, and (b) introspection cannot distinguish (e.g.) perception from hallucination, or knowledge from belief. On the other hand, the naturalist, in point of historical fact, is often a behaviorist as well. He wants to argue not only that mental states are individuated by reference to organism/environment relations, but also that such relations constitute the mental. In the context of the present discussion, he is arguing for the abandonment not just of the formality condition, but of the notion of mental representation as well.

If, however, we take the computational theory of the mind as what's central to the issue, we can reconstruct the debate between rational psychologists and naturalists in a way that does justice to both their points; in particular, in a way that frees the discussion from involvement with introspectionism on the one side and behaviorism on the other.

Insofar as we think of mental processes as computational (hence as formal operations defined on representations) it will be natural to take the mind to be, inter alia, a kind of computer. That is, we will think of the mind as carrying out whatever symbol manipulations are constitutive of the hypothesized computational processes. To a first approximation, we may thus construe mental operations as pretty directly analogous to those of a Turing machine. There is, for example, a working memory (corresponding to a tape) and there are capacities for scanning and altering the contents of the memory (corresponding to the operations of reading and writing on the tape). If we want to extend the computational metaphor by providing access to information about the environment, we can think of the computer as having access to "oracles" which serve, on occasion, to enter information in the memory. On the intended interpretation of this model, these oracles are analogs to the senses. In particular, they are assumed to be transducers, in that what they write on the tape is determined solely by the ambient environmental energies that impinge upon them. (For elaboration of this sort of account, see Putnam 1960; it is, of course, widely familiar from discussions in the field of artificial intelligence.)

I'm not endorsing this model, but simply presenting it as a natural extension of the computational picture of the mind. Its present interest is that we can use it to see how the formality condition connects with the Cartesian claim that the character of mental processes is somehow independent of their environmental causes and effects. The point is that, so long as we are thinking of mental processes as purely computational, the bearing of environmental information upon such processes is exhausted by the formal character of whatever the oracles write on the tape. In particular, it doesn't matter to such processes whether what the oracles write is *true*; whether, for example, they really are transducers faithfully mirroring the state of the environment, or merely the output end of a typewriter manipulated by a Cartesian demon bent on deceiving the machine. I'm saying, in effect, that the formality condition, viewed in this context, is tantamount to a sort of methodological solipsism. If mental processes are formal, then they have access only to the formal properties of such representations of the environment as the senses provide. Hence, they have no access to the *semantic* properties of such representations, including the property of being true, of having referents, or, indeed, the property of being representations *of the environment.*

That some such methodological solipsism really is implicated in much current psychological practice is best seen by examining what researchers actually do. Consider, for example, the well-known work of Professor Terry Winograd. Winograd was primarily interested in the computer simulation of certain processes involved in the handling of verbal information; asking and answering questions, drawing inferences, following instructions and the like. The form of his theory was a program for a computer which "lives in" and operates upon a simple world of blocklike geometric objects (see Winograd 1971). Many of the capacities that the device exercises vis-à-vis its environment seem impressively intelligent. It can arrange the blocks to order, it can issue "perceptual" reports of the present state of its environment and "memory" reports of its past states, it can devise simple plans for achieving desired environmental configurations, and it can discuss its undertakings (more or less in English) with whoever is running the program.

The interesting point for our purposes, however, is that the machine environment which is the nominal object of these actions and conversations actually isn't there. What actually happens is that the programmer so arranges the memory states of the machine that the available data are whatever they would be *if* there were objects for the machine to perceive and manipulanda for it to operate upon. In effect, the machine lives in an entirely notional world; all its beliefs are false. Of course, it doesn't matter to the machine that its beliefs are false since falsity is a semantic property and, qua computer, the device satisfies the formality condition; viz., it has access only to formal (nonsemantic) properties of the representations that it manipulates. In effect, the device is in precisely the situation that Descartes dreads; it's a mere computer which dreams that it's a robot.

I hope that this discussion suggests how acceptance of the computational theory of the mind leads to a sort of methodological solipsism as a part of the research strategy of contemporary cognitive psychology. In particular, I hope it's clear how you get that consequence from the formality condition alone, without so much as raising the introspection issue. I stress this point because it seems to me that there has been considerable confusion about it among the psychologists themselves. People who do machine simulation, in particular, very often advertise themselves as working on the question how thought (or language) is related to the world. My present point is that, whatever else they're doing, they certainly aren't doing *that*. The very assumption that defines their field—viz., that they study mental processes *qua* formal operations on symbols—guarantees that their studies won't answer the question how the symbols so manipulated are semantically interpreted. You can, for example, build a machine that answers baseball questions in the sense that (e.g.) if you type in "Who had the most wins by a National League pitcher since Dizzy Dean?" it will type out "Robin Roberts, who won 28." But you delude yourself if you think that a machine which in this sense answers baseball questions, is thereby answering questions *about* baseball (or that the machine has somehow referred to Robin Roberts). If the *programmer* chooses to interpret the machine inscription "Robin Roberts won 28" as a statement about Robin Roberts (e.g., as the statement that he won 28), that's all well and good, but it's no business of the machine's. The machine has no access to that interpretation, and its computations are in no way affected by it. The machine doesn't know what it's talking about, it doesn't care; *about* is a semantic relation.[4]

This brings us to a point where, having done some sort of justice to the Cartesian's insight, we can also do some sort of justice to the naturalist's. For, after all, mental processes are supposed to be operations on representations, and it is in the nature of representations to represent. We have seen that a psychology which embraces the formality condition is thereby debarred from raising questions about the semantic properties of mental representations; yet surely such questions ought *somewhere* to be raised. The computer which prints out "RR won 28" is not thereby referring to RR. But, surely, when I think: *RR won 28*, I *am* thinking about RR, and if not in virtue of having performed some formal operations on some representations, then presumably in virtue of something else. It's perhaps borrowing the least tendentious fragment of causal theories of reference to assume that what fixes the interpretation of my mental representations of RR is something about the way that he and I are embedded in the world; perhaps not a causal chain stretching between us, but anyhow *some* facts about how he and I are causally situated; *Dasein*, as you might say. Only a *naturalistic* psychology will do to specify these facts, because here we are explicitly in the realm of organism/environment transactions.

We are on the verge of a bland and ecumenical conclusion: that there is room both for a computational psychology—viewed as a theory of formal processes defined over mental representations—*and* a naturalistic psychology, viewed as a theory of the (presumably causal) relations between representations and the world which fix the semantic interpretations of the former. I think that, in principle, this is the right way to look at things. In practice, however, I think that it's misleading. So far as I can see, it's overwhelmingly likely that computational psychology is the only one that we are going to get. I want to argue for this conclusion in two steps. First, I'll argue for what I've till now only assumed: that we must *at least* have a psychology which accepts the formality condition. Then I'll argue that there's good reason to suppose that that's the most that we can have; that a naturalistic psychology isn't a practical possibility and isn't likely to become one.

The first move, then, is to give reasons for believing that at least *some* part of psychology should honor the formality condition. Here too the argument proceeds in two steps. I'll argue first that it is typically under an *opaque* construal that attributions of propositional attitudes to organisms enter into explanations of their behavior; and second that the formality condition is intimately involved with the explanation of propositional attitudes so construed: roughly, that it's reasonable to believe that we can get such explanations only within computational theories. *Caveat emptor*: the arguments under review are, in large part, nondemonstrative. In particular, they will assume the perfectibility in principle of the kinds of psychological theories now being developed, and it is entirely possible that this is an assumption contrary to fact.

Thesis: when we articulate the generalizations in virtue of which behavior is contingent upon mental states, it is typically an opaque construal of the mental state attributions that does the work; for example, it's a construal under which believing that *a is F* is logically independent from believing that *b is F*, even in the case where a = b. It will be convenient to speak not only of opaque construals of propositional attitude ascriptions, but also of *opaque taxonomies* of mental state types; e.g., of taxonomies which, inter alia, count the belief that the Morning Star rises in the east as type distinct from the belief that the Evening Star does. (Correspondingly, *transparent* taxonomies are such as, inter alia, would count these beliefs as type-identical). So, the claim is that mental states are typically opaquely taxonomized for purposes of psychological theory.[5]

The point doesn't depend upon the examples, so I'll stick to the most informal sorts of cases. Suppose I know that John wants to meet the girl who lives next door, and suppose I know that this is true when "wants to" is construed opaquely. Then, given even rough-and-ready generalizations about how people's behaviors are contingent upon their utilities, I can make some reasonable predictions (guesses) about what John is likely to do: he's likely to say (viz., utter), "I want to meet the girl who lives next door." He's likely to call upon his neighbor. He's likely (at a minimum, and all things being equal) to exhibit next-door-directed behavior. None of this is frightfully exciting, but it's all I need for present purposes, and what more would you expect from folk psychology?

On the other hand, suppose that all I know is that John wants to meet the girl next door where "wants to" is construed transparently; i.e., all I know is that it's true of the girl next door that John wants to meet her. Then there is little or nothing that I can predict about how John is likely to proceed. And this is *not* just because rough and ready psychological generalizations want *ceteris paribus* clauses to fill them in; it's also for the deeper reason that I can't infer from what I know about John to any relevant description of the mental causes of his behavior. For example, I have no reason to predict that John will say such things as "I want to meet the girl who lives next door" since, let John be as cooperative and as truthful as you like, and let him be utterly a native speaker, still, he *may* believe that the girl he wants to meet languishes in Latvia. In which case, "I want to meet the girl who lives next door" is the last thing it will occur to him to say. (The contestant wants to say "suspender," for "suspender" is the magic word. Consider what we can predict about his probable verbal behavior if we take this (a) opaquely and (b) transparently. And, of course, the same sorts of points apply, mutatis mutandis, to the prediction of *non*verbal behavior.)

Ontologically, transparent readings are stronger than opaque ones; for example, the former license existential inferences which the latter do not. But psychologically opaque readings are stronger than transparent ones; they tell us more about the character of the mental causes of behavior. The representational theory of mind offers an explanation of this anomaly. Opaque ascriptions are true in virtue of the way that the agent represents the objects of his wants (intentions, beliefs, etc.) *to himself.* And, by assumption, such representations function in the causation of the behaviors that the agent produces. So, for example, to say that it's true *opaquely* that Oedipus did such-and-such because he wanted to marry Jocasta, is to say something like (though not, perhaps, *very* like; see Fodor [1979]): "Oedipus said to himself, 'I want to marry Jocasta,' and his so saying was among the causes of his behavior." Whereas to say (only) that it's true transparently that O. wanted to marry J. is to say no more than that among the causes of his behavior was O.'s saying to himself "I want to marry ..." where the blank was filled by *some* expression that denotes J.[6] But now, what O. *does*, how he in the proprietary sense behaves, will depend on which description he (literally) had in mind.[7] If it's "Jocasta," courtship behavior follows *ceteris paribus*. Whereas, if it's "my Mum," we have the situation towards the end of the play and Oedipus at Colonus eventually ensues.

I dearly wish that I could leave this topic here, because it would be very convenient to be able to say, without qualification, what I strongly implied above: the opaque readings of propositional attitude ascriptions tell us how people represent the objects of their propositional attitudes. What one would like to say, in particular, is that if two people are identically related to formally identical mental representations, then they are in opaquely type-identical mental states. This would be convenient because it yields a succinct and gratifying characterization of what a computational cognitive psychology is about: such a psychology studies propositional attitudes opaquely taxonomized.

I think, in fact, that this is *roughly* the right thing to say since what I think is *exactly* right is that the construal of propositional attitudes which such a psychology renders is nontransparent. (It's nontransparency that's crucial in all the examples we have been considering.) The trouble is that nontransparency isn't quite the same notion as opacity, as we shall now see.

The question before us is: "What are the relations between the pretheoretic notion of type identity of mental states opaquely construed and the notion of type identity of mental states that you get from a theory which strictly honors the formality condition?" And the answer is: complicated. For one thing, it's not clear that we have *a* pretheoretic notion of the opaque reading of a propositional attitude ascription: I doubt that the two standard tests for opacity (failure of existential generalization and failure of substitutivity of identicals) even pick out the same class of cases. But what's more important are the following considerations. While it's notorious that extensionally identical thoughts may be opaquely type distinct (e.g., thoughts about the Morning Star and thoughts about the Evening Star) there are nevertheless some semantic conditions on opaque type identification. In particular:

(a) there are some cases of formally distinct but coextensive token thoughts which count as tokens of the same (opaque) type (and hence as identical in content at least on one way of individuating contents); and
(b) *non*coextensive thoughts are ipso facto, type-distinct (and differ in content, at least on one way of individuating contents).

Case of type (a): 1. I think I'm sick and you think I'm sick. What's running through my head is "I'm sick"; what's running through your head is "he's sick." But we are both having thoughts of the same (opaque) type (and hence of the same content).

2. You think: "that one looks edible"; I think: "this one looks edible." Our thoughts are opaquely type-identical if we are thinking about the same one.

It connects with the existence of such cases that pronouns and demonstratives are typically (perhaps invariably) construed as referring, even when they occur in what are otherwise opaque constructions. So, for example, it seems to me that I can't report Macbeth's hallucination by saying: "Macbeth thinks that's a dagger" if Macbeth is staring at nothing at all. Which is to say that "that's a dagger" doesn't report Macbeth's mental state even though "that's a dagger" may be precisely what is running through Macbeth's head (precisely the representation his relation to which is constitutive of his belief).

Cases of type (b): 1. Suppose that Sam feels faint and Misha knows he does. Then what's running through Misha's head may be "he feels faint." Suppose too that Misha feels faint and Alfred knows he does. Then what's running through Alfred's head, too, may be "he feels faint." I have no, or rather no univocal, inclination to say, in this case, that Alfred and Misha are having type identical thoughts even though the principle of type individuation is, by assumption, opaque and even though Alfred and Misha have the same things running through their heads. But if this is right, then formal identity of mental representations cannot be sufficient for type identity of opaquely taxonomized mental states.[8] (There is an interesting discussion of this sort of case in Geach 1957. Geach says that Aquinas says that there is no "intelligible difference" between Alfred's thought and Misha's. I don't know whether this means that they are having the same thought or that they aren't.)

2. Suppose that there are two Lake Eries (two bodies of water so-called). Consider two tokens of the thought "Lake Erie is wet," one of which is, intuitively speaking about the Lake Erie in North America and one of which is about the other one. Here again, I'm inclined to say that the aboriginal, uncorrupted pretheoretical notion of type-wise same thought wants these to be tokens of *different* thoughts and takes these thoughts to differ in content. (Though in this case, as in the others, I think there's also a countervailing inclination to say that they count as type-identical—and as identical in content—for some relevant purposes and in some relevant respects. How like aboriginal, uncorrupted, pretheoretical intuition!)

I think, in short, that the intuitive opaque taxonomy is actually what you might call "semitransparent." On the one hand, certain conditions on coreference are in force. (Misha's belief that he's ill is type distinct from Sam's belief that *he's* ill and my thought *this is edible* may be type identical to your thought *that is edible*.) On the other hand, you don't get free substitution of coreferring expressions (beliefs about the Morning Star are type-distinct from beliefs about the Evening Star) and existential generalization doesn't go through for beliefs about Santa Claus.

Apparently, then, the notion of same mental state that we get from a theory which honors the formality condition is related to, but not identical to, the notion of same mental state that unreconstructed intuition provides for opaque construals. And it would certainly be reasonable to ask whether we actually need both. I think the answer is probably: yes, if we want to capture *all* the intuitions. For if we restrict ourselves to either one of the taxonomies, we get consequences that we don't like. On the one hand, if we taxonomize *purely* formally, we get identity of belief compatible with difference of truth value. (Misha's belief that he's ill will be type-identical to Sam's belief that *he's* ill, but one may be true while the other is false.) On the other hand, if we taxonomize solely according to the pretheoretic criteria, we get trouble with the idea that people act out of their beliefs and desires. We need, in particular, some taxonomy according to which Sam and Misha have the *same* belief in order to explain why it is that they exhibit the same behaviors. It is, after all, *part* of the pretheoretic notion of belief that difference in belief ought *ceteris paribus* to show up in behavior *somewhere* ("ceteris paribus" means "given relevant identities among other mental states"). Whereas, it's possible to construct cases where differences like the one between Misha's belief and Sam's can't show up in behavior even in principle (see note 8). What we have, in short, is a tension between a partially semantic taxonomy and an entirely functional one, and the recommended solution is to use both.

Having said all this, I now propose largely to ignore it and use the term "opaque taxonomy" for principles of type individuation according to which Misha and Sam are in the same mental state when each believes himself to be ill. When I need to distinguish this sense of opaque taxonomy from the pretheoretic one, I'll talk about *full* opacity and fully opaque type identification.

My claim has been that, in doing our psychology, we want to attribute mental states fully opaquely because it's the fully opaque reading which tells us what the agent has in mind, and it's what the agent has in mind that causes his behavior. I now need to say something about how, precisely, all this is supposed to constitute an argument for the formality condition.

Point one: it's just as well that it's the fully opaque construal of mental states that we need since, patently, that's the only one that the formality condition permits us. This is because the formality condition prohibits taxonomizing psychological states by reference to the semantic properties of mental representations and, at bottom, transparency is a semantic (viz., nonformal; viz., nonsyntactic) notion. The point is sufficiently obvious: if we count the belief that the Evening Star is F as (type) identical to the belief that the Morning Star is F, that must be because of the coreference of such expressions as "the Morning Star" and "the Evening Star." But coreference is a semantic property, and not one which could conceivably have a formal doppelganger; it's inconceivable, in particular, that there should be a system of mental representations such that, in the general case, coreferring expressions are formally identical in that system. (This might be true for God's mind, but not, surely, for anybody else's [and not for God's either unless he is an Extensionalist; which I doubt.]) So if we want transparent taxonomies of mental states, we will have to give up the formality condition. So it's a good thing for the computational theory of the mind that it's not transparent taxonomies that we want.

What's harder to argue for (but might, nevertheless, be true) is point two: that the formality condition *can* be honored by a theory which taxonomizes mental states according to their content. For, barring caveats previously reviewed, it may be that mental states are distinct in content only if they are relations to formally distinct mental representations; in effect, that aspects of content can be reconstructed as aspects of form, at least insofar as appeals to content figure in accounts of the mental causation of behavior. The main thing to be said in favor of this speculation is that it allows us to explain, within the context of the representational theory of mind, how beliefs of different content *can* have different behavioral effects, even when the beliefs are transparently type-identical. The form of explanation goes: it's because different content implies formally distinct internal representations (via the formality condition) and formally distinct internal representations can be functionally different; can differ in their causal role. Whereas, to put it mildly, it's hard to see how internal representations could differ in causal role *unless* they differed in form.

To summarize: transparent taxonomy is patently incompatible with the formality condition; whereas taxonomy in respect of content *may* be compatible with the formality condition, plus or minus a bit. That taxonomy in respect of content *is* compatible with the formality condition, plus or minus a bit, is perhaps *the* basic idea of modern cognitive theory. The representational theory of mind and the computational theory of mind merge here for, on the one hand, it's claimed that psychological states differ in content only if they are relations to type-distinct mental representations; and, on the other, it's claimed that only formal properties of mental representations contribute to their type individuation for the purposes of theories of mind/body interaction. Or, to put it the other way 'round, it's allowed that mental representations affect behavior in virtue of their content, but it's maintained that mental representations are distinct in content only if they are also distinct in form. The first clause is required to make it plausible that mental states are relations to mental representations and the second is required to make it plausible that mental processes are computations. (Computations just *are* processes in which representations have their causal consequences in virtue of their form.) By thus exploiting the notions of content and computation *together*, a cognitive theory seeks to connect the *intensional* properties of mental states with their *causal* properties vis-à-vis behavior. Which is, of course, exactly what a theory of the mind ought to do.

At must be evident from the preceding, I'm partial to programmatic arguments: ones that seek to infer the probity of a conceptual apparatus from the fact that it plays a role in some prima facie plausible research enterprise. So, in particular, I've argued that a taxonomy of mental states which honors the formality condition seems to be required by theories of the mental causation of behavior, and that that's a reason for taking such taxonomies very seriously.

But there lurks, within the general tradition of representational theories of mind, a deeper intuition: that it is not only *advisable* but actually *mandatory* to assume that mental processes have access only to formal (nonsemantic) properties of mental representations; that the contrary view is not only empirically fruitless but also conceptually unsound. I find myself in sympathy with this intuition, though I'm uncertain precisely how the arguments ought to go. What follows is just a sketch.

I'll begin with a version that I *don't* like, an epistemological version:

> Look, it makes no *sense* to suppose that mental operations could apply to mental representations in virtue of (e.g.) the truth or falsity of the latter. For, consider: truth value is a matter of correspondence to the way the world is. To determine the truth value of a belief would therefore involve what I'll call "directly comparing" the belief with the world; i.e., comparing it with the way the world *is*, not just with the way the world is represented as being. And the representational theory of mind says that we have access to the world only *via* the ways in which we represent it.

There is, as it were, nothing that corresponds to looking around (behind? through? what's the right metaphor?) one's beliefs to catch a glimpse of the things they represent. Mental processes can, in short, compare representations, but they can't compare representations with what they're representations of. Hence mental processes can't have access to the truth value of representations or, mutatis mutandis, to whether they denote. Hence the formality condition.

This line of argument could, certainly, be made a good deal more precise. It has been in, for example, some of the recent work of Nelson Goodman (see especially Goodman 1978). For present purposes, however, I'm content to leave it *im*precise so long as it sounds familiar. For I suspect that all versions of the argument suffer from a common deficiency: they assume that you can't run a *correspondence* theory of truth together with a *coherence* theory of evidence. Whereas I see nothing compelling in the inference from "truth is a matter of the correspondence of a belief with the way the world is" to "*ascertaining* truth is a matter of 'directly comparing' a belief with the way the world is." Perhaps we ascertain the truth of our beliefs by comparing them with one another, appealing to inference to the best explanation whenever we need to do so.

Anyhow, it would be nice to have a *non*epistemological defence of the formality condition; one which saves the intuition that there's something conceptually wrong with its denial but doesn't acquire the skeptical/relativistic commitments with which the traditional epistemic versions of the argument have been encumbered. Here goes:

Suppose, just for convenience, that mental processes are algorithms. So, we have rules for the transformation of mental representations, and we have the mental representations that constitute their ranges and domains. Think of the rules as being like hypothetical imperatives; they have antecedents which specify conditions on mental representations, and they have consequents which specify what is to happen if the antecedents are satisfied. And now consider rules (a) and (b):

(a) Iff it's the case that P, do such and such.

(b) Iff you believe it's the case that P, do such and such.

Notice, to begin with, that the compliance conditions on these injunctions are quite different. In particular, in the case where P is *false but believed true*, compliance with (b) consists in doing such and such, whereas compliance with (a) consists in *not* doing it. But despite this difference in compliance conditions, there's something *very* peculiar (perhaps *pragmatically* peculiar, whatever precisely that may mean) about supposing that an organism might have different ways of going about attempting to comply with (a) and (b). The peculiarity is patent in (c). To borrow a joke from Professor Robert Jagger, (c) is a little like the advice: "buy low, sell high." One knows just what it would be *like* to comply with either, but somehow knowing that doesn't help much.

(c) Do such and such iff it's the case that P, *whether or not* you believe that it's the case that P.[9]

The idea is this: when one has done what one can to establish that the belief that P is warranted, one has done what one can to establish that the antecedent of (a) is satisfied. And, conversely, when one has done what one can do to establish that the antecedent of (a) is satisfied, one has done what one can to establish the warrant of the belief that P. Now, I suppose that the following is at least *close* to being true: to have the belief that P is to have the belief that the belief that P is warranted; and conversely, to have the belief that the belief that P is warranted is to have the belief that P. And the upshot of *this* is just the formality condition all over again. Given that mental operations have access to the fact that P is believed (and hence that the belief that P is believed to be warranted, and hence that the belief that the belief that P is warranted is believed to be warranted, ... etc.) there's nothing further left to do; there is nothing that corresponds to the notion of a mental operation which one undertakes to perform just in case one's belief that P is *true*.

This isn't, by the way, any form of skepticism, as can be seen from the following: there's nothing wrong with Jones having one mental operation which he undertakes to perform iff it's the case that P and another *quite different* mental operation which he undertakes to perform iff *Smith* (≠ Jones) believes that it's the case that P. (Cf. "I promise ... though I don't intend to ..." vs. "I promise ... though Smith doesn't intend to ...") There's a first person/third person asymmetry here, but it doesn't impugn the semantic distinction between "P is true" and "P is believed true." The suggestion is that it's the tacit recognition of this pragmatic asymmetry that accounts for the traditional hunch that you can't both identify mental operations with transformations on mental representations and at the same time flout the formality condition; that the representational theory of mind and the computational theory of mind are somehow conjoint options.

So much, then, for the formality condition and the psychological tradition which accepts it. What about Naturalism? The first point is that none of the arguments *for* a rational psychology is, in and of itself, an argument *against* a Naturalistic psychology. As I remarked above, to deny that mental operations have access to the semantic properties of mental representations is *not* to deny that mental representations *have* semantic properties. On the contrary, beliefs are *just* the kinds of things which exhibit truth and denotation, and the Naturalist proposes to make science out of the organism/environment relations which (presumably) fix these properties. Why, indeed, should he not?

This all *seems* very reasonable. Nevertheless, I now wish to argue that a computational psychology is the only one that we are likely to get; that qua research strategy, the attempt to construct a *naturalistic* psychology is very likely to prove fruitless. I think that the basis for such an argument is already to be found in the literature, where it takes the form of a (possibly inadvertent) reductio ad absurdum of the contrary view.

Consider, to begin with, a distinction that Professor Hilary Putnam introduces in "The Meaning of 'Meaning'" (1975) between what he calls "psychological states in the wide sense" and "psychological states in the narrow sense." A psychological state in the *narrow* sense is one the ascription of which does not "(presuppose) the existence of any individual other than the subject to whom that state is ascribed" (p. 10). All others are psychological states in the wide sense. So, for example, *x's jealousy of y* is a schema for expressions which denote psychological states in the wide sense since such expressions presuppose the existence, not only of the *x*s who are in the states, but also of the *y*s who are its objects. Putnam remarks that methodological solipsism (the phrase, by the way, is his) can be viewed as the requirement that only psychological states in the narrow sense are allowed as constructs in psychological theories.

Whereas, it's perhaps Putnam's main point that there are at least *some* scientific purposes (e.g., semantics and accounts of intertheoretical reference) which demand the wide construal. Here, rephrased slightly, is the sort of example that Putnam finds persuasive.

There is a planet (call it "Yon") where things are very much like here. In particular, by a cosmic accident, some of the people on Yon speak a dialect indistinguishable from English and live in an urban conglomerate indistinguishable from the Greater Boston Area. Still more, for every one of our Greater Bostonians, there is a doppelganger on Yon who has precisely the same neurological structure down to and including microparticles. We can assume that, so long as we're construing "psychological state" narrowly, this latter condition guarantees type identity of our psychological states with theirs.

However, Putnam argues, it doesn't guarantee that there is a corresponding identity of psychological states, hither and Yon, if we construe "psychological state" *widely*. Suppose that there is this difference between Yon and Earth; whereas, over here, the stuff we call "water" has the atomic structure H_2O, it turns out that the stuff that they call "water" over there has the atomic structure XYZ ($\neq H_2O$). And now, consider the mental state *thinking about water*. The idea is that, so long as we construe that state widely, it's one that we, but not our doppelgängers, can reasonably aspire to. For, construed widely, one is thinking about water only if it is water that one is thinking about. But it's water that one's thinking about only if it is H_2O that one's thinking about; water *is* H_2O. But since, by assumption, they never think about H_2O over Yon, it follows that there's at least one wide psychological state that we're often in and they never are, however neurophysiologically like us they are, and however much our narrow psychological states converge with theirs.

Moreover, if we try to say what they speak about, refer to, mention, etc.; if, in short, we try to supply a semantics for their dialect, we will have to mention XYZ, not H_2O. Hence it would be wrong, at least on Putnam's intuitions, to say that they have a word for water. A fortiori, the chemists who work in what they call "M.I.T." don't have theories about *water*, even though what runs through their heads when they talk about XYZ may be identical to what runs through our heads when we talk about H_2O. The situation is analogous to the one that arises for demonstratives and token reflexives, as Putnam insightfully points out.

Well, what are we to make of this? Is it an argument against methodological solipsism? And, if so, is it a *good* argument against methodological solipsism?

To begin with, Putnam's distinction between psychological states in the narrow and wide sense looks to be very intimately related to the traditional distinction between psychological states ascriptions opaquely and transparently construed. I'm a bit wary about this since what Putnam *says* about wide ascriptions is only that they "presuppose the existence" of objects other than the ascribee; and, of course *a believes Fb and b exists* does not entail *b is such that a believes F of him*, or even $\exists x$ *(a believes Fx)*. Moreover, the failure of such entailments is notoriously important in discussions of quantifying in. For all that, however, I don't *think* that it's Putnam's intention to exploit the difference between the existential generalization test for transparency and the presupposition of existence test for wideness. On the contrary, the burden of Putnam's argument seems to be precisely that "John believes (widely) that water is F" is true only if water (viz., H_2O) is such that John believes it's F. It's thus unclear to me why Putnam gives the weaker condition on wideness when it appears to be the stronger one that does the work.[10]

But whatever the case may be with the wide sense of belief, it's pretty clear that the narrow sense must be (what I've been calling) fully opaque. (This is because only full opacity allows type identity of beliefs that have different truth conditions [Sam's belief that he's ill with Misha's belief that *he* is; Yon beliefs about XYZ with hither beliefs about H_2O.]) I want to emphasize this correspondence between narrowness and full opacity, and not just in aid of terminological parsimony. Putnam sometimes writes as though he takes the methodological commitment to a psychology of narrow mental states to be a sort of vulgar prejudice: "Making this assumption is, of course, adopting a *restrictive program*—a program which deliberately limits the scope and nature of psychology to fit certain mentalistic preconceptions or, in some cases, to fit an idealistic reconstruction of knowledge and the world" (p. 137). But, in light of what we've said so far, it should be clear that this is a methodology with malice aforethought. Narrow psychological states are those individuated in light of the formality condition; viz., without reference to such semantic properties as truth and reference. And honoring the formality condition is part and parcel of the attempt to provide a theory which explains (a) how the belief that the Morning Star is F could be different from the belief that the Evening Star is F despite the well-known astronomical facts; and (b) how the behavioral effects of believing that the Morning Star is F could be different from those of believing that the Evening Star is F, astronomy once again apparently to the contrary notwithstanding. Putnam is, of course, dubious about this whole project: "... The three centuries of failure of mentalistic psychology is tremendous evidence against this procedure, in my opinion" (p. 137). I suppose this is intended to include everybody from Locke and Kant to Freud and Chomsky. I should have such failures.

So much for background. I now need an argument to show that a naturalistic psychology (a psychology of mental states transparently individuated; hence, presumably, a psychology of mental states in the wide sense) is, for practical purposes, out of the question. So far as I can see, however, Putnam has given that argument. For, consider: a naturalistic psychology is a theory of organism/environment transactions. So, to stick to Putnam's example, a naturalistic psychology would have to find some stuff S and some relation R, such that one's narrow thought that water is wet is a thought about S in virtue of the fact that one bears R to S. Well, *which* stuff? The natural thing to say would be: "Water, of course." Notice, however, that if Putnam is right, it may not even be *true* that the narrow thought that water is wet is a thought about water; it *won't* be true of tokens of that thought which occur on Yon. Whether the narrow thought that water is wet is about water depends on whether it's about H_2O; and whether it's about H_2O depends on "how science turns out"—viz., on what chemistry is true. (Similarly, mutatis mutandis, "water" refers to water is *not*, on this view, a truth of any branch of linguistics; it's chemists who tell us what it is that "water" refers to.) Surely, however, characterizing the objects of thought is methodologically prior to characterizing the causal chains that link thoughts to their objects. But the theory which characterizes the objects of thought is the theory of *everything*; it's all of science. Hence, the methodological moral of Putnam's analysis seems to be: the naturalistic psychologists will inherit the Earth, but only after everybody else is finished with it. No doubt it's alright to have a research strategy that says "wait awhile." But who want to wait *forever*?

This sort of argument isn't novel. Indeed, it was anticipated by Bloomfield (1933). Bloomfield argues that, for all practical purposes, you can't do semantics. The reason that you can't is that to do semantics you have to be able to say, for example, what "salt" refers to. But what "salt" refers to is NaCl, and that's a bit of chemistry, not linguistics:

> The situations which prompt people to utter speech include every object and happening in their universe. In order to give a scientifically accurate definition of meaning for every form of a language, we would have to have a scientifically accurate knowledge of everything in the speaker's world. The actual extent of human knowledge is very small compared to this. We can define the meaning of a speech-form accurately when this meaning has to do with some matter of which we possess scientific knowledge. We can define the names of minerals, as when we say that the ordinary meaning of the English word *salt* is "sodium chloride (NaCl)," and we can define the names of plants or animals by means of the technical terms of botany or zoology, but we have no precise way of defining words like *love* or *hate,* which concern situations that have not been accurately classified.... The statement of meanings is therefore the weak point in language-study, and will remain so until knowledge advances very far beyond its present state. (pp. 139–140)

It seems to me as though Putnam ought to endorse all of this *including the moral*: the distinction between wanting a naturalistic semantics (psychology) and not wanting any is real but academic.[11]

The argument just given depends, however, on accepting Putnam's analysis of his example. But suppose that one's intuitions run the other way. Then one is at liberty to argue like this:

1. They do too have water over Yon; all Putnam's example shows is that there could be two kinds of water, our kind (= H_2O) and their kind (= XYZ).
2. Hence, Yon tokens of the thought that water is wet are thoughts about water after all.
3. Hence, the way chemistry turns out is irrelevant to whether thoughts about water are about water.
4. Hence, the naturalistic psychology of thought need not wait upon the sciences of the objects of thought.
5. Hence, a naturalistic psychology may be in the cards after all.

Since the premises of this sort of reply may be tempting (since, indeed, they may be *true*) it's worth presenting a version of the argument which doesn't depend on intuitions about what XYZ is.

A naturalistic psychology would specify the relations that hold between an organism and an object in its environment when the one is thinking about the other. Now, think how such a theory would have to go. Since it would have to define its generalizations over mental states on the one hand and environmental entities on the other, it will need, in particular, some canonical way of referring to the latter. Well, *which* way? If one assumes that what makes my thought about Robin Roberts a thought *about Robin Roberts* is some causal connection between the two of us, then we'll need a description of RR such that the causal connection obtains in virtue of his satisfying that description. And *that* means, presumably, that we'll need a description under which the relation between him and me instantiates a law.

Generally, then, a naturalistic psychology would attempt to specify environmental objects in a vocabulary such that environment/organism relations are law-instantiating when so described. But here's the depressing consequence again: we have no access to such a vocabulary prior to the elaboration (completion?) of the nonpsychological sciences. "What Granny likes with her herring" isn't, for example, a description under which salt is law-instantiating; nor, presumably, is "salt." What we need is something like "NaCl," and descriptions like "NaCl" are available only *after* we've done our chemistry. What this comes down to is that, at a minimum, "*x*'s being F causally explains . . ." can be true only when "F" expresses nomologically necessary properties of the *x*s. Heaven knows it's hard to say what *that* means, but it presumably rules out both "Salt's being what Granny likes with herring . . ." and "Salt's being salt . . ."; the former for want of being necessary, and the latter for want of being nomological. I take it, moreover, that Bloomfield is right when he says (a) that we don't know relevant nomologically necessary properties of most of the things we can refer to (think about) and (b) that it isn't the linguist's (psychologist's) job to find them out.

Here's still another way to put this sort of argument. The way Bloomfield states his case invites the question: "Why *should* a semanticist want a definition of 'salt' that's 'scientifically accurate' in your sense? Why wouldn't a 'nominal' definition do?" There is, I think, some point to such a query. For example, as Hartry Field has pointed out (1972), it wouldn't make much difference to the way that truth-conditional semantics goes if we were to say only "'salt' refers to whatever it refers to." All we need for this sort of semantics is some way or other of referring to the extension of "salt"; we don't, in particular, need a "scientifically accurate" way. It's therefore pertinent to do what Bloomfield notably does not: distinguish between the goals of *semantics* and those of a naturalistic psychology of language. The latter, by assumption, purports to explicate the organism/environment transactions in virtue of which relations like reference hold. It therefore requires, at a minimum, lawlike generalizations of the (approximate) form: *X's utterance of "salt" refers to salt iff X bears relation R to* ______. Since this whole thing *is* supposed to be lawlike, what goes in for "   " must be a projectible characterization of the extension of "salt." But, in general, we discover which descriptions are projectible only *a posteriori*; in light of how the sciences (including the nonpsychological sciences) turn out. We are back where we started. Looked at this way, the moral is that we can do (certain kinds of) semantics if we have a way of referring to the extension of "salt." But we can't do the naturalistic psychology of reference unless we have some way of saying what salt *is*; which of its properties determine its causal relations.

It's important to emphasize that these sorts of arguments do *not* apply against the research program embodied in "Rational psychology"; viz., to the program which envisions a psychology that honors the formality condition. The problem we've been facing is: under what description does the object of thought enter into scientific generalizations about the relations between thoughts and their objects? It looks as though the naturalist is going to have to say: under a description that's law instantiating; e.g., under physical description. Whereas the rational psychologist has a quite different answer. What *he* wants is *whatever description the organism has in mind* when it thinks about the object of thought, construing "thinks about" fully opaquely. So, for a theory of psychological states narrowly construed, we want such descriptions of Venus as, e.g., "the Morning Star," "the Evening Star," "Venus," etc., for it's these sorts of descriptions which we presumably entertain when we think that the Morning Star is *F*. In particular, it's our relation to these sorts of descriptions that determines what psychological state type we're in insofar as the goal in taxonomizing psychological states is explaining how they affect behavior.

A final point under the general head: the hopelessness of naturalistic psychology. Practicing naturalistic psychologists have been at least dimly aware all along of the sort of bind that they're in. So, for example, the "physical specification of the stimulus" is just about invariably announced as a requirement upon adequate formulations of S-R generalizations. We can now see why. Suppose, wildly contrary to fact, that there exists a human population (e.g., English speakers) in which pencils are, in the technical sense of the notion, discriminative stimuli controlling the verbal response "pencil." The point is that, even if some such generalization were true, it wouldn't be among those enunciated by a naturalistic psychology; the generalizations of naturalistic psychology are presumably supposed to be nomological, and there aren't any *laws* about pencils *qua* pencils. That is: expressions like "pencil" presumably occur in no true, lawlike sentences. Of course, there presumably is *some* description in virtue of which pencils fall under the organism/environment laws of a naturalistic psychology, and everybody (except, possibly, Gibson) has always assumed that those descriptions are, approximately, physical descriptions. Hence, the naturalist's demand, perfectly warranted by his lights, that the stimulus should be physically specified.

But though their theory has been consistent, their practice has uniformly not. In practice, and barring the elaborately circumscribed cases that psychophysics studies, the requirement that the stimulus be physically specified has been ignored by just about *all* practitioners. And, indeed, they were well advised to ignore it; how else could they get on with their job? If they really had to wait for the physicists to determine the description(s) under which pencils are law-instantiators, how would the psychology of pencils get off the ground?

So far as I can see, there are really only two ways out of this dilemma:

1. We can fudge, the way that learning theorists usually do. That is, we can "read" the description of the stimulus from the character of the organism's response. In point of historical fact, this has lead to a kind of naturalistic psychology which is merely a solemn paraphrase of what everybody's grandmother knows: e.g., to saying "pencils are discriminative stimuli for the utterance of 'pencil'" where Granny would have said "pencil" refers to pencils. I take it that Chomsky's review of *Verbal Behavior* (1959) demonstrated, once and for all, the fatuity of this course. What *would* be interesting—what would have surprised Grandmother—is a generalization of the form Δ *is the discriminative stimulus for utterances of "pencil"* where Δ is a description which picks out pencils in some projectible vocabulary (e.g., in the vocabulary of physics). Does anybody suppose that such descriptions are likely to be forthcoming in, say, the *next* three hundred years?

2. The other choice is to try for a computational psychology; which is, of course, the burden of my plaint. On this view, what we can reasonably hope for is a theory of mental states fully opaquely type-individuated. We can try to say what the mental representation is, and what the relation to a mental representation is, such that one believes that the Morning Star is F in virtue of bearing the latter to the former. And we can try to say how that representation, or that relation, or both, differ from the representation and the relation constitutive of believing that the Evening Star is F. A naturalistic psychology, by contrast, remains a sort of ideal of pure reason; there must *be*

such a psychology since, presumably, we do sometimes think of Venus and, presumably, we do so in virtue of a causal relation between it and us. But there's no practical hope of making science out of this relation. And, of course, for methodology, practical hope is *everything*.

One final point, and then I'm through. Methodological solipsism isn't, of course, solipsism *tout court*. It's not part of the enterprise to assert, or even suggest, that you and I are actually in the situation of Winograd's computer. Heaven only knows what relation between me and Robin Roberts makes it possible for me to think of him (refer to him, etc.), and I've been doubting the practical possibility of a science whose generalizations that relation instantiates. But I *don't* doubt that there *is* such a relation or that I do sometimes think of him. Still more: I have reasons not to doubt it; precisely the sorts of reasons I'd supply if I were asked to justify my knowledge claims about his pitching record. In short: it's true that Roberts won twenty-eight, and it's true that I know that he did, and nothing in the preceding tends to impugn these truths. (Or, contrariwise, if he didn't and I'm mistaken, then the reasons for my mistake are philosophically boring; they're biographical, not epistemological or ontological.) My point, then, is *of course* not that solipsism is true; it's just that truth, reference and the rest of the semantic notions aren't psychological categories. What they are is: they're modes of *Dasein*. I don't know what *Dasein* is, but I'm sure that there's lots of it around, and I'm sure that you and I and Cincinnati have all got it. What more do you want?

Acknowledgments

I've had a lot of help with this one. I'm particularly indebted to: Professors Ned Block, Sylvain Bromberger, Janet Dean Fodor, Keith Gundersen, Robert Richardson, Judith Thomson; and to Mr. Israel Krakowski.

Notes

1. I shall speak of "type identity" (distinctness) of mental states to pick out the sense of "same mental state" in which, for example, John and Mary are in the same mental state if both believe that water flows. Correspondingly, I shall use the notion of "token identity" (distinctness) of mental state to pick out the sense of "same mental state" in which it's necessary that if x and y are in the same mental state, then $x = y$.

2. For extensive discussion, see Fodor 1975; forthcoming.

3. This is *not*, notice, the same as saying "formal operations are the ones that apply mechanically"; in this latter sense, *formality* means something like *explicitness*. There's no particular reason for using "formal" to mean both "syntactic" and "explicit," though the ambiguity abounds in the literature.

4. Some fairly deep methodological issues in Artifical Intelligence are involved here. See Fodor 1978 where this surface is lightly scratched.

5. I'm told by some of my friends that this paragraph could be read as suggesting that there are *two kinds* of beliefs: opaque ones and transparent ones. That is not, of course, the way that it is intended to be read. The idea is rather that there are two kinds of conditions that we can place on determinations that a pair of belief tokens count as tokens of the same belief type. According to

one set of conditions (corresponding to transparent taxonomy) a belief that the Morning Star is such and such counts as the same belief as a belief that the Evening Star is such and such; whereas, according to the other set of conditions (corresponding to opaque taxonomy), it does not.

6. I'm leaving it open that it may be to say still less than this (e.g., because of problems about reference under false descriptions). For purposes of the present discussion, I don't need to run a line of the truth conditions for transparent propositional attitude ascriptions. Thank Heaven, since I do not have one.

7. It's worth emphasizing that the sense of "behavior" *is* proprietary, and that that's pretty much what you would expect. Not every true description of an act can be such that a theory of the mental causation of behavior will explain the act under that description. (In being rude to Darcy, Elizabeth is insulting the man whom she will eventually marry. A theory of the mental causation of her behavior might have access to the former description, but not, surely, to the latter.)

Many philosophers—especially since Wittgenstein—have emphasized the ways in which the description of behavior may depend upon its context, and it is a frequent charge against modern versions of Rational psychology that they typically ignore such characterizations. So they do, but so what? You can't have explanations of everything under every description, and it's a question for empirical determination which descriptions of behavior reveal its systematicity vis-à-vis its causes. The Rational psychologist is prepared to bet that—to put it *very* approximately—behavior will prove to be systematic under some of the descriptions under which it is intentional.

At a minimum, the present claim goes like this: there is a way of taxonomizing behaviors and a way of taxonomizing mental states such that, given these taxonomies, theories of the mental causation of behavior will be forthcoming. And that way of taxonomizing mental states construes them nontransparently.

8. One might try saying: what counts for opaque type individuation is what's *in* your head, not just what's running through it. So, for example, though Alfred and Misha are both thinking "he feels faint," nevertheless different counterfactuals are true of them: Misha would cash his pronoun as: "he, Sam" whereas Alfred would cash *his* pronoun as: "he, Misha." The problem would then be to decide *which* such counterfactuals are relevant since, if we count all of them, it's going to turn out that there are few, if any, cases of distinct organisms having type-identical thoughts.

I won't, in any event, pursue this proposal since it seems clear that it won't, in principle, cope with all the relevant cases. Two people would be having different thoughts when each is thinking "I'm ill" even if *everything* in their heads were the same.

9. I'm assuming, for convenience that all the Ps are such that either they or their denials are believed. This saves having to relativize to time (e.g., having (b) and (c) read "... you believe or come to believe ...").

10. I blush to admit that I had missed some of these complexities until Sylvain Bromberger kindly rubbed my nose in them.

11. It may be that Putnam *does* accept this moral. For example, the upshot of the discussion around p. 153 of his article appears to be that a Greek semanticist prior to Archimedes *could* not (in practice) have given a correct account of what (the Greek equivalent of) "gold" means; viz., because the theory needed to specify the extension of the term was simply not available. Presumably *we* are in that situation vis-à-vis the objects of many of *our* thoughts and the meanings of many of our terms; and, presumably, we will continue to do so into the indefinite future. But, then, what's the point of defining psychology (semantics) so that there can't be any?

Glossary

The Editor has suggested that I provide a brief glossary for nonphilosophers. The question as to how the technical jargon should be employed is itself often a matter of philosophical dispute, and the following is by no means supposed to be definitive. In fact, it's very rough.

coherence (theory of truth): the doctrine that the truth of a theory is a matter of the way its claims are related to one another (and hence *not* of the way that they are related to the world). A specimen coherence theory of truth might hold that the true theory is the simplest of the consistent ones.

correspondence (theory of truth): the doctrine that the truth of a theory is a matter of the relation that holds between its claims and the world; the true theory is the one whose claims about the world correspond to the way that the world actually is.

Dasein: a term of art owing to the German philosopher Martin Heidegger, about whom I know nothing. *Dasein* is often rendered in English as "Being in the World."

existential generalization: the principle of logic which permits inference from a premise of the form *a is F* (e.g., John is pink) to a conclusion of the form $\exists x\ (Fx)$ (e.g., there exists something that is pink).

extension (of a term): the set of things of which the term is true. So the extension of "female" is the set of females, etc.

nomological: lawful. It is usually said that a true generalization may nevertheless fail to be a law. It's an issue of considerable philosophical concern what properties *other* than truth a general sentence has to have if it is to express a law. Most philosophers agree that among these further properties is the satisfaction of certain constraints on its vocabulary.

opaque (context): to a first approximation: a sentential context in which existential generalization (q.v.) and/or substitutivity of identicals (q.v.) do *not* apply. (For example, the context "John believes —— lives at the North Pole" is opaque since such inferences as "John believes Santa Claus lives at the North Pole, therefore there is someone whom John believes lives at the North Pole" are invalid.) However, see text.

semantic (properties of an expression): for the purposes of this paper, the semantic properties of an expression are among its relational properties; in particular, they are among those of its properties which it has in virtue of its relations to *non*linguistic entities. Truth is a paradigmatic semantic property (assuming that the correspondence theory of truth (q.v.) is true).

substitutivity of identicals: the principle of logic which permits inference from premises of the form $Fa\ \&\ a = b$ (e.g., the Morning Star is pink and the Morning Star is identical to the Evening Star) to a conclusion of the form *Fb* (e.g., the Evening Star is pink). The idea is that if two expressions name (refer to) the same thing, then they can be substituted in a context without changing its truth value.

transparent (context): to a first approximation, a sentential context which is *not* opaque (q.v.). However, see text.

type/token relation: the relation which holds, for example, between a word and an inscription (or utterance) of that word. By analogy, the relation which holds between a kind and anything which is *of* that kind.

References

Bloomfield, L. (1933). *Language.* London: Allen and Unwin.

Chomsky, N. (1959). Review of Skinner's *Verbal Behavior. Language* 35: 26–58

Field, H. (1972). Tarski's Theory of Truth. *Journal of Philosophy* 69: 347–375.

Fodor, J. A. (1975). *The Language of Thought.* New York: Thomas Y. Crowell.

Fodor, J. A. (1978). Tom Swift and His Procedural Grandmother. *Cognition* 6: 229–247.

Fodor, J. A. (1979). *Propositional Attitudes. Monist* 61: 501–523.

Geach, P. (1957). *Mental Acts.* London: Routledge and Kegan Paul.

Goodman, N. (1978). *Ways of World Making.* Indianapolis: Hackett.

James, W. (1890). *Principles of Psychology,* vol. I. New York: Henry Holt. (Repr., New York: Dover, 1950.)

Putnam, H. (1960). Minds and Machines. In S. Hook (ed.), *Dimensions of Mind.* New York: New York Univ. Press.

Putnam, H. (1975). The Meaning of "Meaning". In K. Gunderson (ed.), *Minnesota Studies in the Philosophy of Science, 7: Language, Mind, and Knowledge.* Minneapolis: Univ. of Minnesota Press.

Winograd, T. (1972). *Understanding Natural Language.* New York: Academic Press.

54 Misrepresentation

Fred Dretske

Epistemology is concerned with knowledge: how do we manage to get things right? There is a deeper question: how do we manage to get things wrong? How is it possible for physical systems to *misrepresent* the state of their surroundings?

The problem is not how, for example, a diagram, *d*, can misrepresent the world, *w*. For if we have another system, *r*, already possessed of representational powers, *d* can be used as an expressive extension of *r*, thereby participating in *r*'s representational successes and failures. When this occurs, *d* can come to mean that *w* is *F* when, in fact, *w* is not *F*, but *d*'s meaning derives, ultimately, from *r*. A chart depicting unemployment patterns over the past ten years can misrepresent this condition, but the chart's capacity for misrepresentation is derived from its role as an expressive instrument for agents, speakers of the language, who already have this power.

No, the problem is, rather, one of a system's powers of representation in so far as these powers do not derive from the representational efforts of another source. Unless we have some clue to how this is possible, we do not have a clue how naturally-evolving biological systems could have acquired the capacity for belief. For belief is, or so I shall assume, a *non-derived* representational capacity the exercise of which *can* yield a misrepresentation.

The capacity for misrepresentation is a part, perhaps only a small part, of the general problem of meaning or intentionality. Once we have meaning, we can, in our descriptions and explanations of human, animal, and perhaps even machine behaviour, lavish it on the systems we describe. Once we have intentionality, we can (to use Dennett's language) adopt the intentional stance.[1] But what (*besides* intentionality) gives us (and not, say, machines) the power to adopt this stance? Our ability to adopt this stance is an *expression*, not an analysis, of intentionality. The borrowed meaning of systems towards which we adopt appropriate attitudes tells us no more about the original capacity for misrepresentation than does a misplaced pin on a military map. What we are after, so to speak, is *nature*'s way of making a mistake, the place where the misrepresentational buck stops. Only when we understand this shall we understand how grey matter can misrepresent the weather for tomorrow's picnic.

1 Natural Signs

Naturally-occurring signs mean something, and they do so without any assistance from us.[2] Water does not flow uphill; hence, a northerly-flowing river means there is a downward gradient in that direction. Shadows to the east mean that the sun is in the west. A sudden force on the passengers in one direction means an acceleration of the train in the opposite direction. The power of these events or conditions to mean what they do is independent of the way we interpret them—or, indeed, of whether we interpret or recognize them at all. The dentist may *use* the X-ray to diagnose the condition of your upper right molar, but the dark shadows mean extensive decay has occurred whether or not he, or anyone else, appreciates this fact. Expanding metal indicates a rising temperature (and in this sense means that the temperature is rising) whether or not anyone, upon observing the former, comes to believe the latter. It meant that *before* intelligent organisms, capable of exploiting this fact (by building thermometers), inhabited the earth. If we are looking for the ultimate source of meaning, and with it an understanding of a system's power of misrepresentation, here, surely, is a promising place to begin.

Natural signs are indicators, more or less reliable indicators, and what they mean is what they indicate to be so. The power of a natural sign to mean something—for example, that Tommy has measles—is underwritten by certain objective constraints, certain lawful relations, between the sign (or the sign's having a certain property) and the condition that constitutes its meaning (Tommy's having measles). In most cases this relation is causal or lawful, one capable of supporting a counterfactual assertion to the effect that if the one condition had not obtained (if Tommy did not have measles), neither would the other (he would not have those red spots all over his face). Sometimes there are merely regularities, non-lawful but none the less pervasive, that help secure the connection between sign and significance. It is partly the fact, presumably not itself lawful, that animals (for example, squirrels or woodpeckers) do not regularly ring doorbells while foraging for food that makes the ringing bell *mean* that someone (i.e. some *person*) is at the door. If squirrels changed their habits (because, say, doorbells were made out of nuts), then a ringing doorbell would no longer mean what it now does. But as things *now* stand, we can (usually) say that the bell would not be ringing unless someone was at the door, that the bell indicates someone's presence at the door, and that, therefore, that is what it means. But this subjunctively expressed dependency between the ringing bell and someone's presence at the door is a reflection of a regularity which, though not conventional, is not fully lawful either. None the less, the doorbell retains its natural meaning as long as this regularity persists.

Beyond this I have nothing very systematic to say about what constitutes the natural meaning of an event or a condition.[3] I shall proceed with what I hope is a reasonably familiar notion, appealing (when necessary) to concrete examples. The project is to see how far one can go in understanding misrepresentation, the power of a condition (state, event, situation) r to mean (say, indicate) *falsely* that w is F (thereby misrepresenting w), in terms of a natural sign's meaning that w is F. Only when (or if) this project succeeds, or shows reasonable prospects of succeeding, will it, or might it, be necessary to look more carefully at what got smuggled in at the beginning.

Though natural meaning is a promising point of departure, it is hard to see how to get under way. Natural signs, though they mean something, though they can (in this sense) represent w (by indicating or meaning that w is F) are powerless to *misrepresent* anything. Either they do their job right or they don't do it at all. The spots on Tommy's face certainly can mean that he has measles, but they mean this *only* when he has measles. If he doesn't have measles, then the spots don't mean this. Perhaps all they mean is that Tommy has been eating too many sweets.

Grice expresses this point by saying that an occurrence (a tokening of some natural sign) means (in what he calls the natural sense of "meaning"—hereafter meaning_n) that *P* only if *P*.[4] He contrasts this sense of meaning with non-natural meaning where a sign can mean that *P* even though *P* is false. If we reserve the word "meaning" (minus subscripts) for that species of meaning in which something can mean that *w* is *F* when *w* isn't *F*, the kind of meaning in which misrepresentation is possible, then meaning_n seems a poorly-qualified candidate for understanding meaning.

In speaking of signs and their natural meaning I should always be understood as referring to *particular* events, states or conditions: *this* track, *those* clouds, and *that* smoke. A sign type (for example, smoke) may be said to mean, in some natural sense, that there is fire even when every token of that type fails to mean_n this (because, occasionally, there is no fire). But this type-associated meaning, whatever its proper analysis, does *not* help us understand misrepresentation unless the individual tokens of that type *have* the type-associated meaning, unless particular puffs of smoke mean_n that there is fire when there is no fire. This, though, is not the case. A petrol gauge's registration of "empty" (this *type* of event) can signify an empty tank, but when the tank is not empty, no particular registration of "empty" by the gauge's pointer means_n that the tank is empty. Hence, no particular registration of the gauge misrepresents the amount of gas in the tank (by meaning_n that it is empty when it is not).

The inability of (particular) natural signs to misrepresent anything is sometimes obscured by the way we exploit them in manufactured devices. Interested as we may be in whether, and if so when, *w* becomes *F*, we concoct a device *d* whose various states are designed to function as natural signs of *w*'s condition. Since this is how we use the device, we tend to say of some particular registration that *d*'s being *G* (assuming this is the natural sign of *w*'s being *F*) means that *w* is *F* even when, through malfunction or misuse, the system is failing to perform satisfactorily and *w* is not *F*. But this, clearly, is not what the particular pointer position means_n. This is what it is *supposed* to mean_n, what it was *designed* to mean_n, what (perhaps) tokens of type *normally* mean_n, but not what it *does* mean_n.

When there is a short circuit, the ring of the doorbell (regardless of what it was designed to indicate, regardless of what it normally indicates) does not indicate that the bellpush is being pressed. It still means_n (indicates) that there is electric current flowing in the doorbell circuit (one of the things it always meant_n), but the latter no longer means_n that the bellpush is being pressed. What the flow of current *now* means_n—and this is surely how we would judge it if we could *see* the bellpush, *see that* it was *not* being pressed—is that the system is malfunctioning or that there is a short circuit somewhere in the wiring. The *statement*, "There is someone at the door," can mean that there is someone at the door even when no one is there, but the ringing doorbell cannot mean this when no one is there. Not, at least, if we are talking about meaning_n. If the bellpush is not being pressed, then we must look for something else for the ringing bell to mean_n. Often, we withdraw to some more proximal meaning_n, some condition or state of affairs in the normal chain of causal antecedents that *does* obtain (for example, the flow of current or the *cause* of the flow of current—for example, a short circuit) and designate it as the meaning_n of the ringing bell.

2 Functional Meaning

Granted, one may say, the doorbell's ringing cannot $mean_n$ that someone is at the door when no one is there; still, in some related sense of meaning, it means this whether or not anyone is there. If this is not natural meaning ($meaning_n$), it is a close cousin.

Whether it is a cousin or not, there certainly is a kind of meaning that attaches to systems, or components of systems, for which there are identifiable *functions*. Consider, once again, the fuel gauge. It has a function: to pass along information about the amount of petrol in the tank. When things are working properly, the position of the needle is a natural sign of the contents of the tank. Its pointing to the left $means_n$ that the tank is empty. Its pointing to the right $means_n$ that the tank is full. And so on for the intermediate positions. But things sometimes go wrong: connections work loose, the battery goes dead, wires break. The gauge begins to register "empty" when the tank is still full. When this happens there is a tendency to say that the gauge misrepresents the contents of the tank. It *says* the tank is empty when it is not. It *means* (not, of course, $means_n$, but still means in *some* sense) that the tank is empty.

When *d*'s being *G* is, normally, a natural sign of *w*'s being *F*, when this is what it normally $means_n$, then there is a sense in which it means this whether or not *w* is *F if it is the function of d to indicate the condition of w*. Let us call this kind of meaning *$meaning_f$*—the subscript indicating that this is a functionally derived meaning.

(M_f) *d*'s being *G* $means_f$ that *w* is $F =$ *d*'s function is to indicate the condition of *w*, and the way it performs this function is, in part, by indicating that *w* is F by its (*d*'s) being *G*

The position of the needle on the broken fuel gauge $means_f$ that the tank is empty because it is the gauge's function to indicate the amount of remaining fuel, and the way it performs this function is, in part, by indicating an empty tank when the gauge registers "empty."[5] And, for the same reason and in the same sense, the ringing doorbell says (i.e. $means_f$) that someone is at the door even when no one is there.

Whether or not M_f represents any progress in our attempt to naturalize meaning (and thus understand a system's non-derivative power to misrepresent) depends on whether the functions in question can themselves be understood in some natural way. If these functions are (what I shall call) *assigned* functions, then $meaning_f$ is tainted with the purposes, intentions, and beliefs of those who assign the function from which $meaning_f$ derives its misrepresentational powers.[6] We shall not have tracked meaning, in so far as this involves the power of misrepresentation, to its original source. We shall merely have worked our way back, somewhat indirectly, to *our own* mysterious capacity for representation.

To understand what I mean by an *assigned* function, and the way *we* (our intentions, purposes and beliefs) are implicated in a system's having such a function, consider the following case. A sensitive spring-operated scale, calibrated in fractions of a gram, is designed and used to determine the weight of very small objects. Unknown to both designers and users, the instrument is a sensitive indicator of altitude. By registering a reduced weight for things as altitude increases (note: a thing's weight is a function of its height above sea level), the instrument *could* be used as a crude altimeter if the user attached a standard weight and noted the instrument's variable registration as altitude changed. Suppose, now, that under normal use in the laboratory the instrument malfunctions and registers 0.98 g. for an object weighing 1 g. Is it misrepresenting the *weight* of the object? Is it misrepresenting the *altitude* of the object? What does the reading of 0.98 g. mean? If we are talking about meaning$_n$, it clearly does not mean$_n$ that the object weighs 0.98 g. Nor does it mean$_n$ that the laboratory is 40,000 ft. above sea level. If we ask about meaning$_f$, though, it seems reasonable to say that the instrument's pointer says or indicates (i.e. means$_f$) that the object weighs 0.98 g. It is the function of this instrument to tell us what objects weigh, and it is telling us (incorrectly, as it turns out) that this object weighs 0.98 g.

But is the altitude being misrepresented? No. It should be noticed that the instrument cannot be misrepresenting *both* the altitude and the weight since a representation (or misrepresentation) of one presupposes a *fixity* (hence, *non*-representation) of the other.[7] Although the instrument *could* be used as an altimeter, it *is not* used that way. That is not its function. Its function is to register weight. That is the function we assign to it, the reason it was built and the explanation why it was built the way it was. Had our purposes been otherwise, it might have meant$_f$ something else. But they were not and it does not.

We sometimes change an instrument's assigned function. When we calibrate it, for example, we do not use it to measure what it is normally used to measure. Instead, we apply it to known quantities in order to use its indication as a (natural) sign of possible malfunction or inaccuracy in the instrument itself. In this case, a reading of 0.98 g. (for a weight *known* to be 1 g.) indicates that the spring has changed its characteristics, the pointer is bent, or some other component is out of adjustment. We get a new functional meaning because our altered background knowledge (normally a result of different intentions and purposes) changes what the pointer's behaviour means$_n$. With *assigned* functions, the meanings$_f$ change as *our* purposes change.[8]

We sometimes use animals in the same way that we use instruments. Dogs have an acute sense of smell. Exploiting this fact, customs officers use dogs to detect concealed marijuana. When the dog wags its tail, barks, or does whatever it is trained to do when it smells marijuana, the dog's behaviour serves as a natural sign—a sign that the luggage contains marijuana. But this does not mean that the dog's behaviour (or the neural condition that triggers this behaviour) can misrepresent the contents of the luggage. The dog's behaviour may make the customs officer believe (falsely) that there is marijuana in the suitcase, but the dog's behaviour means$_f$ this only in a derived way. If the dog is particularly good at its job, barking only when there is marijuana present, we can say that its bark indicates (i.e. means$_n$) that there is marijuana present. Furthermore, it means$_n$ this whether or not anyone interprets it as meaning$_n$ this, whether or not we *use* this natural sign for our own investigative purposes. But when there is no marijuana present, when the dog barks at an innocent box of herbs, the bark does *not* mean$_n$ that there is marijuana present. Nor does it mean$_f$ this in any sense that is independent of *our* interpretative activities. We can, of course, say what the bark means *to us* (that there is marijuana in the suitcase), but this way of talking merely reveals our own involvement in the meaning assigned to the dog's behaviour. *We* assign this meaning because this is the information we are *interested* in obtaining, the information we *expect* to get by using the dog in this way, the information the dog was trained to deliver. But if we set aside our interests and purposes, then, *when there is no marijuana present*, there is *no* sense in which the dog's bark means that there is marijuana in the suitcase. The only kind of misrepresentation occurring here is of the derived kind we are familiar with in maps, instruments, and language.

Therefore, if M_f is to serve as a naturalized account of representation, where this is understood to include the power of *mis*representation, then the functions in question must be *natural* functions, functions a thing has which are independent of *our* interpretative intentions and purposes. What we are looking for are functions involving a system of natural signs that give these signs a content, and therefore a meaning (i.e. a meaning_f), that is not parasitic on the way *we* exploit them in our information-gathering activities, on the way we choose to interpret them.[9]

We need, then, some characterization of a system's natural functions. More particularly, since we are concerned with the function a system of natural signs might have, we are looking for what a sign is *supposed* to mean_n where the "supposed to" is cashed out in terms of the function of that sign (or sign system) in the organism's *own* cognitive economy. We want to know how *the dog* represents the contents of the luggage—what (if anything) the smell of the box means_f *to it*.

3 Needs

The obvious place to look for natural functions is in biological systems having a variety of organs, mechanisms, and processes that were developed (flourished, preserved) *because* they played a vital information-gathering role in the species' adaptation to its surroundings. An information-gathering function, essential in most cases to the satisfaction of a biological need, can only be successfully realized in a system capable of occupying states that serve as natural signs of external (and sometimes *other* internal) conditions. If that cluster of photoreceptors we call the retina is to perform its function (whatever, exactly, we take this function to be), the various states of these receptors must mean_n something about the character and distribution of one's optical surroundings. Just what the various states these receptors mean_f will (in accordance with M_f) be determined by two things: (1) what it is the function of this receptor system to indicate, and (2) the meaning_n of the various states that enable the system to perform this function.

To illustrate the way M_f is supposed to work it is convenient to consider simple organisms with obvious biological needs—some thing or condition without which they could not survive. I say this is convenient because this approach to the problem of misrepresentation has its most compelling application to cognitive mechanisms subserving some basic biological need. And the consideration of *primitive* systems gives us the added advantage of avoiding that kind of circularity in the analysis that would be incurred by appealing to those kinds of "needs" (for example, my need for a word processor) that are derived from desires (for example, my desire to produce faster, cleaner copy). We cannot bring desires in at this stage of the analysis since they already possess the kind of representational content that we are trying to understand.

Some marine bacteria have internal magnets (called magnetosomes) that function like compass needles, aligning themselves (and, as a result, the bacteria) parallel to the earth's magnetic field.[10] Since these magnetic lines incline downwards (towards geomagnetic north) in the northern hemisphere (upwards in the southern hemisphere), bacteria in the northern hemisphere, oriented by their internal magnetosomes, propel themselves towards geomagnetic north. The survival value of magnetotaxis (as this sensory mechanism is called) is not obvious, but it is reasonable to suppose that it functions so as to enable the bacteria to avoid surface water. Since these organisms are capable of living only in the absence of oxygen, movement towards geomagnetic north will take the bacteria away from oxygen-rich surface water and towards the comparatively oxygen-free sediment at the bottom. Southern-hemispheric bacteria have their magnetosomes reversed, allowing them to swim towards geomagnetic south with the same beneficial results. Transplant a southern bacterium in the North Atlantic and it will destroy itself—swimming upwards (towards magnetic south) into the toxic, oxygen-rich surface water.

If a bar magnet oriented in the opposite direction to the earth's magnetic field is held near these bacteria, they can be lured into a deadly environment. Although I shall return to the point in a moment (in order to question this line of reasoning), this appears to be a plausible instance of misrepresentation. Since, in the bacteria's normal habitat, the internal orientation of their magnetosomes $means_n$ that there is relatively little oxygen in *that* direction, and since the organism needs precisely this piece of information in order to survive, it seems reasonable to say that it is the function of this sensory mechanism to serve the satisfaction of this need, to deliver this piece of information, to indicate that oxygen-free water is in *that* direction. If this is what it is *supposed* to $mean_n$, this is what it $means_f$. Hence, in the presence of the bar magnet and in accordance with M_f, the organism's sensory state misrepresents the location of oxygen-free water.

This is not to say, of course, that bacteria have *beliefs*, beliefs to the effect that there is little or no oxygen in *that* direction. The capacity for misrepresentation is only *one* dimension of intentionality, only *one* of the properties that a representational system must have to qualify as a belief system. To qualify as a belief, a representational content must also exhibit (among other things) the familiar opacity characteristic of the propositional attitudes, and, unless embellished in some way, $meaning_f$ does not (yet) exhibit *this* level of intentionality. Our project, though, is more modest. We are looking for a naturalized form of misrepresentation and, if we do not yet have an account of false *belief*, we do, it seems, have a naturalized account of false *content*.

Apart from some terminological flourishes and a somewhat different way of structuring the problem, nothing I have said so far is particularly original. I have merely been retracing steps, some very significant steps, already taken by others. I am thinking especially of Stampe's seminal analysis of linguistic representation in which the (possibly false) content of a representation is identified with what would cause the representation to have the properties it has under conditions of well-functioning;[11] Enc's development of functional ideas to provide an account of the intentionality of cognitive states;[12] Fodor's application of teleological notions in supplying a semantics for his "language of thought;"[13] and Millikan's powerful analysis of meaning in terms of the variety of proper functions a reproducible event (such as a sound or a gesture) might have.[14] I myself have tried to exploit (vaguely) functional ideas in my analysis of belief by defining a structure's semantic content in terms of the information it was developed to carry (hence, acquired the function of carrying).[15]

4 The Indeterminacy of Function

Though this approach to the problem of meaning—and, hence, misrepresentation—has been explored in some depth, there remain obstacles to regarding it as even a promising sketch, let alone a finished portrait, of nature's way of making a mistake.

There is, first, the question of how to understand a system's ability to misrepresent something for which it has no biological need. If *O* does not need (or need to avoid) *F*, it cannot (on the present account) be the *natural* function of any of *O*'s cognitive systems to alert it to the presence (absence, location, approach, identity) of *F*. And without this, there is no possibility of *mis*representing something *as F*. Some internal state could still mean_n that an *F* was present (in the way the state of Rover's detector system means_n that the luggage contains marijuana), but this internal state cannot $\textit{mean}_f$ this. What we have so far is a way of understanding how an organism might misrepresent the presence of food, an obstacle, a predator, or a mate (something there is a biological need to secure or avoid),[16] but no way of understanding how *we* can misrepresent things as, say, can-openers, tennis-rackets, tulips, or the jack of diamonds. Even if we suppose our nervous systems sophisticated enough to indicate (under normal conditions) the presence of such things, it surely cannot be the *natural* function of these neural states to signal the presence—much less, specific kinds—of kitchen utensils, sporting equipment, flowers, and playing cards.

I think this is a formidable, but *not* an insuperable, difficulty. For it seems clear that a cognitive system might develop so as to service, and hence have the natural function of servicing, some biological need without its representational (*and* misrepresentational) efforts being confined to these needs. In order to identify its natural predator, an organism might develop detectors of colour, shape, and movement of considerable discriminative power. Equipped, then, with this capacity for differentiating various colours, shapes, and movements, the organism acquires, as a fringe benefit so to speak, the ability to identify (and, hence, misidentify) things for which it has no biological need. The creature may have no need for green leaves, but its need for pink blossoms has led to the development of a cognitive system whose various states are capable, because of their need-related meaning_f, to mean_f that there are green leaves present. Perhaps, though having no need for such things, it has developed a taste for them and hence a way of representing them with elements that already have a meaning_f.

There is, however, a more serious objection to this approach to the problem of misrepresentation. Consider, once again, the bacteria. It was said that it was the function of their magnetotactic system to indicate the whereabouts of oxygen-free environments. But why describe the function of this system in this way? Why not say that it is the function of this system to indicate the direction of geomagnetic north? Perhaps, to be even more modest, we should assign to this sensor the function of indicating the whereabouts (direction) of magnetic (not necessarily *geo*magnetic) north. This primitive sensory mechanism is, after all, functioning perfectly well when, under the bar magnet's influence, it leads its possessor into a toxic environment. *Something* is going wrong in this case, of course, but I see no reason to place the blame on the sensory mechanism, no reason to say it is not performing *its* function. One may as well complain that a fuel gauge is not performing its function when the petrol tank is filled with water (and the driver is consequently misled about the amount of *petrol* he has left).

Under such abnormal circumstances, the instrument is performing its duties in a perfectly satisfactory way—i.e., indicating the amount of liquid in the tank. What has gone wrong is something for which the instrument itself is not responsible: namely, a breakdown in the normal correlations (between the quantity of liquid in the tank and the quantity of petrol in the tank) that make the gauge serviceable as a *fuel* gauge, that allow it (when conditions are normal) to mean_n that there is petrol in the tank. Similarly, there is nothing wrong with one's perceptual system when one consults a slow-running clock and is, as a result, misled about the time of day. It is the function of one's eyes to tell one what *the clock says*; it is the function of *the clock to* say what the time is. Getting things right about what you need to know is often a *shared* responsibility. You have to get *G* right and *G* has to get *F* right. Hence, even if it is *F* that you need, or need to know about, the function of the perceptual system may be only to inform you of *G*.

If we think about the bacterium's sensory system in this way, then *its* function is to align the organism with the prevailing magnetic field. It is, so to speak, the job of magnetic north to be the direction of oxygen-free water. By transplanting a northern bacterium in the southern hemisphere we can make things go awry, but *not* because a hemispheric transplant undergoes *sensory* disorientation. No, the magnetotactic system functions as it is supposed to function, as it was (presumably) evolved to function. The most that might be claimed is that there is some *cognitive* slip (the bacterium mistakenly "infers" from its sensory condition that *that* is the direction of oxygen-free water). This sort of reply, however, begs the question by presupposing that the creature *already* has the conceptual or representational capacity to represent something *as* the direction of oxygen-free water. Our question is *whether* the organism has this capacity and, if so, where it comes from.[17]

Northern bacteria, it is true, have no need to live in northerly climes *qua* northerly climes. So to describe the function of the bacterium's detectors in terms of the role they play in identifying geomagnetic north is not to describe them in ways that reveal *how* this function is related to the satisfaction of its needs. But we do not have to describe the function of a mechanism in terms of its possessor's ultimate biological needs.[18] It is the function of the heart to circulate the blood. Just *why* the blood needs to be circulated may be a mystery.

So the sticky question is: *given* that a system needs *F*, and *given* that mechanism *M* enables the organism to detect, identify or recognize *F*, *how* does the mechanism carry out this function? Does it do so by representing nearby *F*s *as nearby F*s or does it, perhaps, represent them merely *as nearby G*s, trusting to nature (the correlation between *F* and *G*) for the satisfaction of its needs? To describe a cognitive mechanism as an *F*-detector (and, therefore, as a mechanism that plays a vital role in the satisfaction of an organism's needs) is not *yet* to tell the functional story by means of which this mechanism does its job. All we known when we know that *O* needs *F* and that *m* enables *O* to detect *F* is that *M either* means_f that *F* is present *or* it means_f that *G* is present where *G* is, in *O*'s natural surroundings, a natural sign of *F*'s presence (where *G* means_n *F*).[19] If I need vitamin C, my perceptual–cognitive system should not automatically be credited with the capacity for recognizing objects *as* containing vitamin C (as meaning_f that they contain vitamin C) just because it supplies me with the information required to satisfy this need. Representing things as oranges and lemons will do quite nicely.

The problem we face is the problem of accounting for the misrepresentational capacities of a system *without* doing so by artificially *inflating* the natural functions of such a system. We need some *principled* way of saying what the natural function of a mechanism is, what its various states not only mean_n, but what they $\textit{mean}_f$. It sounds a bit far-fetched (to my ear at least) to describe the bacteria's sensory mechanism as indicating, and having the function of indicating, the whereabouts of oxygen. For this makes it sound as though it is not performing its function under deceptive conditions (for example, in the presence of a bar magnet). This is, after all, a *magneto*tactic, not a *chemo*tactic, sensor. But if we choose to describe the function of this sensor in this more modest way, we no longer have an example of a system with misrepresentational powers. A northern bacterium (transplanted in the southern hemisphere) will not be misrepresenting anything when, under the guidance of its magnetotactic sensor, it moves upwards (towards geomagnetic north) into the lethal surface water. The alignment of its magnetosomes will mean_n what it has always meant_n, what it is its function to mean_n, what it is supposed to mean_n: namely, that *that* is the direction of magnetic north. The disaster can be blamed on the abnormal surroundings. Nor can we salvage some residual misrepresentational capacity by supposing that the bacterium, under the influence of a bar magnet, at least misrepresents the direction of geomagnetic north. For, once again, the same problem emerges: why suppose it is the function of this mechanism to indicate the direction of *geo*magnetic north rather than, simply, the direction of the surrounding magnetic field? If we describe the function only in the latter way, it becomes impossible to fool the organism, impossible to make it misrepresent anything. For its internal states only mean_f that the magnetic field is pointing in *that* direction and (like a compass) this is always accurate.

5 Functional Determination

For the purpose of clarifying issues, I have confined the discussion to simple organisms with primitive representational capacities. It is not surprising, then, to find no clear and unambiguous capacity for misrepresentation at this level. For this power—and, presumably, the dependent capacity for belief—requires a certain threshold of complexity in the information-processing capabilities of a system. Somewhere between the single cell and man we cross that threshold. It is the purpose of this final section to describe the character of this threshold, to describe the *kind* of complexity responsible for the misrepresentational capabilities of higher organisms.

Suppose an organism (unlike our bacterium) has *two* ways of detecting the presence of some toxic substance F. This may be because the organism is equipped with two sense modalities, each (in their different way) sensitive to F (or some modally specific natural sign of F), or because a single sense modality exploits different external signs (or symptoms) of F. As an example of the latter, consider the way we might identify oak trees visually by either one of two ways: by the distinctive leaf pattern (in the summer) or by the characteristic texture and pattern of the bark (in winter). We have, then, two internal states or conditions, I_1 and I_2, each produced by a different chain of antecedent events, that are natural signs of the presence of F. Each means_n that F is present. Suppose, furthermore, that, having a need to escape from the toxic F, these internal states are harnessed to a third state, call it R, which triggers or releases a pattern

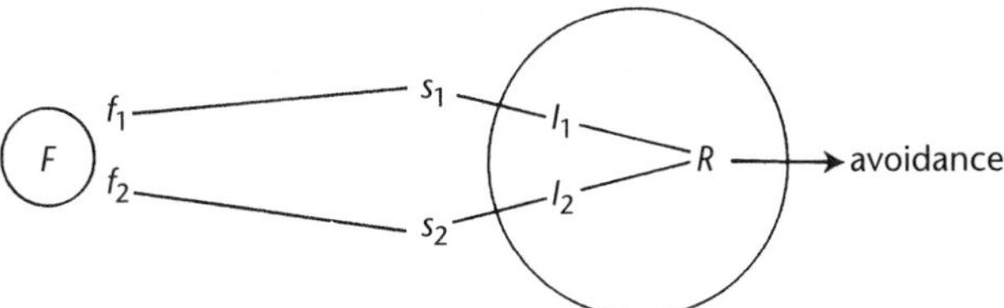

Figure 54.1

of avoidance behaviour. Figure 54.1 assembles the relevant facts. *R*, of course, is also a natural sign of *F*. Under normal circumstances, *R* does not occur unless *F* is present. f_1 and f_2 are properties typical of normal *F*s. s_1 and s_2 are proximal stimuli.

If, now, we present the system with some ersatz *F* (analogous to the bar magnet with the bacteria), something exhibiting *some* of the properties of the real *f* (say f_1), we trigger a chain of events (s_1, I_1, *R* and avoidance) that normally occurs, and is really only appropriate, in the presence of *F*. If we look at the internal state *R* and ask what it means_f under these deceptive conditions, we find ourselves unable to say (as we could in the case of the bacteria) that it means_f anything short of (i.e. more proximal than) *F* itself. Even though s_1 (by means of I_1) is triggering the occurrence of *R*, *R* does not mean_n (hence, cannot mean_f) that s_1 (or f_1) is occurring. *R* is analogous to a light bulb connected to switches wired in parallel *either* of whose closure will turn the light on. When the bulb lights up, it does not mean_n that switch no. 1 is closed even when it is this switch's closure that causes the light to go on. It does not mean_n this, because there is no regular correlation between the bulb lighting up and switch no. 1 being closed (50 per cent of the time it it switch no. 2).

If we think of the detection system described above as having the function of enabling the organism to detect *F*, then the multiplicity of ways of detecting *F* has the consequence that certain internal states (for example, *R*) can indicate (hence mean_f) that *F* is present without indicating anything about the intermediate conditions (i.e. f_1 or s_1) that "tell" it that *F* is present. Our problem with the bacteria was to find a way of having the orientation of its magnetosomes mean_f that oxygen-free water was in a certain direction without *arbitrarily* dismissing the possibility of its meaning_f that the magnetic field was aligned in that direction. We can now see that, with the multiple resources described in Figure 54.1, this possibility can be *non*-arbitrarily dismissed. *R cannot* mean_f that f_1 or s_1 is occurring, because it *does not*, even under optimal conditions, mean_n this. We can therefore claim to have found a non-derivative case of misrepresentation (i.e., *R*'s meaning_f that *F* is present when it is not) which cannot be dismissed by redescribing what *R* means_f so as to eliminate the appearance of misrepresentation. The threatened inflation of possible meanings_f, arising from the variety of ways a system's natural function might be described, has been blocked.

Still, it will be said, we *need not* accept this as a case of genuine misrepresentation *if* we are prepared to recognize that *R* has a *disjunctive* meaning_n. The lighting up of the bulb (connected to switches wired in parallel) does not mean_n that any particular switch is on, but it does indicate that *one* of the switches is on. Similarly, it may be said, even though it is the function of the mechanism having *R* as its terminal state to alert the organism to the presence of *F*, it does so by *R*'s indicating, and having the function of indicating, the occurrence of a certain disjunctive condition—namely, that either f_1 or f_2 (or s_1 or s_2). Our hypothetical organism mistakenly withdraws from *F*, *not* because it misrepresents the ersatz *F* as *F*, but because what it correctly indicates (i.e. that the ersatz *f* is either f_1 or f_2) is no longer correlated in the normal way with something's being *F*.

No matter how versatile a detection system we might design, no matter how many routes of informational access we might give an organism, the possibility will always exist of describing its function (and therefore the meaning$_f$ of its various states) as the detection of some highly disjunctive property of the proximal input. At least, this will always be possible *if* we have a determinate set of disjuncts to which we can retreat.

Suppose, however, that we have a system capable of some form of associative learning. Suppose, in other words, that through repeated exposures to *cs* (a conditioned stimulus) in the presence of *F*, a change takes place. *R* (and, hence, avoidance behaviour) can now be triggered by the occurrence of *cs* alone. Furthermore, it becomes clear that there is virtually no limit to the kind of stimulus that can acquire this "displaced" effectiveness in triggering *R* and subsequent avoidance behaviour. Almost any *s* can become a *cs*, thereby assuming "control" over *R*, by functioning (in the "experience" of the organism) as a sign of *F*.

We now have a cognitive mechanism that not only transforms a variety of different sensory inputs (the s_i) into *one* output-determining state (*R*), but is capable of modifying the character of this many–one mapping over time. If we restrict ourselves to the sensory inputs (the s_i of Figure 54.1), *R* means$_n$ one thing at t_1 (for example, that either s_1 or s_2), something else at t_2 (for example, that either s_1 or s_2 or, through learning, cs_3), and something still different at a later time. Just *what R* means$_n$ will depend on the individual's learning history—on *what* s_i became cs_i *for it*. There is no *time-invariant* meaning$_n$ for *R*; hence, nothing that, through time, could be its function to indicate. In terms of the s_i that produce *R*, *R* can have no time-invariant meaning$_f$.

Of course, throughout this process, *R* continues to indicate the presence of *F*. It does so because, by hypothesis, any new s_i to which *R* becomes conditioned is a natural sign of *F*. Learning is a process in which stimuli that indicate the presence of *F* are, in their turn, indicated by some relevant internal state of the organism (*R* in this case). Therefore, if we are to think of these cognitive mechanisms as having a time-invariant function at all (something that is implied by their continued—indeed, as a result of learning, more efficient—servicing of the associated need), then we *must* think of their function, not as indicating the nature of the proximal (even distal) conditions that trigger positive responses (the s_i and f_1), but as indicating the condition (*F*) for which these diverse stimuli are signs. The mechanism just described has, then, as its natural function, the indication of the presence of *F*. Hence, the occurrence of *R* means$_f$ that *F* is present. It does not mean$_f$ that s_1 or s_2 or ... s_x obtains, even though, at any given stage of development, it will mean$_n$ this for some definite value of *x*.

A system at this level of complexity, having not only multiple channels of access to what it needs to know about, but the resources for expanding its information-gathering resources, possesses, I submit, a genuine power of misrepresentation. When there is a breakdown in the normal chain of natural signs, when, say, cs_7 occurs (a learned sign of *F*) under circumstances in which it does not mean$_n$ that *F* is present (in the way that the broken clock does not mean_n that it is 3.30 a.m.), *R* still means_f (though not, of course, means_n) that *F* is present. It means_f this because that is what it is *supposed* to mean_n, what it is its natural function to mean_n, and there is available no other condition it can mean_f.[20]

Notes

1. D. C. Dennett, "Intentional Systems," *Journal of Philosophy*, 68 (1971), 87–106, reprinted in *Brainstorms* (Montgomery, Vt., 1978).

2. This needs some qualification, but it will do for the moment. What a natural sign means often does depend on us, on what we *know* about relevant alternative possibilities or on how we *use* an associated device. But if we don't know anything, or if the sign occurs in the operation of a device having no normal use, the sign still means something—just not, specifically, what we say it means under epistemically (or functionally) richer conditions. I return to this point in n. 8 below.

3. I give a fuller account of it in F. Dretske, *Knowledge and the Flow of Information* (MIT Press, 1981), chs. 1 and 2.

4. P. Grice, "Meaning," *Philosophical Review*, 66 (1957), 377–88.

5. I hope it is clear, that I am not here concerned with the word "empty" (or the letter "E") that might appear on the gauge. This symbol means empty whatever the gauge is doing, but this is purely conventional. I am concerned with what the pointer's position means_n *whatever* we choose to print on the face of the instrument.

6. L. Wright calls these "conscious" functions; see his "Functions," *Philosophical Review*, 82.2 (Apr. 1973), 142.

7. A doorbell, for example, cannot mean_n *both* that there is someone at the door *and* that there is a short circuit.

8. It isn't the change of purpose *alone* that changes what something means_n (hence, means_f). It is the fact that this change in use is accompanied by altered background knowledge, and meaning_n changes as background knowledge changes. If, for example, *A* depends on both *B* and *C*, a changing *A* can mean_n that *C* is changing *if* we know that *B* is constant. If we know that *C* is constant, it can mean_n that *B* is changing. If we know nothing, it only means that either *B* or *C* is changing. Natural meaning is relative in this sense, but derelativizing it (by ignoring what we know and how we use a device) does not eliminate natural meaning. It merely makes *less determinate* what things mean_n. For a fuller discussion of this point, see ch. 3 in Dretske, *Knowledge and the Flow of Information.*

9. I think much of our talk about the representational capacities of computers is of this assigned, hence derived, kind. It tells us nothing about the intrinsic power of a machine to represent or misrepresent anything. Hence, nothing about the cognitive character of its internal states. R. Cummins, I think, gets it exactly right by distinguishing *cognition (a version of *assigned* meaning) from genuine cognition. See his *Psychological Explanation* (MIT Press, 1983).

10. My source for this example is R. P. Blakemore and R. B. Frankel, "Magnetic Navigation in Bacteria," *Scientific American*, 245. 6 (Dec. 1981).

11. D. Stampe, "Toward a Causal Theory of Linguistic Representation," in P. French, T. Uehling, and H. Wettstein (eds.), *Midwest Studies in Philosophy*, Vol. 2 (University of Minnesota Press, 1977).

12. B. Enç, "Intentional States of Mechanical Devices," *Mind*, 91 (Apr. 1982), 362. Enç identified the content of a functional state with the (construction of the) properties of the event to which the system has the function of responding.

13. J. Fodor, "Psychosemantics, or Where Do Truth Conditions Come From?" *manuscript*.

14. R. Millikan, *Language, Thought, and Other Biological Categories* (MIT Press, 1984).

15. Dretske, *Knowledge and the Flow of Information*, part 3.

16. Something for which there is, in Dennett's (earlier) language, an "appropriate efferent continuation": see his *Content and Consciousness* (London, 1969).

17. Fodor (in a circulated draft of "Why Paramecia Don't Have Mental Representations") distinguishes organisms for which a representational theory of mind is not appropriate (paramecia, for example) and ones for which it is (us, for example) in terms of the latter's ability to respond to non-nomic stimulus properties (properties that are not transducer-detectable). We, but not paramecia, are capable of representing something as, say, a crumpled shirt, and *being a crumpled shirt* is not a projectible property. In this article, Fodor is not concerned with the question of *where* we get this extraordinary representational power from (he suggests it requires inferential capacities). He is concerned only with offering it as a way of distinguishing us from a variety of other perceptual and quasi-cognitive systems.

I agree with Fodor about the importance and relevance of this distinction, but my present concern is to understand *how* a system could acquire the power to represent something in this way. The power to represent something *as* a crumpled shirt (where this implies the correlative ability to misrepresent it as such) is certainly not innate.

18. Enç, "Intentional States of Mechanical Devices," p. 168, says that a photoreceptor in the fruitfly has the function of enabling the fly to reach humid spots (in virtue of the correlation between dark spots and humid spots). I have no objection to describing things in this way. But the question remains: *how* does it perform this function? We can answer this question without supposing that there is any mechanism of the fly whose function it is to indicate the degree of humidity. The sensory mechanism can perform this function if there is merely something to indicate the luminosity—i.e. a photoreceptor. *That* will enable the fly to reach humid spots. Likewise, the bacteria's magnetotactic sense *enables* (and, let us say, has the *function* of enabling) the bacteria to avoid oxygen-rich water. But the way it does it (it may be argued) is by having a sensor that indicates, and has the function of indicating, the direction of the magnetic field.

19. In Fodor's way of putting the point (in "Psychosemantics"), this is merely a way of saying that his identification of the semantics of *M* (some mental representation) with entry conditions (relative to a set of normalcy conditions) still leaves some slack. We can say that the entry condition is the absence (presence) of oxygen *or* a specific orientation of the magnetic field. Appeal to the selectional history of this mechanism won't decide *which* is the right specification of entry conditions—hence, won't tell us whether the bacteria are capable of *mis*representing anything. Fodor, I think, realizes this residual indeterminacy and makes the suggestive remark (n. 9) that this problem is an analogue of the problems of specifying the perceptual object for theories of perception.

20. I am grateful to Berent Enç, Dennis Stampe, and Jerry Fodor for their helpful criticisms, both constructive and destructive, of earlier drafts of this essay.

55 From "(Nonsolipsistic) Conceptual Role Semantics"

Gilbert Harman

What Is (Nonsolipsistic) Conceptual Role Semantics?

In this paper I will defend what I shall call "(nonsolipsistic) conceptual role semantics." This approach involves the following four claims:

(1) The meanings of linguistic expressions are determined by the contents of the concepts and thoughts they can be used to express;

(2) the contents of thoughts are determined by their construction out of concepts; and

(3) the contents of concepts are determined by their "functional role" in a person's psychology, where

(4) functional role is conceived nonsolipsistically as involving relations to things in the world, including things in the past and future.

"Thoughts" here include beliefs, hopes, desires, fears, and other attitudes, in addition to thoughts properly so called. "Functional role" includes any special roles a concept may play in perception and in inference or reasoning, including practical reasoning that leads to action.

I include the parenthetical modifier "(nonsolipsistic)" in the phrase "(nonsolipsistic) conceptual role semantics" to contrast this approach with that of some recent authors (Field, 1977; Fodor, 1980; Loar, 1981) who think of conceptual role solipsistically as a completely internal matter. I put parentheses around "nonsolipsistic" because, as I will argue below, the term is redundant: conceptual role must be conceived nonsolipsistically.

Commenting on Harman (1982), Loewer (1982) takes this nonsolipsistic aspect to be an important *revision* in an earlier solipsistic theory. This is not so. Conceptual role semantics derives from nonsolipsistic behaviorism. It was originally and has until recently been a nonsolipsistic theory (e.g., Sellars, 1954; Harman, 1973). This is discussed further below.

(Nonsolipsistic) conceptual role semantics represents one thing that might be meant by the slogan "meaning is use." But a proper appreciation of the point requires distinguishing (at least) two uses of symbols, their use in calculation, as in adding a column of figures, and their use in communication, as in telling someone the result.

Two Uses of Symbols: Communication and Calculation

Symbols that are being used in calculation are typically not being used at that time for communication. When you add a column of figures you are not normally communicating anything even to yourself. A similar point holds in reverse. Normally you communicate the results of your calculation to someone else only after you are done calculating. There are, of course, mixed cases. You might go through a calculation on the blackboard, intending your audience to see how things come out.

(Nonsolipsistic) conceptual role semantics may be seen as a version of the theory that meaning is use, where the basic use of symbols is taken to be in calculation, not in communication, and where concepts are treated as symbols in a "language of thought." Clearly, the relevant use of such "symbols," the use of which determines their content, is their use in thought and calculation rather than in communication. If thought is like talking to yourself, it is the sort of talking involved in figuring something out, not the sort of talking involved in communication. Thinking is not communicating with yourself.

However, it would be more accurate to say content is use than to say meaning is use; strictly speaking, thoughts and concepts have content, not meaning.

The Meaning of "Meaning"

I assume, following Grice (1959), that we can distinguish what he calls natural meaning (smoke means fire) from what he calls nonnatural meaning (the German word "Feuer" means fire), and we can also distinguish (nonnatural) speaker or user meaning (what a speaker or user of certain symbols means) from what certain words, expressions, or other symbols mean.

Grice proposes to analyze expression meaning in terms of speaker meaning; and he proposes, more controversially, to analyze speaker meaning in terms of a speaker's intentions to communicate something. This last proposal appears to overlook the meaningful use of symbols in calculation. You might invent a special notation in order to work out a certain sort of problem. It would be quite proper to say that by a given symbol you meant so-and-so, even though you have no intentions to use these symbols in any sort of communication.

There does seem to be some sort of connection between speaker or user meaning and the speaker's or user's intentions. Suppose you use your special notation to work out a specific problem. You formulate the assumptions of the problem in your notation, do some calculating, and end up with a meaningful result in that notation. It would be correct to say of you that, when you wrote down a particular assumption in your notation, you meant such and such by what you wrote: but it would be incorrect to say of you that, when you wrote the conclusion you reached in your notation, you meant so and so by what you wrote. This seems connected with the fact that, in formulating the assumption as you did in your notation, you intended to express such and such an assumption; whereas, in writing down the conclusion you reached in your notation, your intention was not to express such and such a conclusion but rather to reach whatever conclusion in your notation followed from earlier steps by the rules of your calculus. This suggests that you mean that so and so in using certain symbols if and only if you use those symbols to express the thought that so and so, with the intention of expressing such a thought.

Unexpressed thoughts (beliefs, fears, desires, etc.) do not have meaning. We would not ordinarily say that in thinking as you did you meant that so and so. If thoughts are in a language of thought, they are not (normally) also expressed in that language.

I say "normally" because sometimes one has thoughts in English or some other real language. Indeed, I am inclined to think a language, properly so called, is a symbol system that is used both for communication and thought. If one cannot think in a language, one has not yet mastered it. A symbol system used only for communication, like Morse code, is not a language.

Concepts and other aspects of mental representation have content but not (normally) meaning (unless they are also expression in a language used in communication). We would not normally say that your concept of redness meant anything in the way that the word "red" in English means something. Nor would we say that you meant anything by that concept on a particular occasion of its exercise.

Thoughts and Concepts

It is sometimes suggested that words have meaning because of the way they are used; the meaning of a word is its use in the language. Ryle (1953, 1961) observes that it would be a mistake to try to extend this idea directly to sentences. There are indefinitely many sentences. Obviously, most of them are never used at all, and most sentences that are used are used only once. Sentences do not normally have regular uses in the way that words do. Sentences have meaning because of the words they contain and the way these words are put together. A use theory of meaning has to suppose it is words and ways of putting words together that have meaning because of their uses, not sentences.

Similarly, it is concepts that have uses or functions or roles in thought, not the possible attitudes in which those concepts occur. There are indefinitely many possible attitudes. Most possible attitudes are never taken by anyone, and most attitudes that are at some point taken by someone are taken by someone only once. Possible beliefs, desires, and other attitudes do not normally have regular uses or functions or roles that make them the possible attitudes they are. Consider, for example, what use or role or function there might be for the possible belief of yours that you have bathed in coca cola. This belief would have a certain content, but no obvious use or role or function. The content of a belief does not derive from its own role or function but rather from the uses of the concepts it exercises....

Content and Inferential Role

Types of Role

Assuming conceptual role semantics as a basic framework, it is plausible that all concepts have a function in reasoning that is relevant to their content. No doubt, some concepts have the content they have primarily because of a special role they play in perception, color concepts for example. But the content of even these concepts depends to some extent on inferential role. A given color concept is the concept of a normally persisting characteristic of objects in the world, a characteristic that can be used both to keep track of objects and as a sign of other things. For example, greenness is a sign of unripeness in certain fruits. Moreover, there are various internal relations among colors. From the premise that an object is red at a certain place at a certain time one can infer that the object is not also green at that place and time.

In the case of concepts of shape and number, inferential connections play a larger role. Perceptual connections are still relevant; to some extent your concept of a triangle involves your notion of what a triangle looks like and your concept of various natural numbers is connected with your ability to count objects you perceive. But the role these notions play in inference looms larger.

The concept expressed by the word "because" plays an important role in one's understanding of phenomena and has (I believe) a central role in inference, since inference is often inference to the best explanation. This role makes the concept expressed by "because" the concept it is, I believe. Is perception relevant at all here? Perhaps. It may be that you sometimes directly perceive causality or certain explanatory relations, and it may be that this helps to determine the content of the concept you express with the word "because." Or perhaps not. Maybe the perception of causality and other explanatory relations is always mediated by inference.

Logical words like "and," "not," "every," and "some" express concepts whose function in inference seems clearly quite important to their content, which is why it seems plausible to say that these words do not mean in intuitionistic logic and quantum logic what they mean in so called classical logic, although even here there may be crucial perceptual functions. It may, for example, be central to your concept of negation that you can sometimes perceive that certain things are not so, as when you perceive that Pierre is not in the cafe, for instance. It may be central to your concept of generality or universal quantification that you can sometimes perceive that everything of a certain sort is so and so, for instance that everyone in the room is wearing a hat.

It is possible that there are certain sorts of theoretical term, like "quark," that play no role in perception at all, so that the content of the concepts they express is determined entirely by inferential role. (But maybe it is important to the concept of a quark that the concept should play a role in the perception of certain pictures or diagrams!) ...

Conceptual Role and External World

In the most elementary cases, possession of a concept of something is connected with perceiving that thing and acting appropriately towards it. What one perceives the thing *as* is reflected in the way one acts. For example, an animal perceives something as food if it treats what it perceives as food, for example by eating what it perceives. Of course, there are complications to this simple story and things can go wrong. But this represents the most elementary case and more complex cases must be conceived in terms of it. So for example, we can describe a creature as mistakenly thinking that something is food when it tries to treat it as food. In so describing the animal, we appeal to a conception of what happens in the normal case when nothing goes wrong and there is no mistake.

In Harman (1973) I emphasize how the appeal to a background of normality figures in all identifications of representational states, even those in an artifact such as a radar aimer. A radar aimer interprets data from radar and calculates where to fire guns in order to shoot down enemy planes. We can describe the device as representing the present and future locations of the planes because radar waves reflected from the planes are received and interpreted to form a representation of the future locations of the planes, and that representation is used in the aiming and firing of the guns that shoot down the planes. We can describe the device as representing the locations of planes even if something goes wrong and the guns miss, because we have a conception of the *normal operation* of the radar aimer. We can even treat the device as representing enemy planes when it is being tested in the laboratory, unconnected to radar and guns, since in our testing we envision it *as* connected in the right way. However, given a different conception of normal context, we could not describe the device as representing planes at all.

The moral is that (nonsolipsistic) conceptual role semantics does not involve a "solipsistic" theory of the content of thoughts. There is no suggestion that content depends only on functional relations among thoughts and concepts, such as the role a particular concept plays in inference. Of primary importance are functional relations to the external world in connection with perception, on the one hand, and action, on the other. The functions of logical concepts can be specified "solipsistically," in terms of the inner workings of one's conceptual system, without reference to things in the "external world." But this is not true for the functions of other concepts.

Concepts include individual concepts and general concepts, where an individual concept functions in certain contexts to pick out a particular object in the external world to which a general concept applies, in the simplest case to enable one to handle the object as a thing of the appropriate sort (cf. Strawson, 1974, pp. 42–51). To repeat an earlier example, it is an important function of the concept of food that in certain circumstances one can recognize particular stuff as food, this recognition enabling one to treat that thing appropriately as food by eating it (Dennett, 1969, p. 73). What makes something the concept red is in part the way in which the concept is involved in the perception of red objects in the external world. What makes something the concept of danger is in part the way in which the concept is involved in thoughts that affect action in certain ways.

The Division of Linguistic Labor

The content of certain concepts appears to depend crucially on functional relations between those concepts and certain words in a public language. You might have a concept of an oak tree by virtue of which you have thoughts about oak trees where the crucial functional relation is a relation between your concept and the word "oak" in English. You might, for example, wonder whether there were any oak trees in your back yard even if you cannot distinguish oak trees from elm trees and do not know any of the distinguishing properties of these two sorts of trees (Putnam, 1975; Kripke, 1972).

(Nonsolipsistic) conceptual role semantics asserts that an account of the content of thoughts is more basic than an account of communicated meaning and the significance of speech acts. In this view, the content of linguistic expressions derives from the contents of thoughts they can be used to express. However, allowance must also be made for cases in which the content of your thoughts depends in part on the content of certain words, such as "oak" and "elm."

Of course, in this case, there are other people who can recognize oaks and distinguish them from elms and who know various distinguishing properties of the trees.

These other people may have a concept of an oak tree which has functional roles that are sufficient to make it the concept of an oak tree apart from any relations the concept has with the word "oak." It is plausible

(1) that their concept acquires its content from this aspect of its functional role, i.e. its role apart from its relation to the word "oak,"
(2) that the word "oak" as they use it has the meaning it has because of its connection with their concept of an oak tree
(3) that the word "oak" as used by a more ignorant person can have the same meaning by virtue of connections between that person's ignorant use of the word and the expert's use, and
(4) that the content of the more ignorant person's concept of an oak tree derives from its connection to his or her use of the word and its meaning as he or she uses it.

Of course, the content of the more ignorant person's concept of an oak tree is not as rich as, so not the same as, the content of the expert's concept. But the ignorant person's concept is still a concept of an oak tree, by virtue of its connection with the word "oak."

(1)–(4) would still allow one to say that the meanings of words derive ultimately from the contents of concepts the words are used to express, where the contents of these concepts do not themselves derive from the meanings of words; however the meanings of a particular person's words may not derive in this way from the contents of that person's concepts. . . .

Twin Earth

Putnam imagines a world, which he calls "Twin Earth," which is just like Earth except for certain minor differences. There are on Twin Earth duplicates of all the people on Earth and the people on Twin Earth speak the same languages as on Earth, using expressions in the same way, except that, because of the minor differences between Earth and Twin Earth, they sometimes refer to different things by their words. In particular, the main difference between Twin Earth and Earth is that where there is water on Earth there is on Twin Earth a liquid with the same macro properties as water but a different chemical structure, which Putnam calls "XYZ."

Now, comparing Earth in 1750 (before the micro-structure of water has been investigated) with Twin Earth at the corresponding time, we find that the English word "water" means something different in the two places, simply because the word is used on Earth to refer to what is in fact H_2O and is used on Twin Earth to refer to what is in fact XYZ. Similarly, where Earthlings think about H_2O, Twin Earthlings think about XYZ. This difference is not in 1750 reflected in any difference in dispositions to react to various perceptual situations, in any difference in inferences that people in the respective places would make, nor in any differences in the actions which people undertake as the result of thoughts involving the relevant concept.

The difference is also not simply a difference in context of utterance or context of thought. Suppose an Earthling were to travel by spaceship and land on an ocean of XYZ in Twin Earth. Looking around, the Earthling comes to believe there is water all around. This belief is false, since the Earthling's concept of water is a concept of something that is in fact H_2O. The Earthling's concept of water remains a concept of the same thing that is referred to by "water" on Earth even though the Earthling is now located in a different context. The context of the thoughts of the Earthling and the context of the thoughts of the Twin Earthlings are now the same; but their thoughts are about XYZ where his are still about water. So this difference in the content of the thoughts of Earthlings and Twin Earthlings cannot be simply a difference in the context in which they have their thoughts.

The difference is due rather to the fact that the content of a person's concept is determined by its functional role in some normal context. The normal context for an Earthling's thoughts about what he or she calls "water" is here on Earth, while the normal context for a Twin Earthling's thoughts about what he or she calls "water" is on Twin Earth.

The normal context can change. If the traveler from Earth to Twin Earth stays on, after a while the normal context for the concepts he or she uses will be properly taken to be the Twin Earth contexts. Thoughts about what he or she calls "water" will be properly considered thoughts about XYZ rather than H_2O. There is, of course, a certain amount of arbitrariness in any decision about when this change has occurred. It will sometimes be possible with equal justice to consider a given thought a thought about H_2O or a thought about XYZ.

A similar arbitrariness would arise concerning a person created spontaneously in outer space as the improbable result of random events at the quantum level, supposing the person were saved from space death by a fortuitously passing space ship, and supposing the person spoke something that sounded very much like English. Suppose, indeed, that this person is a duplicate of you and also (of course) of your Twin Earth counterpart. When the person has thoughts that he or she would express using the term "water," are these thoughts about water (H_2O) or thoughts about XYZ? If we interpret this person's thoughts against a normal background on Earth, we will interpret the relevant thoughts as thoughts about water. If we take the normal background to be Twin Earth, they are thoughts about XYZ. Clearly it is quite arbitrary what we say here.

Qualia

According to (nonsolipsistic) conceptual role semantics, then, the content of a thought is not a matter of the "intrinsic nature" of either that thought or other mental states and experiences but is rather a matter of how mental states are related to each other, to things in the external world, and to things in a context understood as a normal context. There is a familiar objection (Block and Fodor, 1972; Nagel, 1974) to this which claims that content is not determined always by such functions or relations. In this view the intrinsic qualities or "qualia" of certain experiences are sometimes relevant. It is said that your concept of red involves your notion of what it is like to see something red, where what it is like to see something red is not just a matter of the functional or relational characteristics of the relevant experience but of its intrinsic character as well.

One argument for this is that it is possible to imagine a person whose spectrum was inverted with respect to yours, so that the quality of experience you have in seeing something red is the quality this other person has in seeing something green, the quality of experience you have in seeing something blue is the quality this other person has in seeing something orange, and similarly for other colors, although in all relevant respects your color experiences function similarly, so that each of you is just as good as the other in applying the public color words to colored objects. According to this argument, the two of you would have different concepts which you would express using the word "red," although it might be difficult or even impossible to discover this difference, since it is not a functional difference.

I speak of an "argument" here, although (as Lewis [1980] observes in a similar context), the "argument" really comes down simply to denying the functionalist account of the content of concepts and thoughts, without actually offering any reason for that denial. This makes the "argument" difficult to answer. All one can do is look more closely at a functionalist account of the content of color concepts in order to bring out the way in which, according to functionalism, this content does not depend on the intrinsic character of experiences of color.

How could you imagine someone whose spectrum was inverted with respect to yours? One way would be to imagine this happening to yourself. Suppose there were color-inverting contact lenses. You put on a pair of lenses and the colors things seem to have are reversed. The sky now looks orange rather than blue, ripe apples look green, unripe apples look red, and so on. Suppose you keep these lenses on and adapt your behavior. You learn to say "green" rather than "red" when you see something that looks the way red things used to look; you learn to treat what you used to consider a green appearance of apples as a sign of ripeness, and so on. The years pass and your adaption becomes habitual. Would not this be an intelligible case in which someone, the imagined future you, has a notion of what it is like to have the experience of seeing something to which the term "red" applies, where the notion functions in exactly the way in which your notion of what such an experience is like functions, although your notions are different? The functionalist must deny this and say that the imagined you associates the same concept with the word "red" as the actual you does now and indeed sees the world as you now do.

Consider an analogous case. There actually exist lenses that are spatially inverting. With these lenses on, things that are up look down and vice versa. At first it is very difficult to get around if you are wearing such lenses, since things are not where they seem to be. But after a while you begin to adapt. If you want to grab something that looks high, you reach low, and vice versa. If you want to look directly at something that appears in the bottom of your visual field you raise your head, and so on. Eventually, such adaption becomes more or less habitual.

Now functionalism implies that if you become perfectly adapted to such space inverting lenses, then your experience will be the same as that of someone who is not wearing the inverting lenses (who has adapted to not wearing them if necessary), because now the normal context in relation to which your concepts function will have become a context in which you are wearing the inverting lenses. And in fact, people who have worn such lenses do say that, as they adapt to the lenses, the world tends to look right side up again (Taylor, 1962; Pitcher, 1971; Thomas, 1978).

Similarly, functionalism implies that if you become perfectly adapted to color inverting lenses, the world will come to look to you as it looked before in the sense that given such perfect adaption the normal context in which your color concepts function will be a context in which you are wearing the color inverting lenses. According to functionalism, the way things look to you is a relational characteristic of your experience, not part of its intrinsic character.

In order to get a feel for this aspect of (nonsolipsistic) conceptual role semantics, it may be useful to consider certain further cases. Consider Inverted Earth, a world just like ours, with duplicates of us, with the sole difference that there the actual colors of objects are the opposite of what they are here. The sky is orange, ripe apples are green, etc. The inhabitants of Inverted Earth speak something that sounds like English, except that they say the sky is "blue," they call ripe apples "red," and so on. Question: what color does their sky look to them? Answer: it looks orange. The concept they express with the word "blue" plays a relevantly special role in the normal perception of things that are actually orange.

Suppose there is a distinctive physical basis for each different color experience. Suppose also that the physical basis for the experience of red is the same for all normal people not adapted to color inverting lenses, and similarly for the other colors. According to (nonsolipsistic) conceptual role semantics this fact is irrelevant. The person who has perfectly adapted to color inverting lenses will be different from everyone else as regards the physical basis of his or her experience of red, but that will not affect the quality of his or her experience.

Consider someone on Inverted Earth who perfectly adapts to color inverting lenses. Looking at the sky of Inverted Earth, this person has an experience of color whose physical basis is the same as that of a normal person on Earth looking at Earth's sky. But the sky looks orange to the person on Inverted Earth and blue to normal people on Earth. What makes an experience the experience of something's looking the color it looks is not its intrinsic character and/or physical basis but rather its functional characteristics within an assumed normal context.

Consider a brain spontaneously created in space as the improbable result of random events at the quantum level. The physical events in the brain happen to be the same as those in you on Earth looking at the sky on a clear day and also the same as those in a person adapted to color inverting spectacles looking at the sky of Inverted Earth. What is it like for the brain? Is it having an experience of orange or of blue? According to (nonsolipsistic) conceptual role semantics, there is no nonarbitrary way to answer this question; it depends on what is taken as the normal context for assessing the functional *role* of events in that brain. If the normal context is taken to be the normal context for perception of color on Earth, the brain is having an experience of blue. If the normal context is taken to be the normal context for a wearer of inverted spectacles on Inverted Earth, the brain is having an experience of orange.

Inner and Outer Aspects of Conceptual Role

It is sometimes suggested that we need to distinguish inner and outer aspects of conceptual role, counting only the inner solipsistically specifiable side as conceptual role proper, taking the outer aspects to be part of context (Field, 1977; Loar, 1981). The suggestion is that a theory of the content of attitudes must have two parts: (1) a theory of conceptual role proper, solipsistically conceived, and (2) a theory of context that would indicate how content is a function of inner conceptual role and outer context.

But this distinction is unmotivated and the suggestion is unworkable. The distinction is unmotivated because there is no natural border between inner and outer.

Should the inner realm be taken to include everything in the local environment that can be perceived, or should it stop at the skin, the nerve ends, the central nervous system, the brain, the central part of the brain, or what? The suggestion is unworkable because, for most concepts, inner conceptual role can only be specified in terms of conceptual role in a wider sense, namely the function a concept has in certain contexts in relation to things in the so called "external world" (Harman, 1973, pp. 62–65).

To be sure, there are cases of illusion in which one mistakes something else for food. From a solipsistic point of view, these cases may be quite similar to veridical cases, but clearly the cases of mistake are not cases that bring out the relevant function of the concept of food. They are cases of *mis*functioning. We can see these as cases of mistake precisely because the function of concept of food is specified with reference to real and not just apparent food.

Mental states and processes are functional states and processes, that is, they are complex relational or dispositional states and processes, and it is useful to consider simpler dispositions, like fragility or solubility. Water solubility cannot be identified with possession of a particular molecular structure, because (a) different sorts of molecular structure underlie the water solubility of different substances and, more importantly, (b) attributions of water solubility are relative to a choice of background or *normal* context. Rate of dissolving is affected by such things as the presence or absence of electrical, magnetic, or gravitational fields, the amount of vibration, varying degrees of atmospheric pressure, the purity and temperature of the water, and so forth. Whether it is proper to say a given substance is water soluble will depend on what the normal set of conditions for mixing the substance with water is taken to be. A substance is soluble in water if it would dissolve at a fast enough rate if mixed with water in a certain way under certain conditions. Solubility is a relational state of a substance, relating it to potential external things—water and various conditions of mixture and the process of dissolving under those conditions.

Notice that we cannot say that for a substance to be water soluble is for it to be such that, if it receives certain "stimuli," at its surface, it reacts in a certain way. We must also mention water and various external conditions. There is a moral here for Quine's (1960) account of language in terms of "stimulus meaning" and of the related later attempts I have been discussing to develop a purely solipsistic notion of conceptual role.

We are led to attribute beliefs, desires, and so on to a creature only because the creature is able to attain what we take to be its goals by being able to detect aspects of its environment. In the first instance, we study its capacity for mental representation by discovering which aspects of the environment it is sensitive to. Only after that can we investigate the sorts of mistakes it is capable of that might lead to inappropriate behavior. This gives us further evidence about the content of its concepts. But we could never even guess at this without considering how the creature's mental states are connected with things in the outside world.

But the point is not merely one of evidence, since concepts have the content they have because of the way they function in the *normal case* in relation to an external world. If there were no external constraints, we could conceive of anything as instantiating any system of purely solipsistic "functional" relations and *processes*. We could think of a pane of glass or a pencil point as instantiating Albert Einstein or George

Miller, solipsistically conceived. But that does not count. Concepts really must be capable of functioning appropriately. No one has ever described a way of explaining what beliefs, desires, and other mental states are except in terms of actual or possible relations to things in the external world (Dennett, 1969, pp. 72–82; Harman, 1973, pp. 62–65; Bennett, 1976, pp. 36–110).

The most primitive psychological notions are not *belief* and *desire* but rather *knowledge* and *successful intentional action*. Belief and intention are generalizations of knowledge and success that allow for mistake and failure. We conceive a creature as believing things by conceiving it as at least potentially knowing things, and similarly for intention.

Does this show a theory of truth plays a role in semantics? To be sure, in my view the content of a concept is determined by the way in which the concept functions in paradigm or standard cases in which nothing goes wrong. In such cases, one has true beliefs that lead one to act appropriately in the light of one's needs and other ends. But an account of correct functioning is not itself a full account of the truth of beliefs, since beliefs can be true by accident in cases where there is some misfunctioning. And there are no serious prospects for a theory of content that significantly involves an account of truth conditions....

Conclusion

To summarize there are two uses of symbols, in communication and speech acts and in calculation and thought. (Nonsolipsistic) conceptual role semantics takes the second use to be the basic one. The ultimate source of meaning or content is the functional role symbols play in thought.

The content of a concept depends on its role in inference and sometimes in perception. Particularly important for inference are a term's implications. Implication is relevant to inference and therefore to meaning, because implication is explanatory and inference aims at explanatory coherence. Accounts of truth conditions can shed light on meaning to the extent that they bring out implications; it is doubtful whether such accounts have any further bearing on meaning, although they may have heuristic value for studies of logical form....

Allowance must be made for various connections between concepts and the external world. Some concepts have the content they have because of the words they are associated with, although (according to conceptual role semantics) this content ultimately always derives from someone's use of concepts. The content of concepts is often relative to a choice of a normal context of functioning. This is true of color concepts, despite the unargued view of some philosophers that these concepts depend on the intrinsic character of experience....

References

Bennett, J., *Linguistic Behaviour*. Cambridge: Cambridge University Press, 1976.

Block, N. and Fodor, J. A., What Psychological States Are Not. *Philosophical Review*, 1972, 81, 159–181.

Dennett, D. C., *Content and Consciousness*. London: Routledge and Kegan Paul, 1969.

Field, H., Probabilistic Semantics. *Journal of Philosophy*, 1977, 74, 379–409.

Fodor, J. A., Methodological Solipsism as a Research Strategy in Psychology. *Behavioral and Brain Sciences*, 1980, 3, 63–73.

Grice, H. P., Meaning. *Philosophical Review*, 1959, 68, 377–388.

Harman, G., *Thought*. Princeton, NJ: Princeton University Press, 1973.

Harman, G., Conceptual Role Semantics. *Notre Dame Journal of Formal Logic*, 1982, 28, 252–256.

Kripke, S., Naming and Necessity. In D. Davidson and G. Harman (eds.), *Semantics of Natural Language*. Dordrecht: Reidel, 1972.

Lewis, D., Mad Pain and Martian Pain. In N. Block (ed.), *Readings in Philosophy of Psychology*. Cambridge, MA: Harvard University Press, 1980.

Loar, B., *Mind and Meaning*. Cambridge: Cambridge University Press, 1981.

Loar, B., Must Beliefs Be Sentences? In P. D. Asquith and T. Nickles (eds.), *PSA* 1982, vol. 2. East-Lansing, MI: Philosophy of Science Association, 1983a.

Loewer, B., The Role of "Conceptual Role Semantics." *Notre Dame Journal of Formal Logic*, 1982, 23, 305–332.

Nagel, T., What Is It Like to Be a Bat? *Philosophical Review*, 1974, 83, 435–450.

Pitcher, G., *A Theory of Perception*. Princeton, NJ: Princeton University Press, 1971.

Putnam, H., The Meaning of "Meaning." In H. Putnam (ed.), *Mind, Language, and Reality: Philosophical Papers*, vol. 2. Cambridge: Cambridge University Press, 1975.

Quine, W. V., *Word and Object*. Cambridge, MA: MIT Press, 1960.

Ryle, G., Ordinary Language. *Philosophical Review*, 1953, 62. (Reprinted in Ryle 1971.)

Ryle, G., Use, Usage, and Meaning. *Proceedings of the Aristotelian Society*, 1961. Suppl. vol. 35. (Reprinted in Ryle 1971.)

Ryle, G., *Collected Papers*, vol. II. London: Hutchinson, 1971.

Sellars, W., Some Reflections on Language Games. *Philosophy of Science*, 1954, 21, 204–228.

Strawson, P. F., *Subject and Predicate in Logic and Grammar*. London: Methuen, 1974.

Taylor, J. G., *The Behavioral Basis of Perception*. New Haven, CT: Yale University Press, 1962.

Thomas, S., *The Formal Mechanics of Mind*. Ithaca, NY: Cornell University Press, 1978.

56 Social Content and Psychological Content

Brian Loar

By *psychological content* I shall mean whatever individuates beliefs and other propositional attitudes in commonsense psychological explanation, so that they explanatorily interact with each other and with other factors such as perception in familiar ways. In discussions of what appropriately individuates propositional attitudes there occurs the following kind of argument. Some thesis about psychological content is proposed, about, say, what constitutes it in general or constitutes some aspect of it. The reply is made that the thesis fails to capture the correct individuation conditions because correct ascriptions of attitudes using *that-clauses* count them the same when the proposed thesis distinguishes them or vice versa. Here are some examples.

1. There is the idea that the perceptual ability to discriminate objects of a given kind, cats say, may constitute a concept of that kind of object. Think of "concept" here as meaning a certain abstraction from the individuation conditions of certain beliefs and other attitudes, about cats, say. Then the capacity to have certain beliefs about cats, beliefs that have certain psychological contents, would involve the ability perceptually to discriminate cats. Variants of this idea have seemed natural to empiricists and recently to certain functionalists: what better criterion for having certain ordinary concepts than the ability systematically to pick out their instances?

But there is a problem when we consider how apparently we individuate beliefs, as Stephen Stich points out. "Suppose I tell a blind person and a sighted person that there is a cat in the next room, and they believe my report. It seems natural to say that they both come to have the same belief: the belief that there is a cat in the next room. Our intuitions remain the same if we change the example by replacing the merely blind subject with a person like Helen Keller whose perceptual deficiencies are staggering."[1] On these grounds Stich regards as false any theory that implies that the sighted and the blind person's beliefs have distinct contents.

The premise appears correct, for "believes that there is a cat in the next room" does seem univocally assertible of both the sighted person and Helen Keller. For if each were sincerely to assert "there is a cat in the next room" their words conventionally would *mean* the same; and so by ordinary criteria the belief ascription would be true of each on an *oblique* or *de dicto* univocal reading. (The sameness of belief ascription is not then merely a function of a common *de re* reference to the kind *cat*.)

2. There is the very general thesis that the psychological content of a person's attitudes consists in their conceptual or cognitive-functional roles, thus presupposing that our commonsense system of psychological explanation individuates attitudes

along non-social, individualistic lines. Tyler Burge has mounted an imposing counter-argument.[2] He has two objections: that the individualist conceptual role theory counts beliefs as different which common sense counts the same; and that the conceptual role theory counts beliefs as the same which common sense counts different. Both objections rest on the following well-known example of Burge's.

Suppose that a person who is otherwise a normal English speaker believes that he has arthritis in his thigh, and that he also has many true beliefs about arthritis, for example, that he has it in his wrists and ankles. When a doctor tells him that arthritis cannot occur in the thigh ("arthritis means an ailment of the joints") he is surprised but takes the doctor's word for it. Now consider that earlier belief which he would have expressed as "I have arthritis in my ankles." On the conceptual role theory, that belief should count as distinct from the doctor's belief that his patient has arthritis in his ankles. For the two have, or had, crucially different ideas about what "arthritis" means, and consequently the two beliefs have (should on a conceptual role theory be counted as having) crucially different conceptual links to other beliefs. But as Burge argues, common sense ascribes the same belief to both: the belief that the patient has arthritis in his ankles. Thus sameness of conceptual role is not *necessary* for sameness of psychological content.[3] Now it seems clear that Burge is right that the belief ascription applies both to the doctor and to the patient in his uncorrected state on a univocal reading, one that is, moreover, oblique or *de dicto*.

That sameness of conceptual role is not *sufficient* for sameness of content is argued as follows. Suppose the patient (whom we'll now call Bert) had lived in a world much like this one, but one in which doctors apply "arthritis" not to a disease specifically of joints but to a broader class of rheumatoid ailments including one that can occur in thighs. Suppose that Bert's history in that world had from an individualistic point of view been identical with what it is in the real world, and that therefore before visiting the doctor Bert had had a belief he would have expressed as "I have arthritis in my thigh." As we see things, would that have been a belief that he had *arthritis* in his thigh? Burge says no, and again I believe he is right. In that world Bert may have had a belief that he had *tharthritis* (as we may choose to say) in his thigh, for there "arthritis" does not mean what it means among us. So in the actual and the counterfactual situations, the individualistic facts about the conceptual roles of Bert's beliefs are the same, but distinct belief ascriptions are true of him. Burge draws the strong conclusion that the content of a person's beliefs depends in part on social facts that are independent of his cognitive make-up, social facts of which he may not be aware.

Stich's point and the first of Burge's points have a common structure: it is said to be false that discriminative abilities are partially constitutive of psychological contents, and that individual conceptual roles are constitutive of psychological contents, because those theses would count beliefs as distinct to which the same *de dicto* or oblique ascription univocally applies.

3. Metalinguistic contents have often been invoked for beliefs that normally would not be expressed metalinguistically. Thus suppose a person asserts "there are elms in Spain" but knows of no non-metalinguistic distinguishing features of elms among trees or of Spain among countries. It could be said that the content of this person's belief involves the conception of elms as "those trees which among us are called 'elms'" and of Spain as "that country which among us is called 'Spain.'"

One objection (there are others I shall not discuss) is the following. Suppose an Italian who would assert "Ci sono olmi in Spagna" is in the same situation as our English speaker; he does not know elms ("olmi") from other trees or Spain ("Spagna") from other countries. To be consistent we then say that his beliefs involve metalinguistic reference to those Italian nouns. But of course if everything else is normal we should rather say that the two speakers believe the same thing, namely that there are elms in Spain. This holds of them *de dicto* and univocally. They have the same belief, while the metalinguistic analysis counts them as having distinct beliefs. Once again, I find the premise about the oblique or *de dicto* ascription correct, not open to an unforced denial; it would be misguided to insist that we must throw out the univocal that-clause and substitute a pair of metalinguistic that-clauses in order to describe those beliefs correctly.

The question then to be addressed is the relation between *de dicto* or oblique ascriptions of beliefs and their psychological contents, between such ascriptions and their individuation in commonsense psychological explanation. I shall argue that psychological content is not in general identical with what is captured by oblique that-clauses, that commonsense constraints on individuation induce only a loose fit between contents and that-clauses, and that this does not make contents ineffable or even especially elusive. Let me emphasize that the topic is not some theoretical refinement of commonsense psychology, but ordinary everyday psychological explanation.

Behind the three arguments—against recognitional concept theories, conceptual role theories, and metalinguistic concept analyses—lies something like the following assumption:

(*) Sameness of *de dicto* or oblique ascription implies sameness of psychological content.

Perhaps there are facts about the occurrence of indexicals and demonstratives which would generally be perceived nowadays as counterexamples to (*) in its unqualified form. But it is pretty evident, I think, that the above arguments presuppose a version of (*) restricted to general terms (including also proper names; cf. "Spain"). So we have something like:

(A) Sameness of the *de dicto* or oblique occurrence of a general term in two belief ascriptions implies, if everything else is the same, sameness of the psychological content of the two beliefs thus ascribed.

My reply to the above arguments involves denying (A): sameness of the general terms in a pair of belief ascriptions does not (even though all else is equal) ensure that the ascribed beliefs are individuated as the same belief in commonsense psychological explanation.

I shall also argue the falsity of the converse of (A), viz.

(B) Differences in *de dicto* or oblique ascription imply differences in psychological content.

This is important again in connection with Burge's anti-individualism, for it seems to be required for his argument that sameness in the conceptual roles of thoughts is not sufficient for their sameness in psychological content.

A variant of a well-known example of Kripke's may serve to introduce the reason for rejecting (A). In the original example[4] Pierre grew up monolingual in France, where he had heard of a pretty city called "Londres"; he was moreover disposed to assert "Londres est jolie." Subsequently he was taken to live in London, not knowing it to be the Londres he had heard of; the part he lived in was unattractive and he was disposed to assert "London is not pretty." Our ordinary principles of belief ascription lead us then to say, as Kripke points out, both that Pierre believes that London is pretty and that Pierre believes that London is not pretty. These ascriptions are true on an oblique reading[5] and "London" is univocal as we use it.

Now Pierre might have been more fortunate; he might have been taken to an attractive part of London and thus been happy to assert "London is pretty," still unaware that this was the Londres he had heard of. The upshot is interesting: "Pierre believes that London is pretty" is true by virtue of the earlier facts about Pierre, and it is true by virtue of the later facts. And its double truth is on a univocal oblique reading. The point does not depend on translation; parallel cases arise in which someone mistakenly thinks a name names two things, and ascribes the same predicate twice.

But how many beliefs does Pierre have? In other words, how many belief-types are involved, as that is individuated by commonsense psychology? Clearly there are two beliefs, and they are as distinct as my beliefs that Paris is pretty and that Rio is pretty. Those beliefs would interact differently with other beliefs in ordinary psychological explanation. Perhaps in France Pierre came to believe that were he ever to live in "Londres" he would live in the same city as Oscar Wilde, and he retains this belief. But he does not draw from the conjunction of this belief and his later beliefs the conclusion that he now lives in a pretty city also inhabited by Oscar Wilde; and this is not because he has not bothered to put them together.

These beliefs not only are individuated by commonsense psychology as distinct in their psychological roles; it also seems quite appropriate to regard them as distinct in *content*. The differences in their interactive properties flow from differences in how Pierre conceives things, in how he takes the world to be, in what he regards the facts as being—that is, differences in some semantic or intentional dimension. And yet one and the same oblique belief description is true of Pierre univocally by virtue of these beliefs that are distinct in their psychological content.

Let us now look at some beliefs involving general terms. Suppose that Paul, an English speaker, has been raised by a French nanny in a sheltered way. She speaks English with Paul, but amuses herself by referring to the cats around them as "chats" (she says "shahs," pronouncing the "s") and never as "cats." Paul acquires thereby a perfectly good recognitional acquaintance with cats and many beliefs about them, but he does not know that in English they are properly called "cats." Suppose he forms the belief he would express as "All chats have tails"; it seems we are then justified in asserting that Paul believes that all cats have tails, on an oblique reading.[6] As it happens, he occasionally sees his parents, who speak of animals called "cats." Because no cats are ever present, nor any pictures of cats, Paul does not realize that cats are his familiar "chats." Now Paul's parents tell him various things about cats, in particular that they all have tails. On this basis it is again true of Paul that he believes that all cats have tails. And it seems clear that Paul has two beliefs, with distinct psychological contents. For they interact potentially with other beliefs in different ways despite their common univocal ascription.

Had Paul's parents told him of Manx cats, it would have been true that Paul believes that all cats have tails and believes that not all cats have tails, on oblique unequivocal readings. But we should say that those beliefs are not inconsistent in their psychological contents,[7] and this means that these oblique ascriptions do not individuate Paul's beliefs in a way that reflects their psychological relations.

Stephen Stich's reply to the general thesis that recognitional abilities may be crucial to the individuation of beliefs was that Helen Keller and a sighted person both may believe that there is a cat in the next room. Now suppose that Paul had had a slightly different phonological history. His nanny used the English "cat," but somehow Paul got the idea that there are two different meanings of "cat," each referring to a distinct kind of animal (cf. "crab"), the kind he recognizes at a glance and the kind his parents speak of. This idea is so entrenched that when his nanny and his parents, on one of their rare joint appearances, both say "there's a cat in the next room," Paul believes that there are two animals in the next room and is interested to see finally one of the unfamiliar "cats." Now Helen Keller has conveniently dropped by, and she overhears Paul's parents' remark. It seems that she thereby acquires only one belief that there's a cat in the next room, but that Paul has two such beliefs, distinct as types in their psychological individuation. Helen Keller's belief is then identical in type with at most one of Paul's beliefs. And so it is left open that the content of the other belief is constituted in part by Paul's ability to recognize cats. Naturally (A) is thereby falsified.

Now consider again Tyler Burge's first thesis, that two beliefs may differ in their conceptual roles (by virtue of different understandings of some concept) and nevertheless have the same content. Suppose that when Paul leaves home he lives in France for a while, learns about a rheumatoid ailment called "arthrite," and comes to believe that he has it both in his thigh and in his ankles. He would be surprised to learn that you can't have "arthrite" in your thigh. As it happens Paul has a perfectly good understanding of the English "arthritis," which he does not realize is renderable in French as "arthrite" (perhaps he never sees them written down). He is unfortunately given to hypochondria, and comes to believe that he has two problems with his ankles, in his words "arthrite" and "arthritis." It seems that "believes that he has arthritis in his ankles" is doubly but univocally true of Paul, by virtue of beliefs with distinct psychological contents. Had he been less inclined to hypochondria his English belief could have instead been that he does not have arthritis in his ankles. Now that belief would clearly have been psychologically consistent with his French belief that he has arthritis in his ankles, but not with his *actual* English belief. The latter two therefore must be distinct in psychological content—unless, that is, you want to deny that the relevant sort of consistency is consistency in content.[8]

So Burge's observation that "believes that Bert has arthritis in his ankles" is true of the doctor and Bert on an oblique univocal reading, which I have agreed is correct, does not imply that their beliefs have the same content as that is individuated in commonsense psychological explanation.

I shall not go into the third argument, the one against metalinguistic analyses. But it should by now be clear that it does not follow from the fact that "believes that there are elms in Spain" is univocally true of those English and Italian speakers that their beliefs are not metalinguistic with regard to their respective languages and therefore distinct in their psychological contents.

It may be useful to distinguish two theses in what I have been arguing, namely, a thesis about how beliefs are *individuated* in commonsense psychological explanation, and a thesis about *content*, the former being more minimal than the latter.

Commonsense psychological explanation appeals to various elementary *structures* in the relations among beliefs, wants and so on. There are motivational structures: *x*'s believing something, *x*'s believing something else to the effect that given the first thing doing *A* would have a certain result, and *x*'s desire for that result may explain *x*'s doing *A*. There are inferential structures: *x*'s believing something and *x*'s believing something else to the effect that the first thing is sufficient for a certain further thing may explain *x*'s believing that further thing. There are structures of irrationality: *x*'s believing something, *x*'s desire for a certain thing and *x*'s belief to the effect that the first thing could rule out the second may conjointly explain *x*'s compartmentalizing or suppressing the first belief. And so on.[9]

These structures apply to beliefs and desires only as they are appropriately individuated. The simple cases I have been discussing can be spun out in obvious ways to show that the appropriate individuation conditions are not captured by oblique readings of ordinary belief ascriptions. For example, imagine Paul's English belief that he has arthritis in his ankles interacting with a French belief of his that if he has arthritis in his ankles he should apply heat: not much happens as a result. The correct individuation transcends, in some crucial respects at least, what ordinary ascriptions capture. And I am speaking always of commonsense explanation.

As for psychological *content*, if it is not captured by that-clauses, what constitutes it? Are we entitled to regard my alleged underlying psychological individuation as determining a kind of content? I shall return to this question.

Let us take up the second strong Burgean thesis. Suppose "arthritis" had meant *tharthritis*: even if Bert's non-socially-described ruminations remained the same it would not have been true that Bert believed that he had arthritis in his ankles and thigh. *Therefore* sameness of individualist conceptual role is not sufficient for sameness of psychological content.

Now Burge's premise, that our old belief ascription would not then be true of Bert, is correct; and it is an important discovery that belief ascriptions are thus sensitive to social facts which may not be reflected in believers' own versions of things. But the further thesis, that content as it is individuated in psychological explanation depends on independent social factors, is I think not correct.

The anti-individualist conclusion depends on (B), that differences in oblique ascription imply differences in psychological content. But the intuitions which in the cases of Paul and Pierre led us to reject (A) ought also to bring us to reject (B). We should hold that despite their different ascriptions Bert's belief that he has arthritis in his ankles and his belief that he has tharthritis in his ankles have the same psychological content, because they have the same potential for explanatory interaction with other beliefs; what intuitively appeared to determine that potential in the case of Paul and Pierre was how they, as it were, personally conceived things. But let me give some new arguments directed specifically against (B) and the Burgean thesis that sameness of individualist conceptual role is not sufficient for sameness of psychological content.

That (B) is false is already accepted by whoever takes a certain widespread view of Twin Earth cases. Although those Twin Earthling thoughts which they express using "water" are, as the story goes,[10] like ours in their personal conceptual roles, we cannot ascribe to them the thought that, say, they bathe in water. Twin Earthlings have referential contact not with H_2O but with a chemically distinct if phenomenally indistinguishable substance, and so we cannot translate their "water" into English as "water" and hence cannot assert of them anything of the form "believes that ... water...." Conceding these facts about belief *ascriptions*, many have found it intuitive, indeed have taken it to be the point of Twin Earth cases, that Twin Earthlings' thoughts have the same content as ours as that is individuated in psychological explanation, the same "narrow content."

Such intuitions appear to be vindicated by two rather different thought experiments. (1) Suppose Bert is a full member of two English-speaking communities that differ linguistically in small ways of which he is unaware. The first is ours, where "arthritis" means arthritis; but in the second "arthritis" means tharthritis. Let the individual facts about Bert be as in Burge's case. How are we to describe him? If there is no reason to choose just one of the languages as his language, then apparently the best thing for us to say is that Bert believes that he has arthritis in his ankles and believes that he has tharthritis in his ankles. But in explaining Bert psychologically the natural thing to say is that he has just one belief, one way of conceiving what is wrong with his ankles. Similarly, we may imagine a commuter between Earth and Twin Earth who is biworldly in his language without knowing of the systematic referential differences between English and Twin English. He would assert "Water quenches thirst." Again it seems that two belief ascriptions are in order, but that they should be seen as merely different extrinsic descriptions of what is, as regards psychological explanation, the commuter's one way of conceiving things.

(2) Here is a different thought experiment. One is given a diary and told that it is by either an Earthling or a Twin Earthling but not which. An entry says: "No swimming today; we think the water is too rough." This reports a psychological explanation, one that loses nothing from our ignorance of the diary's provenance, that is, from our ignorance of whether it would be correct, in reporting that thought obliquely in a that-clause, to use "water" or "twin-water." It is not that we switch rapidly back and forth between two explanations, one in terms of water and the other in terms of twin-water; all we have to have been told is that the diary was written in one of a class of worlds that resemble Earth in the relevant respects. Or, again, suppose that I do not know whether in Bert's linguistic community "arthritis" means arthritis or tharthritis, but that I know all the relevant individualist facts about Bert. I read in his diary: "I fear I have arthritis, and so today I have made an appointment with a specialist." It is difficult to accept that we do not fully understand the psychological explanation given here, despite our not being in a position to produce the correct that-clause. We understand the diarists' explanations because we know how they conceive things.

What is there to be said against these intuitions in favor of "narrow content"? Two objections could be thought to have force. The first is that so-called narrow content cannot capture an *intentional* property; for the two beliefs in the Burge case and those in the Twin Earth case do not share *truth conditions*. "Content" should mean intentionality, and intentionality is a certain *directedness* of thoughts onto things, properties, states of affairs, in short, truth conditions and the components of truth conditions. The second objection is that there is no appropriate way to *specify* the common content in those pairs of beliefs; and thus the notion of narrow content is just hand-waving.

I shall not say in response to either objection that there *are* that-clauses which do not contain "water" or "arthritis" and which capture the common content of those pairs of beliefs. I am quite prepared to concede that that-clauses are so generally shot through with social and causal presuppositions that narrow content cannot in general be captured thus.

There is a kind of reply to the objection concerning intentionality and truth conditions which I believe is important but shall not develop at length here. Put sketchily the idea is this: the conceptual roles of thoughts are distinct from their truth conditions, and in more than one sense do not determine truth-conditions (except perhaps for certain demonstrative judgments involving perceptual discriminative concepts).[11] But commonsense psychological explanation of the sort we have intuitively appealed to in discussing Paul and Pierre individuates attitudes according to their conceptual roles, the specification of truth conditions having some further function—on which more anon. How can there be *content* without truth conditions? This is, I think, not merely a terminological question, for it involves intuitions about the apparent intentionality of one's own thoughts as judged from a first-person perspective. The point is that the conceptual roles of one's thoughts determine *how* one *conceives* things, and it is difficult to see how one can consider how one oneself conceives things without that in some sense involving what one's thoughts are "about." And that is appropriately called content, by a Principle of the Transparency of Content: if something from an unconfused perspective appears to be content then it is a kind of content. As I say, this is sketchy, but I mention it to register that the defender of "narrow content" has more than one line of defense: it would not matter that narrow content does not determine truth conditions if there is a kind of content that does not involve truth conditions.

Furthermore the demand for a narrow or individualist account of intentionality, in the sense of the outward directedness of thoughts onto states of affairs, is not unanswerable. Consider Bert's diary again. I do not know whether Bert's use of "arthritis" involves a misconception because I do not know the social facts about it. But I do know this: how the world *would* be if Bert's conceptions are or were not misconceptions. How Bert thinks of things—as that is described from an individualist perspective—appears to determine a set of possible worlds, namely, those in which Bert's thoughts are or would be true if they are or were not misconceptions. Call that set of worlds the *realization conditions* of Bert's beliefs. If my ability to explain Bert psychologically presupposes a grasp of something "intentional," something like truth conditions, then it would seem that my grasp of the realization conditions of Bert's beliefs is sufficient. The diary thought experiment supports this.

Realization conditions are of course not truth conditions in our official sense. The truth conditions of a belief depend on some that-clause which correctly ascribes it, and as Burge has shown that is not in general determined by individualist facts. Thus I am not saying that the *real* truth conditions of thoughts are their realization conditions. I am not proposing a redefinition of anything. Rather I am saying that if psychological explanation involves a mapping of thoughts onto possible states of affairs, then realization conditions are there for the taking. There is nothing recondite in the idea; our commonsense understanding of others delivers the realization conditions of their beliefs without our having a name for them.[12]

An adjustment to this suggestion is needed. Suppose I find a diary with the entry: "Hot and sunny today; phoned Maria to invite her to the beach." Now, the date has been torn off the page. Still I appear to understand the diarist's explanation of his/her phoning Maria, despite not knowing the truth conditions (in one sense) of the thought expressed by "hot and sunny today." Is there not, however, a sense in which I do know the truth conditions? Suppose on Tuesday one thinks "it is hot and sunny today," and on Friday one thinks "it is hot and sunny today." They have the same truth conditions in the sense of conditions of truth in abstraction from context. Call them *context-indeterminate*, by contrast with the context-determinate truth conditions that determine sets of possible worlds. Then if understanding the psychological explanation given in the diary requires in some sense knowing truth conditions, they need merely be context-indeterminate.

To put this together with the former point, we may say this: if psychological explanation involves intentionality, then *context-indeterminate realization conditions* are all the intentionality required.[13]

There is still the objection that we cannot in general *specify* the narrow content of thoughts. Now if this means merely that narrow content is not in general captured by ordinary that-clauses, it is difficult to see why it is an objection. We have perfectly sound intuitions about when to distinguish the beliefs of Paul, Pierre, and Bert, despite the fact that that-clauses do not make the right distinctions. If we then lack specifications of narrow content, in the sense in which we have specifications of wide, social content, that must mean that psychological explanation does not require such specifications. We get along perfectly well without them; we individuate beliefs and understand their realization conditions without an official system of generating such specifications. Narrow contents are not ineffable; we get at them in context via various devices. (a) We use that-clauses with one eye on the background facts: different narrow contents are implied by "Paul believes that cats have tails" in the "chat" context and in the "cat" context. (b) We report a person's words, or approximations thereto, together with other utterances which help us to interpret his words: Bert says "I have arthritis in my ankles," but he also says "I have arthritis in my thigh." The second helps one to understand the narrow content expressed by the first. (c) We ascribe narrow content by producing words that have the same narrow content for us. Imagine a Twin Earthling whose language is Twin German; it may help to render one of his beliefs as "I bathe in water" even though there is no water there and those are not the words he would utter. Not that we have much opportunity for interpreting Twin Earthlings, but interpretation by approximately matching narrow contents is one of our fundamental techniques in psychological explanation.

It now seems to me somewhat extraordinary that we should have thought that psychological states are captured by a neat set of content-specifications. But what then are that-clauses for? Of course they play a central role in psychological explanation, given suitable background information; but we have been misconceiving that role in thinking that they define precisely the individuation conditions of psychological states. That-clauses on their oblique readings are sensitive, either directly or indirectly via translation, to how beliefs would linguistically be expressed, and that is, as the examples of Paul and Pierre show, only loosely related to psychological content. Now, as Burge's cases show, that-clauses capture how a belief would be expressed by exhibiting something that is equivalent in *social content* (as we might say) to what the subject would utter, given his deference to the usage of his linguistic community. This enables that-clauses to capture certain extrapsychological relations of propositional attitudes to independent states of affairs, what we may think of as their *socially determined truth conditions*. The fundamental usefulness of this is that we may then describe people as conveyors of more or less determinate information, which remains constant even when the psychological contents of their states vary. That-clauses enable us to impose a grid of socially regularized information on the vagaries of individual psychology. Presumably the system of propositional attitude ascription is part of a larger framework of *restraints*, even, on the centrifugal tendencies of the thoughts of each of us.

Notes

1. Stephen P. Stich, *From Folk Psychology to Cognitive Science: The Case Against Belief* (Cambridge, Mass.: MIT Press/Bradford Books, 1983), 66–67.

2. Tyler Burge, "Individualism and the Mental," in *Midwest Studies in Philosophy, Vol. IV: Studies in Metaphysics*, ed. Peter French, *et al.* (Minneapolis: University of Minnesota Press, 1979), 73–122.

3. It is fair to say that many have taken this to be the message of Burge's paper, that is, that beliefs are not individuated in commonsense explanation by their conceptual roles. Of course Burge's direct point is about the presuppositions of *ascriptions* of beliefs. But because of the widespread supposition that the significance of this point lies in the stronger point, I am taking the stronger point to be the consequential burden of Burge's paper. He writes: "It is expressions at oblique occurrences within content clauses that primarily do the job of providing the content of mental states or events, and in characterizing the person" (*op. cit.*, 76). And again he writes of "the idea that the distinctively mental aspects can be understood fundamentally in terms of the individual's abilities, dispositions, states, and so forth, considered in isolation from his social surroundings" as follows: "our argument undermines this latter suggestion. Social context infects even the distinctively mental features of mentalistic attributions. No man's intentional mental phenomena are insular" (*op. cit.*, 87). More recently, Burge has argued for an apparently less stringent position, namely, that even though there *might* be a level of scientific psychology which is individualist, (a) there are important examples of scientific psychology which cannot be construed individualistically, (b) such non-individualist explanation is legitimate as regards scientific methodology, and (c) commonsense psychological explanation is non-individualist. In this paper I am concerned to argue that Burge's observations about belief ascriptions may be accepted while denying (c).

4. Saul Kripke, "A Puzzle about Belief," in *Meaning and Use*, ed. Avishai Margalit (Dordrecht: Reidel, 1979), 239–83.

5. This assumes that when we ascribe beliefs obliquely to speakers of other languages, the correct way to do so is (roughly) to translate how they would be expressed.

6. How else to represent the belief obliquely than by translating "chats" as "cats"? Keep in mind that the point does not depend on translation.

7. In "Names in Thought," *Philosophical Studies* 51 (1987): 169–85, I discuss the significance of the phenomenon in connection with Saul Kripke's "puzzle about belief."

8. Perhaps it is some sort of "formal" consistency. But then beliefs would not be individuated in commonsense psychological explanation by their *content*, which seems implausible.

9. The circumlocutory wording is meant to avoid propositional variables which appear to presuppose that-clauses. For a way of understanding these structures of rationality and irrationality, see sections 4 and 6 of my accompanying paper "A New Kind of Content."

10. Hilary Putnam, "The Meaning of 'Meaning,'" in *Mind, Language and Reality: Philosophical Papers, Vol. 2* (Cambridge: Cambridge University Press, 1975), 215–71.

11. See Brian Loar, "Must Beliefs be Sentences?" in *PSA 1982: Proceedings of the 1982 Biennial Meeting of the Philosophy of Science Association*, ed. Peter D. Asquith and Thomas Nickles (East Lansing, Michigan: Philosophy of Science Association, 1983), 627–42.

12. This is perhaps similar to what David Lewis proposes in "What Puzzling Pierre Does Not Believe," *Australasian Journal of Philosophy* 59 (1981): 283–89.

As several people have pointed out to me, my "context-independent realization conditions" are quite similar, including their detachment from that-clauses, to Daniel Dennett's *notional worlds* (see "Beyond Belief," in *Thought and Object*, ed. Andrew Woodfield (Oxford: Clarendon Press, 1982), 1–95). I discuss the relation between my account, as that is elaborated in section 6 of "A New Kind of Content," and Dennett's theory in footnote 6 of that paper.

13. Jerry Fodor has recently proposed that narrow content be construed in terms of functions from contexts to sets of possible worlds (in a paper given at UCLA, Spring 1985). And in correspondence he has suggested that this would preclude the need for the realization conditions I propose here. But I do not think that Kaplanesque characters will in fact do the job of capturing the narrow content of general terms, or not unless I am missing something. The reason is that, if you treat natural kind terms as if they are pure indexicals whose semantic values are determined by context, then "water" and "alcohol" would count as having the same narrow content—viz. that function which maps a natural kind term onto a natural kind in accordance with certain causal facts in its history of use. A Kaplanesque "character," a function of that kind, may well individuate the narrow content of a very special feature of thought such as the first-person pronoun, for it can be argued that self-ascription is the only aspect of narrow content whose reference-function always maps the belief onto the believer. But in the narrow individuation of beliefs involving "water" and "alcohol" we want their contributions to be different, in accordance with their conceptual roles. That combination of indexicality and substantive conceptual content is what context-indeterminate realization conditions are supposed to capture.

57 Wide Computationalism

Robert A. Wilson

1 Introduction

It has often been thought that individualism in psychology, the view that psychological states must be taxonomized so as to supervene on the intrinsic, physical properties of individuals,[1] receives supports from the computational theory of mind, a view taken by many philosophers and cognitive scientists to be a foundational assumption of contemporary research in cognitive science.[2] The computational theory of mind, or computationalism, can be summarized as the view that psychological processes and mental states are essentially computational. It makes an empirical claim about the nature of cognitive processing and suggests to many a methodological claim about how cognitive psychology, or cognitive science more generally, ought to proceed.

This paper offers a challenge to those who have either argued from computationalism to individualism or thought such an inference plausible by identifying a possibility that has either been overlooked or not treated seriously by proponents of this family of arguments. The possibility is that of *wide computationalism*, and I shall defend both the possibility and the plausibility of wide computationalism in parts of cognitive psychology.

To get a clearer fix both on the type of argument for individualism I have in mind and the nature of the objection I shall pose to it, consider the following explicit argument, which I shall refer to as the *computational argument* for individualism:

(1) Cognitive psychology taxonomically individuates mental states and processes only *qua* computational states and processes.

(2) The computational states and processes that an individual instantiates supervene on the intrinsic, physical states of that individual.

Therefore,

(3) Cognitive psychology individuates only states and processes that supervene on the intrinsic, physical states of the individual who instantiates those states and processes.

While the "only" in (1) gives this argument the necessary strength for its conclusion, this will make (1) seem implausibly strong to many who adopt a more pluralistic view of psychological taxonomy. Although I think that individualism in psychology as it has been articulated and defended by some of its leading proponents is adequately expressed by (3) above, and so *any* argument from computationalism to individualism so conceived requires a strong, exclusionary premise such as (1), I do not wish to defend this claim here. In fact, make (1) (and so (3)) as weak or as qualified as you like. Still, the computational argument for individualism should be rejected because its perhaps innocent-sounding second premise is false, and *it* is false because of the possibility of wide computationalism in psychology.

2 The Possibility of Wide Computationalism

Suppose that cognitive processing is computational, at least from the point of view of those seeking systematic, scientific, psychological explanations. The states (and the processes which are the transitions between such states) over which a computational psychology quantifies need not be individualistic because the cognitive system to which they belong could be part of a *wide computational* system. That is, the corresponding computational system could transcend the boundary of the individual and include parts of that individual's environment. If this were so, then the computational states of such a cognitive system would not supervene on the intrinsic, physical states of the individual; likewise, the resulting computational psychology would involve essential reference to the environment beyond the individual. The states and processes of a wide computational system are not taxonomized individualistically.

In this section I will concentrate on explaining the coherence of the idea of wide computationalism, i.e., with defending the *possibility* of wide computationalism. I consolidate this defence by considering two objections to wide computationalism in §4, going on in §5 to identify examples of existing research in computational psychology that can be plausibly understood in terms of wide computationalism.

Wide computational systems are computational systems that are not fully instantiated in any individual. Since they literally extend beyond the boundary of the individual, not all of the states they contain can be taxonomized individualistically. Within a wide computational system much of the processing that takes place may well be instantiated fully within the boundary of the individual, but what makes it a wide system is that not all of the computational processes that make up the system are so instantiated. If there are computational (formal) descriptions of both an organism's environment and its mental states, and causal transitions from the former to the latter that can be thought of as computations, there is a process beginning in the environment and ending in the organism which can be viewed as a computation, a wide computation.

To some, the coherence of wide computationalism, its mere possibility, will seem unproblematic. For example, in responding to Martin Davies' claim that "cognitive psychology treats information processing systems (modules) and whole creatures *qua* embedded in particular larger systems and ultimately particular environments" (Davies 1991, p. 482), Gabriel Segal says

> the supervenience base of a representation's content is some larger system in which the representation is embedded. This could be: the whole creature plus its environment, the whole creature, the largest module in which the representation occurs, a sub-processor of that module, a sub-sub-processor of that module, a sub-sub-sub.... Individualism is the thesis that the representational states of a system are determined by intrinsic properties of that system. It seems likely that whole subjects (or whole brains) make up large, integrated, computational systems. Whole subjects plus embedding environments do not make up integrated, computational systems. That is one reason

why individualists draw the line where they do: the whole subject is the largest acceptable candidate for the supervenience base because it is the largest integrated system available. (1991, p. 492, ellipsis in original)[3]

Here Segal seems to be conceding the coherence of wide computationalism, claiming that, as a matter of fact, we don't find computational, cognitive systems larger than the individual. This passage identifies precisely where a proponent of wide computationalism disagrees with the proponent of the computational argument: she rejects the claim that the "whole subject," the individual, is, as a matter of fact, "the largest integrated physical system available" for computational, psychological explanation.

Given the coherence of wide computationalism implicit in this passage, it is not surprising that in Segal's surrounding discussion he notes that the disagreement here is properly resolved by an examination of empirical research in computational psychology. Segal himself thinks that the crucial claim that "whole subjects plus embedding environments do not make up integrated, computational systems, can be defended on a posteriori grounds. One would expect, then, an individualist of Segal's persuasion also to consider (2) in the computational argument to have an a posteriori justification, one which while allowing for the mere possibility of wide computational systems shows why *our* computational, cognitive systems are individualistic.

Not all individualists adopt this view of (2). For example, Frances Egan (1992) has argued that computational taxonomies are individualistic of their nature: there is something general about taxonomy in computational psychology, or perhaps about computational theory more generally still, which entails that cognitive, computational states and processes are individualistic. If Egan is right, then wide computationalism is inconsistent with some more general feature of computational psychology or computational theory, and (2) is not something which simply happens to be true of the computational systems that we instantiate; rather, it says something true about computational systems per se, and can be defended on a priori grounds.[4]

To bring out the contrast between these two types of defence of (2), and to see why the more a priori defence is problematic in this context, consider the details of Egan's argument. It begins with the claim that the goal of computational theories of cognition is "to characterize the mechanisms underlying our various cognitive capacities" (pp. 444–445).[5] And such theories "construe cognitive processes as formal operations defined over symbol structures" (p. 446). Now,

Symbols are just functionally characterized objects whose individuation conditions are specified by a *realization function* f_R which maps equivalence classes of physical features of a system to what we might call "symbolic" features. Formal operations are just those physical operations that are differentially sensitive to the aspects of symbolic expressions that under the realization function f_R are specified as symbolic features. The mapping f_R allows a causal sequence of physical state transitions to be interpreted as a *computation*.

Given this method of individuating computational states, two systems performing the same operations over the same symbol structures are computationally indistinguishable. (p. 446)

From this, claims Egan, it follows that "if two systems are molecular duplicates then they are computational duplicates. Computational descriptions are individualistic: they type-individuate states without reference to the subject's environment or social context" (p. 446).

Egan's final conclusion here does not follow, unless one equates computational systems with *subjects*, i.e., with individuals. Yet doing so would beg the question against the wide computationalist, for the wide computationalist endorses precisely the claim that there can be computational systems which extend beyond the boundary of the individual. There is nothing in the method of computational individuation itself to which Egan points which implies that the class of physical features mapped by a realization function cannot include members that are part of the environment of the individual. This being so, Egan has not provided a sound argument for why individualism (about computational psychology) follows from the very nature of computational psychology, and so her view does not point to some internal incoherence in the idea of wide computationalism.

Wide computationalism is analogous to wide *functionalism*, the view that the conceptual role defining mental states extends into the world (Harman 1987, 1988; Kitcher 1991). Yet wide computationalism is both more modest and more radical than wide functionalism, and provides the basis for a stronger case against individualism. It is more modest in that it concedes that individualism is true of at least some mental processes and rejects only its all-encompassing nature; it is more radical because it denies something about the notion of a formal or computational system—that it be instantiated in an individual—which is almost without exception taken for granted by individualists, and so undermines the computational argument for individualism in a fundamental way. And it is a more decisive objection to individualism, supposing the "radical" claim to be established, because it not only removes computationalism as one of the major supports of individualism without rejecting computationalism but also provides the basis for arguing from computationalism to a distinctly non-individualistic view of computational psychology itself.

The challenge to the computational argument is not posed by directly defending the claim that psychological states require a broad construal but, rather, by arguing that *the formal* or *computational systems* in which they are instantiated or of which they are a part extend beyond the individual. The distinction between an individual and a cognitive, computational system is central to an understanding of wide computationalism. Even if one thinks that many computational, cognitive systems are fully instantiated in the individual, wide computationalism is a possibility because the boundaries of the individual and those of the computational, cognitive system need not be identical.

An example of a possible wide computational process is the familiar process of multiplication.[6] Typically, apart from multiplication problems that are included in one's "times table," one multiplies numbers by storing intermediate solutions in some written form, usually on paper, and then solving the next component of the problem, storing the result on paper, and so on. The actual process that one goes through in multiplying numbers together typically involves the storage of symbols *on paper*. The problem solving activity itself need not and does not take place solely in one's head; it involves, rather, the use of symbols (and conventions) which are not stored exclusively in the head. A description of the process of multiplication must include a description of mathematical symbols, and for most human beings such a description presupposes a reference to something external to the individual organism. A crucial part of the process of multiplication, namely, the storage of mathematical symbols, extends beyond the boundary of the individual. Considered as multipliers, we are part of wide computational systems.

To show the coherence of wide computationalism, this need only be taken as an account of a possible computational, cognitive process, perhaps not one that *we* instantiate. Yet I have described the example in terms of our cognitive processing because I think that human mathematical problem solving, as well as much problem solving more generally, involves (indeed, *essentially* involves) the exploitation of representations in one's environment. The more complex the computational process we engage in—for example, non-trivial mathematical proofs—the more plausible this stronger claim is. Proofs of complex theorems in quantificational logic are rarely carried out entirely in one's head: at least *some* of the symbols are stored externally. What are stored are *pointers* to the symbols that one uses, and while such pointers may be stored inside the head, the symbols to which they point are not stored internally at all: that is why one *needs* a blackboard, pen and paper, or even a calculator.

Not only can a case be made for conceiving of mathematical and logical processes as wide computational processes: the same is true of perceptual and behavioural processes. Wide computationalism is appropriate in cases in which the interaction between an individual and something external to that individual is a crucial part of the computational process being described as an *explanans* in psychology. In the case of perception, it is an intrinsic part of that process that the system accept input from the environment and process it so that further mental processing can proceed. The perceptual process involves an interaction between an individual and her environment. This is in no way incompatible with providing a *computational* account of perception (see §5 below).

Since perception is a process which begins with environmental inputs, inputs which themselves may have a formal description and so be accessible to a computational, cognitive system, all components of the perceptual process can be described as part of a wide computational system. An individualist may object that this characterization of the process of perception simply begs the question. The relevant objects of perception are not external but internal to an individual; for example they are 2-D retinal images, not some type of environmental input. A wide computational account of perception presupposes a view of perception which an individualist should reject.

This objection in effect concedes a weak or negative point I want to make in this section, namely, that the formal or computational nature of mental processing *itself* doesn't entail individualism: one also needs to make a substantial claim about, for example, the objects of perception in order to derive individualism from computationalism. The same is true for any area of cognition which is claimed to be computational. The formality of cognition itself does not entail individualism.

Insofar as this points to a gap between computationalism and individualism in psychology, it allows for the *possibility* of wide computationalism. But a stronger claim about wide computationalism can be formulated and, I think, ultimately defended. Psychological states are computational only insofar as they are part of an implemented formal *system*. (For those who find this controversial, see my discussion in the next section.) But the formal systems of which at least some psychological states are a part are not fully instantiated in any natural individual, i.e., in an organism. So, qua computational states, such psychological states are not instantiated in any individual. Stated in this way, the argument allows one to draw not only the conclusion that a wide computational psychology is possible, but, assuming the truth of computationalism, the conclusion that, for at least some psychological states, such a psychology is *necessary*.

Thus far I have said little about the central notion of *formality*; to further demystify wide computationalism I turn to discuss this notion more explicitly.

3 The Notion of Formality

Computationalism is sometimes expressed as the view that, since cognition is *formal*, cognitive psychology should be restricted to positing and quantifying over the formal properties of mental states. This expression of computationalism, what Fodor (1981, pp. 226–228) has called the *formality condition*, may make the argument from computationalism to individualism in psychology appear compelling, for the formal properties that mental states have are often thought of as *intrinsic* properties of mental symbols, such as their *shape* and *size*.[7] This conception of computationalism allows one to think of formal properties as a particular species of mental *causal powers*, properties which supervene on the intrinsic, physical properties of the individual, and makes it tempting to view computationalism as providing a general theoretical framework for further specifying the nature of such powers. The task of a cognitive psychology which presupposes computationalism, on this conception of formality, is to discover the intrinsic properties of tokens in the language of thought. In senses that I shall explain below, such properties are both *non-semantic* and *non-physical*.[8]

It should be emphasized first, however, that the formality condition is an *interpretation* of computationalism, or a claim about what the acceptance of computationalism entails or involves, not simply a statement of computationalism itself. While the notion of formality is often used in computational theory, talk of formal properties as intrinsic *properties* of the individual components of computational systems is, in certain respects, misleading. The conception of formality used in logic, mathematics and computer science, the disciplines which provide the ultimate foundations for computationalism in psychology, is quite distinct from that expressed by the formality condition. In these disciplines the focus is on the properties and behaviour of formal *systems*. A formal system consists of primitives, formation rules, formulae, axioms, and rules of inference. The foundations of logic is concerned, in part, with the relationship between the notions of a formal system, an effective procedure, an algorithm, a computation, and the set of recursive functions. On this conception of formality, what I shall call the *systemic conception of formality*, a given formal system could be expressed in alternative notations and, in principle, could be realized by a nation of people related to each other as the rules of the system specify (cf. Block 1990, Searle 1981). In this sense, the intrinsic, physical properties of symbols in a formal system are arbitrary.[9]

On the systemic conception of formality, there is little talk of the formal properties that *particular* symbols have. The sorts of "formal properties" which are primarily discussed, properties such as being closed under modus ponens, being transitive, being compact, and being sound and complete, are properties of formal systems or, derivatively, properties of symbols as elements of formal systems. Computational processes, operations and instructions are often thought of as formal, but this is to say only that they can be adequately described as the result of the application of rules or algorithms which constitute the system to which they belong. Insofar as particular symbols in a formal system have formal properties, it is not clear whether such properties are intrinsic or extrinsic properties of the symbols themselves. For example, an instance of the symbol "A" will lead to an instance of the symbol "B" and do so in virtue of its "shape" in a formal system containing only the rule "A ⇒ B." But since this formal property, having that particular shape, has that effect only in a formal system with a rule of that type, one should be wary of identifying such formal properties with intrinsic causal powers that symbols possess. In any case, what is clear is that such properties have the causal significance that they do only insofar as the symbols to which they are attributed are part of a formal system.

The systemic conception of formality, which I shall rely on in the remainder of the paper, makes it natural to express computationalism as the view that cognitive psychology ought to be pitched at a computational *level of description*. I said above that the formal properties of mental states are supposed to be both non-semantic and non-physical, and I want to explain what these two contrasts imply about the (narrow) computationalist's conception of cognition by looking at the two different conditions that a computational level of description of psychological states and processes must satisfy.

In contrast to the *physical* level of description, the computational level is distinct from and irreducible to the levels of description which characterize the physical realizations of a particular formal system. The same computational program, the same formal system, can be instantiated in many physically distinct ways. Given computationalism, this is the sense in which psychology is autonomous of the physical sciences. It is this autonomy, and so the contrast between the formal and the physical, which, I think, underlies the first premise of the computational argument.

In contrast to the *semantic* or representational level of description, the computational level specifies the properties of mental symbols and the rules constituting the formal system of which those mental tokens are a part without reference to what, if anything, those symbols represent. The proponent of the computational argument for individualism claims that, perhaps unlike the semantic level of description, the computational level specifies properties which are determined by the intrinsic, physical states of the organism in which they are instantiated.[10] This feature of the properties specified at the formal level of description makes the second premise of the computational argument intuitively plausible.

4 Two Objections to Wide Computationalism

One prima facie strength of wide computationalism is that it is fairly non-committal regarding the precise computational character of cognition. For example, it would seem to be compatible with both "classical" and connectionist conceptions of computationalism in psychology. Yet this potential strength of wide computationalism may be seen as its Achilles' heel by someone pressing the issue of the degree to which wide computationalism is a *realist* view of computational psychology: to what extent does the plausibility or even the possibility of wide computationalism turn on a view of computationalism that is committed to little more than the utility of the computational *metaphor* in psychology? To put it slightly differently: does wide computationalism presuppose that computational explanations in psychology only *model* the phenomena they purport to explain, in the same way that there are computational models of other phenomena, such as the motions of planetary systems? If so, then wide computationalism will be a view of little significance for computational *psychology*. Central to the computational paradigm in psychology is the idea that an individual's mind is not simply described or modelled by a computer program; cognition is *rule-guided*, not simply *regular* (Bennett 1989). Wide computationalism is possible only if one relies on a weak reading of the computational metaphor, a reading which does not to justice to computationalist commitments in contemporary cognitive psychology.

To understand how a wide computational system could produce rule-guided behaviour, consider how a *narrow* computational system could do so. Since standard personal computers are paradigm cases of narrow computational systems, we can make our discussion more concrete by asking how *they* produce behaviour by actually following rules. Computers follow rules by instantiating or implementing programs constituted by such rules. So what is it to implement a program? For a physical device to be *capable* of implementing a given program is for it to have its physical states configured in such a way that transitions between those states are isomorphic to transitions between states that the program specifies, i.e., there is a mapping from equivalence classes of physical states to the symbolic states that constitute the program. Since implementational power is characterized in terms of the mathematical notion of isomorphism, there is a large number of actual programs and an infinite number of possible programs which any given physical device can implement. One closes the gap between the power to implement and actual implementation by identifying the appropriate causal interaction between the physical storehouse for the program (e.g., a physical disk) and the computer itself. So, in response to the grand epistemological, scepticism-mongering question,"Of the infinite number of programs that a computer could be implementing, how do you know that it is implementing *this* program?", we say: "It implements this one because it is this one that is encoded on the disk we inserted." (And since a physical disk is simply one type of storehouse for a program, we could replace reference to a physical disk here by reference to anything else a program is stored on.)

This view of implementation may make it sound as though the program is *epiphenomenal* to the physical operation of the computer, raising doubts about it as an account of rule-guided behaviour: in what sense is the behaviour that the computer generates anything more than *regular* behaviour, behaviour that appears to be rule-governed but, in fact, is not? I should make it clear that I think that the program *does* play a causal role in the behaviour of the physical device, and that the behaviour it produces is thus rule-governed and not merely regular. But while we may wish to say that the machine behaves in the way it does *because* of how it was programmed (i.e., because of the program it instantiates), we should be sure to distinguish this sort of "downward" causation from that which exists between the physical states themselves. Unless there is massive causal pre-emption "from above", symbolic states can't be viewed as the direct causal antecedents (the efficient causes) of later physical states. In general, to understand the causal role that higher-level states play in the production of behaviour, we need a broader conception of the notion of a causal role than is typically assumed (see Wilson 1993, 1994, 1995).

Although I have stated this view of how computers produce rule-guided behaviour in terms of familiar narrow computational systems, the narrowness of the system plays no significant role in the view; much the same story can be told of a *wide* computational system. The account of implementational power is precisely the same: the wide computational system has the power to implement just those programs for which there is an isomorphism between the system's physical states and the symbolic states the program specifies. The account of actual implementation is a generalization of that in the case of narrow computational systems: a wide computational system implements the "program" physically stored in the environment with which it causally interacts. Determining the proper symbolic description of aspects of an organism's environment is an a posteriori matter, much as doing so with respect to an organism's *internal* structure is.

"Program" occurs in scare-quotes here because of two important differences between the programs that run on standard computers and those that (narrow or wide) computationalists claim run on us: (i) unlike the programs that *we* encode on physical disks, precisely what symbolic interpretations can be given either to aspects of an organism's environment or to its internal structure (or both) are things that must be *discovered*; (ii) these interpretations may not turn out to be elaborate enough themselves to warrant the label "program." Significantly, (i) and (ii) distinguish what we know (and love?) as actual computers from organisms. We simply are not in the appropriate epistemological position to claim either that our brains or our brains plus our environments instantiate programs in precisely the sense that computers do. And in light of the similarities and differences between us and computers that emerge from empirical research, we will be able to decide whether "programs" or "internal languages" are appropriate categories with which to develop psychological explanations. None of this involves adopting a weak understanding of the computational metaphor in psychology, only some epistemic caution that should be adopted whether one defends narrow or wide computationalism.

The idea that by going wide one gives up on something crucial about computationalism reflects a deeply Cartesian view of the mind, a vestige of thinking of the mind and body as distinct substances, which survives within contemporary materialist and naturalistic views of the mind. This vestige is the idea that there is something special about the mind, about what is "in the head," that justifies the ascription of computational states to it, which is not shared with extra-cranial reality; there is a bifurcation between mind and mere matter which makes *only* narrow computationalism a serious option within psychology (cf. Segal 1991, p. 492, quoted above). I shall refer to this idea as *Cartesian computationalism* and will say more about it in my conclusion.

Let me turn to a second objection to wide computationalism, one which introduces broadly empirical grounds for doubting that we are wide computational systems. As Egan (1992, pp. 446, 457) notes, citing examples of research in early vision and in syntactic and morphological analysis in linguistics, the psychological processes for which there are the most satisfying computational accounts are *modular*: they are domain-specific and informationally encapsulated.[11] That is, we have had our greatest empirical successes in computational psychology in explaining the character of psychological processes which function with relative independence from even much of the *internal* workings of the cognitive system, let alone the external environment of the individual.

If empirical success has come within computational psychology only or even predominantly with the correctness of the presumption of modularity, then that should cast doubt on the idea of developing an empirically adequate *wide* computational psychology.

Fodor (1983) makes this point about the relationship between modularity and computational psychology more poignantly by arguing that "global systems are per se bad domains for computational models" (p. 128). Specifically, what he calls *central* processes, such as problem solving and belief-fixation, are unlikely to have computational models precisely because they are, in his view, non-modular. The non-modularity of central processes gives one reason to be sceptical about the real (versus mere) possibility of an adequate computational psychology explaining them. And what is true of central processes, processes which have access to a variety of representational inputs, is also true of wide computational processes, processes which access representations that are *outside* the individual.

Suppose we agree that, by and large, the empirical successes that cognitive science has had thus far have involved highly modular systems, such as those employed in visual perception and phoneme recognition. Perhaps this is for a deep reason, such as its only being highly modular systems which *are* computational; alternatively, it could be due to a relatively shallow reason, such as its being only highly modular computational processes that theorists can readily understand as computational. In either case, there is nothing here that allows for the application of a point about central processes to wide computational processes *since the latter can also be modular*. As I hope the discussion in the next section indicates, contemporary research in cognitive psychology that is properly considered as positing wide computational systems involves highly modular systems.[12]

The implicit premise in the argument from modularity to individualism sketched above—that modular systems are taxonomized individualistically—is false because modular systems may well encapsulate information that is in the individual's *environment*, not elsewhere in the individual. Thus, the module may be a part of a computational system all right, but a *wide* computational system. Neither of the chief two features of modular cognitive systems, their domain-specificity and informational encapsulation, implies that such systems cannot be properly viewed as parts of wide computational systems. Being wide and being modular are compatible properties for a cognitive system to possess—and so modularity does not entail individualism—because the location of the information with respect to which that system is encapsulated does not affect that system's domain-specificity. The real question to be answered is this: are narrow computational accounts of given modular systems always *explanatorily richer* than their wide rivals? It is only if the answer to this question is "Yes" that wide computationalism can be rejected as less plausible in general than narrow computationalism.

5 Wide Computationalism in Cognitive Psychology

Although the possibility of wide computationalism suffices to show that the second premise of the computational argument is false, for those antecedently disposed to think that wide computationalism is coherent the real interest in the computational argument lies in the claim that *we* are plausibly seen as wide computational systems. I think that wide computationalism *is* made plausible by recent computational research in both human and animal cognition. Showing wide computationalism to be not only a coherent but a plausible view of our cognitive processing would both consolidate and broaden my objection to the computational argument. I shall discuss two examples of research in cognitive psychology which show wide computationalism in action.[13]

Sekuler and Blake (1990) devote a significant section of their chapter on spatial vision and form perception to a discussion of an approach to form perception pioneered in the work of Campbell and Robson (1968), an approach known as *multiple spatial channels theory*. The basic idea of the approach is that there are specific stimuli which individual sets of neurons are sensitive to, these stimuli being decomposable into sinusoidal *gratings*. These gratings are relatively simple, having only four relevant parameters: spatial frequency, contrast, orientation, and spatial phase. Any figure composed of these gratings is definable formally in terms of these four parameters. The bold and controversial claim of this research program is that *any* natural scene in an organism's environment can be decomposed into its gratings, and this fact explains a great deal of human form perception, including its limitations.

On this conception of form perception, part of the task of the perceptual psychologist is to identify formal primitives that adequately describe the visual environment, and to specify algorithms which apply to these primitives to determine complete visual scenes. To see what this means, take a case simpler than human vision, that of a lens projecting an image of an object onto a piece of white paper. Figure 57.1 shows the *transfer function* for two lenses, which plots how contrast is transferred through the lens from object to image, and is defined over a range of spatial frequencies. As input, it takes contrast in an object, producing as output contrast in the image. We can likewise define a *contrast sensitivity function* for the human visual system, which takes the same inputs from the world to produce a visual output (see Figure 57.2). The formal system that perceptual psychologists working within this paradigm study is not instantiated in any individual: it includes but is not restricted to the intrinsic properties of an

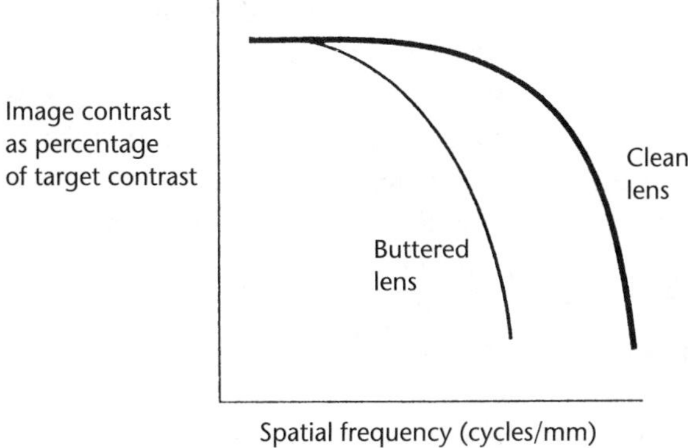

Figure 57.1
Two transfer functions for a lens. The curves specify how contrast in the image formed by the lens is related to contrast in the object. (Reproduced from Sekuler, R. and Blake, R., 1990: *Perception*, with permission of McGraw Hill.)

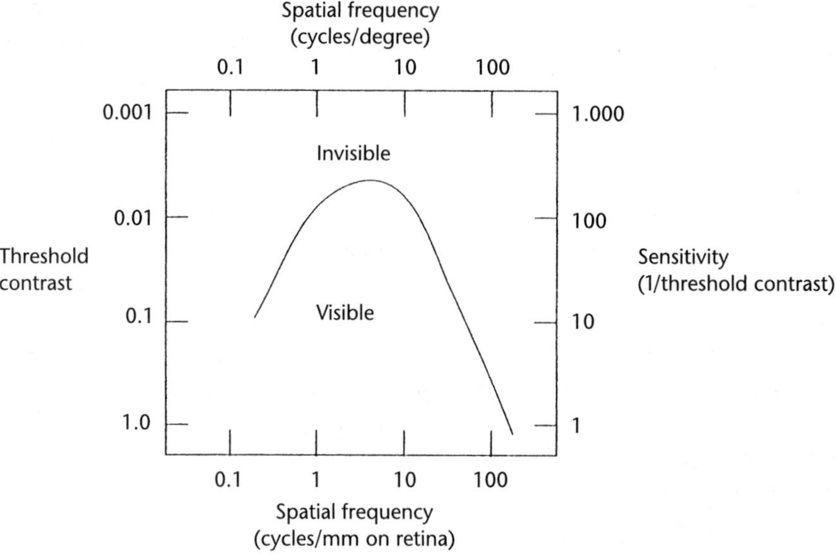

Figure 57.2
A contrast sensitivity function for an adult human. The upper horizontal axis is scaled in units specifying the number of pairs of light and dark bars of the grating falling within one degree of visual angles on the retina. (Reproduced from Sekuler, R. and Blake, R., 1990: *Perception*, with permission of McGraw Hill.)

individual. This is reflected in the actual methodology employed by such psychologists, which involves the extensive and complex mathematical analysis of natural scenes into their computational primitives. Such analysis appears to be an intrinsic part of the multiple spatial channels paradigm, not simply something preliminary to real perceptual psychology.

Gallistel (1989a) reports research on the conceptions of space, time and number that a variety of animals have, including bees, rats, and ants. One of Gallistel's primary conclusions is that purely sensory-based models of a range of animal behaviour are inadequate. Rather, the evidence overwhelmingly suggests that these animals construct quite complex representations of their environments and use these to guide their behaviour. Gallistel argues that such representations are computational, that there is strong evidence that these animals instantiate modules which are sensitive to the formal (e.g., the geometric) structure of their environments, and that this sensitivity is responsible for their navigation through their physical environments. For example, in ants and bees the computational process of *dead reckoning* (which integrates velocity with respect to time) takes as inputs the animal's solar heading, forward speed, and a representation of the solar azimuth, producing as output a representation of the creature's position relative to some landmark, such as a nest. The *ephemeris function*, which produces the third of these inputs, takes as its inputs a sighting of the sun and time on some endogenous clock (see Gallistel 1989b, pp. 70–76). In both of these cases, the computational process extends beyond the boundary of the individual.

Gallistel calls his view a *computational representational* perspective on animal cognition. Of animal navigation, Gallistel says:

> routine animal movements are governed by a navigational process closely analogous to everyday marine practice. This practice rests on an extensive isomorphism between the geometry of motion and position and the computational processes that underlie navigation. At the neurophysiological level of analysis, the hypothesis implies that the mathematical description of the processes in the animal brain that function during animal navigation parallels the mathematical description of the computations a human or computerized navigation system makes. (1989a, pp. 176–177)

This quotation suggests that Gallistel, like those working in the multi-channels paradigm in form perception, does not see anything mysterious in positing an extensive isomorphism between the formally described properties of an environment and those of mental processes.[14]

Two central postulates of these otherwise diverse research programmes is that the environment of the organism has a certain formal structure to it, and that the organism's sensitivity to this structure explains core parts of its cognitive performance. Characterizing the specific nature of the environment in computational terms appears to be a central part of the implicit conception of cognitive psychology in these research programmes. Despite some of Gallistel's own claims about the view he advocates (see below), I see no way in which this is merely additional or peripheral to these research programmes, and in the remainder of this section I shall defend the view that both research programmes support the view that we and our biological kin are parts of wide computational systems.

Recall Segal's view of the relationship between computationalism and individualism, discussed in §2: that, as it turns out, our cognitive systems are narrow, not wide, computational systems. Thus, wide computationalism should be rejected because although it is a coherent view there is *no* research which, in Segal's words, treats "whole subjects plus embedding environments" as "integrated, computational systems." This is a strong empirical claim, one to which in this section I have provided two prima facie counter-examples. The individualist who wishes to defend Segal's claim needs to explain away the appearances. Once the coherence of wide computationalism is conceded—its mere possibility—there are likely to be many such appearances to explain away, and so such an individualist faces a prima facie difficult task.

I think that the most promising way to defend the computational argument from the line of objection I have developed is to concede that even if one *can* view the individual as embedded within a wide computational system, there is no *explanatory* motivation for doing so. For we can also view the individual itself (or, more accurately, a *part of* that individual) as a computational system, a narrow computational system, and *doing so is always adequate for computational, psychological explanation*. Consider the two examples that I have given of purportedly wide computational research. Even if the multi-channels paradigm does seem to posit a formal structure to the environment, it could also be viewed as claiming that the retinal image has such a structure. If this view of the paradigm is correct, then while one *could* view the paradigm as being computationally wide, there is no need to adopt this view of it. Likewise, while the computational representational view that Gallistel defends might seem to view an individual as part of a wide computational system, a system which includes features of that individual's environment, one could also see his view as positing an interesting isomorphism between *two* formal systems, one of which is fully instantiated in the individual. Crucially, cognitive psychology is the study of this *narrow* computational system. Since the form of this defence of the computational argument is the same in each of these two cases, I shall develop it and respond to it by focusing only on Gallistel's view.

A general feature of Gallistel's view of animal cognition that might be thought difficult to reconcile with my interpretation of it is that much animal behaviour is governed by internal maps and mathematical representations of the environment rather than direct sensory input. This view ascribes to an animal a high degree of autonomy from its environment, and this aspect to Gallistel's view at least *sounds* individualistic: animals navigate, for example, by *internal maps,* not by sensory tracing, homing, or other environmentally interactive methods. In characterizing how an animal navigates, we abstract away from its actual environment and concentrate on the intrinsic features of its map or model of that environment.

Several of Gallistel's comments about his own project offer support for this type of individualistic interpretation. Gallistel says that his "agenda is a reductionist one: to understand learning as a neuronal phenomenon" (1989b, p. 24), going on to say that studying the total [wide] computational system is simply a "necessary prelude to understanding what the system does in terms of what its elements do" (1989b, p. 24). Figuring out the computational structure to an organism's environment, while *methodologically* necessary, is peripheral to an understanding of the nature of learning itself, and suggests that there is no deep sense in which Gallistel advocates a view of learning as a wide computational process. In addition, in the conclusion to his book Gallistel says that "[t]he structure of the computational mechanisms is dictated by the formal structure of the representations to be computed and by the sensory or mnemonic data from which they are computed" (1989b, p. 581), suggesting that he sees the *computational* system of interest to the psychologist as fully instantiated in the individual organism.

One response to this interpretation corresponds to and reinforces the weak or negative claim that I made in §2. Even if one *can* see Gallistel's view as a narrow computational approach, the fact that it also can be given a wide computational interpretation shows that computationalism itself does not entail individualism: computational systems need not be individualistic. Yet this response does not address the issue of which of these interpretations of Gallistel's view has greater explanatory adequacy. A second response, corresponding to one of the stronger claims made in §2—about the plausibility or even necessity of wide computationalism in psychology—addresses this issue.

There are two aspects to this second response, one elaborating on the concepts of explanation and explanatory adequacy, the other concentrating on the application of these concepts so understood to particular examples within computational, cognitive psychology. Let me say something brief about the first of these aspects. Were the individualist to claim, in effect, that there is no explanatory need to posit wide computational systems because whenever we can do so we can also identify a corresponding, narrow computational system,[15] she would be presupposing *some* conception of explanatory adequacy, although one yet to be explicitly articulated. Elsewhere (Wilson 1994) I have developed a concept of explanatory adequacy in terms of the notions of *causal depth* and *theoretical appropriateness* and argued that wide psychological explanations are sometimes causally deeper and more theoretically appropriate than individualistic psychological explanations. I think that this argument can be adapted to apply specifically to show that wide *computational* explanations are sometimes more explanatorily adequate than narrow computational explanations in psychology, though I shall not argue this point here. What I want to do instead is make several points pertinent to the second aspect of the issue of explanatory adequacy, points about the research reported by Gallistel discussed above.

The sorts of behaviour that Gallistel is trying to explain involve a flow of information from the environment to the organism. One of Gallistel's main points is that this is not a constant flow of information, as suggested by simple sensory accounts. Yet it would be a mistake to think of his view as denying that (formal) properties of the environment play any significant role in a complete, cognitive explanation of animal navigation.

First, even if an animal's behaviour in navigation is primarily governed by internal maps, these maps are updated by periodically acquired information about the organism's movement and the relative position of objects in the environment. An account of these updates ("fix-taking", in Gallistel's terms) is a necessary part of a complete psychological explanation of the behaviour. If one takes the computational representational view to provide a comprehensive paradigm for the investigation of animal learning and cognition, then fix-taking must be accommodated within that paradigm. The narrow computationalist view allows that relations between psychological states themselves can be computational. The wide computationalist proposes a natural extension of this view to allow organism-environment interactions, such as fix-taking, to be subject to a (wide) computational approach. The individualist must explain processes such as fix-taking in some other way, since her claim is that computational systems are fully instantiated in individuals. The wide computationalist is able to offer a view of fix-taking that has greater explanatory unity than that available to the individualist.

Second, as shown by the above examples of environmental inputs in Gallistel's account, characterizing cognitive, computational states *as representations* sometimes requires non-individualistic descriptions. If a representational psychology may violate individualism in the descriptions it offers of psychological states, then why must a computational psychology be individualistic? This question is not rhetorical, for (i) whether representational psychology violates individualism in particular cases is a substantial question, and (ii) the width of representational content might be thought compatible with the narrowness of computational psychology because of the different functions that intentional and computational ascriptions serve. Egan (1992) has argued that the role of semantics in computational psychology is to provide explanatory *models*, models which may be either narrow or wide, for individualistic computations. If Egan is right about the different explanatory roles that content and computational ascriptions play, then this provides a principled reason for distinguishing between computational and representational aspects of psychology with respect to individualism. To discuss this issue further one would need to re-examine the often-invoked trichotomy between the physical, the syntactic (formal, computational), and the semantic (representational). My own view is that it is most plausible to see the computational and representational levels of description as playing very similar explanatory roles in psychology. Again, however, the issue here cannot be suitably resolved without some discussion of the notion of explanatory adequacy and its application to computational psychology.

6 Conclusion

The computational argument for individualism should be rejected because its second premise, the assumption that computational processes in general are individualistic, is false in light of the possibility and plausibility of wide computationalism in cognitive psychology. Much of my discussion of the second premise of the computational argument aims to explain the coherence of wide computationalism, what I have been calling its mere possibility. I think, however, that the most interesting issue concerns not the coherence of wide computationalism but the extent to which a wide computational research strategy is and could be employed within cognitive psychology. Given that, why have I concentrated on the mere possibility of wide computationalism, rather than its plausibility in cognitive psychology?

The central idea behind wide computationalism is extremely simple. However, fleshing out the idea and being explicit about the implications it has for issues in philosophical psychology allow one to see the respects in which it represents a radical departure from the conception of the mind underlying much contemporary research in computational psychology, what I have called Cartesian computationalism. Precisely because Cartesian computationalism is typically unidentified and unexamined, even the basic idea behind wide computationalism is likely to produce knee-jerk puzzlement. It is for this reason that I have spent so much time in §§2–4 demystifying wide computationalism by articulating what the mere possibility of wide computationalism amounts to.

The more interesting issue of the plausibility of wide computationalism as a perspective on research in cognitive psychology is one whose resolution, as we have seen, turns partially on further discussion of general notions, such as that of explanatory adequacy and causal role, as well as an analysis of notions more specific to computational psychology, such as modularity and formality. Of particular importance is further discussion of the relationship between the notion of formality and *representationalism* in psychology. Such discussion and analysis ought to shed further light on the purported examples of wide computational research that I provided in §5, though I am far from suggesting that the illumination will be unidirectional. The examination of actual research in computational psychology on which the issue of the plausibility of wide computationalism in psychology turns should also facilitate the more conceptual work that remains to be done.

While I think that much contemporary research in computational psychology and (especially) artificial intelligence operates within a Cartesian computational framework, I am not offering an external, a priori critique of such research. Rather, accepting the assumption that psychological states are computational, I am questioning another assumption—that computational, cognitive systems are always completely instantiated in individuals—that usually goes along with it. If I am correct in thinking both that this assumption is typically unquestioned and that it is, in some cases, false, then wide computational psychology would seem worth further investigation. If wide computationalism is not only coherent but a plausible view of at least some existing research within the computational paradigm, then the computational argument can be turned on its head: individualism does not impose a constraint on the individuation of mental states precisely because, in at least some cases, psychological states *are* considered as (wide) computational states for the purposes of psychological explanation.[16]

Notes

1. Following Stich (1983), I employ a supervenience formulation of individualism, rather than Fodor's (1981) "methodological solipsism" formulation, which says that the taxonomy of an individual's psychological states should not presuppose any essential reference to that individual's environment. I am not concerned here with differences between the two formulations and shall use both in my discussion. Individualism characterized in either way is not a view specifically or only about mental representation or mental content. (Hence there are individualists, such as Stich (1983, Ch. 8), who are sceptical about mental representation.)

2. Those who have seen computationalism as offering support for forms of individualism in psychology include Devitt (1990, 1991), Egan (1992), Fodor (1981, 1987), and Segal (1989, 1991). The papers by Egan and Segal offer the most explicit arguments from computationalism to some form of individualism.

3. Segal characterizes individualism here as a thesis about mental representation, although individualists have typically defended a view about psychological states in general (see note 1). Individualists also adopt a more specific view of the nature of the subvenient base than Segal suggests: it is constituted by the intrinsic, physical properties of *the individual.* As we will see, one cannot simply equate individual and computational system, or assume that the latter will be part of the former.

4. Two points about calling this position Egan's: (a) as we will see, there are strands to Egan's discussion which suggest that she accepts a view of the relationship between computationalism and individualism closer to Segal's; (b) the position is one which I think many individualist find appealing. My concern here is to identify an individualistic position alternative to Segal's; I return to discuss Segal's view in §5 below.

5. Egan continues: "this goal is best served by theories which taxonomize states individualistically" (p. 445). This may suggest that she sees computational psychology as individualistic for instrumental or pragmatic reasons rather than because of the nature of computational individuation. But, as I hope will be clear from what follows, her actual argument does not appeal at all to whether individualistic or wide taxonomies "best serve" the goal she has identified; rather, it claims that individualism is strictly implied by the *method* by which computational states are individuated.

6. Thanks to Sydney Shoemaker here; see also Clark (1989, Chs. 4, 7, and 1993, Ch. 6).

7. As Fodor says, "formal operations apply in terms of the, as it were, shapes of the objects in their domains" (1981, p. 227, footnote omitted). It is unclear how literally Fodor intends this suggestion, though he relies on it in many places, including more recent work; for example, see his 1987, p. 18.

8. I thank Robert Stalnaker for emphasizing this point in discussion. The formality condition focuses on only the first of these contrasts, the contrast between formal and semantic properties.

9. Interestingly, Rollins (1989) and Devitt (1990, 1991) both draw something like the distinction I am drawing here between the formality condition and the systemic conception of formality, although neither seems to think the formality condition misleading in the way in which I am claiming it is.

10. This contrast between computational and intentional taxonomies is clear in Egan (1992), where a defence of individualism about computational psychology is combined with a defence of wide intentional content. One could, I suppose, hold just the reverse of this: that computational taxonomies may be wide but intentional taxonomies must be narrow. Exploring this option should be of interest to those who accept wide computationalism but wish to defend an individualistic view of intentionality.

11. The notion of modularity at work here is that articulated by Fodor (1983). While Fodor lists other features of modular systems (e.g., they are fast and mandatory), domain-specificity and informational encapsulation are the two most central. Although these notions themselves warrant some conceptual elaboration (see Wilson 1995), let me here simply provide an intuitive gloss on each. A *domain-specific* system is one which operates on some particular type of information (a domain). An *informationally encapsulated* cognitive system acts as an input-output function on a specifiable and specific set of informational inputs and outputs: it encapsulates some kind or kinds of information, and is insensitive to other information.

12. In fact, I think that there is no conceptual problem in even central processes, such as inference, being modular: even *they* may be domain-specific and informationally encapsulated. Dan Sperber (1994) has argued for this view, and I take the work of Cosmides and Tooby in evolutionary psychology to provide empirical support for it; see, for example, Cosmides (1989) and Cosmides and Tooby (1987).

13. Thanks to both David Field and Frank Keil for useful discussion of the material in this section; they should not, however, be saddled with the conclusions I draw here.

14. Cf. Gallistel's claim that the isomorphism between computational processes instantiated in the head and certain "formal properties" in the environment is responsible for the successful navigation behaviour that many animals exhibit: "there is a rich formal correspondence between processes and relations in the environment and the operations the brain performs. Brain processes and relations recapitulate world processes and relations. The recapitulation is not fortuitous. To fit behaviour to the environment, the brain creates models of the behaviour-relevant aspects of the environment, the formal properties of the processes that realize these models reflect the formal properties of the corresponding external reality because these processes have been subject to evolution by natural selection. Selection has been based on the fidelity of these processes to the external reality. Evolution by natural selection creates rich functioning isomorphisms between brain processes and the environment, and learning is to be understood in terms of these isomorphisms (1989b, p. 27)."

15. This claim is very similar to one that proponents of the narrow content program in psychology have sometimes made: that whatever explanatory work a wide taxonomy of psychological states (e.g., that of folk psychology) does can also be done by a corresponding narrow taxonomy of those states. This claim has sometimes been expressed as the view that wide taxonomies, insofar as they are explanatory, can be factored into narrow taxonomies, plus some external remainder, in much the way that the concept of weight can be factored into the concept of mass, plus that of gravitational force (see Field 1981; Fodor 1987, Ch. 2). I have argued against such views (1992, 1993, 1995).

16. An early version of this paper was presented at the 1992 meeting of the Canadian Philosophical Association and the Society for Philosophy and Psychology; I would like to thank my commentators on those occasions, Wayne Henry and Brian Smith, respectively, as well as the audiences there for useful feedback. Thanks also to Frances Egan, Sydney Shoemaker, Robert Stalnaker, and J. D. Trout for written comments on earlier drafts as well as helpful discussion; and to an anonymous referee for *Mind*.

References

Bennett, Jonathan 1989: *Rationality*. Indianapolis, Indiana: Hackett Publishing.

Block, Ned 1990: "Troubles with Functionalism," excerpted in Lycan 1990, pp. 444–468.

Campbell, F. W. and Robson, J. G. 1968: "Application of Fourier Analysis to the Visibility of Gratings." *Journal of Physiology* 197, pp. 151–166.

Clark, Andy 1989: *Microcognition*. Cambridge, MA: MIT Press.

——— 1993: *Associative Engines*. Cambridge, MA: MIT Press.

Cosmides, Leda 1989: "The Logic of Social Exchange: Has Natural Selection Shaped How Humans Reason? Studies with the Wason Selection Task." *Cognition* 31, pp. 187–276.

Cosmides, Leda and Tooby, John 1987: "From Evolution to Behaviour: Evolutionary Psychology as the Missing Link," in John Dupré, ed., *The Latest on the Best*. Cambridge, MA: MIT Press, pp. 277–306.

Davies, Martin 1991: "Individualism and Perceptual Content." *Mind* 100, pp. 461–484.

Devitt, Michael 1990: "A Narrow Representational Theory of the Mind," in Lycan 1990, pp. 371–398.

——— 1991: "Why Fodor Can't Have it Both Ways," in Barry Loewer and George Rey, eds., *Meaning in Mind*. Cambridge, MA: Basil Blackwell, pp. 95–118.

Egan, Frances 1992: "Individualism, Computation, and Perceptual Content." *Mind* 101, pp. 443–459.

Field, Hartry 1981: "Mental Representation," in Ned Block, ed., *Readings in Philosophy of Psychology*, vol. 2. Cambridge, MA: Harvard University Press, pp. 78–114.

Fodor, Jerry 1981: "Methodological Solipsism Considered as a Research Strategy in Cognitive Psychology," in his *Representations*. Brighton, Sussex: Harvester Press, pp. 225–253.

——— 1983: *The Modularity of Mind*. Cambridge, MA: MIT Press.

——— 1987: *Psychosemantics*. Cambridge, MA: MIT Press.

Gallistel, C. R. 1989a: "Animal Cognition: The Representation of Space, Time and Number." *Psychology Annual Reviews* 40, pp. 155–189.

——— 1989b: *The Organization of Learning*. Cambridge, MA: MIT Press.

Harman, Gilbert 1987: "(Nonsolipsistic) Conceptual Role Semantics," in Ernie LePore, ed., *New Directions in Semantics*. London: Academic Press, pp. 55–81.

——— 1988: "Wide Functionalism," in Stephen Schiffer and Diane Steele, eds., *Cognition and Representation*. Boulder, CO: Westview Press, pp. 1–12.

Kitcher, Patricia 1991: "Narrow Psychology and Wide Functionalism," in Richard Boyd, Phil Gasper, and J. D. Trout, eds., *The Philosophy of Science*. Cambridge, MA: MIT Press, pp. 671–685.

Lycan, William, ed., 1990: *Mind and Cognition*. Cambridge, MA: Basil Blackwell.

Rollins, Mark 1989: *Mental Imagery*. New Haven, CT: Yale University Press.

Searle, John 1981: "Minds, Brains, and Programs," in John Haugeland, ed., *Mind Design*. Cambridge, MA: MIT Press, pp. 282–306.

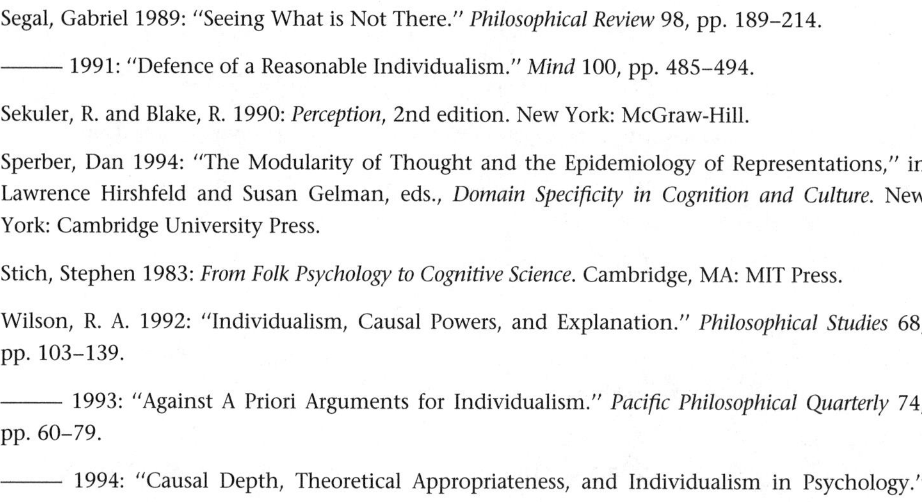

Segal, Gabriel 1989: "Seeing What is Not There." *Philosophical Review* 98, pp. 189–214.

——— 1991: "Defence of a Reasonable Individualism." *Mind* 100, pp. 485–494.

Sekuler, R. and Blake, R. 1990: *Perception*, 2nd edition. New York: McGraw-Hill.

Sperber, Dan 1994: "The Modularity of Thought and the Epidemiology of Representations," in Lawrence Hirshfeld and Susan Gelman, eds., *Domain Specificity in Cognition and Culture*. New York: Cambridge University Press.

Stich, Stephen 1983: *From Folk Psychology to Cognitive Science*. Cambridge, MA: MIT Press.

Wilson, R. A. 1992: "Individualism, Causal Powers, and Explanation." *Philosophical Studies* 68, pp. 103–139.

——— 1993: "Against A Priori Arguments for Individualism." *Pacific Philosophical Quarterly* 74, pp. 60–79.

——— 1994: "Causal Depth, Theoretical Appropriateness, and Individualism in Psychology." *Philosophy of Science*, 61, pp. 55–75.

——— 1995: *Cartesian Psychology and Physical Minds*. New York: Cambridge University Press.

58 From *A Slim Book on Narrow Content*

Gabriel Segal

World Dependence and Empty Concepts

Water and Twater

Here is the original Twin Earth experiment from Putnam 1975a. We consider a time prior to modern chemistry, say 1750. We consider a typical Earthling, Oscar. We consider a Twin Earth that is just like Earth except that where Earth has water, Twin Earth has twater, a substance with a chemical composition different from Earth water, which we can abbreviate "XYZ." XYZ looks, feels, and tastes like water and is similar to it in observable macroscopic respects. But it is not H_2O. On Twin Earth there is an exact duplicate of Oscar, Twin Oscar. Now suppose that both Oscar and Twin Oscar say something using the word (or word form) "water," e.g., "Water is thirst-quenching." Do they mean the same thing by their words?

Putnam argued "No." Water, scientists tell us, is H_2O. XYZ is not H_2O. So XYZ is not water. Our word "water" is not true of XYZ. When Oscar used the word "water," he referred to the same substance as we do now. So Oscar's word "water" referred only to H_2O. But Twin Oscar's word "water" of course referred to the substance in his local environment, which is not H_2O, and hence is not water. So Oscar and Twin Oscar referred to different kinds of substance. And, assuming that a difference in extension entails a difference in meaning, what Oscar and Twin Oscar meant was different as well.

Thus far we have an externalist conclusion about the meaning of a word. But it is a short step to a similar conclusion about the contents of the twins' psychological states; their beliefs, desires, and so on. Sentences express psychological states. What the twins say is what they mean, i.e., the content of the belief they express is just the content of the sentence they utter. So what the twins believe is different too. (Putnam [1975a] did not pursue the conclusion about psychological states, but others, such as Colin McGinn [1982] and Tyler Burge [1982] did, although not always by the short step just described.) . . .

. . . There are two main versions of radical externalism. The extreme version simply identifies broad content with extension.[1] The less extreme version does not. It allows for something like sense. It allows that coextensive concepts can differ in content.[2] But it denies that what distinguishes coextensive concepts is narrow content. What distinguishes coextensive contents might itself be relational. Or, on a more standard view, what distinguishes coextensive contents is not a separable factor at all. Perhaps one could think of it as how the subject is related to the extension, or how the extension is presented to the subject in thought. On this view, these matters cannot be specified in abstraction from the extension, but rather essentially involve it.[3]

I call the radical externalist position, as applied to natural-kind concepts, "the thesis of world dependence of kind concepts" (TWD)....

I will argue that TWD cannot account for the existence of empty kind terms and concepts, kind terms and concepts that do not refer to anything....

... There are numerous empty kind terms that we must take to express concepts. I will dwell on this point, the importance of which is typically underestimated. Empty concepts, whether of kinds or individuals, cannot be swept under the rug. Far from being a rarity, they are a pervasive and significant feature of human cognition.

Religion and spiritual belief play very important roles in our world. All over the world, since the earliest periods of human existence of which we have knowledge, people have worshiped gods and lesser spirits, tried to appease them, blamed them for disasters, and used them to explain features of the world around them. Here is a brief summary of common religious ideas from Pascal Boyer, an anthropologist who specializes in the topic:

> In all human groups one can find a set of ideas concerning nonobservable, extra-natural agencies and processes.... It is assumed in many (but not all) human groups that a nonphysical component of persons can survive after death.... It is often assumed that certain people are especially likely to receive direct inspiration or messages from extra-natural agencies such as gods or spirits.... In most (not all) human groups it is assumed that certain salient events (e.g. illness or misfortune) are symptoms of underlying causal connections between supernatural beings and the world of the living. (Boyer 1994)

Most human groups believe in ghosts: nonphysical entities endowed with various psychological characteristics and powers to affect the physical world. But ghosts do not exist. The terms "ghost" and "spirit" and the various specific terms used by particular cultures for particular kinds of ghosts are empty. Interestingly enough, though, "ghost" has the basic character of a natural-kind term. In a way, of course, it is precisely an *un*natural-kind term, in the sense that while some characteristics of ghosts are familiar intuitive ones (such as their psychological characteristics: ghosts perform modus ponens, just as we living people do, etc.), many of their properties run precisely counter to intuitive expectations (Boyer 1994). Nevertheless, the terms typically used to pick out specific kinds of ghosts by specific cultures exhibit the core features of kind terms. For example, the properties of ghosts are learned by inductive generalizations over the kind. Here is Boyer, discussing bekong, the ancestor ghosts of the Fang (a people who live mainly in Gabon and Cameroon): "Subjects spontaneously assume that all or most ghosts have the powers that are exemplified in particular anecdotes or stories. This would not be possible, without the prior assumption, that ghosts are, precisely, a kind, that one can safely produce instance-based general principles" (1994, 400). Presumably, although Boyer does not discuss this, other core features of natural-kind terms are also present. Bekong do not form an observational or artifactual or nominal kind. Rather, I presume, the Fang regard them as real entities with natures that are partly unknown but to an extent discoverable. Externalist Fang would regard the extension of the term "bekong" as determined by the facts about bekong, not by stipulation or subjective judgement. If it turned out the Fang were right, then "bekong" would also generate Putnam's Twin Earth intuitions, much as "tiger" does.

It is not a serious option to doubt that the Fang have an empty concept *bekong*. It certainly appears that the concept plays an important role in their thought. It features in their explanations of various phenomena (sickness and so on). And it features in beliefs, desires, and other cognitive states that motivate many of their activities. Moreover, Boyer spends some time discussing how Fang children acquire the concept *bekong*. Boyer begins to disentangle the contributions of innate components, inductive generalizations, explicit teaching, and so on, just as developmental psychologists do when they study the acquisition of concepts in other cases....

... [T]he Fang and their concept *bekong*, far from being an unusual case, are typical of human cultures. Think of the time and energy spent by the ancient Egyptians on their temples to the gods and their preparations for life after death in the spirit world. We can make sense of their activities if, but only if, we allow that they have genuine concepts (*god*, *spirit*) that play a major role in their cognition and action.

The same moral applies to scientific thought. There is, for example, the ether, described by the *Oxford Concise Science Dictionary* as follows: "[A] hypothetical medium once believed to be necessary to support the propagation of electromagnetic radiation. It is now regarded as unnecessary.... The existence of the aether was first called into question as a result of the Michelson-Morley experiment." If scientists had no concept of the ether, then it is hard indeed to see how they could once have *believed* that it was necessary for the propagation of electromagnetic radiation, later *called into question* its existence, and then come to *regard* it as unnecessary.

And, to cite another standard example, we have "terra pinguis" or "phlogiston," which was supposed to explain combustion. Here is the *Oxford Concise Science Dictionary* again:

> The existence of this hypothetical substance was proposed in 1669 by Johann Becher.... For example, according to Becher, the conversion of wood to ashes by burning was explained on the assumption that the original wood consisted of ash and *terra pinguis*, which was released during burning. In the 18th century George Stahl renamed the substance *phlogiston* ... and extended the theory to include the calcination (and corrosion) of metals. Thus metals were thought to be composed of *calx* (a powdery residue) and phlogiston.

The theory was finally overthrown by Antoine Lavoisier in the late eighteenth century. Again, it would be difficult to explain the evolution of the theory of combustion without attributing a concept of phlogiston to the scientists involved....

The main argument for attributing empty concepts in all these cases (ghosts, ether, etc.) is simply that by so doing, and only by so doing, can we make psychological sense of a very wide variety of human activity and cognition. Anthropologists, historians of culture and science, psychoanalysts, and others actually do this. In so doing, they provide what appear to be perfectly cogent psychological explanations. If these explanations have apparent flaws, these flaws are not traceable to the attribution of empty concepts. So well entrenched and successful is this practice that it would require a powerful argument indeed to show that it was deeply problematic or incoherent.

Moreover, not only do we standardly offer explanations involving attributions of empty kind concepts. We have no viable alternative. One cannot simply dispense with such attributions and be left with any workable intentional explanations of the various phenomena. Nor can any nonintentional theory address the phenomena. Appeal to neurology or purely syntactic computational theory would be an expression of pure faith. We have no idea how such research programs could bear significantly on the psychological, cultural, anthropological, and historical phenomena that we seek to describe and explain. Nor have we any reason to suppose that one day they will.

Let us allow, then, that humans have or have had concepts of phlogiston, ether, immaterial souls, etc. This conclusion, which appears mandatory, already invites a strong argument against TWD. For if these terms express concepts, why shouldn't it make perfect sense to suppose that "quark," "helium," "Gila monster," "polio," or even "water" might, counterfactually, be empty yet express a concept?...

From the Empty to the Full

The next phase of the argument is best developed in the context of a specific example. Myalgic encephalomyelitis (ME, also known as "chronic fatigue syndrome" or "CFS") is a condition characterized by chronic tendency to extreme fatigue. Symptoms include dizziness, rashes, aches, sensitivity to light and sound, cold sores, swellings, forgetfulness and many others. At the time of writing, there is disagreement in the medical profession about whether ME is caused by a virus and, if it is, how the process occurs.

Let us suppose that it is epistemically possible that there is no such thing as ME. The following is then an epistemically possible future. It turns out that there are a wide variety of different causes of the symptomatology associated with ME: viruses, stress, hysteria, dental amalgam, educational practice (all of which have been seriously suggested). The medical establishment stops using the term "ME," since it is unhelpful for taxonomic purposes. Not only is there no common underlying ailment, but there is also no reason to count ME as worthy of recognition as a syndrome. Doctors become disposed to say: "Some people used to talk about a condition called 'ME,' but it turned out that there wasn't really any such thing."

But it is also epistemically possible that "ME" will become a natural-kind term. Doctors might discover that there is a single virus responsible for most of the diagnosed cases, that most of the diagnosed patients that turned out not to suffer from the viral infection had a different symptomatology, and so on. "ME" could come to refer to the disease caused by the virus, and to nothing else.

In both cases doctors and patients use the term "ME" to engage in apparently cogent conversations. For example, a typical subject, Peter, finds that he is becoming more prone to fatigue. He becomes worried and goes to his doctor. After consultation, the doctor says, "You have ME," and goes on to explain the current wisdom. Psychological explanation of both doctor and patient requires attributing the concept of ME. We might say, "Peter took some time off work because he believed that he suffered from ME and he desired to alleviate the symptoms of ME and he believed that by taking time off work," etc. And we can explain why the doctor thought that Peter had ME and why she went on to prescribe action that she thought might alleviate the symptoms of ME.

Let TE_1 be the empty case and TE_2 the nonempty one. Let our twin subjects be $Peter_1$ and $Peter_2$. We must allow that $Peter_1$, in TE_1, expresses a genuine concept by his term "ME." If we do not, then we will have no adequate explanation of his words and deeds. Call this concept "C_1." Let C_2 be $Peter_2$'s concept and let "ME_2" be our word for expressing C_2. So "ME_2" means just what "ME" actually means if our world happens to be TE_2. And let C_1 and C_2 be individuated by their cognitive content....

... The cognitive role of a concept is its causal role, as specified by a psychological theory, its causal role relative to other psychological states and actions. Here are some aspects of the cognitive role of C_2: Peter$_2$ came to believe that he was suffering from ME$_2$, because his doctor said, "I fear you have ME," and Peter$_2$ believed his doctor. Peter$_2$'s belief that he has ME$_2$, along with his belief that sufferers from ME$_2$ often need to take time off from work, caused him to fear that he would need to take some time off from work. Peter$_2$'s desire to be cured of ME$_2$, or at least to have some of its symptoms alleviated, caused him to seek further advice from his doctor.

Now suppose that a psychologist studying both Peters simply assumes that $C_2 = C_1$. That is, she assumes that whatever concept it is that Peter$_1$ has, with its particular cognitive content, is the very concept that Peter$_2$ has and expresses with his term "ME." The assumption would work perfectly well because C_1 is just the sort of concept that can play the required cognitive role. We know this because that is exactly the role it does play in Peter$_1$'s psychological economy. If, as the psychologist hypothesizes, Peter$_2$ did indeed possess the concept C_1, then he would reason and act exactly as he does. Attributing the concept C_1 to Peter$_2$ would therefore work perfectly well in psychological explanations. And this provides a reason for thinking that the attribution would be correct.

Of course, the subjects' exercises of their concepts do have different effects in their different environments. For example, Peter$_1$ consults one doctor on TE$_1$, and Peter$_2$ consults a numerically distinct doctor on TE$_2$. But it is natural to explain this in terms of the differences between the twins' locations rather than in terms of differences between their concepts. For if Peter$_1$ were to take Peter$_2$'s place on TE$_2$, he would interact with the environment exactly as Peter$_2$ would have if Peter$_2$'s place hadn't been usurped (see Fodor 1987, chap. 2)....

... [T]he point of the argument is that standard psychological explanations, such as belief-desire explanations of action or of the formation of further beliefs and goals, could be successfully formulated in terms of a cognitive content that is common across the twins. And the hypothesis has an obvious virtue. For it offers a compelling explanation of the twins' evident psychological similarities. The reason that the twins' "ME" concepts have the same cognitive roles would be that they have the same cognitive content. If the two concepts had only wide contents, then it is not at all obvious why their cognitive roles should be the same. TWD would therefore have a lot of explaining to do.

The argument is not conclusive, since the success and virtue of an explanation do not guarantee its truth. The explanations are successful because Peter$_2$ thinks and acts just as he would if he had C_1. It does not follow from this that he actually does have C_1. But I think it follows that we have good reason to think that he does: there would be considerable evidence in favor the hypothesis. Further substantiation of the claim would depend on an account of the shared cognitive content. If we could formulate a good account of a kind of cognitive content that would be shared across twins and show how such content could feature successfully in psychological explanation, then the claim would be largely vindicated. If, by contrast, attempts to formulate the account were perpetually to run into difficulty, then we would have reason to think that the hypothesis was on the wrong track....

The argument runs more or less as before. Consider Peter$_1$. How did he acquire his "ME" concept? He learned about ME from the doctor. But that is only the last part of a long story. When he encountered the doctor, he was already in a position rapidly to acquire the concept simply by hearing a few words. In order to explain this, we would have to develop a complex theory of his innate endowment and his developmental history: how he learned about diseases and so on. But the key point is, whatever the truth of the matter, everything specified by that theory would be present on TE_2. There is nothing available on TE_1 to explain how $Peter_1$ acquired C_1, his empty concept of ME, that is not also present on TE_2.

It follows that a theory specifying conditions sufficient for the acquisition of C_1 is applicable to $Peter_2$. But then $Peter_2$ has C_1 as well. And C_1 is the concept he expresses by his word "ME." So the difference between $Peter_1$'s C_1 and $Peter_2$'s C_2 concerns at most the extension....

... Developmental psychologists do not usually care whether the concepts they study are empty or not. If they believe that a concept is empty, they do not typically mention this fact. I doubt, for example, that Boyer ever explicitly points out that ghosts do not exist. And Henry Wellman, studying the acquisition of mentalistic concepts (concepts of belief, desire, perception, and so on) specifically states that he abstains on the question of whether these folk-psychological concepts are empty (1990, 151–153)....

Deferential Dispositions and Cognitive Content

... We turn now to a variety of social externalism, which holds that the content of many kinds of concepts, not merely those of natural kinds, depends in part on the social environment, on the way other people use words....

Putnam's "Elm" and "Beech"

We begin, once again, with an example of Putnam's (1975a). Putnam tells us he cannot distinguish elms from beeches. He cannot tell them apart by sight, nor does he know anything that is true of one but not the other—barring, of course, their names. But when he says "elm," his word is true of elms and not beeches. When he says "beech" his word applies only to beeches, not to elms. Twin Earth is again very like Earth. The difference now is that the Twin word "elm" is used to talk about beeches, while the word "beech" is used to talk about elms. When Twin Putnam says "elm," he is speaking Twin English, so he refers to elms not beeches. Hence Putnam and Twin Putnam mean different things by "elm." Thus argued Putnam. Again, this conclusion seems naturally to extend to the concepts expressed by the words. So we have an apparent counterexample to internalism.

Why is it that Putnam refers to elms and elms only when he says "elm"? Because he intends his usage of the word to conform with that of the experts, he means to refer to those trees called "elms" by those who know what they are talking about. So an important determinant in fixing the extension of Putnam's "elm" concept is the linguistic practice of experts. On Twin Earth, the experts use the words differently, and so Twin Putnam's "elm" concept gets hooked up to beeches, not elms. Cut the pie any way you like, meanings just ain't in the head. Thus argued Putnam.

In Kaplan's terms, Putnam is a "consumer" of language, rather than a "creator," when it comes to "elm." The word "elm" that Putnam uses comes "prepackaged with a semantic value" that has been created by others.[4] It is this prepackaged semantic value that provides what Putnam himself means by "elm" and the concept he expresses by it. So let us call this brand of social externalism "consumerism."

Burge's "Arthritis"

Tyler Burge introduced a different kind of example in support of consumerism. These cases also involve a subject who has only partial information about the meaning of the term involved. But these examples draw on the possibility of the subject believing an analytic falsehood.

A subject, Alf, appears to have a number of mundane beliefs about arthritis. It seems that he believes that he has had arthritis for years, that his arthritis in his wrists and fingers is more painful than his arthritis in his ankles, that there are various kinds of arthritis, and so on. It also seems that he believes, falsely, that he has developed arthritis in his thigh. He goes to the doctor, who tells him that, by definition, arthritis is an inflammation of the joints, and that therefore he cannot have it in his thigh. Alf accepts the doctor's informed opinion and goes on to ask what is wrong with his thigh.

Burge then tells a counterfactual story, which I will rephrase as a tale of Twin Earth. This time the key difference between Earth and Twin Earth is that on the latter planet, the medical profession uses the term "arthritis" more generally than it is used on Earth. It applies not only to inflammations of the joints, but also to certain related conditions, including, as it happens, what Alf and Twin Alf have in their thighs.

Twin Alf, according to Burge, lacks some, probably all, of the propositional attitudes that Alf has about arthritis. Twin Alf has no word which means *arthritis*; his word "arthritis" does not mean *arthritis*, but applies to the more general cluster of ailments. But Alf has the concept of arthritis, even though, for a period of one morning, he entertains an analytic falsehood: that he has arthritis in his thigh. Alf has the concept of arthritis because, like Putnam with "elm," he has some competence with the term and he defers to the relevant experts. When he comes to learn the truth, he might have thought to himself: *Ah, I thought I had arthritis in my thigh, but I was wrong*. Thus, when he knows the facts, he regards himself as having previously deployed the same concept he has now, the concept that applies only to inflammations of the joints.

Part of the interest of this example lies in the fact that "arthritis" is not a natural kind term. If Burge is correct, then the example shows that externalism has a broad range of application that extends far beyond natural kind concepts. Given this, it is very important not to treat the case as if "arthritis" were a natural kind term, as does sometimes happen in the literature.

"Arthritis" just means *inflammation of the joints*, full stop. It comes from the Greek, "arthron" meaning *joint* and "itis," connoting inflammatory conditions. Arthritis can be caused by over 200 different conditions of widely different sorts. The causes include ordinary wear and tear, injury, auto-immune problems, sickle cell anemia, lupus, gout, syphilis, tuberculosis and ankylosis. Since "arthritis" is not a natural kind term, it is important not to let one's intuitions be guided by experience of thinking about examples like "water" or "topaz."

Burge's own discussion of the case does not always fit very well with the true meaning of "arthritis." At one point, he calls it a "family of diseases." This is slightly misleading. Rather, it is a symptom of any of a large selection of diseases that do not form a family in any other sense. Moreover, Burge's description of Alf's state of mind imputes a similar misconception to him (Burge 1979, 95):

> He will be relieved when he is told that one cannot have arthritis in the thigh. His relief is bound up with a network of assumptions that he makes about his arthritis: that it is a kind of disease.

It is of course possible that this is how Alf would react. But if so, then Alf, even after discussion with his doctor, would be under a misapprehension about "arthritis." It is only a kind of disease in the very loose sense in which itchy spots or grazed knees are kinds of diseases. There is no special reason why Alf should be relieved to learn that it is not arthritis in his thigh. After all, the doctor knew without investigation that Alf's arthritis had not spread to his thigh, since as matter of definition, one cannot have arthritis outside the joints. But matters of definition are unlikely to herald good news about a person's health. Alf's worry should be whether the condition causing his arthritis had deteriorated. And, indeed, it might have. Whatever was causing the arthritis might now be causing the pain in his thigh. (My investigations have revealed that Alf suffered from rheumatoid arthritis in the hip which had deteriorated, causing a referred pain in the thigh.) ...

Once one has the definition of "arthritis" firmly in mind, it becomes difficult to make sense of Alf's initial state of mind. Since "arthritis" just means "inflammation of the joints," it is hard to understand how anyone could believe that he has arthritis in the thigh. Burge would probably point out that the apparent conceptual difficulty here should be resolved once one realizes that Alf does not fully grasp what he believes. The internalist might reply that the notion of believing a thought one does not fully grasp is itself not easy to fathom. At any rate, the semantic proximity of "arthritis" to "inflammation of the joints" makes it impossible for the externalist to give an acceptable account of Alf's state of mind. The following argument exploits this difficulty.

Alf does not seem to believe that he has an inflammation of the joints in his thigh, knowing, as he does, that his thigh is not a joint. Indeed, he positively believes that he does not have an inflammation of the joints in his thigh. Or at least he would if he thought about it. But he does not positively believe that he does not have arthritis in his thigh. Alf therefore has two different concepts that he expresses by "arthritis" and "inflammation of the joints." But it would seem that the expert has only one concept expressed by the two expressions: for the expressions are synonymous, and the expert is expert. So it cannot be that Alf is able to deploy the same concept as the experts merely in virtue of his partial competence with the word and his deferential dispositions. If he did, then he would only have one concept, the unique concept expressed by both expressions in the experts' vernacular. So either Alf and the experts express different concepts by "arthritis" or by "inflammation of the joints" or both. Clearly the former is the most likely.

We have here the kernel of a good argument against consumerism....

The core of the argument is the claim that there could be two words that the misinformed subject uses to express different concepts, but that express just one concept of the expert's. Cases like this can be constructed involving a unique expert who does not even have the relevant words in her repertoire. There are two words in the misinformed subject's vocabulary, but only one in the expert's. Let us look at some examples. . . .

Mary is a consultant rheumatologist. In 1999 she writes a definitive article about arthritis. In 2005 she unfortunately dies. In 2010 a publisher publishes it in a volume. In 2010 Bert happens to browse the volume and as a result forms the belief that "arthritis" applies to any disorder in which aches and pains affect muscles and joints. In 2015 he happens to come across a rather inferior photocopy of a section of Mary's article and begins to browse. His eyesight is not very good, so the *r*'s and *n*'s in this inferior photocopy look rather similar to him. He thinks he is reading about a condition called "anthnitis." He reads a crucial paragraph in the article that defines "arthritis" and comes to believe that "anthnitis" just means$_{df}$ *inflammation of the joints*. If asked, he would say, "Anthnitis is not arthritis."

In this example, it is surely correct to say that the experts have just one concept where the subject has two. For no expert has the word "anthnitis" in her repertoire. There are two words in Bert's repertoire, but the deferential paths associated with both of them lead back to the experts' unique term "arthritis" and the unique concept it expresses. . . .

Many general terms in fact have two meanings one of which is a generalization of the other. For example "psychopathy" can either apply to mental illness in general or it can apply to a specific form of social dysfunction involving lack of conscience. "Tea" as applied to drinks can either denote infusions of tea leaves or, more generally, infusions of various fragrant leaves. "Grog" in Australian English can either denote any alcoholic drink, or a specific kind of drink made from spirits. Given this, it easy to imagine someone who falsely believes that a certain word form has two related but different meanings. Generalizing from "tea," for example, Cath might believe that "coffee" can either mean a drink made from ground coffee beans, or any dark, bitter tasting drink. She might then believe that not all coffee (general sense) is coffee (specific sense). Don might believe (incorrectly) that "optician" can either denote any specialist in optics, or, more specifically, a specialist in optics who is commercially involved in the correction of people's sight. Thus Don believes that not all opticians (general sense) are opticians (specific sense). And Bert might believe that "arthritis" can denote either a family of diseases causing inflammations of the joints, or, more generally, any rheumatoid condition involving aches and pains of the joints, muscles, tendons or ligaments. Thus Bert believes that not all arthritis is arthritis. . . .

All of these examples could be spelled out so that the subjects involved had the kind of partial understanding and deferential dispositions that would, according to the consumerist, allow them to express the experts' concept by their use of words. In each case the subjects have two words that express different concepts of theirs. These two words are at the ends of deferential paths that lead back to just one concept of the experts. If one were to deny this, then one would be committed to the claim that any time any subject suffered a misunderstanding of the relevant kind, all the experts (hence all the rest of us) would immediately acquire a new concept. This is not an acceptable result. . . .

I have argued that the social externalist does not draw the right conclusions from Putnam's and Burge's examples. Nevertheless, the intuitions underlying the view can seem compelling. I think that there are two different kinds of intuition at work here, a first personal one and a third personal one. I think that both can be diagnosed. We begin with the former.

The first person intuition centers on the manner in which the ill-informed protagonists accept correction. After Alf has conversed with the doctor, he regards himself as having previously believed that he had arthritis in the thigh. This goes against my internalist claim that Alf did not, prior to the conversation, have the concept of arthritis. I suggest that to understand Alf's view of the matter, we need to think of concepts as organic entities that can persist through changes of extension. Alf takes it that after correction he still deploys the same concept he had earlier. In a sense he is perfectly correct. It is the same concept in the sense that it is the same organic unity that has survived the conversation with the doctor. However, it has undergone a change of cognitive content and even of extension-conditions.

Post Fregean philosophers might find this use of "concept" strange or unacceptable. But really the matter is just terminological. Developmental psychologists frequently discuss the natural evolution of a concept over time. For example, a number of psychologists studying the development of mentalistic concepts (concepts of belief, desire, perception, etc.) hold that typical three-year-olds do not have the adult concept of belief. Rather, they possess a simplified concept that represents states that are something like copies of real situations in people's minds, or perhaps nonrepresentational states that relate people directly to situations in the world. (See, e.g., Gopnik and Wellman 1992, Perner 1991, Wellman 1990.) Call the original concept *s-belief* ("s" for simple) and the mature concept *belief*. The s-belief concept evolves into the belief concept. It doesn't matter whether we describe this as one concept changing its semantics over time or as an ancestor concept ceasing to be and being replaced by a descendent concept. The point is that there is a natural process that involves some kind of mental entity persisting through a semantic change. We could choose to call this evolving mental entity a concept.

The third person intuition is simply that we find it natural to say of Alf that he believes he has arthritis in his thigh. To understand this, it will help to consider some more (brief) examples. Alf says "I have a hippopotamus in my fridge." We incline to the view that Alf believes he has a hippopotamus in his fridge. But he goes on: "It is approximately the size and shape of a tennis ball, has an orange, wrinkly skin, and moist flesh with a pleasant, tart flavor." We revise our view, and decide that when he says "hippopotamus" he means *orange*. (The example is from Davidson 1984, 100–101.)

Fred says, "I have rheumatism in my wrists." We incline to the view that he believes he has rheumatism in his wrists. But he goes on: "I used to work in a factory, and was constantly having to rotate my hands. This caused an inflammation of the joints. 'Rheumatism' just means *inflammation of the joints*, you know." We revise our view, and conclude that by "rheumatism" he means *arthritis*.

The first case illustrates the uncontroversial point that we are not always averse to reinterpreting a subject's words. Alf says "hippopotamus." Once we learn that the concept he thereby expresses is expressed by our word "orange," we use the latter in our ascriptions of contents to him. The second case illustrates that we are not averse to doing this in cases where the word the subject has chosen does not mean exactly what he thinks it does, but still has a closely related meaning. In both cases, the subject misunderstands the word he uses. But the concept he associates with it is one that we happen to know and that we can express by a single word of our language.

Burge's original subject says, "My grandfather had arthritis. Now I have it in my hands and wrists. My joints get inflamed. It is painful." We incline to the view that Alf thinks his grandfather had arthritis, etc. Then he says "My arthritis may have spread to my thigh." Again, the subject misunderstands the word he is using. But now we do not find it so natural to reinterpret his words. Rather, we incline to say that he believes he has arthritis in his thigh. Why is this?

Two features appear to distinguish this case from the previous one. First, we don't know exactly what Alf takes "arthritis" to mean. Since we don't know that, we are not well situated to find an expression that means in our mouths what Alf takes "arthritis" to mean in his. Second, given what we do know, no relatively short expression, no word or simple phrase, springs to mind as a good candidate for the reinterpretation. By contrast, in the "rheumatism" example, Alf conveniently provided us with an account of what he takes the word to mean. And, it so happened, that very account coincided with the definition of a single word in our vocabulary: "arthritis." Thus we knew what content we needed to capture and we had a convenient word for capturing it.

Another example should help us tease apart these two factors. This time Alf says, "I have arthritis in my thigh. Arthritis is a specific kind of rheumatism. It has something to do with the auto-immune system. White blood cells attack the bones and muscles. It is a hereditary condition. There is no known cure." Now we know a fair amount about what Alf takes "arthritis" to mean. How do we report what he thinks he has in his thigh? My feeling is that it is no longer natural to say "He thinks he has arthritis in his thigh." In this case our minds are focused on the nature of Alf's idiosyncratic conception and on the difference between that and our concept of arthritis. On the other hand, we also find ourselves unwilling or unable to reinterpret. We have no word or short phrase that captures Alf's idiolectic meaning. There is the possibility of something like "He thinks he has in his thigh a certain kind of hereditary auto-immune disease involving white blood-cells attacking bones and muscles." But only a pedant would say that.

Thus, although we find it acceptable to say "Alf believes he has arthritis in his thigh" it does not follow that Alf has the concept of arthritis. He doesn't have the concept—our concept, the expert concept—of arthritis. Rather, our acceptance of that report is due to two factors. First, we do not know in any detail what his concept is like. Hence we are not forced to take notice of the precise nature of his concept and how it differs from our concept of arthritis. So we are not averse to accepting "arthritis" in our reports of his beliefs. Second, we don't have a ready alternative word or short phrase by which to reinterpret. So even if we were not happy to stick with "arthritis," we would not have any better option.

The diagnosis is thus that consumerism misconstructs an artefact of our practice of attitude reporting. Since we are not conscious of all of the principles underlying that practice, this misconstruction is understandable. However, the first two examples of this section indicate that it really is a misconstruction. We do reinterpret the subject's words in order to find the best match between his concepts and our vocabulary, when we know how to do so. Given this, our failure to reinterpret and our willingness to use the subject's own words in our reports of his attitudes in Burgean examples is predictable from the factors discussed. The alternative, after all, would be not to attempt to report on the subject's attitudes at all. And it is no surprise that we are not drawn to that option....

Now we can understand how "Alf believes that arthritis is not an inflammation of the joints" can be true, while "Alf believes that an inflammation of the joints is not an inflammation of the joints" is false. Since we can make sense of these reports, it seems that we must associate different concepts with "arthritis" and "inflammation of the joints." ... But I suggest that what is really going is this. "Arthritis is not an inflammation of the joints" and "An inflammation of the joints is not an inflammation of the joints" normally express the same thought for us. But they can cease to so in the specific context of a belief report. In that context, the words are used as sample representations for the purpose of representing what someone else believes. When used as samples, the words need not retain their normal senses. As with Pierre, so with Alf. When we use the terms in the belief report, we ask our audience to interpret the words not as usual, but in a way that makes sense of the reportee. At that point, in the context of talking about Alf, our synonymous expressions cease to be synonymous and are used to express different concepts on our part. But these are really just Alf's concepts that we have adopted for the purposes of understanding him.

So when I say (as I indeed believe), "Nobody could believe that arthritis is not inflammation of the joints," I say something true. For I am using the words as I normally use them. Nothing has arranged the context so that I can use them with someone else's senses. But were Burge to say "Alf believes that arthritis is not an inflammation of the joints" he might speak truly, using "arthritis" in Alf's way.[5] ...

Narrow Content and Psychology

... There is, indeed, a tendency to think that Oscar believes that water is good for plants, while Twin Oscar does not and that Alf believes that he has arthritis in his thigh, while Twin Alf does not. The mistake is to take this tendency too seriously and then to draw from it a general conclusion about the extensions of concepts: either cognitive content is at least sometimes wide, or cognitive content does not determine extension. Generalizing from such twin cases, then, the conclusion is that psychology (at least ordinary common-sense psychology) is either externalist or in need of radical revision. The only move left for the internalist is then to try to develop and defend some revisionist picture of psychology.

The view I recommend is quite different. I think that psychology as it is practiced by the folk and by the scientists, is already, at root, internalist. The externalist intuitions generated by the focal Twin Earth experiments are simply misleading. They reveal only an accidental and adventitious strand of our psychological thinking. The basic apparatus of psychology does not mandate externalism. So ascriptions of content that are made when practicing good, correct psychology are already internalist: the contents they attribute are already narrow....

However, if we are correctly, precisely and explicitly to describe Oscar's and Alf's minds, then we do need to revise certain of the particular ascriptions offered by externalists. In Oscar's case the ascriptions are wrong: he does not have the concept *water*, so he has no *water* beliefs. And I think it is simply wrong for us to use the word "water" in the content sentences of our discourse on his thoughts. In Alf's case the ascriptions are perhaps not wrong. But they are misleading. Alf does not have the concept *arthritis*. As I argued [above], if we can say truly that Alf believes he has arthritis in his thigh, then we are using "arthritis" in Alf's way and not attributing the thought that he has arthritis in his thigh.

So, if we are correctly, precisely and explicitly to describe these particular subjects' minds, then we would do well to adopt neologisms. We can say that the Oscars believe that "dwater" is good for plants, and that the Alfs believe they have "tharthritis" in their thighs. The reason we need to adopt neologisms in these cases is not that the contents we attribute are narrow. It is simply that our words "water" and "arthritis" do not express Oscar's and Alf's concepts. So if we are to use straightforward propositional attributions correctly, precisely and explicitly, we need some new words.

Do we really understand "dwater" and "tharthritis"? What is in the extensions these concepts? How are we to find out?...

I think we probably understand "dwater" rather well. It means roughly "waterlike substance" or "hydroid stuff." "Tharthritis" *per se* is not really an issue, since there are many ways of expanding Alf's biography that would endow him with different concepts. Perhaps "tharthritis" means roughly the same as "rheumatism." Or perhaps Alf has a more detailed misconception. He might, for example, think that tharthritis is a specific kind of hereditary auto-immune disease. The details are not so important.

"Dwater" includes both XYZ and H_2O in its extension. It includes very unhydroid things like oil, alcohol, sugar, electricity and oxygen in its anti-extension. And there are probably many substances that are in neither, such as heavy water (D_2O) and other substances that resemble normal water in some ways but not others. "Dwater" is neither true, nor false of these. The concept Oscar expressed by the term "water" is therefore substantially different from the concept I, and probably you, dear reader, express by that term. Unlike Oscar, my "water" concept is crucially conditioned by my belief that water is H_2O: I think that it is a deep truth that if anything is not H_2O, then it is not water. If I understood metaphysical necessity, I would probably think that it was a metaphysically necessary truth. Mine is a genuine natural kind concept, one that applies to an extension defined in terms of deep structural properties, as discovered by science. Oscar's is not. It is a motley concept that applies in virtue of relatively superficial features.

The extension of "tharthritis" depends upon how the character of Alf is fleshed out. If he had the articulated misconception mentioned above, then a decent first hypothesis about the extension would be that it includes any hereditary auto-immune diseases that can cause at least some of the kinds of symptoms that Alf has in his joints and thigh. It would exclude, for example, influenza, broken bones and sunstroke. And, like "dwater," "tharthritis" probably generates an area of indeterminacy. This might include, say, non-hereditary auto-immune diseases that produce the same symptomatology as paradigm cases. We would find out more about the details of Oscar's and Alf's concepts just by doing psychology. We could make a start by interviewing them.

I am not going to offer an algorithm for discovering the extension conditions of a concept. I know of no such algorithm. Nor am I going to offer any philosophical theory of content.... Cognitive content is the subject matter of psychology. So one good way to discover the cognitive contents of people's concepts is to do correct psychology. And, although there is no known algorithm for doing psychology correctly, there are certainly some substantial heuristics....

Prior to that, I want to adjust the dialectical balance. For it may seem that the externalist has an advantage, offering more satisfactory answers to questions about the extensions of concepts than I can offer. It can seem that Putnam and Burge have offered principled and complete answers to questions about the extensions of Oscar's and Alf's concepts, answers, moreover, that do not leave inelegant areas of indeterminacy. This is all an illusion.

The considerations that Putnam and Burge offer do not lead to algorithms for finding out what is in the extension of a concept.... I will argue that in general we are all in the same boat (or rather similar boats, anyway) when it comes to addressing questions like "What is *x*'s concept of *Y*?" and "How do we find out?" ...

Interestingly, Putnam (1975a) did not really give an argument for the conclusion that "water" in 1750 had the same extension as it does now, referring only to H_2O. Rather he assumed it, perhaps on the basis of intuition. He then gave a sketchy model of how extensions of natural kind terms are fixed. It is a sort of "just so" story with an air of plausibility to it. Humans encounter some number of samples of the kind. They use a word, *W*, to refer to the samples. And they intend the word to generalize beyond encountered samples to future and counterfactual cases, roughly as follows: "*W* is to be true of anything that has the same underlying nature as these instances, and of nothing else." In the case of water, the underlying nature is of the sort appropriate to liquids. Thus, "water" applies to this stuff (pointing to some samples) and to all and only other samples of the same liquid. What makes something the same liquid as these samples, what fixes the appropriate underlying principle of classification, is to be decided by science. Science is in the business of carving nature at its joints, and so, when it succeeds, finds the correct instantiation for "same liquid."[6]

This is an initially appealing story, and it does fit with some intuitions as well as with some aspects of scientific practice. However, Putnam's model cannot be quite right. A second example will show why. It is adapted from LaPorte (1996).

In the 1920s, a group of Earth scientists are sent to a twin Earth. They find that a certain kind of liquid is common there. It looks rather like typical Earth water. Interested, the scientists wonder whether what they have found is water. On examination, they find that while it resembles typical Earth water in many respects, there are some important differences. For example, it boils and freezes at slightly different temperatures than does normal H_2O. And, importantly, it is not conducive to terrestrial life, but rather is fatal to plants and animals from Earth.

The scientists go on to examine its internal constitution. They find that this, too, is interestingly different from typical water. Rather than being composed of normal hydrogen and oxygen, it is composed of oxygen plus a hitherto unknown component, which, like, normal hydrogen, has only one proton and one electron, but has an additional neutron. They decide that they have found a new element, which they call "deuterium" and give the hydroid substance the chemical description "D_2O." Having discovered that this stuff is both macroscopically and chemically different from water, and being somewhat Putnamian in their views about kind terms, they feel they have established that it is definitely not water. They call it "deutroxide."

When they return to Earth they report on their discovery, emphasizing how they had established that deutroxide is not water. Earth scientists, having already discovered deuterium oxide themselves and regarded it as a variety of water, heavy water, are unimpressed.

LaPorte points out that neither group of scientists is right and neither wrong.[7] Nothing about the nature of the world, nor the initial usage of "water," determines whether D_2O should or should not have been called "water" when it was discovered. We should conclude that "water" was neither true nor false of D_2O prior to 1920. The fact that scientists classified D_2O as a kind of water, rather than not, was presumably due in part to contingencies concerning the distribution of D_2O relative to H_2O (small amounts of D_2O tend to occur in normal water and do not occur separately in large volumes).[8]

We can already see that Putnam's initially appealing account of the extension of natural kind terms cannot be quite right. It is not as if we had initially pointed to some samples of water and said "These samples and all and only samples of the same kind of liquid will be called 'water'" and left it up to science, carving nature at its joints, to tell us what the same kind of liquid really is. Or, to the extent that we do use terms with some such idea in mind, we do not thereby succeed in fixing their extensions.

Mark Wilson (1983) provides other examples of adventitious factors affecting the evolution of natural kind terms. Here is one. "Grant's zebra" was originally applied to a particular species of zebras native to Kenya. A different subspecies of the same species of zebra found in Rhodesia was called "Chapman's zebra." It was discovered that the two subspecies interbred near the Zambezi river. "Grant's zebra" is still used only to refer to the Kenyan subspecies and not to the Rhodesian one. But suppose that Chapman's zebras had not been given a special name and had first been investigated near the Zambezi. Then it would have been natural for the scientists to say: "There are two subspecies of Grant's zebra." The term would then have ended up applying to the whole species. We should conclude that "Grant's zebra" was, originally, neither true nor false of Chapman's zebras.

In Wilson's example, it is simply the order of discovery that determines the developments in usage. But there are many further reasons why Putnam's model is inaccurate. Many terms that might have ended up extending over a natural kind in fact did not. Our taxonomies reflect a wide variety of contingencies that have nothing to do with nature's own joints. The expectations of scientists constitute one obvious factor. And beyond that, there are a whole variety of human interests, the whole plethora of nonscientific activities for which we develop our taxonomies.

Neither "cat" (in its broadest use) nor "whale" picks out a biological kind, even though in both cases one is at hand. Whales are large cetaceans (the order containing whales, dolphins and porpoises).[9] Size matters. But the term could easily have come to cover the other cetaceans as well, just as "water" came to cover D_2O. "Cat," in its broadest use, covers the family Felidae, but includes also members of other families, such as civet cats and polecats.

The great heterogeneity of the development of usage is nicely illustrated by gems.[10] Diamonds have the same chemical composition as coal. But since diamonds and coal are so different in ways that matter to us, we don't call coal "diamonds" nor diamonds "coal." "Sapphire," in its broader use, applies to all gem varieties of corundum (Al_2O_3) except ruby, according to most authorities. The original Greek term probably referred not to sapphires, but to lapis lazuli. "Ruby" applies only to red corundum. "Topaz" applies to aluminum silicate ($Al_2(SiO_4)(OH, F)_2$), no matter what the color. However, the original term, used by Greeks and Romans, applied not to aluminum silicate, but to yellow corundum, i.e. yellow sapphire. Emeralds and aquamarines are both beryl ($Be_3Al_2Si_6O_{18}$), the former green, the latter blue. Jade (as Putnam pointed out) comes in two varieties, jadeite and nephrite. But "jade" almost became a natural kind term. LaPorte found the following entry in an old reference book:

> *Jade,* a name applied to certain ornamental stones ... belonging to at least two distinct species, one termed nephrite and the other jadeite. While the term jade is popularly used in this sense, *it is now usually restricted by mineralogists to nephrite.* (*Encyclopaedia Brittanica,* 1911, 122; quoted in LaPorte 1996; emphasis is LaPorte's)

So, even if most or all of the samples to which a prescientific term is applied happen to belong to a natural kind, there are various possibilities for the development of usage over time. First: there will often be more than one natural kind subsuming all the samples ("water," "Grant's zebra"), and nothing makes one a more likely candidate than some others. Maybe there will always be more than one kind available, since natural kinds come in hierarchies: e.g., subspecies, species, genus and so on. Second: the term may well end up applying to an arbitrary subclass of a natural kind ("emerald," "sapphire," "whale"). Third: the term may end up applying to a motley of two or more natural kinds ("jade," "cat"). Last (and perhaps of least significance), it may even end up applying to a kind that the original samples didn't belong to ("topaz").[11]

Putnam's model is evidently far too simple. It just is not the case that by using a term to apply to samples of a natural kind, the term gets to have that kind in its extension. And this shows, at the very least, that the question of what a prescientific term extends over is extremely difficult for a Putnam style externalist to answer. There is no more reason to suppose that all and only varieties of H_2O were in the extension of prescientific "water,"[12] than that all and only cetaceans were in the extension of prescientific "whale," or felidae in the extension of "cat," or beryl in the extension of "emerald," etc.

Indeed it does not seem that there is any good reason to think that a pre-scientific term ever extends over a natural kind. It is true that, as in the case of "water," a term may end up applying to a specific natural kind after pivotal scientific discoveries. But any such term might have ended up either not applying to a natural kind at all, or applying to a different one.

What I propose as a more plausible view than Putnam's is that prescientific terms for natural phenomena apply to motleys. A motley may consist in several natural kinds, or in a collection that includes some, but not all, samples of a plurality of natural kinds. Motley terms are common: "tree," "river," "rock," "metal," "fish," "influenza." When a term becomes a natural kind term with the development of science, its extension alters. Competent users come to regard some particular scientific principle of classification as correct, and so begin to use the term in line with that. When this happens, the extension may enlarge, or shrink or alter its boundaries in both directions. But before the scientific principle is known and more or less explicitly adopted, there is nothing that ties the word to a unique natural kind....

What is in the extension of "tharthritis"? How could we tell? Burge's account suggests that experts can pin down Alf's apparently rather nebulous personal conception to a clear and determinate extension. I will now argue that experts cannot in general play such an extension-fixing role. For many concepts, when it comes to answering questions of the form "what is in the extension of concept C?," "how are we to tell?" we are all in the same boat....

Here is a variant on Burge's story. Fred apparently has many ordinary beliefs about pies. He believes that pies have an outer crust, that they can have sweet or savory fillings, that pork pies are cheap and highly calorific, and so on. He begins to learn to cook. One day he buys some pre-mixed pastry, lines a baking tin with it, fills it with an apple and sugar based paste and places it in the oven. Delia, a famous chef and author of culinary textbooks, drops by. Fred produces the dish and says, "Would you like some apple pie?" Delia says, "Actually, that's not a pie. With a pie, the pastry must either completely enclose the filling, or the filling must be enclosed by a receptacle and have a pastry upper crust." Fred accepts the correction and goes on to ask what kind of dish he has produced. "A tart, I suppose," said Delia.

On Twin Earth, the word "pie" is used more widely, to cover various baked dishes, including, as it happens, the tart Fred has produced. When Twin Fred offers his friend Delia some apple pie, she merely accepts, having no dispute with Fred's description of the dish.

Now I'll let you in on some secrets: "Earth" is England and "Twin Earth" is the United States. The usage of "pie" does indeed vary across the Atlantic: witness American "pecan pie," "pumpkin pie," and "lemon meringue pie." The two versions of the story are both possible futures concerning Fred, who, although originally English, spends equal time in England and the United States.

What is the extension of the concept Fred expresses with "pie"? What does it depend on? The social externalist's position is that the extensions of one's concepts are partly determined by the views of the experts to whom one does and ought to defer. But here, two sets of experts seems equally suited. Fred would defer just as readily to American Delia as he would to English Delia. And it doesn't seem to be the case that one has more claim to Fred's allegiance than the other. Surely, the case could be fleshed out so that any non-arbitrary criteria of proper allegiance would apply equally to both candidates. Even if one could motivate the idea that it depends on what country Fred is in when he speaks, that would not help. Fred travels on the QE2 and spends much time mid-Atlantic. (Cases of this kind, in which the protagonist has allegiance to different communities, were offered in Loar 1987.)

The social externalist is in a difficult position. How many concepts does Fred have? Two, because he defers to two sets of experts? None, because of his confused pattern of deference? Neither of these answers is plausible. Fred has exactly one concept that he expresses by "pie."

We can run a somewhat similar variant of Putnam's "elm" and "beech" case. The term "Milky Way" in England refers to a certain kind of rather light chocolate bar with a soft praliné like filling. In the United States, it refers to a type of chocolate bar with a soft nougat and caramel center, closely resembling what in England are called "Mars Bars." The closest American counterpart to what the English call "Milky Way" are in the United States called "Three Musketeers."

Fred is no expert in confections, and rarely eats chocolate. He believes that "Mars" and "Milky Way" denote different kinds of chocolate bars, but he does not know what distinguishes them. He is on the QE_2, and fancies something sweet. "I think they have Milky Ways," says Delia. "Oh, fine, that's just what I want. Will you get me one?" What has Fred asked for? What does he want? As with the pie case, we can assume that neither English nor American usage dominates. We cannot motivate the idea that he wants an English Milky Way as opposed to an American one, nor an American Milky Way as opposed to an English one. Nor does the idea that he has two quite distinct desires glow with plausibility. Does he then have no concept at all? Of course he has a concept. He has a whole cluster of desires and beliefs that he expresses with the help of the expression "Milky Way." If he did not, it would be hard to explain his speaking as he does, his reaching into his pocket to give Delia some money, the fact that his actions are related to his being hungry, his wanting something sweet and so forth....

The difficulty I have raised for the social externalist is this. The social externalist holds that provided one has a minimal competence with a term and is disposed suitably to defer to the right experts, then one can deploy the concept expressed by the term. But suppose there are two sets of appropriate experts. The externalist then faces a choice. He could hold that since there are two concepts made available by experts, and the subject has minimal competence with the word, and would defer to an expert of either of the two expert camps, he has two concepts. But this is not a good choice. First, it is obviously counterintuitive. Second, it ignores what the externalist should see as a confused pattern of deferential relations leading the subject to a confused state of mind. Third, it makes for poor psychological explanation: why attribute two concepts when there is only need for one?

Alternatively, the externalist could appeal to the abnormality and unsuitability of the social environment, and hold that the subject therefore lacks an expert concept. This leads to a further choice. Either the subject has no concept, or he has a different one from the experts. The former option is unacceptable, since we can and should attribute some concept to the protagonist, in order to explain his behavior and other cognitive processes.

And the latter option is problematic as well. If the subject does not have the expert concept, then what does he have? How do we find out? The problem now is not that these questions are unanswerable. Rather, it is that the social externalist now faces the same kind of questions as the internalist. For he must now give an account of how a subject can have a concept that does not depend upon his allegiance to any coherent group of experts.

The same problem arises in many other ways as well. Most obviously, it comes up in relation to the experts themselves. What is in the extension of the expert's concept of arthritis? Arthritis is inflammation of the joints. But what is the extension of the concepts *inflammation* and *joints*? It can't be experts all the way down. Something other than the opinion of experts must fix the extension of the experts' concepts.

Further, in real life, experts often fail to agree, and nothing determines which experts an individual does or should defer to. For example, in France "foie gras" has a legal meaning: the liver of any edible bird, including chicken. The important legal constraint on foie gras products is that they cannot include the livers of too many different types of bird. And it has a different culinary one: fresh or preserved liver of goose or duck (see the *Larousse Gastronomique*). The meaning of "chocolate" is at the time of writing in dispute between Brussels and chocolate manufacturers, and has a third dictionary meaning.

Dictionaries disagree too. Compare for example, the entries for "sapphire" in the *OED* (2nd edition) with the *Random House* (2nd edition). *OED* (entry b): "Min. Used as a general name for all the precious transparent varieties of native crystalline alumina, including the ruby." Random House: "Any gem variety of corundum other than the ruby, esp. one of the blue varieties." This disagreement is due neither to national differences nor to a difference between lay and scientific usage, because the *Oxford Concise Scientific Dictionary* (2nd edition) sides with the Random House, offering, "Any of the gem varieties of corundum except ruby, especially the blue variety, but other colors of sapphire include yellow, brown, green, pink, orange and purple." . . .

Finally, dictionaries often contain multiple entries of a single polysemous word, specifying extensionally different but closely related meanings. Compare, for example, the *OED*'s entry b for "sapphire," given above, with its entry a: "A precious stone of a beautiful transparent blue." Again, nothing determines which of various entries in a dictionary deserves the allegiance of a reasonably competent but inexpert lay speaker.

It should be clear now that neither samples of natural kinds, nor experts, nor the conjunction of the two, can provide adequate constraints that can be fruitfully exploited by a completely general account of concepts. On any theory, many concepts do not have determinate extensions fixed by either. An internalist account of Oscar's *dwater* and Alf's *tharthritis* concepts is therefore not likely to face any special difficulties of its own. Rather, it is likely to face just the same difficulties that the externalist faces with concepts like "tree" or "fish," with the concepts of experts, with the concepts of inexpert transatlantic errants, with concepts associated with many polysemous words and so on. . . .

Neologisms are likely to be of use for psychologists studying subjects that differ in some important and general way from the academics themselves, such as children, subjects from non-scientific cultures, or people (e.g., scientists and philosophers) from history. Here, the relevant generalizations will be over groups, not individuals, and the neologisms will signal important differences between the subject group's concepts and those of the scientists who study them. In these cases, the use of neologisms seems to be a rather good idea. The point warrants a little discussion.

The use of neologisms already has some currency. Some psychologists (e.g., Perner 1991) already use the term "prelief" to denote a concept of three-year olds', which they see as an undifferentiated concept that, on maturing, differentiates into our concepts of belief and pretence.

According to many developmental psychologists, small children have many concepts that we lack. For example, as Piaget claimed some time ago, children have a single concept that differentiates into our concepts of weight and density. It is not simply that they have the concept of weight and later acquire the concept of density. Rather, the ancestor concept runs together features of both in a way that makes it implausible that it is either the concept *weight* or the concept *density*. (This is argued in Carey 1985.) We do not have this undifferentiated concept, nor do we have a word to express or denote it.

Carey (1985) also argues at some length that children lack the adult concept of living thing. The concept that children express by "alive" contrasts not with inanimate, but with "dead." Moreover, this contrasting pair of concepts itself runs together the contrasts between "real" and "imaginary," "existent" and "nonexistent," and "functional" and "broken." For example, children tend to say such things as, "A button is alive because it can fasten a blouse," "A table is alive because you can see it." And if you ask children to list things that are not alive, they tend to list only the dead: George Washington, ghosts, dinosaurs. . . .

The history of science provides similar examples. Thus, before the time of Black, scientists had not distinguished heat from temperature. The Experimenters of the Florentine Academy, for example, had a single concept that ran together elements of both heat and temperature: sometimes they treated the quantity as intensive, sometimes as extensive. Here, it certainly seems right to attribute to the early scientists an incoherent concept that we lack. There is no particular reason why externalists should wish to deny this.

In all these cases we would do well to adopt neologisms. We could say, for example, that small children believe that they are "shalive," not that they are alive, and that the Experimenters of the Academy believed that "hemperature" had both strength and intensity. It is true that coining neologisms is not the standard practice of psychologists and historians of science, Perner notwithstanding. Carey, for example, uses the term "*heat*," in italics, for the concept of the experimenters of the Academy. But she clearly intends this term not to express our concept of heat. In effect, she adopts the policy that I claimed was standard in everyday propositional attitude reporting. She uses a word of her vocabulary in opaque contexts in a nonstandard way, with a nonstandard meaning. The context of discussion makes it clear that she is doing this, and provides us with enough clues to get something of a handle on the experimenters' concept. There is nothing wrong with this practice. But it would be clearer and less prone to induce confusion if one adopted two terms rather than using one ambiguously.

Methodology

In this concluding subsection I want briefly to sketch how psychology might look from an internalist perspective. None of what follows is supposed to be an argument for internalism. It is supposed merely to present a sketch of psychology that is compatible with internalism and independently plausible.

Jerry Fodor (1987, chap. 1) elegantly captured a fundamental feature of psychology. Psychological states have both representational properties (content properties) and causal powers. These mirror one another. One can predict the causal powers of a psychological state from its content and type (belief, desire, etc.). Psychology, both folk and scientific, specifies principles that allow us to exploit this correspondence.

Two simple cases will illustrate. Beth believes that either Brazil or Argentina will win the soccer world cup. When Argentina lose in the semi finals, she comes to believe that they will not win the world cup. Now we can predict who she thinks will win. When we describe her beliefs, we do so in terms of their contents. And, on the basis of this, we can predict the causal relations among them.

Beth believes that Brazil will win the world cup. She also believes that anybody who bets a hundred pounds on the winning team stands to win a lot of money. Beth wishes to win a lot of money. She has no reason not to place a bet on Brazil and believes she is in a position to do so. We predict that she will try to place a bet on Brazil.

Beth's desires and beliefs tend to cause what they tend to rationalize.[13] This coordination of causality and rationalization lies at the heart of psychology. And it offers us an obvious heuristic for ascribing contents: charity. We can get a lot right, if we attribute psychological states to subjects that would render their behavior rational: if the individual were subject to the states we posit, then she would behave as she does, given that the states tend to cause what they tend to rationalize.

Charity is certainly not the be all and end all of psychology. People often fail to draw logical conclusions from what they already believe, even when these consequences would matter to them. And people often fail to do what it would be rational for them to do, given what they believe and what they want. There are many different reasons for these limitations. There are heavy constraints of time and processing resources, such as memory. Moreover, people don't always use valid principles of reasoning when they do make inferences. Sometimes they use fallacious ones. Sometimes they fail to use valid ones, even if they are aware of them. And sometimes people are simply overwhelmed by the power of their desires, felt needs and addictions and go right ahead and do what they know to be the wrong thing.

For those and many other reasons, it is not always the case that the most charitable interpretation of a subject is the correct one. Nevertheless, charitable interpretation is a good basic heuristic, and one that plays a central role in common sense psychology.

Charity also applies to causal relations between the environment and psychological states. We get a lot of practically indispensable evidence about people's psychological states by looking at how they are situated in their environments. If we see a person running rapidly away from a manifestly enraged dog, we might hypothesize that he is afraid of it. But we have to be careful how we see the role of the environment. For it is not even approximately true that people believe all and only truths about the world they inhabit. Rather, we know that humans typically have five senses, and we know a fair amount about the ranges and limitations of these senses. For example, we know that in good light, a normal subject with her eyes open will form largely accurate visual representations of the shapes, sizes and locations of middle-sized objects in front of her. But we also know that she can't see objects that are in the dark, or too small, or too far away. And we know some of the conditions under which she will form false visual representations. We are thus in a position to make decent hypotheses about cognitive states that are caused by the environment.

Even with all its limitations taken into account and catered for, the charitable strategies of common sense psychology are only heuristics. They provide only a rough and preliminary guide to true ascriptions. This is in part because charitable interpretation doesn't require us to look inside the heads of our subjects, which is where the crucial causal activity takes place. The ideal common sense psychologist could be fooled by a giant look-up table or a good actor (see Block 1981 for discussion). Nevertheless, it is pretty good heuristic and it allows us to formulate and partially confirm psychological attributions.

Now there is nothing in the basic principles of common sense psychology, in the charitable principles of interpretation that it deploys, that entails externalism. It is perfectly possible that the best interpretations of a subject would not distinguish twins. So a first shot at an answer to the question of how we could find what the narrow contents (i.e., the contents) of a subject's concepts are, is that we can do so by the normal methods.

It Oscar were brought forward in time, we could begin to find out about his concept of dwater simply by using the normal methods. For example, we would look at what kinds of samples he is willing to call "water." And we would, of course, consider not just actual causes, but counterfactual ones too. What would cause him to assent to "water"? Since XYZ would cause him so to assent, we have a little evidence already that it is in the extension of the concept.

Commonsense interpretation tells us a great deal about what is not in the extension of a concept. If Oscar, in full command of the situation and apprised of all relevant facts, insists that a sample of oil is not what he calls "water," then this is good evidence that dwater does not include oil. We could pursue the matter. We might ask him why this sample isn't dwater (by saying, "Why isn't this water?" in Oscar's language). He might examine the sample and say, "Water is typically colorless, odorless, tasteless and not at all viscous: this sample is black, smelly, tastes awful and it is slightly viscous. I'd say this is oil and definitely not water." Excellent evidence that oil is not in the extension of Oscar's concept of dwater, wouldn't you say?...

So we could make considerable progress towards finding out what is in the extension of "dwater" just by using the standard means. *Dwater* is the concept that fits best into our best overall interpretation of the subject's behavior, taking into account all the relevant counterfactuals about what they would say and do under various circumstances....

The important point is that the basic principles of folk psychology can be applied in a way that is compatible with internalism. There is nothing about the basic apparatus of charitable interpretation, exploiting the parallel between causal and rational properties, that dictates that it would yield externalist interpretations, ones that would distinguish twins. Rather we should expect the reverse.

Folk psychology is just the beginning. To learn more about concepts, we would have to proceed to science. But scientific psychology exploits the same basic apparatus as do the folk. Cognitive science with its computational models and cognitive psychology and psycholinguistics with their attributions of complex tacit theories, all rely on something like the basic principle of charity. They ascribe representations and bodies of knowledge on the assumption that subjects, modules and cognitive systems behave in ways that make reasonable sense. In this way, they exploit the parallel between causal and representational properties of psychological states, events, and processes.[14]

Scientific psychology of course revises and extends the folk apparatus in many different ways, bringing in many further constraints on attributions of content, constraints from acquisition, deficits, computational models, neural scans and so on and on. To be sure that none of these constraints brings in externalist principles of attribution would require examination of the various different branches of psychology. This would be a most worthwhile pursuit.[15] But prima facie there is not the slightest reason to suppose that any of them do. Scientific psychology as it is actually practiced appears to be perfectly compatible with internalism. So the right way to find out about narrow contents is just the right way to find out about cognitive content generally: do psychology.

Notes

1. Fodor (1994) tentatively endorses this version.

2. To be precise, it allows that coextensive atomic concepts can differ in content. The point is that the difference in content cannot be put down to a difference in the extension of component concepts. Water and H_2O might be held to differ in content in that the latter has a component concept of hydrogen, say, while the former does not. The view at issue allows for distinctions of content that do not involve any such differences in extension.

3. I think Burge (1982), McDowell (1984, 1986), Evans (1982), and Wiggins (1980) hold something along those lines.

4. Kaplan 1989, 602. See Mercier 1994 for discussion.

5. As mentioned above, we are not conscious of the semantic mechanisms we use in belief reporting, so there is no reason why what I am saying should be obvious to any of us.

6. See Kripke 1980 for a similar story.

7. He now prefers to say that if one group is right, then so is the other (LaPorte, p.c.).

8. In fact, the chemical terms "H" and "H_2O" are ambiguous. Deuterium (D) and tritium (T, 1 proton, 2 neutrons) are hydrogen isotopes. In chemical classification, the isotopes of an element are varieties of that element. So D and T are varieties of hydrogen. "H" can be used either to denote hydrogen, hence to extend over deuterium and tritium, or it can be used in contrast to "D" and "T" to denote just normal hydrogen. "H_2O" is similarly ambiguous. The usage that is most consistent with chemical vernacular in general allows "H" and "H_2O" their wider meanings.

9. For detailed discussion of "whale," see Dupré 1999. For more general discussion of folk and scientific biological taxonomies, see Dupré 1990. Our views on these matters are much the same.

10. I have borrowed some of the examples from LaPorte and dug out the others from the *Oxford Concise Science Dictionary* and the *Oxford English Dictionary*.

11. For attempts to deal with some of these cases from a roughly Putnamian standpoint, see Sterelny 1983, Devitt and Sterelny 1987, Miller 1992, and Brown 1998. None of the accounts deals with all of the cases. I think that they would all have trouble with, e.g., "Grant's zebra," "sapphire," and "water." I doubt that any account retaining basic Putnamian intuitions could deliver plausible results across a broad range of cases without getting other ones wrong. But that is for you to judge, dear reader.

12. In fact it is not clear that in ordinary contemporary English (as described in dictionaries) "water" is true of steam and ice, although it is in my idiolect. That is another case that could have gone either way (and may in fact have gone both ways).

13. In fact, as I said in chapter three, I believe that representational properties are themselves causally efficacious: it is because a state represents what it does that it causes what it does. I also believe that causally efficacious properties must be intrinsic. This leads to a short argument for

internalism. However, I can't offer any non-question-begging defense of the premises, so the argument is of little polemical value.

14. For a different view, see Chomsky 1995, 2003.

15. Rather, it is a worthwhile pursuit. There is a lot of literature on this topic, with arguments offered on both sides. See, for example, Patterson 1991 on developmental psychology; Chomsky 1995, 2003, and Mercier 1994 on psycholinguistics; Cummins 1983, Wilson 1995 and Segal 1997 on cognitive science. There has been in particular a detailed debate about David Marr's computational theory of vision, with Segal (1989c, 1991) and Butler (1996a, 1996b) arguing that it is internalist, and Burge (1986a, 1986b), Davies (1991, 1992), and Egan (1995) arguing that it is externalist.

References

Almog, J., Perry, J., and Wettstein, H. 1989. *Themes from Kaplan.* Oxford: Oxford University Press.

Block, N. 1981. "Psychologism and Behaviorism." *Philosophical Review* 90: 5–43.

Boyer, P. 1994. "Cognitive Constraints on Cultural Representations: Natural Ontologies and Religious Ideas." In Hirschfield and Gelman 1994.

Brown, J. 1998. "Natural Kind Terms and Recognitional Capacities." *Mind* 107: 275–303.

Burge, T. 1979. "Individualism and the Mental." In P. French, T. Uehling, and H. Wettstein, eds., *Studies in Epistemology,* Midwest Studies in Philosophy, no. 4, pp. 73–121. Minneapolis: University of Minnesota Press.

Burge, T. 1982. "Other Bodies." In Woodfield 1982, pp. 97–120.

Burge, T. 1986a. "Individualism and Psychology." *Philosophical Review* 95: 3–45.

Burge, T. 1986b. "Intellectual Norms and the Foundation of Mind." *Journal of Philosophy* 83: 697–720.

Butler, K. 1996a. "Individualism and Marr's Computational Theory of Vision." *Mind and Language* II: 313–337.

Butler, K. 1996b. "Content, Computation, and Individualism in Vision Theory." *Analysis* 56: 146–154.

Carey, S. 1985. *Conceptual Change in Childhood.* Cambridge, MA: MIT Press.

Chomsky, N. 1995. "Language and Nature." *Mind* 104: 1–61.

Chomsky, N. 2003. "Internalist Explorations." In M. Hahn and B. Ramberg, eds., *Reflections and Replies: Essays on the Philosophy of Tyler Burge.* Cambridge, MA: MIT Press.

Cummins, R. 1983. *The Nature of Psychological Explanation.* Cambridge, MA: MIT Press.

Davidson, D. 1984. *Inquiries into Truth and Interpretation.* Oxford: Clarendon Press.

Davies, M. 1991. "Individualism and Perceptual Content." *Mind* 100: 461–484.

Davies, M. 1992. "Perceptual Content and Local Supervenience." *Proceedings of the Aristotelian Society* 92: 21–45.

Devitt, M., and Sterelny, K. 1987. *Language and Reality.* Oxford: Blackwell.

Dupré, J. 1990. "Natural Kinds and Biological Taxa." *Philosophical Review* 99: 66–99.

Dupré, J. 1999. "Are Whales Fish?" In D. L. Medin and S. Atran, eds., *Folk Biology*. Cambridge, MA: MIT Press.

Egan, F. 1995. "Computation and Content." *Philosophical Review* 104: 181–203.

Evans, G. 1982. *The Varieties of Reference*. Oxford: Oxford University Press.

Fodor, J. 1987. *Psychosemantics*. Cambridge, MA: MIT Press.

Fodor, J. 1990a. "A Theory of Content, II." In Fodor 1990b, pp. 89–136.

Fodor, J. 1990b. *A Theory of Content and Other Essays*. Cambridge, MA: MIT Press.

Fodor, J. 1994. *The Elm and the Expert*. Cambridge, MA: MIT Press.

Gopnik, A., and Wellman, H. 1992. "Why the Child's Theory of Mind Really Is a Theory." *Mind and Language* 7: 145–172.

Hirschfield, L. A., and Gelman, S. A., eds. 1994. *Mapping the Mind: Domain Specificity in Cognition and Culture*. Cambridge: Cambridge University Press.

Kaplan, D. 1989. "Afterthoughts." In Almog, Perry, and Wettstein 1989, pp. 565–614.

Kripke, S. 1980. *Naming and Necessity*. Cambridge, MA: Harvard University Press. Originally published in D. Davidson and G. Harman, eds., *Semantics of Natural Language*, pp. 253–355. Dordrecht: Reidel, 1972.

LaPorte, J. 1996. "Chemical Kind Term Reference and the Discovery of Essence." *Noûs* 30, no. I: 112–132.

Loar, B. 1987. "Social Content and Psychological Content." In R. Grimm and D. Merrill, eds., *Contents of Thought: Proceedings of the 1985 Oberlin Colloquium in Philosophy*, pp. 99–139. Includes comments by Akeel Bilgrami, pp. 110–121.

McDowell, J. 1984. "*De Re* Senses." In C. Wright, ed., *Frege: Tradition and Influence*, pp. 283–294. Oxford: Basil Blackwell.

McDowell, J. 1986. "Singular Thought and the Extent of Inner Space." In Pettit and McDowell 1986, pp. 137–168.

McGinn, C. 1982. "The Structure of Content." In Woodfield 1982, pp. 207–258.

Mercier, A. 1994. "Consumerism and Language Acquisition." *Linguistics and Philosophy* 17: 499–519.

Miller, R. B. 1992. "A Purely Causal Solution to One of the *Qua* Problems." *Australasian Journal of Philosophy* 70: 425–434.

Patterson, S. 1991. "Individualism and Semantic Development." *Philosophy of Science* 58: 15–31.

Perner, J. 1991. *Understanding the Representational Mind*. Cambridge, MA: MIT Press.

Putnam, H. 1975a. "The Meaning of 'Meaning.'" In K. Gunderson, ed., *Language, Mind, and Knowledge*, Minnesota Studies in the Philosophy of Science, no. 7. Reprinted in Putnam 1975b, pp. 215–271.

Putnam, H. 1975b. *Mind, Language, and Reality*. Vol. 2 of *Philosophical Papers*. Cambridge: Cambridge University Press.

Segal, G. 1989. "Seeing What Is Not There." *Philosophical Review* 98: 189–214.

Segal, G. 1991. "Defense of a Reasonable Individualism." *Mind* 100: 485–493.

Segal, G. 1997. Review of Wilson, *Cartesian Psychology and Physical Minds: Individualism and the Sciences of Mind. British Journal for the Philosophy of Science* 48: 151–157.

Sterelny, K. 1983. "Natural Kind Terms." *Pacific Philosophical Quarterly* 64: 110–125.

Wellman, H. 1990. *The Child's Theory of Mind.* Cambridge, MA: MIT Press.

Wiggins, D. 1980. *Sameness and Substance.* Oxford: Oxford University Press.

Wilson, M. 1983. "Predicate Meets Property." *Philosophical Review* 91: 549–589.

Wilson, R. A. 1995. *Cartesian Psychology and Physical Minds: Individualism and the Sciences of Mind.* Cambridge: Cambridge University Press.

Woodfield, A. 1982. *Thought and Object.* Oxford: Clarendon Press.

IV Innateness and Modularity

Introduction

The problem of innate ideas and innate knowledge is among the most celebrated in the history of philosophy. In its original form (already discussed in the time of Plato and Aristotle), the debate over "innateness" centered around whether certain bodies of concepts and knowledge were built into the mind, or if instead all our concepts and knowledge are acquired from experience. Yet (as the two-part title of this section illustrates) the original discussion of innate ideas has in modern times mutated into a slightly different and more complicated question. Very roughly, the current debate focuses not simply on whether there are *concepts* and *knowledge* built into the mind, but in addition whether the mind possesses specialized *faculties* dedicated to a specific area of knowledge—for example, a special faculty devoted to language, or one devoted to mathematics. Historically, writers who have argued for innate knowledge of (for example) mathematics did not suppose that a unique mathematical *faculty* was involved in having or exercising that knowledge; reasoning about mathematics would be performed by a generic "intellect," just as reasoning about birds or rocks would be. The more recent discussion fuses together the older question of innate knowledge and concepts, with the newer question of whether the mind possesses specialized faculties, or mental organs—called *modules*—devoted to a particular domain or subject matter.

We begin with a famous passage from Plato (circa 428–348 B.C.E.) in which Socrates demonstrates to Meno that even an uneducated boy has innate knowledge of geometry. Of course, there is a long-standing dispute as to whether Socrates coaxes the knowledge from the boy or essentially supplies the correct answer by skillful use of leading questions. In any case, Plato's thesis is that all of our knowledge is innate, and that sensory experience is simply the occasion for the recollection of that knowledge.

Aristotle (384–322 B.C.E.) approaches the question of innate ideas and knowledge by way of a puzzle over science. In Aristotle's theory, scientific knowledge amounts to argumentation that deduces new conclusions from absolutely certain evidence. But the question then arises of how we come to know such evidence in the first place. Since this evidence must be at least as certain as the conclusions deduced from it, it would be strange if this knowledge were innate—for then even children would have knowledge more certain than science, without realizing it. On the other hand, if we have to deduce this evidence from further evidence, we only push the problem back a step—for then the question would be where that *further* evidence came from. Aristotle's solution is to claim that our minds have a power to take in particular sensory experiences, store them, and (after sufficient repetition), *generalize from them*. For example, after seeing Callias, and many other men as well, my mind can generalize to the universal concept, *man*; and likewise, presumably, I can generalize facts about particular men to the universal (perhaps essential) truths about all men. While Aristotle's discussion here is brief, it serves as a model for later critics of innate ideas: in order to explain how our minds can possess general concepts and truths, such a critic will argue for a mental faculty capable of generalizing from particular experiences.

While René Descartes (1596–1650) acknowledges that a child learns, for example, geometry by starting with specific examples, he follows Plato in denying that this proves the child somehow built up the general laws of geometry from experience of specific cases. On the contrary, Descartes argues that since the senses supply only particular, imperfect examples, these would never be adequate to yield the perfect figures and general laws of mathematics. In the same way, assuming that stimulation of the sense organs amounts ultimately to minute motions (vibrations caused by the impact of physical stimuli), he argues that motion is so unlike the sensory ideas we possess—pains, colors, sounds—that these cannot be "copied" from the sense organs; and ideas of nonphysical objects (such as the ideas of God, and the soul) likewise cannot in turn be built up from sensory ideas. Descartes concludes that these ideas (and knowledge, such as mathematical truths) must be innate in our minds. He adds, however, that calling them "innate" only means that our intellect (our "faculty of thought") has the *potential* to think such ideas on the right occasion—not that the ideas exist preformed in our minds, or that anyone was actually thinking of God or geometry in the womb.

John Locke (1632–1704) provides a classical empiricist criticism of innate ideas and knowledge, arguing that innateness of certain truths requires, at a minimum, *universal agreement* about them; and that even if such agreement were found, it would still not prove such knowledge is innate, so long as an alternative explanation of its origins is possible. As a matter of fact, he argues, even the most minimal truths of logic or metaphysics that are claimed to be innate—such as that "Nothing can both exist and not exist"—are not agreed to by the very young, or the mentally impaired; and he rejects the defense that such truths might be in the mind without an individual realizing it, objecting that it is incoherent to claim something can be in the mind without our ever being aware of it. Noting that the innatist often claims that such truths are evident once we reach the "age of reason," Locke offers an alternative explanation of this fact: the child learns certain truths as part of learning the meaning of the terms in her language. While the mind begins as an empty container, the child learns about particular objects, and their names, from sensory experience; and then, through the mental power of "abstraction," the child builds general concepts from these particular experiences, and (again) the appropriate words for these concepts. Since a fairly minimal mental endowment—involving only sensation, memory, and abstraction—is taken to account for the facts, Locke concludes that there is no evidence supporting the more extravagant mental architecture of the innatists.

Gottfried Wilhelm Leibniz (1646–1716) responds to some of Locke's points, suggesting that the disagreement between innatists such as Plato and Descartes, and critics such as Aristotle and Locke, is not as large as it might seem. Like Descartes, Leibniz points to the human grasp of mathematics, and other "necessary truths," as knowledge incapable of being acquired from sensory information alone. And like Descartes, he argues that calling such knowledge "innate" implies only that it is contained within the mind potentially, as a tendency or disposition that develops in the right circumstances. Against Locke's claim that we are aware of anything in our minds, Leibniz points to counterexamples of potential knowledge that is not always accessible to consciousness. For instance, memory and habits sometimes fail us, only to reemerge later when we're thinking of something else—thus illustrating that they were in our minds even when we had no conscious access to them.

The work of Johann Gaspar Spurzheim (1776–1832) marks an interesting development in the debate over innatism, helping to set the stage for the contemporary discussion. Spurzheim was cofounder (with Franz Gall) of *phrenology*, an early nineteenth-century theory of mental faculties (also discussed by Comte, in chapter 7). Central to this theory were the twin views that the mind possesses distinct faculties applying to specific domains, and that each of these faculties is realized in a distinct brain structure—making the brain a collection of such mental "organs." Unlike traditional, generic faculties such as intellect and memory, the faculties in Spurzheim's speculative list include, for example, those for love of one's children, religious awe, self-esteem, and causal connections. He notes that we believe in different sensory faculties (with distinct physical organs) because we find that each can be impaired independently of how the others function (what, in chapter 73, Smith calls "double dissociation"). So, likewise, the fact that individuals excel in specific areas; that mental illness can impair some abilities while leaving others intact; and that different abilities develop at different ages, all argue against a homogeneous brain structure and in favor of distinct mental organs. Spurzheim is willing to agree with Locke that *specific ideas* are not innate. But because the structure of the human mind has remained the same across cultures, and over thousands of years, and individuals develop specific talents even when external conditions work against them, he insists that these mental faculties are innate.

Jerry Fodor continues the classical philosophical case for innate ideas, arguing for a strong, and entirely general, innatism of concepts. Fodor holds that in order to learn the meaning of a term in a natural language like English, one must state a rule for its meaning—this rule itself being formulated in a "language of thought." But since this language of thought is capable of stating the meaning rule of any term we can learn, this suggests that the language of thought must already have built into it the conceptual resources to express all such meaning.

Much of the current debate over innate ideas and knowledge focuses not so much on general arguments over the need for innate knowledge, as on specific case studies in the cognitive sciences suggesting that the mind has innate parts, or "faculties," devoted to a particular subject matter—one particularly well-known example (though certainly not the only one) being the linguistic theory of Noam Chomsky and his associates. The innateness debate then becomes a discussion of whether there are such innate mental organs, or "modules."

Jean Piaget (1896–1980) thinks there is a middle ground between the bare empiricism of someone like Locke, and a view advocating powerful innate mental structures. Piaget rejects the claim that ideas are innate, but he also denies that that ideas and knowledge come from pure "unprocessed" perception. He holds instead that our minds always organize experience by fitting it into conceptual structures; but, Piaget claims, rather than possessing these structures from birth, the child develops them in the course of performing increasingly sophisticated *actions*. Beginning with general intelligence, and interacting with the world in the normal way, the child goes through a series of progressively more complex and sophisticated conceptual structures, or "schemata." Arguing against Chomsky's views on language, Piaget suggests that an innate language organ would be "inexplicable" from the perspective of evolutionary biology, and that language acquisition can be accounted for on the basis of general intelligence alone.

Noam Chomsky responds to Piaget's remarks on the plausibility of an innate linguistic capacities. To the claim of biological inexplicability, Chomsky argues that the development of a language organ is no more problematic than the development of the mammalian eye or the cerebral cortex. On the question of whether general intelligence would suffice for language acquisition, Chomsky describes a rule of English syntax and argues that it is not the rule that a general learning mechanism would select. He concludes that beings who can learn English do not rely solely on general learning mechanisms.

Hilary Putnam argues against Chomsky, suggesting that general intelligence is enough to account for acquisition of the rule Chomsky has in mind if the learner has semantic knowledge—that is, if the learner understands that the string is being used to communicate something about an object, and knows which part of the string is being used to refer to the object. Putnam also takes issue with Chomsky on the question of the plausibility of a language organ, suggesting that the development of the mammalian eye appears to be much more gradual than Chomsky claims. Putnam agrees with Piaget that a language organ would be anomalous from the perspective of evolutionary theory.

In a further discussion, Chomsky considers how our theorizing about other biological endowments can shed light on what is the most reasonable hypothesis about language. In cases of bodily development such as an embryo growing arms and legs, or a person going through puberty, no one finds it unusual to suppose that this is a biological program unfolding in a manner predetermined by genetic coding. And while environmental input can certainly affect how this biological program is enacted—proper nutrition, for example, is needed for normal development of the embryo, and onset of puberty at a normal age—we are not tempted to claim that, for example, puberty is a learned response to environmental input. Chomsky argues that this is because such input is obviously too minimal, and too different among individuals, to account for the uniform result. For the same reason, he claims, mental endowments such as language should not be forced into a model of learned skills, on analogy with a pigeon trained through behavioral conditioning, but rather should be understood as genetically encoded. Just as it is uncontroversial that we have different biological organs (heart, stomach, eyes, etc.), since these serve different functions and operate in significantly different ways, Chomsky argues it is sensible to conclude that our different cognitive capacities (e.g., for language, or vision) are served by different specialized *mental organs*, or *modules*.

Chomsky also offers some useful observations about the link between the older question of *innatism*, and the newer focus on *modularity*. He stresses that innate knowledge is not the same as modularity of mind, since a homogeneous, nonmodular mind could still have innate knowledge. But he adds that supporters of one tend to support the other as well—so that contemporary researchers tend to argue *for* both modularity and innatism, or *against* both.

In a very influential work, Jerry Fodor presents his theory of mental modules. According to Fodor, the philosophical discussion of innatism, from Plato to Chomsky, has focused on whether we have innate *bodies of knowledge* concerning a *specific domain*—say, knowledge of mathematics or language. At the same time, tradition also recognizes mental faculties, or "mechanisms," such as memory or imagination, that are characterized by the way they operate (memory stores and recovers mental representations) and *not* by their subject matter (memory stores information about mathematics, music, and God equally). But Fodor proposes a kind of overlap of these two mental structures: while traditional mental mechanisms, such as memory, are what he calls "horizontal faculties" (because they stretch out "horizontally" across many different areas of information), he argues that we also have "vertical faculties," or *modules*, which are mental mechanisms devoted to specific domains of knowledge. Moreover, he holds that such modules will be what he terms "input systems"—faculties such as linguistic or visual processors that act as "middle-men" between sense organs (or "transducers") and the "central processes" of conscious thought and reasoning.

Fodor offers a list of nine features that, taken together, provide something like a definition of modular "input systems." (1) They are domain specific (applying to a specific subject, such as grammar or visual shape). (2) Their operation is mandatory (since we cannot help but hear a sentence of our native language as a sentence, or see the visual scene before us). (3) The "central processes" of conscious mental states have access only to the final output of such systems (not to the intermediate computational steps they use). (4) Such input systems are unusually fast. (5) They are "informationally encapsulated," appealing only to their specific sensory input, not to general knowledge (so that classic visual illusions, for instance, cannot be corrected by our knowledge that the image is illusory). (6) The outputs of these systems are "shallow," not revealing the intermediate computational steps involved in reaching this final product. (7) Input systems are associated with fixed, specific neural structures. (8) They exhibit specific and characteristic types of breakdown, such as aphasia of linguistic comprehension and production. (9) Their development exhibits a characteristic schedule—language, for instance, following a definite schedule of normal acquisition. While Fodor allows that modularity is not an all-or-nothing affair, and that not all of these features are equally important—he believes that informational encapsulation is the central feature of modularity—his list of features, and the notion of modularity it constitutes, has been the focus of considerable debate and controversy in the literature that follows.

William Marslen-Wilson and Lorraine K. Tyler examine the "input system" for language that Fodor includes in his list of modules, arguing that experimental evidence shows how computation of sentence grammar includes pragmatic factors (using contextual background knowledge) and information on discourse structure (information on the normal structure of conversation). Since, on Fodor's view, pragmatics and discourse analysis study objects of "central processing," outside the domain of his language module, Marslen-Wilson and Tyler conclude that language processing is not "informationally encapsulated" from such central resources in the way Fodor assumes.

Moreover, since linguistic processing is extremely fast even when appealing to background knowledge, they argue that fast processing is no evidence for Fodor's grammar module. Ultimately, the authors suggest that Fodor's language input system is an attempt to give a psychological role to the sort of grammatical theory developed by Chomskyan linguists; and with the elimination of a separate module devoted just to computing grammatical structure, the separate level of grammatical representation such linguists have argued for should likewise be swept away.

Daniel Sperber returns to evolutionary considerations to argue, against Fodor, that even the "central processes" of conceptual reasoning are modular. While we can understand how Fodor's peripheral "input systems" might evolve, Sperber thinks it would be an evolutionary mystery how humans developed the holistic, unconstrained reasoning powers that Fodor claims for the central processes. Instead, Sperber argues for conceptual modules applying to specific domains (for example, physical objects, living creatures, human psychology), and of various sizes—possibly even "micromodules" the size of a single concept. In particular, as part of a module for understanding other peoples' minds, humans would have the power to represent *representations*—enabling us to think about representations in others' minds, but also about our own concepts. With such a "meta-representational" module, he argues, we can make sense, within an evolutionary framework, of the human ability to reason about abstract domains (such as theoretical physics) that offer no initial evolutionary advantage. On this picture, the mind would be a patchwork of different conceptual modules whose interaction would no doubt be complex, but which would still not defy theoretical explanation in the way Fodor's unconstrained central processes do. In addition, Sperber notes, conceptual modules would provide an explanation for the development and variation of human *cultures*: concepts that either fit a conceptual module well, or flatly contradict it, would stand out, and so stand a greater chance of spreading throughout a society.

Neil Smith considers in more detail how Chomsky's case for a special, innate language faculty relates to Fodor's theory of modules, arguing that Chomsky's language faculty is at least a close relative of Fodorian modules. As evidence that things are genuinely distinct, Smith cites *dissociation*—where one thing can appear or occur without the other. If each can appear without the other, we have a case of *double dissociation*. As applied to the debate over innate faculties—specifically, whether the mind has a specialized language faculty, distinct from general intelligence—he considers evidence that each ability can occur without the other. While it is generally accepted that intelligence can exist in the absence of linguistic capacities—for example, in stroke patients—it is more controversial whether the reverse is also the case. Smith holds that a striking illustration of this is found in *savants*—individuals remarkably skilled in one area (e.g., music or mathematics), but with severely impaired skills almost everywhere else. Smith focuses on a linguistic savant named Christopher, who has (varying degrees of) fluency in a wide number of languages, while exhibiting an IQ only in the mid-50s. On the basis of this sort of evidence, Smith argues that language is a "*quasi-module*": a fast, domain-specific mechanism, but (unlike Fodor's modules) applying to conceptual (rather than perceptual) tasks, and allowing some use of information from other areas. In fact, Smith claims, evidence from more specific linguistic impairments (with one patient excelling at words and word-formation rules but exhibiting limited grammar, and other patients exhibiting the reverse) suggests that the language faculty contains several smaller "quasi-modules" as parts. In closing, Smith presents some critical observations on other approaches to modularity—including Sperber's theory (chapter 72) and connectionist approaches (examined in part V).

Further Readings

A selection of historical and philosophical works are included in Stephen Stich, ed., *Innate Ideas* (Berkeley: University California Press, 1975).

M. Piatelli-Palmerini, ed., *The Debate between Noam Chomsky and Jean Piaget* (Cambridge, Mass.: Harvard University Press, 1980) includes essays by many important writers on the question of Chomskyan linguistics and innatism.

Jay L. Garfield, ed., *Modularity in Knowledge Representation and Natural-Language Understanding* (Cambridge, Mass.: MIT Press, 1987) offers essays for and against Fodor's concept of modularity, drawing on evidence from language and vision.

Lawrence Hirshfield and Susan Gelman, eds., *Domain Specificity in Cognition and Culture* (New York: Cambridge University Press, 1994) provides recent perspectives, from a variety of human sciences, on specialized mental faculties and innateness.

Annette Karmiloff-Smith, *Beyond Modularity: A Developmental Perspective on Cognitive Science* (Cambridge, Mass.: MIT Press, 1992), proposes an alternative to Fodor's view, in which the distinction between modules and central processes is weakened, and modules are not innate but develop over time.

Steven Pinker, *The Language Instinct* (New York: Harper Collins, 1994) presents a readable survey of topics related to language, including innateness, modularity, and their relation to biology and evolutionary theory, arguing for a largely Chomskyan position.

59 From *The Meno*

Plato

Meno. And how will you enquire, Socrates, into that which you do not know? What will you put forth as the subject of enquiry? And if you find what you want, how will you ever know that this is the thing which you did not know?

Socrates. I know, Meno, what you mean; but just see what a tiresome dispute you are introducing. You argue that a man cannot enquire either about that which he knows, or about that which he does not know; for if he knows, he has no need to enquire; and if not, he cannot; for he does not know the very subject about which he is to enquire.

Men. Well, Socrates, and is not the argument sound?

Soc. I think not.

Men. Why not?

Soc. I will tell you why: I have heard from certain wise men and women who spoke of things divine that—

Men. What did they say?

Soc. They spoke of a glorious truth, as I conceive.

Men. What was it? and who were they?

Soc. Some of them were priests and priestesses, who had studied how they might be able to give a reason of their profession: there have been poets also, who spoke of these things by inspiration, like Pindar, and many others who were inspired. And they say—mark, now, and see whether their words are true—they say that the soul of man is immortal, and at one time has an end, which is termed dying, and at another time is born again, but is never destroyed. And the moral is, that a man ought to live always in perfect holiness. "*For in the ninth year Persephone sends the souls of those from whom she has received the penalty of ancient crime back again from beneath into the light of the sun above, and these are they who become noble kings and mighty men and great in wisdom and are called saintly heroes in after ages.*" The soul, then, as being immortal, and having been born again many times, and having seen all things that exist, whether in this world or in the world below, has knowledge of them all; and it is no wonder that she should be able to call to remembrance all that she ever knew about virtue, and about everything; for as all nature is akin, and the soul has learned all things, there is no difficulty in her eliciting or as men say learning, out of a single recollection all the rest, if a man is strenuous and does not faint; for all enquiry and all learning is but recollection. And therefore we ought not to listen to this sophistical argument about the impossibility of enquiry: for it will make us idle and is sweet only to the sluggard; but the other saying will make us active and inquisitive. In that confiding, I will gladly enquire with you into the nature of virtue.

Men. Yes, Socrates; but what do you mean by saying that we do not learn, and that what we call learning is only a process of recollection? Can you teach me how this is?

Soc. I told you, Meno, just now that you were a rogue, and now you ask whether I can teach you, when I am saying that there is no teaching, but only recollection; and thus you imagine that you will involve me in a contradiction.

Men. Indeed, Socrates, I protest that I had no such intention. I only asked the question from habit; but if you can prove to me that what you say is true, I wish that you would.

Soc. It will be no easy matter, but I will try to please you to the utmost of my power. Suppose that you call one of your numerous attendants, that I may demonstrate on him.

Men. Certainly. Come hither, boy.

Soc. He is Greek, and speaks Greek, does he not?

Men. Yes, indeed; he was born in the house.

Soc. Attend now to the questions which I ask him, and observe whether he learns of me or only remembers.

Men. I will.

Soc. Tell me, boy, do you know that a figure like this is a square?

Boy. I do.

Soc. And you know that a square figure has these four lines equal?

Boy. Certainly.

Soc. And these lines which I have drawn through the middle of the square are also equal?

Boy. Yes.

Soc. A square may be of any size?

Boy. Certainly.

Soc. And if one side of the figure be of two feet, and the other side be of two feet, how much will the whole be? Let me explain: if in one direction the space was of two feet, and in the other direction of one foot, the whole would be of two feet taken once?

Boy. Yes.

Soc. But since this side is also of two feet, there are twice two feet?

Boy. There are.

Soc. Then the square is of twice two feet?

Boy. Yes.

Soc. And how many are twice two feet? count and tell me.

Boy. Four, Socrates.

Soc. And might there not be another square twice as large as this, and having like this the lines equal?

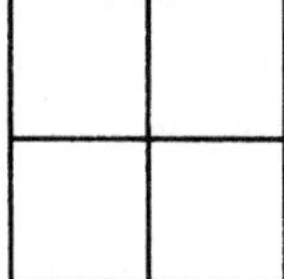

Figure 59.1

Boy. Yes.

Soc. And of how many feet will that be?

Boy. Of eight feet.

Soc. And now try and tell me the length of the line which forms the side of that double square: this is two feet—what will that be?

Boy. Clearly, Socrates, it will be double.

Soc. Do you observe, Meno, that I am not teaching the boy anything, but only asking him questions; and now he fancies that he knows how long a line is necessary in order to produce a figure of eight square feet; does he not?

Men. Yes.

Soc. And does he really know?

Men. Certainly not.

Soc. He only guesses that because the square is double, the line is double.

Men. True.

Soc. Observe him while he recalls the steps in regular order. (*To the Boy.*) Tell me, boy, do you assert that a double space comes from a double line? Remember that I am not speaking of an oblong, but of a figure equal every way, and twice the size of this—that is to say of eight feet; and I want to know whether you still say that a double square comes from a double line?

Boy. Yes.

Soc. But does not this line become doubled if we add another such line here?

Boy. Certainly.

Soc. And four such lines will make a space containing eight feet?

Boy. Yes.

Soc. Let us describe such a figure: Would you not say that this is the figure of eight feet?

Boy. Yes.

Soc. And are there not these four divisions in the figure, each of which is equal to the figure of four feet?

Boy. True.

Soc. And is not that four times four?

Boy. Certainly.

Soc. And four times is not double?

Boy. No, indeed.

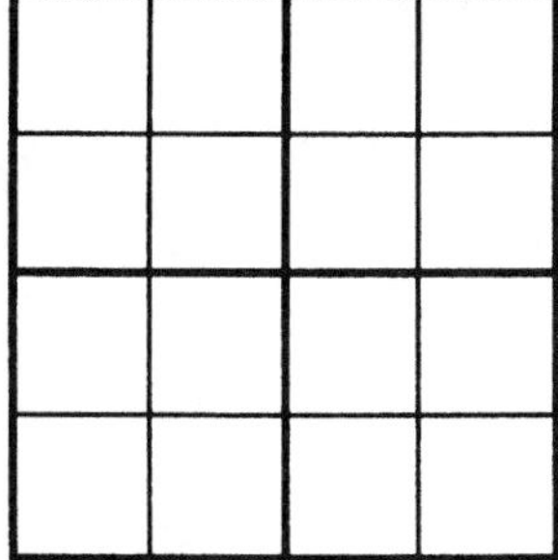

Figure 59.2

Soc. But how much?

Boy. Four times as much.

Soc. Therefore the double line, boy, has given a space, not twice, but four times as much.

Boy. True.

Soc. Four times four are sixteen—are they not?

Boy. Yes.

Soc. What line would give you a space of eight feet, as this gives one of sixteen feet;—do you see?

Boy. Yes.

Soc. And the space of four feet is made from this half line?

Boy. Yes.

Soc. Good; and is not a space of eight feet twice the size of this, and half the size of the other?

Boy. Certainly.

Soc. Such a space, then, will be made out of a line greater than this one, and less than that one?

Boy. Yes; I think so.

Soc. Very good; I like to hear you say what you think. And now tell me, is not this a line of two feet and that of four?

Boy. Yes.

Soc. Then the line which forms the side of eight feet ought to be more than this line of two feet, and less than the other of four feet?

Boy. It ought.

Soc. Try and see if you can tell me how much it will be.

Boy. Three feet.

Soc. Then if we add a half to this line of two, that will be the line of three. Here are two and there is one; and on the other side, here are two also and there is one: and that makes the figure of which you speak?

Boy. Yes.

Soc. But if there are three feet this way and three feet that way, the whole space will be three times three feet?

Boy. That is evident.

Soc. And how much are three times three feet?

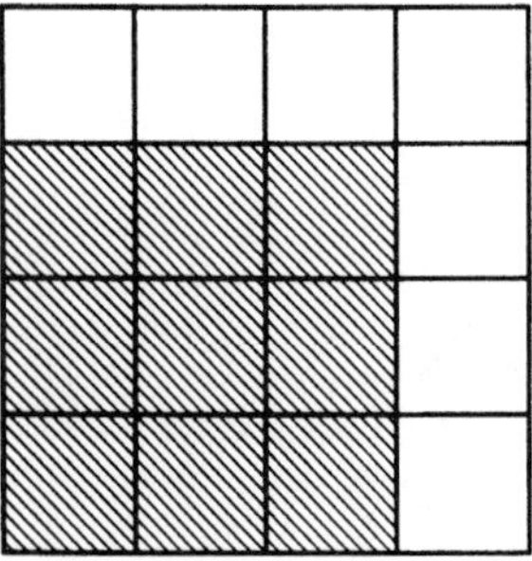

Figure 59.3

Boy. Nine.

Soc. And how much is the double of four?

Boy. Eight.

Soc. Then the figure of eight is not made out of a line of three?

Boy. No.

Soc. But from what line?—tell me exactly; and if you would rather not reckon, try and show me the line.

Boy. Indeed, Socrates, I do not know.

Soc. Do you see, Meno, what advances he has made in his power of recollection? He did not know at first, and he does not know now, what is the side of a figure of eight feet: but then he thought that he knew, and answered confidently as if he knew, and had no difficulty; now he has a difficulty, and neither knows nor fancies that he knows.

Men. True.

Soc. Is he not better off in knowing his ignorance?

Men. I think that he is.

Soc. If we have made him doubt, and given him the "torpedo's shock," have we done him any harm?

Men. I think not.

Soc. We have certainly, as would seem, assisted him in some degree to the discovery of the truth; and now he will wish to remedy his ignorance, but then he would have been ready to tell all the world again and again that the double space should have a double side.

Men. True.

Soc. But do you suppose that he would ever have enquired into or learned what he fancied that he knew, though he was really ignorant of it, until he had fallen into perplexity under the idea that he did not know, and had desired to know?

Men. I think not, Socrates.

Soc. Then he was the better for the torpedo's touch?

Men. I think so.

Soc. Mark now the farther development. I shall only ask him, and not teach him, and he shall share the enquiry with me: and do you watch and see if you find me telling or explaining anything to him, instead of eliciting his opinion. Tell me, boy, is not this a square of four feet which I have drawn?

Boy. Yes.

Soc. And now I add another square equal to the former one?

Boy. Yes.

Soc. And a third, which is equal to either of them?

Boy. Yes.

Soc. Suppose that we fill up the vacant corner?

Boy. Very good.

Soc. Here, then, there are four equal spaces?

Boy. Yes.

Soc. And how many times larger is this space than this other?

Boy. Four times.

Soc. But it ought to have been twice only, as you will remember.

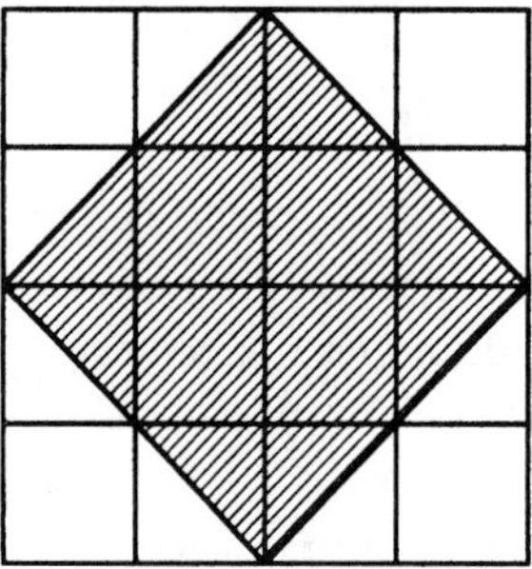

Figure 59.4

Boy. True.

Soc. And does not this line, reaching from corner to corner, bisect each of these spaces?

Boy. Yes.

Soc. And are there not here four equal lines which contain this space?

Boy. There are.

Soc. Look and see how much this space is.

Boy. I do not understand.

Soc. Has not each interior line cut off half of the four spaces?

Boy. Yes.

Soc. And how many spaces are there in this section?

Boy. Four.

Soc. And how many in this?

Boy. Two.

Soc. And four is how many times two?

Boy. Twice.

Soc. And this space is of how many feet?

Boy. Of eight feet.

Soc. And from what line do you get this figure?

Boy. From this.

Soc. That is, from the line which extends from corner to corner of the figure of four feet?

Boy. Yes.

Soc. And that is the line which the learned call the diagonal. And if this is the proper name, then you, Meno's slave, are prepared to affirm that the double space is the square of the diagonal?

Boy. Certainly, Socrates.

Soc. What do you say of him, Meno? Were not all these answers given out of his own head?

Men. Yes, they were all his own.

Soc. And yet, as we were just now saying, he did not know?

Men. True.

Soc. But still he had in him those notions of his—had he not?

Men. Yes.

Soc. Then he who does not know may still have true notions of that which he does not know?

Men. He has.

Soc. And at present these notions have just been stirred up in him, as in a dream; but if he were frequently asked the same questions, in different forms, he would know as well as any one at last?

Men. I dare say.

Soc. Without any one teaching him he will recover his knowledge for himself, if he is only asked questions?

Men. Yes.

Soc. And this spontaneous recovery of knowledge in him is recollection?

Men. True.

Soc. And this knowledge which he now has must he not either have acquired or always possessed?

Men. Yes.

Soc. But if he always possessed this knowledge he would always have known; or if he has acquired the knowledge he could not have acquired it in this life, unless he has been taught geometry; for he may be made to do the same with all geometry and every other branch of knowledge. Now, has any one ever taught him all this? You must know about him, if, as you say, he was born and bred in your house.

Men. And I am certain that no one ever did teach him.

Soc. And yet he has the knowledge?

Men. The fact, Socrates, is undeniable.

Soc. But if he did not acquire the knowledge in this life, then he must have had and learned it at some other time?

Men. Clearly he must.

Soc. Which must have been the time when he was not a man?

Men. Yes.

Soc. And if there have been always true thoughts in him, both at the time when he was and was not a man, which only need to be awakened into knowledge by putting questions to him, his soul must have always possessed this knowledge, for he always either was or was not a man?

Men. Obviously.

60 From *Posterior Analytics*, Book II, Chapter 19

Aristotle

... As regards syllogism and demonstration, the definition of, and the conditions required to produce each of them, are now clear, and with that also the definition of, and the conditions required to produce, demonstrative knowledge, since it is the same as demonstration. As to the basic premisses, how they become known and what is the developed state of knowledge of them is made clear by raising some preliminary problems.

We have already said that scientific knowledge through demonstration is impossible unless a man knows the primary immediate premisses. But there are questions which might be raised in respect of the apprehension of these immediate premisses: one might not only ask whether it is of the same kind as the apprehension of the conclusions, but also whether there is or is not scientific knowledge of both; or scientific knowledge of the latter, and of the former a different kind of knowledge; and, further, whether the developed states of knowledge are not innate but come to be in us, or are innate but at first unnoticed. Now it is strange if we possess them from birth; for it means that we possess apprehensions more accurate than demonstration and fail to notice them. If on the other hand we acquire them and do not previously possess them, how could we apprehend and learn without a basis of preexistent knowledge? For that is impossible, as we used to find, in the case of demonstration. So it emerges that neither can we possess them from birth, nor can they come to be in us if we are without knowledge of them to the extent of having no such developed state at all. Therefore we must possess a capacity of some sort, but not such as to rank higher in accuracy than these developed states. And this at least is an obvious characteristic of all animals, for they possess a congenital discriminative capacity which is called sense-perception. But though sense-perception is innate in all animals, in some the sense-impression comes to persist, in others it does not. So animals in which this persistence does not come to be have either no knowledge at all outside the act of perceiving, or no knowledge of objects of which no impression persists; animals in which it does come into being have perception and can continue to retain the sense-impression in the soul: and when such persistence is frequently repeated a further distinction at once arises between those which out of the persistence of such sense-impressions develop a power of systematizing them and those which do not. So out of sense-perception comes to be what we call memory, and out of frequently repeated memories of the same thing develops experience; for a number of memories constitute a single experience. From experience again—i.e. from the universal now stabilized in its entirety within the soul, the one beside the many which is a single identity within them all—originate the skill of the craftsman and the knowledge of the man of science, skill in the sphere of coming to be and science in the sphere of being.

We conclude that these states of knowledge are neither innate in a determinate form, nor developed from other higher states of knowledge, but from sense-perception. It is like a rout in battle stopped by first one man making a stand and then another, until the original formation has been restored. The soul is so constituted as to be capable of this process.

Let us now restate the account given already, though with insufficient clearness. When one of a number of logically indiscriminable particulars has made a stand, the earliest universal is present in the soul: for though the act of sense-perception is of the particular, its content is universal—is man, for example, not the man Callias. A fresh stand is made among these rudimentary universals, and the process does not cease until the indivisible concepts, the true universals, are established: e.g. such and such a species of animal is a step towards the genus animal, which by the same process is a step towards a further generalization.

Thus it is clear that we must get to know the primary premisses by induction; for the method by which even sense-perception implants the universal is inductive. Now of the thinking states by which we grasp truth, some are unfailingly true, others admit of error—opinion, for instance, and calculation, whereas scientific knowing and intuition are always true: further, no other kind of thought except intuition is more accurate than scientific knowledge, whereas primary premisses are more knowable than demonstrations, and all scientific knowledge is discursive. From these considerations it follows that there will be no scientific knowledge of the primary premisses, and since except intuition nothing can be truer than scientific knowledge, it will be intuition that apprehends the primary premisses—a result which also follows from the fact that demonstration cannot be the originative source of demonstration, nor, consequently, scientific knowledge of scientific knowledge. If, therefore, it is the only other kind of true thinking except scientific knowing, intuition will be the originative source of scientific knowledge. And the originative source of science grasps the original basic premiss, while science as a whole is similarly related as originative source to the whole body of fact.

61 From *Replies to Objections* V and "Notes Directed against a Certain Program"

René Descartes

... But the greater error here is our critic's assumption that the knowledge of particular truths is always deduced from universal propositions in consonance with the order of the sequence observed in the syllogism of dialectic. This shows that he is but little acquainted with the method by which truth should be investigated. For it is certain that in order to discover the truth we should always start with particular notions, in order to arrive at general conceptions subsequently, though we may also in the reverse way, after having discovered the universals, deduce other particulars from them. Thus in teaching a child the elements of geometry we shall certainly not make him understand the general truth that "*when equals are taken from equals the remainders are equal,*" or that "*the whole is greater than its parts,*" unless by showing him examples in particular cases....

Meanwhile, moreover, I do not admit *that the ideas of these figures have at any time entered our minds through the senses,* as is the common persuasion. For though, doubtless, figures such as the Geometers consider can exist in reality, I deny that any can be presented to us except such minute ones that they fail altogether to affect our senses. For, let us suppose that these figures consist as far as possible of straight lines; yet it will be quite impossible for any really straight part of the line to affect our senses, because when we examine with a magnifying glass those lines that appear to us to be most straight, we find them to be irregular and bending everywhere in an undulating manner. Hence when first in infancy we see a triangular figure depicted on paper, this figure cannot show us how a real triangle ought to be conceived, in the way in which geometricians consider it, because the true triangle is contained in this figure, just as the statue of Mercury is contained in a rough block of wood. But because we already possess within us the idea of a true triangle, and it can be more easily conceived by our mind than the more complex figure of the triangle drawn on paper, we, therefore, when we see that composite figure, apprehend not it itself, but rather the authentic triangle. This is exactly the same as when we look at a piece of paper on which little strokes have been drawn with ink to represent a man's face; for the idea produced in us in this way is not so much that of the lines of the sketch as of the man. But this could not have happened unless the human face had been known to us by other means, and we had been more accustomed to think of it than of those minute lines, which indeed we often fail to distinguish from each other when they are moved to a slightly greater distance away from us. So certainly we should not be able to recognize the Geometrical triangle by looking at that which is drawn on paper, unless our mind possessed an idea of it derived from other sources....

In article twelve he appears to dissent from me only in words, for when he says that *the mind has no need of innate ideas, or notions, or axioms*, and at the same time allows it the faculty of thinking (to be considered natural or innate), he makes an affirmation in effect identical with mine, but denies it in words. For I never wrote or concluded that the mind required innate ideas which were in some sort different from its faculty of thinking; but when I observed the existence in me of certain thoughts which proceeded, not from extraneous objects nor from the determination of my will, but solely from the faculty of thinking which is within me, then, that I might distinguish the ideas or notions (which are the forms of these thoughts) from other thoughts *adventitious* or *factitious*, I termed the former *"innate."* In the same sense we say that in some families generosity is innate, in others certain diseases like gout or gravel, not that on this account the babes of these families suffer from these diseases in their mother's womb, but because they are born with a certain disposition or propensity for contracting them.

The conclusion which he deduces in *article* XIII from the preceding article is indeed wonderful. *"For this reason,"* he says (i.e. because the mind has no need of innate ideas, but the faculty of thinking of itself is sufficient), *"all common notions, engraven on the mind, owe their origin to the observation of things or to tradition"*—as though the faculty of thinking could of itself execute nothing, nor perceive nor think anything save what it received from observation or tradition, that is, from the senses. So far is this from being true, that, on the contrary, any man who rightly observes the limitations of the senses, and what precisely it is that can penetrate through this medium to our faculty of thinking must needs admit that no ideas of things, in the shape in which we envisage them by thought, are presented to us by the senses. So much so that in our ideas there is nothing which was not innate in the mind, or faculty of thinking, except only these circumstances which point to experience—the fact, for instance, that we judge that this or that idea, which we now have present to our thought, is to be referred to a certain extraneous thing, not that these extraneous things transmitted the ideas themselves to our minds through the organs of sense, but because they transmitted something which gave the mind occasion to form these ideas, by means of an innate faculty, at this time rather than at another. For nothing reaches our mind from external objects through the organs of sense beyond certain corporeal movements, as *our author* himself affirms, in *article* XIX, taking the doctrine from my *Principles*; but even these movements, and the figures which arise from them, are not conceived by us in the shape they assume in the organs of sense, as I have explained at great length in my *Dioptrics*. Hence it follows that the ideas of the movements and figures are themselves innate in us. So much the more must the ideas of pain, colour, sound and the like be innate, that our mind may, on occasion of certain corporeal movements, envisage these ideas, for they have no likeness to the corporeal movements. Could anything be imagined more preposterous than that all common notions which are inherent in our mind should arise from these movements, and should be incapable of existing without them? I should like *our friend* to instruct me as to what corporeal movement it is which can form in our mind any common notion, e.g. the notion that *"things which are equal to the same thing are equal to one another,"* or any other he pleases; for all these movements are particular, but notions are universal having no affinity with movements and no relation to them....

... And surely it is manifest to every man that sight, of itself and by its proper function, presents nothing beyond pictures, and hearing nothing beyond voices or sounds, so that all these things that we think of, beyond these voices or pictures, as being symbolised by them, are presented to us by means of ideas which come from no other source than our faculty of thinking, and are accordingly together with that faculty innate in us, that is, always existing in us potentially; for existence in any faculty is not actual but merely potential existence, since the very word "faculty" designates nothing more or less than a potentiality. But that with regard to God we can comprehend nothing beyond a name or a bodily effigy, no one can affirm, save a man who openly professes himself an atheist, and moreover destitute of all intellect....

... Thereafter he enumerates, among the species of perception, nothing but *sense*, *memory*, and *imagination*; from which one may gather that he admits no *pure intellection* (i.e. intellection which deals with no corporeal images), and, accordingly, that he himself believes that no cognition is possessed of God, or of the human mind, or of other immaterial things. Of this I can imagine but one cause, namely, that the thoughts he has concerning these things are so confused that he never observes in himself a pure thought, different from every corporeal image....

... By innate ideas I never understood anything other than that which he himself, on page 6 of his second pamphlet, affirms in so many words to be true, viz. that "*there is innate in us by nature a potentiality whereby we know God*"; but that these ideas are *actual*, or that they are some kind of species different from the faculty of thought I never wrote nor concluded. On the contrary, I, more than any other man, am utterly averse to that empty stock of scholastic entities—so much so, that I cannot refrain from laughter when I see that mighty heap which our hero—a very inoffensive fellow no doubt—has laboriously brought together to prove that *infants have no notion of God so long as they are in their mother's womb*—as though in this fashion he was bringing a magnificent charge against me....

62 From *An Essay Concerning Human Understanding*

John Locke

It is an established opinion amongst some men, that there are in the understanding certain *innate principles*; some primary notions, *κοιναὶ ἔννοιαι*, characters, as it were stamped upon the mind of man; which the soul receives in its very first being, and brings into the world with it. It would be sufficient to convince unprejudiced readers of the falseness of this supposition, if I should only show (as I hope I shall in the following parts of this Discourse) how men, barely by the use of their natural faculties, may attain to all the knowledge they have, without the help of any innate impressions; and may arrive at certainty, without any such original notions or principles. For I imagine any one will easily grant that it would be impertinent to suppose the ideas of colours innate in a creature to whom God hath given sight, and a power to receive them by the eyes from external objects: and no less unreasonable would it be to attribute several truths to the impressions of nature, and innate characters, when we may observe in ourselves faculties fit to attain as easy and certain knowledge of them as if they were originally imprinted on the mind.

But because a man is not permitted without censure to follow his own thoughts in the search of truth, when they lead him ever so little out of the common road, I shall set down the reasons that made me doubt of the truth of that opinion, as an excuse for my mistake, if I be in one; which I leave to be considered by those who, with me, dispose themselves to embrace truth wherever they find it.

There is nothing more commonly taken for granted than that there are certain *principles*, both *speculative* and *practical*, (for they speak of both), universally agreed upon by all mankind: which therefore, they argue, must needs be the constant impressions which the souls of men receive in their first beings, and which they bring into the world with them, as necessarily and really as they do any of their inherent faculties.

This argument, drawn from universal consent, has this misfortune in it, that if it were true in matter of fact, that there were certain truths wherein all mankind agreed, it would not prove them innate, if there can be any other way shown how men may come to that universal agreement, in the things they do consent in, which I presume may be done.

But, which is worse, this argument of universal consent, which is made use of to prove innate principles, seems to me a demonstration that there are none such: because there are none to which all mankind give an universal assent. I shall begin with the speculative, and instance in those magnified principles of demonstration, "Whatsoever is, is," and "It is impossible for the same thing to be and not to be"; which, of all others, I think have the most allowed title to innate. These have so settled a reputation of maxims universally received, that it will no doubt be thought strange if any one should seem to question it. But yet I take liberty to say, that these propositions are so far from having an universal assent, that there are a great part of mankind to whom they are not so much as known.

For, first, it is evident, that all children and idiots have not the least apprehension or thought of them. And the want of that is enough to destroy that universal assent which must needs be the necessary concomitant of all innate truths: it seeming to me near a contradiction to say, that there are truths imprinted on the soul, which it perceives or understands not: imprinting, if it signify anything, being nothing else but the making certain truths to be perceived. For to imprint anything on the mind without the mind's perceiving it, seems to me hardly intelligible. If therefore children and idiots have souls, have minds, with those impressions upon them, *they* must unavoidably perceive them, and necessarily know and assent to these truths; which since they do not, it is evident that there are no such impressions. For if they are not notions naturally imprinted, how can they be innate? and if they are notions imprinted, how can they be unknown? To say a notion is imprinted on the mind, and yet at the same time to say, that the mind is ignorant of it, and never yet took notice of it, is to make this impression nothing. No proposition can be said to be in the mind which it never yet knew, which it was never yet conscious of. For if any one may, then, by the same reason, all propositions that are true, and the mind is capable ever of assenting to, may be said to be in the mind, and to be imprinted: since, if any one can be said to be in the mind, which it never yet knew, it must be only because it is capable of knowing it; and so the mind is of all truths it ever shall know. Nay, thus truths may be imprinted on the mind which it never did, nor ever shall know; for a man may live long, and die at last in ignorance of many truths which his mind was capable of knowing, and that with certainty. So that if the capacity of knowing be the natural impression contended for, all the truths a man ever comes to know will, by this account, be every one of them innate; and this great point will amount to no more, but only to a very improper way of speaking; which, whilst it pretends to assert the contrary, says nothing different from those who deny innate principles. For nobody, I think, ever denied that the mind was capable of knowing several truths. The capacity, they say, is innate; the knowledge acquired. But then to what end such contest for certain innate maxims? If truths can be imprinted on the understanding without being perceived, I can see no difference there can be between any truths the mind is *capable* of knowing in respect of their original: they must all be innate or all adventitious: in vain shall a man go about to distinguish them. He therefore that talks of innate notions in the understanding, cannot (if he intend thereby any distinct sort of truths) mean such truths to be in the understanding as it never perceived, and is yet wholly ignorant of. For if these words "to be in the understanding" have any propriety, they signify to be understood. So that to be in the understanding, and not to be understood; to be in the mind and never to be perceived, is all one as to say anything is and is not in the mind or understanding. If therefore these two propositions, "Whatsoever is, is," and "It is impossible for the same thing to be and not to be," are by nature imprinted, children cannot be ignorant of them: infants, and all that have souls, must necessarily have them in their understandings, know the truth of them, and assent to it.

To avoid this, it is usually answered, that all men know and assent to them, *when they come to the use of reason*; and this is enough to prove them innate. I answer:

Doubtful expressions, that have scarce any signification, go for clear reasons to those who, being prepossessed, take not the pains to examine even what they themselves say. For, to apply this answer with any tolerable sense to our present purpose, it must signify one of these two things: either that as soon as men come to the use of reason these supposed native inscriptions come to be known and observed by them; or else, that the use and exercise of men's reason, assists them in the discovery of these principles, and certainly makes them known to them.

If they mean, that by the use of reason men may discover these principles, and that this is sufficient to prove them innate; their way of arguing will stand thus, viz. that whatever truths reason can certainly discover to us, and make us firmly assent to, those are all naturally imprinted on the mind; since that universal assent, which is made the mark of them, amounts to no more but this,—that by the use of reason we are capable to come to a certain knowledge of and assent to them; and, by this means, there will be no difference between the maxims of the mathematicians, and theorems they deduce from them: all must be equally allowed innate; they being all discoveries made by the use of reason, and truths that a rational creature may certainly come to know, if he apply his thoughts rightly that way.

But how can these men think the use of reason necessary to discover principles that are supposed innate, when reason (if we may believe them) is nothing else but the faculty of deducing unknown truths from principles or propositions that are already known? That certainly can never be thought innate which we have need of reason to discover; unless, as I have said, we will have all the certain truths that reason ever teaches us, to be innate. We may as well think the use of reason necessary to make our eyes discover visible objects, as that there should be need of reason, or the exercise thereof, to make the understanding see what is originally engraven on it, and cannot be in the understanding before it be perceived by it. So that to make reason discover those truths thus imprinted, is to say, that the use of reason discovers to a man what he knew before: and if men have those innate impressed truths originally, and before the use of reason and yet are always ignorant of them till they come to the use of reason, it is in effect to say, that men know and know them not at the same time.

It will here perhaps be said that mathematical demonstrations, and other truths that are not innate, are not assented to as soon as proposed, wherein they are distinguished from these maxims and other innate truths. I shall have occasion to speak of assent upon the first proposing, more particularly by and by. I shall here only, and that very readily, allow, that these maxims and mathematical demonstrations are in this different: that the one have need of reason, using of proofs, to make them out and to gain our assent; but the other, as soon as understood, are, without any the least reasoning, embraced and assented to. But I withal beg leave to observe, that it lays open the weakness of this subterfuge, which requires the use of reason for the discovery of these general truths: since it must be confessed that in their discovery there is no use made of reasoning at all. And I think those who give this answer will not be forward to affirm that the knowledge of this maxim, "That it is impossible for the same thing to be and not to be," is a deduction of our reason. For this would be to destroy that bounty of nature they seem so fond of, whilst they make the knowledge of those principles to depend on the labour of our thoughts. For all reasoning is search, and casting about, and requires pains and application. And how can it with any tolerable sense be supposed, that what was imprinted by nature, as the foundation and guide of our reason, should need the use of reason to discover it?

Those who will take the pains to reflect with a little attention on the operations of the understanding, will find that this ready assent of the mind to some truths, depends not, either on native inscription, or the use of reason, but on a faculty of the mind quite distinct from both of them, as we shall see hereafter. Reason, therefore, having nothing to do in procuring our assent to these maxims, if by saying, that "men know and assent to them, when they come to the use of reason," be meant, that the use of reason assists us in the knowledge of these maxims, it is utterly false; and were it true, would prove them not to be innate.

If by knowing and assenting to them "when we come to the use of reason," be meant, that this is the time when they come to be taken notice of by the mind; and that as soon as children come to the use of reason, they come also to know and assent to these maxims; this also is false and frivolous. First, it is false; because it is evident these maxims are not in the mind so early as the use of reason; and therefore the coming to the use of reason is falsely assigned as the time of their discovery. How many instances of the use of reason may we observe in children, a long time before they have any knowledge of this maxim, "That it is impossible for the same thing to be and not to be?" And a great part of illiterate people and savages pass many years, even of their rational age, without ever thinking on this and the like general propositions. I grant, men come not to the knowledge of these general and more abstract truths, which are thought innate, till they come to the use of reason; and I add, nor then neither. Which is so, because, till after they come to the use of reason, those general abstract ideas are not framed in the mind, about which those general maxims are, which are mistaken for innate principles, but are indeed discoveries made and verities introduced and brought into the mind by the same way, and discovered by the same steps, as several other propositions, which nobody was ever so extravagant as to suppose innate. This I hope to make plain in the sequel of this Discourse. I allow therefore, a necessity that men should come to the use of reason before they get the knowledge of those general truths; but deny that men's coming to the use of reason is the time of their discovery.

In the mean time it is observable, that this saying, that men know and assent to these maxims "when they come to the use of reason," amounts in reality of fact to no more but this,—that they are never known nor taken notice of before the use of reason, but may possibly be assented to some time after, during a man's life; but when is uncertain. And so may all other knowable truths, as well as these; which therefore have no advantage nor distinction from others by this note of being known when we come to the use of reason; nor are thereby proved to be innate, but quite the contrary.

But, secondly, were it true that the precise time of their being known and assented to were, when men come to the use of reason; neither would that prove them innate. This way of arguing is as frivolous as the supposition itself is false. For, by what kind of logic will it appear that any notion is originally by nature imprinted in the mind in its first constitution, because it comes first to be observed and assented to when a faculty of the mind, which has quite a distinct province, begins to exert itself? And therefore the coming to the use of speech, if it were supposed the time that these maxims are first assented to, (which it may be with as much truth as the time when men come to the use of reason,) would be as good a proof that they were innate, as to say they are innate because men assent to them when they come to the use of reason. I agree then with these men of innate principles, that there is no knowledge of these general and self-evident maxims in the mind, till it comes to be exercise of reason: but I deny that the coming to the use of reason is the precise time when they are first taken notice of; and if that were the precise time, I deny that it would prove them innate. All that can with any truth be meant by this proposition, that men "assent to them when they come to the use of reason," is no more but this,—that the making of general abstract ideas, and the understanding of general names, being a concomitant of the rational faculty, and growing up with it, children commonly get not those general ideas, nor learn the names that stand for them, till, having for a good while exercised their reason about familiar and more particular ideas, they are, by their ordinary discourse and actions with others, acknowledged to be capable of rational conversation. If assenting to these maxims, when men come to the use of reason, can be true in any other sense, I desire it may be shown; or at least, how in this, or any other sense, it proves them innate.

The senses at first let in *particular* ideas, and furnish the yet empty cabinet, and the mind by degrees growing familiar with some of them, they are lodged in the memory and names got to them. Afterwards, the mind proceeding further, abstracts them, and by degrees learns the use of general names. In this manner the mind comes to be furnished with ideas and language, the *materials* about which to exercise its discursive faculty. And the use of reason becomes daily more visible as these materials that give it employment increase. But though the having of general ideas and the use of general words and reason usually grow together, yet I see not how this any way proves them innate. The knowledge of some truths, I confess, is very early in the mind; but in a way that shows them not to be innate. For, if we will observe, we shall find it still to be about ideas, not innate, but acquired; it being about those first which are imprinted by external things, with which infants have earliest to do, which make the most frequent impressions on their senses. In ideas thus got, the mind discovers that some agree and others differ, probably as soon as it has any use of memory; as soon as it is able to retain and perceive distinct ideas. But whether it be then or no, this is certain, it does so long before it has the use of words; or comes to that which we commonly call "the use of reason." For a child knows as certainly before it can speak the difference between the ideas of sweet and bitter (i.e., that sweet is not bitter), as it knows afterwards (when it comes to speak) that wormwood and sugarplums are not the same thing.

A child knows not that three and four are equal to seven, till he comes to be able to count seven, and has got the name and idea of equality; and then, upon explaining those words, he presently assents to, or rather perceives the truth of that proposition. But neither does he then readily assent because it is an innate truth, nor was his assent wanting till then because he wanted the use of reason; but the truth of it appears to him as soon as he has settled in his mind the clear and distinct ideas that these names stand for. And then he knows the truth of that proposition upon the same grounds and by the same means, that he knew before that a rod and a cherry are not the same thing; and upon the same grounds also that he may come to know afterwards "That it is impossible for the same thing to be and not to be," as shall be more fully shown hereafter. So that the later it is before any one comes to have those general ideas about which those maxims are; or to know the signification of those general terms that stand for them; or to put together in his mind the ideas they stand for; the later also will it be before he comes to assent to those maxims;—whose terms, with the ideas they stand for, being no more innate than those of a cat or a weasel, he must stay till time and observation have acquainted him with them; and then he will be in a capacity to know the truth of these maxims, upon the first occasion that shall make him put together those ideas in his mind, and observe whether they agree or disagree, according as is expressed in those propositions. And therefore it is that a man knows that eighteen and nineteen are equal to thirty-seven, by the same self-evidence that he knows one and two to be equal to three: yet a child knows this not so soon as the other; not for want of the use of reason, but because the ideas the words eighteen, nineteen, and thirty-seven stand for, are not so soon got, as those which are signified by one, two, and three.

This evasion therefore of general assent when men come to the use of reason, failing as it does, and leaving no difference between those supposed innate and other truths that are afterwards acquired and learnt, men have endeavoured to secure an universal assent to those they call maxims, by saying, they are generally assented to as soon as proposed, and the terms they are proposed in understood: seeing all men, even children, as soon as they hear and understand the terms, assent to these propositions, they think it is sufficient to prove them innate. For, since men never fail after they have once understood the words, to acknowledge them for undoubted truths, they would infer, that certainly these propositions were first lodged in the understanding, which, without any teaching, the mind, at the very first proposal immediately closes with and assents to, and after that never doubts again.

In answer to this, I demand whether ready assent given to a proposition, upon first hearing and understanding the terms, be a certain mark of an innate principle? If it be not, such a general assent is in vain urged as a proof of them: if it be said that it is a mark of innate, they must then allow all such propositions to be innate which are generally assented to as soon as heard, whereby they will find themselves plentifully stored with innate principles. For upon the same ground, viz. of assent at first hearing and understanding the terms, that men would have those maxims pass for innate, they must also admit several propositions about numbers to be innate; and thus, that one and two are equal to three, that two and two are equal to four, and a multitude of other the like propositions in numbers, that everybody assents to at first hearing and understanding the terms, must have a place amongst these innate axioms. Nor is this the prerogative of numbers alone, and propositions made about several of them; but even natural philosophy, and all the other sciences, afford propositions which are sure to meet with assent as soon as they are understood. That "two bodies cannot be in the same place" is a truth that nobody any more sticks at than at these maxims, that "it is impossible for the same thing to be and not to be," that "white is not black," that "a square is not a circle," that "bitterness is not sweetness." These and a million of such other propositions, as many at least as we have distinct ideas of, every man in his wits, at first hearing, and knowing what the names stand for, must necessarily assent to. If these men will be true to their own rule, and have assent at first hearing and understanding the terms to be a mark of innate, they must allow not only as many innate propositions as men have distinct ideas, but as many as men can make propositions wherein different ideas are denied one of another. Since every proposition wherein one different idea is denied of another, will as certainly find assent at first hearing and understanding the terms as this general one, "It is impossible for the same thing to be and not to be," or that which is the foundation of it and is the easier understood of the two, "The same is not different"; by which account they will have legions of innate propositions of this one sort, without mentioning any other. But, since no proposition can be innate unless the *ideas* about which it is be innate, this will be to suppose all our ideas of colours, sounds, tastes, figure, etc., innate, then which there cannot be anything more opposite to reason and experience. Universal and ready assent upon hearing and understanding the terms is, I grant, a mark of self-evidence; but self-evidence, depending not on innate impressions, but on something else, (as we shall show hereafter,) belongs to several propositions which nobody was yet so extravagant as to pretend to be innate.

Nor let it be said, that those more particular self-evident propositions, which are assented to at first hearing, as that "one and two are equal to three," that "green is not red," etc., are received as the consequences of those more universal propositions which are looked on as innate principles; since any one, who will but take the pains to observe what passes in the understanding, will certainly find that these, and the like less general propositions, are certainly known, and firmly assented to by those who are utterly ignorant of those more general maxims; and so, being earlier in the mind than those (as they are called) first principles, cannot owe to them the assent wherewith they are received at first hearing.

If it be said, that these propositions, viz. "two and two are equal to four," "red is not blue," etc., are not general maxims, nor of any great use, I answer, that makes nothing to the argument of universal assent upon hearing and understanding. For, if that be the certain mark of innate, whatever proposition can be found that receives general assent as soon as heard and understood, that must be admitted for an innate proposition, as well as this maxim, "That it is impossible for the same thing to be and not to be," they being upon this ground equal. And as to the difference of being more general, that makes this maxim more remote from being innate; those general and abstract ideas being more strangers to our first apprehensions than those of more particular self-evident propositions; and therefore it is longer before they are admitted and assented to by the growing understanding. And as to the usefulness of these magnified maxims, that perhaps will not be found so great as is generally conceived, when it comes in its due place to be more fully considered.

But we have not yet done with "assenting to propositions at first hearing and understanding their terms." It is fit we first take notice that this, instead of being a mark that they are innate, is a proof of the contrary; since it supposes that several, who understand and know other things, are ignorant of these principles till they are proposed to them; and that one may be unacquainted with these truths till he hears them from others. For, if they were innate, what need they be proposed in order to gaining assent, when, by being in the understanding, by a natural and original impression, (if there were any such,) they could not but be known before? Or doth the proposing them print them clearer in the mind than nature did? If so, then the consequence will be, that a man knows them better after he has been thus taught them than he did before. Whence it will follow that these principles may be made more evident to us by others' teaching than nature has made them by impression: which will ill agree with the opinion of innate principles, and give but little authority to them; but, on the contrary, makes them unfit to be the foundations of all our other knowledge; as they are prentended to be. This cannot be denied, that men grow first acquainted with many of these self-evident truths upon their being proposed: but it is clear that whosoever does so, finds in himself that he then begins to know a proposition, which he knew not before, and which from thenceforth he never questions; not because it was innate, but because the consideration of the nature of the things contained in those words would not suffer him to think otherwise, how, or whensoever he is brought to reflect on them. [And if whatever is assented to at first hearing and understanding the terms must pass for an innate principle, every well-grounded observation, drawn from particulars into a general rule, must be innate. When yet it is certain that not all, but only sagacious heads, light at first on these observations, and reduce them into general propositions: not innate, but collected from a preceding acquaintance and reflection on particular instances. These, when observing men have made them, unobserving men, when they are proposed to them, cannot refuse their assent to.]

If it be said, the understanding hath an *implicit* knowledge of these principles, but not an *explicit*, before this first hearing (as they must who will say "that they are in the understanding before they are known,") it will be hard to conceive what is meant by a principle imprinted on the understanding implicitly, unless it be this,—that the mind is capable of understanding and assenting firmly to such propositions. And thus all mathematical demonstrations, as well as first principles, must be received as native impressions on the mind; which I fear they will scarce allow them to be, who find it harder to demonstrate a proposition than assent to it when demonstrated. And few mathematicians will be forward to believe, that all the diagrams they have drawn were but copies of those innate characters which nature had engraven upon their minds.

There is, I fear, this further weakness in the foregoing argument, which would persuade us that therefore those maxims are to be thought innate, which men admit at first hearing; because they assent to propositions which they are not taught, nor do receive from the force of any argument or demonstration, but a bare explication or understanding of the terms. Under which there seems to me to lie this fallacy, that men are supposed not to be taught nor to learn anything *de novo*; when, in truth, they are taught, and do learn something they were ignorant of before. For, first, it is evident that they have learned the terms, and their signification; neither of which was born with them. But this is not all the acquired knowledge in the case: the ideas themselves, about which the proposition is, are not born with them, no more than their names, but got afterwards. So that in all propositions that are assented to at first hearing, the terms of the proposition, their standing for such ideas, and the ideas themselves that they stand for, being neither of them innate, I would fain know what there is remaining in such propositions that is innate. For I would gladly have any one name that proposition whose terms or ideas were either of them innate. We *by degrees* get ideas and names, and *learn* their appropriated connexion one with another; and then to propositions made in such terms, whose signification we have learnt, and wherein the agreement or disagreement we can perceive in our ideas when put together is expressed, we at first hearing assent; though to other propositions, in themselves as certain and evident, but which are concerning ideas not so soon or so easily got, we are at the same time no way capable of assenting. For, though a child quickly assents to this proposition, "That an apple is not fire," when by familiar acquaintance he has got the ideas of those two different things distinctly imprinted on his mind, and has learnt that the names apple and fire stand for them; yet it will be some years after, perhaps, before the same child will assent to this proposition, "That it is impossible for the same thing to be and not to be"; because that, though perhaps the words are as easy to be learnt, yet the signification of them being more large, comprehensive, and abstract than of the names annexed to those sensible things the child hath to do with, it is longer before he learns their precise meaning, and it requires more time plainly to form in his mind those general ideas they stand for. Till that be done, you will in vain endeavour to make any child assent to a proposition made up of such general terms; but as soon as ever he has got those ideas, and learned their names, he forwardly closes with the one as well as the other of the forementioned propositions: and with both for the same reason; viz. because he finds the ideas he has in his mind to agree or disagree, according as the words standing for them are affirmed or denied one of another in the proposition. But if propositions be brought to him in words which stand for ideas he has not yet in his mind, to such propositions, however evidently true or false in themselves, he affords neither assent nor dissent, but is ignorant. For words being but empty sounds, any further than they are signs of our ideas, we cannot but assent to them as they correspond to those ideas we have, but no further than that. But the showing by what steps and ways knowledge comes into our minds; and the grounds of several degrees of assent, being the business of the following Discourse, it may suffice to have only touched on it here, as one reason that made me doubt of those innate principles.

To conclude this argument of universal consent, I agree with these defenders of innate principles,—that if they are innate, they must needs have universal assent. For that a truth should be innate and yet not assented to, is to me as unintelligible as for a man to know a truth and be ignorant of it at the same time. But then, by these men's own confession, they cannot be innate; since they are not assented to by those who understand not the terms; nor by a great part of those who do understand them, but have yet never heard nor thought of those propositions; which, I think, is at least one half of mankind. But were the number far less, it would be enough to destroy universal assent, and thereby show these propositions not to be innate, if children alone were ignorant of them.

But that I may not be accused to argue from the thoughts of infants, which are unknown to us, and to conclude from what passes in their understandings before they express it; I say next, that these two general propositions are not the truths that first possess the minds of children, nor are antecedent to all acquired and adventitious notions: which, if they were innate, they must needs be. Whether we can determine it or no, it matters not, there is certainly a time when children begin to think, and their words and actions do assure us that they do so. When therefore they are capable of thought, of knowledge, of assent, can it rationally be supposed they can be ignorant of those notions that nature has imprinted, were there any such? Can it be imagined, with any appearance of reason, that they perceive the impressions from things without, and be at the same time ignorant of those characters which nature itself has taken care to stamp within? Can they receive and assent to adventitious notions, and be ignorant of those which are supposed woven into the very principles of their being, and imprinted there in indelible characters, to be the foundation and guide of all their acquired knowledge and future reasonings? This would be to make nature take pains to no purpose; or at least to write very ill; since its characters could not be read by those eyes which saw other things very well: and those are very ill supposed the clearest parts of truth, and the foundations of all our knowledge, which are not first known, and without which the undoubted knowledge of several other things may be had. The child certainly knows, that the nurse that feeds it is neither the cat it plays with, nor the blackmoor it is afraid of: that the wormseed or mustard it refuses, is not the apple or sugar it cries for: this it is certainly and undoubtedly assured of: but will any one say, it is by viture of this principle, "That it is impossible for the same thing to be and not to be," that it so firmly assents to these and other parts of its knowledge? Or that the child has any notion or apprehension of that proposition at an age, wherein yet, it is plain, it knows a great many other truths? He that will say, children join in these general abstract speculations with their sucking bottles and their rattles, may perhaps, with justice, be thought to have more passion and zeal for his opinion, but less sincerity and truth, than one of that age.

Though therefore there be several general propositions that meet with constant and ready assent, as soon as proposed to men grown up, who have attained the use of more general and abstract ideas, and names standing for them; yet they not being to be found in those of tender years, who nevertheless know other things, they cannot pretend to universal assent of intelligent persons, and so by no means can be supposed innate;—it being impossible that any truth which is innate (if there were any such) should be unknown, at least to any one who knows anything else. Since, if they are innate truths, they must be innate thoughts: there being nothing a truth in the mind that it has never thought on. Whereby it is evident, if they be any innate truths, they must necessarily be the first of any thought on; the first that appear.

That the general maxims we are discoursing of are not known to children, idiots, and a great part of mankind, we have already sufficiently proved: whereby it is evident they have not an universal assent, nor are general impressions. But there is this further argument in it against their being innate: that these characters, if they were native and original impressions, should appear fairest and clearest in those persons in whom yet we find no footsteps of them; and it is, in my opinion, a strong presumption that they are not innate, since they are least known to those in whom, if they were innate, they must needs exert themselves with most force and vigour. For children, idiots, savages, and illiterate people, being of all others the least corrupted by custom, or borrowed opinions; learning and education having not cast their native thoughts into new moulds; nor by superinducing foreign and studied doctrines, confounded those fair characters nature had written there; one might reasonably imagine that in *their* minds these innate notions should lie open fairly to every one's view, as it is certain the thoughts of children do. It might very well be expected that these principles should be perfectly known to naturals; which being stamped immediately on the soul, (as these men suppose,) can have no dependence on the constitution or organs of the body, the only confessed difference between them and others. One would think, according to these men's principles, that all these native beams of light (were there any such) should, in those who have no reserves, no arts of concealment, shine out in their full lustre, and leave us in no more doubt of their being there, than we are of their love of pleasure and abhorrence of pain. But alas, amongst children, idiots, savages, and the grossly illiterate, what general maxims are to be found? what universal principles of knowledge? Their notions are few and narrow, borrowed only from those objects they have had most to do with, and which have made upon their senses the frequentest and strongest impressions. A child knows his nurse and his cradle, and by degrees the playthings of a little more advanced age; and a young savage has, perhaps, his head filled with love and hunting, according to the fashion of this tribe. But he that from a child untaught, or a wild inhabitant of the woods, will expect these abstract maxims and reputed principles of science, will, I fear, find himself mistaken. Such kind of general propositions are seldom mentioned in the huts of Indians: much less are they to be found in the thoughts of children, or any impressions of them on the minds of naturals. They are the language and business of the schools and academies of learned nations, accustomed to that sort of conversation or learning, where disputes are frequent; these maxims being suited to artifical argumentation and useful for conviction, but not much conducing to the discovery of truth or advancement of knowledge. But of their small use for the improvement of knowledge I shall have occasion to speak more at large.

I know not how absurd this may seem to the masters of demonstration. And probably it will hardly go down with anybody at first hearing. I must therefore beg a little truce with prejudice, and the forbearance of censure, till I have been heard out in the sequel of this Discourse, being very willing to submit to better judgments. And since I impartially search after truth, I shall not be sorry to be convinced, that I have been too fond of my own notions; which I confess we are all apt to be, when application and study have warmed our heads with them.

Upon the whole matter, I cannot see any ground to think these two speculative Maxims innate: since they are not universally assented to; and the assent they so generally find is no other than what several propositions, not allowed to be innate, equally partake in with them: and since the assent that is given them is produced another way, and comes not from natural inscription, as I doubt not but to make appear in the following Discourse. And if *these* "first principles" of knowledge and science are found not to be innate, no *other* speculative maxims can (I suppose), with better right pretend to be so. . . .

63 From *New Essays on Human Understanding*

Gottfried Wilhelm Leibniz

The *Essay on the Understanding,* produced by an illustrious Englishman, is one of the finest and most admired works of the age. Since I have thought at length about the same subject and about most of the topics which are dealt with in it, I have decided to comment upon it. I thought that this would be a good opportunity to publish something entitled *New Essays on the Understanding* and to gain a more favourable reception for my thoughts by putting them in such good company. I thought too that I might benefit from someone else's labour, not only to lessen mine (since it is easier to follow the thread of a good author than to do everything by one's own efforts), but also to add something to what he has produced for us, which is always easier than to start from the beginning. It is true that my opinions frequently differ from his, but far from denying the merit of this famous writer I testify in his favour by showing where and why I differ from him, when I find that on certain significant points I have to prevent his authority from prevailing over reason.

Indeed, although the author of the *Essay* says hundreds of fine things which I applaud, our systems are very different. His is closer to Aristotle and mine to Plato, although each of us parts company at many points from the teachings of both of these ancient writers. He is more popular whereas I am sometimes forced to be a little more esoteric and abstract—which is no advantage for me, particularly when writing in a living language....

Our disagreements concern points of some importance. There is the question whether the soul in itself is completely blank like a writing tablet on which nothing has as yet been written—a *tabula rasa*—as Aristotle and the author of the *Essay* maintain, and whether everything which is inscribed there comes solely from the senses and experience; or whether the soul inherently contains the sources of various notions and doctrines, which external objects merely rouse up on suitable occasions, as I believe and as do Plato and even the Schoolmen and all those who understand in this sense the passage in St. Paul where he says that God's law is written in our hearts (*Romans,* 2: 15). The Stoics call these sources Prolepses, that is fundamental assumptions or things taken for granted in advance. Mathematicians call them common notions or *koinai ennoiai.* Modern philosophers give them other fine names and Julius Scaliger, in particular, used to call them "seeds of eternity" and also "*zopyra*"—meaning living fires or flashes of light hidden inside us but made visible by the stimulation of the senses, as sparks can be struck from a steel. And we have reason to believe that these flashes reveal something divine and eternal: this appears especially in the case of necessary truths. That raises another question, namely whether all truths depend on experience, that is on induction and instances, or if some of them have some other foundation. For if some events can be foreseen before any test has been made of them, it is obvious that we contribute something from our side. Although the senses are necessary for all our actual knowledge, they are not sufficient to provide it all, since they never give us anything but instances, that is particular or singular truths. But however many instances confirm a general truth, they do not suffice to establish its universal necessity; for it does not follow that what has happened will always happen in the same way. For instance, the Greeks and Romans and all the other nations on earth always found that within the passage of twenty-four hours day turns into night and night into day. But they would have been mistaken if they had believed that the same rule holds everywhere, since the contrary was observed during a stay in Novaya Zemlya. And anyone who believed that it is a necessary and eternal truth at least in our latitudes would also be mistaken, since we must recognize that neither the earth nor even the sun exist necessarily, and that there may come a time when this beautiful star no longer exists, at least in its present form, nor its whole system. From this it appears that necessary truths, such as we find in pure mathematics and particularly in arithmetic and geometry, must have principles whose proof does not depend on instances nor, consequently, on the testimony of the senses, even though without the senses it would never occur to us to think of them. This distinction must be thoroughly observed, and Euclid understood that so well that he demonstrates by reason things that experience and sense-images make very evident. Logic also abounds in such truths, and so do metaphysics and ethics, together with their respective products, natural theology and natural jurisprudence; and so the proof of them can only come from inner principles, which are described as innate. It would indeed be wrong to think that we can easily read these eternal laws of reason in the soul, as the Praetor's edict can be read on his notice-board, without effort or inquiry; but it is enough that they can be discovered within us by dint of attention: the senses provide the occasion, and successful experiments also serve to corroborate reason, somewhat as checks in arithmetic help us to avoid errors of calculation in long chains of reasoning. It is in this same respect that man's knowledge differs from that of beasts: beasts are sheer empirics and are guided entirely by instances. While men are capable of demonstrative knowledge [*science*], beasts, so far as one can judge, never manage to form necessary propositions, since the faculty by which they make sequences is something lower than the reason which is to be found in men. The sequences of beasts are just like those of simple empirics who maintain that what has happened once will happen again in a case which is similar in the respects that they are impressed by, although that does not enable them to judge whether the same reasons are at work. That is what makes it so easy for men to ensnare beasts, and so easy for simple empirics to make mistakes. Even people made cunning by age and experience are not proof against this when they trust too much to their past experience; as has happened to various people engaged in civil or military affairs, through their not taking sufficiently to heart that the world changes and that men become cleverer and find hundreds of new tricks—whereas the deer and hares of our time are not becoming craftier than those of long ago. The sequences of beasts are only a shadow of reasoning, that is, they are nothing but a connection in the imagination—a passage from one image to another; for when a new situation appears similar to its predecessor, it is expected to have the same concomitant features as before, as though things were linked [*liaison*] in reality just because their images are linked in the memory. It is true, moreover, that reason counsels us to expect ordinarily that what we find in the future will conform to long experience of the past; but even so, this is no necessary and infallible truth, and it can fail us when we least expect it to, if there is a change in the reasons which have been maintaining it. This is why the wisest men do not trust it so implicitly that they neglect to probe somewhat, where possible, into the reason for such regularities, in order to know when they will have to allow exceptions. For only reason is capable of establishing reliable rules, of making up the deficiencies of those which have proved unreliable by allowing exceptions to them, and lastly of finding unbreakable links in the cogency of necessary inferences. This last often provides a way of foreseeing events without having to experience sensible links between images, as beasts must. Thus what shows the existence of inner sources of necessary truths is also what distinguishes man from beast.

Perhaps our gifted author will not entirely disagree with my view. For after devoting the whole of his first book to rejecting innate illumination, understood in a certain sense, he nevertheless admits at the start of his second book, and from there on, that ideas which do not originate in sensation come from reflection. But reflection is nothing but attention to what is within us, and the senses do not give us what we carry with us already. In view of this, can it be denied that there is a great deal that is innate in our minds, since we are innate to ourselves, so to speak, and since we include Being, Unity, Substance, Duration, Change, Action, Perception, Pleasure, and hosts of other objects of our intellectual ideas? And since these objects are immediately related to our understanding and always present to it (although our distractions and needs prevent us being always aware of them), is it any wonder that we say that these ideas, along with what depends on them, are innate in us? I have also used the analogy of a veined block of marble, as opposed to an entirely homogeneous block of marble, or to a blank tablet—what the philosophers call a *tabula rasa*. For if the soul were like such a blank tablet then truths would be in us as the shape of Hercules is in a piece of marble when the marble is entirely neutral as to whether it assumes this shape or some other. However, if there were veins in the block which marked out the shape of Hercules rather than other shapes, then that block would be more determined to that shape and Hercules would be innate in it, in a way, even though labour would be required to expose the veins and to polish them into clarity, removing everything that prevents their being seen. This is how ideas and truths are innate in us—as inclinations, dispositions, tendencies, or natural potentialities, and not as actions; although these potentialities are always accompanied by certain actions, often insensible ones, which correspond to them.

Our gifted author seems to claim that there is nothing *potential* in us, in fact nothing of which we are not always actually aware. But he cannot hold strictly to this; otherwise his position would be too paradoxical, since, again, we are not always aware of our acquired dispositions [*habitude*] or of the contents of our memory, and they do not even come to our aid whenever we need them, though often they come readily to mind when some idle circumstance reminds us of them, as when hearing the opening words of a song is enough to bring back the rest. So on other occasions he limits his thesis to the statement that there is nothing in us of which we have not at least previously been aware. But no one can establish by reason alone how far our past and now perhaps forgotten awarenesses may have extended, especially if we accept the Platonists' doctrine of recollection which, though sheer myth, is entirely consistent with unadorned reason. And furthermore, why must we acquire everything through awareness of outer things and not be able to unearth anything from within ourselves? Is our soul in itself so empty that unless it borrows images from outside it is nothing? I am sure that our judicious author could not approve of such a view. Where could tablets be found which were completely uniform? Will a perfectly homogeneous and even surface ever be seen? So why could we not also provide ourselves with objects of thought from our own depths, if we take the trouble to dig there? Which leads me to believe that fundamentally his view on this question is not different from my own or rather from the common view, especially since he recognizes two sources of our knowledge, the senses and reflection. . . .

64 From *Phrenology*

J. G. Spurzheim

The Brain Is an Aggregate of Organs

The brain is exclusively the organ of the manifestations of the mind; but it remains for us to investigate, whether the whole of that viscus is to be considered as one single organ, or as an aggregate of as many particular and independent organs, as there are particular and independent species of manifestations of the mind. On this subject, philosophical writings contain the most absurd and contradictory opinions. Those, who believe in the singleness of the soul, conclude that its organ must be single also; others, who examine the particular faculties of the soul, maintain that every special faculty must appertain to a particular organ.

As soon as philosophers began to pay attention to the beings of nature, it became necessary to divide them into numerous classes. Moses speaks of the brutes which live and feel, and those which reason. The Greek philosophers, calling the cause of every phenomenon—soul, spoke of a soul of plants, a soul of animals, and a soul of man. They also admitted a vegetative and a sensitive soul. The inclinations were regarded as the result of the *animus*, and the intellect and reason as the apanage of the *mens*. Pythagoras, St. Paul, Galen, Gilbert, Gassendi, Bacon, Van Helmont, Wepfer, Leibnitz, Fr. Hoffmann, Haller, Blumenbach, Soemmerring, Reil, Barthez, &c., all suppose the various phenomena of animals and man, as dependent on the existence of different causes. Plato and several ancient writers speak of an unreasonable and of a reasonable soul. Those who admit only one soul in man, as Anaxagoras, Aristotle, Thomas Aquinas, Descartes, Stahl, &c., are obliged to acknowledge it possessed of, at least, several faculties. St. Augustin, determined with great exactness the faculties which are common to man and animal, and those which are proper to man. Malebranche, and many other philosophers, speak of principal and secondary faculties; the principal, are understanding and will; the secondary, are subdivisions of understanding: perception, memory, judgment, and imagination; and of will: inclination, desire, affections, and passions. Some authors have even further subdivided these special faculties; Vieussens speaks of two kinds of imagination; and others admit several kinds of memory, as a local memory, a verbal memory, a memory of facts, and a memory of time. Thus it is clear that various principles, or various faculties of the same principle, have been admitted at all times to account for the phenomena of mind....

These quotations, which might be greatly multiplied, show that the idea of a plurality of mental organs as well as faculties is very old, and that they who call it an invention of Gall are in error.

Let us then examine in a general way the proofs which must convince every reflective mind that the brain is a congeries or aggregate of different organs.

It is a general observation that nature, to produce dissimilar effects, has varied the material condition of bodies. This is seen throughout the world: every salt and every metal has its own crystallization; every plant has its particular structure; even the parts of the same tree performing different offices, as wood, bark, leaves, flowers, and fruit, have varying qualities. The organization of every variety of animal, and of every part of the same animal, is also modified; there is a particular organ for every function: the liver for the secretion of bile, the heart for circulation, and the lungs for respiration. The five external senses are separate and independent of each other. There are special nerves for voluntary motion, and others for each sort of sensation. Hence, nature is not so strongly attached to simplicity and unity as certain speculative philosophers are pleased to maintain. This plurality and independent existence of the organs of automatic life and the external senses, renders it probable that the different internal sensations and functions of the mind, are also manifested by different organs.

Besides analogy there are still other proofs of this furnished by the psychology of animals and man in the state of health and disease. The brains of different animals should be different, because their faculties vary. The beaver which builds a hut, the dog which hunts, the blackbird which sings, the swallow which migrates, must have brains whose organization differs widely. Thus it is not a matter of indifference to have a brain of this or of that kind. Even individuals of the same species do not possess all faculties in the same degree: some excel generally, others are middling in all things; some are geniuses, others are idiots. The organization of the brain in all these cases cannot be equally perfect. Moreover, if the brain were not composed of different organs, why should understanding increase as it becomes complicated? The cerebral organization of the different sexes at least should be modified; for certain faculties are more active in females, and others in males. These modified manifestations are easily understood, if we admit that certain organs are more developed in males, and others in females.

Further, in the same individual, certain propensities, sentiments, and intellectual faculties are manifested with great energy, while others scarcely appear. One may excel in verbal memory, and be incapable of combining two philosophical ideas; another may be a great painter, and a bad musician, or a miserable poet; and a third, a great poet, and a bad general; piety and stupidity and piety and intelligence, may be conjoined. Every one has his peculiar gifts. Hence the same mass of brain cannot preside over dissimilar functions. If there were but one organ of sense for all impressions, all should be felt as soon as one was experienced; but the external senses, being attached to different organs, one of them may be weak and another strong. It is the same with the internal senses: if the same part were the organ of every faculty, how could the mind, by means of a single instrument, manifest one faculty in perfection, and another in a very limited manner?

Nor are all the propensities and intellectual faculties manifested simultaneously; several appear at an earlier, several at a later period. Some are very energetic in children, others appear only in adult age; some disappear at the age of fifty or sixty, and others last till ninety or a hundred. Now if every faculty were dependent on the same organ, all ought to appear and disappear simultaneously. All these difficulties are removed, if we admit different organs which are developed, and which diminish, at different periods, as happens amongst the external senses. Smell and taste appear earlier than sight and hearing, because their organs are sooner developed....

Disease also contributes to prove the plurality of the cerebral organs; for how is it possible to combine the fact of partial insanities with the idea of unity of the brain? It is with the cerebral parts as with the nerves of the external senses. Any nerve may be diseased, while the others remain healthy; we may be blind and hear, or be deaf and see. Dr. Parry, of Bath, told me, that in one of his patients while the motion of the whole tongue was perfect, the taste of one side was impaired. Analogous facts are generally known to medical men; why should not the cerebral parts be similarly affected? One faculty of the mind is often deranged, while all the others remain unimpaired. Monomaniæ, or fixed ideas, may be explained by this consideration. There are also madmen, who are reasonable only in one kind of mental manifestation. I know the case of a chemist who is mad in everything except chemistry; and of an embroiderer, who, during her fits, and in the midst of the greatest absurdities, calculates precisely how much stuff is necessary for any particular piece of work. From all these considerations it follows, that there are as many organs as special and independent faculties; and consequently that the brain cannot be a single organ, but must be composed of several....

Division of the Faculties of the Mind, and Nomenclature

Philosophers have, at all times, thought it necessary to make divisions and subdivisions among the faculties of the mind. Gall rejects all which have hitherto been conceived or admitted: the division into instinct in animals, and understanding in man; that of the human mind into understanding and will, and the subdivision of understanding into attention, memory, judgment, and imagination; and of will into inclination, propensity, desire and passion. He admits various faculties of the mind, but thinks that all manifest the same modes of action; he therefore denied the possibility of classing the mental powers in kinds, according to their distinctive nature. He first speaks of the external senses and their apparatus, and then of the internal faculties and their organs, beginning at the basis of the brain and finishing at its summit, taking only the situation of the respective organs as a guide to the order of his descriptions.

I agree with Gall, that the divisions of the mental faculties, as hitherto established by philosophers, are incorrect, but I do not think with him, that the cerebral organs are susceptible of the same modes of action. I conceive it possible to divide them, and to establish a new classification according to their special and characteristic functions.

Gall, being unacquainted with the special faculties, and not being able to find out organs for the powers which philosophers consider as such, observed man in action, and named the organs accordingly. This kind of denomination is still perceptible in his last publication. Actions, however, seldom result from one single power, and often proceed from abuses of the faculties; the nomenclature, therefore, assumed and modified by Gall, was, in my opinion, always very defective. No organ should be named after any action, and certainly not after the abuse of its function. The names of theft and murder, given to two organs, allowed fair play to the opponents. It is true, that individuals who steal from infancy, notwithstanding the most careful education and the severest punishment, have one portion of the brain particularly developed, but all persons in whom the same part is large, are not thieves in the common acceptation of the word. It is the same with the organ, formerly called, that of murder; those who from infancy have a strong propensity to destroy and to kill have a part of the brain highly developed, but all those who have that organ large, do not necessarily murder. Gluttony and drunkenness depend on some organic cause; but we cannot speak of special organs of those disorders. The abuses of physical love depend on a certain organization, but no one speaks of an organ of adultery. Theft and murder then are abuses of two faculties, as I shall explain hereafter. . . .

All the functions of man which take place with consciousness, are ascribed to the mind, and constitute *animal* life. They may be divided into two orders, a division admitted from the remotest antiquity, and known under the names Soul and Spirit; moral and intellectual faculties; understanding and will; heart and head. I shall designate them by feelings and intellect, or by *affective* and *intellectual* faculties.

Both orders of the cerebral functions may be subdivided into several genera, and each genus into several species. Some *affective* powers produce only desires, inclinations or instincts; I denominate them by the general title *propensities*. The name *propensities*, then, is only applied to indicate internal impulses which invite to certain actions. They correspond with the instincts, or instinctive powers of animals. There are other *affective* faculties which are not confined to inclination alone, but have something superadded that may be styled *sentiment*. Self-esteem, for instance, produces a certain propensity to act; but, at the same time, feels another emotion or affection which is not merely propensity. All the faculties which I call *propensities* are common to man and animals, but those of which I now speak, and which I shall name *sentiments*, are partly common to man and animals, and partly proper to man.

The second order of mental powers is destined to make us acquainted with the existence of the external world, with the qualities of the bodies that surround us, and, also, with their relations; I call them *intellectual*. They may be subdivided into four genera. The first includes the functions of the external senses and of voluntary motion; the second, those faculties, which make man and animals acquainted with external objects, and their physical qualities; and the third, the functions connected with the knowledge of relation between objects or their qualities; these three genera, I name *perceptive faculties*; the fourth genus comprises the faculties which act on all the other sensations and notions, and these I style *reflective* faculties.

Each genus of faculties, both affective and intellectual, consists of several species, and each species offers several modifications, or varieties, even idiosyncrasies, or monstrosities. The essential, however, of the faculties always remains, and is even unaltered by disease. The essential nature of the faculties is that which must be determined, and the result of this proceeding is a new philosophy of the mind. . . .

. . . In my opinion there is no organ of cunning, of religion, of poetry, mathematics, mechanics, &c. I consider these mental operations, as compound, and think that their elements must be determined. I consequently do not give names to the organs according to actions, but solely according to the nature of faculties. I shall elucidate my meaning by means of the external senses. There is a power of seeing, and an organ of sight, but there is no organ of seeing red, blue, yellow, or squares, triangles, or other colors, or forms. We speak of a sense of hearing, and not of a sense of hearing the song of birds, the music of man, or the noise of a cannon, &c. In the same way, there is an organ of the propensity to conceal, but none of hypocrisy; an organ of the desire of applause, but none of emulation, or glory; a sense of reverence, but none of this or that mode of worship, and so on.

This distinction between the faculty itself and its application, explains how the same organization, in different individuals, may be accompanied by good or bad actions, for the essence of the faculty is preserved, and its application alone differs, and is good or bad. The feeling of reverence, being directed to the God of Christians, to saints, angels, or to natural objects, or being satisfied by all sorts of actions, by singing of psalms, by fastings, burning candles, or by charity and peacefulness, &c., is always one and the same.

The nomenclature of Phrenology, therefore, is to be established according to the fundamental powers themselves, and by no means according to their application. I am aware that neither English philologists, nor the English public, like to admit new words, and I must apologize for having introduced several. The English language presents very few single words, which express my conceptions of the peculiar faculties of the mind. Hence, I had to choose between speaking by circumlocution, and adopting new names. Now, I think with Locke, that we have still the same rights as our predecessors, and I, therefore, proposed new single names, formed as much as possible, in conformity with the spirit of the language. Having established different propensities, as peculiar faculties of the mind, in order to designate *propensity*, I have taken the termination *ive*, which shows the quality of producing, and *ness*, which indicates the abstract state; *iveness* is therefore joined to different roots; the preference being always given to English words generally admitted; but when such were not to be found, to Latin participles, so commonly used in English to express meanings similar to those I was in search of, as destructiveness, productiveness, &c.

The termination *ous*, indicates a *sentiment*, as anxious, cautious, pious, conscientious, &c. and I should have been very glad to have found similar adjectives for every primitive sentiment of the mind; when they occurred, I have added *ness*, in order to express the abstract state, as cautiousness, conscientiousness, marvellousness, &c.

The names of the intellectual faculties are easily understood, and do not require particular explanation....

Before I enter into details upon the organs of the mind, I shall answer a question which may be put in regard to every organ, viz.: *Why do you admit a particular organ of this, and not of another function?* When actions alone are spoken of, it is certainly difficult to conceive the necessity of particular organs; yet the answer is decisive when we can say: experience demonstrates it. Moreover as I look for fundamental powers and not merely for their organs, the necessity of every one may be proved even by reasoning, that is, by the general proofs which confirm the plurality of the powers and organs. In considering these proofs, in relation to every faculty, we may be sure in our proceeding. Every faculty is fundamental, and a particular organ must be pointed out for it:

1. Which exists in one kind of animal and not in another;
2. Which varies in the sexes of the same species;
3. Which is not proportionate to the other faculties of the same individual;

4. Which does not manifest itself simultaneously with the other faculties, that is, which appears or disappears earlier or later than they;
5. Which may act or repose singly;
6. Which individually is propagated in a distinct manner from parents to children; and
7. Which singly may preserve its proper state of health, or be affected by disease.

Gall did not determine any of the organs in conformity with these views. He followed an empirical method only, looking for organs according to the actions of man. But I have no hesitation to maintain that in pointing out the special or fundamental powers of the mind, my proceeding is philosophical, founded on principles, and adequate to refute the following objections made against the object of our investigations.

Some adversaries say that too many, others that too few, organs are acknowledged, and that they might be multiplied infinitely. The former should know, however, that each is admitted by the same proofs which demonstrate their plurality generally, and that it is verified by experience. The independent existence of one organ is neither more nor less certain than that of any other; and if similar proofs be admitted confirmatory of one, they must be agreed to in regard to every other. On the other hand the opponents who think that enough organs are not admitted, should consider, that every faculty may be applied to an infinite number of objects. Seeing is always seeing, but to what an infinity of objects may the power be directed! Hearing is always hearing, but how various the impressions perceived by this sense! It is the same with the internal faculties. Constructing is always constructing, but how infinite in number and variety the objects that may be produced! Moreover, it is to be observed, that a great number of actions result from combinations of different powers; and, therefore, it is not surprising to see so many effects produced by a small number of primitive faculties. Are not twenty-four letters of the alphabet sufficient to compose all imaginable words? The muscles of the face are not very numerous, yet almost every individual of the human kind has a different physiognomy. There are few primitive sounds; few primitive colors; only ten primitive signs of numbers; but what an infinity of combinations do not each of these furnish? Let us suppose from thirty to forty primitive faculties of the mind, and then consider all possible combinations, with their modifications; and we shall not feel surprised that we observe such a number of modified functions. I repeat that the organs are not multiplied unnecessarily, but that determinate principles are followed in establishing each of them, such only as nature presents being recognised.

Some opponents have a peculiar turn of mind. They rely on their saying that Phrenology is not complete, as if this imperfect state could refute that which is discovered and confirmed. The physical analysis of matter is not yet complete; shall therefore all discoveries of modern chemists be denied: such a conclusion would be evidently erroneous. In the same way this incomplete state of Phrenology does not refute that which is certain in it. . . .

The following new classification of the fundamental phenomena of the mind is the result of all physiological inquiries, contained in my work entitled Phrenology, and constitutes a summary of its philosophy.

Order I

Affective Faculties or Feelings

The essential nature of the affective faculties is to feel emotions. I shall indicate their nature, the aim of their existence, the disorders to which they dispose, and the consequences of their inactivity.

Genus I—*Feelings Common to Man and Animals*

Hunger and thirst are desires felt and known by means of the brain, and there is a special organ in which these impressions inhere.

(*Alimentiveness*)
Aim: The preservation of the individual.
Disorders: Gluttony—Drunkenness.
Its inactivity is accompanied by want of appetite.

Destructiveness
Aim: Destruction, and the violent death of animals, for the sake of living on their flesh.
Disorders: Murder, cruelty.
Its inactivity prevents destruction.

Physical love—(*Amativeness*)
Aim: The propagation of the species.
Disorders: Fornication, adultery, incest and other illegitimate modes of satisfaction.
Its inactivity predisposes to passive continency.

Love of offspring—(*Philoprogenitiveness*)
Aim: The preservation of the offspring.
Disorders: Too active; it spoils children, or causes their loss to be felt as an insupportable calamity.
Its inactivity disposes to neglect, or to abandon the progeny.

Inhabitiveness
Aim: Animals have peculiar instincts to dwell in determinate localities. Nature destined all places to be inhabited.
Disorder: Nostalgia.

Attachment—(*Adhesiveness*)
Aim: Attachment to all around us. It appears variously modified, and produces friendship, marriage, society, habit, and general attachment.
Disorders: Inconsolable grief for the loss of a friend.
Its inactivity predisposes to carelessness about others.

Courage—(*Combativeness*)
Aim: Intrepidity and defence.
Disorders: Quarrelsomeness, disputation, attack, anger.
Its inactivity predisposes to cowardice, timidity, and fear.

Secretiveness
Aim: To conceal.
Disorders: Cunning, duplicity, falsehood, hypocrisy, dissimulation, intriguing, lying.
Its inactivity predisposes to be deceived by others.

Acquisitiveness
Aim: To acquire that which is necessary to our preservation.
Disorders: Theft, fraud, usury, corruptibility.
Its inactivity makes one's own interest be neglected.

Constructiveness
Aim: Construction in general.

Cautiousness
Aim: To be cautious and circumspect.
Disorders: Uncertainty, irresolution, anxiety, fear, melancholy.
Its inactivity predisposes to levity.

Self-Esteem
Aim: Self-esteem.
Disorders: Pride, haughtiness, disdain, arrogance, insolence.
Its inactivity predisposes to humility.

Love of Approbation
Aim: Love of approbation and distinction.
Disorders: Vain glory, vanity, ambition, titles, distinctions.
Its inactivity predisposes to indifference about the opinion of others.

Genus II—*Affective Faculties Proper to Man*[1]

Benevolence
Aim: Benevolence in general.
Disorders: Benevolence to the undeserving, or at the expense of others.
Its inactivity predisposes to selfishness, and not to regard others.

Reverence
Aim: To respect what is venerable.
Disorders: Idolatry, bigotry.
Its inactivity predisposes to irreverence.

Firmness
Aim: Firmness.
Disorders: Stubbornness, obstinacy, and disobedience.
Its inactivity predisposes to inconstancy and changeableness.

Conscientiousness
Aim: Justice, conscientiousness, and duty.
Disorders: Remorse for actions which are innocent, or of no importance.
Its inactivity predisposes to forgetfulness of duty.

Hope
Aim: Hope.
Disorders: Love of scheming.
Its inactivity predisposes to despair.

Marvellousness
Aim: Admiration, and belief in supernaturality.

Disorders: Sorcery, astrology, the belief in demons.
Its inactivity predisposes to incredulity in revealed ideas.

Ideality
Aim: Perfection.
Disorders: Too great exaltation, eccentricity.
Its inactivity predisposes to taking things as they are.

Mirthfulness
Aim: Glee, mirth, laughter.
Disorders: Raillery, mockery, irony, satire.
Its inactivity predisposes to seriousness.

Imitation
Aim: Imitation, expression in the arts.
Disorders: Buffoonery, grimaces.
Its inactivity hinders expression in the arts, and imitation in general.

Order II

Intellectual Faculties
The essential nature of the intellectual faculties is to procure knowledge.

Genus I ***External senses.***

Genus II ***Internal senses,*** or perceptive faculties, which procure knowledge of external objects, their physical qualities, and various relations.

Individuality.	Order.
Configuration.	Calculation.
Size.	Eventuality.
Weight and resistance.	Time.
Coloring.	Tune.
Locality.	Language.

Genus III ***Reflective Faculties***
Comparison.
Causality. . . .

On the Innateness of the Mental Dispositions

Let us see now what is innate. The fundamental powers of the mind, as well as the organization on which their manifestations depend, are given to man by the Creator. The constancy of human nature affords the first proof of this position. The human kind, in as far as its history is known, has ever been the same, not only as regards organic, but also as concerns phrenic life. The skeletons of ancient mummies are the very same as those of the men at the present day; and all ages have exhibited virtues and vices essentially similar. Thus, the special faculties of man have ever been the same; the only difference observable at different times, is, that they have been more or less active, and variously modified in individuals. Here one has unjustly seized a piece of ground, there a place of distinction; here mistresses have been celebrated on an oaten-reed, there on a harp; conquerors in one quarter have been decorated with feathers, in another with purple and crowns, and so on; these modifications are, however, all grounded upon primitive faculties essentially the same. And man, though endowed with proper and peculiar faculties, still receives them from creation; the truly human nature is as determinate as the nature of every other being. Though man compares his sensations and ideas, inquires into the causes of phenomena, draws consequences, discovers laws and general principles, measures immense distances and times, and circumnavigates the globe; though he acknowledges culpability and worthiness, bears a monitor in his interior, and raises his mind to conceive and to adore a God,—yet none of the faculties which cause these acts result either from accidental external influences or from his own will. How indeed could the Creator abandon and give man up to chance in the noblest and most important of all his doings? Impossible! Here, as in all besides, he has prescribed laws to man, and guided his steps in a determinate path. He has secured the continuance of the same essential faculties in the human kind,—faculties whose existence we should never have conceived had the Creator not bestowed them upon us.

The uniformity of the essential faculties of mankind, notwithstanding the influence of society, climate, modes of living, laws, religion, education, and fortuitous events, affords another great proof that nothing can change the institutions of nature. We every where find the same species; whether man clothe himself or go naked, fight with slings or artillery, stain his skin, or powder his hair, dance to the sound of a drum or the music of a concert, adore the sun, moon, and stars, or in his religion be guided by Christian principles, his special faculties are universally the same.

I have also spoken of genius, in order to prove that education does not produce our faculties, and mentioned that children often show peculiar faculties before they have received any kind of instruction. External circumstances are sometimes very unfavorable to the exhibition of genius; but gifted individuals do not always wait for opportunities, they even make them, and leave parents, professions, and all behind, to be at liberty to follow their natural inclinations. Moses, David, Tamerlane, and Pope Sixtus the Fifth, were shepherds; Socrates, Pythagoras, Theophrastus, Demosthenes, Molière, Rousseau, and a thousand others, who have lived to adorn the world, were the sons of artificers. Geniuses sometimes surmount great difficulties, and vanquish innumerable impediments, before their character prevails and they assume their natural place. Such individuals, prevented by circumstances from following their natural bent, still find their favorite amusement in pursuing it. Hence peasants, shepherds, and artisans, have become astronomers, poets, and philosophers; and, on the other hand, kings, and prime ministers, employed themselves in the mechanical arts; all, indeed, unites to prove the innateness of the primitive mental faculties.

Men of genius, however, have been said to form a particular class, and to be incomparable with persons whose faculties are of middling excellence.

This, however, is the same as saying that hunger and circulation do not depend on organization, because all have not immoderate appetite and fever; or that the mole does not see with its eyes, because the stag sees better; or that man has no smell, since the dog's is superior. But, if we admit that organization causes the highest degree of activity of the different faculties, the lowest degree must also depend on it. Moreover, the greatest genius in one particular is often very weak in others. William Crotch, at six years of age, astonished all who heard him by his musical talents; but in every other respect he was a child. Cæsar could never have become a Horace or a Virgil, nor Alexander a Homer. Newton could not have been changed into so great a poet as he was an astronomer; nor Milton into so great an astronomer as he was a poet. Nay, Michael Angelo could not have composed the pictures of Raphael, or the contrary; nor Albano those of Titian, and so on.

The mental faculties again must be innate, since, although essentially the same in both sexes, they present modifications in each. Some are more energetic in women, others in men. . . .

We may add, that in every nation, notwithstanding the uniformity of its opinions, customs, professions, arts, sciences, laws, religion, and all its positive institutions, each individual composing it differs from every other by some peculiarity of character. Each has greater capacity and inclination in one than in another direction, and even in childhood manifests his own manner of thinking and feeling. Every one excuses his frailties by saying, it is my nature; it is stronger than I; I cannot help it, &c. Even brothers and sisters often differ extremely, though their education is uniform. The cause of difference must, therefore, be internal.

The innateness of the faculties must also be admitted, because there is a direct relation between their manifestations and a certain organic apparatus.

Finally, if we believe that man is a being of creation, it is only rational to suppose that his faculties are determinate and ordained. I consequently, with all these considerations in view, contend for the innateness of every faculty of the mind. But here it is of importance to notice an observation of Locke upon innateness. He, to show that ideas are not innate, stated that children do not manifest certain qualities, and that different nations have different, nay, opposite principles of morality. This position, however, in relation to the innateness of ideas and moral principles, must not be confounded with the innateness of the faculties. No sensation, no idea, no principle, is innate. Sensations and ideas of external objects follow from external impressions, and these being accidental, ideas of them cannot be innate; but the faculties which perceive impressions, and conceive ideas, are innate. Thus the idea of a stone, plant, or animal, is not innate; but these objects make impressions on the senses, which produce sensations or ideas in the mind, and both the senses and the mental faculties are innate. In the same manner, sensations and ideas of external and accidental events, and, in general, determinate actions of the faculties, are not innate. The propensity to love, and not the object of love; the faculty of speaking, not the peculiar language; the faculty of comparing and judging, not the determinate judgment; the faculty of poetry, not the particular poem, &c., is innate. There is, therefore, a great difference between innate faculties and innate ideas and sensations.

It is also true that children do not manifest all the faculties, but we cannot from this conclude that these are not innate. Birds do not make nests, the hamster and marmot do not collect provisions, the swallow does not migrate immediately after birth; neither do animals propagate, nor females give suck, when they come into the world; yet all these qualities are innate. This difficulty is easily explained. Every faculty has its own organ, in proportion to whose development are its manifestations. Now in childhood several organs are very little, and in adult age very greatly developed; and while some are proportionately larger in children than in the grown-up, others are fully developed in both. The manifestations of the faculties being, as I have stated, always proportionate to the development and activity of their organs, it becomes evident why some of them do not appear in infancy.

Why moral principles differ in different nations is also obvious. I agree with Locke that they are not innate, but maintain that the faculties which form them are. I shall afterwards show that moral principles depend on several faculties, and vary in nations in consequence of different combinations of their organs; the justice of a libertine without benevolence and veneration must differ entirely from that of a charitable, modest, and continent person. The same fundamental faculties exist every where, but their manifestations are universally modified. Men every where adore a Supreme Being; they every where have marks of honor and of infamy; there are every where masters and servants; all nations make war, whether with clubs and arrows, or with muskets and artillery; and every where the dead are lamented, and their remembrance cherished, whether it be by embalming their bodies, by putting their ashes into an urn, or by depositing their remains in the tomb. Hence, though the functions of the faculties in general are modified in different nations, and of those consequently which determine the moral principles also, the same fundamental powers still appear in the customs, manners, and laws of all.

An essential part of the study of man, therefore, is to show that his nature is determinate, that all his faculties are innate, and that nature's first prerogative is to maintain the number and the essence of his special powers, whilst she permits many modifications of the functions of all, in the same way precisely as she preserves species, but continually sacrifices individuals.

The second right of nature is to allow more or less activity to individual faculties in different persons; that is, she endows all with the same faculties, but gives them in very different degrees. Some few are geniuses, but the majority are middling in all respects. Nature then produces genius, and the individual dispositions of every one....

These are facts which observation proves. Philosophers, therefore, can only examine how nature produces such phenomena, and see whether it is possible to imitate and to assist her.

Thus, the principle of Phrenology—that the faculties of the mind are innate—is indubitable.

Note

1. The rudiments of some of them exist also in animals; but they are much stronger and more extensive in their sphere of application in man.

65 From *The Language of Thought*

Jerry A. Fodor

The first objection I want to consider is an allegation of infinite regress. It can be dealt with quickly (but for a more extensive discussion, see the exchange between Harman, 1969, and Chomsky, 1969).

Someone might say: "According to you, one cannot learn a language unless one already knows a language. But now consider *that* language, the metalanguage in which representations of the extensions of object language predicates are formulated. Surely, learning *it* must involve prior knowledge of a meta-metalanguage in which its truth definitions are couched. And so on ad infinitum. Which is unsatisfactory." There is, I think, a short and decisive answer. My view is that you can't learn a language unless you already *know* one. It isn't that you can't learn a language unless you've already *learned* one. The latter claim leads to infinite regress, but the former doesn't; not, at least by the route currently being explored. What the objection has in fact shown is that *either* my views are false *or* at least one of the languages one knows isn't learned. I don't find this dilemma embarrassing because the second option seems to me to be entirely plausible: the language of thought is known (e.g., is the medium for the computations underlying cognitive processes) but not learned. That is, it is innate. (Compare Atherton and Schwartz, 1974, which commits explicitly the bad argument just scouted.)

There is, however, another way of couching the infinite regress argument that is more subtle: "You say that understanding a predicate involves representing the extension of that predicate in some language you already understand. But now consider understanding the predicates of the metalanguage. Doesn't that presuppose a representation of *its* truth conditions in some meta-metalanguage previously understood? And, once again, so on ad infinitum?" This argument differs from the first one in that the regress is run on "understand" rather than on "learn," and that difference counts. For, while I am not committed to the claim that the language of thought is *learned,* I am committed to the claim that it is, in a certain sense, understood: e.g., that it is available for use as the vehicle of cognitive processes. Nevertheless, this objection, like the other one, commits the fallacy of *ignoratio elenchi*: The position attacked is not the one defended.

What I said was that learning what a predicate means involved representing the extension of that predicate; not that understanding the predicate does. A sufficient condition for the latter might be just that one's use of the predicate is always in fact conformable to the truth rule. To see what's at issue here, consider the case of real computers.

Real computers characteristically use at least two different languages: an input/output language in which they communicate with their environment and a machine language in which they talk to themselves (i.e., in which they run their computations). "Compilers" mediate between the two languages in effect by specifying biconditionals whose left-hand side is a formula in the input/output code and whose right-hand side is a formula in the machine code. Such biconditionals are, to all intents and purposes, representations of truth conditions for formulae in the input/output language, and the ability of the machine to use that language depends on the availability of those definitions. (All this is highly idealized, but it's close enough for present purposes.)[1] My point is that, though the machine must have a compiler if it is to use the input/output language, it doesn't *also* need a compiler for the machine language. What avoids an infinite regression of compilers is the fact that the machine is *built* to use to machine language. Roughly, the machine language differs from the input/output language in that its formulae correspond directly to computationally relevant physical states and operations of the machine: The physics of the machine thus guarantees that the sequences of states and operations it runs through in the course of its computations respect the semantic constraints on formulae in its internal language. What takes the place of a truth definition for the machine language is simply the engineering principles which guarantee this correspondence.

I shall presently return to this point in some detail. For the moment, suffice it to suggest that there are two ways in which it can come about that a device (including, presumably, a person) understands a predicate. In one case, the device has and employs a representation of the extension of the predicate, where the representation is itself given in some language that the device understands. In the second case, the device is so constructed that its use of the predicate (e.g., in computations) comport with the conditions that such a representation would specify. I want to say that the first is true of predicates in the natural languages people learn and the second of predicates in the internal language in which they think.

"But look," you might reply, "you admit that there is at least one language whose predicates we understand without the internal representation of truth conditions. You admit that, for that language, the answer to: 'How do we use its predicates correctly?' is that we just do; that we are just built that way. This saves you from infinite regress, but it suggests that even the regress from the natural language to the inner language is otiose. You argue that we learn 'is a chair' only if we learn that is falls under the truth rule ⌜*y is a chair*⌝ *is true iff x is G* and then you say that the question of learning a truth rule for *G* doesn't arise. Why not stop a step sooner and save yourself trouble? Why not say that the question of how we learn 'is a chair' doesn't arise either? Explanation has to stop somewhere."

The answer is that explanation has to stop somewhere but it doesn't have to—and it better not—stop *here*. The question of how we learn "is a chair" *does* arise precisely because English *is* learned. The question of how *G* is learned does not arise precisely because, by hypothesis, the language in which *G* is a formula is innate. Once again, thinking about computers is likely to be illuminating.

The critical property of the machine language of computers is that its formulae can be paired directly with the computationally relevant physical states of the machine in such fashion that the operations the machine performs respect the semantic constraints on formulae in the machine code. Token machine states are, in this sense, interpretable as tokens of the formulae. Such a correspondence can *also* be effected between physical states of the machine and formulae of the input/output code, but only by first compiling these formulae: i.e., only by first translating them into the machine language. This expresses the sense in which machines *are* "built to use" their machine language and are *not* "built to use" their input/output codes. It also suggests an empirical theory: When you find a device using a language it was not built to use (e.g., a language that it has *learned*), assume that the way it does it is by translating the formulae of that language into formulae which correspond directly to its computationally relevant physical states. This would apply, in particular, to the formulae of the natural languages that speaker/hearers learn, and the correlative assumption would be that the truth rules for predicates in the natural language function as part of the translation procedure.

Admittedly this is just a *theory* about what happens when someone understands a sentence in a language he has learned. But at least it *is* a theory, and one which makes understanding a sentence analogous to computational processes whose character we roughly comprehend. On this view, what happens when a person understands a sentence must be a translation process basically analogous to what happens when a machine "understands" (viz., compiles) a sentence in its programming language. I shall try to show that there are broadly empirical grounds for taking this sort of model seriously. My present point, however, is just that it is at least *imaginable* that there should be devices which need truth definitions for the languages they speak but not for the language that they compute in. If *we* are such devices, then there is point to asserting that learning English involves learning that ⌜*y* is a chair⌝ is true iff *x* is *G*, even though one denies that learning that requires learning that ⌜*y* is *G*⌝, *is true iff x* is Ψ for any Ψ other than *G* or "is a chair."

I don't, in short, think that the view of language learning so far sketched leads to infinite regress. It does lead to a one-stage regress; viz., from the natural language to the internal code—and that one stage is empirically rather than conceptually motivated. That is, we can imagine an organism which is born speaking and born speaking whatever language its nervous system uses for computing. For such an organism, the question of how it learns its language would, *ex hypothesi*, not arise; and the view that its use of the language is controlled by an internal representation of the truth conditions upon the predicates of that language might well be otiose. All we would need to suppose is that the organism is so constructed that its use of the expressions in the language conforms to the conditions that a truth definition for the language would articulate. But we are not such organisms and, so far as I know, for us no alternative to the view that we learn rules which govern the semantic properties of the expressions in our language is tenable....

To begin with, it may be felt that I have been less than fair to the view that natural language *is* the language of thought. It will be recalled that the main objection to this view was simply that it cannot be true for those computational processes involved in the acquisition of natural language itself. But, though it might be admitted that the *initial* computations involved in first language learning cannot themselves be run in the language being learned, it could nevertheless still be claimed that, a foothold in the language having once been gained, the child then proceeds by extrapolating his bootstraps: The fragment of the language first internalized is itself somehow essentially employed to learn the part that's left. This process eventually leads to the construction of a representational system more elaborate than the one the child started with, and this richer system mediates the having of thoughts the child could not otherwise have entertained.

Surely something that *looks* like this does sometimes happen. In the extreme case, one asks a dictionary about some word one doesn't understand, and the dictionary tells one, in one's own language, what the word means. That, at least, *must* count as using one part of one's language to learn another part. And if the adult can do it by the relatively explicit procedure of consulting a dictionary, why shouldn't the child do it by the relatively implicit procedure of consulting the corpus that adults produce? In particular, why shouldn't he use his observations of how some term applies to confirm hypotheses about the extension of that term? And why should not these hypotheses be couched in a fragment of the very language that the child is learning; i.e., in that part of the language which has been mastered to date?

This begins to seem a dilemma. On the one hand, it sometimes *does* help, in learning a language, to use the language that one is trying to learn. But, on the other hand, the line of argument that I have been pursuing appears to show that it *couldn't* help. For I have been saying that one can't learn *P* unless one learns something like "$\ulcorner P_y \urcorner$ is true iff *Gx*," and that one can't learn *that* unless one is able to use G. But suppose G is a predicate (not of the internal language but) in the same language that contains *P*. Then G must itself have been learned and, *ex hypothesi*, learning G must have involved learning (for some predicate or other) that G applies iff *it* applies. The point is that this new predicate must either be a part of the internal language or "traceable back" to a predicate in the internal language by iterations of the present argument. In neither case however does any predicate which belongs to the same language as *P* play an essential role in mediating the learning of *P*.

What makes the trouble is of course that the biconditional is *transitive*. Hence, if I can express the extension of G in terms of, say, H, and I can express the extension of *P* in terms of G, then I can express the extension of *P* in terms just of H (namely, $\ulcorner y$ is $P \urcorner$) is true iff *Hx*. So, introducing G doesn't seem to have gained us any leverage. There doesn't seem to be any way in which the part of a natural language one knows could play an essential role in mediating the learning of the part of the language that one doesn't know. Paradox.

In fact, two closely related paradoxes. We want to make room for the possibility that there is *some* sense in which you can use one part of a language to learn other parts, and we want to make room for the possibility that there is *some* sense in which having a language might permit the thinking of thoughts one could not otherwise entertain. But the views we have so far been propounding seem not to admit of either possibility: Nothing can be expressed in a natural language that can't be expressed in the language of thought. For if something could, we couldn't learn the natural language formula that expresses it.[2]

Fortunately, both paradoxes are spurious and for essentially the same reasons. To begin with the learning case, what the argument thus far shows is this. Suppose *F* is a (proper) fragment of English such that a child has mastered *F* and only *F* at time *t*. Suppose that F' is the rest of English. Then the child can use the vocabulary and syntax of F to express the truth conditions for the predicates of F' only insofar as the semantic properties of F' terms is already expressible in F. What the child cannot do, in short, is use the fragment of the language that he knows to increase the expressive power of the concepts at his disposal. But he may be able to use it for *other* purposes, and doing so may, in brute empirical fact, be essential to the mastery of F'. The most obvious possibility is to use F for mnemonic purposes.

It is a commonplace in psychology that mnemonic devices may be essential to a memory-restricted system in coping with learning tasks. If, as it seems reasonable to suppose, relatively simple natural language expressions are often coextensive only with quite elaborate formulae in the internal code, it becomes easy to see how learning one part of a natural language could be an essential precondition for learning the rest: The first-learned bits might serve to abbreviate complicated internal formulae, thus allowing the child to reduce the demands on computing memory implicit in projecting, confirming, and storing hypotheses about the truth conditions on the later-learned items. This sort of thing is familiar from teaching the vocabulary of formal systems. Complex concepts are typically not introduced directly in terms of primitives, but rather by a series of interlinking definitions. The point of this practice is to set bounds on the complexity of the formulae that have to be coped with at any given stage in the learning process.[3]

Essentially similar considerations suggest how it might after all be the case that there are thoughts that only someone who speaks a language can think. True, for every predicate in the natural language it must be possible to express a coextensive predicate in the internal code. It does not follow that for every natural language predicate *that can be entertained* there is an *entertainable* predicate of the internal code. It is no news that single items in the vocabulary of a natural language may encode concepts of extreme sophistication and complexity. If terms of the natural language can become incorporated into the computational system by something like a process of abbreviatory definition, then it is quite conceivable that learning a natural language may increase the complexity of the thoughts that we can think. To believe this, it is only necessary to assume that the complexity of thinkable thoughts is determined (*inter alia*) by some mechanism whose capacities are sensitive to the form in which the thoughts are couched. As we remarked above, memory mechanisms are quite plausibly supposed to have this property.

So, I am not committed to asserting that an articulate organism has *no* cognitive advantage over an inarticulate one. Nor, for that matter, is there any need to deny the Whorfian point that the kinds of concepts one has may be profoundly determined by the character of the natural language that one speaks. Just as it is necessary to distinguish the concepts that can be expressed in the internal code from the concepts that can be entertained by a memory-restricted system that computes with the code, so, too, it is necessary to distinguish the concepts that *can* be entertained (*salve* the memory) from the ones that actually get employed. This latter class is obviously sensitive to the particular experiences of the code user, and there is no principled reason why the experiences involved in learning a natural language should not have a specially deep effect in determining how the resources of the inner language are exploited.[4]

What, then, *is* being denied? Roughly, that one can learn a language whose expressive power is greater than that of a language that one already knows. Less roughly, that one can learn a language whose predicates express extensions not expressible by those of a previously available representational system. Still less roughly, that one can learn a language whose predicates express extensions not expressible by predicates of the representational system *whose employment mediates the learning.*

Now, while this is all compatible with there being a computational advantage associated with knowing a natural language, it is *in*compatible with this advantage being, as it were, principled. If what I have been saying is true, than all such computational advantages—all the facilitatory effects of language upon thought—will have to be explained away by reference to "performance" parameters like memory, fixation of attention, etc. Another way to put this is: If an angel is a device with infinite memory and omnipresent attention—a device for which the performance/competence distinction is vacuous—then, on my view, there's no point in angels learning Latin; the conceptual system available to them by virtue of having done so can be no more powerful than the one they started out with.

It should now be clear why the fact that we can use part of a natural language to learn another part (e.g., by appealing to a monolingual dictionary) is no argument against the view that no one can learn a language more powerful than some language he already knows. One cannot use the definition *D* to understand the word W unless (a) "*W* means *D*" is true and (b) one understands *D*. But if (a) is satisfied, D and W must be at least coextensive, and so if (b) is true, someone who learns W by learning that it means *D* must already understand at least one formula coextensive with W, viz., the one that *D* is couched in. In short, learning a word can be learning what a dictionary definition says about it *only for someone who understands the definition.* So appeals to dictionaries do not, after all, show that you can use your mastery of a part of a natural language to learn expressions you could not otherwise have mastered. All they show is what we already know: Once one is able to express an extension, one is in a position to learn that *W* expresses that extension.

Notes

1. Someone might point out that, if the compiler formulae are biconditional, they could be read as specifying truth conditions for formulae in the *machine language* with the input/output code providing the metalinguistic vehicles of representation. In fact, however, the appearance of symmetry is spurious even if the two languages are entirely intertranslatable. For while the machine uses the machine code formulae without appealing to the compiler, it has no access to formulae in the input/output language except via the translations that the compiler effects. There is thus a useful sense in which, so far as the machine is concerned, machine language formulae express the meanings of formulae in the input/output code but not vice versa.

2. I know of only one place in the psychological literature where this issue has been raised. Bryant (1974) remarks: "the main trouble with the hypothesis that children begin to take in and use relations to help them solve problems because they learn the appropriate comparative terms like 'larger' is that it leaves unanswered the very awkward question of how they learned the meaning of these words in the first place" (p. 27). This argument generalizes, with a vengeance, to *any* proposal that the learning of a word is essential to mediate the learning of the concept that the word expresses.

3. I am assuming—as many psychologists do—that cognitive processes exploit at least two kinds of storage: a "permanent memory" which permits relatively slow access to essentially unlimited amounts of information and a "computing memory" which permits relatively fast access to at most a quite small number of items. Presumably, in the case of the latter system, the ability to display a certain body of information may depend critically on the form in which the information is coded. For extensive discussions see Neisser (1967). Suffice it to remark here that one way in which parts of a natural language might mediate further language learning is by providing the format for such encoding.

4. It should nevertheless be stressed that there is a fundamental disagreement between the kinds of views I have been proposing and those that linguistic relativists endorse. For such writers as Whorf, the psychological structure of the neonate is assumed to be diffuse and indeterminate. The fact about development that psychological theories are required to explain is thus the emergence of the adult's relatively orderly ontological commitments from the sensory chaos that is supposed to characterize the preverbal child's experience. This order has, to put it crudely, to come from somewhere, and the inventory of lexical and grammatical categories of whatever language the child learns would appear to be a reasonable candidate if a theorist is committed to the view that cognitive regularities must be reflexes of *environmental* regularities. On this account, the cognitive systems of adults ought to differ about as much as, and in about the ways that, the grammars and lexicons of their languages do and, so far as the theory is concerned, languages may differ without limit.

On the internal code story, however, all these assumptions are reversed. The child (indeed, the infraverbal organism of whatever species) is supposed to bring to the problem of organizing its experiences a complexly structured and endogenously determined representational system. Similarities of cognitive organization might thus be predicted even over wide ranges of environmental variation. In particular, the theorist is not committed to discovering environmental analogues to such structural biases as the adult ontology exhibits. He is thus prepared to be unsurprised by the prima facie intertranslatability of natural languages, the existence of linguistic universals, and the broad homologies between human and infrahuman psychology. (For further discussion, see Fodor et al., 1974.)

Bibliography

Atherton, M., and Schwartz, R., 1974. "Linguistic Innateness and Its Evidence." *Journal of Philosophy*, 71: 155–168.

Bryant, P. E., 1974. *Perception and Understanding in Young Children*. New York: Basic Books.

Chomsky, N., 1969. "Linguistics and Philosophy." In S. Hook, ed. *Language and Philosophy*. New York: NYU Press.

Fodor, J. A., Bever, T., and Garrett, M., 1974. *The Psychology of Language: An Introduction to Psycholinguistics and Generative Grammar*. New York: McGraw-Hill.

Harman, G., 1969. "Linguistic Competence and Empiricism." In S. Hook. ed. *Language and Philosophy*. New York: NYU Press.

Neiser, U., 1967. *Cognitive Psychology*. New York: Appleton.

66 The Psychogenesis of Knowledge and Its Epistemological Significance

Jean Piaget

Fifty years of experience have taught us that knowledge does not result from a mere recording of observations without a structuring activity on the part of the subject. Nor do any a priori or innate cognitive structures exist in man; the functioning of intelligence alone is hereditary and creates structures only through an organization of successive actions performed on objects. Consequently, an epistemology conforming to the data of psychogenesis could be neither empiricist nor preformationist, but could consist only of a constructivism, with a continual elaboration of new operations and structures. The central problem, then, is to understand how such operations come about, and why, even though they result from nonpredetermined constructions, they eventually become logically necessary.

Empiricism

The critique of empiricism is not tantamount to negating the role of experimentation, but the "empirical" study of the genesis of knowledge shows from the onset the insufficiency of an "empiricist" interpretation of experience. In fact, no knowledge is based on perceptions alone, for these are always directed and accompanied by schemes of action. Knowledge, therefore, proceeds from action, and all action that is repeated or generalized through application to new objects engenders by this very fact a "scheme," that is, a kind of practical concept. The fundamental relationship that constitutes all knowledge is not, therefore, a mere "association" between objects, for this notion neglects the active role of the subject, but rather the "assimilation" of objects to the schemes of that subject. This process, moreover, prolongs the various forms of biological "assimilations," of which cognitive association is a particular case as a functional process of integration. Conversely, when objects are assimilated to schemes of action, there is a necessary "adaptation" to the particularities of these objects (compare the phenotypic "adaptations" in biology), and this adaptation results from external data, hence from experience. It is thus this exogenous mechanism that converges with what is valid in the empiricist thesis, but (and this reservation is essential) adaptation does not exist in a "pure" or isolated state, since it is always the adaptation of an assimilatory scheme; therefore this assimilation remains the driving force of cognitive action.

These mechanisms, which are visible from birth, are completely general and are found in the various levels of scientific thought. The role of assimilation is recognized in the fact that an "observable" or a "fact" is always interpreted from the moment of its observation, for this observation always and from the beginning requires the utilization of logico-mathematical frameworks such as the setting up of a relationship or a correspondence, proximities or separations, positive or negative quantifications leading to the concept of measure—in short, a whole conceptualization on the part of the subject that excludes the existence of pure "facts" as completely external to the activities of this subject, all the more as the subject must make the phenomena vary in order to assimilate them.

As for the learning processes invoked by the behaviorist empiricists on behalf of their theses, Inhelder, Sinclair, and Bovet have shown that these processes do not explain cognitive development but are subject to its laws, for a stimulus acts as such only at a certain level of "competence" (another biological notion akin to assimilation). Briefly, the action of a stimulus presupposes the presence of a scheme, which is the true source of the response (which reverses the *SR* schema or makes it symmetrical [$S \rightleftarrows R$]). Besides, Pribram has demonstrated a selection of inputs existing even at the neurological level.

Preformation

Is it necessary, then, to turn in the direction of the preformation of knowledge? I will return later to the problem of innateness and will limit myself for the moment to the discussion of the hypothesis of determination. If one considers the facts of psychogenesis, one notes first the existence of stages that seem to bear witness to a continual construction. In the first place, in the sensorimotor period preceding language one sees the establishment of a logic of actions (relations of order, interlocking of schemes, intersections, establishment of relationships, and so on), rich in discoveries and even in inventions (recognition of permanent objects, organization of space, of causality). From the ages of 2 to 7, there is a conceptualization of actions, and therefore representations, with discovery of functions between covariations of phenomena, identities, and so forth, but without yet any concept of reversible operations or of conservation. These last two concepts are formed at the level of concrete operations (ages 7 to 10), with the advent of logically structured "groupings," but they are still bound to the manipulation of objects. Finally, around the age of 11 to 12, a hypothetico-deductive propositional logic is formed, with a combinatorial lattice, "sums of parts," algebraic four-groups, and so on.

However, these beautiful successive and sequential constructions (where each one is necessary to the following one) could be interpreted as the progressive actualization (related to factors such as neurological maturity) of a set of preformations, similar to the way in which genetic programming regulates organic "epigenesis" even though the latter continues to interact with the environment and its objects. The problem is therefore to choose between two hypotheses: authentic constructions with stepwise disclosures to new possibilities, or successive actualization of a set of possibilities *existing from* the beginning. First, let us note that the problem is similar in the history of science: are the clearly distinct periods in the history of mathematics the result of the successive creations of mathematicians, or are they only the achievement through progressive thematizations of the set of all possibilities corresponding to a universe of Platonic ideas? Now, the set of all possibilities is an antinomic notion like the set of all sets, because the set is itself only a possibility. In addition, today's research shows that, beyond the transfinite number "kappa zero" (which is the limit of predicativity), some openings into new possibilities are still taking place, but are in fact unpredictable since they cannot be founded on a combinatorial lattice. Thus, either mathematics is a part of nature, and then it stems from human constructions, creative of new concepts; or mathematics originates in a Platonic and suprasensible universe, and in this case, one would have to show through what psychological means we acquire knowledge of it, something about which there has never been any indication.

This brings us back to the child, since within the space of a few years he spontaneously reconstructs operations and basic structures of a logico-mathematical nature, without which he would understand nothing of what he will be taught in school. Thus, after a lengthy preoperative period during which he still lacks these cognitive instruments, he reinvents for himself, around his seventh year, the concepts of reversibility, transitivity, recursion, reciprocity of relations, class inclusion, conservation of numerical sets, measurements, organization of spatial references (coordinates), morphisms, some connectives, and so on—in other words, all the foundations of logic and mathematics. If mathematics were preformed, this would mean that a baby at birth would already possess virtually everything that Galois, Cantor, Hilbert, Bourbaki, or MacLane have since been able to realize. And since the child is himself a consequence, one would have to go back as far as protozoa and viruses to locate the seat of "the set of all possibilities."

In a word, the theories of preformation of knowledge appear, for me, as devoid of concrete truth as empiricist interpretations, for the origin of logico-mathematical structures in their infinity cannot be localized either in objects or in the subject. Therefore, only constructivism is acceptable, but its weighty task is to explain both the mechanisms of the formation of new concepts and the characteristics these concepts acquire in the process of becoming logically necessary.

Reflective Abstraction

If logico-mathematical structures are not preformed, one must, in contrast, go far back to discover their roots, that is, the elementary functioning permitting their elaboration; and as early as the sensorimotor stages, that is to say, much before language, one finds such points of departure (though without any absolute beginning, since one must then go back as far as the organism itself; see the section on the biological roots of knowledge). What are the mechanisms, then, that provide the constructions from one stage to the other? The first such mechanism I will call "reflective abstraction."

It is, in fact, possible to distinguish three different kinds of abstraction. (1) Let us call "empirical abstraction" the kind that bears on physical objects external to the subject. (2) Logico-mathematical abstraction, in contrast, will be called "reflective" because it proceeds from the subject's actions and operations. This is even true in a double sense; thus we have two interdependent but distinct processes: that of a projection onto a higher plane of what is taken from the lower level, hence a "reflecting," and that of a "reflection" as a reorganization on the new plane—this reorganization first utilizing, only instrumentally, the operations taken from the preceding level but aiming eventually (even if this remains partially unconscious) at coordinating them into a new totality. (3) We will speak finally of "reflected abstraction" or "reflected thought" as the thematization of that which remained operational or instrumental in (2); phase (3) thus constitutes the natural outcome of (2) but presupposes in addition a set of explicit comparisons at a level above the "reflections" at work in the instrumental utilizations and the constructions in process of (2). It is essential, therefore, to distinguish the phases of reflective abstractions, which occur in any construction at the time of the solution of new problems, from reflected abstraction, which adds a system of explicit correspondences among the operations thus thematized.

Reflective and reflected abstractions, then, are sources of structural novelties for the following reasons: In the first place, the "reflecting" on a higher plane of an element taken from a lower level (for example, the interiorization of an action into a conceptualized representation) constitutes an establishment of correspondences, which is itself already a new concept, and this then opens the way to other possible correspondences, which represents a new "opening." The element transferred onto the new level is then constituted from those that were already there or those that are going to be added, which is now the work of the "reflection" and no longer of the "reflecting" (although initially elicited by the latter). New combinations thus result which can lead to the construction of new operations operating "on" the preceding ones, which is the usual course of mathematical progress (an example in the child: a set of additions creating multiplication).[1] As a rule, all reflecting on a new plane leads to and necessitates a *reorganization*, and it is this reconstruction, productive of new concepts, that we call "reflection"; yet well before its general thematization, reflection comes into action through a set of still instrumental assimilations and coordinations without any conceptual awareness of structures as such (this is to be found all through the history of mathematics). Finally reflected abstraction or retrospective thematization become possible, and although they are found only on preconstructed elements, they naturally constitute a new construction in that their transversal correspondences render simultaneous that which was until now elaborated by successive longitudinal linkings (compare, in scientific thought, the thematization of "structures" by Bourbaki).

Constructive Generalization

Abstraction and generalization are obviously interdependent, each founded on the other. It results from this that only inductive generalization, proceeding from "some" to "all" by simple extension, will correspond to empirical abstraction, whereas constructive and "completive" generalizations in particular will correspond to reflective and reflected abstractions.

The first problem to be solved, then, is that of the construction of successive steps that have been established in the preceding paragraphs. Now, each one of them results from a new assimilation or operation aimed at correcting an insufficiency in the previous level and actualizing a possibility that is opened by the new assimilation. A good example is the passage of action to representation due to the formation of the semiotic function. Sensorimotor assimilation consists only of assimilating objects to schemes of action, whereas representative assimilation assimilates objects to each other, hence the construction of conceptual schemes. Now, this new form of assimilation already was virtual in sensorimotor form since it bore on multiple but successive objects; it was then sufficient to complete these successive assimilations by a simultaneous act of setting into transversal correspondence before passing to the next level. But such an action implies the evocation of objects not presently perceived, and this evocation requires the formation of a specific instrument, which is the semiotic function (deferred imitations, symbolic play, mental image which is an interiorized imitation, sign language, and so on, in addition to vocal and learned language). Now, sensorimotor signifiers already exist in the form of cues or signals, but they constitute only one aspect or a part of the signified objects; on the contrary, the semiotic function commences when signifiers are differentiated from what is thereby signified and when signifiers can correspond to a multiplicity of things signified. It is clear, then, that between the conceptual assimilation of objects between themselves and semiotization, there is a mutual dependence and that both proceed from a completive generalization of sensorimotor assimilation. This generalization embeds a reflective abstraction bearing on elements directly borrowed from sensorimotor assimilation.

Likewise, it would be easy to show that the new concepts inherent in the levels of initially concrete, then hypothetico-deductive operations proceed from completive generalizations as well. It is thus that concrete operations owe their new abilities to the acquisition of reversibility, which has already been prepared by preoperative reversibility; but the reversibility, in addition, requires a systematic adjustment of affirmations and negations, that is to say, an autoregulation which, by the way, is always working within the constructive generalizations (I will return to the subject of autoregulation in the section on necessity and equilibration). As for the hypothetico-deductive operations, these are made possible by the transition from the structures of "groupings" devoid of a combinatorial lattice (the elements of which are disjoint), to the structures of the "set of components" embedding a combinatorial lattice and full generalization of partitions.[2]

These last advances are due to a particularly important form of constructive generalizations, which consist of raising an operation to its own square or a higher power: thus, combinations are classifications of classifications, permutations are seriations of seriations, the sets of components are partitions of partitions, and so on.

Finally, let us call attention to a simpler but equally important form which consists of generalizations by synthesis of analogous structures, such as the coordination of two systems of references, internal and external to a spatial or cinematic process (the 11- to 12-year-old level).

The Biological Roots of Knowledge

What we have seen so far speaks in favor of a systematic constructivism. It is nonetheless true that its sources are to be sought at the level of the organism, since a succession of constructions could not admit of an absolute beginning. But before offering a solution, we should first ask ourselves what a preformationist solution would mean biologically; in other words, what *a priorism* would look like after having been rephrased in terms of innateness.

A famous author has demonstrated this quite clearly: it is Konrad Lorenz, who considers himself a Kantian who maintains a belief in a hereditary origin of the great structures of reason as a precondition to any acquisition drawn from experience. But as a biologist, Lorenz is well aware that, except for "general" heredity common to all living beings or major groups, specific heredity varies from one species to another: that of man, for instance, remains special to our own particular species. As a consequence, Lorenz, while believing as a precondition that our major categories of thought are basically inborn, cannot, for that very reason, assert their generality: hence his very enlightening formula according to which the *a prioris* of reason consist simply of "innate working hypotheses." In other words, Lorenz, while retaining the point of departure of the *a priori* (which precedes the constructions of the subject), sets aside necessity which is more important, whereas we are doing exactly the opposite, that is, insisting on necessity (see the next section), but placing it at the end of constructions, without any prerequisite hereditary programming.

Lorenz's position is therefore revealing: if reason is innate, either it is general and one must have it go back as far as the protozoa, or it is specific (species-specific or genus-specific, for instance) and one must explain (even if it is deprived of its essential character of necessity) through which mutations and under the influence of which natural selections it developed. Now, as research stands at present, current explanations would be reduced for this particular problem to a pure and simple verbalism; in fact, they would consist of making reason the product of a random mutation, hence of mere chance.

But what innatists surprisingly seem to forget is that there exists a mechanism which is as general as heredity and which even, in a sense, controls it: this mechanism is autoregulation, which plays a role at every level, as early as the genome, and a more and more important role as one gets closer to higher levels and to behavior. Autoregulation, whose roots are obviously organic, is thus common to biological and mental processes, and its actions have, in addition, the great advantage of being directly controllable. It is therefore in this direction, and not in mere heredity, that one has to seek the biological explanation of cognitive constructions, notwithstanding the fact that by the interplay of regulations of regulations, autoregulation is eminently constructivist (and dialectic) by its very nature.[3]

It is understandable, therefore, that while fully sympathizing with the transformational aspects of Chomsky's doctrine, I cannot accept the hypothesis of his "innate fixed nucleus." There are two reasons for this. The first one is that this mutation particular to the human species would be biologically inexplicable; it is already very difficult to see why the randomness of mutations renders a human being able to "learn" an articulate language, and if in addition one had to attribute to it the innateness of a rational linguistic structure, then this structure would itself be subject to a random origin and would make of reason a collection of mere "working hypotheses," in the sense of Lorenz. My second reason is that the "innate fixed nucleus" would retain all its properties of a "fixed nucleus" if it were not innate but constituted the "necessary" result of the constructions of sensorimotor intelligence, which is prior to language and results from those joint organic and behavioral autoregulations that determine this epigenesis. It is indeed this explanation of a noninnate fixed nucleus, produced by sensorimotor intelligence, that has been finally admitted by authors such as Brown, Lenneberg, and McNeill. This is enough to indicate that the hypothesis of innateness is not mandatory in order to secure the coherence of Chomsky's beautiful system.

Necessity and Equilibration

We still have to look for the reason why the constructions required by the formation of reason become progressively necessary when each one begins by various trials that are partly episodic and that contain, until rather late, an important component of irrational thought (non-conservations, errors of reversibility, insufficient control over negations, and so on). The hypothesis naturally will be that this increasing necessity arises from autoregulation and has a counterpart with the increasing, parallel equilibration of cognitive structures. Necessity then proceeds from their "interlocking."

Three forms of equilibration can be distinguished in this respect. The most simple, and therefore the most precocious, is that of assimilation and accommodation. Already at the sensorimotor level, it is obvious that in order to apply a scheme of actions to new objects, this scheme must be differentiated according to the properties of these objects; therefore one obtains an equilibrium aimed at both preserving the scheme and taking into account the properties of the object. If however, these properties turn out to be unexpected and interesting, the formation of a subscheme or even of a new scheme has to prove feasible. Such new schemes will then necessitate an equilibration of their own. But these functional mechanisms are found at all levels. Even in science, the assimilation between linear and angular speeds involves two joint operations: common space-time relationships are assimilated while one accommodates for these nonetheless distinct solutions; similarly, the incorporation of open systems to general thermodynamic systems requires differentiating accommodation as well as assimilations.

A second form of equilibrium imposes itself between the subsystems, whether it is a question of subschemes in a scheme of action, subclasses in a general class, or subsystems of the totality of operations that a subject has at his disposal, as for example, the equilibration between spatial numbers and measurement during calculations in which both can intervene. Now, since subsystems normally evolve at different speeds, there can be conflicts between them. Their equilibration presupposes in this case a distinction between their common parts and their different properties, and consequently a compensatory adjustment between partial affirmations and negations as well as between direct or inverted operations, or even the utilization of reciprocities. One can see, then, how equilibration leads to logical necessity: the progressive coherence, sought and finally attained by the subject, first comes from a mere causal regulation of actions of which the results are revealed, after the fact, to be compatible or contradictory; this progressive coherence then achieves a comprehension of linkings or implications that have become deductible and thereby necessary.

The third form of equilibration relies upon the previous one but distinguishes itself by the construction of a new global system: it is the form of equilibration required by the very process of differentiation of new systems, which requires then a compensatory step of integration into a new totality. Apparently, there is here a simple balance of opposing forces, the differentiation threatening the unity of the whole and the integration jeopardizing the necessary distinctions. In fact, the originality of the cognitive equilibrium (and, by the way, further down in the hierarchy, also of organic systems) is to ensure, against expectations, the enrichment of the whole as a function of the importance of these differentiations and to ensure their multiplication (and not only their consistency) as a function of intrinsic (or having become such) variations of the totality of its own characteristics. Here again one clearly sees the relationship between equilibration and progressive logical necessity, that is, the necessity of the *terminus ad quem* resulting from the final integration or "interlocking" of the systems.

In summary, cognitive equilibration is consequently "accretive" (*majorante*); that is to say, the disequilibria do not lead back to the previous form of equilibrium, but to a better form, characterized by the increase of mutual dependencies or necessary implications.

As for experimental knowledge, its equilibration admits, in addition to the previous laws, of a progressive transfer (*passage*) from the exogenous to the endogenous, in the sense that perturbations (falsifications of expectations) are first nullified or neutralized, then progressively integrated (with displacement of equilibrium), and finally incorporated into the system as deducible intrinsic variations reconstructing the exogenous by way of the endogenous. The biological equivalent of this process (compare "from noise to order" in von Foerster)[4] is to be sought in the "phenocopy," as I have endeavored to interpret and to generalize this notion in a recent paper.[5]

Psychogenesis and History of Science

As Holton said, one can recognize certain convergences between psychogenesis and the historical development of cognitive structures;[6] this is what I will attempt to define in an upcoming work with the physicist Rolando Garcia.

In some cases, before seventeenth-century science, one can even observe a stage-by-stage parallelism. For instance, in regard to the relationship between force and movement, one can distinguish four periods: (1) the Aristotelian theory of the two motors with, as a consequence, the model of *antiperistasis*; (2) an overall explanation in which force, movement, and impetus remain undifferentiated; (3) the theory of impetus (or *élan*), conceived by Buridan as a necessary intermediary between force and movement; and (4) a final and pre-Newtonian period in which impetus tends to conflate with acceleration. Now, one notes a succession of four very similar stages in the child. The first one is that one in which the two motors remain rather systematic as residues of animism, but with a large number of spontaneous examples of *antiperistasis* (and this often occurs in very unexpected situations, and not only for the movement of projectiles). During a second stage, an overall notion comparable to "action" intervenes and can be symbolized by *mve*, in which *m* represents the weight, *v* the speed, and *e* the distance covered. During a third period (ages 7 to 10), the "impetus" in the sense of Buridan's middle term spontaneously appears, but with, in addition, the power of "passing through" motionless intermediaries by passing through their "interior" when a movement is transmitted through their mediation. Finally, in a fourth phase (around the age of 11 to 12), the first inklings of the notion of acceleration appear.

For larger periods of history, obviously one does not find any stage-by-stage parallelism, but one can search for common mechanisms. For instance, the history of Western geometry bears witness to a process of structuration whose steps are those of a centration on an emphasis by Euclid on simply intrafigural relationships, then a construction of interfigural relationships with Cartesian coordinate systems, and then finally a progressive algebrization by Klein. Now one finds, on a small scale, a similar process in children, who naturally begin with the "intrafigural," but who discover around their seventh year that in order to determinate a point on a plane, one measurement is not sufficient, but two are necessary, and they must be orthogonally arranged. After this "interfigural" stage (which is necessary also for the construction of horizontal lines) follows that which we can call the "transfigural" stage, in which the properties to be discovered cannot be read on a single diagram, but necessitate a deduction or a calculation (for example, mechanical curves, relative motions, and so on).

Now, these analogies with the history of science assuredly speak in favor of my constructivism. *Antiperistasis* was not transmitted hereditarily from Aristotle to the little Genevans, but Aristotle began by being a child; for childhood precedes adulthood in all men, including cavemen. As for what the scientist keeps from his younger years, it is not a collection of innate ideas, since there are tentative procedures in both cases, but a constructive ability; and one of us went so far as to say that a physicist of genius is a man who has retained the creativity inherent to childhood instead of losing it in school.

Notes

1. Considering the number of these additions and not only their result.

2. Let us recall that completive generalization is a constructive process essential in mathematics: for example, the transition from passages of groupoids to semigroups, then from there to monoids, then to groups, to rings, and to bodies.

3. It is true that autoregulation is in part innate, but more in terms of functioning than in terms of structures.

4. H. von Foerster, "On Self-organizing Systems and Their Environments," in *Self-organizing Systems*, ed. M. Yovitz and S. E. Cameron (Elmsford, N.Y.: Pergamon Press, 1960).

5. J. Piaget, *Adaptation vitale et psychologie de l'intelligence: Sélection organique et phénocopie* (Paris: Hermann, 1974).

6. G. Holton, *Thematic Origins of Scientific Thought* (Cambridge, Mass.: Harvard University Press, 1973), p. 102.

67 On Cognitive Structures and Their Development: A Reply to Piaget

Noam Chomsky

In his interesting remarks on the psychogenesis of knowledge and its epistemological significance, Jean Piaget formulates three general points of view as to how knowledge is acquired: empiricism, "preformation" ("innatism"), and his own "constructivism." He correctly characterizes my views as, in his terms, a variety of "innatism." Specifically, investigation of human language has led me to believe that a genetically determined language faculty, one component of the human mind, specifies a certain class of "humanly accessible grammars." The child acquires one of the grammars (actually, a system of such grammars, but I will abstract to the simplest, ideal case) on the basis of the limited evidence available to him. Within a given speech-community, children with varying experience acquire comparable grammars, vastly underdetermined by the available evidence. We may think of a grammar, represented somehow in the mind, as a system that specifies the phonetic, syntactic, and semantic properties of an infinite class of potential sentences. The child knows the language so determined by the grammar he has acquired. This grammar is a representation of his "intrinsic competence." In acquiring language, the child also develops "performance systems" for putting this knowledge to use (for example, production and perception strategies). So little is known about the general properties of performance systems that one can only speculate as to the basis for their development. My guess would be that, as in the case of grammars, a fixed, genetically determined system of some sort narrowly constrains the forms that they can assume. I would also speculate that other cognitive structures developed by humans might profitably be analyzed along similar lines.

Against this conception Piaget offers two basic arguments: (1) the mutations, specific to humans, that might have given rise to the postulated innate structures are "biologically inexplicable"; (2) what can be explained on the assumption of fixed innate structures can be explained as well as "the 'necessary' result of constructions of sensorimotor intelligence."

Neither argument seems to me compelling. As for the first, I agree only in part. The evolutionary development is, no doubt, "biologically unexplained." However, I know of no reason to believe the stronger contention that it is "biologically inexplicable." Exactly the same can be said with regard to the physical organs of the body. Their evolutionary development is "biologically unexplained," in exactly the same sense. We can, *post hoc*, offer an account as to how this development might have taken place, but we cannot provide a theory to select the actual line of development, rejecting others that appear to be no less consistent with the principles that have been advanced concerning the evolution of organisms. Although it is quite true that we have no idea how or why random mutations have endowed humans with the specific capacity to learn a human language, it is also true that we have no better idea how or why random mutations have led to the development of the particular structures of the mammalian eye or the cerebral cortex. We do not therefore conclude that the basic nature of these structures in the mature individual is determined through interaction with the environment (though such interaction is no doubt required to set genetically determined processes into motion and of course influences the character of the mature organs). Little is known concerning evolutionary development, but from ignorance, it is impossible to draw any conclusions. In particular, it is rash to conclude either (A) that known physical laws do not suffice in principle to account for the development of particular structures, or (B) that physical laws, known or unknown, do not suffice in principle. Either (A) or (B) would seem to be entailed by the contention that evolutionary development is literally "inexplicable" on biological grounds. But there seems to be no present justification for taking (B) seriously, and (A), though conceivably true, is mere speculation. In any event, the crucial point in the present connection is that cognitive structures and physical organs seem to be comparable, as far as the possibility of "biological explanation" is concerned.

The second argument seems to me a more important one. However, I see no basis for Piaget's conclusion. There are, to my knowledge, no substantive proposals involving "constructions of sensorimotor intelligence" that offer any hope of accounting for the phenomena of language that demand explanation. Nor is there any initial plausibility to the suggestion, as far as I can see. I might add that although some have argued that the assumption of a genetically determined language faculty is "begging the question," this contention is certainly unwarranted. The assumption is no more "question-begging" in the case of mental structures than is the analogous assumption in the case of growth of physical organs. Substantive proposals regarding the character of this language faculty are refutable if false, confirmable if true. Particular hypotheses have repeatedly been challenged and modified in the light of later research, and I have no doubt that this will continue to be the case.

It is a curiosity of our intellectual history that cognitive structures developed by the mind are generally regarded and studied very differently from physical structures developed by the body. There is no reason why a neutral scientist, unencumbered by traditional doctrine, should adopt this view. Rather, he would, or should, approach cognitive structures such as human language more or less as he would investigate an organ such as the eye or heart, seeking to determine: (1) its character in a particular individual; (2) its general properties, invariant across the species apart from gross defect; (3) its place in a system of such structures; (4) the course of its development in the individual; (5) the genetically determined basis for this development; (6) the factors that gave rise to this mental organ in the course of evolution. The expectation that constructions of sensorimotor intelligence determine the character of a mental organ such as language seems to me hardly more plausible than a proposal that the fundamental properties of the eye or the visual cortex or the heart develop on this basis. Furthermore, when we turn to specific properties of this mental organ, we find little justification for any such belief, so far as I can see.

I will not attempt a detailed argument here, but will merely sketch the kind of reasoning that leads me to the conclusions just expressed.

Suppose that we set ourselves the task of studying the cognitive growth of a person in a natural environment. We may begin by attempting to delimit certain cognitive domains, each governed by an integrated system of principles of some sort. It is, surely, a legitimate move to take language to be one such domain, though its exact boundaries and relations to other domains remain to be determined. In just the same way, we might proceed to study the nature and development of some organ of the body. Under this quite legitimate assumption, we observe that a person proceeds from a genetically determined initial state S_0 through a sequence of states $S_1, S_2, \ldots$, finally reaching a "steady state" S_s which then seems to change only marginally (say, by the addition of new vocabulary). The steady state is attained at a relatively fixed age, apparently by puberty or somewhat earlier. Investigating this steady state, we can construct a hypothesis as to the grammar internally represented. We could try to do the same at intermediate stages, thus gaining further insight into the growth of language.

In principle, it is possible to obtain as complete a record as we like of the experience available to the person who has achieved this steady state. We make no such attempt in practice, of course, but we can nevertheless focus on particular aspects of this experience relevant to specific hypotheses as to the nature of S_s and S_0. Assuming a sufficient record E of relevant experience, we can then proceed to construct a second-order hypothesis as to the character of S_0. This hypothesis must meet certain empirical conditions: It cannot be so specific as to rule out attested steady states, across languages; it must suffice to account for the transition from S_0 to S_s, given E, for any (normal) person. We may think of this hypothesis as a hypothesis with regard to a function mapping E into S_s. For any choice of E sufficient to give rise to knowledge of some human language L, this function must assign an appropriate S_s in which the grammar of L is represented. We might refer to this function as "the learning theory for humans in the domain language"—call it LT(H, L). Abstracting away from individual differences, we may take S_0—which specifies LT(H, L)—to be a genetically determined species character. Refinements are possible, as we consider stages of development more carefully.

More generally, for any species O and cognitive domain D that have been tentatively identified and delimited, we may, correspondingly, investigate LT(O, D), the "learning theory" for the organism O in the domain D, a property of the genetically determined initial state. Suppose, for example, that we are investigating the ability of humans to recognize and identify human faces. Assuming "face-recognition" to constitute a legitimate cognitive domain F, we may try to specify LT(H, F), the genetically determined principles that give rise to a steady state (apparently some time after language is neurally fixed, and perhaps represented in homologous regions of the right hemisphere, as some recent work suggests). Similarly, other cognitive domains can be studied in humans and other organisms. We would hardly expect to find interesting properties common to LT(O, D) for arbitrary O, D; that is, we would hardly expect to discover that there exists something that might be called "general learning theory." As far as I know, the prospects for such a theory are no brighter than for a "growth theory," intermediate in level between cellular biology and the study of particular organs, and concerned with the principles that govern the growth of arbitrary organs for arbitrary organisms.

Again, we may refine the investigation, considering intermediate states as well.

Returning to the case of language, to discover the properties of S_0 we will naturally focus attention on properties of later states (in particular, S_s) that are not determined by E, that is, elements of language that are known but for which there appears to be no relevant evidence. Consider a few examples.

The Structure-Dependent Property of Linguistic Rules

Consider the process of formation of simple yes-or-no questions in English. We have such declarative-question pairs as (1):

(1) The man is here.—Is the man here?
The man will leave.—Will the man leave?

Consider the following two hypotheses put forth to account for this infinite class of pairs:

H_1: process the declarative from beginning to end (left to right), word by word, until reaching the first occurrence of the words *is*, *will*, etc.; transpose this occurrence to the beginning (left), forming the associated interrogative.

H_2: same as H_1, but select the first occurrence of *is*, *will*, etc., following the first noun phrase of the declarative.

Let us refer to H_1 as a "structure-independent rule" and H_2 as a "structure-dependent rule." Thus, H_1 requires analysis of the declarative into just a sequence of words, whereas H_2 requires an analysis into successive words and also abstract phrases such as "noun phrase." The phrases are "abstract" in that their boundaries and labeling are not in general physically marked in any way; rather, they are mental constructions.

A scientist observing English speakers, given such data as (1), would naturally select hypothesis H_1 over the far more complex hypothesis H_2, which postulates abstract mental processing of a nontrivial sort beyond H_1. Similarly, given such data as (1) it is reasonable to assume that an "unstructured" child would assume that H_1 is valid. In fact, as we know, it is not, and H_2 is (more nearly) correct. Thus consider the data of (2):

(2) The man who is here is tall.—Is the man who is here tall?
The man who is tall will leave.—Will the man who is tall leave?

These data are predicted by H_2 and refute H_1, which would predict rather the interrogatives (3):

(3) Is the man who here is tall?
Is the man who tall will leave?

Now the question that arises is this: how does a child know that H_2 is correct (nearly), while H_1 is false? It is surely not the case that he first hits on H_1 (as a neutral scientist would) and then is forced to reject it on the basis of data such as (2). No child is taught the relevant facts. Children make many errors in language learning, but none such as (3), prior to appropriate training or evidence. A person might go through much or all of his life without ever having been exposed to relevant evidence, but he will nevertheless unerringly employ H_2, never H_1, on the first relevant occasion (assuming that he can handle the structures at all). We cannot, it seems, explain the preference for H_2 on grounds of communicative efficiency or the like. Nor do there appear to be relevant analogies of other than the most superficial and uninformative sort in other cognitive domains. If humans were differently designed, they would acquire a grammar that incorporates H_1, and would be none the worse for that. In fact, it would be difficult to know, by mere passive observation of a person's total linguistic performance, whether he was using H_1 or H_2.

Such observations suggest that it is a property of S_0—that is, of LT(H, L)—that rules (or rules of some specific category, identifiable on quite general grounds by some genetically determined mechanism) are structure-dependent. The child need not consider H_1; it is ruled out by properties of his initial mental state, S_0. Although this example is very simple, almost trivial, it illustrates the general problem that arises when we attend to the specific properties of attained cognitive states.

68 What Is Innate and Why: Comments on the Debate

Hilary Putnam

I can say in a nutshell what I think about Chomsky and Piaget; neither has good arguments, but there is almost certainly something to what each one says. In this paper I am first going to say why the arguments are not good, and then discuss the more important question of why there is something right to what they say.

I shall begin with Chomsky's arguments. When one reads Chomsky, one is struck by a sense of great intellectual power; one knows one is encountering an extraordinary mind. And this is as much a matter of the spell of his powerful personality as it is of his obvious intellectual virtues: originality; scorn for the faddish and the superficial; willingness to revive (and the ability to revive) positions (such as the "doctrine of innate ideas") that had seemed passé; concern with topics, such as the structure of the human mind, that are of central and perennial importance. Yet I want to claim that his individual arguments are *not good.* I will examine only one example here, but I claim that a similar examination could be carried out on any of the arguments he has offered at this conference, with similar results.

The argument concerns "the process of formation of simple yes-or-no questions in English." In his paper, Chomsky considers "such declarative-question pairs" as:

(1) The man is here.—Is the man here?
The man will leave.—Will the man leave?

And he considers two hypotheses "put forth to account for this infinite class of pairs" (of course, H_1 has never been "put forth" by anyone, nor would any sane person put it forth):

H_1: process the declarative from beginning to end (left to right), word by word, until reaching the first occurrence of the words *is, will,* etc.; transpose this occurrence to the beginning (left), forming the associated interrogative.

H_2: same as H_1, but select the first occurrence of *is, will,* etc., following the first noun phrase of the declarative.

Chomsky then writes:

> Let us refer to H_1 as a "structure-independent rule" and H_2 as a "structure-dependent rule." Thus, H_1 requires analysis of the declarative into just a sequence of words, whereas H_2 requires an analysis into successive words and also abstract phrases such as "noun phrase." The phrases are "abstract" in that their boundaries and labeling are not in general physically marked in any way; rather, they are mental constructions.

A scientist observing English speakers, given such data as (1), would naturally select hypothesis H_1 over the far more complex hypothesis H_2, which postulates abstract mental processing of a nontrivial sort beyond H_1. Similarly, given such data as (1) it is reasonable to assume that an "unstructured" child would assume that H_1 is valid. In fact, as we know, it is not, and H_2 is (more nearly) correct. Thus consider the data of (2):

(2) The man who is here is tall.—Is the man who is here tall?
The man who is tall will leave.—Will the man who is tall leave?

These data are predicted by H_2 and refute H_1, which would predict rather the interrogatives (3):

(3) Is the man who here is tall?
Is the man who tall will leave?

Now the question that arises is this: how does a child know that H_2 is correct (nearly), while H_1 is false? It is surely not the case that he first hits on H_1 (as a neutral scientist would) and then is forced to reject it on the basis of data such as (2).

Chomsky's conclusion from all this is the following:

Such observations suggest that it is a property of S_0—that is, of LT(H, L)—that rules (or rules of some specific category, identifiable on quite general grounds by some genetically determined mechanism) are structure-dependent. The child need not consider H_1; it is ruled out by properties of his initial mental state, S_0.

I wish to discuss this example by considering two different questions: (1) can we account for the child's selection of "structure-dependent" hypotheses and concepts in the course of language learning on the basis of general intelligence, without postulating that the preference for H_2 over H_1 is built in, or that a template of a typical human language is built in, as Chomsky wishes us to do; and (2) can we account specifically for the preference of H_2 over H_1 without assuming that such a specific preference is built in? Before discussing these questions, however, I want to consider the vexed question, "What is a grammar?"

The Nature of Grammars

A grammar is some sort of system which—ideally—generates the "grammatical sentences" of a language and none of the ungrammatical ones. And a grammatical sentence is one generated by *the* grammar of the language (or by any adequate one, if one believes as Zellig Harris does that there is no such thing as *the* grammar of a language).[1] This is obviously a circular definition. But how does one break the circularity?

Chomsky suggested long ago (in "Explanatory Models in Linguistics")[2] that a child *hears* people classing sentences as "grammatical" or "ungrammatical"—not, of course, in those words, but by hearing them correct each other or the child—and that he projects a grammar as a simplest extrapolation from such data satisfying some innate constraints.

The trouble with this view is that the factual premise is clearly false. People don't object to all and only *ungrammatical* sentences. If they object at all, it is to *deviant* sentences—but they do not, when they correct each other, clearly say (in a way that a child can understand) whether the deviance was syntactic, semantic, discourse-theoretic, or whatever.

Chomsky asserts that the child is, in effect, supplied with "a list of grammatical sentences" and "a list of ungrammatical sentences" and has to extrapolate from these two lists. But this is surely false. If anything, he is supplied rather with a list of acceptable sentences and a list of sentences that are deviant-for-some-reason-or-other; a grammar of his language will generate (idealizing somewhat) all of the acceptable sentences in the first list, but unfortunately, it will not be the case that it generates none of the deviant sentences in the other list. On the contrary, the grammatical sentences will be a superset of the (finite list of) acceptable sentences, which is *not disjoint from* the (finite list of) deviant sentences.

Moreover, the second list does not have to exist at all. Chomsky has cited evidence that children can learn their first language without being corrected; and I am sure he also believes that they don't need to hear anyone else corrected either. Chomsky might reply to this by scrapping the hypothetical second list (the list of "ungrammatical," or at least, "unacceptable" sentences). He might say that the grammar of an arbitrary language is the simplest projection of any suitable finite set of acceptable sentences satisfying some set of innate constraints. This throws the whole burden of defining what a grammar is on the innate constraints. I want to suggest a different approach: one that says, in quite traditional fashion, that the grammar of a language is a property of the *language*, not a property of the brain of *Homo sapiens*.

Propositional Calculus

Let us start with a simple and well-understood example: the artificial language called "propositional calculus" with its standard interpretation. The grammar of propositional calculus can be stated in many different but equivalent ways. Here is a typical one:

(I) A propositional variable standing alone is a well-formed formula.

(II) If A and B are well-formed formulas, so are ~A, (A & B), (A ∨ B) and (A ⊃ B).[3]

(III) Nothing is a well-formed formula unless its being so follows from (I) and (II).

The fact that a perfectly grammatical sentence may be deviant for semantic reasons, which is a feature of natural languages, is possessed also by this simple language, since "p & ~p" (for example) is perfectly grammatical but would not be "uttered" for obvious semantic reasons.

Now consider the "semantics" of propositional calculus as represented by the following inductive definition of *truth* in terms of *primitive truth* (truth for propositional variables, which is left undefined). The fact that primitive truth is left undefined means that this can be thought of as an *interpretation-schema*, which becomes an interpretation when joined to any definition of primitive truth.

Definition:

(i) ~A is true if and only if A is not true.

(ii) (A & B) is true if and only if A and B are both true.

(iii) (A ∨ B) is true if and only if at least one of A, B is true.

(iv) (A ⊃ B) is true unless A is true and B is not true.

Notice that the inductive definition of *truth* in propositional calculus parallels (in a sense which could be made precise, but which I will not attempt to make precise here) the inductive definition of *grammatical* in propositional calculus. Now, there are other ways of defining grammatical in propositional calculus with the property that corresponding to them there exist parallel inductive definitions of truth in propositional calculus. But if we limit ourselves to those that are computationally feasible (that is, the corresponding decision program is short, when written in any standard format, and the typical computation is also short), not a great many are known, and they are all extremely similar. In this sense, propositional calculus as an interpreted system possesses an *intrinsic* grammar and semantics.

Let me elaborate on this a little. If Martians exist, very likely they have hit upon propositional calculus, and it may be that when they use propositional calculus their logicians' brains employ different heuristics than our logicians' brains employ. But that does not mean that propositional calculus has a different grammar when used by a Martian and when used by a Terrestrian. The grammar is (any one of) the simplest inductive definition(s) of the set of strings in the alphabet of propositional calculus for which truth is defined—that is, the simplest inductive definition(s) with the property that there exist parallel inductive definitions of truth. Given the semantics of propositional calculus (and no information about the brains of speakers), the class of reasonable grammars is fixed by that semantics, *not* by the structure of the brains that do the processing.

It may seem that I have begged too many questions by introducing the predicate "true"; but it is not essential to my argument. Suppose we do not define "true," but rather "follows from." Any reasonably simple definition of the relation "x follows from y" in propositional calculus will have the property that it presupposes a syntactic analysis of the standard kind. In other words, checking that something is an axiom or a proof, etc., will involve checking that strings and components of strings have the forms (p & q), ~p, (p ∨ q), (p ⊃ q). The grammar (I), (II), (III) not only generates the set of strings over which the relation "follows from" is defined, but it generates it in a way that corresponds to properties of strings referred to in the definition of "follows from."

Coming to natural language: suppose we think of a natural language as a very complicated formalized language whose formalization is unknown. (This seems to be how Chomsky thinks of it.) Suppose we think of the speaker as a computer that, among other things, computes whether certain strings are "true," given certain inputs, or if you don't like "true," as a computer that computes whether certain sequences of strings are "proofs," or computes the "degree of confirmation" of certain strings, and so forth. The fact is that any one of these semantic, or deductive logical, or inductive logical notions will have an *inductive definition* whose clauses parallel or at least presuppose a syntactic analysis of the language.

To come right out with it: I am suggesting (1) that the declarative grammar of a language is the inductive definition of a set of strings which is the set over which semantic, deductive-logical, inductive-logical (and so on) predicates are defined;[4] (2) that it must be in such a form that the inductive definitions of these predicates can easily "parallel" it; (3) that the corresponding decision program must be as computationally feasible as is consistent with (1) and (2). If a language is thought of in this way—as a system of strings with a semantics, with a deductive logic, with an inductive logic, and so on—then it is easy to see how the grammar can be a property of the *language* and not of the speakers' *brains*.

The Nature of Language Learning

Let us consider the linguistic abilities of Washoe (the chimpanzee brought up to use a certain amount of deaf-mute sign language by Alan and Beatrice Gardner). No doubt Chomsky will point out that Washoe lacks many of the syntactic abilities that humans have, and on these grounds he would claim that it is wrong to apply the term "language" to what she has learned. But the application of this term is not what is important. What is important is the following:

1. There is a certain class of words, which I will call *nouns-for-Washoe*, which Washoe associates with (classes of) *things*. For example, Washoe associates the word "grape" (in sign language) with more-or-less stereotypical grapes, "banana" with more-or-less stereotypical bananas, and so forth.
2. There is a *frame*, ______ gives ______ (to) ______, which Washoe has acquired (for example, "Alan gives apple to Trixie").
3. She can project *new* uses of this frame. If you teach her a new word, say "date," she will figure out herself the use she is expected to make of "______ gives *date* (to) ______."
4. She can use the word "and" to combine sentences. She can figure out the expected use of *p* and *q* from the uses of p and q separately.[5]

Actually Washoe's abilities go far beyond these four capacities; but let us just consider these for now. The only plausible account of what has occurred is that Washoe has "internalized" a rule to the effect that if X is a *noun-for-Washoe*, and A, B, and C are people's names—counting Washoe (of course) as a person—then "A gives X to B" is a sentence, and a rule to the effect that if p, q are sentences so is *p and q*. And these are *structure-dependent rules* which Washoe has learned *without benefit of an innate template for language*.

Nor is this really surprising. Let us introduce a semantic predicate to describe the above tiny fragment of Washoe's "language" (where the "shudder-quotes" are inserted to avoid the accusation of question-begging), say, the predicate "corresponds to the condition that." Here are the "semantic rules" for the fragment in question:

(I) If X is a *noun-for-Washoe* and B, C are people-names, and X corresponds to things of kind K, and b, c are the people corresponding to B, C, then "B gives X (to) C" corresponds to the condition that b gives something of kind K to c.

(II) If p, q are *sentences-for-Washoe, p and q* corresponds to the condition that the condition corresponding to p and the condition corresponding to q both obtain.

Now, I submit that Washoe is not really interested in learning that certain *uninterpreted* strings of gestures have a certain *uninterpreted* property called "grammaticality." She is interested for practical reasons—reward, approval, and so forth—in learning (I) and (II). But learning (I) and (II) automatically involves learning the grammatical facts that:

(i) If B, C are people-names and X is a *noun-for-Washoe*, "B gives X (to) C" is a sentence-for-Washoe.

(ii) If p, q are sentences-for-Washoe, so is *p and q*.

For the set of sentences "generated" by the "grammar" (i), (ii) is precisely the set over which the semantic predicate—"corresponds to the condition that ______"—is defined by the inductive definition (I), (II); and the clauses (I), (II) presuppose precisely the syntactic analysis given by (i), (ii). Given that Washoe is trying to learn the *semantics* of Washoe-ese, and the syntax is only a *means* to this end, there are only two possibilities: either her intelligence will be too low to internalize "structure-dependent" rules like (I), (II), and she will fail; or her intelligence will be high enough, and as a corollary we will be able to ascribe to Washoe "implicit knowledge" of the syntactic rules (i), (ii)—not because she "knows" (I), (II) *and in addition* "knows" (i), (ii), but because having the "know-how" that constitutes implicit knowledge of (I), (II) *includes* implicit knowledge of (i), (ii).

But the same thing is true of the child. The child is not trying to learn a bunch of *syntactic* rules as a kind of crazy end-in-itself. He is learning, and he wants to learn, *semantic* rules, and these *cannot* be stated without the use of structure-dependent notions. There aren't even plausible candidates for structure-independent semantic rules. So *of course* (given that his intelligence is high enough to learn language), *of course* the child "internalizes" structure-dependent rules. And given that he must be building up an "inner representation" of abstract structural notions such as *sentence*, *noun*, *verb phrase*, and so on in learning to understand the language, the mere fact that H_2 uses such notions and H_1 does not, does *not* make H_2 so much less plausible than H_1.

Chomsky has, so to speak, "pulled a fast one" on us. He presents us with a picture of the child as being like an insanely scientistic linguist. Both are looking at language as a stream of uninterpreted noises; both are interested in an occult property of "grammaticality." From this (crazy) point of view, it is not surprising that H_1 seems infinitely "simpler" than H_2. So—Chomsky springs his carefully prepared trap—"Why doesn't the child try the simpler-but-false hypothesis H_1 *before* the correct hypothesis H_2?"

But this isn't what children (or sane linguists) are like at all. The child is in the process of trying to understand English. He has already tumbled (if Washoe can, so can he!) to the fact that he needs to internalize structure-dependent notions to do this. So the mere fact that H_2 *uses* such notions doesn't at all make it implausible or excessively complex. The point is that the *learning of grammar is dependent on the learning of semantics*. And there aren't even any candidates for structure-independent semantic rules (if there are, they get knocked out pretty early, even by a chimpanzee's brain).

H_1 Considered More Closely

So far I have argued that H_2 is not nearly as weird from the point of view of the intelligent brain unaided by an innate template of language as Chomsky wants to make it seem. But I haven't argued against H_1. So still the question remains, why doesn't the child try H_1?

Let us try applying to this problem the conception of grammar we just sketched (grammar as, so to speak, semantics minus the semantic predicates). H_1 will only be "tried" by the child if the child "tries" some *semantic* hypotheses that correspond to H_1. The child wants to *understand* questions, not just to "flag" them as questions. But it is plausible to assume (and Chomsky himself would assume) that understanding questions involves recovering the underlying declarative. This means that the question-transformation must have an *inverse* the child can perform. H_1 is indeed simple, but *its inverse is horribly complicated.* Moreover, *its inverse uses the full resources of the grammar*; all the notions, such as "noun phrase," that H_1 does not employ have to be employed in recovering the declarative from the output of our application of H_1. So it is no mystery that the child (or its brain) never "tries" such an unworkable semantic theory, and hence never "tries" H_1.

Incidentally, H_1 itself employs "abstract" notions, since it contains the phrase-structure concept "declarative," and applying it, if it were a rule of English, would therefore involve working with notions such as "noun phrase," since these have to be used to recognize declaratives. And some languages do have question-transformations that are as "structure-independent" as H_1 is; for example, in Hebrew one can form a question from a declarative by just prefixing *na im*. But this prefixing operation *does* have a simple inverse, namely, deleting *na im.*

I would like now to discuss Chomsky's more abstract remarks at the beginning of his paper. Let me begin with what he says about intelligence.

Chomsky on General Intelligence

So far I have assumed that there is such a thing as general intelligence; that is, that whatever else our innate cognitive repertoire may include, it *must* include *multipurpose* learning strategies, heuristics, and so forth. But Chomsky appears to deny this assumption explicitly. I quote:

> More generally, for any species O and cognitive domain D that have been tentatively identified and delimited, we may, correspondingly, investigate LT(O, D), the "learning theory" for the organism O in the domain D, a property of the genetically determined initial state. Suppose, for example, that we are investigating the ability of humans to recognize and identify human faces. Assuming "face-recognition" to constitute a legitimate cognitive domain F, we may try to specify LT(H, F), the genetically determined principles that give rise to a steady state (apparently some time after language is neurally fixed, and perhaps represented in homologous regions of the right hemisphere, as some recent work suggests). Similarly, other cognitive domains can be studied in humans and other organisms. We would hardly expect to find interesting properties common to LT(O, D) for arbitrary O, D; that is, we would hardly expect to discover that there exists something that might be called "general learning theory." As far as I know, the prospects for such a theory are no brighter than for a "growth theory," intermediate in level between cellular biology and the study of particular organs, and concerned with the principles that govern the growth of arbitrary organs for arbitrary organisms.

The key notion in this argument is the notion of a "domain." How wide is a domain? Is all of mathematics one domain? If so, what about empirical science? Or are physics, chemistry, and so on, all *different* domains?

If Chomsky admits that a domain can be as wide as empirical science (that there can be a "learning theory for empirical science"), then he has granted that something exists that may fittingly be called "general intelligence." (Chomsky might retort that only exceptionally intelligent individuals can discover new truths in empirical science, whereas everyone learns his native language. But this is an extraordinarily elitist argument: the abilities of exceptionally intelligent men must be *continuous* with those of ordinary men, after all, and the relevant mechanisms must be present at some level of functioning in all human brains.) Even if only physics, or just all of solid-state physics, or just all of the solid-state physics of crystals is one domain, the same point holds: heuristics and strategies capable of enabling us to learn new facts in these areas must be extraordinarily multipurpose (and we have presently no idea what they are). Once it is granted that such multipurpose learning strategies exist, the claim that they *cannot* account for language learning becomes highly dubious, as I argued long ago.[6] (Consider Washoe!)

On the other hand, if domains become so small that each domain can use only learning strategies that are highly specific in purpose (such as "recognizing faces," "learning a grammar"), then it becomes really a miracle that evolution endowed us with all these skills, most of which (for example, higher mathematics, nuclear physics) were not used at all until *after* the evolution of the race was complete (some 100,000-odd years ago). And the analogy with organ growth does not then hold at all: the reason there does not have to be a multipurpose learning mechanism is that there are only limited numbers of organs, whereas there are virtually unlimited numbers of "domains."

The Prospects of General Learning Theory

Chomsky feels that the "prospects" of "general learning theory" are bad. I tend to agree. I see no reason to think that the detailed functioning of the human mind will ever be transparent to the human mind.[7] But the existence of general intelligence is one question; the prospect for a revealing *description* of it is another.

Incidentally, if the innateness hypothesis is right, I am also not optimistic about the prospects for a revealing description of the innate template of language. The examples Chomsky has given us of how to go about inferring the structure of the template (such as the argument about H_1 and H_2) are such bad arguments that they cast serious doubt on the feasibility of the whole program, at least at this point in history (especially if there exist *both* general intelligence *and* an innate template).

On the other hand, we may well be able to discover interesting facts and laws about general intelligence without being able to describe it completely, or to model it by, say, a computer program. There may be progress in studying general intelligence without its being the case that we ever succeed in writing down a "general learning theory" in the sense of a mathematical model of multipurpose learning.

Chomsky on Evolution

Chomsky dismisses Piaget's question regarding how such a thing as an innate template for language might have evolved. But he should not dismiss it. One answer he might have given is this: primitive language first appeared as an *invention*, introduced by some extraordinary member of the species and learned by the others as Washoe learns her fragment of language. Given such a beginning of the instrument, genetic changes to enable us to use the instrument better (including the enlargement of the so-called speech center in the left lobe of normal humans) could have occurred, and would be explained, if they did occur, by natural selection. Presumably Chomsky did not give this answer because (1) he wants to deny that there exists such a thing as general intelligence, and to deny that even the simplest grammar could be internalized by general intelligence alone; and (2) he wants to deny that Washoe's performance is continuous with language learning, and to deny that it has any interest for the study of language learning. But this is surely perverse. If the first language user *already* had a complete innate template, then this could only have been a miraculous break in the evolutionary sequence, as Piaget in effect points out.

Chomsky remarks that we don't know the details of the development of the motor organs either, and this is surely true. We do postulate that they developed bit by bit. This poses difficulties, however, since there are no creatures with two thirds of a wing! But there have been impressive successes in this direction (for example, working out the evolution of the eye). We have found creatures with gliding membranes which are, in a sense, "two thirds of a wing." And we have found eyes with only rods (no cones) and eyes with only cones (no rods). Since the first draft of this paper was written, there have been exciting new suggestions in evolutionary theory.[8]

It is one thing to say that we cannot scientifically explain how certain structures were produced (and the theory of natural selection does not even claim that those structures were *probable*), and quite another to say that we now have scientific reason to postulate a large number of "mental organs" as specific as the various domains and subdomains of human knowledge. Such a mental organization would not be scientifically explicable at all; it would mean that God simply decided to produce these structures at a certain point in time because they were the ones we would need a half a million (or whatever) years later. (Although I don't doubt that God is ultimately responsible for what we are, it is bad scientific methodology to invoke Him as a *deus ex machina*. And, in any case, this is such a *messy* miracle to attribute to Him! Why should He pack our heads with a billion different "mental organs," rather than just making us smart?) On the other hand, if our language capacity did develop bit by bit, even with "jumps," a description of the first bit will almost certainly sound like a description of Washoe. But then we will have conceded that *some* internalization of linguistic rules (at least in prototype form) can be accounted for without innateness.

A Better Argument

But this suggests that there *is* an argument for *some* "innateness" that Chomsky might have used. Consider the phenomenon called "echo-location" in the bat. The bat emits supersonic "noises," which are reflected from the prey (or whatever—for example, a single insect), and the bat can "steer" by these sound-reflections as well as if it had sight (that is, it can avoid fine wires, catch the mosquito that is trying to avoid it, and so forth). Now, examination of the bat's brain shows that there has been a tremendous enlargement of the centers connected with hearing (they fill about seven-eighths of the bat's brain), as compared to other mammals (including, presumably, those in its evolutionary past). Clearly, a lot of the bat's echo-locating ability is *now* "innate."

Suppose Chomsky were to grant that Washoe has protospeech, and thereby grant that general intelligence can account for *some* language learning. He could then *use evolution as an argument for (some) "innateness."* In other words, we could argue that, given the enormous value of the language ability (as central to human life as echolocation is to bat life), it is *likely* that genetic changes have occurred to make the instrument better—for example, the development of the "speech center" in the left lobe. (But caution is needed: if the left lobe is damaged early, speech *can* develop in the right lobe.) This argument is the only one I know of that makes it plausible that there is *some* innate structuring of human language that is not simply a corollary to the innate (that is, genetically predetermined) structuring of human cognition in general. But the argument is not very strong: it could be *general intelligence* that has been genetically refined bit by bit and not a hypothetical language template. Indeed, even species-specific and functionally useless aspects of all human languages could be the product of unknown but genetically predetermined aspects of the overall functioning of the human brain and not clues to the character of a language template; so the mere existence of such aspects is no evidence at all for the template hypothesis.

I think there is an answer that Chomsky can make to this objection; but I will defer it until I have discussed Piaget.

Piaget's "Constructivism"

The view I have been putting forward—that everything Chomsky ascribes to an innate template of language, a "mental organ" specifically designed to enable us to *talk*, can, for all we know, be explained by general intelligence—agrees in broad outline with the view of Piaget. However, there seem to me to be serious conceptual difficulties with this view when it is combined with Piaget's specific account of what general intelligence is like.

Piaget supposes that human intelligence develops in stages, each stage depending on biological maturation (that is, the age of the child) and on the successful attainment of the previous stages. At a certain stage, certain concepts characteristically appear, for example, the concept of "conservation." But what is it to have such a concept as conservation?

I submit that the only coherent account presently available for having the concept of conservation is this: to have the concept is to have mastered a bit of *theory*, that is, to have acquired the characteristic uses of such expressions as "same amount," and some key *beliefs*, expressed by sentences involving such expressions, or equivalent symbolism. I don't claim that all concepts are abilities to use symbolism; an animal that *expects* the water to reach the same height when it is poured from a pot back into the glass might be said to have a minimal concept of conservation, but I claim that anything like the *full* concept of conservation involves the ability to use symbolism with the complexity of language in certain ways. (I don't claim that this is a "tautology"; rather that it is the only coherent account presently available for what full-blown concepts *are*. And I don't claim to have argued this here, but I have discussed this elsewhere;[9] and, of course, this insight is not mine but Wittgenstein's—indeed, it is the main burden of *Philosophical Investigations*.)

But if a maturational schedule *involving the development of concepts* is innate, and *concepts are essentially connected with language*,[10] then Piaget's hypothesis would seem to imply Chomsky's; "constructivism" would entail "nativism."

Of course, Piaget does not commit so crude an error. He does not suppose that the maturational *schedule* is given (that is, innate); what he takes as given is "reflective abstraction"—it is this that "precedes language" and that is supposed to take us from one "step" to the next.

But "reflection" and "abstraction" have *no literal meaning* apart from *language*! If "reflective abstraction" is not literally meant, it is either a metaphor for empiricist "generalization," which is insufficient to account for language learning and use, or a metaphor for we-know-not-what.

It seems to me that Piaget should take the view that "reflective abstraction" is something *like* the use of language in the making of hypothetico-deductive inferences, as Chomsky and Fodor urge, and hence conclude that something *like* the use of language is "innate." This position would have brought him into convergence with Chomsky, instead of into an unnecessary sectarian squabble. Moreover, his own suggestion in 1958 that formal logic is the best model for human reasoning[11] is very consonant with such a position.

Fodor's "Tautology"

In the discussion Fodor said some things that were a little careless. I want to rectify some of these errors, not for the sake of being "picky," but because the discussion becomes hopelessly confused at the critical point if we let them stand.

First a quibble: Fodor and Chomsky are simply wrong when they say that it is a "tautology" that we can't learn anything, unless some innate "prejudices" are "built in." It is not *logically* impossible that our heads should be as empty as the Tin Woodman's and we should still talk, love, and so on; it would just be an extreme example of a *causal anomaly* if it ever happened that a creature with no internal structure did these things. I don't doubt for one moment that our dispositions *do* have a causal explanation, and of course the functional organization of our brains is where one might look for a causal explanation (although I myself think that we won't be able to describe this in very much detail in the foreseeable future).[12] But this still is not a tautology.

Second, it is true that we can't learn how to learn unless we have some prior learning-dispositions: we have to have some dispositions to learn that are not themselves learned, on pain of infinite regress (however, the impossibility of an infinite regress in the real world is hardly a tautology!); but that does not mean that it is *logically necessary* (a "tautology") that the unlearned dispositions be innate. We might (*logically possibly*) acquire a new *unlearned* disposition every five minutes for no cause at all, for example, or for some cause that does not count as a form of "learning." There just aren't any significant tautologies in this area.

The reason this is not *just* a quibble is this: once we pare down Fodor's and Chomsky's big "tautology" to something like this: *as a matter of fact* (not logic!), *no learning without some laws of learning,* we see that no one, least of all the empiricists, has ever denied it. Chomsky's and Fodor's claim that there is a big, mysterious tautology that no one appreciated until Nelson Goodman and that everyone they dislike fails to appreciate is mere rhetoric....

Fodor's Argument for the Innateness of All Concepts

My aim in the remainder of this paper is to develop a modest a priori argument for the Fodor-Chomsky view that something *like* a language-processing capacity must be innate. But if Fodor's argument in *The Language of Thought* were acceptable, *my* work would be all done. So I must first explain why I reject Fodor's argument.

Fodor's argument has two parts. First, he contends that the only model we have presently available for the brain is the all-purpose digital computer. He contends, moreover, that such a computer, if it "learns" at all, must have an innate "program" for making generalizations in its built-in computer language. (Here he goes too fast—this is precisely what I think we need an *argument* for.) Second, he concludes that every predicate that a brain could learn to use must have a *translation* into the computer language of that brain. So no "new" concepts can be acquired: all concepts are innate!

I want to examine this second part of the argument, which is fallacious even if the first part is granted. Fodor's reasoning is as follows: Learning the meaning of a predicate is inferring what the semantic properties of that predicate are, that is, concluding (inductively) to some such generalization as:

(A) For every x, P is true of x if and only if Q(x).

But if (A) is in brain language, so is Q. (P need not be; P is mentioned, not used in (A). But Q is *used*, not mentioned.) And if (A) is correct, Q is coextensive with P, and is so by virtue of what P *means* (otherwise (A) is not a correct semantic characterization of the meaning of P). So Q is *synonymous* with P; P is not a *new* concept, because there is a predicate (namely, Q) in "brain language" that is synonymous with it. But P is an *arbitrary* predicate the brain can learn to understand—so no new concepts can be learned!

What is wrong with this argument is clear. The assumption is as strong as what Fodor wishes to prove. So all we have to do is show how it could be false, even given Fodor's general outlook, and nothing is left but a simple case of begging the question.

First a point of terminology: Every computer does have a built-in "computer language," but *not* a language that contains quantifiers (that is, the words "all" and "some," or synonyms thereof). Let me explain.

A digital computer is a device that stores its own program and that consults its own program in the course of a computation. It is not at all necessary that the brain be a digital computer in *this* sense. The brain does not, after all, have to be reprogrammed as an all-purpose digital computer does. (One might reply that learning is "reprogramming"; but Fodor is talking about the program *for* learning, not about what is learned, and this program might be stored as the brain's *structure,* not as a code.) Waiving this objection: the program that a digital computer stores consists of "instructions" such as "add the two numbers in address 12" and "go back to step 6"—none of which use the word "all." So generalization (A) *cannot ever be stated* in "machine language," even if the computer's program is a program for making inductive inferences in some formalized language (for example, if the program is that of the hypothetico-deductive machine mentioned earlier). Moreover, machine language does not contain (nor can one introduce into it by definition) such notions as "tree," "cow," "jumps," "spontaneous," "pert," and so on—it only contains such notions as "add," "subtract," "0," "1," "put result in address 17," "go back to instruction so-and-so," and "print out contents of address blah-blah."

Let us suppose, however (what needs to be proved) that our brain is a hypothetico-deductive machine, and that it carries out inference in a formalized language ILL (for Inductive Logic Language) according to some program for eliminative induction. And let us suppose that Fodor is not really talking about the brain's *machine language* when he postulates his "language of thought," but about ILL. Even if so strong an assumption is conceded, his argument still does not work.

To see why it does not work, let us recall that when the speaker has finally mastered the predicate P, on Fodor's model, he is supposed to have acquired a new "subroutine." Even if this subroutine is described initially in ILL or in some special "programming language," or both, it has to have a translation into machine language that the brain's "compiler" can work out, or the brain won't "execute" this subroutine. Let S be the description of the subroutine in question *in machine language*; then even if we grant that the brain learns P by making an induction, it need not be an induction with the conclusion (A). It would suffice that the brain instead conclude:

(B) I will be doing OK with P if subroutine S is employed.

And *this* can be stated in ILL provided ILL has the concept "doing OK with an item," and ILL contains machine language. But this does *not* require ILL to contain (synonyms for) "face," "cow," "jumps," "spontaneous," "pert," and so on. Fodor's argument has failed.

Fodor suggests that he would claim that the machine language description of how to use, say, "tree" *is* (a form of) the predicate *tree*. But this is simply an extension of use designed to make his thesis an uninteresting "tautology."

Of course, the predicate "doing OK with P" may arouse suspicion. But it should not. The "machine" (the brain) doesn't have to understand this predicate as linguists and philosophers would! The generalization (B) is simply a signal to the machine to add subroutine S to its repertoire of subroutines. (We should keep in mind Dennett's caution that talk of "machine language" is dangerous because we are tempted to confuse *our* abilities with the formalism in question with the machine's abilities.)

Notes

1. Z. S. Harris, *Methods in Structural Linguistics* (Chicago: University of Chicago Press, 1951).

2. N. Chomsky, "Explanatory Models in Linguistics," in *Logic, Methodology and Philosophy of Science*, ed. E. Nagel, P. Suppes, and A. Tarsk (Stanford, Calif.: Stanford University Press, 1962).

3. Each formula can be associated with a corresponding statement expressed in ordinary language, namely, "not-A," "A and B," "A or B," "if A, then B."

4. By "declarative grammar" I mean that part of the grammar that generates the declarative sentences of the language. The usual assumption—made also by Chomsky—is that interrogatives, imperatives, and so on are somehow derived from declaratives.

5. What I have given here is a very oversimplified account of Washoe's actual abilities. The interested reader should consult the following works: B. Gardner and R. A. Gardner, "Two-Way Communication with an Infant Chimpanzee," in *Behavior of Non-Human Primates,* ed. A. Schrier and F. Stollnitz (New York and London: Academic Press, 1971), vol. 4, pp. 117–184; B. Gardner and R. A. Gardner, "Teaching Sign Language to the Chimpanzee Washoe" (16-mm sound film), State College of Pennsylvania, Psychological Cinema Register, 1974; B. Gardner and R. A. Gardner, "Comparing the Early Utterances of Child and Chimpanzee," in *Minnesota Symposia on Child Psychology,* ed. A. Pick (Minneapolis, Minn.: University of Minnesota Press, 1974); B. Gardner and R. A. Gardner, "Evidence for Sentence Constituents in the Early Utterances of Child and Chimpanzee," *Journal of Experimental Psychology: General* 104: 244–267, 1975. The last of these references bears directly on Washoe's ability to learn "structure-dependent" rules.

6. See chapter 5 of my *Mind, Language, and Reality* (Cambridge: Cambridge University Press, 1975).

7. I discuss this in my 1976 John Locke Lectures, *Meaning and the Moral Sciences* (London: Routledge and Kegan Paul, 1978).

8. For an account of some of these suggestions, I recommend Stephen Gould's *Ontogeny and Phylogeny* (Cambridge, Mass.: Harvard University Press, 1977).

9. See chapter 1 of my *Mind, Language, and Reality.*

10. It is worth noting in this connection that Piaget's research method (in all but a few experiments) consists of studying *verbal* behavior.

11. J. Piaget and B. Inhelder, *The Growth of Logical Thinking from Childhood to Adolescence* (London: Routledge and Kegan Paul, 1958).

12. This is argued in my John Locke Lectures.

69 From *Rules and Representations*

Noam Chomsky

... What is currently understood even in a limited way seems to me to indicate that the mind is a highly differentiated structure, with quite distinct subsystems. If so, an understanding of the properties of one of these systems should not be expected to provide the principles by which others are organized and function. Even an account of knowledge of language that is overflowing with insights is unlikely to contribute directly to the study of factors that enter into our understanding of the nature of the visual world, or conversely. This is not to deny, of course, that these systems interact and may share some general properties. But we should remain open to the possibility —even the strong likelihood—that they are organized in quite different ways.... Granting all of this, I still can think of no way to undertake the study of mind except by investigating the specific character of particular systems, such as the language faculty. The principles cannot be expected to carry over, but the results attained and the mode of successful inquiry may prove suggestive elsewhere, much as the study of vision has proven suggestive for the study of language. And any results attained are direct contributions to the theory of mind.

Throughout the discussion I have been referring to *human* language and *human* cognition. I have in mind certain biological properties, the most significant of these being properties that are genetically-determined and characteristic of the human species, which I will assume for the purposes of this discussion to be genetically uniform, a further idealization. These properties determine the kinds of cognitive systems, language among them, that can develop in the human mind. In the case of language, I will use the term "universal grammar" to refer to these properties of human biological endowment. Thus the properties of universal grammar are "biologically necessary," but in the interesting cases not logically necessary elements of what someone might choose to call a language. If, indeed, the mind is modular in character, a system of distinct though interacting systems, then language-like systems might be acquired through the exercise of other faculties of mind, though we should expect to find empirical differences in the manner of acquisition and use in this case. The actual systems called "languages" in ordinary discourse are undoubtedly not "languages" in the sense of our idealizations, if only because of the nonhomogeneity of actual speech communities, and might also be "impure" in the sense that they incorporate elements derived by faculties other than the language faculty and hence depart in certain respects from principles of universal grammar. These again are possibilities that are neither particularly surprising nor unique to this inquiry....

An inquiry into universal grammar in the sense of the term that I am adopting here falls within what Hume called "moral philosophy," that is, "the science of human nature," which is concerned with "the secret springs and principles, by which the human mind is actuated in its operations," and most importantly, those "parts of [our] knowledge" that are derived "from the original hand of nature." Descartes took this to be the most useful inquiry in which we can engage: "to determine the nature and the scope of human knowledge."[1] The problem has run through the history of human thought from the earliest times. Some have argued that the frame of reference I am assuming is so different that it is improper to regard the current inquiry as concerned with the traditional problems. For Descartes, mind is not a part of the biological world. Furthermore, he appears to regard the mind as uniform and undifferentiated: "there is within us but one soul, and this soul has not in itself any diversity of parts"; "the mind is entirely indivisible."[2] One might then argue that we are not studying Descartes's problem when we consider the human mind as a specific biological system, one with components and elements of varied kinds, to be explored as we would study any other aspect of the physical world. This conclusion holds, however, only if we regard Descartes as an irrational dogmatist, that is, as putting forth doctrines that define the domain of inquiry, rather than as arguing for principles that he believed he had established within an inquiry more broadly construed. That seems to me a questionable move.

As for Hume, I think he was wrong in his empirical assumptions about the principles by which the mind is actuated, innate and acquired, but right in the way he formulated the question, particularly, in taking his inquiry to be analogous to physics. I do not mean to suggest that other concerns and other questions are illegitimate, but rather that these central concerns of the philosophical tradition are legitimate and important, whatever current terminology one may choose to clothe them in.

From this point of view, we can proceed to approach the study of the human mind much in the way that we study the physical structure of the body. In fact, we may think of the study of mental faculties as actually being a study of the body—specifically the brain—conducted at a certain level of abstraction. It may be useful, as a point of departure, to consider for a moment how we do proceed to study the human body.

We assume, no doubt correctly, that the human species is characterized by a certain biological endowment. The embryo grows ultimately to the adult as its genetic program unfolds under the triggering and shaping effect of the environment. These effects are worth distinguishing. Take the standard conditioning paradigm, in which a course of behavior is constructed in a step-by-step process by manipulation of reinforcement contingencies, that is, contingencies that for some reason or another change the probability of behavior. This is an example of a shaping effect of the environment. Or suppose that there is some domain, however narrow, in which traditional empiricist psychology is valid; say that a child receives simultaneously a visual and an auditory impression and associates them, the residue of the auditory impression serving as the name of the object taken to have caused the visual impression. There are notorious problems in working any of this out, crucially, the problem of how we can have sensory experience uninformed by conceptual judgment.[3] That this is possible has often been denied, by seventeenth-century Cartesians for example. Schopenhauer, who develops a post-Kantian version, attributes this view to "the ancients," citing for example "the famous verse of the philosopher Epicharmus": "Only the mind can see and hear; everything else is deaf and blind."[4] But suppose that we put these problems aside. Then the empiricist paradigm can serve as an example of the shaping effect of the environment on knowledge, furthermore a case in which there is some sort of "resemblance" between what is in the mind and what it perceives.

Suppose, in contrast, that certain environmental conditions are required to set in operation an intrinsically determined process, as nutrition is required for cellular growth to take place in predetermined ways. It has been reported, for example, that handling of rats induces lateralization for spatial and affective processes.[5] In such cases, the processes that take place are not shaped by the environment; they do not reflect the course of interchange with it or somehow "resemble" the stimulus, any more than a child is a reflection of the food he eats. When external conditions are necessary for, or facilitate the unfolding of, an internally controlled process, we can speak of their "triggering" effect. If institutionalized children do not learn a language, the reason may be that a crucial triggering factor, appropriate social interchange, is lacking, as in the case of Harlow's deprived monkeys; but we would not therefore say that attention, care and love shape the growth of language in the sense that a schedule of reinforcement shapes the behavior of a pigeon. The distinction between the two kinds of effects of the environment is not sharp, but it is conceptually useful. My own suspicion is that a central part of what we call "learning" is actually better understood as the growth of cognitive structures along an internally directed course under the triggering and partially shaping effect of the environment. In the case of human language, there evidently is a shaping effect; people speak different languages which reflect differences in their verbal environment.[6] But it remains to be seen in what respects the system that develops is actually shaped by experience, or rather reflects intrinsic processes and structures triggered by experience.

Returning to the analogy to the physical body, we take for granted that the organism does not learn to grow arms or to reach puberty—to mention an example of genetically determined maturation that takes place long after birth. Rather, these developments are determined by the genetic endowment, though the precise manner in which the genetic plan is realized depends in part on external factors, both triggering and shaping. For example, nutritional level can apparently affect the time of onset of puberty over a considerable range. As the biological plan unfolds, a system of interacting organs and structures matures—the heart, the visual system, and so on, each with its specific structures and functions, interacting in largely predetermined ways.

Our biological endowment determines both the scope and limits of physical growth. On the one hand, it permits the growth of a complex system of highly articulated physical organs, intrinsically determined in their essential properties. Were it not for this highly specific innate endowment, each individual would grow into some kind of an amoeboid creature, merely reflecting external contingencies, one individual quite unlike another, each utterly impoverished and lacking the intricate special structures that make possible a human existence and that differentiate one species from another. Our biological endowment permits a vast potential for development, roughly uniform for the species. At the same time, it in fact narrowly limits what each individual can become; the human embryo presumably cannot become a bird by modification of the external environment. Scope and limits of development are intimately related. Innate factors permit the organism to transcend experience, reaching a high level of complexity that does not reflect the limited and degenerate environment. These very same factors rule out many possible courses of development and limit drastically the final states that can be attained in physical growth.

Now all of this should be transparent and hardly controversial. Apparently very little is known about how any of it happens, but no one really doubts that something of this sort is roughly true. If it were proposed that we "make" our physical constitution, or are "taught" to pass through puberty, or "learn" to have arms rather than wings, no one would take the suggestion very seriously, even in the present state of ignorance concerning the mechanisms involved. Why is this so? Presumably, the reason derives from the vast qualitative difference between the impoverished and unstructured environment, on the one hand, and the highly specific and intricate structures that uniformly develop, on the other. In essence, this is a variant of a classical argument in the theory of knowledge, what we might call "the argument from poverty of the stimulus." Socrates' success in eliciting knowledge from the slave boy is a classical example. To take a variant of this argument that seems to me quite relevant to contemporary concerns, consider Descartes's argument for innate ideas in the perceptual domain. Descartes argues in the *Dioptrics* that

> there is no need to suppose that anything material passes from objects to our eyes to make us see colors and light, nor that there is anything in these objects that is similar to the ideas or the sensations that we have of them: just as nothing moves from the objects that a blind man senses that must pass along his stick to his hand, and the resistance or the movement of these bodies which is the only cause of the sensations that he has of them, is in no way similar to the ideas that he conceives of them. And in this way, your mind will be freed of all those little images flying through the air, called *intentional species*, which so exercise the imagination of the philosophers.[7]

Experience conforms to our mode of cognition, as his immediate successors, and later Kant, were to say. This mode of cognition must, Descartes argued, involve such innate ideas as geometrical figures, as well as all the "common notions," since the stimulus does not resemble what the mind produces on the occasion of stimulation. As he suggested elsewhere, we take a presented figure to be a distorted triangle, not a perfect example of what it is, presumably because the mind is organized in terms of principles of geometry.[8] Hume, in contrast held that we have no concept at all of regular geometrical figures, indeed that it is absurd to imagine that we have any such concept beyond what the senses convey,[9] a conclusion that should be interpreted, I think, as a *reductio ad absurdum* argument against empiricist beliefs as to the shaping effect of stimulation on the mental structures they evoke. Descartes's argument, in effect, relies on the observation that the stimulus does not contain the elements that constitute our knowledge, though it may serve as the occasion for the mind to produce an interpretation of experience in terms of conceptual structures drawn from its own inner resources. "The book of nature is legible only to an intellectual eye," as Cudworth wrote.[10]

While the argument is controversial in the case of the mind, more so than I think it should be, it is not discussed at all in the case of the physical body, but rather assumed without notice as the basis for scientific inquiry. There have, however, been intriguing discussions of similar issues in other domains of biology. I will return to some of these later, in discussing the question of learning and growth. Note that the argument is of course nondemonstrative. It is what is sometimes called an inference to the best explanation, in this case, that what the stimulus lacks is produced by the organism from its inner resources; in other words, organisms endowed with different modes of cognition might interpret the stimulus quite differently, so that our attention is directed to these modes of cognition and their origin, if we are concerned to understand the organism-environment interaction and the essential nature of the organism involved.

Descartes's arguments for innate ideas, when they are considered at all, are generally regarded as somehow missing the point or as "a ludicrous failure" if understood as offering "a general causal principle."[11] But I think the objections miss the point. It is quite true, as Roy Edgley says in an interesting discussion of the issues, that "An idea in the mind would be attributable entirely to an external object only, so to speak, if there were no mind there at all." This is, in effect, Hume's position, as expressed, for example, in his image of the mind as "a kind of theatre, where several perceptions successively make their appearance; pass, repass, glide away, and mingle in an infinite variety of postures and situations," though "The comparison of the theatre must not mislead us" since there is no stage: "They are the successive perceptions only, that constitute the mind."[12] ...

We may usefully think of the language faculty, the number faculty, and others, as "mental organs," analogous to the heart or the visual system or the system of motor coordination and planning. There appears to be no clear demarcation line between physical organs, perceptual and motor systems, and cognitive faculties in the respects in question. In short, there seems little reason to insist that the brain is unique in the biological world in that it is unstructured and undifferentiated, developing on the basis of uniform principles of growth or learning—say those of some learning theory, or of some yet-to-be conceived general multipurpose learning strategy—that are common to all domains.

David Hubel, who has pioneered some of the most exciting work of recent years on the physical basis for mammalian vision, concludes that

> we are led to expect that each region of the central nervous system has its own special problems that require different solutions. In vision we are concerned with contours and directions and depth. With the auditory system, on the other hand, we can anticipate a galaxy of problems relating to temporal interactions of sounds of different frequencies, and it is difficult to imagine that the same neural apparatus deals with all of these phenomena ... for the major aspects of the brain's operation no master solution is likely.[13]

There may well be properties common to diverse systems. For example, experience is necessary for "fine tuning" in the case of the visual and auditory systems as in other systems that develop in accordance with fixed genetic instructions. Recent work on motor coordination in monkeys seems to show "that many motor programs are part of a primate's genetic endowment. No sensory feedback or spinal reflex loops are necessary for learning the repertoire of movements ... [though] ... sensory feedback is necessary for 'fine tuning' ..."[14] Perceptual and motor systems are no doubt in part "set" by the shaping effect of some aspects of the environment,[15] but the systems that emerge seem to be highly specialized, intrinsically programmed in quite different ways. In short, what is taken for granted without direct evidence in the case of physical growth on the basis of an implicit argument from poverty of the stimulus is also being found in the study of the brain and nervous system; unsurprisingly, one would think.

In the case of cognitive faculties, it is widely assumed that development is uniform across domains and that the intrinsic properties of the initial state are homogeneous and undifferentiated, an assumption found across a spectrum of opinion reaching from Skinner to Piaget, who differ on much else, and common in contemporary philosophy as well. Notice that there are two issues here: the issue of innate structure and of modularity. One might hold that there is rich innate structure, but little or no modularity. But there is a relation between the views, in part conceptual. Insofar as there is little in the way of innate structure, what develops in the mind of an individual will be a homogeneous system derived by the application to experience of common principles that constitute the innate endowment. Such differentiation as there may be will reflect differentiation in the environment. Correspondingly, the belief that various systems of mind are organized along quite different principles leads to the natural conclusion that these systems are intrinsically determined, not simply the result of common mechanisms of learning or growth. It is not surprising, then, to find that opinions "cluster." Those who tend toward the assumption of modularity tend also to assume rich innate structure, while those who assume limited innate structure tend to deny modularity.

Once we begin to take seriously the actual states attained in particular cases, we are, I believe, led to the conclusion that intrinsic structure is rich (by the argument from poverty of the stimulus) and diverse (by virtue of the apparent diversity in fundamental principles of capacities and mental structures attained). These conclusions are, I think, to be expected in the case of systems that have any significant function in the life of an organism. As noted, they are taken for granted without much thought or evidence in the study of physical development; no one doubts that the instructions for a liver and a visual system will be quite different. Insofar as anything is known about cognitive systems—which is not very far—the related assumptions of poverty of initial structure and homogeneity do not seem tenable, and the general line of argument that keeps analogous assumptions from being considered at all in the case of physical growth seems applicable. The more we learn about specific systems, the more applicable it becomes, and I would hazard a guess that this will continue to be so. In the case of human conceptual systems, for example, intrinsic even to such apparently elementary notions as "thing" or "object" there is a subtle interaction between conditions of spatio-temporal contiguity, the willed acts of an agent responsible for the object, and other factors.[16] It is difficult to interpret this except in terms of our intrinsic modes of cognition. When we turn to language, many examples have been studied of shared knowledge that appears to have no shaping stimulation—knowledge without grounds, from another point of view—and that seems to be based on principles with only the most superficial resemblance to those operative in other cognitive domains. ...

It seems reasonable to assume that the language faculty—and, I would guess, other mental organs—develops in the individual along an intrinsically determined course under the triggering effect of appropriate social interaction and partially shaped by the environment—English is not Japanese, just as the distribution of horizontal and vertical receptors in the visual cortex can be modified by early visual experience. The environment provides the information that questions are formed by movement of a question word and that "each other" is a reciprocal expression; in other languages this is not the case, so that these cannot be properties of biological endowment in specific detail. Beyond such information, much of our knowledge reflects our modes of cognition, and is therefore not limited to inductive generalization from experience, let alone any training that we may have received. And just as the visual system of a cat, though modified by experience, will never be that of a bee or a frog, so the human language faculty will develop only one of the human languages, a narrowly constrained set.

A familiar argument against a modular approach to the study of mind is that it "reduces the possibility of viewing language as an aspect of the total corpus of behavior" and "obscures the connections between language and other aspects of cognition."[17] By parity of argument, we should conclude that the belief that the eye and the ear work on different principles reduces the possibility of viewing vision as an aspect of behavior and obscures the relations between vision and hearing. It is a sad commentary on the field that such arguments can even be advanced.

Consider again the question whether cognitive functions are both diverse, and determined in considerable detail by a rich innate endowment. If the answer is positive, for some organism, that organism is fortunate indeed. It can then live in a rich and complex world of understanding shared with others similarly endowed, extending far beyond limited and varying experience. Were it not for this endowment, individuals would grow into mental amoeboids, unlike one another, each merely reflecting the limited and impoverished environment in which he or she develops, lacking entirely the finely articulated, diverse and refined cognitive organs that make possible the rich and creative mental life that is characteristic of all individuals not seriously impaired by individual or social pathology—though once again we must bear in mind that the very same intrinsic factors that permit these achievements also impose severe limits on the states that can be attained; to put it differently, that there is an inseparable connection between the scope and limits of human knowledge.

Finally, let me emphasize the limits on the enterprise I have been outlining. Two individuals with the same genetic endowment and common experience will attain the same state, specifically, the same state of knowledge of language (random elements aside). But this does not preclude the possibility of diversity in the exercise of this knowledge, in thought or action. The study of acquisition of knowledge or of interpretation of experience through the use of acquired knowledge still leaves open the question of the causation of behavior, and more broadly, our ability to choose and decide what we will do.

Notes

1. "Rules for the Direction of the Mind," Rule VIII, Haldane and Ross, p. 26.

2. "The Passions of the Soul," Article XLVII, *ibid.*, p. 353; "Meditation VI," *ibid.*, p. 196.

3. For a recent discussion, see Michael Williams, *Groundless Belief* (New Haven, Conn.: Yale University Press, 1977).

4. Arthur Schopenhauer, *On The Fourfold Root of the Principle of Sufficient Reason* (La Salle, Ill.: Open Court, 1974), p. 109.

5. V. H. Denenberg, J. Garbanati, G. Sherman, D. A. Yutzey, R. Kaplan, "Infantile Stimulation Induces Brain Lateralization in Rats," *Science* (September 1978), 201(22):1150–51.

6. Harry J. Jerison exploits this fact as one part of an argument that the exigencies of communication were not the primary factors responsible for the evolution of the language faculty. See his "Discussion Paper: The Paleoneurology of Language," in S. R. Harnad, H. D. Steklis, and J. Lancaster, eds., *Origins and Evolution of Language and Speech,* New York Academy of Sciences, *Annals* (1976), 280. See also his "Paleoneurology and the Evolution of Mind," *Scientific American* (January 1976).

7. Charles Adam and Paul Tannery, eds., *Oeuvres de Descartes* (Paris, 1897 to 1913), 6:85. My translation.

8. "Reply to Objections V," in Haldane and Ross, 2:227–28.

9. See chapter 6, p. 247, below.

10. For discussion, see my *Cartesian Linguistics* (New York: Harper & Row, 1966), part 4; and *Reflections on Language,* ch. 1. One of the examples that Descartes uses is face recognition: "... when we look at a piece of paper on which little strokes have been drawn with ink to represent a man's face ... the idea produced in us ... is not so much that of the lines of the sketch as of the man. But this could not have happened unless the human face had been known to us by other means, and we had been more accustomed to think of it than of these minute lines, which indeed we often fail to distinguish from each other when they are moved to a slightly greater distance away from us." See reference of note [8]. Face recognition appears to be a "right hemisphere" task involving neural structures that mature rather late, perhaps about age ten or beyond. There has been considerable study of the task of recognizing objects on the basis of partial sketches. Performance tends to be impaired more by right hemisphere than left hemisphere lesions, and there are individual differences. Thus artists tend to do much better than others. Whether the differences result from experience or are innate, perhaps a factor in career choice, is unknown. On some cross-cultural and cross-group differences, see Andrea Lee Thompson, Joseph E. Bogen, John F. Marsh, "Cultural Hemisphericity: Evidence from Cognitive Tests," *International Journal of Neuroscience* (1979), 9:37–43, and references cited there.

Note that to sharpen the discussion, we should distinguish between the role of intrinsic structures in perception, on the one hand, and in the growth and development of cognitive structures, on the other. In each of these two distinct cases, we can discern applications of the argument from poverty of the stimulus.

11. Edgley, p. 9.

12. David Hume, *A Treatise of Human Nature,* Book I, Part IV, section 6; (London: Everyman's Library, J. M. Dent & Sons Ltd., 1911), 1:239–40.

13. David H. Hubel, "Vision and the Brain," *Bulletin* of the American Academy of Arts and Sciences, (April 1978), 31(7):28.

14. Gina Bari Kolata, "Primate Neurobiology: Neurosurgery with Fetuses," *Science* (3 March 1978), 199:960–61, citing Edward Taub.

15. For a review of some relevant work, see Colin Blakemore, "Developmental Factors in the Formation of Feature Extracting Neurons," in F. O. Schmitt and F. G. Worden, eds., *The Neurosciences: Third Study Program,* (Cambridge: MIT Press, 1973), pp. 105–13.

16. See *Reflections on Language,* pp. 44f., 203, for discussion.

17. Jane H. Hill and Robert B. Most, Review of Harnad, Steklis and Lancaster, *Language* (September 1978), 54(3):651–52. The authors (an anthropological linguist and cognitive psychologist) note correctly that similar arguments are commonly offered by Piagetians. They assert that "there is

no question that the kinds of behaviors which can be elicited from laboratory chimpanzees ... become more understandable if language is seen as but one manifestation of cognitive development, and not as a 'separate organ.'" This is a curious argument against modularity. Since advocates of modularity, at least those they mention, believe (correctly, to my knowledge) that recent work substantiates the familiar view that even the most elementary properties of human language (say, the use of recursive embedding to generate a discrete infinity of sentences) are beyond the capacities of apes, they would agree that no concept of "language faculty" will help to make the behavior of chimpanzees more understandable. (On this matter see John Limber, "Language in Child and Chimp?," *American Psychologist* [1977], 32:280–94; Herbert Terrace, "Is Problem Solving Language? A Review of Premack's Intelligence in Apes and Man," *Journal of the Experimental Analysis of Behavior* 31 [1979]:161–175; and my "Human Language and Other Semiotic Systems," *Semiotica* 25, nos. 1, 2 [1979]:31–44 [reprinted in S. Kasem and N. M. AbuZeid, eds., *Introduction to Semiotics: Translated Papers and Studies* (Cairo: Elias, 1986)].) There are other confusions in the review that are typical of much recent literature, for example, the belief that one who concludes that apes lack the capacity for human language is committed to a "discontinuity theory" (whatever that is); as are, by the same logic, those who harbor the strange belief that humans can't fly and that the mammalian eye operates differently from the insect eye. Again, this notion is widespread. For example, a panel on human language and symbolic systems of apes at the February 1978 meetings of the American Association for the Advancement of Science (AAAS) was entitled: "Emergence of Language: Continuities and Discontinuities," on the implicit assumption that lack of homology between human language and ape symbol systems entails "discontinuities" in evolution. It would be equally reasonable to entitle a program devoted to the mammalian and insect eye: "Emergence of the Mammalian Visual System: Continuities and Discontinuities." Plainly, a separate course of evolution implies nothing about "discontinuity."

70 From *Modularity of Mind*

Jerry A. Fodor

Chomsky likes to speak of mental structures on anatomical analogy to hearts, limbs, wings and so forth. "We may usefully think of the language faculty, the number faculty, and others as 'mental organs,' analogous to the heart or the visual system or the system of motor coordination and planning. There appears to be no clear demarcation line between physical organs, perceptual and motor systems and cognitive faculties in the respects in question" (Chomsky 1980, p. 3). There is, of course, a point to this analogy. It rests largely in the contention (entirely plausible, in my view) that for mental faculties, as for bodily organs, ontogenetic development is to be viewed as the unfolding of an "intrinsically determined process." In particular: "... we take for granted that the organism does not learn to grow arms or to reach puberty.... When we turn to the mind and its products, the situation is not qualitatively different from what we find in the case of the body" (ibid., pp. 2–3). But though Chomsky's point is well taken, his terminology is in some respects misleading; important distinctions are obscured by a use of "structure" that applies promiscuously to bodily organs and psychological faculties as Neocartesians construe the latter. It is, indeed, only when we insist upon these distinctions that we can see clearly what the Neocartesian account of mental structure actually amounts to.

It turns out, upon examination, that what Chomsky thinks is innate is primarily a certain *body of information*: the child is, so to speak, "born knowing" certain facts about universal constraints on possible human languages. It is the integration of this innate knowledge with a corpus of "primary linguistic data" (e.g., with the child's observations of utterances produced by adult members of its speech community) that explains the eventual assimilation of mature linguistic capacities....

It is, I think, the essence of the Neocartesian style in psychology to assume that mental structure should be explicated largely by reference to the propositional contents of mental states. In this respect, no doubt, the new Cartesianism bears the imprint of Descartes' own largely epistemological concerns. Descartes was, after all, mainly interested in determining what sorts of things can be known, and with what degree of certainty. In his epistemology, the primary explicandum is our ability to recognize certain truths (of geometry, of theology, of metaphysics, or whatever); and the prototypical form of explanation is to exhibit these truths as identical to, or deducible from, propositions that are innately given and self-evident. Where the overriding motive is the explanation of propositional knowledge, it is perhaps hardly surprising that one should come to view mental structure largely in terms of the organization of propositional content.

I say that this strategy is prototypically Cartesian but, of course, it is on display as early as Plato's *Meno*, where the slave boy's ability to answer questions of geometry that Socrates puts to him is explained by reference to "opinions" that were always "somewhere in him." ...

There are aspects of mental organization for which Chomsky's version of the Cartesian story is, in my view, extremely persuasive. But, precisely for that reason, it is important to emphasize that there are other, quite different, sorts of things that a theorist may have in mind when he talks of endogenous psychological structures. For example, consider memory. If one is going to postulate innately specified faculties, memory is, surely, a plausible candidate. Yet *memory isn't a faculty in the Neocartesian sense of that notion*. Having a memory isn't a matter of having one or another set of beliefs, and if memory is an innate capacity, that couldn't be because there is some set of propositions that organisms are born cognizing. There isn't, in short, the remotest temptation to identify the structure of memory with the inferential structure of a body of propositions. Memory is, so one supposes, some sort of *mechanism*, analogous to a hand or a liver or a heart. Viewed hypostatically at least, memory really does seem to be a kind of mental *organ* in ways that the putative language faculty, even viewed hypostatically, really does not....

We turn, then, to a different notion of mental structure, one according to which a psychological faculty is par excellence a sort of mechanism. Neocartesians individuate faculties by reference to their typical propositional contents (so that, for example, the putative language organ is so identified in virtue of the information about linguistic universals that it contains). By contrast, according to the present account, a faculty is individuated *by reference to its typical effects*, which is to say that it is functionally individuated. If there is a language faculty in this sense of faculty, then it is whatever piece of (presumably neurological) machinery functions to mediate the assimilation and employment of verbal capacities.

One way to appreciate this distinction between faculties-cum-belief-structures and faculties-cum-psychological-mechanisms is to notice that even theorists who are blatantly Empiricist in respect of the former may nevertheless be (anyhow, closet) Nativists in respect of the latter. This was, in fact, John Locke's position according to some authorities.

> ... Locke thought too obvious to mention explicitly in the *Essay* ... the existence of natural faculties such as perception, understanding and memory, and innate mental powers like those of abstraction, comparison and discernment. The "white paper" metaphor is meant to indicate that the understanding (and hence the mind) is originally empty of *objects* of thought like ideas; but it has whatever apparatus is necessary to acquire them through experience, and then to derive knowledge by comparing and contrasting them with each other.[1] [Harris, 1977]

So, then, the (noncartesian) faculty psychologist is per se interested in the analysis of mind into interacting component mechanisms.[2] However, the history of this kind of faculty psychology exhibits two variants of the doctrine according to the axis along which the mind is sliced. According to the most familiar version—which I shall call "horizontal" faculty psychology—cognitive processes exhibit the interaction of such faculties as, e.g., memory, imagination, attention, sensibility, perception, and so forth; and the character of each such process is determined by the particular mix of faculties that it recruits. However, the character of mentation is more or less *in*dependent of its subject matter; the faculties are supposed to be invariant from one topic of thought to the next.[3]

For example, traditional accounts of the mind often acknowledged a faculty of *judgment*, whose characteristic function was supposed to be the recognition of identities and differences among mental contents (in one terminology among Ideas). A very refined judgment is one which can distinguish between even very similar Ideas (in the manner, say, of John Austin distinguishing a mere accident from a full-blooded inadvertence). Judgment found work to do in (e.g.) perceptual recognition, where the categorization of current sensory data is supposed to require comparing it with information from memory; but the details needn't concern us here.

Now, this faculty of judgment might get exercised in respect of matters aesthetic, legal, scientific, practical, or moral, and this list is by no means exhaustive. The point is that, according to the horizontal treatment of mental structure, *it is the self-same faculty of judgment every time.* The discrimination of identity and difference among aesthetic ideas is thus performed by precisely the same psychological mechanism that distinguishes, as it might be, weight from mass or torts from misdemeanors. On this view, then, aesthetic judgment is simply the application of the faculty of judgment to the process of drawing aesthetic distinctions. It follows that there is no such thing as a faculty-of-aesthetic-judgment per se. A fortiori, there is no such thing as an aesthetic faculty....

Horizontal faculty psychology has been with us always; it seems to be the common-sense theory of the mind. By contrast, the "vertical" tradition in faculty psychology has specifiable historical roots. It traces back to the work of Franz Joseph Gall (1758–1828), the founding father of phrenology and a man who appears to have had an unfairly rotten press.

According to Gall, the traditional census of horizontal mental faculties is largely a fiction. There is, in particular, no such thing as judgment, no such thing as attention, no such thing as volition, no such thing as memory; in fact, there are no horizontal faculties at all. Instead, there is a bundle of what Gall variously describes as propensities, dispositions, qualities, aptitudes, and fundamental powers; of these an aptitude for music will do as an example. (I should emphasize that Gall does *not* himself speak of "vertical faculties." I have coined that term to suggest a certain reading of Gall's text—viz., that he agrees with traditional faculty theories that the mind is structured into functionally distinguishable subsystems, but disagrees about how the divisions between these systems should be drawn.) ...

Anyhow, in the case of what Gall sometimes calls the "intellectual" capacities, it is useful to identify an aptitude with competence in a certain cognitive domain; in which case, the intellectual aptitudes (unlike, n.b., the horizontal faculties) are distinguished by reference to their subject matter. It is of central importance to understand that, in thus insisting upon domain specificity, Gall is not simply making the conceptual point that if music (e.g.) is distinct from mathematics, then musical aptitude is correspondingly distinct from mathematical aptitude. Gall is also claiming that the psychological mechanisms which subserve the one capacity are different, de facto, from those that subserve the other. I take it that this claim is the heart of Gall's theory.

In fact, some of Gall's favorite analogies for aptitudes are ethological. Nest-building and bird song are presumably not to be viewed as applications of a general intellectual capacity to the accomplishment of specific ends; it would thus be a mistake to postulate a horizontal faculty of avian intellect of which competence in singing and nesting are among the manifestations. Similarly with man: "There are as many different kinds of intellect as there are distinct qualities.... One individual may have considerable intellect relative to one fundamental power, but a very narrow one in reference to every other.... A special faculty of intellect or understanding is as entirely inadmissible as a special faculty of instinct" (p. 240) (all Gall quotations are from Hollander, 1920). Intellect per se could not, therefore, be neurologically localizable, any more than instinct per se could be subserved by a specific brain mechanism.

Gall's point is precisely analogous to one that could be made by denying that there is such a thing as *acuity*. There are, no doubt, visual acuity, auditory acuity, and perhaps gustatory and intellectual acuity as well. And one might add that a given individual may have considerable acuity relative to one fundamental power, but very narrow acuity in reference to every other. However, since visual, auditory, gustatory, and intellectual acuity are surely just parameters of vision, audition, taste, and intellect respectively, it follows that there could be no such things as a *faculty of acuity*; that would be the wrong way to carve things up. Acuity, to put it in trendy terms, is syncategorematic; and so, for Gall, is intellect....

... We can then distinguish four major ingredients of Gall's notion of a fundamental power: vertical faculties are *domain specific*, they are *genetically determined*, they are associated with *distinct neural structures*, and—to introduce a new point—they are *computationally autonomous*. The relevant consideration about computational autonomy is that Gall's fundamental powers do not share—and hence do not compete for—such horizontal resources as memory, attention, intelligence, judgment or whatever. This view of vertical faculties as not merely distinct in the functions they perform, but also relatively independent in the performance of their functions, will be important later when we turn to consider the notion of a cognitive module.

Suffice it, for present purposes, to note that his emphasis upon the computational autonomy of vertical faculties is one of the chief points that distinguishes Gall's theorizing from Chomsky's. For example, Chomsky (1980) suggests that there is perhaps a mathematical faculty. But, as one might expect in the light of the [previous] discussion ... what he appears to mean by this is only part of what Gall would have meant. Chomsky's claim is primarily that some mathematical information (specifically, the idea that you can generate the natural numbers by adding one indefinitely) is innately specified. Gall would quite probably have liked that, but he would have claimed considerably more. *Qua architectural* nativist, Gall's view would be that the psychological *mechanisms* of memory, judgment, imagination, will, or whatever that mediate mathematical reasoning are themselves innately specified. *Qua vertical faculty theorist*, Gall's view would be that these mechanisms, insofar as they come into play when you do mathematics, are only nominally related to the memory, judgment, imagination ... etc. that are engaged when you talk or commit homocides.[4] And, *qua autonomy theorist*, Gall's view would be that the mental operations that go on when you do mathematics do not much interact with and, specifically, do not much interfere with others of one's mental capacities. That we can, most of us, count and chew gum at the same time would have struck Gall as a fact that offers significant perspectives upon our mental organization.

It is important to emphasize that innateness and computational autonomy, in particular, are quite *different* properties of cognitive systems, only the first being at play in Chomsky's notion of a mental organ. Suppose, to take an extreme case, that knowledge of Peano's axioms is innate; they are not learned but genetically transmitted. It wouldn't follow, even from this radical thesis, that there is an arithmetic faculty in Gall's sense. For, the hypothesis that arithmetic knowledge is genetically transmitted is—but the vertical faculty thesis for arithmetic is not—compatible with the possibility that the psychological mechanisms that mediate arithmetic reasoning are the same ones that underlie the capacity for abstract thought in general. It is thus compatible with Chomsky's notion of a mental organ, but not with Gall's notion of a vertical faculty, that arithmetic reasoning shares (horizontal) psychological resources with jurisprudential reasoning, aesthetic reasoning, or filling out one's income tax.[5]

It is worth adding that, just as the innateness thesis for fundamental powers does not imply their organization into computationally autonomous vertical faculties, so the horizontal analysis of a cognitive capacity would not imply that that capacity is learned. Most faculty psychologists have, in point of historical fact, been nativists of the horizontal persuasion. It may be that there is use for the notion of horizontal cognitive organization, particularly in light of the possibility of a mixed model which includes both vertical and horizontal elements. It would not follow that there is much use for (or much sense to be made of) the notion that mental structures are learned. (See Fodor, 1975.) It is thus important to disentagle the horizontal faculty story from any form of Empiricism....

... One would ... expect—what anyhow seems to be desirable—that the notion of modularity ought to admit of degrees. The notion of modularity that I have in mind certainly does. When I speak of a cognitive system as modular, I shall therefore always mean "to some interesting extent." Second, I am not, in any strict sense, in the business of "defining my terms." I don't think that theoretical terms usually have definitions (for that matter, I don't think that nontheoretical terms usually do either).... [W]hat I take to be perhaps the most important aspect of modularity—something that I shall call "informational encapsulation"—has yet to appear.... Roughly, modular cognitive systems are domain specific, innately specified, hardwired, autonomous, and not assembled. Since modular systems are domain-specific computational mechanisms, it follows that they are species of vertical faculties....

... [A]s we have already had reason to observe, Turing machines are also very simple devices; their functional architecture is exhaustively surveyed when we have mentioned a small number of interacting subsystems (tape, scanner, printer, and executive) and a small inventory of primitive machine operations (stop, start, move the tape, read the tape, change state, print). Moreover—and this is the point of present concern—Turing machines are *closed* computational systems; the sole determinants of their computations are the current machine state, the tape configuration, and the program, the rest of the world being quite irrelevant to the character of their performance; whereas, of course, organisms are forever exchanging information with their environments, and much of their psychological structure is constituted of mechanisms which function to mediate such exchanges. If, therefore, we are to start with anything like Turing machines as models in cognitive psychology, we must think of them as embedded in a matrix of subsidiary systems which affect their computations in ways that are responsive to the flow of environmental events. The function of these subsidiary systems is to provide the central machine with information about the world; information expressed by mental symbols in whatever format cognitive processes demand of the representations that they apply to....

Pylyshyn and I (1981) have called these subsidiary systems "compiled transducers," using the "compiled" part to indicate that they have an internal computational structure and the "transducer" part to indicate that they exhibit a certain sort of informational encapsulation that will presently loom large in this discussion. I think that usage is all right given the explication, but it admittedly hasn't much to do with the conventional import of these terms and thus probably produces as much confusion as it avoids.

It is, perhaps, not surprising that computer theory provides no way of talking that does precisely the job I want to do. Computers generally interface with their environments *via some human being* (which is what makes them computers rather than robots). The programmer thus takes on the function of the subsidiary computational systems that I have been struggling to describe—viz., by providing the machine with information about the world in a form in which the machine can use it. Surprising or not, however, it is a considerable nuisance. Ingenuity having failed me completely, I propose to call them variously "input systems," or "input analyzers" or, sometimes, "interface systems." At least this terminology emphasizes that they operate relatively early on. I rely on the reader to keep it in mind, however, that input systems are *post*-transductive mechanisms according to my usage. Also that switches from one of the epithets to another usually signify no more than a yen for stylistic variation.

So, then, we are to have a trichotomous functional taxonomy of psychological processes; a taxonomy which distinguishes transducers, input systems, and central processors, with the flow of input information becoming accessible to these mechanisms in about that order. These categories are intended to be exclusive but not, of course, to exhaust the types of psychological mechanisms that a theory of cognition might have reason to postulate....

Input Systems as Modules

The modularity of the input systems consists in their possession of most or all of the properties now to be enumerated. If there are other psychological systems which possess most or all of these properties then, of course, they are modular too. It is, however, a main thesis of this work that the properties in virtue of which input systems are modular are ones which, in general, central cognitive processes do not share.

1 Input Systems Are Domain Specific

Let's start with this: how many input systems are there? The discussion thus far might be construed so as to suggest an answer somewhere in the vicinity of six—viz., one for each of the traditional sensory/perceptual "modes" (hearing, sight, touch, taste, smell) and one more for language. This is *not*, however, the intended doctrine; what is proposed is something much more in the spirit of Gall's bumps. I imagine that within (and, quite possibly, across)[6] the traditional modes, there are highly specialized computational mechanisms in the business of generating hypotheses about the distal sources of proximal stimulations. The specialization of these mechanisms consists in constraints either on the range of information they can access in the course of projecting such hypotheses, or in the range of distal properties they can project such hypotheses about, or, most usually, on both.

Candidates might include, in the case of vision, mechanisms for color perception, for the analysis of shape, and for the analysis of three-dimensional spatial relations.[7] They might also include quite narrowly task-specific "higher level" systems concerned with the visual guidance of bodily motions or with the recognition of faces of conspecifics. Candidates in audition might include computational systems that assign grammatical descriptions to token utterances; or ones that detect the melodic or rhythmic structure of acoustic arrays; or, for that matter, ones that mediate the recognition of the *voices* of conspecifics. There is, in fact, some evidence for the domain specificity of several of the systems just enumerated, but I suggest the examples primarily by way of indicating the levels of grain at which input systems might be modularized.

What, then, are the arguments for the domain specificity of input systems? To begin with, there is a sense in which input systems are ipso facto domain specific in a way in which computational systems at large are not....

... [H]ow good is the inference from the eccentricity of the stimulus domain to the specificity of the corresponding psychological mechanisms? I am, in fact, not boundlessly enthusiastic about such inferences; they are clearly a long way from apodictic. Chess playing, for example, exploits a vast amount of eccentric information, but nobody wants to postulate a chess faculty. (Well, *almost* nobody. It is of some interest that recent progress in the artificial intelligence of chess has been achieved largely by employing specialized hardware. And, for what it's worth, chess is notably one of those cognitive capacities which breeds prodigies; so it is a candidate for modularity by Gall's criteria if not by mine.) Suffice it, for the present to suggest that it is probably characteristic of many modular systems that they operate in eccentric domains, since a likely motive for modularizing a system is that the computations it performs are idiosyncratic. But the converse inference—from the eccentricity of the domain to the modularity of the system—is warranted by nothing stronger than the maxim: specialized systems for specialized tasks. The most transparent situation is thus the one where you have a mechanism that computes an eccentric domain and is also modular by independent criteria; the eccentricity of the domain rationalizes the modularity of the processor and the modularity of the processor goes some way towards explaining how the efficient computation of eccentric domains is possible.

2 The Operation of Input Systems Is Mandatory

You can't help hearing an utterance of a sentence (in a language you know) as an utterance of a sentence, and you can't help seeing a visual array as consisting of objects distributed in three-dimensional space. Similarly, mutatis mutandis, for the other perceptual modes: you can't, for instance, help feeling what you run your fingers over as the surface of an object.[8] Marslen-Wilson and Tyler (1981), discussing word recognition, remark that "... even when subjects are asked to focus their attention on the acoustic-phonetic properties of the input, they do not seem to be able to avoid identifying the words involved.... This implies that the kind of processing operations observable in spoken-word recognition are mediated by automatic processes which are obligatorily applied ..." (p. 327).

The fact that input systems are apparently constrained to apply whenever they can apply is, when one thinks of it, rather remarkable. There is every reason to believe that, in the general case, the computational relations that input systems mediate—roughly, the relations between transducer outputs and percepts—are quite remote. For example, on all current theories, it requires elaborate processing to get you from the representation of a proximal stimulus that the retina provides to a representation of the distal stimuli as an array of objects in space.[9] Yet we apparently have no choice but to take up this computational burden whenever it is offered. In short, the operation of the input systems appears to be, in this respect, inflexibly insensitive to the character of one's utilities. You can't hear speech as noise *even if you would prefer to*....

3 There Is Only Limited Central Access to the Mental Representations That Input Systems Compute

It is worth distinguishing the claim that input operations are mandatory (you can't but hear an utterance of a sentence *as* an utterance of a sentence) from the claim that what might be called "interlevels" of input representation are, typically, relatively inaccessible to consciousness. Not only must you hear an utterance of a sentence as such, but, to a first approximation, you can hear it *only* that way.

What makes this consideration interesting is that, according to all standard theories, the computations that input systems perform typically proceed via the assignment of a number of intermediate analyses of the proximal stimulation. Sentence comprehension, for example, involves not only acoustic encoding but also the recovery of phonetic and lexical content and syntactic form. Apparently an analogous picture applies in the case of vision, where the recognition of a distal array as, say, a-bottle-on-a-table-in-the-corner-of-the-room proceeds via the recovery of a series of preliminary representations (in terms of visual frequencies and primal sketches inter alia. For a review of recent thinking about interlevels of visual representation, see Zucker, 1981).

The present point is that the subject doesn't have equal access to all of these ascending levels of representation—not at least if we take the criterion of accessibility to be the availability for explicit report of the information that these representations encode. Indeed, as I remarked above, the lowest levels (the ones that correspond most closely to transducer outputs) appear to be completely *in*accessible for all intents and purposes. The rule seems to be that, even if perceptual processing goes from "bottom to top" (each level of representation of a stimulus computed being more abstractly related to transducer outputs than the one that immediately preceded), still *access* goes from top down (the further you get from transducer outputs, the more accessible the representations recovered are to central cognitive systems that presumably mediate conscious report)....

4 Input Systems Are Fast

Identifying sentences and visual arrays are among the fastest of our psychological processes. It is a little hard to quantify this claim because of unclarities about the individuation of mental activities. (What precisely are the boundaries of the processes to be compared? For example, where does sentence (/scene) *recognition* stop and more central activities take over? Compare the discussion in section 6, below.) Still, granting the imprecision, there are more than enough facts around to shape one's theoretical intuitions.

Among the simplest of voluntary responses are two-choice reactions (push the button if the *left*-hand light goes on). The demands that this task imposes upon the cognitive capacities are minimal, and a practiced subject can respond reliably at latencies on the low side of a quarter of a second. It thus bears thinking about that the recovery of semantic content from a spoken sentence can occur at speeds quite comparable to those achieved in the two-choice reaction paradigm. In particular, appreciable numbers of subjects can "shadow" continuous speech with a quarter-second latency (shadowing is repeating what you hear as you hear it) and, contrary to some of the original reports, there is now good evidence that such "fast shadowers" understand what they repeat. (See Marslen-Wilson, 1973.) Considering the amount of processing that must go on in sentence comprehension (unless all our current theories are *totally* wrong-headed), this finding is mind-boggling. And, mind-boggling or otherwise, it is clear that shadowing latency is an extremely conservative measure of the speed of comprehension. Since shadowing requires *repeating* what one is hearing, the 250 msec. of lag between stimulus and response includes not only the time required for the perceptual analysis of the message, but also the time required for the subject's integration of his verbalization....

5 Input Systems Are Informationally Encapsulated

Some of the claims that I'm now about to make are in dispute among psychologists, but I shall make them anyway because I think that they are true. I shall run the discussion in this section largely in terms of language, though, as usual, it is intended that the morals should hold for input systems at large.

I remarked above that, almost certainly, understanding an utterance involves establishing its analysis at several different levels of representation: phonetic, phonological, lexical, syntactic, and so forth. Now, in principle, information about the probable structure of the stimulus at any of these levels could be brought to bear upon the recovery of its analysis at any of the others. Indeed, in principle *any* information available to the hearer, including meteorological information, astrological information, or—rather more plausibly—information about the speaker's probable communicative intentions could be brought to bear at any point in the comprehension process. In particular, it is entirely possible that, in the course of computing a structural description, information that is specified only at relatively high levels of representation should be "fed back" to determine analyses at relatively lower levels.[10] But though this is possible in principle, the burden of my argument is going to be that the operations of input systems are in certain respects unaffected by such feedback.

I want to emphasize the "in certain respects." For there exist, in the psychological literature, dramatic illustrations of the effects of information feedback upon some input operations. Consider, for example, the "phoneme restoration effect" (Warren, 1970). You make a tape recording of a word (as it might be, the word "legislature") and you splice out one of the speech sounds (as it might be, the "s"), which you then replace with a tape recording of a cough. The acoustic structure of the resultant signal is thus /legi(cough)lature/. But what a subject will *hear* when you play the tape to him is an utterance of /legislature/ with a cough "in the background." It surely seems that what is going on here is that the perceived phonetic constituency of the utterance is determined not just by the transduced information (not just by information specified at *sub*phonetic levels of analysis) but also by higher-level information about the probable lexical representation of the utterance (i.e., by the subject's guess that the intended utterance was probably /legislature/).

It is not difficult to imagine how this sort of feedback might be achieved. Perhaps, when the stimulus is noisy, the subject's mental lexicon is searched for a "best match" to however much of the phonetic content of the utterance has been securely identified. In effect, the lexicon is queried by the instruction "Find an entry some ten phones long, of which the initial phone sequence is /legi/ and the terminal sequence is /lature/." The reply to this query constitutes the lexical analysis under which the input is heard.

Apparently rather similar phenomena occur in the case of visual scotoma (where neurological disorders produce a "hole" in the subject's visual field). The evidence is that scotoma can mask quite a lot of the visual input without creating a phenomenal blind spot for the subject. What happens is presumably that information about higher-level redundancies is fed back to "fill in" the missing sensory information. Some such process also presumably accounts for one's inability to "see" one's retinal blind spot.

These sorts of considerations have led to some psychologists (and many theorists in AI) to propose relentlessly top-down models of input analysis, in which the perceptual encoding of a stimulus is determined largely by the subject's (conscious or unconscious) beliefs and expectations, and hardly at all by the stimulus information that transducers provide. Extreme examples of such feedback-oriented approaches can be found in Schank's account of language comprehension, in Neisser's early theorizing about vision, and in "analysis by synthesis" approaches to sentence parsing. Indeed, a sentimental attachment to what are known generically as "New Look" accounts of perception (Bruner, 1973) is pervasive in the cognitive science community. It will, however, be a main moral of this discussion that the involvement of certain sorts of feedback in the operation of input systems would be incompatible with their modularity, at least as I propose to construe the modularity thesis. One or other of these doctrines will have to go.

In the long run, which one goes will be a question of how the data turn out. Indeed, a great deal of the empirical interest of the modularity thesis lies in the fact that the experimental predictions it makes tend to be diametrically opposed to the ones that New Look approaches license. But experiments to one side, there are some prima facie reasons for doubting that the computations that input systems perform could have anything like unlimited access to high-level expectations or beliefs. These considerations suggest that even if there are *some* perceptual mechanisms whose operations are extensively subject to feedback, there must be others that compute the structure of a percept largely, perhaps solely, in isolation from background information.

For one thing, there is the widely noted persistence of many perceptual illusions (e.g., the Ames room, the phi phenomenon, the Muller-Lyre illusion in vision; the phoneme restoration and click displacement effects in speech) even in defiance of the subject's explicit knowledge that the percept is illusory. The very same subject who can tell you that the Muller-Lyre arrows are identical in length, who indeed has seen them measured, still finds one looking longer than the other. In such cases it is hard to see an alternative to the view that at least *some* of the background information at the subject's disposal is inaccessible to at least some of his perceptual mechanisms....

The informational encapsulation of the input systems is, or so I shall argue, the essence of their modularity. It's also the essence of the analogy between the input systems and reflexes; reflexes are informationally encapsulated with bells on.

Suppose that you and I have known each other for many a long year (we were boys together, say) and you have come fully to appreciate the excellence of my character. In particular, you have come to know perfectly well that under no conceivable circumstances would I stick my finger in your eye. Suppose that this belief of yours is both explicit and deeply felt. You would, in fact, go to the wall for it. Still, if I jab my finger near enough to your eyes, and fast enough, you'll blink. To say ... that the blink reflex is mandatory is to say, inter alia, that it has no access to what you know about my character or, for that matter, to any other of your beliefs, utilities and expectations. For this reason the blink reflex is often produced when sober reflection would show it to be uncalled for; like panther-spotting, it is prepared to trade false positives for speed.

That is what it is like for a psychological system to be informationally encapsulated. If you now imagine a system that is encapsulated in the way that reflexes are, but also computational in a way that reflexes are not, you will have some idea of what I'm proposing that input systems are like....

6 Input Analyzers Have "Shallow" Outputs

The question where to draw the line between observation and inference (in the psychological version, between perception and cognition) is one of the most vexed, and most pregnant, in the philosophy of science. One finds every opinion from the extreme "foundationalist" view, which restricts observation to processes that issue in infallible introspective reports, to the recent revisionism which denies that the distinction is in any respect principled. (Hanson, 1958, for example, holds that a physicist can *see* that the cloud chamber contains a proton track in the same sense of "see" that is operative when Smith sees that there's a spot on Jones' tie.) Sometimes the argument for this sort of view is based explicitly on accounts of perception borrowed from New Look psychology, which suggests that *all* perception is ineliminably and boundlessly theory laden; see Goodman (1978)....

... [T]he corresponding psychological problem of saying where perceptual processes interface with cognitive ones must be addressed by anyone who takes the postulation of modular input systems seriously. For one thing, it is a point of definition that distinct functional components cannot interface *everywhere* on pain of their ceasing to be distinct. It is this consideration that flow-chart notation captures by drawing boxes around the processing systems it postulates. That only the inputs and outputs of functionally individuated systems can mediate their information exchanges is tautological....

In general, the more constrained the information that the outputs of perceptual systems are assumed to encode—the shallower their outputs, the more plausible it is that the computations that effect the encoding are encapsulated. If, for example, the visual analysis system can report only upon the shapes and colors of things (all higher-level integrations being post-perceptual) it is correspondingly plausible that all the information that system exploits may be represented internal to it. By contrast, if the visual system can deliver news about protons (as a psychologized version of the Hanson story would suggest), then the likelihood that visual analysis is informationally encapsulated is negligible. Chat about protons surely implies free access to quite a lot of what I have been calling "background knowledge." ...

7 Input Systems Are Associated with Fixed Neural Architecture

Martin Gardner has a brief discussion of Gall in his *In the Name of Science* (1952). Gardner remarks that "Modern research on the brain has, as most everyone knows, completely demolished the old 'faculty psychology.' Only sensory centers are localized" (p. 293). The argument moves breathtakingly fast. Is faculty psychology literally incompatible with, say, an equipotential brain? Remember that faculties are, in the first instance, functionally rather than physiologically individuated. And perhaps *localization* isn't precisely the notion that Gardner wants, since, after all, there might be neural specificity of some functions that aren't localized in the sense of being associated with large, morphologically characterizable brain regions. Still, if you read "perceptual" for "sensory," and if you add language, and if you don't worry about the localization of motor and other noncognitive functions, there is something to what Gardner says. In particular, it seems that there is characteristic neural architecture associated with each of what I have been calling the input systems. Indeed, the following, stronger, claim seems to be approximately true: *all* the cases of massive neural structuring to which a content-specific cognitive function can confidently be assigned appear to be associated with input analysis, either with language or with perception. There is, to put it crudely, no known brain center for *modus ponens*....

8 Input Systems Exhibit Characteristic and Specific Breakdown Patterns

The existence of—and analogies between—relatively well defined pathological syndromes in the perceptual systems on the one hand and the language-processing mechanisms on the other has been too frequently noted to require much discussion here. There seems to be general agreement that the agnosias and aphasias constitute patterned failures of functioning—i.e., they cannot be explained by mere quantitative decrements in global, horizontal capacities like memory, attention, or problem-solving. This is hardly surprising if, on the one hand, input analysis is largely effected by specific, hardwired neural circuitry and, on the other, the pathologies of the input systems are caused by insult to these specialized circuits.

Contrast the central processes, which do not appear to be intimately associated with specific neural architecture and also do not appear to be prone to well defined breakdown syndromes. (It used to be thought that schizophrenia is a "pathology of thought," but I gather this view is no longer very popular.)

I don't, however, wish to overplay this point. Any psychological mechanism which is functionally distinct may presumably be selectively impaired, horizontal faculties included. There may thus quite possibly be pathologies of, say, memory or attention that are not domain specific in the way that the aphasias and agnosias are supposed to be; see, e.g., Milner, Corbin, and Teuber (1968). If so, then that is evidence (*contra* Gall) that such capacities are mediated by bona fide faculties and that they are horizontally organized. As previously remarked, the possibility of advancing mixed models in this area ought not to be ignored.

9 The Ontogeny of Input Systems Exhibits a Characteristic Pace and Sequencing

The issues here are so very moot, and the available information is so fragmentary, that I offer this point more as a hypothesis than a datum. There are, however, straws in the wind. There is now a considerable body of findings about the ontogenetic sequencing of language acquisition, and there are some data on the very early visual capacities of infants. These results are compatible, so far, with the view that a great deal of the developmental course of the input systems is endogenously determined. On the one hand, the capacity of infants for visual categorization appears to have been very seriously underestimated by empiricist theorizing (see the recent work of Spelke, 1982; Meltzoff, 1979; Bower, 1974; and others). And, on the other hand, linguistic performance—though obviously not present in the neonate—appears to develop in an orderly way that is highly sensitive to the maturational state of the organism, and surprisingly insensitive to deprivation of environmental information. (Goldin-Meadow and Feldman, 1977; Gleitman, 1981.) Moreover, language development appears to respect many of the universals of adult grammatical organization even at quite early stages (see Brown, 1973, and, papers in Takavolian, 1981)....

Notes

1. I'm not at all sure, by the way, that Harris' reading of Locke is right in this respect. The direction of Locke's thought on these matters seems to have been away from faculty psychology and toward a doctrine of intrinsic mental *capacities* or dispositions. The postulation of these latter he appears to have viewed as, as it were, explanatory bedrock; specifically, the exercise of such mental "powers" is *not* viewed—even implicitly—as mediated by a corresponding apparatus of psychological mechanisms. (Shades of Gilbert Ryle.) Thus Locke says about memory that "this laying up of our ideas in the repository of memory signifies no more but this—that the mind has a power, in many cases, to revive perceptions which it once had ..." (Locke, *Essay*, Book 2, chapter 10, par. 2). It is of interest that this positivistic disclaimer was new in the second edition of the *Essay*, talk of a "repository to lay up ... Ideas" having been unabashed in the earlier version of the text. This rather suggests (contrary to Harris) that the incompatibility, at least in spirit, between a thoroughgoing Empiricism and any acknowledgment of endogenous psychological mechanisms was becoming clear to Locke. On this reading, Locke was far from viewing the existence of "natural faculties" as "too obvious to mention," anathema having been, at least by the second edition of the *Essay*, fairly explicitly pronounced.

2. It may be worth reemphasizing that the *non*cartesian faculty psychologist need not be an *anti*cartesian faculty psychologist. On the contrary, it is perfectly possible to take the view that the typical cognitive faculty is a mechanism for the manipulation of mental representations. These latter may in turn be viewed as endowed with propositional contents, hence as vehicles for encoding the informational structures with which Neocartesian theories are primarily concerned. Most serious contemporary cognitive science is, I think, committed to some such account. More of this later.

3. Spearman (1927, p. 29) lists seven mental faculties which he claims were traditionally acknowledge: sense, intellect, memory, imagination, attention, speech, and movement. "Any further increase in the number of faculties beyond these seven has, in general, only been attained by subdividing some or other of these." Of the faculties enumerated in Spearman's census, only the first five are clearly "horizontal" in the sense of the present discussion, and "speech" is a vertical faculty par excellence. This sort of indifference to the horizontal/vertical distinction is, by the

way, practically universal in the faculty psychology literature, Franz Joseph Gall being, as we shall see, perhaps the only major figure to insist upon it.

Spearman's views on the history of psychology will, by the way, be frequently referred to in what follows; he is the one major experimental psychologist in this century to take the faculty tradition seriously.

4. This puts the case a little too strongly. Gall does, of course, think there are functional homologies between, say, mathematical memory and musical memory; both mediate the recall of things. The two memory systems are, however, supposed to be distinct by neurological criteria and by the criterion of autonomy of operation.

5. Even this may overestimate the similarity between Gall's views and Chomsky's. Gall doesn't actually seem to be very interested in innate *information*, the major burden of his plaint being the existence of innate *mental capacities*. As we've seen, it takes a special—Cartesian—view of how mental capacities are to be explained to see the second of these issues as crucially involving the first.

6. The "McGurk effect" provides fairly clear evidence for cross-modal linkages in at least one input system for the modularity of which there is independent evidence. McGurk has demonstrated that what are, to all intents and purposes, hallucinatory speech sounds can be induced when the subject is presented with a visual display of a speaker making vocal gestures appropriate to the production of those sounds. The suggestion is that (within, presumably, narrowly defined limits) mechanisms of phonetic analysis can be activated by—and can apply to—*either* accoustic *or* visual stimuli. (See McGurk and MacDonald, 1976.) It is of central importance to realize that the McGurk effect—though cross-modal—is itself domain specific—viz., specific to language. A motion picture of a bouncing ball does not induce bump, bump, bump hallucinations. (I am indebted to Professor Alvin Liberman both for bringing McGurk's results to my attention and for his illuminating comments on their implications.)

7. Generally speaking, the more peripheral a mechanism is in the process of perceptual analysis—the earlier it operates, for example—the better candidate for modularity it is likely to be. In the limit, it is untendentious—even traditional—to view the functioning of psychophysical (/sensory) mechanisms as largely autonomous with respect to central processes and largely parallel with respect to one another.

There is recent, striking evidence owing to Treisman and her colleagues that the detection of such stimulus "features" as shape and color is typically parallel, preattentive, and *prior* to the identification of the object in which the features, as it were, inhere: "... features are registered early, automatically, and in parallel across the visual field, while objects are identified separately only at a later stage, which requires focused attention" (Treisman and Gelade, 1980, p. 98). There is analogous evidence for the modularity of phonetic feature detectors that operate in speech perception (see Eimas and Corbet, 1973), though its interpretation is less than univocal (see Ganong, 1977).

8. I won't, in general, have much to say about input processes other than those involved in vision and language, since these are by far the areas in which the available psychology is most developed. But I hope, and believe, that the points I'll be making apply pretty well to all of the perceptual mechanisms.

9. Strictly speaking, I suppose I should say that this is true according to all current non-Gibsonian accounts. For reasons given elsewhere, however (see Fodor and Pylyshyn, 1981), I am deeply unmoved by the Gibsonian claim to have devised a noncomputational theory of perception. I propose simply to ignore it in this discussion.

10. A sufficient, but not a necessary, condition for the level of representation n being "higher" than the level of representation m is that the entities specified at n contain the entities specified

at *m* as constituents (in the way that words have syllables as constituents, for example). It would be nice if there proved to be a well-ordering of the interlevels of representation computed by each input system, but nothing in the present discussion depends on assuming that this is so. Still less is there reason to assume, in cases where the computations that a system performs are affected by data fed into it from outside, that the exogenous information can always be ordered, with respect to abstractness, relative to the levels of representation that the system computes. I shall conform to the prevalent usage in which *all* effects of background beliefs and expectations in perceptual processing are described as the feedback of information from "higher levels." But it is far from clear that either "higher" or "level" should be taken very seriously when so employed.

References

Bower, T. (1974). *Development in Infancy*. San Francisco, W. H. Freeman.

Brown, R. (1958). "How Shall a Thing Be Called?" *Psychological Review* 65: 14–21.

Bruner, J. (1957). "On Perceptual Readiness." *Psychological Review* 64: 123–152.

Chomsky, N. (1980). "Rules And Representations." *Behavorial and Brain Sciences* 3: 1–15.

Fodor, J. (1975). *The Language of Thought*. New York, Thomas Y. Crowell.

Fodor, J., and Pylyshyn, Z. (1981). "How Direct Is Visual Perception?" *Cognition* 9: 139–196.

Gardner, M. (1952). *In the Name of Science*. New York, Putnam.

Gleitman, L. (1981). "Maturational Determinants of Language Growth." *Cognition* 10: 103–114.

Goldin-Meadow, S., and Feldman, H. (1977). "The Development of Language-Like Communication without a Language Model." *Science* 197: 401–403.

Goodman, N. (1978). *Ways of Worldmaking*. Indianapolis, Hackett.

Hanson, N. (1958). *Patterns of Discovery*. Cambridge, Cambridge University Press.

Harris, J. (1977). "Leibniz and Locke on Innate Ideas." In I. C. Tipton (ed.), *Locke on Human Understanding*. Oxford Readings in Philosophy, Oxford University Press.

Hollander, B. (1920). *In Search of the Soul*. New York, E. P. Dutton.

Marslen-Wilson, W. (1973). "Speech Shadowing and Speech Perception." Ph.D. thesis, M.I.T.

Marslen-Wilson, W., and Tyler, L. (1981). "Central Processes in Speech Understanding." *Philosophical Transactions of the Royal Society* B 295: 317–322.

Meltzoff, A., and Bonton, R. (1979). "Intermodal Matching." *Nature* 282: 403–404.

Milner, B., Corbin, S., and Teuber, H.-L. (1968). "Further Analysis of the Hippocampal Amnesic Syndrome: 14-Year Follow-Up Study of H. M." *Neuropsychologia* 6: 215–234.

Spelke, E. (1982). "Perceptual Knowledge of Objects in Infancy." In J. Mehler, E. Walker, and M. Garrett (eds.), *Perspectives on Mental Representation*. Hillsdale, N.J., N. Lawrence Erlbaum Associates.

Takavolian, S. (ed.) (1981). *Language Acquisition and Linguistic Theory*. Cambridge, Mass., MIT Press.

Warren, R. (1970). "Perceptual Restoration of Missing Speech Sounds." *Science* 167: 392–393.

Zucker, S. (1981). "Computer Vision and Human Perception." Technical report 81-10, Computer Vision and Graphics Laboratory, McGill University.

71 Against Modularity

William Marslen-Wilson and Lorraine Komisarjevsky Tyler

The fundamental claim of the modularity hypothesis (Fodor 1983) is that the process of language comprehension—of mapping from the speech signal onto a message-level interpretation—is not a single, unitary process but involves at least two different kinds of process.[1] There is a modular, highly constrained, automatized "input system" that operates blindly on its bottom-up input to deliver, as rapidly as neurally possible, a shallow linguistic representation to a second kind of process, labeled by Fodor a "central process." This second type of process relates the output of the modular input system to the listener's knowledge of the world, of the discourse content, and so on. In particular, these central processes are responsible for the fixation of perceptual belief.

To justify this dichotomy between kinds of mental process, Fodor marshals a list of properties that input systems have and that central processes do not have. These include domain specificity, mandatoriness, speed, informational encapsulation, and a number of less critical properties. We do not dispute that there are some "central processes" that do not share these properties. Our argument here, nonetheless, is that those processes that map onto discourse representations and that also participate in the fixation of perceptual belief in fact share many of the special properties that Fodor treats as diagnostic of modular input systems.

We will argue on this basis that the modularity hypothesis gives the wrong kind of account of the organization of the language-processing system. This system does have fixed properties, and it does seem to be domain specific, mandatory, and fast in its operations. It is also, in a restricted sense, informationally encapsulated, because top-down influences do not control its normal first-pass operations. But its boundaries do not neatly coincide, as Fodor and others would have us believe, with the boundaries conventionally drawn between the subject matter of linguistic theory (construed as formal syntax) and the subject matter of disciplines such as pragmatics and discourse analysis.

In other words, we will argue, Fodor has misidentified the basic phenomenon that needs to be explained. Our comprehension of language, as he repeatedly stresses, is of the same order of immediacy as our perception, say, of the visual world. The modularity hypothesis tries to explain this by arguing that the primary processes of language analysis must operate with the blindness and the immunity to conscious control of the traditional reflex. Only in this way can we buy the brute speed with which the system seems to work.

But what is compelling about our real-time comprehension of language is not so much the immediacy with which linguistic form becomes available as the immediacy

Table 71.1
Diagnostic features for modularity.

	Target of mapping process	
Diagnostic feature	Logical form	Discourse model
Domain specificity	Yes	Yes
Mandatory	Yes	Yes
Limited access to intermediate representations	Yes	Yes
Speed	Yes	Yes
Informational encapsulation	No	No
Shallow output	—	—

with which interpreted meaning becomes available. It is this that is the target of the core processes of language comprehension, of the processes that map from sound onto meaning.

In the next section we will discuss the diagnostic properties assigned to input systems. We will then go on to present some experimental evidence for the encroachment of "modular" properties into processing territories reserved for central processes. This will be followed by a discussion of the implications of this failure of the diagnostic features to isolate a discontinuity in the system at the point where Fodor and others want to place it. We do not claim that there are no differences between input systems and central processes; but, the differences that do exist are not distributed in the way that the modularity hypothesis requires.

Diagnostic Features

Table 71.1 lists the principal diagnostic features that, according to Fodor, discriminate input systems from central processes.[2] We will go through these six features in order, showing how each one fails to support a qualitative discontinuity at the fracture point indicated by Fodor and by most other modularity theorists, e.g., Forster (1979 and 1987), Garrett (1978), and Frazier et al. (1983b). In each case the question is the same: Does the feature distinguish between a mapping process that terminates on a specifically linguistic, sentence-internal form of representation (labeled "logical form" in the table) and a process that terminates on some form of discourse representation or mental model?

Domain Specificity

The argument here is that when one is dealing with a specialized domain—that is, a domain that has its own idiosyncratic computations to perform—one would expect to find a specialized processor. However, as Fodor himself points out (1983, p. 52), the inference from domain idiosyncracy to modular processor is not by itself a strong one. Furthermore, he presents neither evidence nor arguments that the process of mapping linguistic representations onto discourse models is any less domain specific (i.e., less idiosyncratic or specialized) than the processes required to map onto "shallow" linguistic representations.

Mandatory Processing

Mandatory processing is what we have called *obligatory processing* (Marslen-Wilson and Tyler 1980a, 1981), and what others have called *automatic* (as opposed to controlled) processing (e.g., Posner and Snyder 1975; Shiffrin and Schneider 1977). The claim here is that modular processes apply mandatorily and that central processes do not. Fodor's arguments for this are entirely phenomenological. If we hear an utterance in a language we know, we are forced to perceive it as a meaningful, interpretable string, and not as a sequence of meaningless noises.

But there is no reason to suppose that this mandatory projection onto higher-level representations stops short at logical form. Indeed, one's phenomenological experience says quite distinctly otherwise. Consider the following pair of utterances, uttered in normal conversation after a lecture: "Jerry gave the first talk today. He was his usual ebullient self." Hearing this, it seems just as cognitively mandatory to map the pronoun *He* at the beginning of the second sentence onto the discourse representation of *Jerry* set up in the course of the first sentence as it does, for example, to hear *All Gaul is divided into three parts* as a sentence and not as an acoustic object (see Fodor 1983, p. 55).

In other words, in what we call *normal first-pass processing* the projection onto an interpretation in the discourse model can be just as mandatory as the projection onto "shallower" levels of linguistic analysis.[3] And if there is a distinction here between mapping onto logical form and mapping onto a discourse model, it probably isn't going to be picked up by this kind of introspective analysis.

Limited Central Access to Intermediate Representations

The underlying assumption here is that the perceptual process proceeds through the assignment of a number of intermediate levels of representation, culminating in the final output of the system. Fodor claims that these "interlevels" are relatively less accessible to central processes than the output representation. There are two points we can make here.

First, there is nothing in Fodor's discussion of this (1983, pp. 55–60) that specifically implicates a shallow linguistic level as *the* level of representation that is more accessible to central processes. Second, if one is dealing with a series of automatized processes, tracking obligatorily through the processing sequence, then one is surely going to get a form of overwriting of the perceptual representations at each level intermediate to the final one. This will make the interlevels less accessible to the perceiver, but without the need to assign a special status to this final level—other than that, because it is the final level, it will not be overwritten by subsequent levels.

At this point one is returned to the phenomenological issues raised in the preceding section: What is the level of perceptual representation onto which the process obligatorily maps, and is this the form of representation that is most readily accessible to other processes?

Speed

The speed of language processing is central to Fodor's argument. The projection from signal onto message seems to be carried out as rapidly as is either neurally or informationally possible. Close shadowers, as he points out, with repetition delays of around

250 msec, seem to be operating at the limit of the ability of the speech signal to deliver information. In fact (as we argue in Marslen-Wilson 1985), close shadowers are outrunning even the abilities of their processing system to deliver its products to conscious awareness; they start to initiate their repetition of what they hear before they are fully aware of what they are saying.

But why does this speed matter? How does it help to diagnose an input system with its boundaries somewhere in the region of logical form?

Fodor's argument is simply that speech processing can only be this fast if it is domain specific, mandatory, and informationally encapsulated—if, in other words, it is like a reflex.[4] And for a process to be reflexive it cannot also be reflective—or, as Fodor puts it, "sicklied o'er with the pale cast of thought" (p. 64). This means, in particular, that this primary rapid analysis process must be restricted to properties of utterances that can largely be computed from the bottom up and without reference to background knowledge, problem-solving mechanisms, and the like. These properties, Fodor believes, are the grammatical and logical structure of an utterance: the abstract representation of utterance *form*.

Fodor's argument fails on two counts: because the available evidence shows that mapping onto a discourse model can be at least as fast as any putative mapping onto logical form, and because discourse mapping is not necessarily slowed down even when it does involve pragmatic inference (which is just the kind of open-ended process that Fodor argues must be excluded from rapid first-pass processing).

Informational Encapsulation

Informational encapsulation is the claim that input systems are informationally isolated from central processes, in the sense that information derived from these central processes cannot directly affect processing within the input system. This claim lies at the empirical core of Fodor's thesis.

Informational encapsulation is not a diagnostic feature that functions in the same way as the previous four we have discussed. Although it is a property that modular language processes are assumed to have and that central processes do not, it is definable as such only in terms of the relationship between the two of them. To defeat Fodor's argument, we do not need to show whether or not central and modular processes share the property of encapsulation, but simply that they are not isolated from each other in the ways the modularity hypothesis requires. Exactly what degree of isolation does the hypothesis require?

The notion of informational encapsulation, as deployed by Fodor, is significantly weaker than the general notion of autonomous processing, argued for by Forster (1979) and others. This general notion states that the output of each processing component in the system is determined solely by its bottom-up input. Fodor, however, makes no claims for autonomous processing within the language module. Top-down communication between levels of linguistically specified representation does not violate the principle of informational encapsulation (Fodor 1983, pp. 76–77). The language module as a whole, however, is autonomous in the standard sense. No information that is not linguistically specified—at the linguistic levels up to and including logical form—can affect operations within the module. Fodor believes that the cost of fast, mandatory operation in the linguistic input system is isolation from everything else the perceiver knows.

As stated, this claim cannot be completely true. When listeners encounter syntactically ambiguous strings, where only pragmatic knowledge can resolve the ambiguity, they nonetheless seem to end up with the structural analysis that best fits the context.[5] To cope with this, Fodor does allow a limited form of interaction at the syntactic interface between the language module and central processes. The central processes can give the syntactic parser feedback about the semantic and pragmatic acceptability of the structures it has computed (Fodor 1983, pp. 134–135). Thus, in cases of structural ambiguity, extramodular information does affect the outcome of linguistic analysis.

How is this limited form of interaction to be distinguished, empirically, from a fully interactive, unencapsulated system? Fodor's position is based on the exclusion of top-down predictive interaction: "What the context analyzer is *prohibited* from doing is telling the parser *which* line of analysis it ought to try next—i.e., semantic information can't be used predictively to guide the parse" (Fodor 1983, p. 135; emphases in original). What this means, in practice, is that context will not be able to guide the normal first-pass processing of the material; it will come into play only when the first-pass output of the syntactic parser becomes available for semantic and pragmatic interpretation. This, in turn, means that the claim for informational encapsulation depends empirically on the precise timing of the contextual resolution of syntactic ambiguities—not whether context can have such effects, but when. Is there an exhaustive computation of all readings compatible with the bottom-up input, among which context later selects, or does context intervene early in the process, so that only a single reading needs to be computed? Fodor presents no evidence that bears directly on this issue. But let us consider the arguments he does present, bearing in mind that he does not regard these arguments as proving his case, but simply as making it more plausible.

The first type of argument is frankly rhetorical. It is based on an analogy between input systems and reflexes. If (as Fodor suggests on pages 71–72) input systems are computationally specified reflexes, then, like reflexes, they will be fully encapsulated. The language module will spit out its representation of logical form as blindly and as impenetrably as your knee will respond to the neurologist's rubber hammer. But this is not in itself evidence that the language input system actually is informationally encapsulated. It simply illustrates what input systems might be like if they really were a kind of cognitive reflex. By the same token, the apparent cognitive impenetrability of certain phenomena in visual perception is also no evidence *per se* for the impenetrability of the language module (Fodor, pp. 66–67).

Fodor's second line of argument is teleological in nature: If an organism knows what is good for it, then it will undoubtedly want to have its input systems encapsulated. The organism needs to see or hear what is actually there rather than what it expects should be there, and it needs its first-pass perceptual assignments to be made available as rapidly as possible. And the only way to guarantee this kind of fast, unprejudiced access to the state of the world is to encapsulate one's input systems.

It is certainly true that organisms would do well to ensure themselves fast, unprejudiced input. But this is not evidence that encapsulation is the optimal mechanism for achieving this, nor, specifically, is it evidence that the language input system has these properties—or even that it is subject to this kind of stringent teleological constraint.

The third line of argument is more germane to the issues at hand, since it deals directly with the conventional psycholinguistic evidence for interaction and autonomy in the language-processing system. But even here, Fodor has no evidence that the relationship between syntactic parsing and central processes is restricted in the ways his analysis requires. What he does instead is show that many of the results that are usually cited as evidence for interaction need not be interpreted in this way—although, as noted above, it is only by significantly diluting the concept of autonomy that he can defend the modularity hypothesis against its major counterexamples.

In any case, despite Fodor's caveats, the evidence we will report below suggests that context does guide the parser on-line, and not solely in the "after-the-event" manner Fodor predicts. Hence the entry in table 71.1. Informational encapsulation does not separate the processes that map onto logical form from those that map onto discourse models.

Shallow Output

Fodor claims that the output of the language input system is restricted to whatever can be computed without reference to "background data." This, however, is not a diagnostic feature at all—it is the basic point at issue.

It is our position that the diagnostics discussed by Fodor, and briefly analyzed here, do not select out an output level corresponding to logical form. Rather, they select an output level that is at least partially nonlinguistic in nature. Although the output of the class of mandatory, fast processes may be relatively "shallow," it does not fall at a level of the system that distinguishes either modular processes from central processes (as defined by Fodor) or the linguistic from the nonlinguistic.

Experimental Evidence

In this section we will review some of the evidence supporting our position. In particular, we will argue for three main claims, each of which is in conflict with one or more of the major assumptions upon which Fodor has based the modularity hypothesis. These claims are the following:

(i) that the mapping of the incoming utterance onto a discourse model is indistinguishable in its rapidity from the mapping onto "logical form" (or equivalently shallow levels)

(ii) that the discourse mapping process is not significantly slowed down even when the correct mapping onto discourse antecedents requires pragmatic inference (showing that speed *per se* does not distinguish processes involving only bottom-up linguistic computation from processes involving, at least potentially, "everything the perceiver knows")

(iii) that, if we do assume a representational difference in on-line processing between a level of logical form and a post-linguistic level situated in a discourse model, then there is clear evidence for top-down influences on syntactic choice during first-pass processing and not only after the event.

Table 71.2
Sample word-monitoring materials.

Normal prose
The church was broken into last night.
Some thieves stole most of the *lead* off the roof.
Anomalous prose
The power was located in great water.
No buns puzzle some in the *lead* off the text.
Scrambled prose
In was power water the great located.
Some the no puzzle buns in *lead* text the off.

The evidence for these claims derives from a variety of different experiments. We will proceed here by describing each class of experiment separately, showing in each case how it bears on the three claims.

Word-Monitoring Experiments

This research provides evidence for the speed of discourse mapping and for the rapid on-line computation of pragmatic inferences. The first of these experiments (Marslen-Wilson and Tyler 1975, 1980a) was designed to track the availability of different types of processing information as these became available during the processing of an utterance.

The experiment used three types of prose materials (see table 71.2). The Normal Prose strings were normal sentences that could be analyzed both semantically and syntactically. The second prose type, Anomalous Prose, was syntactically still relatively normal but had no coherent semantic interpretation. The third condition, Scrambled Prose, could not be analyzed syntactically or semantically. Sentences of each of these three types were presented either in isolation or preceded by a lead-in sentence. This allowed us to observe the effects of the presence or absence of a discourse context. Each test sentence also contained a monitoring target word, such as *lead* in the sample set given in table 71.2. These target words occurred in different serial positions across the test sentences, varying from the second to the tenth position. By measuring the monitoring response time at different points across each type of test material, we could determine the time course with which syntactic and semantic processing information became available, and how this was affected by whether or not a discourse context was available.

We will concentrate here on the relationship between Normal Prose and the other two prose conditions at the early target positions as a function of the presence or absence of a discourse context. The upper panel of figure 71.1 gives the response curves for the discourse condition, where the lead-in sentence is present. Here, targets in Normal Prose are responded to faster than those in Anomalous or Scrambled Prose even at the earliest word positions. The average difference in intercept between Normal Prose and the other conditions (for Identical and Rhyme monitoring[6]) is 53 msec. This means that the extra processing information that Normal Prose provides is being developed by the listener right from the beginning of the utterance.

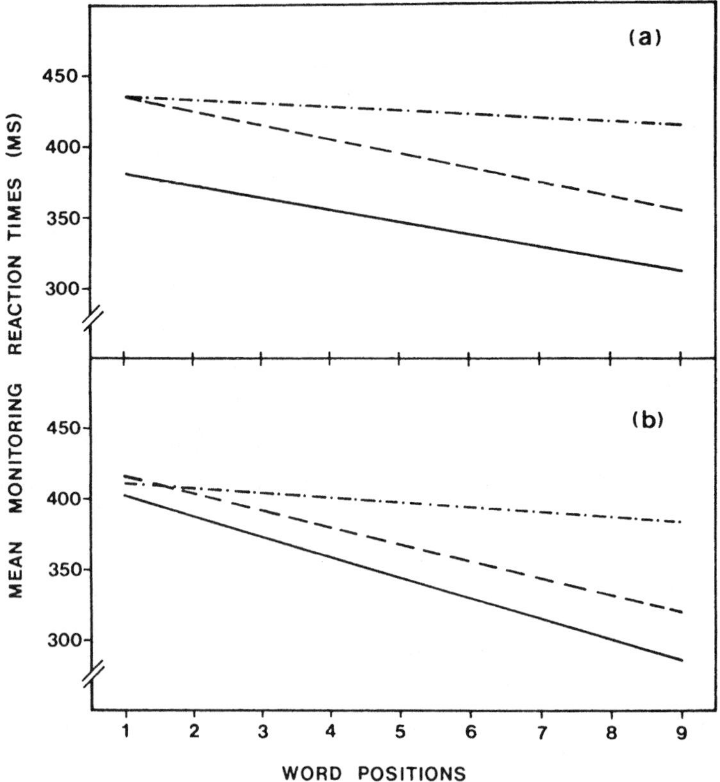

Figure 71.1
Mean reaction times (in milliseconds) for word monitoring in three prose contexts, presented either with a preceding context sentence (a) or without one (b) and plotted across word positions 1–9. The unbroken lines represent responses in normal prose, the broken lines responses in anomalous prose, and the dotted lines responses in scrambled prose.

The critical point, illustrated by the lower panel of figure 71.1, is that this early advantage of Normal Prose depends on the presence of the lead-in sentence. When no lead-in sentence is present, the extra facilitation of monitoring responses in Normal Prose contexts develops later in the utterance, and the mean intercept difference between Normal Prose and the other two conditions falls to a nonsignificant 12 msec.

We can take for granted that the on-line interpretability of the early words of the test sentence depends on their syntactic well-formedness, so that the early advantage of Normal Prose reflects in part the speed and earliness with which a syntactic analysis of the incoming material is being computed. But the effects of removing the lead-in sentence show that the mapping onto a discourse model must be taking place at least as early and at least as rapidly as any putative mapping onto logical form. There is nothing in the data to suggest the sort of temporal lag in the accessibility of these two kinds of perceptual target that would support the modularity hypothesis.

It is possible to devise modular systems in which predictions about the differential speed of different types of process do not play a role, so that the absence of a difference here is not fatal. But what it does mean is that speed of processing cannot be used as a

Table 71.3
Sample materials for local-anomaly experiment.

Condition A
The crowd was waiting eagerly.
The young man carried the *guitar*....
Condition B
The crowd was waiting eagerly.
The young man buried the *guitar*....
Condition C
The crowd was waiting eagerly.
The young man drank the *guitar*....
Condition D
The crowd was waiting eagerly.
The young man slept the *guitar*....

diagnostic criterion for distinguishing processes that map onto purely linguistic levels of representation from those that map onto mental models. This, in turn, undermines Fodor's basic assumption that speed requires modular processing. If you can map onto a discourse level as rapidly as you can map onto a shallow linguistic level, then modularity and encapsulation cannot be the prerequisites for very fast processing.

A second word-monitoring experiment (Brown, Marslen-Wilson, and Tyler, in preparation) again illustrates the speed of processing and, in particular, the rapidity with which pragmatic inferences can be made during on-line processing. Instead of the global disruption of prose context in the previous experiment, this experiment used only Normal Prose sentence pairs containing local anomalies of different types. A typical stimulus set, illustrated in table 71.3, shows a neutral lead-in sentence followed by four different continuation sentences. The same target word (*guitar*) occurs in all four sentences. Variation of the preceding verb creates four different context conditions.

In condition A there are no anomalies; the sentence is normal. In condition B there is no syntactic or semantic violation, but the combination of critical verb and target is pragmatically anomalous—whatever one does with guitars, one does not normally bury them. Conditions C and D involve stronger violations—in C of semantic-selection restrictions, and in D of subcategorization constraints. Presented to subjects in a standard monitoring task, these materials produce a steady increase in mean response time across conditions, from 241 msec for targets in the normal sentences to 320 msec for the subcategorization violations.

We are concerned here with the significant effects of pragmatic anomaly (mean: 267 msec) and what these imply for the speed with which representations of different sorts can be computed. The point about condition B is that the relative slowness to respond to *guitar* in the context of burying, as opposed to the context of carrying in condition A, cannot be attributed to any *linguistic* differences between the two conditions. It must instead be attributed to the listeners' inferences about likely actions involving guitars. The implausibility of burying guitars as opposed to carrying them is something that needs to be deduced from other things that the listener knows about guitars, burying, carrying, and so on. And yet, despite the potential unboundedness of the inferences

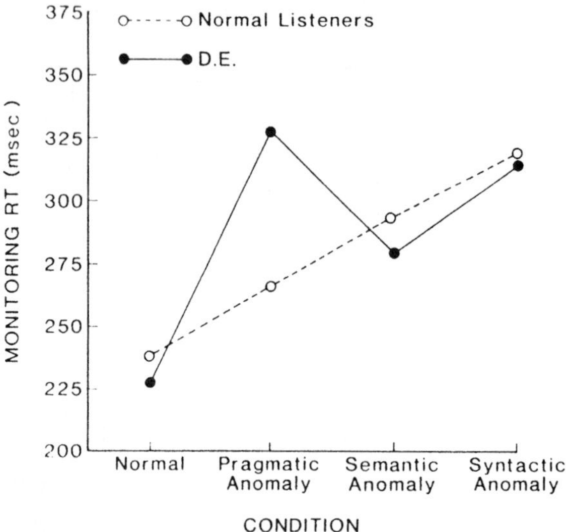

Figure 71.2
Mean word-monitoring reaction times for four experimental conditions for the patient D. E. and for a group of normal controls.

that might have to be drawn here, the listener can apparently compute sufficient consequences, in the interval between recognizing the verb and responding to the target, for these inferences to significantly affect response time.[7]

The possibility of very rapid pragmatic inferencing during language processing is also supported by the on-line performance of certain aphasic patients. In one case of classic agrammatism (Tyler 1985, 1986) we found a selective deficit in syntactic processing such that the patient could not construct global structural units. When this patient was tested on the set of contrasts described above, we found a much greater dependency on pragmatic information, as reflected in his greatly increased latencies to the pragmatic anomaly condition relative to normal subjects and relative to his own performance in the other conditions (see figure 71.2). Again, the pragmatically plausible relationship between verb and potential object was being computed very rapidly as the utterance was being heard.

Resolution of Syntactic Ambiguity

The research described in this section bears on all three of the claims at issue, but it speaks most directly to the on-line contextual guidance of syntactic parsing. It does so by looking at the processing of phrasal fragments (such as *landing planes*) when they are placed in different kinds of discourse contexts.

Ambiguous fragments of this type have two different readings, which we will refer to here, following Townsend and Bever (1982), as the *adjectival* and the *gerund* reading. The question at issue is whether prior nonlinguistic context can resolve such ambiguities, and the timing with which this contextual disambiguation might occur. The crucial claim for the modularity hypothesis is that context cannot act predictively, so that the first-pass analysis of such structures will be conducted on the basis of purely linguistic considerations.

In our first examination of this question (Tyler and Marslen-Wilson 1977) we placed the ambiguous fragments in disambiguating contexts of the following types.

Adjectival bias: If you walk too near the runway, landing planes. . . .
Gerund bias: If you've been trained as a pilot, landing planes. . . .

The subjects heard one of the two context clauses, followed by the ambiguous fragment. Immediately after the acoustic offset of the fragments (e.g., at the end of the /s/ of *planes*), a visual probe was flashed up, which was either an appropriate or an inappropriate continuation of the fragment. The probe was always either the word *is* or the word *are*, and its appropriateness depended on the preceding context. For the cases above, *is* is an appropriate continuation of *landing planes* when this has the gerund reading, but not when it has the adjectival reading. The opposite holds for the probe *are*.

The results of the experiment seemed clear-cut. There was a significantly faster naming latency to appropriate probes. These on-line preferences, we argued at the time, could be explained only if we assumed that the listener was rapidly evaluating the structural readings of the ambiguous fragments relative to the meanings of the words involved and relative to the pragmatic plausibility of each reading in the given context. Furthermore, since the inappropriateness effects were just as strong for these ambiguous fragments as they were for a comparison group of unambiguous fragments (e.g., *smiling faces*), we argued in favor of a single computation. Instead of arguing that both analyses were being computed and that one was later selected, we argued that context affected the parsing process directly, so that only one reading was ever computed.

This first experiment was criticized, primarily on methodological grounds, by Townsend and Bever (1982) and by Cowart (1983), who pointed out that the stimuli contained a number of potential confounds, of which the most serious was the distribution of singular and plural cataphoric pronouns in the context sentences. Examination of the stimulus materials shows that the adjectival contexts tended to contain such pronouns as *they* and *them*, whereas the gerund contexts contained pronouns such as *it*. For example, for the ambiguous phrase *cooking apples*, the adjectival context was *Although they may be very tart . . .*; the gerund context was *Although it doesn't require much work . . . .*

Given that these sentences appear in isolation, such pronouns tend to be treated as cataphoric—that is, as co-referential with an entity that has not yet been mentioned. They may create, therefore, the expectation that either singular or plural potential referents will be occurring later in the text. This is a type of contextual bias that could potentially be handled within the syntactic parser, without reference to pragmatic variables. Although this pronoun effect can just as easily be attributed to an interaction with discourse context, it is nonetheless important to show whether or not a discourse bias can still be observed when the pronoun effect is neutralized.

To this end, a further experiment was carried out (W. Marslen-Wilson and A. Young, manuscript in preparation) with pairs of context sentences having exactly parallel structures, containing identical pronouns, and differing only in their pragmatic implications—for example, the following.

Adjectival bias: If you want a cheap holiday, visiting relatives . . . .
Gerund bias: If you have a spare bedroom, visiting relatives . . . .

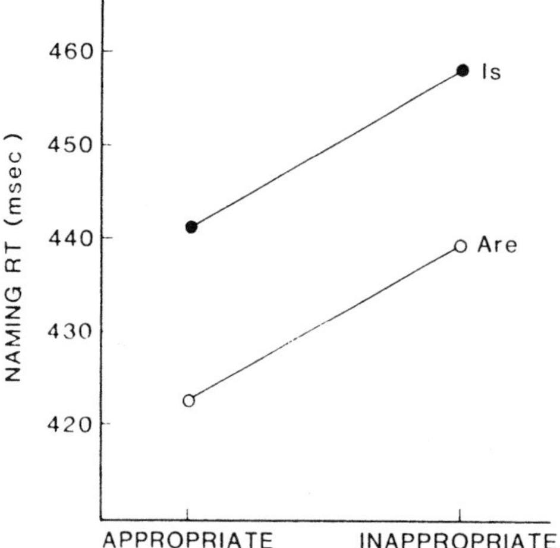

Figure 71.3
Mean naming latencies for appropriate and inappropriate *is* and *are* targets.

The results, summarized in figure 71.3, show that there was still a significant effect of contextual appropriateness on response times to the *is* and *are* probes. Responses were slower for *is* when it followed an ambiguous phrase heard in an adjectival context, and slower for *are* when the same phrase followed a gerund context. Even when all forms of potential syntactic or lexical bias were removed from the context clauses, we still saw an immediate effect on the structure assigned to these ambiguous fragments.

These results confirm that nonlinguistic context affects the assignment of a syntactic analysis, and they tell us that it does so very early. The probe word comes immediately after the end of the fragment, at the point where the ambiguity of the fragment first becomes fully established—note that the ambiguity of these sequences depends on knowing both words in the fragment; sequences like *landing lights* are not ambiguous in the same way. This means that we are finding significant context effects at what is effectively the earliest point at which we can measure.

What does this mean for the modularity hypothesis and its claims for informational encapsulation? The results do not force a single-computation account. No matter how early context effects are detected, it is always possible to argue that multiple readings were nonetheless computed, so that what we are picking up are after-the-event selection effects rather than direct control of the initial syntactic parse. But the cost of this move is that it makes it very difficult to discriminate the modular version of interaction from an account that allows continuous or even predictive interactions between levels. The modular account simply fails to make empirically distinct predictions. And if this is the case, then the claim for informational encapsulation cannot help us to distinguish modular from central processes.

Pragmatic Inference in Anaphor Resolution

A third class of experiments, using the same naming task, looked at the processing relationship between an utterance and its discourse context. They were specifically designed to test the claim that even when the linkage between an utterance and its dis-

Table 71.4
Sample materials for anaphora experiment.

Context sentences
As Philip was walking back from the shop he saw an old woman trip and fall flat on her face in the street. She seemed unable to get up again.
Continuation fragments
(1) Philip ran towards....
(2) He ran towards....
(3) Running towards....

course context can only be based on pragmatic inference, this will not slow down the on-line mapping process.

In the first of these experiments (Marslen-Wilson and Tyler 1980b; Tyler and Marslen-Wilson 1982), two context sentences were followed by one of three continuation fragments (see table 71.4). Each of these fragments contained an anaphoric device linking the fragments to the preceding discourse. In fragment 1 the device was the name of some individual previously mentioned; in fragment 2 it was an unambiguous personal pronoun; in fragment 3 (an example of zero anaphora) there were no explicit lexical cues at all.

In each case, to interpret the fragment, it is necessary to determine who is the agent of the action denoted by the verb, and to evaluate this with respect to the preceding discourse. In fragments 1 and 2 the agent is directly lexically specified (*Philip*; *He*), and can be unambiguously related to possible antecedents on the basis of this lexical information alone. It is case 3 that concerns us here. The only way in which agency can be assigned is on the basis of differential pragmatic inference that matches the properties of *Running towards* ... to the properties of the potential antecedents in the discourse. It is necessary to infer who is most likely running towards whom.

To measure the timing of anaphoric linkage in these three conditions, we used the naming technique described in the preceding section. The subjects heard the context sentences together with one of the three continuation fragments. At the acoustic offset of the fragment (e.g., at the end of *towards*), a visual probe word was presented to them, which they had to name as quickly as possible. For the examples given in table 71.4, the probe word would have been either *him* or *her*. For each case, *her* is a more appropriate continuation than *him*. The critical experimental question was whether the size of the expected preference effect (slower naming of inappropriate probes) would be the same for all three continuations.

This bears upon the claims of the modularity hypothesis in two ways. First, it measures the speed and the on-line effectiveness of discourse linkages based on pragmatic inference, in direct comparison with linkages that can be based on less computationally costly search and matching processes. Second, it asks whether top-down context can act upon the syntactic parser in ways that are prohibited by the modularity hypothesis.[8] If the appropriateness effect is as strong in the zero case as in the other two, then, on our analysis, the missing subject of the verb will have been filled in, on-line, on the basis of a process of differential pragmatic inference. This will mean that contextual considerations can determine the assignment of predicate-argument relations

Table 71.5
Results of anaphora experiment.

	Mean naming latencies (msec)		
Type of anaphor	Appropriate	Inappropriate	Difference
Repeated name	379	429	50
Pronoun	385	434	49
Zero anaphor	384	420	36

in logical form. But the modularity hypothesis specifically excludes central processes from having this kind of influence on syntactic representations. Context can give the parser Yes/No feedback, but it can never directly tell the parser what the content of its analyses should be.

The results, summarized in table 71.5, show that there is a marked appropriateness effect in each condition, and that the size of the effect does not vary significantly. This confirms that utterances are immediately integrated with their discourse contexts, since the inappropriateness of *him* or *her*, in all three conditions, depends on the relationship between the discourse properties of the antecedent and the properties assigned to that antecedent in the continuation sentence. It also shows that when the linkage can depend only on pragmatic inference, as in the Zero Anaphor case, this does not significantly impair or slow down the on-line integration process.

The speed of these integration processes is underlined by the outcome of another manipulation in the experiment. This was a variation in the length of the verb phrase in the continuation fragment, so that, in the zero case, the probe could appear anywhere from the second to the fifth word of the fragment. These variations had no effect on the size of the inappropriateness effect for the Zero Anaphor conditions. The difference between appropriate and inappropriate probes averaged 36 msec for the shortest verb phrases and 33 msec for the longest verb phrases.

As we noted above, the effects for the zero condition suggest a form of top-down effect on syntactic representations that is incompatible with the claim for informational encapsulation. The appropriateness effect depends on the inferral of agency; to the extent that this leads to the top-down filling of the empty subject slot in the argument structure of the verb, then context is specifying the actual content of a representation within the linguistic input system.

The results of this first study were elaborated and confirmed in a subsequent experiment using similar materials and techniques. The first goal of this second experiment (Marslen-Wilson, Tyler, and Koster, in preparation) was to ensure that the effects we have attributed here to differential pragmatic inference had not been confounded with the effects of discourse focus. In a narrative discourse, a particular individual may become salient—or "in focus"—and this can lead listeners to expect that this individual will continue to be mentioned, especially as subject, in subsequent utterances (see Karmiloff-Smith 1980, 1985; Marslen-Wilson and Tyler 1980b; Marslen-Wilson, Levy, and Tyler 1982). This possibility was not fully controlled for in the first experiment.

To deal with this problem, and to look more specifically at how different sources of constraint were integrated to determine the mapping of an utterance onto its discourse

Table 71.6
Materials for factorial anaphora experiment.

Condition 1: Discourse bias with congruent verb bias
After the surgeon had examined the 12-year old girl with the badly broken leg, he decided he would have to take immediate action. He'd had a lot of experience with serious injuries. He knew what he had to do next.
A. He quickly injected . . .
B. She quickly injected . . .   HER/HIM
C. Quickly injecting . . .

Condition 2: Discourse bias with neutral verb
As Bill was buying popcorn at the movies, he saw an old girl-friend get in line for a ticket. He had arrived at the movies especially early. He wanted to be sure of getting a good seat.
A. He waved at . . .
B. She waved at . . .   HER/HIM
C. Waving at . . .

Condition 3: Discourse bias with opposing verb bias
Mary lost hope of winning the race to the ocean when she heard Andrew's footsteps approaching her from behind. The deep sand was slowing her down. She had trouble keeping her balance.
A. She overtook . . .
B. He overtook . . .   HIM/HER
C. Overtaking . . .

context, the second experiment co-varied in a semi-factorial manner three different factors: discourse focus, the pragmatic implications of the verb, and the lexical specificity of anaphors. The subset of these contrasts that concern us here are given in table 71.6, which lists some sample context stories and (in capitals) their associated continuation fragments and visual probes.

For all three main conditions, a strong discourse bias was set up. Each context story always contained two protagonists, with one foregrounded and the other not. The principal actor appeared in subject position in the first sentence and continued to function as the main actor for at least two subsequent sentences. Pretests of these materials showed that listeners expected the following sentence to have the main actor continuing in subject position. This was the manipulation of *discourse focus*.

The second manipulation, also applying to all three conditions, was the variation in the *lexical specificity* of the anaphor in subject position in the continuation fragments. The contrast here was between lexically unambiguous anaphors (for these examples, the pronouns *He* and *She*) and the lexically empty Zero Anaphor case. The two pronouns co-varied with discourse focus. For the A continuations, the pronoun was always consistent with the discourse bias, so that it selected as subject the individual who was salient in the preceding context. For the B continuations, the pronoun selected the individual who was not in discourse focus (the second of the two protagonists).

The third manipulation was the *pragmatic implications of the verb*—that is the congruence of the actions denoted by the verb with what was already known in the discourse about the two protagonists. This was co-varied with the other two factors. Thus, in condition 1, the verb bias fitted the discourse bias. These two together were also congruent with the pronoun for continuation 1A, but not for 1B. In continuation 1C, verb bias and discourse bias worked together. In condition 2, the pragmatics of the verb were neutral and were designed to be equally compatible with both potential antecedents. This allowed us to measure, in continuation 2C, the effects of discourse bias when no other cues were available.

Finally, in condition 3, the verb bias was in conflict with discourse bias. The crucial test was in 3C, the Zero Anaphor condition. If verb semantics can be interpreted on-line to select the pragmatically appropriate antecedent, then we should detect this effect even here, where discourse focus favored a different antecedent in subject position.

To test for the effects of these variations, we again used the naming task. Subjects heard the context story together with one of the continuation fragments, and were asked to name as rapidly as possible a visual probe that appeared at the acoustic offset of the fragment. The relative speed of their responses to the probes—which were always unambiguously coreferential with one of the two protagonists in the preceding context story—were taken to reflect the way in which the listeners had linked the continuation fragment to the discourse context.

The probes were not labeled "appropriate" or "inappropriate" in advance, since for many conditions the appropriateness of a given probe was itelf the question at issue. Instead, we adopted the convention of referring to probe 1 and probe 2. Probe 1 was always the probe that was consistent with the discourse bias and with the subject pronoun in continuation A—in table 71.6, for example, probe 1 is *her* for conditions 1A and 2A, and *him* for 3A. The term *consistent* means here that a given pronoun probe in object position is consistent with a given assignment of an agent to subject position. A probe will be consistent with a source of constraint, such as discourse bias, if this favors the instantiation in subject position of a suitable agent.

The results of this experiment, listed in table 71.7, bear upon the modularity hypothesis in two ways. First, there is the confirmation that pragmatic inference, operating alone, can link utterances to discourses as effectively as pronouns and names. In condi-

Table 71.7
Results of factorial anaphora experiment.

	Mean naming latency (msec)		
Condition	Probe 1	Probe 2	Difference
Discourse bias and congruent verb			
1A: Congruent pronoun	481	535	+54
1B: Incongruent pronoun	532	506	−26
1C: Zero anaphor	500	536	+36
Discourse bias and neutral verb			
2A: Congruent pronoun	472	528	+56
2B: Incongruent pronoun	527	467	−60
2C: Zero anaphor	496	543	+47
Discourse bias and incongruent verb			
3A: Congruent pronoun	511	506	−5
3B: Incongruent pronoun	549	482	−67
3C: Zero anaphor	530	482	−48

tion 3C, where the pragmatic implications of the verb actually go against discourse bias—therefore ruling out any possibility of a confounding with discourse effects—there is an appropriateness effect of 48 msec.

Consider the example in table 71.6, where the discourse in condition 3 sets up the character Mary in discourse focus. In our pretests of this context, listeners produced continuation sentences that kept Mary in focus as subject and main actor. In the experimental materials, however, the verb in the continuation fragment (*Overtaking*) is inconsistent with the listener's mental model of the relationship between Mary and her competitor Andrew. Mary, slipping and stumbling, is in no position to be overtaking someone, and it is this that determines who the listener instantiates as agent of the action. It is probe 2 (*her*) that is treated as appropriate, and not the probe that is consistent with the discourse bias. The size of the effect compares favorably with cases like 1A and 2A, where a congruent pronoun is present as well.

Equally significant, the results show that discourse focus on its own can also control the on-line intepretation of utterance fragments. Discourse bias is the weakest of the three variables, and its effects are usually obscured by the other two sources of constraint. But when these other sources are neutralized (as in condition 2C, where there is no pronoun and the verb is pragmatically neutral) there is a clear discourse-based appropriateness effect, which is just as strong as the effects produced by pronouns or verbs in other conditions. Once again agency is being assigned under conditions where the parser could have no basis for doing so on purely linguistic grounds. It is only in the representation of the discourse that any basis exists for choosing between one actor or the other as subject of the verb in the continuation fragment. If the way the effect operates is by affecting the assignment of predicate-argument relations in logical form, then it is doing so in contradiction to the crucial predictions of the modularity hypothesis.

The effect of discourse bias in 2C demonstrates, in addition, that these assignment processes take place as the continuation fragment is being heard—in particular, before the presentation of the visual probe. If an assignment of agency had not already been made before the subject knew what the visual probe was, there would not have been any inappropriateness effect. The effects in 2A and 2B show that the assignment of either protagonist as agent is equally acceptable here—the probe *her* is named just as rapidly after *He waved at....* as the probe *him* after *She waved at....* Equally, there is nothing about the sequence *Waving at him* (with the female actor as agent) that makes it any less appropriate in the given discourse context than *Waving at her* (with the male as subject).

To explain the appropriateness effects, we have to assume a particular ordering of processing events. At the moment when the continuation fragment starts, the manipulation of discourse focus has led to the expectation that the actor in focus will continue in subject position. Unless the subject pronoun is inconsistent with this expectation (as in 2B), and unless the semantics of the verb select the other protagonist (as in 3C), the listener will go ahead and assign agency on this basis. He or she can do this as soon as the information becomes available that the verb is pragmatically neutral. Evidence from other studies (see the subsection on word-monitoring experiments) shows that this occurs while the verb is still being heard. Thus, by the time the visual probe appears, a commitment has already been made to the discourse mapping of the continuation fragment. Given this assignment, probe 2 will be perceived as inappropriate.

More generally, the results over the nine conditions reveal a pattern of dependencies between the discourse model and the current utterance that is difficult to handle within a system based on the rigidly bottom-up communication paths that characterize the modularity hypothesis. In particular, we are dealing here with a system that is highly flexible, even opportunistic, in its use of different types of processing information to achieve the perceptual goal of relating an utterance to its discourse context.

We see in the results that all three types of constraint—pronoun constraint, discourse bias, and pragmatic coherence—are equally capable, under the right conditions, of controlling the outcome of this process, and we see this occurring within the kind of on-line time frame that is supposed to characterize modular processes. This flexibility in using different sources of constraint, as and when they are available, means that the process of discourse linkage is not dependent on information being made available to it in a fixed order or in a fixed format. This stands in opposition to the central argument of the modularity thesis: that language comprehension is centered around a system that is entirely fixed in its properties and that is entirely insensitive to the changing informational circumstances within which utterances occur.

Implications

The evidence presented in the preceding section, and the analyses discussed earlier, lead to a view of language processing that is in many ways quite similar to the approach put forward by Fodor. It shares Fodor's emphasis on the remarkable speed and efficiency of real-time language processing, and it accepts that these processes normally operate in a mandatory fashion. It also accepts a certain degree of functional encapsulation, in the sense that contextual influences do not operate in a top-down manner in normal first-pass processing.

But it diverges from Fodor's approach in two major respects. First, it does not attempt to explain the special properties of language processing by postulating a distinct type of cognitive entity called an input system or a module. Second, it includes within the domain of these special processes the aspect of language comprehension that Fodor is most eager to exclude: the computing of inferences that draw upon nonlinguistic knowledge.

What is the nature of the approach we are advocating, and how does it accommodate the kinds of phenomena that Fodor hoped to explain with the concept of a module? How, in particular, does it accommodate the kinds of phenomena that behave as if they were modular, on Fodor's account, but nonetheless involve extramodular processes? We repeat below the view of language processing that we began to lay out in our 1980a, 1980b, and 1981 papers.

- We assume that language comprehension is mediated by a stable set of highly skilled, automatized processes that apply obligatorily to their characteristic inputs. Such a system has fixed properties in the sense that there is a mandatory sequence of operations that must always apply to a given input.

We leave open the question of whether this system has fixed properties in the sense intended by Fodor—that is, because its properties are in some way genetically specified and therefore "hardwired." At present there seems to be no very convincing way of discriminating those fixed properties of language processing that derive from genetic constraints on the system from those that derive from the automatization of highly practiced skills (see Jusczyk and Cohen 1985; Sternberg 1985).

- The function of this set of core processes is to project the speech input onto a representation in the world—onto, for example, a mental model in the sense defined by Johnson-Laird (1983). It achieves this as rapidly as is informationally and neurally possible. There is no processing hiatus, no detectable change of cognitive means of transport, that coincides with the transition from the strictly linguistic to the discourse-representation or mental model. Nor is there evidence of any lag that might correspond to the requirement to map onto some linguistic level before mapping onto the discourse model. On the contrary, there is evidence (see our subsection on pragmatic inference) that the input can be mapped onto the discourse level even when the assumed linguistic level is still incomplete.
- These obligatory core processes operate on the principle of *bottom-up priority*. It is the bottom-up input to the system that sets it into motion and that determines what its possible outputs can be. We see this very clearly in the behavior of the word-recognition process. The membership of the initial cohort of word candidates is determined by the sensory input alone, and it is this initial cohort that defines the universe of possible candidates (Marslen-Wilson 1984; Tyler and Wessels 1983). Such a system cannot produce an output that is incompatible with its bottom-up input.

This is not the same as informational encapsulation, although it has many of the same effects. So long as the bottom-up input is phonologically and morphosyntactically unambiguous, it will uniquely determine the output of the system, and contextual influences will be difficult to detect—in other words, the system will give the appearance of encapsulated modularity. But when the input to the system is ambiguous or incomplete (as in the *landing planes* experiments or the Zero Anaphora studies), one can see clearly the on-line consequences of contextual factors. (For a further discussion of the conditions under which "predictive" context effects can be observed, see [Altmann 1987])

- Finally, and most controversial, these core processes permit no top-down effects in normal first-pass processing. This is because the concept of a top-down effect is defined in terms of a relationship between different representational levels arranged in a hierarchy. In Fodor's psycholinguistic ontology, a level of something like logical form exists as a representational level in the processing system, and this stands in a hierarchical relationship to some further level (or levels) of representation corresponding to the pragmatic interpretation of the utterance. The notion of informational encapsulation, forbidding certain kinds of top-down interaction, is defined by Fodor in terms of these ordered levels.

To be able to evaluate the modularity hypothesis on its own terms, and to construct tests that would be intelligible within its particular frame of reference, we have up to this point in the chapter gone along with these assumptions about levels of representation. We turn now to an alternative ontology, in which we recognize no distinct level of representation corresponding to logical form—or to any other purely syntactic analytic level.

We assume, instead, that there is no level of symbolic representation mediating between lexical representations and mental models. Instead, there are procedures and mechanisms for mapping the one onto the other; for using the information provided by what the speaker is saying to construct a representation of his intended message. The apparatus of syntactic theory is a description of the properties of this construction procedure—as Crain and Steedman (1985, p. 323) put it, the rules of syntax "describe what a processor *does* in assembling a semantic interpretation." Notions such as logical form, therefore, are part of a description of a process; they are not themselves the process they are describing.

Where does this leave the context effects, and the violations of informational encapsulation, that we discussed above? The answer is, in part, that the issue disappears. If there are not two levels standing in the necessary hierarchical relationship to each other, there cannot be interactions between them. The true implication of evidence for interaction may be, in the end, that there is no interaction.

In particular, it becomes meaningless to infer "interaction" from the filling in of insufficiencies at one level on the basis of information available at a higher level. For a two-level, hierarchical system, the implication of the Zero Anaphor effects discussed above was that the lower level was penetrable by the higher level. But where there is no lower level of structural representation, and where the basic processing act performed by the system is the mapping onto pragmatically coherent locations in the discourse model, then the concept of interaction simply fails to apply.

We have, instead, multiple potential sources of cues for correct mapping, one of which (in the experiment in question) is the explicit lexical cues provided by the subject pronouns, but which also include the expectations derived from the structure of the discourse, and the differential inferences drawn from the relationship between input semantics and the state of the discourse model and the entities it contains. If the subject slot is lexically empty, as in our Zero Anaphor cases, the listener will assume that the speaker intends him to recover the intended agent from some other property of the message and its discourse environment. The end result is the same: an instantiation of the appropriate agent in the discourse model. But this involves no top-down influences, no creation at a lower level of mental contents that are derivable only at a higher level. There is no lower level of the appropriate sort, only the ability to integrate diverse information in the construction of the discourse.

By the same token, the arguments for interaction based on the resolution of structural ambiguity will also dissolve. In a system of the type Fodor envisages, the existence of an early preference for the contextually appropriate reading of a phrase like *landing planes* is *prima facie* evidence for a top-down effect on the operation of the syntactic parser. But again, if there is no autonomous syntactic level of representation, and if the basic operation of the system is to construct coherent interpretations in the domain of the discourse model, then there is no "interaction" here, and in effect, no ambiguity either. In terms of the on-line functioning of the system, the bottom-up input is ambiguous only to the extent that the interpretative target in the discourse model permits it to be. And cooperative speakers will not present their addressees with irresolvable ambiguities.

In fact, we might speculate, it is the cooperativeness of speakers and listeners that goes the furthest in explaining how the speech process can be so rapid, and how, in particular, inputs can be projected with such immediacy onto the listener's discourse model: It is because speakers prepare their utterances so that they cohere with what has been said before, and because listeners run their processing systems on this assumption. This is what gives language processing its seemingly ballistic property—that the speaker constructs a communicative packet that is already configured to map onto the receptive configuration of the listener.[9]

Concluding Remarks

We end with some comments on what can be regarded as the hidden agenda of the modularity discussion—namely, the underlying question of the kind of role that syntactic theory should play in a psychological model of language processing. From this perspective, the modularity hypothesis can be regarded as the very strong psychological claim for the direct participation of the constructs of linguistic analysis in the process of language comprehension, up to and including the level of logical form. It saves a central role for syntactic analysis and representation, safely encapsulated within the language module.

This is one reason why it is so important for the modularity hypothesis that the dividing line between modular and extramodular processes falls at the interface between the linguistic and the nonlinguistic. Unfortunately, as we have tried to show here, the diagnostic features that are supposed to place the dividing line at just this crucial point fail to do so. The central processes of language comprehension do not conveniently stop dead at the level of logical form. This means not only that the hypothesis itself fails, but that so do the assumptions it tries to smuggle in about the role of linguistic theory in a model of psycholinguistic processing.

It is at this level of the discussion that we are "against modularity." We reject it as a claim about the relationship between linguistic construct and psychological process. The facts of psycholinguistic performance simply do not support the rigid dichotomy between the domains of the syntactic and the non-syntactic that is the central claim of the modularity thesis. The thesis is seductive, entertaining, perhaps even heuristically useful. But as a basis for the construction of explanatory theories of human psycholinguistic performance it is, we believe, fundamentally misleading. It misconstrues the nature of the problem that is set for us by the extraordinary speed and immediacy of on-line language comprehension, and it invites us to accept, as a solution to this problem, a view of the organization of the language-processing system that obscures rather than clarifies the questions we now need to be asking.

Notes

1. We exclude from consideration here the immediate sensory transducers.

2. We will not discuss here three additional features that Fodor mentions: neural hardwiring, characteristic breakdown patterns, and ontogenetic uniformity. The evidence in these domains is hardly crisp enough, at the moment, to seriously distinguish the opposing views we are contrasting.

3. This is not to say that all discourse mapping is phenomenologically mandatory. Consider the following discourse pair: *John couldn't decide whether to eat steak or hamburger. In the end he went for*

the less expensive meat. Here one has to stop and think before deciding on the referent for *less expensive meat.* It is worth considering how this might differ from cases where the mapping goes more smoothly.

4. It is important, nonetheless, to keep clear the relationship between speed and automaticity. Very fast processes will almost certainly be mandatory processes, but the converse does not hold. Some mandatory processes—growing old, getting hungry—are really quite slow.

5. These are cases like *The detective watched the policeman with the walking-stick,* where the prepositional phrase *with the walking-stick* is more plausibly attached to *the policeman* than to *the detective.*

6. In Identical monitoring the actual target word is specified in advance to the subjects; in Rhyme monitoring the subjects listen for a target that rhymes with a cue word given in advance.

7. These arguments hold even if one tries to take the view of monitoring performance proposed by Tanenhaus, Carlson, and Seidenberg (1985), in which the effects of context on monitoring performance are written off as a form of sophisticated guessing. Even if this is the way context effects are mediated, the difference between conditions A and B still depends on the on-line computation of the differential pragmatic plausibility of the target appearing as the object of the different verbs in these two conditions. And it is the speed of pragmatic inferencing that is at issue here.

8. We are indebted to Jerry Fodor and Merrill Garrett for extensive discussions of this aspect of the research.

9. For a detailed illustration of the extent to which a speaker fits the design of his utterances to the informational requirements of his addressee, see Marslen-Wilson et al. 1982.

References

Altmann, G. 1987. "Modularity and Interaction in Sentence Processing." In J. Garfield, ed., *Modularity in Knowledge Representation and Natural Language Understanding* (Cambridge, Mass.: MIT Press).

Cowart, W. 1983. "Reference Relations and Syntactic Processing: Evidence of Pronoun's Influence on a Syntactic Decision that Affects Naming." Indiana University Linguistics Club.

Crain, S., and M. Steedman. 1985. "On Not Being Led Up the Garden Path." In D. Dowty, L. Kartunnen, and A. M. Zwickey, eds., *Natural Language Parsing: Psycholinguistic, Computational, and Theoretical Perspectives* (Cambridge: Cambridge University Press).

Fodor, J. A. 1983. *Modularity of Mind* (Cambridge, Mass.: MIT Press).

Forster, K. I. 1979. "Levels of Processing and the Structure of the Language Processor." In W. E. Cooper and E. C. T. Walker, eds., *Sentence Processing: Psycholinguistics Studies Presented to Merrill Garrett* (Mahwah, N.J.: Lawrence Erlbaum).

Forster, K. I. 1987. "Binding, Plausibility, and Modularity." In J. L. Garfield, ed., *Modularity in Knowledge Representation and Natural-Language Understanding* (Cambridge, Mass.: MIT Press).

Frazier, L., C. Clifton, and J. Randall. 1983[b]. "Filling Gaps: Decision Principles and Structure in Sentence Comprehension." *Cognition* 13: 187–222.

Garrett, M. F. 1978. "Word and Sentence Perception." In R. Held, H. L. Teuber, and H. Leibowitz, eds., *Handbook of Sensory Physiology*, vol. 8: *Perception* (Academic).

Johnson-Laird, P. N. 1983. *Mental Models* (Cambridge: Cambridge University Press).

Jusczyk, P. W., and A. Cohen. 1985. "What Constitutes a Module?" *Behavioral and Brian Sciences* 8: 20–21.

Karmiloff-Smith, A. 1980. "Psychological Processes Underlying Pronominalization and Non-Pronominalization in Children's Connected Discourse." In J. Kreiman and A. E. Ojeda, eds., *Papers from the Parasession on Pronouns and Anaphora* (Chicago Linguistic Society).

Karmiloff-Smith, A. 1985. "Language and Cognitive Processes from a Developmental Viewpoint." *Language and Cognitive Processes* 1: 61–85.

Marslen-Wilson, W. D. 1984. "Function and Process in Spoken Word Recognition: A Tutorial Review." In H. Bouma and D. G. Bouwhuis, eds., *Attention and Performance X: Control of Language Processes* (Mahwah, N.J.: Lawrence Erlbaum).

Marslen-Wilson, W. D. 1985. "Speech Shadowing and Speech Communication." *Speech Communication* 4: 55–73.

Marslen-Wilson, W. D., E. Levy, and L. K. Tyler. 1982. "Producing Interpretable Discourse: The Establishment and Maintenance of Reference." In R. J. Jarvella and W. Klein, eds., *Speech Place and Action* (New York: Wiley).

Marslen-Wilson, W. D., and L. K. Tyler. 1975. "Processing Structure of Sentence Perception." *Nature* 257: 784–786.

Marslen-Wilson, W. D., and L. K. Tyler. 1980a. "The Temporal Structure of Spoken Language Understanding." *Cognition* 8: 1–71.

Marslen-Wilson, W. D., and L. K. Tyler. 1980b. "Towards a Psychological Basis for a Theory of Anaphora." In J. Kreiman and A. Ojeda, eds., *Papers from the Parasession on Pronouns and Anaphora* (Chicago Linguistics Society, 1983).

Marslen-Wilson, W. D., and L. K. Tyler. 1981. "Central Processes in Speech Understanding." *Philosophical Transactions of the Royal Society* B 295: 317–322.

Posner, M., and C. Snyder. 1975. "Attention and Cognitive Control." In R. L. Solso, ed., *Information Processing and Cognition* (Mahwah, N.J.: Lawrence Erlbaum).

Shiffrin, R., and W. Schneider. 1977. "Controlled and Automatic Human Information Processing: 2. Perceptual Learning, Automatic Attending, and a General Theory." *Psychological Review* 84: 127–190.

Sternberg, R. J. 1985. "Controlled versus Automatic Processing." *Behavioral and Brain Sciences* 8: 32–33.

Tanenhaus, M. K., G. N. Carlson, and M. S. Seidenberg. 1985. "Do Listeners Compute Linguistic Representations?" In D. Dowty, L. Kartunnen, and A. M. Zwickey, eds., *Natural Language Parsing: Psycholinguistic, Computational, and Theoretical Perspectives* (Cambridge: Cambridge University Press).

Townsend, D. J., and T. G. Bever. 1982. "Natural Units Interact During Language Comprehension." *Journal of Verbal Learning and Verbal Behavior* 28: 681–703.

Tyler, L. K. 1985. "Real-Time Comprehension Processes in Agrammatism: A Case Study." *Brain and Language* 26: 259–275.

Tyler, L. K. 1986. "Spoken Language Comprehension in Aphasia: A Real-Time Processing Perspective." In M. Coltheart, R. Job, and G. Sartori, eds., *The Cognitive Neuropsychology of Language* (Mahwah, N.J.: Lawrence Erlbaum).

Tyler, L. K., and W. D. Marslen-Wilson. 1977. "The On-Line Effects of Semantic Context on Syntactic Processing." *Journal of Verbal Learning and Verbal Behavior* 16: 683–692.

Tyler, L. K., and W. D. Marslen-Wilson. 1982. "The Resolution of Discourse Anaphors: Some On-Line Studies." *Text* 2: 263–291.

Tyler, L. K., and J. Wessels. 1983. "Quantifying Contextual Contributions to Word-Recognition Processes." *Perception and Psycholinguistics* 34: 409–420.

72 The Modularity of Thought and the Epidemiology of Representations

Dan Sperber

Ten years ago, Jerry Fodor published *The Modularity of Mind*, a book that received much well-deserved attention. His target was the then-dominant view according to which there are no important discontinuities between perceptual processes and conceptual processes. Information flows freely, "up" and "down," between these two kinds of processes, and beliefs inform perception as much as they are informed by it. Against this view, Fodor argued that perceptual processes (and also linguistic decoding) are carried out by specialized, rather rigid mechanisms. These "modules" each have their own proprietary data base, and do not draw on information produced by conceptual processes.

Although this was probably not intended and has not been much noticed, "modularity of mind" was a paradoxical title, for, according to Fodor, modularity is to be found only at the periphery of the mind, in its input systems.[1] In its center and bulk, Fodor's mind is decidedly *non*modular. Conceptual processes—that is, thought proper—are presented as a big holistic lump lacking joints at which to carve. Controversies have focused on the thesis that perceptual and linguistic decoding processes are modular, much more than on the alleged nonmodularity of thought.[2]

In this chapter, I have two aims. The first is to defend the view that thought processes might be modular too (what Fodor [1987: 27] calls "modularity theory gone mad"—oh well!). Let me however echo Fodor and say that, "when I speak of a cognitive system as modular, I shall ... always mean 'to some interesting extent'" (Fodor, 1983: 37). My second aim is to articulate a modular view of human thought with the naturalistic view of human culture that I have been developing under the label "epidemiology of representations" (Sperber, 1985b). These aims are closely related: Cultural diversity has always been taken to show how plastic the human mind is, whereas the modularity of thought thesis seems to deny that plasticity. I want to show how, contrary to the received view, organisms endowed with truly modular minds might engender truly diverse cultures.

Two Commonsense Arguments against the Modularity of Thought

Abstractly and roughly at least, the distinction between perceptual and conceptual processes is clear: Perceptual processes have, as input, information provided by sensory receptors and, as output, a conceptual representation categorizing the object perceived. Conceptual processes have conceptual representations both as input and as output. Thus seeing a cloud and thinking "here is a cloud" is a perceptual process. Inferring from this perception "it might rain" is a conceptual process.

The rough idea of modularity is also clear: A cognitive module is a genetically specified computational device in the mind/brain (henceforth: the mind) that works pretty much on its own on inputs pertaining to some specific cognitive domain and provided by other parts of the nervous systems (e.g., sensory receptors or other modules). Given such notions, the view that perceptual processes might be modular is indeed quite plausible, as argued by Fodor. On the other hand, there are two main commonsense arguments (and several more technical ones) that lead one to expect conceptual thought processes not to be modular.

The first commonsense argument against the modularity of thought has to do with integration of information. The conceptual level is the level at which information from different input modules, each presumably linked to some sensory modality, gets integrated into a modality-independent medium. A dog can be seen, heard, smelled, touched, and talked about. The percepts are different; the concept is the same. As Fodor points out,

> the general form of the argument goes back at least to Aristotle: the representations that input systems deliver have to interface somewhere, and the computational mechanisms that affect the interface must ipso facto have access to information from more than one cognitive domain. (Fodor, 1983: 101–102)

The second commonsense argument against the modularity of thought has to do with cultural diversity and novelty. An adult human's conceptual processes range over an indefinite variety of domains, including party politics, baseball history, motorcycle maintenance, Zen Bhuddism, French cuisine, Italian opera, chess playing, stamp collecting, and Fodor's chosen example, modern science. The appearance of many of these domains in human cognition is very recent and not relevantly correlated with changes in the human genome. Many of these domains vary dramatically in content from one culture to another, or are not found at all in many cultures. In such conditions, it would be absurd to assume that there is an ad hoc genetically specified preparedness for these culturally developed conceptual domains.

These two commonsense arguments are so compelling that Fodor's more technical considerations (having to do with "isotropy," illusions, rationality, etc.) look like mere nails in the coffin of a dead idea. My goal will be to shake the commonsense picture and to suggest that the challenge of articulating conceptual integration, cultural diversity, and modularity may be met and turns out to be a source of psychological and anthropological insights.

Notice, to begin with, that both the informational integration argument and the cultural diversity argument are quite compatible with *partial* modularity at the conceptual level.

True, it would be functionally self-defeating to reproduce at the conceptual level the same domain partition found at the perceptual level, and have a different conceptual module treat separately the output of each perceptual module. No integration whatsoever would take place, and the dog seen and the dog heard could never be one and the very same mastiff Goliath. But who says conceptual domains have to match perceptual domains? Why not envisage, at the conceptual level, a wholly different, more or less orthogonal domain partition, with domain-specific conceptual mechanisms, each getting their inputs from several input mechanisms? For instance, all the conceptual outputs of perceptual modules that contain the concept MASTIFF might be fed into a specialized module (say a domain-specific inferential device handling living-kind concepts), which takes care (inter alia) of Goliath qua mastiff. Similarly, all the conceptual outputs of input modules that contain the concept THREE might be fed into a specialized module, which handles inference about numbers, and so forth. In this way, information from different input devices might get genuinely integrated, though not into a single conceptual system, but into several such systems.

Of course, if you have, say, a prudential rule that tells you to run away when you encounter more than two bellicose dogs, you would not really be satisfied to be informed by the living-kinds module that the category BELLICOSE DOG is instantiated in your environment, and by the numerical module that there are more than two of something. Some further, at least partial, integration had better take place. It might even be argued—though *that* is by no means obvious—that a plausible model of human cognition should allow for *full* integration of all conceptual information at some level. Either way, partial or full integration might take place further up the line, among the outputs of conceptual rather than of perceptual modules. Conceptual integration is not incompatible with at least some conceptual modularity.

Similarly, the conceptual diversity argument implies that some conceptual domains (chess, etc.) could not be modular. It certainly does not imply that none of them could be. Thus, in spite of superficial variations, living-kind classification exhibits strong commonalities across cultures (see Berlin, 1978) in a manner that does suggest the presence of a domain-specific cognitive module (see Atran, 1987, 1990).

The thesis that some central thought processes might be modular gets support from a wealth of recent work (well illustrated in [Hirschfeld and Gelman 1994]) tending to show that many basic conceptual thought processes, found in every culture and in every fully developed human, are governed by domain-specific competences. For instance, it is argued that people's ordinary understanding of the movements of an inert solid object, of the appearance of an organism, or of the actions of a person are based on three distinct mental mechanisms: a naive physics, a naive biology, and a naive psychology (see for instance Atran, 1987; Keil, 1989; Leslie, 1987, 1988; Spelke, 1988, and their contributions to [Hirschfeld and Gelman 1994]—see Carey, 1985, for a dissenting view). It is argued moreover that these mechanisms, at least in rudimentary form, are part of the equipment that makes acquisition of knowledge possible, rather than being acquired competences.

Accepting as a possibility some degree of modularity in conceptual systems is innocuous enough. Jerry Fodor himself recently considered favorably the view that "intentional folk psychology is, essentially, an innate, *modularized* database" (Fodor, 1992: 284—italics added) without suggesting that he was thereby departing from his former views on modularity. But what about the possibility of *massive* modularity at the conceptual level? Do the two commonsense arguments, integration and diversity, really rule it out?

Modularity and Evolution

If modularity is a genuine natural property, then what it consists of is a matter of discovery, not stipulation. Fodor himself discusses a number of characteristic and diagnostic features of modularity. Modules, he argues, are "domain-specific, innately specified, hardwired, autonomous" (1983: 36). Their operations are mandatory (p. 52) and fast (p. 61); they are "informationally encapsulated" (p. 64), that is, the only background information available to them is that found in their proprietary data base. Modules are "associated with fixed neural architecture" (p. 98). Fodor discusses still other features that are not essential to the present discussion.

There is one feature of modularity that is implied by Fodor's description, but that he does not mention or discuss. If, as Fodor argues, a module is innately specified, hardwired, and autonomous, then it follows that *a cognitive module is an evolved mechanism with a distinct phylogenetic history*. This is a characteristic, but hardly a diagnostic feature, because we know close to nothing about the actual evolution of cognitive modules. But I have been convinced by Leda Cosmides and John Tooby (see Cosmides, 1989; Cosmides & Tooby, 1987; Tooby & Cosmides, 1989, 1992, [1994])[3] that we know enough about evolution on the one hand and cognition on the other to come up with well-motivated (though, of course, tentative) assumptions as to when to expect modularity, what properties to expect of modules, and even what modules to expect. This section of the chapter owes much to their ideas.

Fodor himself does mention evolutionary considerations, but only in passing. He maintains that, phylogenetically, modular input systems should have preceded nonmodular central systems:

> Cognitive evolution would thus have been in the direction of gradually freeing certain sorts of problem-solving systems from the constraints under which input analyzers labor—hence of producing, as a relatively late achievement, the comparatively domain-free inferential capacities which apparently mediate the higher flights of cognition. (Fodor, 1983: 43)

Let us spell out some of the implications of Fodor's evolutionary suggestion. At an early stage of cognitive evolution we should find modular sensory input analyzers directly connected to modular motor controllers. There is no level yet where information from several perceptual processes would be integrated by a conceptual process. Then there emerges a conceptual device, that is, an inferential device that is not itself directly linked to sensory receptors. This conceptual device accepts input from two or more perceptual devices, constructs new representations warranted by these inputs, and transmits information to motor control mechanisms.

Initially, of course, this conceptual device is just another module: It is specialized, innately wired, fast, automatic, and so forth. Then, so the story should go, it grows and becomes less specialized, possibly it merges with other similar conceptual devices, to the point where it is a single big conceptual system, able to process all the outputs of all the perceptual modules, and able to manage all the conceptual information available to the organism. This true central system cannot, in performing a given cognitive task, activate all the data accessible to it, or exploit all of its many procedures. Automaticity and speed are no longer possible. Indeed, if the central system automatically did what it is capable of doing, this would trigger a computational explosion with no end in sight.[4]

An evolutionary account of the emergence of a conceptual module in a mind that had known only perceptual processes is simple enough to imagine. Its demodularization would be much harder to explain.

A toy example might go like this: Organisms of a certain species, call them "protorgs," are threatened by a danger of a certain kind. This danger (the approach of elephants that might trample the orgs, as it might be) is signaled by the co-occurrence of a noise N and soil vibrations V. Protorgs have an acoustic perception module that detects instances of N and a vibration-perception module that detects instances of V. The detection either of N by one perceptual module, or of V by the other activates an appropriate flight procedure. Fine, except that when N occurs alone, or when V occurs alone, it so happens that there is no danger. So protorgs end up with a lot of "false positives," uselessly running away, and thus wasting energy and resources.

Some descendants of the protorgs, call them "orgs," have evolved another mental device: a conceptual inference mechanism. The perceptual modules no longer directly activate their flight procedure. Rather their relevant outputs, that is, the identification of noise N and that of vibrations V, go to the new device. This conceptual mechanism acts essentially as an AND-gate: When, and only when both N and V have been perceptually identified, does the conceptual mechanism get into a state that can be said to represent the presence of danger, and it is this state that activates the appropriate flight procedure.

Orgs, so the story goes, competed successfully with protorgs for food resources, and that is why you won't find protorgs around.

The orgs' conceptual mechanism, though not an *input* module, is nevertheless a clear case of a module: It is a domain-specific problem solver; it is fast, informationally encapsulated, associated with fixed neural architecture, and so forth. Of course, it is a tiny module, but nothing stops us from imagining it becoming larger: Instead of accepting just two bits of information from two simple perceptual modules, the conceptual module could come to handle more from more sources, and to control more than a single motor procedure, but still be domain-specific, automatic, fast, and so on.

At this juncture, we have two diverging evolutionary scenarios on offer. According to the scenario suggested by Fodor, the conceptual module should evolve toward less domain specificity, less informational encapsulation, less speed, and so on. In other words, it would become less and less modular, possibly merge with other demodularized devices, and end up like the kind of central system with which Fodor believes we are endowed ("Quineian," "isotropic," etc.). There are two gaps in this scenario. The first gap has to do with mental mechanisms and is highlighted by Fodor himself in his "First Law of the Nonexistence of Cognitive Science." This law says in substance that the mechanisms of nonmodular thought processes are too complex to be understood. So, just accept that there are such mechanisms and don't ask how they work.

The second gap in Fodor's scenario has to do with the evolutionary process itself that is supposed to bring about the development of such a mysterious mechanism. No doubt, it might be advantageous to trade a few domain-specific inferential micromodules for an advanced all-purpose macrointelligence, if there is any such thing. For instance, superorgs endowed with general intelligence might develop technologies to eradicate the danger once and for all instead of having to flee again and again. But evolution does not offer such starkly contrasted choices. The available alternatives at any one time are all small departures from the existing state. Selection, the main force driving evolution, is near-sighted (whereas the other forces, genetic drift, etc., are blind). An immediately advantageous alternative is likely to be selected from the narrow available range, and this may bar the path to highly advantageous long-term outcomes. A demodularization scenario is implausible for this very reason.

Suppose indeed the conceptual danger analyzer is modified in some mutant orgs, not in the direction of performing better at its special task, but in that of less domain specificity. The modified conceptual device processes not just information relevant to the orgs' immediate chances of escape, but also information about innocuous features of the dangerous situation, and about a variety of innocuous situations exhibiting these further features; the device draws inferences not just of an urgent practical kind, but also of a more theoretical character. When danger is detected, the new, less modular system does not automatically trigger flight behavior, and when it does, it does so more slowly—automaticity and speed go with modularity—but it has interesting thoughts that are filed in memory for the future ... if there is any future for mutant orgs endowed with this partly demodularized device.

Of course, speed and automaticity are particularly important for danger analyzers, and less so for other plausible modules, for instance, modules governing the choice of sexual partners. However, the general point remains: Evolved cognitive modules are likely to be answers to specific, usually environmental problems. Loosening the domain of a module will bring about, not greater flexibility, but greater slack in the organism's response to the problem. To the extent that evolution goes toward improving a species' biological endowments, then we should generally expect improvements in the manner in which existing modules perform their task, emergence of new modules to handle other problems, but not demodularization.

True, it is possible to conceive of situations in which the marginal demodularization of a conceptual device might be advantageous, or at least not detrimental, in spite of the loss of speed and reliability involved. Imagine, for instance, that the danger the conceptual module was initially selected to analyze has vanished from the environment; then the module is not adapted any more and a despecialization would do no harm. On the other hand why should it do any good? Such odd possibilities fall quite short of suggesting a positive account of the manner in which, to repeat Fodor's words, "cognitive evolution would ... have been in the direction of gradually freeing certain sorts of problem-solving systems from the constraints under which input analyzers labor." It is not that this claim could not be right, but it is poorly supported. In fact the only motivation for it seems to be the wish to integrate the belief that human thought processes are nonmodular in some evolutionary perspective, however vague. Better officialize the explanatory gap with a "Second Law of the Nonexistence of Cognitive Science," according to which the forces that have driven cognitive evolution can never be identified.[5] Just accept that cognitive evolution occurred (and resulted in the demodularization of thought) and don't ask how.

Instead of starting from an avowedly enigmatic view of homo sapiens's thought processes and concluding that their past evolution is an unfathomable mystery, one might start from evolutionary considerations plausible in their own right and wonder what kind of cognitive organization these might lead one to expect in a species of which we know that it relies heavily on its cognitive abilities for its survival. This yields our second scenario.

As already suggested, it is reasonable to expect conceptual modules to gain in complexity, fine-grainedness, and inferential sophistication *in the performance of their function*. As with any biological device, the function of a module may vary over time, but there is no reason to expect new functions to be systematically more general than old ones. It is reasonable, on the other hand, to expect new conceptual modules to appear in response to different kinds of problems or opportunities. Thus more and more modules should accumulate.

Because cognitive modules are each the result of a different phylogenetic history, there is no reason to expect them all to be built on the same general pattern and elegantly interconnected. Though most if not all conceptual modules are inferential devices, the inferential procedures that they use may be quite diverse. Therefore, from a modular point of view, it is unreasonable to ask what is the general form of human inference (logical rules, pragmatic schemas, mental models, etc.) as is generally done in the literature on human reasoning (see Manktelow and Over, 1990, for a recent review).

The "domains" of modules may vary in character and in size: There is no reason to expect domain-specific modules to handle each a domain of comparable size. In particular there is no reason to exclude micromodules the domain of which is the size of a concept rather than that of a semantic field. In fact, I will argue that many human concepts are individually modular. Because conceptual modules are likely to be many, their interconnections and their connections with perceptual and motor control modules may be quite diverse too. As argued by Andy Clark (1987, 1990), we had better think of the mind as kludge, with sundry bits and components added at different times, and interconnected in ways that would make an engineer cringe.

Modularity and Conceptual Integration

The input to the first conceptual modules to have appeared in cognitive evolution must have come from the perceptual modules. However, once some conceptual modules were in place, their output could serve as input to other conceptual modules.

Suppose the orgs can communicate among themselves by means of a small repertoire of vocal signals. Suppose further that the optimal interpretation of some of these signals is sensitive to contextual factors. For instance, an ambiguous danger signal indicates the presence of a snake when emitted by an org on a tree, and approaching elephants when emitted by an org on the ground. Identifying the signals and the relevant contextual information is done by perceptual modules. The relevant output of these perceptual modules is processed by an ad hoc conceptual module that interprets the ambiguous signals. Now, it would be a significant improvement if the conceptual module specialized in inferring the approach of elephants would accept as input not only perceptual information on specific noises and soil vibrations but also interpretations of the relevant signals emitted by other orgs. If so, this danger-inferring conceptual module would receive input not just from perceptual modules but also from another conceptual module, the context-sensitive signal interpreter.

In the human case, it is generally taken for granted that domain-specific abilities can handle not just primary information belonging to their domain and provided by perception but also verbally or picturally communicated information. Thus experiments on the development of zoological knowledge use as material, not actual animals, but pictures or verbal descriptions. Though this practice deserves more discussion than it usually gets, it may well be sound. If so, its being sound is itself quite remarkable.

Then too, some conceptual modules might get *all* of their input from other conceptual modules. Imagine for instance that an org emits a danger signal only when two conditions are fulfilled: It must have inferred the presence of a danger on the one hand, and that of friendly orgs at risk on the other hand. Both inferences are performed by conceptual modules. If so, then the conceptual module that decides whether or not to emit the danger signal gets all of its input from other conceptual modules, and none from perceptual ones.

We are now envisaging a complex network of conceptual modules: Some conceptual modules get all of their input from perceptual modules, other modules get at least some of their input from conceptual modules, and so forth. Every information may get combined with many others across or within levels and in various ways (though overall conceptual integration seems excluded). What would be the behavior of an organism endowed with such complex modular thought processes? Surely, we don't know. Would it behave in a flexible manner like humans do? Its responses could at least be extremely fine-grained. Is there more to flexibility than this fine-grainedness? "Flexibility" is a metaphor without a clear literal interpretation, and therefore it is hard to tell. Still, when we think of flexibility in the human case, we particularly have in mind the ability to learn from experience. Can a fully modular system learn?

Imprinting is a very simple form of modular learning. What, for instance, do orgs know about one another? If orgs are nonlearning animals, they might be merely endowed with a conspecific detector and detectors for some properties of other orgs such as sex or age, but they might otherwise be unable to detect any single individual as such, not even, say, their own mothers. Or, if they are very primitive learners, they might have a mother-detector module that will be "initialized" (i.e., have its parameters fixed or its empty slots filled) once and for all by the newborn org's first encounter with a large moving creature in its immediate vicinity (hopefully its real mum). As a result of this encounter the initialized module becomes a detector for the particular individual who caused the imprinting.

If they are slightly more sophisticated learners, orgs may have the capacity to construct several detectors for different individual conspecifics. They might have a template module quite similar to a mother-detector, except that it can be "initialized" several times, each time projecting a differently initialized copy of itself that is specialized for the identification of a different individual. Would the initialized copies of the template module be modules too? I don't see why not. The only major difference is that these numerous projected modules seem less likely to be hardwired than a single mother-detector module.[6] Otherwise, both kinds of modules get initialized and operate in exactly the same manner. Of our more sophisticated orgs, we would want to say, then, that they had a modular domain-specific ability to represent mentally conspecific individuals, an ability resulting in the generation of micromodules for each represented individual.

Consider in this light the human domain-specific ability to categorize living kinds. One possibility is that there is an initial template module for living-kind concepts that gets initialized many times, producing each time a new micromodule corresponding to one living-kind concept (the dog module, the cat module, the goldfish module, etc.).

Thinking of such concepts as modules may take some getting used to, I admit. Let me help: Concepts are domain-specific (obviously), they have a proprietary data-basis (the encyclopedic information filed under the concept), and they are autonomous computational devices (they work, I will argue, on representations in which the right concept occurs, just as digestive enzymes work on food in which the right molecule occurs). When, on top of all that, concepts are partly genetically specified (via some domain-specific conceptual template), they are modular at least to some interesting extent, no?

The template–copy relationship might sometimes involve more levels. A general living-kind-categorization metatemplate could project, not directly concepts, but other, more specific templates for different domains of living kinds. For instance, a fundamental parameter to be fixed might concern the contrast between self-propelled and non-self-propelled objects (Premack, 1990), yielding two templates, one for zoological concepts and another one for botanical concepts.

Another possibility still is that the initial metatemplate has three types of features: (1) fixed features that characterize living kinds in general, for instance, it might be an unalterable part of any living-kind concept that the kind is taken to have an underlying essence (Atran, 1987; Gelman and Coley, 1991; Gelman and Markman, 1986, 1987; Keil, 1989; Medin and Ortony, 1989); (2) parameters with default values that can be altered in copies of the template, for instance, "self-propelled" and "nonhuman" might be revisable features of the initial template; (3) empty slots for information about individual kinds. If so, then, the default-value template could serve as such for nonhuman animal concepts. To use the template for plant concepts, or to include humans in a taxonomy of animals would involve changing a default value of the initial template.

How is the flow of information among modules actually governed? Is there a regulating device? Is it a pandemonium? A market economy? Many types of models can be entertained. Here is a simple possibility.

The output of perceptual and conceptual modules is in the form of conceptual representations. Perceptual modules categorize distal stimuli and must each have therefore the conceptual repertoire needed for the output categorizations of which they are capable. Conceptual modules may infer new output categorizations from the input conceptual representations they process; they must have an input and an output conceptual repertoire to do so. Let us assume that modules accept as input any conceptual representation in which a concept belonging to their input repertoire occurs. In particular single-concept micromodules process all and only representations where their very own concept occurs. These micromodules generate transformations of the input representation by replacing the concept with some inferentially warranted expansion of it. They are otherwise blind to the other conceptual properties of the representations they process (in the manner of the "calculate" procedure in some word processor, which scans the text but "sees" only numbers and mathematical signs). Generally, the presence of specific concepts in a representation determines what modules will be activated and what inferential processes will take place (see Sperber and Wilson, 1986, chap. 2).

A key feature of modularity in Fodor's description is informational encapsulation: A full-fledged module uses a limited data base and is not able to take advantage of information relevant to its task if that information is in some other data base. Central processes on the other hand are not so constrained. They are characterized, on the contrary, by free flow of information. Thus beliefs about Camembert cheese might play a role in forming conclusions about quarks, even though they hardly belong to the same conceptual domain. This is a fact, and I wouldn't dream of denying it. What does it imply regarding the modularity of conceptual processes? It implies that one particular modular picture cannot be right: Imagine a single layer of a few large mutually unconnected modules; then an information treated by one module won't find its way to another. If, on the other hand, the output of one conceptual module can serve as input to another one, modules can each be informationally encapsulated while chains of inference can take a conceptual premise from one module to the next and therefore integrate the contribution of each in some final conclusion. A holistic effect need not be the outcome of a holistic procedure.

Once a certain level of complexity in modular conceptual thought is reached, modules can emerge whose function it is to handle problems raised, not externally by the environment, but internally by the workings of the mind itself. One problem that a rich modular system of the kind we are envisaging would encounter as surely as Fodor's nonmodular central processes is the risk of computational explosion.

Assume that a device would have emerged, the function of which is to put up on the board, so to speak, some limited information for actual processing. Call this device "attention." Think of it as a temporary buffer. Only representations stored in that buffer are processed (by the modules whose input conditions they satisfy), and they are processed only as long as they stay in the buffer. There is, so to speak, competition among representations for attention. The competition tends to work out so as to maximize cognitive efficiency, that is, it tends to select for a place in the buffer, and thus for inferential processing, the most relevant information available at the time. There is a much longer story to be told: read *Relevance* (Sperber and Wilson, 1986).

Attention is of course not domain-specific. On the other hand it is a clear adaptation to an internal processing problem: the problem encountered by any cognitive system able to identify much more information perceptually than it can fully process conceptually. Such a system must be endowed with a means of selecting the information to be conceptually processed. Relevance-guided attention is such a means. Whether or not it should be called a module does not really matter: Attention fits snugly into a modular picture of thought.

I don't expect these speculations to be convincing—I am only half convinced myself, though I will be a bit more by the end of this chapter—but I hope they are intelligible. If so, this means that one can imagine a richly modular conceptual system that integrates information in so many partial ways that it is not obvious any more that we, human beings, genuinely integrate it in any fuller way. The argument against the modularity of thought based on the alleged impossibility of modular integration should lose at least its immediate commonsense appeal.

Actual and Proper Domains of Modules

Modules are domain-specific, and many, possibly most domains of modern human thought are too novel and too variable to be the specific domain of a genetically specified module. This second commonsense argument against the modularity of thought is reinforced by adaptationist considerations: In many domains, cultural expertise is hard to see as a biological adaptation. This is true not just of new domains such as chess, but also of old domains such as music. Expertise in these domains is unlikely therefore to be based on an ad hoc evolved mechanism. Of course, one can always try to concoct some story showing that, say, musical competence is a biological adaptation. However, merely assuming the adaptive character of a trait without a plausible demonstration is an all too typical misuse of the evolutionary approach.

Let me try an altogether different line. An adaptation is, generally, an adaptation to given environmental conditions. If you look at an adaptive feature just by itself, inside the organism, and forget altogether what you know about the environment and its history, you cannot tell what its function is, what it is an adaptation to. The function of a giraffe's long neck is to help it eat from trees, but in another environment—make it on another planet to free your imagination—the function of an identical body part on an identical organism could be to allow the animal to see farther, or to avoid breathing foul air near the ground, or to fool giant predators into believing that its flesh was poisonous.

A very similar point—or, arguably, a special application of the very same point—has been at the center of major recent debates in the philosophy of language and mind between "individualists" and "externalists." Individualists hold that the content of a concept is in the head of the thinker, or, in other terms, that a conceptual content is an intrinsic property of the thinker's brain state. Externalists maintain—rightly, I believe—that the same brain state that realizes a given concept might realize a different concept in another environment, just as internally identical biological features might have different functions.[7]

The content of a concept is not an intrinsic but a relational property[8] of the neural realizer of that concept, and is contingent upon the environment and the history (including the phylogenetic prehistory) of that neural object. This extends straightforwardly to the case of domain-specific modules. A domain is semantically defined, that is, by a concept under which objects in the domain are supposed to fall. The domain of a module is therefore not a property of its internal structure (whether described in neurological or in computational terms).

There is no way a specialized cognitive module might pick its domain just in virtue of its internal structure, or even in virtue of its connections to other cognitive modules. All that the internal structure provides is, to borrow an apt phrase from Frank Keil [Keil 1994], a *mode of construal*, a disposition to organize information in a certain manner and to perform computations of a certain form. A cognitive module also has structural relations to other mental devices with which it interacts. This determines in particular its *input conditions*: through which other devices the information must come, and how it must be categorized by these other devices. But, as long as one remains within the mind and ignores the connections of perceptual modules with the environment, knowledge of the brain-internal connections of a specialized cognitive module does not determine its domain.

Pace Keil, the fact that the mode of construal afforded by a mental module might fit many domains does *not* make the module any less domain-specific, just as the fact that my key might fit many locks does not make it any less the key to my door. The mode of construal and the domain, just like my key and my lock, have a long common history. How, then, do interactions with the environment over time determine the domain of a cognitive module? To answer this question, we had better distinguish between the *actual* and the *proper* domain of a module.

The *actual domain* of a conceptual module is all the information in the organism's environment that may (once processed by perceptual modules, and possibly by other conceptual modules) satisfy the module's input conditions. Its *proper domain* is all the information that it is the module's biological function to process. Very roughly, the function of a biological device is a class of effects of that device that contributes to making the device a stable feature of an enduring species. The function of a module is to process a specific range of information in a specific manner. That processing contributes to the reproductive success of the organism. The range of information that it is the function of a module to process constitutes its proper domain. What a module actually processes is information found in its actual domain, whether or not it also belongs to its proper domain.

Back to the orgs. The characteristic danger that initially threatened them was being trampled by elephants. Thanks to a module, the orgs reacted selectively to various signs normally produced, in their environment, by approaching elephants. Of course, approaching elephants were sometimes missed, and other, unrelated and innocuous events did sometimes activate the module. But even though the module failed to pick out all and only approaching elephants, we describe its function as having been to do just that (rather than doing what it actually did). Why? Because it is its relative success at that task that explains its having been a stable feature of an enduring species. Even though they were not exactly coextensive, the actual domain of the module overlapped well enough will the approaching-elephants domain. Only the latter, however, was the proper domain of the module.

Many generations later, elephants had vanished from the orgs' habitat, while hippopotamuses had multiplied, and now *they* trampled absent-minded orgs. The same module that had reacted to most approaching elephants and a few sundry events now reacted to most approaching hippos and a few sundry events. Had the module's proper domain become that of approaching hippos? Yes, and for the same reasons as before: Its relative success at reacting to approaching hippos explains why this module remained a stable feature of an enduring species.[9]

Today, however, hippopotamuses too have vanished and there is a railway passing through the orgs' territory. Because orgs don't go near the rails, trains are no danger. However the same module that had reacted selectively to approaching elephants and then to approaching hippos now reacts to approaching trains (and produces a useless panic in the orgs). The *actual* domain of the module includes mostly approaching trains. Has its *proper* domain therefore become that of approaching trains? The answer should be "no" this time: Reacting to trains is what it does, but it is not its function. The module's reacting to trains does not explain its remaining a stable feature of the species. In fact, if the module and the species survive, it is in spite of this marginally harmful effect.[10]

Still, an animal psychologist studying the orgs today might well come to the conclusion that they have a domain-specific ability to react to trains. She might wonder how they have developed such an ability given that trains have been introduced in the area too recently to allow the emergence of a specific biological adaptation (the adaptive value of which would be mysterious anyhow). The truth, of course, is that the earlier proper domains of the module, approaching elephants and then hippos, are now empty, that its actual domain is, by accident, roughly coextensive with the set of approaching trains, and that the explanation of this accident is the fact that the input conditions of the module, which had been positively selected in a different environment, happen to be satisfied by trains and hardly anything else in the orgs' present environment.

Enough of toy examples. In the real world, you are not likely to get elephants neatly replaced by hippos and hippos by trains, and to have each kind in turn satisfying the input conditions of some specialized module. Natural environments, and therefore cognitive functions, are relatively stable. Small shifts of cognitive function are more likely to occur than radical changes. When major changes occur in the environment, for instance as the result of a natural cataclysm, some cognitive functions are just likely to be lost: If elephants go, so does the function of your erstwhile elephant-detector. If a module loses its function, or equivalently if its proper domain becomes empty, then it is unlikely that its actual domain will be neatly filled by objects all falling under a single category, such as passing trains. More probably, the range of stimuli causing the module to react will end up being such an awful medley as to discourage any temptation to describe the actual domain of the module in terms of a specific category. Actual domains are usually not conceptual domains.

Cultural Domains and the Epidemiology of Representations

Most animals get only highly predictable kinds of information from their conspecifics, and not much of it at that. They depend therefore on the rest of the environment for their scant intellectual kicks. Humans are special. They are naturally massive producers, transmitters, and consumers of information. They get a considerable amount and variety of information from fellow humans, and they even produce and store some for their own private consumption. As a result, I will argue, the actual domain of human cognitive modules is likely to have become much larger than their proper domain. Moreover these actual domains, far from being uncategorizable chaos, are likely to be partly organized and categorized by humans themselves. So much so, I will argue, that we should distinguish the *cultural domains* of modules from both their proper and actual domains.

Just a quick illustration before I give a more systematic sketch and a couple of more serious examples: Here is the infant in her cradle, endowed with a domain-specific, modular, naive physics. The proper domain of that module is a range of physical events that typically occur in nature, and the understanding of which is crucial to the organism's later survival. Presumably, other primates are endowed with a similar module. The naive physics module of the infant chimp (and of the infant Pleistocene homo not-yet-sapiens) reacts to the odd fruit or twig falling, to the banana peel being thrown away, to occasional effects of the infant's own movement, and it may be challenged by the irregular fall of a leaf. Our human infant's module, on the other hand, is stimulated not just by physical events happening incidentally, but also by an "activity center" fixed to the side of her cradle, a musical merry-go-round just above her head, balls bounced by elder siblings, moving pictures on a television screen, and a variety of educational toys devised to stimulate her native interest in physical processes.

What makes the human case special? Humans change their own environment at a rhythm that natural selection cannot follow, so that many genetically specified traits of the human organism are likely to be adaptations to features of the environment that have ceased to exist or have greatly changed. This may be true not just of adaptations to the nonhuman environment, but also of adaptations to earlier stages of the hominid social environment.

In particular, the actual domain *of any* human cognitive module is unlikely to be even approximately coextensive with its proper domain. The actual domain of any human cognitive module is sure, on the contrary, to include a large amount of cultural information that meets its input conditions. This results neither from accident, nor from design. It results from a process of social distribution of information.

Humans not only construct individually *mental* representations of information, but they also produce information for one another in the form of *public* representations (e.g., utterances, written texts, pictures), or in the form of other informative behaviors and artifacts. Most communicated information, though, is communicated to one person or a few people on a particular occasion, and that is the end of it. Sometimes, however, addressees of a first act of communication communicate the information received to other addressees who communicate it in turn to others, and so on. This process of repeated transmission may go on to the point where we have a chain of mental and public representations both causally linked and similar in content—similar in content because of their causal links—instantiated throughout a human population. Traditions and rumors spread in this particular manner. Other types of representations may be distributed by causal chains of a different form (e.g., through imitation with or without instruction, or through broadcast communication). All such causally linked, widely distributed representations are what we have in mind when we speak of culture.

I have argued (Sperber, 1985b, 1990a, 1992) that to explain culture is to explain why some representations become widely distributed: A naturalistic science of culture should be an *epidemiology of representations*. It should explain why some representations are more successful—more contagious—than others.[11]

In this epidemiological perspective, all the information that humans introduce into their common environment can be seen as competing[12] for private and public space and time, that is, for attention, internal memory, transmission, and external storage. Many factors affect the chances of some information being successful and reaching a wide and lasting level of distribution, of being stabilized in a culture. Some of these factors are psychological, others are ecological. Most of these factors are relatively local, others are quite general. The most general psychological factor affecting the distribution of information is its compatibility and fit with human cognitive organization.

In particular, relevant information, the relevance of which is relatively independent from the immediate context, is *ceteris paribus*, more likely to reach a cultural level of distribution: Relevance provides the motivation both for storing and for transmitting the information, and independence from an immediate context means that relevance will be maintained in spite of changes of local circumstances, that is, it will be maintained on a social scale. Relevance is, however, always relative to a context; independence from the immediate context means relevance in a wider context of stable beliefs and expectations. On a modular view of conceptual processes, these beliefs, which are stable across a population, are those that play a central role in the modular organization and processing of knowledge. Thus information that either enriches or contradicts these basic modular beliefs stands a greater chance of cultural success.

I have argued (Sperber, 1975, 1980, 1985b) that beliefs that violate head-on module-based expectations (e.g., beliefs in supernatural beings capable of action at a distance, ubiquity, metamorphosis, etc.) thereby gain a salience and relevance that contribute to their cultural robustness. Pascal Boyer (1990) has rightly stressed that these violations of intuitive expectations in the description of supernatural beings are in fact few and take place against a background of satisfied modular expectations. Kelly and Keil (1985) have shown that cultural exploitation of representations of metamorphoses are closely constrained by domain-based conceptual structure. Generally speaking, we should expect culturally successful information essentially to resemble that found in some proper domain, and at the same time to exhibit sufficient originality so as to avoid mere redundancy.

A cognitive module stimulates in every culture the production and distribution of a wide array of information that meets its input conditions. This information, being artifactually produced or organized by the people themselves, is from the start conceptualized and therefore belongs to conceptual domains that I propose to call the module's *cultural domain(s)*. In other terms, cultural transmission causes, in the actual domain of any cognitive module, a proliferation of parasitic information that mimics the module's proper domain.

Let me first illustrate this epidemiological approach with speculations on a nonconceptual case, that of music. This is intended to be an example of a way of thinking suggested by the epidemiological approach rather than a serious scientific hypothesis, which I would not have the competence to develop.

Imagine that the ability and propensity to pay attention to, and analyze certain complex sound patterns became a factor of reproductive success for a long enough period in human prehistory. The sound patterns would have been discriminable by pitch variation and rhythm. What sounds would have exhibited such patterns? The possibility that springs to mind is human vocal communicative sounds. It need not be the sounds of homo sapiens speech, though. One may imagine a human ancestor with much poorer articulatory abilities and relying more than modern humans do on rhythm and pitch for the production of vocal signals. In such conditions, a specialized cognitive module with the required disposition might well have evolved.

This module would have had to combine the necessary discriminative ability with a motivational force to cause individuals to attend to the relevant sound patterns. The motivation would have to be on the hedonistic side: pleasure and hopeful expectation rather than pain and fear. Suppose that the relevant sound pattern co-occurred with noise from which it was hard to discriminate. The human ancestor's vocal abilities may have been quite poor, and the intended sound pattern may have been embedded in a stream of parasitic sounds (a bit like when you speak with a sore throat, a cold, and food in your mouth). Then the motivational component of the module should have been tuned so that detecting a low level of the property suffices to procure a significant reward.

The proper domain of the module we are imagining is the acoustic properties of early human vocal communications. It could be that this proper domain is now empty: Another adaptation, the improved modern human vocal tract, may have rendered it obsolete. Or it may be that the relevant acoustic properties still play a role in modern human speech (in tonal languages in particular) so that the module is still functional. The sounds that the module analyzes thereby causing pleasure to the organism of which it is a part—that is, the sounds meeting the module's input conditions—are not often found in nature (with the obvious exception of bird songs). However, such sounds can be artificially produced. And they have been, providing this module with a particularly rich cultural domain: music. The relevant acoustic pattern of music is much more detectable and delectable than that of any sound in the module's proper domain. The reward mechanism, which was naturally tuned for a hard-to-discriminate input, is now being stimulated to a degree that makes the whole experience utterly addictive.

The idea is, then, that humans have created a cultural domain, music, which is parasitic on a cognitive module, the proper domain of which preexisted music and had nothing to do with it. The existence of this cognitive module has favored the spreading, stabilization, and progressive diversification and growth of a repertoire meeting its input conditions: First pleasing sounds were serendipitously discovered, then sound patterns were deliberately produced and became music proper. These bits of culture compete for mental and public space and time, and ultimately for the chance to stimulate the module in question in as many individuals as possible for as long as possible. In this competition, some pieces of music do well, at least for a time, whereas others are selected out, and thus music, and musical competence, evolve.

In the case of music, the cultural domain of the module is much more developed and salient than its proper domain, assuming that it still has a proper domain. So much so that it is the existence of the cultural domain and the domain-specificity of the competences it manifestly evokes that justifies looking, in the present or in the past, for a proper domain that is not immediately manifest.

In other cases, the existence of a proper domain is at least as immediately manifest as that of a cultural one. Consider zoological knowledge. The existence of a domain-specific competence in the matter is not hard to admit, if the general idea of domain specificity is accepted at all. One way to think of it, as I have suggested, is to suppose that humans have a modular template for constructing concepts of animals. The biological function of this module is to provide humans with ways of categorizing animals they may encounter in their environment and of organizing the information they may gather about them. The proper domain of this modular ability is the living local fauna. What happens however is that you end up, thanks to cultural input, constructing many more animal concepts than there are animals with which you will ever interact. If you are a twentieth-century Westerner, you may, for instance, have a well-stocked cultural subdomain of dinosaurs. You may be a dinosaur expert. In another culture you might have been a dragon expert.

This invasion of the actual domain of a conceptual module by cultural information occurs irrespective of the size of the module. Consider a micromodule such as the concept of a particular animal, say the rat. Again, you are likely to have fixed, in the data base of that module, culturally transmitted information about rats, whether of a folkloristic or of a scientific character, that goes well beyond the proper domain of that micromodule, that is, well beyond information derivable from, and relevant to, interactions with rats (though, of course, it may be of use for your interactions with other human beings, e.g., by providing a data base exploitable in metaphorical communication).

On the macromodular side of things, accept for the sake of this discussion that the modular template on which zoological concepts are constructed is itself an initialized version (maybe the default version) of a more abstract living-kinds metatemplate. That metatemplate is initialized in other ways for other domains (e.g., botany), projecting several domain-specific templates, as I have suggested here. What determines a new initialization is the presence of information that (1) meets the general input conditions specified in the metatemplate, but (2) does not meet the more specific conditions found in the already initialized templates. That information need not be in the proper domain of the metatemplate module. In other words, the metatemplate might get initialized in a manner that fits no proper domain at all but only a cultural domain. A cultural domain that springs to mind in this context is that of representations of supernatural beings (see Boyer, 1990, 1993, [1994]). But there may also be less apparent cases.

Consider in this light the problem raised by Hirschfeld ([Hirschfeld 1994]; see also Hirschfeld, 1988, 1993). Children are disposed to categorize humans into "racial" groups conceived in an essentialist manner. Do children possess a domain-specific competence for such categorization? In other terms, are humans naturally disposed to racism? In order to avoid such an unappealing conclusion, it has been suggested (Atran, 1990; Boyer, 1990) that children transfer to the social sphere a competence that they have first developed for living kinds, and that they do so in order to make sense of the regularities in human appearance (e.g., skin color) that they have observed. However, Hirschfeld's experimental evidence shows that racial categorization develops without initially drawing on perceptually relevant input. This strongly suggests that there is a domain-specific competence for racial classification.

What the epidemiological approach adds is the suggestion that racial classification might result from an ad hoc template derived from the living-kinds metatemplate, through an initialization triggered by cultural input. Indeed, recent experiments suggest that, in certain conditions, the mere encounter with a nominal label used to designate a living thing is enough to tilt the child's categorization of that thing toward an essentialist construal (Davidson and Gelman, 1990; Gelman and Coley, 1991; Markman, 1990; Markman and Hutchinson, 1984). It is quite possible then that being presented with nominal labels for otherwise undefined and undescribed humans is enough (given an appropriate context) to activate the initialization of the ad hoc template. If so, then perception of differences among humans is indeed not the triggering factor.

There is, as Hirschfeld suggested, a genetically specified competence that determines racial classification without importing its models from another concrete domain. However, the underlying competence need not have racial classification as its proper domain. Racial classification may be a mere cultural domain, based on an underlying competence that does not have any proper domain. The initialization of an ad hoc template for racial classification could well be the effect of parasitic, cultural input information on the higher-level learning module the function of which is to generate ad hoc templates for genuine living-kind domains such as zoology and botany. If this hypothesis is correct—mind you, I am not claiming that it is, merely that it may be—then no racist disposition has been selected *for* (Sober, 1984) in humans. However the dispositions that have been selected for make humans all too easily susceptible to racism given minimal, innocuous-looking cultural input.

The relationship between the proper and the cultural domains of the same module is not one of transfer. The module itself does not have a preference between the two kinds of domains, and indeed is blind to a distinction that is grounded in ecology and history.

Even when an evolutionary and epidemiological perspective is adopted, the distinction between the proper and the cultural domain of a module is not always easy to draw. Proper and cultural domains may overlap. Moreover, because cultural domains are things of this world, it can be a function of a module to handle a cultural domain, which ipso facto becomes a proper domain.

Note that the very existence of a cultural domain is an effect of the existence of a module. Therefore, initially at least, a module cannot be an adaptation to its own cultural domain. It must have been selected because of a preexisting proper domain. In principle, it might *become* a function of the module to handle its own cultural domain. This would be so when the ability of the module to handle its cultural domain contributed to its remaining a stable feature of an enduring species. The only clear case of an adaptation of a module to its own effects is that of the linguistic faculty. The linguistic faculty in its initial form cannot have been an adaptation to a public language that could not exist without it. On the other hand it seems hard to doubt that language has become the proper domain of the language faculty.[13]

If there are modular abilities to engage in specific forms of social interaction (as claimed by Cosmides, 1989), then, as in the case of the language faculty, the cultural domains of these abilities should at least overlap with their proper one. Another interesting issue in this context is the relationship between numerosity—the proper domain of a cognitive module—and numeracy, an obvious cultural domain dependent on language (see Dehaene, 1992; Gallistel and Gelman, 1992; Gelman and Gallistel, 1978). In general, however, there is no reason to expect the production and maintenance of cultural domains to be a biological function of all, or even most, human cognitive modules.

If this approach is correct, it has important implications for the study of domain specificity in human cognition. In particular it evaporates, I believe, the cultural diversity argument against the modularity of thought. For even if thought were wholly modular, we should nevertheless find many cultural domains, varying from culture to culture, and whose contents are such that it would be preposterous to assume that they are the proper domain of an evolved module. The cultural idiosyncrasy and lack of relevance to biological fitness of a cognitive domain leaves entirely open the possibility that it might be a domain of a genetically specified module: its cultural domain.

Metarepresentational Abilities and Cultural Explosion

If you are still not satisfied that human thought could be modular through and through, if you feel that there is more integration taking place than I have allowed for so far, if you can think of domains of thought that don't fit with any plausible module, well then we agree. It is not just that beliefs about Camembert cheese might play a role in forming conclusions about quarks, it is that we have no trouble at all entertaining and understanding a conceptual representation in which Camembert and quarks occur simultaneously. You have just proved the point by understanding the previous sentence.

Anyhow, with or without Camembert, beliefs about quarks are hard to fit into a modular picture. Surely, they don't belong to the actual domain of naive physics; similarly, beliefs about chromosomes don't belong to the actual domains of naive biology, beliefs about lycanthropy don't belong to the actual domain of folk zoology, beliefs about the Holy Trinity or about cellular automata seem wholly removed from any module.

Is this to say that there is a whole range of extramodular beliefs, of which many religious or scientific beliefs would be prime examples? Not really. We have not yet exhausted the resources of the modular approach.

Humans have the ability to form mental representations of mental representations; in other words, they have a metarepresentational ability. This ability is so particular, both in terms of its domain and of its computational requirements that anybody willing to contemplate the modularity of thought thesis will be willing to see it as modular. Even Fodor does (Fodor, 1992). The metarepresentational module[14] is a special conceptual module, however, a second-order one, so to speak. Whereas other conceptual modules process concepts and representations of things, typically of things perceived, the metarepresentational module processes concepts of concepts and representations of representations.

The actual domain of the metarepresentational module is clear enough: It is the set of all representations of which the organism is capable of inferring or otherwise apprehending the existence and content. But what could be the proper domain of that module? Much current work (e.g., Astington et al., 1989) assumes that the function of the ability to form and process metarepresentations is to provide humans with a naive psychology. In other terms, the module is a "theory of mind module" (Leslie, [1994]), and its proper domain is made of the beliefs, desires, and intentions that cause human behavior. This is indeed highly plausible. The ability to understand and categorize behavior, not as mere bodily movements, but in terms of underlying mental states, is an essential adaptation for organisms that must cooperate and compete with one another in a great variety of ways.

Once you have mental states in your ontology, and the ability to attribute mental states to others, there is but a short step, or no step at all, to your having desires about these mental states—desiring that she should believe this, desiring that he should desire that—and to forming intentions to alter the mental states of others. Human communication is both a way to satisfy such metarepesentational desires, and an exploitation of the metarepresentational abilities of one's audience. As suggested by Grice (1957) and developed by Deirdre Wilson and myself (1986), a communicator, by means of her communicative behavior, is deliberately and overtly helping her addressee to infer the content of the mental representation she wants him to adopt (Sperber and Wilson, 1986).

Communication is, of course, radically facilitated by the emergence of a public language. A public language is rooted in another module, the language faculty. We claim, however, that the very development of a public language is not the cause, but an effect of the development of communication made possible by the metarepresentational module.

As a result of the development of communication, and particularly of linguistic communication, the actual domain of the metarepresentational module is teeming with representations made manifest by communicative behaviors: intentions of communicators and contents communicated. Most representations about which there is some interesting epidemiological story to be told are communicated in this manner and therefore enter people's minds via the metarepresentational module.

As already suggested, many of the contents communicated may find their way to the relevant modules: What you are told about cats is integrated with what you see of cats, in virtue of the fact that the representation communicated contains the concept CAT. But now you have the information in two modes: as a representation of cats, handled by a first-order conceptual module, and as a representation of a representation of cats, handled by the second-order metarepresentational module. That module knows nothing about cats but it may know something about semantic relationships among representations; it may have some ability to evaluate the validity of an inference, the evidential value of some information, the relative plausibility of two contradictory beliefs, and so forth. It may also evaluate a belief, not on the basis of its content, but on the basis of the reliability of its source. The metarepresentational module may therefore form or accept beliefs about cats for reasons that have nothing to do with the kind of intuitive knowledge that the CAT module (or whatever first-order module handles cats) delivers.

An organism endowed with perceptual and first-order conceptual modules has beliefs delivered by these modules, but has no beliefs about beliefs, either its own or those of others, and no reflexive attitude to them. The vocabulary of its beliefs is limited to the output vocabulary of its modules, and it cannot conceive or adopt a new concept nor criticize or reject old ones. An organism also endowed with a metarepresentational module can represent concepts and beliefs qua concepts and beliefs, evaluate them critically, and accept them or reject them on metarepresentational grounds. It may form representations of concepts and of beliefs pertaining to all conceptual domains, of a kind that the modules specialized in those domains might be unable to form on their own, or even to incorporate. In doing so, however, the better endowed organism is merely using its metarepresentational module within the module's own domain, that is, representations.

Humans, with their outstanding metarepresentational abilities, may thus have beliefs pertaining to the same conceptual domain rooted in two quite different modules: The first-order module specialized in that conceptual domain, or the second-order metarepresentational module, specialized in representations. These are, however, two different kinds of beliefs, "intuitive beliefs" rooted in first-order modules, and "reflective beliefs" rooted in the metarepresentational module (see Sperber, 1985a, chap. 2, 1985b, 1990a). Reflective beliefs may contain concepts (e.g., "quarks," "Trinity") that do not belong in the repertoire of any module, and that are therefore available to humans only reflectively, via the beliefs or theories in which they are embedded. The beliefs and concepts that vary most from culture to culture (and that often seem unintelligible or irrational from another culture's perspective) are typically reflective beliefs and the concepts they introduce.

Reflective beliefs can be counterintuitive (more exactly, they can be counterintuitive with respect to our intuitions about their subject matter, while, at the same time, our metarepresentational reasons for accepting them are intuitively compelling). This is relevant to the most interesting of Fodor's technical arguments against the modularity of central processes. The informational encapsulation and mandatory character of perceptual modules is evidenced, Fodor points out, by the persistence of perceptual illusions, even when we are apprised of their illusory character. There is, he argues, nothing equivalent at the conceptual level. True, perceptual illusions have the feel, the vividness of perceptual experiences, that you won't find at the conceptual level. But what you do find is that we may give up a belief and still feel its intuitive force, and feel also the counterintuitive character of the belief we adopt in its stead.

You may believe with total faith in the Holy Trinity, and yet be aware of the intuitive force of the idea that a father and son cannot be one and the same. You may understand why black holes cannot be seen, and yet feel the intuitive force of the idea that a big solid, indeed dense object cannot but be visible. The case of naive versus modern physics provides many other blatant examples.[15] What happens, I suggest, is that the naive physics module remains largely unpenetrated by the ideas of modern physics, and keeps delivering the same intuitions, even when they are not believed any more (or at least not reflectively believed).

More generally the recognition of the metarepresentational module, of the duality of beliefs that it makes possible, and of the gateway it provides for cultural contagion, plugs a major gap in the modular picture of mind I have been trying to outline. The mind is here pictured as involving three tiers: a single thick layer of input modules, just as Fodor says, then a complex network of first-order conceptual modules of all kinds, and then a second-order metarepresentational module. Originally, this metarepresentational module is not very different from the other conceptual modules, but it allows the development of communication and triggers a cultural explosion of such magnitude that its actual domain is blown up and ends up hosting a multitude of cultural representations belonging to several cultural domains.

This is how you can have a truly modular mind playing a major causal role in the generation of true cultural diversity.

Acknowledgments

I thank Lawrence Hirschfeld, Pierre Jacob, and Deirdre Wilson for their useful comments on an earlier version of this paper.

Notes

1. Fodor also mentions the possibility that output, i.e., motor systems might be modular too. I assume that it is so, but will not discuss the issue here.

2. Howard Gardner's *Frames of Mind* (1983) defends a modular theory of central processes with a concern that I share for the cultural aspect of the issue. My approach is otherwise quite different from his.

3. See also Barkow (1989), Barkow, Cosmides, and Tooby (1992), Brown (1991), Rozin (1976), Rozin and Schull (1988), and Symons (1979).

4. This is, of course, the "frame problem," the very existence of which Fodor (1987) sees as indissolubly linked to the nonmodularity and to the rationality of thought. The frame problem, qua

psychological problem, is being overestimated. Two psychological hypotheses allow us to reduce it to something tractable. First the modularity of thought hypothesis, as pointed out by Tooby and Cosmides (1992) considerably reduces the range of data and procedures that may be invoked in any given conceptual task. Second, the hypothesis that cognitive processes tend to maximize relevance (Sperber and Wilson, 1986) radically narrows down the actual search space for any conceptual task.

5. The point cannot just be that the forces that have driven cognitive evolution cannot be identified for certain; that much is trivially true. The claim must be that these forces cannot be even tentatively and reasonably identified, unlike the forces that have driven the evolution of, say, organs of locomotion. See Piatelli-Palmarini (1989) and Stich (1990) for clever but unconvincing arguments in favor of this Second Law.

6. Note that if apparent lack of hardwiring was an obstacle to acknowledging modularity, this would be an obstacle in the case of Fodor's linguistic input modules too. Take the case of a bilingual. Surely she has two modules, one for each language. Both result from fixing parameters and filling a lexicon in a template module, the language acquisition device. However we should be reluctant to imagine that there were (at least) two hardwired templates in place, waiting to be initialized. Hence, at least one of the initialized templates results from a projection of the initial structure onto new sites.

7. Burge (1979) and Putnam (1975) offered the initial arguments for externalism (I myself am convinced by Putnam's arguments but not by Burge's). For a sophisticated discussion, see Recanati (1993).

8. Arguably, content is a biological function in an extended sense—see Dretske (1988), Millikan (1984), and Papineau (1987). My views have been influenced by Millikan's.

9. There are of course conceptual problems here (see Dennett, 1987; Fodor, 1988). It could be argued, for instance, that the module's proper domain was neither elephants nor hippos, but something else, say, "approaching big animals that might trample orgs." If so, we would want to say that its proper domain had *not* changed with the passing of the elephants and the coming of the hippos. I side with Dennett in doubting that much of substance hinges on which of these descriptions we choose: The overall explanation remains exactly the same.

10. That is why it would be a mistake to say that the function of a device is to react to whatever might satisfy its input conditions and to equate its actual and proper domains. Though there may be doubt about the correct assignment of the proper domain of some device (see note 9), the distinction between actual and proper domains is as solid as that between effect and function.

11. Comparable evolutionary or epidemiological views of culture have been put forward by Boyd and Richerson (1985), Cavalli-Sforza and Feldman (1981), Dawkins (1976), and myself (in addition to some very different evolutionary approaches by many others). The epidemiology of representations that I have been advocating differs from other approaches (1) by stressing the importance of individual cognitive mechanisms in the overall explanation of culture, and (2) by arguing that information is transformed every time it is transmitted to such an extent that an analogy with biological reproduction or replication is inappropriate. See also Tooby and Cosmides (1992) for important new developments in this area.

12. Here, as in talk of representations competing for attention, the term "competition" is only a vivid metaphor. Of course, no intention or disposition to compete is implied. What is meant is that, out of all the representations present in a human group at a given time, some, at one extreme, will spread and last, whereas, as the opposite extreme, others will occur only very briefly

and very locally. This is not a random process, and it is assumed that properties of the information itself play a causal role in determining its wide or narrow distribution.

13. See Pinker and Bloom (1990) and my contribution to the discussion of their paper (Sperber, 1990b).

14. The capacity to form and process metarepresentations could be instantiated not in a single, but in several distinct modules, each, say, metarepresenting a different domain or type of representations. For lack of space and compelling arguments, I will ignore this genuine possibility.

15. And a wealth of subtler examples have been analyzed in a proper cognitive perspective by Atran (1990).

References

Astington, J. W., Harris, P., and Olson, D. (1989). *Developing theories of mind.* New York: Cambridge University Press.

Atran, S. (1987). Ordinary constraints on the semantics of living kinds. *Mind and Language, 2*(1), 27–63.

Atran, S. (1990). *Cognitive foundations of natural history.* New York: Cambridge University Press.

Barkow, J. H. (1989). *Darwin, sex and status: Biological approaches to mind and culture.* Toronto: University of Toronto Press.

Barkow, J., Cosmides, L., and Tooby, J. (Eds.). (1992). *The adapted mind: Evolutionary psychology and the generation of culture.* New York: Oxford University Press.

Berlin, B. (1978). Ethnobiological classification. In E. Rosch and B. Lloyd (Eds.), *Cognition and categorization.* Hillsdale, NJ: Erlbaum.

Boyd, Robert, and Richerson, Peter J. (1985). *Culture and the evolutionary process.* Chicago: The University of Chicago Press.

Boyer, P. (1990). *Tradition as truth and communication.* New York: Cambridge University Press.

Boyer, P. (1993). *The naturalness of religious ideas.* Berkeley: University of California Press.

Boyer, P. (1994). Cognitive constraints on cultural representations: Natural ontologies and religious ideas. In Hirschfeld and Gelman (1994).

Brown, D. (1991). *Human universals.* New York: McGraw-Hill.

Burge, T. (1979). Individualism and the mental. *Midwest Studies in Philosophy, 5,* 73–122.

Carey, S. (1985). *Conceptual development in childhood.* Cambridge, MA: MIT Press.

Cavalli-Sforza, L. L., and Feldman, M. W. (1981). *Cultural transmission and evolution: A quantitative approach.* Princeton: Princeton University Press.

Clark, A. (1987). The kludge in the machine. *Mind and Language, 2*(4), 277–300.

Clark, A. (1990). *Microcognition: Philosophy, cognitive science, and parallel distributed processing.* Cambridge, MA: MIT Press.

Cosmides, L. (1989). The logic of social exchange: Has natural selection shaped how humans reason? Studies with the Wason selection task. *Cognition, 31,* 187–276.

Cosmides, L., and Tooby, J. (1987). From evolution to behavior: Evolutionary psychology as the missing link. In J. Dupré (Ed.), *The latest on the best: Essays on evolution and optimality*. Cambridge, MA: MIT Press.

Cosmides, L. and Tooby, J. (1994). Origins of domain specificity: The evolution of functional organization. In Hirschfeld and Gelman (1994).

Davidson, N. S., and Gelman, S. (1990). Induction from novel categories: The role of language and conceptual structure. *Cognitive Development, 5*, 121–152.

Dawkins, Richard. (1976). *The selfish gene*. Oxford: Oxford University Press.

Dehaene, S. (1992). Varieties of numerical abilities. *Cognition, 44*(1–2), 1–42.

Dennett, D. (1987). *The intentional stance*. Cambridge, MA: MIT Press.

Dretske, F. (1988). *Explaining behavior*. Cambridge, MA: MIT Press.

Fodor, J. (1983). *The modularity of mind*. Cambridge, MA: MIT Press.

Fodor, J. (1987). Modules, frames, fridgeons, sleeping dogs, and the music of the spheres. In J. Garfield (Ed.), *Modularity in knowledge representation and natural-language understanding* (pp. 26–36). Cambridge, MA: MIT Press.

Fodor, J. (1988). *Psychosemantics*. Cambridge, MA: MIT Press.

Fodor, J. (1992). A theory of the child's theory of mind. *Cognition, 44*, 283–296.

Gallistel, C. R., and Gelman, R. (1992). Preverbal and verbal counting and computation. *Cognition, 44*(1–2), 43–74.

Gardner, H. (1983). *Frames of mind: The theory of multiple intelligences*. New York: Basic Books.

Gelman, R., and Gallistel, C. R. (1978). *The child's understanding of number*. Cambridge, MA: Harvard University Press.

Gelman, S., and Coley, J. D. (1991). The acquisition of natural kind terms. In S. Gelman and J. Byrnes (Eds.), *Perspectives on language and thought*. New York: Cambridge University Press.

Gelman, S., and Markman, E. (1986). Categories and induction in young children. *Cognition, 23*, 183–209.

Gelman, S., and Markman, E. (1987). Young children's inductions from natural kinds: The role of categories and appearances. *Child Development, 58*, 1532–1541.

Grice, H. P. (1957). Meaning. *Philosophical Review, 66*, 377–388.

Hirschfeld, L. (1988). On acquiring social categories: Cognitive development and anthropological wisdom. *Man, 23*, 611–638.

Hirschfeld, L. (1993). Discovering social difference: The role of appearance in the development of racial awareness. *Cognitive Psychology, 25*, 317–350.

Hirschfeld, L. (1994). Is the acquisition of social categories based on domain-specific competence or on knowledge transfer? In Hirschfeld and Gelman (1994).

Hirschfeld, L., and S. Gelman (Eds.) (1994). *Mapping the Mind: Domain Specificity in Cognition and Culture*. Cambridge: Cambridge University Press.

Keil, F. C. (1989). *Concepts, kinds, and cognitive development*. Cambridge, MA: Bradford Books/MIT Press.

Keil, F. (1994). The birth and nurturance of concepts by domains: The origins of concepts of living things. In Hirschfeld and Gelman (1994).

Kelly, M., and Keil, F. C. (1985). The more things change . . . : Metamorphoses and conceptual development. *Cognitive Science, 9,* 403–416.

Leslie, A. (1987). Pretense and representation: The origins of "theory of mind." *Psychological Review, 94,* 412–426.

Leslie, A. (1988). The necessity of illusion: Perception and thought in infancy. In L. Weiskrantz (Ed.), *Thought without language.* Oxford: Clarendon Press.

Leslie, A. (1994). ToMM, ToBY, and Agency: Core architecture and domain specificity. In Hirschfeld and Gelman (1994).

Manktelow, K., and Over, D. (1990). *Inference and understanding: A philosophical and psychological perspective.* London: Routledge.

Markman, E. M. (1990). The whole-object, taxonomic, and mutual exclusivity assumptions as initial constraints on word meanings. In S. Gelman and J. Byrnes (Eds.), *Perspectives on language and thought.* New York: Cambridge University Press.

Markman, E. M., and Hutchinson, J. E. (1984). Children's sensitivity to constraints on word meaning: Taxonomic versus thematic relations. *Cognitive Psychology, 16,* 1–27.

Medin, D., and Ortony, A. (1989). Psychological essentialism. In S. Vosniadou and A. Ortony (Eds.), *Similarity and analogical reasoning.* Cambridge: Cambridge University Press.

Millikan, R. G. (1984). *Language, thought, and other biological categories.* Cambridge, MA: MIT Press.

Papineau, D. (1987). *Reality and representation.* Oxford: Blackwell.

Piatelli-Palmarini, M. (1989). Evolution, selection and cognition: From "learning" to parameter setting in biology and the study of language. *Cognition, 31,* 1–44.

Pinker, S., and Bloom, P. (1990). Natural language and natural selection. *Behavioral and Brain Sciences, 13*(4), 703–784.

Premack, D. (1990). The infant's theory of self-propelled objects. *Cognition, 36,* 1–16.

Premack, D., and Woodruff, G. (1978). Does the chimpanzee have a theory of mind? *Behavioral and Brain Sciences, 1*(4), 515–526.

Putnam, H. (1975). The meaning of "meaning." In *Mind, language and reality: Philosophical papers, volume II.* Cambridge: Cambridge University Press.

Recanati, F. (1993). *Direct reference, meaning and thought.* Oxford: Blackwell.

Rozin, P. (1976). The evolution of intelligence and access to the cognitive unconscious. In J. M. Sprague and A. N. Epstein (Eds.), *Progress in psychobiology and physiological psychology.* New York: Academic Press.

Rozin, P., and Schull, J. (1988). The adaptive-evolutionary point of view in experimental psychology. In R. Atkinson, R. Herrnstein, G. Lindzey, and R. Luce (Eds.), *Steven's handbook of experimental psychology.* New York: John Wiley and Sons.

Sober, E. (1984). *The nature of selection.* Cambridge, MA: MIT Press.

Spelke, E. S. (1988). The origins of physical knowledge. In L. Weiskrantz (Ed.), *Thought without language.* Oxford: Clarendon Press.

Sperber, D. (1975). *Rethinking symbolism.* Cambridge: Cambridge University Press.

Sperber, D. (1980). Is symbolic thought prerational? In Mary Foster and Stanley Brandes (Eds.), *Symbol as sense.* New York: Academic Press.

Sperber, D. (1985a). *On anthropological knowledge.* New York: Cambridge University Press.

Sperber, D. (1985b). Anthropology and psychology: Towards an epidemiology of representations (The Malinowski Memorial Lecture 1984). *Man* (N.S.) *20,* 73–89.

Sperber, D. (1990a). The epidemiology of beliefs. In C. Fraser and G. Gaskell (Eds.), *The social psychological study of widespread beliefs.* Oxford: Clarendon Press.

Sperber, D. (1990b). The evolution of the language faculty: A paradox and its solution. *Behavioral and Brain Sciences, 13*(4), 756–758.

Sperber, D. (1992). Culture and matter. In J.-C. Gardin and C. S. Peebles (Eds.), *Representations in archeology.* Bloomington: Indiana University Press.

Sperber, D., and Wilson, D. (1986). *Relevance: Communication and cognition.* Oxford: Blackwell.

Stich, S. (1990). *The fragmentation of reason.* Cambridge, MA: MIT Press.

Symons, D. (1979). *The evolution of human sexuality.* New York: Oxford University Press.

Tooby, J., and Cosmides, L. (1989). Evolutionary psychology and the generation of culture, Part I: Theoretical considerations. *Ethology and Sociobiology, 10,* 29–49.

Tooby, J., and Cosmides, L. (1992). The psychological foundations of culture. In J. Barkow, L. Cosmides, and J. Tooby (Eds.), *The adapted mind: Evolutionary psychology and the generation of culture.* New York: Oxford University Press.

73 Dissociation and Modularity: Reflections on Language and Mind

Neil Smith

It would be presumptuous to imagine that one could do more than scratch the surface of a subject as vast as that indicated by the subtitle of this chapter. Language, mind, and the relationship of one to the other have preoccupied many of the best thinkers for millennia, and I can hope neither to summarize nor to replace their conclusions in a few pages. There are, however, clear generalizations to be made, and I can at least gesture in what I think is the right direction. The essence is modularity; the evidence is dissociation.

Modularity

I adopt a view of cognitive architecture on which the mind is pervasively modular in the sense of Chomsky (1975, 1984) and Fodor (1983). There are significant differences between their positions, some of which I spell out here, but there is sufficient overlap to make a unified summary feasible. I begin with Fodor's now classical position, as put forward in *The Modularity of Mind.* Fodor differentiates the central system, which is responsible for higher cognitive activities, such as general problem solving and the fixation of belief, from the input systems, which provide grist for the central mill. He then argues that these input systems, which correspond in the first instance to the sensorium, but crucially also include the language faculty, share a number of further properties, and any component with these properties is then, by definition, a module. For instance, modules are *domain specific,* in that their operations are sensitive only to a subset of impinging stimuli—light waves for vision, sound waves for audition, and likewise for the other senses. They are relatively *fast,* in that it takes minimal time to see a person as a person, but much longer to decide what to buy one's mother as a birthday present. Modules operate *mandatorily*—you have no choice but to see a face as a face, or to understand a sentence of your native language; but you may choose to ignore what you have seen and heard. They are *ontogenetically deterministic,* in that their development typically unfolds in the same way across the species without the benefit of overt instruction. The visual systems of children from all over the world appear to grow in much the same way, irrespective of culture, and their linguistic systems characteristically go through comparable stages at comparable ages, irrespective of the language being acquired. Modules are subject to *idiosyncratic pathological breakdown,* in that brain damage can cause deafness or blindness or aphasia. This suggests further that modules are *subserved by specific neural architecture* which is probably genetically determined. Finally, the operations of modules seem to be largely impervious to

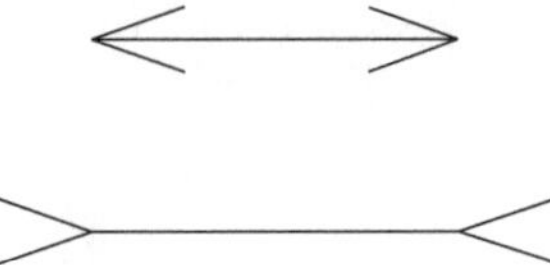

Figure 73.1
The Müller–Lyer illusion.

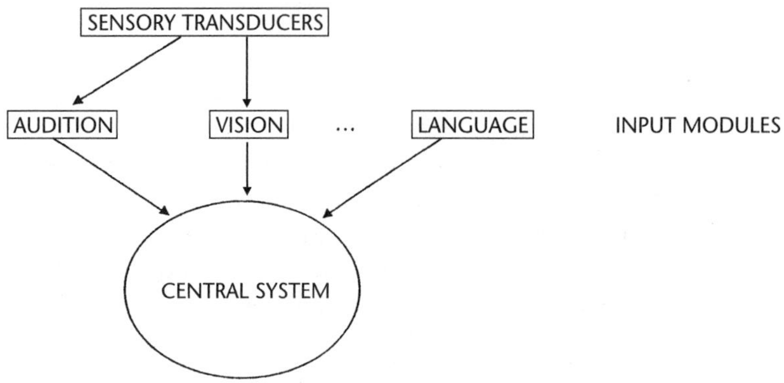

Figure 73.2a
Schematic representation of Fodor's Model.

the influence of the central system; they are "informationally encapsulated." The classic example is provided by the Müller-Lyer optical illusion, in which two lines, flanked by inward or outward pointing arrowheads are displayed as in Fig. 73.1. The visual system perceives the lower line as longer than the upper line. Even if you take a ruler and convince yourself that the two lines are indeed of identical length, your eyes still interpret them as being different. That is, the working of the visual system is impervious to the explicit knowledge provided by the central system.

All of these properties are, of course, the subject of debate and controversy, but it is generally agreed that the most important of them are domain specificity and informational encapsulation (Carston, 1996; Coltheart, 1999). As this is a position with which I disagree, it is also worth noting Fodor's claim that the central system is largely inaccessible to scientific investigation; hence he attributes to it virtually no internal structure. More recently, however (Fodor, 1992), he admitted some putative structure into the central system as well. A simplified schematic representation of Fodor's view is given in Fig. 73.2a. The transducers convert a physical stimulus, such as light waves, into a neural signal; the input systems then interpret transduced information for the central system to work on.

For Chomsky, the language faculty cannot be a Fodorian module for two reasons. First, we use language to speak as well as to understand, and if Fodor is correct in identifying modules with "input systems," then language, which is also an output system, cannot be a module. Second, and more importantly, the language faculty must in some respects be "central" to accommodate the basic fact that it is a system of knowledge. Moreover, this knowledge constitutes a common store that is neutral as between

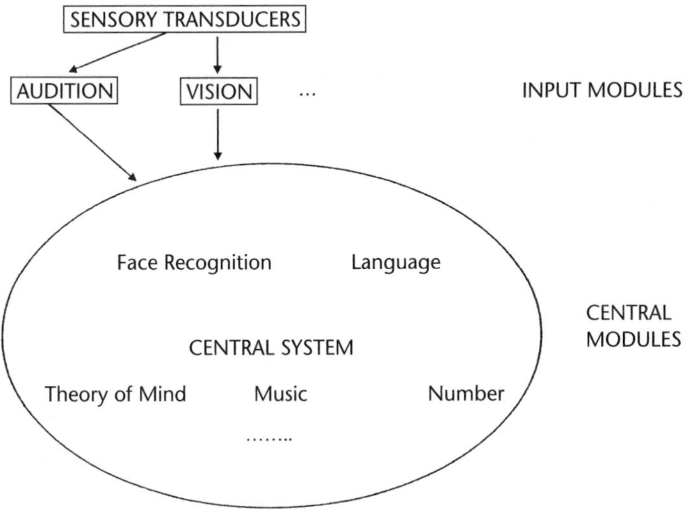

Figure 73.2b
Schematic representation of Chomsky's Model.

speaker and hearer. That is, we draw on largely the same knowledge whether we are producing an utterance of our own or interpreting that of someone addressing us. If understanding (parsing) and production deployed different systems, we would expect it to be the case that someone could speak one language and understand only a different one. Moreover, Chomsky does not share Fodor's pessimism that the central system is essentially inscrutable, suggesting that a range of functions from moral judgment to face recognition falls within its purview, and language is just one such domain, albeit the one about which we know most. (For discussion, see Levy and Kavé, 1999, and Smith, 1999.) A simplified schematic representation of Chomsky's view is given in Fig. 73.2b. I return later to different kinds of modules.

Note that Chomsky has not committed himself to anything like this simplistic diagram, which is intended only to highlight some of the differences between him and Fodor. In Smith and Tsimpli (1995, p. 170) we propose and defend a more complex model of the mind in which the language faculty is partly inside and partly outside the central system. The "Central modules" here correspond to our "Quasi-modules."

Dissociation

Although dissociation does not entail modularity, it is the case that modularity entails (possible) dissociation. Accordingly, a major kind of evidence for modularity is functional autonomy, as seen most obviously in dissociative pathology. If a system's operation is independent of other systems, that system is prima facie a candidate for having modular status. Such autonomy is characteristic of the senses: One can be deaf without being blind, blind without being deaf. Although there are conditions in which both afflictions occur simultaneously, they can in principle dissociate, with the implication that the functions are independent of each other, subserved by different mechanisms, characterized by different generalizations, and liable to breakdown under different conditions. Not all dissociations are "double" or absolute in this way. Consider the incidence of hemophilia in the population. There are four logical possibilities—males with or without hemophilia, and females with or without hemophilia. In fact, the category of "females with hemophilia" is essentially nonexistent. Although females can carry the disease, they cannot suffer from it. Sex and hemophilia are only singly dissociable, not doubly dissociable, indicating that one property is dependent on the other.

This kind of dependency has been of central importance in discussions of the relation between language and other properties of mind, in particular of intelligence. It is (relatively) uncontroversial that three of the four logical possibilities are found: normal people exhibit the coexistence of language and intelligence; anencephalic subjects (those born with an absent or poorly developed cerebrum) develop neither language nor intelligence; and some aphasic conditions can result in the loss of language with intelligence unimpaired. An interesting example is given by Sloboda (1985, p. 260), who reported that after a stroke, the Russian composer Shebalin had severe difficulties with understanding and reproducing speech, but continued to compose and to teach his music students to the same high level as before. Such cases involving aphasia are hard to evaluate, as the inability to make manifest one's intelligence via one's linguistic ability may give a grossly misleading impression of one's competences. An extreme example is provided by "locked-in syndrome" of the kind poignantly described by Bauby in his autobiography (1997). Bauby suffered a devastating stroke, resulting in mutism and quadriplegia, yet his book shows that his knowledge of French and his intelligence were obviously intact. Furthermore, the spontaneous intelligent behavior of the permanently language-less makes it plausible that the third category exists. Whether the fourth possibility occurs, where people manifest linguistic ability in the absence of (some specifiable level of) intelligence, has been less obvious.

If the category does not exist, and if there is therefore a crucial link between language and intelligence, we have two possibilities: Either the acquisition of language is dependent on the antecedent presence of particular conceptual abilities, or particular conceptual contrasts are available only in the presence of particular linguistic ability. The second of these views was put forward by Quine, who claimed that cognitive development is parasitic on language. His claim (1960, section 19) is that the syntax of quantification is prerequisite to understanding the difference between individuals and substances. For example, until children have mastered the syntactic differences between count and mass nouns, their grasp of the ontological distinction between substances like *water* and individuals such as *people* or *sticks* cannot be comparable with the adult's conception. Meticulous experimentation (Soja, Carey, and Spelke, 1991) has refuted this claim, demonstrating that from the very earliest stages of language acquisition, children exploit conceptual categories of substance and individual essentially equivalent to those that adults use. Because Quine's claim would seem to suggest that speakers of languages like Chinese, which make minimal or no use of the count/mass distinction, would be unable to conceptualize the contrast (which they can), this refutation came as no surprise to linguists and psychologists. More interestingly, such findings make the contrary claim, that intelligence is necessary for first language acquisition, even more plausible. This position has indeed been widely defended.

There is a long tradition, best exemplified by the work of the Genevan psychologist Piaget and his associates, that claims that the acquisition of language is dependent on

Figure 73.3
Seriation.

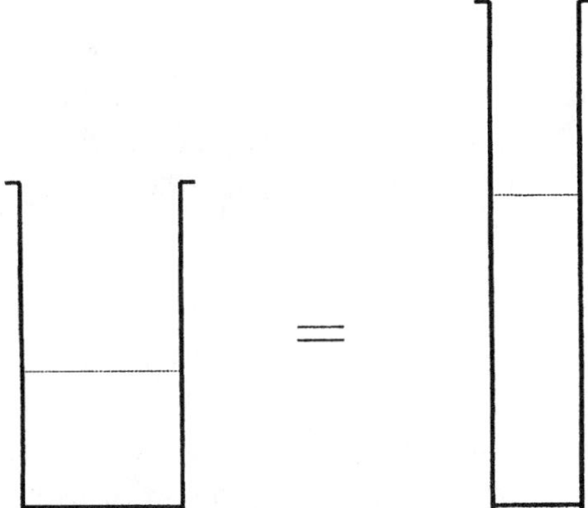

Figure 73.4
Conservation of volume.

the prior attainment of a particular level of cognitive ability; there are "cognitive prerequisites for the development of grammar," in Slobin's (1973) phrase. A typical observation from within this paradigm is that "Genevan psycholinguists tend to find the reason for [the late acquisition of the passive] in difficulties of a cognitive nature" (Inhelder, 1980, p. 135). To take a specific example, Piagetians hold that there is a correlation between the acquisition of comparatives and passives and the attainment of the "concrete operational" stage of cognitive development. This stage is marked by the achievement of the ability to pass "seriation" and "conservation" tasks. By seriation is meant the ability correctly to put in ascending or descending order the elements in an array of the kind seen in Fig. 73.3; by conservation is meant the ability to recognize the equivalence of two perceptually distinct stimuli—for instance, that a liquid poured from a tall thin glass into a short wide glass, as in Fig. 73.4, retains a constant volume. It appears that the mastery of comparatives presupposes seriation, and the mastery of passives presupposes conservation.

If such Piagetian views were correct, they would constitute evidence against the autonomy, and hence the modularity, of the language faculty. In fact, there is evidence from children with Williams syndrome that such views are simply wrong. Williams syndrome, or infantile hypercalcemia, is a genetically determined condition that results in a variety of physical and psychological characteristics. Affected children suffer from hypertension and heart defects, and they have "an elfin-like face, with heavy orbital ridge, temporal dimples, full cheeks, retroussé nose, flat nasal bridge, flared nostrils, stellate iris pattern, wide mouth, and irregular dentition" (Karmiloff-Smith, Klima, Grant, and Baron-Cohen, 1995, p. 198). Psychologically, they are characterized by severe deficits in spatial cognition, number, and problem solving, but by proficiency in face recognition, theory of mind, rote memory, and language. Of relevance here is that Bellugi and her colleagues (Bellugi, Marks, Bihrle, and Sabo, 1993) showed persuasively that Williams syndrome children have mastery of the syntactic constructions (passives and comparatives) whose acquisition is supposedly dependent on the achievement of the ability successfully to carry out seriation and conservation tasks, but that they consistently fail in these cognitive tasks. It is thus clear that in this population, language and intelligence dissociate.

Further evidence for such dissociation of language and intelligence, and for the putative modularity of the language faculty, comes from the "savant" syndrome, in particular from a man (Christopher) whom Ianthi Tsimpli and I have been studying for the past decade (Smith and Tsimpli, 1995, 1997; Tsimpli and Smith, 1991, 1998).

Christopher

Savants are people who have an island of talent in an ocean of disability. Typical examples are provided by calendrical calculators, who can tell you instantly the day of the week on which any named date falls; by athetoid musicians, who can play music while being unable to manipulate a spoon; and by retarded artists, who can draw magnificent animals or buildings while being unable to look after themselves. The traditional wisdom is that such people typically have minimal or no language ability (Treffert, 1989), so it was of great interest when we came across a savant whose talent is precisely in manipulating languages.

Born in January 1962, Christopher lives in sheltered accommodation because he is unable to look after himself. He is right-handed, but his hand–eye coordination is so impaired that everyday tasks like dressing or hanging a cup on a hook are serious chores for him; his psychological profile, outlined in Fig. 73.5, shows a pattern of mod-

Raven's Matrices:		75
WISC-R, UK:	Verbal:	89
	Performance:	42
Goodenough "Draw a Man":		40

Peabody Picture Vocabulary Test
English—121, German—114, French—110, Spanish—89

Columbia Greystone Mental Maturity Scale: Score 68; Mental Age 9.2; IQ 56

Embedded Figures Test (Witkin): Responses random (perhaps 1/12 correct)

Figure 73.5
Christopher's psychological background. Christopher's performance varied somewhat on different occasions of testing. For details, see Smith and Tsimpli 1995 and O'Connor and Hermelin 1991. In all cases except the last, the norm is 100.

erate to severe disability in performance tasks, but results close to normal in verbal tasks.

In addition, he is quite unable to master tick tack toe (noughts and crosses), and he fails Piagetian conservation-of-number tasks. For example, presented with two rows of beads, arranged either so that the beads on each string matched each other or so that those on one string were spread out to form a longer line as in Fig. 73.6, Christopher was consistent in claiming that whichever string the beads were spread out on contained more items than the other. Children usually conserve number correctly between the ages of 4 and 5 years.

Christopher also shows some, but not all of the signs of autism. On the "Sally-Anne" task, designed to test the subject's ability to impute false belief to others, Christopher usually fails, but on the superficially comparable Smarties test he is usually successful. In one version of the Sally-Anne test, the subject and another observer watch while the experimenter hides a toy. The observer is then sent out of the room and, in full view of the subject, the toy is moved from its first position and hidden in a new position. After ensuring that the subject was aware of where the toy was first hidden and of when the observer was last present, he or she is then asked where the observer will look for the toy on returning to the room. From about the age of 4, normal people indicate the first hiding place. Children under the age of 4, and autistic subjects, usually indicate the second hiding place, *where the toy actually is*. That is, they are unable to entertain the idea that someone else could have a representation of the world which deviates from reality; they cannot understand "false belief." In the Smarties test, subjects are shown a Smarties container (a well-known chocolate candy) and asked what they think is in it. When they reply "Smarties," they are shown that it really contains a pencil, and are then asked what their friends across the room will think is in it when they are asked. Again, autistic and very young children typically reply "a pencil"; older children, of course, reply correctly "Smarties." The standard explanation for this phenomenon is in terms of the absence or malfunctioning of a "theory-of-mind module" (more accurately a theory of other minds), a component of the mind that enables you to take someone else's point of view irrespective of whether that point of view conforms to reality. (For extensive discussion, including an explanation for Christopher's differential success, see Smith and Tsimpli, 1995, and especially Tsimpli and Smith, 1998.)

Despite his poor or mixed performance on tests of this kind, Christopher has considerable encyclopedic and linguistic knowledge. He defined correctly such terms as *baht* (the unit of currency used in Thailand) and *han'gul* (the name of the Korean script); he identified the nationality and affiliation of various footballers (telling us, for instance, that Koeman used to play for Barcelona); and he recognizes public figures such as Margaret Thatcher, Saddam Hussein, and Melina Mercouri. On the linguistic side, he

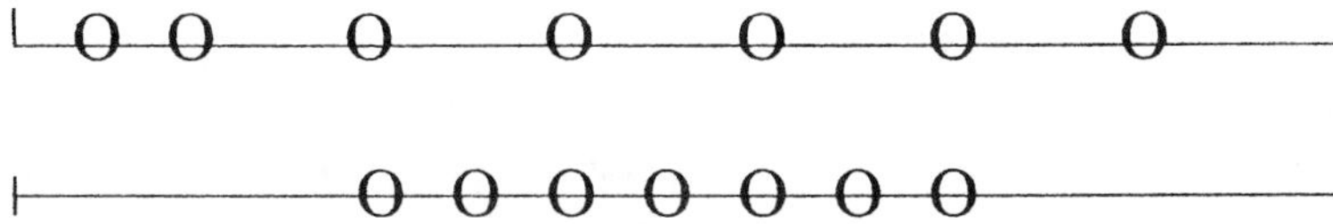

Figure 73.6
Conservation of number.

shows normal command of English syntax, as tested in production, comprehension, and wellformedness judgments of examples including relatives, clefts, questions, negatives, *that*-trace effects, control relations, and parasitic gaps. That is, he shows normal command of even the most complicated syntax, giving appropriate judgments on the acceptability of such examples as those in (1):

(1a) Who do you think that arrived?

(1b) Which book did you throw away without reading?

He correctly rejects as ungrammatical "*that*-trace effect" sentences like that in (1a), and he correctly accepts "parasitic gap" sentences like that in (1b). Moreover, despite the psychological profile given above, he can also integrate this linguistic knowledge into simple patterns of inferencing, correctly using both logical and contextual information in answering questions based on dialogues such as that in (2):

(2) John said, "Would you like some coffee?"
Mary replied, "Coffee would keep me awake."
Do you think Mary accepted the coffee?
(Christopher's response: "No")

That this is not simply some kind of learned response is clear from his ability to vary his judgment for more complex examples, as illustrated in (3):

(3) Mary said, "I have to work all night tonight."
John said, "Would you like some coffee?"
Mary replied, "Coffee would keep me awake."
Do you think Mary accepted the coffee?
(Christopher's response: "Yes")

What is most striking about Christopher is his considerable polyglot ability. He has some knowledge, ranging from a smattering to that of an average undergraduate, of Danish, Dutch, Finnish, French, German, Greek, Hindi, Italian, Norwegian, Polish, Portuguese, Russian, Spanish, Swedish, Turkish, and Welsh. He may have some ability in several others on which we have not tested him. He has recently been exposed to speakers of Hungarian, Serbo-Croatian, and a variety of other languages, and is reportedly assimilating them rapidly, and we are currently giving him intensive instruction in British Sign Language (Morgan et al., 2002). His knowledge of these various languages has been gleaned in a variety of ways. For some, such as the Scandinavian languages, it has been derived mainly from pedagogical grammar books; for others, such as Greek and Polish, it has arisen from reading and interacting with native speakers; for yet others, such as French and Spanish, it has come from all of these in combination with some formal school instruction. In every case we have consulted native speakers of the various languages to corroborate our judgment of his varying abilities. Detailed discussion and examples of his translational prowess in the languages listed above can be found in Smith and Tsimpli (1995:12–17).

It is worth noting that the languages he controls belong to groups that are unrelated historically or structurally, and that they are written in a variety of different scripts. It is also remarkable that Christopher is not a particularly good judge of his own abilities. After first asserting and then denying that he knew Russian, he was able to give a rough translation of the opening of a Russian short story written in Cyrillic script. It may be that his claims to "know X" are best interpreted as the ability—common to most linguists—to recognize that a passage comes from a particular language: He has correctly identified dozens of languages in this way, including, but not limited to, Arabic, Bengali, Chinese, Finnish, Georgian, Hungarian, Icelandic, Japanese, Korean, Letzeburgesch, and Mongolian.

His talent is impressive, but what is most remarkable about Christopher's second-language acquisition is the speed with which he masters the lexicon and the morphology. As part of our investigations we taught him two new languages under conditions of controlled input. That is, we controlled the nature and order of the input data, so that we had a complete record of every detail of the language to which he was exposed. One of these languages was Berber (Smith, Tsimpli, and Ouhalla, 1993), an Afro-Asiatic language of North Africa with a rich morphology, that is, with a wide variety of inflectional endings. On the basis of sets of sentences presented both orally (by a native speaker) and in written form, Christopher mastered the Berber system of subject agreement rapidly and with enthusiasm. It is noteworthy that both in Berber and in other languages, Christopher's mastery of morphology is characterized by the kind of overgeneralization that indicates that he is using inferred rules rather than just a prodigious memory. For instance, in Portuguese, abstract nouns typically end in *-ação,* where in English they end in *-ation*. Accordingly, in providing us with examples in Portuguese, he produced the "regular" but nonexistent form *examinação* ("examination") instead of the correct word *examen*. Similarly, he used the regularized sequence *Ime vlemmenos* ("I am seen") in Modern Greek, even though *vlemmenos* does not exist.

In contrast with his prodigious vocabulary and impressive morphological knowledge, and in contrast with his essentially flawless knowledge of the complexities of English syntax, Christopher's syntax in the various languages he has tackled seems soon to reach a plateau, beyond which he never proceeds. This suggests that the syntax of these languages is being somehow "filtered" through his native English. For instance, his Modern Greek is fluent, but after several years of exposure to a wide variety of data, and even to explicit teaching, he still makes systematic errors both in his performance and in his judgments of well-formedness on sentences involving the null subject parameter. That is, Greek—like Spanish and Italian, but unlike French and English—allows subject pronouns to be freely omitted if the referent is contextually recoverable. This phenomenon generally correlates with a wide variety of other syntactic characteristics, such as the *that*-trace effects mentioned earlier, and although Christopher can cope with the missing subject, he has persistent difficulty with the related constructions. Thus, although the Greek equivalent of (1a) is acceptable, Christopher judges it to be ungrammatical—as in English—despite his fluency in the language.

The mixture of talent and disability documented here is already evidence of the kind of dissociation of language and intelligence that was discussed earlier. Further evidence of a more striking kind is provided by two of the tests we carried out with him. The first of these is Christopher's reaction to a kind of fixed-ratio deletion cloze test; the second is his learning of an "impossible" invented language called Epun. Let us look at each in turn. For the first, we constructed anomalous prose passages by taking *n* consecutive words from a text, deleting the next *n* words, and so on repeatedly, producing second-order, fifth-order, seventh-order and 10-order approximations to

English (Smith and Tsimpli, 1995, p. 73). We then presented these passages to Christopher to see what his reaction would be. Given the rather automaton-like manner in which he translates, we predicted that he would balk only at the most extreme divergences from coherent text. In fact, it was only with second-order approximations that he gave any indication that he found the examples anything but normal. Given the seventh-order sequence in (4), his reaction was immediately to try to translate it into French, as in (5), adding the comment in (6). A translation back into English of his translation is given in (5′)—the item italicized was left in English.

(4) The Pharaohs had enough stone to build enough papyrus, too, so there was nothing as large as floating islands. The papyrus a modest fifth of the Sphinx's length. Of the underworld of mummies and stood it made us realize what giant structures.

(5) Les Pharaohs ont beaucoup de pierres pour, pour construire des papyrus, aussi, so il n'y était pas si grand comme le île flottante. Le papyrus, un modeste quinze—cinq de le longueur du Sphinx. Et je ne sais pas.

(5′) The pharaohs have many stones to, to build some papyrus, also *so* it wasn't as big as the floating island. The papyrus, a modest fifteen—five of the length of the Sphinx. And I don't know.
[Note that "le île" should have been "l'île"; "cinq" should have been "cinquième"; "de le" should have been "du," as in the (correct) phrase "du Sphinx" immediately following.]

(6) NVS What did you think of that passage?
C Très bon, très bon. ["Very good, very good"].

I take it that this reaction is abnormal and indicates at the very least an insensitivity to violations of coherence or rationality. His translation is not without mistakes (Smith and Tsimpli, 1995, p. 169), but it is clear from his linguistic profile, especially his expertise in providing grammaticality judgments, that his language faculty is operating more efficiently than his faculty of common sense, which here seems to be switched off.

Corroboration of the dissociation between his linguistic and general intellectual abilities came from the second area already mentioned—the acquisition of Epun. As well as teaching Berber to Christopher, we decided to teach him an invented language in which we could manipulate variables of interest. We were stimulated by Chomsky's (1991, p. 40) observation that "knowing something about UG [Universal Grammar—the innate endowment that the child brings to first language acquisition—NS], we can readily design "languages" that will be unattainable by the language faculty." Accordingly, after several months of teaching Christopher (and a group of controls) aspects of a perfectly possible if nonexistent language, we gradually introduced linguistically "impossible" but logically simple constructions. The hypothesis we wished to test was that although Christopher's remarkable language faculty should enable him to cope with anything natural languages could confront him with, his limited intelligence would prevent him coming up with the logically simple solutions to the problems we presented him. In contrast, normal undergraduate controls should be able to use their intelligence to learn what, by hypothesis, was beyond their language faculty.

To investigate this possibility we used the pervasive and fundamental property of "structure dependence." Consider the example in (7):

(7) The man who is tall is in the room

and the task of working out how to form questions from statements. Given a pair of sentences of the kind in (8):

(8a) The man is tall.

(b) Is the man tall?

a range of logically possible solutions is available. You could try moving the third word to the front; this works with (8a), but with "John is tall" it would give the impossible "tall John is?". You could try moving the first auxiliary verb to the front (auxiliaries are things like *is*, *can*, and *might*; in the present example *is* is the auxiliary), but with (7) this would give the ungrammatical result "Is the man who tall is in the room?" Mentioning the auxiliary is all right, but what is needed is a rule which refers not to mathematical notions like first and third, but exclusively to *structural* notions like "subject" and "auxiliary." To form a question in English you move the auxiliary immediately following the subject to the front of the sentence. The subject of (8a) is "*The man*"; the subject of (7) is "*The man who is tall*," not just "*The man*." The example is trivial, but the moral is vital: All rules in all languages are "structure dependent" in this way.

We constructed a series of both structure-dependent and structure-independent examples and submitted them to Christopher and the controls (Smith et al., 1993; Smith and Tsimpli, 1995). A simple example of a structure-independent operation is given by the process of emphasis formation in (9), in which the element *-nog* is suffixed to the *third word* of the corresponding nonemphatic sentence: that is, the position of the suffix is arithmetically rather than structurally determined.

(9a) Chi h-u-pat Lodo-p to miza kakol
Who Past-3MS-Pos Lodo-Obl and I see[1]
Who saw Lodo and me?

(b) Chi h-u-pat Lodo-p-*nog* to miza kakol
Who Past-3MS-Pos Lodo-Obl-Emph and I see
Who did see Lodo and me?

Examples of structure-dependent, but nonetheless impossible, processes are provided by the syntax of tense and negation. Epun has the basic word order Subject Verb Object (SVO), but this changes depending first on whether the sentence is positive or negative, and second on the tense, so that we have the possibilities in (10):

(10) SV(O)Positive (present and future)
VS(O)Negative (present and future)
(O)SVPositive (past)
(O)VSNegative (past)

The intuitive generalizations implicit here are that in negative sentences the verb moves to presubject position, and in transitive past-tense sentences the object is moved to initial position. The processes are "impossible" because in no language can negation be marked solely by a change in word order—it is always necessary that there be an overt negative morpheme such as "*not*" in English—and because there is no motivation for the movement of the object to initial position. In current linguistic theory (Chomsky, 1995), all movement has to be motivated by the presence of some morphological driving force, and we deliberately constructed the language so that this was absent. That is, the relations among the array of word orders in (10) are logically extremely simple, but they are nonetheless linguistically impossible. The idea was that controls would be able to induce these simple generalizations by a form of elementary problem solving, that is, by processes external to the language faculty, whereas Christopher would fail to induce them because his "central" problem-solving abilities were inadequate, and his linguistic abilities were (by hypothesis) irrelevant in a domain that lay outside the scope of linguistic theory.

The results provided partial confirmation of these predictions. Structure-independent operations of the kind shown in (9) proved impossible for Christopher, but they proved impossible for everyone else as well. Although the controls could solve such quasi-arithmetic problems in a nonlinguistic domain, in a linguistic context they appeared to be unable to suppress the architectural constraints of the language faculty and remained baffled by the process of emphasis formation. As we show in the discussion of connectionism that follows; this result has wider implications than might at first appear. Structure dependent, but linguistically impossible, operations were within the abilities of the control group but proved beyond Christopher in the initial stages, although he made some progress after prolonged exposure. Specifically, he showed partial mastery of the syntax of negation, but the peculiarities of the past tense proved totally insuperable, whereas the controls performed essentially flawlessly in both domains. I take it that these results support modularist claims about the dissociability of the cognitive and the linguistic systems.

Modified Modularity

The language faculty is clearly domain specific and it is, at least in part, independent of other aspects of mind. But it is not just an input system in Fodor's sense, and it is furthermore necessary to attribute greater structure to the "central" system than Fodor allows for, so we need a more subtle ontology than one that just differentiates modules and the central system. Accordingly, Ianthi Tsimpli and I have suggested that it is desirable to draw a distinction between modules and what we call "quasi-modules" (Smith and Tsimpli, 1995; Tsimpli and Smith, 1998). Like Fodorian modules, quasi-modules are domain-specific, fast, and mandatory, but they are not informationally encapsulated and their vocabulary, which may differ from case to case, is conceptual not perceptual. We have argued extensively elsewhere (Tsimpli and Smith, 1998) for the claim that theory of mind is a quasi-module in this sense; other domains that partake of at least some of the same properties include face recognition, moral judgment, music, common sense, the number sense, the senses of social structure and of personality structure, and perhaps folk physics and folk biology. In addition, it is still necessary to maintain the notion of the "submodular" structure characteristic of the language faculty (and other domains) in which, for instance, we have Chomskyan modules[2] of Theta theory, Binding theory, Case theory, and so on. A full explanation of these theories is not essential to an understanding of the current discussion of modules and quasi-modules, but to give a flavor of the enterprise, consider Case theory. This module of the grammar accounts for the contrast between *he* and *him*, in "he saw him," and the dependence of such forms on differences of finiteness, as illustrated in (11):

(11a) I believe him to be a werewolf.

(b) I believe he is a werewolf.

In each of these examples *he/him* is the subject of the clause *be a werewolf*, but it has to appear in the oblique (accusative) form *him* when the verb (*be*) is nonfinite (that is, not marked for tense), and in the nominative form *he* when the verb (*is*) is finite.

In every case where a module or quasi-module is postulated, there arises the possibility of double dissociation. Concentrating on the case of Christopher, we can see a number of dissociations. Christopher illustrates the situation in which linguistic ability is generally spared and general intelligence is impaired, while aphasia provides evidence for the converse—impaired linguistic ability and spared general intelligence. A developmental parallel to such aphasia, where aspects of the language faculty are impaired but general intelligence is within the normal range, is provided by specific language impairment (SLI; for an overview, see Joanisse and Seidenberg, 1998). In this condition children fail to develop age-appropriate knowledge of language despite being cognitively normal in all or most other respects. In fact, this simple characterization is itself controversial: Many researchers have claimed that the deficit is not language specific but is rather a reflex of a general deficit in the processing of rapid sequential information (Tallal, 1990). Although some SLI subjects may show such deficits in addition to language problems, it is becoming clear that there is a population in whom the only difficulty is linguistic (Bishop, 1997; van der Lely, 1997; van der Lely and Stollwerck, 1997), where moreover the epidemiology shows that the deficit is genetically determined (Gopnik, 1997). Such cases provide an interesting contrast to that of Christopher, both in the double dissociation of the deficits involved, and also in the details of the putative linguistic problem. In addition to those like Joanisse and Seidenberg (1998), who argue that SLI is characterized by a general processing deficit rather than a purely linguistic one, there have been a number of attempts to pinpoint the precise nature of what the linguistic deficit in SLI is. The "Agreement Deficit" of Clahsen, Bartke, and Gollner (1997) predicts inter alia that there should be problems with person and number agreement on verbs, but not on nouns; Gopnik's (1994) "Implicit Rule Formation Deficit" claims that SLI children cannot construct grammatical rules; van der Lely's (1996) "Representational Deficit with Dependent Relationships" predicts specific problems with particular aspects of adjectival versus verbal passives—the difference between "*The girl was very frightened*" and "*The girl was cruelly frightened*" (for a comprehensive overview, see Levy and Kavé, 1999).

All of these suggestions have had difficulty in accounting for the fact that the production of SLI children is characteristically a mixture of the correct and the incorrect. That is, their utterances often give evidence that they have knowledge of the linguistic constructions on which they usually fail. In brief, they appear to obey linguistic constraints optionally. The most plausible explanation for this pattern seems currently to be that there is conflict between the principles of "Last Resort" and "Procrastinate" in the sense of Chomsky (1995). Last Resort stipulates that a grammatical operation of a particular kind, such as movement, can take place only if there is no alternative which will give rise to an acceptable output; Procrastinate stipulates that movement should be delayed as long as possible, with the result that it takes place preferentially at LF—the level of Logical Form—where its effects are largely invisible. The idea is that the incorporation of one but not the other of these principles in the pathologically developing grammar leads to the possibility of a range of optional choices that are normally excluded (Davies, 2002; van der Lely, 1998). What is of most current relevance is that the SLI population provides a double dissociation with regard to Christopher. SLI children may be of normal intelligence but have problems with that part of language—the inflectional morphology—at which Christopher, despite his intellectual impairment, is best.

Other dissociations abound. Just as intelligence and language are dissociable, so also is it possible to separate linguistic ability and "theory of mind" in the sense of Frith and her colleagues (Frith, 1989; Frith and Happé, 1994; Frith, Morton and Leslie, 1991; Leslie, 1987). Autistic subjects probably lack a theory of mind but—especially in the case of Asperger's syndrome (Frith, Smith, in press)—may control language within normal limits. Some Down syndrome children provide a contrary scenario, with their theory of mind being intact, so that they characteristically succeed on "false belief" tasks, but with their linguistic ability moderately to severely degraded.

That the language faculty and the number faculty dissociate can be seen from different kinds of savants. Uniquely, Christopher's ability is in language, and his numerical talent is minimal. By contrast, calendrical calculators and other mathematical prodigies are characteristically severely linguistically impoverished, often being unable to communicate more than basic needs (Hermelin and O'Connor, 1990; O'Connor and Hermelin, 2001). In the case of number, it appears that there is also evidence for submodular dissociation (Dehaene, 1997; Wynn, 1998), with addition and subtraction being both differentially affected in pathology and separately localized in imaging studies. Language and face recognition dissociate, with Williams syndrome children being remarkable at both (Karmiloff-Smith et al., 1995),[3] whereas Christopher's performance on face recognition tasks is (typically for someone who has autistic characteristics) extremely weak.

If we look at the linguistic domain, similar "submodular" dissociations within the language faculty are also manifest, providing corroborative support for any linguistic theory that postulates the kind of modules characteristic of most versions of a Principles and Parameters model. The most obvious of these dissociations is between the lexicon and the "computational system" (Chomsky, 1995; Clahsen, 1999), roughly, the contrast between vocabulary and grammar. As we saw earlier, Christopher's first language, English, is entirely normal, but it is striking that his talent in his numerous "second" languages is restricted largely to mastery of the morphology and the lexicon, while his syntactic ability rapidly peaks and then plateaus. This dissociation is significant in that it is precisely the syntax, the main domain of parametric variation, that is the subpart of the language faculty that is most likely to be genetically specified and develop or unfold during a particular "critical period" (Smith, 1998). If Christopher's "second" languages have all been learned after the end of this critical period, it suggests that his talent, however remarkable, is necessarily flawed. It also suggests that in interesting respects, Christopher's abilities are only partly "linguistic." Unlike first-language acquisition, second-language learning may crucially involve the deployment of general learning strategies that are ultimately correlated with attributes of the central system (Tsimpli and Smith, 1991). Christopher is then able to "relexify" the particular syntactic template of his first language, but he cannot modify that original template itself—a large proportion of his second-language activity consists in introducing items of vocabulary from a wide variety of languages into English syntactic structures. This makes Christopher strikingly different from talented second-language learners whose "ultimate attainment" is close to that of native speakers (Birdsong, 1992). Assuming nonetheless that there is an obvious linguistic component to Christopher's learning of "second" languages, the dissociation between morphology and syntax is reminiscent of the reverse dissociation found in the case of children with spinal muscular atrophy, who seem to develop a proficient syntactic rule system but have correspondingly greater difficulty with lexical development (Sieratzki and Woll, 1998).

Alternatives

Modularity is frequently adduced as support for the "innateness" of the language faculty, but, as has been frequently pointed out, modularity (as also sub-modularity and quasi-modularity) is compatible with a variety of noninnatist positions, and the boundaries of what constitutes a module (or submodule, quasi-module, etc.) are definable in a variety of ways. In this section I wish to look briefly at one or two alternatives to the position I have already outlined.

Karmiloff-Smith (1992) argued extensively for the view that modules are a function of constructivist, epigenetic development rather than of simple genetic determination. That is, "cognitive development is the outcome of a self-organizing system that is structured and shaped by its interaction with the environment" (Carston, 1996, p. 78), with the mind of the newborn being largely unstructured and knowledge free. She supports her position with a series of elegant explanations for developmental patterns in terms of the "Representational Redescription Hypothesis," where redescription involves the transfer from implicit, unconscious, representation to explicit—hence potentially conscious—representation. Her thesis is compatible with some patterns of meta-linguistic development in children, but it is inadequate for dealing with the regular emergence of the functional categories of syntax (at around the 2 years stage). Functional categories of the kind exemplified by determiners, such as "*the*," inflectional elements, such as the plural "*-s*," and complementizers, such as "*that*" and "*if*," seem to emerge at about the same age in all children learning all languages, largely independently of intelligence, context, and environment (Smith, 1994). Although it is obvious that triggering input is necessary, this uniform emergence points strongly to a genetic, rather than an epigenetic, etiology—a conclusion that is supported by two other considerations. First, many phonological parameters are set in the first year of life (Jusczyk 1997 and 2003), and syntactic choices have been argued by Wexler (1998) to be available to the child from a stage before representational redescription can even get under way. Second, her account leaves mysterious why brain functions, in particular linguistic functions, should develop in such a way that they are localized similarly from person to person and from language to language. It is hard to see any appreciable role for the environment in such development.

A second alternative account of modularity is provided by Sperber (1994), who developed a position that also assigns considerable structure to the "central system" and that also makes a tripartite distinction among types of modules, but whose boundaries are somewhat different and which, I suspect, is flawed. His first division is into modules the size of concepts—the CAT module, the GOLDFISH module, and other "micromodules" for every concept we have. Second, he postulates modules à la Fodor that are sensitive to particular kinds of percept: vision, audition, and so on. Third, he suggests that the central system is best characterized by a metarepresentational module (or modules), devoted to "representations of representations." There is no provision in this system for submodules of the kind found within the language faculty or within the number sense, but it is likely that Sperber would happily add such structure to his model. Where we differ is in the apparent equation of "concept" with "micromodule" and in the assumption that all of the central system is metarepresentational. There are two problems. The first is whether there are any identity criteria for "module" under his system, or whether it is simply an allusive "loose use" of terminology (Sperber and Wilson, 1986) with no definable content. The second is whether the central systems—"quasi-modules" in my terminology—all involve "metarepresentation"; that is, the second-order representation of another representation. If all quasi-modules were necessarily metarepresentational, Sperber could plausibly accommodate them within a suggested (1994, p. 64) extension of his system allowing his metarepresentational module to be fragmented into a number of sub-components. However, although moral judgment and a sense of social structure are plausibly metarepresentational in this way, it is not obvious that music, the number sense or face recognition are. For instance, face recognition is itself not unitary, as it involves at least two components—face recognition proper, and the emotional response to the retrieved percept. These components are independently subject to breakdown, as in prosopagnosia (the specific inability to recognize faces) and Capgras' Delusion (the failure to register an emotional response to the face recognized) respectively (Coltheart, Langdon, and Breen, 1997). Although the latter may be metarepresentational, it is not clear why one should consider the former to be so. If this interpretation is correct, then it removes one possible basis for the unification inherent in Sperber's model. (For further discussion, see Tsimpli and Smith, 1998.)

The most radical alternative to modularist theories is provided by Connectionism (Plaut 2003). This approach denies the need for symbolic representations at all. All the complexities of human thought and language can emerge from interactions among a set of processing units which can take on different activation values. A connectionist network consists of a set of nodes that collect inputs from a variety of sources (both inside and outside the system), and transmit inputs to other nodes, thereby activating them in turn. The connections may be unidirectional or bidirectional, and are differently weighted so that the next node along may be either inhibited or excited. "Learning" results from training a network by repeatedly exposing it to vast numbers of examples of the pattern to be acquired. Importantly, there is no need to postulate any kind of initial domain-specific structure to the network, as the framework denies the need either for the innate schemata which are held to underlie modular accounts of linguistic ability, be these Fodorian or Chomskyan, or indeed for symbolic representation more generally. In this section I want to highlight what I perceive to be a serious problem for the spirit of connectionist accounts, and thereby lend indirect support to a modularist view (Bechtel and Abrahamson, 1991; Elman, 1993; Elman; 1996; for further discussion, see Clahsen, 1999; Marcus, 2001; Smith, 1997, 1999. Plaut 2003 provides a radically different viewpoint on connectionist accounts of language).

It is not controversial that connectionist networks can serve as one possible form of implementation for symbolic theories, nor that the sophistication of current networks is sufficient to model almost anything one cares to throw at them, even though their achievements in rendering the complexities of syntax are so far minimal. Whether they have anything at all to offer in the way of a replacement for symbolic theories, however, is a matter of heated controversy. Whichever view one takes, there are several claimed advantages of connectionist systems that are worth listing: They are explicit, they have neural correlates, they are "interactive," statistically based, and self-organizing, they manifest graceful degradation, and they allow for plasticity. Some of these properties are clearly desirable, some are irrelevant, and others may be pernicious. Let us look at them in turn.

The first property, explicitness, is uncontroversially beneficial, but it does not provide a principled distinction between symbolic systems, such as formal grammars and connectionist systems. The second characteristic, the fact that neural networks are modeled on one aspect of the structure of the brain is of no greater relevance than it would be to model them on physicists' superstring models of the universe, on the grounds that they are ultimately realized in terms of quarks and the like. What is important is the nature of the generalizations that can be expressed in alternative systems, and there are few, if any, syntactic generalizations statable in terms of networks. Next, connectionist networks are interactive, in that their final properties emerge from interaction among component parts of the system. This may or may not be an advantage. There are interesting issues concerning the relations among input systems and what we have called quasi-modules (e.g., informational encapsulation), but what precisely these relations are is an open empirical issue, not one to be decided in advance by fiat. Similar remarks obtain with regard to the property of being self-organizing: If the organization that emerges is the same as that found in human beings, then it is an advantage, but to the extent that the organization has to be built in by ascribing initial weights to the various connections, it is an admission of the correctness of innatist assumptions. Likewise with plasticity: The fact that "region *x* can be co-opted to carry out the function usually effected by region *y*" is sometimes used as an argument against modular systems (e.g., by Elman et al., 1996). The idea is that the claimed innateness of modularity is undermined by the brain's ability to compensate for injury in one area by "redeploying" its forces. For example, if a child suffers damage to the language area (e.g., in the form of a left hemispherectomy), the language function may be taken over by the right hemisphere. It is supposed to follow that modularity cannot be (innately) prespecified but must emerge. But it is not clear why this is problem for innateness hypotheses: invoking plasticity implicitly presupposes that regions *x* and *y* are, in the absence of pathological conditions, prespecified for the particular (modular) functions that connectionists are at pains to deny.

Although these critical observations should be taken into consideration in evaluating connectionist models, none of them provides particularly strong counterevidence to the theory. But there are two major objections to connectionism, relating to the other properties mentioned, which seem to me to be more problematic. The first is that connectionism is in principle inadequate for handling certain sorts of linguistic phenomena; the second is that it is in principle well designed to do things that it should not be able to do—that is, it is intrinsically too powerful. Networks typically use the method of gradient descent, but this militates against providing a sensible explanation for certain linguistic processes. Consider the phenomenon of "retreat," where a child who has internalized a grammar that overgenerates—as in Bowerman's (1987) example "don't giggle me"—retreats to a grammar in which this is, correctly, ungrammatical. That is, the child has to change its grammar from more general to less general. According to Elman, gradient descent "makes it difficult for a network to make dramatic changes in its hypotheses. Once a network is committed to an erroneous generalization it may be unable to escape" (Elman, 1993, p. 94). This unfortunately seems to make the problem of retreat insoluble.

It may be possible to alleviate this problem by modifying the learning rate or the momentum of the network, but the second kind of problem is more serious. It is of the essence of connectionist networks that they are sensitive to statistical data, and that structure emerges as a function of the frequency of elements of the input. I pointed out earlier that in the experiment in which Christopher and the controls had to learn Epun, none of them were able to infer the simple rule that emphatic sentences were produced by suffixing some element to the third word. This is something that connectionist networks are extremely good at doing, but which they ought not to be good at if they are accurately to replicate the normal abilities of human learners. Unlike networks, grammars can't count. That is, there is no phonological or syntactic rule in any of the world's languages, which requires reference to such notions as the third word, or the fourth segment. Rather, all rules of grammar refer either to structural configurations or to adjacency, and the course of linguistic development in the child seems to indicate that "structure dependence is the prerequisite to, not the outcome of, language acquisition" (Smith, 1997, p. 7). It is possible to impose additional constraints on a network so that it could not learn structure independent operations, correctly replicating the behaviour of human subjects. But such manipulation is contrary to the spirit of the enterprise and requires building in the "innate" structure that networks are supposed to be able to do without.

Conclusion

The mind is modular, but to put flesh on that skeletal statement it is necessary to distinguish different notions of "module." Input systems are modular in Fodor's sense, being sensitive to a subset of perceptually available stimuli; but *pace* Fodor, language is not just an input system, and it is also necessary to assign some structure to the "central" system, compartmentalizing it into a number of conceptual "quasi-modules" one of which is language. Both kinds of entities may be characterised by further "submodular," structure, corresponding to traditional notions such as morphology and syntax, and addition and multiplication, as well as some of the more recent constructs of linguistic theory, giving rise to the subtheories of a generative grammar, such as case and binding.

Modularity is in part genetically determined, but if language is modular, then the existence of different languages shows that it must also be in part the product of external input. The demarcations between what is learned and what is innate is contentious and the subject of ongoing research, but no one seriously doubts that both components are needed. There is ongoing healthy disagreement as to what the defining properties of modules are. I have suggested that some of the confusion and disagreement in the literature has arisen from a failure to make enough distinctions, and I have proposed a distinction between modules of the kind made famous by Fodor and quasi-modules, corresponding somewhat more closely to Chomsky's conception of the mind. I have defended these ideas on the basis of a wealth of dissociationist data, paying particular attention to the case of the polyglot savant, Christopher. Finally, I have argued that nonmodular (and nonsymbolic) rivals to modularity, specifically connectionist models, seem to have serious problems as replacements for theories of language and mind, even though they may remain viable as implementations for such theories. As of today, a modular conception of language, and of the structure of the mind more generally, is the most powerful and the most explanatory one available.

Acknowledgments

I am grateful to the organizers of the conference "Mind, Brain, and Language," which was sponsored by the Center for Advanced Study at the University of Illinois at Urbana–Champaign. I am particularly indebted to both of the organizers and to the other participants in the conference for a variety of comments and questions. The work on Christopher has all been done in collaboration with Ianthi Tsimpli, and with the support of the Leverhulme Trust under grant number F.134.

Notes

1. The term "h-u-pat" is a positive auxiliary inflected for past and third person masculine singular; "-p" is the marker of oblique case. The word order is a function of tense and transitivity. Details can be found in the references cited.

2. It is worth making explicit that Chomsky's use of the term *modular* varies according to context between an interpretation in which the language faculty is a module, and one in which, e.g., Case theory is a module.

3. Williams syndrome children appear to achieve their remarkable feats of face recognition by processes distinct from those of normals, focussing on one trait rather than the whole facial gestalt.

References

Bates, E., and Elman, J. 1996. Learning rediscovered. *Science, 274*, 1849–1850.

Bauby, J. D. (1997). *The diving-bell and the butterfly.* New York: Vintage Books.

Bechtel, W., and Abrahamson, A. (1991). *Connectionism and the mind: An introduction to parallel processing in networks.* Oxford: Blackwell.

Bellugi, U., Marks, S., Bihrle, A., and Sabo, H. (1993). Dissociation between language and cognitive functions in Williams syndrome. In D. Bishop and K. Mogford (Eds.), *Language development in exceptional circumstances* (pp. 177–189). Hillsdale, NJ: Lawrence Erlbaum Associates.

Birdsong, D. (1992). Ultimate attainment in second language learning. *Language, 68,* 706–755.

Bishop, D. V. M. (1997). *Uncommon understanding: Development and disorders of language comprehension in children.* London: Psychology Press.

Bowerman, M. (1987). The "no negative evidence" problem. How do children avoid constructing an overly general grammar? In J. Hawkins (Ed.), *Explaining language universals* (pp. 73–101). Oxford: Blackwell.

Carston, R. (1996). The architecture of the mind: Modularity and modularization. In D. Green and others (Eds.), *Cognitive Science: An Introduction* (pp. 53–83). Oxford, Blackwell.

Chomsky, N. (1975). *Reflections on language.* New York: Pantheon.

Chomsky, N. (1984). *Modular approaches to the study of mind.* San Diego: San Diego State University Press.

Chomsky, N. (1991). Linguistics and cognitive science: Problems and mysteries. In A. Kasher (Ed.), *The Chomskyan turn* (pp. 26–53). Oxford, Blackwell.

Chomsky, N. (1995). *The minimalist program.* Cambridge, MA: MIT Press.

Clahsen, H. (1999). Lexical entries and rules of language: A multidisciplinary study of German inflection. *Behavioral and Brain Sciences, 22,* 991–1060.

Clahsen, H., Bartke, S., and Gollner, S. (1997). Formal features in impaired grammars: A comparison of English and German SLI children. *Essex Research Reports in Linguistics, 14,* 42–75.

Coltheart, M. (1999). Modularity and cognition. *Trends in Cognitive Sciences, 3,* 115–120.

Coltheart, M., Langdon, R., and Breen, N. (1997). Misidentification syndromes and cognitive neuropsychiatry. *Trends in Cognitive Sciences, 1,* 157–158.

Davies, L. (2002). Specific language impairment as principle conflict: Evidence from negation. *Lingua, 112,* 281–300.

Dehaene, S. (1997). *The number sense.* London: Allen Lane.

Elman, J. (1993). Learning and development in neural networks: The importance of starting small. *Cognition, 48,* 71–99.

Elman, J., Bates, E., Johnson, M., Karmiloff-Smith, A., Parisi, D., and Plunkett, K. (1996). *Rethinking innateness: A connectionist perspective on development.* Cambridge, MA: MIT Press.

Fodor, J. (1983). *The modularity of mind.* Cambridge, MA: MIT Press.

Fodor, J. (1992). A theory of the child's theory of mind. *Cognition, 44,* 283–296.

Frith, U. (1989). *Autism: Explaining the enigma.* Oxford: Blackwell.

Frith, U. (1991). Asperger and his syndrome. In U. Frith (Ed.), *Autism and Asperger syndrome* (pp. 1–36). Cambridge: Cambridge University Press.

Frith, U., and Happé, F. (1994). Language and communication in autistic disorders. *Philosophical Transactions of the Royal Society of London B, 346*, 97–104.

Frith, U., Morton, J., and Leslie, A. (1991). The cognitive basis of a biological disorder. *Trends in Neuroscience, 14*, 433–438.

Gopnik, M. (1997). Language deficits and genetic factors. *Trends in Cognitive Sciences, 1*, 5–9.

Hermelin, B. (2001). *Bright splinters of the mind*. London: Jessica Kinglsey Publishers.

Hermelin, B., and O'Connor, N. (1990). Factors and primes: A specific numerical ability. *Psychological Medicine, 20*, 163–169.

Inhelder, B. (1980). Language and knowledge in a constructivist framework. In M. Piattelli-Palmarini (Ed.), *Language and learning: The debate between Jean Piaget and Noam Chomsky* (pp. 132–141). Cambridge MA: Harvard University Press.

Joanisse, M., and Seidenberg, M. (1998). Specific language impairment: A deficit in grammar or processing? *Trends in Cognitive Sciences, 2*, 240–247.

Jusczyk, P. (1997). *The discovery of spoken language*. Cambridge, MA: MIT Press.

Jusczyk, P. (2003). The role of speech perception capacities in early language acquisition. In M. Mack and M. Banich (Eds.), *Mind, Brain, and Language*. Mahwah, N.J.: Erlbaum.

Karmiloff-Smith, A. (1992). *Beyond modularity*. Cambridge, MA: MIT Press.

Karmiloff-Smith, A., Klima, E., Grant, J., and Baron-Cohen, S. (1995). Is there a social module? Language, face processing, and theory of mind in individuals with Williams syndrome. *Journal of Cognitive Neuroscience, 7*, 196–208.

Leslie, A. (1987). Pretense and representation: The origins of "Theory of Mind." *Psychological Review, 94*, 412–426.

Levy, Y., and Kavé, G. (1999). Language breakdown and linguistic theory: A tutorial overview. *Lingua, 107*, 95–143.

Marcus, G. (2001). *The algebraic mind: Reflections on connectionism and cognitive science*. Cambridge, MA: MIT Press.

Morgan, G., Smith, N. V., Tsimpli, I. M., and Woll, B. (2002). Language against the odds: The learning of British Sign Language by a polyglot savant. *Journal of Linguistics, 38*, 1–41.

O'Connor, N., and Hermelin, B. (1984). Idiot savant calendrical calculators: Maths or memory? *Psychological Medicine, 14*, 801–806.

O'Connor, N., and Hermelin, B. (1991). A specific linguistic ability. *American Journal of Mental Retardation, 95*, 673–680.

Piaget, J., and Inhelder, B. (1968). *The psychology of the child*. London: Routledge.

Plaut, D. C. (2003). Connectionist modeling of language: Examples and implications. In M. Mack and M. Banich (Eds.), *Mind, Brain, and Language*. Mahwah, N.J.: Erlbaum.

Quine, W. V. O. (1960). *Word and object*. Cambridge, MA: MIT Press.

Sieratzki, J. S., and Woll, B. (1998). *Toddling into language: Precocious language development in motor-impaired children with spinal muscular atrophy*. In A. Greenhill, M. Hughes, H. Littlefield, and H. Walsh (Eds.), Proceedings of the 22nd annual Boston University Conference on Language Development, (Vol. 2, pp. 684–694). Somerville, MA: Cascadilla Press.

Slobin, D. (1973). Cognitive prerequisites for the development of grammar. In C. Ferguson and D. Slobin (Eds.), *Studies of child language development* (pp. 175–208). New York: Holt Rinehart and Winston.

Sloboda, J. (1985). *The musical mind: The cognitive psychology of music.* Oxford: Clarendon Press.

Smith, N. V. (1994). Review article on A. Karmiloff-Smith (1992). *European Journal of Disorders of Communication, 29,* 95–105.

Smith, N. V. (1997). Structural eccentricities. *Glot International, 2,* 8. Reprinted in Smith, 2002, pp. 110–115.

Smith, N. V. (1998). Jackdaws, sex and language acquisition. *Glot International, 3,* 7. Reprinted in Smith, 2002, pp. 95–99.

Smith, N. V. (1999). Chomsky: Ideas and ideals. Cambridge: Cambridge University Press.

Smith, N. V. (2002). *Language, bananas and bonobos.* Oxford: Blackwell.

Smith, N. V. (in press). Wonder. *Glot International,* 6.

Smith, N. V., and Tsimpli, I.-M. (1995). The mind of a savant: Language-learning and Modularity. Oxford: Blackwell.

Smith, N. V., and Tsimpli, I.-M. (1997). Reply to Bates: Review of Smith and Tsimpli, 1995. *The International Journal of Bilingualism, 2,* 180–186.

Smith, N. V., Tsimpli, I.-M., and Ouhalla, J. (1993). Learning the impossible: The acquisition of possible and impossible languages by a polyglot *savant. Lingua, 91,* 279–347.

Soja, N., Carey, S., and Spelke, E. (1991). Ontological categories guide young children's inductions of word meaning: Object terms and substance terms. *Cognition, 38,* 179–211.

Sperber, D. (1994). The modularity of thought and the epidemiology of representations. In L. Hirschfeld and S. Gelman (Eds.), *Mapping the mind: Domain specificity in cognition and culture* (pp. 39–67). Cambridge: Cambridge University Press.

Sperber, D., and Wilson, D. (1986). Loose talk. *Proceedings of the Aristotelian Society, NS LXXXVI,* 153–171.

Tallal, P. (1990). Fine-grained discrimination deficits in language learning impaired children are specific neither to the auditory modality nor to speech perception. *Journal of Speech and Hearing Research, 33,* 616–617.

Treffert, D. A. (1989). *Extraordinary people.* London: Black Swan.

Tsimpli, I.-M., and Smith, N. V. (1991). Second language learning: Evidence from a polyglot savant. *University College London Working Papers in Linguistics, 3,* 171–183.

Tsimpli, I.-M., and Smith, N. V. (1998). Modules and quasi-modules: language and theory of mind in a polyglot savant. *Learning and individual differences, 10,* 193–215.

van der Lely, H. K. J. (1996). Specifically language impaired and normally developing children: Verbal passive *vs.* adjectival passive sentence interpretation. *Lingua, 98,* 243–272.

van der Lely, H. K. J. (1997). Language and cognitive development in a grammatical SLI boy: Modularity and innateness. *Journal of Neurolinguistics, 10,* 75–107.

van der Lely, H. K. J. (1998). SLI in children: Movement, economy and deficits in the computational syntactic system. *Language Acquisition, 72,* 161–192.

van der Lely, H. K. J., and Stollwerck, L. (1997). Binding theory and grammatical specific language impairment in children. *Cognition, 62*, 245–290.

Wexler, K. (1998). The unique checking constraint and the extended projection principle as the explanation for the optional infinitive stage: very early parameter-setting, maturational mechanisms and variation in grammatical development. *Lingua, 106*, 23–79.

Wynn, K. (1998). Psychological foundations of number: Numerical competence in human infants. *Trends in Cognitive Sciences, 2*, 296–303.

V Associationism and Connectionism

Introduction

Connectionism is a loosely organized research program involving researchers in computer science, psychology, and in some cases neurobiology. The research program has received considerable attention both in academia and the popular press, and is sometimes touted as a radical breakthrough in our understanding of the human mind. On the other hand, there are those who argue that connectionism is nothing more than "high-tech" Lockean associationism. It is probably too soon to say with certainty where the truth lies; careful study of earlier associationist and contemporary connectionist writings reveals not only marked differences, but a number of fundamental similarities as well.

The basic idea underlying associationism certainly is not new. We begin with Thomas Hobbes (1588–1679), who is interested in giving an account of our train of thinking. The section contains a famous passage in which Hobbes shows how the discussion of a civil war could be causally related to someone asking the price of a Roman penny. The idea of the war triggers a sequence of related or connected ideas, resulting in the seemingly anomalous question.

John Locke (1637–1704) develops the associationist doctrine somewhat, arguing that some ideas come to be associated by natural connections holding between them while other ideas come to be associated through custom (education, interests, etc.). Locke also argues that association can account for certain kinds of pathological thinking. For example, if one has a bad experience in a particular room, one might be unable to enter the room again without thinking of the experience. This is because the ideas of the room and the experience will have become inextricably associated.

John Stuart Mill (1806–1873) offers an associationist account that at first glance seems not to move beyond that of Locke. But Mill draws an interesting distinction between the ways factors can combine to yield an effect—specifically, how several mental representations ("ideas") can combine to yield another idea. If the effect is simply the additive sum of the individual causes (so that the effect is what would be had by applying the causes separately), Mill calls such a relation *mechanical*. But he holds that in some cases the effect resulting from combined causes is *more than* the contribution to be had from those causes individually—what he calls a *chemical* relation, or law, between a complex cause and its effect. The existence of such "chemical laws" has an important consequence for a theory of association: whereas direct introspection of some ideas (for example, of an orange) reveals the more basic ideas it has as constituents, with other ideas (e.g., of shape, or extension) first-person examination of the idea *does not reveal the parts* that go to make up that idea. (In fact, since the complex idea in this case is not a simple sum of the contributing ideas, Mill prefers to say that the various contributing ideas *generate* the complex idea, rather than simply constitute it.) Since the laws of association hold for these complex ideas, just as with simpler ones, Mill notes (with some reservation) that even when associated ideas seem quite different, the association can be appealed to as evidence that the subsequent idea is chemically "composed" of the earlier "parts."

William James (1842–1910) gives a helpful survey of work in associationist psychology and addresses two very important issues: the question of whether any general associative principle might underlie the proposed associationist laws, and the question of whether neural mechanisms underlie associationist psychology. James thus anticipates those contemporary philosophers who take connectionism to be grounded in neural mechanisms.

We begin the contemporary debate with an introduction by James McClelland, David Rumelhart, and Geoffrey Hinton of a version of connectionism known as *parallel distributed processing* (PDP). Although these writers do not make explicit reference to the early associationist psychologists, it is clear that they share certain fundamental views. In PDP models of memory, for example, properties might be associated with mutually excitatory units (processors). So, if a unit representing René Descartes were activated, there might be a corresponding excitation of a unit representing the property of *being a philosopher*, or the property of *being French*. The connection strengths between units within the network are set by training the network with a general learning algorithm that may be considered a descendant of the principles first enunciated by Locke, Hume, and subsequent associationists.

The PDP perspective stands in marked contrast to what is sometimes called the classical theory of computation, in which computation consists of formal operations on complex syntactic objects. For example, on the classical view the inference from the sentence P&Q to the sentence P is executed by a formal mechanism sensitive only to the syntactic (grammatical) form of P&Q. Jerry Fodor and Zenon Pylyshyn take strong exception to the PDP paradigm, suggesting that there are several reasons for preferring the classical theory. They argue that PDP models, by giving up structure-sensitive processes, give up as well the ability to account for a number of phenomena including (i) the *productivity* of human linguistic processes (i.e., the ability to create and comprehend sentences of unbounded length like "This is the cat that ate the rat that lived in the house that ..."); (ii) *systematicity* (the ability to understand "Jack likes Jill" is always accompanied by the ability to understand "Jill likes Jack"); (iii) *compositionality* (the meaning of a sentence is a function of the meaning of its parts); and (iv) *inferential coherence* (inferences from, e.g., P&Q to P). In general, they argue, connectionist models are bound to fall before one of these two problems: *either* the system will be so weak (through lack of productivity and systematicity) that it cannot accurately model and explain the features of human cognition; *or*, if it does have all these features (and thus mirrors the classical theory of mind), it will count as a mere *implementation* (instantiation) of the classical model of the mind, providing no alternative (or challenge) to the classical model.

In his response to Fodor and Pylyshyn, Paul Smolensky stresses the paradoxical features of cognition: it can exhibit the "hard," rule-governed aspect, which they stress, but it also has a "soft" flexibility that a set of unbending rules fails to capture. Since the soft features seem biologically prior and more common, Smolensky recommends taking them as basic to cognition, and getting what cases of hard rules as do exist to arise as side effects, "emergent properties" of the soft system. Using a simple example, he argues that a connectionist system can exhibit a sort of constituent structure—for example, where a concept "coffee" is a cluster of microfeatures (such as "burnt smell," "brown liquid," "touching porcelain"), it can act as part of a larger concept "cup with coffee." But a somewhat different concept of coffee (with microfeature "touching metal," rather than "touching porcelain") may act as part of the representation "coffee in a can"—so that which cluster of microfeatures means "coffee" varies, depending on the larger concept it is a component of. What all the different context-dependent "coffee" representations have in common, Smolensky notes, is only a rough "family resemblance"; but this loose family of similar representations may *approximately* mirror the general, everyday concept of "coffee." While he admits that research into some of these topics is just getting started, Smolensky concludes that such microlevel representation can provide a sufficient approximation of ordinary, higher-level concepts, capturing the existing degree of "systematicity" that Fodor and Pylyshyn emphasize.

Jerry Fodor and Brian McLaughlin insist that the classical "language of thought" model can explain the systematicity of human cognition in a way not possible under Smolensky's proposals. Central to their criticism is the notion of a "classical constituent": a part of a larger whole that is present whenever that larger whole is. (The word "John," for instance, is a "classical constituent" of the sentence "John loves the girl," because whenever that sentence is present, the word "John" must be as well.) The classical model explains the systematicity of thought by assuming that larger symbols in a language of thought are composed of smaller ones (just as "John" is a part of "John loves the girl"), and that these constituent symbols exert causal effects on the behavior of the larger whole. By contrast, while the overall activation vector of Smolensky's network can be *mathematically* analyzed into different components, these components won't be "classical constituents" exerting causal powers on the behavior of the network—Smolensky himself calls them "imaginary" components, emphasizing that they are not actual parts of the network. Fodor and McLaughlin note, by analogy, that although the number 6 can be mathematically analyzed into the factors 3 and 2, these mathematical factors need not play any *causal* role in my thought about the number 6; and in the same way, they insist, the purely mathematical components of tensor analysis can't make any causal contribution in accounting for the systematicity of thought. The authors conclude that the connectionist systems Smolensky promotes will not be able to explain systematicity in the way the "language of thought" view can.

Tim van Gelder considers what might be the most important or "defining" features required for a viable alternative to the classical "computational theory of mind." That more traditional approach has typically been called "symbolic" computing, and alternatives to it such as connectionism have been dubbed "nonsymbolic"; but since the term "symbolic" has never been clearly defined, "nonsymbolic" likewise does not carve out a definite approach. Van Gelder finds appeal to "distributed" representations, as opposed to "symbolic," likewise unhelpful, until a clear understanding of "distributed" is made available. After an instructive survey of numerous key terms, van Gelder settles on two central candidates for what "distributed representation" might involve:

either *superposition* or *equipotentiality* of representation. *Superposition* involves having the same computational "unit" with several different contents—for example, having one holograph depicting several different scenes (each of which can be separately accessed and viewed), or a set of nodes in a connectionist network that represents several different objects. With superposed representations there is no limit to how many contents can be represented; but as more are added, each content degrades—for example, as more scenes are represented by the same holograph, each scene will be represented more poorly. (This permits the "graceful degradation" mentioned in connectionist theory.) *Equipotentiality* involves having a certain representation, R, where the parts of R have the same content as R itself. (Roughly: superposition involves one representation having two or more different contents, while equipotentiality involves subparts of a representation having the same content as the whole.) As van Gelder notes, getting clear on when we have a case equipotentiality involves a certain amount of judgment on the part of the viewer. In particular, *how clearly* each part has to represent its content, in order to count as having the *same* content as the whole—rather than just something vaguely similar—depends on our interests.

The fact that superposition is not interest-sensitive in this way is, for van Gelder, one advantage it offers over equipotentiality, in terms of providing a clear interpretation of "distributed" representation. But he cites several other advantages of superposed representation as well: it provides a powerful means of representation that fits most of the favored examples of distributed representation from computing, optics, and psychology; and it makes clear the difference between distributed and local representations. Moreover, van Gelder argues that superposed representation, as a model of human cognition, is faithful to the details of neural networks, yet general enough to be implemented in various ways—thus providing the more general and abstract level of computing called for by the classical computational theory of mind. (As evidence of this generality, he cites research on memory that makes use of distributed representations, without ever specifying any concrete implementation for those representations.) Reading "distributed representation" in this way, van Gelder suggests, provides it with a means of avoiding the criticism that connectionism systems are mere "implementation" models.

William Ramsey, Stephen Stich, and Joseph Garon consider possible implications of connectionist theory for the mind–body problem—in particular, whether connectionist theory, if it does provide an accurate model of human cognition, also provides evidence in favor of eliminative materialism (discussed by Paul Churchland in chapter 16). The authors argue that connectionism proposes to explain the same domain of evidence handled by our commonsense psychology of beliefs, desires, and other "propositional attitudes"; and although they concede that in some cases of theory-change objects from the older theory are retained, or reduced, they deny this will be a possibility for commonsense psychology. Beliefs, desires, and the like are ordinarily taken to be *functionally discrete* (distinct objects, separable from one another); *semantically interpretable* (each having its own meaning); and *playing distinct causal roles* in the workings of the mind. For instance, a desire for coffee and a desire to talk to a friend are ordinarily taken to be different mental objects, with different mental content, and playing different roles in, for example, the causation of action. But because the representations in connectionist systems are distributed over numerous activation units, with internal "hidden units" having no clear symbolic interpretation, they seem to exhibit nothing like the discrete, interpretable objects of commonsense psychology. So the authors offer a conditional conclusion: while they cannot be sure that such connectionist systems will ultimately account for human cognition, they hold that *if* connectionism does prove successful, then eliminative materialism will be true, and traditional psychological objects such as beliefs and desires will turn out not to exist.

Further Reading

The following five texts provide classical works in associationist psychology.

David Hartley, *Observations on Man, His Frame, His Duty, and His Expectations* (London: 1749).

James Mill, *Analysis of the Phenomena of the Human Mind* (London: 1829).

E. L. Thorndike, *Connectionism* (New York: Macmillan, 1940).

C. O. Hebb, *The Organization of Behavior* (New York: John Wiley, 1949).

G. Mandler and J. Mandler, eds., *Thinking: From Association to Gestalt* (New York: John Wiley, 1964).

The current debate over connectionism is explored in the following five works.

Marvin Minsky and Seymour Papert, *Perceptrons*, expanded edition (Cambridge, Mass.: MIT Press, 1986).

David Rumelhart, James McClelland, and the PDP Research Group, *Parallel Distributed Processing*, 2 volumes (Cambridge, Mass.: MIT Press, 1986).

William Bechtel and A. Abrahamson, *Connectionism and the Mind: An Introduction to Parallel Processing Networks* (Oxford: Basil Blackwell, 1990).

Terence Horgan and John Tienson, eds., *Connectionism and the Philosophy of Mind* (Dordrecht: Kluwer, 1991).

William Ramsey, Stephen Stich, and David E. Rumelhart, *Philosophy and Connectionist Theory* (Hillsdale, N.J.: Lawrence Erlbaum, 1991).

A connectionist approach to the topic of innatism is presented in J. L. Elman, E. A. Bates, A. Karmiloff-Smith, D. Parisi, and K. Plunkett, *Rethinking Innateness: A Connectionist Perspective on Development* (Cambridge, Mass.: MIT Press, 1996).

74 From *Leviathan*

Thomas Hobbes

By *consequence,* or *train of thoughts,* I understand that succession of one thought to another, which is called, to distinguish it from discourse in words, *mental discourse.*

When a man thinks on any thing whatsoever, his next thought after, is not altogether so casual as it seems to be. Not every thought to every thought succeeds indifferently. But as we have no imagination, whereof we have not formerly had sense, in whole, or in parts; so we have no transition from one imagination to another, whereof we never had the like before in our senses. The reason whereof is this. All fancies are motions within us, relics of those made in the sense: and those motions that immediately succeeded one another in the sense, continue also together after sense: insomuch as the former coming again to take place, and be predominant, the latter follows, by coherence of the matter moved, in such manner, as water upon a plane table is drawn which way any one part of it is guided by the finger. But because in sense, to one and the same thing perceived, sometimes one thing, sometimes another succeeds, it comes to pass in time, that in the imagining of any thing, there is no certainty what we shall imagine next; only this is certain, it shall be something that succeeded the same before, at one time or another.

Train of Thoughts Unguided

This train of thoughts, or mental discourse, is of two sorts. The first is *unguided, without design,* and inconstant; wherein there is no passionate thought, to govern and direct those that follow, to itself, as the end and scope of some desire, or other passion: in which case the thoughts are said to wander, and seem impertinent one to another, as in a dream. Such are commonly the thoughts of men, that are not only without company, but also without care of any thing; though even then their thoughts are as busy as at other times, but without harmony; as the sound which a lute out of tune would yield to any man; or in tune, to one that could not play. And yet in this wild ranging of the mind, a man may oft-times perceive the way of it, and the dependence of one thought upon another. For in a discourse of our present civil war, what could seem more impertinent, than to ask, as one did, what was the value of a Roman penny? Yet the coherence to me was manifest enough. For the thought of the war, introduced the thought of the delivering up the king to his enemies; the thought of that, brought in the thought of the delivering up of Christ; and that again the thought of the thirty pence, which was the price of that treason; and thence easily followed that malicious question, and all this in a moment of time; for thought is quick.

Train of Thoughts Regulated

The second is more constant; as being *regulated* by some desire, and design. For the impression made by such things as we desire, or fear, is strong, and permanent, or, if it cease for a time, of quick return: so strong it is sometimes, as to hinder and break our sleep. From desire, arises the thought of some means we have seen produce the like of that which we aim at; and from the thought of that, the thought of means to that mean; and so continually, till we come to some beginning within our own power. And because the end, by the greatness of the impression, comes often to mind, in case our thoughts begin to wander, they are quickly again reduced into the way: which observed by one of the seven wise men, made him give men this precept, which is now worn out, *Respice finem*; that is to say, in all your actions, look often upon what you would have, as the thing that directs all your thoughts in the way to attain it.

Remembrance

The train of regulated thoughts is of two kinds; one, when of an effect imagined we seek the causes, or means that produce it: and this is common to man and beast. The other is, when imagining any thing whatsoever, we seek all the possible effects, that can by it be produced; that is to say, we imagine what we can do with it, when we have it. Of which I have not at any time seen any sign, but in man only; for this is a curiosity hardly incident to the nature of any living creature that has no other passion but sensual, such as are hunger, thirst, lust, and anger. In sum, the discourse of the mind, when it is governed by design, is nothing but *seeking*, or the faculty of invention, which the Latins called *sagacitas*, and *solertia*; a hunting out of the causes, of some effect, present or past; or of the effects, of some present or past cause. Sometimes a man seeks what he has lost; and from that place, and time, wherein he misses it, his mind runs back, from place to place, and time to time, to find where, and when he had it; that is to say, to find some certain, and limited time and place, in which to begin a method of seeking. Again, from thence, his thoughts run over the same places and times, to find what action, or other occasion might make him lose it. This we call *remembrance*, or calling to mind: the Latins call it *reminiscentia*, as it were a *re-conning* of our former actions.

Sometimes a man knows a place determinate, within the compass whereof he is to seek; and then his thoughts run over all the parts thereof, in the same manner as one would sweep a room, to find a jewel; or as a spaniel ranges the field, till he find a scent; or as a man should run over the alphabet, to start a rhyme.

Prudence

Sometimes a man desires to know the event of an action; and then he thinks of some like action past, and the events thereof one after another; supposing like events will follow like actions. As he that foresees what will become of a criminal, re-cons what he has seen follow on the like crime before; having this order of thoughts, the crime, the officer, the prison, the judge, and the gallows. Which kind of thoughts, is called *foresight*, and *prudence*, or *providence*; and sometimes *wisdom*; though such conjecture, through the difficulty of observing all circumstances, be very fallacious. But this is certain; by how much one man has more experience of things past, than another, by so much also he is more prudent, and his expectations the seldomer fail him. The *present* only has a being in nature; things *past* have a being in the memory only, but things *to come* have no being at all; the *future* being but a fiction of the mind, applying the sequels of actions past, to the actions that are present; which with most certainty is done by him that has most experience, but not with certainty enough. And though it be called prudence, when the event answers our expectation; yet in its own nature, it is but presumption. For the foresight of things to come, which is providence, belongs only to him by whose will they are to come. From him only, and supernaturally, proceeds prophecy. The best prophet naturally is the best guesser; and the best guesser, he that is most versed and studied in the matters he guesses at: for he has most *signs* to guess by.

Signs

A *sign* is the evident antecedent of the consequent; and contrarily, the consequent of the antecedent, when the like consequences have been observed, before: and the oftener they have been observed, the less uncertain is the sign. And therefore he that has most experience in any kind of business, has most signs, whereby to guess at the future time; and consequently is the most prudent: and so much more prudent than he that is new in that kind of business, as not to be equalled by any advantage of natural and extemporary wit: though perhaps many young men think the contrary.

Nevertheless it is not prudence that distinguisheth man from beast. There be beasts, that at a year old observe more, and pursue that which is for their good, more prudently, than a child can do at ten.

Conjecture of the Time Past

As prudence is a *presumption* of the *future*, contracted from the *experience* of time *past*: so there is a presumption of things past taken from other things, not future, but past also. For he that hath seen by what courses and degrees a flourishing state hath first come into civil war, and then to ruin; upon the sight of the ruins of any other state, will guess, the like war, and the like courses have been there also. But this conjecture, has the same uncertainty almost with the conjecture of the future; both being grounded only upon experience.

There is no other act of man's mind, that I can remember, naturally planted in him, so as to need no other thing, to the exercise of it, but to be born a man, and live with the use of his five senses. Those other faculties, of which I shall speak by and by, and which seem proper to man only, are acquired and increased by study and industry; and of most men learned by instruction, and discipline; and proceed all from the invention of words, and speech. For besides sense, and thoughts, and the train of thoughts, the mind of man has no other motion; though by the help of speech, and method, the same faculties may be improved to such a height, as to distinguish men from all other living creatures.

Infinite

Whatsoever we imagine is *finite*. Therefore there is no idea, or conception of any thing we call *infinite*. No man can have in his mind an image of infinite magnitude; nor conceive infinite swiftness, infinite time, or infinite force, or infinite power. When we say any thing is infinite, we signify only, that we are not able to conceive the ends, and bounds of the things named; having no conception of the thing, but of our own inability. And therefore the name of God is used, not to make us conceive him, for he is incomprehensible; and his greatness, and power are unconceivable; but that we may honour him. Also because, whatsoever, as I said before, we conceive, has been perceived first by sense, either all at once, or by parts; a man can have no thought, representing any thing, not subject to sense. No man therefore can conceive any thing, but he must conceive it in some place; and endued with some determinate magnitude; and which may be divided into parts; nor that any thing is all in this place, and all in another place at the same time; nor that two, or more things can be in one, and the same place at once: for none of these things ever have, nor can be incident to sense; but are absurd speeches, taken upon credit, without any signification at all, from deceived philosophers, and deceived, or deceiving Schoolmen.

75 From *An Essay Concerning Human Understanding*

John Locke

There is scarce any one that does not observe something that seems odd to him, and is in it self really Extravagant in the Opinions, Reasonings, and Actions of other Men. The least flaw of this kind, if at all different from his own, every one is quick-sighted enough to espie in another, and will by the Authority of Reason forwardly condemn, though he be guilty of much greater Unreasonableness in his own Tenets and Conduct, which he never perceives, and will very hardly, if at all, be convinced of.

This proceeds not wholly from Self-love, though that has often a great hand in it. Men of fair Minds, and not given up to the over weening of Self-flattery, are frequently guilty of it; and in many Cases one with amazement hears the Arguings, and is astonish'd at the Obstinacy of a worthy Man, who yields not to the Evidence of Reason, though laid before him as clear as Day-light.

This sort of Unreasonableness is usually imputed to Education and Prejudice, and for the most part truly enough, though that reaches not the bottom of the Disease, nor shews distinctly enough whence it rises, or wherein it lies. Education is often rightly assigned for the Cause, and Prejudice is a good general Name for the thing it self: But yet, I think, he ought to look a little farther who would trace this sort of Madness to the root it springs from, and so explain it, as to shew whence this flaw has its Original in very sober and rational Minds, and wherein it consists.

I shall be pardon'd for calling it by so harsh a name as *Madness*, when it is considered, that opposition to Reason deserves that Name, and is really Madness; and there is scarce a Man so free from it, but that if he should always on all occasions argue or do as in some cases he constantly does, would not be thought fitter for *Bedlam*, than Civil Conversation. I do not here mean when he is under the power of an unruly Passion, but in the steady calm course of his Life. That which will yet more apologize for this harsh Name, and ungrateful Imputation on the greatest part of Mankind is, that enquiring a little by the bye into the Nature of Madness, I found it to spring from the very same Root, and to depend on the very same Cause we are here speaking of. This consideration of the thing it self, at a time when I thought not the least on the Subject which I am now treating of, suggested it to me. And if this be a Weakness to which all Men are so liable; if this be a Taint which so universally infects Mankind, the greater care should be taken to lay it open under its due Name, thereby to excite the greater care in its Prevention and Cure.

Some of our *Ideas* have a natural Correspondence and Connexion one with another: It is the Office and Excellency of our Reason to trace these, and hold them together in that Union and Correspondence which is founded in their peculiar Beings. Besides this there is another Connexion of *Ideas* wholly owing to Chance or Custom; *Ideas* that in themselves are not at all of kin, come to be so united in some Mens Minds, that 'tis very hard to separate them, they always keep in company, and the one no sooner at any time comes into the Understanding but its Associate appears with it; and if they are more than two which are thus united, the whole gang always inseparable shew themselves together.

This strong Combination of *Ideas*, not ally'd by Nature, the Mind makes in it self either voluntarily, or by chance, and hence it comes in different Men to be very different, according to their different Inclinations, Educations, Interests, *etc.* Custom settles habits of Thinking in the Understanding, as well as of Determining in the Will, and of Motions in the Body; all which seems to be but Trains of Motion in the Animal Spirits, which once set a going continue on in the same steps they have been used to, which by often treading are worn into a smooth path, and the Motion in it becomes easy and as it were Natural. As far as we can comprehend Thinking, thus *Ideas* seem to be produced in our Minds; or if they are not, this may serve to explain their following one another in an habitual train, when once they are put into that tract, as well as it does to explain such Motions of the Body. A Musician used to any Tune will find that let it but once begin in his Head, the *Ideas* of the several Notes of it will follow one another orderly in his Understanding without any care or attention, as regularly as his Fingers move orderly over the Keys of the Organ to play out the Tune he has begun, though his unattentive Thoughts be elsewhere a wandering. Whether the natural cause of these *Ideas*, as well as of that regular Dancing of his Fingers be the Motion of his Animal Spirits, I will not determine, how probable soever by this Instance it appears to be so: But this may help us a little to conceive of Intellectual Habits, and of the tying together of *Ideas*.

That there are such Associations of them made by Custom in the Minds of most Men, I think no Body will question who has well consider'd himself or others; and to this, perhaps, might be justly attributed most of the Sympathies and Antipathies observable in Men, which work as strongly, and produce as regular Effects as if they were Natural, and are therefore called so, though they at first had no other Original but the accidental Connexion of two *Ideas*, which either the strength of the first Impression, or future Indulgence so united, that they always afterwards kept company together in that Man's Mind, as if they were but one *Idea*. I say most of the Antipathies, I do not say all, for some of them are truly Natural, depend upon our original Constitution, and are born with us; but a great part of those which are counted Natural, would have been known to be from unheeded, though, perhaps, early Impressions, or wanton Phancies at first, which would have been acknowledged the Original of them if they had been warily observed. A grown Person surfeiting with Honey, no sooner hears the Name of it, but his Phancy immediately carries Sickness and Qualms to his Stomach, and he cannot bear the very *Idea* of it; other *Ideas* of Dislike and Sickness, and Vomiting presently accompany it, and he is disturb'd, but he knows from whence to date this Weakness, and can tell how he got this Indisposition: Had this happen'd to him, by an over dose of Honey, when a Child, all the same Effects would have followed, but the Cause would have been mistaken, and the Antipathy counted Natural.

I mention this not out of any great necessity there is in this present Argument, to distinguish nicely between Natural and Acquired Antipathies, but I take notice of it for another purpose, (*viz.*) that those who have Children, or the charge of their Education, would think it worth their while diligently to watch, and carefully to prevent the undue Connexion of *Ideas* in the Minds of young People. This is the time most susceptible of lasting Impressions, and though those relating to the Health of the Body, are by discreet People minded and fenced against, yet I am apt to doubt, that those which relate more peculiarly to the Mind, and terminate in the Understanding, or Passions, have been much less heeded than the thing deserves; nay, those relating purely to the Understanding have, as I suspect, been by most Men wholly over-look'd.

This wrong Connexion in our Minds of *Ideas* in themselves, loose and independent one of another, has such an influence, and is of so great force to set us awry in our Actions, as well Moral as Natural, Passions, Reasonings, and Notions themselves, that, perhaps, there is not any one thing that deserves more to be looked after.

The *Ideas* of *Goblines* and *Sprights* have really no more to do with Darkness than Light; yet let but a foolish Maid inculcate these often on the Mind of a Child, and raise them there together, possibly he shall never be able to separate them again so long as he lives, but Darkness shall ever afterwards bring with it those frightful *Ideas*, and they shall be so joined that he can no more bear the one than the other.

A Man receives a sensible Injury from another, thinks on the Man and that Action over and over, and by ruminating on them strongly, or much in his Mind, so cements those two *Ideas* together, that he makes them almost one; never thinks on the Man, but the Pain and Displeasure he suffered comes into his Mind with it, so that he scarce distinguishes them, but has as much an aversion for the one as the other. Thus Hatreds are often begotten from slight and almost innocent Occasions, and Quarrels propagated and continued in the World.

A Man has suffered Pain or Sickness in any Place, he saw his Friend die in such a Room; though these have in Nature nothing to do one with another, yet when the *Idea* of the Place occurs to his Mind, it brings (the Impression being once made) that of the Pain and Displeasure with it, he confounds them in his Mind, and can as little bear the one as the other.

When this Combination is settled and whilst it lasts, it is not in the power of Reason to help us, and relieve us from the Effects of it. *Ideas* in our Minds, when they are there, will operate according to their Natures and Circumstances; and here we see the cause why Time cures certain Affections, which Reason, though in the right, and allow'd to be so, has not power over, nor is able against them to prevail with those who are apt to hearken to it in other cases. The Death of a Child, that was the daily delight of his Mother's Eyes, and joy of her Soul, rends from her Heart the whole comfort of her Life, and gives her all the torment imaginable; use the Consolations of Reason in this case, and you were as good preach Ease to one on the Rack, and hope to allay, by rational Discourses, the Pain of his Joints tearing asunder. Till time has by disuse separated the sense of that Enjoyment and its loss from the *Idea* of the Child returning to her Memory, all Representations, though never so reasonable, are in vain; and therefore some in whom the union between these *Ideas* is never dissolved, spend their Lives in Mourning, and carry an incurable Sorrow to their Graves.

A Friend of mine knew one perfectly cured of Madness by a very harsh and offensive Operation. The Gentleman, who was thus recovered, with great sense of Gratitude and Acknowledgment, owned the Cure all his Life after, as the greatest Obligation he could have received; but whatever Gratitude and Reason suggested to him, he could never bear the sight of the Operator: That Image brought back with it the *Idea* of that Agony which he suffer'd from his Hands, which was too mighty and intolerable for him to endure.

Many Children imputing the Pain they endured at School to their Books they were corrected for, so joyn those *Ideas* together, that a Book becomes their Aversion, and they are never reconciled to the study and use of them all their Lives after; and thus Reading becomes a torment to them, which otherwise possibly they might have made the great Pleasure of their Lives. There are Rooms convenient enough, that some Men cannot Study in, and fashions of Vessels, which though never so clean and commodious they cannot Drink out of, and that by reason of some accidental *Ideas* which are annex'd to them, and make them offensive; and who is there that hath not observed some Man to flag at the appearance, or in the company of some certain Person not otherwise superior to him, but because having once on some occasion got the Ascendant, the *Idea* of Authority and Distance goes along with that of the Person, and he that has been thus subjected is not able to separate them.

76 From *A System of Logic*

John Stuart Mill

The subject, then, of Psychology is the uniformities of succession, the laws, whether ultimate or derivative, according to which one mental state succeeds another—is caused by, or at least is caused to follow, another. Of these laws, some are general, others more special. The following are examples of the most general laws.

First, whenever any state of consciousness has once been excited in us, no matter by what cause, an inferior degree of the same state of consciousness, a state of consciousness resembling the former, but inferior in intensity, is capable of being reproduced in us, without the presence of any such cause as excited it at first. Thus, if we have once seen or touched an object, we can afterwards think of the object though it be absent from our sight or from our touch. If we have been joyful or grieved at some event, we can think of or remember our past joy or grief, though no new event of a happy or painful nature has taken place. When a poet has put together a mental picture of an imaginary object, a Castle of Indolence, a Una, or a Hamlet, he can afterwards think of the ideal object he has created without any fresh act of intellectual combination. This law is expressed by saying, in the language of Hume, that every mental *impression* has its *idea*.

Secondly, these ideas, or secondary mental states, are excited by our impressions, or by other ideas, according to certain laws which are called Laws of Association. Of these laws the first is, that similar ideas tend to excite one another. The second is, that when two impressions have been frequently experienced (or even thought of), either simultaneously or in immediate succession, then whenever one of these impressions, or the idea of it, recurs, it tends to excite the idea of the other. The third law is, that greater intensity in either or both of the impressions is equivalent, in rendering them excitable by one another, to a greater frequency of conjunction. These are the laws of ideas, on which I shall not enlarge in this place, but refer the reader to works professedly psychological, in particular to Mr. James Mill's *Analysis of the Phenomena of the Human Mind*, where the principal laws of association, along with many of their applications, are copiously exemplified, and with masterly hand.[1]

These simple or elementary Laws of Mind have been ascertained by the ordinary methods of experimental inquiry; nor could they have been ascertained in any other manner. But a certain number of elementary laws having thus been obtained, it is a fair subject of scientific inquiry how far those laws can be made to go in explaining the actual phenomena. It is obvious that complex laws of thought and feeling not only may, but must be generated from these simple laws. And it is to be remarked that the case is not always one of Composition of Causes: the effect of concurring causes is not always precisely the sum of the effects of those causes when separate, nor even always an effect of the same kind with them. Reverting to the distinction which occupies so prominent a place in the theory of induction, the laws of the phenomena of mind are sometimes analogous to mechanical, but sometimes also to chemical laws. When many impressions or ideas are operating in the mind together, there sometimes takes place a process of a similar kind to chemical combination. When impressions have been so often experienced in conjunction that each of them calls up readily and instantaneously the ideas of the whole group, those ideas sometimes melt and coalesce into one another, and appear not several ideas, but one, in the same manner as, when the seven prismatic colours are presented to the eye in rapid succession the sensation produced is that of white. But as in this last case it is correct to say that the seven colours when they rapidly follow one another *generate* white, but not that they actually *are* white; so it appears to me that the Complex Idea, formed by the blending together of several simpler ones, should, when it really appears simple, (that is, when the separate elements are not consciously distinguishable in it,) be said to *result from*, or *be generated by*, the simple ideas, not to *consist* of them. Our idea of an orange really *consists* of the simple ideas of a certain colour, a certain form, a certain taste and smell, etc., because we can, by interrogating our consciousness, perceive all these elements in the idea. But we cannot perceive, in so apparently simple a feeling as our perception of the shape of an object by the eye, all that multitude of ideas derived from other senses, without which it is well ascertained that no such visual perception would ever have had existence; nor, in our idea of Extension, can we discover those elementary ideas of resistance derived from our muscular frame in which it had been conclusively shown that the idea originates. These, therefore, are cases of mental chemistry, in which it is proper to say that the simple ideas generate, rather than that they compose, the complex ones.

With respect to all the other constituents of the mind, its beliefs, its abstruser conceptions, its sentiments, emotions, and volitions, there are some (among whom are Hartley and the author of the *Analysis*) who think that the whole of these are generated from simple ideas of sensation by a chemistry similar to that which we have just exemplified. These philosophers have made out a great part of their case, but I am not satisfied that they have established the whole of it. They have shown that there is such a thing as mental chemistry; that the heterogeneous nature of a feeling A, considered in relation to B and C, is no conclusive argument against its being generated from B and C. Having proved this, they proceed to show that where A is found B and C were or may have been present; and why, therefore, they ask, should not A have been generated from B and C? But even if this evidence were carried to the highest degree of completeness which it admits of; if it were shown (which hitherto it has not, in all cases, been) that certain groups of associated ideas not only might have been, but actually were present whenever the more recondite mental feeling was experienced, this would amount only to the Method of Agreement, and could not prove causation until confirmed by the more conclusive evidence of the Method of Difference. If the question be whether Belief is a mere case of close association of ideas, it would be necessary to examine experimentally if it be true that any ideas whatever, provided they are associated with the required degree of closeness, give rise to belief. If the inquiry be into the origin of moral feelings, the feeling, for example, of moral reprobation, it is necessary to compare all the varieties of actions or states of mind which are ever morally disapproved, and see whether in all these cases it can be shown, or reasonably surmised, that the action or state of mind had become connected by association, in the disapproving mind, with some particular class of hateful or disgusting ideas; and the method employed is, thus far, that of Agreement. But this is not enough. Supposing this proved, we must try further by the Method of Difference whether this particular kind of hateful or disgusting ideas, when it becomes associated with an action previously indifferent, will render that action a subject of moral disapproval. If this question can be answered in the affirmative, it is shown to be a law of the human mind that an association of that particular description is the generating cause of moral reprobation. That all this is the case has been rendered extremely probable, but the experiments have not been tried with the degree of precision necessary for a complete and absolutely conclusive induction.[2]

It is further to be remembered, that even if all which this theory of mental phenomena contends for could be proved, we should not be the more enabled to resolve the laws of the more complex feelings into those of the simpler ones. The generation of one class of mental phenomena from another, whenever it can be made out, is a highly interesting fact in psychological chemistry; but it no more supersedes the necessity of an experimental study of the generated phenomenon, than a knowledge of the properties of oxygen and sulphur enables us to deduce those of sulphuric acid without specific observation and experiment. Whatever, therefore, may be the final issue of the attempt to account for the origin of our judgments, our desires, or our volitions, from simpler mental phenomena, it is not the less imperative to ascertain the sequences of the complex phenomena themselves by special study in conformity to the canons of Induction. Thus, in respect to Belief, psychologists will always have to inquire what beliefs we have by direct consciousness, and according to what laws one belief produces another; what are the laws in virtue of which one thing is recognised by the mind, either rightly or erroneously, as evidence of another thing. In regard to Desire, they will have to examine what objects we desire naturally, and by what causes we are made to desire things originally indifferent, or even disagreeable to us; and so forth. It may be remarked, that the general laws of association prevail among these more intricate states of mind, in the same manner as among the simpler ones. A desire, an emotion, an idea of the higher order of abstraction, even our judgments and volitions when they have become habitual, are called up by association, according to precisely the same laws as our simple ideas.

Notes

1. When this chapter was written, Professor Bain had not yet published even the first part (*The Senses and the Intellect*) of his profound *Treatise on the Mind*. In this the laws of association have been more comprehensively stated and more largely exemplified than by any previous writer; and the work, having been completed by the publication of *The Emotions and the Will*, may now be referred to as incomparably the most complete analytical exposition of the mental phenomena, on the basis of a legitimate induction, which has yet been produced. More recently still, Mr. Bain has joined with me in appending to a new edition of the *Analysis* notes intended to bring up the analytic science of Mind to its latest improvements.

Many striking applications of the laws of association to the explanation of complex mental phenomena are also to be found in Mr. Herbert Spencer's *Principles of Psychology*.

2. In the case of the moral sentiments, the place of direct experiment is to a considerable extent supplied by historical experience, and we are able to trace with a tolerable approach to certainty the particular associations by which those sentiments are engendered. This has been attempted, so far as respects the sentiment of justice, in a little work by the present author, entitled *Utilitarianism*.

77 From *The Principles of Psychology*

William James

I shall try to show, in the pages which immediately follow, that there is no other *elementary* causal law of association than the law of neural habit. All the *materials* of our thought are due to the way in which one elementary process of the cerebral hemispheres tends to excite whatever other elementary process it may have excited at some former time. The number of elementary processes at work, however, and the nature of those which at any time are fully effective in rousing the others, determine the character of the total brain-action, and, as a consequence of this, they determine the object thought of at the time. According as this resultant object is one thing or another, we call it a product of association by contiguity or of association by similarity, or contrast, or whatever other sorts we may have recognized as ultimate. Its production, however, is, in each one of these cases, to be explained by a merely quantitative variation in the elementary brain-processes momentarily at work under the law of habit, so that *psychic* contiguity, similarity, etc., are derivatives of a single profounder kind of fact.

My thesis, stated thus briefly, will soon become more clear; and at the same time certain disturbing factors, which co-operate with the law of neural habit, will come to view.

Let us then assume as the *basis* of all our subsequent reasoning this law: *When two elementary brain-processes have been active together or in immediate succession, one of them, on reoccurring, tends to propagate its excitement into the other.*

But, as a matter of fact, every elementary process has found itself at different times excited in conjunction with *many* other processes, and this by unavoidable outward causes. Which of these others it shall awaken now becomes a problem. Shall *b* or *c* be aroused next by the present *a*? We must make a further postulate, based, however, on the fact of *tension* in nerve-tissue, and on the fact of summation of excitements, each incomplete or latent in itself, into an open resultant. The process *b*, rather than *c*, will awake, if in addition to the vibrating tract *a* some other tract *d* is in a state of sub-excitement, and formerly was excited with *b* alone and not with *a*. In short, we may say:

The amount of activity at any given point in the brain-cortex is the sum of the tendencies of all other points to discharge into it, such tendencies being proportionate (1) *to the number of times the excitement of each other point may have accompanied that of the point in question;* (2) *to the intensity of such excitements; and* (3) *to the absence of any rival point functionally disconnected with the first point, into which the discharges might be diverted.*

Expressing the fundamental law in this most complicated way leads to the greatest ultimate simplification. Let us, for the present, only treat of spontaneous trains of thought and ideation, such as occur in revery or musing. The case of voluntary thinking toward a certain end shall come up later.

Take, to fix our ideas, the two verses from "Locksley Hall":

"I, the heir of all *the ages* in the foremost files of time,"

and—

"For I doubt not through *the ages* one increasing purpose runs."

Why is it that when we recite from memory one of these lines, and get as far as *the ages*, that portion of the *other* line which follows, and, so to speak, sprouts out of *the ages*, does not also sprout out of our memory, and confuse the sense of our words? Simply because the word that follows *the ages* has its brain-process awakened not simply by the brain-process of *the ages* alone, but by it *plus* the brain-processes of all the words preceding *the ages*. The word *ages* at its moment of strongest activity would, *per se*, indifferently discharge into either "in" or "one." So would the previous words (whose tension is momentarily much less strong than that of *ages*) each of them indifferently discharge into either of a large number of other words with which they have been at different times combined. But when the processes of "*I, the heir of all the ages*," simultaneously vibrate in the brain, the last one of them in a maximal, the others in a fading phase of excitement; then the strongest line of discharge will be that which they *all alike* tend to take. "*In*" and not "*one*" or any other word will be the next to awaken, for its brain-process has previously vibrated in unison not only with that of *ages*, but with that of all those other words whose activity is dying away.

But if some one of these preceding words—"heir," for example—had an intensely strong association with some brain-tracts entirely disjoined in experience from the poem of "Locksley Hall"—if the reciter, for instance, were tremulously awaiting the opening of a will which might make him a millionaire—it is probable that the path of discharge through the words of the poem would be suddenly interrupted at the word "heir." His *emotional interest in that word* would be such that its *own special associations would prevail* over the combined ones of the other words. He would, as we say, be abruptly reminded of his personal situation, and the poem would lapse altogether from his thoughts.

The writer of these pages has every year to learn the names of a large number of students who sit in alphabetical order in a lecture-room. He finally learns to call them by name, as they sit in their accustomed places. On meeting one in the street, however, early in the year, the face hardly ever recalls the name, but it may recall the place of its owner in the lecture-room, his neighbors' faces, and consequently his general alphabetical position; and then, usually as the common associate of all these combined data, the student's name surges up in his mind.

A father wishes to show to some guests the progress of his rather dull child in Kindergarten instruction. Holding the knife upright on the table, he says, "What do you call that, my boy?" "I calls it a *knife*, I does," is the sturdy reply, from which the child cannot be induced to swerve by any alteration in the form of question, until the father recollecting that in the Kindergarten a pencil was used, and not a knife, draws a long one from his pocket, holds it in the same way, and then gets the wished-for answer, "I calls it *vertical*." All the concomitants of the Kindergarten experience had to recombine their effect before the word "vertical" could be reawakened.

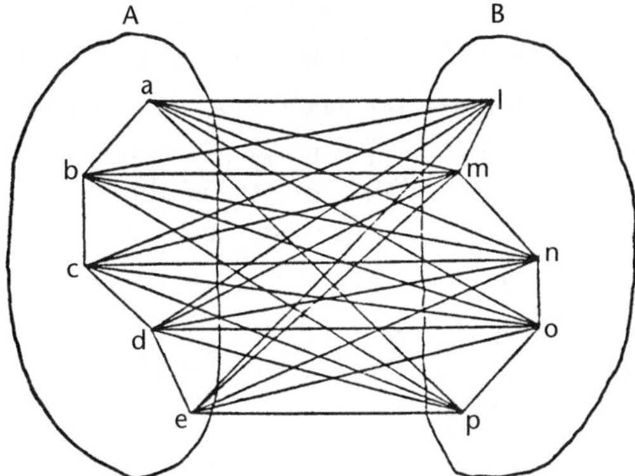

Figure 77.1

Impartial Redintegration

The ideal working of the law of compound association, were it unmodified by any extraneous influence, would be such as to keep the mind in a perpetual treadmill of concrete reminiscences from which no detail could be omitted. Suppose, for example, we begin by thinking of a certain dinner-party. The only thing which all the components of the dinner-party could combine to recall would be the first concrete occurrence which ensued upon it. All the details of this occurrence could in turn only combine to awaken the next following occurrence, and so on. If *a, b, c, d, e,* for instance, be the elementary nerve-tracts excited by the last act of the dinner-party, call this act A, and *l, m, n, o, p* be those of walking home through the frosty night, which we may call B, then the thought of A must awaken that of B, because *a, b, c, d, e,* will each and all discharge into *l* through the paths by which their original discharge took place. Similarly they will discharge into *m, n, o,* and *p;* and these latter tracts will also each reinforce the other's action because, in the experience B, they have already vibrated in unison. The lines in figure 77.1 symbolize the summation of discharges into each of the components of B, and the consequent strength of the combination of influences by which B in its totality is awakened.

Hamilton first used the word "redintegration" to designate all association. Such processes as we have just described might in an emphatic sense be termed redintegrations, for they would necessarily lead, if unobstructed, to the reinstatement in thought of the *entire* content of large trains of past experience. From this complete redintegration there could be no escape save through the irruption of some new and strong present impression of the senses, or through the excessive tendency of some one of the elementary brain-tracts to discharge independently into an aberrant quarter of the brain. Such was the tendency of the word "heir" in the verse from "Locksley Hall," which was our first example. How such tendencies are constituted we shall have soon to inquire with some care. Unless they are present, the panorama of the past, once opened, must unroll itself with fatal literality to the end, unless some outward sound, sight, or touch divert the current of thought.

Let us call this process *impartial redintegration.* Whether it ever occurs in an absolutely complete form is doubtful. We all immediately recognize, however, that in some minds there is a much greater tendency than in others for the flow of thought to take this form. Those insufferably garrulous old women, those dry and fanciless beings who spare you no detail, however petty, of the facts they are recounting, and upon the thread of whose narrative all the irrelevant items cluster as pertinaciously as the essential ones, the slaves of literal fact, the stumblers over the smallest abrupt step in thought, are figures known to all of us. Comic literature has made her profit out of them. Juliet's nurse is a classical example. George Eliot's village characters and some of Dickens's minor personages supply excellent instances.

Perhaps as successful a rendering as any of this mental type is the character of Miss Bates in Miss Austen's "Emma." Hear how she redintegrates:

"But where could *you* hear it?" cried Miss Bates. "Where could you possibly hear it, Mr. Knightley? For it is not five minutes since I received Mrs. Cole's note—no, it cannot be more than five—or at least ten—for I had got my bonnet and spencer on, just ready to come out—I was only gone down to speak to Patty again about the pork—Jane was standing in the passage—were not you, Jane?—for my mother was so afraid that we had not any salting-pan large enough. So I said I would go down and see, and Jane said: 'Shall I go down instead? for I think you have a little cold, and Patty has been washing the kitchen.' 'Oh, my dear,' said I—well, and just then came the note. A Miss Hawkins—that's all I know—a Miss Hawkins, of Bath. But, Mr. Knightley, how could you possibly have heard it? for the very moment Mr. Cole told Mrs. Cole of it, she sat down and wrote to me. A Miss Hawkins—"

But in every one of us there are moments when this complete reproduction of all the items of a past experience occurs. What are those moments? They are moments of emotional recall of the past as something which once was, but is gone forever—moments, the interest of which consists in the feeling that our self was once other than it now is. When this is the case, any detail, however minute, which will make the past picture more complete, will also have its effect in swelling that total contrast between *now* and *then* which forms the central interest of our contemplation.

Ordinary or Mixed Association

This case helps us to understand why it is that the ordinary spontaneous flow of our ideas does not follow the law of impartial redintegration. *In no revival of a past experience are all the items of our thought equally operative in determining what the next thought shall be. Always some ingredient is prepotent over the rest.* Its special suggestions or associations in this case will often be different from those which it has in common with the whole group of items; and its tendency to awaken these outlying associates will deflect the path of our revery. Just as in the original sensible experience our attention focalized itself upon a few of the impressions of the scene before us, so here in the reproduction of those impressions an equal partiality is shown, and some items are emphasized above the rest. What these items shall be is, in most cases of spontaneous revery, hard to determine beforehand. In subjective terms we say that *the prepotent items are those which appeal most to our* INTEREST.

Expressed in brain-terms, the law of interest will be: *some one brain-process is always prepotent above its concomitants in arousing action elsewhere.*

"Two processes," says Mr. Hodgson,[1] "are constantly going on in redintegration. The one a process of corrosion, melting, decay; the other a process of renewing, arising, becoming.... No object of representation remains long before consciousness in the same state, but fades, decays, and becomes indistinct. Those parts of the object, however, which possess an interest resist this tendency to gradual decay of the whole object.... This inequality in the object—some parts, the uninteresting, submitting to decay; others, the interesting parts, resisting it—when it has continued for a certain time, ends in becoming a new object."

Only where the interest is diffused equally over all the parts (as in the emotional memory just referred to, where, as all *past*, they all interest us alike) is this law departed from. It will be least obeyed by those minds which have the smallest variety and intensity of interests—those who, by the general flatness and poverty of their aesthetic nature, are kept forever rotating among the literal sequences of their local and personal history.

Most of us, however, are better organized than this, and our musings pursue an erratic course, swerving continually into some new direction traced by the shifting play of interest as it ever falls on some partial item in each complex representation that is evoked. Thus it so often comes about that we find ourselves thinking at two nearly adjacent moments of things separated by the whole diameter of space and time. Not till we carefully recall each step of our cogitation do we see how naturally we came by Hodgson's law to pass from one to the other. Thus, for instance, after looking at my clock just now (1879), I found myself thinking of a recent resolution in the Senate about our legal-tender notes. The clock called up the image of the man who had repaired its gong. He suggested the jeweller's shop where I had last seen him; that shop, some shirt-studs which I had bought there; they, the value of gold and its recent decline; the latter, the equal value of greenbacks, and this, naturally, the question of how long they were to last, and of the Bayard proposition. Each of these images offered various points of interest. Those which formed the turning-points of my thought are easily assigned. The gong was momentarily the most interesting part of the clock, because, from having begun with a beautiful tone, it had become discordant and aroused disappointment. But for this the clock might have suggested the friend who gave it to me, or any one of a thousand circumstances connected with clocks. The jeweller's shop suggested the studs, because they alone of all its contents were tinged with the egoistic interest of possession. This interest in the studs, their value, made me single out the material as its chief source, etc., to the end. Every reader who will arrest himself at any moment and say, "How came I to be thinking of just this?" will be sure to trace a train of representations linked together by lines of contiguity and points of interest inextricably combined. This is the ordinary process of the association of ideas as it spontaneously goes on in average minds. *We may call it* ORDINARY, *or* MIXED, ASSOCIATION.

Another example of it is given by Hobbes in a passage which has been quoted so often as to be classical:

In a discourse of our present civil war, what could seem more impertinent than to ask (as one did) what was the value of a Roman penny? Yet the coherence to me was manifest enough. For the thought of the war introduced the thought of the delivering up the King to his enemies; the thought of that brought in the thought of the delivering up of Christ; and that again the thought of the thirty pence, which was the price of that treason: and thence easily followed that malicious question; and all this in a moment of time; for thought is quick.[2]

Can we determine, now, when a certain portion of the going thought has, by dint of its interest, become so prepotent as to make its own exclusive associates the dominant features of the coming thought—can we, I say, determine *which* of its own associates shall be evoked? For they are many. As Hodgson says:

The interesting parts of the decaying object are free to combine again with any objects or parts of objects with which at any time they have been combined before. All the former combinations of these parts may come back into consciousness; one must; but which will?

Mr. Hodgson replies:

There can be but one answer: that which has been most *habitually* combined with them before. This new object begins at once to form itself in consciousness, and to group its parts round the part still remaining from the former object; part after part comes out and arranges itself in its old position; but scarcely has the process begun, when the original law of interest begins to operate on this new formation, seizes on the interesting parts and impresses them on the attention to the exclusion of the rest, and the whole process is repeated again with endless variety. I venture to propose this as a complete and true account of the whole process of redintegration.

In restricting the discharge from the interesting item into that channel which is simply most *habitual* in the sense of most frequent, Hodgson's account is assuredly imperfect. An image by no means always revives its most frequent associate, although frequency is certainly one of the most potent determinants of revival. If I abruptly utter the word *swallow*, the reader, if by habit an ornithologist, will think of a bird; if a physiologist or a medical specialist in throat diseases, he will think of deglutition. If I say *date*, he will, if a fruit-merchant or an Arabian traveller, think of the produce of the palm; if an habitual student of history, figures with A.D. or B.C. before them will rise in his mind. If I say *bed, bath, morning*, his own daily toilet will be invincibly suggested by the combined names of three of its habitual associates. But frequent lines of transition are often set at naught. The sight of C. Göring's "*System der kritischen Philosophie*" has most frequently awakened in me thoughts of the opinions therein propounded. The idea of suicide has never been connected with the volumes. But a moment since, as my eye fell upon them, suicide was the thought that flashed into my mind. Why? Because but yesterday I received a letter from Leipzig informing me that this philosopher's recent death by drowning was an act of self-destruction. Thoughts tend, then, to awaken their most recent as well as their most habitual associates. This is a matter of notorious experience, too notorious, in fact, to need illustration. If we have seen our friend this morning, the mention of his name now recalls the circumstances of that interview, rather than any more remote details concerning him. If Shakespeare's plays are mentioned, and we were last night reading "Richard II," vestiges of that play rather than of "Hamlet" or "Othello" float through our mind. Excitement of peculiar tracts, or peculiar modes of general excitement in the brain, leave a sort of tenderness or exalted sensibility behind them which takes days to die away. As long as it lasts, those tracts or those modes are liable to have their activities awakened by causes which at other times might leave them in repose. Hence, *recency* in experience is a prime factor in determining revival in thought.

Vividness in an original experience may also have the same effect as habit or recency in bringing about likelihood of revival. If we have once witnessed an execution, any subsequent conversation or reading about capital punishment will almost certainly suggest images of that particular scene. Thus it is that events lived through only once, and in youth, may come in after-years, by reason of their exciting quality or emotional intensity, to serve as types or instances used by our mind to illustrate any and every occurring topic whose interest is most remotely pertinent to theirs. If a man in his boyhood once talked with Napoleon, any mention of great men or historical events, battles or thrones, or the whirligig of fortune, or islands in the ocean, will be apt to draw to his lips the incidents of that one memorable interview. If the word *tooth* now suddenly appears on the page before the reader's eye, there are fifty chances out of a hundred that, if he gives it time to awaken any image, it will be an image of some operation of dentistry in which he has been the sufferer. Daily he has touched his teeth and masticated with them; this very morning he brushed them, chewed his breakfast and picked them; but the rarer and remoter associations arise more promptly because they were so much more intense.

A fourth factor in tracing the course of reproduction is *congruity in emotional tone* between the reproduced idea and our mood. The same objects do not recall the same associates when we are cheerful as when we are melancholy. Nothing, in fact, is more striking than our utter inability to keep up trains of joyous imagery when we are depressed in spirits. Storm, darkness, war, images of disease, poverty, and perishing afflict unremittingly the imaginations of melancholiacs. And those of sanguine temperament, when their spirits are high, find it impossible to give any permanence to evil forebodings or to gloomy thoughts. In an instant the train of association dances off to flowers and sunshine, and images of spring and hope. The records of Arctic or African travel perused in one mood awaken no thoughts but those of horror at the malignity of Nature; read at another time they suggest only enthusiastic reflections on the indomitable power and pluck of man. Few novels so overflow with joyous animal spirits as "The Three Guardsmen" of Dumas. Yet it may awaken in the mind of a reader depressed with sea-sickness (as the writer can personally testify) a most dismal and woeful consciousness of the cruelty and carnage of which heroes like Athos, Porthos, and Aramis make themselves guilty.

Habit, recency, vividness, and emotional congruity are, then, all reasons why one representation rather than another should be awakened by the interesting portion of a departing thought. We may say with truth that *in the majority of cases the coming representation will have been either habitual, recent, or vivid, and will be congruous*. If all these qualities unite in any one absent associate, we may predict almost infallibly that that associate of the going thought will form an important ingredient in the coming thought. In spite of the fact, however, that the succession of representations is thus redeemed from perfect indeterminism and limited to a few classes whose characteristic quality is fixed by the nature of our past experience, it must still be confessed that an immense number of terms in the linked chain of our representations fall outside of all assignable rule. Take the instance of the clock. Why did the jeweller's shop suggest the shirt-studs rather than a chain which I had bought there more recently, which had cost more, and whose sentimental associations were much more interesting? Both chain and studs had excited brain-tracts simultaneously with the shop. The only reason why the nerve-stream from the shop-tract switched off into the stud-tract rather than into the chain-tract must be that the stud-tract happened at that moment to lie more open, either because of some accidental alteration in its nutrition or because the incipient sub-conscious tensions of the brain as a whole had so distributed their equilibrium that it was more unstable here than in the chain-tract. Any reader's introspection will easily furnish similar instances. It thus remains true that to a certain extent, even in those forms of ordinary mixed association which lie nearest to impartial redintegration, *which* associate of the interesting item shall emerge must be called largely a matter of accident—accident, that is, for our intelligence. No doubt it is determined by cerebral causes, but they are too subtle and shifting for our analysis.

Notes

1. *Time and Space,* p. 266. Compare Coleridge: "The true practical general law of association is this: that whatever makes certain parts of a total impression more vivid or distinct than the rest will determine the mind to recall these, in preference to others equally linked together by the common condition of contemporaeity or of *contiguity*. But the will itself, by confining and intensifying the attention, may arbitrarily give vividness or distinctness to any object whatsoever" (*Biographia Litteraria,* Chap. V.).

2. *Leviathan,* pt. I, chap. III [chap. 74 in this volume].

78 The Appeal of Parallel Distributed Processing

James L. McClelland, David E. Rumelhart, and Geoffrey E. Hinton

What makes people smarter than machines? They certainly are not quicker or more precise. Yet people are far better at perceiving objects in natural scenes and noting their relations, at understanding language and retrieving contextually appropriate information from memory, at making plans and carrying out contextually appropriate actions, and at a wide range of other natural cognitive tasks. People are also far better at learning to do these things more accurately and fluently through processing experience.

What is the basis for these differences? One answer, perhaps the classic one we might expect from artificial intelligence, is "software." If we only had the right computer program, the argument goes, we might be able to capture the fluidity and adaptability of human information processing.

Certainly this answer is partially correct. There have been great breakthroughs in our understanding of cognition as a result of the development of expressive high-level computer languages and powerful algorithms. No doubt there will be more such breakthroughs in the future. However, we do not think that software is the whole story.

In our view, people are smarter than today's computers because the brain employs a basic computational architecture that is more suited to deal with a central aspect of the natural information processing tasks that people are so good at. We will show through examples that these tasks generally require the simultaneous consideration of many pieces of information or constraints. Each constraint may be imperfectly specified and ambiguous, yet each can play a potentially decisive role in determining the outcome of processing. After examining these points, we will introduce a computational framework for modeling cognitive processes that seems well suited to exploiting these constraints and that seems closer than other frameworks to the style of computation as it might be done by the brain. We will review several early examples of models developed in this framework, and we will show that the mechanisms these models employ can give rise to powerful emergent properties that begin to suggest attractive alternatives to traditional accounts of various aspects of cognition. We will also show that models of this class provide a basis for understanding how learning can occur spontaneously, as a by-product of processing activity.

Multiple Simultaneous Constraints

The Mutual Influence of Syntax and Semantics Multiple constraints operate ... strongly in language processing.... Rumelhart (1977) has documented many of these multiple constraints. Rather than catalog them here, we will use a few examples from language to illustrate the fact that the constraints tend to be reciprocal: The example shows that they do not run only from syntax to semantics—they also run the other way.

It is clear, of course, that syntax constrains the assignment of meaning. Without the syntactic rules of English to guide us, we cannot correctly understand who has done what to whom in the following sentence:

The boy the man chased kissed the girl.

But consider these examples (Rumelhart 1977; Schank 1973):

I saw the grand canyon flying to New York.
I saw the sheep grazing in the field.

Our knowledge of syntactic rules alone does not tell us what grammatical role is played by the prepositional phrases in these two cases. In the first, "flying to New York" is taken as describing the context in which the speaker saw the Grand Canyon—while he was flying to New York. In the second, "grazing in the field" could syntactically describe an analogous situation, in which the speaker is grazing in the field, but this possibility does not typically become available on first reading. Instead we assign "grazing in the field" as a modifier of the sheep (roughly, "who were grazing in the field"). The syntactic structure of each of these sentences, then, is determined in part by the semantic relations that the constituents of the sentence might plausibly bear to one another. Thus, the influences appear to run both ways, from the syntax to the semantics and from the semantics to the syntax.

In these examples, we see how syntactic considerations influence semantic ones and how semantic ones influence syntactic ones. We cannot say that one kind of constraint is primary.

Mutual constraints operate, not only between syntactic and semantic processing, but also within each of these domains as well. Here we consider an example from syntactic processing, namely, the assignment of words to syntactic categories. Consider the sentences:

I like the joke.
I like the drive.
I like to joke.
I like to drive.

In this case it looks as though the words *the* and *to* serve to determine whether the following word will be read as a noun or a verb. This, of course, is a very strong constraint in English and can serve to force a verb interpretation of a word that is not ordinarily used this way:

I like to mud.

On the other hand, if the information specifying whether the function word preceding the final word is *to* or *the* is ambiguous, then the typical reading of the word that follows it will determine which way the function word is heard. This was shown in an experiment by Isenberg, Walker, Ryder, and Schweikert (1980). They presented sounds halfway between *to* (actually /t^/) and *the* (actually /ꟈ^/) and found that words like *joke*, which we tend to think of first as nouns, made subjects hear the marginal stimuli

Figure 78.1
Some ambiguous displays. The first one is from Selfridge 1955. The second line shows that three ambiguous characters can each constrain the identity of the others. The third, fourth, and fifth lines show that these characters are indeed ambiguous in that they assume other identities in other contexts. (The ink-blot technique of making letters ambiguous is due to Lindsay and Norman, 1972.)

as *the*, while words like *drive*, which we tend to think of first as verbs, made subjects hear the marginal stimuli as *to*. Generally, then, it would appear that each word can help constrain the syntactic role, and even the identity, of every other word.

Simultaneous Mutual Constraints in Word Recognition Just as the syntactic role of one word can influence the role assigned to another in analyzing sentences, so the identity of one letter can influence the identity assigned to another in reading. A famous example of this, from Selfridge, is shown in figure 78.1. Along with this is a second example in which none of the letters, considered separately, can be identified unambiguously, but in which the possibilities that the visual information leaves open for each so constrain the possible identities of the others that we are capable of identifying all of them.

At first glance, the situation here must seem paradoxical: The identity of each letter is constrained by the identities of each of the others. But since in general we cannot know the identities of any of the letters until we have established the identities of the others, how can we get the process started?

The resolution of the paradox, of course, is simple. One of the different possible letters in each position fits together with the others. It appears then that our perceptual system is capable of exploring all these possibilities without committing itself to one until all of the constraints are taken into account.

Understanding Through the Interplay of Multiple Sources of Knowledge It is clear that we know a good deal about a large number of different standard situations. Several theorists have suggested that we store this knowledge in terms of structures called variously: *scripts* (Schank 1976), *frames* (Minsky 1975), or *schemata* (Norman and

Bobrow 1976; Rumelhart 1975). Such knowledge structures are assumed to be the basis of comprehension. A great deal of progress has been made within the context of this view.

However, it is important to bear in mind that most everyday situations cannot be rigidly assigned to just a single script. They generally involve an interplay between a number of different sources of information. Consider, for example, a child's birthday party at a restaurant. We know things about birthday parties, and we know things about restaurants, but we would not want to assume that we have explicit knowledge (at least, not in advance of our first restaurant birthday party) about the conjunction of the two. Yet we can imagine what such a party might be like. The fact that the party was being held in a restaurant would modify certain aspects of our expectations for birthday parties (we would not expect a game of Pin-the-Tail-on-the-Donkey, for example), while the fact that the event was a birthday party would inform our expectations for what would be ordered and who would pay the bill.

Representations like scripts, frames, and schemata are useful structures for encoding knowledge, although we believe they only approximate the underlying structure of knowledge representation that emerges from the class of models we consider elsewhere. Our main point here is that any theory that tries to account for human knowledge using script-like knowledge structures will have to allow them to interact with each other to capture the generative capacity of human understanding in novel situations. Achieving such interactions has been one of the greatest difficulties associated with implementing models that really think generatively using script- or frame-like representations.

Parallel Distributed Processing

In the examples we have considered, a number of different pieces of information must be kept in mind at once. Each plays a part, constraining others and being constrained by them. What kinds of mechanisms seem well suited to these task demands? Intuitively, these tasks seem to require mechanisms in which each aspect of the information in the situation can act on other aspects, simultaneously influencing other aspects and being influenced by them. To articulate these intuitions, we and others have turned to a class of models we call *Parallel Distributed Processing* (PDP) models. These models assume that information processing takes place through the interactions of a large number of simple processing elements called units, each sending excitatory and inhibitory signals to other units. In some cases, the units stand for possible hypotheses about such things as the letters in a particular display or the syntactic roles of the words in a particular sentence. In these cases, the activations stand roughly for the strengths associated with the different possible hypotheses, and the interconnections among the units stand for the constraints the system knows to exist between the hypotheses. In other cases, the units stand for possible goals and actions, such as the goal of typing a particular letter, or the action of moving the left index finger, and the connections relate goals to subgoals, subgoals to actions, and actions to muscle movements. In still other cases, units stand not for particular hypotheses or goals, but for aspects of these things. Thus a hypothesis about the identity of a word, for example, is itself distributed in the activations of a large number of units.

PDP Models: Cognitive Science or Neuroscience?

One reason for the appeal of PDP models is their obvious "physiological" flavor: They seem so much more closely tied to the physiology of the brain than are other kinds of information-processing models. The brain consists of a large number of highly interconnected elements which apparently send very simple excitatory and inhibitory messages to each other and update their excitations on the basis of these simple messages. The properties of the units in many of the PDP models we will be exploring were inspired by basic properties of the neural hardware.

Though the appeal of PDP models is definitely enhanced by their physiological plausibility and neural inspiration, these are not the primary bases for their appeal to us. We are, after all, cognitive scientists, and PDP models appeal to us for psychological and computational reasons. They hold out the hope of offering computationally sufficient and psychologically accurate mechanistic accounts of the phenomena of human cognition which have eluded successful explication in conventional computational formalisms; and they have radically altered the way we think about the time-course of processing, the nature of representation, and the mechanisms of learning.

Examples of PDP Models

In what follows, we review a number of recent applications of PDP models to problems in perception, memory, and language. In many cases, as we shall see, parallel distributed processing mechanisms are used to provide natural accounts of the exploitation of multiple, simultaneous, and often mutual constraints. We will also see that these same mechanisms exhibit emergent properties which lead to novel interpretations of phenomena which have traditionally been interpreted in other ways.

Perception

Perceptual Completion of Familiar Patterns Perception, of course, is influenced by familiarity. It is a well-known fact that we often misperceive unfamiliar objects as more familiar ones and that we can get by with less time or with lower-quality information in perceiving familiar items than we need for perceiving unfamiliar items. Not only does familiarity help us determine what the higher-level structures are when the lower-level information is ambiguous; it also allows us to fill in missing lower-level information within familiar higher-order patterns. The well-known *phonemic restoration effect* is a case in point. In this phenomenon, perceivers hear sounds that have been cut out of words as if they had actually been present. For example, Warren (1970) presented *legi#lature* to subjects, with a click in the location marked by the #. Not only did subjects correctly identify the word legislature; they also heard the missing /s/ just as though it had been presented. They had great difficulty localizing the click, which they tended to hear as a disembodied sound. Similar phenomena have been observed in visual perception of words since the work of Pillsbury (1897).

Two of us have proposed a model describing the role of familiarity in perception based on excitatory and inhibitory interactions among units standing for various hypotheses about the input at different levels of abstraction (McClelland and Rumelhart 1981, Rumelhart and McClelland 1982). The model has been applied in detail to the role of familiarity in the perception of letters in visually presented words, and has proved to provide a very close account of the results of a large number of experiments.

The model assumes that there are units that act as detectors for the visual features which distinguish letters, with one set of units assigned to detect the features in each of the different letter-positions in the word. For four-letter words, then, there are four such sets of detectors. There are also four sets of detectors for the letters themselves and a set of detectors for the words.

In the model, each unit has an activation value, corresponding roughly to the strength of the hypothesis that what that unit stands for is present in the perceptual input. The model honors the following important relations which hold between these "hypotheses" or activations: First, to the extent that two hypotheses are mutually consistent, they should support each other. Thus, units that are mutually consistent, in the way that the letter *T* in the first position is consistent with the word *TAKE*, tend to excite each other. Second, to the extent that two hypotheses are mutually inconsistent, they should weaken each other. Actually, we can distinguish two kinds of inconsistency: The first kind might be called between-level inconsistency. For example, the hypothesis that a word begins with a *T* is inconsistent with the hypothesis that the word is *MOVE*. The second might be called mutual exclusion. For example, the hypothesis that a word begins with *T* excludes the hypothesis that it begins with *R* since a word can only begin with one letter. Both kinds of inconsistencies operate in the word perception model to reduce the activations of units. Thus, the letter units in each position compete with all other letter units in the same position, and the word units compete with each other. This type of inhibitory interaction is often called *competitive inhibition*. In addition, there are inhibitory interactions between incompatible units on different levels. This type of inhibitory interaction is simply called *between-level inhibition*.

The set of excitatory and inhibitory interactions between units can be diagrammed by drawing excitatory and inhibitory links between them. The whole picture is too complex to draw, so we illustrate only with a fragment: Some of the interactions between some of the units in this model are illustrated in figure 78.2.

Let us consider what happens in a system like this when a familiar stimulus is presented under degraded conditions. For example, consider the display shown in figure 78.3. This display consists of the letters *W*, *O*, and *R*, completely visible, and enough of a fourth letter to rule out all letters other than *R* and *K*. Before onset of the display, the activations of the units are set at or below 0. When the display is presented, detectors for the features present in each position become active (i.e., their activations grow above 0). At this point, they begin to excite and inhibit the corresponding detectors for letters. In the first three positions, *W*, *O*, and *R* are unambiguously activated, so we will focus our attention on the fourth position where *R* and *K* are both equally consistent with the active features. Here, the activations of the detectors for *R* and *K* start out growing together, as the feature detectors below them become activated. As these detectors become active, they and the active letter detectors for *W*, *O*, and *R* in the other positions start to activate detectors for words which have these letters in them and to inhibit detectors for words which do not have these letters. A number of words are partially consistent with the active letters, and receive some net excitation from the letter level, but only the word *WORK* matches one of the active letters in all four

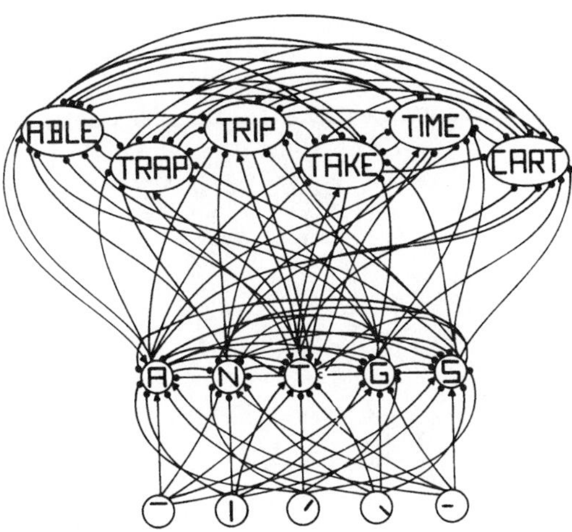

Figure 78.2
The unit for the letter *T* in the first position of a four-letter array and some of its neighbors. Note that the feature and letter units stand only for the first position; in a complete picture of the units needed from processing four-letter displays, there would be four full sets of feature detectors and four full sets of letter detectors. (From "An Interactive Activation Model of Context Effects in Letter Perception: Part I. An Account of Basic Findings" by J. L. McClelland and D. E. Rumelhart, 1981, *Psychological Review*, 88, p. 380. Copyright 1981 by the American Psychological Association. Reprinted by permission.)

positions. As a result, *WORK* becomes more active than any other word and inhibits the other words, thereby successfully dominating the pattern of activation among the word units. As it grows in strength, it sends feedback to the letter level, reinforcing the activations of the *W*, *O*, *R*, and *K* in the corresponding positions. In the fourth position, this feedback gives *K* the upper hand over *R*, and eventually the stronger activation of the *K* detector allows it to dominate the pattern of activation, suppressing the *R* detector completely.

This example illustrates how PDP models can allow knowledge about what letters go together to form words to work together with natural constraints on the task (i.e. that there should only be one letter in one place at one time), to produce perceptual completion in a simple and direct way.

Completion of Novel Patterns However, the perceptual intelligence of human perceivers far exceeds the ability to recognize familiar patterns and fill in missing portions. We also show facilitation in the perception of letters in unfamiliar letter strings which are word-like but not themselves actually familiar.

One way of accounting for such performances is to imagine that the perceiver possesses, in addition to detectors for familiar words, sets of detectors for regular subword units such as familiar letter clusters, or that they use abstract rules, specifying which classes of letters can go with which others in different contexts. It turns out, however, that the model we have already described needs no such additional structure to produce perceptual facilitation for word-like letter strings; to this extent it acts as if it "knows" the orthographic structure of English. We illustrate this feature of the

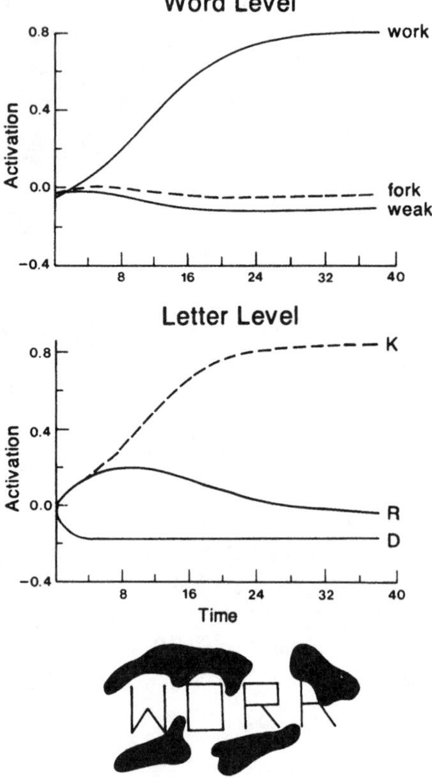

Figure 78.3
A possible display that might be presented to the interactive activation model of word recognition, and the resulting activations of selected letter and word units. The letter units are for the letters indicated in the fourth position of a four-letter display.

model with the example shown in figure 78.4, where the nonword *YEAD* is shown in degraded form so that the second letter is incompletely visible. Given the information about this letter, considered alone, either *E* or *F* would be possible in the second position. Yet our model will tend to complete this letter as an *E*.

The reason for this behavior is that, when *YEAD* is shown, a number of words are partially activated. There is no word consistent with *Y*, *E* or *F*, *A*, and *D*, but there are words which match *YEA_* (*YEAR*, for example) and others which match *_EAD* (*BEAD*, *DEAD*, *HEAD*, and *READ*, for example). These and other near misses are partially activated as a result of the pattern of activation at the letter level. While they compete with each other, none of these words gets strongly enough activated to completely suppress all the others. Instead, these units act as a group to reinforce particularly the letters *E* and *A*. There are no close partial matches which include the letter *F* in the second position, so this letter receives no feedback support. As a result, *E* comes to dominate, and eventually suppress, the *F* in the second position.

The fact that the word perception model exhibits perceptual facilitation to pronounceable nonwords as well as words illustrates once again how behavior in accordance with general principles or rules can emerge from the interactions of simple

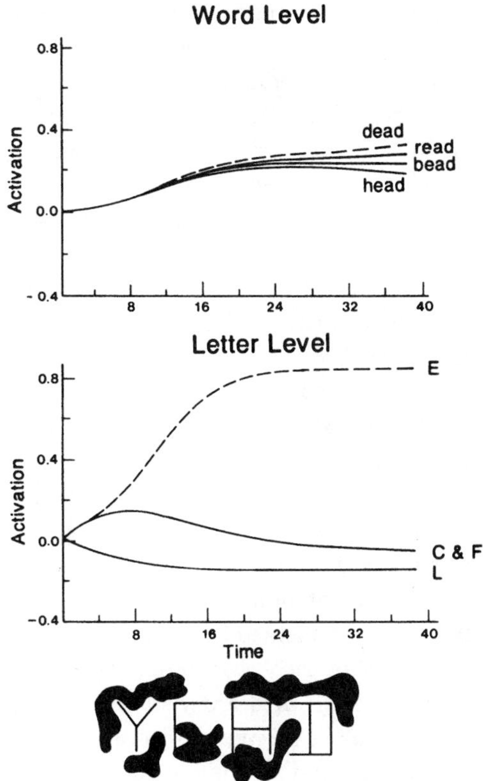

Figure 78.4
An example of a nonword display that might be presented to the interactive activation model of word recognition and the response of selected units at the letter and word levels. The letter units illustrated are detectors for letters in the second input position.

processing elements. Of course, the behavior of the word perception model does not implement exactly any of the systems of orthographic rules that have been proposed by linguists (Chomsky and Halle 1968, Venesky 1970) or psychologists (Spoehr and Smith 1975). In this regard, it only approximates such rule-based descriptions of perceptual processing. However, rule systems such as Chomsky and Halle's or Venesky's appear to be only approximately honored in human performance as well (Smith and Baker 1976). Indeed, some of the discrepancies between human performance data and rule systems occur in exactly the ways that we would predict from the word perception model (Rumelhart and McClelland 1982). This illustrates the possibility that PDP models may provide more accurate accounts of the details of human performance than models based on a set of rules representing human competence—at least in some domains.

Retrieving Information From Memory

Content Addressability One very prominent feature of human memory is that it is content addressable. It seems fairly clear that we can access information in memory based on nearly any attribute of the representation we are trying to retrieve.

Of course, some cues are much better than others. An attribute which is shared by a very large number of things we know about is not a very effective retrieval cue, since it does not accurately pick out a particular memory representation. But, several such cues, in conjunction, can do the job. Thus, if we ask a friend who goes out with several women, "Who was that woman I saw you with?", he may not know which one we mean—but if we specify something else about her—say the color of her hair, what she was wearing (insofar as he remembers this at all), where we saw him with her—he will likely be able to hit upon the right one.

It is, of course, possible to implement some kind of content addressability of memory on a standard computer in a variety of different ways. One way is to search sequentially, examining each memory in the system to find the memory or the set of memories which has the particular content specified in the cue. An alternative, somewhat more efficient, scheme involves some form of indexing—keeping a list, for every content a memory might have, of which memories have that content.

Such an indexing scheme can be made to work with error-free probes, but it will break down if there is an error in the specification of the retrieval cue. There are possible ways of recovering from such errors, but they lead to the kind of combinatorial explosions which plague this kind of computer implementation.

But suppose that we imagine that each memory is represented by a unit which has mutually excitatory interactions with units standing for each of its properties. Then, whenever any property of the memory became active, the memory would tend to be activated, and whenever the memory was activated, all of its contents would tend to become activated. Such a scheme would automatically produce content addressability for us. Though it would not be immune to errors, it would not be devastated by an error in the probe if the remaining properties specified the correct memory.

As described thus far, whenever a property that is a part of a number of different memories is activated, it will tend to activate all of the memories it is in. To keep these other activities from swamping the "correct" memory unit, we simply need to add initial inhibitory connections among the memory units. An additional desirable feature would be mutually inhibitory interactions among mutually incompatible property units. For example, a person cannot both be single and married at the same time, so the units for different marital states would be mutually inhibitory.

McClelland (1981) developed a simulation model that illustrates how a system with these properties would act as a content addressable memory. The model is obviously oversimplified, but it illustrates many of the characteristics of the more complex models....

Consider the information represented in figure 78.5, which lists a number of people we might meet if we went to live in an unsavory neighborhood, and some of their hypothetical characteristics. A subset of the units needed to represent this information is shown in figure 78.6. In this network, there is an "instance unit" for each of the characters described in figure 78.5, and that unit is linked by mutually excitatory connections to all of the units for the fellow's properties. Note that we have included property units for the names of the characters, as well as units for their other properties.

Now, suppose we wish to retrieve the properties of a particular individual, say Lance. And suppose that we know Lance's name. Then we can probe the network by activat-

The Jets and The Sharks

Name	Gang	Age	Edu	Mar	Occupation
Art	Jets	40s	J.H.	Sing.	Pusher
Al	Jets	30s	J.H.	Mar.	Burglar
Sam	Jets	20s	COL.	Sing.	Bookie
Clyde	Jets	40s	J.H.	Sing.	Bookie
Mike	Jets	30s	J.H.	Sing.	Bookie
Jim	Jets	20s	J.H.	Div.	Burglar
Greg	Jets	20s	H.S.	Mar.	Pusher
John	Jets	20s	J.H.	Mar.	Burglar
Doug	Jets	30s	H.S.	Sing.	Bookie
Lance	Jets	20s	J.H.	Mar.	Burglar
George	Jets	20s	J.H.	Div.	Burglar
Pete	Jets	20s	H.S.	Sing.	Bookie
Fred	Jets	20s	H.S.	Sing.	Pusher
Gene	Jets	20s	COL.	Sing.	Pusher
Ralph	Jets	30s	J.H.	Sing.	Pusher
Phil	Sharks	30s	COL.	Mar.	Pusher
Ike	Sharks	30s	J.H.	Sing.	Bookie
Nick	Sharks	30s	H.S.	Sing.	Pusher
Don	Sharks	30s	COL.	Mar.	Burglar
Ned	Sharks	30s	COL.	Mar.	Bookie
Karl	Sharks	40s	H.S.	Mar.	Bookie
Ken	Sharks	20s	H.S.	Sing.	Burglar
Earl	Sharks	40s	H.S.	Mar.	Burglar
Rick	Sharks	30s	H.S.	Div.	Burglar
Ol	Sharks	30s	COL.	Mar.	Pusher
Neal	Sharks	30s	H.S.	Sing.	Bookie
Dave	Sharks	30s	H.S.	Div.	Pusher

Figure 78.5

Characteristics of a number of individuals belonging to two gangs, the Jets and the Sharks. (From "Retrieving General and Specific Knowledge from Stored Knowledge of Specifics" by J. L. McClelland, 1981, *Proceedings of the Third Annual Conference of the Cognitive Science Society*, Berkeley, CA. Copyright 1981 by J. L. McClelland. Reprinted by permission.)

ing Lance's name unit, and we can see what pattern of activation arises as a result. Assuming that we know of no one else named Lance, we can expect the Lance name unit to be hooked up only to the instance unit for Lance. This will in turn activate the property units for Lance, thereby creating the pattern of activation corresponding to Lance. In effect, we have retrieved a representation of Lance. More will happen than just what we have described so far, but for the moment let us stop here.

Of course, sometimes we may wish to retrieve a name, given other information. In this case, we might start with some of Lance's properties, effectively asking the system, say "Who do you know who is a Shark and in his 20s?" by activating the Shark and 20s units. In this case it turns out that there is a single individual, Ken, who fits the description. So, when we activate these two properties, we will activate the instance unit for Ken, and this in turn will activate his name unit, and fill in his other properties as well.

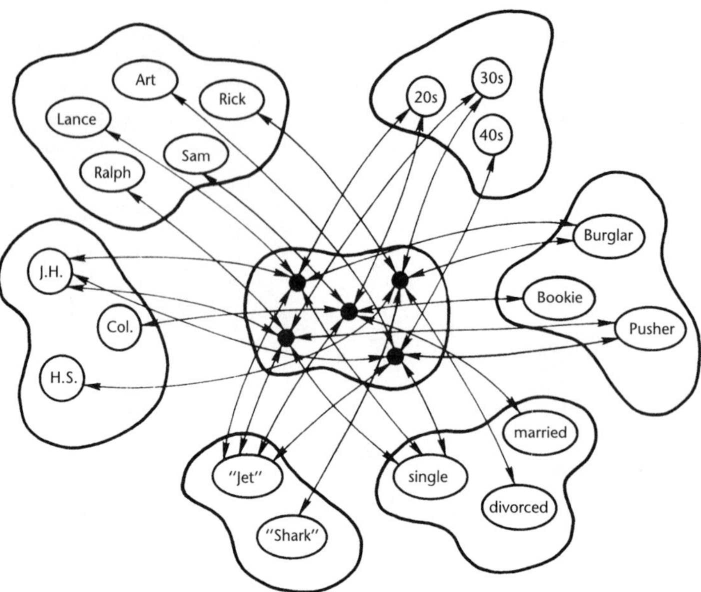

Figure 78.6
Some of the units and interconnections needed to represent the individuals shown in 78.5. The units connected with double-headed arrows are mutually excitatory. All the units within the same cloud are mutually inhibitory. (From "Retrieving General and Specific Knowledge from Stored Knowledge of Specifics" by J. L. McClelland, 1981, *Proceedings of the Third Annual Conference of the Cognitive Science Society*, Berkeley, CA. Copyright 1981 by J. L. McClelland. Reprinted by permission.)

Graceful Degradation A few of the desirable properties of this kind of model are visible from considering what happens as we vary the set of features we use to probe the memory in an attempt to retrieve a particular individual's name. Any set of features which is sufficient to uniquely characterize a particular item will activate the instance node for that item more strongly than any other instance node. A probe which contains misleading features will most strongly activate the node that it matches best. This will clearly be a poorer cue than one which contains no misleading information—but it will still be sufficient to activate the "right answer" more strongly than any other, as long as the introduction of misleading information does not make the probe closer to some other item. In general, though the degree of activation of a particular instance node and of the corresponding name nodes varies in this model as a function of the exact content of the probe, errors in the probe will not be fatal unless they make the probe point to the wrong memory. This kind of model's handling of incomplete or partial probes also requires no special error-recovery scheme to work—it is a natural by-product of the nature of the retrieval mechanism that it is capable of graceful degradation.

Default Assignment It probably will have occurred to the reader that in many of the situations we have been examining, there will be other activations occurring which may influence the pattern of activation which is retrieved. So, in the case where we retrieved the properties of Lance, those properties, once they become active, can begin to activate the units for other individuals with those same properties. The memory unit for Lance will be in competition with these units and will tend to keep their activation down, but to the extent that they do become active, they will tend to activate their own properties and therefore fill them in. In this way, the model can fill in properties of individuals based on what it knows about other, similar instances.

To illustrate how this might work we have simulated the case in which we do not know that Lance is a Burglar as opposed to a Bookie or a Pusher. It turns out that there are a group of individuals in the set who are very similar to Lance in many respects. When Lance's properties become activated, these other units become partially activated, and they start activating their properties. Since they all share the same "occupation," they work together to fill in that property for Lance. Of course, there is no reason why this should necessarily be the right answer, but generally speaking, the more similar two things are in respects that we know about, the more likely they are to be similar in respects that we do not, and the model implements this heuristic.

Spontaneous Generalization The model we have been describing has another valuable property as well—it tends to retrieve what is common to those memories which match a retrieval cue which is too general to capture any one memory. Thus, for example, we could probe the system by activating the unit corresponding to membership in the Jets. This unit will partially activate all the instances of the Jets, thereby causing each to send activations to its properties. In this way the model can retrieve the typical values that the members of the Jets have on each dimension—even though there is no one Jet that has these typical values. In the example, 9 of 15 Jets are single, 9 of 15 are in their 20s, and 9 of 15 have only a junior high school education; when we probe by activating the Jet unit, all three of these properties dominate. The Jets are evenly divided between the three occupations, so each of these units becomes partially activated. Each has a different name, so that each name unit is very weakly activated, nearly cancelling each other out.

In the example just given of spontaneous generalization, it would not be unreasonable to suppose that someone might have explicitly stored a generalization about the members of a gang. The account just given would be an alternative to "explicit storage" of the generalization. It has two advantages, though, over such an account. First, it does not require any special generalization formation mechanism. Second, it can provide us with generalizations on unanticipated lines, on demand. Thus, if we want to know, for example, what people in their 20s with a junior high school education are like, we can probe the model by activating these two units. Since all such people are Jets and Burglars, these two units are strongly activated by the model in this case; two of them are divorced and two are married, so both of these units are partially activated.[1]

The sort of model we are considering, then, is considerably more than a content addressable memory. In addition, it performs default assignment, and it can spontaneously retrieve a general concept of the individuals that match any specifiable probe. These properties must be explicitly implemented as complicated computational extensions of other models of knowledge retrieval, but in PDP models they are natural by-products of the retrieval process itself.

Representation and Learning in PDP Models

In the Jets and Sharks model, we can speak of the model's *active representation* at a particular time, and associate this with the pattern of activation over the units in the system. We can also ask: What is the stored knowledge that gives rise to that pattern of activation? In considering this question, we see immediately an important difference between PDP models and other models of cognitive processes. In most models, knowledge is stored as a static copy of a pattern. Retrieval amounts to finding the pattern in long-term memory and copying it into a buffer or working memory. There is no real difference between the stored representation in long-term memory and the active representation in working memory. In PDP models, though, this is not the case. In these models, the patterns themselves are not stored. Rather, what is stored is the *connection strengths* between units that allow these patterns to be re-created. In the Jets and Sharks model, there is an instance unit assigned to each individual, but that unit does not contain a copy of the representation of that individual. Instead, it is simply the case that the connections between it and the other units in the system are such that activation of the unit will cause the pattern for the individual to be reinstated on the property units.

This difference between PDP models and conventional models has enormous implications, both for processing and for learning. We have already seen some of the implications for processing. The representation of the knowledge is set up in such a way that the knowledge necessarily influences the course of processing. Using knowledge in processing is no longer a matter of finding the relevant information in memory and bringing it to bear; it is part and parcel of the processing itself.

For learning, the implications are equally profound. For if the knowledge is the strengths of the connections, learning must be a matter of finding the right connection strengths so that the right patterns of activation will be produced under the right circumstances. This is an extremely important property of this class of models, for it opens up the possibility that an information processing mechanism could learn, as a result of tuning its connections, to capture the interdependencies between activations that it is exposed to in the course of processing.

In recent years, there has been quite a lot of interest in learning in cognitive science. Computational approaches to learning fall predominantly into what might be called the "explicit rule formulation" tradition, as represented by the work of Winston (1975), the suggestions of Chomsky, and the ACT* model of J. R. Anderson (1983). All of this work shares the assumption that the goal of learning is to formulate explicit rules (propositions, productions, etc.) which capture powerful generalizations in a succinct way. Fairly powerful mechanisms, usually with considerable innate knowledge about a domain, and/or some starting set of primitive propositional representations, then formulate hypothetical general rules, e.g., by comparing particular cases and formulating explicit generalizations.

The approach that we take in developing PDP models is completely different. First, we do not assume that the goal of learning is the formulation of explicit rules. Rather, we assume it is the acquisition of connection strengths which allow a network of simple units to act *as though* it knew the rules. Second, we do not attribute powerful computational capabilities to the learning mechanism. Rather, we assume very simple connection strength modulation mechanisms which adjust the strength of connections between units based on information locally available at the connection.

Local vs. Distributed Representation Before we turn to an explicit consideration of this issue, we raise a basic question about representation. Once we have achieved the insight that the knowledge is stored in the strengths of the interconnections between units, a question arises. Is there any reason to assign one unit to each pattern that we wish to learn? Another possibility—one that we explore extensively...—is the possibility that the knowledge about any individual pattern is not stored in the connections of a special unit reserved for that pattern, but is distributed over the connections among a large number of processing units. On this view, the Jets and Sharks model represents a special case in which separate units are reserved for each instance.

Models in which connection information is explicitly thought of as distributed have been proposed by a number of investigators. The units in these collections may themselves correspond to conceptual primitives, or they may have no particular meaning as individuals. In either case, the focus shifts to patterns of activation over these units and to mechanisms whose explicit purpose is to learn the right connection strengths to allow the right patterns of activation to become activated under the right circumstances.

In the rest of this section, we will give a simple example of a PDP model in which the knowledge is distributed. We will first explain how the model would work, given preexisting connections, and we will then describe how it could come to acquire the right connection strengths through a very simple learning mechanism. A number of models which have taken this distributed approach have been discussed in Hinton and J. A. Anderson's (1981) *Parallel Models of Associative Memory.* We will consider a simple version of a common type of distributed model, a *pattern associator.*

Pattern associators are models in which a pattern of activation over one set of units can cause a pattern of activation over another set of units without any intervening units to stand for either pattern as a whole. Pattern associators would, for example, be capable of associating a pattern of activation on one set of units corresponding to the appearance of an object with a pattern on another set corresponding to the aroma of the object, so that, when an object is presented visually, causing its visual pattern to become active, the model produces the pattern corresponding to its aroma.

How a Pattern Associator Works For purposes of illustration, we present a very simple pattern associator in figure 78.7. In this model, there are four units in each of two pools. The first pool, the A units, will be the pool in which patterns corresponding to the sight of various objects might be represented. The second pool, the B units, will be the pool in which the pattern corresponding to the aroma will be represented. We can pretend that alternative patterns of activation on the A units are produced upon viewing a rose or a grilled steak, and alternative patterns on the B units are produced upon sniffing the same objects. Figure 78.8 shows two pairs of patterns, as well as sets of interconnections necessary to allow the A member of each pair to reproduce the B member.

The details of the behavior of the individual units vary among different versions of pattern associators. For present purposes, we'll assume that the units can take on positive or negative activation values, with 0 representing a kind of neutral intermediate

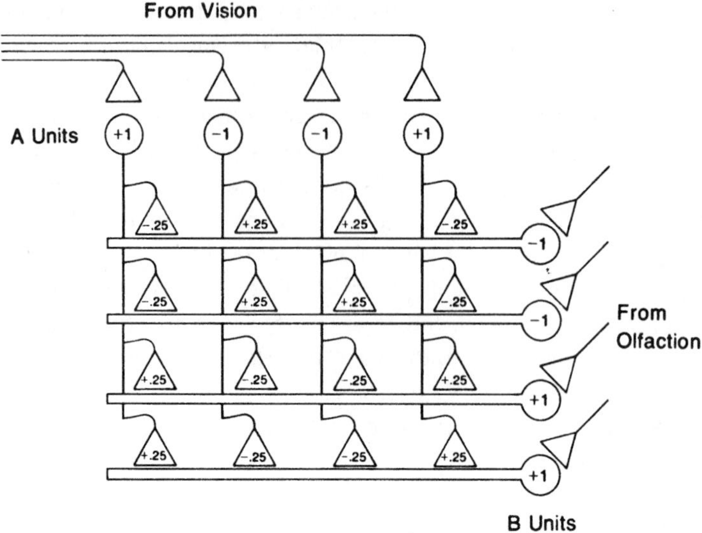

Figure 78.7
A simple pattern associator. The example assumes that patterns of activation in the A units can be produced by the visual system and patterns in the B units can be produced by the olfactory system. The synaptic connections allow the outputs of the A units to influence the activation of the B units. The synaptic weights linking the A units to the B units were selected so as to allow the patterns of activation shown on the A units to reproduce the pattern of activation shown on the B units without the need for any olfactory input.

value. The strengths of the interconnections between the units can be positive or negative real numbers.

The effect of an A unit on a B unit is determined by multiplying the activation of the A unit times the strength of its synaptic connection with the B unit. For example, if the connection from a particular A unit to a particular B unit has a positive sign, when the A unit is excited (activation greater than 0), it will excite the B unit. For this example, we'll simply assume that the activation of each unit is set to the sum of the excitatory and inhibitory effects operating on it. This is one of the simplest possible cases.

Suppose, now, that we have created on the A units the pattern corresponding to the first visual pattern shown in figure 78.8, the rose. How should we arrange the strengths of the interconnections between the A units and the B units to reproduce the pattern corresponding to the aroma of a rose? We simply need to arrange for each A unit to tend to excite each B unit which has a positive activation in the aroma pattern and to inhibit each B unit which has a negative activation in the aroma pattern. It turns out that this goal is achieved by setting the strength of the connection between a given A unit and a given B unit to a value proportional to the product of the activation of the two units. In figure 78.7, the weights on the connections were chosen to allow the A pattern illustrated there to produce the illustrated B pattern according to this principle. The actual strengths of the connections were set to $\pm.25$, rather than ±1, so that the A pattern will produce the right magnitude, as well as the right sign, for the activations of the units in the B pattern. The same connections are reproduced in matrix form in figure 78.8A.

+1	−1	−1	+1	
−.25	+.25	+.25	−.25	−1
−.25	+.25	+.25	−.25	−1
+.25	−.25	−.25	+.25	+1
+.25	−.25	−.25	+.25	+1

(a)

−1	+1	−1	+1	
+.25	−.25	+.25	−.25	−1
−.25	+.25	−.25	+.25	+1
−.25	+.25	−.25	+.25	+1
+.25	−.25	+.25	−.25	−1

(b)

Figure 78.8
Two simple associators represented as matrices. The weights in the first two matrices allow the A pattern shown above the matrix to produce the B pattern shown to the right of it. Note that the weights in the first matrix are the same as those shown in the diagram in figure 78.7.

Pattern associators like the one in figure 78.7 have a number of nice properties. One is that they do not require a perfect copy of the input to produce the correct output, though its strength will be weaker in this case. For example, suppose that the associator shown in figure 78.7 were presented with an A pattern of (1, −1, 0, 1). This is the A pattern shown in the figure, with the activation of one of its elements set to 0. The B pattern produced in response will have the activations of all of the B units in the right direction; however, they will be somewhat weaker than they would be, had the complete A pattern been shown. Similar effects are produced if an element of the pattern is distorted—or if the model is damaged, either by removing whole units, or random sets of connections, etc. Thus, their pattern retrieval performance of the model degrades gracefully both under degraded input and under damage.

How a Pattern Associator Learns So far, we have seen how we as model builders can construct the right set of weights to allow one pattern to cause another. The interesting thing, though, is that we do not need to build these interconnection strengths in by hand. Instead, the pattern associator can teach itself the right set of interconnections through experience processing the patterns in conjunction with each other.

A number of different rules for adjusting connection strengths have been proposed. One of the first—and definitely the best known—is due to D. O. Hebb (1949). Hebb's actual proposal was not sufficiently quantitative to build into an explicit model. However, a number of different variants can trace their ancestry back to Hebb. Perhaps the simplest version is:

When unit A and unit B are simultaneously excited, increase the strength of the connection between them.

A natural extension of this rule to cover the positive and negative activation values allowed in our example is:

Adjust the strength of the connection between units A and B in proportion to the product of their simultaneous activation.

In this formulation, if the product is positive, the change makes the connection more excitatory, and if the product is negative, the change makes the connection more inhibitory. For simplicity of reference, we will call this the *Hebb rule*, although it is not exactly Hebb's original formulation.

With this simple learning rule, we could train a "blank copy" of the pattern associator shown in figure 78.7 to produce the B pattern for rose when the A pattern is shown, simply by presenting the A and B patterns together and modulating the connection strengths according to the Hebb rule. The size of the change made on every trial would, of course, be a parameter. We generally assume that the changes made on each instance are rather small, and that connection strengths build up gradually. The values shown in figure 78.8A, then, would be acquired as a result of a number of experiences with the A and B pattern pair.

It is very important to note that the information needed to use the Hebb rule to determine the value each connection should have is *locally available* at the connection. All a given connection needs to consider is the activation of the units on both sides of it. Thus, it would be possible to actually implement such a connection modulation scheme locally, in each connection, without requiring any programmer to reach into each connection and set it to just the right value.

It turns out that the Hebb rule as stated here has some serious limitations, and, to our knowledge, no theorists continue to use it in this simple form. More sophisticated connection modulation schemes have been proposed by other workers; most important among these are the delta rule, the competitive learning rule, and the rules for learning in stochastic parallel models. All of these learning rules have the property that they adjust the strengths of connections between units on the basis of information that can be assumed to be locally available to the unit. Learning, then, in all of these cases, amounts to a very simple process that can be implemented locally at each connection without the need for any overall supervision. Thus, models which incorporate these learning rules train themselves to have the right interconnections in the course of processing the members of an ensemble of patterns.

Learning Multiple Patterns in the Same Set of Interconnections Up to now, we have considered how we might teach our pattern associator to associate the visual pattern for one object with a pattern for the aroma of the same object. Obviously, different patterns of interconnections between the A and B units are appropriate for causing the visual pattern for a different object to give rise to the pattern for its aroma. The same principles apply, however, and if we presented our pattern associator with the A and B patterns for steak, it would learn the right set of interconnections for that case instead (these are shown in figure 78.8B). In fact, it turns out that we can actually teach the same pattern associator a number of different associations. The matrix representing the set of interconnections that would be learned if we taught the same pattern associator both the rose association and the steak association is shown in figure 78.9. The reader can verify this by adding the two matrices for the individual patterns together. The reader can also verify that this set of connections will allow the rose A pattern to produce the rose B pattern, and the steak A pattern to produce the steak B pattern: when either input pattern is presented, the correct corresponding output is produced.

The examples used here have the property that the two different visual patterns are completely uncorrelated with each other. This being the case, the rose pattern produces no effect when the interconnections for the steak have been established, and the steak pattern produces no effect when the interconnections for the rose association

$$\begin{bmatrix} - & + & + & - \\ - & + & + & - \\ + & - & - & + \\ + & - & - & + \end{bmatrix} + \begin{bmatrix} + & - & + & - \\ - & + & - & + \\ - & + & - & + \\ + & - & + & - \end{bmatrix} = \begin{bmatrix} & & ++ & -- \\ -- & ++ & & \\ & & -- & ++ \\ ++ & -- & & \end{bmatrix}$$

Figure 78.9
The weights in the third matrix allow either A pattern shown in figure 78.8 to recreate the corresponding B pattern. Each weight in this case is equal to the sum of the weight for the A pattern and the weight for the B pattern, as illustrated.

are in effect. For this reason, it is possible to add together the pattern of interconnections for the rose association and the pattern for the steak association, and still be able to associate the sight of the steak with the smell of a steak and the sight of a rose with the smell of a rose. The two sets of interconnections do not interact at all.

One of the limitations of the Hebbian learning rule is that it can learn the connection strengths appropriate to an entire ensemble of patterns only when all the patterns are completely uncorrelated. This restriction does not, however, apply to pattern associators which use more sophisticated learning schemes.

Attractive Properties of Pattern Associator Models Pattern associator models have the property that uncorrelated patterns do not interact with each other, but more similar ones do. Thus, to the extent that a new pattern of activation on the A units is similar to one of the old ones, it will tend to have similar effects. Furthermore, if we assume that learning the interconnections occurs in small increments, similar patterns will essentially reinforce the strengths of the links they share in common with other patterns. Thus, if we present the same pair of patterns over and over, but each time we add a little random noise to each element of each member of the pair, the system will automatically learn to associate the central tendency of the two patterns and will learn to ignore the noise. What will be stored will be an average of the similar patterns with the slight variations removed. On the other hand, when we present the system with completely uncorrelated patterns, they will not interact with each other in this way. Thus, the same pool of units can extract the central tendency of each of a number of pairs of unrelated patterns.

Extracting the Structure of an Ensemble of Patterns The fact that similar patterns tend to produce similar effects allows distributed models to exhibit a kind of spontaneous generalization, extending behavior appropriate for one pattern to other similar patterns. This property is shared by other PDP models, such as the word perception model and the Jets and Sharks model described above; the main difference here is in the existence of simple, local, learning mechanisms that can allow the acquisition of the connection strengths needed to produce these generalizations through experience with members of the ensemble of patterns. Distributed models have another interesting property as well: If there are regularities in the correspondences between pairs of patterns, the model will naturally extract these regularities. This property allows distributed models to acquire patterns of interconnections that lead them to behave in ways we ordinarily take as evidence for the use of linguistic rules.

Here, we describe [such a] model very briefly. The model is a mechanism that learns how to construct the past tenses of words from their root forms through repeated presentations of examples of root forms paired with the corresponding past-tense form. The model consists of two pools of units. In one pool, patterns of activation representing the phonological structure of the root form of the verb can be represented, and, in the other, patterns representing the phonological structure of the past tense can be represented. The goal of the model is simply to learn the right connection strengths between the root units and the past-tense units, so that whenever the root form of a verb is presented the model will construct the corresponding past-tense form. The model is trained by presenting the root form of the verb as a pattern of activation over the root units, and then using a simple, local, learning rule to adjust the connection strengths so that this root form will tend to produce the correct pattern of activation over the past-tense units. The model is tested by simply presenting the root form as a pattern of activation over the root units and examining the pattern of activation produced over the past-tense units.

The model is trained initially with a small number of verbs children learn early in the acquisition process. At this point in learning, it can only produce appropriate outputs for inputs that it has explicitly been shown. But as it learns more and more verbs, it exhibits two interesting behaviors. First, it produces the standard *ed* past tense when tested with pseudo-verbs or verbs it has never seen. Second, it "overregularizes" the past tense of irregular words it previously completed correctly. Often, the model will blend the irregular past tense of the word with the regular *ed* ending, and produce errors like *CAMED* as the past of *COME*. These phenomena mirror those observed in the early phases of acquisition of control over past tenses in young children.

The generativity of the child's responses—the creation of regular past tenses of new verbs and the overregularization of the irregular verbs—has been taken as strong evidence that the child has induced the rule which states that the regular correspondence for the past tense in English is to add a final *ed* (Berko 1958). On the evidence of its performance, then, the model can be said to have acquired the rule. However, no special rule-induction mechanism is used, and no special language-acquisition device is required. The model learns to behave in accordance with the rule, not by explicitly noting that most words take *ed* in the past tense in English and storing this rule away explicitly, but simply by building up a set of connections in a pattern associator through a long series of simple learning experiences. The same mechanisms of parallel distributed processing and connection modification which are used in a number of domains serve, in this case, to produce implicit knowledge tantamount to a linguistic rule. The model also provides a fairly detailed account of a number of the specific aspects of the error patterns children make in learning the rule. In this sense, it provides a richer and more detailed description of the acquisition process than any that falls out naturally from the assumption that the child is building up a repertoire of explicit but inaccessible rules.

There is a lot more to be said about distributed models of learning, about their strengths and their weaknesses, than we have space for in this preliminary consideration. For now we hope mainly to have suggested that they provide dramatically different accounts of learning and acquisition than are offered by traditional models of these processes. We saw earlier that performance in accordance with rules can emerge from the interactions of simple, interconnected units. Now we can see how the acquisition of performance that conforms to linguistic rules can emerge from a simple, local, connection strength modulation process.

Acknowledgments

This research was supported by Contract N00014-79-C-0323, NR 667-437 with the Personnel and Training Research Programs of the Office of Naval Research, by grants from the System Development Foundation, and by a NIMH Career Development Award (MH00385) to the first author.

Note

1. In this and all other cases, there is a tendency for the pattern of activation to be influenced by partially activated, near neighbors, which do not quite match the probe. Thus, in this case, there is a Jet Al, who is a Married Burglar. The unit for Al gets slightly activated, giving Married a slight edge over Divorced in the simulation.

References

Anderson, J. R. 1983. *The architecture of cognition.* Cambridge, MA: Harvard University Press.

Berko, J. 1958. The child's learning of English morphology. *Word, 14,* 150–177.

Chomsky, N., and Halle, M. 1968. *The sound pattern of English.* New York: Harper and Row.

Hebb, D. O. 1949. *The organization of behavior.* New York: Wiley.

Hinton, G. E., and Anderson, J. A., eds. 1981. *Parallel models of associative memory.* Hillsdale, NJ: Erlbaum.

Isenberg, D., Walker, E. C. T., Ryder, J. M., and Schweikert, J. 1980, November. *A top-down effect on the identification of function words.* Paper presented at the Acoustical Society of America, Los Angeles.

Lindsay, P. H., and Norman, D. A. 1972. *Human information processing: An introduction to psychology.* New York: Academic Press.

McClelland, J. L. 1981. Retrieving general and specific information from stored knowledge of specifics. *Proceedings of the Third Annual Meeting of the Cognitive Science Society,* 170–172.

McClelland, J. L., and Rumelhart, D. E. 1981. An interactive activation model of context effects in letter perception: Part 1. An account of basic findings. *Psychological Review, 88,* 375–407.

Minsky, M. 1975. A framework for representing knowledge. In P. H. Winston, ed., *The psychology of computer vision* (pp. 211–277). New York: McGraw-Hill.

Norman, D. A., and Bobrow, D. G. 1976. On the role of active memory processes in perception and cognition. In C. N. Cofer, ed., *The structure of human memory* (pp. 114–132). Freeman: San Francisco.

Pillsbury, W. B. 1897. A study in apperception. *American Journal of Psychology, 8,* 315–393.

Rumelhart, D. E. 1975. Notes on a schema for stories. In D. G. Bobrow and A. Collins, eds., *Representation and understanding* (pp. 211–236). New York: Academic Press.

Rumelhart, D. E. 1977. Toward an interactive model of reading. In S. Dornic, ed., *Attention and Performance VI*. Hillsdale, NJ: Erlbaum.

Rumelhart, D. E., and McClelland, J. L. 1982. An interactive activation model of context effects in letter perception: Part 2. The contextual enhancement effect and some tests and extensions of the model. *Psychological Review, 89*, 60–94.

Schank, R. C. 1973. Identification of conceptualizations underlying natural language. In R. C. Schank, and K. M. Colby, eds., *Computer models of thought and language* (pp. 187–247). San Francisco: Freeman.

Schank, R. C. 1976. The role of memory in language processing. In C. N. Cofer, ed., *The structure of human memory* (pp. 162–189). Freeman: San Francisco.

Selfridge, O. G., and Neisser, U. 1960. Pattern recognition by machine. *Scientific American, 203*, 60–68.

Smith, P. T., and Baker, R. G. 1976. The influence of English spelling patterns on pronounciation. *Journal of Verbal Learning and Verbal Behavior, 15*, 267–286.

Spoehr, K., and Smith, E. 1975. The role of orthographic and phonotactic rules in perceiving letter patterns. *Journal of Experimental Psychology: Human Perception and Performance, 1*, 21–34.

Venesky, R. L. 1970. *The structure of English orthography*. The Hague: Mouton.

Warren, R. M. 1970. Perceptual restoration of missing speech sounds. *Science, 167*, 393–395.

Winston, P. H. 1975. Learning structural descriptions from examples. In P. H. Winston, ed., *The psychology of computer vision* (pp. 157–209). New York: McGraw-Hill.

79 Connectionism and Cognitive Architecture: A Critical Analysis

Jerry A. Fodor and Zenon W. Pylyshyn

1 Introduction

Connectionist or *PDP* models are catching on. There are conferences and new books nearly every day, and the popular science press hails this new wave of theorizing as a breakthrough in understanding the mind (a typical example is the article in the May issue of *Science 86*, called "How we think: A new theory"). There are also, inevitably, descriptions of the emergence of Connectionism as a Kuhnian "paradigm shift." (See Schneider, 1987, for an example of this and for further evidence of the tendency to view Connectionism as the "new wave" of Cognitive Science.)

The fan club includes the most unlikely collection of people. Connectionism gives solace both to philosophers who think that relying on the pseudoscientific intentional or semantic notions of folk psychology (like goals and beliefs) mislead psychologists into taking the computational approach (e.g., P. M. Churchland, 1981; P. S. Churchland, 1986; Dennett, 1986); and to those with nearly the opposite perspective, who think that computational psychology is bankrupt because it doesn't address issues of intentionality or meaning (e.g., Dreyfus and Dreyfus, 1988). On the computer science side, Connectionism appeals to theorists who think that serial machines are too weak and must be replaced by radically new parallel machines (Fahlman and Hinton, 1986), while on the biological side it appeals to those who believe that cognition can only be understood if we study it as neuroscience (e.g., Arbib, 1975; Sejnowski, 1981). It is also attractive to psychologists who think that much of the mind (including the part involved in using imagery) is not discrete (e.g., Kosslyn and Hatfield, 1984), or who think that cognitive science has not paid enough attention to stochastic mechanisms or to "holistic" mechanisms (e.g., Lakoff, 1986), and so on and on. It also appeals to many young cognitive scientists who view the approach as not only anti-establishment (and therefore desirable) but also rigorous and mathematical (see, however, note 2). Almost everyone who is discontent with contemporary cognitive psychology and current "information processing" models of the mind has rushed to embrace "the Connectionist alternative."

When taken as a way of modeling *cognitive architecture*, Connectionism really does represent an approach that is quite different from that of the Classical cognitive science that it seeks to replace. Classical models of the mind were derived from the structure of Turing and von Neumann machines. They are not, of course, committed to the details of these machines as exemplified in Turing's original formulation or in typical commercial computers; only to the basic idea that the kind of computing that is relevant to understanding cognition involves operations on symbols (see Fodor, 1976, 1987; Newell, 1980, 1982; Pylyshyn, 1980, 1984a,b). In contrast, Connectionists propose to design systems that can exhibit intelligent behavior without storing, retrieving, or otherwise operating on structured symbolic expressions. The style of processing carried out in such models is thus strikingly unlike what goes on when conventional machines are computing some function.

Connectionist systems are networks consisting of very large numbers of simple but highly interconnected "units." Certain assumptions are generally made both about the units and the connections: Each unit is assumed to receive real-valued activity (either excitatory or inhibitory or both) along its input lines. Typically the units do little more than sum this activity and change their state as a function (usually a threshold function) of this sum. Each connection is allowed to modulate the activity it transmits as a function of an intrinsic (but modifiable) property called its "weight." Hence the activity on an input line is typically some non-linear function of the state of activity of its sources. The behavior of the network as a whole is a function of the initial state of activation of the units and of the weights on its connections, which serve as its only form of memory.

Numerous elaborations of this basic Connectionist architecture are possible. For example, Connectionist models often have stochastic mechanisms for determining the level of activity or the state of a unit. Moreover, units may be connected to outside environments. In this case the units are sometimes assumed to respond to a narrow range of combinations of parameter values and are said to have a certain "receptive field" in parameter-space. These are called "value units" (Ballard, 1986). In some versions of Connectionist architecture, environmental properties are encoded by the pattern of states of entire populations of units. Such "coarse coding" techniques are among the ways of achieving what Connectionists call "distributed representation."[1] The term "Connectionist model" (like "Turing Machine" or "van Neumann machine") is thus applied to a family of mechanisms that differ in details but share a galaxy of architectural commitments. We shall return to the characterization of these commitments below.

Connectionist networks have been analysed extensively—in some cases using advanced mathematical techniques.[2] They have also been simulated on computers and shown to exhibit interesting aggregate properties. For example, they can be "wired" to recognize patterns, to exhibit rule-like behavioral regularities, and to realize virtually any mapping from patterns of (input) parameters to patterns of (output) parameters—though in most cases multiparameter, multi-valued mappings require very large numbers of units. Of even greater interest is the fact that such networks can be made to learn; this is achieved by modifying the weights on the connections as a function of certain kinds of feedback (the exact way in which this is done constitutes a preoccupation of Connectionist research and has lead to the development of such important techniques as "back propagation").

In short, the study of Connectionist machines has led to a number of striking and unanticipated findings; it's surprising how much computing can be done with a uniform network of simple interconnected elements. Moreover, these models have an appearance of neural plausibility that Classical architectures are sometimes said to lack. Perhaps, then, a new Cognitive Science based on Connectionist networks should replace the old Cognitive Science based on Classical computers. Surely this is a proposal that ought to be taken seriously: if it is warranted, it implies a major redirection of research.

Unfortunately, however, discussions of the relative merits of the two architectures have thus far been marked by a variety of confusions and irrelevances. It's our view that when you clear away these misconceptions what's left is a real disagreement about the nature of mental processes and mental representations. But it seems to us that it is a matter that was substantially put to rest about thirty years ago; and the arguments that then appeared to militate decisively in favor of the Classical view appear to us to do so still.

In the present paper we will proceed as follows. First, we discuss some methodological questions about levels of explanation that have become enmeshed in the substantive controversy over Connectionism. Second, we try to say what it is that makes Connectionist and Classical theories of mental structure incompatible. Third, we review and extend some of the traditional arguments for the Classical architecture. Though these arguments have been somewhat recast, very little that we'll have to say here is entirely new. But we hope to make it clear how various aspects of the Classical doctrine cohere and why rejecting the Classical picture of reasoning leads Connectionists to say the very implausible things they do about logic and semantics.

1.1 Levels of Explanation

There are two major traditions in modern theorizing about the mind, one that we'll call "Representationalist" and one that we'll call "Eliminativist." Representationalists hold that postulating representational (or "intentional" or "semantic") states is essential to a theory of cognition; according to Representationalists, there are states of the mind which function to encode states of the world. Eliminativists, by contrast, think that psychological theories can dispense with such semantic notions as representation. According to Eliminativists the appropriate vocabulary for psychological theorizing is neurological or, perhaps behavioral, or perhaps syntactic; in any event, not a vocabulary that characterizes mental states in terms of what they represent. (For a neurological version of eliminativism, see P. S. Churchland, 1986; for a behavioral version, see Watson, 1930; for a syntactic version, see Stich, 1983.)

Connectionists are on the Representationalist side of this issue. As Rumelhart and McClelland (1986a, p. 121) say, PDPs "are explicitly concerned with the problem of internal representation." Correspondingly, the specification of what the states of a network *represent* is an essential part of a Connectionist model. Consider, for example, the well-known Connectionist account of the bistability of the Necker cube (Feldman and Ballard, 1982). "Simple units representing the visual features of the two alternatives are arranged in competing coalitions, with inhibitory ... links between rival features and positive links within each coalition.... The result is a network that has two dominant stable states." Notice that, in this as in all other such Connectionist models, the commitment to mental representation is explicit: the label of a node is taken to express the representational content of the state that the device is in when the node is excited, and there are nodes corresponding to monadic and to relational properties of the reversible cube when it is seen in one way or the other.

There are, to be sure, times when Connectionists appear to vacillate between Representationalism and the claim that the "cognitive level" is dispensable in favor of a more precise and biologically-motivated level of theory. In particular, there is a lot of talk in the Connectionist literature about processes that are "sub-symbolic"—and therefore presumably *not* representational. But this is misleading: Connectionist modeling is consistently Representationalist in practice, and Representationalism is generally endorsed by the very theorists who also like the idea of cognition "emerging from the subsymbolic." Thus, Rumelhart and McClelland (1986a, p. 121) insist that PDP models are "... strongly committed to the study of representation and process." Similarly, though Smolensky (1988, p. 2) takes Connectionism to articulate regularities at the "sub-symbolic level" of analysis, it turns out that sub-symbolic states do have a semantics, though it's not the semantics of representations at the "conceptual level." According to Smolensky, the semantical distinction between symbolic and sub-symbolic theories is just that "entities that are typically represented in the symbolic paradigm by [single] symbols are typically represented in the sub-symbolic paradigm by a large number of sub-symbols."[3] Both the conceptual and the sub-symbolic levels thus postulate representational states, but sub-symbolic theories slice them thinner.

We are stressing the Representationalist character of Connectionist theorizing because much Connectionist methodological writing has been preoccupied with the question "What level of explanation is appropriate for theories of cognitive architecture?" (see, for example, the exchange between Broadbent, 1985, and Rumelhart and McClelland, 1985). And, as we're about to see, what one says about the levels question depends a lot on what stand one takes about whether there are representational states.

It seems certain that the world has causal structure at very many different levels of analysis, with the individuals recognized at the lowest levels being, in general, very small and the individuals recognized at the highest levels being, in general, very large. Thus there is a scientific story to be told about quarks; and a scientific story to be told about atoms; and a scientific story to be told about molecules ... ditto rocks and stones and rivers ... ditto galaxies. And the story that scientists tell about the causal structure that the world has at any one of these levels may be quite different from the story that they tell about its causal structure at the next level up or down. The methodological implication for psychology is this: If you want to have an argument about *cognitive* architecture, you have to specify the level of analysis that's supposed to be at issue.

If you're *not* a Representationalist, this is quite tricky since it is then not obvious what makes a phenomenon cognitive. But specifying the level of analysis relevant for theories of cognitive architecture is no problem for either Classicists or Connectionists. Since Classicists and Connectionists are both Representationalists, for them any level at which states of the system are taken to encode properties of the world counts as a *cognitive* level; and no other levels do. (Representations of "the world" include of course, representations of symbols; for example, the concept WORD is a construct at the cognitive level because it represents something, namely words.) Correspondingly, it's the architecture of representational states and processes that discussions of *cognitive architecture* are about. Put differently, the architecture of the cognitive system consists of the set of basic operations, resources, functions, principles, etc. (generally the sorts of properties that would be described in a "user's manual" for that architecture if it were available on a computer), whose domain and range are the *representational states* of the organism.[4]

It follows that, if you want to make good the Connectionist theory *as a theory of cognitive architecture*, you have to show that the processes which operate on *the representational states* of an organism are those which are specified by a Connectionist architecture. It is, for example, *no use at all*, from the cognitive psychologist's point of view, to show that the *non*representational (e.g., neurological, or molecular, or quantum mechanical) states of an organism constitute a Connectionist network, because that would *leave open* the question whether the mind is such a network *at the psychological level*. It is, in particular, perfectly possible that nonrepresentational neurological states are interconnected in the ways described by Connectionist models *but that the representational states themselves are not*. This is because, just as it is possible to implement a *Connectionist* cognitive architecture in a network of causally interacting nonrepresentational elements, so too it is perfectly possible to implement a *Classical* cognitive architecture in such a network.[5] In fact, the question whether Connectionist networks should be treated as models at some level of implementation is moot.

It is important to be clear about this matter of levels on pain of simply trivializing the issues about cognitive architecture. Consider, for example, the following remark of Rumelhart's: "It has seemed to me for some years now that there must be a unified account in which the so-called rule-governed and [the] exceptional cases were dealt with by a unified underlying process—a process which produces rule-like and rule-exception behavior through the application of a single process ... [In this process] ... both the rule-like and non-rule-like behavior is a product of the interaction of a very large number of 'sub-symbolic' processes" (Rumelhart, 1984, p. 60). It's clear from the context that Rumelhart takes this idea to be very tendentious; one of the Connectionist claims that Classical theories are required to deny.

But in fact it's not. For, *of course* there are "sub-symbolic" interactions that implement both rule-like and rule-violating behavior; for example, quantum mechanical processes do. *That's* not what Classical theorists deny; indeed, it's not denied by anybody who is even vaguely a materialist. Nor does a Classical theorist deny that rule-following and rule-violating behaviors are both implemented by the very same neurological machinery. For a Classical theorist, neurons implement *all* cognitive processes in precisely the same way: viz., by supporting the basic operations that are required for symbol-processing.

What *would* be an interesting and tendentious claim is that there's no distinction between rule-following and rule-violating mentation *at the cognitive or representational or symbolic level*; specifically, that it is not the case that the etiology of rule-following behavior is mediated by the representation of explicit rules.[6] We will argue that it too is *not* what divides Classical from Connectionist architecture; Classical models *permit* a principled distinction between the etiologies of mental processes that are explicitly rule-governed and mental processes that aren't; but they don't demand one.

In short, the issue between Classical and Connectionist architecture is not about the explicitness of rules; as we'll presently see, Classical architecture is not, per se, committed to the idea that explicit rules mediate the etiology of behavior. And it is not about the reality of representational states; Classicists and Connectionists are all Representational Realists. And it is not about nonrepresentational architecture; a Connectionist neural network can perfectly well implement a Classical architecture at the cognitive level.

So, then, what *is* the disagreement between Classical and Connectionist architecture about?

2 The Nature of the Dispute

Classicists and Connectionists all assign semantic content to *something*. Roughly, Connectionists assign semantic content to "nodes" (that is, to units or aggregates of units; see note 1)—i.e., to the sorts of things that are typically labeled in Connectionist diagrams; whereas Classicists assign semantic content to *expressions*—i.e., to the sorts of things that get written on the tapes of Turing machines and stored at addresses in von Neumann machines.[7] But Classical theories disagree with Connectionist theories about what primitive relations hold among these content-bearing entities. Connectionist theories acknowledge *only causal connectedness* as a primitive relation among nodes: when you know how activation and inhibition flow among them, you know everything there is to know about how the nodes in a network are related. By contrast, Classical theories acknowledge not only causal relations among the semantically evaluable objects that they posit, but also a range of structural relations, of which constituency is paradigmatic.

This difference has far reaching consequences for the ways that the two kinds of theories treat a variety of cognitive phenomena, some of which we will presently examine at length. But, underlying the disagreements about details are two architectural differences between the theories:

(1) *Combinatorial syntax and semantics for mental representations* Classical theories—but not Connectionist theories—postulate a "language of thought" (see, for example, Fodor, 1975); they take mental representations to have *a combinatorial syntax and semantics*, in which (a) there is a distinction between structurally atomic and structurally molecular representations; (b) structurally molecular representations have syntactic constituents that are themselves either structurally molecular or structurally atomic; and (c) the semantic content of a (molecular) representation is a function of the semantic contents of its syntactic parts, together with its constituent structure. For purposes of convenience, we'll sometime abbreviate (a)–(c) by speaking of Classical theories as committed to "complex" mental representations or to "symbol structures."[8]

(2) *Structure sensitivity of processes* In Classical models, the principles by which mental states are transformed, or by which an input selects the corresponding output, are defined over structural properties of mental representations. Because Classical mental *representations* have combinatorial structure, it is possible for Classical mental *operations* to apply to them by reference to their form. The result is that a paradigmatic Classical mental process operates upon any mental representation that satisfies a given structural description, and transforms it into a mental representation that satisfies another structural description. (So, for example, in a model of inference one might recognize an operation that applies to any representation of the form *P&Q* and transforms it into a representation of the form *P*.) Notice that since formal properties can be defined at a variety of levels of abstraction, such an operation can apply equally to representations that differ widely in their structural complexity. The operation that applies to representations of the form *P&Q* to produce *P* is satisfied by, for example, an expression like "(AvBvC) & (DvEvF)", from which it derives the expression "(AvBvC)".

We take (1) and (2) as the claims that define Classical models, and we take these claims quite literally; they constrain the physical realizations of symbol structures. In particular, the symbol structures in a Classical model are assumed to correspond to real physical structures in the brain and the *combinatorial structure* of a representation is supposed to have a counterpart in structural relations among physical properties of the brain. For example, the relation "part of," which holds between a relatively simple symbol and a more complex one, is assumed to correspond to some physical relation among brain states.[9] This is why Newell (1980) speaks of computational systems such as brains and Classical computers as "*physical symbol systems*."

This bears emphasis because the Classical theory is committed not only to there being a system of physically instantiated symbols, but also to the claim that the physical properties onto which the structure of the symbols is mapped *are the very properties that cause the system to behave as it does*. In other words the physical counterparts of the symbols, and their structural properties, *cause* the system's behavior. A system which has symbolic expressions, but whose operation does not depend upon the structure of these expressions, does not qualify as a Classical machine since it fails to satisfy condition (2). In this respect, a Classical model is very different from one in which behavior is caused by mechanisms, such as energy minimization, that are not responsive to the physical encoding of the structure of representations.

From now on, when we speak of "Classical" models, we will have in mind *any* model that has complex mental representations, as characterized in (1) and structure-sensitive mental processes, as characterized in (2). Our account of Classical architecture is therefore neutral with respect to such issues as whether or not there is a separate executive. For example, Classical machines can have an "object-oriented" architecture, like that of the computer language *Smalltalk*, or a "message passing" architecture, like that of Hewett's (1977) *Actors*—so long as the objects or the messages have a combinatorial structure which is causally implicated in the processing. Classical architecture is also neutral on the question whether the operations on the symbols are constrained to occur one at a time or whether many operations can occur at the same time.

Here, then, is the plan for what follows. In the rest of this section, we will sketch the Connectionist proposal for a computational architecture that does away with complex mental representations and structure sensitive operations. (Although our purpose here is merely expository, it turns out that describing exactly what Connectionists are committed to requires substantial reconstruction of their remarks and practices. Since there is a great variety of points of view within the Connectionist community, we are prepared to find that some Connectionists in good standing may not fully endorse the program when it is laid out in what we take to be its bare essentials.) Following this general expository (or reconstructive) discussion, Section 3 provides a series of arguments favoring the Classical story. Then the remainder of the paper considers some of the reasons why Connectionism appears attractive to many people and offers further general comments on the relation between the Classical and the Connectionist enterprise.

2.1 Complex Mental Representations

To begin with, consider a case of the most trivial sort; two machines, one Classical in spirit and one Connectionist.[10] Here is how the Connectionist machine might reason.

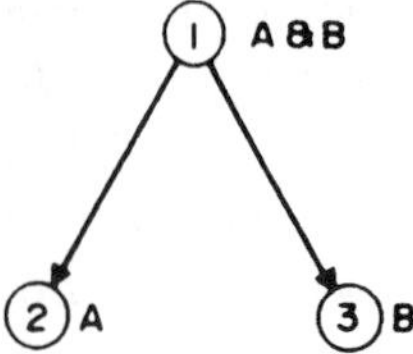

Figure 79.1
A possible Connectionist network for drawing inferences from A & B to A or to B.

There is a network of labelled nodes as in figure 79.1. Paths between the nodes indicate the routes along which activation can spread (that is, they indicate the consequences that exciting one of the nodes has for determining the level of excitation of others). Drawing an inference from A&B to A thus corresponds to an excitation of node 2 being caused by an excitation of node 1 (alternatively, if the system is in a state in which node 1 is excited, it eventually settles into a state in which node 2 is excited; see note 7).

Now consider a Classical machine. This machine has a tape on which it writes expressions. Among the expressions that can appear on this tape are: "A", "B", "A&B", "C", "D", "C&D", "A&C&D" ... etc. The machine's causal constitution is as follows: whenever a token of the form P&Q appears on the tape, the machine writes a token of the form P. An inference from A&B to A thus corresponds to a tokening of type "A&B" on the tape causing a tokening of type "A".

So then, what does the architectural difference between the machines consist in? In the Classical machine, the objects to which the content A&B is ascribed (viz., tokens of the expression "A&B") literally contain, as proper parts, objects to which the content A is ascribed (viz., tokens of the expression "A".) Moreover, the semantics (e.g., the satisfaction conditions) of the expression "A&B" is determined in a uniform way by the semantics of its constituents.[11] By contrast, in the Connectionist machine none of this is true; the object to which the content A&B is ascribed (viz., node 1) is causally connected to the object to which the content A is ascribed (viz., node 2); but there is no structural (e.g., no part/whole) relation that holds between them. In short, it is characteristic of Classical systems, but not of Connectionist systems, to exploit arrays of symbols some of which are atomic (e.g., expressions like "A") but indefinitely many of which have other symbols as syntactic and semantic parts (e.g., expressions like "A&B").

It is easy to overlook this difference between Classical and Connectionist architectures when reading the Connectionist polemical literature or examining a Connectionist model. There are at least four ways in which one might be lead to do so: (1) by failing to understand the difference between what arrays of symbols do in Classical machines and what node labels do in Connectionist machines; (2) by confusing the question whether the nodes in Connectionist networks have *constituent* structure with the question whether they are *neurologically distributed*; (3) by failing to distinguish between a representation having semantic and syntactic constituents and a concept being encoded in terms of microfeatures, and (4) assuming that since representations of Connectionist networks have a graph structure, it follows that the nodes in the networks have a corresponding constituent structure. We shall now need rather a long digression to clear up these misunderstandings.

2.1.1 The Role of Labels in Connectionist Theories In the course of setting out a Connectionist model, intentional content will be assigned to machine states, and the expressions of some language or other will, of course, be used to express this assignment; for example, nodes may be labelled to indicate their representational content. Such labels often have a combinatorial syntax and semantics; in this respect, they can look a lot like Classical mental representations. The point to emphasize, however, is that it doesn't follow (and it isn't true) that the nodes to which these labels are assigned have a combinatorial syntax and semantics. "A&B", for example, can be tokened on the tape of the Classical machine *and can also appear as a label in a Connectionist machine* as it does in figure 79.1. And, of course, the expression "A&B" is syntactically and semantically complex: it has a token of "A" as one of its syntactic constituents, and the semantics of the expression "A&B" is a function of the semantics of the expression "A". But it isn't part of the intended reading of the diagram that node 1 itself has constituents; the node—unlike its label—has no semantically interpreted parts.

It is, in short, important to understand the difference between Connectionist labels and the symbols over which Classical computations are defined. The difference is this: Strictly speaking, the labels play *no role at all* in determining the operation of a Connectionist machine; in particular, the operation of the machine is unaffected by the syntactic and semantic relations that hold among the expressions that are used as labels. To put this another way, the node labels in a Connectionist machine are not part of the causal structure of the machine. Thus, the machine depicted in figure 79.1 will continue to make the same state transitions regardless of what labels we assign to the nodes. Whereas, by contrast, the state transitions of Classical machines are causally determined *by the structure—including the constituent structure—of the symbol arrays that the machines transform*: change the symbols and the system behaves quite differently. (In fact, since the behavior of a Classical machine is sensitive to the syntax of the representations it computes on, even interchanging *synonymous*—semantically equivalent—representations affects the course of computation.) So, although the Connectionist's labels and the Classicist's data structures both constitute languages, only the latter language constitutes a medium of computation.[12]

2.1.2 Connectionist Networks and Graph Structures The *second* reason that the lack of syntactic and semantic structure in Connectionist representations has largely been ignored may be that Connectionist networks look like general graphs; and it is, of course, perfectly possible to use graphs to describe the internal structure of a complex symbol. That's precisely what linguists do when they use "trees" to exhibit the constituent structure of sentences. Correspondingly, one could imagine a graph notation that expresses the internal structure of mental representations by using arcs and labelled nodes. So, for example, you might express the syntax of the mental representation that corresponds to the thought that John loves the girl like this:

John → loves → the girl

Under the intended interpretation, this would be the structural description of a mental representation whose content is that John loves the girl, and whose constituents are: a mental representation that refers to *John*, a mental representation that refers to *the girl*, and a mental representation that expresses the two-place relation represented by "→ loves →".

But although graphs can sustain an interpretation as specifying the logical syntax of a complex mental representation, this interpretation is inappropriate for graphs of Connectionist networks. Connectionist graphs are not structural descriptions of mental representations; they're specifications of causal relations. All that a Connectionist can mean by a graph of the form X → Y is: *states of node X causally affect states of node Y*. In particular, the graph can't mean *X is a constituent of Y* or *X is grammatically related to Y* etc., since these sorts of relations are, in general, not defined for the kinds of mental representations that Connectionists recognize.

Another way to put this is that the links in Connectionist diagrams are not generalized pointers that can be made to take on different functional significance *by an independent interpreter*, but are confined to meaning something like "sends activation to." The intended interpretation of the links as causal Connections is intrinsic to the theory. If you ignore this point, you are likely to take Connectionism to offer a much richer notion of mental representation than it actually does.

2.1.3 Distributed Representations The *third* mistake that can lead to a failure to notice that the mental representations in Connectionist models lack combinatorial syntactic and semantic structure is the fact that many Connectionists view representations as being *neurologically distributed*; and, presumably, whatever is distributed must have parts. It doesn't follow, however, that whatever is distributed must have *constituents*; being neurologically distributed is very different from having semantic or syntactic constituent structure.

You have constituent structure when (and only when) the parts of semantically evaluable entities are themselves semantically evaluable. Constituency relations thus hold among objects all of which are at the representational level; they are, in that sense, *within* level relations.[13] By contrast, neural distributedness—the sort of relation that is assumed to hold between "nodes" and the "units" by which they are realized—is a *between* level relation: The nodes, but not the units, count as representations. To claim that a node is neurally distributed is presumably to claim that its states of activation correspond to patterns of neural activity—to aggregates of neural "units"—rather than to activations of single neurons. The important point is that nodes that are distributed in this sense can perfectly well be syntactically and semantically atomic: Complex spatially-distributed implementation in no way implies constituent structure.

There is, however, a different sense in which the representational states in a network might be distributed, and this sort of distribution also raises questions relevant to the constituency issue.

2.1.4 Representations as "Distributed" over Microfeatures Many Connectionists hold that the mental representations that correspond to commonsense concepts (CHAIR, JOHN, CUP, etc.) are "distributed" over galaxies of lower level units which themselves have representational content. To use common Connectionist terminology (see Smolensky, 1988), the higher or "conceptual level" units correspond to vectors in a "sub-conceptual" space of microfeatures. The model here is something like the relation between a defined expression and its defining feature analysis: thus, the concept BACHELOR might be thought to correspond to a vector in a space of features that includes ADULT, HUMAN, MALE, and MARRIED; i.e., as an assignment of the value + to the first two features and—to the last. Notice that distribution over microfeatures (unlike distribution over neural units) is a relation among representations, hence a relation at the cognitive level.

Since microfeatures are frequently assumed to be derived automatically (i.e., via learning procedures) from the statistical properties of samples of stimuli, we can think of them as expressing the sorts of properties that are revealed by multivariate analysis of sets of stimuli (e.g., by multidimensional scaling of similarity judgments). In particular, they need not correspond to English words; they can be finer-grained than, or otherwise atypical of, the terms for which a non-specialist needs to have a word. Other than that, however, they are perfectly ordinary semantic features, much like those that lexicographers have traditionally used to represent the meanings of words.

On the most frequent Connectionist accounts, theories articulated in terms of microfeature vectors are supposed to show how concepts are *actually* encoded, hence the feature vectors are intended to *replace* "less precise" specifications of macrolevel concepts. For example, where a Classical theorist might recognize a psychological state of entertaining the concept CUP, a Connectionist may acknowledge only a *roughly analogous* state of tokening the corresponding feature vector. (One reason that the analogy is only rough is that which feature vector "corresponds" to a given concept may be viewed as heavily context dependent.) The generalizations that "concept level" theories frame are thus taken to be only approximately true, the exact truth being stateable only in the vocabulary of the microfeatures. Smolensky, for example (p. 11), is explicit in endorsing this picture: "Precise, formal descriptions of the intuitive processor are generally tractable not at the conceptual level, but only at the subconceptual level."[14] This treatment of the relation between commonsense concepts and microfeatures is exactly analogous to the standard Connectionist treatment of rules; in both cases, macrolevel theory is said to provide a vocabulary adequate for formulating generalizations that roughly approximate the facts about behavioral regularities. But the contructs of the macrotheory do *not* correspond to the causal mechanisms that generate these regularities. If you want a theory of these mechanisms, you need to replace talk about rules and concepts with talk about nodes, connections, microfeatures, vectors and the like.[15]

Now, it is among the major misfortunes of the Connectionist literature that the issue about whether commonsense concepts should be represented by sets of microfeatures has gotten thoroughly mixed up with the issue about combinatorial structure in mental representations. The crux of the mixup is the fact that sets of microfeatures can overlap, so that, for example, if a microfeature corresponding to "+ has-a-handle" is part of the array of nodes over which the commonsense concept CUP is distributed, then you might think of the theory as representing "+ has-a-handle" as a *constituent* of the concept CUP; from which you might conclude that Connectionists have a notion of constituency after all, contrary to the claim that Connectionism is not a language-of-thought architecture (see Smolensky, 1988).

A moment's consideration will make it clear, however, that even on the assumption that concepts are distributed over microfeatures, "+ has-a-handle" is not a constituent of CUP in anything like the sense that "Mary" (the word) is a constituent of (the sentence) "John loves Mary." In the former case, "constituency" is being (mis)used to refer to a semantic relation between predicates; roughly, the idea is that macrolevel predicates like CUP are defined by sets of microfeatures like "has-a-handle," so that it's some sort of semantic truth that CUP applies to a subset of what "has-a-handle" applies to. Notice that while the extensions of these predicates are in a set/subset relation, the predicates themselves are not in any sort of part-to-whole relation. The expression "has-a-handle" isn't *part of* the expression CUP any more than the English phrase "is an unmarried man" is part of the English phrase "is a bachelor."

Real constituency does have to do with parts and wholes; the symbol "Mary" is literally a part of the symbol "John loves Mary." It is because their symbols enter into real-constituency relations that natural languages have both atomic symbols and complex ones. By contrast, the definition relation can hold in a language where *all* the symbols are syntactically atomic; e.g., a language which contains both "cup" and "has-a-handle" as atomic predicates. This point is worth stressing. The question whether a representational system has real-constituency is independent of the question of microfeature analysis; it arises both for systems in which you have CUP as semantically primitive, and for systems in which the semantic primitives are things like "+ has-a-handle" and CUP and the like are defined in terms of these primitives. It really is very important not to confuse the semantic distinction between primitive expressions and defined expressions with the syntactic distinction between atomic symbols and complex symbols.

So far as we know, there are no worked out attempts in the Connectionist literature to deal with the syntactic and semantical issues raised by relations of real-constituency. There is, however, a proposal that comes up from time to time: viz., that what are traditionally treated as complex symbols should actually be viewed as just sets of units, with the role relations that traditionally get coded by constituent structure represented by units belonging to these sets. So, for example, the mental representation corresponding to the belief that John loves Mary might be the feature vector {+*John-subject*; +*loves*; +*Mary-object*}. Here "John-subject," "Mary-object" and the like are the labels of units; that is, they are atomic (i.e., micro-) features, whose status is analogous to "has-a-handle." In particular, they have no internal syntactic analysis, and there is no structural relation (except the orthographic one) between the feature "Mary-object" that occurs in the set {John-subject; loves; Mary-object} and the feature "Mary-subject" that occurs in the set {Mary-subject; loves; John-object}. (See, for example, the discussion in Hinton, 1987 of "role-specific descriptors that represent the conjunction of an identity and a role [by the use of which] we can implement part-whole hierarchies using set intersection as the composition rule." See also, McClelland, Rumelhart and Hinton, 1986, p. 82–85, where what appears to be the same treatment is proposed in somewhat different terms.)

Since, as we remarked, these sorts of ideas aren't elaborated in the Connectionist literature, detailed discussion is probably not warranted here. But it's worth a word to make clear what sort of trouble you would get into if you were to take them seriously.

As we understand it, the proposal really has two parts: On the one hand, it's suggested that although Connectionist representations cannot exhibit real-constituency, nevertheless the Classical distinction between complex symbols and their constituents can be replaced by the distinction between feature sets and their subsets; and, on the other hand, it's suggested that role relations can be captured by features. We'll consider these ideas in turn.

(1) Instead of having complex symbols like "John loves Mary" in the representational system, you have feature sets like {+*John-subject*; +*loves*; +*Mary-object*}. Since this set has {+*John-subject*}, {+*loves*; +*Mary-object*} and so forth as sub-sets, it may be supposed that the force of the constituency relation has been captured by employing the subset relation.

However, it's clear that this idea won't work since not all subsets of features correspond to genuine constituents. For example, among the subsets of {+*John-subject*; +*loves*; +*Mary-object*} are the sets {+*John-subject*; +*Mary-object*} and the set {+*John-subject*; +*loves*} which do not, of course, correspond to constituents of the complex symbol "John loves Mary."

(2) Instead of defining roles in terms of relations among constituents, as one does in Classical architecture, introduce them as microfeatures.

Consider a system in which the mental representation that is entertained when one believes that John loves Mary is the feature set {+*John-subject*; +*loves*; +*Mary-object*}. What representation corresponds to the belief that John loves Mary and Bill hates Sally? Suppose, pursuant to the present proposal, that it's the set {+*John-subject*; +*loves*; +*Mary-object*; +*Bill-subject*; +*hates*; +*Sally-object*}. We now have the problem of distinguishing that belief from the belief that John loves Sally and Bill hates Mary; and from the belief that John hates Mary and Bill loves Sally; and from the belief that John hates Mary and Sally and Bill loves Mary; etc., since these other beliefs will all correspond to precisely the same set of features. The problem is, of course, that nothing in the representation of Mary as +*Mary-object* specifies whether it's the loving or the hating that she is the object of; similarly, mutatis mutandis, for the representation of John as +*John-subject*.

What has gone wrong isn't disastrous (yet). All that's required is to enrich the system of representations by recognizing features that correspond not to (for example) just being a subject, but rather to being the subject of a loving of Mary (the property that John has when John loves Mary) and being the subject of a hating of Sally (the property that Bill has when Bill hates Sally). So, the representation of John that's entertained when one believes that John loves Mary and Bill hates Sally might be something like +*John-subject-hates-Mary-object*.

The disadvantage of this proposal is that it requires rather a lot of microfeatures.[16] How many? Well, a number of the order of magnitude of the *sentences* of a natural language (whereas one might have hoped to get by with a vocabulary of basic expressions that is not vastly larger than the *lexicon* of a natural language; after all, natural languages do). We leave it to the reader to estimate the number of microfeatures you would need, assuming that there is a distinct belief corresponding to every grammatical sentence of English of up to, say, fifteen words of length, and assuming that there is an average of, say, five roles associated with each belief. (Hint: George Miller once estimated that the number of well-formed 20-word sentences of English is of the order of magnitude of the number of seconds in the history of the universe.)

The alternative to this grotesque explosion of atomic symbols would be to have *a combinatorial syntax and semantics for the features*. But, of course, this is just to give up the game since the syntactic and semantic relations that hold among the parts of the complex feature *+((John subject) loves (Mary object))* are the very same ones that Classically hold among the constituents of the complex symbol "John loves Mary"; these include the role relations which Connectionists had proposed to reconstruct using just sets of atomic features. It is, of course, no accident that the Connectionist proposal for dealing with role relations runs into these sorts of problems. Subject, object and the rest are Classically defined *with respect to the geometry of constituent structure trees*. And Connectionist representations don't have constituents.

The idea that we should capture role relations by allowing features like *John-subject* thus turns out to be bankrupt; and there doesn't seem to be any other way to get the force of structured symbols in a Connectionist architecture. Or, if there is, nobody has given any indication of how to do it. This becomes clear once the crucial issue about structure in mental representations is disentangled from the relatively secondary (and orthogonal) issue about whether the representation of commonsense concepts is "distributed" (i.e., from questions like whether it's CUP or "has-a-handle" or both that is semantically primitive in the language of thought).

It's worth adding that these problems about expressing the role relations are actually just a symptom of a more pervasive difficulty: A consequence of restricting the vehicles of mental representation to sets of atomic symbols is a notation that fails quite generally to express the way that concepts group into propositions. To see this, let's continue to suppose that we have a network in which the nodes represent concepts rather than propositions (so that what corresponds to the thought that John loves Mary is a distribution of activation over the set of nodes {JOHN; LOVES; MARY} rather than the activation of a single node labelled JOHN LOVES MARY). Notice that it cannot plausibly be assumed that all the nodes that happen to be active at a given time will correspond to concepts that are constituents of the *same* proposition; least of all if the architecture is "massively parallel" so that many things are allowed to go on—many concepts are allowed to be entertained—simultaneously in a given mind. Imagine, then, the following situation: at time t, a man is looking at the sky (so the nodes corresponding to SKY and BLUE are active) and thinking that John loves Fido (so the nodes corresponding to JOHN, LOVES, and FIDO are active), and the node FIDO is connected to the node DOG (which is in turn connected to the node ANIMAL) in such fashion that DOG and ANIMAL are active too, We can, if you like, throw it in that the man has got an itch, so ITCH is also on.

According to the current theory of mental representation, this man's mind at t is specified by the vector {+JOHN, +LOVES, +FIDO, +DOG, +SKY, +BLUE, +ITCH, +ANIMAL}. And the question is: *which subvectors of this vector correspond to thoughts that the man is thinking?* Specifically, what is it about the man's representational state that determines that the simultaneous activation of the nodes, {JOHN, LOVES, FIDO} constitutes his thinking that John loves Fido, but the simultaneous activation of FIDO, ANIMAL and BLUE does *not* constitute his thinking that Fido is a blue animal? It seems that we made it too easy for ourselves when we identified the thought that John loves

Mary with the vector {+JOHN, +LOVES, +MARY}; at best that works only on the assumption that JOHN, LOVES and MARY are the only nodes active when someone has that thought. And that's an assumption to which no theory of mental representation is entitled.

It's important to see that this problem arises precisely because the theory is trying to use sets of atomic representations to do a job that you really need complex representations for. Thus, the question we're wanting to answer is: Given the total set of nodes active at a time, what distinguishes the subvectors that correspond to propositions from the subvectors that don't? This question has a straightforward answer if, contrary to the present proposal, complex representations are assumed: When representations express concepts that belong to the same proposition, they are not merely simultaneously active, but also *in construction with each other*. By contrast, representations that express concepts that don't belong to the same proposition may be simultaneously active; but, they are ipso facto *not* in construction with each other.

In short, you need two degrees of freedom to specify the thoughts that an intentional system is entertaining at a time: one parameter (active vs inactive) picks out the nodes that express concepts that the system has in mind; the other (in construction vs not) determines how the concepts that the system has in mind are distributed in the propositions that it entertains. For symbols to be "in construction" in this sense is just for them to be constituents of a complex symbol. Representations that are in construction form parts of a geometrical whole, *where the geometrical relations are themselves semantically significant.* Thus the representation that corresponds to the thought that John loves Fido is not a *set* of concepts but something like a *tree* of concepts, and it's the geometrical relations in this tree that mark (for example) the difference between the thought that John loves Fido and the thought that Fido loves John.

We've occasionally heard it suggested that you could solve the present problem consonant with the restriction against complex representations if you allow networks like this:

The intended interpretation is that the thought that Fido bites corresponds to the simultaneous activation of these nodes; that is, to the vector {+FIDO, +SUBJECT OF, +BITES}—with similar though longer vectors for more complex role relations.

But, on second thought, this proposal merely begs the question that it set out to solve. For, if there's a problem about what justifies assigning the proposition *John loves Fido* as the content of the set {JOHN, LOVES, FIDO}, there is surely the same problem about what justifies assigning the proposition *Fido is the subject of bites* to the set {FIDO, SUBJECT-OF, BITES}. If this is not immediately clear, consider the case where the simultaneously active nodes are {FIDO, SUBJECT-OF, BITES, JOHN}. Is the propositional content that Fido bites or that John does?[17]

Strikingly enough, the point that we've been making in the past several paragraphs is very close to one that Kant made against the Associationists of his day. In "Transcendental Deduction (B)" of The First Critique, Kant remarks that:

> ... if I investigate ... the relation of the given modes of knowledge in any judgement, and distinguish it, as belonging to the understanding, from the relation according to laws of the reproductive imagination [e.g., according to the principles of association], which has only subjective validity, I find that a judgement is nothing but the manner in which given modes of knowledge are brought to the objective unity of apperception. This is what is intended by the copula "is." It is employed to distinguish the objective unity of given representations from the subjective.... Only in this way does there arise from the relation a *judgement,* that is a relation which is *objectively valid,* and so can be adequately distinguished from a relation of the same representations that would have only subjective validity—as when they are connected according to laws of association. In the latter case, all that I could say would be "If I support a body, I feel an impression of weight"; I could not say, "It, the body, is heavy." Thus to say "The body is heavy" is not merely to state that the two representations have always been conjoined in my perception,... what we are asserting is that they are combined *in the object*... (CPR, p. 159; emphasis Kant's)

A modern paraphrase might be: A theory of mental representation must distinguish the case when two concepts (e.g., THIS BODY, HEAVY) are merely *simultaneously entertained* from the case where, to put it roughly, the property that one of the concepts expresses is predicated of the thing that the other concept denotes (as in the thought: THIS BODY IS HEAVY). The relevant distinction is that while both concepts are "active" in both cases, in the latter case but *not* in the former the active concepts are in construction. Kant thinks that "this is what is intended by the copula 'is.'" But of course there are other notational devices that can serve to specify that concepts are in construction; notably the bracketing structure of constituency trees.

There are, to reiterate, two questions that you need to answer to specify the content of a mental state: "Which concepts are 'active'" and "Which of the active concepts are in construction with which others?" Identifying mental states with sets of active nodes provides resources to answer the first of these questions but not the second. That's why the version of network theory that acknowledges sets of atomic representations but no complex representations fails, in indefinitely many cases, to distinguish mental states that are in fact distinct.

But we are *not* claiming that you can't reconcile a Connectionist architecture with an adequate theory of mental representation (specifically with a combinatorial syntax and semantics for mental representations). On the contrary, of course you can: All that's required is that you use your network to implement a Turing machine, and specify a combinatorial structure for its computational language. What it appears that you can't do, however, is have both a combinatorial representational system and a Connectionist architecture *at the cognitive level.*

So much, then, for our long digression. We have now reviewed one of the major respects in which Connectionist and Classical theories differ; viz., their accounts of mental *representations*. We turn to the second major difference, which concerns their accounts of mental *processes*.

2.2 Structure Sensitive Operations

Classicists and Connectionists both offer accounts of mental processes, but their theories differ sharply. In particular, the Classical theory relies heavily on the notion of the logico/syntactic form of mental representations to define the ranges and domains of mental operations. This notion is, however, unavailable to orthodox Connectionists since it presupposes that there are nonatomic mental representations.

The Classical treatment of mental processes rests on two ideas, each of which corresponds to an aspect of the Classical theory of computation. Together they explain why the Classical view postulates at least three distinct levels of organization in computational systems: not just a physical level and a semantic (or "knowledge") level, but a syntactic level as well.

The first idea is that it is possible to construct languages in which certain features of the syntactic structures of formulas correspond systematically to certain of their semantic features. Intuitively, the idea is that in such languages the syntax of a formula encodes its meaning; most especially, those aspects of its meaning that determine its role in inference. All the artificial languages that are used for logic have this property and English has it more or less. Classicists believe that it is a crucial property of the Language of Thought.

A simple example of how a language can use syntactic structure to encode inferential roles and relations among meanings may help to illustrate this point. Thus, consider the relation between the following two sentences:

(1) John went to the store and Mary went to the store.

(2) Mary went to the store.

On the one hand, from the semantic point of view, (1) entails (2) (so, of course, inferences from (1) to (2) are truth preserving). On the other hand, from the syntactic point of view, (2) is a constituent of (1). These two facts can be brought into phase by exploiting the principle that sentences with the *syntactic structure* "(S1 and S2)$_S$" entail their sentential constituents. Notice that this principle connects the syntax of these sentences with their inferential roles. Notice too that the trick relies on facts about the grammar of English; it wouldn't work in a language where the formula that expresses the conjunctive content *John went to the store and Mary went to the store* is *syntactically* atomic.[18]

Here is another example. We can reconstruct such truth preserving inferences as *if Rover bites then something bites* on the assumption that (a) the sentence "Rover bites" is of the syntactic type **F**a, (b) the sentence "something bites" is of the syntactic type ∃x (**F**x) and (c) every formula of the first type entails a corresponding formula of the second type (where the notion "corresponding formula" is cashed syntactically; roughly the two formulas must differ only in that the one has an existentially bound variable at the syntactic position that is occupied by a constant in the other). Once again the point to notice is the blending of syntactical and semantical notions: The rule of existential generalization applies to formulas in virtue of their syntactic form. But the salient property that's preserved under applications of the rule is semantical: What's claimed for the transformation that the rule performs is that it is *truth* preserving.[19]

There are, as it turns out, examples that are quite a lot more complicated than these. The whole of the branch of logic known as proof theory is devoted to exploring them.[20] It would not be unreasonable to describe Classical Cognitive Science as an extended attempt to apply the methods of proof theory to the modeling of thought (and similarly, of whatever other mental processes are plausibly viewed as involving inferences; preeminently learning and perception). Classical theory construction rests on the hope that syntactic analogues can be constructed for nondemonstrative inferences (or informal, commonsense reasoning) in something like the way that proof theory has provided syntactic analogues for validity.

The second main idea underlying the Classical treatment of mental processes is that it is possible to devise machines whose function is the transformation of symbols, and whose operations are sensitive to the syntactical structure of the symbols that they operate upon. This is the Classical conception of a computer: it's what the various architectures that derive from Turing and von Neumann machines all have in common.

Perhaps it's obvious how the two "main ideas" fit together. If, in principle, syntactic relations can be made to parallel semantic relations, and if, in principle, you can have a mechanism whose operations on formulas are sensitive to their syntax, then it may be possible to construct a *syntactically* driven machine whose state transitions satisfy *semantical* criteria of coherence. Such a machine would be just what's required for a mechanical model of the semantical coherence of thought; correspondingly, the idea that the brain *is* such a machine is the foundational hypothesis of Classical cognitive science.

So much for the Classical story about mental processes. The Connectionist story must, of course, be quite different: Since Connectionists eschew postulating mental representations with combinatorial syntactic/semantic structure, they are precluded from postulating mental processes that operate on mental representations in a way that is sensitive to their structure. The sorts of operations that Connectionist models do have are of two sorts, depending on whether the process under examination is learning or reasoning.

2.2.1 Learning If a Connectionist model is intended to learn, there will be processes that determine the weights of the connections among its units as a function of the character of its training. Typically in a Connectionist machine (such as a "Boltzman Machine") the weights among connections are adjusted until the system's behavior comes to model the statistical properties of its inputs. In the limit, the stochastic relations among machine states recapitulates the stochastic relations among the environmental events that they represent.

This should bring to mind the old Associationist principle that the strength of association between "Ideas" is a function of the frequency with which they are paired "in experience" and the Learning Theoretic principle that the strength of a stimulus–response connection is a function of the frequency with which the response is rewarded in the presence of the stimulus. But though Connectionists, like other Associationists, are committed to learning processes that model statistical properties of inputs and outputs, the simple mechanisms based on co-occurrence statistics that were the hallmarks of old-fashioned Associationism have been augmented in Connectionist models by a number of technical devices. (Hence the "new" in "New Connectionism.") For example, some of the earlier limitations of associative mechanisms are overcome by allowing the network to contain "hidden" units (or aggregates) that are not directly connected to the environment and whose purpose is, in effect, to detect statistical patterns in the activity of the "visible" units including, perhaps, patterns that are more abstract or more "global" than the ones that could be detected by old-fashioned perceptrons.[21]

In short, sophisticated versions of the associative principles for weight-setting are on offer in the Connectionist literature. The point of present concern, however, is what all versions of these principles have in common with one another and with older kinds of Associationism: viz., these processes are all *frequency*-sensitive. To return to the example discussed above: if a Connectionist learning machine converges on a state where it is prepared to infer A from A&B (i.e., to a state in which when the "A&B" node is excited it tends to settle into a state in which the "A" node is excited) the convergence will typically be caused by statistical properties of the machine's training experience: e.g., by correlation between firing of the "A&B" node and firing of the "A" node, or by correlations of the firing of both with some feedback signal. Like traditional Associationism, Connectionism treats learning as basically a sort of statistical modeling.

2.2.2 Reasoning Association operates to alter the structure of a network *diachronically* as a function of its training. Connectionist models also contain a variety of types of "relaxation" processes which determine the *synchronic* behavior of a network; specifically, they determine what output the device provides for a given pattern of inputs. In this respect, one can think of a Connectionist model as a species of analog machine constructed to realize a certain function. The inputs to the function are (i) a specification of the connectedness of the machine (of which nodes are connected to which); (ii) a specification of the weights along the connections; (iii) a specification of the values of a variety of idiosyncratic parameters of the nodes (e.g., intrinsic thresholds; time since last firing, etc.) (iv) a specification of a pattern of excitation over the input nodes. The output of the function is a specification of a pattern of excitation over the output nodes; intuitively, the machine chooses the output pattern that is most highly associated to its input.

Much of the mathematical sophistication of Connectionist theorizing has been devoted to devising analog solutions to this problem of finding a "most highly associated" output corresponding to an arbitrary input; but, once again, the details needn't concern us. What is important, for our purposes, is another property that Connectionist theories share with other forms of Associationism. In traditional Associationism, the probability that one Idea will elicit another is sensitive to the strength of the association between them (including "mediating" associations, if any). And the strength of this association is in turn sensitive to the extent to which the Ideas have previously been correlated. Associative strength was not, however, presumed to be sensitive to features of the content or the structure of representations per se. Similarly, in Connectionist models, the selection of an output corresponding to a given input is a function of properties of the paths that connect them (including the weights, the states of intermediate units, etc.). And the weights, in turn, are a function of the statistical properties of events in the environment (or of relations between patterns of events in the environment and implicit "predictions" made by the network, etc.). But the syntactic/semantic structure of the representation of an input is *not* presumed to be a factor in determining the selection of a corresponding output since, as we have seen, syntactic/semantic structure is not defined for the sorts of representations that Connectionist models acknowledge.

To summarize: Classical and Connectionist theories disagree about the nature of mental representation; for the former, but not for the latter, mental representations characteristically exhibit a combinatorial constituent structure and a combinatorial semantics. Classical and Connectionist theories also disagree about the nature of mental processes; for the former, but not for the latter, mental processes are characteristically sensitive to the combinatorial structure of the representations on which they operate.

We take it that these two issues define the present dispute about the nature of cognitive architecture. We now propose to argue that the Connectionists are on the wrong side of both.

3 The Need for Symbol Systems: Productivity, Systematicity, Compositionality and Inferential Coherence

Classical psychological theories appeal to the constituent structure of mental representations to explain three closely related features of cognition: its productivity, its compositionality and its inferential coherence. The traditional argument has been that these features of cognition are, on the one hand, pervasive and, on the other hand, explicable only on the assumption that mental representations have internal structure. This argument—familiar in more or less explicit versions for the last thirty years or so—is still intact, so far as we can tell. It appears to offer something close to a demonstration that an empirically adequate cognitive theory must recognize not just causal relations among representational states but also relations of syntactic and semantic constituency; hence that the mind cannot be, in its general structure, a Connectionist network.

3.1 Productivity of Thought

There is a classical productivity argument for the existence of combinatorial structure in any rich representational system (including natural languages and the language of thought). The representational capacities of such a system are, by assumption, unbounded under appropriate idealization; in particular, there are indefinitely many propositions which the system can encode.[22] However, this unbounded expressive power must presumably be achieved by finite means. The way to do this is to treat the system of representations as consisting of expressions belonging to a generated set. More precisely, the correspondence between a representation and the proposition it expresses is, in arbitrarily many cases, built up recursively out of correspondences between parts of the expression and parts of the proposition. But, of course, this strategy can operate only when an unbounded number of the expressions are non-atomic. So linguistic (and mental) representations must constitute *symbol systems* (in the sense of note 8). So the mind cannot be a PDP.

Very often, when people reject this sort of reasoning, it is because they doubt that human cognitive capacities are correctly viewed as productive. In the long run there can be no a priori arguments for (or against) idealizing to productive capacities; whether you accept the idealization depends on whether you believe that the inference from finite performance to finite capacity is justified, or whether you think that finite performance is typically a result of the interaction of an unbounded competence with resource constraints. Classicists have traditionally offered a mixture of methodological and empirical considerations in favor of the latter view.

From a methodological perspective, the least that can be said for assuming productivity is that it precludes solutions that rest on inappropriate tricks (such as storing all the pairs that define a function); tricks that would be unreasonable in practical terms even for solving finite tasks that place sufficiently large demands on memory. The idealization to unbounded productive capacity forces the theorist to separate the finite specification of a method for solving a computational problem from such factors as the resources that the system (or person) brings to bear on the problem at any given moment.

The empirical arguments for productivity have been made most frequently in connection with linguistic competence. They are familiar from the work of Chomsky (1968) who has claimed (convincingly, in our view) that the knowledge underlying linguistic competence is generative—i.e., that it allows us *in principle* to generate (/understand) an unbounded number of sentences. It goes without saying that no one does, or could, *in fact* utter or understand tokens of more than a finite number of sentence types; this is a trivial consequence of the fact that nobody can utter or understand more than a finite number of sentence tokens. But there are a number of considerations which suggest that, despite de facto constraints on performance, ones knowledge of ones language supports an unbounded productive capacity in much the same way that ones knowledge of addition supports an unbounded number of sums. Among these considerations are, for example, the fact that a speaker/hearer's performance can often be improved by relaxing time constraints, increasing motivation, or supplying pencil and paper. It seems very natural to treat such manipulations as affecting the transient state of the speaker's memory and attention rather than what he knows about—or how he represents—his language. But this treatment is available only on the assumption that the character of the subject's performance is determined by interactions between the available knowledge base and the available computational resources.

Classical theories are able to accommodate these sorts of considerations because they assume architectures in which there is a functional distinction between memory and program. In a system such as a Turing machine, where the length of the tape is not fixed in advance, changes in the amount of available memory *can be affected without changing the computational structure of the machine*; viz., by making more tape available. By contrast, in a finite state automaton or a Connectionist machine, adding to the memory (e.g., by adding units to a network) alters the connectivity relations among nodes and thus does affect the machine's computational structure. Connectionist cognitive architectures cannot, by their very nature, support an expandable memory, so they cannot support productive cognitive capacities. The long and short is that if productivity arguments are sound, then they show that the architecture of the mind can't be Connectionist. Connectionists have, by and large, acknowledged this; so they are forced to reject productivity arguments.

The test of a good scientific idealization is simply and solely whether it produces successful science in the long term. It seems to us that the productivity idealization has more than earned its keep, especially in linguistics and in theories of reasoning. Connectionists, however, have not been persuaded. For example, Rumelhart and McClelland (1986a, p. 119) say that they "... do not agree that [productive] capabilities are of the essence of human computation. As anyone who has ever attempted to process sentences like 'The man the boy the girl hit kissed moved' can attest, our ability to process even moderate degrees of center-embedded structure is grossly impaired relative to an ATN [Augmented Transition Network] parser.... What is needed, then, is not a mechanism for flawless and effortless processing of embedded constructions ... The challenge is to explain how those processes that others have chosen to explain in terms of recursive mechanisms can be better explained by the kinds of processes natural for PDP networks."

These remarks suggest that Rumelhart and McClelland think that the fact that center-embedding sentences are hard is somehow an *embarrassment* for theories that view linguistic capacities as productive. But of course it's not since, according to such theories, performance is an effect of interactions between a productive competence and restricted resources. There are, in fact, quite plausible Classical accounts of why center-embeddings ought to impose especially heavy demands on resources, and there is a reasonable amount of experimental support for these models (see, for example, Wanner and Maratsos, 1978).

In any event, it should be obvious that the difficulty of parsing center-embeddings can't be a consequence of their recursiveness per se since there are many recursive structures that are strikingly easy to understand. Consider: "this is the dog that chased the cat that ate the rat that lived in the house that Jack built." The Classicist's case for productive capacities in parsing rests on the transparency of sentences like these.[23] In short, the fact that center-embedded sentences are hard perhaps shows that there are some recursive structures that we can't parse. But what Rumelhart and McClelland need if they are to deny the productivity of linguistic capacities is the much stronger claim that there are no recursive structures that we can parse; and this stronger claim would appear to be simply false.

Rumelhart and McClelland's discussion of recursion (pp. 119–120) nevertheless repays close attention. They are apparently prepared to concede that PDPs can model recursive capacities only indirectly—viz., by implementing Classical architectures like ATNs; so that *if* human cognition exhibited recursive capacities, that would suffice to show that minds have Classical rather than Connectionist architecture at the psychological level. "We have not dwelt on PDP implementations of Turing machines and recursive processing engines *because we do not agree with those who would argue that such capacities are of the essence of human computation*" (p. 119, our emphasis). Their argument that recursive capacities *aren't* "of the essence of human computation" is, however, just the unconvincing stuff about center-embedding quoted above.

So the Rumelhart and McClelland view is apparently that if you take it to be independently obvious that some cognitive capacities are productive, then you should take the existence of such capacities to argue for Classical cognitive architecture and hence for treating Connectionism as at best an implementation theory. We think that this is quite a plausible understanding of the bearing that the issues about productivity and recursion have on the issues about cognitive architecture....

In the meantime, however, we propose to view the status of productivity arguments for Classical architectures as moot; we're about to present a different sort of argument for the claim that mental representations need an articulated internal structure. It is closely related to the productivity argument, but it doesn't require the idealization to unbounded competence. Its assumptions should thus be acceptable even to theorists who—like Connectionists—hold that the finitistic character of cognitive capacities is intrinsic to their architecture.

3.2 Systematicity of Cognitive Representation

The form of the argument is this: Whether or not cognitive capacities are really *productive*, it seems indubitable that they are what we shall call "systematic." And we'll see that the systematicity of cognition provides as good a reason for postulating combinatorial structure in mental representation as the productivity of cognition does: You get, in effect, the same conclusion, but from a weaker premise.

The easiest way to understand what the systematicity of cognitive capacities amounts to is to focus on the systematicity of language comprehension and production. In fact, the systematicity argument for combinatorial structure in *thought* exactly recapitulates the traditional Structuralist argument for constituent structure in sentences. But we pause to remark upon a point that we'll re-emphasize later; linguistic capacity is a paradigm of systematic cognition, but it's wildly unlikely that it's the only example. On the contrary, there's every reason to believe that systematicity is a thoroughly pervasive feature of human and infrahuman mentation.

What we mean when we say that linguistic capacities are *systematic* is that the ability to produce/understand some sentences is *intrinsically* connected to the ability to produce/understand certain others. You can see the force of this if you compare learning languages the way we really do learn them with learning a language by memorizing an enormous phrase book. The point isn't that phrase books are finite and can therefore exhaustively specify only *non*-productive languages; that's true, but we've agreed not to rely on productivity arguments for our present purposes. Our point is rather that you can learn *any part of a phrase book without learning the rest.* Hence, on the phrase book model, it would be perfectly possible to learn that uttering the form of words "Granny's cat is on Uncle Arthur's mat" is the way to say (in English) that Granny's cat is on Uncle Arthur's mat, and yet have no idea at all how to say that it's raining (or, for that matter, how to say that Uncle Arthur's cat is on Granny's mat). Perhaps it's self-evident that the phrase book story must be wrong about language acquisition because a speaker's knowledge of his native language is never like that. You don't, for example, find native speakers who know how to say in English that John loves the girl but don't know how to say in English that the girl loves John.

Notice, in passing, that systematicity is a property of the mastery of the syntax of a language, not of its lexicon. The phrase book model really does fit what it's like to learn the *vocabulary* of English since when you learn English vocabulary you acquire a lot of basically *independent* capacities. So you might perfectly well learn that using the expression "cat" is the way to refer to cats and yet have no idea that using the expression "deciduous conifer" is the way to refer to deciduous conifers. Systematicity, like productivity, is the sort of property of cognitive capacities that you're likely to miss if you concentrate on the psychology of learning and searching lists.

There is, as we remarked, a straightforward (and quite traditional) argument from the systematicity of language capacity to the conclusion that sentences must have syntactic and semantic structure: If you assume that sentences are constructed out of words and phrases, and that many different sequences of words can be phrases of the same type, the very fact that one formula is a sentence of the language will often imply that other formulas must be too: in effect, systematicity follows from the postulation of constituent structure.

Suppose, for example, that it's a fact about English that formulas with the constituent analysis "NP VP NP" are well formed; and suppose that "John" and "the girl" are NPs and "loves" is a VP. It follows from these assumptions that "John loves the girl," "John loves John," "the girl loves the girl," and "the girl loves John" must all be sentences. It follows too that anybody who has mastered the grammar of English must have linguistic capacities that are systematic in respect of these sentences; he *can't but* assume that all of them are sentences if he assumes that any of them are. Compare the situation on the view that the sentences of English are all atomic. There is then no structural analogy between "John loves the girl" and "the girl loves John" and hence no reason why understanding one sentence should imply understanding the other; no more than understanding "rabbit" implies understanding "tree."[24]

On the view that the sentences are atomic, the systematicity of linguistic capacities is a mystery; on the view that they have constituent structure, the systematicity of linguistic capacities is what you would predict. So we should prefer the latter view to the former.

Notice that you can make this argument for constituent structure in sentences without idealizing to astronomical computational capacities. There are productivity arguments for constituent structure, but they're concerned with our ability—in principle—to understand sentences that are arbitrarily long. Systematicity, by contrast, appeals to premises that are much nearer home; such considerations as the ones mentioned above, that no speaker understands the form of words "John loves the girl" except as he also understands the form of words "the girl loves John." The assumption that linguistic capacities are productive "in principle" is one that a Connectionist might refuse to grant. But that they are systematic *in fact* no one can plausibly deny.

We can now, finally, come to the point: the argument from the systematicity of linguistic capacities to constituent structure in sentences is quite clear. *But thought is systematic too,* so there is a precisely parallel argument from the systematicity of thought to syntactic and semantic structure in mental representations.

What does it mean to say that thought is systematic? Well, just as you don't find people who can understand the sentence "John loves the girl" but not the sentence "the girl loves John," so too you don't find people who can *think the thought* that John loves the girl but can't think the thought that the girl loves John. Indeed, in the case of verbal organisms the systematicity of thought *follows from* the systematicity of language if you assume—as most psychologists do—that understanding a sentence involves entertaining the thought that it expresses; on that assumption, nobody *could* understand both the sentences about John and the girl unless he were able to think both the thoughts about John and the girl.

But now if the ability to think that John loves the girl is intrinsically connected to the ability to think that the girl loves John, that fact will somehow have to be explained. For a Representationalist (which, as we have seen, Connectionists are), the explanation is obvious: Entertaining thoughts requires being in representational states (i.e., it requires tokening mental representations). And, just as the systematicity of language shows that there must be structural relations between the sentence "John loves the girl" and the sentence "the girl loves John," so the systematicity of thought shows that there must be structural relations between the mental representation that corresponds to the thought that John loves the girl and the mental representation that corresponds to the thought that the girl loves John;[25] namely, the two mental representations, like the two sentences, *must be made of the same parts*. But if this explanation is right (and there don't seem to be any others on offer), then mental representations have internal structure and there is a language of thought. So the architecture of the mind is not a Connectionist network.[26]

To summarize the discussion so far: Productivity arguments infer the internal structure of mental representations from the presumed fact that nobody has a *finite* intellectual competence. By contrast, systematicity arguments infer the internal structure of mental representations from the patent fact that nobody has a *punctate* intellectual competence. Just as you don't find linguistic capacities that consist of the ability to understand sixty-seven unrelated sentences, so too you don't find cognitive capacities that consist of the ability to think seventy-four unrelated thoughts. Our claim is that this isn't, in either case, an accident: A linguistic theory that allowed for the possibility of punctate languages would have gone not just wrong, but *very profoundly* wrong. And similarly for a cognitive theory that allowed for the possibility of punctate minds.

But perhaps not being punctate is a property only of the minds of language users; perhaps the representational capacities of infraverbal organisms do have just the kind of gaps that Connectionist models permit? A Connectionist might then claim that he can do everything "up to language" on the assumption that mental representations lack combinatorial syntactic and semantic structure. Everything up to language may not be everything, but it's a lot. (On the other hand, a lot may be a lot, but it isn't everything. Infraverbal cognitive architecture mustn't be so represented as to make the eventual acquisition of language in phylogeny and in ontogeny require a miracle.)

It is not, however, plausible that only the minds of verbal organisms are systematic. Think what it would mean for this to be the case. It would have to be quite usual to find, for example, animals capable of representing the state of affairs *a*R*b*, but incapable of representing the state of affairs *b*R*a*. Such animals would be, as it were, *a*R*b* sighted but *b*R*a* blind since, presumably, the representational capacities of its mind affect not just what an organism can think, but also what it can perceive. In consequence, such animals would be able to learn to respond selectively to *a*R*b* situations but quite *un*able to learn to respond selectively to *b*R*a* situations. (So that, though you could teach the creature to choose the picture with the square larger than the triangle, you couldn't for the life of you teach it to choose the picture with the triangle larger than the square.)

It is, to be sure, an empirical question whether the cognitive capacities of infraverbal organisms are often structured that way, but we're prepared to bet that they are not. Ethological cases are the exceptions that prove the rule. There *are* examples where salient environmental configurations act as "gestalten"; and in such cases it's reasonable to doubt that the mental representation of the stimulus is complex. But the point is precisely that these cases are *exceptional*; they're exactly the ones where you expect that there will be some special story to tell about the ecological significance of the stimulus: that it's the shape of a predator, or the song of a conspecific ... etc. Conversely, when there is no such story to tell you expect structurally similar stimuli to elicit correspondingly similar cognitive capacities. That, surely, is the least that a respectable principle of stimulus generalization has got to require.

That infraverbal cognition is pretty generally systematic seems, in short, to be about as secure as any empirical premise in this area can be. And, as we've just seen, it's a premise from which the inadequacy of Connectionist models as cognitive theories follows quite straightforwardly; as straightforwardly, in any event, as it would from the assumption that such capacities are generally productive.

3.3 Compositionality of Representations

Compositionality is closely related to systematicity; perhaps they're best viewed as aspects of a single phenomenon. We will therefore follow much the same course here as in the preceding discussion: first we introduce the concept by recalling the standard arguments for the compositionality of natural languages. We then suggest that parallel arguments secure the compositionality of mental representations. Since compositionality requires combinatorial syntactic and semantic structure, the compositionality of thought is evidence that the mind is not a Connectionist network.

We said that the systematicity of linguistic competence consists in the fact that "the ability to produce/understand some of the sentences is intrinsically connected to the ability to produce/understand certain of the others." We now add that which sentences are systematically related is not arbitrary from a semantic point of view. For example, being able to understand "John loves the girl" goes along with being able to understand "the girl loves John," and there are correspondingly close semantic relations between these sentences: in order for the first to be true, John must bear to the girl the very same relation that the truth of the second requires the girl to bear to John. By contrast, there is no intrinsic connection between understanding either of the John/girl sentences and understanding semantically unrelated formulas like "quarks are made of gluons" or "the cat is on the mat" or "$2 + 2 = 4$"; it looks as though semantical relatedness and systematicity keep quite close company.

You might suppose that this covariance is covered by the same explanation that accounts for systematicity per se; roughly, that sentences that are systematically related are composed from the same syntactic constituents. But, in fact, you need a further assumption, which we'll call the "principle of compositionality": insofar as a language is systematic, a lexical item must make approximately the same semantic contribution to each expression in which it occurs. It is, for example, only insofar as "the," "girl," "loves" and "John" make the same semantic contribution to "John loves the girl" that they make to "the girl loves John" that understanding the one sentence implies understanding the other. Similarity of constituent structure accounts for the semantic relatedness between systematically related sentences only to the extent that the semantical properties of the shared constituents are context-independent.

Here it's idioms that prove the rule: being able to understand "the," "man," "kicked" and "bucket" isn't much help with understanding "the man kicked the bucket," since "kicked" and "bucket" don't bear their standard meanings in this context. And, just as you'd expect, "the man kicked the bucket" is *not* systematic even with respect to syntactically closely related sentences like "the man kicked over the bucket" (for that matter, it's not systematic with respect to the "the man kicked the bucket" read literally).

It's uncertain exactly how compositional natural languages actually are (just as it's uncertain exactly how systematic they are). We suspect that the amount of context induced variation of lexical meaning is often overestimated because other sorts of context sensitivity are misconstrued as violations of compositionality. For example, the difference between "feed the chicken" and "chicken to eat" must involve an *animal/food* ambiguity in "chicken" rather than a violation of compositionality since if the context "feed the ..." could *induce* (rather than select) the meaning *animal*, you would expect "feed the veal," "feed the pork" and the like.[27] Similarly, the difference between "good book," "good rest" and "good fight" is probably not meaning shift but syncategorematicity. "Good *NP*" means something like *NP that answers to the relevant interest in NPs:* a good book is one that answers to our interest in books (viz., it's good to read); a good rest is one that answers to our interest in rests (viz., it leaves one refreshed); a good fight is one that answers to our interest in fights (viz., it's fun to watch or to be in, or it clears the air); and so on. It's because the meaning of "good" is syncategorematic and has a variable in it for relevant interests, that you can know that a good flurg is a flurg that answers to the relevant interest in flurgs without knowing what flurgs are or what the relevant interest in flurgs is (see Ziff, 1960).

In any event, the main argument stands: systematicity depends on compositionality, so to the extent that a natural language is systematic it must be compositional too. This illustrates another respect in which systematicity arguments can do the work for which productivity arguments have previously been employed. The traditional argument for compositionality is that it is required to explain how a finitely representable language can contain infinitely many nonsynonymous expressions.

Considerations about systematicity offer one argument for compositionality; considerations about entailment offer another. Consider predicates like "... is a brown cow." This expression bears a straightforward semantical relation to the predicates "... is a cow" and "... is brown"; viz., that the first predicate is true of a thing if and only if both of the others are. That is, "... is a brown cow" severally entails "... is brown" and "... is a cow" and is entailed by their conjunction. Moreover—and this is important—this semantical pattern is not peculiar to the cases cited. On the contrary, it holds for a very large range of predicates (see "... is a red square," "... is a funny old German soldier," "... is a child prodigy"; and so forth).

How are we to account for these sorts of regularities? The answer seems clear enough; "... is a brown cow" entails "... is brown" because (a) the second expression is a constituent of the first; (b) the syntactical form "(adjective noun)$_N$" has (in many cases) the semantic force of a conjunction, and (c) "brown" retains its semantical value under simplification of conjunction. Notice that you need (c) to rule out the possibility that "brown" means *brown* when it modifies a noun but (as it might be) *dead* when it's a predicate adjective; in which case "... is a brown cow" wouldn't entail "... is brown" after all. Notice too that (c) is just an application of the principle of composition.

So, here's the argument so far: you need to assume some degree of compositionality of English sentences to account for the fact that systematically related sentences are always semantically related; and to account for certain regular parallelisms between the syntactical structure of sentences and their entailments. So, beyond any serious doubt, the sentences of English must be compositional to some serious extent. But the principle of compositionality governs the semantic relations between words *and the expressions of which they are constituents*. So compositionality implies that (some) expressions *have* constituents. So compositionality argues for (specifically, presupposes) syntactic/semantic structure in sentences.

Now what about the compositionality of mental representations? There is, as you'd expect, a bridging argument based on the usual psycholinguistic premise that one uses language to express ones thoughts: Sentences are used to express thoughts; so if the ability to use some sentences is connected with the ability to use certain other, semantically related sentences, then the ability to think some thoughts must be correspondingly connected with the ability to think certain other, semantically related thoughts. But you can only think the thoughts that your mental representations can express. So, if the ability to think certain thoughts is interconnected, then the corresponding representational capacities must be interconnected too; specifically, the ability to be in some representational states must imply the ability to be in certain other, semantically related representational states.

But then the question arises: *how could* the mind be so arranged that the ability to be in one representational state is connected with the ability to be in others that are semantically nearby? What account of mental representation would have this consequence? The answer is just what you'd expect from the discussion of the linguistic material. Mental representations must have internal structure, just the way that sentences do. In particular, it must be that the mental representation that corresponds to the thought that John loves the girl contains, as its parts, the same constituents as the mental representation that corresponds to the thought that the girl loves John. That would explain why these thoughts are *systematically* related; *and, to the extent that the semantic value of these parts is context-independent, that would explain why these systematically related thoughts are also semantically related*. So, by this chain of argument, evidence for the compositionality of sentences is evidence for the compositionality of the representational states of speaker/hearers.

Finally, what about the compositionality of infraverbal thought? The argument isn't much different from the one that we've just run through. We assume that animal thought is largely systematic: the organism that can perceive (hence learn) that *a***R***b* can generally perceive (/learn) that *b***R***a*. But, systematically related thoughts (just like systematically related sentences) are generally semantically related too. It's no surprise that being able to learn that the triangle is above the square implies being able to learn that the square is above the triangle; whereas it would be *very* surprising if being able to learn the square/triangle facts implied being able to learn that quarks are made of gluons or that Washington was the first President of America.

So, then, what explains the correlation between systematic relations and semantic relations in infraverbal thought? Clearly, Connectionist models don't address this question; the fact that a network contains a node labelled X has, so far as the constraints imposed by Connectionist architecture are concerned, *no implications at all* for the labels of the other nodes in the network; in particular, it doesn't imply that there will be nodes that represent thoughts that are semantically close to X. This is just the semantical side of the fact that network architectures permit arbitrarily punctate mental lives.

But if, on the other hand, we make the usual Classicist assumptions (viz., that systematically related thoughts share constituents and that the semantic values of these shared constituents are context independent) the correlation between systematicity and semantic relatedness follows immediately. For a Classicist, this correlation is an "architectural" property of minds; it couldn't but hold if mental representations have the general properties that Classical models suppose them to.

What have Connectionists to say about these matters? There is some textual evidence that they are tempted to deny the facts of compositionality wholesale. For example, Smolensky (1988) claims that: "Surely ... we would get quite a different representation of 'coffee' if we examined the difference between 'can with coffee' and 'can without coffee' or 'tree with coffee' and 'tree without coffee'; or 'man with coffee' and 'man without coffee'... context insensitivity is not something we expect to be reflected in Connectionist representations...."

It's certainly true that compositionality is not generally a feature of Connectionist representations. Connectionists can't acknowledge the facts of compositionality because they are committed to mental representations that don't have combinatorial structure. But to give up on compositionality is to take "kick the bucket" as a model for the relation between syntax and semantics; and the consequence is, as we've seen, that you make the systematicity of language (and of thought) a mystery. On the other hand, to say that "kick the bucket" is aberrant, and that the right model for the syntax/semantics relation is (e.g.) "brown cow," is to start down a trail which leads, pretty inevitably, to acknowledging combinatorial structure in mental representation, hence to the rejection of Connectionist networks as cognitive models.

We don't think there's any way out of the need to acknowledge the compositionality of natural languages and of mental representations. However, it's been suggested (see Smolensky, op cit.) that while the principle of compositionality is false (because content isn't context invariant) there is nevertheless a "family resemblance" between the various meanings that a symbol has in the various contexts in which it occurs. Since such proposals generally aren't elaborated, it's unclear how they're supposed to handle the salient facts about systematicity and inference. But surely there are going to be serious problems. Consider, for example, such inferences as

(i) Turtles are slower than rabbits.

(ii) Rabbits are slower than Ferraris.

....

(iii) Turtles are slower than Ferraris.

The soundness of this inference appears to depend upon (a) the fact that the same relation (viz., *slower than*) holds between turtles and rabbits on the one hand, and rabbits and Ferraris on the other; and (b) the fact that that relation is transitive. If, however, it's assumed (contrary to the principle of compositionality) that "slower than" means something different in premises (i) and (ii) (and presumably in (iii) as well)—so that, strictly speaking, the relation that holds between turtles and rabbits is *not* the same one that holds between rabbits and Ferraris—then it's hard to see why the inference should be valid.

Talk about the relations being "similar" only papers over the difficulty since the problem is then to provide a notion of similarity that will guaranty that if (i) and (ii) are true, so too is (iii). And, so far at least, no such notion of similarity has been forthcoming. Notice that it won't do to require just that the relations all be similar in respect of their *transitivity*, i.e., that they all be transitive. On that account, the argument from "turtles are slower than rabbits" and "rabbits are furrier than Ferraris" to "turtles are slower than Ferraris" would be valid since "furrier than" is transitive too.

Until these sorts of issues are attended to, the proposal to replace the compositional principle of context invariance with a notion of "approximate equivalence ... across contexts" (Smolensky, 1988) doesn't seem to be much more than hand waving.

3.4 The Systematicity of Inference

In Section 2 we saw that, according to Classical theories, the syntax of mental representations mediates between their semantic properties and their causal role in mental processes. Take a simple case: It's a "logical" principle that conjunctions entail their constituents (so the argument from *P&Q* to *P* and to *Q* is valid). Correspondingly, it's a psychological law that thoughts that *P&Q* tend to cause thoughts that *P* and thoughts that *Q* all else being equal. Classical theory exploits the constituent structure of mental representations to account for both these facts, the first by assuming that the combinatorial semantics of mental representations is sensitive to their syntax and the second by assuming that mental processes apply to mental representations in virtue of their constituent structure.

A consequence of these assumptions is that Classical theories are committed to the following striking prediction: inferences that are of similar logical type ought, pretty generally,[28] to elicit correspondingly similar cognitive capacities. You shouldn't, for example, find a kind of mental life in which you get inferences from *P&Q&R* to *P* but you don't get inferences from *P&Q* to *P*. This is because, according to the Classical account, this logically homogeneous class of inferences is carried out by a correspondingly homogeneous class of psychological mechanisms: The premises of both inferences are expressed by mental representations that satisfy the same syntactic analysis (viz., $S_1\&S_2\&S_3\& \ldots S_n$); and the process of drawing the inference corresponds, in both cases, to the same formal operation of detaching the constituent that expresses the conclusion.

The idea that organisms should exhibit similar cognitive capacities in respect of logically similar inferences is so natural that it may seem unavoidable. But, on the contrary: there's nothing in principle to preclude a kind of cognitive model in which inferences that are quite similar from the logician's point of view are nevertheless computed by quite different mechanisms; or in which some inferences of a given logical type are computed and other inferences of the same logical type are not. Consider, in particular, the Connectionist account. A Connectionist can certainly model a mental life in which, if you can reason from *P&Q&R* to *P*, then you can also reason from *P&Q* to *P*. For example, the network in (Figure 79.2) would do.

But notice that *a Connectionist can equally model a mental life in which you get one of these inferences and not the other*. In the present case, since there is no structural relation between the *P&Q&R* node and the *P&Q* node (remember, all nodes are atomic; don't be misled by the node *labels*) there's no reason why a mind that contains the first should also contain the second, or vice versa. Analogously, there's no reason why you shouldn't get minds that simplify the premise *John loves Mary and Bill hates Mary* but no others; or minds that simplify premises with 1, 3, or 5 conjuncts, but don't simplify

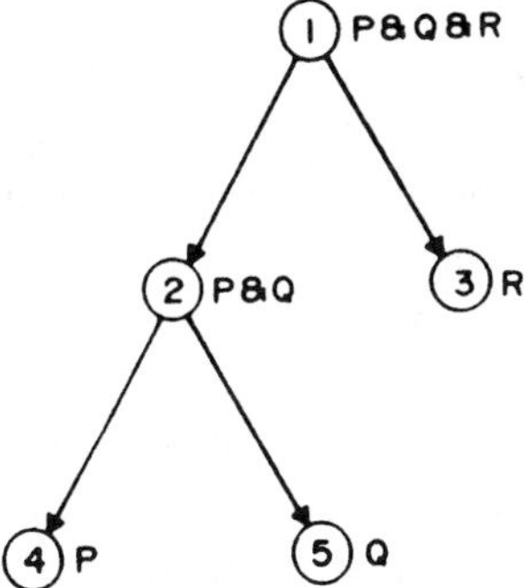

Figure 79.2
A possible Connectionist network which draws inferences from P & Q & R to P and also draws inferences from P & Q to P.

premises with 2, 4, or 6 conjuncts; or, for that matter, minds that simplify only premises that were acquired on Tuesdays ... etc.

In fact, the Connectionist architecture is *utterly indifferent* as among these possibilities. That's because it recognizes no notion of syntax according to which thoughts that are alike in inferential role (e.g., thoughts that are all subject to simplification of conjunction) are expressed by mental representations of correspondingly similar syntactic form (e.g., by mental representations that are all syntactically conjunctive). So, the Connectionist architecture tolerates gaps in cognitive capacities; it has no mechanism to enforce the requirement that logically homogeneous inferences should be executed by correspondingly homogeneous computational processes.

But, we claim, you don't find cognitive capacities that have these sorts of gaps. You don't, for example, get minds that are prepared to infer *John went to the store* from *John and Mary and Susan and Sally went to the store* and from *John and Mary went to the store* but not from *John and Mary and Susan went to the store*. Given a notion of logical syntax—the very notion that the Classical theory of mentation requires to get its account of mental processes off the ground—it is a *truism* that you don't get such minds. Lacking a notion of logical syntax, it is a *mystery* that you don't.

3.5 Summary

It is perhaps obvious by now that all the arguments that we've been reviewing—the argument from systematicity, the argument from compositionality, and the argument from inferential coherence—are really much the same: If you hold the kind of theory that acknowledges structured representations, it must perforce acknowledge representations with *similar* or *identical* structures. In the linguistic cases, constituent analysis implies a taxonomy of sentences by their syntactic form, and in the inferential cases, it implies a taxonomy of arguments by their logical form. So, if your theory also acknowledges mental processes that are structure sensitive, then it will predict that similarly structured representations will generally play similar roles in thought. A theory that says that the sentence "John loves the girl" is made out of the same parts as the sentence "the girl loves John," and made by applications of the same rules of composition, will have to go out of its way to explain a linguistic competence which embraces one sentence but not the other. And similarly, if a theory says that the mental representation that corresponds to the thought that *P&Q&R* has the same (conjunctive) syntax as the mental representation that corresponds to the thought that *P&Q* and that mental processes of drawing inferences subsume mental representations in virtue of their syntax, it will have to go out of its way to explain inferential capacities which embrace the one thought but not the other. Such a competence would be, at best, an embarrassment for the theory, and at worst a refutation.

By contrast, since the Connectionist architecture recognizes no combinatorial structure in mental representations, gaps in cognitive competence should proliferate arbitrarily. It's not just that you'd expect to get them from time to time; it's that, on the "no-structure" story, *gaps are the unmarked case*. It's the *systematic* competence that the theory is required to treat as an embarrassment. But, as a matter of fact, inferential competences are *blatantly* systematic. So there must be something deeply wrong with Connectionist architecture.

What's deeply wrong with Connectionist architecture is this: Because it acknowledges neither syntactic nor semantic structure in mental representations, it perforce treats them not as a generated set but as a list. But lists, qua lists, have no structure; any collection of items is a possible list. And, correspondingly, on Connectionist principles, any collection of (causally connected) representational states is a possible mind. So, as far as Connectionist architecture is concerned, there is nothing to prevent minds that are arbitrarily unsystematic. But that result is *preposterous*. Cognitive capacities come in structurally related clusters; their systematicity is pervasive. All the evidence suggests that *punctate minds can't happen*. This argument seemed conclusive against the Connectionism of Hebb, Osgood and Hull twenty or thirty years ago. So far as we can tell, nothing of any importance has happened to change the situation in the meantime.[29]

A final comment to round off this part of the discussion. It's possible to imagine a Connectionist being prepared to admit that while systematicity doesn't *follow from*—and hence is not explained by—Connectionist architecture, it is nonetheless *compatible* with that architecture. It is, after all, perfectly possible to follow a policy of building networks that have *a***R***b* nodes only if they have *b***R***a* nodes ... etc. There is therefore nothing to stop a Connectionist from stipulating—as an independent postulate of his theory of mind—that all biologically instantiated networks are, de facto, systematic.

But this misses a crucial point: It's not enough just to stipulate systematicity; one is also required to specify a mechanism that is able to enforce the stipulation. To put it another way, it's not enough for a Connectionist to agree that all minds are systematic; he must also explain *how nature contrives to produce only systematic minds*. Presumably there would have to be some sort of mechanism, over and above the ones that Connectionism per se posits, the functioning of which insures the systematicity of biologically instantiated networks; a mechanism such that, in virtue of its operation, every network that has an *a***R***b* node also has a *b***R***a* node ... and so forth. There are, however, no proposals for such a mechanism. Or, rather, there is just one: The only mechanism that is known to be able to produce pervasive systematicity is Classical architecture. And, as we have seen, Classical architecture is not compatible with Connectionism since it requires internally structured representations.

Notes

1. The difference between Connectionist networks in which the state of a single unit encodes properties of the world (i.e., the so-called "localist" networks) and ones in which the pattern of states of an entire population of units does the encoding (the so-called "distributed" representation networks) is considered to be important by many people working on Connectionist models. Although Connectionists debate the relative merits of localist (or "compact") versus distributed representations (e.g., Feldman, 1986), the distinction will usually be of little consequence for our purposes, for reasons that we give later. For simplicity, when we wish to refer indifferently to either single unit codes or aggregate distributed codes, we shall refer to the "nodes" in a network. When the distinction is relevant to our discussion, however, we shall explicitly mark the difference by referring either to units or to aggregate of units.

2. One of the attractions of Connectionism for many people is that it does employ some heavy mathematical machinery, as can be seen from a glance at many of the chapters of the two volume collection by Rumelhart, McClelland and the PDP Research Group (1986). But in contrast to many other mathematically sophisticated areas of cognitive science, such as automata theory or parts of Artificial Intelligence (particularly the study of search, or of reasoning and knowledge representation), the mathematics has not been used to map out the limits of what the proposed class of mechanisms can do. Like a great deal of Artificial Intelligence research, the Connectionist approach remains almost entirely experimental; mechanisms that look interesting are proposed and explored by implementing them on computers and subjecting them to empirical trials to see what they will do. As a consequence, although there is a great deal of mathematical work within the tradition, one has very little idea what various Connectionist networks and mechanisms are good for in general.

3. Smolensky seems to think that the idea of postulating a level of representations with a semantics of subconceptual features is unique to network theories. This is an extraordinary view considering the extent to which *Classical* theorists have been concerned with feature analyses in every area of psychology from phonetics to visual perception to lexicography. In fact the question whether there are "sub-conceptual" features is *neutral* with respect to the question whether cognitive architecture is Classical or Connectionist.

4. Sometimes, however, even Representationalists fail to appreciate that it is *representation* that distinguishes cognitive from noncognitive levels. Thus, for example, although Smolensky (1988) is clearly a Representationalist, his official answer to the question "What distinguishes those dynamical systems that are cognitive from those that are not?" makes the mistake of appealing to complexity rather than intentionality: "A river ... fails to be a cognitive dynamical system only because it cannot satisfy a *large* range of goals under a *large* range of conditions." But, of course, that depends on how you individuate goals and conditions; the river that wants to get to the sea wants first to get half way to the sea, and then to get half way more, ..., and so on; quite a lot of goals all told. The real point, of course, is that states that represent goals play a role in the etiology of the behaviors of people but not in the etiology of the "behavior" of rivers.

5. That Classical architectures can be implemented in networks is not disputed by Connectionists; see for example Rumelhart and McClelland (1986a, p. 118): "... one can make an arbitrary computational machine out of linear threshold units, including, for example, a machine that can carry out all the operations necessary for implementing a Turing machine; the one limitation is that real biological systems cannot be Turing machines because they have finite hardware."

6. There is a different idea, frequently encountered in the Connectionist literature, that this one is easily confused with: viz., that the distinction between regularities and exceptions is merely

stochastic (what makes "went" an irregular past tense is just that the *more frequent* construction is the one exhibited by "walked"). It seems obvious that if this claim is correct it can be readily assimilated to Classical architecture.

7. This way of putting it will do for present purposes. But a subtler reading of Connectionist theories might take it to be total machine *states* that have content, e.g., the state of *having such and such a node excited.* Postulating connections among labelled nodes would then be equivalent to postulating causal relations among the corresponding content bearing machine states: To say that the excitation of the node labelled "dog" is caused by the excitation of nodes labelled [d], [o], [g] is to say that the machine's representing its input as consisting of the phonetic sequence [dog] causes it to represent its input as consisting of the word "dog." And so forth. Most of the time the distinction between these two ways of talking does not matter for our purposes, so we shall adopt one or the other as convenient.

8. Sometimes the difference between simply postulating representational states and postulating representations with a combinatorial syntax and semantics is marked by distinguishing theories that postulate *symbols* from theories that postulate *symbol systems.* The latter theories, but not the former, are committed to a "language of thought." For this usage, see Kosslyn and Hatfield (1984) who take the refusal to postulate symbol systems to be the characteristic respect in which Connectionist architectures differ from Classical architectures. We agree with this diagnosis.

9. Perhaps the notion that relations among physical properties of the brain instantiate (or encode) the *combinatorial structure* of an expression bears some elaboration. One way to understand what is involved is to consider the conditions that must hold on a mapping (which we refer to as the "physical instantiation mapping") from expressions to brain states if the causal relations among brain states are to depend on the combinatorial structure of the encoded expressions. In defining this mapping it is not enough merely to specify a physical encoding for each symbol; in order for the *structures* of expressions to have causal roles, structural relations must be encoded by physical properties of brain states (or by sets of functionally equivalent physical properties of brain states).

Because, in general, Classical models assume that the expressions that get physically instantiated in brains have a generative syntax, the definition of an appropriate physical instantiation mapping has to be built up in terms of (a) the definition of a primitive mapping from atomic symbols to relatively elementary physical states, and (b) a specification of how the structure of complex expressions maps onto the structure of relatively complex or composite physical states. Such a structure-preserving mapping is typically given recursively, making use of the combinatorial syntax by which complex expressions are built up out of simpler ones. For example, the physical instantiation mapping **F** for complex expressions would be defined by recursion, given the definition of **F** for *atomic* symbols and given the *structure* of the complex expression, the latter being specified in terms of the "structure building" rules which constitute the generative syntax for complex expressions. Take, for example, the expression "(A&B)&C." A suitable definition for a mapping in this case might contain the statement that for any expressions *P* and *Q*, $\mathbf{F}[P\&Q] = \mathrm{B}(\mathbf{F}[P], \mathbf{F}[Q])$, where the function B specifies the physical relation that holds between physical states $\mathbf{F}[P]$ and $\mathbf{F}[Q]$. Here the property B serves to physically encode, (or "instantiate") the relation that holds between the expressions *P* and *Q*, on the one hand, and the expressions *P&Q* on the other.

In using this rule for the example above *P* and *Q* would have the values "A&B" and "C" respectively, so that the mapping rule would have to be applied twice to pick the relevant physical structures. In defining the mapping recursively in this way we ensure that the relation between the expressions "A" and "B," and the composite expression "A&B," is encoded in terms of a physical relation between constitutent states that is identical (or functionally equivalent) to the physical relation used to encode the relation between expressions "A&B" and "C," and their composite expression "(A&B)&C." This type of mapping is well known because of its use in Tarski's definition of an interpretation of a language in a model. The idea of a mapping from symbolic expressions to a structure of physical states is discussed in Pylyshyn (1984a, pp. 54–69), where it is referred to as an "instantiation function" and in Stabler (1985), where it is called a "realization mapping."

10. This illustration has not any particular Connectionist model in mind, though the caricature presented is, in fact, a simplified version of the Ballard (1987) Connectionist theorem proving system (which actually uses a more restricted proof procedure based on the *unification* of Horn clauses). To simplify the exposition, we assume a "localist" approach, in which each semantically interpreted node corresponds to a single Connectionist unit; but nothing relevant to this discussion is changed if these nodes actually consist of patterns over a cluster of units.

11. This makes the "compositionality" of data structures a defining property of Classical architecture. But, of course, it leaves open the question of the degree to which *natural* languages (like English) are also compositional.

12. Labels aren't part of the *causal structure* of a Connectionist machine, but they may play an essential role in its *causal history* insofar as designers wire their machines to respect the semantical relations that the labels express. For example, in Ballard's (1987) Connectionist model of theorem proving, there is a mechanical procedure for wiring a network which will carry out proofs by unification. This procedure is a function from a set of node labels to a wired-up machine. There is thus an interesting and revealing respect in which node labels are relevant to the operations that get performed when the function is executed. But, of course, the machine on which the labels have the effect is not the machine whose states they are labels of; and the effect of the labels occurs at the time that the theorem-proving machine is constructed, not at the time its reasoning process is carried out. *This* sort of case of labels "having effects" is thus quite different from the way that symbol tokens (e.g., tokened data structures) can affect the causal processes of a Classical machine.

13. Any relation specified as holding among representational states is, by definition, within the "cognitive level." It goes without saying that relations that are "within-level" by this criterion can count as "between-level" when we use criteria of finer grain. There is, for example, nothing to prevent hierarchies of levels of representational states.

14. Smolensky (1988, p. 14) remarks that "unlike symbolic tokens, these vectors lie in a topological space, in which some are close together and others are far apart." However, this seems to radically conflate claims about the Connectionist model and claims about its implementation (a conflation that is not unusual in the Connectionist literature). If the space at issue is *physical*, then Smolensky is committed to extremely strong claims about adjacency relations in the brain; claims which there is, in fact, no reason at all to believe. But if, as seems more plausible, the space at issue is *semantical* then what Smolensky says isn't true. Practically any cognitive theory will imply distance measures between mental representations. In Classical theories, for example, the distance between two representations is plausibly related to the number of computational steps it takes to derive one representation from the other. In Connectionist theories, it is plausibly related to the number of intervening nodes (or to the degree of overlap between vectors, depending on the version of Connectionism one has in mind). The interesting claim is not that an architecture offers *a* distance measure but that it offers the *right* distance measure—one that is empirically certifiable.

15. The primary use that Connectionists make of microfeatures is in their accounts of generalization and abstraction (see, for example, Hinton, McClelland, and Rumelhart, 1986). Roughly, you

get generalization by using overlap of microfeatures to define a similarity space, and you get abstraction by making the vectors that correspond to *types* be subvectors of the ones that correspond to their *tokens*. Similar proposals have quite a long history in traditional Empiricist analysis; and have been roundly criticized over the centuries. (For a discussion of abstractionism see Geach, 1957; that similarity is a primitive relation—hence not reducible to partial identity of feature sets—was, of course, a main tenet of Gestalt psychology, as well as more recent approaches based on "prototypes.") The treatment of microfeatures in the Connectionist literature would appear to be very close to early proposals by Katz and Fodor (1963) and Katz and Postal (1964), where both the idea of a feature analysis of concepts and the idea that relations of semantical containment among concepts should be identified with set-theoretic relations among feature arrays are explicitly endorsed.

16. Another disadvantage is that, strictly speaking it doesn't work; although it allows us to distinguish the belief that John loves Mary and Bill hates Sally from the belief that John loves Sally and Bill hates Mary, we don't yet have a way to distinguish believing that (John loves Mary because Bill hates Sally) from believing that (Bill hates Sally because John loves Mary). Presumably nobody would want to have microfeatures corresponding to these.

17. It's especially important at this point not to make the mistake of confusing diagrams of Connectionist networks with constituent structure diagrams (see section 2.1.2). Connecting SUBJECT-OF with FIDO and BITES does not mean that when all three are active FIDO is the subject of BITES. A network diagram is not a specification of the internal structure of a complex mental representation. Rather, it's a specification of a pattern of causal dependencies among the states of activation of nodes. Connectivity in a network determines which sets of simultaneously active nodes are possible; but it has no *semantical* significance.

The difference between the paths between nodes that network diagrams exhibit and the paths between nodes that constituent structure diagrams exhibit is precisely that the latter but not the former specify parameters of mental representations. (In particular, they specify part/whole relations among the constituents of complex symbols.) Whereas network theories define semantic interpretations over sets of (causally interconnected) representations of concepts, theories that acknowledge complex symbols define semantic interpretations over sets of representations of concepts *together with specifications of the constituency relations that hold among these representations*.

18. And it doesn't work uniformly for English conjunction. Compare: *John and Mary are friends* → **John are friends*; or *The flag is red, white and blue* → *The flag is blue*. Such cases show either that English is not the language of thought, or that, if it is, the relation between syntax and semantics is a good deal subtler for the language of thought than it is for the standard logical languages.

19. It needn't, however, be strict truth-preservation that makes the syntactic approach relevant to cognition. Other semantic properties might be preserved under syntactic transformation in the course of mental processing—e.g., warrant, plausibility, heuristic value, or simply *semantic non-arbitrariness*. The point of Classical modeling isn't to characterize human thought as supremely logical; rather, it's to show how a family of types of semantically coherent (or knowledge-dependent) reasoning are mechanically possible. Valid inference is the paradigm only in that it is the best understood member of this family; the one for which syntactical analogues for semantical relations have been most systematically elaborated.

20. It is not uncommon for Connectionists to make disparaging remarks about about the relevance of logic to psychology, even thought they accept the idea that inference is involved in reasoning. Sometimes the suggestion seems to be that it's all right if Connectionism can't reconstruct the theory of inference that formal deductive logic provides since it has something even better on

offer. For example, in their report to the U.S. National Science Foundation, McClelland, Feldman, Adelson, Bower and McDermott (1986) state that "... connectionist models realize an evidential logic *in contrast to* the symbolic logic of conventional computing (p. 6; our emphasis)" and that "evidential logics are becoming increasingly important in cognitive science and have a natural map to connectionist modeling" (p. 7). It is, however, hard to understand the implied contrast since, on the one hand, evidential logic must surely be a fairly conservative extension of "the symbolic logic of conventional computing" (i.e., most of the theorems of the latter have to come out true in the former) and, on the other, there is not the slightest reason to doubt that an evidential logic would "run" on a Classical machine. Prima facie, the problem about evidential logic isn't that we've got one that we don't know how to implement; it's that we haven't got one.

21. Compare the "little s's" and "little r's" of neo-Hullean "mediational" Associationists like Charles Osgood.

22. This way of putting the productivity argument is most closely identified with Chomsky (e.g., Chomsky, 1965; 1968). However, one does not have to rest the argument upon a basic assumption of infinite generative capacity. Infinite generative capacity can be viewed, instead, as a consequence or a corollary of theories formulated so as to capture the greatest number of generalizations with the fewest independent principles. This more neutral approach is, in fact, very much in the spirit of what we shall propose below. We are putting it in the present form for expository and historical reasons.

23. McClelland and Kawamoto (1986) discuss this sort of recursion briefly. Their suggestion seems to be that parsing such sentences doesn't really require recovering their recursive structure: "... the job of the parser [with respect to right-recursive sentences] is to spit out phrases in a way that captures their *local* context. Such a representation may prove sufficient to allow us to reconstruct the correct bindings of noun phrases to verbs and prepositional phrases to *nearby* nouns and verbs" (p. 324; emphasis ours). It is, however, by no means the case that all of the semantically relevant grammatical relations in readily intelligible embedded sentences are local in surface structure. Consider: "*Where* did the man who owns the cat that chased the rat that frightened the girl say that he was going to move to (X)?" or "*What* did the girl that the children loved to listen to promise your friends that she would read (X) to them?" Notice that, in such examples, a binding element (italicized) can be arbitrarily displaced from the position whose interpretation it controls (marked "X") without making the sentence particularly difficult to understand. Notice too that the "semantics" doesn't determine the binding relations in either example.

24. See Pinker (1984, Chapter 4) for evidence that children never go through a stage in which they distinguish between the internal structures of NPs depending on whether they are in subject or object position; i.e., the dialects that children speak are always systematic with respect to the syntactic structures that can appear in these positions.

25. It may be worth emphasizing that the structural complexity of a mental representation is not the same thing as, and does *not* follow from, the structural complexity of its propositional content (i.e., of what we're calling "the thought that one has"). Thus, Connectionists and Classicists can agree to agree that *the thought that P&Q* is complex (and has the thought that *P* among its parts) while agreeing to diagree about whether mental representations have internal syntactic structure.

26. These considerations throw further light on a proposal we discussed in Section 2. Suppose that the mental representation corresponding to the thought that John loves the girl is the feature vector {*+John-subject; +loves; +the-girl-object*} where "*John-subject*" and "*the-girl-object*" are atomic features; as such, they bear no more structural relation to "*John-object*" and "*the-girl-subject*" than they do to one another or to, say, "*has-a-handle.*" Since this theory recognizes no structural relation between "*John-subject*" and "*John-object,*" it offers no reason why a representational system

that provides the means to express one of these concepts should also provide the means to express the other. This treatment of role relations thus makes a mystery of the (presumed) fact that anybody who can entertain the thought that John loves the girl can also entertain the thought that the girl loves John (and, mutatis mutandis, that any natural language that can express the proposition that John loves the girl can also express the proposition that the girl loves John). This consequence of the proposal that role relations be handled by "role specific descriptors that represent the conjunction of an identity and a role" (Hinton, 1987) offers a particularly clear example of how failure to postulate internal structure in representations leads to failure to capture the systematicity of representational systems.

27. We are indebted to Steve Pinker for this point.

28. The hedge is meant to exclude cases where inferences of the same logical type nevertheless differ in complexity in virtue of, for example, the length of their premises. The inference from (A ∨ B ∨ C ∨ D ∨ E) and (–B&–C&–D&–E) to A is of the same logical type as the inference from A ∨ B and –B to A. But it wouldn't be very surprising, or very interesting, if there were minds that could handle the second inference but not the first.

29. Historical footnote: Connectionists are Associationists, but not every Associationist holds that mental representations must be unstructured. Hume didn't, for example. Hume thought that mental representations are rather like pictures, and pictures typically have a compositional semantics: the parts of a picture of a horse are generally pictures of horse parts.

On the other hand, allowing a compositional semantics for mental representations doesn't do an Associationist much good so long as he is true to this spirit of his Associationism. The virtue of having mental representations with structure is that it allows for structure sensitive operations to be defined over them; specifically, it allows for the sort of operations that eventuate in productivity and systematicity. Association is not, however, such an operation; all *it* can do is build an internal model of redundancies in experience by altering the probabilities of transitions among mental states. So far as the problems of productivity and systematicity are concerned, an Associationist who acknowledges structured representations is in the position of having the can but not the opener.

Hume, in fact, cheated: he allowed himself not just Association but also "Imagination," which he takes to be an "active" faculty that can produce new concepts out of old parts by a process of analysis and recombination. (The idea of a unicorn is pieced together out of the idea of a horse and the idea of a horn, for example.) Qua associationist Hume had, of course, no right to active mental faculties. But allowing imagination in gave Hume precisely what modern Connectionists don't have: an answer to the question how mental processes can be productive. The moral is that if you've got structured representations, the temptation to postulate structure sensitive operations and an executive to apply them is practically irresistible.

References

Arbib, M. (1975). Artificial intelligence and brain theory: Unities and diversities. *Biomedical Engineering, 3*, 238–274.

Ballard, D. H. (1986). Cortical connections and parallel processing: Structure and function. *The Behavioral and Brain Sciences, 9*, 67–120.

Ballard, D. H. (1987). Parallel Logical Inference and Energy Minimization. Report TR142, Computer Science Department, University of Rochester.

Broadbent, D. (1985). A question of levels: Comments on McClelland and Rumelhart. *Journal of Experimental Psychology: General, 114*, 189–192.

Chomsky, N. (1965). *Aspects of the theory of syntax*. Cambridge, MA: MIT Press.

Chomsky, N. (1968). *Language and mind*. New York: Harcourt, Brace and World.

Churchland, P. M. (1981). Eliminative materialism and the propositional attitudes. *Journal of Philosophy, 78*, 67–90.

Churchland, P. S. (1986). *Neurophilosophy*. Cambridge, MA: MIT Press.

Dennett, D. (1986). The logical geography of computational approaches: A view from the east pole. In Brand, M. and Harnish, M. (Eds.), *The representation of knowledge*. Tuscon, AZ: The University of Arizona Press.

Dreyfus, H., and Dreyfus, S. (1988). Making a mind vs modelling the brain: A. I. back at a branch point. *Daedalus, 117*, 15–43.

Fahlman, S. E., and Hinton, G. E. (1987). Connectionist architectures for artificial intelligence. *Computer, 20*, 100–109.

Feldman, J. A. (1986). Neural representation of conceptual knowledge. Report TR189. Department of Computer Science, University of Rochester.

Feldman, J. A., and Ballard, D. H. (1982). Connectionist models and their properties. *Cognitive Science, 6*, 205–254.

Fodor, J. (1975). *The language of thought*. Harvester Press, Sussex. (Harvard University Press paperback).

Fodor, J. D. (1977). *Semantics: Theories of meaning in generative grammar*. New York: Thomas Y. Crowell.

Fodor, J. (1987). *Psychosemantics*. Cambridge, MA: MIT Press.

Geach, P. (1957). *Mental acts*. London: Routledge and Kegan Paul.

Hewett, C. (1977). Viewing control structures as patterns of passing messages. *Artificial Intelligence Journal, 8*, 232–364.

Hinton, G. (1987). Representing part-whole hierarchies in connectionist networks. Unpublished manuscript.

Hinton, G. E., McClelland, J. L., and Rumelhart, D. E. (1986). Distributed representations. In Rumelhart, D. E., McClelland, J. L. and the PDP Research Group, *Parallel distributed processing: Explorations in the microstructure of cognition. Volume I: Foundations*. Cambridge, MA: MIT Press/Bradford Books.

Kant, I. (1929). *The critique of pure reason*. New York: St. Martins Press.

Katz, J. J., and Fodor, J. A. (1963). The structure of a semantic theory, *Language, 39*, 170–210.

Katz, J., and Postal, P. (1964). *An integrated theory of linguistic descriptions*. Cambridge, MA: MIT Press.

Kosslyn, S. M., and Hatfield, G. (1984). Representation without symbol systems. *Social Research, 51*, 1019–1054.

Lakoff, G. (1986). Connectionism and cognitive linguistics. Seminar delivered at Princeton University, December 8, 1986.

McClelland, J. L., Feldman, J., Adelson, B., Bower, G., and McDermott, D. (1986). *Connectionist models and cognitive science: Goals, directions and implications*. Report to the National Science Foundation, June, 1986.

McClelland, J. L., and Kawamoto, A. H. (1986). Mechanisms of sentence processing: Assigning roles to constituents. In McClelland, Rumelhart and the PDP Research Group (Eds.), *Parallel distributed processing: volume 2*. Cambridge, MA: MIT Press/Bradford Books.

McClelland, J. L., Rumelhart, D. E., and Hinton, G. E. (1986). The appeal of parallel distributed processing. In Rumelhart, McClelland and the PDP Research Group (Eds.), *Parallel distributed processing: volume 1*. Cambridge, MA: MIT Press/Bradford Books.

Newell, A. (1980). Physical symbol systems. *Cognitive Science, 4*, 135–183.

Newell, A. (1982). The knowledge level. *Artifical Intelligence, 18*, 87–127.

Pinker, S. (1984). *Language, learnability and language development*. Cambridge: Harvard University Press.

Pylyshyn, Z. W. (1980). Cognition and computation: Issues in the foundations of cognitive science. *Behavioral and Brain Sciences, 3:1*, 154–169.

Pylyshyn, Z. W. (1984a). *Computation and cognition: Toward a foundation for cognitive science*. Cambridge, MA: MIT Press/Bradford Books.

Pylyshyn, Z. W. (1984b). Why computation requires symbols. *Proceedings of the Sixth Annual Conference of the Cognitive Science Society, Boulder, Colorado, August, 1984*. Hillsdale, NJ: Erlbaum.

Rumelhart, D. E. (1984). The emergence of cognitive phenomena from sub-symbolic processes. In *Proceedings of the Sixth Annual Conference of the Cognitive Science Society, Boulder, Colorado, August, 1984*. Hillsdale, NJ: Erlbaum.

Rumelhart, D. E., and McClelland, J. L. (1985). Levels indeed! A response to Broadbent. *Journal of Experimental Psychology: General, 114*, 193–197.

Rumelhart, D. E., and McClelland, J. L. (1986a). PDP Models and general issues in cognitive science. In Rumelhart, McClelland and the PDP Research Group (Eds.), *Parallel distributed processing, volume 1*. Cambridge, MA: MIT Press/Bradford Books.

Rumelhart, D. E., and McClelland, J. L. (1986b). On learning the past tenses of English verbs. In Rumelhart, McClelland and the PDP Research Group (Eds.), *Parallel distributed processing, volume 1*. Cambridge, MA: MIT Press/Bradford Books.

Schneider, W. (1987). Connectionism: Is it a paradigm shift for psychology? *Behavior Research Methods, Instruments, and Computers, 19*, 73–83.

Sejnowski, T. J. (1981). Skeleton filters in the brain. In Hinton, G. E., and Anderson, A. J. (Eds.), *Parallel models of associative memory*. Hillsdale, NJ: Erlbaum.

Smolensky, P. (1988). On the proper treatment of connectionism. *Behavioral and Brain Sciences, 11*, 1–74.

Stabler, E. (1985). How are grammars represented? *Behavioral and Brain Sciences, 6*, 391–420.

Stich, S. (1983). *From folk psychology to cognitive science*. Cambridge, MA: MIT Press/Bradford Books.

Wanner, E., and Maratsos, M. (1978). An ATN approach to comprehension. In Halle, M., Bresnan, J., and Miller, G. A. (Eds.), *Linguistic theory and psychological reality*. Cambridge, MA: MIT Press.

Watson, J. (1930). *Behaviorism*. Chicago: University of Chicago Press.

Ziff, P. (1960). *Semantic analysis*. Ithaca, NY: Cornell University Press.

80 The Constituent Structure of Connectionist Mental States: A Reply to Fodor and Pylyshyn

Paul Smolensky

The primary purpose of this article is to reply to the central point of Fodor and Pylyshyn's critique of connectionism. The direct reply to their critique comprises section 2 of this paper. In short, I argue that Fodor and Pylyshyn are simply mistaken in their claim that connectionist mental states lack the necessary constituent structure, and that the basis of this mistake is a failure to appreciate the significance of distributed representations in connectionist models. Section 3 is a broader response to the bottom line of their critique, which is that connectionists should re-orient their work towards *implementation* of the classical symbolic cognitive architecture. I argue instead that connectionist research should develop *new formalizations* of the fundamental computational notions that have been given one particular formal shape in the traditional symbolic paradigm.

My response to Fodor and Pylyshyn's critique presumes a certain meta-theoretical context that is laid out in section 1. In this first section I argue that any discussion of the choice of some framework for cognitive modeling (e.g., the connectionist framework) must admit that such a choice embodies a response to a fundamental cognitive paradox, and that this response shapes the entire scientific enterprise surrounding research within that framework. Fodor and Pylyshyn are implicitly advocating one class of response to the paradox over another, and I wish to analyze their critique in this light.

1 The Paradox and Several Responses

In this section, I want to consider the question of what factors go into the decision about what cognitive modeling formalism to adopt, given the choice between the symbolic formalism and the connectionist formalism. I want to argue that the crucial move in deciding this question is to take a stance on the issue that I will refer to as "the Paradox of Cognition," or more simply, "the Paradox."

The Paradox is simple enough to identify. On the one hand, cognition is *hard*: characterized by the rules of logic, by the rules of language. On the other hand, cognition is *soft*: if you write down the rules, it seems that realizing those rules in automatic formal systems (which AI programs are) gives systems that are just not sufficiently fluid, not robust enough in performance, to constitute what we want to call true intelligence. That, quite simply, is the Paradox. In attempting to characterize the laws of cognition, we are pulled in two different directions: when we focus on the rules governing high-level cognitive competence, we are pulled towards structured, symbolic representations and processes; when we focus on the variance and complex detail of real intelligent performance, we are pulled towards statistical, numerical descriptions. The Paradox could be called, somewhat more precisely, The Structure/Statistics Dilemma.[1] The stance one adopts towards the Paradox strongly influences the role that can be played by symbolic and connectionist modeling formalisms. At least five noteworthy stances have been taken on the Paradox, and I will now quickly review them. I will consider each in its purest form; these extreme stances can be viewed as caricatures of the more subtle positions actually taken by cognitive scientists.

The first stance one should always consider when confronted with a paradox is *denial*. In fact, that is probably the most popular choice. The denial option comes in two forms. The first is to *deny the soft*. A more reputable name for this might be *rationalism*. In this response to the Paradox one insists that the essence of intelligence is logic and following rules—everything else is inessential. This can be identified as the motivation behind the notion of ideal competence in linguistics (Chomsky 1965), where soft behavior and performance variability are regarded as mere noise. The fact that there is tremendous regularity in this noise is to be ignored—at least in the purest version of this stance.

The other denial stance is obviously to *deny the hard*. According to this view, rule following is really characteristic of *novice*, not expert, behavior; the essence of real intelligence is its *evasion* of rule-following (Dreyfus and Dreyfus 1986). Indeed, some of the strongest advocates of this position are connectionists who claim "there are no rules" in cognition.

If one rejects the denial options, one can go for the opposite extreme, which I will call *the split brain*.[2] On this view, the head contains both a soft machine and hard machine, and they sit right next to each other. This response to the Paradox is embodied in talk about systems that have "connectionist modules" and "rule-based modules" and some sort of communication between them. There is the right, connectionist brain doing soft, squishy processing, and the left, von Neumann brain doing the hard rule-based processing. Rather than "the split brain," this scene of a house divided—right and left working side-by-side despite their profound differences—might better be called by its French name: *cohabitation*.

Advocates of this response presumably feel they are giving both sides of the Paradox equal weight. But does this response really grapple with the full force of the Paradox? In the split brain, there is a *hard line* that surrounds and isolates the softness, and there is no soft line that demarks the hardness. The softness is neatly tucked away in an overall architecture characterized by a hard distinction between hard and soft processing. The full force of the Paradox insists that the soft and hard aspects of cognition are so intimately intertwined that such a hard distinction is not viable. Not to mention the serious problem of getting the two kinds of systems to intimately cooperate when they speak such different languages.

The third approach to the Paradox is *the fuzzy approach* (Gupta, Ragade, and Yager 1979). Here the basic idea is take a hard machine and coat its parts with softness. One takes a rule-based system for doing medical diagnosis and attaches a number to every rule that says how certain the inference is (Shortliffe 1976; Zadeh 1975, 1983); or one takes a set, and for every member in the set attaches a number which says how much of member of the set it is (Zadeh 1965). In this response to the Paradox, softness is defined to be degrees of hardness. One takes the ontology of the problem that comes out of the hard approach, and one affixes numbers to all the elements of this ontology rather than reconceptualizing the ontology in a new way that intrinsically reflects the softness in the system.

On such ontological grounds, the fourth approach is starting to get rather more sophisticated. On this view, the cognitive machine is at bottom a hard machine; fundamentally, everything works on rules—but the machine is so complex that it *appears soft* when you look at it on a higher level. *Softness emerges from hardness*. This response to the Paradox is implicit in a comment such as, "O.k., maybe my expert system *is* brittle, but that is because it is just a toy system with only 10,000 rules ... if I had the resources, I would build the *real* system with 10^{10} rules, and it would just be as intelligent as the human expert." In other words, if there are enough hard rules sloshing around in the system, fluid behavior will be an emergent property.

In terms of levels of description, here is the picture. There is a level of description at which the cognitive system is hard: the lower level. And there is a level of description at which it is soft: the higher level. That is the sense in which this approach is getting more sophisticated: it uses *levels of analysis* to reconcile the hard and soft sides of the Paradox.

The question here is whether this approach will ever work. The effort to liberate systems built of large numbers of hard rules from the brittleness that is intrinsic to such rules has been underway for some time now. Whether the partial successes constitute a basis for optimism or pessimism is clearly a difficult judgment call.

The fifth and final approach I want to consider is the one that I have argued (Smolensky 1988a) forms the basis of the proper treatment of connectionism. On this view, which I have called the *subsymbolic* approach, the cognitive system is fundamentally a soft machine that is so complex that it sometimes appears hard when viewed at higher levels. As in the previous approach, the Paradox is addressed through two levels of analysis—but now it is the lower level that is soft and the upper level that is hard: now *hardness emerges from softness*.

Having reviewed these five responses to the Paradox, we can now see why the decision of whether to adopt a symbolic computational formalism or a connectionist one is rooted in a stance on the Paradox. The issue is whether to assume a formalism that *gives for free* the characteristics of the hard side of the Paradox, or one that gives for free the characteristics of the soft side. If you decide not to go for combining both formalisms (*cohabitation*), but to take one as fundamental, then whichever way you go, you have got to either *ignore* the other side, or *build it* in the formalism you have chosen.

So what are the possible motivations for taking the soft side as the fundamental substrate on which to build the hard—whatever hard aspects of cognition need to be built? Here are some reasons for giving the soft side priority in that sense.

- A fundamentally soft approach is appealing if you view *perception*, rather than *logical inference*, as the underpinning of intelligence. In the subsymbolic approach, the fundamental basis of cognition is viewed as categorization and other perceptual processes of that sort.

- In overall cognitive performance, hardness seems more the exception than the rule. That cuts both ways, of course. The denial option is always open to say it is only the 3% that is not soft that really characterizes intelligence, and that is what we should worry about.
- An evolutionary argument says that the hard side of the cognitive paradox evolved later, on top of the soft side, and that your theoretical ontogeny should recapitulate phylogeny.
- Compared to the symbolic rule-based approaches, it is much easier to see how the kind of soft systems that connectionist models represent could be implemented in the nervous system.
- If you are going to base your whole solution to the Paradox on the emergence of one kind of computation from the other, then it becomes crucially important to be able to analyze the higher level properties of the lower level system. That the mathematics governing connectionist networks can be analyzed for emergent properties seems a considerably better bet than extremely complex rule-based systems being analyzable for their emergent properties. The enterprise of analyzing the emergent properties of connectionist systems is rather closely related to traditional kinds of analysis of dynamical systems in physics; it has already shown signs that it may ultimately be as successful.
- Finally, the hard side has had priority for several decades now with disappointing results. It is time to give the soft side a few decades to produce disappointing results of its own.

The choice of adopting a fundamentally soft approach and building a hard level on top of that has serious costs—as pointed out in some detail by Kirsh (1987). The power of symbols and symbolic computation is not given to you for free; you have to construct them out of soft stuff, and this is really very difficult. At this point, we do not know how to pull it off. As Kirsh points out, if you do not have symbols in the usual sense, it is not clear that you can cope with a number of problems. Fodor and Pylyshyn's critique is basically a statement of the same general sort: that the price one has to pay for going connectionist is the failure to account for certain regularities of the hard side, regularities that the symbolic formalism gives you essentially for free.

If the force of such critiques is taken to be that connectionism does not *yet* come close enough to providing the capabilities of symbolic computation to do justice to the hard side of the Paradox, then I personally think that they are quite correct. Adopting the subsymbolic stance on the Paradox amounts to taking out an enormous loan—a loan that has barely begun to be paid off.

If, on the other hand, the force of such critiques is taken to be that connectionism can *never* come close enough to providing the capabilities of symbolic computation without merely implementing the symbolic approach, then, as I will argue in the remainder of this article, I believe such critiques must be rejected.

Where are the benefits of going with the subsymbolic approach to the Paradox? Why is this large loan worth taking out? In my view, the principal justification is that if we succeed in building symbols and symbol manipulation out of "connectoplasm" then we will have an explanation of *where symbols and symbol manipulation come from*—and that is worth the risk and the effort; very much so. With any luck we will even have an explanation how the *brain* builds symbolic computation. But even if we do not get that directly, it will be the first theory of how to get symbols out of anything that remotely resembles the brain—and that certainly will be helpful (indeed, I would argue, crucial) in figuring out how the brain actually does it.

Another potential payback is a way of explaining *why* those aspects of cognition that exhibit hardness should exhibit hardness: why the area of hardness falls where it does; why it is limited as it is; why the symbolic approach succeeds where it succeeds and fails where it fails.

Finally, of course, if the subsymbolic approach succeeds, we will have a truly unified solution to the Paradox: no denial of one half of the problem, and no profoundly split brain.

We can already see contributions leading towards these ultimate results. The connectionist approach is producing new concepts and techniques for capturing the regularities in cognitive performance both at the lower level where the connectionist framework naturally applies and at the higher level where the symbolic accounts are important. (For recent surveys, see McClelland, Rumelhart, and the PDP Research Group 1986; Rumelhart, McClelland, and the PDP Research Group 1986; Smolensky, forthcoming.) The theoretical repertoire of cognitive and computer science is being enriched by new conceptions of how computation can be done.

As far as where we actually stand on achieving the ultimate goals, in my opinion, what we have are interesting techniques and promising suggestions. Our current position in the intellectual history of connectionist computation, in my view, can be expressed by this analogy:

$$\frac{\text{current understanding of connectionist computation}}{\text{current understanding of symbolic computation}} : : \frac{\text{Aristotle}}{\text{Turing}}$$

We are somewhere approximating Aristotle's position in the intellectual development of this new computational approach. If there are any connectionist enthusiasts who think that we can really model cognition from such a position, they are, I fear, sadly mistaken. And if we cannot get from Aristotle to (at least) Turing in our understanding of subsymbolic computation, we are not going to get much closer to real cognition than we are now.

One final comment before proceeding to Fodor and Pylyshyn's critique. The account given here relating the choice of a connectionist framework to the hard/soft paradox sheds some light on the question, often asked by observers of the sociology of connectionism: "Why does the connectionist fan club include such a strange assortment of people?" At least in the polite reading of this question, "strange assortment" refers to a philosophically quite heterogenous group of cognitive scientists whose views have little more in common than a rejection of the mainstream symbolic paradigm. My answer to this question is that the priority of the hard has made a lot of people very unhappy for a long time. The failure of mainstream formal accounts of cognitive processes to do justice to the soft side of the Paradox has made people from a lot of different perspectives feel alienated from the endeavor. By assigning to the soft the position of priority, by making it the basis of the formalism, connectionism has given a lot of people who have not had a formal leg to stand on a formal leg to stand on. And they *should* be happy about that.

At this point, "connectionism" refers more to a formalism than a theory. So it is not appropriate to paraphrase the question of the previous paragraph as "What kind of theory would have as its adherents such a disparate group of people?" It is not really a question of a *theory* at all—it is really a question of what kind of *formalism* allows people with different theories to say what they need to say.

Having made my case that understanding the choice of a connectionist formalism involves considering alternative stances towards the Paradox of Cognition, I now proceed to consider Fodor and Pylyshyn's critique in this light.

2 Fodor and Pylyshyn on the Constituent Structure of Mental States

Here is a quick summary of the central argument of Fodor and Pylyshyn (1988).

(1) Thoughts have composite structure.

By this they mean things like: the thought that *John loves the girl* is not atomic; it is a composite mental state built out of thoughts about *John*, *loves*, and *the girl*.

(2) Mental processes are sensitive to this composite structure.

For example, from any thought of the form p & q—regardless of what p and q are—we can deduce p.

Fodor and Pylyshyn elevate (1) and (2) to the status of defining the Classical View of Cognition, and they want to say that this is what is being challenged by the connectionists. I will later argue that they are wrong, but now we continue with their argument.

Having identified claims (1) and (2) as definitive of the Classical View, Fodor and Pylyshyn go on to argue that there are compelling arguments for these claims. [They admit up front that these arguments are a rerun updated for the '80s, a colorized version of a film that was shown in black and white some time ago—with the word "behaviorism" replaced throughout by "connectionism."] Mental states have, according to these arguments, the properties of productivity, systematicity, compositionality, and inferential coherence. Without going into all these arguments, let me simply state that for present purposes I am willing to accept that they are convincing enough to justify the conclusion that (1) and (2) must be taken quite seriously. Whatever the inclinations of other connectionists, these and related arguments convince me that denying the hard is a mistake. They do not convince me that I should deny the soft—nor, presumably, are they intended to.

Now for Fodor and Pylyshyn's analysis of connectionism. They assert that in (standard) connectionism, *all representations are atomic*; mental states have no composite structure, violating (1). Furthermore, they assert, (standard) *connectionist processing is association* which is sensitive only to *statistics*, not to *structure*—in violation of (2). Therefore, they conclude, (standard) connectionism is maximally non-Classical; it violates both the defining principles. Therefore connectionism is defeated by the compelling arguments in favor of the Classical View.

What makes Fodor and Pylyshyn say that connectionist represention are atomic? The second figure of their paper says it all—it is rendered here as figure 80.1. This network is supposed to illustrate the standard connectionist account of the inference from

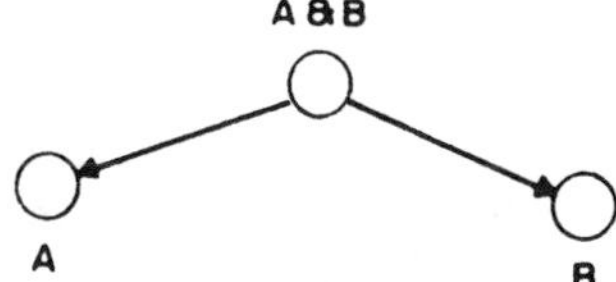

Figure 80.1
Fodor and Pylyshyn's network.

A & *B* to *A* and to *B*. It is true that Ballard and Hayes wrote a paper (Ballard and Hayes 1984) about using connectionist networks to do resolution theorem proving in which networks like this appear. However, it is a serious mistake to view this as the paradigmatic connectionist account for anything like human inferences of this sort. This kind of *ultra-local* connectionist representation, in which entire propositions are represented by individual nodes, is far from typical of connectionist models, and certainly not to be taken as *definitive* of the connectionist approach.

My central counter-argument to Fodor and Pylyshyn starts with the claim that any critique of the connectionist approach must consider the consequences of using *distributed representations*, in which the representations of high level conceptual entities such as propositions are distributed over many nodes, and the same nodes simultaneously participate in the representation of many entities. Their response, in Section 2.1.3, is as follows. The distributed/local representation issue concerns (they assume) whether each of the nodes in figure 80.1 refers to something complicated and lower level (the distributed case) or not (the local case). But, they claim, this issue is irrelevant, because it pertains to a *between level* issue, and the compositionality of mental states is a *within level* issue.

My response is that they are correct that compositionality is a within level issue, and correct that the distributed/local distinction is a between level issue. Their argument presumes that because of this difference, one issue cannot influence the other. But this is a fallacy. It assumes that the between-level relation in distributed representations cannot have any consequences on the *within level* structure of the relationships between the representations of *A* & *B* and the representation of *A*. And that is simply false. There are implications of distributed representations for compositionality, which I am going to bring out in the rest of this section through an extended example. In particular it will turn out that figure 80.1 is no more relevant to a distributed connectionist account of inference than it is to a symbolic account. In the hyper-local case, figure 80.1 is relevant and their critique stands; in the distributed case, figure 80.1 is a bogus characterization of the connectionist account and their critique completely misses its target. It will further turn out that a valid analysis of the actual distributed case, based on suggestions of Pylyshyn himself, leads to quite the opposite conclusion: connectionist models using distributed representations describe mental states with a relevant kind of (within level) constituent structure.

Before developing this counter-argument, let me summarize the bottom line of the Fodor and Pylyshyn paper. Since they believe *standard* connectionism to be fatally flawed, they advocate that connectionists pursue instead a *nonstandard connectionism*. Connectionists should embrace principles (1) and (2); they should accept the classical view and should design their nets to be implementations of classical architectures. The logic implicit here is that connectionist models that respect (1) and (2) must necessarily be implementations of a classical architecture; this is their second major fallacy, which I will return to in section 3. Fodor and Pylyshyn claim that connectionism should be used to implement classical architectures, and that having done this, connectionism will provide not a new cognitive architecture but an implementation for the old cognitive architecture—that what connectionism can provide therefore is not a new paradigm for cognitive science but rather some new information about "implementation science" or possibly, neuroscience.

If connectionists were to follow the implementation strategy that Fodor and Pylyshyn advocate, I do believe these consequences concerning cognitive architecture *would* indeed follow. But I do not believe that it follows from accepting (1) and (2) that connectionist networks must be implementations. In section 3, I argue that connectionists can consistently accept (1) and (2) while rejecting the implementationalist approach Fodor and Pylyshyn advocate.

For now, the goal is to show that connectionist models using *distributed* representations ascribe to mental states the kind of compositional structure demanded by (1), contrary to Fodor and Pylyshyn's conclusion based on the network of figure 80.1 embodying a hyper-local representation.

My argument consists primarily in carrying out an analysis that was suggested by Zenon Pylyshyn himself at the 1984 Cognitive Science Meeting in Boulder. A sort of debate about connectionism was held between Geoffrey Hinton and David Rumelhart on the one hand, and Zenon Pylyshyn and Kurt Van Lehn on the other. While pursuing the nature of connectionist representations, Pylyshyn asked Rumelhart: "Look, can you guys represent a cup of coffee in these networks?" Rumelhart's reply was "Sure" so Pylyshyn continued: "And can you represent a cup without coffee in it?" Waiting for the trap to close, Rumelhart said "Yes" at which point Pylyshyn pounced: "Ah-hah, well, the difference between the two is just the representation of *coffee* and you have just built a representation of *cup with coffee* by combining a representation of *cup* with a representation of *coffee*."

So, let's carry out exactly the construction suggested by Pylyshyn, and see what conclusion it leads us to. We will take a *distributed* representation of *cup with coffee* and substract from it a distributed representation of *cup without coffee* and we will call what is left "the connectionist representation of *coffee*."

To generate these distributed representations I will use a set of "microfeatures" (Hinton, McClelland, and Rumelhart 1986) that are not very micro—but that is always what happens when you try to create examples that can be intuitively understood in a nontechnical exposition. These microfeatures are shown in figure 80.2.

Figure 80.2 shows a distributed representation of *cup with coffee*: a pattern of activity in which those units that are active (black) are those that correspond to microfeatures present in the description of a cup containing coffee. Obviously, this is a crude, nearly sensory-level representation, but again that helps make the example more intuitive—it is not essential.

Given the representation of *cup with coffee* displayed in figure 80.2, Pylyshyn suggests we subtract the representation of *cup without coffee*. The representation of *cup without coffee* is shown in figure 80.3, and figure 80.4 shows the result of subtracting it from the representation of *cup with coffee*.

Units	Microfeatures
●	upright container
●	hot liquid
○	glass contacting wood
●	porcelain curved surface
●	burnt odor
●	brown liquid contacting porcelain
●	porcelain curved surface
○	oblong silver object
●	finger-sized handle
●	brown liquid with curved sides and bottom

Figure 80.2
Representation of *cup* with *coffee*.

Units	Microfeatures
●	upright container
○	hot liquid
○	glass contacting wood
●	porcelain curved surface
○	burnt odor
○	brown liquid contacting porcelain
●	porcelain curved surface
○	oblong silver object
●	finger-sized handle
○	brown liquid with curved sides and bottom

Figure 80.3
Representation of *cup without coffee*.

So what does this procedure produce as "the connectionist representation of *coffee*"? Reading off from figure 80.4, we have a burnt odor and hot brown liquid with curved sides and bottom surfaces contacting porcelain. This is indeed a representation of *coffee*, but in a very particular context: the context provided by *cup*.

What does this mean for Pylyshyn's conclusion that "the connectionist representation of *cup with coffee* is just the representation of *cup without coffee* combined with the representation of *coffee*"? What is involved in combining the representations of figures 80.3 and 80.4 back together to form that of figure 80.2? We assemble the representation of *cup with coffee* from a representation of a *cup*, and a representation of *coffee*, but it is a rather strange combination. It has also got representation of the *interaction* of the cup with coffee—like *brown liquid contacting porcelain*. Thus the composite representation is built from coffee *extracted* from the situation *cup with coffee*, together with *cup* extracted from the situation *cup with coffee*, together with their interaction.

Units	Microfeatures
○	upright container
●	hot liquid
○	glass contacting wood
○	porcelain curved surface
●	burnt odor
●	brown liquid contacting porcelain
○	porcelain curved surface
○	oblong silver object
○	finger-sized handle
●	brown liquid with curved sides and bottom

Figure 80.4
Representation of *coffee.*

So the compositional structure is there, but it is there in an *approximate* sense. It is *not* equivalent to taking a context-independent representation of *coffee* and a context-independent representation of *cup*—and certainly not equivalent to taking a context-independent representation of the relationship *in* or *with*—and sticking them all together in a symbolic structure, concatenating them together to form the kinds of syntactic compositional structures that Fodor and Pylyshyn think connectionist nets should implement.

To draw this point out further, let's consider the representation of *coffee* once the cup has been subtracted off. This, suggests Pylyshyn, is the connectionist representation of *coffee*. But as we have already observed, this is really a representation of *coffee* in the particular context of being inside a cup. According to Pylyshyn's formula, to get the connectionist representation of *coffee* it should have been in principle possible to take the connectionist representation of *can with coffee* and subtract from it the connectionist representation of *can without coffee*. What would happen if we actually did this? We would get a representation of ground brown burnt smelling granules stacked in a cylindrical shape, together with granules contacting tin. This is the connectionist representation of *coffee* we get by starting with *can with coffee* instead of *cup with coffee*. Or we could start with the representation of *tree with coffee* and subtract off *tree without coffee*. We would get a connectionist representation for *coffee* which would be a representation of brown beans in a funny shape hanging suspended in mid air. Or again we could start with *man with coffee* and get still another connectionist representation of *coffee*: one quite similar to the entire representation of *cup with coffee* from which we extracted our first representation of *coffee*.

The point is that the representation of *coffee* that we get out of the construction starting with *cup with coffee* leads to a different representation of *coffee* than we get out of other constructions that have equivalent status a priori. That means if you want to talk about the connectionist representation of *coffee* in this distributed scheme, you have to talk about a *family of distributed activity patterns*. What knits together all these particular representations of *coffee* is nothing other than a *family resemblance*.

The first moral I want to draw out of this *coffee* story is this: unlike the hyper-local case of figure 80.1, with distributed representations, complex representations *are* composed of representations of constituents. The constituency relation here is a *within level* relation, as Fodor and Pylyshyn require: the pattern or *vector* representing *cup with coffee* is composed of a *vector* that can be identified as a distributed representation of *cup without coffee* together with a *vector* that can be identified as a particular distributed representation of *coffee*. In characterizing the constituent vectors of the vector representing the composite, we are *not* concerned with the fact that the vector representing *cup with coffee* is a vector comprised of the activity of individual microfeature units. The *between level* relation between the vector and its individual numerical elements is *not* the constituency relation, and so section 2.1.4 of Fodor and Pylyshyn (this volume) is irrelevant—there they address a mistake that is not being made.

The second moral is that the constituency relation among distributed representations is one that is important for the analysis of connectionist models, and for explaining their behavior, but it is *not* a part of the causal mechanism within the model. In order to process the vector representing *cup with coffee*, the network does not have to decompose it into constituents. For processing, it is the *between level* relation, not the within level relation, that matters. The processing of the vector representing *cup with coffee* is determined by the individual numerical activities that make up the vector: it is over these lower-level activities that the processes are defined. Thus the fact that there is considerable arbitrariness in the way the constituents of *cup with coffee* are defined introduces no ambiguities in the way the network processes that representation—the ambiguities exist only for us who analyze the model and try to explain its behavior. Any particular definition of constituency that gives us explanatory leverage is a valid definition of constituency; lack of uniqueness is not a problem.

This leads directly to the third moral, that the decomposition of composite states into their constituents is not precise and uniquely defined. The notion of constituency is important but attempts to formalize it are likely to crucially involve *approximation*. As discussed at some length in Smolensky (1988a), this is the typical case: notions from symbolic computation provide important tools for constructing higher-level accounts of the behavior of connectionist models using distributed representation—but these notions provide approximate, not precise, accounts.

Which leads to the fourth moral, that while connectionist networks using distributed representations *do* describe mental states with the type of constituency required by (1), they do *not* provide a literal implementation of a syntactic language of thought. The context dependency of the constituents, the interactions that must be accomodated when they are combined, the inability to uniquely, precisely identify constituents, the need to take seriously the notion that the representation of *coffee* is a collection of vectors knit together by family resemblance—all these entail that the relation between connectionist constituency and syntactic constituency is *not* one of literal implementation. In particular, it would be absurd to claim that even if the connectionist story is correct then that would have no implications for the cognitive architecture, that it would merely fill in lower level details without important implications for the higher level account.

These conclusions all address (1) without explicitly addressing (2). Addressing (2) properly is far beyond the scope of this paper. To a considerable extent, it is beyond the scope of current connectionism. Let me simply point out that the Structure/Statistics Dilemma has an attractive possible solution that the connectionist approach is perfectly situated to pursue: *the mind is a statistics-sensitive engine operating on structure-sensitive numerical representations*. The previous arguments have shown that distributed representations do possess constituency relations, and that, properly analyzed, these representations can be seen to encode structure. Extending this to grapple with the full complexity of the kinds of rich structures implicated in complex cognitive processes is a research problem that has been attacked with some success but which remains to be definitively concluded (see Smolensky 1987 and section 3). Once we have complex structured information represented in distributed numerical patterns, statistics-sensitive processes can proceed to analyze the statistical regularities in a fully structure-sensitive way. Whether such processes can cope with the full force of the Structure/Statistics Dilemma is apt to remain an open question for some time yet.

The conclusion, then, is that distributed models *can* satisfy both (1) and (2). Whether (1) and (2) can be satisfied to the point of providing an account adequate to cover the *full demands of cognitive modeling* is of course an open empirical question—just as it is for the symbolic approach to satisfying (1) and (2). Just the same, distributed connectionist models do *not* amount to an implementation of the symbolic instantiations of (1) and (2) that Fodor and Pylyshyn are committed to.

Before summing up, I would like to return to figure 80.1. In what sense can figure 80.1 be said to describe the relation between the distributed representation of *A&B* and the distributed representations of *A* and *B*? It was the intent of the *coffee* example to show that the distributed representations of the constituents are, in an approximate but explanation-relevant sense, part of the representation of the composite. Thus, in the distributed case, the relation between the node of figure 80.1 labelled *A & B* and the others is a sort of whole/part relation. An inference mechanism that takes as input the vector representing *A & B* and produces as output the vector representing *A* is a mechanism that extracts a part from a whole. And in this sense it is no different from a symbolic inference mechanism that takes the syntactic structure **A & B** and extracts from it the syntactic constituent **A**. The connectionist mechanisms for doing this are of course quite different than the symbolic mechanisms, and the approximate nature of the whole/part relation gives the connectionist computation different overall characteristics: we do not have simply a new implementation of the old computation.

It is clear that, just as figure 80.1 offers a crude summary of the symbolic process of passing from **A & B** to **A**, a summary that uses the labels to encode hidden internal structures within the nodes, *exactly the same is true of the distributed connectionist case*. In the distributed case, just as in the symbolic case, the links in figure 80.1 are crude summaries of complex processes and not simple-minded causal channels that pass activity from the top node to the lower nodes. Such a causal story applies only to the hyper-local connectionist case, which here serves as the proverbial straw man.

Let me be clear: there is no distributed connectionist model, as far as I know, of the kind of formal inference Fodor and Pylyshyn have in mind here. Such formal inference is located at the far extreme of the hard side of the Paradox, and is not at this point a cognitive process (or abstraction thereof) that the connectionist formalism can be said to have built upon its soft substrate. But at root the Fodor and Pylyshyn critique revolves around the constituent structure of mental states—formal inference is just one setting in which to see the importance of that constituent structure. So the preceeding discussion of the constituent structure of distributed representations does address the heart of their critique, even if a well-developed connectionist account of formal inference remains unavailable.

So, let's summarize the overall picture at this point. We have got principles (1) and (2), and we have got a symbolic instantiation of these in a language of thought using syntactic constituency. According to Fodor and Pylyshyn, what connectionists should do is take that symbolic language of thought as a higher level description and then produce a connectionist implementation in a literal sense. The syntactic operations of the symbolic language of thought then provide an exact formal higher level account.

By contrast, I argue that the distributed view of connectionist compositionality allows us to instantiate the same basic principles of (1) and (2) *without* going through a symbolic language of thought. By going straight to distributed connectionist models we get *new instantiations of compositionality principles*.

I happen to believe that the symbolic descriptions *do* provide useful approximate higher level accounts of how these connectionist models compute—but in no sense do these distributed connectionist models provide a literal implementation of a symbolic language of thought. The approximations require a willingness to accept context sensitive symbols and interactional components present in compositional structures, and the other funny business that came out in the *coffee* example. If you are willing to live with all those degrees of approximation then you can usefully view these symbolic level descriptions as approximate higher level accounts of the processing in a connectionist network.

The overall conclusion, then, is that *the classical and connectionist approaches differ not in whether they accept principles (1) and (2), but in how they formally instantiate them*. To confront the real classical/connectionist dispute, one has to be willing to descend to the level of the particular formal instantiations they give to these nonformal principles. To fail to descend to this level of detail is to miss the issue. In the classical approach, principles (1) and (2) are formalized using syntactic structures for thoughts and symbol manipulation for mental processes. In the connectionist view (1) or (2) are formalized using distributed vectorial representations for mental states, and the corresponding notion of compositionality, together with association-based mental processes that derive their structure sensitivity from the structure sensitivity of the vectorial representations engaging in those processes.

In terms of research methodology, this means that the agenda for connectionism should not be to develop a connectionist implementation of the symbolic language of thought but rather to develop formal analyses of vectorial representations of complex structures and operations on those structures that are sufficiently structure-sensitive to do the required work.

In summary: distributed representations provide a description of mental states with semantically interpretable constituents, but there is no precise formal account of the construction of composites from context-independent semantically interpretable constituents. On this account, there *is* a language of thought—but only approximately; the language of thought does not provide a basis for an exact formal account of mental structure or processes—it cannot provide a precise formal account of the cognitive architecture.[3]

3 Connectionism and Implementation

In section 2 I argued that connectionist research should be directed toward structure-sensitive representations and processes but not toward the implementation of a symbolic language of thought. In this section I want to consider this middle ground between implementing symbolic computation and ignoring structure. Many critics of connectionism do not seem to understand that this middle ground exists. (For further discussion of this point, and a map that explicitly locates this middle ground, see Smolensky 1988b.)

A rather specific conclusion of section 2 was that connectionists need to develop the analysis of distributed (vectorial) representations of composite structures and the kinds of processes that operate on them with the necessary structure sensitivity. More generally, my characterization of the goal of connectionist modeling is to develop formal models of cognitive processes that are based on the mathematics of dynamical systems continuously evolving in time: complex systems of numerical variables governed by differential equations. These formal accounts live in the category of continuous mathematics rather than relying on the discrete mathematics that underlies the traditional symbolic formalism. This characterization of the goal of connectionism is far from universal: it is quite inconsistent with the definitive characterization of Feldman and Ballard (1982), for example. In Smolensky (1988a) I argue at some length that my characterization, called *PTC*, constitutes a Proper Treatment of Connectionism.

A central component of PTC is the relation hypothesized between connectionist models based on continuous mathematics and classical models based on discrete, symbolic computation. That relationship, which entered briefly in the Fodor and Pylyshyn argument of section 2, might be called the *cognitive correspondence principle*: When connectionist computational systems are analyzed at higher levels, elements of symbolic computation appear as emergent properties.

Figure 80.5 illustrates the cognitive correspondence principle. At the top we have nonformal notions: the central hypotheses that the principles of cognition consist in principles of memory, of inference, of compositionality and constituent structure, etc. In the Fodor and Pylyshyn argument, the relevant nonformal principles were their compositionality principles (1) and (2).

The nonformal principles at the top of figure 80.5 have certain formalizations in the discrete category, which are shown one level down on the right branch. For example, memory is formalized as standard location-addressed memory or some appropriately more sophisticated related notion. Inference gets formalized in the discrete category as logical inference, a particular form of symbol manipulation. And so on.

The PTC agenda consists in taking these kinds of cognitive principles and finding new ways to instantiate them in formal principles based on the mathematics of dynamical systems; these are shown in figure 80.5 at the lowest level on the left branch. The concept of memory retrieval is reformalized in terms of the continuous evolution of a dynamical system towards a point attractor whose position in the state

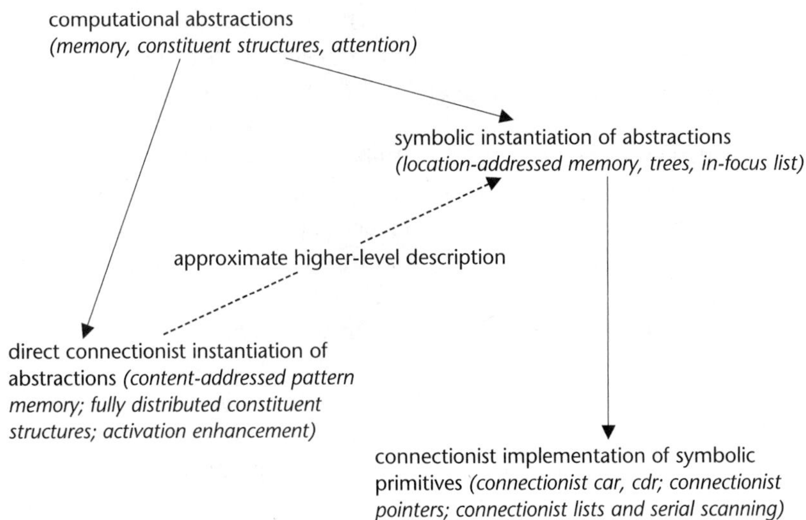

Figure 80.5
PTC versus implementationalism (reprinted with permission of *The Behavioral and Brain Sciences*).

space is the memory; you naturally get content-addressed memory instead of location-addressed memory. (Memory storage becomes modification of the dynamics of the system so that its attractors are located where the memories are supposed to be; thus the principles of memory storage are even more unlike their symbolic counterparts than those of memory retrieval.) When reformalizing inference principles, the continuous formalism leads naturally to principles of statistical inference rather than logical inference. And so on.

The cognitive correspondence principle states that the general relationship between the connectionist formal principles and the symbolic formal principles—given that they are both instantiations of common nonformal notions—is that if you take a higher level analysis of what is going on in the connectionist systems you find that it matches, to some kind of approximation, what is going on in the symbolic formalism. This relation is indicated in figure 80.5 by the dotted arrow.

This is to be contrasted with an implementational view of connectionism which Fodor and Pylyshyn advocate. As portrayed in figure 80.5, the implementational methodology is to proceed from the top to the bottom not directly, via the left branch, but indirectly, via the right branch; connectionists should take the symbolic instantiations of the nonformal principles and should find ways of implementing *them* in connectionist networks.

The PTC methodology is contrasted not just with the implementational approach, but also with the eliminitivist one. In terms of these methodological considerations, eliminitivism has a strong and a weak form. The weak form advocates taking the left branch of figure 80.5 but ignoring altogether the symbolic formalizations, on the belief that the symbolic notions will confuse rather than enlighten us in our attempts to understand connectionist computation. The strong eliminitivist position states that even viewing the nonformal principles at the top of figure 80.5 as a starting point for thinking about cognition is a mistake; e.g., that it is better to pursue a blind bottom-up strategy in which low-level connectionist principles are taken from neuroscience and we see where they lead us without being prejudiced by archaic prescientific notions such as those at the top of figure 80.5.

In rejecting both the implementationalist and eliminitivist positions, PTC views connectionist accounts as reducing and explaining symbolic accounts. Connectionist accounts serve to refine symbolic accounts, to reduce the degree of approximation required, to enrich the computational notions from the symbolic and discrete world, to fill them out with notions of continuous computation. Primarily that is done by descending to a lower level of analysis, by focussing on the microstructure implicit in these kinds of symbolic operations.

I call this the cognitive correspondence principle because I believe it has a role to play in the developing microtheory of cognition that is analogous to the role that the quantum correspondence principle played in the development of microtheory in physics. The case from physics embodies the structure of figure 80.5 quite directly. There are certain physical principles that arch over both the classical and quantum formalisms: the notions of space and time and associated invariance principles, the principles of energy and momentum conservation, force laws, and so on. These principles at the top of figure 80.5 are instantiated in particular ways in the classical formalism, corresponding to the point one level down on the right branch. To go to a lower level of physical analysis requires the development of a new formalism. In this quantum formalism, the fundamental principles are reinstantiated: they occupy the bottom of the left branch. The classical formalism can be looked at as a higher level description of the same principles operating at the lower quantum level: the dotted line of figure 80.5. Of course, quantum mechanics does not *implement* classical mechanics: the accounts are intimately related, but classical mechanics provides an approximate, not an exact, higher-level account.[4] In a deep sense, the quantum and classical theories are quite incompatible: according to the ontology of quantum mechanics, the ontology of classical mechanics is quite impossible to realize in this world. But there is no denying that the classical ontology and the accompanying principles are theoretically essential, for at least two reasons: (a) to provide explanations (in a literal sense, approximate ones) of an enormous range of classical phenomena for which direct explanation from quantum principles is hopelessly infeasible, and (b), historically, to provide the guidance necessary to discover the quantum principles in the first place. To try to develop lower level principles without looking at the higher level principles for guidance, given the insights we have gained from those principles, would seem, to put it mildly, inadvisable. It is basically this pragmatic consideration that motivates the cognitive correspondence principle and the PTC position it leads to.

In the PTC methodology, it is essential to be able to analyze the higher level properties of connectionist computation in order to relate them to properties of symbolic computation, e.g., to see whether they have the necessary computational power. I now want to summarize what I take to be the state of the art in the mathematical analysis of computation in connectionist systems, and how it relates to Fodor and Pylyshyn's critique. This summary is presented in figure 80.6.

Figure 80.6 shows the pieces of a connectionist model and elements of their analysis. The connectionist model basically has four parts. There is the task that the model is

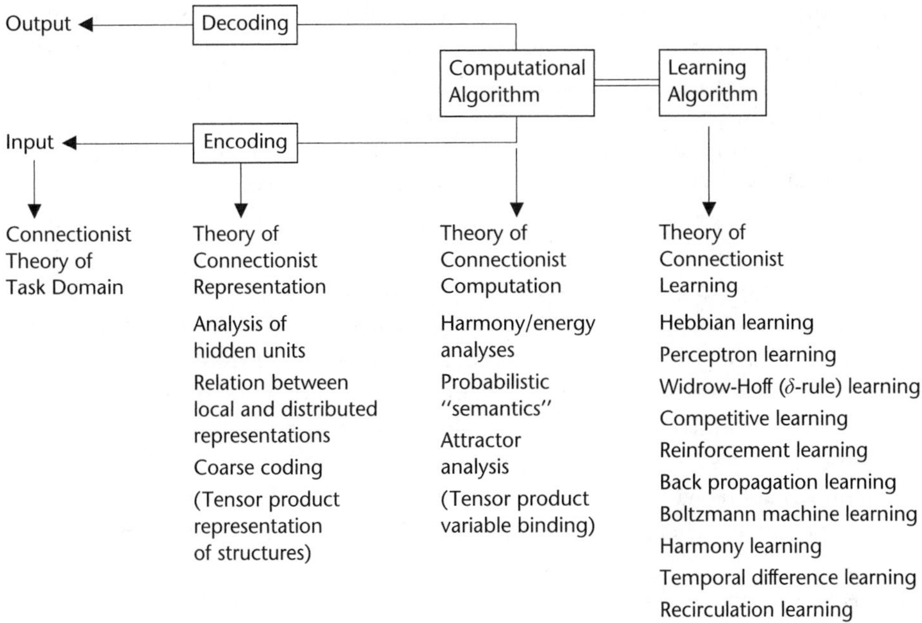

Figure 80.6
Theory of Connectionst models.

supposed to perform—for example, to take some set of inputs into a set of outputs described in the terms characteristic of the problem domain. Then there is an actual connectionist network which will perform that mapping from input to output; but between the original task and the model we need methods for encoding and decoding. The encoding must take the problem domain characterization of an input and code it into a form that the network can process, namely, activities of certain input processors. Similarily, the activity of the output processors has to be decoded into some problem domain statement which can be construed as the output of the network. The input-to-output mapping inside the network is the computational algorithm embodied in the network and, more often than not, in addition, there is a learning algorithm which modifies the parameters in the computational algorithm in order to get it to converge on the correct input/output behavior of the correct computation.

In terms of analyzing these four elements of connectionist modeling, things get progressively worse as we move from right to left. In the area of connectionist learning, there are lots of analyses: algorithms for tweaking lower-level connection strengths which will produce reasonable higher level convergence towards the correct input/output mapping. The figure shows as many as would fit conveniently and there are many more.[5]

So, if you think that the problem with connectionism is that a particular learning algorithm has some characteristic you do not like, then chances are there is another learning algorithm that will make you happy. Relative to the rest, the learning theory is in good shape, even though when it comes to theorems about what functions can be learned by a given algorithm, there is very little.

With respect to analyzing the higher-level properties of the algorithms for computing outputs from inputs, there is considerably less theory. The technique of analyzing convergence using a function that measures the "energy" or "harmony" of network states (Ackley, Hinton, and Sejnowski 1985; Cohen and Grossberg 1983; Geman and Geman 1984; Hinton and Sejnowski 1983; Hopfield 1982; Smolensky 1983, 1986a) get us somewhere, as do a few other techniques[6] but it seems rather clear that the state of analysis of connectionist computation is considerably less developed than that of connectionist learning.

After this things get *very* thin. What about the theory behind encoding and decoding, the theory of how to take the kinds of inputs and outputs that have to be represented for cognitive processes and turn them into actual patterns of activity? By and large, it is a black art: there is not much in the way of analysis. People have been getting their hands dirty exploring the representations in hidden units (e.g., Hinton 1986; Rosenberg 1987), but so far I see little reason to believe our understanding of these representations will go further than understanding an occasional node or a few statistical properties. There are a few other simple analyses[7] but they do not take us very far.

At the far left of figure 80.6 is the theory of the task environment that comes out of a connectionist perspective. This is essentially nonexistent. To many, I believe, that is really the ultimate goal: the theory of the domain in connectionist terms.

As figure 80.6 makes clear, there is a very important weak leg here: the connectionist theory of representation. In particular, until recently we have not had any systematic ideas about how to represent complex structures. In fact, it was Fodor and Pylyshyn who really got me thinking about this, and ultimately convinced me. The result was the tensor product technique for generating fully distributed representations of complex structures (Smolensky 1987). For this reason the tensor product representation is dedicated to Fodor and Pylyshyn. This representational scheme is a formalization and generalization of representational techniques that have been used piecemeal in connectionist models. As others have discussed ..., the tensor product technique provides a systematic and disciplined procedure for representing complex, structured objects. One can prove that the tensor product representation has a number of nice computational properties from the standpoint of connectionist processing. In this sense, it is appropriate to view the tensor product representation as occupying the lower level corner of figure 80.5: it provides a formalization that is natural for connectionist computation of the nonformal notion of constituent structure, and is a likely candidate to play a role in connectionist cognitive science analogous to that played by constituent structure trees in symbolic cognitive science.

The tensor product representation rests on the use of the tensor product operation to perform in the vectorial world the analog of binding together a variable and its value. Figure 80.6 shows where tensor product variable binding and tensor product representations of structures fit into the overall problem of analyzing connectionist cognitive models.

I hope this last section has made more plausible my working hypothesis that between the connectionist view that Fodor and Pylyshyn attack—denying the importance of structured representations and structure-sensitive processes—and the connectionist methodology they advocate—implementation of the classical symbolic cognitive architecture—there is a promising middle ground on which productive and exciting research can be pursued.

Acknowledgments

This work has been supported by NSF grants IRI-8609599 and ECE-8617947 to the author, and by a grant to the author from the Sloan Foundation's computational neuroscience program.

Notes

1. For related discussions, see, e.g., Gerken and Bever 1986, Greeno 1987.

2. For some somewhat spooky empirical results directly bearing on this issue, see Bever, Carrithers, and Townsend 1987.

3. An important open question is whether the kind of story I have given on *cup of coffee* using these hokey microfeatures will carry over to the kind of distributed representations that real connectionist networks create for themselves in their hidden units—if you make the analysis appropriately sophisticated. The resolution of this issue depends on the (as yet inscrutable) nature of these representations for realistic problems. The nature of the problem is important, for it is perfectly likely that connectionist networks will develop compositional representations in their hidden units only when this is advantageous for the problem they are trying to solve. As Fodor and Pylyshyn, and the entire Classical paradigm, argue, such compositional representations are in fact immensely useful for a broad spectrum of cognitive problems. But until such problems—which tend to be considerably more sophisticated than those usually given to connectionist networks—have been explored in some detail with connectionist models, we will not really know if hidden units will develop compositional representations (in the approximate sense discussed in this paper) when they "should."

4. Many cases analogous to "implementation" *are* found in physics. Newton's laws provide an "implementation" of Kepler's laws; Maxwell's theory "implements" Coulomb's law; the quantum principles of the hydrogen atom "implement" Balmer's formula.

5. Here are a smattering of references to these learning rules; rather than giving historically primary references I have cited recent easily accessible expositions that include the original citations. (In fact I have chosen papers in Rumelhart, McClelland, and the PDP Group 1986, when possible.) For an exposition of Hebbian, perceptron, and Widrow-Hoff or delta-rule learning, see Rumelhart, Hinton, and McClelland 1986 and Stone 1986. For competitive learning see Grossberg 1987, and Rumelhart and Zipser 1986. For reinforcement learning, see Barto, Sutton and Anderson 1983, and Sutton 1987. For back propagation learning see Rumelhart, Hinton and Williams 1986. For Boltzmann machine learning, see Hinton and Sejnowski 1986. For harmony learning, see Smolensky 1986a. Temporal difference learning is reported in Sutton 1987. A simple recirculation learning algorithm is discussed in Smolensky 1987; the idea has been under exploration by Hinton and McClelland for several years, and their first paper should appear in 1988.

6. On giving the computation in connectionist networks semantics based on statistical inference, see Shastri and Feldman 1985; Smolensky 1986a; Golden 1988.

7. For some simple explorations of the relation between local and distributed representations, see Smolensky 1986b. For some observations about the power of the distributed representational technique called "coarse coding," see Hinton, McClelland, and Rumelhart 1986.

References

Ackley, D. H., Hinton, G. E., and Sejnowski, T. J. (1985). A learning algorithm for Boltzmann machines. *Cognitive Science*, 9, 147–169.

Ballard, D. and Hayes, P. J. (1984). Parallel logical inference. *Proceedings of the Sixth Annual Conference of the Cognitive Science Society*. Rochester, NY, June.

Barto, A. G., Sutton, R. S., and Anderson, C. W. (1983). Neuronlike elements that can solve difficult learning control problems. *IEEE Transactions on Systems, Man, and Cybernetics* SMC-13, 834–846.

Bever, T. G., Carrithers, C., and Townsend, D. J. (1987). A tale of two brains: The sinistral quasi-modularity of language. *Proceedings of the Ninth Annual Conference of the Cognitive Science Society*. 764–773. Seattle, WA, July.

Chomsky, N. (1965). *Aspects of the Theory of Syntax*. Cambridge, MA: MIT Press.

Cohen, M. A. and Grossberg, S. (1983). Absolute stability of global pattern formation and parallel memory storage by competitive neural networks. *IEEE Transactions on Systems, Man, & Cybernetics* SMC-13, 815–826.

Dreyfus, S. E. and Dreyfus, H. L. (1986). *Mind over machine: The power of human intuition and expertise in the era of the computer*. New York: Free Press.

Fodor, J. A. and Pylyshyn, Z. W. (1988). Connectionism and cognitive architecture: A critical analysis. *Cognition*, 28, 2–71.

Feldman, J. A. and Ballard, D. H. (1982). Connectionist models and their properties. *Cognitive Science* 6, 205–254.

Geman, S. and Geman, D. (1984). Stochastic relaxation, Gibbs distributions, and the Bayesian restoration of images. *IEEE Transactions on Pattern Analysis and Machine Intelligence*, 6, 721–741.

Gerken, L. and Bever, T. G. (1986). Linguistic intuitions are the result of interactions between perceptual processes and linguistic universals. *Cognitive Science* 10, 457–476.

Golden, R. (1988). A unified framework for connectionist systems. *Biological Cybernetics* 59: 109–120.

Greeno, J. G. (1987). The cognition connection. *The New York Times*, Jan. 4, p. 28.

Grossberg, S. (1987). Competitive learning: From interactive activation to adaptive resonance. *Cognitive Science* 11, 23–63.

Gupta, M., Ragade, R., and Yager, R. (eds.) (1979). *Advances in Fuzzy Set Theory and Applications*. Amsterdam: North-Holland.

Hinton, G. E. (1987). Learning distributed representations of concepts. *Proceedings of the Eighth Annual Meeting of the Cognitive Science Society*. Hillsdale, NJ: Erlbaum, 1–12.

Hinton, G. E., McClelland, J. L. and Rumelhart, D. E. (1986). Distributed representations. In J. L. McClelland, D. E. Rumelhart, and the PDP Research Group, *Parallel Distributed Processing: Explorations in the Microstructure of Cognition. Volume 2: Psychological and Biological Models*. Cambridge, MA: MIT Press/Bradford Books.

Hinton, G. E. and Sejnowski, T. J. (1983a). Analyzing cooperative computation. *Proceedings of the Fifth Annual Conference of the Cognitive Science Society*. Rochester, NY.

Hopfield, J. J. (1982). Neural networks and physical systems with emergent collective computational abilities. *Proceedings of the National Academy of Sciences, USA* 79, 2554–2558.

Kirsh, D. (1988). Paying the price for cognition. *The Southern Journal of Philosophy* 26 (supplement): 119–135.

McClelland, J. L., Rumelhart, D. E., and the PDP Research Group (1986). *Parallel Distributed Processing: Explorations in the Microstructure of Cognition. Volume 2: Psychological and Biological Models.* Cambridge, MA: MIT Press/Bradford Books.

Rosenberg, C. R. (1987). Revealing the structure of NETtalk's internal representations. *Proceedings of the Ninth Annual Meeting of the Cognitive Science Society*, 537–554. Seattle, WA, July.

Rumelhart, D. E., Hinton, G. E. and Williams, R. J. (1986). Learning internal representations by error propogation. In D. E. Rumelhart, J. L. McClelland, and the PDP Research Group, *Parallel Distributed Processing: Explorations in the Microstructure of Cognition. Volume 1: Foundations.* Cambridge, MA: MIT Press/Bradford Books.

Rumelhart, D. E., Hinton, G. E., and McClelland, J. L. (1986). A general framework for parallel distributed processing. In D. E. Rumelhart, J. L. McClelland and the PDP Research Group, *Parallel Distributed Processing: Explorations in the Microstructure of Cognition. Volume 1: Foundations.* Cambridge, MA: MIT Press/Bradford Books.

Rumelhart, D. E., McClelland, J. L. and the PDP Research Group (1986). *Parallel Distributed Processing: Explorations in the Microstructure of Cognition. Volume 1: Foundations.* Cambridge, MA: MIT Press/Bradford Books.

Rumelhart, D. E. and Zipser, D. (1986). Feature discovery by competitive learning. In D. E. Rumelhart, J. L. McClelland and the PDP Research Group, *Parallel Distributed Processing: Explorations in the Microstructure of Cognition. Volume 1: Foundations.* Cambridge, MA: MIT Press/Bradford Books.

Shastri, L. and Feldman, J. A. (1985). Evidential reasoning in semantic networks: A formal theory. *Proceedings of the International Joint Conference on Artificial Intelligence.* Los Angeles, CA.

Shortliffe, E. H. (1976). *Computer-based Medical Consultations: MYCIN.* New York: American Elsevier.

Smolensky, P. (1983). Schema selection and stochastic inference in modular environments. *Proceedings of the National Conference on Artificial Intelligence.* Washington, D.C.

Smolensky, P. (1986a). Information processing in dynamical systems: Foundations of harmony theory. In D. E. Rumelhart, J. L. McClelland and the PDP Research Group, *Parallel Distributed Processing: Explorations in the Microstructure of Cognition. Volume 1: Foundations.* Cambridge, MA: MIT Press/Bradford Books.

Smolensky, P. (1986b). Neural and conceptual interpretations of parallel distributed processing models. In J. L. McClelland, D. E. Rumelhart, and the PDP Research Group, *Parallel Distributed Processing: Explorations in the Microstructure of Cognition. Volume 2: Psychological and Biological Models.* Cambridge, MA: MIT Press/Bradford Books.

Smolensky, P. (1987). On variable binding and the representation of symbolic structures in connectionist systems. Technical Report CU-CS-355-87, Department of Computer Science, University of Colorado at Boulder, February. (Revised version to appear in *Artificial Intelligence*.)

Smolensky, P. (1988a). On the proper treatment of connectionism. *Behavioral and Brain Sciences* 11(1): 1–23.

Smolensky, P. (1988b). Putting together connectionism—again. *Behavioral and Brain Sciences* 11(1): 59–74.

Smolensky, P. (forthcoming). *Lectures on connectionist cognitive modeling*. Hillsdale, NJ: Erlbaum.

Stone, G. O. (1986). An analysis of the delta rule and learning statistical associations. In D. E. Rumelhart, J. L. McClelland, and the PDP Research Group, *Parallel Distributed Processing: Explorations in the Microstructure of Cognition. Volume 1: Foundations*. Cambridge, MA: MIT Press/Bradford Books.

Sutton, R. S. (1987). Learning to predict by the methods of temporal differences. Technical Report 87-509.1, GTE Laboratories, Waltham, MA.

Zadeh, L. A. (1965). Fuzzy sets. *Information and Control*, 8, 338–353.

Zadeh, L. A. (1975). Fuzzy logic and approximate reasoning. *Synthese* 30, 407–428.

Zadeh, L. A. (1983). Role of fuzzy logic in the management of uncertainty in expert systems. *Fuzzy Sets and Systems* 11, 199–227.

81 Connectionism and the Problem of Systematicity: Why Smolensky's Solution Doesn't Work

Jerry A. Fodor and Brian P. McLaughlin

Introduction

In two recent papers, Paul Smolensky (1987, 1988b) responds to a challenge Jerry Fodor and Zenon Pylyshyn (Fodor and Pylyshyn, 1988) have posed for connectionist theories of cognition: to explain the existence of systematic relations among cognitive capacities without assuming that cognitive processes are causally sensitive to the constituent structure of mental representations. This challenge implies a dilemma: if connectionism can't account for systematicity, it thereby fails to provide an adequate basis for a theory of cognition; but if its account of systematicity requires mental processes that are sensitive to the constituent structure of mental representations, then the theory of cognition it offers will be, at best, an implementation architecture for a "classical" (language of thought) model. Smolensky thinks connectionists can steer between the horns of this dilemma if they avail themselves of certain kinds of distributed mental representation. In what follows, we will examine this proposal.

Our discussion has three parts. In section I, we briefly outline the phenomenon of systematicity and its Classical explanation. As we will see, Smolensky actually offers two alternatives to this Classical treatment, corresponding to two ways in which complex mental representations can be distributed; the first kind of distribution yields complex mental representations with "weak compositional structure," the second yields mental representations with "strong compositional structure." We will consider these two notions of distribution in turn: in section II, we argue that Smolensky's proposal that complex mental representations have weak compositional structure should be rejected both as inadequate to explain systematicity and on internal grounds; in section III, we argue that postulating mental representations with strong compositional structure also fails to provide for an explanation of systematicity. The upshot will be that Smolensky avoids only one horn of the dilemma that Fodor and Pylyshyn proposed. We shall see that his architecture is genuinely non-Classical since the representations he postulates are not "distributed over" constituents in the sense that Classical representations are; and we shall see that for that very reason Smolensky's architecture leaves systematicity unexplained.

I The Systematicity Problem and Its Classical Solution

The systematicity problem is that cognitive capacities come in clumps. For example, it appears that there are families of semantically related mental states such that, as a matter of psychological law, an organism is able to be in one of the states belonging to the family only if it is able to be in many of the others. Thus, you don't find organisms that can learn to prefer the green triangle to the red square but can't learn to prefer the red triangle to the green square. You don't find organisms that can think the thought that the girl loves John but can't think the thought that John loves the girl. You don't find organisms that can infer P from P&Q&R but can't infer P from P&Q. And so on over a very wide range of cases. For the purposes of this paper, we assume without argument:

(i) that cognitive capacities are generally systematic in this sense, both in humans and in many infrahuman organisms;

(ii) that it is nomologically necessary (hence counterfactual supporting) that this is so;

(iii) that there must therefore be some psychological mechanism in virtue of the functioning of which cognitive capacities are systematic;

(iv) and that an adequate theory of cognitive architecture should exhibit this mechanism.

Any of i–iv may be viewed as tendentious; but, so far as we can tell, all four are accepted by Smolensky. So we will take them to be common ground in what follows.[1]

The Classical account of the mechanism of systematicity depends crucially on the idea that mental representation is language-like. In particular, mental representations have a combinatorial syntax and semantics. We turn to a brief discussion of the Classical picture of the syntax and semantics of mental representations; this provides the basis for understanding the Classical treatment of systematicity.

Classical Syntax and Classical Constituents

The Classical view holds that the syntax of mental representations is like the syntax of natural language sentences in the following respect: both include complex symbols (bracketing trees) which are constructed out of what we will call *Classical constituents*. Thus, for example, the English sentence "John loves the girl" is a complex symbol whose decomposition into Classical constituents is exhibited by some such bracketing tree as:

```
            Sentence
 .   .   .   .   .
 .               .
Subject      Predicate
                     .
 .               .       Object
 .               .          .
 .               .          .
 John          loves      the girl
```

Correspondingly, it is assumed that the mental representation that is entertained when one thinks the thought that John loves the girl is a complex symbol of which the Classical constituents include representations of John, the girl, and loving.

It will become clear in section III that it is a major issue whether the sort of complex mental representations that are postulated in Smolensky's theory have constituent structure. We do not wish to see this issue degenerate into a terminological wrangle. We therefore stipulate that, for a pair of expression types E1, E2, the first is a *Classical* constituent of the second *only if* the first is tokened whenever the second is tokened. For example, the English word "John" is a Classical constituent of the English sentence "John loves the girl" and every tokening of the latter implies a tokening of the former (specifically, every token of the latter *contains* a token of the former; you can't say "John loves the girl" without saying "John").[2] Likewise, it is assumed that a mentalese symbol which names John is a Classical constituent of the mentalese symbol that means that John loves the girl. So again tokenings of the one symbol require tokenings of the other.

It is precisely because Classical constituents have this property that they are always accessible to operations that are defined over the complex symbols that contain them; in particular, it is precisely because Classical mental representations have Classical constituents that they provide domains for structure-sensitive mental processes. We shall see presently that what Smolensky offers as the "constituents" of connectionist mental representations are non-Classical in this respect, and that that is why his theory provides no account of systematicity.

Classical Semantics

It is part of the Classical picture, both for mental representation and for representation in natural languages, that generally when a complex formula (e.g., a sentence) S expresses the proposition P, S's constituents express (or refer to) the elements of P.[3] For example, the proposition that John loves the girl contains as its elements the individuals John and the girl, and the two-place relation "loving." Correspondingly, the formula "John loves the girl," which English uses to express this proposition, contains as constituents the expressions "John," "loves" and "the girl." The sentence "John left and the girl wept," whose constituents include the formulas "John left" and "the girl wept," expresses the proposition that John left and the girl wept, whose elements include the proposition that John left and the proposition that the girl wept. And so on.

These assumptions about the syntax and semantics of mental representations are summarized by condition C:

C: If a proposition P can be expressed in a system of mental representation M, then M contains some complex mental representation (a "mental sentence") S, such that S expresses P and the (Classical) constituents of S express (or refer to) the elements of P.

Systematicity

The Classical explanation of systematicity assumes that C holds by nomological necessity; it expresses a *psychological law* that subsumes all systematic minds. It should be fairly clear why systematicity is readily explicable on the assumptions, first, that mental representations satisfy C, and, second, that mental processes have access to the constituent structure of mental representations. Thus, for example, since C implies that anyone who can represent a proposition can, ipso facto, represent its elements, it implies, in particular, that anyone who can represent the proposition that John loves the girl can, ipso facto, represent John, the girl and the two-place relation *loving*. Notice, however, that the proposition that *the girl loves John* is *also* constituted by these same individuals/relations. So, then, assuming that the processes that integrate the mental representations that express propositions have access to their constituents, it follows that anyone who can represent John's loving the girl can also represent the girl's loving John. Similarly, suppose that the constituents of the mental representation that gets tokened when one thinks that P&Q&R and the constituents of the mental representation that gets tokened when one thinks that P&Q both include the mental representation that gets tokened when one thinks that P. And suppose that the mental processes that mediate the drawing of inferences have access to the constituent structure of mental representations. Then it should be no surprise that anyone who can infer P from P&Q&R can likewise infer P from P&Q.

To summarize: the Classical solution to the systematicity problem entails that (i) systems of mental representation satisfy C (a fortiori, complex mental representations have Classical constituents); and (ii) mental processes are sensitive to the constituent structure of mental representations. We can now say quite succinctly what our claim against Smolensky will be: on the one hand, the cognitive architecture he endorses does not provide for mental representations with Classical constituents; on the other hand, he provides no suggestion as to how mental processes could be structure sensitive unless mental representations have Classical constituents; and, on the third hand (as it were) he provides no suggestion as to how minds could be systematic if mental processes aren't structure sensitive. So his reply to Fodor and Pylyshyn fails.

Most of the rest of the paper will be devoted to making this analysis stick.

II Weak Compositionality

Smolensky's views about "weak" compositional structure are largely inexplicit and must be extrapolated from his "coffee story," which he tells in both of the papers under discussion (and also in 1988a). We turn now to considering this story.

Smolensky begins by asking how we are to understand the relation between the mental representation COFFEE and the mental representation CUP WITH COFFEE.[4] His answer to this question has four aspects that are of present interest:

(i) COFFEE and CUP WITH COFFEE are activity vectors (according to Smolensky's weak compositional account, this is true of the mental representations corresponding to all commonsense concepts; whether it also holds for (for example) technical concepts won't matter for what follows). A vector is, of course, a magnitude with a certain direction. A pattern of activity over a group of "units" is a state consisting of the members of the group each having an activation value of 1 or 0.[5] Activity vectors are representations of such patterns of activity.

(ii) CUP WITH COFFEE representations contain COFFEE representations as (non-Classical)[6] constituents in the following sense: they contain them as *component* vectors. By stipulation, $\mathbf{a}$ is a component vector of $\mathbf{b}$, if there is a vector $\mathbf{x}$ such that $\mathbf{a} + \mathbf{x} = \mathbf{b}$ (where "+" is the operation of vector addition). More generally, according to Smolensky, the relation between vectors and their non-Classical constituents is that the former are derivable from the latter by operations of vector analysis.

(iii) COFFEE representations and CUP WITH COFFEE representations are activity vectors over units which represent microfeatures (units like BROWN, LIQUID, MADE OF PORCELAIN, etc.).

(iv) COFFEE (and, presumably, any other representation vector) is *context dependent.* In particular, the activity vector that is the COFFEE representation in CUP WITH COFFEE *is distinct from* the activity vector that is the COFFEE representation in, as it might be, GLASS WITH COFFEE or CAN WITH COFFEE. Presumably this means that the vector in question, with no context specified, does not give necessary conditions for being *coffee.* (We shall see later that Smolensky apparently holds that it doesn't specify sufficient conditions for being *coffee* either.)

Claims i and ii introduce the ideas that mental representations are activity vectors and that they have (non-Classical) constituents. These ideas are neutral with respect to the distinction between strong and weak compositionality so we propose to postpone discussing them until section III. Claim iii, is, in our view, a red herring. The idea that there are microfeatures is orthogonal both to the question of systematicity and to the issues about compositionality. We therefore propose to discuss it only very briefly. It is claim iv that distinguishes the strong from the weak notion of compositional structure: a representation has weak compositional structure iff it contains context-dependent constituents. We propose to take up the question of context-dependent representation here.

We commence by reciting the coffee story (in a slightly condensed form).

Since, following Smolensky, we are assuming heuristically that units have bivalent activity levels, vectors can be represented by ordered sets of zeros (indicating that a unit is "off") and ones (indicating that a unit is "on"). Thus, Smolensky says, the CUP WITH COFFEE representation might be the following activity vector over microfeatures:

1—UPRIGHT CONTAINER
1—HOT LIQUID
0—GLASS CONTACTING WOOD[7]
1—PORCELAIN CURVED SURFACE
1—BURNT ODOR
1—BROWN LIQUID CONTACTING PORCELAIN
1—PORCELAIN CURVED SURFACE
0—OBLONG SILVER OBJECT
1—FINGER-SIZED HANDLE
1—BROWN LIQUID WITH CURVED SIDES AND BOTTOM[8]

This vector, according to Smolensky, contains a COFFEE representation as a constituent. This constituent can, he claims, be derived from CUP WITH COFFEE by subtracting CUP WITHOUT COFFEE from CUP WITH COFFEE. The vector that is the remainder of this subtraction will be COFFEE.

The reader will object that this treatment presupposes that CUP WITHOUT COFFEE is a constituent of CUP WITH COFFEE. Quite so. Smolensky is explicit in claiming that "the pattern or vector representing *cup with coffee* is composed of a vector that can be identified as a particular distributed representation of *cup without coffee* with a representation with the content *coffee*" (1988b: p. 10).

One is inclined to think that this must surely be wrong. If you combine a representation with the content *cup without coffee* with a representation with the content *coffee*, you get not a representation with the content *cup with coffee* but rather a representation with the self-contradictory content *cup without coffee with coffee*. Smolensky's subtraction procedure appears to confuse the representation of *cup without coffee* (viz. CUP WITHOUT COFFEE) with the representation of *cup* without the representation of *coffee* (viz. CUP). CUP WITHOUT COFFEE expresses the content *cup without coffee*; CUP combines consistently with COFFEE. But nothing does both.

On the other hand, it must be remembered that Smolensky's mental representations are advertised as context dependent, hence non-compositional. Indeed, we are given *no clue at all* about what sorts of relations between the semantic properties of complex symbols and the semantic properties of their constituents his theory acknowledges. Perhaps in a semantics where constituents don't contribute their contents to the symbols they belong to, it's all right after all if CUP WITH COFFEE has CUP WITHOUT COFFEE (or, for that matter, PRIME NUMBER, or GRANDMOTHER, or FLYING SAUCER or THE LAST OF THE MOHICANS) among its constituents.

In any event, to complete the story, Smolensky gives the following features for CUP WITHOUT COFFEE:

1—UPRIGHT CONTAINER
0—HOT LIQUID
0—GLASS CONTACTING WOOD
1—PORCELAIN CURVED SURFACE
0—BURNT ODOR
0—BROWN LIQUID CONTACTING PORCELAIN
1—PORCELAIN CURVED SURFACE
0—OBLONG SILVER OBJECT
1—FINGER-SIZED HANDLE
0—BROWN LIQUID WITH CURVED SIDES AND BOTTOM etc.

Subtracting this vector from CUP WITH COFFEE, we get the following COFFEE representation:

0—UPRIGHT CONTAINER
1—HOT LIQUID
0—GLASS CONTACTING WOOD
0—PORCELAIN CURVED SURFACE
1—BURNT ODOR
1—BROWN LIQUID CONTACTING PORCELAIN
0—PORCELAIN CURVED SURFACE
0—OBLONG SILVER OBJECT
0—FINGER-SIZED HANDLE
1—BROWN LIQUID WITH CURVED SIDES AND BOTTOM

That, then, is Smolensky's "coffee story."

Comments

(i) Microfeatures It's common ground in this discussion that the explanation of systematicity must somehow appeal to relations between complex mental representations and their constituents (on Smolensky's view, to combinatorial relations among vectors). The issue about whether there are microfeatures is entirely orthogonal; it concerns only the question *which properties the activation states of individual units express.* (To put it in more Classical terms, it concerns the question which symbols constitute the *primitive vocabulary* of the system of mental representations.) If there are microfeatures, then the activation states of individual units are constrained to express only (as it might be) "sensory" properties (1987: p. 146). If there aren't, then activation states of individual units can express not only such properties as *being brown* and *being hot,* but also such properties as *being coffee.* It should be evident upon even casual reflection that, whichever way this issue is settled, the constituency question—viz., the question how the representation COFFEE relates to the representation CUP WITH COFFEE—remains wide open. We therefore propose to drop the discussion of microfeatures in what follows.

(iv) Context-Dependent Representation As far as we can tell, Smolensky holds that the representation of *coffee* that he derives by subtraction from CUP WITH COFFEE is context dependent in the sense that it need bear no more than a "family resemblance" to the vector that represents *coffee* in CAN WITH COFFEE, GLASS WITH COFFEE, etc. There is thus no single vector that counts as *the* COFFEE representation, hence no single vector that is a component of all the representations which, in a Classical system, would have COFFEE as a Classical constituent.

Smolensky himself apparently agrees that this is the wrong sort of constituency to account for systematicity and related phenomena. As he remarks, "a true constituent can move around and fill any of a number of different roles in different structures" (1988b: p. 11) and the connection between constituency and systematicity would appear to turn on this. For example, the solution to the systematicity problem mooted in section I depends exactly on the assumption that tokens of the representation type JOHN express the same content in the context LOVES THE GIRL that they do in the context THE GIRL LOVES (viz., that they pick out *John,* who is an element both of the proposition *John loves the girl* and of the proposition *the girl loves John*). It thus appears, prima facie, that the explanation of systematicity requires context-independent constituents.

How, then, does Smolensky suppose that the assumption that mental representations have weak compositional structure, that is, that mental representation is context dependent, bears on the explanation of systematicity? He simply doesn't say. And we don't have a clue. In fact, having introduced the notion of weak compositional structure, Smolensky to all intents and purposes drops it in favor of the notion of strong compositional structure, and the discussion of systematicity is carried out entirely in terms of the latter. What, then, he takes the relation between weak and strong compositional structure to be,—and, for that matter, which kind of structure he actually thinks that mental representations have[9]—is thoroughly unclear.

In fact, quite independent of its bearing on systematicity, the notion of weak compositional structure as Smolensky presents it is of very dubious coherence. We close this section with a remark or two about this point.

It looks as though Smolensky holds that the COFFEE vector that you get by subtraction from CUP WITH COFFEE is not a COFFEE representation when it stands alone. "This representation is indeed a representation of coffee, but [only?] in a very particular context: the context provided by *cup* [i.e. CUP]" (1987: p. 147). If this is the view, it has bizarre consequences. Take a liquid that has the properties specified by the microfeatures that comprise COFFEE in isolation, but that isn't coffee. Pour it into a cup, et voila! it *becomes* coffee by semantical magic.

Smolensky explicitly doesn't think that the vector COFFEE that you get from CUP WITH COFFEE gives necessary conditions for being coffee, since you'd get a different COFFEE vector by subtraction from, say, GLASS WITH COFFEE. And the passage just quoted suggests that he thinks it doesn't give sufficient conditions either. But, then, if the microfeatures associated with COFFEE are neither necessary nor sufficient for being *coffee*[10] the question arises what, according to this story, *does* makes a vector a COFFEE representation; when does a vector have the content *coffee*?

As far as we can tell, Smolensky holds that what makes the COFFEE component of CUP WITH COFFEE a representation with the content *coffee* is that it is distributed over units representing certain microfeatures *and* that it figures as a component vector of a vector which is a CUP WITH COFFEE representation. As remarked above, we are given no details at all about this reverse compositionality according to which the embedding vector determines the contents of its constituents; how it is supposed to work isn't even discussed in Smolensky's papers. But, in any event, a regress threatens since the question now arises: if being a component of a CUP OF COFFEE representation is required to make a vector a *coffee* representation, what is required to make a vector a *cup of coffee* representation? Well, presumably CUP OF COFFEE represents *cup of coffee* because it involves the microfeatures it does *and* because it is a component of still another vector; perhaps one that is a THERE IS A CUP OF COFFEE ON THE TABLE representation. Does this go on forever? If it doesn't, then presumably there are some vectors which aren't constituents of any others. But now, what determines *their* contents? Not the contents of their constituents because, by assumption, Smolensky's semantics isn't compositional (CUP WITHOUT COFFEE is a constituent of CUP WITH COFFEE, etc.). And not the vectors that they are constituents of, because, by assumption, there aren't any of those.

We think it is unclear whether Smolensky has a coherent story about how a system of representations could have weak compositional structure.

What, in light of all this, leads Smolensky to embrace his account of weak compositionality? Here's one suggestion: perhaps Smolensky confuses being a representation of a cup with coffee with being a CUP WITH COFFEE representation. Espying some cup with coffee on a particular occasion, in a particular context, one might come to be in a mental state that represents it as having roughly the microfeatures that Smolensky lists. That mental state would then be a representation of a cup with coffee in this sense: there is a cup of coffee that it's a mental representation of. But it wouldn't, of course, follow, that it's a CUP WITH COFFEE representation; and the mental representation of that cup with coffee might be quite different from the mental representation of the cup with coffee that you espied on some other occasion or in some other context. So *which mental representation a cup of coffee gets is context dependent*, just as Smolensky says. But that doesn't give Smolensky what he needs to make mental representations themselves context dependent. In particular, from the fact that cups with coffee get different representations in different contexts, it patently doesn't follow that the mental symbol that represents something as *being* a cup of coffee in one context might represent something as being something else (a giraffe say, or The Last of The Mohicans) in some other context. We doubt that anything will give Smolensky that, since we know of no reason to suppose that it is true.

In short, it is natural to confuse the true but uninteresting thought that how you mentally represent some coffee depends on the context, with the much more tendentious thought that the mental representation COFFEE is context dependent. Assuming that he is a victim of this confusion makes sense of many of the puzzling things that Smolensky says in the coffee story. Notice, for example, that all the microfeatures in his examples express more or less perceptual properties (cf. Smolensky's own remark that his microfeatures yield a "nearly sensory level representation"). Notice, too, the peculiarity that the microfeature "porcelain curved surface" occurs *twice* in the vector for CUP WITH COFFEE, COFFEE, CUP WITHOUT COFFEE and the like. Presumably, what Smolensky has in mind is that, when you look at a cup, you get to see two curved surfaces, one going off to the left and the other going off to the right.

Though we suspect this really is what's going on, we won't pursue this interpretation further since, if it's correct, then the coffee story is completely irrelevant to the question of what kind of constituency relation a COFFEE representation bears to a CUP WITH COFFEE; and that, remember, is the question that bears on the issues about systematicity.

III Strong Compositional Structure

So much, then, for "weak" compositional structure. Let us turn to Smolensky's account of "strong" compositional structure. Smolensky says that:

> A true constituent can move around and fill any of a number of different roles in different structures. Can *this* be done with vectors encoding distributed representations, and be done in a way that doesn't amount to simply implementing symbolic syntactic constituency? The purpose of this section is to describe research showing that the answer is affirmative. (1988b: p. 11)

The idea that mental representations are activity vectors over units, and the idea that some mental representations have other mental representations as components, is common to the treatment of both weak and strong compositional structure. However, Smolensky's discussion of the latter differs in several respects from his discussion of the former. First, units are explicitly supposed to have continuous activation levels between 0 and 1; second, he does not invoke the idea of microfeatures when discussing strong compositional structure; third, he introduces a new vector operation (multiplication) to the two previously mentioned (addition and subtraction); fourth, and most important, strong compositional structure does not invoke—indeed, would appear to be incompatible with—the notion that mental representations are context dependent. So strong compositional structure does not exhibit the incoherences of Smolensky's theory of context-dependent representation.

We will proceed as follows. First we briefly present the notion of strong compositional structure. Then we shall turn to criticism.

Smolensky explains the notion of strong compositional structure, in part, by appeal to the ideas of a tensor product representation and a superposition representation. To illustrate these ideas, consider how a connectionist machine might represent four-letter English words. Words can be decomposed into roles (viz., ordinal positions that letters can occupy) and things that can fill these roles (viz., letters). Correspondingly, the machine might contain activity vectors over units which represent the relevant roles (i.e., over the *role units*) and activity vectors over units which represent the fillers (i.e., over the *filler units*). Finally, it might contain activity vectors over units which represent *filled roles* (i.e., letters in letter positions); these are the *binding units*. The key idea is that the activity vectors over the binding units might be tensor products of activity vectors over the role units and the filler units. The representation of a word would then be a superposition vector over the binding units; that is, a vector that is arrived at by superimposing the tensor product vectors.

The two operations used here to derive complex vectors from component vectors are vector multiplication in the case of tensor product vectors and vector addition in the case of superposition vectors. These are iterative operations in the sense that activity vectors that result from the multiplication of role vectors and filler vectors might themselves represent the fillers of roles in more complex structures. Thus, a tensor product which represents the word "John" as *"J" in first position, "o" in second position ... etc.* might itself be bound to the representation of a syntactical function to indicate, for example, that "John" has the role subject-of in "John loves the girl." Such tensor product representations could themselves be superimposed over yet another group of binding units to yield a superposition vector which represents the bracketing tree (John) (loves (the girl)).

It is, in fact, unclear whether this sort of apparatus is adequate to represent all the semantically relevant syntactic relations that Classical theories express by using bracketing trees with Classical constituents. (There are, for example, problems about long-distance binding relations, as between quantifiers and bound variables.) But we do not wish to press this point. For present polemical purposes, we propose simply to assume that each Classical bracketing tree can be coded into a complex vector in such fashion that the constituents of the tree correspond in some regular way to components of the vector.

But this is not, of course, to grant that either tensor product or superposition vectors *have* Classical constituent structure. In particular, from the assumptions that bracketing trees have Classical constituents and that bracketing trees can be coded by activity vectors, it does *not* follow that activity vectors have Classical constituents. On the contrary, a point about which Smolensky is himself explicit is vital in this regard: the components of a complex vector need not even correspond to patterns of activity over units actually in the machine. As Smolensky puts it, the activity states of the filler and role units can be "imaginary" even though the ultimate activity vectors—the ones which do not themselves serve as filler or role components of more complex structures—must be actual activity patterns over units in the machine. Consider again our machine for representing four-letter words. The superposition pattern that represents, say, the word "John" will be an activity vector actually realized in the machine.

However, the activity vector representing "J" will be merely imaginary, as will the activity vector representing *the first letter position*. Similarly for the tensor product activity vector representing *"J" in the first letter position*. The only pattern of activity that will be *actually tokened* in the machine is the superposition vector representing "John."

These considerations are of central importance for the following reason. Smolensky's main strategy is, in effect, to invite us to consider the components of tensor product and superposition vectors to be analogous to the Classical constituents of a complex symbol; hence to view them as providing a means by which connectionist architectures can capture the causal and semantic consequences of Classical constituency in mental representations. However, the components of tensor product and superposition vectors differ from Classical constituents in the following way: when a complex Classical symbol is tokened, its constituents are tokened. When a tensor product vector or superposition vector is tokened, its components are not (except per accidens). The implication of this difference, from the point of view of the theory of mental processes, is that whereas the Classical constituents of a complex symbol are, ipso facto, available to contribute to the causal consequences of its tokenings—in particular, they are available to provide domains for mental processes—the components of tensor product and superposition vectors can have no causal status as such. What is merely imaginary can't make things happen, to put this point in a nutshell.

We will return presently to what all this implies for the treatment of the systematicity problem. There is, however, a preliminary issue that needs to be discussed.

We have seen that the components of tensor product/superposition vectors, unlike Classical constituents, are not, in general, tokened whenever the activity vector of which they are the components is tokened. It is worth emphasizing, in addition, the familiar point that there is, in general, no *unique* decomposition of a tensor product or superposition vector into components. Indeed, given that units are assumed to have continuous levels of activation, there will be *infinitely* many decompositions of a given activity vector. One might wonder, therefore, what sense there is in talk of *the* decomposition of a mental representation into significant constituents given the notion of constituency that Smolensky's theory provides.[11]

Smolensky replies to this point as follows. Cognitive systems will be dynamical systems; there will be dynamic equations over the activation values of individual units, and these will determine certain regularities over activity vectors. Given the dynamical equations of the system, certain decompositions can be especially useful for "explaining and understanding" its behavior. In this sense, the dynamics of a system may determine "normal modes" of decomposition into components. So, for example, though a given superposition vector can, in principle, be taken to be the sum of many different sets of vectors, yet it may turn out that we get a small group of sets—even a unique set—when we decompose in the direction of normal modes; and likewise for decomposing tensor product vectors. The long and short is that *it could, in principle, turn out* that, given the (thus far undefined) normal modes of a dynamical cognitive system, complex superposition vectors will have it in common with Classical complex symbols that they have a unique decomposition into semantically significant parts. Of course, it also could turn out that they don't, and no ground for optimism on this point has thus far been supplied.

Having noted this problem, however, we propose simply to ignore it. So here is where we now stand: by assumption (though quite possibly contrary to fact), tensor product vectors and superposition vectors can code constituent structure in a way that makes them adequate vehicles for the expression of propositional content; and, by assumption (though again quite possibly contrary to fact), the superposition vectors that cognitive theories acknowledge have a unique decomposition into semantically interpretable tensor product vectors which, in turn, have a unique decomposition into semantically interpretable filler vectors and role vectors; so it's determinate which proposition a given complex activity vector represents.

Now, assuming all this, what about the systematicity problem?

The first point to make is this: if tensor product/superposition vector representation solves the systematicity problem, the solution must be quite different from the Classical proposal sketched in section I. True tensor product vectors and superposition vectors "have constituents" in some suitably extended sense: tensor product vectors have semantically evaluable components, and superposition vectors are decomposable into semantically evaluable tensor product vectors. But the Classical solution to the systematicity problem assumes that *the constituents of mental representations have causal roles*; that they provide domains for mental processes. The Classical constituents of a complex symbol thus contribute to determining the causal consequences of the tokening of that symbol, and it seems clear that the "extended" constituents of a tensor product/superposition representation can't do that. On the contrary, the components of a complex vector are typically not even tokened when the complex vector itself is tokened; they are simply constituents into which the complex vector *could be* resolved consonant with decomposition in the direction of normal modes. But, to put it crudely, the fact that six *could be* represented as "3 × 2" cannot, in and of itself, affect the causal processes in a computer (or a brain) in which six *is* represented as "6." Merely counterfactual representations have no causal consequences; only actually tokened representations do.

Smolensky is, of course, sensitive to the question whether activity vectors really do have constituent structure. He defends at length the claim that he has not contorted the notion of constituency in claiming that they do. Part of this defense adverts to the role that tensor products and superpositions play in physical theory:

> The state of the atom, like the states of all systems in quantum theory, is represented by a vector in an abstract vector space. Each electron has an internal state (its "spin"); it also has a role it plays in the atom as a whole: it occupies some "orbital," essentially a cloud of probability for finding it at particular places in the atom. The internal state of an electron is represented by a "spin vector"; the orbital or role of the electron (part) in the atom (whole) is represented by another vector, which describes the probability cloud. The vector representing the electron as situated in the atom is the tensor product of the vector representing the internal state of the electron and the vector representing its orbital. The atom as a whole is represented by a vector that is the sum or superposition of vectors, each of which represents a particular electron in its orbital.... (1988b: pp. 19–20)

"So," Smolensky adds, "someone who claims that the tensor product representational scheme distorts the notion of constituency has some explaining to do" (1988b: p. 20).

The physics lesson is greatly appreciated; but it is important to be clear on just what it is supposed to show. It's not, at least for present purposes, in doubt that tensor products *can represent* constituent structure. The relevant question is whether tensor product representations *have* constituent structure; or, since we have agreed that they may be said to have constituent structure "in an extended sense," it's whether they have the kind of constituent structure to which causal processes can be sensitive, hence the kind of constituent structure to which an explanation of systematicity might appeal.[12] But we have already seen the answer to *this* question: the constituents of complex activity vectors typically aren't "there," so if the causal consequences of tokening a complex vector are sensitive to its constituent structure, that's a miracle.

We conclude that assuming that mental representations are activation vectors does not allow Smolensky to endorse the Classical solution of the systematicity problem. And, indeed, we think Smolensky would grant this since he admits up front that mental processes will not be causally sensitive to the strong compositional structure of mental representations. That is, he acknowledges that the constituents of complex mental representations play no causal role in determining what happens when the representations get tokened. "... Causal efficacy was not my goal in developing the tensor product representation ..." (1988b: p. 21). What are causally efficacious according to connectionists are the activation values of individual units; the dynamical equations that govern the evolution of the system will be defined over these. It would thus appear that Smolensky must have some *non*-Classical solution to the systematicity problem up his sleeve; some solution that does *not* depend on assuming mental processes that are causally sensitive to constituent structure. So then, after all this, what *is* Smolensky's solution to the systematicity problem?

Remarkably enough, *Smolensky doesn't say*. All he does say is that he "hypothesizes ... that ... the systematic effects observed in the processing of mental representations arise because the evolution of vectors can be (at least partially and approximately) explained in terms of the evolution of their components, even though the precise dynamical equations apply [only] to the individual numbers comprising the vectors and [not] at the level of [their] constituents—i.e. even though the constituents are not causally efficacious" (1988b: p. 21).

It is left unclear how the constituents ("components") of complex vectors are to explain their evolution (even partially and approximately) when they are, by assumption, at best causally inert and, at worst, merely imaginary. In any event, what Smolensky clearly does think is causally responsible for the "evolution of vectors" (and hence for the systematicity of cognition) are unspecified processes that affect the states of activation of the individual units (the neuron analogs) out of which the vectors are composed. So, then, as far as we can tell, the proposed connectionist explanation of systematicity (and related features of cognition) comes down to this: Smolensky "hypothesizes" that systematicity is somehow a consequence of underlying neural processes.[13] Needless to say, if that *is* Smolensky's theory, it is, on the one hand, certainly true, and, on the other hand, not intimately dependent upon his long story about fillers, binders, tensor products, superposition vectors and the rest.

By way of rounding out the argument, we want to reply to a question raised by an anonymous *Cognition* reviewer, who asks: "... couldn't Smolensky easily build in mechanisms to accomplish the matrix algebra operations that would make the necessary vector explicit (or better yet, from his point of view, . . . mechanisms that are sensitive to the imaginary components without literally making them explicit in some string of units)?"[14] But this misses the point of the problem that systematicity poses for connectionists, which is not to show that systematic cognitive capacities are *possible* given the assumptions of a connectionist architecture, but to explain how systematicity could be *necessary*—how it could be a *law* that cognitive capacities are systematic—given those assumptions.[15]

No doubt it is possible for Smolensky to wire a network so that it supports a vector that represents aRb if and only if it supports a vector that represents bRa; and perhaps it is possible for him to do that without making the imaginary units explicit[16] (though there is, so far, no proposal about how to ensure this for *arbitrary* a, R and b). The trouble is that, although the architecture permits this, it equally permits Smolensky to wire a network so that it supports a vector that represents aRb if and only if it supports a vector that represents zSq; or, for that matter, if and only if it supports a vector that represents The Last of The Mohicans. The architecture would appear to be absolutely indifferent as among these options.

Whereas, as we keep saying, in the Classical architecture, if you meet the conditions for being able to represent aRb, *YOU CANNOT BUT MEET THE CONDITIONS FOR BEING ABLE TO REPRESENT bRa*; the architecture won't let you do so because (i) the representation of a, R and b are constituents of the representation of aRb, and (ii) you have to token the constituents of the representations that you token, so Classical constituents can't be just imaginary. So then: it is *built into* the Classical picture that you can't think aRb unless you are able to think bRa, but the Connectionist picture is *neutral* on whether you can think aRb even if you can't think bRa. But it is a law of nature that you can't think aRb if you can't think bRa. So the Classical picture explains systematicity and the Connectionist picture doesn't. So the Classical picture wins.

Conclusion

At one point in his discussion, Smolensky makes some remarks that we find quite revealing: he says that, even in cases that are paradigms of Classical architectures (LISP machines and the like), ". . . we normally think of the 'real' causes as physical and far below the symbolic level . . ." Hence, even in Classical machines, the sense in which operations at the symbol level are real causes is just that ". . . there is . . . a complete and precise algorithmic (temporal) story to tell about the states of the machine described . . ." at that level (1988b: p. 20). Smolensky, of course, denies that there is a ". . . comparable story at the symbolic level in the human cognitive architecture . . . that is a difference with the Classical view that I have made much of. *It may be that a good way to characterize the difference is in terms of whether the constituents in mental structure are causally efficacious in mental processing*" (1988b: p. 20; our emphasis).

We say that this is revealing because it suggests a diagnosis: it would seem that Smolensky has succumbed to a sort of generalized epiphenomenalism. The idea is that even Classical constituents participate in causal processes solely by virtue of their physical microstructure, so even on the Classical story it's what happens at the neural level that *really* counts. Though the evolution of vectors can perhaps be explained in a predictively adequate sort of way by appeal to macroprocesses like operations on constituents, still if you want to know what's *really* going on—if you want the *causal* explanation—you need to go down to the "precise dynamical equations" that apply to activation states of units. That intentional generalizations can only approximate these precise dynamical equations is among Smolensky's recurrent themes. By conflating the issue about "precision" with the issue about causal efficacy, Smolensky makes it seem that to the extent that macrolevel generalizations are imprecise, to that extent macrolevel processes are epiphenomenal.

It would need a philosophy lesson to say all of what's wrong with this. Suffice it for present purposes that the argument iterates in a way that Smolensky ought to find embarrassing. No doubt, we do get greater precision when we go from generalizations about operations on constituents to generalizations about operations on units. But if that shows that symbol-level processes aren't really causal, then it must be that unit-level processes aren't really causal either. After all, we get *still more* precision when we go down from unit-sensitive operations to molecule-sensitive operations, and more precision yet when we go down from molecule-sensitive operations to quark-sensitive operations. The moral is not, however, that the causal laws of psychology should be stated in terms of the behavior of quarks. Rather, the moral is that whether you have a level of causal explanation is a question, not just of how much precision you are able to achieve, but also of *what generalizations you are able to express*. The price you pay for doing psychology at the level of units is that you lose causal generalizations that symbol-level theories are able to state. Smolensky's problems with capturing the generalizations about systematicity provide a graphic illustration of these truths.

It turns out, at any event, that there is a crucial caveat to Smolensky's repeated claim that connectionist mechanisms can reconstruct everything that's interesting about the notion of constituency. Strictly speaking, he claims only to reconstruct whatever is interesting about constituents *except their causes and effects*. The explanation of systematicity turns on the causal role of the constituents of mental representations and is therefore among the casualties. Hilary Putnam, back in the days when he was still a Metaphysical Realist, used to tell a joke about a physicist who actually managed to build a perpetual motion machine; all except for a part that goes back and forth, back and forth, back and forth, forever. Smolensky's explanation of systematicity has very much the character of this machine.

We conclude that Fodor and Pylyshyn's challenge to connectionists has yet to be met. We still don't have *even a suggestion* of how to account for systematicity within the assumptions of connectionist cognitive architecture.

Notes

1. Since the two are often confused, we wish to emphasize that taking *systematicity* for granted leaves the question of *compositionality* wide open. The systematicity of cognition consists of, for example, the fact that organisms that can think aRb can think bRa and vice versa. *Compositionality* proposes a certain explanation of systematicity: viz., that the content of thoughts is determined, in a uniform way, by the content of the context-independent concepts that are their constituents: and that the thought that bRa is constituted of the same concepts as the thought that aRb. So the polemical situation is as follows. If you are a Connectionist who accepts systematicity, then you

must argue either that systematicity can be explained without compositionality, or that connectionist architecture accommodates compositional representation. So far as we can tell, Smolensky vacillates between these options: what he calls "weak compositionality" favors the former and what he calls "strong compositionality" favors the latter.

We emphasize this distinction between systematicity and compositionality in light of some remarks by an anonymous *Cognition* reviewer: "By berating the [connectionist] modelers for their inability to represent the common-sense [uncontextualized] notion of 'coffee' ... Fodor and McLaughlin are missing a key point—the models are not supposed to do so. If you buy the ... massive context-sensitivity ... that connectionists believe in." Our strategy is *not*, however, to argue that there is something wrong with connectionism because it fails to offer an uncontextualized notion of mental (or, mutatis mutandis, linguistic) representation. Our argument is that if connectionists assume that mental representations are context sensitive, they will need to offer some explanation of systematicity that does not entail compositionality *and they do not have one.*

We do not, therefore, offer direct arguments for context-insensitive concepts in what follows; we are quite prepared that "coffee" should have a meaning only in context. Only, we argue, *if* it does, then some non-compositional account of the systematicity of coffee-throughts will have to be provided.

2. Though we shall generally consider examples where complex symbols literally *contain* their Classical constituents, the present condition means to leave it open that symbols may have Classical constituents that are not among their (spatio-temporal) parts. (For example, so far as this condition is concerned, it might be that the Classical constituents of a symbol include the values of a "fetch" operation that takes the symbol as an argument.)

3. We assume that the elements of propositions can include, for example, individuals, properties, relations and other propositions. Other metaphysical assumptions are, of course, possible. For example, it is arguable that the constituents of propositions include *individual concepts* (in the Fregian sense) rather than individuals themselves; and so on. Fortunately, it is not necessary to enter into these abstruse issues to make the points that are relevant to the systematicity problem. All we really need is that propositions have internal structure, and that, characteristically, the internal structure of complex mental representations corresponds, in the appropriate way, to the internal structure of the propositions that they express.

4. The following notational conventions will facilitate the discussion: we will follow standard practice and use capitalized English words and sentences as canonical names for mental representations. (Smolensky uses italicized English expressions instead.) We stipulate that the semantic value of a mental representation so named is the semantic value of the corresponding English word or sentence, and we will italicize words or sentences that denote semantic values. So, for example, COFFEE is a mental representation that expresses (the property of being) *coffee* (as does the English word "coffee"); JOHN LOVES THE GIRL is a mental representation that expresses the proposition that *John loves the girl*; and so forth. It is important to notice that our notation allows that the mental representation JOHN LOVES THE GIRL can be atomic and the mental representation COFFEE can be a complex symbol. That is, capitalized expressions should be read as the names of mental representations rather than as structural descriptions.

5. Smolensky apparently allows that units may have continuous levels of activation from 0 to 1. In telling the coffee story, however, he generally assumes bivalence for ease of exposition.

6. As we shall see below, when an activity vector is tokened, its component vectors typically are not. So the constituents of a complex vector are, ipso facto, non-Classical.

7. Notice that this microfeature is "off" in CUP WITH COFFEE, so it might be wondered why Smolensky mentions it at all. The explanation may be this: operations of vector combination

apply only to vectors of the same dimensionality. In the context of the weak constituency story, this means that you can only combine vectors that are activity patterns *over the same units*. It follows that a component vector must contain the same units (though, possibly at different levels of activation) as the vectors with which it combines. Thus if GRANNY combines with COFFEE to yield GRANNY'S COFFEE, GRANNY must contain activation levels for all the units in COFFEE and vice versa. In the present example, it may be that CUP WITH COFFEE is required to contain a 0-activation level for GLASS CONTACTING WOOD to accommodate cases where it is a component of some other vector. Similarly with OBLONG SILVER OBJECT (below) since cups with coffee often have spoons in them.

8. Presumably Smolensky does not take this list to be exhaustive, but we don't know how to continue it. Beyond the remark that although the microfeatures in his examples correspond to "... nearly sensory-level representation[s] ..." that is "not essential," Smolensky provides no account at all of what determines which contents are expressed by microfeatures. The question thus arises why Smolensky assumes that COFFEE is not itself a microfeature. In any event, Smolensky repeatedly warns the reader not to take his examples of microfeatures very seriously, and we don't.

9. They can't have both; either the content of a representation is context dependent or it's not. So, if Smolensky does think that you need strong compositional structure to explain systematicity, and that weak compositional structure is the kind that Connectionist representations have, then it would seem that he *thereby* grants Fodor and Pylyshyn's claim that Connectionist representations can't explain systematicity. We find this all very mysterious.

10. If they were necessary and sufficient, COFFEE wouldn't be context dependent.

11. The function of the brackets in a Classical bracketing tree is precisely to exhibit its decomposition into constituents; and when the tree is well formed this decomposition will be unique. Thus, the bracketing of "(John) (loves) (the girl)" implies, for example, both that "the girl" is a constituent and that "loves the" is not.

12. It's a difference between psychology and physics that whereas psychology is about the casual laws that govern tokenings *of (mental) representations*, physics is about the causal laws that govern (not mental representations but) atoms, electrons and the like. Since *being a representation* isn't a property in the domain of physical theory, the question whether mental representations have constituent structure has no analog in physics.

13. More precisely: we take Smolensky to be claiming that there is some property D, such that if a dynamical system has D its behavior is systematic, and such that human behavior (for example) is caused by a dynamical system that has D. The trouble is that this is a platitude since it is untendentious that human behavior is systematic, that its causation by the nervous system is lawful, and that the nervous system is dynamical. The least that has to happen if we are to have a substantive connectionist account of systematicity is: first, it must be made clear what property D is, and second it must be shown that D is a property that connectionist systems can have by law. Smolensky's theory does nothing to meet either of these requirements.

14. Actually, Smolensky is forced to choose the second option. To choose the first would, in effect, be to endorse the Classical requirement that tokening a symbol implies tokening its constituents; in which case, the question arises once again why such a network isn't an implementation of a language of thought machine. Just as Smolensky mustn't allow the representations of roles, fillers and binding units to be subvectors of superposition vectors if he is to avoid the "implementation" horn of the Fodor/Pylyshyn dilemma, so too he must avoid postulating mechanisms that make role, filler and binding units explicit (specifically, accessible to mental operations) whenever the superposition vectors are tokened. Otherwise he again has symbols with Classical constituents

and raises the question why the proposed device isn't a language of thought machine. Smolensky's problem is that the very feature of his representations that make them wrong for explaining systematicity (viz., that their constituents are allowed to be imaginary) is the one that they have to have to assure that they aren't Classical.

15. Fodor and Pylyshyn were very explicit about this. See, for example, 1988: p. 48.

16. Terence Horgan remarks (personal communication) "... often there are two mathematically equivalent ways to calculate the time-evolution of a dynamical system. One is to apply the relevant equations directly to the numbers that are elements of a single total vector describing the initial state of the system. Another way is to mathematically decompose that vector into component normal-mode vectors, then compute the time-evolution of each [of these] ... and then take the later state of the system to be described by a vector that is the superposition of the resulting normal-mode vectors." Computations of the former sort are supposed to be the model for operations that are "sensitive" to the components of a mental representation vector without recovering them. (Even in the second case, it's the theorist who recovers them in the course of the computations by which he makes his predictions. This does not, of course, imply that the constituents thus "recovered" participate in causal processes in the system under analysis.)

References

Fodor, J., and Pylyshyn, P. (1988). Connectionism and cognitive architecture: A critical analysis. *Cognition, 28*, 3–71.

Smolensky, P. (1987). The constituent structure of mental states: A reply to Fodor and Pylyshyn. *Southern Journal of Philosophy, 26*, 137–160.

Smolensky, P. (1988a). On the proper treatment of connectionism. *Behavioral and Brain Sciences, 11*, 1–23.

Smolensky, P. (1988b). Connectionism, constituency and the language of thought. University of Colorado Technical report; also in Loewer, B., and Rey, G. (Eds.), *Meaning in mind: Fodor and his critics*. Oxford: Blackwell, 1991.

82 What Is the "D" in "PDP"? A Survey of the Concept of Distribution

Tim van Gelder

Suppose there were such a thing as the "computational theory of mind" (CTM); and suppose that, for whatever reason, you were dissatisfied with it. You may well be tempted to ask: What would an alternative look like? Could there be an alternative that was even remotely plausible? Is connectionism in the business of developing such an alternative?

With issues such as these in vogue recently, considerable attention has been given to the preparatory task of succinctly characterizing some version of CTM to which the desired alternative can stand opposed. One point of universal consensus has been that an essential feature of CTM is the use of symbolic representations. Any theory failing to employ such representations automatically falls outside the broad CTM umbrella. This suggests an obvious approach to the questions just raised. Assuming that any remotely plausible theory of mind must be based on manipulation of internal representations of some kind, we need to find some other generic form of representation to play a foundational role in the new theory analogous to that played by symbolic representation in CTM. Having found such a form, we could evaluate the general plausibility of a theory of mind constructed around it. Perhaps connectionist work contains some clues here, both about the form itself and about the kind of theory in which it would be embedded.

The alternative form of representation required by this approach has to satisfy some demanding conditions. It must, of course, be demonstrably nonsymbolic, but it must also be sufficiently general to allow the characterization of a reasonably broad conception of the mind. This means, among other things, that it must be rich enough to encompass a wide variety of particular articulations (just as symbolic representation can be instantiated in a very wide variety of particular ways), and yet characterizable in a way that is sufficiently abstract to transcend all kinds of irrelevant implementation details. Crucially, it will have to be powerful enough to make possible the effective representing of the kinds of information that are essential to human cognitive performance. Preferably, this alternative will have some deep connection with neural network architectures, thereby minimizing future difficulties relating the new theory to the neurobiological details, and in the meantime allowing us to both interpret and learn from connectionist research.

This is a tall order by any account, and a moment's reflection reveals that there are few if any plausible candidates available. The traditional cognitive science literature is of remarkably little help here. In that relatively small portion concerned specifically with the actual form of mental representation, symbolic styles have for the most part been contrasted only with broadly imagistic styles (pictorial, analog, etc.). For a long period the most notable research taking a manifestly nonsymbolic approach was the investigation of mental imagery, and surveys of the field typically treat these two broad categories as the only relevant possibilities. Yet, although the category of imagistic representations might begin to satisfy some of the constraints just listed, it clearly fails to satisfy others; in particular, it is generally accepted that imagistic representations are not powerful enough to underlie central aspects of cognition such as linguistic performance and problem solving. There has even been serious debate over whether mental imagery itself is strictly imagistic.

One response to this apparent lack of plausible alternatives is to accept that representations must be symbolic in some suitably generic sense, and consequently to maintain that any feasible alternative to CTM must differ not in how knowledge is represented but rather in how the representations themselves are manipulated—that is, in the nature of the mental processes. Yet this approach also is unpromising. Representations and processes tend to go hand in hand; the way knowledge is represented largely fixes appropriate processes and vice versa. For this reason, conceding that representations must be generically symbolic places one in a conceptual vortex with the standard CTM at the center.

One reason there appear to be so few alternatives is that the conception of symbolic representation invoked in characterizations of CTM is so very general, and usually rather vague. This suggests a more cautious gambit: fine-tune the conception of symbolic representation itself, articulating some more specific formulation that can fairly be attributed to CTM, thereby making room for some quasi-symbolic alternative between analog anarchy on one hand and the rigors of strictly syntactic structure on the other. However, although headway can certainly be made in this direction, it has an obvious strategic flaw: Major differences in paradigms are unlikely to rest on delicate philosophical distinctions, and if perchance they did, it would be relatively difficult to convince others of the fact. It is vastly preferable to propose a style of representation with unquestionable antisymbolic credentials. If there actually is any quasi-symbolic option of the kind just mentioned, it should be introduced as a special case of a manifestly distinct category, rather than as some subtle variant on the standard symbolic model.

If at this point we look to connectionism, it is difficult to avoid noticing the frequent emphasis on distributed representation, an emphasis evident even in the familiar designation "parallel distributed processing" (PDP). Distributed representation may well satisfy the first of the requirements on an acceptable alternative, because it is often deliberately contrasted with symbolic representation (e.g., as when it is claimed that a network knows how to form the past tense without the benefit of explicit symbolic rules). Moreover, the category appears to be appropriately general; at one time or another, distributed representation has cropped up in areas as diverse as functional neuroanatomy, psychology of memory, image processing, and optical phenomena such as holography; indeed, researchers originally began applying the term *distributed representation* in connectionist contexts precisely because of perceived similarities between connectionist representations and these other cases. Considerations such as these suggest we should inquire into the possibility that distributed representations form the kind of category we are after. Perhaps, in other words, there is here a natural kind of representation, a kind that includes all or most of the cases previously described as distributed, whose members are somehow inherently nonsymbolic, but that is nevertheless sufficiently rich, powerful, and so on, that it might form the basis of some plausible alternative to CTM.

The immediate difficulty with this suggestion is the lack of any clear account of what distributed representation actually is. The concept itself is relatively novel, and though many people have recently offered their preferred brief characterizations, it has had almost no serious treatments as an independent topic of investigation.[1] Worse, there is very little consensus even in such characterizations as are available. The diversity of definitions suggests that there really is no unified category of distributed representations after all. Feldman (1989) for one has concluded "... people have been using the term ["distributed"] to denote everything from a fully holographic model to one where two units help code a concept; thus, the term has lost its usefulness (p. 72). Clearly, before we can even begin to take seriously the idea that a plausible alternative to CTM might be constructed on a distributed foundation, we need to formulate a reasonably clear and comprehensive account of the nature of distributed representation. This task goes vastly beyond what might be achieved here; what follows is simply an exploratory overview of the current concept (or concepts), a disentangling of some of the many themes and issues that have at one time or another been associated with distribution.

Diverse Definitions of Distribution

A useful point of entry is to note the inadequacy of one style of definition common in connectionist work. In perhaps the most authoritative version (Hinton, McClelland, and Rumelhart, 1986), representations are alleged to be distributed if: "Each entity is represented by a pattern of activity distributed over many computing elements, and each computing element is involved in representing many different entities" (p. 77).[2] The most obvious problem here, from the current perspective, is one of narrow focus. A distributed representation is defined as a "pattern of activity" over "computing elements" specifically; but this is too limited even for connectionist purposes, because there at least two species of distributed representation in connectionist networks—the patterns of activity themselves, and the patterns of connectivity that mediate their transformation. It may be that these are in fact essentially interlocked, each needing the other, but there is at least a prima facie distinction, because the two kinds of representation appear to have some significantly different characteristics. Thus this definition would have to be generalized significantly if it were to capture the notion of distribution implicit even in connectionist work, let alone whatever is common to cases as diverse as those mentioned above.

Narrowness is not however the worst of its problems. The intended contrast is with a variety of "localist" representation in which each entity is represented by activity in a single computing element. But in its concern to distinguish distribution from these kinds of localist cases, this definition patently fails to distinguish it from other cases that, surely, are not distributed in any interesting sense. For many familiar kinds of representation count as "patterns of activity" over sets of "computing elements" ("units," "locations," or whatever); in particular, when numbers are encoded as strings of bits in a register of an ordinary pocket calculator, they are being represented by distinctive activity patterns, and each unit or location participates in the representing of many different numbers over the course of a calculation.[3] This leaves two possibilities: either distribution is not an interestingly distinct category after all; or it is, but one whose essence eludes this definition. The latter turns out to be vastly more fertile as a working hypothesis.

Day to day practice often compensates for deficiencies in overt formulation. The real content of this characterization is implicit in the way it is received and guides construction of new connectionist schemes of representation. In this light, the central theme of this version—the representing of entities as different patterns of activity over groups of units—deserves closer scrutiny. Consider first the very simple requirement that entities be represented over many units—or, more generally, over some relatively extended portion of the resources available for representing.[4] Lacking any better term, I will describe representations that are spread out in this sense as *extended*. Clearly, a representation can only be extended by comparison with some normal, minimum or standard form, which can vary from case to case and style to style. Thus in typical connectionist networks the benchmark is one computing unit to every item, and relative to this a representation is extended if it uses many units for every item. In the brain the most plausible minimal unit is presumably the neuron (as in "grandmother" or "yellow Volkswagen" cells). Note however that in some other cases, such as optical holography—generally taken to be a paradigm example of distributed representation—there is no obvious parallel, because the surface of a photographic plate does not come naturally partitioned.

This bare notion of extendedness may seem trivial, but it is a very common theme in characterizations of distribution; indeed, on some occasions distribution is described solely in such terms.[5] It is therefore interesting to see what, if anything, is gained by distributing even in this minimal sense.

An important practical concern is worth mentioning first: extendedness can buy a certain kind of reliability or robustness. If an item is represented over many locations in such a way that no particular location is crucial to overall efficacy, then the system can withstand small and isolated damage or noise relatively well. This point is illustrated by the benefits of redundancy. Duplicating a given representation many times obviously increases the ability of the whole collection to convey the same content under adverse conditions. Thus, one reason for the industrious copying of medieval manuscripts was to ensure that if any one were lost, the same text would be preserved elsewhere—a point with a modern counterpart for users of word processors. An extended representation need not be simply redundant, however. Instead of activating a single neuron to represent a given perceptual item, the brain activates a vast number, forming an overall pattern for the same purpose, but where each neuron is tuned in a slightly different way to the retinal input. Loss of any particular neuron, or noise in the system, has almost no effect on the overall effectiveness of this representation, which is fortunate, given how noisy neurons are and the rate at which we lose them.

Whether this advantage of noise or damage resistance in fact accrues to a given case of extended representation depends very much on the form of encoding involved. A particular number N might be represented in a digital computer either in binary form or, in a more extended fashion, as a string of bits of length N; neither has any particular advantage of reliability over the other, even though the latter uses vastly more resources. This is just to stress again the point that extendedness must be achieved in such a way that no particular unit or location is crucial, a condition violated in both these cases. Further, the portion of the resources involved should be large not only relative to some theoretical minimum (such as the unit, neuron, or location), but also relative to the scale of likely damage or noise in the system itself.

Whether a representation is extended is independent of the stronger requirement that a given representation take the form of a distinctive pattern over that larger portion of the resources. Despite this independence, an important advantage in distributing representations in this sense is that it makes possible the use of a distinctive pattern for each distinct item. Indeed, such an approach will be essential if we want to represent a number of different items over the same set of units. Many authors, especially connectionists and commentators on connectionism, claim that the essence of distribution is to be found in this shift to the level of overall patterns, or, more generally, to characteristic overall states of the network or system. Rosenfeld and Touretzky (1988), for example, have defined schemes of distributed representation as those in which "each entity is represented by a pattern of activity over many units (p. 463).[6]

These patterns might be completely unrelated; they might be chosen at random, or it might suit one's computational purposes to choose patterns simply so as to maximize the distinctness of any two representations. On the other hand, an important reason for moving to characteristic patterns for the representing of each item is that the internal structures of these patterns can be systematically related, both to each other and to the nature of the items to be represented, thereby making the overall scheme more useful in certain ways. There are many ways to develop pattern-based schemes of representation in which the internal structures of the patterns have this kind of systematic semantic significance, but one in particular has been especially popular in connectionism. On this approach individual processing units pick out (micro)features, which are simply aspects of the domain, though usually at a much finer grain than that of the primary items to be represented. In a well known example, in order to represent a kind of room, we first assign to individual units features that are typically found in various kinds of rooms, such as *sofa, TV, ceiling and stove.*[7] Each different kind of room can then be represented by means of a distinctive pattern over these units—that is, that pattern that picks out all and only the relevant features. In this way it is possible to generate patterns for representing items in which semantic differences are built directly into the internal structure.

The popularity of this approach in connectionism has led to a common misconception of distributed representation as somehow essentially related to the notion of a microfeatural semantics for individual units. Thus, some influential commentators, including notably Pinker and Prince, have seized on the deployment of microfeatures as the crucial feature distinguishing genuinely distributed representations from other pattern-based schemes.[8] Meanwhile, others (such as Lloyd, 1989, p. 106) urged precisely the opposite—that is, that the distinguishing mark of genuinely distributed representation is that individual units do not have any semantic significance, microfeatural or otherwise. Though this disagreement is partly terminological, there is an important issue at stake here. As has been pointed out by connectionists in a number of places, it is quite possible to develop a scheme in which every item is represented by means of a semantically significant pattern over a set of units without individual units having any particular microfeatural significance at all.[9] The employment of microfeatures (such as "Wickelfeatures") is just one relatively convenient method for generating such patterns, a method that can readily be discarded if it fails to provide a useful overall scheme of representation. Connectionist work is by no means deeply committed to the existence of microfeatural analyses of task domains, or to simple feature-based semantics for their representations (the failings of which are readily acknowledged on all sides), and the use of microfeatures is best regarded as essentially incidental to the distributedness of representations.

When one wants to model cognitive functions, it is particularly useful to have internal structure in the representations reflecting semantic properties, for differences in internal structure will have direct causal effects that can systematically influence the direction of processing. Thus some connectionists have argued that using patterns of activity over many units, rather than activation in a single unit, makes possible processes that, by virtue of their sensitivity to the internal structure of the representation themselves, are indirectly sensitive to the nature of the represented items.[10] Typically, choosing a strictly localist style of representation will preclude interesting internal structural differences between representations, and so, to compensate, the representations of each item will have to be supplemented by further knowledge about how it should be processed (stored, for example, in symbolic rules, or in the connectivity pattern among units). In one sense, of course, connectionists are here simply reiterating an old familiar point. Thus we use a compositional language rather than an unbounded set of primitives precisely because the internal structure of compositional representations has a systematic semantic and computational significance. If there is anything novel in the connectionist emphasis on using patterns with semantically significant internal structure, it lies in the highly controversial claim that the pattern-based schemes naturally implementable in neural networks are expressively more rich than any feasible compositional language. It is often claimed, for example, that by using patterns of neural activity as the fundamental mode of representation, connectionists are able to represent fine shades of meaning in a way that is fundamentally or at least practically impossible for normal symbolic schemes.

One way to generate representations with both kinds of advantages discussed so far (i.e., robustness and rich internal structure) is by coarse-coding. This places at least two special conditions on the kinds of features assigned to individual units. First, they must be coarse, where again this is always relative to some intuitive or perhaps theoretically defined standard or minimum. One way the notion of a coarse assignment is often expressed is in terms of the size of the receptive field of a unit, that is, those aspects or features of the domain with which activity in a unit is correlated. Coarse assignments are those that give individual units relatively wide receptive fields. Thus, individual neurons in the visual cortex are known to pick up on features present in the visual input such as lines at a certain orientation, but they are often coarse-coded in the sense that the band of orientations to which the neuron will actually react is quite wide. Coarse assignments are often disjunctive; for example, to generate coarse-coded representations of rooms (as in the above example) we could have individual connectionist units standing not for individual features such as sofa, but for disjunctions of features (e.g., sofa or TV). This principle carries over to the example of neurons in the visual system, since neurons generally have wide receptive fields along a number of different dimensions at once (e.g., orientation, location, movement).

The second condition is that the assignments be overlapping; if one unit picks out sofa or TV, the next should pick out TV or ceiling, and so on. Again, visual neurons generally satisfy this condition; if one neuron has as its receptive field a certain portion of the visual field, another will cover an overlapping portion, and so on. A representation of a whole item, such as a room or a visual scene, is then just a distinctive pattern over the full set of units. Such a representation has the advantage of robustness, because the large and overlapping nature of the receptive fields of the units pretty much ensures that no individual unit or group of units is crucial to successful representing. These representations also possess semantically significant internal structure, because the particular pattern used to represent an item is determined by the nature of that item, and so similarities and differences among the items to be represented will be directly reflected in similarities and differences among the representations themselves.

In numerous places in the connectionist literature distribution is seen as identical with, or at least deeply bound up with, coarse coding.[11] Coarse coded representations satisfy the first of the conditions in the standard connectionist definition quoted at the start of this section, because they are characteristic patterns of activity over groups of many units. Moreover, they also satisfy the second requirement, that each unit be involved in representing many different entities, because the representations of other items are simply different patterns of activity over the same group of units. In fact, individual units can even be involved in representing many different entities at the same time, for the characteristic patterns for two different entities can be activated at once over the same set of units. The representings of the two different entities can in this way be superimposed on each other. One might initially suppose that this would introduce all kinds of deleterious interference effects, but—depending very much on the details of the coarse coding scheme in question and the entities being represented—it turns out to be possible to superimpose patterns while preserving the functional independence of the representations. An excellent example is the working memory in Touretzky and Hinton's (1988) Distributed Connectionist Production System.

The fact that representations can be superimposed in this way highlights a crucial ambiguity in the apparently simple notion of "localist" representation with which distribution is often contrasted. When a contrast with extended representation is in order, the relevant sense of "local" is, roughly, that of restriction in extent. When a contrast with superimposed representation is in order, however, the relevant sense of "local" is that of discrete, separated or nonoverlapping. These are quite different and indeed independent properties, and for a clear understanding of distribution it is crucial they be carefully distinguished. One author who does so very clearly is Murdock (1979):

> The idea of distributed storage does not necessarily imply that information is physically spread out over a large area. Rather, the key issue is whether memory traces, whatever their nature, are separate or combined. With localized storage, each trace is separate; so whether it is boxes or bins, there is one trace per location. Distributed memory takes the opposite position, where combined (superimposed) traces can be stored and there is no individual representation for a given item.[12] (p. 111)

He cannot however afford to discount entirely the importance of being spread over a large area, because distribution in this weaker sense turns out in practice to be a necessary condition for representations to be effectively superimposed. If individual memories were encoded in the brain by single neurons, it would be very unlikely that memories could be stored in a superimposed fashion (many memories to one neuron). It is only because each memory is stored across a wide network of neurons that it is possible, in practice, to store many memories over the same set of neurons.

The superimposition of representings, in some form or other, is probably the single most common theme in characterizations of distribution, especially when we look beyond the connectionist literature. In many characterizations it is clearly the dominant theme. According to McClelland and Rumelhart (1986b), for example, "[Distributed] models hold that all memories, old and new, are stored in the same set of connections . . ." (p. 504).[13]

Under what circumstances is it correct to say that two representings are superposed? First, some points of terminology: When two representations are effectively superposed, they become a single new item representing both the original contents. Thus we should avoid thinking of superposed representations, unless for some reason we deliberately want to keep the separate identities of the originals in mind. Rather, we should think of the superposed representings achieved by a single representation. Second, the terms *superimposed* and *superposed* are only largely synonymous. In what follows I will use *superposed* on the ground that it is shorter, although rejecting certain domain-specific connotations such as the notion of wave addition in physics. *Superposed* as I intend it is defined in what follows.

Intuitively, the representings of two distinct items are superposed if they are coextensive—if, in other words, they occupy the same portion of the resources available for representing. Thus in connectionist networks we can have different items stored as patterns of activity over the same set of units, or multiple different associations encoded in one set of weights. This point can be stated a little more precisely as follows. Suppose we have some accurate way to measure the amount of the resources involved in representing a given content item C.[14] Then a representation R of an item C is conservative if the amount of the resources involved in representing C is equal to R itself (no more and no less). A representation R of a series of items c_i is superposed just in case R is a conservative representation of each c_i.

This characterization is completely general, but can easily be fleshed out in many different ways. For example, in developing his tensor product scheme for representing structured items in connectionist networks, Smolensky (1987b) offers a formal definition of superposition in terms of vector addition. The result of adding two vectors is a new vector that, under the scheme in question, is taken to represent the same items as both the originals. Since the portion of the resources implicated in representing each item is now exactly coextensive—that is, just the whole new vector itself—the representings are superposed in exactly the sense just outlined.[15]

Sometimes it is appropriate to say both that a representation has just a single content, and that the representing of that content involves superposition. An example is an optical hologram of a single scene. In this case there is a single content, but, given the way holograms are constructed, each part of scene is represented over the whole surface. Such cases are naturally covered by the above characterization, for the items

c_i that are each conservatively represented by R are now simply the parts of a single overall content C. Superposition is essentially the same, whether it applies to a set of items or to the parts of a single decomposable item. The only different is one of convenience, that is, where we find it natural to think of the primary level for identification of distinct items or contents.

Superposition appears to come in something like degrees in at least three ways. First, R was required above to be a conservative representation of each c_i, with the consequence that the resources involved in representing each item are identical. This is the most interesting case, but various weaker notions can be defined by relaxing this condition, allowing weaker overlapping relations between some or all pairs of representings. This accounts for the intuition that there is some kind of superposition occurring in coarse-coded schemes. In such schemes the receptive field of a given unit generally overlaps significantly with those of its neighbors. Consequently, particular features of the represented item will tend to be represented in overlapping (i.e., partially superposed) regions of the representation itself. However, we do not have full superposition in the representings of the individual various features; it is merely a neighborly overlapping effect.

Second, whether the amounts of resources involved in representing distinct items are the same depends very much on how we measure the resources, and in particular on our choice of dimensions along which to require that the amounts be identical. To take a very simple example: A family photo album captures many scenes, but not in a superposed fashion, for each distinct scene is encoded by a given photograph. This assumes that we are considering the album along the natural spatial dimensions. If we consider the album as extended through time, and ask how much of the album is involved in representing each scene, the answer will be roughly the same for every one, suggesting that the representings are superposed. We could take this as indicating that the degree of superposition in a given case depends on the nature or the number of dimensions along which coextensiveness of representings obtains. A better view is that such examples highlight the requirement, for genuine superposition, that representings be coextensive in all dimensions, or at least in all those dimensions where variation makes a real difference to the semantic significance of the representation.

Finally, a third way superposition comes in degrees is in how many contents or content parts are represented over the same space. It makes intuitive sense that the more distinct contents represented over the same space, the more strongly superposed the representation. Holograms are a good example, because the relevant scene-portions are extremely fine-grained, no larger than point sources; each of these very fine portions is represented over the whole surface of the hologram. The strongest possible notion of superposition, then, would require that R be a conservative representation of arbitrarily fine portions of the overall content. It is not difficult to construct artificial examples of this kind of extreme superposition. Suppose for example we were to treat a function as represented by its Fourier transform. Each point in the transform function is obtained by multiplying the whole function with a distinct trigonometric function and integrating over the result. Each point in the original function, then, is effectively represented over the whole transform; thus there is full superposition of arbitrarily fine slices of the original. This kind of extreme case is however not the norm; indeed, often the idea of arbitrarily fine divisions of the content makes little sense.

A metaphor often used to illustrate the difference between (discrete) localist schemes and superposed schemes is that of a filing cabinet. In the ideal filing cabinet every distinct item to be represented is encoded on a separate sheet of paper, and the sheets are then placed side by side in cabinet drawers. Because every item is stored separately, every item can be accessed independently of all the others, and the modification, removal or destruction of any one piece does not affect any others. If representation in the cabinet were fully superposed, by contrast, there would be no separate location for each discrete item; rather, the whole cabinet would be representing every item without any more fine-grained correspondence of sheets or locations to individual items. Accessing the representation of one item is, in an obvious sense, accessing the representation of all items; and modifying or destroying the representing of one cannot but affect the representing of all (though the effect is not necessarily harmful).

Superposed schemes thus differ fundamentally from more standard localist varieties. In general, schemes of representation define a space of allowable representations and set up a correspondence with the space of items or contents to be represented. We are accustomed to thinking of such schemes as setting up a roughly isomorphic correspondence—that is, there is a distinct representation for every item to be represented, and the structure of the space of representations systematically corresponds (in a way that can only be characterized relative to the scheme in question) to the structure of the space of possible contents. Thus, languages usually define an infinite array of distinct expression types, which are then put in correspondence with distinct items or states of affairs; and standard methods of generating images aim at finding a distinct image for every scene. When this kind of discrete correspondence fails to be the case—when, for example, the representational scheme assigns two distinct contents to the one representation (ambiguity), or two distinct representations to the one content (synonymy, redundancy)—we usually think of it as some kind of aberration or defect in the scheme, to be ironed out if we were to set about improving the scheme.

The notion of superposed representation overthrows this whole familiar picture, for superposition aims precisely at finding one point in the space of representations that can serve as the representation of multiple contents. For schemes in which R is a representation of c only if there is some non-arbitrary structural or functional relationship between R and c (if, for example, c itself or important information about c an be recovered from R) this becomes a formidable requirement, in the sense that actually finding such a point, one that can do double or multiple semantic duty, may be quite difficult. It is a nontrivial requirement on the way a scheme is set up that it be rich enough to be able to generate such representations. Consider the well-known example of a simple linear network incapable of computing the "XOR" function. The fundamental problem here is that no one point in the space of connection weights is capable of performing all the transformations from input to output which define that function. Representing these transformations in a fully superposed fashion requires moving to a different network structure, offering a different space of possible representations in the connections.

Suppose one's aim is to store a number of items. A localist scheme represents each item in its stored form exactly as it was represented previously; this is an essential part of the filing cabinet analogy. A superposed scheme, however, must find a single point in the space that can function properly as the representation of every item to be stored. Hence superposed storage involves transformation, and if an item is to be recovered in its original form, this transformation must be reversed. This brings us to another common theme in characterizations of distributed representation, the notion that although localist schemes store things as they are, distributed schemes must recreate the originals, or something like them, on demand: as Rumelhart and Norman (1981) stated, "Information is better thought of as 'evoked' than 'found'" (p. 3).[16]

It was pointed out just above that finding a point in the space of representations that can do multiple semantic duty is often difficult, and there is no guarantee that there is any one point that can perform its multiple duties perfectly or even at all. A good procedure for producing superposed representations will find a point that performs optimally in representing the full set of items, but such a point may still perform imperfectly with respect to a particular item. Various different schemes for producing superposed representations utilize different encoding processes of varying degrees of complexity and subtlety. It is typically the case, however, that when the representings of various different items are superposed, these various representings influence and perhaps interfere with each other; for example, the superposed recording of two different scenes in one hologram results in partially degraded performance for each. In general, then, whether due to limitations inherent in the representational space, or limitations of the superposing process itself, superposed representations often exhibit imperfections that arise precisely because various representings are being superposed. This, then, is another recurrent feature in descriptions of distribution: "Memory systems in which distinct stored items are spread over the storage elements and in which items can mix with each other are often referred to as 'distributed' or 'holographic'" (Anderson, 1977, p. 30).[17] Although this might pose a technical problem for anyone interested in devising efficient distributed storage methods, it might also be a crucial feature of systems utilizing distributed representations in psychological modeling, because these imperfect performance characteristics may turn out to be useful in explaining certain features of human cognitive performance.

There is one particularly important manner in which this mixing or interference is often manifested. Suppose we have a number of items to be represented, each of which is a variant on a theme (or perhaps a few central themes). Suppose, for example, we wish to store a series of vectors exhibiting a certain structural tendency or pattern in common, though there is significant random variation from one to the next. Then when the representings of all the items are superposed, those respects in which they are similar will naturally be reinforced, and those in which they differ will tend to be in conflict and hence cancel each other out. Though this effect depends very much on both the details of the particular encoding process that generates the superposed representation and the particular items to be stored, what can often happen is that the resulting representation performs well insofar as it is representing the common features of each item, but poorly insofar as it is representing unique variations. The representation, in other words, has generalized; it has emphasized the central tendencies from among a set of exemplars, and now disregards or downplays particular differences.[18] This generalization can be advantageous at a later point, when the representation is evaluated with regard to its performance as a representation of some item it was not originally designed to handle. In such a case, the representation will perform acceptably just insofar as that item can be treated as exemplifying the central tendencies previously extracted.

In any localist scheme, each distinct item is represented by means of a proprietary chunk of the available resources. Because resources are usually finite, this puts a strict upper limit on the number of items that can be represented, and attempts to exceed this limit can have more or less unfortunate consequences. Superposed schemes, by contrast, attempt to find a single state of one (possibly large) chunk of the resources that functions as a representation of all the items to be stored. Storing another item does not take up more resources; rather, it involves transforming the state of the same resources. The issue, then, is not whether there are resources available for storing the item at all; it is rather how well the new state functions as a representation of all the stored items. Depending on the particular scheme in question, it is typically the case that storing more items results in gradual worsening of performance across all or most items rather than an inability to store any particular one. This is the much vaunted *graceful degradation* of distributed systems, and it clearly follows from the nature of superposed representation (or rather, one important aspect of it).[19]

Equipotentiality

I have stressed the fundamental gulf between superposed schemes of representation and more familiar localist schemes, but distribution has on occasion been associated with even more radical possibilities. Consider Lashley's (1950) famous claim about the representation in the brain: "It is not possible to demonstrate the isolated localization of a memory trace anywhere within the nervous system. Limited regions may be essential for learning or retention of a particular activity, but within such regions the parts are functionally equivalent. The engram is represented throughout the area ..." (p. 477). The first sentence appears to be a clear statement of superposition. The second sentence however claims that all memory traces are contained in all parts of the brain region. This is a much stronger claim, for it is easy enough to envisage a case of fully superposed representings, but where parts of the overall representation do not have the same content as the whole. It is clear that Lashley was aware of the difference between these two properties, and in general claimed that the stronger one was true of the brain. Thus, in earlier work, he had formulated the famous principle of neural equipotentiality, "the apparent capacity of any intact part of a functional area to carry out, with or without reduction in efficiency, the functions which are lost by destruction of the whole ..." (Lashley, 1929, p. 25). For current purposes we should modify this principle and think of a representation as equipotential just in case each part of that representation has the same semantic significance as the whole. Every part represents just what the whole represents.

Some have explicitly maintained that equipotentiality is the essence of distributed representation,[20] and this idea is implicit in much other discussion. Thus, insofar as Lashley is regarded as having determined that memories are represented in distributed fashion in the brain—a very common move—distribution is being at least implicitly equated with equipotentiality. The same is true when we regard optical holograms as paradigms of distributed representation, for equipotentiality is one of the most well-known features of at least certain varieties of hologram.[21] It is therefore worth spending some time clarifying this notion of equipotentiality, especially in its relation to superposition.

Equipotentiality requires that the various parts of a representation R have the same content as R itself. There is an obvious symmetry here with the notion of superposition, which required that the various parts of the overall content have the same representing. This suggests the symmetrically opposed definition: R is an equipotential representation of C just in case every part r_i of R is a representation of C.[22] Unfortunately, this form of the definition seems to allow for tedious counterexamples involving the simple duplication or replication of a given self-sufficient representation. An example is Venetian wallpaper, which duplicates hundreds of identical discrete little sketches of the Rialto all across the wall. Every sketch is representing the Rialto (or Venice), and the whole wall certainly represents nothing more, and so it would seem that the wallpaper is equipotential. Surely equipotentiality is a more interesting phenomenon than this!

One problem with these merely redundant representation is that their equipotentiality, such as it is, stops at a certain fixed level: portions of the overall representation smaller than an individual Rialto sketch do not have the same content as the whole. One way to rule out such cases, then, would be to require that arbitrary portions of R have the same content as the whole. Thus, R is equipotential with respect to C just in case every portion r_i of R is a representation of C for every division of R into parts; that is, no matter how you slice it, each part still has the same content as the whole. This suggests an asymmetry between superposition and equipotentiality: because although superposition is an interesting phenomenon for any given discrete division of the content into more than one part, equipotentiality only appears to be interesting for arbitrary divisions.

It is doubtful, however, whether equipotentiality in this sense is ever attained. For one thing, if we take fine enough portions of any representation it is unlikely we will have any content at all, let alone the full original content. Though holograms, for example, are taken to be equipotential, small enough portions fail to encode anything; all we need do is take some portion smaller than the wavelength of the illuminating beam and we cannot possibly recover anything of the original image. On reflection it would be truly remarkable for a nontrivial representation to have the same content in any portion, no matter how small, as is conveyed by the whole. Second, even reasonably large portions of the original representation typically are not identical in content with the original. Lashley himself was careful to qualify his principle of neural equipotentiality with a corresponding principle of mass action, which acknowledged that the smaller the chunk of brain remaining, the worse the performance. Each portion, it would seem, could not have had exactly the same content as the whole; for if it had, it would presumably have been able to generate the same performance. Similarly for the hologram: The whole scene is recoverable from each part, but only with proportionately reduced perspective and image quality.

Rescuing the notion of equipotentiality in the face of these objections requires a two-pronged strategy. On one hand, we need only require that all portions of some sufficient size (an inherently vague notion) represent the same as the whole. Mere redundancy then becomes one trivial way of achieving this effect, practical in some contexts, such as the preservation of medieval wisdom, but manifestly implausible in others, such as encoding memories in the brain. More interesting methods, such as the convolution transformation underlying holography, vary parts of R smoothly and systematically as a function of the whole content. Second, we need to explain some sense in which these sufficiently large portions represent the same as the whole despite slight variation or degradation. Intuitively, the portions are all still in some important sense representing the same thing, regardless of the degradation in performance. Sustaining this intuition means formulating some kind of distinction between what a representation is of and how good it is as a representation of that content; or, in other words, a kind of semantic character versus quality distinction. A representation would then be equipotential insofar as all sufficiently large portions have, not the same "content," but rather the same semantic character as the whole, even if at lower quality.

When do two representations have the same semantic character in the relevant sense? We need here some notion of a privileged or important dimension of the content, such that each part can be seen as semantically coextensive along that dimension, although perhaps varying on others. To illustrate: Why do a hologram and its portion have the same semantic character, even if the portion performs significantly worse in generating the whole scene? The answer is that crudely spatial dimensions of the encoded scene are accorded a certain kind of priority, and what the portion does is recreate the whole scene along these dimensions, albeit in a degraded way. In short, two representations have the same character if their performance is essentially equivalent along what happens to be the intuitively important dimension, though it may vary on others. Lashley regarded regions of the rat brain as equipotential because, with only portions of the region remaining, a rat could perform the same tasks, even if more slowly or clumsily. Hence the important dimension here is simply the fact of performance; speed or agility is relegated to a lesser importance and so is just a matter of quality, not character.

This description of the character versus quality distinction is a start, but it is by no means complete because it does not give any general guidelines for determining what the important dimension is in a particular case. It is unlikely, however, that there could be any such general guidelines, because the relevant dimension changes from case to case according to interests and purposes that can vary greatly in ways that have little or nothing to do with intrinsic properties of the representations themselves. It is natural to be impressed by the fact that each portion of the hologram reproduces the same spatial extent of the image. Yet consider the case of an aerospace engineer devising a holographic display unit for a jet fighter. Here the primary advantage a holographic display has over a regular screen is that the generated image conveys depth effects at sufficiently high resolution to assist the pilot in operating the plane. Both depth effects and resolution would presumably be lost, however, if only a portion of a hologram were employed; hence, from the engineer's point of view, the hologram is not at all equipotential. Though the hologram itself remains the same, from one naive point of view it counts as equipotential, although from another point of view it does not. Because the general character versus quality distinction depends on the notion of a privileged dimension, that distinction itself is rendered inherently flexible, even vague; and consequently the very idea of equipotentiality is without any very firm foundation.

It has already been pointed out that superposition does not entail equipotentiality. Given the symmetry between the concepts, it should not be surprising that the converse is also true: Equipotentiality does not, in general, entail superposition. Thus, consider again the trivial case of Venetian wallpaper. If we consider only parts larger than a certain minimum size, then each part has the same content as the whole. Yet there is clearly one scattered portion of the wall where the Rialto is found multiply depicted, and likewise one portion where the gondola is found, and these portions are entirely discrete, as can be seen by the fact that we could paint over all Rialto depictions while leaving all gondola depictions intact. The wallpaper is therefore trivially equipotential with respect to the whole scene, but not superposed with respect to the Rialto and the gondola.

The relation between these concepts is however more intimate than these independence claims suggest. Notice for example that full equipotentiality (i.e., equipotentiality of arbitrarily fine portions of R) immediately entails full superposition. If the whole content is encoded in every part of the representation, no matter how fine, it follows that every part of the content must be encoded over the whole representation.[23] Further, it turns out that standard methods for generating real instances of equipotential representation do in fact vary every part of the representation as a function of the whole content, thereby guaranteeing superposition. Conversely, common methods for developing superposed representations often produce something akin to equipotentiality as a side-effect. In connectionism, for example, it is common to represent transformations from input to output in the one set of weights. It is a well-known feature of such representations that they are relatively impervious to localized damage or noise; thus, removing units or connections makes relatively little difference to overall performance (Wood, 1978). Another way to describe this situation is in terms of the equipotentiality of the representation: large enough portions effectively represent the same as the whole.

In general, insofar as there is equipotentiality, any portion of a representation can take over the tasks of the whole; in other words, equipotential representations are robust by their very nature. This brings the discussion of themes associated with distribution around a full circle. Robustness was seen to be a desirable consequence of at least some forms of merely extensive representation, but it dropped out of consideration in the discussion of superposition. Although superposed representations are often relatively robust, nothing in the definition of superposition itself guarantees this: although a series of items are represented over the same resources, it might be that all those resources are required for the effective representing of any one item. However, with equipotentiality, which is intuitively the strongest form of distribution of all, robustness is guaranteed.

Distributed systems or representations are often described as *holistic*. This is an extraordinarily vague term, and usually contributes nothing to our understanding of the phenomenon in question; nevertheless, with the above discussion in mind it is possible to sort out some things that might be intended. For example, describing a distributed representation as holistic might be a reference to the fact that, when a representation R is superposed, each part of R is involved in representing a number of items at once, and in that sense reflects the "whole" content. Similarly, in superposed schemes R functions as a representation of a number of items at once; in that sense, one state represents the whole content, or each item is only represented in the context of the whole content. Alternatively, describing distributed representations as holistic might be a reference to equipotentiality, where each part represents the "whole" content. Each of these senses gestures in the direction of some important aspect of distributed representation; however, superimposing them in the one (dare I say, holistic) concept results, in this case, in little more than a blur.[24]

What Is Distribution?

This discussion sketches just the broadest outlines of the current concept of distribution. It reveals something of the multiplicity of themes in the vicinity of distribution, and some of the extraordinary differences among characterizations previously put forward. But how does it bear on the wider project of finding some general kind of representation on the basis of which a genuine alternative to CTM might be constructed? What, after this discussion, can we say that distributed representation actually is?

In view of the multifarious nature of typical instances, and the wide variety of properties thought to be central to distribution, it may be tempting to suppose that distributed representation is really just some kind of "family resemblance" concept, gathering together in a loose way a heterogeneous collection of styles of representation that actually turn out to have no interesting properties in common. Such concepts are bad news for theorizing because they effectively preclude one from making interesting general claims about all members of that type. Consequently if a survey of current usage revealed that distribution was in fact such a concept, the speculative project of investigating alternatives to CTM constructed around a putative category of distributed representation would be stopped in its tracks.

This prospect is not a serious concern, however. Current usage has only a limited claim on our allegiance. The appropriate response, in the interests of conceptual clarification and scientific progress, would be simply to redraw the conceptual boundaries, thereby revising the current muddled use of the term. We would be providing, in other words, an explication of the concept: a new, precise account of distribution, based on the old confused version but displacing it. In the current case, moreover, there is a way of explicating the concept of distribution that is not excessively disruptive of current usage. It turns out that one theme—the superposition of representings—is both common to a large proportion of standard characterizations and true of most cases that intuition counts as paradigm instances. This opens the door to a proposal, still informal and far from precise, but nevertheless substantial: distribution is the superposition of representings, and distributed representations are those which belong to schemes defined around a core method of generating superposed representations.

One reason for supposing that superposition is the heart of distribution is that the various other themes and properties discussed above are either implausibly weak or implausibly strong. Thus, extensiveness alone cannot be what is important about distributed representation, because a wide variety of representations that are obviously not distributed in any interesting sense consume more than some theoretical minimum by way of representational resources. To count as genuinely distributed a representation must be more than simply spread over a large area, whether that be on the page, in the sky, in a computer memory or in the brain. Similarly, a distributed representation must also be more than just a "pattern" over some extended area, for virtually any representation will count as a pattern of some kind. This notion must be tightened somehow, yet various common approaches—such as the requirement that the patterns result from coarse-coding—fail to capture the natural class of distributed representations, for they end up excluding various standard cases to which such an approach is inapplicable. Coming from the other direction, equipotentiality cannot be regarded as a definitive feature of distribution. For one thing, it is not always clear that equipotentiality is a well-defined property: it all depends on whether we can privilege some dimension along which it makes sense to say that the full content is preserved in each portion of the representation. Equipotentiality also suffers the problem of exclusivity; all kinds of representations that appear to be distributed in an important sense fail to exhibit significant equipotentiality.

Superposition has neither of these failings. It is strong enough that very many kinds of representations do not count as superposed, yet it manages to subsume virtually all paradigm cases of distribution, whether these are drawn from the brain, connectionism, psychology, or optics. Moreover, superposition is a satisfying choice in other ways. As a structural feature it seems to be in deep-seated opposition to the standard kinds of localist schemes with which we have long been familiar. As pointed out above, usual forms of representation are designed so that, roughly, the structure of the domain of representations mirrors that of world itself; every different item to be represented is mapped to its own distinctive point or points in the space of representations. Superposed schemes violate this neat order, and do so inherently; thus the distinction between localist and superposed schemes marks a fundamental gulf in kinds of representation, a gulf suggesting that semantic superposition is not some incidental property that merely cross-classifies other forms of representation, but rather is the kind of property that manages to pick out a whole distinct genus of its own.

Much remains to be done if this speculation is to be firmly grounded. The notion of semantic superposition has to be precisely defined, and it must be shown that schemes of distributed representation can be effectively generated in such terms; this includes showing that a sufficient number of the intuitive paradigm cases of distribution are indeed characterizable as falling under superposed schemes. It would also have to be demonstrated that the loose claims of incompatibility made here between superposition and other supposedly localist styles, such as generically symbolic representation, stand up under closer scrutiny. If such elaboration were successful, however, we would be able—indeed, obliged—to investigate the possibility raised at the beginning of this paper: namely, that a theory of cognition might be constructed on a distributed foundation, a theory that would automatically count as an alternative to CTM.

Thorough investigation of this possibility would involve determining whether the generic category of distributed representation, defined in terms of superposition, satisfies the demanding criteria set forth earlier. It is entirely unclear at this stage, for example, whether distributed representations (of whatever particular variety) would be sufficiently powerful to represent effectively the kinds of information that underlie human cognitive performance. Much connectionist work in psychological modeling can be regarded as an empirical investigation of precisely this issue, but it is still much too early to expect any conclusive verdict, especially when we realize that those investigations are being carried out in the absence of any well-developed theory of the nature of distributed representation.

On the other hand, there are some reasons to be optimistic. I have suggested already that, from the preliminary perspective afforded by this overview, it is plausible to suppose that distributed representation is both appropriately general as a category and inherently non-symbolic, features that surely constitute a promising start. Moreover, distributed representations possess the desired deep affiliation with neural networks. Briefly, on the current proposal, a distributed representation is one in which each component of the representation is implicated in the representing of many items at once. The high degree of interconnectedness between processing units in neural networks constitutes excellent conditions for implementing this kind of dependence. This is not to say, of course, that any representation in a neural network must be distributed; on the contrary, it is manifestly possible to impose localist or even symbolic structures on neural mechanisms. It is to say that neural networks provide a very natural medium for implementing distributed representations; or rather, to put the point even more strongly: to insist on utilizing nondistributed representations in a neural network framework would be to stubbornly avoid capitalizing on some of the most important benefits of neural machinery. It would be akin to using digital electronic circuitry while stubbornly refusing to implement general purpose symbol processing.

This deep affiliation makes distributed representation attractive as a possible alternative to symbolic representation. There is, for example, nothing implausible in supposing that there are distributed representations to be found in the brain. Quite the contrary: Distribution is an empirically well-established feature of the neurological substrate in which our cognitive capabilities find their ultimate realization. Indeed, the biological reality of distributed representation is a principle so secure that it cannot even be counted as a discovery, for the concept itself first arose in attempts to describe the unusual kinds of representations found in the brain, and when it was proposed above that there may be a broad natural category of distributed representation, neural representations were taken to be paradigm instances. This intimate association with the actual machinery underlying human cognition stands in plain contrast with the biological remoteness of symbolic representations. Though CTM demands a language of thought, and CTM advocates insist that the expressions of this language are realized in the neural substrate, and consequently predict the eventual discovery of "symbols amongst the neurons," neuroscience has never yet stumbled across syntactically structured representations in the brain. This discrepancy only becomes more embarrassing to CTM as the sum of neuroscientific knowledge increases, and provides at least a prima facie argument in favor of any biologically motivated alternative.

Nevertheless, this proposal does not fall afoul of another quite different methodological constraint based on the supposed autonomy of psychology and neuroscience. CTM orthodoxy maintains that psychological generalizations are only to be found at a certain level of description of a system—roughly, the level at which the system's operation is most usefully understood as cognizing, that is, involving the transformation of representations. When CTM proposes symbolic representation as the form in which information must be stored and processed, symbolic representation is described in a sufficiently general way in which only the abstract structure is important. All kinds of implementational details become irrelevant, and, consequently, systems differing widely in their physical instantiation can be regarded as falling under the same psychological principles. To descend to the level of the system's particular implementation would be to descend to a level from which the true psychological generalizations are no longer visible. An immediate consequence of this view is that theories and models of cognitive functioning are held to be relevantly similar, or seen as falling under the one approach or paradigm, only insofar as they are similar at this relatively abstract level. Thus it becomes possible to maintain that the sole thread binding all CTM (or classical) approaches together is a commitment to symbolic representation together with operations that are sensitive to syntactic structure.

Recently however, with rapid advances in neuroscience and the resurgence of connectionism, it has become popular to maintain that cognitive functioning is not independent of, and can not be understood independently of, the details of the particular way in which cognition happens to be instantiated. Thus, in the case of human cognitive abilities, it is maintained that we must shift the focus of attention from abstract, purely psychological or "top down" investigations to the messy details of the actual neurobiological mechanisms themselves, their evolutionary context, and their very specific capabilities. Meanwhile it is maintained that the crucial feature bringing the wide diversity of approaches within the groundswell of opposition to CTM under a single paradigm is not to be found at the level of a form of representation but rather in terms of a general commitment to neurobiological authenticity.

An articulated concept of distributed representation offers a sound theoretical basis for reconciling these two apparently conflicting strains of thought. It possesses an inherent neurobiological plausibility, but without sacrificing the generality required of a genuinely psychological hypothesis. I have urged that distribution be understood in terms of the superposition of representings, a notion that is completely independent of details of the particular ways in which the superposition might be achieved. The wide variety of instances of distribution already known to exist—and effectively describable in terms of superposition—attests to the breadth of this characterization. Given a well-developed conception of distributed representation, it is possible to determine which kinds of operations are suited to processing distributed representations, and consequently what kinds of distributed mechanisms might subserve various different cognitive functions, without ever needing to descend to descriptions of particular hardware implementations. Arguments for or against such theories can then be formulated at this relatively abstract psychological level. It is in this light that we should understand many connectionist models of cognitive functions that, despite being based on networks of neural units, are highly remote from biological details. This approach can also be seen in the work of psychologists such as Metcalfe, who has proposed distributed mechanisms to account for various memory phenomena quite irrespective of how those mechanisms are in fact instantiated in the head; these proposals are then tested on the basis of straightforwardly psychological experiments. (For examples of Metcalfe's work see Eich, 1982; Metcalfe, 1989; also Murdock, 1979, 1982.) With high level descriptions of distributed mechanisms in hand, it is possible to continue on to construct much more specific models which specify, to some relevant level of detail, how these distributed mechanisms happen to be built up out of human wetware, a process which not only tests the hypotheses themselves but stimulates future developments.

In short, the concept of distributed representation enables us to preserve the insight that a theory of cognition is more than just a theory of how particular mechanisms perform their specific functions; but also, by virtue of its intimate relationship with connectionism and the brain, acknowledges the importance of detailed studies of the actual machinery underlying human cognitive performance. There need be no tension between studying cognition and studying particular neurobiological instantiations of cognition, because the general concept of distributed representation functions as the unifying principle. For this reason, there is also no need to insist that the central feature binding together a wide group of neuroscientific and connectionist alternatives to CTM is a concern with neurobiological plausibility, for we can now see the possibility of a deeper similarity between these various approaches, one that obtains at the level at which they count as theories of cognition.

Notes

1. A notable exception here is work by Walters (see, e.g., Walters, 1987), although her concerns are considerably more restricted than those taken up here. A preliminary account of distributed representation in connectionist contexts is found in Hinton, McClelland, and Rumelhart (1986).

2. Here, to avoid obvious circularity, we should read "distributed" as meaning something like "spread over."

3. Single bit storage locations in a digital memory can be seen as extremely simple computing units, changing state according to their inputs, and outputting their state when accessed. See McEliece 1985.

4. This is the point at which characterizations of distribution in the sense of interest to us here comes closest to the mainstream computer science conception. In this latter usage "distributed" applies to systems where storage or processing responsibilities are not restricted to any single computer but rather are spread through a connected network of machines; coordinating these various computers to achieve a single task then becomes a major design problem.

5. Kosslyn and Hatfield (1984), for example, claim that: "In the brain, the best current guess is that information is not stored in a given location. Rather, information appears to be distributed across numerous locations" (p. 1030). Fodor and Pylyshyn (1988) think that "To claim that a node is distributed is presumably to claim that its states of activation correspond to patterns of neural activity—to aggregates of neural 'units'—rather than to activations of single neurons ..." (p. 19). See also McClelland, Rumelhart, and Hinton 1986, p. 33; Papert 1988, p. 11; P. M. Churchland 1986, p. 289; Tienson 1987, pp. 10–11; Tye 1987, p. 170.

6. Consider also Feldman 1989: "The most compact representation possible would have a unique unit dedicated to each concept. If we assume that a unit corresponds to one neuron, then this is the grandmother cell or pontifical cell theory. The other extreme would have each concept represented as a pattern of activity in all the units in the system. This is well known as the holographic model of memory, and it is the most highly distributed theory that we will consider" (p. 71). Other such characterizations include Bechtel 1987, p. 19; Churchland and Sejnowski 1989, p. 30ff.; P. S. Churchland 1989, p. 118; Cummins 1989, p. 147; Smolensky 1987b, p. 144; Lloyd 1989, p. 110; Touretzky 1986, p. 523.

7. This example is drawn from the Schema model (Rumelhart, Smolensky, McClelland, and Hinton, 1986).

8. Pinker and Prince (1988) claim that "PDP models ... rely on 'distributed' representations: a large scale entity is represented by a pattern of activation over a set of units rather than by turning

on a single unit dedicated to it. This would be a strictly implementational claim, orthogonal to the differences between connectionist and symbol-processing theories, were it not for an additional aspect: the units have semantic content; they stand for (that is, they are turned on in response to) specific properties of the entity, and the entity is thus represented solely in terms of which of those properties it has" (p. 115). There is some precedent in connectionist writings for this position; thus Rumelhart, Hinton, and McClelland (1986) claim that "In some models these units may represent particular conceptual objects such as features, letters, words, or concepts; in others they are simply abstract elements over which meaningful patterns can be defined. When we speak of a distributed representation, we mean one in which the units represent small, feature-like entities. In this case it is the pattern as a whole that is the meaningful level of analysis. This should be contrasted to a one-unit-one-concept representational system in which single units represent entire concepts or other large meaningful entities" (p. 47). See also Clark 1989, p. 94.

9. For example: "Another possibility ... [is] that the knowledge about any individual pattern is not stored in the connections of a special unit reserved for that pattern, but is distributed over the connections among a large number of processing units.... The units in these collections may themselves correspond to conceptual primitives, or they may have no particular meaning as individuals" (McClelland, Rumelhart, and Hinton, 1986, p. 33).

10. For example, Anderson and Hinton (1981, pp. 11–12); Hinton (1981). As Hinton puts it: "the 'direct content' of a concept (its set of microfeatures) interacts in interesting ways with its 'associative content' (its links to other concepts). The reason for this interaction, of course, is that the associative content is caused by the direct content ..." (p. 175).

11. Touretzky and Hinton (1988): "We have rejected this idea in favor of a distributed or "coarse coded" representation ... each particular face is almost certainly encoded as a pattern of activity distributed over quite a large number of units, each of which responds to a subset of the possible faces...." (p. 426–427). See also Sejnowski 1981, p. 191; P. S. Churchland 1986, p. 459; Horgan and Tienson 1987, p. 105.

12. Kohonen (1984) is also clear about the distinction: "the spatial distributedness of memory traces, the central characteristic of holograms, may mean either of the following two facts: (i) Elements in a data set are spread by a transformation over a memory area, but different data sets are always stored in separate areas. (ii) Several data sets are superimposed on the same medium in a distributed form" (p. 81).

13. Kohonen (1984) claims that "In distributed memories, every memory element or fragment of memory medium holds traces from many stored items, i.e., the representations are superimposed on each other. On the other hand, every piece of stored information is spread over a large area." (p. 11). For other examples see McClelland and Rumelhart 1986a, p. 176; Papert 1988, p. 12; Rosenberg and Sejnowski 1986, p. 75; Sejnowski 1981, p. 191.

14. How exactly this amount is determined is not the concern here, but, for a first pass, suppose that it includes any portion of the representational resources such that variation in that portion is systematically correlated with variation in C, where "systematically correlated" is essentially relative to processes and relations privileged by the particular scheme of representation being employed.

15. See Smolensky 1987a, s.2.2.2.

16. A good example is also found in McClelland, Rumelhart, and Hinton 1986: "In most models, knowledge is stored as a static copy of a pattern. Retrieval amounts to finding the pattern in long-term memory and copying it into a buffer or working memory. There is no real difference between the stored representation in long-term memory and the active representation in working memory.

In PDP models, though, this is not the case. In these models, the patterns themselves are not stored. Rather, what is stored is the *connection strengths* between units that allow these patterns to be re-created" (p. 31). For a particularly strong version, compare Murdock 1982: "What is stored is not a 'wax tablet' or graven image; in fact, what is stored is not in any sense any sort of an item at all" (p. 623).

17. The same theme is taken up by Rumelhart and McClelland (1986): "Associations are simply stored in the network, but because we have a *superpositional* memory, similar patterns blend into one another and reinforce each other" (p. 267).

18. Of course, if it is desirable to actually *preserve* these individual differences, encoding schemes can be designed and implemented accordingly.

19. Note that the term *graceful degradation*, like the term *distributed representation*, has many senses; the sense described here is particularly appropriate to a narrow focus on the issue of representation.

20. Westlake (1970): "... the property of distributedness, which is displayed only by holographic processes. This property, an attribute of certain types of holograms, permits any small portion of the hologram to reconstruct the entire original scene recorded by the hologram ..." (p. 129). See also Pribram (1969, p. 75).

21. Leith and Uptanieks (1965): "each part of the hologram, no matter how small, can reproduce the entire image; thus the hologram can be broken into small fragments, each of which can be used to construct a complete image" (p. 31).

22. We cannot require that eachr_i be a *conservative* representation of C, for if r_i is conservative, then r_i would have to include all of the resources involved in representing C—that is, R could only have only been divided into one part. This trivialises equipotentiality.

23. The converse, however, does not in general hold: full superposition does not entail full equipotentiality. This can be seen from the Fourier transform example. Though every point in the original function is represented over the whole transform, it is not possible to recreate the whole original function from any given point in the transform. This difference is due to an asymmetry in the concepts themselves. Equipotentiality requires that each portion of R actually represent the whole content, although superposition requires only that each portion of R be involved in representing each part of the content.

24. The alleged "holism" of distributed representation has nothing to do with the term *hologram*. Denis Gabor coined the term, from the Greek for *whole writing*, to bring out the fact that a hologram records all the information in a given wave of light (i.e., intensity and phase).

References

Anderson, J. A. (1977). Neural models with cognitive implications. In D. Laberge and S. J. Samuels (Eds.), *Basic processes in reading* (pp. 27–90). Hillsdale, NJ: Lawrence Erlbaum Associates.

Anderson, J. A., and Hinton, G. E. (1981). Models of information processing in the brain. In G. E. Hinton and J. A. Anderson (Eds.), *Parallel models of associative memory* (pp. 9–48).

Bechtel, W. (1987). Connectionism and the philosophy of mind: An overview. *Southern Journal of Philosophy, 26* (Suppl.), 17–42.

Churchland, P. M. (1986). Some reductive strategies in cognitive neurobiology. *Mind, 95*, 279–309.

Churchland, P. S. (1986). *Neurophilosophy*. Cambridge, MA: MIT Press.

Churchland, P. S. (1989). From Descartes to neural networks. *Scientific American, 261*(1), 118.

Churchland, P. S., and Sejnowski, T. J. (1989). Neural representation and neural computation. In N. Nadel, L. A. Cooper, P. Culicover, and R. M. Harnish (Eds.), *Neural connections, mental computation* (pp. 15–48). Cambridge, MA: MIT Press.

Clark, A. (1989). *Microcognition: Philosophy, cognitive science and parallel distributed processing*. Cambridge, MA: Bradford Books/MIT Press.

Cummins, R. (1989). *Meaning and mental representation*. Cambridge, MA: MIT Press.

Eich, J. M. (1982). A composite holographic recall memory. *Psychological Review, 89*, 627.

Feldman, J. A. (1989). Neural representation of conceptual knowledge. In L. Nadel, L. A. Cooper, P. Culicover, and R. M. Harnish (Eds.), *Neural connections, mental computation* (pp. 69–103). Cambridge, MA: Bradford/MIT Press.

Fodor, J. A., and Pylyshyn, Z. W. (1988). Connectionism and cognitive architecture: A critical analysis. *Cognition, 28*, 3–71.

Hinton, G. E. (1981). Implementing semantic networks in parallel hardware. In G. E. Hinton and J. A. Anderson (Eds.), *Parallel models of associative memory* (pp. 161–187). Hillsdale, NJ: Lawrence Erlbaum Associates.

Hinton, G. E., McClelland, J. L., Rumelhart, D. E., and the PDP Research Group (1986). *Parallel distributed processing: Explorations in the microstructure of cognition*. Vol. 1: Foundations (pp. 77–109). Cambridge, MA: MIT Press.

Horgan, T., and Tienson, J. (1987). Settling into a new paradigm. *Southern Journal of Philosophy, 26* (Suppl.), 97–113.

Kohonen, T. (1984). *Self-organization and associative memory*. New York: Springer-Verlag.

Kosslyn, S. M., and Hatfield, G. (1984). Representation without symbol systems. *Social Research, 51*, 1019–1045.

Lashley, K. S. (1929). *Brain mechanisms and intelligence*. Chicago: University of Chicago Press.

Leith, E. N., and Uptanieks, J. (1965). Photography by Laser. *Scientific American, 212*, 24–35.

Lloyd, D. (1989). *Simple Minds*. Cambridge, MA: MIT Press.

McClelland, J. L., and Rumelhart, D. E. (1986a). A distributed model of human learning and memory. In J. L. McClelland, D. E. Rumelhart, and the PDP Research Group, *Parallel distributed processing: Explorations in the microstructure of cognition. Vol. 2: Psychological and biological models* (pp. 170–215). Cambridge, MA: MIT Press.

McClelland, J. L., and Rumelhart, D. E. (1986b). Amnesia and distributed memory. In D. E. Rumelhart, J. L. McClelland, and the PDP Research Group, *Parallel distributed processing: explorations in the microstructure of cognition. Vol. 2: Psychological and biological models* (pp. 503–527). Cambridge, Mass.: MIT Press.

McClelland, J. L., Rumelhart, D. E., and Hinton, G. E. (1986). The appeal of parallel distributed processing. In D. E. Rumelhart, J. L. McClelland, and the PDP Research Group, *Parallel distributed processing: explorations in the microstructure of cognition. Vol. 1: Foundations* (pp. 3–34). Cambridge, Mass.: MIT Press.

McEliece, R. J. (1985). The reliability of computer memories. *Scientific American, 252*(1), 88–95.

Metcalfe, J. (1989). Composite Holographic Associative Recall Model (CHARM) and Blended Memories in Eyewitness Testimony. *Proceedings of the 11th Annual Conference on the Cognitive Science Society* (pp. 307–314).

Murdock, B. B. (1979). Convolution and correlation in perception and memory. In L. G. Nilsson (Ed.), *Perspectives on memory research: Essays in honor of Uppsala University's 500th Anniversary* (pp. 609–626). Hillsdale, NJ: Lawrence Erlbaum Associates.

Murdock, B. B. (1982). A theory for the storage and retrieval of item and associative information. *Psychological Review, 89*(6), 609–626.

Papert, S. (1988). One AI or many? *Daedalus, 117*(1), 1–14.

Pinker, S., and Prince, A. (1988). On language and connectionism: Analysis of a parallel distributed processing model of language acquisition. *Cognition, 28*, 73–193.

Pribram, K. H. (1969). The neurophysiology of remembering. *Scientific American, 220*, 75.

Rosenberg, C. R., and Sejnowski, T. J. (1986). The spacing effect on NETtalk, a massively-parallel network. *Proceedings of the Eighth Annual Conference of the Cognitive Science Society* (pp. 72–88).

Rosenfeld, R., and Touretzky, D. S. (1988). Coarse-coded symbol memories and their properties. *Complex Systems, 2*, 463–484.

Rumelhart, D. E., Hinton, G. E., and McClelland, J. L. (1986). A general framework for parallel distributed processing. In McClelland, J. L., Rumelhart, D. E., and the PDP Research Group, *Parallel Distributed Processing: Explorations in the Microstructure of Cognition. Vol 1: Foundations* (pp. 45–76). Cambridge, Mass.: MIT Press.

Rumelhart, D. E., and McClelland, J. L. (1986). On learning the past tenses of English verbs. In D. E. Rumelhart, J. L. McClelland, and the PDP Research Group, *Parallel distributed processing: explorations in the microstructure of cognition. Vol. 2: Psychological and biological models* (pp. 216–271). Cambridge, Mass.: MIT Press.

Rumelhart, D. E., and Norman, D. A. (1981). Introduction. In *Parallel Models of Associative Memory* (pp. 1–8). Hillsdale, NJ: Lawrence Erlbaum Associates.

Rumelhart, D. E., Smolensky, P., McClelland, J. L., and Hinton, G. E. (1986). Schemata and sequential thought processes in PDP models. In D. E. Rumelhart, J. L. McClelland, and the PDP Research Group, *Parallel distributed processing: explorations in the microstructure of cognition. Vol. 2: Psychological and biological models* (pp. 7–57). Cambridge, Mass.: MIT Press.

Sejnowski, T. J. (1981). Skeleton filters in the brain. In G. E. Hinton and A. J. Anderson (Eds.), *Parallel models of associative memory* (pp. 189–212). Hillsdale, NJ: Lawrence Erlbaum Associates.

Smolensky, P. (1987a). On variable binding and the representation of symbolic structure in connectionist systems. (Tech. Rep. CU-CS-355-87.) Department of Computer Science, University of Colorado.

Smolensky, P. (1987b). The constituent structure of mental states: A reply to Fodor and Pylyshyn. *Southern Journal of Philosophy*, 26 (Suppl.), 137–160.

Tienson, J. (1987). Introduction to connectionism. *Southern Journal of Philosophy, 26* (Suppl.), 1–16.

Touretzky, D. S. (1986). BoltzCONS: Reconciling connectionism with the recursive nature of stacks and trees. *Proceedings of the Eighth Annual Conference of the Cognitive Science Society* (pp. 265–273).

Touretzky, D. S., and Hinton, G. E. (1988). A distributed connectionist production system. *Cognitive Science, 12,* 423–466.

Tye, M. (1987). Representation in Pictorialism and Connectionism. *Southern Journal of Philosophy, 26* (Suppl.), 163–184.

Walters, D. (1987). Properties of connectionist variable representations. *Proceedings of the Ninth Annual Conference of the Cognitive Science Society* (pp. 265–273).

Westlake, P. R. (1970). The possibilities of neural holographic processes within the brain. *Kybernetik, 7,* 129–153.

Wood, C. C. (1978). Variations on a theme by Lashley: Lesion experiments on the neural model of Anderson, Silverstein, Ritz and Jones. *Psychological Review, 85,* 582–591.

83 Connectionism, Eliminativism, and the Future of Folk Psychology

William Ramsey, Stephen P. Stich, and Joseph Garon

1 Introduction

In the years since the publication of Thomas Kuhn's *Structure of Scientific Revolutions*, the term "scientific revolution" has been used with increasing frequency in discussions of scientific change, and the magnitude required of an innovation before someone or other is tempted to call it a revolution has diminished alarmingly. Our thesis in this paper is that if a certain family of connectionist hypotheses turn out to be right, they will surely count as revolutionary, even on stringent pre-Kuhnian standards. There is no question that connectionism has already brought about major changes in the way many cognitive scientists conceive of cognition. However, as we see it, what makes certain kinds of connectionist models genuinely revolutionary is the support they lend to a thoroughgoing eliminativism about some of the central posits of common sense (or "folk") psychology. Our focus in this paper will be on beliefs or propositional memories, though the argument generalizes straightforwardly to all the other propositional attitudes. If we are right, the consequences of this kind of connectionism extend well beyond the confines of cognitive science, since these models, if successful, will require a radical reorientation in the way we think about ourselves.

Here is a quick preview of what is to come. Section 2 gives a brief account of what eliminativism claims, and sketches a pair of premises that eliminativist arguments typically require. Section 3 says a bit about how we conceive of common sense psychology, and the propositional attitudes that it posits. It also illustrates one sort of psychological model that exploits and builds upon the posits of folk psychology. Section 4 is devoted to connectionism. Models that have been called "connectionist" form a fuzzy and heterogeneous set whose members often share little more than a vague family resemblance. However, our argument linking connectionism to eliminativism will work only for a restricted domain of connectionist models, interpreted in a particular way; the main job of Section 4 is to say what that domain is and how the models in the domain are to be interpreted. In Section 5 we will illustrate what a connectionist model of belief that comports with our strictures might look like, and go on to argue that if models of this sort are correct, then things look bad for common sense psychology. Section 6 assembles some objections and replies. The final section is a brief conclusion.

Before plunging in we should emphasize that the thesis we propose to defend is a *conditional* claim: *If* connectionist hypotheses of the sort we will sketch turn out to be right, so too will eliminativism about propositional attitudes. Since our goal is only to show how connectionism and eliminativism are related, we will make no effort to argue for the truth of falsity of either doctrine. In particular, we will offer no argument in favor of the version of connectionism required in the antecedent of our conditional. Indeed our view is that it is early days yet—too early to tell with any assurance how well this family of connectionist hypotheses will fare. Those who are more confident of connectionism may, of course, invoke our conditional as part of a larger argument for doing away with the propositional attitudes.[1] But, as John Haugeland once remarked, one man's ponens is another man's tollens. And those who take eliminativism about propositional attitudes to be preposterous or unthinkable may well view our arguments as part of a larger case against connectionism. Thus, we'd not be at all surprised if trenchant critics of connectionism, like Fodor and Pylyshyn, found both our conditional and the argument for it to be quiet congenial.[2]

2 Eliminativism and Folk Psychology

"Eliminativism," as we shall use the term, is a fancy name for a simple thesis. It is the claim that some category of entities, processes or properties exploited in a common sense or scientific account of the world do not exist. So construed, we are all eliminativists about many sorts of things. In the domain of folk theory, witches are the standard example. Once upon a time witches were widely believed to be responsible for various local calamities. But people gradually became convinced that there are better explanations for most of the events in which witches had been implicated. There being no explanatory work for witches to do, sensible people concluded that there were no such things. In the scientific domain, phlogiston, caloric fluid and the luminiferous ether are the parade cases for eliminativism. Each was invoked by serious scientists pursuing sophisticated research programs. But in each case the program ran aground in a major way, and the theories in which the entities were invoked were replaced by successor theories in which the entities played no role. The scientific community gradually came to recognize that phlogiston and the rest do not exist.

As these examples suggest, a central step in an eliminativist argument will typically be the demonstration that the theory in which certain putative entities or processes are invoked should be rejected and replaced by a better theory. And that raises the question of how we go about showing that one theory is better than another. Notoriously, this question is easier to ask than to answer. However, it would be pretty widely agreed that if a new theory provides more accurate predictions and better explanations than an old one, and does so over a broader range of phenomena, and if the new theory comports as well or better with well established theories in neighboring domains, then there is good reason to think that the old theory is inferior, and that the new one is to be preferred. This is hardly a complete account of the conditions under which one theory is to be preferred to another, though for our purposes it will suffice.

But merely showing that a theory in which a class of entities plays a role is inferior to a successor theory plainly is not sufficient to show that the entities do not exist. Often a more appropriate conclusion is that the rejected theory was wrong, perhaps seriously wrong, about some of the properties of the entities in its domain, or about the laws governing those entities, and that the new theory gives us a more accurate account *of those very same entities*. Thus, for example, pre-Copernican astronomy was very wrong about the nature of the planets and the laws governing their movement. But it would be something of a joke to suggest that Copernicus and Galileo showed that the planets Ptolemy spoke of do not exist.[3]

In other cases the right thing to conclude is that the posits of the old theory are reducible to those of the new. Standard examples here include the reduction of temperature to mean molecular kinetic energy, the reduction of sound to wave motion in the medium, and the reduction of genes to sequences of polynucleotide bases.[4] Given our current concerns, the lesson to be learned from these cases is that even if the common sense theory in which propositional attitudes find their home is replaced by a better theory, that would not be enough to show that the posits of the common sense theory do not exist.

What more would be needed? What is it that distinguishes cases like phlogiston and caloric, on the one hand, from cases like genes or the planets on the other? Or, to ask the question in a rather different way, what made phlogiston and caloric candidates for elimination? Why wasn't it concluded that phlogiston is oxygen, that caloric is kinetic energy, and that the earlier theories had just been rather badly mistaken about some of the properties of phlogiston and caloric?

Let us introduce a bit of terminology. We will call theory changes in which the entities and processes of the old theory are retained or reduced to those of the new one *ontologically conservative* theory changes. Theory changes that are not ontologically conservative we will call *ontologically radical*. Given this terminology, the question we are asking is how to distinguish ontologically conservative theory changes from ontologically radical ones.

Once again, this is a question that is easier to ask than to answer. There is, in the philosophy of science literature, nothing that even comes close to a plausible and fully general account of when theory change sustains an eliminativist conclusion and when it does not. In the absence of a principled way of deciding when ontological elimination is in order, the best we can do is to look at the posits of the old theory—the ones that are at risk of elimination—and ask whether there is anything in the new theory that they might be identified with or reduced to. If the posits of the new theory strike us as deeply and fundamentally different from those of the old theory, in the way that molecular motion seems deeply and fundamentally different from the "exquisitely elastic" fluid posited by caloric theory, then it will be plausible to conclude that the theory change has been a radical one, and that an eliminativist conclusion is in order. But since there is no easy measure of how "deeply and fundamentally different" a pair of posits are, the conclusion we reach is bound to be a judgment call.[5]

To argue that certain sorts of connectionist models support eliminativism about the propositional attitudes, we must make it plausible that these models are not ontologically conservative. Our strategy will be to contrast these connectionist models, models like those set out in Section 5, with ontologically conservative models like the one sketched at the end of Section 3, in an effort to underscore just how ontologically radical the connectionist models are. But here we are getting ahead of ourselves. Before trying to persuade you that connectionist models are ontologically radical, we need to take a look at the folk psychological theory that the connectionist models threaten to replace.

3 Propositional Attitudes and Common Sense Psychology

For present purposes we will assume that common sense psychology can plausibly be regarded as a theory, and that beliefs, desires and the rest of the propositional attitudes are plausibly viewed as posits of that theory. Though this is not an uncontroversial assumption, the case for it has been well argued by others.[6] Once it is granted that common sense psychology is indeed a theory, we expect it will be conceded by almost everyone that the theory is a likely candidate for replacement. In saying this, we do not intend to disparage folk psychology, or to beg any questions about the status of the entities it posits. Our point is simply that folk wisdom on matters psychological is not likely to tell us all there is to know. Common sense psychology, like other folk theories, is bound to be incomplete in many ways, and very likely to be inaccurate in more than a few. If this were not the case, there would be no need for a careful, quantitative, experimental science of psychology. With the possible exception of a few die hard Wittgensteinians, just about everyone is prepared to grant that there are many psychological facts and principles beyond those embedded in common sense. If this is right, then we have the first premise needed in an eliminativist argument aimed at beliefs, propositional memories and the rest of the propositional attitudes. The theory that posits the attitudes is indeed a prime candidate for replacement.

Though common sense psychology contains a wealth of lore about beliefs, memories, desires, hopes, fears and the other propositional attitudes, the crucial folk psychological tenets in forging the link between connectionism and eliminativism are the claims that propositional attitudes are *functionally discrete, semantically interpretable*, states that play a *causal role* in the production of other propositional attitudes, and ultimately in the production of behavior. Following the suggestion in Stich 1983, we'll call this cluster of claims *propositional modularity*.[7] (The reader is cautioned not to confuse this notion of propositional modularity with the very different notion of modularity defended in Fodor 1983.)

There is a great deal of evidence that might be cited in support of the thesis that folk psychology is committed to the tenets of propositional modularity. The fact that common sense psychology takes beliefs and other propositional attitudes to have semantic properties deserves special emphasis. According to common sense:

i. when people see a dog nearby they typically come to believe *that there is a dog nearby*;
ii. when people believe *that the train will be late if there is snow in the mountains*, and come to believe *that there is snow in the mountains*, they will typically come to believe *that the train will be late*;
iii. when people who speak English say "There is a cat in the yard," they typically believe *that there is a cat in the yard*.

And so on, for indefinitely many further examples. Note that these generalizations of common sense psychology are couched in terms of the *semantic* properties of the attitudes. It is in virtue of being the belief *that p* that a given belief has a given effect or cause. Thus common sense psychology treats the predicates expressing these semantic properties, predicates like "believes *that the train is late*," as *projectable* predicates—the sort of predicates that are appropriately used in nomological or law-like generalizations.

Perhaps the most obvious way to bring out folk psychology's commitment to the thesis that propositional attitudes are *functionally discrete* states is to note that it typically makes perfectly good sense to claim that a person has acquired (or lost), a single memory or belief. Thus, for example, on a given occasion it might plausibly be claimed that when Henry awoke from his nap he had completely forgotten that the car keys were hidden in the refrigerator, though he had forgotten nothing else. In saying that folk psychology views beliefs as the sorts of things that can be acquired or lost one at a time, we do not mean to be denying that having any particular belief may presuppose a substantial network of related beliefs. The belief that the car keys are in the refrigerator is not one that could be acquired by a primitive tribesman who knew nothing about cars, keys or refrigerators. But once the relevant background is in place, as we may suppose it is for us and for Henry, it seems that folk psychology is entirely comfortable with the possibility that a person may acquire (or lose) the belief that the car keys are in the refrigerator, while the remainder of his beliefs remain unchanged. Propositional modularity does not, of course, deny that acquiring one belief often leads to the acquisition of a cluster of related beliefs. When Henry is told that the keys are in the refrigerator, he may come to believe that they haven't been left in the ignition, or in his jacket pocket. But then again he may not. Indeed, on the folk psychological conception of belief it is perfectly possible for a person to have a long standing belief that the keys are in the refrigerator, and to continue searching for them in the bedroom.[8]

To illustrate the way in which folk psychology takes propositional attitudes to be functionally discrete, *causally active* states let us sketch a pair of more elaborate examples.

(i) In common sense psychology, behavior is often explained by appeal to certain of the agent's beliefs and desires. Thus, to explain why Alice went to her office, we might note that she wanted to send some e-mail messages (and, of course, she believed she could do so from her office). However, in some cases an agent will have several sets of beliefs and desires each of which *might* lead to the same behavior. Thus we may suppose that Alice also wanted to talk to her research assistant, and that she believed he would be at the office. In such cases, common sense psychology assumes that Alice's going to her office might have been caused by either one of the belief/desire pairs, or by both, and that determining which of these options obtains is an empirical matter. So it is entirely possible that on *this* occasion Alice's desire to send some e-mail played no role in producing her behavior; it was the desire to talk with her research assistant that actually caused her to go to the office. However, had she not wanted to talk with her research assistant, she might have gone to the office anyhow, because the desire to sent some e-mail, which was causally inert in her actual decision making, might then have become actively involved. Note that in this case common sense psychology is prepared to recognize a pair of quite distinct semantically characterized states, one of which may be causally active while the other is not.

(ii) Our second illustration is parallel to the first, but focuses on beliefs and inference, rather than desires and action. On the common sense view, it may sometimes happen that a person has a number of belief clusters, any one of which might lead him to infer some further belief. When he actually does draw the inference, folk psychology assumes that it is an empirical question what he inferred it from, and that this question typically has a determinate answer. Suppose, for example, that Inspector Clouseau believes that the butler said he spent the evening at the village hotel, and that he said he arrived back on the morning train. Suppose Clouseau also believes that the village hotel is closed for the season, and that the morning train has been taken out of service. Given these beliefs, along with some widely shared background beliefs, Clouseau might well infer that the butler is lying. If he does, folk psychology presumes that the inference might be based either on his beliefs about the hotel, or on his beliefs about the train, or both. It is entirely possible, from the perspective of common sense psychology, that although Clouseau has long known that the hotel is closed for the season, this belief played no role in his inference on this particular occasion. Once again we see common sense psychology invoking a pair of distinct propositional attitudes, one of which is causally active on a particular occasion while the other is causally inert.

In the psychological literature there is no shortage of models for human belief or memory which follow the lead of common sense psychology in supposing that propositional modularity is true. Indeed, prior to the emergence of connectionism, just about all psychological models of propositional memory, save for those urged by behaviorists, were comfortably compatible with propositional modularity. Typically, these models view a subject's store of beliefs or memories as an interconnected collection of functionally discrete, semantically interpretable states which interact in systematic ways. Some of these models represent individual beliefs as sentence-like structures—strings of symbols which can be individually activated by transferring them from long term memory to the more limited memory of a central processing unit. Other models represent beliefs as a network of labeled nodes and labeled links through which patterns of activation may spread. Still other models represent beliefs as sets of production rules.[9] In all three sorts of models, it is generally the case that for any given cognitive episode, like performing a particular inference or answering a question, some of the memory states will be actively involved, and others will be dormant.

In Figure 83.1 we have displayed a fragment of a "semantic network" representation of memory, in the style of Collins and Quillian 1972. In this model, each distinct proposition in memory is represented by an oval node along with its labeled links to various concepts. By adding assumptions about the way in which questions or other sorts of memory probes lead to activation spreading through the network, the model enables us to make predictions about speed and accuracy in various experimental studies of memory. For our purposes there are three facts about this model that are of particular importance. First, since each proposition is encoded in a functionally discrete way, it is a straightforward matter to add or subtract a *single* proposition from memory, while leaving the rest of the network unchanged. Thus, for example, Figure 83.2 depicts the result of removing one proposition from the network in Figure 83.1. Second, the model treats predicates expressing the semantic properties of beliefs or memories as *projectable*.[10] They are treated as the sorts of predicates that pick out scientifically genuine *kinds*, rather than mere accidental conglomerates, and thus are suitable for inclusion in the statement of lawlike regularities. To see this, we need only consider the way in which such models are tested against empirical data about memory acquisition and forgetting. Typically, it will be assumed that if a subject is told

SEMANTIC NETWORK

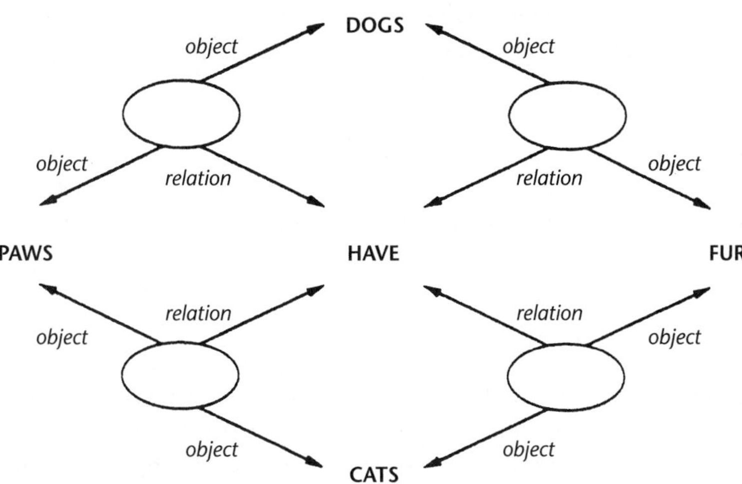

PROPOSITIONS
1. Dogs have fur.
2. Dogs have paws.
3. Cats have fur.
4. Cats have paws.

Figure 83.1

SEMANTIC NETWORK

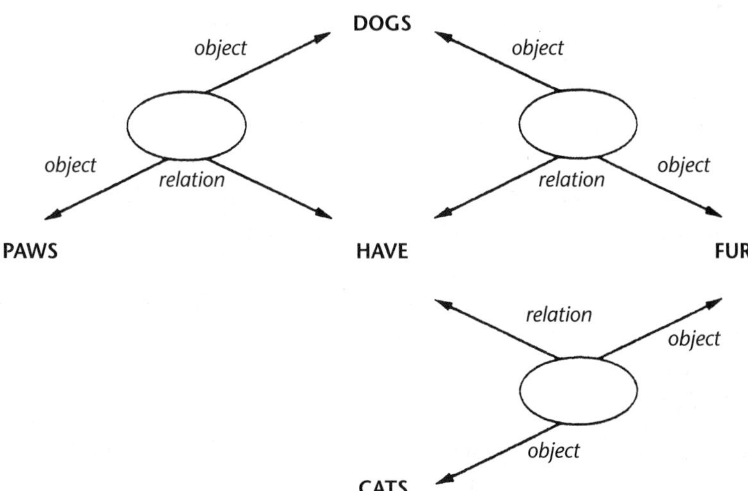

PROPOSITIONS
1. Dogs have fur.
2. Dogs have paws.
3. Cats have fur.

Figure 83.2

(for example) that the policeman arrested the hippie, then the subject will (with a certain probability) remember *that the policeman arrested the hippie.*[11] And this assumption is taken to express a nomological generalization—it captures something lawlike about the way in which the cognitive system works. So while the class of people who *remember that the policeman arrested the hippie* may differ psychologically in all sorts of ways, the theory treats them as a psychologically natural kind. Third, in any given memory search or inference task exploiting a semantic network model, it makes sense to ask which propositions were activated and which were not. Thus, a search in the network of Figure 83.1 might terminate without ever activating the proposition that cats have paws.

4 A Family of Connectionist Hypotheses

Our theme, in the previous section, was that common sense psychology is committed to propositional modularity, and that many models of memory proposed in the cognitive psychology literature are comfortably compatible with this assumption. In the present section we want to describe a class of connectionist models which, we will argue, are *not* readily compatible with propositional modularity. The connectionist models we have in mind share three properties:

i. their encoding of information in the connection weights and in the biases on units is *widely distributed*, rather than being *localist*;
ii. individual hidden units in the network have no comfortable symbolic interpretation; they are *subsymbolic*, to use a term suggested by Paul Smolensky;
iii. the models are intended as *cognitive models*, not merely as *implementations* of cognitive models.

A bit later in this section we will elaborate further on each of these three features, and in the next section we will describe a simple example of a connectionist model that meets our three criteria. However, we are under no illusion that what we say will be sufficient to give a sharp-edged characterization of the class of connectionist models we have in mind. Nor is such a sharp-edged characterization essential for our argument. It will suffice if we can convince you that there is a significant class of connectionist models which are incompatible with the propositional modularity of folk psychology.

Before saying more about the three features on our list, we would do well to give a more general characterization of the sort of models we are calling "connectionist," and introduce some of the jargon that comes with the territory. To this end, let us quote at some length from Paul Smolensky's lucid overview.

> Connectionist models are large networks of simple, parallel computing elements, each of which carries a numerical *activation value* which it computes from neighboring elements in the network, using some simple numerical formula. The network elements or *units* influence each other's values through connections that carry a numerical strength or *weight*....
>
> In a typical ... model, input to the system is provided by imposing activation values on the *input units* of the network; these numerical values represent some encoding or *representation* of the input. The activation on the input units propagates along the connections until some set of activation values emerges on the *output units*; these activation values encode the output the

system has computed from the input. In between the input and output units there may be other units, often called *hidden units*, that participate in representing neither the input nor the output.

The computation performed by the network in transforming the input pattern of activity to the output pattern depends on the set of connection strengths; *these weights are usually regarded as encoding the system's knowledge.*[12] In this sense, the connection strengths play the role of the program in a conventional computer. Much of the allure of the connectionist approach is that many connectionist networks *program themselves*, that is, they have autonomous procedures for tuning their weights to eventually perform some specific computation. Such *learning procedures* often depend on training in which the network is presented with sample input/output pairs from the function it is supposed to compute. In learning networks with hidden units, the network itself "decides" what computations the hidden units will perform; because these units represent neither inputs nor outputs, they are never "told" what their values should be, even during training. . . .[13]

One point must be added to Smolensky's portrait. In many connectionist models the hidden units and the output units are assigned a numerical "bias" which is added into the calculation determining the unit's activation level. The learning procedures for such networks typically set both the connection strengths and the biases. Thus in these networks the system's knowledge is usually regarded as encoded in *both* the connection strengths and the biases.

So much for a general overview. Let us now try to explain the three features that characterize those connectionist models we take to be incompatible with propositional modularity.

(i) In many non-connectionist cognitive models, like the one illustrated at the end of Section 3, it is an easy matter to locate a functionally distinct part of the model encoding each proposition or state of affairs represented in the system. Indeed, according to Fodor and Pylyshyn, "conventional [computational] architecture requires that there be distinct symbolic expressions for each state of affairs that it can represent."[14] In some connectionist models an analogous sort of functional localization is possible, not only for the input and output units but for the hidden units as well. Thus, for example, in certain connectionist models, various individual units or small clusters of units are themselves intended to represent specific properties or features of the environment. When the connection strength from one such unit to another is strongly positive, this might be construed as the system's representation of the proposition that if the first feature is present, so too is the second. However, in many connectionist networks it is not possible to localize propositional representation beyond the input layer. That is, there are no particular features or states of the system which lend themselves to a straightforward semantic evaluation. This can sometimes be a real inconvenience to the connectionist model builder when the system as a whole fails to achieve its goal because it has not represented the world the way it should. When this happens, as Smolensky notes,

[I]t is not necessarily possible to localize a failure of veridical representation. Any particular state is part of a large causal system of states, and failures of the system to meet goal conditions cannot in general be localized in any particular state or state component."[15]

It is connectionist networks of this sort, in which it is not possible to isolate the representation of particular propositions or states of affairs within the nodes, connection strengths and biases, that we have in mind when we talk about the encoding of information in the biases, weights and hidden nodes being *widely distributed* rather than *localist*.

(ii) As we've just noted, there are some connectionist models in which some or all of the units are intended to represent specific properties or features of the system's environment. These units may be viewed as the model's symbols for the properties or features in question. However, in models where the weights and biases have been tuned by learning algorithms it is often not the case that any single unit or any small collection of units will end up representing a specific feature of the environment in any straightforward way. As we shall see in the next section, it is often plausible to view such networks as collectively or holistically encoding a set of propositions, although none of the hidden units, weights or biases are comfortably viewed as *symbols*. When this is the case we will call the strategy of representation invoked in the model *subsymbolic*. Typically (perhaps always?) networks exploiting subsymbolic strategies of representation will encode information in a widely distributed way.

(iii) The third item on our list is not a feature of connectionist models themselves, but rather a point about how the models are to be interpreted. In making this point we must presuppose a notion of theoretical or explanatory level which, despite much discussion in the recent literature, is far from being a paradigm of clarity.[16] Perhaps the clearest way to introduce the notion of explanatory level is against the background of the familiar functionalist thesis that psychological theories are analogous to programs which can be implemented on a variety of very different sorts of computers.[17] If one accepts this analogy, then it makes sense to ask whether a particular connectionist model is intended as a model at the psychological level or at the level of underlying neural implementation. Because of their obvious, though in many ways very partial, similarity to real neural architectures, it is tempting to view connectionist models as models of the implementation of psychological processes. And some connectionist model builders endorse this view quite explicitly. So viewed, however, connectionist models are not *psychological* or *cognitive* models at all, any more than a story of how cognitive processes are implemented at the quantum mechanical level is a psychological story. A very different view that connectionist model builders can and often do take is that their models are at the psychological level, not at the level of implementation. So construed, the models are in competition with other psychological models of the same phenomena. Thus a connectionist model of word recognition would be an alternative to—and not simply a possible implementation of—a non-connectionist model of word recognition; a connectionist theory of memory would be a competitor to a semantic network theory, and so on. Connectionists who hold this view of their theories often illustrate the point by drawing analogies with other sciences. Smolensky, for example, suggests that connectionist models stand to traditional cognitive models (like semantic networks) in much the same way that quantum mechanics stands to classical mechanics. In each case the newer theory is deeper, more general and more accurate over a broader range of phenomena. But in each case the new theory and the old are competing at the same explanatory level. If one is right, the other must be wrong.

In light of our concerns in this paper, there is one respect in which the analogy between connectionist models and quantum mechanics may be thought to beg an important question. For while quantum mechanics is conceded to be a *better* theory than classical mechanics, a plausible case could be made that the shift from classical to quantum mechanics was an ontologically *conservative* theory change. In any event, it is not clear that the change was ontologically *radical*. If our central thesis in this paper is correct, then the relation between connectionist models and more traditional cognitive models is more like the relation between the caloric theory of heat and the kinetic theory. The caloric and kinetic theories are at the same explanatory level, though the shift from one to the other was pretty clearly ontologically radical. In order to make the case that the caloric analogy is the more appropriate one, it will be useful to describe a concrete, though very simple, connectionist model of memory that meets the three criteria we have been trying to explicate.

5 A Connectionist Model of Memory

Our goal in constructing the model was to produce a connectionist network that would do at least some of the tasks done by more traditional cognitive models of memory, and that would perspicuously exhibit the sort of distributed, sub-symbolic encoding described in the previous section. We began by constructing a network, we'll call it Network A, that would judge the truth or falsehood of the sixteen propositions displayed [below] in line in Figure 83.3. The network was a typical three tiered feed-forward network consisting of 16 input units, four hidden units and one output unit, as shown in Figure 83.4. The input coding of each proposition is shown in the center column in Figure 83.3. Outputs close to 1 were interpreted as "true" and outputs close to zero were interpreted as "false." Back propagation, a familiar connectionist learning

	Proposition	Input	Output
1	Dogs have fur.	11000011 00001111	1 true
2	Dogs have paws.	11000011 00110011	1 true
3	Dogs have fleas.	11000011 00111111	1 true
4	Dogs have legs.	11000011 00111100	1 true
5	Cats have fur.	11001100 00001111	1 true
6	Cats have paws.	11001100 00110011	1 true
7	Cats have fleas.	11001100 00111111	1 true
8	Fish have scales.	11110000 00110000	1 true
9	Fish have fins.	11110000 00001100	1 true
10	Fish have gills.	11110000 00000011	1 true
11	Cats have gills.	11001100 00000011	0 false
12	Fish have legs.	11110000 00111100	0 false
13	Fish have fleas.	11110000 00111111	0 false
14	Dogs have scales.	11000011 00110000	0 false
15	Dogs have fins.	11000011 00001100	0 false
16	Cats have fins.	11001100 00001100	0 false
	Added Proposition		
17	Fish have eggs.	11110000 11001000	1 true

Figure 83.3

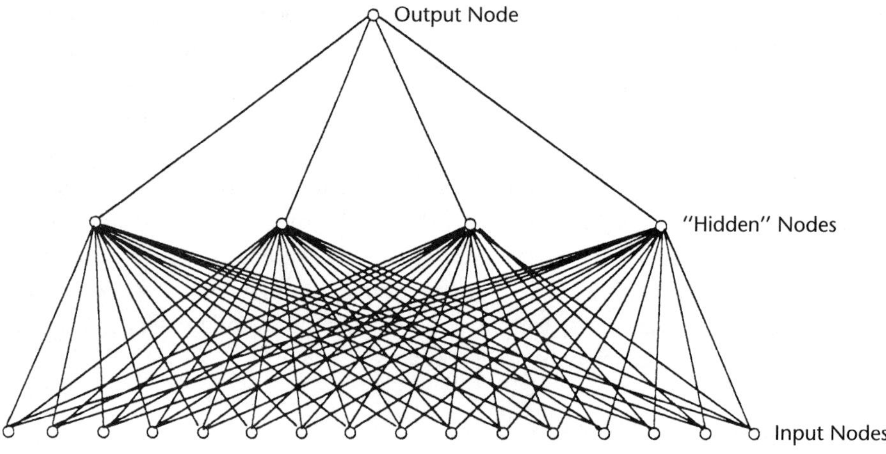

Figure 83.4

Network A

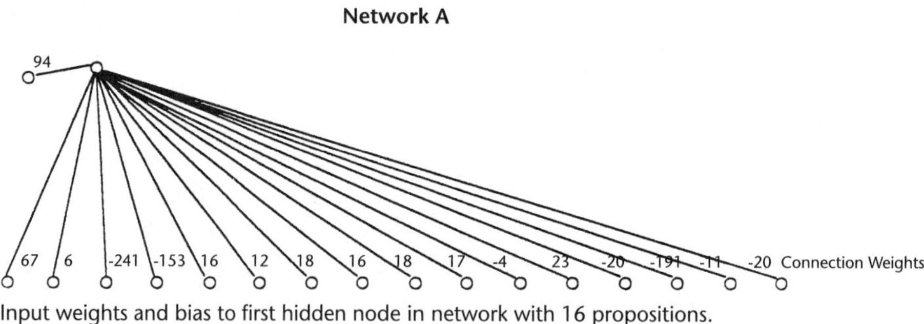

Input weights and bias to first hidden node in network with 16 propositions.

Figure 83.5

algorithm was used to "train up" the network thereby setting the connection weights and biases. Training was terminated when the network consistently gave an output higher than .9 for each true proposition and lower than .1 for each false proposition. Figure 83.5 shows the connection weights between the input units and the leftmost hidden unit in the trained up network, along with the bias on that unit. Figure 83.6 indicates the connection weights and biases further upstream. Figure 83.7 shows the way in which the network computes its response to the proposition *Dogs have fur* when that proposition is encoded in the input units.

There is a clear sense in which the trained up Network A may be said to have stored information about the truth or falsity of propositions (1)–(16), since when any one of these propositions is presented to the network it correctly judges whether the proposition is true or false. In this respect it is similar to various semantic network models which can be constructed to perform much the same task. However, there is a striking difference between Network A and a semantic network model like the one depicted in Figure 83.1. For, as we noted earlier, in the semantic network there is a functionally distinct sub-part associated with each proposition, and thus it makes perfectly good sense to ask, for any probe of the network, whether or not the representation of a specific proposition played a causal role. In the connectionist network by contrast, there is no

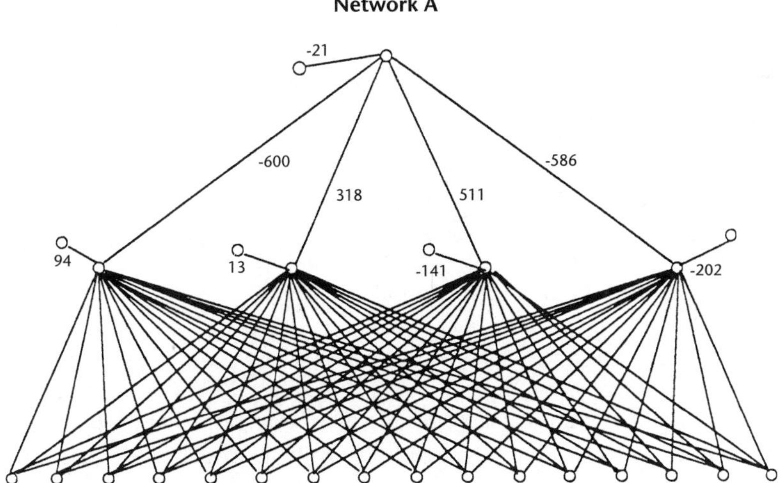

Weights and biases in network with 16 propositions.

Figure 83.6

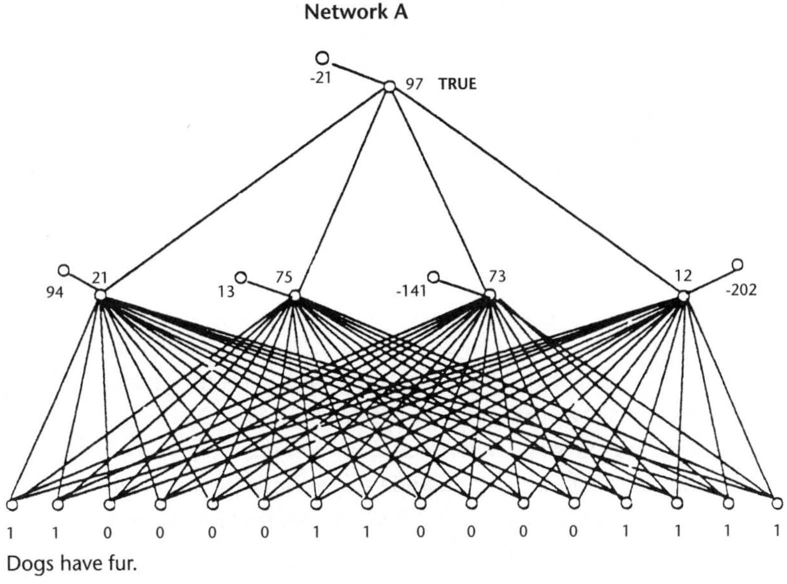

Dogs have fur.

Figure 83.7

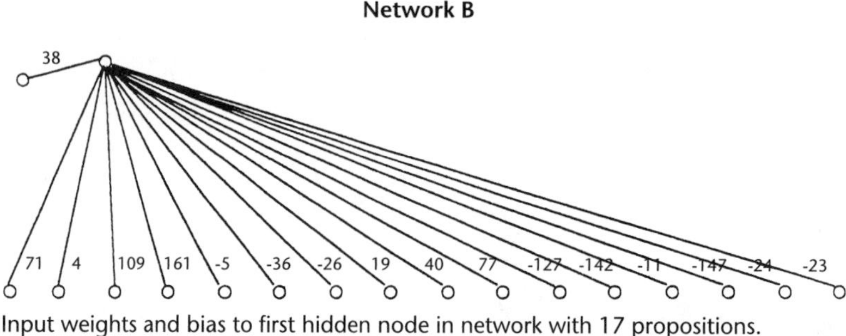

Input weights and bias to first hidden node in network with 17 propositions.

Figure 83.8

distinct state or part of the network that serves to represent any particular proposition. The information encoded in Network A is stored holistically and distributed throughout the network. Whenever information is extracted from Network A, by giving it an input string and seeing whether it computes a high or a low value for the output unit, *many* connection strengths, *many* biases and *many* hidden units play a role in the computation. And any particular weight or unit or bias will help to encode information about *many* different propositions. It simply makes no sense to ask whether or not the representation of a particular proposition plays a causal role in the network's computation. It is in just this respect that our connectionist model of memory seems radically incongruent with the propositional modularity of common sense psychology. For, as we saw in Section 3, common sense psychology seems to presuppose that there is generally some answer to the question of whether a particular belief or memory played a causal role in a specific cognitive episode. But if belief and memory are subserved by a connectionist network like ours, such questions seem to have no clear meaning.

The incompatibility between propositional modularity and connectionist models like ours can be made even more vivid by contrasting Network A with a second network, we'll call it Network B, depicted in Figures 83.8 and 83.9. Network B was trained up just as the first one was, except that one additional proposition was added to the training set (coded as indicated below the line in Figure 83.3). Thus Network B encodes all the same propositions as Network A plus one more. In semantic network models, and other traditional cognitive models, it would be an easy matter to say which states or features of the system encode the added proposition, and it would be a simple task to determine whether or not the representation of the added proposition played a role in a particular episode modeled by the system. But plainly in the connectionist network those questions are quite senseless. The point is not that there are no differences between the two networks. Quite the opposite is the case; the differences are many and widespread. But these differences do not correlate in any systematic way with the functionally discrete, semantically interpretable states posited by folk psychology and by more traditional cognitive models. Since information is encoded in a highly distributed manner, with each connection weight and bias embodying information salient to many propositions, and information regarding any given proposition scattered throughout the network, the system lacks functionally distinct, identifiable sub-structures that are semantically interpretable as representations of individual propositions.

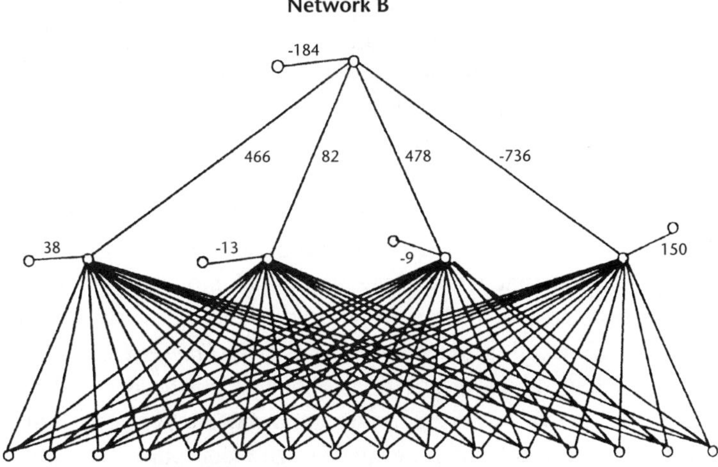

Weights and biases in network with 17 propositions.

Figure 83.9

The contrast between Network A and Network B enables us to make our point about the incompatibility between common sense psychology and these sorts of connectionist models in a rather different way. We noted in Section 3 that common sense psychology treats predicates expressing the semantic properties of propositional attitudes as projectable. Thus "believes that dogs have fur" or "remembers that dogs have fur" will be projectable predicates in common sense psychology. Now both Network A and Network B might serve as models for a cognitive agent who believes that dogs have fur; both networks store or represent the information that dogs have fur. Nor are these the only two. If we were to train up a network on the 17 propositions in Figure 83.3 plus a few (or minus a few) we would get yet another system which is as different from Networks A and B as these two are from each other. The moral here is that though there are *indefinitely* many connectionists networks that represent the information that dogs have fur just as well as Network A does, these networks have no projectable features in common that are describable in the language of connectionist theory. From the point of view of the connectionist model builder, the class of networks that might model a cognitive agent who believes that dogs have fur is not a genuine kind at all, but simply a chaotically disjunctive set. Common sense psychology treats the class of people who believe that dogs have fur as a psychologically natural kind; connectionist psychology does not.[18]

6 Objections and Replies

The argument we've set out in the previous five sections has encountered no shortage of objections. In this section we will try to reconstruct the most interesting of these, and indicate how we would reply.

Objection (i): Models like A and B are not serious models for human belief or propositional memory.

Of course, the models we've constructed are tiny toys that were built to illustrate the features set out in Section 4 in a perspicuous way. They were never intended to model any substantial part of human propositional memory. But various reasons have been offered for doubting that *anything like* these models could ever be taken seriously as psychological models of propositional memory. Some critics have claimed that the models simply will not scale up—that while teaching a network to recognize fifteen or twenty propositions may be easy enough, it is just not going to be possible to train up a network that can recognize a few thousand propositions, still less a few hundred thousand.[19] Others have objected that while more traditional models of memory, including those based on sentence-like storage, those using semantic networks, and those based on production systems, all provide some strategy for *inference* or *generalization* which enables the system to answer questions about propositions it was not explicitly taught, models like those we have constructed are incapable of inference and generalization. It has also been urged that these models fail as accounts of human memory because they provide no obvious way to account for the fact that suitably prepared humans can easily acquire propositional information one proposition at a time. Under ordinary circumstances, we can just *tell* Henry that the car keys are in the refrigerator, and he can readily record this fact in memory. He doesn't need anything like the sort of massive retraining that would be required to teach one of our connectionist networks a new proposition.

Reply: If this were a paper aimed at defending connectionist models of propositional memory, we would have to take on each of these putative shortcomings in some detail. And in each instance there is at least something to be said on the connectionist side. Thus, for example, it just is not true that networks like A and B don't generalize beyond the propositions on which they've been trained. In Network A, for example, the training set included:

Dogs have fur   Cats have fur.
Dogs have paws   Cats have paws.
Dogs have fleas   Cats have fleas.

It also included

Dogs have legs.

but not

Cats have legs.

When the network was given an encoding of this last proposition, however, it generalized correctly and responded affirmatively. Similarly, the network responded negatively to an encoding of

Cats have scales

though it had not previously been exposed to this proposition.

However, it is important to see that this sort of point by point response to the charge that networks like ours are inadequate models for propositional memory is not really required, given the thesis we are defending in this paper. For what we are trying to establish is a *conditional* thesis: *if* connectionist models of memory of the sort we describe in Section 4 are right, *then* propositional attitude psychology is in serious trouble. Since conditionals with false antecedents are true, we win by default if it turns out that the antecedent of our conditional is false.

Objection (ii): Our models do not really violate the principle of propositional modularity, since the propositions the system has learned are coded in functionally discrete ways, though this may not be obvious.

We've heard this objection elaborated along three quite different lines. The first line—let's call it Objection (iia)—notes that functionally discrete coding may often be *very* hard to notice, and can not be expected to be visible on casual inspection. Consider, for example, the way in which sentences are stored in the memory of a typical von Neuman architecture computer—for concreteness we might suppose that the sentences are part of an English text and are being stored while the computer is running a word processing program. Parts of sentences may be stored at physically scattered memory addresses linked together in complex ways, and given an account of the contents of all relevant memory addresses one would be hard put to say where a particular sentence is stored. But nonetheless each sentence is stored in a *functionally discrete* way. Thus if one knew enough about the system it would be possible to erase any particular sentence it is storing by tampering with the contents of the appropriate memory addresses, while leaving the rest of the sentences the system is storing untouched. Similarly, it has been urged, connectionist networks may in fact encode propositions in functionally discrete ways, though this may not be evident from a casual inspection of the trained up network's biases and connection strengths.

Reply (iia): It is a bit difficult to come to grips with this objection, since what the critic is proposing is that in models like those we have constructed there *might* be some covert functionally discrete system of propositional encoding that has yet to be discovered. In response to this we must concede that indeed there might. We certainly have no argument that even comes close to demonstrating that the discovery of such a covert functionally discrete encoding is impossible. Moreover, we concede that if such a covert system were discovered, then our argument would be seriously undermined. However, we're inclined to think that the burden of argument is on the critic to show that such a system is not merely possible but *likely*; in the absence of any serious reason to think that networks like ours do encode propositions in functionally discrete ways, the mere logical possibility that they might is hardly a serious threat.

The second version of Objection (ii)—we'll call it Objection (iib)—makes a specific proposal about the way in which networks like A and B might be discretely, though covertly, encoding propositions. The encoding, it is urged, is to be found in the pattern of activation of the hidden nodes, when a given proposition is presented to the network. Since there are four hidden nodes in our networks, the activation pattern on presentation of any given input may be represented as an ordered 4-tuple. Thus, for example, when network A is presented with the encoded proposition *Dogs have fur*, the relevant 4-tuple would be (21, 75, 73, 12), as shown in Figure 83.7. Equivalently, we may think of each activation pattern as a point in a four dimensional hyperspace. Since each proposition corresponds to a unique point in the hyperspace, that point may be viewed as the encoding of the proposition. Moreover, that point represents a functionally discrete state of the system.[20]

Reply (iib): What is being proposed is that the pattern of activation of the system on presentation of an encoding of the proposition *p* be identified with the belief that *p*. But this proposal is singularly implausible. Perhaps the best way to see this is to note that in common sense psychology beliefs and propositional memories are typically of substantial duration; and they are the sorts of things that cognitive agents generally have lots of even when they are not using them. Consider an example. Are kangaroos marsupials? Surely you've believed for years that they are, though in all likelihood this is the first time today that your belief has been activated or used.[21] An activation pattern, however, is not an enduring state of a network; indeed, it is not a state of the network at all except when the network has had the relevant proposition as input. Moreover, there is an enormous number of other beliefs that you've had for years. But it makes no sense to suppose that a network could have many activation patterns continuously over a long period of time. At any given time a network exhibits at most one pattern of activation. So activation patterns are just not the sorts of things that can plausibly be identified with beliefs or their representations.

Objection (iic): At this juncture, a number of critics have suggested that long standing beliefs might be identified not with activation patterns, which are transient states of networks, but rather with *dispositions to produce activation patterns*. Thus, in network A, the belief that dogs have fur would not be identified with a location in activation hyperspace but with the network's *disposition* to end up at that location when the proposition is presented. This *dispositional state* is an enduring state of the system; it is a state the network can be in no matter what its current state of activation may be, just as a sugar cube may have a disposition to dissolve in water even when there is no water nearby.[22] Some have gone on to suggest that the familiar philosophical distinction between dispositional and occurrent beliefs might be captured, in connectionist models, as the distinction between dispositions to produce activation patterns and activation patterns themselves.

Reply (iic): Our reply to this suggestion is that while dispositions to produce activation patterns are indeed *enduring* states of the system, they are not the right sort of enduring states—they are not the discrete, independently causally active states that folk psychology requires. Recall that on the folk psychological conception of belief and inference, there will often be a variety of quite different underlying causal patterns that may lead to the acquisition and avowal of a given belief. When Clouseau says that the butler did it, he may have just inferred this with the help of his long standing belief that the train is out of service. Or he may have inferred it by using his belief that the hotel is closed. Or both long standing beliefs may have played a role in the inference. Moreover, it is also possible that Clouseau drew this inference some time ago, and is now reporting a relatively long standing belief. But it is hard to see how anything like these distinctions can be captured by the dispositional account in question. In reacting to a given input, say *p*, a network takes on a specific activation value. It may also have dispositions to take on other activation values on other inputs, say *q* and *r*. But there is no obvious way to interpret the claim that these further dispositions play a causal role in the network's reaction to *p*—or, for that matter, that they do not play a role. Nor can we make any sense of the idea that on one occasion the encoding of *q* (say, the proposition that the train is out of service) played a role while the encoding of *r* (say, the proposition that the hotel is closed) did not, and on another occasion, things went the other way around. The propositional modularity presupposed by common sense psychology requires that belief tokens be functionally discrete states capable of causally interacting with one another in some cognitive episodes and of remaining causally inert in other cognitive episodes. However, in a distributed connectionist system like Network A, the dispositional state which produces one activation pattern is functionally inseparable from the dispositional state which produces another. Thus it is impossible to isolate some propositions as causally active in certain cognitive episodes, while others are not. We conclude that reaction pattern dispositions won't do as belief tokens. Nor, so far as we can see, are there any other states of networks like A and B that will fill the bill.

7 Conclusion

The thesis we have been defending in this paper is that connectionist models of a certain sort are incompatible with the propositional modularity embedded in common sense psychology. The connectionist models in question are those which are offered as models at the *cognitive* level, and in which the encoding of information is widely distributed and subsymbolic. In such models, we have argued, there are no *discrete, semantically interpretable* states that play a *causal role* in some cognitive episodes but not others. Thus there is, in these models, nothing with which the propositional attitudes of common sense psychology can plausibly be identified. If these models turn out to offer the best accounts of human belief and memory, we will be confronting an *ontologically radical* theory change—the sort of theory change that will sustain the conclusion that propositional attitudes, like caloric and phlogiston, do not exist.

Acknowledgments

Thanks are due to Ned Block, Paul Churchland, Gary Cottrell, Adrian Cussins, Jerry Fodor, John Heil, Frank Jackson, David Kirsh, Patricia Kitcher and Philip Kitcher for useful feedback on earlier versions of this paper. Talks based on the paper have been presented at the UCSD Cognitive Science Seminar and at conferences sponsored by the Howard Hughes Medical Foundation and the University of North Carolina at Greensboro. Comments and questions from these audiences have proved helpful in many ways.

Notes

1. See, for example, Churchland 1981 and 1986, where explicitly eliminativist conclusions are drawn on the basis of speculations about the success of cognitive models similar to those we shall discuss.

2. Fodor, J. and Pylyshyn, Z. 1988.

3. We are aware that certain philosophers and historians of science have actually entertained ideas similar to the suggestion that the planets spoken of by pre-Copernican astronomers do not exist. See, for example, Kuhn 1970, Ch. 10, and Feyerabend 1981, Ch. 4. However, we take this suggestion to be singularly implausible. Eliminativist arguments can't be that easy. Just what has gone wrong with the accounts of meaning and reference that lead to such claims is less clear. For further discussion on these matters see Kuhn 1983, and Kitcher 1978 and 1983.

4. For some detailed discussion of scientific reduction, see Nagel 1961; Schaffner 1967; Hooker 1981; and Kitcher 1984. The genetics case is not without controversy. See Kitcher 1982 and 1984.

5. It's worth noting that judgments on this matter can differ quite substantially. At one end of the spectrum are writers like Feyerabend 1981, and perhaps Kuhn 1962, for whom relatively small differences in theory are enough to justify the suspicion that there has been an ontologically radical change. Toward the other end are writers like Lycan, who writes:

> I am at pains to advocate a very liberal view ... I am entirely willing to give up fairly large chunks of our commonsensical or platitudinous theory of belief or of desire (or of almost anything else) and decide that we were just wrong about a lot of things, without drawing the inference that we are no longer talking about belief or desire ... I think the ordinary word "belief" (qua theoretical term of folk psychology) points dimly toward a natural kind that we have not fully grasped and that only mature psychology will reveal. I expect that "belief" will turn out to refer to some kind of information bearing inner state of a sentient being ..., but the kind of state it refers to may have only a few of the properties usually attributed to beliefs by common sense. (Lycan 1988, pp. 31–2)

On our view, both extreme positions are implausible. As we noted earlier, the Copernican revolution did not show that the planets studied by Ptolemy do not exist. But Lavosier's chemical revolution *did* show that phlogiston does not exist. Yet on Lycan's "very liberal view" it is hard to see why we should not conclude that phlogiston really does exist after all—it's really oxygen, and prior to Lavosier "we were just very wrong about a lot of things."

6. For an early and influential statement of the view that common sense psychology is a theory, see Sellars 1956. More recently the view has been defended by Churchland 1970 and 1979, Chs. 1 and 4; and by Fodor 1988, Ch. 1. For the opposite view, see Wilkes 1978; Madell 1986; Sharpe 1987.

7. See Stich 1983, pp. 237 ff.

8. Cherniak 1986, Ch. 3, notes that this sort of absent mindedness is commonplace in literature and in ordinary life, and sometimes leads to disastrous consequences.

9. For sentential models, see John McCarthy 1968, 1980, and 1986; and Kintsch 1974. For semantic networks, see Quillian 1969; Collins and Quillian 1972; Rumelhart, Lindsay and Norman 1972; Anderson and Bower 1973; and Anderson 1976 and 1980, Ch. 4. For production systems, see Newell and Simon 1972; Newell 1973; Anderson 1983; and Holland, et. al. 1986.

10. For the classic discussion of the distinction between projectable and non-projectable predicates, see Goodman 1965.

11. See, for example, Anderson and Bower 1973.

12. Emphasis added.

13. Smolensky 1988, p. 1.

14. Fodor and Pylyshyn 1988, p. 57.

15. Smolensky 1988, p. 15.

16. Broadbent, D. 1985; Rumelhart and McClelland 1985; Rumelhart and McClelland 1986, Ch. 4; Smolensky 1988; Fodor and Pylyshyn 1988.

17. The notion of program being invoked here is itself open to a pair of quite different interpretations. For the right reading, see Ramsey 1989.

18. This way of making the point about the incompatibility between connectionist models and common sense psychology was suggested to us by Jerry Fodor.

19. This point has been urged by Daniel Dennett, among others.

20. Quite a number of people have suggested this move, including Gary Cottrell, and Adrian Cussins.

21. As Lycan notes, on the commons sense notion of belief, people have lots of them "even when they are asleep" (Lycan 1988, p. 57).

22. Something like this objection was suggested to us by Ned Block and by Frank Jackson.

References

Anderson, J. and Bower, G. (1973). *Human Associative Memory*. Washington, DC: Winston.

Anderson, J. (1976). *Language, Memory and Thought*. Hillsdale, NJ: Lawrence Erlbaum Associates.

Anderson, J. (1980). *Cognitive Psychology and Its Implications*. San Francisco, CA: W. H. Freeman and Co.

Anderson, J. (1983). *The Architecture of Cognition*. Cambridge, MA: Harvard University Press.

Broadbent, D. (1985). A question of levels: Comments on McClelland and Rumelhart. *Journal of Experimental Psychology: General*, 114: 189–192.

Cherniak, C. (1986). *Minimal Rationality*. Cambridge, MA: Bradford Books.

Churchland, P. (1970). The logical character of action explanations. *Philosophical Review, 79*(2): 214–236.

Churchland, P. (1979). *Scientific Realism and the Plasticity of Mind*. Cambridge, England: Cambridge University Press.

Churchland, P. (1981). Eliminative Materialism and Propositional Attitudes. *Journal of Philosophy, 78*(2): 67–90.

Churchland, P. (1986). Some Reductive Strategies in Cognitive Neurobiology. *Mind, 95*(379): 279–309.

Collins, A. and Quillian, M. (1972). Experiments on semantic memory and language comprehension. In L. Gregg (Ed.), *Cognition in Learning and Memory* (pp. 117–137). New York: Wiley.

Feyerabend, P. (1981). *Realism, Rationalism and Scientific Method: Philosophical Papers: Vol. 1*. Cambridge, England: Cambridge University Press.

Fodor, J. and Pylyshyn, Z. (1988). Connectionism and cognitive architecture: A critical analysis. *Cognition, 28*, 3–71.

Fodor, J. (1987). *Psychosemantics: The Problem of Meaning in the Philosophy of Mind*. Cambridge, MA: MIT Press.

Goodman, N. (1965). *Fact, Fiction, and Forecast*. Indianapolis, IN: Bobbs-Merrill.

Holland, J., Holyoak, K., Nisbett, R. and Thagard, P. (1986). *Induction: Processes of Inference, Learning and Discovery*. Cambridge, MA: MIT Press.

Hooker, C. (1981). Towards a general theory of reduction: (Parts I, II and III). *Dialogue, 20*, 38–59, 201–236, 496–529.

Kintsch, W. (1974). *The Representation of Meaning in Memory*. Hillsdale, NJ: Lawrence Erlbaum Associates.

Kitcher, P. (1978). Theories, theorists and theoretical change. *Philosophical Review, 87*(4): 519–547.

Kitcher, P. (1982). Genes. *British Journal for the Philosophy of Science, 82*(33): 337–359.

Kitcher, P. (1983). Implications of incommensurability, PSA 1982. In P. Asquith and T. Nickles (Eds.), *Proceedings of the 1982 Biennial Meeting of the Philosophy of Science Association: Vol. 2* (pp. 689–703). East Lansing, MI: Philosophy of Science Association.

Kitcher, P. (1984). 1953 and all that: A tale of two sciences. *Philosophical Review, 93*, 335–373.

Kuhn, T. (1962). *The Structure of Scientific Revolutions*. Chicago, IL: University of Chicago Press.

Kuhn, T. (1983). Commensurability, Comparability, Communicability, PSA 1982. In P. Asquith and T. Nickles (Eds.), *Proceedings of the 1982 Biennial Meeting of the Philosophy of Science Association: Vol. 2*. (pp. 669–688). East Lansing, MI: Philosophy of Science Association.

Lycan, W. (1988). *Judgment and Justification*. Cambridge, England: Cambridge University Press.

Madell, G. (1986). Neurophilosophy: A principled skeptic's response. *Inquiry, 29*(2): 153–168.

McCarthy, J. (1968). Programs with common sense. In M. Minsky (Ed.), *Semantic Information Processing*. Cambridge, MA: MIT Press.

McCarthy, J. (1980). Circumscription: A form of non-monotonic reasoning. *Artificial Intelligence, 13*(1,2): 27–41.

McCarthy, J. (1986). Applications of Circumscription to Formalizing Common-Sense Knowledge. *Artificial Intelligence, 28*, 89–116.

Nagel, E. (1961). *The Structure of Science*. New York: Harcourt, Brace and World.

Newell, A. and Simon, H. (1972). *Human Problem Solving*. Englewood Cliffs, NJ: Prentice Hall.

Newell, A. (1973). Production systems: Models of control structures. In W. Chase (Ed.), *Visual Information Processing*. New York: Academic Press.

Quillian, M. (1966). *Semantic Memory*. Cambridge, MA: Bolt, Branak and Newman.

Ramsey, W. (1989). Parallelism and functionalism. *Cognitive Science, 13*, 139–144.

Rumelhart, D. and McClelland, J. (1985). Levels indeed! A response to Broadbent. *Journal of Experimental Psychology: General, 114*(2): 193–197.

Rumelhart, D., Lindsay, P. and Norman, D. (1972). A process model for long term memory. In E. Tulving and W. Donaldson (Eds.), *Organization of Memory*. New York: Academic Press.

Rumelhart, D., McClelland, J. and the PDP Research Group. (1986). *Parallel Distributed Processing: Vols. I and II*. Cambridge, MA: MIT Press.

Sellars, W. (1956). Empiricism and the philosophy of mind. In H. Feigl and M. Scriven (Eds.), *Minnesota Studies in the Philosophy of Science: Vol. 1*. Minneapolis, MN: University of Minnesota Press.

Schaffner, K. (1967). Approaches to reduction. *Philosophy of Science, 34*, 137–147.

Sharp, R. (1987). The very idea of folk psychology. *Inquiry, 30*, 381–193.

Smolensky, P. (1988). On the proper treatment of connectionism. *Behavioral and Brain Sciences, 11*, 1–74.

Stich, S. (1983). *From Folk Psychology to Cognitive Science*. Cambridge, MA: MIT Press.

Wilkes, K. (1978). *Physicalism*. London: Routledge and Kegan Paul.

Index